# ADVERTISING COMMUNICATIONS & PROMOTION MANAGEMENT

# McGraw-Hill Series in Marketing

Anderson, Hair, and Bush: *Professional Sales Management*

Bennett: *Marketing*

Bovee, Houston, and Thill: *Marketing.*

Bovee, Thill, Dovel, and Wood: *Advertising Excellence*

Bowersox and Closs: *Logistical Management: The Integrated Supply Chain Process*

Bowersox and Cooper: *Strategic Marketing Channel Management*

Buskirk and Buskirk: *Selling: Principles and Practices*

Dobler, Burt, and Lee: *Purchasing and Materials Management: Text and Cases*

Douglas and Craig: *Global Marketing Strategy*

Etzel, Walker, and Stanton: *Marketing*

Guiltinan and Paul: *Cases in Marketing Management*

Guiltinan and Paul: *Marketing Management Strategies and Programs*

Hasty: *Retail Management*

Johnson, Kurtz, and Scheuing: *Sales Management: Concepts, Practices, and Cases*

Kinnear and Taylor: *Marketing Research: An Applied Approach*

Loudon and Della Bitta: *Consumer Behavior: Concepts and Applications*

Lovelock and Weinberg: *Marketing Challenges: Cases and Exercises*

Monroe: *Pricing*

Moore and Pessemier: *Product Planning and Management: Designing and Delivering Value*

Oliver: *Satisfaction: A Behavioral Perspective On The Consumer*

Rossiter and Percy: *Advertising Communications and Promotion Management*

Ulrich and Eppinger: *Product Design and Development*

Zeithaml and Bitner: *Services Marketing*

# ADVERTISING COMMUNICATIONS & PROMOTION MANAGEMENT

SECOND EDITION

- - - - - - - - - - - - - - - - - - - - - - - - - - - - - - - - -

## JOHN R. ROSSITER

Australian Graduate School of Management

## LARRY PERCY

Communications Advertising Consultant

Boston, Massachusetts   Burr Ridge, Illinois   Dubuque, Iowa
Madison, Wisconsin   New York, New York   San Francisco, California   St. Louis, Missouri

*Irwin/McGraw-Hill*

**A Division of The McGraw·Hill Companies**


ADVERTISING COMMUNICATIONS AND PROMOTION MANAGEMENT
International Editions 1998

10 09
20 09 08 07 06 05 04 03 02
UPE BJE

This book was set in Times Roman by Graphic World, Inc.
The editors were Karen Westover, Dan Alpert, and Sharla Volkersz.
The production supervisor was Richard DeVitto.
The art editor was Jane Brundage.
Illustrations were by Graphic World, Inc. and Terry Domzal.
The cover was designed by Juan Vargas.


**Library of Congress Cataloging-in-Publication Data**
Advertising communications and promotion management / John R.
    Rossiter, Larry Percy. – 2nd ed.
        p.    cm.
    Includes bibliographical references and index.
    ISBN 0-07-053943-X
    1. Advertising.    2. Communication in marketing.    3. Sales
promotion.    I. Rossiter, John R.    II. Percy, Larry.
HF5821.A293      1996
659.1–dc20                                                    96-25413
                                                                  CIP


http://www.mhcollege.com


**When ordering this title, use ISBN 0-07-115514-7**

Printed in Singapore

# ABOUT THE AUTHORS

JOHN R. ROSSITER is an "Aussie" with 15 years of United States marketing experience. He is Professor of Marketing at the Australian Graduate School of Management (AGSM) at the University of New South Wales, in Sydney, Australia, where he teaches buyer behavior and advertising management. Before joining the AGSM, he was Assistant Professor of Marketing at The Wharton School, University of Pennsylvania; Associate Professor of Business in the Graduate School of Business at Columbia University in New York; and Head of the School of Marketing at the University of Technology, Sydney.

Dr. Rossiter has coauthored three other books and has contributed more than 50 conference papers and journal articles to the field, with his work appearing in the *Journal of Consumer Research,* the *Journal of Marketing Research,* and the *Journal of Advertising Research.* He has been a marketing and advertising consultant to Ogilvy & Mather advertising agency and to numerous client companies in the United States, Europe, and Australia.

LARRY PERCY is an American, an experienced advertising research manager, and a jazz and art connoisseur. Now Visiting Professor at Oxford, and an advertising communications consultant, he was previously Vice President and Director of Strategic Research at Lintas: USA advertising agency in Detroit and New York. He began his advertising career at Young & Rubicam in New York and has been director of advertising research for several other leading agencies. In a part-time capacity, he has taught at Carnegie-Mellon University and the University of Pittsburgh, offering courses in marketing theory, advertising strategy, and advertising research.

Mr. Percy is author of a book on integrated marketing communications, coauthor and coeditor of two previous books on advertising theory, and has contributed over 50 conference papers and journal articles to the field. He has served as Industry Director of the Association for Consumer Research and sits on the editorial board of a number of journals, including the *Journal of Marketing Research.* He has also conducted numerous executive seminars, both throughout the United States and in Europe and Asia, on advertising communications management.

*To my father, a scientist who encouraged me to question
conventional wisdom and, by thinking and testing, to replace it
with something better.*

*—JRR*

*To all those who over the years have challenged and encouraged
me, most especially my friend and coauthor.*

*—LP*

# CONTENTS

**Preface**                                    **xiii**

---
## PART ONE
---

# AC&P and Marketing Objectives

### 1. ADVERTISING COMMUNICATIONS AND PROMOTIONS                                    3
Advertising Communications and
Promotions Defined                             3
AC&P and Strategic Marketing
Management                                     8
The Six-Step Effects Sequence                  11
Buyer Response Steps                           12
The Six Steps from the Manager's
Viewpoint                                      14
Summary                                        20
Notes                                          21
Discussion Questions                           23
Further Reading                                24

### 2. MARKETING OBJECTIVES AND BUDGET                                        25
Marketing Objectives for the Campaign          25
Three Avenues to Profit and Three Time
Horizons                                       26
Selling Price Objectives                       28
Cost Objectives                                29

Sales Volume Objectives                        30
Setting the Overall AC&P Budget                32
The Task Method                                34
The Management-Jury IAF/5Q Method              35
Budgeting for a New Product Category           37
Budgeting for a New Brand                      37
Budgeting for an Established Brand             40
Quality of Advertising Spending               43
Summary                                        44
Appendix                                       45
  2A. Strategies Based On Upside and
      Downside Elasticity                      45
  2B. When to Use Market Share Objectives      46
Notes                                          47
Discussion Questions                           52
Further Reading                                52

---
## PART TWO
---

# Target Audience Action Objectives

### 3. TARGET AUDIENCE SELECTION AND ACTION OBJECTIVES                             57
Target Audience Options                        57
Target Audience Selection via Leverage         61
Action Objectives                              63

Trial Objectives 64

Repeat Purchase Objectives 68

Distributors as Target Audiences 71

Summary 72

Appendix 74
   3A. *Universality of the Brand Loyalty Approach* 74
   3B. *Trial and Repeat Purchase Goals for*
     *Regularly Purchased Products and Services* 75

Notes 77

Discussion Questions 81

Further Reading 81

**4. BEHAVIORAL SEQUENCE MODEL FOR
SPECIFIC TARGETING** 83

Constructing a Behavioral Sequence Model 83

Profiling the Decision Participant 91

Summary 99

Notes 100

Discussion Questions 104

Further Reading 105

**PART THREE**

# Communication Objectives and Positioning

**5. COMMUNICATION OBJECTIVES** 109

The Five Communication Effects 109

1. Category Need 110

2. Brand Awareness 113

3. Brand Attitude 120

4. Brand Purchase Intention 126

5. Purchase Facilitation 128

Summary 129

Appendix 130
   5A. *Further Considerations for Brand Attitude* 130
   5B. *Purchase Inhibitors Must Be Facilitated* 132

Notes 132

Discussion Questions 138

Further Reading 139

**6. POSITIONING** 140

Positioning and Brand Position 140

The X-YZ Macromodel of Positioning
Location 141

The I-D-U Mesomodel of Benefit Emphasis 147

The a-b-e Micromodel of Benefit Focus 152

Positioning Statement 159

Summary 160

Appendix 161
   6A. *Target-Audience I-D-U Analysis* 161
   6B. *I-D-U and Multiattribute Strategies* 163
   6C. *Subliminal Sexual Imagery in Ads* 165

Notes 166

Discussion Questions 174

Further Reading 174

**PART FOUR**

# Creative Strategy

**7. THE CREATIVE IDEA** 177

Creative Strategy Sequence 177

The Creative Idea 178

Theory of Random Creativity 184

I-G-I Method of Brainstorming 191

RAM-Conveyor Theory of Creative Ideas 192

Long-Term Management of Creativity for the
Brand 198

Summary 199

Appendix 200
   7A. *Examples of Great Creative Ideas* 200
   7B. *Mathematical Basis of the Theory of Random*
     *Creativity* 202
   7C. *Random Creativity Benefits Everyone* 205

Notes 207

Discussion Questions 211

Further Reading 211

**8. CREATIVE EXECUTION TACTICS: BRAND
AWARENESS AND LOW-INVOLVEMENT
PERSUASION** 212

The Rossiter-Percy Grid 212

Learning: The Basis of Brand Awareness and
Low-Involvement Brand Attitude 214

Brand Awareness Tactics (Branding) 216

Brand Attitude Tactics (Persuasion) 224

Low-Involvement/Informational Tactics 224

Low-Involvement/Transformational Tactics 227

Summary 230

Appendix 231

8A. *Brand Recognition Versus Brand Recall
from TV Advertising* 231

8B. *Brand Name Recallability* 231

8C. *How Do You Make Claims "Extreme"?* 232

Notes 233

Discussion Questions 243

Further Reading 243

### 9. CREATIVE EXECUTION TACTICS: HIGH-INVOLVEMENT PERSUASION 244

Acceptance and the ALEA Model of
Processing: The Basis of High-Involvement
Brand Attitude 244

High-Involvement/Informational Tactics 246

High-Involvement/Transformational Tactics 255

The VisCAP Model of Presenter Selection 260

Summary 268

Appendix 269

9A. *Cognitive Response Theory* 269

9B. *Explicit Comparative Advertising—
Research Results* 269

9C. *Legal Requirements and Objectivity* 270

Notes 271

Discussion Questions 278

Further Reading 278

### 10. CREATIVE EXECUTION: ATTENTION AND THE STRUCTURE OF ADS 279

Attention: Its Function and Importance 279

TV Commercials 280

Radio Commercials 284

Print Ads: An Overview 288

Newspaper Ads 289

Consumer and General Business Magazine
Ads 292

Industrial Magazine Ads 298

Yellow Pages and Directory Display Ads 300

Outdoor and Poster Ads 303

Direct Response Ads 305

Summary 312

Notes 312

Discussion Questions 319

Further Reading 319

### PART FIVE

# Integrated Communications Strategy

### 11. CORPORATE ADVERTISING COMMUNICATIONS 323

Integrated Communications Strategy 323

Budget Allocation for IMC Activities 328

Corporation's Perspective 331

Corporate Identity and PR 333

Corporate Image Advertising 334

Sponsorships (Including Event Marketing
and Publicity) 339

Summary 341

Appendix 342

11A. *Avon's New IMC Strategy* 342

11B. *Corporate Design—Examples* 343

11C. *Crisis and Rumor Management* 343

11D. *Planning and Evaluating Sponsorships* 346

Notes 347

Discussion Questions 350

Further Reading 351

### 12. MANUFACTURER'S PROMOTIONS 352

Sales-Force Promotions 352

Trade Promotions 354

Customer or Consumer Trial Promotions 356

Repeat-Purchase Promotions 367

Summary 373

Appendix 375

12A. *Factors in Trade Show Promotion* 375

12B. *Direct Price-Off Presentation Tactics* 375

12C. *Social Reinforcement in Service
Transactions* 376

12D. *The Cusp-Catastrophe Model of High-
Involvement Repeat Purchases* 376

Notes 377

Discussion Questions 381

Further Reading 381

### 13. RETAILER'S PROMOTIONS 382

The Retailer's Marketing Perspective 382

Retail Layout and Atmosphere — 384
Retail Feature Ads — 388
POP Displays — 390
Price-Off Promotions — 391
Private Labeling — 392
TV or PC Interactive Shopping — 393
Summary — 395
Appendix — 396
  *13A. Grocery Store Shopping Statistics* — 396
  *13B. Who Responds to the Retail Price-Off?* — 397
  *13C. Implementing Retailer's Price-Offs* — 399
Notes — 400
Discussion Questions — 403
Further Reading — 403

**14. DIRECT MARKETING PROMOTIONS** — 404
Database Marketing — 404
Loyalty Programs — 411
Summary — 413
Notes — 414
Discussion Questions — 415
Further Reading — 415

**PART SIX**

# Media Strategy

**15. ADVERTISING AND IMC MEDIA SELECTION** — 419
Media Selection Based on Communication Objectives — 419
The Concepts of Primary and Secondary Media — 428
National Consumer Advertising — 430
Retail Advertising — 434
Industrial Advertising — 436
Corporate Image Advertising — 438
Direct Response Advertising — 439
Summary — 442
Notes — 444
Discussion Questions — 444
Further Reading — 445

**16. MEDIA STRATEGY: THE REACH PATTERN AND EFFECTIVE FREQUENCY** — 446
The Importance of Media Strategy and Its Parameters — 446
The Reach Pattern — 451
Effective Frequency — 457
Estimating Minimum Effective Frequency — 461
Scheduling Over Time: Short-Term Tactical Adjustments — 468
Summary — 469
Notes — 471
Discussion Questions — 475
Further Reading — 476

**17. MEDIA PLAN IMPLEMENTATION** — 477
First-Stage Selection of Media Vehicles by Direct Matching — 477
Adjustment Factors for Second-Stage Media Vehicle Selection — 481
Scheduling Insertions in the Vehicles — 489
Profit and the Media Schedule — 492
Summary — 493
Appendix — 495
  *17A. Schedule Implementation for the Smaller Advertiser* — 495
  *17B. Schedule Implementation for the Larger Advertiser* — 497
Notes — 498
Discussion Questions — 501
Further Reading — 502

**PART SEVEN**

# Advertising Research and Evaluation

**18. ADVERTISING STRATEGY RESEARCH** — 505
Situation Audit — 505
Qualitative Research — 519
Quantitative Research — 524
Advertising Strategy Summary — 532
Notes — 534
Further Reading — 537

**19. CONCEPT DEVELOPMENT RESEARCH, MJTs, AND AD TESTING** 538

An Example: AT&T's "Cost of Visit" Campaign 538
Concept Development Research 540
Management Judgment Tests (MJTs) 548
The Purpose of Ad Testing and the Decision to Test 550
Syndicated Ad Testing: MSW and ARS 553
Custom-Designed Ad Test (Rossiter-Percy Method) 555
Screening Questions and Pre-Measures 563
Processing Measures 564
Communication Effects Measures 566
Communication Failure 571
Buyer Behavior Measures 572
Testing Promotion Offers 572
Notes 576
Further Reading 584

**20. CAMPAIGN TRACKING AND EVALUATION** 585

Measures Used in Tracking 585
Methodology for Tracking Studies 590
Applications of Tracking 596
How Often to Track 597
What Is "Wearout"? 598
First Check: The Marketing Plan 599
Second Check: The Media Plan 601
Final Check: The Advertisements Themselves 602
Summary of Advertising Wearout Solutions 605
Notes 606
Discussion Questions 609
Further Reading 609

**Appendix: AC&P Plan** 611
**Index** 625

# PREFACE

*Advertising Communications and Promotion Management,* Second Edition, builds on the previous Rossiter and Percy book, *Advertising and Promotion Management,* which many regard as the definitive text in the field. Like the previous book, the new one is written for:

- MBA students taking a marketing course in advertising management or marketing communications management, and undergraduate students in managerial, as opposed to merely descriptive, advertising courses.
- Managers in client companies and advertising agencies who wish to update and advance their on-the-job planning for advertising communications and promotion.

However, the main reason this new book is much more than a revision of the earlier one is its accommodation of the "integrated marketing communications" (IMC) revolution. Shortly after the appearance of the earlier text in 1987, the whole field of advertising and promotion changed radically and irrevocably, becoming conceived much more broadly than before. We took the time to observe and reflect about where the new integrated advertising communications and promotion (AC&P) field should be heading. Therefore, you will find:

- A new name for the book—*Advertising Communications and Promotion Management*—reflecting the integration of mainstream advertising with corporate communications, direct response advertising, and promotions.
- A completely new section of the book (Part Five) covering integrated communications strategy.
- The section on media strategy (Part Six) appropriately expanded to incorporate both traditional advertising media *and* the new media.
- A broader perspective taken throughout, with more emphasis on corporate communications and business products and services in addition to the traditional focus on consumer packaged goods.

Advertising is more important than ever under the new advertising *communications* approach. As we explain in this book, advertising planning and execution skills have experienced greater demand in the new integrated communications era. Two observations, one from creative strategy and one from media strategy, underscore the increased role of advertising. The first observation is that the two largest IMC activities (in other words, activities *not* regarded as traditional advertising), telemarketing and direct response advertising, depend the *most* on advertising copywriting skills. For agencies, their advertising copywriting skills are called upon much more than in the previous era of TV advertising dominance. The second observation is that the most visible achievement of the IMC revolution is to vastly expand the media options available to the advertiser: Now, almost every contact with customers, from packaging to public relations, has to be considered as a potential advertising medium. This much greater range of options requires the media planner to have much better skills than in the past—but they are an expansion of the same skills of advertising media selection and scheduling that have always been required. These and other realizations confirm that advertising has become much more important in the new era. We call the new field *advertising communications,* rather than simply advertising, to signify the broader perspective incorporating related communications.

In this book, we contribute some very new developments to advertising communications and promotion theory. You will find, in addition to the aforementioned general changes:

- A new and advanced method of choosing a positioning strategy (Chapter 6).
- A provocative chapter on "the creative idea" (Chapter 7), which includes our new random creativity procedure for commissioning an advertising campaign and a new model of effective creativity in advertising.
- Updated Rossiter-Percy grid tactics (Chapters 8 and 9) for brand awareness and low- and high-involvement persuasion.
- A new chapter on "attention and the structure of ads" (Chapter 10), which enables the small advertiser, and students working in project teams, to construct their own ads.
- A breakthrough chapter on media strategy (Chapter 16), which introduces our new concept of reach patterns as well as effective frequency in the new media environment.
- Updated and decisive coverage of concept development research, management judgment tests, and ad testing (Chapter 19) and campaign tracking and evaluation (Chapter 20).

*Advertising Communications and Promotion Management,* Second Edition, is much expanded in coverage but retains the successful framework of our previous book. We believe that this new book can guide your advertising communications and promotion planning for the foreseeable future.

Although much of its content is radically new, this book covers all the standard, major topics in advertising communications and promotion management. Questions covered in the seven parts of the book include the following.

- What are the purposes of advertising communications and promotion? How should the manager plan, overall, for these activities? (AC&P and Marketing Objectives)
- How does a target audience differ from a market segment, and how is the target audience selected? Should the behavioral objective for the campaign be purchase action, or should it be prior, purchase-related action? (Target Audience Action Objectives)
- What overall communication objectives have to be addressed to produce the desired action? In terms of communication content, in what category will the brand be positioned, and how is the target audience decision maker to be addressed? Which benefits should be emphasized, which only mentioned, and which perhaps omitted in the brand's advertising and promotions? (Communication Objectives and Positioning)
- How vital is the creative idea for the campaign? Do ads have to be believable and likable in order to be effective? When should creative techniques such as comparative advertising, a special presenter, or humor be used? (Creative Strategy)
- Which other forms of advertising communications—such as corporate image advertising, sponsorships, and publicity—will work best for the company and the brand? How can promotions be integrated with advertising communications not only to create short-term sales increases but also to contribute to long-term sales? (Integrated Communications Strategy)
- Which primary and secondary media should be selected for consumer, retail, industrial, corporate, or direct response campaigns? Why are the reach pattern and minimum effective frequency the dual keys to media scheduling? (Media Strategy)
- How can qualitative research be used in conjunction with quantitative research to develop an advertising communication strategy for the brand? How should ads and promotion offers be developed and tested? How should campaigns be tracked and evaluated? (Advertising Research)

We discuss and recommend answers to all these questions, and many more. And at the end of the book, to summarize our approach, we also provide an advertising communications and promotion checklist plan for use by managers.

We'd again like to thank everyone who helped on our earlier book (see the Preface to *Advertising and Promotion Management*). The first book established the Rossiter-Percy framework. In this new book, which builds on that framework, most of the new thinking was done by the authors themselves. But we would particularly like to thank our esteemed German colleague, the late Werner Kroeber-Riel, for his inspiring work in advertising theory and advertising expert systems (we know he'll hear these thanks); Lawrence Ang, John Rossiter's doctoral student at the AGSM, for his major contributions to the new creativity model; Sharat Mathur of AGSM and Rosemary Kalapurakal of Women, Ink., New York, for their contributions to our random creativity theory; Don Schultz of Northwestern University for his kind advice on the integrated marketing communications perspective; Glenn Myatt of the Australian Tourist Commission for enhancing the managerial relevance of the sections on positioning research and media strategy; Kevin Keller of University of North Carolina, Chapel Hill, and Gary Lilien of Pennsylvania State Univeristy, for their advice and encouragement with the new book; and Vicki Staudte, then of Campbell-Mithun-Esty, Minneapolis, for valuable comments on the early drafts.

We would like to thank our reviewers: Avery Abernethy, Auburn University; Simeon Chow, Boston University; Cornelia Droge, Michigan State University; David Eppright, University of West Florida; Don Granbois, Indiana University; Douglas Hausknecht, University of Akron; Dan Putler, Purdue University; Bonnie Reece, Michigan State University; Jane Reid, Youngstown State University; and, Doug Stayman, Cornell University.

We would especially like to thank Terry Domzal of George Mason University for her expert help with the final draft and for finding pertinent examples; Tonette Tokura, Sacha Homan, Celest Kenny, and Tracey Dourlay for their diligent research assistance; and Mary O'Sullivan and Marijn van den Heiden for their exemplary skills in bringing the manuscript to completion. The first author thanks the Unilever-Erasmus Foundation and his colleagues, including Ale Smidts, Fred van Raaij, and Berend Wierenga, at the Rotterdam School of Management, where he visited in 1995–1996, for their generous support. We'd also like to thank Bonnie Binkert and Karen Westover, as well as Dan Alpert and Jane Brundage, our keen editors at McGraw-Hill. Sharla Volkersz of McGraw-Hill deserves special thanks for her superb management of the text's production stages as does our copyeditor, Brian Jones, for his fine editing of its expression and prose.

John R. Rossiter
Larry Percy
*December 1996*

## PART ONE

# AC&P AND MARKETING OBJECTIVES

**CHAPTER 1: ADVERTISING COMMUNICATIONS AND PROMOTIONS**

**CHAPTER 2: MARKETING OBJECTIVES AND BUDGET**

# Advertising Communications and Promotions

This chapter defines the nature and purpose of advertising communications and promotions[1] in accordance with an integrated marketing communications perspective, and shows how they fit into the general process of marketing management. We introduce a six-step advertising communications and promotion (AC&P) plan for the manager to follow. After reading this chapter, you should be able to:

- Distinguish the basic purposes of advertising communications and promotions.
- Appreciate how they can be "integrated" in an overall marketing communications program.
- Learn the six-step AC&P effects sequence.
- Learn the four buyer response steps.
- See how the manager proceeds "from the top down" in formulating the AC&P plan.

## ADVERTISING COMMUNICATIONS AND PROMOTIONS DEFINED

Advertising communications and promotions are viewed by marketing managers as highly interrelated yet specialized means of informing prospective and current customers about products and services, and persuading them to buy. Advertising communications and promotions are highly interrelated in that they both rely on the communication process for their effects and are so often used together—especially in integrated marketing communications (IMC) programs.

Yet they are specialized because of the specific effectiveness of the techniques available for each. These techniques are introduced in overview in Figure 1.1.

The differences and similarities between advertising communications and promotions can be defined from both conceptual and practical perspectives.

### Conceptual Perspective

The basic conceptual *difference* between advertising communications and promotions is suggested by the Latin origins of the two terms (Table 1.1).

- *Advertising communications* are often regarded as a relatively *indirect* form of persuasion, based on information or emotional appeals about product benefits, designed to create favorable mental impressions that "turn the mind toward" purchase.
- *Promotions* are often regarded as a more *direct* form of persuasion, based frequently on external incentives rather than inherent product benefits, designed to stimulate immediate purchase and to "move sales forward" more rapidly than would otherwise occur.

The main conceptual *similarity* between advertising communications and promotions is that both are forms of marketing communication: they can be used to achieve the same communication objectives for the brand. As we shall see later, not only advertising communications but also promotions can be used

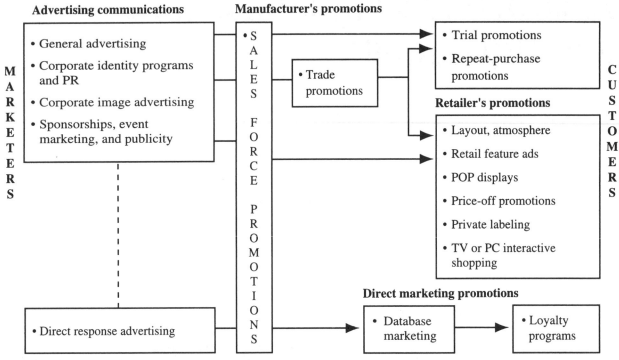

**FIGURE 1.1**
Advertising communications and promotions: an overview.

to generate awareness, establish or change attitudes, and stimulate purchase intentions. Both advertising communications and promotions have the potential for building *brand equity* in the form of a "customer franchise" of people with a relatively permanent preference for the brand, as well as for creating "nonfranchise" effects in the form of temporary buyers of the brand.[2] The extent to which they can do so by using the same message gives rise to IMC: *integrating marketing communications.*

**Practical Perspective**

Managers, in practice, regard advertising communications and promotion as consisting of a set of *techniques* from which they can select one or several for a particular campaign. These sets of techniques mix advertising communications and promotions, depending on the manager's purpose, which differs according to whether the manager is a business advertiser, a consumer advertiser, or a retail advertiser. In providing the list for each, we have tried to use the names that

| TABLE 1.1 | | |
|---|---|---|
| **LATIN ORIGINS OF THE TERMS "ADVERTISING COMMUNICATIONS" AND "PROMOTIONS"[a]** | | |
| **Term** | **Latin origin** | **Functional translation** |
| Advertising communications | *Advertere* = to turn toward | Advertising communications aim to turn the buyer or consumer's mind toward purchase. |
| Promotions | *Promovere* = to move forward or advance | Promotions aim to immediately stimulate purchase. |

[a]As far as we can tell, the famous marketing researcher and former Harvard professor of advertising Daniel Starch was the first to mention advertising's Latin root as a means of explaining the term (D. Starch, *Principles of Advertising,* Chicago: A. W. Shaw, 1926). The notion of advertising "turning the *mind* toward" purchase was suggested by Dirksen and Kroeger (C. J. Dirksen and A. Kroeger, *Advertising Principles, Problems, and Cases,* Homewood, IL: Irwin, 1960).

each type of manager would use, regardless of conceptual overlaps in the techniques.

The *business* advertising manager, who advertises and promotes to other businesses, mainly chooses from 10 techniques:[3]

1. Media advertising (TV, radio, newspaper, business or consumer magazines)
2. Trade journal advertising
3. Directories
4. Direct response advertising (main media, direct mail, interactive TV or PC)
5. Brochures, sales literature, audiovisual presentation tapes
6. Telemarketing
7. Loyalty programs
8. Sponsorships or event marketing
9. Exhibitions, trade shows, and conventions
10. Publicity and public relations

The *consumer* advertising manager, who advertises and promotes the company's products or services to consumers, mainly chooses from eight techniques:

1. Media advertising (TV, radio, newspaper, magazines, and, in many countries, cinema)
2. Direct response advertising (usually in main media but sometimes via direct mail or interactive TV or PC)
3. Outdoor advertising (billboards, posters)
4. On-package or point-of-purchase (POP) advertising
5. Trade promotions (sales promotions that favor distributors)
6. Consumer promotions (sales promotions that favor consumers)
7. Sponsorships or event marketing
8. Publicity and public relations

The *retail* advertising manager, who also advertises and promotes to consumers, mainly chooses from 10 techniques:[4]

1. Local media advertising (TV, radio, local newspapers, regional editions of magazines, or cinema, where available)
2. Local direct response advertising (catalogs, interactive TV or PC shopping, brochures, flyers)
3. Retail coupons (usually co-op with manufacturer) distributed in local print media or door-to-door

4. Local outdoor advertising (billboards, posters, signs)
5. In-store displays
6. Displays with feature price
7. Shelf tags
8. Store events
9. Local sponsorships
10. Private labeling

We will see that the various techniques of advertising communication and promotion can be linked by a common set of communication objectives in reaching designated target audiences and influencing their actions. The manager's task is to *select* the best one or several techniques for the communication objectives to be achieved by the campaign. Also, given the diversity of techniques, the manager should attempt to *integrate* the marketing communication messages if more than one advertising or promotion technique is used in a given campaign.

### Increased Importance of Advertising

Overall in the United States, it is estimated that about $180 billion is spent on advertising communications and about $160 billion on promotions, a ratio of 53 percent to 47 percent.[5] However, the relative figures are fuzzy because of the increased emphasis on *integrated* marketing communications. (For instance, consider the Arm & Hammer Detergent exhibit in Figure 1.2: Is it an ad, or is it a promotion offer?) We believe that the actual breakdown is more like a ratio of 75 percent advertising communications to 25 percent promotions, heavily emphasizing advertising when advertising is more broadly defined, as explained next.

We emphasize advertising in this book and downplay the alleged shift over to promotion. Our reasons are twofold: (1) There has, in fact, been an *increase,* not a decrease, in use of the general media of advertising in the last decade; what has changed is the *number of media options available* for advertising, which makes it *appear* that the main advertising media are being favored less by marketers. (2) Most of the growth in promotion, apart from "forced" trade promotions, has been *additional*—and mostly in *adlike* promotions.

In support of the first point, it is instructive to compare U.S. advertising expenditures for 1993, the most recent year for which detailed data are available, with those of a decade earlier, before the alleged swing

**FIGURE 1.2**
Arm & Hammer detergent promotion offer—or is it an advertisement? *Courtesy:* Church & Dwight Co., Inc., Arm & Hammer Division.

away from traditional advertising.[6] Newspaper advertising spending grew from $20.6 billion in 1983 to $31.8 billion in 1993; TV (noncable) from $16.4 billion to $28.1 billion, and cable TV from $0.3 billion to $2.5 billion; radio from $5.2 billion to $9.4 billion; magazines from $4.2 billion to $7.4 billion; and so forth. Even allowing for inflation over the decade, it is simply not true that the traditional media have experienced a defection by advertisers. Moreover, advertising expenditures are expected to increase at an annual rate of over 6 percent during the next 5 years.[7] The new reality is that the *number and variety of media options* for both advertising and advertised promotions have increased. As we shall demonstrate in Chapter 15, these newer IMC media are best regarded from the manager's perspective *as if they were additional advertising media,* just like the traditional ad-

vertising media, and not as nonadvertising means of communicating about the brand.

The second point debunks the myth that sales promotions are displacing advertising. If anything, the reverse of this myth is true. For instance, freestanding inserts in newspapers (FSIs) have virtually taken over in coupon promotions, with 80 to 85 percent of all coupons now distributed via FSIs.[8] There's no doubt that FSIs are *ads:* they advertise both the brand *and* a promotion. Furthermore, telemarketing, which is by far the biggest ($60 million in 1993) and fastest-growing form of promotion, is *advertising-like,* even though it's technically classified as promotion because it "moves sales forward" more quickly than traditional advertising does. Essentially, telemarketing is direct response advertising over the phone. Relatedly, the enormous growth of direct mail, the third largest medium of advertising (or the fourth if you include telemarketing as advertising, which we do), has produced an increased demand for *traditional* advertising (read: copywriting) skills. And finally, the emergence of interactive TV or PC advertising also increases demand for traditional copywriting. Advertising is in very good shape indeed.

Most of the promotional (and IMC) revolution, therefore, has been toward *more advertising.* Table 1.2 shows our estimate of the incidence of advertising versus promotion, with the former defined as *advertising or advertising-like communications* and the latter defined as *price-related promotions.* The ratio is 75 percent to 25 percent in favor of advertising broadly defined.

There's no doubt that the *planning and management* of advertising and promotion have changed in the past decade. This is best reflected in the concept of integrated marketing communications (IMC), discussed next. But advertising principles—particularly as embodied in creative strategy and media strategy—have only become *more* important in the new era.

### Integrated Marketing Communications (IMC)

The emphasis in contemporary advertising management is on *integrated marketing communications*—IMC—for a brand. (Throughout this book we will use the word "brand" to stand for whatever is being promoted. As indicated in Figure 1.2, this may be a company, institution, product, service, issue or cause or idea, or person.) By "integrated marketing communications" or simply "integrated communications" we

## TABLE 1.2

**ESTIMATED 1993 U .S. AC&P EXPENDITURES**

(*Three-quarters of expenditures comprise advertising or advertising-like communications* (*indicated by* +) *and only one-quarter comprises promotions.*)

| Advertising or advertising-like communications (+) | Expenditures (billions) | Price-related promotions | Expenditures (billions) |
|---|---|---|---|
| Telemarketing (+) | $60 | Trade promotions | $38 |
| Newspaper advertising | $32 | Consumer promotions[b] | $18 |
| TV (including cable TV) | $31 | POP price-offs, displays | $16 |
| Direct mail | $27 | Total | $72 |
| Miscellaneous[a] | $27 | Percentage | 25% |
| *Yellow Pages* | $10 | | |
| Radio | $9 | | |
| Trade shows (+) | $9 | | |
| Magazine | $7 | | |
| Sponsorships (+) | $3 | | |
| Outdoor | $1 | | |
| Place-based ads | $1 | | |
| Publicity (+) | n.a. | | |
| Total | $217 | | |
| Percentage | 75% | | |

[a]Miscellaneous includes directories (other than the *Yellow Pages*), weekly shoppers, pamphlets, and other nonmeasured media, including the Internet.
[b]Consumer promotions include FSIs, which are arguably advertising and are certainly adlike.
*Sources: Marketer's Guide to Media,* 1994; Shergill, 1993; and other specialized references (see note 6).

mean the (1) selective combination of appropriate types of advertising and promotion, (2) meeting a *common set of communication objectives* for the brand and, more particularly, to support a *singular "macropositioning"* for the brand, and (3) integration *over time* with regard to customers. Selective combination is pursued, for instance, by Volvo, which is advertised as an upscale automobile in the United States and sponsors professional tennis and golf tournaments, both upscale sports. The singular macropositioning of McDonald's, as a family-appeal company, sees it advertising only in noncontroversial media and gaining image-appropriate publicity for its investment in a chain of children's play centers. Integration over time with regard to customers is important, too; for instance, in the timing of trade and consumer promotions, and especially in one-on-one (direct) database marketing.

The new emphasis on IMC has changed advertising communications and promotion (AC&P) planning in at least four ways:[9]

**1.** *Locating the Responsibility for Overall AC&P Coordination.* On the client side, it is usually the advertising manager (or marketing manager or product manager if there is not a specialized advertising man-

ager) who is responsible for coordinating integrated marketing communications for the brand. On the agency side, it is *sometimes* the advertising agency that does the coordination of media advertising, direct response, sales promotion, and PR; these latter functions may be located within one full-service agency or hired by the agency as services from external subcontractors. But it is far more common for separate specialist firms to be hired by the client for each function. It seems likely that the IMC approach to AC&P planning will continue to be dominated by the advertiser rather than the agency, and we basically endorse this.[10] A practical reason for advertiser dominance is that advertisers can best control the problem of different compensation methods among the various functions, and most are doing this with a fee system. But the main reason is conceptual: IMC strategy should be coordinated by the *advertiser* (the client advertising manager), as should all strategy, in our view. Agencies and other specialist suppliers should recommend and perform the tactical implementation.

**2.** *Deciding the Point of Entry.* Although advertising will usually be the main component of an IMC campaign, this does not mean that the campaign must necessarily begin with advertising.[11] New prestige brands may choose to launch with exclusive distribution (for example, Perrier launched in the United States originally by distributing to trendy restaurants, and Redken launched via hairdressing salons—then both brands broadened their distribution and used mass media advertising later). Or the launch may be by planned publicity (for example, Paul Newman's "Newman's Own" salad dressing was launched via news items in magazines and was only later advertised). Small brands may use trade promotions to get distribution and shelf space, and employ clever packaging on the shelf, perhaps combined with in-store samples if appropriate (for example, Smartfood Popcorn, now owned by Frito-Lay, entered the market this way). In Chapter 4, we show how the construction of a *behavioral sequence model* for the brand can identify the best point of entry from among marketing communications options, and various points of contact from among subsequent options, to stimulate and maintain sales with the target audience. Following the point of entry, IMC requires integration *over time* when contacting the prospective customer.

3. *Much Wider Intermedia Coordination.* In IMC, the media choices extend beyond conventional advertising media and may include sales promotion media, such as sampling, coupons, or loyalty programs; corporate PR media, such as press releases, special events, or sponsorships; and direct response media, such as direct response ads in mass media, or by mail, by telephone, in home, or at the point of purchase. Indeed, for many companies, the product's *distribution outlets* themselves have virtually become an advertising medium.[12] For instance, McDonald's golden-arches signs serve as a reminder ad, and point-of-purchase promotions within the McDonald's store also contribute to McDonald's overall advertising presence. In Chapter 15, we offer a systematic way to select among *all* IMC media. Increased intermedia coordination is now required of managers in buying and scheduling these wider media options.

4. *Consistency of Positioning in Campaigns Aimed at Multiple Target Audiences.* Most IMC campaigns in the true sense of *integrated communications* will be reaching multiple target audiences: the company's own employees, its sales force, the trade, buyers or consumers, and often government officials as well. The action objectives and particular communication objectives for these target audiences may differ, but

IMC's purpose is to keep the macropositioning of the brand—as reflected in the *broad content* of its communication objectives—as consistent as possible. Chapter 6 conceptualizes positioning with consistency in mind, and Chapter 11 specifically examines IMC's functions with regard to the extent of consistency of positioning that should be applied.

Having defined what advertising communications and promotions (AC&P) are about, we now look at how they fit into marketing.

## AC&P AND STRATEGIC MARKETING MANAGEMENT

### Marketing Strategy Principles

It is useful now to put advertising communications and promotions in context by reviewing their role in strategic marketing management. Marketing management can be conceptualized in a strategic framework that identifies four basic principles (Figure 1.3).[13]

First, the manager makes an assessment of *company resources*—financial, technical, and managerial—vis-à-vis the major competitors' resources. The strategic principle in this assessment is to identify *differen-*

**FIGURE 1.3**
Marketing strategy framework. The capitalized phrases denote the four strategy components, with their strategy principles in parentheses.

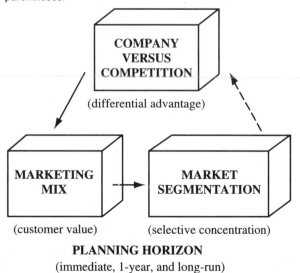

COMPANY VERSUS COMPETITION
(differential advantage)

MARKETING MIX
(customer value)

MARKET SEGMENTATION
(selective concentration)

**PLANNING HORIZON**
(immediate, 1-year, and long-run)

*tial advantages,* which can be parlayed into superior marketplace performance and financial success. The competitive orientation is frequently as vital to success as the customer orientation which underlies the marketing concept.[14] A great deal of advertising communications and promotion planning is competitor-oriented rather than customer-oriented, and in competitive situations, the manager does not have to generate the best (or ideal) plan but rather a plan that is better than those of competitors. Most managers have to simultaneously adopt a customer orientation and a competitor orientation.

Second, the manager reviews the controllable inputs to the market, most importantly the company's product or products (or services) but also the other three Ps, which together make up the famous 4Ps of the *marketing mix:* price, place (distribution), and promotion. The strategic principle underlying marketing mix management is the provision of *customer value,* which is a set of utilities deriving from the 4Ps: product and service benefits; price-value and payment terms; distribution convenience and store image; and promotional rewards.[15]

Third, customer value is packaged to appeal to particular *target markets.* Target markets include trade distributors as well as ultimate buyers and consumers. This introduces the third facet of marketing strategy: target market selection. The strategic principle here is *selective concentration* (market segmentation and concentration of financial and marketing resources) on markets that represent the best profit potential. The marketing mix, one for each target market, is fine-tuned to deliver maximal customer value to the target market.

Fourth, marketing strategy must be formulated in relation to a particular *planning horizon.* Immediate, 1-year, and long-run objectives and strategies must be planned in terms of anticipated changes in the future environment. Technical, economic, political, legal, and sociocultural trends must be estimated while adhering to the three principles of differential advantage in relation to competitors, customer value in the marketing mix, and selective concentration on target markets.

Advertising communications and promotion planning, as part of marketing strategy, should be conducted in accordance with these four basic principles of strategic marketing management. General illustrations follow.

**1.** *Differential Advantage.* Advertising budgets and superior advertising creativity are sources of differential advantage for the firm. So too are promotion budgets, especially during price wars, and also the correct selection of promotion techniques for new and existing products.

**2.** *Customer Value.* Advertising can provide customer value and build brand equity by signifying brand reliability, informing customers about product and service benefits and availability, or conferring a desired image or status upon the user. Promotions can provide customer value by providing rewards for immediate purchase, most often monetary rewards in the form of discounts or savings, but also participatory rewards as in promotional contests and sweepstakes.

**3.** *Selective Concentration.* Advertising is most often selectively aimed at target customers who are prospectively or currently loyal to the brand. Promotions are most often aimed at target customers on the fringe of the loyal segment, to induce them to try or rebuy the brand.

**4.** *Time Factor.* Advertising generally has a longer planning (and effects) horizon than do promotions, although both can be used as elements of immediate, 1-year, and long-run marketing strategies.

These are the general strategic considerations for advertising communications and promotion planning. In the next several sections, we examine more specific considerations.

### The New Marketing Mix

The new emphasis on integrated marketing communications (IMC) has produced a new marketing mix (Figure 1.4). The traditional 4Ps of product, price, place, and promotion are all there—but reconfigured.

**FIGURE 1.4**

The new marketing mix. Integrated marketing communications (IMC) are viewed as promoting the 4Ps overall. *Sources:* see note 16.

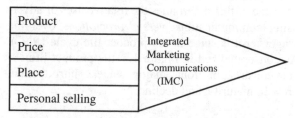

The fourth P becomes just personal selling, which all companies have in their marketing mix to some degree; and promotion in the broad sense becomes "integrated marketing communications," which promote the *total* marketing mix.[16] Marketing communication of the *product or service* occurs through its packaging or design, and of course through advertising and publicity. Marketing communication of the *price* is through the selection of prestige, competitive, or value pricing, and through retail ads. Marketing communication of the *place* is through the distribution channel as a promotional vehicle, such as store atmosphere and point-of-purchase ads and promotions. Marketing communication of *personal selling* is through exhibits such as trade shows and, increasingly, preselling via a commercial Web page on the Internet. Thus, all of the 4Ps are promoted by integrated marketing communications.

However, whereas "integrated marketing communications" is an appropriate overall description, managers still make decisions between "advertising" (now including advertising communications more broadly) and "promotions" (meaning *price-related* promotions, or simply, sales promotions). Accordingly, we will maintain the distinction between advertising communications, broadly considered, and promotions, meaning price-related promotions. When we don't need or wish to differentiate, we will use the joint term AC&P.

**Overall Emphasis.** The overall emphasis on AC&P versus *personal selling* differs by type of business. An early study by Udell[17] asked managers to judge the importance of advertising communications and promotion relative to personal selling. Udell's results indicated that industrial product managers place less importance (31 percent) on AC&P than on personal selling; that consumer durable goods managers place about equal emphasis (52 percent) on AC&P and personal selling; and that, as expected, for consumer packaged goods managers, AC&P is more important (62 percent) than personal selling.

**Emphasis Over the Product Life Cycle.** The main factor that determines the relative uses of advertising communications *versus* promotions over the longer term is stage in the product life cycle (PLC). As conceptualized in Figure 1.5, the product life cycle consists of four major stages: introduction, growth, maturity, and decline.[18]

**Market performance**

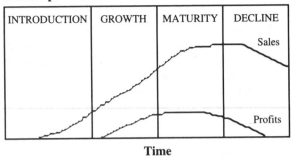

**FIGURE 1.5**
Product life cycle (PLC) stages.

Advertising communications and promotion expenditures in the *introduction* stage are typically both high (Table 1.3).[19] A high level of advertising is needed to make people aware of the newly introduced product and to communicate its benefits for prospective buyers' considerations. However, a high level of promotion is also needed to further build awareness and to induce people to try the new product.

Advertising communications and promotion strategies in the *growth* stage may differ depending on whether the brand is (a) either the market share leader or well-differentiated from other brands in the product category, or (b) an imitative, "me-too" brand. In

**TABLE 1.3**

**RELATIVE ROLES OF ADVERTISING COMMUNICATIONS AND PROMOTIONS ACCORDING TO PRODUCT LIFE CYCLE (PLC) STAGES[a]**

| PLC stage | Advertising communications | Promotions |
|---|---|---|
| 1. Introduction | High | High |
| 2. Growth | | |
|   (a) Leader or differentiated | High | Low |
|   (b) Me-too product | Low | High |
| 3. Maturity | | |
|   (a) High brand loyalty | High | Low |
|   (b) Low brand loyalty | Low | High |
| 4. Decline | None | Low (trade) |

[a]After R. A. Strang, *The Promotional Planning Process*, New York: Praeger, 1980, p. 82. Reprinted with permission of Greenwood Publishing Group, Inc., Westport, CT.

the former instance, advertising is emphasized as a means of maintaining brand identity and differentiation. In the latter instance, advertising can be lower because the imitator can capitalize on the leader's advertising. Correspondingly, promotion is higher so as to induce trial of, and switching to, the me-too brand.

Advertising communications and promotion strategies in the *maturity* stage may also differ, this time depending on whether the brand has managed to engender (a) high or (b) low brand loyalty. Brands with high loyalty usually will emphasize advertising to maintain the successful brand image. Brands with a low degree of loyalty, on the other hand, usually will have to emphasize promotions as a means of attracting and holding buyers.

Advertising communications and promotions in the *decline* stage of the product life cycle are phased out as the manager tries to minimize marketing costs. Advertising is discontinued. Promotions, however, are continued at a low level—to distributors—to keep the product in stock while the manufacturer's inventory is reduced to zero.

Altogether, though, marketing managers make strategic use of *both* advertising communications and promotions. It is not sufficient to regard advertising and promotion as independent. Rather, advertising and promotion embrace sets of specialized techniques to achieve *integrated* marketing purposes with the choice of techniques varying according to the factors we have outlined.

## THE SIX-STEP EFFECTS SEQUENCE

Advertising communications and promotions, and indeed the policy of integrating AC&P, have one ultimately desired effect—to contribute to company profits. A firm would not, or should not, spend money on advertising communications or promotions unless the expenditure more than pays for itself by ultimately increasing or protecting profit. Things are not as simple as this, however. Advertising communications and promotions have to produce a series of *prior* effects which, if successfully accomplished, *lead* to profit.

Our approach identifies a six-step effects sequence for AC&P (Figure 1.6): exposure → processing → communication effects and brand position → target audience action → sales or market share and brand

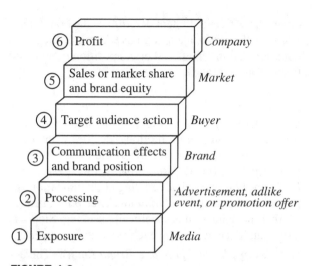

**FIGURE 1.6**
Six-step effects sequence. The effects are in the boxes. The levels at which the effects operate are shown in italics.

equity → profit. We will now explain each of these six steps in turn.

**1.** *Exposure.* In order for advertising communications or promotions to be successful, the prospective buyer must first be *exposed* to the advertisement, adlike event, or promotion offer. This means that the ad, adlike event, or promotion offer must be placed so that the prospective buyer can see, read, or hear it, as appropriate. Exposure takes place via advertising or promotion *media*. Step 1 is exposure (via media).

**2.** *Processing.* The prospective buyer must next *process* (respond to) one or more elements in the ad, adlike event, or promotion offer if it is to have an effect. Processing consists of *immediate* responses to elements of an ad, adlike event, or promotion offer— namely, attention, learning, emotional responses, and acceptance. Step 2 is processing (of the ad or adlike event or promotion offer).

**3.** *Communication Effects and Brand Position.* Immediate responses to an ad, adlike event, or promotion offer have to produce more permanent responses—associated with the *brand*. These more permanent, brand-connected responses are called *communication effects.* Two universally necessary communication effects are *brand awareness* and *brand attitude.* (We will discuss other communication effects later.) Their content determines the brand's *position* in the target audience buyer's mind. Step 3 is communication effects and brand position (connected to and for the brand).

**4.** *Target Audience Action.* Communication effects and the brand's position are elicited when the prospective buyer—a member of the *target audience* for the advertising or promotion—decides whether or not to take *action* with regard to the brand, such as purchasing the brand. More broadly, this is *buyer behavior,* although in an advertising communications or promotion context, it is *target audience buyer behavior* that the campaign is specifically seeking. Step 4 is target audience action (by each prospective buyer).

**5.** *Sales or Market Share and Brand Equity.* The actions of individual buyers of the brand cumulate to produce *sales.* In comparison with the sales of competing brands in a category or market, sales can be expressed as *market share.* More recently, brand equity (the brand's strength as measured by its price elasticity of demand) has been added to this step. Step 5 is sales or market share as well as brand equity (in a market).

**6.** *Profit.* From the company's standpoint, sales are worthwhile only insofar as they lead to profit. If advertising communications and promotions are supposed to produce sales, then they must be accountable for producing *profit* too. Step 6 is profit (for the company).

Briefly, these are the six steps that form the six-step effects sequence for advertising communications and promotions. We now examine these steps from the potential buyer's perspective, and then from the manager's perspective.

## BUYER RESPONSE STEPS

The first four steps (exposure → processing → communication effects and brand position → target audience action) are called the *buyer response steps* (Figure 1.7). All advertising communications and promotion campaigns attempt to influence this sequence of steps. An example will help to illustrate why the four buyer response steps are necessary for advertising, adlike events, or promotion to be successful.

Exposure, processing, communication effects and brand position, and action are the steps that you yourself go through when you buy a product as a result of

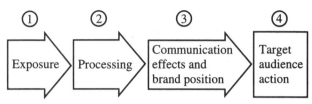

**FIGURE 1.7**
Buyer response steps. Note that these are the first four steps in the overall six-step effects sequence.

advertising communications (or promotion). Think of the TV advertising campaign that introduced Healthy Choice frozen dinners not so long ago. (Later we will use more business and services examples. But Healthy Choice was the most successful consumer packaged goods brand launched since Coca-Cola a hundred years ago, and most readers, Americans anyway, are familiar with it.)

**1.** *Exposure.* The ConAgra Company, makers of Healthy Choice, ran a very heavy TV ad campaign to introduce this brand. So unless you were an absolute non–TV watcher, you were undoubtedly *exposed* to one or more commercials for Healthy Choice dinners.

**2.** *Processing.* You probably paid attention to some parts, such as the visuals of the package or the name of the spokesperson, of at least one of the commercials. So you probably *processed* the Healthy Choice ads to some, or perhaps a considerable, degree.

**3.** *Communication Effects and Brand Position.* There are usually several communication effects. If you learned the brand name from the advertising and remembered what the new brand looks like, you attained *brand awareness.* If you also formed an opinion for or against Healthy Choice dinners, you attained *brand attitude.* The learned contents of brand awareness and brand attitude largely determine the brand's *position* in your mind. If the brand's position is favorable, then you may take the final step intended for the target audience—action.

**4.** *Target Audience Action.* The relevant action for Healthy Choice dinners is purchase. If you purchased a Healthy Choice dinner, then the advertising influenced you successfully.

Of course, advertising is rarely responsible, by itself, for purchase. You may have received a coupon in your Sunday newspaper for a Healthy Choice dinner, inviting you to try the product at 50¢ off. This coupon promotion would have had to have attained exactly the same four buyer response steps as the advertisement if it influenced your purchase. (The buyer response steps apply to *all* types of marketing communications.) Other elements of the marketing mix probably contributed too: product performance, such as taste, which is especially important for repeat purchase following trial of the brand; price, assuming price is similar to that of other frozen dinners; distribution, assuming you could find the brand in the frozen-foods section of a store where you shop; and other publicity forms of promotion, such as favorable comments from dieticians in magazine articles or perhaps passed on to you by friends. But the advertising undoubtedly played a large part.

### Buyer Response Steps As "Gates"

The buyer response steps can be regarded as a series of "gates" which an ad, adlike event, or promotion offer must get through to influence target audience action and thus lead to sales.[20] Getting through these gates is by no means guaranteed! As the remaining chapters make clear, thorough planning is required for each step.

A TV ad campaign for a new food product like Healthy Choice, for instance, might expect success in getting through each of the gates as follows, by the end of the first year:[21]

- *Step 1:* About 90 percent of consumers will have the opportunity to see the TV ads (exposure). That is, 90 percent get through the first gate (.9 probability).
- *Step 2:* Of these consumers, only about 60 percent will pay enough attention to the ads to register the message (processing). Thus, 60 percent of the 90 percent means that 54 percent of consumers get through the second gate (.9 × .6 = .54 probability).
- *Step 3:* Of those who processed the TV campaign's message, about 33 percent will be sufficiently aware of the brand and sufficiently impressed by its benefits to intend to try it (communication effects and brand position). Thus, only 18 percent of consumers get through the third gate (.9 × .6 × .33 = .18 probability).
- *Step 4:* Assuming that the brand achieves very wide distribution in stores and that those who would respond to trial-promotion offers receive

them, about 70 percent *of the 18 percent* will actually try the brand (target audience action). Thus, the net result is that only 13 percent of consumers get through all four gates (.9 × .6 × .33 × .7 ≈ .13 probability).

Thirteen percent of households is in fact the norm for trial of new food products in the first year.[22] Healthy Choice may have exceeded this trial rate— but only by getting higher percentages of people through the different buyer response gates. For example, better communication of benefits or a stronger introductory promotion at step 3 might raise the communication-effects and brand-position probability to 0.5; if so, the trial purchase incidence would be .9 × .6 × .5 × .7 ≈ .19 probability, or 19 percent of households.

The example above is for an entire ad campaign. What about a single ad exposed once, such as one newspaper ad intended to produce immediate purchase? Bogart and his colleagues[23] have shown that a typical consumer product advertised in a quarter-page newspaper ad will be bought by only 0.6 percent (six one-hundredths of a percent) of consumers that day or the day after the ad appeared. The gate probabilities for this type of ad might be .6 for exposure; .2 for processing, because of having to notice the ad among other ads on the page; .1 for communication effects and brand position, because there has been only one exposure; and a low .05 for target audience action, which presumes that consumers visit the store within the 2-day period and are not distracted by competing brands. Overall, .6 × .2 × .1 × .05 = .0006 probability, which means that only 0.6 percent of households take action.

These more-or-less realistic examples illustrate how important it is to plan for each step to maximize the proportion of potential buyers who get through each gate. The chain of probabilities means that the proportion of potential buyers has diminished considerably by the last step. (These probabilities will be revisited in the next chapter, where we demonstrate the *task method* of budget-setting.)

To summarize: The first four steps of the six-step effects sequence are the buyer response steps. Advertising communications and promotions must positively influence each of the four steps on each of their four corresponding levels: (1) exposure (media); (2) processing (ad, adlike event, or promotion offer);

(3) communication effects and brand position (brand); and (4) target audience action (buyer). If any one of these steps is not achieved for an individual buyer (or for enough buyers), the advertising, adlike event, or promotion won't work—And, going beyond the four buyer response steps, the AC&P campaign therefore will not contribute to (5) sales or market share and brand equity; and (6) profit.

## THE SIX STEPS FROM THE MANAGER'S VIEWPOINT

The manager views the six-step effects sequence in reverse. Going back to Figure 1.6, the manager must plan "from the top down," beginning with step 6 (profit) and concluding with step 1 (exposure). This is because objectives at the top end must be set before strategies at the lower end can be devised. To put it plainly, you don't advertise first and then devise a purpose for the advertising later!

The *manager's planning stages* are depicted in Figure 1.8. As the figure illustrates, the manager "descends" the six steps in six main stages (the manager's first stage corresponds to the last two steps of the effects sequence, and there is an additional final stage for the manager that traces through all six steps to evaluate the campaign). We will now explain these six stages; the organization of this book corresponds to them.[24]

**FIGURE 1.8**
The six steps as seen from the manager's viewpoint. The manager proceeds "from the top down," in six main stages, to develop the advertising communication and promotion plan.

### Marketing Objectives and Budget

In planning for advertising communications and promotions, and in planning an IMC campaign, the manager first has to consider the *marketing objectives* for the brand[25] and decide on the overall purpose for advertising it or promoting it from the *company's* point of view. Marketing objectives most often center on alternative avenues for contributing to the advertiser's profit, which we will examine in more detail in the next chapter. At this initial stage, too, the overall budget or appropriation for AC&P is usually decided.

The marketing manager for Healthy Choice dinners, for example, would expect Healthy Choice's advertising to contribute to *profit*. If it does not, the brand should be marketed without advertising, which is possible for some store brands and generic items but not for a national brand like Healthy Choice hoping to do well in the fiercely competitive frozen

dinner market. Of course, there is a time allowance for profit payback. The marketing manager for Healthy Choice would not expect the advertising to pay back in terms of profits immediately. Many new products are advertised at a loss for a year or two because they have to repay the costs of product development, which include capital equipment and management time invested in the product up to this point.

Most likely, sales (absolute volume) and possibly market share (relative volume in the category) goals were set for Healthy Choice dinners for the initial launch period and beyond, with these goals set at an esitmated price level that would pay back in terms of positive profits after a year or so. The marketing or product manager would estimate, or be given as a goal by higher management, the expected profit payout from the launch date onward, and would then estimate the volume of sales, at the most likely price and cost levels, that would meet the successive profit targets for the time period of the launch and the first several years of the brand's performance. Also at this stage, Healthy Choice's brand equity in terms of price elasticity of demand may be set as an objective concurrent with the sales to be generated.[26]

The manager must then estimate the amount of advertising that will be needed to guarantee the required sales volume for the first year—the overall advertising budget (promotions such as introductory consumer trial promotions are usually estimated separately and are therefore discussed later). To provide some hypothetical but realistic figures, let us assume that the Healthy Choice dinner line was intended to attain a 5 percent market share of the $3.4 billion frozen dinner-and-entree market in 1990, its first year. This represents approximately $170 million of retail sales in one year. Let us further assume an average price for the single-serving dinners of $2.50. This means that 68 million units of Healthy Choice dinners would have to be sold in the first year. Healthy Choice reportedly spent almost $26 million on advertising in 1990. If our estimate of 5 percent market share, representing $170 million worth of retail sales is near correct, this would represent an advertising-to-sales ratio (A/S) of approximately 15 percent—which would be fairly typical for a new product launch in this category.

The manager has estimated that an advertising budget of $26 million is needed to guarantee a sales volume of 68 million units for the first year. (Note also, therefore, that the advertising cost per unit is 38¢, which is 15 percent of the retail selling price; this is another way of arriving at the A/S ratio.) However, this advertising budget cannot simply be interpreted to mean that advertising contributes "15 percent of sales." Because of advertising's *interaction with,* or dependence on, other marketing-mix inputs—such as distribution, shelf display, brand name, price, and price promotions—the sales volume might have been *much* lower without the catalyst of advertising. Accordingly, it is best to think of overall advertising budgets as "assisting necessarily to produce" or "assuring" the required level of sales; that is, the advertising assists all 100 percent of sales and not just 15 percent of them.

We examine marketing objectives and overall budgeting in the next chapter.

## Target Audience Selection and Action Objectives

The manager now has to consider where sales are going to come from in response to advertising communications and promotions. The question of who is most likely to respond to advertising communications and perhaps separately to promotions focuses on *target audience selection.* Concurrent with target audience selection is the task of setting behavioral *action objectives* for advertising communications and promotions. Target audience action, you will remember, is the final step (step 4) of the buyer response steps. Depending on the target audience, the action objectives will normally be trial or repeat purchase, although other behavioral objectives could be purchase-related actions that are converted to purchase by the rest of the marketing mix. Trade target audience objectives may be purchase-related, such as to give the brand good visibility in the store. For now, however, we will concentrate on the consumer target audience.

In the Healthy Choice example, our manager faces a considerable task in selecting a target audience for the brand. The manager must have expected that Healthy Choice dinners would cannibalize some of ConAgra's other frozen dinner sales (the company's main frozen dinner brand at the time of the launch was Banquet, although the company subsequently launched another line of frozen dinners under its Ultra Slim-Fast label). However, the main target in the "competitive set" was clearly Stouffer's Lean Cuisine brand. In converting Lean Cuisine purchasers to Healthy Choice, the target audience would be defined as "brand switchers."

But would brand switchers from Lean Cuisine and other frozen dinners be sufficient to meet the sales goal established for Healthy Choice dinners? Healthy Choice very cleverly selected the name, "Healthy Choice," and packaging (the green packaging suggesting natural and healthy) to appeal additionally to nonusers of frozen dinners who may be persuaded to try the product because of the healthy attribute inherent in the product concept. Thus, a second target audience, "new category users," was quite likely an additional target audience selected by the marketing manager.

Recall that our estimated sales goal for Healthy Choice dinners for the first year was 68 million units. Behaviorally, how might this sales goal be achieved? There are approximately 70 million households in the

United States. If all of these households purchased a Healthy Choice dinner just once during the year, their actions would achieve the sales goal. More realistically, the sales goal could be achieved by inducing 15 percent of households—perhaps consisting of 10 percent brand switchers and 5 percent new category users—to buy a Healthy Choice dinner an average of 6.5 times during the year. Alternatively again, if Healthy Choice dinners were expected to develop brand loyalty quickly (which they may have done, being the first "heart-healthy" entry into the frozen dinner market), then the sales goal could have been attained by inducing as few as 1 percent of U.S. households to buy Healthy Choice dinners *twice a week,* which would easily exceed the 68 million-unit sales goal. The manager has to estimate the most likely combination of trial incidence and repeat-purchase incidence that will yield the sales goal. For as we will see, the advertising and promotion strategies are quite different depending on whether the sales are to be achieved with a high trial and a low repeat rate or a low trial and a very high repeat rate, as in the last alternative above.

For both target audiences, new category users and brand switchers, the action objective at the launch of the Healthy Choice campaign would be *trial.* However, in the case of new category users, a more refined description would be "category trial," whereas for brand switchers, a more refined description would be "brand trial based on brand switching." The action objective for both groups thereafter would become *repeat purchase,* assuming that further advertising is required or further promotions offered.

In Part Two of this book, we show how to select target audiences and how to set specific behavioral action objectives for advertising communications and promotions.

## Communication Objectives and Positioning

**Communication Objectives.** Advertising communications and promotions work via communication effects (step 3 of the buyer response steps) to cause action. The manager's corresponding planning stage is to determine which communication effects (brand associations) need to be established in the prospective buyer's mind in order to establish the brand's position and cause the buyer to take action. In determining the relevant communication effects, the manager sets *communication objectives* for each AC&P campaign.

Communication objectives are selected from options within the five basic communication effects: category need, brand awareness, brand attitude, brand purchase intention, and purchase facilitation.

When Healthy Choice dinners were first launched, the manager probably set several communication objectives for the advertising.

**1.** The introductory advertising probably tried to stimulate the frozen dinner category as a whole by creating a new subcategory or partition within the market—the subcategory of heart-healthy[27] frozen dinners. Being the first brand entry into this new subcategory, Healthy Choice would benefit from an increase in "primary demand" for heart-healthy frozen dinners (category need).

**2.** Potential new consumers of Healthy Choice (either new category users or brand switchers) have to learn the new brand name and associate it with the product category of frozen dinners. They also have to learn to recognize the new package—a bold green box with white lettering, a food product picture, and a "flag" prominently announcing the low number of calories (Figure 1.9). Ideally, the advertising would cause potential triers, when contemplating frozen or convenience dinners, to recall the brand name and then look for it by recognizing the package in stores (brand awareness).

**3.** Further, before trying Healthy Choice dinners, potential new triers would have to develop a favorable (if tentative before trial) opinion of the brand. The attractive food picture on the package would be instrumental in generating "good taste" expectations, but the main stimuli inducing trial would undoubtedly be the descriptive name, "Healthy Choice," and the specific attributes shown just below the name—namely, "low fat," "low cholesterol," and "low sodium meal," all of which are supposed to be healthy for the heart. The taste proviso and health attributes would combine—as benefit beliefs—to influence the prospective trier's overall opinion of the brand (brand attitude).

**4.** Also, a definite intention for the potential trier to try Healthy Choice dinners at the first opportunity would be a likely advertising communication objective. It would also be a likely *promotion* communication objective, for which trial coupons would be used to stimulate a definite decision to try the product (brand purchase intention).

**FIGURE 1.9A**
Healthy Choice package (front).

**FIGURE 1.9B**
Healthy Choice package (back). *Courtesy:* ConAgra Frozen Foods.

**5.** Potential consumers would know where to buy Healthy Choice dinners—in the frozen-foods section of their local supermarket—so the fifth communication effect (purchase facilitation) would *not,* in this case, be an advertising communication objective.[28]

**Positioning.** *Positioning* requires the strategic application of the first three communication effects with regard to a particular target audience. More precisely, the brand is positioned, for the target audience, into a *category* (by linking brand awareness with category need) with emphasis on a specific *brand benefit* or set of benefits (to influence brand attitude). For example, the positioning statement for Healthy Choice dinners for *new category users* might be "To people who don't usually buy frozen dinners / Healthy Choice is the brand of frozen dinner / that is 'healthy for your heart'"; whereas the positioning statement for *brand switchers* might be: "To people who buy Lean Cuisine frozen dinners / Healthy Choice is the brand of *low-calorie* frozen dinners / that is 'healthy for your heart.'"[29] By using the benefit "healthy for your heart," Healthy Choice is attempting to create a new

subcategory need, but initially it competes within the broader category of "frozen dinners," or "low-calorie frozen dinners," depending on the target audience.

From the prospective buyer's perspective, the target audience aspect of positioning is implicit. Explicitly, the buyer learns the category membership and main benefit or benefits of the brand as the brand's position.

In Part Three of this book, we describe these communication effects, show how to set appropriate communication objectives for the brand, and show how to select a specific brand position to be communicated.

### Creative Strategy and Integrated Communications Strategy

Once the communication objectives and positioning for the brand have been determined, the manager next has to ask the advertising agency to devise a *creative strategy* that will effectively convey the brand's positioning and achieve the communication objectives. Full achievement of the brand's communication objectives is likely also to require a more extensive *integrated communications strategy* which coordinates advertising and other adlike events with promotions.

**Creative Strategy.** The creative strategy requires the agency to generate a "creative idea" (presented to the client-manager as a "creative concept") for the advertising that, once executed in the form of a particular advertisement or set of advertisements, will be processed (step 2 in the buyer response steps) by the target audience in the intended manner to produce the desired communication effects and brand position (step 3 in the buyer response steps). The manager's role (in the client company) is to approve the creative strategy and, in most instances, test the creative executions (the ads) to ensure that they are capable of attaining the brand's communication objectives and specific position, which they must do when delivered by the media plan.

In the example of Healthy Choice dinners, the manager probably had several creative strategies (in the form of creative concepts) offered by the agency, Campbell-Mithun-Esty. There are *many possible creative ideas* that may have been able to achieve the "heart-healthy frozen dinner" positioning together with the specific communication objectives for Healthy Choice dinners (which were category need, brand awareness, brand attitude, and brand purchase intention). The agency could, for instance, have focused on the low-fat, low-cholesterol, and low-sodium attributes of the product and taken a scientific approach (much as was done on the back of the package—see Figure 1.9, panel B). However, that was not the approach selected.

The brand manager and the agency chose to use the *dramatic* creative idea of having Mr. Mike Harper, Chairman and CEO of ConAgra, deliver the communication objectives via the revelation of his own health problem—a heart attack—and his initially unsuccessful search for healthy-yet-convenient meals while recovering. This true story led to Harper's development of the Healthy Choice product. A summary (storyboard) of the introductory commercial is shown in Figure 1.10. While this turned out to be a highly effective creative strategy, again it is important to note that there are many other *potential* creative ideas and executions that may have achieved the specific communication objectives and positioning equally well. Nevertheless, the "CEO spokesperson" approach in this case was a very effective selection, as was probably confirmed by ad testing (pretesting) of this versus several other alternative creative concepts suggested by the agency.

**FIGURE 1.10**
Launch commercial for Healthy Choice frozen dinners.
*Courtesy:* ConAgra Frozen Foods.

As we will see in Part Four of this book, creative strategy has two components: a creative idea and creative executions of the idea in the form of particular commercials or advertisements. It is in these two components that the "magic" of advertising—the creativity provided by the agency—is vital. Although there is a good deal of mystique associated with the creative process, it is important that the client manager control its outcome with the brand's objectives firmly in mind. We will have more to say in Parts Four and Seven (on advertising research) on how this is best achieved.

**Integrated Communications Strategy.** Achievement of the brand's communication objectives and brand position may be assisted by an integrated communications strategy which incorporates adlike events and of course promotions. Earlier in the chapter, we mentioned many techniques, ranging from sales promotions to various special events and forms of publicity.

Healthy Choice dinners were launched with two *consumer promotion* techniques. One was a sales promotion offer—an introductory trial coupon distributed during Heart Month via Sunday newspapers and direct mail. The other was a PR event—free cholesterol tests in stores. Both these promotions contributed to the brand's communication objectives—and were consistent (integrated with) the brand's positioning. In particular, the coupons helped to increase brand awareness and to stimulate immediate (trial-purchase) intentions among those who received them. The timing of the coupon promotion and the nature of the PR event probably helped to build brand attitude, too. Just as there are potentially many alternative *creative* strategies that could have been used, so too are there many potential *promotion* strategies. For example, free taste samples could have been distributed via retail stores or, more simply, a price-off promotion could have been used at the point of purchase for a limited period.

We must not forget promotions to retailers as well. ConAgra would normally have had to use quite extensive *trade promotions,* in the form of buying allowances or cooperative advertising deals or both, to get the new product into the already-crowded supermarket freezer cases. However, the innovativeness and evident consumer appeal of Healthy Choice (reinforced in a sales video shown to retailers) in this instance served to reduce the company's expenditure on trade promotion.

In Part Five of this book, we discuss integrated communications strategy. We will see how various forms of promotions—which work best when integrated with advertising—can be used to achieve the target audience action objectives of trial and repeat purchase (step 4 in the buyer response steps). These action objectives may include retailers or distributors as target audiences as well as ultimate buyers or consumers.

### Media Strategy

Next, the manager has to plan a media strategy for the advertising communications, and for promotions if both are used in an IMC campaign. Basically, media strategy centers on the exposure step (step 1) of the buyer response steps, although processing (step 2) is also implicated.

In planning media strategy, the manager makes two main decisions: media selection (*where* to most efficiently reach the target audience) and media scheduling (*how often* the target audience needs to be reached to produce the intended communication effects and action). The principles of media planning are exactly the same for the various types of promotions as they are for advertising. Promotions often employ delivery "vehicles" that should be thought of as media, such as point-of-purchase displays or in-home, on-pack promotions. An integrated marketing communications (IMC) approach requires that we consider these as media.

The Healthy Choice manager, to return to our example, had to plan together with the agency to select and then schedule media for Healthy Choice dinners. For the advertising of a new supermarket product such as this, the primary medium would probably be television and the secondary medium would be magazines, especially those aimed at women as the household decision makers for food selection. For the launch, Healthy Choice used only television—but lots of it.

Media must also be selected for the promotional activities. Healthy Choice was launched with three IMC promotion media: freestanding inserts (FSIs) in newspapers; direct mail; and in-store publicity. FSIs are a good example of the integration of advertising with promotion. Newspaper FSIs are like magazine ads (and probably *substituted* for magazine ads, which would normally be used in a new product launch such as this); FSIs are also treated as *coupons.* The in-store cholesterol test, too, is a good example of an IMC promotion based on the singular macropositioning of the product as heart-healthy.

The second media strategy decision, media scheduling, is quite complicated. Difficult scheduling questions had to be answered for Healthy Choice. How many times would the Healthy Choice advertising have to be exposed to a nonbuyer of frozen dinners to entice him or her to try not only the brand but the category itself? And, once tried, assuming a favorable opinion of the product, how often, between typical home-use dinner purchase occasions, would the "continuing" advertising have to be seen or heard in order to keep the new trier aware of and intending to rebuy the brand? When should the trial coupons be issued—*before* the advertising is likely to be seen, or at some time *afterward* so that new category triers have already become aware of and learned something about the Healthy Choice product? The media budget then has to be allocated in accordance with these media strategy decisions.

In Part Six of this book, we provide answers to complex media questions like those posed for Healthy Choice dinners above. Media strategy is difficult but crucial: it is where most of the manager's budget will be spent.

### Campaign Tracking and Evaluation

As the final stage, the manager has to plan (yes—in advance) how to monitor, or "track," the campaign and evaluate it. Early planning of the campaign tracking and evaluation phase is required because a benchmark reading of the marketplace must be taken *before* the campaign begins, so that the campaign's effects can be measured against this pre-campaign baseline.

We advocate continuous tracking of advertising communications and promotion campaigns so that the manager always knows how the campaign is progressing. Essentially, what is monitored or tracked are the buyer response steps—exposure (the media plan's delivery of the advertisements, adlike events, or promotions), processing (such as self-reported attention to the advertising), communication effects (such as brand awareness and brand attitude) and brand position, and action (in the form of trial, usage, or other relevant target audience behaviors). These are then related to company records of sales, market share, and profit. Thus, all six steps of the effects sequence are covered.

The manager of Healthy Choice dinners, in our example, would want to know that the advertising and promotion offers are working as planned. A survey—perhaps a weekly survey—was probably commissioned. Its purpose would be to track consumer exposure, both to the advertising and to the introductory coupons; registration of the intended communication effects and brand position in consumers' minds; and trial- and repeat-purchase behaviors, both with and without coupons, as well as consumer satisfaction with the new product. The introductory coupon promotion would also be tracked at a general level by records of the number of redemptions, but note that this information would have to be supplemented by

individual-level data to determine whether coupon redemptions represented trial purchases only or came also from consumers who used the coupons to make repeat purchases after they had already tried the product.

Because of the many factors *besides* advertising communications and promotion activities that can affect sales, the campaign tracking and evaluation stage of advertising planning is never easy or straightforward. This phase is too often avoided but it certainly should be done. For the vast amounts of money spent on advertising and promotion—for instance, $26 million on advertising alone for the launch of Healthy Choice dinners in the first year—the manager should provide an account and an assessment of the effectiveness of such expenditures.

In Part Seven of this book, we review the best techniques available to managers, for both business and consumer products and services, for keeping track of the progress of advertising and promotion or IMC campaigns and for arriving at an assessment of how well the campaign has performed.

To review, the advertising manager has six stages to plan: marketing objectives and budget; target audience selection and action objectives; communication objectives and positioning; creative strategy and integrated communications strategy; media strategy; and campaign tracking and evaluation. The only stages that are occasionally omitted are integrated communications strategy, if the campaign is exclusively advertising-based, and the final stage, campaign tracking and evaluation. However, omitting the final stage is unwise, and we see an increasing trend toward evaluating campaigns through continuous measurement.

### SUMMARY

Advertising communications and promotions are best regarded practically as alternative sets of techniques, often used in combination (AC&P), to meet the marketing objectives for the brand. Advertising communications *tend* to take an indirect ("turn the mind toward" purchase), longer-term approach to gaining customers; whereas promotions *tend* to take a direct ("buy now"), shorter-term approach to gaining customers. However, advertising and promotions are both forms of marketing communication designed to make prospective buyers aware of the brand, create or change brand attitudes, and stimulate purchase intentions. The extent to which they do this by providing the same basic message gives rise to integrated marketing communications.

The real differences between advertising communications and promotions lie in their relative use in strategic marketing management. We have seen how the emphasis differs, in the longer term, according to the brand's stage in the product life cycle and the extent of brand loyalty it has attained. Whereas the techniques of advertising communications and promotions differ, their use has to be integrated for the brand centrally and over time.

Advertising communications and promotions work via a six-step effects sequence: (1) exposure (via media), (2) processing (of the ad, adlike event, or promotion offer), (3) communication effects and brand position (connected to and for the brand), (4) target audience action (by the buyer), (5) sales or market share (resulting from cumulative buyer actions in a market) and brand equity, leading to (6) profit (for the company).

The first four of these steps are called the buyer response steps. Each prospective buyer of the brand, in response to AC&P, must be exposed via media; must process the ad, adlike event, or promotion offer in the manner intended by the advertiser; must acquire communication effects associated with the brand and learn its brand position; and, based on these prior effects, must take action and buy the brand.

The manager plans for AC&P campaigns according to the six steps, but in reverse, and in six main stages. The manager first considers marketing objectives and budget (corresponding to profit, sales or market share, and brand equity); then target audience selection and action objectives; then communication objectives and positioning; then creative strategy and integrated communications strategy, including promotions; then media strategy; and finally, campaign tracking and evaluation. This hierarchical, "from the top down" process progressively narrows the alternatives until a complete AC&P plan is constructed.

In the Appendix to this book, we include a checklist AC&P plan. But how is this checklist filled out? That is the subject of the rest of the book.

## NOTES

1. Throughout this book, "promotion" refers to *sales* promotion in its many forms. "Promotions" is practitioners' shorthand way of referring to sales promotions.
2. R. M. Prentice, How to split your marketing funds between advertising and promotion, *Advertising Age,* January 10, 1977, p. 41.
3. Updates from an original list compiled by P. N. Hague, *The Industrial Market Research Handbook,* 2nd ed., London, UK: Kogan Page, 1987, Chp. 11.
4. The list includes suggestions given in W. T. Moran, Advertising and promotion processes, Working paper, Greenwich, CT: Moran & Tucker, Inc., ca. 1989.
5. Our source is the forecast for 1996 by Veronis, Suhler & Associates reported in J. Mandese and S. Donaton, Media, promotion gap to narrow, *Advertising Age,* June 29, 1992, p. 16, and in C. Goerne, Communications spending expected to grow 7.1 percent in next five years, *Marketing News,* August 3, 1992, p. 5. Because the estimates are for 1996, the total expenditure is higher than in the 1993 estimates in Table 1.2, which follows.

   V, S & A surveys the total U.S. market, unlike the widely reported surveys by Donnelly Marketing, which concentrate on the 100 leading consumer packaged goods companies. Donnelly's figures show a much lower ratio of advertising to promotion for these companies, with consumer advertising at 31 percent, consumer promotion at 25 percent, and trade promotion at 44 percent; see C. Miller, Trade promotion spending in 1990 hits record level, *Marketing News,* May 13, 1991, p. 6. We use the V, S & A results because they include not only national consumer advertisers but also business and retail advertisers, who use much more narrow-audience and local advertising in the "nonmeasured media," such as outdoor, direct mail, local newspapers, directories, and specialty ads in calendars and flyers.
6. Estimation for 1993 by McCann-Erickson, Inc., and reported in ADWEEK's *Marketer's Guide to Media,* 1994, *17* (1), pp. 9–12. The other reference in Table 1.2 is S. Shergill, The changing U.S. media and marketing environment: Implications for media advertising expenditures, *International Journal of Advertising,* 1993, *12* (2), pp. 95–115.
7. R. J. Fox and G. L. Geissler, Notes and comments: Crisis in advertising? *Journal of Advertising,* 1994, *23* (4), pp. 79–82. We agree with the predictions in their article.
8. In 1992, 80 percent by Nielsen's estimate and 86 percent by CMS estimate; *Marketers' Guide to Media,* 1994, *17* (1), p. 128.

9. See M. Snyder, Re-thinking "integrated," *Advertising Age,* October 28, 1991, p. 32, and E. Thorson, Announcement of 11th annual Advertising and Consumer Psychology conference on "integrated communications," *Association for Consumer Research Newsletter,* Provo, UT: Association for Consumer Research, December 1991, p. 7.

10. A U.S. survey reported in *Marketing,* March 1994, p. 8, found that 83 percent of advertisers believe it is their responsibility to coordinate strategy for IMC. But 77 percent of their agencies claim to have done so in the clients' most recent campaigns.

11. H. Hastings, Introducing new products without advertising, *Journal of Consumer Marketing,* 1990, *7* (3), pp. 19–25.

12. D. W. Stewart, Speculations on the future of advertising research, *Journal of Advertising,* 1992, *21* (3), pp. 1–18.

13. The strategic framework owes a debt to various marketing theorists, including Peter Drucker and Abe Shuchman. This version is used in Columbia University's marketing management course.

14. For a worthwhile assessment of why the competitor orientation is equal in importance to the customer orientation, see A. R. Oxenfeldt and W. L. Moore, Customer or competitor: Which guideline for marketing? *Management Review,* 1978, *67* (8), pp. 43–48. A broader view of the importance of competitive advantage in business strategy is given in R. S. Achrol and D. L. Appel, New developments in corporate strategy planning, *AMA Marketing Educators Conference Proceedings,* Chicago, IL: American Marketing Association, 1983, pp. 305–310.

15. James Culliton, of Harvard, in the 1940s began referring to the business executive as a "mixer of ingredients." The idea was borrowed by his colleague Neil Borden, who popularized the term "marketing mix." If the chemical analogy is followed closely, the marketing mix is really a "marketing compound," since the elements of the mix (such as advertising communications and promotion) interact with each other to produce the final result. See N. H. Borden, *Advertising Text and Cases,* Homewood, IL: Irwin, 1964.

16. In academia, Northwestern University was perhaps the first to recognize the change and incorporate the new marketing mix in its teaching, via Don Schultz and later also Bob Blattberg, who joined Northwestern from Chicago, where another leading theorist of IMC, John Deighton, was a professor. Deighton also worked closely with Larry Percy at Lintas. And see W. van Waterschoot and C. Van den Bulte, The 4P classification of the marketing mix revisited, *Journal of Marketing,* 1992, *56* (4), pp. 83–93. We thank Grahame Dowling for suggesting this diagram of the new mix.

17. J. G. Udell. The perceived importance of the elements of strategy, *Journal of Marketing,* 1968, *32* (1), pp. 34–40.

18. The product life cycle concept was introduced by Columbia University's business economics professor Joel Dean. See J. Dean, Pricing policies for new products, *Harvard Business Review,* 1950, *28* (6), 45–53. For a more specific breakdown of PLC stages, see C. W. Hofer and D. Schendel, *Strategy Formulation: Analytical Concepts,* St. Paul, MN: West, 1978.

Some writers have expressed doubts about the product life cycle phenomenon. For a convenient summary of the main issues and main references, see G. S. Day, The product life cycle: Analysis and applications issues, *Journal of Marketing,* 1981, *45* (4), pp. 60–67. However, in a comprehensive review across industries, it has been shown that the classic PLC curve is the most common: see D. R. Rink and J. E. Swan, Product life cycle research: A literature review, *Journal of Business Research,* 1979, *7* (3), pp. 219–242.

An important article by David Midgley demonstrates that both the classic PLC curve and exceptions to it, such as the cycle-recycle pattern, can be closely predicted by separating sales into first-time purchases and repeat or replacement purchases: the curves can be predicted for product classes, product forms, and brands. See D. F. Midgley, Toward a theory of the product life cycle: Explaining diversity, *Journal of Marketing,* 1981, *45* (4), pp. 109–115. The first-purchase or "penetration" pattern for product classes, not to be confused with the total sales pattern, can be early-peaked, relatively continuous, or late-peaked, as demonstrated in an interesting analysis by C. J. Easingwood, Early product life cycle forms for infrequently purchased major products, *International Journal of Research in Marketing,* 1987, *4*, pp. 3–9.

The classic PLC holds almost universally for product classes, very well for product forms, but less often for particular brands, largely because brand managers try to manage their way *out* of the life cycle, especially in the late growth and decline stages. Claims that some brands last forever are usually deceptive. For example, M. Lubliner compared the top 25 consumer package goods brands from 1923 and found that 19 were still brand leaders in 1983 (Old standbys hold their own, *Advertising Age,* September 19, 1983, p. 32). However, these results conceal the many model (product form) changes within the brand names. For instance the leading Gillette razor "brand" in 1923 is not the same as Sensor, the leading Gillette razor on the market now.

19. Here we are addressing not just the absolute emphasis on advertising communications and promotion but also the relative use of advertising communications versus promotions during the product life cycle. For a review

of factors affecting the absolute emphasis on advertising and promotion, see P. W. Farris and R. D. Buzzell, Why advertising and promotion costs vary: Some cross-sectional analyses, *Journal of Marketing,* 1979, *43* (4), pp. 112–122.

20. The "gates" or probability-chaining approach first came to our attention from W. J. McGuire, The nature of attitudes and attitude change, in G. Lindzey and E. Aronson, eds., *The Handbook of Social Psychology,* vol. 3, Reading, MA: Addison-Wesley, 1969, pp. 136–314. For more recent applications in marketing, see G. L. Urban and J. R. Hauser, *Design and Marketing of New Products,* 2nd ed., Englewood Cliffs, NJ: Prentice-Hall, 1993.

21. We emphasize that these figures are entirely hypothetical because we did not have access to appropriate research data. However, they are within reason. Healthy Choice achieved a 4.4 percent market share (in dollars) of frozen dinners-and-entrees in 1991, its first year, which is consistent with the 13 percent trial rate. See Brand scoreboard, *Advertising Age,* November, 1992, p. 16.

22. J. Rubinson, Update on trial and repeat trends for new products, *Proceedings: Advertising and Promotion Effectiveness Workshop,* New York, NY: Advertising Research Foundation, 1989, pp. 255–265.

23. L. Bogart, B. S. Tolley, and F. Orenstein, What one little ad can do, *Journal of Advertising Research,* 1970, *10* (4), pp. 3–13.

24. In the manager's planning sequence, creative strategy and integrated communications strategy theoretically occur together. In this book, however, and most often in reality, creative strategy *precedes* integrated communication strategy.

25. Throughout the book we will use the term "brand" to refer to any advertisable or promotable entity which the manager is responsible for. Most often, this will indeed be a brand—of either a product or service. However, a brand could also be a company, as in corporate-image advertising or public relations; an institution, such as the International Red Cross; or even a person, such as a political candidate, or an idea, such as free enterprise. Sometimes, too, an unbranded commodity, such as produce or raw materials, may be the focus of advertising communications or promotions. Unless otherwise specified, "brand" could refer to any of these things.

26. The remarkable equity of the Healthy Choice brand name was proved in 1994 when ConAgra licensed the name to Kellogg's. Sales of the three Kellogg's cereals that adopted the Healthy Choice name immediately rose. Fittingly, they were low-fat, high-fiber cereals that could be linked with a healthy lifestyle. See: Year was no bust, *Advertising Age,* December 13, 1994, p. 17.

27. The advertising for Healthy Choice dinners refers to "heart-healthy," but it is likely that many consumers generalize from the name and think of the new subcategory as simply "healthy" frozen dinners, as distinct from low-calorie or diet frozen dinners such as Lean Cuisine or Weight Watchers. We will return to this example in Chapter 5 of the book.

28. Healthy Choice, according to our assumptions, was launched at a moderate and competitive price ($2.50, on average), and many triers also used trial coupons worth 50¢ off the purchase price. Had the brand been launched with a very *high* initial price, the communication effect of purchase facilitation may have been an objective. The introductory promotion offer would be seen not only as speeding up trial-purchase intention but also as overcoming the high price inhibition and thereby facilitating purchase. Although purchase facilitation, which addresses potential problems with the 4Ps of the marketing mix, would not be a communication objective for consumers, it may well have been a communication objective for the *trade,* to aid the brand's distribution. Heavy introductory consumer advertising is often used to try to "pull" the brand through the distribution channel, coupled with trade promotions to "push" it through. See any introductory marketing management text for a discussion of "push" versus "pull" promotion in distribution strategy.

29. See note 27. Lean Cuisine buyers have already selected themselves into the subcategory of low-calorie or diet frozen dinners.

## DISCUSSION QUESTIONS

**1.1.** Look at the Arm & Hammer Heavy Duty Detergent exhibit again (Figure 1.2) and answer the following questions:
   a. Given the conceptual definition of advertising communications as (indirectly) "turning the buyer or consumer's mind toward purchase," which elements of the message execution seem to do this, and why?
   b. Given the conceptual definition of promotions as (directly) trying to "immediately stimulate purchase," which elements seem to do this, and why?
   c. Overall, how would you classify the exhibit? Pick a ratio to summarize your conclusion, for example, 50 percent AC and 50 percent P.

**1.2.** You are probably already quite familiar with marketing strategy, but it is worthwhile to emphasize that both advertising communications and promotions must be consistent with marketing strategy principles. Some refresher questions:
   a. What are IBM's differential advantages in the personal computer market?

**b.** What customer value or values do designer-label clothes offer for their premium price?

**c.** Which demographic market (or markets) appears to have been [targeted] by the marketer of Lexus cars?

**d.** "Avon ladies" selling Avon cosmetics door to door do not seem to be as prevalent as they once were. Do you think this represents a change in planning by the company, and if so, how and why?

**1.3.** Why do you think industrial product managers, in general, rely less on AC&P than do managers of consumer goods?

**1.4.** Visit a local supermarket and look at the brand displays for (a) detergent and (b) paper towels. What is the approximate proportion of brands in each category using in-store promotions? Relate your findings to the discussion of product life cycle factors that affect the relative use of advertising communications versus promotions.

**1.5.** What do you believe to be the purpose of integrated marketing communications (IMC), and what challenges does it pose for the manager?

**1.6.** What was your personal experience with the TV advertising for Healthy Choice dinners? Write a two-page description of how you personally remember going through the four buyer response steps, concluding with whether you purchased a Healthy Choice dinner or not, and why.

**1.7.** Could Healthy Choice dinners (the first product for this brand) have been launched successfully *without* any advertising communications or promotions? How could the four buyer response steps have been achieved using *other elements* of the marketing mix, that is, product, price, distribution, and personal selling (exclude publicity or PR)?

## FURTHER READING

Drucker, P. F. *Management: Tasks, Responsibilities, Practices.* New York: Harper & Row, 1973.

This book contains an excellent and highly readable discussion of the basic principles of strategic marketing management, including differential advantage, customer value, and selective concentration.

Kotler, P. *Marketing Management,* 8th ed. Englewood Cliffs, NJ: Prentice-Hall, 1993.

We expect that many readers will have read this leading marketing textbook. It provides a handy reference for terms in our first chapter (such as marketing mix, market segmentation, planning, and product life cycle) as well as marketing concepts used later in our text.

Dickson, P. R. *Marketing Management.* Fort Worth, TX: Dryden, 1994.

A new and highly original textbook on marketing management, this book provides strong economic and psychological inputs to marketing theory and implementation and is a welcome alternative to clones of the McCarthy and Kotler texts.

Ambler, T. *Need-to-Know Marketing: An Accessible A to Z Guide.* London, UK: Century Business, 1992.

This is an excellent practical book on marketing management. It is delightful to read and full of the wisdom of experience.

Colley, R. H. *Defining Advertising Goals for Measured Advertising Results.* New York, NY: Association of National Advertisers, Inc., 1961.

The classic DAGMAR approach to advertising (an acronym from the title) is worth reading even though the specific steps in Colley's approach do not exactly match the steps described in our book.

Schultz, D. E., Tannenbaum, S. I., and Lauterborn, R. F. *Integrated Marketing Communications.* Lincolnwood, IL: NTC Business Books, 1992.

The first book entirely on IMC, it contains useful planning concepts and two recent applications of integrated campaigns. However, these authors recommend IMC completely without providing what we see as necessary qualifications.

# CHAPTER 2

# Marketing Objectives and Budget

This chapter has two aims: to show how advertising communications and promotions must contribute to the brand's marketing objectives, and to show how to set the overall AC&P budget. After reading this chapter, you should:

- Appreciate that the ultimate marketing objective is profit (which can be economically or socially defined).
- See that there are three ways in which advertising communications and promotions can affect profit: by affecting price, cost, and sales volume.
- Be able to establish immediate, 1-year, and long-run marketing objectives for advertising communications and promotions.
- Know how to set the overall AC&P budget.

In terms of the six-step effects sequence, this chapter covers steps 5 and 6. In terms of the manager's planning stages, it covers the first stage of the AC&P plan. (Refer back to Figure 1.8.)

## MARKETING OBJECTIVES FOR THE CAMPAIGN

The manager's first stage of planning for advertising communications and promotion is to set marketing objectives *for the campaign* (where the campaign refers to the year's plan or a shorter-term plan). This means making sure that the advertising communications and promotions overall can assure the marketing objectives that have *already been decided for the*

brand. However, an AC&P campaign can sometimes have *its own objectives* in the sense of being primarily responsible for a major change in marketing performance. With a product that is sold only by direct response advertising, for instance, the advertising is almost completely responsible for attaining the marketing objectives; besides the advertising, all that is needed is distribution by mail or courier to deliver the ordered product to the customer.

We will shortly present a convenient framework for classifying the major ways in which advertising communications and promotions can contribute to the attainment of marketing objectives. The focus will be on *profit*—the alternative avenues to which are selling price, unit cost, and sales volume. Before we turn to this framework, however, we will comment briefly on the use of objectives and the nature of profit.

### Objectives and Goals

We define "objective" as a broad aim or general description of a desired outcome, and a "goal" as an objective made specific as to degree and time. (For other useful definitions, see Table 2.1.) It should be evident that goals provide more precise performance targets for managers to aim for and are therefore preferable to objectives.[1] However, it is not always possible to forecast all types of performance precisely and thereby set goals. Similarly, an overly precise goal does not mean much unless the company is willing and able to *measure* goal attainment.

| TABLE 2.1 | |
| --- | --- |

**DEFINITIONS FOR AC&P PLANNING**

| Term | Definition |
| --- | --- |
| Strategic planning | The formulation of objectives (ends) and strategies (means) for attaining them |
| Objective | A broad aim or general description of a desired outcome |
| Goal | An objective made specific as to degree and time |
| Strategy | A broad plan of action with an objective or goal in mind |
| Tactics | The specific details or components of a strategy showing how it can be implemented |

When goal estimation is not possible, or when goal attainment is not measurable, it is still worthwhile to set *objectives*. Although objectives are broad aims that do not specify either the degree of performance required or the expected attainment period, they can still serve as directional guides for management and are better than no guides at all. For example, knowledge that the company is trying to increase sales rather than hold sales at their present level (two possible objectives) provides a useful guide for managers even though the amount and timing of the targeted sales increase are not specified.

Marketing objectives—stated explicitly in the AC&P plan—greatly facilitate campaign planning and evaluation.[2]

### Profit, Broadly Defined

The ultimate purpose of advertising communications and promotions, and of all other business functions, is to maximize profit. This is why profit is shown as the final step in the six-step effects sequence. The time horizon for profit maximization is usually, but not always, long-run profit. We shall consider some short-run examples as well.

Whereas the profit maximization purpose is evident for most business and consumer products and services, it can be obscure for some types of advertising communications, especially with integrated communications campaigns. Corporate image advertising, for instance, is often thought to have *only* the objective of making people feel good about the company.

However, if these good feelings do not translate into tangible, accountable results such as a higher stock price for the company or a higher rate of attracting good employees—in other words, profit—then the organization should not be investing in corporate image advertising. The same argument applies to other integrated communications activities such as sponsorship, event marketing, and public relations. The profit results of these integrated communications may not be easy to quantify, but profit remains their objective.

Profit can also be considered in human, rather than solely monetary, terms. Public service advertising is often justified on the basis of this broader definition of profit, which includes social utility. In Australia, for instance, there have been several carefully documented studies showing that recent government anti–drink-and-drive campaigns have led to a very profitable reduction in the rate of automobile accidents, with profit measured objectively in terms of savings—to the public—of millions of dollars in medical and insurance costs. Additionally, the road-safety campaigns undoubtedly produced a difficult-to-measure but equally real profit in terms of human lives saved and the anguish of family members and friends avoided.

The most commonly used (monetary) measures of profit are given in Chapter 18.

### THREE AVENUES TO PROFIT AND THREE TIME HORIZONS

A useful way of deciding on marketing objectives for advertising communications and promotions is to realize that there are three ways in which AC&P can contribute to the ultimate objective of profit. If we chart these three avenues to profit vis-à-vis the three time horizons for AC&P planning, we get a 3 × 3 matrix of potential marketing objectives, as shown in Figure 2.1.

### Avenues to Profit

Generally defined, profit = (price − cost) × sales volume. From this equation, we see that there are three potential ways in which advertising communications and promotions can contribute to the brand's profit:

1. By *increasing* the brand's *price*, provided price can be raised without a completely offsetting loss of sales volume.

## THREE AVENUES TO PROFIT

| | Increasing selling price | Lowering cost | Increasing sales volume |
|---|---|---|---|
| **Immediate** | *Advertising*—Justify high introductory price or price increase.<br>*Promotion*—Temporarily discount high introductory price. | *Advertising*—None (immediate cost is increased).<br>*Promotion*—None (immediate cost is increased). | *Advertising*—Use direct response advertising; retail advertising; or classified ads.<br>*Promotion*—Use sales promotions (trade,retail, or consumer). |
| **1-year** | *Advertising*—Increase upside price elasticity and decrease downside price elasticity (thereby increasing brand equity).<br>*Promotion*—"Ratchet" promotions after successful advertising bursts (less price reduction needed). | *Advertising*—Partially substitute advertising for sales calls; reduce trade promotion ("pull" strategy).<br>*Promotion*—Increase "switching costs" and thus lower cost to retain customer. | *Advertising*—Use media advertising.<br>*Promotion*—Use trial promotions (for frequent repeat products); achieve decycling; motivate sales force. |
| **Long-run** | *Advertising*—Protect brand equity and thus raise average selling price.<br>*Promotion*—Offer loyalty promotions (less price reduction needed) and maintain value positioning. | *Advertising*—Lower unit cost via experience curve.<br>*Promotion*—Lower unit cost via experience curve. | *Advertising*—Defend attained sales rate.<br>*Promotion*—None (beyond increasing pool of triers initially). |

**FIGURE 2.1**

A 3 × 3 matrix of possible marketing objectives for advertising and promotion based on the assumption that profit = (selling price − cost) × sales volume.

**2.** By *lowering costs.*

**3.** By *increasing sales volume.*

Usually, we think only of the third avenue—increasing sales volume—but the other two avenues to increased profit are just as important. Of course, if the objective is to *maintain* profit rather than necessarily increase it, then maintaining the brand's price, cost, and present sales volume would be sufficient. For brands facing heavy competition or an industry-wide recession, profit maintenance may be a sufficient objective. Here, however, we will assume that the objective is to increase profit, when we examine, shortly, the ways in which AC&P can do so.

### Time Horizons

Alternative time horizons for AC&P planning—practically speaking—can be:

**1.** *Immediate,* with the desired results to be achieved as soon as possible.

**2.** *1-year,* which is the typical medium-run AC&P planning period and also the typical budgeting period.

**3.** *Long-run,* extending beyond a year and into the foreseeable future.

As we shall see, these three planning horizons cover most of the situations the manager faces in setting marketing objectives for advertising communications and promotions.

Corresponding to the cells of the matrix in Figure 2.1, we suggest under the next three main headings the major ways in which advertising communications and promotions, respectively, can contribute to profit through each of the avenues to profit and for each time horizon. The suggestions are comprehensive but not necessarily exhaustive. Rather, our intent is to provide a useful framework for thinking about marketing objectives for a specific campaign. We will order our discussion of the matrix by working down the columns under each of the three avenues to profit. We have deliberately left the discussion of sales volume until last because, whereas "increasing sales" is the most obvious marketing objective, the manager should seriously examine the other two alternatives, raising price and lowering costs, as well.

## SELLING PRICE OBJECTIVES

Profit can be increased by increasing the selling price of the product or service so that it provides a greater profit margin per unit than previously. Total profit will increase as long as the number of units sold at the higher price does not decline too much. Selling-price "elasticity," defined shortly, is an important aspect of the price avenue to profit. We will now consider the immediate, 1-year, and long-run price objectives for advertising (including advertising-like communications) and promotion (price promotions).

### Immediate Price Objectives

**Advertising.** In the immediate term, advertising can be used to explain or justify a high selling price, such as for an expensive new-product introduction, or a substantial price increase for an existing product. Advertising for Piaget watches, for example, has boasted that the Piaget is the "highest-priced watch in the world." Another example is when utility companies propose rate hikes and attempt to explain to customers, via advertising, why the price increase is necessitated, and thereby achieve the price increase without losing customers or sales volume.

**Promotion.** Promotion, too, can be used, though slightly differently, to ease resistance to a high introductory price by announcing a discount that is strictly a limited-time, introductory offer. In this way, using integrated communications, the marketer may be able to maintain a high-price image and indeed charge a higher price later while offering, in effect, a penetration price. However, as with other price-off promotions, the profit must come from additional volume sold, because the profit margin per unit has actually been reduced via the lower promotional selling price.

### 1-Year Price Objectives

**Advertising.** An insightful analysis by marketing consultant William T. Moran[3] contends that the most important marketing objective for advertising is to increase the selling price of the product and, more precisely, to influence its *price elasticity of demand* in two particular ways. Price elasticity of demand refers to changes in the brand's sales rate in response to changes in price. In Moran's analysis, price is defined in terms of *relative* price within the product category, that is, the brand's selling price relative to the average selling price of all brands in the category. Price elas-

ticity is separated into "upside" elasticity, which is how much the brand's sales go up in response to a price cut by the brand, and "downside" elasticity, which is how much the brand's sales go down in response to a price increase by the brand—or, because we are considering relative price, in response to price cuts or price-off promotions by competing brands. (We show how to calculate these elasticities in Chapter 18.)

In the 1-year planning period, the price-relevant objectives of advertising are to increase the brand's upside elasticity and decrease its downside elasticity. In other words, when our brand promotes by reducing price, its sales should shoot sharply upward (high upside elasticity) because advertising has given our brand high *perceived worth,* such that the price reduction increases its *value* to the customer (value being utility divided by price, or "benefits per dollar"). At the same time, our brand should be relatively immune to price-off promotions by competitors, meaning that when they promote their brands, our sales should not go down by much if at all (low downside elasticity). If our sales go down when competitors cut their prices or promote, then our brand—while it may have value equity on the upside—is not *unique* enough on the downside, meaning that there are other brands out there that are seen as good value when they cut their price and are then too readily substituted for our brand.

As Moran notes, a brand's medium-run or "dynamic" *brand equity* can be measured in terms of the *ratio* of its upside elasticity to its downside elasticity: a high number in the numerator and a low number in the denominator reflects strong brand equity. It is important to realize that the two factors are affected *independently* and, in particular, that a high upside elasticity does not guarantee a low downside elasticity.[4] This is examined further in chapter appendix 2A, Strategies Based on Upside and Downside Elasticity.

**Promotion.** In the 1-year planning period, the advertising objectives of increasing upside price elasticity and decreasing downside price elasticity can be assisted by scheduling promotion *after* each burst of advertising, to produce a "ratchet effect." This is described in Chapter 16.

Price support (in the relative-price, upward-and-downward-elasticity sense identified by Moran) is therefore a very important marketing objective for both advertising and promotion. In a competitive market, it is a vital contributor to profit. An everyday example of this is seen in supermarkets, where shoppers are willing to pay, on average, about 14 percent more for nationally advertised brands than for store brands.[5] However, the 14 percent premium has to pay for the national brands' higher advertising and trade promotion costs if they are to be profitable.

### Long-Run Price Objectives

**Advertising.** Advertising's long-run objective with regard to selling price is, or should be, the consolidation and protection of brand equity (a continuation of the 1-year price objective). In the long run, brand equity is the "asset value" of the brand,[6] reflected in the long-run average selling price of the brand *relative to its particular product category's* average selling price. Thus, McDonald's is not high-priced as far as restaurants go, but it does command a price premium in its particular category of fast-food hamburger restaurants.

The same objective holds for corporate "equity" via corporate image advertising, recognizing that we are defining the term "brand" broadly to include corporations. A study conducted for Bozell & Jacobs, a New York advertising agency, suggests that corporate image advertising has a small but significant and positive effect on company stock prices, which reflect investors' perceptions of corporations' equity. This finding is clarified in two further very long-run studies which show that the company's *total advertising in the most recent year* causes most of the effect. The effect of advertising on stock price is larger for consumer product companies than for industrial product companies but is still clearly profitable for both.[7]

At the brand level, there is now substantial evidence that the brand's advertising spending relative to competing brands is critically related to its brand equity in the long run,[8] and that this effect is causal in that *advertising causes brand equity* rather than the other way round. By and large, well-advertised brands are perceived by buyers as better value for a comparable price.

**Promotion.** In some special circumstances, promotions can contribute to long-run brand or corporate equity. Many marketers now offer integrated "continuity" promotions, such as frequent-flier programs, which reward long-term customer loyalty (although there is a question here as to whether these programs

merely "buy" equity for as long as they are in effect rather than "building" it more permanently). In business-to-business marketing, so-called *strategic alliances* may be formed between buyers and sellers, which frequently involve jointly-offered special prices or price-off promotions. Continuity programs and special joint discounts are promotions that can make customers less price sensitive to *later* price increases.

The promotional route to brand or corporate equity means that it is not always necessary to pursue a "highest quality" positioning. At the corporate level, the equity of some companies resides in a long-term "value" positioning (or "reasonable quality at low prices equals good value"). Kmart, Target, and Radio Shack electronics stores all occupy this position. For these retailers, a long history of price-off promotions can help to preserve their equity. Once established, this value positioning tends to retain all but the most discerning customers even when price is raised or competitors lower their prices.

## COST OBJECTIVES

A second way in which advertising communications and promotions can contribute to profit is by *lowering the cost* of manufacturing or marketing the brand. If the unit cost of the product can be lowered, then the unit profit margin, representing the difference between unit selling price and unit cost, will be larger and, even with constant volume, total profit will increase. As with price objectives, we will consider immediate, 1-year, and long-run objectives for reducing cost via advertising and promotion.

### Immediate Cost Objectives

**Advertising and Promotion.** Both advertising and promotion are costs in the short term, and therefore no immediate cost reduction is possible. The opposite occurs, in fact, because the unit cost of selling the brand is immediately increased by having to pay for the advertising or promotion campaign. The cost situation may be quite different over a longer period, however, as we will shortly see.

### 1-Year Cost Objectives

**Advertising.** Advertising plays a well-known role in business-to-business marketing by substituting, to some extent, for sales calls.[9] The average cost of an industrial sales call is currently about $295, and it takes an average of four calls to close a sale[10]—whereas the average cost to reach a business prospect through business-publication advertising is only about 20¢.[11] Although it is most unlikely that advertising could substitute for all four sales calls and close the sale, it is often the case that preliminary sales calls can be replaced by advertising that introduces the company and its products or services. Indeed, this has been known for many years, so it is likely that the average of four business sales calls to close a sale *already allows* for prior advertising. Nevertheless, those businesses that do not advertise may have a higher sales call frequency than average, which advertising could reduce.

We caution here that increased advertising, beyond the point of substituting for sales calls, could actually *raise* selling costs. Extra salespeople may have to be added to service the additional business generated by advertising. This caveat is noted, for example, in a survey of advertising elasticities (responsiveness to advertising) by Sethuraman and Tellis[12] in which they found that the average advertising elasticity for durable products was twice as high as for fast-moving consumer goods but that the extra sales volume, if this elasticity were to be exploited, would not necessarily result in greater profits if the size of the sales force had to be increased.

Advertising also can be used to reduce selling costs in a related way by generating qualified prospects for subsequent personal selling. Direct response advertising is often used for this purpose—at much lower cost than if the prospects had been obtained through cold-call personal selling visits.

Advertising can reduce selling costs for fast-moving consumer goods (fmcg) sold through grocery and drugstores by reducing ongoing trade promotion expenditures. Manufacturers can adopt a "pull" strategy of so successfully advertising their products to consumers that retailers are obliged to stock the manufacturer's new products. The retailer is then not in a position to demand as high a trade promotion contribution, if any, from the manufacturer.

**Promotion.** Promotions can lower *relative* costs in the medium-run by raising the potential "switching costs" for current customers. In consumer marketing, this may be achieved by loyalty programs or sometimes by the judicious choice of premium promotions. For instance, razors are often virtually given away with blades so that the user will feel compelled to buy the same blades to fit the razor for the lifetime of the razor. In business marketing, many business promotions to customers incorporate a contract such that the cost of breaking the contract is a large disincentive for switching to another supplier. If the cost of retaining present customers is lower than the cost of acquiring new customers,[13] these "lock-in" promotions will lower the company's costs for the year and perhaps longer.

### Long-Run Cost Objectives

**Advertising and Promotion.** In the longer term, some industries may be characterized by an "experience curve" whereby a large sales volume allows the firm to attain economies of scale in production and also perhaps economies from experience in marketing the product.[14] This translates into lower average unit costs. Advertising and promotion, by spurring sales volume, can move the firm more quickly down the experience curve. At a constant selling price per unit, profit would therefore increase.

However, it should be noted that economies of scale or of experience are hard to demonstrate in many industries.[15] Lower average costs are either very small or nonexistent for early entrants in most industrial and consumer product categories nowadays, according to several recent analyses.[16] Therefore, the reality of long-run cost reduction should be *directly investigated* rather than loosely assumed.

### SALES VOLUME OBJECTIVES

By far the most common marketing objective for advertising communications and promotions is to increase or maintain sales volume. (More precisely, the objective is to increase or maintain the sales *rate*, since what matters is the number of units sold per time period. For example, selling 1,000 cases per month is better than selling only 1,000 cases per year! However, "volume" has become more widely used than the precise term "rate" and we will stay with the former except when we want to draw attention to the rate itself.) According to the profit equation given earlier, an increase in sales volume, at constant selling price and cost, will produce greater total profit. Consistent with our framework, we will consider immediate, 1-year, and long-run time horizons for sales volume objectives.

## Immediate Sales Volume Objectives

**Advertising.** There are many situations in which advertising campaigns are designed to increase sales volume immediately; indeed, many campaigns are designed to do *only* this, having a very short-run sales volume objective and associated profit objective. Direct response advertising is an obvious example, but there are many others. Retail advertising, classified advertising, and special event advertising, such as for a movie or an upcoming concert, have immediate sales volume increase as their objective. Political campaign advertising, to influence voting behavior in terms of "volume" of voters, could also be classified as the use of advertising to achieve an immediate volume objective.

**Promotion.** Promotions—particularly price promotions—provide numerous instances of immediate sales volume increase as the marketing objective. What more immediacy can there be than the typical sales-promotion offer urging consumers to "act now"? Trade promotions, consumer price promotions, and retail promotions all have this objective.

Trade promotions can help to increase the sales volume of product bought by retailers. However, due to the prevalent practice of "forward buying," whereby retailers stock up when the promotion is on and fail to buy when it is not, trade promotions are very often not profitable for the manufacturer while being very profitable for the retailer.

Consumer price promotions are quite often employed in a volume sense to temporarily or more permanently increase the consumer's inventory. When a competitor launches a new product, for instance, other brands may run consumer promotions to try to "load" consumers so that they will be temporarily removed from the market while the new competitive product is being introduced and may therefore not ever try it.

Interestingly—or perversely, depending on your perspective—certain types of fmcg products are actually *consumed* at a higher rate when greater inventory is held at home. Beer, soft drinks, cookies, and other impulse snacks are examples. For these types of products, consumer promotions increase sales volume in the short run without a completely offsetting fall-off in the rate of buying afterward.

Stock clearance promotions by retail stores are another example of immediate sales volume being sought; here, the profit may come not so much from the retailer's profit margin, since products' prices may actually be slashed below cost in order to clear them, but from the opportunity cost savings of being able to put new, higher-priced stock in inventory once the old inventory is cleared.

Price promotions, therefore, are often used to increase buyers' purchase quantity in the short run. They are a *short-run* volume builder but may not always be profitable.[17] The exception is trial promotions, discussed below, which introduce new buyers to the brand. Trial promotions are not profitable in the short run but can produce 1-year and longer-run profit if the new triers stay with the brand.

## 1-Year Sales Volume Objectives

**Advertising.** As outlined in the manager's planning stages, advertising budgets are most often set for the 1-year period. The budget is based on the forecast volume of sales for the year. Here, advertising is being used to produce, support, or "assure" a given sales volume (again, more correctly, a given sales rate) for the year. The sales volume objective could be set in relation to a fast sales rate for a new product launch; maintenance of the sales rate for a current product; or a sales rate increase for a "re-staged" product.

**Promotion.** Promotions can be used in a number of ways to produce a sales volume increase over the 1-year planning period. *Trial promotions,* for instance, are designed to increase the number of new customers for the brand, who may subsequently provide increased business during the remainder of the year. Trade trial promotions are used to increase the volume of sales to new distributors or retailers. Distribution usually has an *accelerating,* not simply a linear, effect on the rate of sales,[18] so trade promotion to increase distribution (trade sales volume) is therefore an important marketing objective for most manufacturers.

All types of promotions can be used to attempt to even out the purchase cycle or to reduce seasonal or other time-related fluctuations for products subject to uneven sales. This evening-out or "de-cycling" of sales volume is an important objective for production and inventory profitability. Off-peak discounts for long-distance telephone calls or off-peak airline or train fares are everyday examples of this objective.

Both advertising (consumer or customer "pull") and promotion (sales incentives) can be used to motivate the company's sales force to "push" for more sales volume in selling to retailers or direct to business users or consumers. This is another, albeit indirect, way in which advertising and promotion can increase sales volume over the year and thereby contribute to profit.

### Long-Run Sales Volume Objectives

**Advertising But Rarely Promotion.** It is almost a truism that advertising is expected to contribute to sales volume in the long run. Some interesting evidence that it can do this comes from a meta-analysis survey by Sethuraman and Tellis[19] showing that advertising elasticity (the measured responsiveness of sales volume to advertising) is larger if the advertising and sales relationship is analyzed over an annual period than if it is examined only in the short run, that is, at monthly or shorter periods. Promotion, we should note, does not generally have this very long run sales objective beyond its initial role of increasing the pool of triers for the product.

For established brands, the realistic long-run objective is to *maintain* the rate of sales. British advertising theorists, notably Ehrenberg and more recently Stewart and Jones,[20] have contended that the most frequent long-run purpose of advertising is *defensive*. Because the great majority of product categories' sales are flat or slightly declining, these theorists argue that advertising's main role is to maintain or reinforce current customers' patronage so as to prevent a sales or market share decline that might otherwise occur in the absence of advertising. Competitively considered, advertising is thus seen as insurance: it is a price the brand must pay to stay in the market. For established brands, therefore, advertising is seen as a "weak force" in that it mainly helps to retain current users rather than to attract new ones. Indeed, as the British commentators have remarked, if the success of advertising campaigns were based solely on sales increases rather than preventing sales losses, we would see product *category* volumes expanding dramatically, which they have not. In flat markets, sales volume maintenance is a very important and much more realistic objective than a sales volume increase. In response to this British view, U.S. advertising expert William D. Wells has commented that advertising may well be a "weak market force," but it is also very inexpensive relative to personal selling, direct marketing, and other forms of marketing communications.[21]

In summary, we have seen that the marketing objectives for advertising communications and promotions can be much more comprehensive and specific than simply to increase sales. The $3 \times 3$ matrix of marketing objectives presented and discussed above shows that advertising and promotion can contribute—often in an integrated manner—to those marketing objectives that *ultimately* cause profit: namely, increasing selling price, lowering cost, and increasing sales volume. Moreover, we have seen that the marketing objectives of an AC&P campaign can have an immediate focus, can be established with regard to a 1-year time horizon (the typical planning period), or can take a long-run perspective. These alternatives form a comprehensive set of options for the manager in considering the overall purpose of a particular campaign.

Chapter appendix 2B, When to Use Market Share Objectives, provides a cautionary note on sales versus market share. In our discussion of marketing objectives, we have referred only to sales. The commonly used term "market share" has a more specific interpretation and purpose.

To achieve the brand's marketing objectives with AC&P, an overall budget must be decided (discussed in this chapter) and allocated (see Chapter 11). For most companies, the AC&P budget amount is a very difficult figure to arrive at. Few have the $4.3 billion[22] that the world's largest advertiser, Procter & Gamble, chooses to spend! The remainder of this chapter addresses the overall AC&P budget-setting decision.

### SETTING THE OVERALL AC&P BUDGET

In the remainder of this chapter, our purpose is to show how to set the *overall* AC&P budget for the planning year. The overall budget amount can then be allocated to one or more specific campaigns after the advertising communications and promotions strategies are decided in the subsequent planning stages (see Chapter 11). We view overall budget setting as a logical conclusion to the process of deciding the marketing objectives for the brand's advertising communications and promotions. Thus, it completes the first of the manager's planning stages.

The establishment of an overall AC&P budget for a brand requires that profit, sales, or market share now be considered as advertising and promotion *goals*. The manager has to estimate the contribution of

AC&P expenditures, to be fixed at the beginning of the planning year, to profit, sales, or market share *expected* by the end of the year.

### Our Approach to Budget Setting

Accurate budget setting for advertising communications and promotion is a complicated process. We make several overall recommendations which should make the process easier for the manager. We describe two general methods that can be used in any budget-setting situation: the objective-and-task method (which we will abbreviate as the task method) and the management-jury "independent averaged forecast/ five questions method (IAF/5Q method). Then, we propose some specialized budgeting methods for use in new-product situations and some for established-product situations. We conclude with an important reminder on the quality versus the quantity of spending in determining the budget.

### Overall Budget-Setting Recommendations

There are three recommendations that we believe will help the manager to arrive at a reasonable determination of the overall AC&P budget:

1. Think of the entire budget initially in terms of general advertising expenditure.
2. Use at least two methods.
3. Realize that the overall budget can be flexibly implemented during the campaign.

These recommendations are explained next.

**Think Initially in Terms of General Advertising Expenditure.** Initially, the overall budget should be set as though it consisted entirely of *general advertising* expenditure. (The exception is for companies in product categories where *trade promotion* is entrenched, such as products sold through grocery or drugstores. Unless this practice lessens in the future, which we think it will, then the manager in such a company has no option but to allocate first to trade promotion.[23] This allocation should be roughly proportional to the brand's target market share or, more precisely, target distribution share. The manager can then proceed as we outline in deciding how much to spend on advertising.) It is much easier for the manager to envision how general advertising affects sales than how all marketing communications would do so. Once the general advertising budget is determined, the manager

can later decide (using an extension of the *task method,* described below) how this total should best be spent between various types and media of advertising communications and consumer or customer promotions (see Chapter 11 for a discussion of IMC decisions and Chapter 15 for a discussion of media choices).

**Use At Least Two Methods.** The estimation of the general advertising budget, let alone subbudgets for specific campaigns, can rarely be perfectly accurate. This is because the causal relationship between advertising exposures and action (through the buyer response steps) is usually not fully known and, of course, because the future (usually a 1-year time horizon for the overall budget) cannot be predicted with certainty. Accordingly, it is wise to make the overall budget estimation by using at least two methods. If one method contains faulty reasoning, the other may compensate.[24] The final budget should be based on a progressively achieved "convergence" of the two methods' estimates, with the primary method given most of the weight. We will suggest which pair of methods seems best in the various new product and established product budgeting situations.

**Allow for Flexible Implementation of the Budget.** Our concern here is with setting the overall, *initial* AC&P budget for the year (the usual planning period). However, the budget is a forecast. The initial budget amount, realistically, will be *revised* a number of times during the year—in response to the relative effectiveness of general advertising vis-à-vis other AC&P activities, the quality of the advertising, competitors' actions, and corporate decisions on the advertising budget. Also, the manager should increase the budget when the AC&P activities are working and decrease or even eliminate it when they aren't. The need for flexibility is worth emphasizing because, in practice, overall 1-year budgets are too often regarded as fixed, preventing companies from taking advantage of an upward-trending advertising campaign or a winning promotion—or from wasting money on bad campaigns.

Two generally applicable budgeting methods— recommended for large and small companies both— are described next. (They will be recommended either as primary or backup methods in the specific marketing situations to follow.) These are the task method and the IAF/5Q method.

## THE TASK METHOD

The task method (full name: the objective-and-task method[25]) is based on the buyer response steps. The task method is reportedly now the budgeting method most widely used by *leading* advertisers.[26] The main reason it is not routinely used by *all* advertisers, we would surmise, is that the task method is quite difficult to apply properly. It requires:

- Clear identification, and operational measurement, of the buyer response steps (the steps again are: exposure → processing → communication effects and brand position → target audience action).
- Willingness to measure, or at least thoughtfully estimate, the transitions or "conversion ratios" from one buyer response step to the next.

The rationale for the task method is straightforward. Basically, the method asks how many advertising *exposures* (step 1) are required to deliver a given level of *processing* of the brand's ad or ads (step 2), which in turn will deliver a given number of prospects

with fully acquired *communication effects and brand position* in mind (step 3), which in turn will deliver the desired number of prospects taking *action* (step 4), thus achieving the sales goal.

In applying the task method, the manager *calculates backward* through the buyer response steps. A worked example is shown in Table 2.2 and Figure 2.2. In the example, we have used the more everyday names for each step: "insertions" (for the exposure step), "exposed" (for the processing step), "aware" (for the communication effects and brand position step), and "triers and repeaters" (for the action step). Later in the book, we will use more precise definitions and measures of the steps.

The table and figure show an example: the conversion ratios (transitions from one step to the next) are *for illustrative purposes only*. In practice, these have to be measured or carefully estimated by the manager. The conversion ratios in this example are: for insertions to exposures, .2; for exposures to awareness, .5; for awareness to trial, .2; and for trial to repeat, .5 (in this example, we have separated two different buying

---

### TABLE 2.2

**EXAMPLE OF THE TASK METHOD OF SETTING THE OVERALL AC&P BUDGET**

| Steps in the method | Example |
|---|---|
| 1. State the *sales volume goal* (in units) for the year. | 4,000,000 units |
| 2. Estimate (if applicable) the repeat incidence and repeat rate, and calculate the number of *triers*[a] needed to produce the sales level. | 2,000,000 triers, of whom 1,000,000 buy once and 1,000,000 buy again (trial-to-repeat ratio of 0.5) an average of three times (repeat rate of 3/year) |
| 3. Estimate the proportion of trial resulting among those who are made *aware*[b] of the product through advertising, and calculate the number of aware consumers required to produce the trial level. | 10,000,000 aware consumers if the awareness-to-trial conversion ratio is 0.2 |
| 4. Estimate the proportion of aware consumers resulting from those who receive sufficient *exposures*[c] to the advertising, and calculate the number of sufficiently exposed consumers needed to produce the awareness level. | 20,000,000 effectively exposed consumers if the exposures-to-awareness conversion ratio is 0.5, when "sufficient exposures" are estimated at 4+ |
| 5. Estimate the number of advertising *insertions*[d] needed to produce the sufficiently exposed level. | 20 insertions placed in three trade journals in the first 6 months will produce 20,000,000 consumers reached at 4+ frequency, the insertion frequency that will be needed if it is assumed that only 1 in every 5 insertions is actually seen and read, that is, an insertion-to-exposure ratio of 0.2 |
| 6. Calculate the *cost* of the advertising insertions which—with creative production and any other costs added—provides the estimated budget. | $600,000 if the average insertion costs $30,000; plus $30,000 for creative production and $15,000 for research = a total budget of $645,000 |

[a] "Number of triers" corresponds with "target audience action" (step 4 in the buyer response steps).
[b] "Awareness" is used loosely here and will later in the book be replaced by "attained the communication effects and brand position" (step 3 in the buyer response steps).
[c] "Sufficiently exposed," similarly, will be replaced by "processed the advertisement" (step 2 in the buyer response steps).
[d] "Insertions" here are the same as "exposure" (step 1 in the buyer response steps).

| $600,000 spent on media for 20 ad *insertions* | x 0.2 insertion-to-exposure conversion ratio |

| = | 20,000,000 consumers *exposed* at 4+ frequency | x 0.5 exposure-to-awareness conversion ratio |

| = | 10,000,000 consumers *aware* | x 0.2 awareness-to-trial conversion ratio |

| = | 2,000,000 *triers* | x 0.5 trial-to-*repeat* (3/year) conversion ratio |

= 1,000,000 single sales + (1,000,000 x 3) repeat sales

= 4,000,000 units in one year

Total budget = $600,000 media + $30,000 creative
production + $15,000 research

= $645,000

**FIGURE 2.2**
The task method. Results of the calculations in Table 2.2 shown in flowchart form.

behaviors, trial and repeat buying, in the action step). Conversion ratios are usually quite difficult to estimate accurately. However, as we emphasize further in Chapter 20, these ratios *must* be estimated if the manager wants to know whether and *how* the campaign worked. For now, this example will suffice to illustrate the task method as referred to in the remainder of this chapter.

## THE MANAGEMENT-JURY IAF/5Q METHOD

The second generally applicable budget-setting method is based on management judgment and is also known as the "jury of management opinion." We will therefore refer to it as the *management-jury* method. The management-jury method is the easiest and least expensive method of setting budgets (or of making *any* forecast in business). However, in the way it is *typically* implemented, it also tends to be the least accurate. To increase the accuracy of the management-jury method, we recommend that it be implemented by the "independent averaged forecast"

(IAF) and "five questions" (5Q) procedures described below.

### Independent Averaged Forecast (IAF)

Armstrong[27] has extensively studied the management-jury method of forecasting and has shown that it can be improved considerably by using an independent averaged forecast derived from the panel of jurors. The procedure is as follows (we will refer to the participating managers as jurors):

**1.** *Have five to ten jurors make independent forecasts.* You need a minimum of five to six jurors for their efforts to start canceling themselves out and a more accurate aggregated forecast to emerge, but beyond ten jurors the accuracy of such forecasts does not improve much. Each juror should make his or her forecast independently, that is, without discussion with other jurors.

**2.** *The jurors need not be advertising experts.* Surprising as it may seem, experts do no better than general managers in terms of forecast accuracy; anyone who is basically familiar with the product and market can act as a juror. However, the jurors should be selected from diverse areas within the company, not just from the marketing department. The more diverse the jurors in terms of background, the more likely it is that their errors will cancel themselves out and the average of their estimates will converge on a good forecast.[28]

**3.** *Provide the jurors with a short list of the main factors that affect sales.* Better solutions to the complex task of sales forecasting emerge when the problem is broken down into smaller components; however, only a short list should be used because jurors will rely on only a small amount of information even if more is provided. This short list would be a good start: (a) overall product-category sales trends, (b) competing brands' sales trends, and (c) the main marketing variables that influence sales. The causal direction of each factor's influence on sales is sufficient; the magnitude of its effect is not needed.

**4.** *Remind the jurors of potential interactions.* In the management-jury method, jurors must allow or control for the above factors mentally. The jurors should therefore be reminded that the factors in the list may be interdependent—particularly advertising and other marketing inputs such as distribution or price.

**5.** *Obtain independent estimates and then average them* (*using the median*) *to yield the forecast.* Do not use group discussion or feedback methods such as Delphi:[29] these lead to group biases which destroy the random canceling effect and lead to a less accurate forecast. The average of independent estimates is best. And the median is the appropriate average statistic as it is not influenced by extreme estimates.

The management-jury method of independent averaged forecast (IAF) can now be employed to set the overall AC&P budget by having the jurors make their estimates using the "five questions" (5Q) procedure, described next.

### The "Five Questions" (5Q) Procedure

Lodish[30] has developed a relatively simple and justifiable procedure for estimating the sales response to various levels of advertising expenditure. Look at Figure 2.3 and then consider these five questions (5Q):

**1.** What is the level of sales, in dollars, at the *current* level of advertising expenditure (established brand)? Or what would sales be at the *most likely* level of advertising expenditure (new brand)? ($A_{current}$)

**2.** What would sales be if advertising expenditure were *zero?* ($A_0$)

**3.** What would *maximum* sales be if you could spend as much as you wished on advertising, and what would this expenditure have to be? ($S_{max}$, $A_{max}$)

**4.** What would sales be if the current (or most likely) level of advertising were *halved?* ($A_{-50\%}$)

**5.** What would sales be if the current (or most likely) level of advertising were *increased half* as much again? ($A_{+50\%}$)

The sales levels estimated in response to these five questions allow us to plot five points on the sales response function, as shown in the figure. The management-jury method of IAF can be used to provide the estimates. (The estimates may be easier to make if the sales are in *units* of sales volume, but they then need to be converted to *dollars;* the advertising budget is in *dollars.*) Each point on the graph would then represent the average—specifically, the median —of all jurors' sales forecasts of unit volume for the five advertising expenditure amounts. Note that in question 3, you want the median of the jurors' *two* estimates ($S_{max}$ then $A_{max}$) because $A_{max}$ has to be estimated on the horizontal axis and $S_{max}$ on the vertical

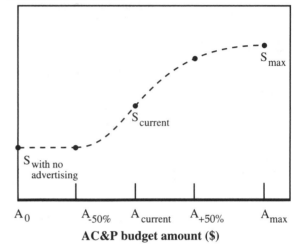

**Sales estimates (units)**

**FIGURE 2.3**

Sales response function for AC&P budget levels estimated from the "five questions" (5Q) procedure.

axis. The median is used because, unlike the mean, it is not affected by extreme estimates that may occur when using a small number of jurors.

Of course, the sales response curve may not look exactly like the one shown in the figure (S-shaped). It may, for instance, be concave (like the top part of an S). For established brands, the curvature of the figure is probably somewhat exaggerated, but this is to illustrate the procedure more clearly. For a new brand, sales may be estimated to be as low as zero with zero advertising. These situations are easily shown graphically.

The 5Q procedure will yield enough data points to derive the brand's "advertising-to-sales response function" reasonably well. Whereas it might be contended that the resulting graph is "only based on judgment," it does reflect managers' assumptions about reality. Each manager as a juror implicitly uses (his or her version of) this curve, often unknowingly, when making advertising budget recommendations. The five-questions procedure has the value of making the assumed response function explicit.

The *actual budget amount* is then chosen by considering the marketing objectives for the brand. If the objective is to *maximize sales,* then the budget amount would be read off the bottom axis of the graph at the point where the sales curve *first* reaches its peak. If, however, as we advise in most situations, the objective is to *maximize profit,* the sales response function should be estimated first, and then the following three costs subtracted from the sales (dollars) curve: the "cost of goods sold" (unit variable cost $\times$ volume), any additional fixed costs (such as a new factory to produce enough products), *and* the advertising cost. Direct estimation of a "profit response function" is too difficult;[31] the profit-maximizing budget is best derived by cost subtraction from the sales response function.

With these two general budgeting methods—the task method and the (management-jury) IAF/5Q method—now explained, we examine these and some additional specialized methods for new product category introductions, for new brand introductions, and for established brands.

## BUDGETING FOR A NEW PRODUCT CATEGORY

The most difficult budgeting situation of all is when the brand is the first to enter a completely new-to-the-world product category. The original manufacturers of such major innovations as television sets, contact lenses, and industrial robots must have faced this budgeting decision. The main difficulty is that there is no history from related products to use as a budget-setting guideline. Another very real difficulty is that the time from the innovation's introduction to its "takeoff" into the growth phase of the product life cycle, when the budget will need to be radically increased, can be very long. For instance, color TVs were introduced in 1952 but sales didn't take off until 1961; VCRs were introduced in 1972 but sales didn't take off until 1979–80; really new consumer durables take an average of 12 years before entering the growth phase.[32] However, whereas the life cycle is almost impossible to predict for the long run, the sales prospects on a year-to-year basis (a year being the normal budgeting period) are somewhat more predictable. In any event, the budget forecast is largely judgmental.

We recommend the task method as the primary method for new product category budget estimation, with the IAF/5Q method as the backup.

### Task Method

The most justifiable budgeting procedure in the totally-new-product-category advertising situation is the task method. Indeed, there really is no alternative

method to use other than guesswork. The risky aspect of the task method in this situation is that it does require some educated guesswork in estimating the "conversion ratios" linking each step. The advantage of the task method is that by thinking through a series of estimations in a causal chain, the final answer is likely to be more accurate than an overall guess.

For a completely new product category, error in estimating the ratios can be substantial. Overestimates, of course, are the real problems since underestimates (with one exception, effective frequency on the exposure step) mean that you are going to do better than you planned, for the same budget amount. If available, product test market and advertising pretest information should be used to assist in these estimates.

**IAF Assistance.** If no test market or advertising pretest information is available, the conversion ratios for new product category introductions can be estimated *in* the task method by using *just the IAF procedure.* That is, use a jury panel of managers to estimate the first conversion ratio, average the estimates, and then repeat the process for the subsequent conversion ratios.

### IAF/5Q Method

The *full* IAF/5Q method, in which the sales response function is estimated, can then be *additionally* applied after the task method, since we recommend the use of at least two methods. However, with no history for completely new products, the IAF/5Q method is not as reliable in this situation. The most weight should therefore be placed on the task method's budget estimate.

## BUDGETING FOR A NEW BRAND

This situation refers to a new brand entering an *existing* product category. With existing product categories, there is the experience of the industry or of competitors to draw upon. However, this is *partial* information only; we should not assume that competitors are budgeting correctly, although we might surmise that the market leaders are closer than others to being correct.

### Task Method

The task method should be used as the primary method for new brand budgeting, but given the complexity of estimating the conversion ratios, whose accuracy can greatly affect the resulting budget, we would recommend using at least one competitor-oriented method as a backup method and comparing that estimate with the task method's estimate. These backup methods, described next, are industry A/S ratio comparison, and Peckham's 1.5 rule / order-of-entry method.

### Industry A/S Ratio Comparison

The first of the backup budgeting approaches for new brands entering existing product categories is for the manager to examine the industry advertising-to-sales (A/S) ratio for the industry most closely related to the product category. These figures, calculated for each Standard Industrial Classification (SIC) code, are available in most countries from trade sources or industry analysts such as, in the United States, the Schonfeld & Associates Company. Many of them are reported each year in the trade press. With a little per-

sistence, even the small advertiser can get hold of industry-appropriate figures.

Table 2.3 shows selected industry A/S ratios in the United States for 1991 (a stable year for the U.S. economy). In established industries, these ratios don't change much from year to year. In most cases, promotion is included as well, so the figures represent the "overall advertising" expense that we have been considering.

**Budget Higher for a New Brand.** Because the budget is to be for a new brand in the category, it should be set *higher* than the industry average by at least half again (double would be even safer for the first year). Keying off the industry A/S ratio, while crude, can at least help the manager get into the competitive ballpark of what should be spent.

More specific figures on *particular competitors'* advertising budgets can often be obtained by careful monitoring of the trade press. For instance, you could

---

| TABLE 2.3 |
|---|

**ADVERTISING[a]-TO-SALES RATIOS IN THE UNITED STATES FOR SELECTED INDUSTRIES (1991)**

| Industry | A/S % | Industry | A/S % |
|---|---|---|---|
| **Business products** | | **Consumer products** | |
| Chemicals (wholesale) | 4.2 | Confectionery (chocolate, candy) | 10.5 |
| Adhesives and sealants | 2.7 | Perfumes, toiletries, and cosmetics | 10.1 |
| Lumber and building materials | 1.9 | Soap and detergents | 7.8 |
| Textile mill products | 1.8 | Pharmaceutical products | 6.1 |
| Computers and office equipment | 1.6 | Beer | 4.9 |
| Engines and turbines | 1.3 | Soft drinks | 3.0 |
| Farm machinery and equipment | 1.1 | Tobacco | 1.4 |
| **Business services** | | **Consumer services** | |
| Airlines | 1.9 | Investment advice | 8.0 |
| Professional consulting services | 1.4 | Movie theaters | 5.7 |
| Air couriers | 1.2 | Urban buses and trains | 1.6 |
| **Retail stores** | | Savings institutions | 0.7 |
| | | Consumer durables | |
| Furniture stores | 7.6 | Furniture manufacturers | 3.8 |
| Consumer electrical product stores | 5.8 | Motor vehicles | 2.2 |
| Video-rental stores | 4.7 | Household appliances | 2.1 |
| Eating places | 3.4 | | |
| Department stores | 2.8 | | |
| Drugstores | 1.6 | | |
| Grocery stores | 1.2 | | |
| **Miscellaneous** | | | |
| Mail-order and catalog houses | 6.9 | | |
| Dairy products | 4.1 | | |

[a]"Advertising" budgets include promotion expenditures in most cases.
*Source:* As reported in *Advertising Age,* September 16, 1991, p. 32. Used by permission of Schonfeld & Associates, Inc., Lincolnshire, IL 60069.

learn that Nike (the athletic footwear and clothing company) spent $33 million on advertising in the first quarter of 1991 alone, or that Ralph Lauren spent $10 million to launch its Polo Crest line of men's cologne.[33] Advertising budgets for *corporate image* advertising are also frequently reported in the trade press.

Research industry averages or significant competitors' spending figures is, however, only a starting point to provide a rough idea of the approximate amount that the new brand should anticipate having to spend. A second and more refined method to supplement the task method is available should the right conditions hold.

### Peckham's 1.5 Rule/Order-of-Entry Method

The new-brand budgeting rule proposed by J. O. Peckham, a respected consultant who worked for many years with the A. C. Nielsen Company, is worth investigating because of his extensive observation of advertising budgets and their effects.[34] We should note that his Nielsen experience would be mainly with consumer products sold through supermarkets and drugstores. (To apply the rule to *other* types of products and services is an extrapolation beyond Peckham's data. However, as a *backup* to the task method, it's worth investigating, especially for larger advertisers who have access to the relevant figures needed to apply this method.) We call his method "the 1.5 rule" and supplement it with an "order-of-entry" refinement.

There is one important qualification to using Peckham's 1.5 rule, namely, that it is applicable only in product categories where there is a demonstrable correlation between "share of voice," or SOV (the brand's advertising expenditure as a percentage or "share" of the total product category advertising expenditure), and "share of market," or SOM (the brand's sales units as a percentage of the total product category sales units). The manager can obtain an approximate indication of whether this correlation holds by obtaining brand-specific spending figures for the product category and relating these to the various brands' market shares. Of course, it should be cautioned that this correlation may not be causal, because other brands in the category may set their budgets *based on* SOV and thus spuriously produce the relationship. However, with the *yearly periods* for which we are budgeting, there is a strong relationship between SOV and SOM across a broad range of industries, for industrial as well as consumer products.[35]

If the SOV-SOM correlation can be reasonably verified, Peckham recommends setting the new brand's SOV at *1.5 times the target SOM* desired by the end of the brand's first 2 years. Assuming that the industry total advertising expenditure amount is known and the industry sales volume is known, it is easy to translate the SOV figure into a specific advertising budget. It is also easy to translate the target SOM into a specific sales volume figure (and we recommend always specifying the sales goal) for the 2-year period following launch.

But how does the manager set the target level of market share (SOM)? Here, it is advisable to consider the new brand's *order of entry* into the market, as explained next.

**To Set Target Share, Consider the Order of Entry.** In nearly all product categories, for consumer and business products alike, there is an enduring market share advantage that goes along with the brand's order of entry. This advantage pertains to market share expressed in *units,* not dollars. For various reasons,[36] the first, or "pioneer," brand in most product categories enjoys an enduring market share leadership; the second brand to enter tends to gain the second largest market share; the third, the third largest; and so forth.

The general size-of-share ratio (of the $n^{th}$ brand-to-enter's share as a fraction of the previous, $n^{th} - 1$, brand's share) for business products and consumer products appears to be about 0.71; although, for frequently purchased consumer products, the size ratio increases from 0.71 to about 0.92 as further, similar brands enter.[37] Let us explain the general case and then the latter modification will be easy to follow. Given that the first brand into a category has, by definition, 100 percent market share, the next brand entering can expect to reduce the pioneer's share down to 58 percent and take 42 percent for itself (thus producing the $42/58 = 0.72 \approx 0.71$ size-of-share ratio). Other things being equal—that is, parity brands with parity advertising—the third brand to enter can expect to force the first and second brands down to 45 percent and 32 percent while itself acquiring 23 percent (note that 23 percent is 0.71 of 32 percent, which in turn is 0.72 of 44 percent). The expected shares of subsequent entrants can be calculated similarly. These "par shares" are shown in Table 2.4, for slow- and

**EXPECTED MARKET SHARES ("PAR SHARES") BASED ON ORDER OF ENTRY INTO THE PRODUCT CATEGORY**

(*Note: market share in units, not dollars.*)

| Industrial products and consumer durables[a] | | | | | | |
|---|---|---|---|---|---|---|
| Number of competing brands in category | | | | | | |
| Order of entry | 1 | 2 | 3 | 4 | 5 | 6 | Total market |
| 1st | 100 | | | | | | 100 |
| 2nd | 58 | 42 | | | | | 100 |
| 3rd | 45 | 32 | 23 | | | | 100 |
| 4th | 39 | 28 | 20 | 14 | | | 101[b] |
| 5th | 35 | 25 | 18 | 13 | 9 | | 100 |
| 6th | 33 | 24 | 17 | 12 | 8 | 6 | 100 |

| Consumer packaged goods[c] | | | | | | |
|---|---|---|---|---|---|---|
| Number of competing brands in category | | | | | | |
| Order of entry | 1 | 2 | 3 | 4 | 5 | 6 | Total market |
| 1st | 100 | | | | | | 100 |
| 2nd | 58 | 42 | | | | | 100 |
| 3rd | 44 | 31 | 25 | | | | 100 |
| 4th | 36 | 25 | 21 | 18 | | | 100 |
| 5th | 31 | 22 | 18 | 15 | 14 | | 100 |
| 6th | 27 | 19 | 16 | 14 | 12 | 11 | 99[b] |

[a]Based on Robinson and Fornell, 1985. For more detailed estimates based on concentrated versus nonconcentrated business and consumer categories, see Parry and Bass, 1990. (See note 37 for more complete references.)
[b]Rounded.
[c]Based on Urban et al., 1986. (See note 37 for the complete reference.)

fast-moving products, respectively. These figures are very important because they represent *possible limits* to the market share that subsequent brand entrants into a product category can expect to attain *if* they enter with a parity product and parity advertising, hence the term "par share."[38]

**Overcoming Order of Entry.** Order-of-entry effects can be overcome by later entrants in either or both of two main ways: by entering with a superior product whose higher quality is evident to consumers; or by spending a lot more than normal on good advertising, which is our main concern here. For instance, Tide was the second brand to enter the detergent market behind Oxydol—but, with perhaps a better product and almost certainly superior advertising, Tide was able to surpass Oxydol's market share by twofold. Similarly, Rolaids was the third brand to enter the stomach remedy (antacid) market, but with perhaps a better product and heavy advertising spending behind its long-running theme ("How do you spell

'relief'? R-O-L-A-I-D-S") was able to take market leadership from the pioneer brand, Tums, and the second brand, Digel.[39]

For business products and consumer durables, where advertising plays a lesser role in the marketing mix than does personal selling, a superior product is more likely to overcome a late entry disadvantage than is more and better advertising.[40] Nevertheless, a large-budget "burst" of advertising with a good advertising message is worth trying for a year (assuming that any resulting increased sales can be serviced by the sales force at a low enough cost to make the increased sales bring in extra profit).

However, in most product categories—about 76 percent of categories according to Buzzell[41]—order-of-entry advantages attained in market share are *never* overcome. It is therefore wise to consider this fact when budgeting for a new brand. The nature of the product or service category might be such as to impose a quite unshakable structure on the market in accordance with order of entry.

We have taken this detour into the evidence on order of entry and market share to emphasize two points. First, the evidence suggests that market share goals for new brands entering established categories cannot be set in a vacuum. The data provided in Table 2.4 serve as a benchmark which the new entrant can then try to beat either with a better-quality product, if technically possible, or with better—and usually more—advertising. Second, the evidence emphasizes that budget size *alone* cannot simplistically "buy share" in an unlimited amount. The order-of-entry analysis should help to make SOM target setting for new brands entering an established category a more realistic process. If you have the data, and if an SOV-SOM relationship is demonstrable, then the Peckham's 1.5 rule / order-of-entry method can be applied to estimate the budget required to attain the target share.

**BUDGETING FOR AN ESTABLISHED BRAND**

Budgeting for established brands in established product categories is the most frequent budget setting situation for managers. Budgeting in this situation is somewhat easier than for the new brands because the manager can take advantage of historical data on the brand's previous spending and sales performance.

We will describe two accurate but difficult methods of budget setting that have been used successfully by some, usually larger, companies: the spending test and statistical projection. The alternative to these difficult methods is the IAF/5Q method, usable by all companies. Then we will describe a rule-of-thumb method, called Schroer's method, that appears to us to have sufficient validity for most companies to be worth trying, as long as they are multiregional companies. Specifically, we recommend this as the primary method for multiregional established brands.

### Spending Test

The textbook way to estimate advertising's contribution to sales for an established brand (and sometimes for a new brand) is to conduct an "investment spending" test in the actual marketplace. In the spending test procedure, a set of typical, closely matched markets is selected and different levels of advertising are allocated to each market. These levels represent experimental budget amounts—which may be higher *or lower* than last year's level. Then the actual sales results in each market are compared. The expenditure level that exhibits the highest sales rate or profit, depending on the firm's objectives, is then used as the budget for the total market. For grocery and drugstore products, scanner test markets (as offered by Information Resources' BehaviorScan or Nielsen's Scan-Trak, for instance) are often used for these experiments, although these services provide limited coverage of the total U.S. market.

*Advantages.* The experimental method in a properly conducted spending test controls for other factors that influence sales, and which may differ between markets, through randomization. If the trial budget levels are assigned randomly to markets, it can be assumed that other factors will average out, leaving advertising spending as the differentiating causal factor. Even if the assignment is not entirely random, differences in other factors can often be controlled statistically after the results are in (for example, by analysis of covariance), thus allowing for a cleaner interpretation of the experimental results.

*Disadvantages.* Although spending tests are *potentially* the most valid way to estimate advertising's contribution to sales, they have several disadvantages which deter their use: (1) they are costly—the best experiments use multiple markets for each spending level so as to better control for other factors, a step which few companies can afford and where risky compromises are often made; (2) they take time—the firm has to wait for the experimental results

before setting the budget, and it becomes tempting to compromise on the length and thus the reliability of the experiment; (3) they could be radical—many companies are reluctant to test extreme conditions, such as zero advertising, for fear of permanent or lasting damage to sales in those areas; (4) they could be sabotaged—competitors may realize when a test is being conducted and try to sabotage it by altering their own spending or marketing inputs, thus "de-randomizing" the other factors in the experiment and making the results questionable; and (5) the local market differences, which nearly always exist, *remain* as differences—which is the most serious danger in trying to set a single, total-market budget from experiments, as we shall see shortly.

### Statistical Projection

For established brands, statistical projections of previous advertising-to-sales relationships to the forthcoming planning period can be an economical alternative to the spending test's marketplace experiments. In this procedure, historical spending levels and historical sales levels are compared over time (best done in terms of months, quarters, and years, to gauge short- and longer-term effects), and a statistical technique (most often regression analysis) is used to compute the relationship between the two. The size of the relationship provides an estimate for determining the advertising budget size in relation to expected sales.

*Advantages.* Statistical projection controls for other factors statistically rather than experimentally, although they could be regarded as inputs to an "experiment over time" if their levels have been varied. A multiple regression equation can be developed, for example, which includes statistics on these other variables, such as distribution coverage and price levels, in addition to advertising and promotion. Regression techniques should be based on models which estimate not only within-period relationships but also carry-over effects from previous periods.[42]

*Disadvantages.* There are three main disadvantages of statistical projection: (1) it is for well-established brands only—obviously, for newer brands there is not a sufficient historical advertising and sales trend from which to project; (2) it assumes continuity, perhaps mistakenly—statistical projections assume that conditions that applied in past periods will continue into the current budgeting period so that the relationship between advertising and sales will stay the same, which is a risky assumption if the market is volatile, with new brands entering or old brands leaving, though the regression prediction can and should be modified by management judgment to take account of expected changes in market conditions;[43] (3) and it requires in-depth knowledge of statistics—frankly, this is the biggest problem with statistical projection, because the use of regression has technical difficulties that even the experts don't always agree on how to solve.

In summary, spending test and statistical projection are accurate but difficult budgeting techniques for established brands. We suggest they be tried (as one of the two or more methods) by *only* the most statistically sophisticated managers. For *most* companies, large or small, the IAF/5Q method is adequate instead of these methods. (Also, remember, the budget for an *established* brand is unlikely to be *way* off, and it can always be adjusted as the campaign progresses, as explained in Chapter 20.)

To be used as the *primary* method for established brands sold in a *number* of regions, we are impressed by the logic of a newly proposed method, described next, which we call Schroer's method.

### Schroer's Method

Managers of established brands distributed multiregionally should consider the budgeting procedure proposed by Schroer, a consumer goods strategist with the consulting firm of Booz, Allen & Hamilton.[44] Schroer's method has a good deal of logic behind it and also is mindful of empirical evidence on the difficulty of achieving large sales or market share gains in established, mature product categories.

Schroer's method assumes that the product category has reached maturity in the product category life cycle—that is, primary demand cannot be increased and therefore a market share increase (presuming this increases profit) is the only available objective for our brand. His procedure is as follows:

**1.** Budgets should not be set nationally but rather locally, market by market. ("Locally" means geographically; for instance, Campbell Soup Company reportedly divides the U.S. market into 22 strategic geographic regions. However, the market-by-market divisions could be applied to different end-use markets or market segments *if* the media plan can reach them separately. We will stay with the term "local," however, for easier exposition.)

**2.** The two aspects to examine in each local market are: (a) the largest competitor's share of total advertising spending in the category (SOV) in relation to the largest competitor's market share (SOM); and (b) our brand's market share (SOM) in that local market and, specifically, whether we are the leader or a follower in that market.

**3.** If the largest competitor's SOV is below its SOM, this signals an opportunity for our brand to attack. (Of course, we may *be* the largest-share brand and would therefore wish to maintain our market share; see Figure 2.4.) If our brand is going to successfully attack

**FIGURE 2.4**

Budgeting strategies (in each local market) according to the largest competitor's advertising spending and our brand's market share. Key: SOV = "share of voice," the percentage of total advertising spending; SOM = "share of market," that is, market share; and LC = largest competitor in that market.
*Source:* Schroer, 1990. See note 44.

| Our Brand's SOM in local market | **Largest Competitor (LC) in local market** | |
| | Low SOV/SOM (below 1.0) | High SOV/SOM (1.0 or higher) |
| --- | --- | --- |
| Follower | *Attack*—with a large SOV premium, approximately twice that of the LC, and sustain it for a year or more. | *Follow niche strategy*—retreat and focus, reduce spending. |
| Leader | *Maintain*—set our SOV/SOM at 1.0. | *Follow defensive strategy*—increase spending to match that of the LC. |

the largest competitor (LC), then we must be prepared to make a massive increase in spending (in that local market) and be prepared to sustain the expenditure increase *for 12 months or more.* The required expenditure increase is estimated to be equal to 20 to 30 percentage points of share of voice *above* the largest competitor's spending, which is usually approximately double the competitor's budget in that market.

**4.** In other markets, where the largest competitor's SOV is equal to or greater than its SOM, our brand may choose to resort to a defensive strategy, which requires matching expenditure, or even retreat to a niche strategy, which requires reduced expenditure.

The established-brand spending strategies—for each local market—are summarized in the figure. The *local market focus* is the key to the success of this budgeting approach. As Schroer points out, few market leaders would be willing to allow another brand to outspend them by double on a national basis. However, when expenditures and market shares are analyzed on a *local* basis, plenty of opportunities for attack exist.[45] And, even if the largest competitor is astute enough and quick enough to pick up the pattern, the chances of retaliation are surprisingly low. Schroer gives a number of case history examples of this budgeting approach being used with great success. We believe this procedure deserves close examination by the manager of an established, multiregional brand. (However, because of the crucial consequence if competitors retaliate, it is not appropriate for a *single-region* local advertiser. Such an advertiser should use the task method for budget setting as the primary method.)

Overall, then, we have explained and recommended a number of budgeting methods for various advertising situations. For convenient reference, we summarize these methods in Table 2.5.

## QUALITY OF ADVERTISING SPENDING

In setting the overall AC&P budget, we have assumed that the *quality* of advertising spending is a constant and that the sales results of advertising are dependent solely on the *amount* spent. Of course, this is a vastly oversimplified assumption, but it is necessary because in most cases the manager does not yet *know* the quality of spending.

Quality of spending is represented by factors such as accurate media placement (one budget may be

**TABLE 2.5**

**SUMMARY OF RECOMMENDED AC&P BUDGET-SETTING METHODS**

| Advertising situation | Primary method | Backup or check methods |
|---|---|---|
| New product category introduction (first brand in "new-to-the-world" product category) | • Task method (with test market data or IAF manage-ment jury) | • IAF/5Q method |
| New brand in existing category | • Task method (with test market data or IAF manage-ment jury) | • Industry A/S ratio compari-son (basic)<br>• Peckham's 1.5 rule / order-of-entry method |
| Established brand in existing category | • Schroer's method (if brand is multi-regional; other-wise, use task method) | • Spending test<br>• Statistical pro-jection<br>• IAF/5Q method |

partly wasted on nonprospects whereas another might be accurately directed at the target audience) and of course the creative quality of the AC&P campaign itself (a "real winner" campaign versus an equally expensive but mediocre one). In fact, quality is a consideration all the way through the buyer response steps: (1) accuracy of *exposure,* (2) correctness of *processing* of the ads, adlike events, or promotion offers, (3) attainment and appropriateness of the brand's *communication effects and position,* and (4) concentration on the right *target audience action.*

Figure 2.5 shows a hypothetical example of how advertising spending *quality* can affect sales results. Lest the reader think these curves exaggerated, the graph is confirmed by actual though smoothed data published by Blair[46] showing variations in sales results as a function of the *creative quality* ("persuasiveness") of the advertisement. There is now plenty of evidence that differences in the persuasive (or communication) effectiveness of advertisements can produce large differences in sales results. For new brands, for instance, from equivalent budgets, a "real winner" creative campaign can produce many times higher sales than a poor one.

Although much less often studied, the quality of *media plans,* too, can be greatly improved from the standard types of plans that are in operation at present, as we will see in Chapters 15 to 17 of the book.

**Sales (units)**

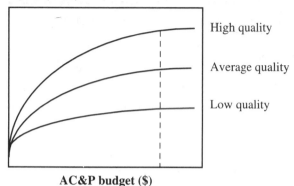

**AC&P budget ($)**

**FIGURE 2.5**
Sales effects of the same quantity but different "qualities" of spending on AC&P. Although not shown in this simplified diagram, quality differences may occur all the way through the buyer response steps leading to sales.

Media plans all too commonly suffer from loose matching of media vehicles with the target audience—a problem which is compounded when using integrated marketing campaigns—and from failure to estimate the reach pattern and the frequency needed at the individual level to accomplish the communication objectives of the campaign.

Nevertheless, at this stage of the manager's planning, the concern is with setting the *initial* AC&P budget. The quality of the advertising communications, and of promotion offers when these are used, as represented by the media strategy and the creative strategy for both advertising communications and promotions, are, at this stage, unknown factors. Thus, we must assume an *average* level of creative and media spending quality and concentrate on setting the budget based on *quantity* of spending. In Chapter 20, where we address campaign tracking and evaluation, we will see that the budget can be, and frequently is, altered to take into account differences in actual media plan quality and actual creative quality (these quality differences apply not only to advertising but also to promotion). The manager should track the campaign to determine the best spending rate *during* it and thus how much of the initial budget to finally spend.

## SUMMARY

The first stage of AC&P planning is to decide on the marketing objectives that the brand's campaign or campaigns must address and also to set the overall advertising communications and promotion (AC&P) budget. Advertising communications and promotions can be planned with the purpose of supporting or "guaranteeing" a previously established marketing objective, such as designated sales goal; or the campaign can have its own marketing objectives if it is intended to be largely responsible for a major change in the brand's marketing performance.

Profit (usually defined as economic profit but sometimes additionally defined in terms of social utility) is the ultimate objective of every advertising communications or promotion campaign. However, it is important to realize that the three avenues to profit—increasing selling price, lowering unit cost, and increasing sales volume—are vital subsidiary marketing objectives. Advertising and promotion can maintain or increase profit by maintaining or increasing the brand's price differential over other brands; maintaining or lowering the cost per unit sold; or maintaining or increasing sales volume, which is the rate at which units are sold.

Advertising, using the term here broadly to encompass advertising communications in general, can effectively increase the brand's relative selling price in two ways: (1) by increasing its perceived benefits and thus increasing its upside price elasticity (so sales go up faster when the brand offers a price reduction or a promotion), and (2) by increasing its perceived uniqueness and thereby decreasing its downside price elasticity (so sales do not go down as much when the brand raises its price or when its relative price is raised due to competitors' price cuts or promotions). A useful dynamic indicator of brand equity, suggested by Moran, is the ratio of upside to downside price elasticity of demand for the brand.

Advertising and promotion may be able to lower unit costs by helping to presell the brand and partially replacing expensive sales calls. For some products, advertising and promotion may be able to reduce long-run average cost if an "experience curve" is demonstrable with volume of units produced.

Advertising and promotion can also affect profit, of course, by increasing sales. If price and unit cost remain the same while the volume (rate) of sales increases, total profit will increase. However, "maximizing sales" is not a wise objective if the unit cost to reach the extra customers increases such that profit actually declines. Sales are often used as an objective in the form of market share, but sales and market share are different measures. Market share is a relative measure whereas sales are an absolute measure, and market share critically depends on correct definition of the market. Assuming correct market definition, market share is a useful primary objective in growing markets (introductory or growth phases of the product category's life cycle) because it indicates how well your sales are progressing relative to those of the average brand. However, market share, and also sales, are less useful objectives in mature or declining markets, where the emphasis should be on profit.

In the chapter, we describe possible marketing objectives for AC&P campaigns in terms of the three avenues to profit—increasing price, lowering cost, and increasing sales volume. We further organize this discussion in terms of three planning horizons: immediate, 1-year (the usual planning period), and longer-run. The possible marketing objectives are too numerous to summarize here, but the summary point is that the manager should consider *all three* contributors to profit as well as the planning horizon when establishing marketing objectives for the campaign.

Establishing the overall budget for a brand's advertising and promotion is a difficult process that can be made less so by following three recommendations: begin by thinking in terms of *general* advertising (the budget can be subdivided into types of advertising communications and types of promotion later, when the target audience and communciation objectives are decided, as shown in Chapter 11); use at least two budgeting methods (a primary method and a backup method as a check); and realize that the overall budget can be flexible when implemented during the campaign (at this stage we are setting only the *initial* AC&P budget; it can be adjusted up or down as the results of the campaign or campaigns progressively become evident).

Two generally applicable AC&P budget-setting methods are (1) the task method, which is the best method overall but difficult to apply properly; and (2) the management-jury IAF/5Q method, which is easy to apply and more accurate than many other methods commonly in use.

When budgeting for the introduction of a completely new product category, where ours is the innovating brand, we recommend the use of *both* these methods. With no historical data to go on, there are no alternatives in this situation.

When budgeting for the introduction of a new brand into an existing product category, we again recommend the task method as the primary method, backed up by at least the basic method of industry A/S ratio comparison (for smaller advertisers) but preferably by the much more precise Peckham's 1.5 rule / order-of-entry method (for larger advertisers with the requisite data). The latter method is based on realistically attainable market share which, for a new brand entering an existing category, is sensible to consider.

When budgeting for an established (continuing) brand in an existing category that is sold in multiple regions, we recommend Schroer's method, which is based on *local* market shares and associated competitive strategies, backed up by (if affordable and if the statistical sophistication of the manager is high) the spending test method or statistical projection, or (if neither conditions are met) by the management-jury IAF/5Q method. For a one-market, local advertiser, we recommend the task method as primary and the IAF/5Q method as a backup.

Money alone does not buy sales; obviously, the quality of spending is as much or more important than the quantity of money spent. However, at this initial stage of planning, the manager does not yet know the quality of the media plan, for advertising or promotion, nor, usually, the quality of the advertising or promotion offers, so *average* quality must be assumed. The initial AC&P budget can be adjusted to reflect actual quality as that quality is revealed during implementation of the campaign.

## APPENDIX

# 2A. Strategies Based on Upside and Downside Elasticity

Moran's theory suggests different (marketing and) marketing communications strategies according to where the brand is located in terms of its upside and downside price elasticities of demand. Since these strategies bear on the integrative relationship between advertising, communications and promotions, they are worth reviewing here even though our present concern is with marketing objectives rather than with issues of strategy. To simplify the concepts of elasticity, we will refer to upside elasticity as "value" and to downside elasticity as "uniqueness," meaning low substitutability in buyers' minds. Thus, a brand should strive for high value *and* high uniqueness (low substitutability). Strategies for the four combinations of value and uniqueness are shown in Figure 2.6.

**Value**

| Uniqueness | High | Low |
|---|---|---|
| **High** | • Promote<br>• Ratchet on advertising | • Broaden distribution<br>• Extend product line<br>• Raise price |
| **Low** | • Sharpen product<br>positioning<br>• Advertise (U) | • Improve product<br>• Advertise (V and U) |

U = Uniqueness
V = Value

**FIGURE 2.6**

Marketing strategies based on the brand's upside demand elasticity (value) and downside demand elasticity (substitutability—here considered inversely as uniqueness).
*Source:* Adapted from W.T. Moran, The advertising-promotion balance, Paper presented to the Association of National Advertisers' Advertising Research Workshop, New York, NY, 1978.

Beginning with the upper left-hand cell and moving clockwise, we see that the following strategies apply:

- *High Value / High Uniqueness.* Our brand is in an ideal position: sales respond well to our own price reductions and are insulated against competitors' price reductions. *Strategy:* Increase frequency of promotions in between bursts of further equity-building advertising (the "ratchet effect"; see Chapter 16 on media scheduling).
- *Low Value / High Uniqueness.* Our brand is in an "inelastic" market, which is also a good (but rare) position to be in. Our sales are not affected if we raise our price, and competitors cannot hurt us with their price reductions. *Strategy:* Broaden distribution, extend the product line, and *raise* price since sales will stay constant and unit revenue and thus profit will increase.
- *High Value / Low Uniqueness.* Our brand's sales respond well to our own price reductions but are vulnerable to competitors' price reductions. Our brand has value equity but is not unique. *Strategy:* Reposition the product more uniquely, then readvertise its *uniqueness.*
- *Low Value / Low Uniqueness.* Our brand is in the worst position: sales do not respond to our own price reductions and sales are also lost to competitors when they reduce prices. *Strategy:* Improve the product, then advertise (or readvertise with much better advertising) to build value equity *and* perceived uniqueness as quickly as possible. Obviously, this is an expensive and difficult task.

## 2B. When to Use Market Share Objectives

When setting marketing objectives, the terms "sales" and "market share" are too often used interchangeably. Sales are *absolute sales* (the number of units sold or dollars generated in a specified time period). Market share, on the other hand, refers to *relative sales* (your sales as a percentage of the total product category or industry sales). Since total category or industry sales volume is the denominator of market share, it follows that the only situation in which "sales" and "market share" are identical is when category or industry sales are perfectly flat, that is, in the mature stage of the product category's or industry's life cycle. Use of the terms interchangeably in other situations can be misleading for the manager. Both have their correct use as objectives, as explained next.

Sales objectives (absolute sales in units *and* dollars[47]) should *always* be set—simply because a sales objective is clear and unambiguous. However, market share (relative sales) has superior diagnostic value in a growing market—assuming a strategically correct definition of the "market" upon which to estimate market share (see Chapter 5's discussion of the *category need* communication objective and Chapter 18 concerning *market partitioning*). But in a mature or declining market, profit, rather than sales or market share, has the most diagnostic value.

- In *growing markets,* the emphasis should be on *market share* rather than absolute sales. Market share indicates how fast your sales are rising relative to competitors' sales and is an important indicator of growth-phase performance.

- In *mature or declining markets,* the emphasis should be on *profit* rather than either sales or market share, for reasons given below. In a declining market, you may actually gain market share while experiencing falling sales, because other competitors are leaving the market.

Recently, there has been a substantial rethinking of the ubiquitous marketing objective of attempting to *maximize* long-run market share. For instance, Urban and Star[48] conclude that "aggressive strategies that seek maximum market share rarely turn out to be the most profitable." This is because maximum *profit* usually occurs *before* the point of maximum market share and thus before the point of maximum sales (Figure 2.7).[49] The average costs to attract the last few customers' sales or the last few points of market share are typically much higher than the average costs preceding them (although not shown in the figure, the cost line can actually curve upward at this point). An objective of

trying to squeeze out maximum sales or market share can, via a rapidly upturning cost curve, cut substantially into profits that would have been obtained had the extra market share or sales not been sought. Simon and Arndt[50] also provide strong evidence for a diminishing rate of sales increase as advertising and promotion expenditures increase, which supports the conclusion that maximum profits are reached *below* the level of maximum sales.

When setting marketing objectives for a brand, the manager should focus on *profit maximization* as the ultimate objective rather than sales or market share maximization. Market share maximization is a useful objective for a new brand in a new product category (introduction or growth phase) but only to attain a more profitable position. Once there (maturity phase), maximum profit will usually be maintained by *not* seeking to maximize market share or sales, which are equivalent in a mature market, but rather by keeping market share and sales at a level that is known to produce optimal profit. Instrumental in maintaining the brand's market share and sales rate is continuous attention to its equity—its value and uniqueness—as reflected by its price demand elasticity.

**FIGURE 2.7**

Maximum profit usually occurs *before* the peak of sales, at a *lower* level of advertising communications and promotion expenditure than the level that maximizes sales. (Reprinted by permission from the *Journal of Advertising Research,* March 1961.)

**Financial performance ($)**

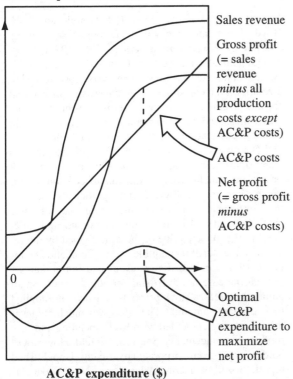

Sales revenue

Gross profit (= sales revenue *minus* all production costs *except* AC&P costs)

AC&P costs

Net profit (= gross profit *minus* AC&P costs)

Optimal AC&P expenditure to maximize net profit

**AC&P expenditure ($)**

## NOTES

1. Evidence on the value of setting explicit advertising objectives comes from studies by S. H. Britt, Are so-called successful advertising campaigns really successful? *Journal of Advertising Research,* 1969, *9* (2), pp. 3–9; S. Majaro, Advertising by objectives, *Management Today,* 1970, January, pp. 71–73; and D. C. Marshner, DAGMAR revisited—eight years later, *Journal of Advertising Research,* 1971, *11* (27), pp. 27–33.

    Interestingly, too, individuals perform better when they are accountable to challenging, explicit objectives (that is: goals). A review of 110 studies of goal setting on individual performance found higher performance in 90 percent of the studies. See E. A. Locke, K. N. Shaw, L. M. Saari, and G. P. Latham, Goal setting and task performance, *Psychological Bulletin,* 1981, *90* (1), pp. 125–152.

    More generally, an important meta-analysis of the relationship between strategic planning (explicit objectives, generation of strategies, evaluation of strategies, seeking commitment to chosen strategy, and monitoring results) and firms' performance found conservatively estimated correlations of .25 with sales growth and .28 with earnings-per-share growth, with some suggestion of a stronger relationship in turbulent environments (though see the final paragraph of this note regarding highly turbulent environments). See B. K. Boyd, Strategic planning and financial performance:

A meta-analytic review, *Journal of Management Studies,* 1991, *28* (4), pp. 353–374.

MBA students using the MARKSTRAT marketing simulation game, which includes advertising decisions, also perform better when using formal planning (objectives, strategy, review, and iterate) in a normal marketing environment.

However, rigid adherence to a formal plan can be dysfunctional if the market is *highly* turbulent, as occurs in the early phase with some high-tech products. See R. Glazer and A. M. Weiss, Marketing in turbulent environments: Decision processes and the time-sensitivity of information, *Journal of Marketing Research,* 1993, *30* (4), pp. 509–521.

2. In the case of advertising communications and promotions, this is evidenced in three areas:

   **a.** *Company Coordination.* Managers in other functional areas—such as finance and production—are able to coordinate with the marketing manager much more effectively if all managers are working with a common written set of marketing objectives for the product.

   **b.** *Agency Coordination.* Similarly, many disputes and errors can be avoided if everyone within the advertising agency concerned with the account—account executives, researchers, creative group, and media planners—has the same set of client-approved objectives to work toward.

   **c.** *Performance Evaluation.* The presence of written objectives makes performance evaluation—both by the company and the agency—much less ambiguous, particularly if the objectives are expressed as goals.

3. William T. Moran's theory and analysis were first outlined in W. T. Moran, Insights from price research, Paper presented at the Marketing Conference, the Conference Board, New York, NY, 1976; and W. T. Moran, The advertising-promotion balance, Paper presented at the Association of National Advertiser's Advertising Research Workshop, New York, NY, 1978.

4. For example, an analysis of 19 beverage brands by Ogilvy & Mather found no relationship between upside and downside elasticity for 17 of them. O & M call their technique "Brand/Price Trade-Off" but it is actually Moran's idea implemented by using Gabor's buy-response methodology. See M. Blackston, Price trade-offs as a measure of brand value, *Journal of Advertising Research,* 1990, *30* (4), pp. RC-3 to RC-6; and also A. Gabor, *Pricing Principles and Practices,* London: Heineman Educational Books, 1977. Another study showed that advertising exposures during the purchase cycle increased consumers' price sensitivity, although the authors did not examine upside and downside elasticity separately. The advertising effect on price sensitivity (elasticity) was observed for three of the 11 brands of dog food and two of the three brands of aluminum foil in the study, implying that only good advertising, rather than just any advertising, has this effect. See V. Kanetkar, C. B. Weinberg, and D. L. Weiss, Price sensitivity and television advertising exposures: Some empirical findings, *Marketing Science,* 1992, *11* (4), pp. 359–371.

5. C. Anson and R. F. Silverstone, Supermarket strategy summary, in the *Maryland Center for Public Broadcasting's Consumer Survival Kit,* Owing Hills, MD: Maryland Center for Public Broadcasting, 1975.

6. Actually, in a financial sense, equity is assets minus liabilities, which fits Moran's dual perspective rather well. In a thoughtful monograph on brand valuation from an accounting perspective, Barwise and his coauthors summarize seven factors used by the Interbrand company to assess a brand's asset value: market share, life of brand (how long on market), long-run sales trend, market stability, internationality, amount and quality of marketing support, and legal protection. In our opinion, in the absence of standard objective criteria, this is a valid list. See P. Barwise, C. Higson, A. Likierman, and P. Marsh, *Accounting for Brands,* London Business School, UK, 1989. The list is on p. 33.

7. For the original study, see E. P. Schonfeld and J. H. Boyd, The financial payoff in corporate advertising, *Journal of Advertising Research,* 1982, *22* (1), pp. 45–55. This study is further discussed in Chapter 11: Niefeld conducted a follow-up analysis showing a 33 to 1 return on the corporate image advertising investment for the average corporate advertiser. Schonfeld and Boyd measured only corporate image advertising in business publications. In the more recent studies, Cooil and Devinney found very large effects of the previous year's *total* advertising spending (A/S ratio) on stock price, and smaller but significant effects on profit; while Simon and Sullivan found significant effects for the current year's advertising and 2-year share-of-voice (SOV, defined later in this chapter) on brand equity, defined as the market value of the firm divided by the replacement costs of its tangible assets. Cooil and Devinney used a more sensitive analysis and found that a 1 percent increase in advertising spending (a very small amount) increases stock prices by 1.1 percent (applied to a very large amount). The effect was much bigger if the advertising coincided with R&D spending and new product announcements. See J. S. Niefeld, How stockholders profit from corporate advertising, Unpublished report, Bozell & Jacobs Advertising, New York, NY,

1984; B. Cooil and T. Devinney, The return to advertising expenditure, *Marketing Letters,* 1992, *3* (2), pp. 137–145; and C. J. Simon and M. M. Sullivan, The measurement and determinants of equity: A financial approach, *Marketing Science,* 1993, *12* (1), pp. 28–52. The authors acknowledge the assistance of Tim Devinney in interpreting this research.

8. See A. Biel, Strong brand, high spend, *Admap,* 1990, November, pp. 35–40; S. Hume, Brand loyalty study, *Advertising Age,* March 2, 1982, p. 19, reporting the research from NPD's results; and W. A. Kamakura and G. J. Russell, Measuring brand value with scanner data, *International Journal of Research in Marketing,* 1993, *10* (1), pp. 9–22.

9. S. Gopalakrishna and R. Chaterjee, A communications response model for a mature industrial product: Applications and implications, Working paper, College of Business Administration, Pennsylvania State University, 1991.

10. Cahners Advertising Research Report #452.1F, 1992. The average for 1992 was $292, so we have rounded upward slightly. Note that there are wide variations in the average cost and number of calls, by industry.

11. R. W. Haas, *Industrial Marketing Management,* 4th ed., Boston, MA: Kent Publishing Company, 1989.

12. R. Sethuraman and G. Tellis, An analysis of the trade-off between advertising and price discounting, *Journal of Marketing Research,* 1991, *29* (2), pp. 160–174. Their analysis examined overall advertising elasticity and price elasticity and did not distinguish, as we have, between upside and downside elasticities. The average advertising elasticity for durable products was 0.23 while the average advertising elasticity for frequently purchased products was 0.09.

13. F. F. Reichheld and W. E. Sasser, Jr., Zero defects quality comes to services, *Harvard Business Review,* 1990, *68* (5), pp. 105–111.

14. Economies of scale are a well-known phenomenon in economics; see, for example, W. S. Comanor and T. A. Wilson, *Advertising and Marketing Power,* Cambridge, MA: Harvard University Press, 1974. The broader concept of an "experience curve," reflecting "expertise" efficiency as well as production efficiency, was popularized by The Boston Consulting Group, *Perspectives on Experience,* Cambridge, MA: The Boston Consulting Group, 1968.

15. M. E. Porter, *Competitive Strategy,* New York, NY: The Free Press, 1980.

16. See W. T. Robinson and C. Fornell, Sources of market pioneer advantages in consumer goods industries, *Journal of Marketing Research,* 1985, *22* (3), pp. 305–317; W. T. Robinson, Sources of market pioneer advantages: The case of industrial goods industries, *Journal of Marketing Research,* 1988, *25* (1), pp. 87–94; and M. Parry and F. M. Bass, When to lead or follow? It depends, *Marketing Letters,* 1989, *1* (3), pp. 187–198.

17. M. Abraham and L. Lodish, Getting the most out of advertising and promotion, *Harvard Business Review,* 1990, *90* (3), pp. 50–60.

18. P. Farris, J. Olver, and C. de Kluyver, The relationship between distribution and market share, *Marketing Science,* 1989, *8* (2), pp. 107–127.

19. Same reference as note 12. Sethuraman and Tellis found that the advertising elasticity coefficient was 0.19 for yearly interval studies compared with 0.08 for monthly or shorter study intervals. Kim and Lehmann, studying a typical consumer food product, found that TV advertising did not affect sales over a 1-week period but had a significant effect over a 4-month period; see D. Kim and D. R. Lehmann, The long and short run impacts of advertising, price and promotion, Working paper, School of Management, State University of New York, Buffalo, 1991. Also, research from Information Resources, Inc., supports the reality of the long-run positive sales volume effects of advertising; see the Abraham and Lodish reference in note 17.

20. See A. S. C. Ehrenberg, whose views were first outlined in Repetitive advertising and the consumer, *Journal of Advertising Research,* 1974, *14* (2), pp. 25–34; and in Advertising: Reinforcing not persuading? in S. S. Bell, ed., *Evaluating the Effects of Consumer Advertising on Market Position over Time: How to Tell Whether Advertising Ever Works,* Cambridge, MA: Marketing Science Institute, 1988, pp. 18–19; M. J. Stewart, The long term effect of econometrics, *Admap,* February 1978, pp. 64–70; and J. P. Jones, Advertising: Strong force or weak force? Two views an ocean apart, *International Journal of Advertising,* 1990, *9* (3), pp. 223–246.

21. W. D. Wells' comment was made in a discussion session following the Ehrenberg presentation: see the reference to Ehrenberg's 1988 paper in note 20.

22. In 1993, the most recent year for which figures were available, Procter & Gamble spent $4.3 billion on AC&P worldwide ($2.4 billion in the United States alone), followed by Unilever at $2.6 billion and Johnson & Johnson at $1.0 billion. In the United States, ↑ noteworthy that two non–packaged goods adver↑ General Motors and Sears, were among the spenders. The largest U.S. advertising ag↑ year were Leo Burnett, J. Walter Thomp↑ McCann-Erickson, and DDB Needham ↑ each billing (gross) about $2 billion. See ↑ *Age,* September 28, 1994; and March 20, ↑ the worldwide figures.

23. G. S. Low and J. J. Mohr, The advertising sales promotion trade-off: Theory and practice, Working paper no. 92-127, Marketing Science Institute, Cambridge, MA, 1992.

24. A recent survey of 100 leading advertisers in each of three countries, the United States, the United Kingdom, and Canada, indicates that 51 percent of them use more than one method to estimate advertising budgets. It is not known, however, how many use multiple methods in *each* brand-budgeting situation, as we recommend here. See C. L. Hung and D. C. West, Advertising budgeting methods in Canada, the UK and the USA, *International Journal of Advertising,* 1991, *10* (3), pp. 239–250.

25. The objective-and-task method, or the task method, was apparently developed, or at least popularized, by G. M. Ule, A media plan for "Sputnik" cigarettes, in *How to Plan Media Strategy,* New York: American Association of Advertising Agencies, 1957, pp. 41–52, and has been summarized in most editions of P. Kotler's *Marketing Management* text.

26. Internationally, about two-thirds of "leading" advertisers report using the task method, a figure that has increased markedly in the last decade. See Hung and West, referenced in note 24, where 61 percent of leading advertisers reported using the task method; a 15-country survey conducted in 1985, in N. E. Synodinos, C. F. Keown, and L. W. Jacobs, Transnational advertising practices: A survey of leading brand advertisers in fifteen countries, *Journal of Advertising Research,* 1989, *29* (2), pp. 43–50, where 64 percent reported using it; and a British survey conducted in 1987, in J. E. Lynch and G. J. Hooley, Increasing sophistication in advertising budget setting, *Journal of Advertising Research,* 1990, *30* (1), pp. 67–75, where a broader (not just "leading") sample of consumer and industrial companies reported 50 percent usage of the task method, with more profitable companies using it more often than less profitable ones, by 63 percent versus 48 percent. The sample sizes were large enough in the latter study to allow comparisons across broad product types, with the resulting reported incidence of usage of the task method as follows: repeat-purchase consumer goods, 56 percent; consumer durables, 49 percent; repeat-purchase industrial goods, 59 percent; and capital industrial goods, 39 percent. Thus, the method is generally applicable.

27. J. S. Armstrong, *Long-Range Forecasting: From Crystal Ball to Computer,* 2nd ed., New York, NY: Wiley-Interscience, 1985; and J. S. Armstrong, R. J. Brodie, and S. McIntire, Forecasting methods for marketing: A review of empirical research, *Singapore Marketing Review,* 1987, *2,* pp. 7–23.

28. D. G. Morrison and D. C. Schmittlein, How many forecasters do you really have? Mahalanobis provides the intuition for the surprising Clemen and Winkler result, *Operations Research,* 1991, *39* (3), pp. 519–523.

29. The Delphi Method, named after the fabled Oracle of Delphi, uses individual judgments but employs successive rounds of judgments in which individuals are given the group average judgment from the previous round, thus providing feedback and reducing independence.

30. The "Five Questions" (5Q) approach was developed by Len Lodish for his CALLPLAN model and used by John Little in his ADBUDG model. See L. M. Lodish, CALLPLAN: An interactive salesman's call planning system, *Management Science,* 1971, *18* (4), Part II, pp. 25–40; J. D. C. Little, Models and managers: The concept of a decision calculus, *Management Science,* 1970, *16* (8), pp. B466–B485; J. D. C. Little and L. M. Lodish, Commentary on "Judgment based marketing decision models," *Journal of Marketing,* 1981, *45* (4), pp. 24–29; and E. Anderson, L. M. Lodish, and B. A. Weitz, Resource allocation behavior in conventional channels, *Journal of Marketing Research,* 1987, *24* (1), pp. 85–97.

31. Most companies estimate the sales response function and then subtract costs to estimate profit, rather than trying to estimate the profit response function directly. Kraft General Foods, for instance, recently reported using this indirect method; see R. Stone and M. Duffy, Measuring the impact of advertising, *Journal of Advertising Research,* 1993, *33* (6), pp. RC-8 to RC-12. Budget "optimizing" methods almost invariably use a simpler proxy for profit; see, for example, P. J. Danaher and R. T. Rust, Determining the optimal level of media spending, *Journal of Advertising Research,* 1994, *34* (1), pp. 28–34.

32. P. N. Golder and G. J. Tellis, Evaluating new product categories: Will sales ever take-off? Abstract, Marketing Science conference, University of New South Wales, Sydney, Australia, July 2–5, 1995.

33. These figures were obtained from *Advertising Age,* September 19, 1991, p. 18, and October 7, 1991, p. 4, respectively.

34. J. O. Peckham, *The Wheel of Marketing,* Scarsdale, NY: Self-published, 1981.

35. C. J. Simon and M. M. Sullivan, same reference as note 7, studying 638 firms across 20 industries, found an accounted-for variation, $R^2$, of .71 with SOV current year, SOV previous year, and order-of-entry (see several paragraphs ahead in the text) as the main predictor variables. However, we will see in the media chapters that SOV should not be applied to all campaigns indiscriminately when absolute spending is more theoret-

ically appropriate and various advertising spending inputs can be tracked.

36. See G. S. Carpenter, Marketing pioneering and competitive positioning strategy, Working paper, Graduate School of Business, Columbia University, New York, 1987; and M. B. Lieberman and D. B. Montgomery, First-mover advantages, *Strategic Management Journal,* 1988, *9* (Summer), pp. 41–58. For products sold competitively through retailers, an important fact is that retailers favor the innovator most, the first follower moderately, and are neutral toward subsequent followers. With increasing retailer domination of channels, this tends to reinforce the early-entry advantage. See F. H. Alpert, M. A. Kamins, and J. L. Graham, An examination of reseller buyer attitudes toward order of brand entry, *Journal of Marketing,* 1992, *56* (3), pp. 25–37. The emphasis by retailers on newness also fits earlier findings by D. B. Montgomery, New product distribution: An analysis of supermarket buyer decisions, *Journal of Marketing Research,* 1978, *12* (3), pp. 255–264.

37. Compiled from the following sources: W. T. Robinson and C. Fornell, Sources of market pioneer advantages in consumer goods industries, *Journal of Marketing Research,* 1985, *22* (3), pp. 305–317; W. T. Robinson, Sources of market pioneer advantages: The case of industrial goods industries, *Journal of Marketing Research,* 1988, *25* (1), pp. 87–94; and M. Parry and F. M. Bass, When to lead or follow? It depends, *Marketing Letters,* 1990, *1* (3), pp. 187–198. The modification for frequently purchased consumer products (fast-moving consumer goods, or fmcg) comes from G. Urban, T. Carter, S. Gaskin, and Z. Mucha, Market share rewards to pioneering brands: An empirical analysis and strategic implications, *Management Science,* 1986, *32* (6), pp. 645–659.

38. Size ratios were popularized by The Boston Consulting Group, *Perspectives on Experience,* Cambridge, MA: The Boston Consulting Group, 1968; see also R. D. Buzzell, Are there "natural" market structures? *Journal of Marketing,* 1981, *45* (1), pp. 42–51. The "par share" concept was introduced by The Hendry Corporation, *Speaking of Hendry,* New York: The Hendry Corporation, 1976.

39. For fast-moving consumer goods, an intriguing analysis by Urban and his colleagues demonstrated that the second brand entering the market, if it wishes to attain the same market share as the pioneer, must enter either:

   a. with a 36 percent *perceived* better product (meaning that if, for example, the average brand is rated by consumers as 60 on a 0-to-100 scale of overall quality, then the new brand must achieve a rating of at least 96), *or*

   b. by spending 3.4 times as much as the pioneer, the pioneer being usually the leading competitor, which is a very expensive proposition, *or*

   c. by having advertising which, in terms of communication quality, is 3.4 times more effective than the pioneer's advertising, which is quite possible, *or*

   d. by having a combination of more spending and better quality advertising, which is very possible.

   Third and later brands would have (slightly) increasingly larger numbers in their "overcoming" tasks.
   Urban et al.'s measure of "perceived quality" was brand preference *conditional on brand awareness* (see Chapter 5 of our book for an interpretation that is entirely consistent with their approach). For a new brand, brand awareness is highly dependent on attained distribution. However, advertising can play a major role in increasing brand awareness (whereas product preference may be based more on the product itself and somewhat less influenced by advertising), and so there may be slight double-counting here with the advertising quality variable. See the reference in note 37.

40. R. G. Cooper, The dimensions of industrial new product success and failure, *Journal of Marketing,* 1979, *43* (2), pp. 93–103.

41. R. D. Buzzell, same reference as in note 38.

42. Excellent though advanced coverage of regression techniques in advertising budget determination is given in D. M. Hanssens, L. J. Parsons, and R. L. Schultz, *Market Response Models: Econometric and Time Series Analysis,* Boston, MA: Kluwer, 1990. See also M. G. Dekimpe and D. M. Hanssens, The persistence of marketing effects on sales, *Marketing Science,* 1995, *14* (1), pp. 1–21.

43. R. C. Blattberg and S. J. Hoch, Database models and managerial intuition: 50% model + 50% manager, *Management Science,* 1990, *36* (8), pp. 887–899.

44. J. C. Schroer, Ad spending: Growing market share, *Harvard Business Review,* 1990, *68* (1), pp. 44–48.

45. For example, Schlitz beer, a market leader itself about 20 years ago until it changed its brewing method and slipped to be a minor brand, launched a comeback in 1992 by attacking larger competitors in geographic regions, mainly in the South and Southeast, where the name still has high value (upside) equity. For these loyal local markets, Schlitz reverted to its original advertising theme, "The beer that made Milwaukee famous." Many of those consumers still saw Schlitz as a premium brand—now offered at a popular price and taking advantage of value equity. In these regional markets, sales of Schlitz have increased at a double-digit rate. See J. P. Cortez, Schlitz

rebounds as lower-price brew, *Advertising Age,* September 14, 1992, p. 62.

46. M. H. Blair, An empirical investigation of advertising wearin and wearout, *Journal of Advertising Research,* 1988, *28* (6), pp. 45–50. We return to her results in Chapter 6.

47. For forecasting and planning purposes, *unit* sales (and likewise *unit* market share) are more important than dollar sales or market share. The two often differ. Dollars are mainly useful for calculating profit, whereas units show unambiguously how sales or market share is doing. See S. P. Schnaars, Unit of measurement effects on the relative accuracy of extrapolations or: Do dollar sales forecasts insure trends? *AMA Educators' Conference Proceedings,* Chicago: American Marketing Association, 1986, pp. 407–412.

48. G. L. Urban and S. H. Star, *Advanced Marketing Strategy,* Englewood Cliffs, NJ: Prentice-Hall, 1991. The quotation is from p. 183. The same warning about blind pursuit of maximum sales or market share, but this time from a brand equity perspective, is issued by W. T. Moran, Marketplace measurement of brand equity, *Journal of Brand Management,* 1994, *1* (5), pp. 272–282.

49. The diagram is taken from an article by R. J. Jessen, A switch-over experimental design to measure advertising effect, *Journal of Advertising Research,* 1961, *1* (3), pp. 15–22. It has been widely reproduced in similar form elsewhere.

50. J. L. Simon and J. Arndt, The shape of the advertising response function, *Journal of Advertising Research,* 1980, *20* (4), pp. 11–28.

## DISCUSSION QUESTIONS

**2.1. a.** "The purpose of all advertising and promotion . . . is to maximize profit." Discuss what we meant by this statement and whether or not you agree with it.

**b.** What is the difference between a *sales* objective and a *market share* objective, and when are these objectives appropriate?

**c.** Why are goals preferable to objectives, and objectives preferable to no plan at all?

**2.2.** At the beginning of the chapter, we said that the role of advertising communications or promotions in a given campaign is either to *assure* marketing objectives already set for the brand or to *achieve* marketing objectives set especially for the campaign. Now that you have read the chapter, discuss, with examples, these two roles of advertising communications, and of promotions, in relation to marketing objectives.

**2.3.** Give a real (or realistic) campaign example of:

**a.** An immediate selling price objective for promotion.

**b.** 1-year price objective for advertising.

**c.** A 1-year cost objective for advertising.

**d.** An immediate sales volume objective for promotion.

**e.** A long-run sales volume objective for advertising.

**2.4.** With regard to Moran's analysis of upside and downside demand elasticity, describe and explain your marketing and AC&P recommendations in the following two scenarios:

**a.** Competitors never change their prices; when you raise your price, your sales rate doesn't change appreciably, and when you lower your price, your sales rate still doesn't change.

**b.** When you offer price promotions, your sales go up sharply; but when your competitors offer price promotions, your sales go down sharply.

**2.5. a.** Why did we recommend setting the AC&P budget initially in terms of general advertising only, and using at least two methods to do so?

**b.** What is meant by "quality" of advertising spending, and how does it affect the budget-setting process?

**2.6.** Discuss how Rollerblade, Inc., may have used the task method to set its advertising budget in 1991 if it was aiming for a 70 percent share of the purchases to be made by the 3,000,000 people in the United States who were expected to buy in-line skates that year. (Note: There is no need to produce an actual budget. However, the conversion ratio estimates at each step should be discussed and justified.)

**2.7.** Assume that American Express currently is spending $50 million on advertising for its Green Card and that current sales are $5,000 million annualiy. Working in teams of five classmates, go through the management-jury IAF/5Q procedure and estimate the sales response function for the Green Card. What should the advertising budget amount be, and why?

**2.8.** Discuss the main budgeting methods Healthy Choice dinners could employ, now that it is an established brand in a mature category.

## FURTHER READING

Armstrong, J.S. *Long-Range Forecasting: From Crystal Ball to Computer,* 2nd ed. New York: Wiley-Interscience, 1985.

The easiest-to-read book on forecasting (including the management-jury method) ever written. Worthwhile shelf reference for any manager who has to make sales forecasts.

Broadbent, S. *The Advertiser's Handbook for Budget Determination,* Lexington, MA: Lexington Books (in association with the Association of National Advertisers, Inc.), 1988.

Offers a detailed, real-world discussion of budget setting. Misses some recent U.S. ideas, but is very good on the trade-offs necessary to "negotiate" the budget and have it accepted by upper management (an aspect we have bypassed in the interest of an idealized perspective).

Moran, W. T. Insights from pricing research, 1976; The advertising-promotion balance, 1978; and Marketplace measurement of brand equity, *Journal of Brand Management,* 1994, *1* (5), pp. 272–282.

The two early papers by leading marketing consultant William T. Moran were published in conference proceedings (by The Conference Board and the Association of National Advertisers, respectively, in the years shown) and are somewhat difficult to obtain, but they are well worth reading before his 1994 journal article. The two early papers explain his concepts of "upside" and "downside" price elasticity of demand (related later to brand equity) and associated brand strategies as summarized in our chapter. The 1994 article, we should note, refers to upside elasticity as "relative price" and downside (in)elasticity as "durability."

Schroer, J. C. Ad spending: Growing market share. *Harvard Business Review,* 1990, *68* (1), pp. 44–48.

We've recommended Schroer's budgeting method for multiregional established brands. Managers contemplating using this method will find it informative to read the original article.

Urban, G. L., and Star, S. H. *Advanced Marketing Strategy.* Englewood Cliffs, NJ: Prentice-Hall, 1991.

Whereas Kotler's *Marketing Management* remains a standard reference in marketers' libraries, this text by Urban and Star is a welcome addition. Their book is very strong on competitive strategy and the dynamics of product management, and is useful supplementary reading for our Chapter 2. Throughout, the authors demonstrate convincingly how appropriate market research can improve marketing decisions.

## PART TWO

# TARGET AUDIENCE ACTION OBJECTIVES

**CHAPTER 3: TARGET AUDIENCE SELECTION AND ACTION OBJECTIVES**

**CHAPTER 4: BEHAVIORAL SEQUENCE MODEL FOR SPECIFIC TARGETING**

# Target Audience Selection and Action Objectives

Target audience selection and action objectives represent the second of the manager's planning stages. In the first stage, marketing objectives were established for the campaign (most often a sales goal) and a budget decided. The manager now needs to decide, from the potential market, *who* are the best prospects for the campaign and *what action* the campaign should encourage them to take. This chapter describes the five general target audience options for AC&P campaigns and the behavioral action objectives for each. (In the next chapter, we will look at *who*, specifically, within the target audience we want to target and *what*, specifically, we want them to *do*—as participants in the purchase decision.) After reading this chapter, you should:

- Understand the awareness-attitude-behavior or "brand loyalty" approach to target audience definition and see how it identifies five buyer groups which are potential target audiences for a particular advertising, promotion, or IMC campaign.
- Know how to select one (or occasionally two) of these groups for the campaign by estimating the "leverage" of each prospective target audience.
- Learn the action objectives (trial or repeat purchase behaviors) that are appropriate for each target audience.
- Know how to establish a trial goal and a repeat purchase goal for the campaign.

## TARGET AUDIENCE OPTIONS

### The Awareness-Attitude-Behavior Approach

To determine which prospective buyers represent the best sales potential, it is useful to think of "our" sales as being dependent on product category sales and our brand's performance within that category. We can see that our brand potentially could be purchased by any of five buyer groups:

1. *New category users (NCUs),* who enter the category by buying our brand.
2. *Brand loyals (BLs),* who regularly buy our brand.
3. *Favorable brand switchers (FBSs),* who occasionally buy our brand and also buy other brands.
4. *Other-brand switchers (OBSs),* who buy other brands but *not* ours.
5. *Other-brand loyals (OBLs),* who regularly buy a brand other than ours.

These potential buyer groups are shown schematically in Figure 3.1. Brand loyals represent the core of our sales, our most frequent buyers. Favorable brand switchers are the "fringe" of our sales: they include our brand in their brand-switching behavior but they buy it less frequently than do our loyal customers. Sales also may be gained by attracting new category users to our brand, by inducing other-brand switchers to include our brand in their repertoire, or by drawing loyal customers away from other brands—an often difficult task.

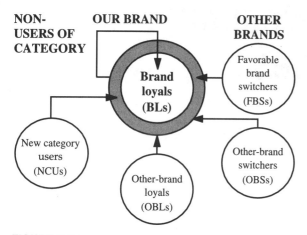

**FIGURE 3.1**

Five buyer groups as sources of sales. Our brand's sales are represented by the loyal core (inside circle) and the switching fringe (shaded area).

A good way to understand the five groups is to think of a well-known brand such as Maxwell House Instant Coffee. How would you classify yourself? You may be (1) a non–category user and thus potentially a *new* category user, an NCU, who has never tried instant coffee or doesn't like instant coffee; (2) a loyal Maxwell House drinker, a BL, who rarely drinks any other brand of instant coffee; (3) a favorable brand switcher, an FBS, who drinks Maxwell House but also other brands such as Nescafé and Taster's Choice; (4) an other-brand switcher, an OBS, who drinks other brands such as Nescafé and Taster's Choice but *not* Maxwell House; or (5) an other-brand loyal, an OBL, who primarily drinks some brand other than Maxwell House, such as Nescafé mainly or Taster's Choice mainly. Notice that everyone can be classified into one of these five groups.

**Brand Loyalty is the Key.** Our classification of buyer groups relies heavily on the phenomenon of brand loyalty. Brand loyalty can be defined as regular (repeat) purchase of the brand based on (a) continued awareness and (b) a favorable price- and promotion-resistant attitude toward it. Brand loyalty is therefore an awareness-attitude-behavior concept.[1]

Why do we introduce awareness and attitude here when our focus in this chapter is on buyer behavior? The answer is that the would-be buyer's awareness and attitude have to be known in addition to his or her

behavior in order to assess sales potential. Consider the following.

**1.** *New category users (NCUs)* may or may not represent good sales potential depending on their awareness of the *category* (it may cost a lot to make them aware) and especially on their attitude toward the *category* and not just our brand. In the instant coffee example, children may be quite favorable toward instant coffee before they are allowed to drink it, whereas many adults may be neutral or negative toward instant coffee. Note that behavior is not sufficient to assess the NCUs' sales potential because those with favorable attitudes toward the category are no different behaviorally from those with neutral or negative attitudes (they are all nonusers). We have to know their category awareness and attitudes in order to assess NCUs' sales potential.

**2.** *Brand loyals (BLs)* already have maximum awareness of, and a strongly favorable attitude toward, our brand and are the core of our current and future expected sales. They may not, however, represent good potential for *increased* sales beyond the rate at which they are buying now. For instance, loyal drinkers of Maxwell House instant coffee may not wish to drink it, or any other coffee for that matter, more often than they now do.

**3.** *Favorable brand switchers (FBSs)* include our brand in their switching behavior and thus presumably have at least a moderately favorable attitude toward it because otherwise they would not buy it at all. Their awareness, however, may slip over time and may be a cause of their less-frequent purchase of our brand. Also, we have to know their attitudes to see if they could be made loyal or whether they will always be just moderately favorable, attracted to our brand from time to time for variety ("rotators") or whenever it offers a promotion ("deal-selectors").[2] Maxwell House's strategy would heavily depend on the extent of these different attitudes among its FBS buyers.

**4.** *Other-brand switchers (OBSs)* do not include our brand in their switching behavior. This could be because they are unaware of it, or have fluctuating awareness so that too often our brand is forgotten or not noticed; or because of a neutral or negative attitude toward our brand even though they *are* aware of it; or because our brand is priced too high for them. Maxwell House would have to know the source of their exclusion of the brand in order to assess OBSs' sales potential.

*5. Other-brand loyals (OBLs)* usually have the least sales potential because they are satisfied with, and are therefore committed attitudinally to, another brand. They may or may not be aware of our brand. Although their behavior looks more promising than that of the NCU because they already purchase within the category, the attitudes of OBLs, which often are decidedly neutral or more often actively negative toward us, may make them our worst prospects.[3] Trier-rejectors of Maxwell House, for instance, would be very hard to win away from their loyalty to another brand without reformulating our product.

In Chapter 18, on advertising strategy research, we show how to more finely divide the five buyer groups into 12 subgroups based on their awareness, attitudes, and behavior. The 12 subgroups, which are very useful for precise targeting, are Unaware NCU, Positive NCU, and Negative NCU; Single-BL and Multi-BL; Experimental FBS and Routinized FBS; Experimental OBS and Routinized OBS; and Neutral OBL, Favorable OBL, and Unfavorable OBL. However, this level of target-audience classification is not always necessary, and we will refer to it only occasionally until Chapter 18. For present purposes, it is more important to understand the five major groups.

Sales come from one or more of the five awareness-attitude-behavior groups: new category users, brand loyals, favorable brand switchers, other-brand switchers, or other-brand loyals. These five buyer groups are mutually exclusive and exhaustively define our potential customers. Awareness-attitude-behavior, or "brand loyalty," is the most appropriate way to define the target audience for advertising communications or promotions. For a particular campaign, however, some *further* delineation of the target audience is often appropriate, explained next.

### Geographic, Demographic, or Psychographic Delineation Within a Buyer Group

Geographic, demographic, or psychographic factors are often *additionally* used to narrow down or delineate a target audience from one of the five buyer groups for a particular campaign. "Geographics" refers to the buyer's area of residence or place of work. "Demographics" refers to objective descriptive characteristics of the buyer, such as age, sex, or occupation. And "psychographics" refers to subjective descriptive characteristics such as lifestyle, personality, or general attitudes. Geographic descriptions are always appropriate, as we shall see, and are usually properly used. But demographic or psychographic descriptions are frequently misunderstood and misused in target audience definitions: they are not alone sufficient. We now explain the correct roles of geographics, demographics, and psychographics in target audience definition.

**Geographic Delineation of the Target Audience.** Geographic delineation of the target audience is always appropriate. Every advertising communications or promotion campaign has a geographic constraint. Even "global" campaigns are, in reality, "multicountry" campaigns, with many geographic exclusions. (Of course, a truly global campaign is theoretically possible in the future via satellite TV—but only if everyone could afford, and were willing to buy, a satellite-reception TV set!) Similarly, when a campaign is described as "national," it may be truly national or may just cover geographic "major markets." However, national advertisers *also* conduct regional or local campaigns. Indeed, these were recommended in Schroer's method of local-market budgeting in the previous chapter. And, of course, many regional or local advertisers have *only* regional or local distribution, and thus their target audiences are geographically constrained.

Unless the campaign is evidently national, the geographic specification should be stated in the target audience definition. Thus, for instance, an electrical appliance retailer in Solon, Ohio, may define the target audience for a radio advertising campaign as "Favorable brand switchers within a 50-mile radius of Solon, Ohio." On the other hand, GE, as an electrical-appliance marketer, might define the target audience for a national TV campaign as simply "Favorable brand switchers," with the implied geographic definition being the whole of the United States. However, with so many campaigns being intended for "global" or multicountry use, it is advisable these days to *specify* the geographic definition of the campaign.

**Demographic or Psychographic Delineation Within a Buyer Group.** Demographics or psychographics are *not sufficient* to define a target audience. However, a particular campaign may be intended to appeal to a specific demographic or psychographic group *within* one of the five buyer groups.

An application example of demographic delineation is provided by Anheuser-Busch's superpremium

Michelob beer brand.[4] For the past several years, Michelob has relied on its "Night belongs to Michelob" campaign targeted at the traditional "young drinker" target, the 21-to-26 year-old age group. Recognizing that the U.S. population is aging, Michelob's marketing manager asked its new agency, D'Arcy Masius Benton & Bowles, to "aim for an older audience." The new campaign, which was launched in January 1992, depicts somewhat older actors in the commercials and uses the theme-line "Some days are better than others." However, to state that Michelob's target audience for the campaign is "adults 27 and older" would be a vast over-simplification. In the first place, approximately 50 percent of U.S. adults do not drink beer! To have a target audience that includes 50 percent NCUs (inducing non–beer-drinking adults to take up beer drinking) would be naive. Thus, age is *not* a sufficient descriptor of Michelob's target audience. Prior to the new campaign, Michelob's market share had slipped to 1.4 percent nationally. Besides retaining the rather few brand loyals (BLs) that the brand apparently has, Michelob probably intends to target the very large pool of "older" *brand switchers,* particularly favorable brand switchers (FBSs) who occasionally buy Michelob. Alternatively or additionally, Michelob could target Miller Lite loyals (OBLs for Michelob), who also are aging.[5] So brand loyalty segmentation is necessary first and age then becomes a delineating descriptor.

An application of psychographic delineation might have occurred with the launch of Healthy Choice frozen dinners. The brand-loyalty target audiences were OBSs and NCUs but it appeared that within these buyer groups, the brand was specially targeting those consumers who feared heart trouble. We could infer this from the brand's "heart-healthy" positioning.

The brand loyalty (awareness-attitude-behavior) approach should always be primary and *may* then be narrowed by a further demographic (or psychographic or any other descriptive) delineation if desired. Figure 3.2 shows this for the general case of an additional variable intersecting a brand-loyalty buyer group as the target audience. Managers should thereby be able to see that demographic (or even geographic or psychographic) definitions of the target audience alone are insufficient. The brand loyalty approach (five buyer groups) is the starting point—and then further

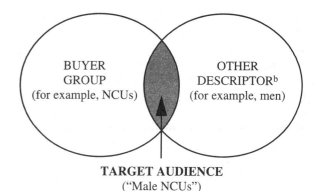

**TARGET AUDIENCE**
("Male NCUs")

[a]It is optional, not mandatory, to delineate within a buyer group.
[b]Other descriptors are usually a geographic, demographic or psychographic subgroup of the total population.

**FIGURE 3.2**
Optional[a] delineation of a buyer group by another descriptor variable to define the target audience.

refinements (usually for a specific campaign) can be used to narrow down the target audience to the best sales-potential group.

### Applicability to All Products and Services

The awareness-attitude-behavior or brand loyalty approach, with its identification of the five buyer groups as potential target audiences, is applicable to *all* types of products and services. So far, the examples we have used have been for consumer packaged goods, or fmcg (fast-moving consumer goods), whose frequent purchase allows loyalty to be readily observed in actual behavior. However, as Gensch[6] and others have pointed out, the brand loyalty approach is even *more necessary* in the case of *infrequently purchased* products and services. This is because the brand loyalty approach is essentially based on *attitudes* (hence "loyalty") which cause repeat purchase behavior in the future. For products with long purchase cycles, such as industrial equipment or consumer durables, the marketer has to rely *primarily* on attitudes to assess target audience potential because the purchase behavior is so infrequent.

Chapter appendix 3A, Universality of the Brand Loyalty Approach, provides examples for industrial, consumer-durable, retail, and service marketers.

## TARGET AUDIENCE SELECTION VIA LEVERAGE

### Target Audience Versus Target Market

The term "target audience" distinguishes those to whom *a particular advertising communications or promotion campaign* is directed, whereas the term "target market" refers to those to whom *the entire marketing mix* is directed. For a particular campaign, the target audience may thus be a subset of the target market.

One or more of the five prospective buyer groups becomes a *target audience* only when the marketer decides to direct advertising communications or promotions to that group. A prospect group becomes a *target* for advertising communications or promotions and, in the communication sense, becomes an *audience* for a particular advertising communications or promotion campaign.

### Primary and Secondary Target Audiences

Usually, only one prospect group will be chosen as the target audience for a particular campaign. However, it is sometimes appropriate to identify a *primary* target audience and (usually one other) *secondary* target audience. For instance, Gensch's industrial campaign for ABB Electric (see chapter appendix 3A) probably identified favorable brand switchers (FBSs) as the primary target audience and other-brand switchers (OBSs) as the secondary target. Also, it is quite common for a campaign to try to attract "new" sales from another group while protecting "existing" sales to its own brand loyals. The Michelob campaign discussed earlier, for instance, was trying to attract older drinkers while not losing loyal younger drinkers. The brand's own BLs are a common secondary target audience for a new campaign aimed at another group. Most such campaigns are designed to secondarily reinforce loyalty and only rarely would an advertiser risk alienating the brand's current BLs.

The words "primary" and "secondary" refer, not to the target audiences' sizes, but to their relative *leverage,* a concept explained next.

### Selecting a Target Audience via Leverage

Advertising communications or promotions directed to a particular prospect group must be considered in terms of *cost* as well as expected revenue. Another way of saying this is that each prospect group's sales potential should be evaluated on the basis of its advertising or promotion *leverage:* the expected increase in our brand's sales (in dollars) divided by the advertising or promotion expenditure we would have to make to get those increased sales.

The likely advertising and promotion leverage of the five general prospect groups depends on the product category life cycle, as follows. Here, it may be useful to refer, where appropriate, to the various target audience subgroups that can be identified using the research procedure given in Chapter 18. [We will indicate these subgroups in brackets in the numbered paragraphs that follow.]

**1.** *New category users (NCUs)* have *decreasing* leverage as the product category matures. Early in the product category life cycle, NCUs offer good sales potential [Unaware NCUs], but it may also cost a considerable amount to get them to try our brand because lengthy "educational" advertising may be required, as well as a substantial promotion offer, to induce trial of the category. By the maturity stage, those who are still NCUs have virtually zero leverage because their sales potential is now very small and the cost of converting them to buying in a product category that they have already decided against [Negative NCUs] would be very high, if indeed they could be converted at all. Leverage for NCUs therefore proceeds from *moderate to low* during the product category life cycle.

**2.** *Brand loyals (BLs)* have the highest potential for our future sales (at their current per capita buying rate) and they are also comparatively inexpensive to retain. They like the brand, so it will tend to sell itself without heavy additional advertising or promotion. BLs' leverage for the *current sales rate* is thus *very high* throughout the product category life cycle. This high leverage is very important when, as in most product categories, the maturity stage is long-lasting. However, although most of the current sales rate is coming from this group, it may *decline* if we *stop* advertising for too long a period, that is, if we advertise too infrequently. Continuous low-frequency advertising to BLs, or occasional bursts spaced not too far apart, may be required to stay in business. Advertising to BLs has to have some continuity over the long term because, contrary to prevailing wisdom, consumers' brand loyalty does *not* increase as they grow older.[7]

Notice that the BLs' leverage for *continuing* the current sales is not the same as their leverage for *increasing* the sales rate. If we consider a single branded item, most BLs (per capita) are buying at near a maximum rate now (especially if they are Single-BLs); an increase in the sales rate from BLs would be small, if achievable at all, and it would be quite expensive to persuade an already loyal customer to become even more loyal (from Multi-BL status). Thus, as a sales *increase* target, BLs typically have *low* leverage throughout the product category life cycle.[8] If, however, the "brand" is the *company* (for instance, a bank), then BLs may have high leverage for *other items* (for instance, other services) sold by the company.

**3.** *Favorable brand switchers* (*FBSs*) have relatively *high* leverage *early* in the product category life cycle [Experimental FBSs] since most BLs will come from this group. After they experiment with various new brands, their purchases of our brand will increase if they include it in their "acceptable set" [thereby becoming Routinized FBSs]. Their leverage will increase also because the costs of "trial" advertising and promotion will have already been incurred. As the product life cycle matures, FBSs move to *moderate* leverage: their "switching in" is usually responsive to advertising and especially promotion, but it costs a lot to retain them (more than to retain BLs) because the effects of promotions are often temporary.

**4.** *Other-brand switchers* (*OBSs*) have a similar life cycle pattern to FBSs but at a *lower* leverage level. They are always harder to attract, especially if they have tried and rejected us, and more so as the product category matures [Routinized OBSs]. Furthermore, the cost to attract OBSs increases as more and more promotion is needed to "buy" their patronage, if indeed it can be bought. OBSs' leverage therefore goes from *moderate to low* during the product category life cycle.

**5.** *Other brand loyals* (*OBLs*) in most cases have very low sales potential. Those who are not 100 percent loyal to another brand [and are Favorable OBSs, having not definitely rejected our brand] may be converted temporarily by heavy promotion, but this would be at high cost. The OBL group therefore has *low* leverage throughout the product category life cycle. We should note, however, that a small brand (such as R-C Cola) in a category dominated by large-brand OBLs (consumers loyal to Coke or Pepsi) may have little option but to target OBLs if its objective is a large increase in sales [more precisely, the target

would be Neutral OBLs or Favorable OBLs, with Negative OBLs avoided].

**Measuring Advertising or Promotion Leverage.** Advertising or promotion leverage—or IMC leverage, if advertising and promotion are used together—can be best grasped intuitively on a per capita basis. Think of how much of our brand the average individual in the group is buying now—for example, two packages a year at $2.00 per package = $4.00. Then think of by how much our advertising communications or promotion campaign could increase the sales level—for example, to three packages a year at $2.00 per package = $6.00; that is, an average per capita increase of $2.00. (Note that for BLs, and even FBSs, the campaign objective may be simply *maintaining* and not necessarily increasing the rate of sales. If so, the sales increase should be calculated as *the addition above the decline you would expect to occur* if you did *not* run the campaign. For example, if the group's buying rate would decline to one package a year *without* advertising, then the average per capita increase if the current sales rate is maintained is *also* $2.00. These may be referred to as *unlost* sales due to the campaign.) Overall leverage is then easily calculated by considering the number of buyers in the group and the cost of the advertising, promotion, or IMC campaign needed to produce or support the sales increment. Thus,

$$\text{Advertising, promotion, or IMC leverage} = \frac{\substack{\text{Number of buyers} \\ \text{in prospect group}} \times \substack{\text{Average per capita extra} \\ \text{or unlost sales (in dollars)}}}{\text{Cost of campaign (in dollars)}}$$

In our example, if there are 10 million buyers in the prospect group and we estimate that a campaign to induce them to buy an extra (or unlost) $2.00 worth of our brand per year would cost $10 million, then the leverage of this group is

$$\frac{10{,}000{,}000 \times \$2.00}{\$10{,}000{,}000} = 2$$

In other words, this target audience as a group would be returning $2.00 of sales for every $1.00 spent on advertising or promotion.

**Profit Leverage.** Leverage, of course, should be fully calculated as *profit leverage*. This is achieved via the leverage formula given above by substituting *per capita profit* for per capita sales. It should be obvious that we would normally consider pursuing a prospect group as a target audience *only* if its advertising or promotion *profit leverage* were larger than 1—meaning that the returns to be gained from the campaign outweigh its costs. In our example, it can be seen that if the cost of manufacturing and distributing the extra $2.00 worth of sales is $1.00 or more per capita, on top of the $1.00 per capita of advertising cost, then it would not be worth advertising for the increased sales, as the profit would be exactly negated by the cost.

The higher the profit leverage, the more attractive is the prospect group as a target audience.[9] All five prospect groups should be evaluated in terms of their leverage, and a primary and perhaps a secondary target audience chosen on this basis.

### ACTION OBJECTIVES

Once the target audience has been selected, action objectives for that target audience have to be specified. Action objectives are the behavior(s) expected to result from the campaign: observable, measurable, *actual behavior.*[10] In the present chapter, we consider the action objectives associated with each of the five buyer groups (if each were to be selected as a target audience) in terms of purchase behavior. In the next chapter, we will show how the manager may further specify *purchase-related behaviors* when relevant.

Target audience action objectives in terms of purchase behavior are fundamentally just two: trial and repeat purchase. However, these come with finer gradations, based on the following behavioral parameters: *occurrence,* such as whether or not to try a new product category or new brand, or to retry it; *rate,* such as how often to buy a particular brand; *amplitude* or *amount,* such as how much to buy per purchase occasion; *timing,* such as when to buy; and *persistence,* or more technically "resistance to extinction," which becomes important later, in media planning, as explained in Chapter 16, when the manager needs to know for how long the advertising or promotion can be delayed or "flighted" before purchase behavior begins to decline.

We will first present the applicable action objectives for each of the five buyer groups. Then we will consider important facts pertaining to trial and repeat purchase behaviors which will help the manager set precise trial or repeat purchase action objectives (goals) for a particular campaign.

### Action Objectives for the Five Buyer Groups

In Table 3.1, we list the typical action objectives for each of the five buyer groups when that group serves as a target audience for a campaign. The action objectives are divided into trial objectives and repeat purchase objectives. Note that we have placed the

**TABLE 3.1**

**ACTION OBJECTIVES FOR THE FIVE BUYER GROUPS**

| | Target audience | | | | |
| --- | --- | --- | --- | --- | --- |
| | New category users (NCUs) | Other-brand loyals (OBLs) | Other-brand switchers (OBSs) | Favorable brand switchers (FBSs) | Brand loyals (BLs) |
| **Trial objectives** | | | | | |
| Category trial | ✔ | | | | |
| Brand trial | ✔ | ✔ | ✔ | | |
| Brand retrial | | ✔ | ✔ | | |
| **Repeat purchase objectives** | | | | | |
| Maintain repeat rate | | | | | ✔ |
| Increase repeat rate | | ✔ | ✔ | ✔ | |
| Buy more per occasion (stock up) | | | | ✔ | ✔ |
| Buy less per occasion[a] | | | | ✔ | ✔ |
| Accelerate timing | | | | ✔ | ✔ |
| Delay timing[a] | | | | ✔ | ✔ |

[a]Sometimes employed as an objective (see text).

potential target audiences in approximate order of loyalty to our brand, from lowest (NCUs) at the left to highest (BLs) at the right.

For NCUs, the action objectives are category trial and brand trial. We want NCUs to try the category *via* our brand. Of course, we hope that thereafter they will not need to try any other brands in the category, but we may not have too much control over that! In Chapter 5, where we consider communication objectives, we will see that the communication task for category trial is considerably more elaborate than for brand trial alone. This is because NCUs have to be educated about the benefits of the product category itself before they can evaluate the benefits of our brand.

For OBLs, the initial action objectives would be brand trial or, if they have already tried our brand in the past, brand retrial. Thereafter, the action objective would be an increased repeat-purchase rate. Interestingly (though not shown in the table), the "increase repeat rate" objective may shift to "maintain repeat rate" quite quickly for OBLs because, if they can be won over, they are likely to transfer their loyalty from their previous brand to their new one.

For OBSs, the same action objectives apply as for OBLs. However, since they are switchers rather than loyal to another brand, there is somewhat more chance that they have tried our brand previously, so the trial objective will more often be brand *retrial* for the OBS target audience. The action objective subsequently would be to increase their repeat purchase rate in the course of their switching behavior. Early in the product category life cycle, following exploration, OBSs may increase their repeat purchase rate and become BLs. Later in the product category life cycle, switching will have become a habitual pattern for OBSs, and we would look for them to increase their repeat rate, from not buying our brand at all to at least buying it occasionally.

For FBSs, the emphasis is on repeat purchase. FBSs already buy our brand but are occasional buyers whose purchase rate we usually wish to increase. In addition to increased repeat rate, we have identified a number of other repeat-purchase behaviors (for FBSs *and* BLs) to illustrate the behavioral parameters noted previously. These include:

- *Buying more per purchase occasion* (known as "stocking up" or "stockpiling" from the buyer's viewpoint and as "loading customers" from the marketer's viewpoint).
- *Buying less per purchase occasion,* which is often the action objective of social marketing or "de-marketing," as in an energy conservation or anti-drug campaign.
- *Accelerated timing of purchase,* which is another way to load buyers with your brand when new competitors are entering a growing category, or which is applicable when the manufacturer or retailer wishes to quickly clear inventory.
- *Delayed timing of purchase,* which may be an action objective for financial institutions in the business of providing credit, such as banks and credit card companies, where profit is made from slow payment and thus higher total interest paid.

For BLs, the most typical action objective—and it's not necessarily an easy one—is simply to *maintain* their repeat purchase rate. As the concept of leverage indicates, the marketer hopes to maintain the purchase rate of BLs at the lowest possible cost. BLs, as shown in the table, may also be a target for other repeat-purchase action objectives—not so much for a permanently increased repeat purchase rate, since they are presumably buying at close to a maximum rate now from a long-term perspective, but rather for *short-term* increases in the form of buying more per purchase occasion (temporary stocking up) or accelerating the timing of their purchases. Again, in some circumstances, reduced purchase amount or delayed timing may be an objective.

We now show how the manager can establish trial and repeat purchase *goals* once the target audience has been selected. We have retained the word "objectives" in our headings below for trial and repeat purchase because the manager may be content to set a broad objective. But it is preferable to set *goals,* which identify the degree and time period for the objective, to increase campaign accountability.

## TRIAL OBJECTIVES

Trial is the *initial* action objective for:

- New product categories
- New brands
- New target audiences (new users or new use) for an established brand

### Trial Goal for a New Product Category

The most difficult objective-setting situation facing the manager is setting a trial goal for a new product category where our brand is the *first entry* in the new category. The newer the product category, particularly if it is a discontinuous innovation,[11] the more difficult the task.

When the new product category is *similar to an existing* category, such as the introduction of Healthy Choice as the first brand into the "heart-healthy" frozen dinner-and-entree category, the manager's task is easier because the historically attained trial for comparable categories can be used to help set a realistic trial goal for the new category. For instance, the brand manager for Healthy Choice could have studied carefully the trial attained earlier by Lean Cuisine, which was the first brand to enter the "gourmet" low-calorie frozen entree category.[12]

In contrast, when the new category is discontinuous or *very different* from anything that has gone before it, imitation of other categories can be misleading. For example, consider the introduction of *interactive CDs* (such as Philips' CD-I). This new product does not "compete with" or replace existing CDs; it is a unique additional product. In this "totally new product" situation, the manager could take a survey of buying intentions based on the new product concept. (In Chapter 19, as part of advertising research, we show how to measure and "weight" purchase intentions.) An awareness-to-trial conversion ratio can then be estimated, as in the task method of Chapter 2. This estimate may then have to be corrected for a possible positive (or negative) word-of-mouth diffusion effect from early triers to later triers. For durables, various quantitative forecasting models, such as the Bass model, and an even better model by Horsky, are available to assist the manager in making these estimates.[13]

Difficult as it may be to estimate trial and set a realistic trial goal for the first brand entry into a very new product category, this judgment must be made. For products with long purchase cycles, the first year's sales will be made up almost entirely of trial purchases. Thus, an estimate of trial (here equal to sales) will be necessary if the manager is employing the recommended task method for setting the AC&P budget (see Chapter 2). Here, as always, the independent-averaged-forecast procedure from the IAF/5Q method is very useful, since it does not put total reliance on the one manager. If you are setting a trial objective for a new product category, it is worth reviewing the steps in the task method and the IAF part of the IAF/5Q method described in Chapter 2.

### Trial Goal for a New Brand (or New Target Audience)

A trial goal is considerably easier to set when a new brand is being introduced into an existing category or an established brand is being targeted to new users. (A difficulty arises, however, if the product category is very new and is still rapidly expanding in the *growth* phase of the product category life cycle, since trial norms are not yet applicable. In this situation, the manager would do better to regard the task as being more like a *new product category* introduction and use the task method as described above.)

When the product category is established or *mature,* as are the great majority of product categories in which managers operate, then the trial goal for the new or newly repositioned brand can be quite accurately set by using either *norms,* which are widely available for consumer packaged goods but not other products, or by using *Ehrenberg's method,* which is universally applicable as long as the repeat purchase rate in the category is known, as it would be if the product category is established. We describe each of these methods next.

**Trial Norms for Consumer Packaged Goods.** An incredible number of new consumer packaged goods are launched into the nation's food stores and drugstores each year. For supermarkets alone, Wascoe[14] estimates that, whereas there were 1,365 new entries in 1970, this number had increased to 13,244 (a tenfold increase) by 1990. He estimates that in 1990 there were about 10,000 new food products introduced and about 3,000 non–food products introduced, such as health and beauty aids, paper products, and pet foods. Of course, most of these new entries are not new brands in the sense of a new brand *name.* Rather, most are *brand extensions* (a brand name transferred from one product category to another, such as Healthy Choice Soups, transferring the Healthy Choice name from frozen dinners and entrees) or *line extensions* (new varieties offered by an existing brand, such as a *new flavor* of Healthy Choice soup) or simply new package sizes. Nevertheless, for the brand manager, a trial goal must be set for each.

From the *retailer's* perspective, about one-third of the items carried by supermarkets each year are new. This is based on the statistic that a large chain supermarket (for instance, CUB or Safeway) stocks about 30,000 different items and that manufacturers introduce about 13,000 new items each year, as just mentioned. Thus, as brand managers well know, trial is a vital action objective for *retail* target audiences as well. We will return to retail target audiences later in the chapter and focus on consumers here.

The NPD Group, Inc., has provided norms for the trial of supermarket products from NPD/Nielsen panel data over the last 15 years.[15] "Trial" is measured by exposing panel members to the new item's concept and then, at the end of the interview, allowing panelists to take home the product (trial) or to accept an equivalent cash incentive (nontrial). This "simulated test market" procedure generally provides a quite accurate prediction of actual, in-market trial.

Trial norms (1-year) are shown in Table 3.2, for 1986–88, for broad consumer packaged goods (fmcg) categories. Household products appear to attract the highest household willingness to try, although the typical new brand of household item is tried by only 29 percent of the nation's households in its first year. Health and beauty aids, being "personal" products, have a considerably lower average trial incidence,

only 16 percent—and, as shown in the table, for really personal products, trial is 8 percent or less. New brands of food items have a trial incidence that also suggests conservatism in personal tastes: about 13 percent of households will try the average new food item in its first year.

These trial incidence figures are, of course, *averages* across many specific product categories within the broad categories shown in the table. Nevertheless, for the manager, these types of norms are a better starting point than the pure guesswork that we have seen in some consumer product marketing plans! Moreover, the figures are averages for the average new item introduction—with, of course, the average amount of new item distribution, and average advertising and promotion.

*Order-of-Entry Refinement.* The manager should also pay attention to the *order-of-entry effect* described in Chapter 2's discussion of budgeting. Depending on how late the new brand enters the product category (in terms of the number of previous competitors, not in terms of time per se), the likely attainable trial incidence will be reduced. The order-of-entry figures for consumer packaged goods provided in Chapter 2 were actually for market share rather than for trial incidence. Rubinson provides some order-of-entry market share estimates from his panel data which we can extrapolate to trial. The *first brand* to enter a product category will, by definition, have 100 percent market share, which represents about *40 percent* trial by all households; the next brand can expect to attain about 30 percent trial (by all households); the third brand about 18 percent; and so on down to the ninth brand to enter being able to expect only about 4 percent trial. Indeed, Rubinson's data suggest that the *fifth* brand to enter will attain the average new-item trial incidence of 13 percent but that later entrants will fall below this.[16] Again note that these are all-product averages and that the absolute levels, and the order-of-entry ratio, will depend on the particular product category.

*Length of Trial Period.* For a new fmcg brand entry, trial can be an objective for a considerable period *after* the initial introduction. Given strong distribution, it takes about 2 years for trial to reach its peak (that is, for the pool of available triers to be used up in response to the original positioning for the brand). Approximately two-thirds of the trial level is attained within the first 6 months, assuming a normal rollout

---

**TABLE 3.2**

**TRIAL NORMS FOR A NEW ITEM IN BROAD CONSUMER PACKAGED GOODS PRODUCT CATEGORIES**

| Broad product category | 1-Year trial incidence (% of households) |
|---|---|
| Household products | 29 |
| Food products[a] | 13 |
| Health and beauty aids | 16 |
| • Soap | 22 |
| • Feminine-hygiene products | 8 |
| • Over-the-counter drugs | 5 |
| Pet food (all households) | 6 |
| Average of all products | 13 |

[a]The food-products norm excludes carbonated beverages, which have an exceptionally high trial incidence.
*Source:* J. Rubinson, Update on trial and repeat trends for new products, *Proceedings: Advertising and Promotion Effectiveness Workshop,* New York: Advertising Research Foundation, 1989, pp. 255–265. Based on 153 cases from NPD/Nielsen panel, 1986–88.

schedule in the new item's distribution. Although the rate of trial undoubtedly slows after the first year, and we do not have precise figures available, Artzt[17] of Procter & Gamble reports that, for new P&G products, trial typically continues to build by approximately one-third for the second year after introduction. Putting these two figures together, as shown in Figure 3.3, we see that trial forms a negatively accelerated curve: if the peak is at 2 years, then the 6-month goal is 50 percent; and the 1-year goal is 75 percent, of the maximum 2-year trial level.

For the 2-year trial goal, therefore, simply multiply the norms in Table 3.2 by 1.33. It may be remembered that Peckham's 1.5 rule (described in Chapter 2) uses a 2-year trial goal for setting the new brand's budget.

We must reemphasize that these norms, including the "trial curve" in the figure, are strictly *averages*. Individual products almost surely will differ. But, in the absence of better information, these norms give the manager a good starting point.

**Ehrenberg's Method: Penetration × Average Frequency.** An even more precise method of estimating a trial goal for a new brand in an established product category is provided by Ehrenberg.[18] Ehrenberg's method applies to any product or service category *as long as there is repeat purchase.* (However, it can't be used for *single*-purchase products or services, for which the manager should use the task method to set the trial goal.) Ehrenberg's method is thus relevant for many industrial products, for industrial and consumer services that are patronized with some regularity, for retailers (to estimate trial patronage of their stores), and also for consumer packaged goods. Applications of the method range from industrial oil purchases, to patronage of supermarkets, to consumer purchase of instant coffee.

Ehrenberg's method is based on the fact that sales in a given year are made up of the brand's *penetration* (the number of triers in that year, who could be new triers or retriers) multiplied by the brand's *average repeat purchase rate* (the yearly rate with which *those triers* buy the brand). Based on observations of brands in hundreds of product and service categories, Ehrenberg and his colleagues have found that average repeat purchase rates differ relatively little across brands. Therefore, if we know the repeat purchase rate for the *average* brand, then the target sales level for our new brand divided by this average repeat purchase rate will give us the *minimum* trial incidence we need to shoot for (the actual goal is discussed shortly). To give a simple example, if the target sales level for our brand is 200 units per year and the average brand is bought four times a year, then we have to obtain 200 ÷ 4 = 50 trial customers *at least,* to meet our sales goal.

It must be understood that the *target sales level* in the Ehrenberg method is *itself* an estimate. (For determining this estimate, we recommend using the new brand's expected market share based on its order of entry, given in Chapter 2, Table 2.4, converted to sales units.) The main value of Ehrenberg's method is to estimate the required *trial* goal.

Chapter appendix 3B, Trial and Repeat Purchase Goals for Regularly Purchased Products and Services, provides worked examples of Ehrenberg's method.

*Unassisted Trial.* A final caveat in setting a trial objective—or more precisely, a *goal,* since the amount of trial and the time period for trial should be specified—is that the manager should be very careful to estimate "true" trial corrected for introductory aids such as free or discounted samples or generous introductory coupons or price-offs. These will temporarily inflate the trial incidence. The more important figure is the first *unassisted* trial purchase—made voluntarily by the buyer. As a rule of thumb, we suggest that the normal trial goal should be set at *2.5 times* the incidence of the intended eventual penetration. If free

**FIGURE 3.3**

Typical growth of trial for a new brand in an established consumer packaged goods category.

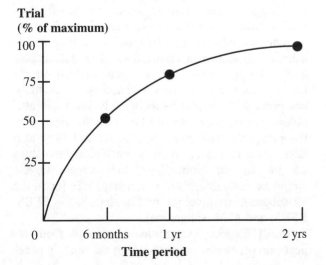

Trial
(% of maximum)

**Time period**

samples or heavily discounted trial-size samples are used to introduce the new brand, set the *sample-assisted* trial goal at *5 times* the intended eventual penetration.[19]

**Direct Response Trial.** In the foregoing discussion, we have assumed that the manager is interested in setting a trial goal that is to be "supported by" the AC&P launch campaign. Mass media campaigns usually make this assumption—that the launch advertising and promotion campaign is playing a supporting role with the rest of the marketing mix in achieving the (total) trial goal. *Direct response campaigns,* in contrast, are often planned in terms of the incremental (usually completely new) trial goal the campaign *itself* would have to attain. For a direct response campaign, the manager has to estimate the trial incidence that could be attributed to the campaign *alone,* that is, without considering the effects of distribution, competitors' pricing, and other marketing variables, whose effects tend to be minor in direct response marketing.

Fortunately, most advertising agencies have norms for the trial incidence that can be expected from a direct response campaign. These norms vary with the selectivity of the mailing list or media vehicle's audience, the price of the item, and the type of offer. Much higher norms are used for selective audiences, for example, than the widely quoted response rate of 1.2 percent for a *mass* mailing. Additionally, as a check, the task method should also be used to estimate the trial goal. Start with the size of the audience reached by the campaign and then estimate the chain of conversion ratios from one buyer response step to the next, as described in Chapter 2, through to target audience action.

## REPEAT PURCHASE OBJECTIVES

After trial, the success of brands in most product or service categories depends on repeat purchase. (The exceptions are one-purchase or very-long-purchase-cycle products or services, such as life insurance or vacation visits to Australia.) Sales of our brand in a given period are due to the number of triers (penetration) of our brand and the average frequency with which they buy it (repeat purchase).

### Unassisted Repeat Purchase for Triers

If we have targeted *trial* as the action objective (such as for an NCU, OBS, or OBL target audience) or retrial (likely for OBS or OBL target audiences later in

our *brand's* life cycle), then attaining an *unassisted first repeat* is a relevant repeat purchase objective before we focus on their future repeat purchase rate. This is just the same as the point we made above about unassisted trial. We emphasize this because the tendency of many managers is to measure only "first repeat" and then try to project this to a future repeat rate. If the brand is launched or restaged with a trial or retrial promotion, it is quite likely that many customers will buy more than once *while* the promotion is in effect.[20] (In Chapter 12, we will see that some promotions can be designed to minimize this.) Under these circumstances, the first repeat purchase can be a misleading indicator of future repeat purchase.

The manager therefore must be very careful to focus on the first *unassisted* repeat purchase as this will be a more valid indicator of future repeat in the absence of promotional incentives.

### Repeat Purchase for Regularly Bought Products and Services

Repeat-purchase rates for *regularly purchased* products and services are very stable (again see chapter appendix 3B). The only difficulty is if ours is the first brand in the category, in which case we will need to rely on test market data or wait until we can observe a stable repeat purchase rate. However, repeat purchase alone, by buyers of the brand, doesn't tell the whole story from a standpoint of target audience action objectives, as we'll see next.

**Brand Attitude as the True Dividing Factor.** Assessment of the extent to which it is possible to increase buyers' repeat-purchase rates requires knowledge of their *attitude* toward the brand. Borrowing from the Hendry Corporation's work, these attitudes usually form a "bathtub" or U-shaped distribution as shown in Figure 3.4.[21] The shaded portion under the curve indicates that the best targets for an increase in repeat purchase are those prospects with neutral to moderately favorable attitudes—because they should be easier to move than the prospects with negative attitude and they also have room to move, whereas the highly favorables do not. In our terminology, the increase targets would be favorable brand switchers, FBSs [or in the 12 subgroup terminology of Chapter 18, the EFBS, RFBS, and MBL subgroups].

**Don't Expect Exceptions.** Deviations from repeat purchase rates proportional to the brand's pene-

Number of
buyers in
product
category

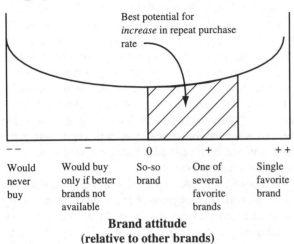

Best potential for
*increase* in repeat purchase
rate

| – – | – | 0 | + | + + |
|-----|---|---|---|-----|
| Would never buy | Would buy only if better brands not available | So-so brand | One of several favorite brands | Single favorite brand |

**Brand attitude
(relative to other brands)**

**FIGURE 3.4**
"Bathtub" or U-shaped distribution of brand attitude across buyers (adapted from the Hendry System; see note 23). Repeat-purchase *increase* potential is best in the shaded portion, among those whose (relative) attitude toward the brand is neutral to moderately favorable.

tration are exceedingly rare. Deviations, when they occasionally occur, take two forms: "niche" brands, with low penetration and high repeat rate (examples: Tab, in the soft-drink category, and Wheaties, among breakfast cereals); or "change-of-pace" brands, with high penetration and low repeat rate (examples: 7-Up and Sprite among soft drinks, and Rice Krispies among cereals). However, contrary to marketing folklore and to many managers' positioning endeavors, *hardly ever* does a frequently purchased product category exhibit either a niche brand or a change-of-pace brand.[22] Ehrenberg's method of setting the brand's repeat purchase goal based on its penetration level (see chapter appendix 3B) is therefore a highly reliable procedure, which we recommend for all regularly purchased product and service categories.

### Repeat Purchase Intentions for Products and Services with Long Purchase Cycles

Many products and services have a very long purchase cycle, which may extend for a year or even 5 or 10 years. Automobiles, an example which we discuss in chapter appendix 3B, are one such product, as are

many other consumer durables such as washing machines and microwave ovens. Many services, too, such as hospital services, are "purchased" infrequently. So also are major capital equipment items in industry. For these products and services, it is inappropriate to use average repeat purchase rate (per year for instance) as a guideline, because the repeat purchase rate is far too low. (Note, however, that *institutional* buyers, such as fleet automobile renters or capital equipment resellers, usually have purchase cycles that are much shorter. For them, average repeat purchase rate is applicable.)

If the purchase cycle is long, the product or service probably will have *changed* by the time the buyer is ready to repeat.[23] It could therefore be contended that the major action objective for products with long purchase cycles is trial rather than repeat purchase. Nevertheless, for many of these products, despite the long interval, there can be a fair amount of brand loyalty and thus a considerable tendency to buy again from the same manufacturer.[24] This tendency can be measured as purchase intentions.

**Purchase Intentions.** For long purchase-cycle products or services, it is more appropriate to use *intentions* to stay loyal or to switch instead of repeat purchase as such. Managers in these product or service categories do, or should, conduct periodic surveys to measure, within the total potential market, the proportion of prospects who intend to stay loyal or switch away from the brand—or to switch *in* to it. These "intended switch-ins" and "intended stays" are better regarded from a marketing communications perspective as requiring *trial* action objectives, because the likelihood is that the product or service will have changed quite substantially over the long interval.

The action objective or goal is then set in terms of the number or proportion of buyers to be *attracted* (FBSs) and *retained* (BLs). The prospective buyers' nomination of our brand for the next intended purchase (intended trial) is the action objective for these products or services.

### Repeat Purchase Amount and Timing Objectives

To this point, we have been discussing repeat purchase rate (and repeat purchase proportion in the case of intentions) while ignoring two further behavioral parameters—the *amount* purchased per purchase occasion by the buyer and the exact *timing* of that purchase.

For most products and services, amount per occasion and purchase timing can be disregarded when setting repeat-purchase action objectives (we discuss three exceptions shortly, two for products and one for services). People are remarkably consistent in both the amount of product they purchase per purchase occasion (usually in accord with well-established habits of family or personal consumption) and in the time interval they leave between purchases (often governed by regular shopping habits in visiting stores[25]). In a study of U.S. retail sales of regular ground caffeinated coffee, for example, Gupta[26] found that when sales increased due to a promotion, only 2 percent of the increase was due to buyers' purchasing multiple cans and 4 percent to their buying a larger can (amount). Some of the sales increase, 14 percent, was due to accelerated purchase to take advantage of the promotion (timing). But most of the increase, 80 percent of it, was caused by brand switching (switching-in) to the promoted brand. Amount and timing, therefore, do not change much, especially when considered over a 1-year period, the usual time horizon for action objectives.

However, increased purchase amount and accelerated purchase timing may be *short-run* action objectives for products that meet two criteria: products that can be *stored easily* and that are *not perishable.* Ground coffee meets *neither* of these criteria very well because most people do not want a large can taking up pantry or freezer space and also they tend to want fresh coffee and thus do not keep it for long periods. On the other hand, products such as plastic wrap and bath soap are reasonably convenient to store and do not have a perceived deterioration problem. Consequently, in such product categories, increased purchase amount and purchase acceleration—both of which tend to result in a stockpile—are more common.[27]

**Stockpiling's Effects on Consumption and Repeat Purchase.** It is well known by marketers of the more "impulse" types of products that if the marketer can induce the consumer to stockpile, it will increase the consumer's rate of usage or consumption. For instance, the more potato chips or soft drinks you have on hand at home, the faster you will eat them or drink them! This relates to the purchase-related action objective of increasing usage per usage occasion, but note that it is contingent upon *first* increasing the amount of purchase per purchase occasion, or on accelerating the timing of purchase, which will have much the same effect.[28]

By offering an appropriate promotion, the manager may be able to increase the target audience's purchase amount or speed of purchase. But unless the consumption rate *also* increases, there will be an equal and opposite *deficit effect* following the promotion. This "peaks and valleys" pattern is observed many times in scanner data for supermarket products, where a sales promotion causes a large increase in sales only to be followed after the promotion by a corresponding decrease.[29] Only for products that consumers are willing and able to *consume* faster will increased purchase amount or accelerated purchase have a positive *long-term* effect on sales.

Of course, the manager may have *short-term*—often competitive—objectives in trying to "load" buyers or consumers temporarily, such as when a new competitor is entering the market; or in trying to accelerate their purchase, such as to clear inventory. These short-term objectives are achieved, usually, without any change in the brand's long-term repeat purchase rate.

**Stockpiling of Services.** Conventional wisdom has it that services, in contrast with most products, are perishable and so cannot be stockpiled. The reasoning is that a service is provided instantly and is not tangible and therefore cannot be stored. This is true from the seller's standpoint but not necessarily from the buyer's. It would be feasible to think of *vouchers or credit for future services* as being stockpilable. For instance, frequent-flier mileage and upgrades can be stored and are nonperishable, usually for about 12 months. Encouraging the buyer to sign a service contract "up front" is a similar type of storage behavior that protects the seller against competitive purchases. Indeed, credit cards themselves are a prime example. Accordingly, purchase amount and timing objectives (stockpiling) can be set for many types of services.

**Long-Term Amount Objectives.** Some advertising and promotion campaigns aimed at *current users* (FBS and BL target audiences) are designed explicitly to increase rate of purchase *and* purchase amount over the long term.[30] Usually, this is a campaign that tries to broaden the usage occasions for the product. Classic advertising campaigns based on this strategy include "Orange juice—it's not just for breakfast any more," "Soup is good food" (from Campbell's, the market leader), and American Express's "Don't leave home without it." More recently, promotional campaigns for airlines' frequent-flier programs have offered mileage credit for using designated hotels and rental-car services while traveling, which have as their action objective for flying with the airline long-term increased rate and amount of purchase behavior.

Finally, there are "de-marketing" situations, where the purpose is to decrease or delay purchase over the long term. Government don't-drink-and-drive campaigns are an example where decreased purchase (and consumption) is the action objective. Campaigns for home loans emphasizing "years to pay" are an example of delayed timing as an action objective. The financial institution would probably prefer you to pay slowly so that the higher total interest payments result in more profit.

## DISTRIBUTORS AS TARGET AUDIENCES

*Distributors (wholesalers or retailers)* also are target audiences for trial and repeat purchase objectives: if distributors will not accept our brand, then the ultimate buyers or consumers cannot buy it (unless we are using direct marketing).

### Importance of Distribution

For those brands seeking to increase market share, distribution is crucial. A recent analysis of frequently purchased consumer goods shows that a brand can't become big until it has achieved approximately 50 percent distribution, whereupon market share *accelerates* with further distribution, as depicted in Figure 3.5.[31] Of course, the causality here is largely two-way, a combination of distribution "push" with demand "pull" if the brand is favorably received by consumers or final customers. However, maximum distribution (few brands achieve over 80 percent) means more opportunities for the consumer to repeat without having to settle for a substitute brand and gives these big brands an extra boost in market share.[32] We should, however, note two exceptions to this relationship. Specialty or "search" goods do not necessarily need or want maximum distribution; indeed, their exclusiveness may partly *depend on* limited, specialized distribution (Gucci apparel, for instance). Also, as we emphasized in Chapter 2, maximizing profit is usually

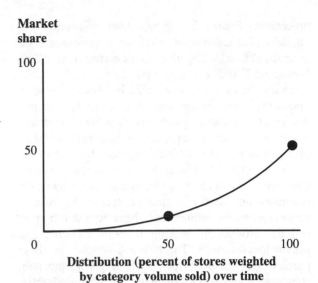

**Market share**

**Distribution (percent of stores weighted by category volume sold) over time**

**FIGURE 3.5**
Typical relationship between distribution and market share achieved over time for frequently purchased products. Note that the causality is two-way (push-pull) but that extra distribution means extra opportunities to buy, and thus "push" is likely to be effective in its own right. Adapted from Farris et al.; see note 31.

more important than maximizing market share, and thus maximum distribution may not be sought. Nevertheless, the "threshold" relationship shown in the figure is one of which managers should be aware.

### Distributor Target Audiences and Action Objectives

Manufacturers can and should classify distributors into the five prospect groups—NCUs, OBLs, OBSs, FBSs, and BLs. For instance, the manufacturer of Apple computers has as prospects Apple-specialized retail outlets (BLs), others that carry Apple but also competing makes of computers (FBSs), and still others that do not carry the Apple brand (OBSs, OBLs, or potential NCUs). Just as with ultimate buyers, the manager should select distributor target audiences, for trade advertising and promotion, according to the estimated leverage of the distributor groups.

The action objectives for distributors are also analogous to those for ultimate customers or consumers, namely trial and repeat purchase in their various forms. Although this takes us ahead into the next chapter's more specific action objectives since it includes purchase-related as well as purchase objectives, Figure 3.6 shows how distributor (or "trade") trial and repeat purchase behaviors are instrumental in attaining ultimate customer (here called "consumer") trial and repeat purchase.

In the figure, trade acceptance has been labeled as "purchase" even though this may not be an accurate description, as with goods consigned to the trade. Trade acceptance, in turn, can be measured in terms of the basic two buyer behaviors: trade trial (stocking the item in the first place) and trade repeat purchase (reordering the item). Usually, though, the marketer is interested not merely in trade acceptance but also in various *purchase-related* trade behaviors that help to sell the product by making it more available and salient to customers. The figure lists some of these purchase-related behaviors, such as giving the item shelf space and special displays, for which advertising and promotion (to the trade) frequently play an important role. These purchase-related trade behaviors follow trade acceptance. Trade acceptance and repeat purchase are discussed further in conjunction with manufacturer's promotions in Chapter 12.

All of these purchase and purchase-related behaviors on the part of distributors—as well as the purchase-related behaviors on the part of consumers—are aimed ultimately at increasing consumer *purchase*

behaviors (seen by following the arrows in Figure 3.6). The consumer marketer is always ultimately concerned with consumer trial and repeat purchase even though other behaviors may constitute vital purchase-related steps along the way.

Listing all the possible purchase-related behaviors that distributors and consumers could engage in would not be a very productive exercise. Fortunately, there is an easier way. By constructing a *behavioral sequence model* as shown in the next chapter, the manager can easily identify those purchase-related behaviors and purchase behaviors that are most relevant to the advertising communications or promotion situation faced by the brand.

### Distributors' Own Target Audience and Action Objectives

Distributors, in turn, have ultimate customers or consumers as their target. Usually, these buyers are the same ultimate target market that the manufacturer is seeking (as in manufacturer's brands sold through grocery and drugstores, but also for the store's own private-label brand if it has one). Whereas the distributor's and the manufacturer's action objectives are the same at the brand level, the distributor is more *broadly* interested in his or her own store or outlet trial and store or outlet repeat patronage. Thus, distributors must consider store loyals, store switchers, store NCUs, and so forth. We consider distributors' objectives further in conjunction with retailer's promotions in Chapter 13.

**FIGURE 3.6**

Purchase and purchase-related behaviors: trade and consumer targets.

**A. Trade behaviors**

PURCHASE ———————→ PURCHASE-RELATED

1. Stock item
   (equivalent of trial)
2. Reorder item (equivalent of repeat purchase)

For example:
- Give item favorable shelf space
- Display and promote item
- Recommend item to customers and other retailers

↓

**B. Consumer behaviors**

PURCHASE-RELATED ——→ PURCHASE

For example:
- Make sales inquiry
- Visit store
- Redeem coupons
- Recommend item to friends

1. Trial
2. Repeat purchase

### SUMMARY

Sales potentially can come from any or all of five groups of buyers: new category users (NCUs), brand loyals (BLs), favorable brand switchers (FBSs), other-brand switchers (OBSs), or other-brand loyals (OBLs). Considering these five prospect groups constitutes the brand loyalty approach or, more precisely, the awareness-attitude-behavior approach, to target audience selection.

Selecting a *target audience* is a process of deciding which prospect group will be most *responsive to advertising communications or promotion,* or to both used together in the case of IMC campaigns, in relation to the cost of the advertising, promotion, or IMC program. Expected extra or unlost sales (number of buyers × their average incremental purchase amount in dollars) divided by the expected cost of the campaign directed to that group defines its leverage. Only high-leverage prospect groups should be chosen as target audiences.

A particular advertising, promotion, or IMC campaign usually is directed at a single target audience (one of the five prospect groups). However, when there is a lesser leverage effect on other prospect groups, it is sometimes meaningful to designate a primary and a secondary target audience. In particular, for campaigns aimed at attracting new prospects as the primary target audience, brand loyals usually will be an implicit secondary target audience to insure that the new campaign will retain them.

For a particular advertising, promotion, or IMC campaign, it is reasonably common to further delineate the target audience from within one of the five buyer groups. Delineation may be dictated practically by geographics, or strategically (in relation to a particular campaign) by demographic or psychographic variables. Geographic delineation is almost always appropriate since most campaigns have geographic constraints. Demographic or psychographic delineation of the target audience *may* be appropriate (for instance, a campaign directed to "NCU women" or to "FBSs who like to travel"), but we caution against the erroneous practice of defining target audiences in terms of demographics or psychographics alone without considering their brand loyalty status. Advertising communications (always) and promotion (ideally) are entirely concerned with establishing, reinforcing, or changing loyalty and, in defining a target audience, this factor cannot be omitted. Although this chapter has been about buyer *behavior,* we noted that brand loyalty—from an advertising communications or promotions standpoint—is defined in terms of awareness, attitude, and behavior. The reason for this loyalty definition will be driven home when we examine the AC&P communication objectives that produce target audience action.

Action objectives for each target audience are set in terms of two types of *behavior:* trial and repeat purchase.

For new products or new target audiences, the manager must set a trial objective (preferably a goal). A trial goal can be set for very new products by employing a purchase diffusion forecasting model in conjunction with management judgment (see Chapter 18). For other products, trial norms are widely available and, for frequently purchased products and services, a method proposed by Ehrenberg provides a precise way of estimating the trial incidence that the brand can be expected to attain.

Repeat purchase is an action objective that follows trial for most products and services. Repeat purchase rates are usually a lot easier to predict than trial, and it is thus relatively simple in most cases to set a realistic repeat purchase goal. For frequently purchased products and services, Ehrenberg's method again can be used. For products and services with very long purchase cycles, such as industrial capital equipment or consumer durables, purchase *intentions* must be used. Here, our manager must estimate or measure the proportion of all buyers who intend to stay loyal to our brand and also the proportion who intend to switch in to our brand.

In addition to repeat purchase rates, some advertising and promotion campaigns (usually promotions) are designed to affect the *amount* purchased per purchase occasion or the *timing* of purchase. These two behavioral parameters are usually short-term action objectives because the stockpiling caused by the larger purchase amount or faster purchase can lead to the deferral of subsequent purchases, and thus the long-term purchase rate doesn't change. However, for extended-usage campaigns or for impulse products or services, magnification or acceleration of purchase can result in a higher rate of consumption. Also, for some products and services, decreased purchase amounts or delayed timing of purchase can be objectives.

Distributor or trade (wholesaler or retailer) action objectives are analogous to trial and repeat purchase. These are essential (indeed prior) action objectives for most marketers. The decision by a distributor to carry our brand is the equivalent of trial; the decision to reorder it is the equivalent of repeat purchase; and decisions to give it more shelf space or to promote it at the retail level are the equivalents of increasing purchase amount and accelerating purchase timing.

In the next chapter, we learn more about the target audience by identifying the participants in the overall decision process that leads to target audience action. We also show how to identify other decision stages and behaviors that precede or follow purchase which, when targeted by an advertising, promotion, or IMC campaign, can increase the likelihood that purchase—and repeat purchase—will occur.

# 3A. Universality of the Brand Loyalty Approach

The awareness-attitude-behavior or brand loyalty approach is applicable to *all* types of products and services, both industrial and consumer. A managerially meaningful "loyalty" measure can always be constructed, as demonstrated in the following examples. Brand loyalty (the five potential buyer groups) should *always* be used as the primary basis of target audience selection for AC&P campaigns.

**Industrial Target Audiences.** Industrial marketers should not hesitate to apply the brand loyalty approach. Gensch[33] applied it to the marketing program for ABB Electric, a marketer of electrical engineering equipment, with great success, winning the Institute of Management Sciences' Edelman prize in 1990 for the best real-world application of management science techniques. Gensch divided the company's total potential market on the basis of "supplier loyalty," using a measure that included the potential customer's attitudinal evaluation of various suppliers (ABB Electric and others) as well as recent past purchases and current intentions to buy from each supplier in the coming year. In this case, because new category users were not considered a realistic target, potential customers were divided into four buyer groups: brand loyals, favorable brand switchers, other-brand switchers, and other-brand loyals. Following Gensch's advice, ABB Electric implemented a direct mail and sales force program that emphasized the benefits rated as most important by the two groups considered to be most switchable, FBSs and OBSs. The experimental program was implemented in two randomly selected geographic areas, with a third area used as the control area, in which the previous marketing program was maintained.

The results of Gensch's experiment are shown in Table 3.3. As can be seen, the experimental program successfully resulted in increased sales to the two targeted buyer groups: sales increased markedly among favorable brand switchers, and to a slightly lesser extent among other-brand switchers. The total sales increase in the first experimental area was 18 percent and in the second experimental area 12 percent, versus a sales decline of 10 percent in the control area. Moreover, these results were achieved despite a 15 percent decline in overall industry sales (much like the decline in the control area). Targeting based on the brand loyalty approach (to FBSs and OBSs) was evidently responsible for the impressive results.

Another industrial application of the brand-loyalty approach is by Segal,[34] who studied the market for high-precision plastics in a chemical industry. Here, brand loyals were defined as those who prefer to buy from a single supply source (90 percent or more of purchases from one supplier), and brand switchers as those customers who prefer to buy from multiple sources of supply (placing less than 90 percent of their orders with a single supplier). Segal provided an interesting analysis of why and under what circumstances buyers may prefer to be single-source loyal or to engage in "controlled" brand switching among multiple suppliers.

**Consumer-Durable Target Audiences.** The brand loyalty approach also applies to consumer durables. For instance, Columbo and Morrison, using 1963 data, divided the U.S. car-buying market into "hard-core loyals" and "potential switchers," as did Chandrasekharan, McCarthy, and Wright in a more recent study. In these studies, brand loyalty was defined in terms of the make and type of car purchased previously, compared with the currently owned car and the make and type that the car buyer intended to purchase next. U.S. manufacturers, of course, are very concerned about loyalty not only to their own makes but to U.S.-made cars over imports. A 1987 study by R. L. Polk & Company, based on 1987 purchases in comparison with the car bought previously, reported the following repeat-purchase loyalties: imports, which would include Japanese and European makes, 59 percent; GM, 55 percent; Ford, 46 percent; and Chrysler, only 36 percent.[35] Quite evidently, automobile manufacturers and the U.S. automobile industry are closely monitoring car buyers' intended loyalty and intended switching in conjunction with current advertising and promotion campaigns.

**Retail Target Audiences.** Retailers, as well, can apply the brand loyalty approach. For instance, Keng and Ehrenberg have studied loyalty patterns for patronage of supermarkets in the United Kingdom, and Wilson and Woodside have applied the Ehrenberg formulation of brand loyalty to patronage of women's specialty clothing stores in the United States.[36] These studies show that store-choice behavior is very much like brand-choice behavior, with some shoppers remaining highly loyal, others engaging in fre-

---

| TABLE 3.3 | | | |
|---|---|---|---|

**GENSCH'S EXPERIMENT FOR AN ELECTRICAL SUPPLY COMPANY: SALES RESULTS OBTAINED USING THE BRAND-LOYALTY APPROACH TO TARGET AUDIENCE SELECTION**

| Target audience | Experimental area 1 | Experimental area 2 | Control area |
|---|---|---|---|
| Brand loyals | + 2% | + 3% | + 3% |
| Favorable brand switchers | + 26% | + 18% | − 9% |
| Other-brand switchers | + 16% | + 8% | − 18% |
| Other-brand loyals | − 4% | − 3% | − 4% |
| Total sales | + 18% | + 12% | − 10% |

*Source:* See note 33.

quent switching between stores, and still others who are not "users" of the category.

**Services Target Audiences.** Business or consumer services also can be productively approached from a brand loyalty perspective. For instance, AT&T's "The right choice" campaign was clearly aimed at preventing previously "forced" brand loyals, due to AT&T's earlier monopoly, from switching to the newer rival long-distance telephone companies such as MCI and U.S. Sprint. Also, new services, like new products, have to attract new category users initially, and then target brand switchers or other-brand loyals while retaining their own loyals.

# 3B. Trial and Repeat Purchase Goals for Regularly Purchased Products and Services

Ehrenberg's method can be used for any product or service category that is regularly purchased. Although it is illustrated for a common consumer product here, it is equally applicable to industrial products.

The purpose of Ehrenberg's method is to set a realistic trial goal and then a suitable repeat purchase goal for the brand.

**Trial Goal.** Ehrenberg provides trial incidence calculations for the U.S. instant coffee market from several years ago, which we will use here to exemplify his method because it is a product category with which most of us are familiar. Table 3.4 shows the relevant data, which managers usually can obtain from diary or scanner panel services, or from a market survey.

Penetration is defined as the percentage of households that will buy a particular brand at least once during the planning period (say, 1 year). Note that this definition allows for retrial as well as completely new trial; penetration is simply the proportion of households that will buy the brand at least once during the year (see second column of table). For the average established brand of instant coffee, penetration is 17 percent of all households. During the course of the year, those triers will buy the brand several times (see third column of table). The typical repeat purchase rate is 2.8 times, based on the average for established brands of instant coffee.

Suppose our brand is about to be launched in this category. To meet the sales goal we have set for it, the brand will have to attain a 2.4 percent market share across *all* households. The total market is about five purchases of instant coffee per household per year (actually, instant coffee–buying households make about nine purchases per year, but not all households are buyers of instant coffee). Five purchases per household per year means 500 purchases per 100 households per year; a 2.4 percent share of these purchases translates to 12 purchases per 100 households per year (that is, 2.4 percent × 500 = 12 purchases). Purchases per 100 households per year (sales) for existing brands are shown in the right column of the table.

These 12 purchases per 100 households could be made up of, at one extreme, 1 percent of households buying the new brand 12 times during the year or, at the other extreme, 12 percent of households buying it once a year. However, the fact is that the new brand is most likely to be purchased at the *average* repeat purchase rate for the instant coffee category, which is 2.8 times per year. Therefore, the desired penetration incidence for the new brand is sales divided by average frequency, which is 12 ÷ 2.8 = 4.3 percent.

---

**TABLE 3.4**

**PENETRATION × AVERAGE REPEAT PURCHASE RATE = SALES**

*(Exemplified for the U.S. instant coffee market several years ago. Time period = 1 year.)*

| Brand | Penetration (% of households buying the brand) | Repeat purchase rate (average number of times the brand was bought) | Sales (number of purchases per 100 households) |
|---|---|---|---|
| Maxwell House | 24 | 3.6 | 86 |
| Sanka | 21 | 3.3 | 69 |
| Taster's Choice | 22 | 2.8 | 62 |
| High Point | 22 | 2.6 | 57 |
| Folger's | 18 | 2.7 | 49 |
| Nescafé | 13 | 2.9 | 38 |
| Brim | 9 | 2.0 | 18 |
| Maxim | 6 | 2.6 | 16 |
| Average | 17 | 2.8 | 48 |

*Source:* MRCA panel data analyzed by A. S. C. Ehrenberg. See note 18.

*Trial Goal = Desired Penetration Incidence × 2.5.* In this example, the manager for the new brand should actually see the first-year trial goal at about *11 percent* in order to ensure penetration of 4 or 5 percent of households. (Why 11 percent? Ehrenberg's figures on penetration and repeat rates are based on *established* brands. To get 4.3 percent "stable penetration," we have conservatively allowed for approximately 60 percent initial-trier *rejection* of the brand, a figure which could be made more precise by test marketing. If the rejection rate is 60 percent, the acceptance rate is only 40 percent and thus the penetration figure needs to be multiplied by 2.5, that is, by 100 ÷ 40 = 2.5, to calculate the trial goal. Here, 4.3 × 2.5 = 10.75 ≈ 11 percent.[37]) To take another example using the same data, a market share goal of 5 percent for the year would translate to 25 purchases per 100 households per year. This would most likely be attained by achieving 25 ÷ 2.8 = 8.9 percent penetration incidence—translating to about a 22 percent trial goal. Any other target market share can be run through the procedure similarly and the trial goal calculated.[38]

**Repeat Purchase Goal.** Let us turn now to repeat-purchase action objectives for those who are already buying our brand. In the U.S. instant coffee example discussed above, we saw that, for the typical brand, the average frequency of purchase of the brand by its buyers was 2.8 times per year. However, this average figure, for most brands, combines the repeat-purchase patterns of two very different groups making up our total buyers: favorable brand switchers and brand loyals. To distinguish these two groups meaningfully as target audiences for our brand, we would need to know the strengths of their *attitude* toward it.

- BLs would regard our brand as their most preferred brand and would be unwilling to accept substitutes except, perhaps, for occasional variety.
- FBSs, on the other hand, would regard our brand as one of several acceptable brands among which they switch quite frequently (they would have a somewhat lower repeat purchase rate).

By relating this attitudinal difference to actual *behavior,* the manager can draw the correct dividing line between "brand loyal" and "favorable switching" repeat purchase. Usually, however, the manager has available only the behavioral data and therefore makes an arbitrary division. The repeat purchase goals for each of the two target audiences of brand buyers are then set as follows.

*"Heavy Half" Indicates BL and FBS Repeat Purchase Goals.* With an arbitrary division of our brand's buyers into two equal-sized groups, the well-known "heavy half" or "20:80" rule will be observed. This means that half of the brand's buyers (mainly FBSs) will account for 20 percent of its purchases, and the other half (mainly BLs—the heavy half) will account for 80 percent of its purchases. Indeed,

whereas the numbers may not be exact for every product category, they are very close for the U.S. instant coffee market in the example provided by Ehrenberg[39] (see Table 3.5). For the typical brand of instant coffee, 49 percent of its buyers buy it only once during the year, accounting for 19 percent of the brand's sales volume. The other 51 percent of the brand's buyers buy it two or more times per year and account for 81 percent of the brand's sales volume. Arbitrarily, we could call the first group of buyers FBSs and the second group BLs.

Alternatively, with another arbitrary division of instant coffee buyers, we could define BLs more tightly as those who make three or more purchases of the brand per year, in which case the BL group would be 32 percent of the brand's buyers, accounting for 65 percent of its sales volume. The FBSs would then be the other 68 percent of the brand's buyers, who buy the brand only once or twice during the year and account for 35 percent of its sales volume.

Again, there is nothing magical about the half or one-third division; the better place to make the division between FBSs and BLs is in conjunction with their *attitude* toward the brand. Regardless of exactly where the division is placed, these typical data indicate that most brands' sales will be made up of a core of BLs who purchase the brand frequently and a fringe of FBSs who purchase the brand less frequently.

Let us suppose, for instance, that the 32 percent of buyers who purchase a particular brand of instant coffee three or more times per year happen to coincide with those who have a "single-preferred brand" attitude and thereby represent "true" BLs [the SBL subgroup in Chapter 18's target audience classification]. The average annual purchase rate for BLs would then be 5.2, and the average annual purchase rate for FBSs would be 1.3 (averages calculated for the heavy third and the other two-thirds from Table 3.5). These would be the initial or "going-in" repeat purchase rates for the two target audiences. The manager may then wish to establish a *target* repeat purchase rate of, for example, 6.0 for the BL group and, again for example only, 2.0 for the FBS group.

The distribution of purchase rates in the table further suggests that these hypothetical repeat purchase goals would be most likely to be achieved, in the first instance, by moving the "slightly less loyal" of the BLs to a higher purchase frequency, since the "highly loyal" BLs are presumably already near a maximum repeat purchase rate; and, in the second instance, by either moving the one-purchase FBSs to two purchases or the two-purchase FBSs into the BL group.[40]

There is much to be learned from arraying brands' data in a form such as shown in the tables. Again, we emphasize that these patterns are characteristic of all (repeat purchase) product categories. Similar repeat rates across brands hold not only for frequently purchased consumer

## TABLE 3.5

### DISTRIBUTION (PERCENTAGE FREQUENCY) OF PURCHASE RATES FOR U.S. INSTANT COFFEE BRANDS

(*Time period = 1 year.*)

| Brand | Purchase rate (number of purchases of brand by its buyers in 1 year) | | | | | | | Average purchase rate |
|---|---|---|---|---|---|---|---|---|
| | 1 | 2 | 3 | 4 | 5 | 6 | 7 + | |
| Maxwell House | 38 | 16 | 11 | 8 | 7 | 5 | 15 | 3.6 |
| Sanka | 40 | 19 | 11 | 6 | 6 | 3 | 15 | 3.3 |
| Folger's | 53 | 18 | 10 | 5 | 3 | 3 | 8 | 2.7 |
| Maxim | 56 | 19 | 6 | 5 | 3 | 1 | 10 | 2.6 |
| Average[a] | 49 | 19 | 9 | 7 | 4 | 3 | 9 | 2.8 |

heavy third

heavy half

[a]The average is calculated across all eight brands listed in Table 3.4. Selected brands are shown here for greater clarity. Sanka is included to demonstrate that decaf brands do not differ from regular brands in their purchase rate.
*Source:* same as for Table 3.4.

products but also for consumer services and industrial products and services. These patterns are extremely typical and therefore allow realistic trial and repeat purchase goals to be set.

## NOTES

1. A number of authors have defined brand loyalty in terms of attitude and behavior. See for example G. S. Day, A two-dimensional concept of brand loyalty, *Journal of Advertising Research,* 1969, *9* (3), pp. 29–35; and J. Jacoby and R. W. Chestnut, *Brand Loyalty Measurement and Management,* New York: Ronald Press, 1978. We define it *also* in terms of brand awareness, for reasons that will become clearer in Part Three, where we discuss communication objectives for advertising communications and promotion.

2. The terms "rotators," who switch for variety, and "deal selectors," who switch for price promotions on their preferred brands, come from Josh McQueen, research director at Leo Burnett U.S.A., and were reported in A. L. Baldinger, What CEOs are saying about brand equity: A call to action for researchers, *Journal of Advertising Research,* 1992, *32* (4), pp. RC-6 to RC-12. Also see A. K. Sylvester, J. McQueen, and S. D. Moore, Brand growth and "Phase 4 marketing," *Admap,* September 1994, pp. 34–36.

3. In a recent study it was shown that consumers loyal to another brand (OBLs) can be vulnerable to brand switching if the product category is a "low risk" one

(see Chapter 4, and Chapter 8's discussion of low-involvement brand decisions). The product category studied was facial tissue. See R. C. Blattberg, T. Buesing, and S. K. Sen, Segmentation strategies for national brands, *Journal of Marketing,* 1980, *44* (4), pp. 59–67.

4. I. Teinowitz, Michelob thinks older, *Advertising Age,* February 3, 1992, p. 47.

5. I. Teinowitz, Can Burnett lift Lite? Miller moves account as brand hits middle age, *Advertising Age,* March 18, 1991, pp. 1, 54.

6. D. H. Gensch, Targeting the switchable industrial customer, *Marketing Science,* 1984, *3* (1), pp. 41–54.

7. See A. S. C. Ehrenberg, Advertising: Reinforcing not persuading?, in S. S. Bell, ed., *Evaluating the Effects of Consumer Advertising on Market Position over Time: How to Tell Whether Advertising Ever Works,* Cambridge, MA: Marketing Science Institute, 1988, pp. 18–19; and M. D. Uncles and A. S. C. Ehrenberg, Brand choice among older consumers, *Journal of Advertising Research,* 1990, *30* (4), pp. 19–22.

8. Of course, this depends on how "loyally" BLs are defined. If very high behavioral loyalty is used as the dividing line between BLs and FBSs, then this statement is true. If loyalty is defined with a lower repeat-purchase rate cutoff, then there is room for an increased purchase rate for BLs.

9. The foregoing discussion of leverage implies that there may be "increasing returns" to advertising for a specific buyer group at a specific stage in the product

category life cycle. The conventional academic conclusion is that advertising virtually always produces diminishing returns, but for an argument supporting our view, see R. L. Steiner, Point of view: The paradox of increasing returns to advertising, *Journal of Advertising Research,* 1987, *27* (1), pp. 45–53.

10. We emphasize the use of *actual behavior* for action objectives because a common error is to identify *communication* objectives rather than *action* objectives at this stage. "To make people aware," for instance, may well be an action by the advertiser but it is *not* an action by the customer! To be aware is a communication effect; it occurs as a mental response, not a behavioral one.

11. T. S. Robertson, The process of innovation and the diffusion of innovation, *Journal of Marketing,* 1967, *31* (1), pp. 14–19.

12. Weight Watchers, the Heinz brand, was available well before Stouffer's Lean Cuisine as a low-calorie entree but Heinz at the time did not adopt a high-end or "gourmet" positioning.

13. An excellent review of first-purchase (trial) diffusion models is provided in G. L. Lilien, P. Kotler, and K. S. Moorthy, *Marketing Models,* Englewood Cliffs, NJ: Prentice-Hall, 1992, chapter 10. The Bass model predicts trial purchases based on an "innovation" effect (the number of people who adopt the new product on their own initiative) and an "imitation" effect (those who adopt based on acquaintance with innovators). In our Chapter 18, we show how it can be applied to forecasting a trial goal. The Horsky model is newer and is not summarized in the Lilien et al. text. The Horsky model explains *why* people adopt products (for either timesaving or pleasure-enhancement reasons, which fit very well with our negative and positive purchase motivations discussed in Chapter 5) and also allows an early forecast of trial. These are its two main improvements over the Bass model. See D. Horsky, A diffusion model incorporating product benefits, price, income and information, *Marketing Science,* 1990, *9* (4), pp. 342–365. Repeat-purchase diffusion is discussed in the same chapter of the Lilien et al. text and also in G. L. Lilien, A. G. Rao, and S. Kalish, Bayesian estimates and control of detailing effort in a repeat purchase diffusion environment, *Management Science,* 1981, *27* (5), pp. 493–506. For a less-mathematical discussion, see G. L. Urban and S. H. Star, *Advanced Marketing Strategy,* Englewood Cliffs, NJ: Prentice-Hall, 1991, chapter 6.

14. The estimates of new entries are from D. Wascoe, Jr., Choices, choices, choices! *Minneapolis Star Tribune,* October 6, 1991, pp. 1D, 5D. The company new-entry figures are from a survey made by *Gorman's New Product News,* reported in R. Fannin, Where are the new brands? *Marketing & Media Decisions,* 1989, *24* (7), pp. 22–24, 26, 27. To look at these figures from another perspective: in 1988, General Foods introduced 137 new items, Kraft introduced 116, H. J. Heinz introduced 106, with Sara Lee's 56 new items being the fewest among the major food companies. Revlon introduced 66 new items that year, Lever/ Cheseborough-Ponds introduced 52, with Pfizer's 23 new items being the fewest among the major nonfood companies.

15. J. Rubinson, Sales simulation—new marketing realities produce new testing needs, *Marketing Review,* 1986, *42* (2), pp. 13–15; and Update on trial and repeat trends for new products, in *Proceedings: Advertising and Promotion Effectiveness Workshop,* New York: Advertising Research Foundation, 1989, pp. 255–266.

16. These data are actually simulated market shares. But, as we shall see shortly, with a minor adjustment, market shares are highly correlated with trial rates, and thus we feel reasonably confident in reporting these figures as "trial" norms. The general point is that the manager should adjust for likely order-of-entry effects in setting trial objectives—unless the new entry is outstandingly different or, as noted in Chapter 2, is launched with superior advertising and a very heavy introductory budget.

17. E. L. Artzt, The lifeblood of brands, *Advertising Age,* November 4, 1991, p. 32.

18. A. S. C. Ehrenberg, Buyer behavior and NBD, Working paper, London Business School, 1987. Available from Professor Ehrenberg at South Bank Business School, London, UK.

19. In Chapter 12's discussion of manufacturer's trial promotions, we estimate that only 15 to 20 percent of consumers who receive a free or heavily discounted trial-size sample for the average new fmcg product will subsequently make a voluntary, full-price purchase. Thus, at least 80 percent will reject it. Therefore, the sample's distribution incidence should be set at 5 times the targeted eventual penetration incidence.

20. See Chapter 12 for other reasons for "false repeat."

21. The Hendry Corporation, *Speaking of Hendry,* New York: The Hendry Corporation, 1976. It should be noted that Hendry's "bathtub" distributions employ repeat purchase *behavior* (the brand's "share of requirements," that is, share of category purchases, for each buyer) as the horizontal axis. To assess potential for *increased* repeat purchase, however, this axis should be *brand attitude.* More on brand attitude can be found in Chapter 5.

22. The examples of "niche"and "change-of-pace" brands come from B. E. Kahn, M. U. Kalwani, and D. G. Morrison, Niching versus change-of-pace brands: Using purchase frequencies and penetration rates to infer

brand positionings, *Journal of Marketing Research,* 1988, *25* (4), pp. 384–390. However, examining a much larger number of product categories, also of frequently purchased supermarket products, a subsequent study showed these "deviant" brands to be extremely rare and not to occur at all in most product categories; see P. S. Fader and D. C. Schmittlein, Excess behavioral loyalty for high-share brands: Deviations from the Dirichlet model for repeat purchasing, *Journal of Marketing Research,* 1993, *30* (4), pp. 478–493. As with Ehrenberg's research, the "double jeopardy" effect (see notes 38 and 40) was almost universally observed, with the larger brands showing the higher repeat rates, due most likely to their much wider distribution. That is, even if smaller brands' buyers wanted to buy them as often, limited distribution prevents them from doing so; see P. Farris, J. Olver, and G. de Kluyver, The relationship between distribution and market share, *Marketing Science,* 1989, *8* (2), pp. 107–127.

23. John A. Howard's model of Extensive Problem Solving applies to buyer behavior for new product categories *and* infrequently purchased product categories, where buyers have to relearn the choice criteria and brand evaluations. See J. A. Howard, *Consumer Behavior: Application of Theory,* New York, NY: McGraw-Hill, 1977.

24. B. L. Bayus, Brand loyalty and marketing strategy: An application to home appliances, *Marketing Science,* 1992, *1* (1), pp. 21–38. For home appliances, such as color TV sets and dishwashers, the longer the consumer has had the old model, the more likely he or she is to buy the same *brand* next time.

25. B. E. Kahn and D. C. Schmittlein, Shopping trip behavior: An empirical investigation, *Marketing Letters,* 1989, *1* (1), pp. 55–69.

26. S. Gupta, Impact of sales promotions on when, what, and how much to buy, *Journal of Marketing Research,* 1988, *25* (4), pp. 342–355. For another detailed study of action objectives in response to promotion that takes into account how much to buy and when to buy, see I. S. Currim and L. G. Schneider, A taxonomy of consumer purchase strategies in a promotion intensive environment, *Marketing Science,* 1991, *10* (2), pp. 91–110.

27. For example, a study of toilet tissues—a storable, nonperishable product category—found that brand-loyal buyers tended to stock up in response to recent TV advertising exposures. See G. J. Tellis, Advertising exposure, loyalty, and brand purchase: A two-stage model of choice, *Journal of Marketing Research,* 1988, *25* (2), pp. 134–144. Also see G. F. Lowenstein, Frames of mind in intertemporal choice, *Management Science,* 1988, *34* (2), pp. 200–214; J. Chiang, A simultaneous approach to whether, what and how much to buy questions, *Marketing Science,* 1991, *10* (4), pp. 297–315;

and R. J. Meyer and J. Assuncao, The optimality of consumer stockpiling strategies, *Marketing Science,* 1990, *9* (1), pp. 18–41, the latter study demonstrating the paradoxical results that, when prices are rising, consumers tend to *under*-stockpile (present losses seem worse) and, when prices are falling, they tend to *over*-stockpile (present gains seem more attractive or perhaps a price rise is feared in the future).

28. An interesting phenomenon related to stockpiling has been identified by Simonson in attempting to explain brand switching due to "variety seeking." In a simulated shopping experiment, he found that a consumer who buys several items in the product category on *one* shopping trip, intending to consume the items sequentially over several consumption occasions, is much more likely to "brand switch," that is, to buy a varied selection of brands and flavors or types, than a consumer in the same product category who buys one item at a time, just before intended consumption. Thus, if you are the sort of shopper who buys three months' worth of frozen dinners, you are considerably more likely to buy a variety of brands and types than if you are the type of last-minute shopper who buys one frozen dinner from the store on the evening of consumption. Simonson's explanation of this phenomenon is that multiple simultaneous purchases lead to instant "mental satiation" on any one particular brand or type, whereas the time-spaced purchases tend to minimize single-brand satiation. It may help also to explain why convenience stores such as 7-Eleven can successfully offer a smaller range of items. See I. Simonson, The effect of purchase quantity and timing on variety-seeking behavior, *Journal of Marketing Research,* 1990, *27* (2), pp. 150–162.

29. See, especially A. S. C. Ehrenberg, K. Hammond, and G. J. Goodhardt, The after-effects of price-related consumer promotions, *Journal of Advertising Research,* 1994, *34* (4), pp. 11–21.

30. B. Wansink and M. L. Ray, How expansion advertising affects brand usage frequency: A programmatic evaluation, Report no. 93-126, Cambridge, MA: Marketing Science Institute, 1993.

31. P. Farris, J. Olver, and G. de Kluyver, same reference as in note 22.

32. P. S. Fader and D. C. Schmittlein, same reference as in note 22.

33. D. H. Gensch, same reference as note 6; and also D. H. Gensch, N. Aversa, and S. P. Moore, A choice-modeling marketing information system that enabled ABB Electric to expand its market share, *Interfaces,* 1990, *20* (1), pp. 6–25.

34. M. N. Segal, Implications of single vs. multiple buying sources, *Industrial Marketing Management,* 1989, *18* (3), pp. 163–178.

35. See R. A. Columbo and D. G. Morrison, A brand switching model with implications for marketing strategies, *Marketing Science,* 1989, *8* (1), pp. 89–99; and R. Chandrasekharan, P. S. McCarthy, and G. P. Wright, Models of brand loyalty in the automobile market, Paper presented at the Sixth International Conference on Travel Behavior, Montreal, Quebec, May 1991. The R. L. Polk & Co. survey was summarized in Shifting car loyalty, *Research Alert,* December 18, 1987, p. 5. For an application of the Columbo-Morrison model to other consumer durables such as refrigerators, washers, and color TV, see B. L. Bayus, Brand loyalty and marketing strategy: An application to home appliances, *Marketing Science,* 1992, *11* (1), pp. 21–38.

36. See K. A. Keng and A. S. C. Ehrenberg, Patterns of store choice, *Journal of Marketing Research,* 1984, *21* (3), pp. 399–409; and E. J. Wilson and A. G. Woodside, A comment on patterns of store choice and customer gain/loss analysis, *Journal of the Academy of Marketing Science,* 1991, *19* (4), pp. 377–382. It should be noted that Ehrenberg's formulation of brand loyalty, used in both the above studies, is based only on behavior.

37. We arrived at the "penetration incidence × 2.5" rule of thumb based on the NPD methodology and results described in the Rubinson 1986 article (see note 15). In the NPD method, consumers, after seeing a concept description, can choose the new item or accept the cash equivalent. Those who choose the new item are then telephoned a short time later and asked if they intend to buy the item in the store—that is, make a real, unassisted trial. Only 43 percent, for the average fmcg product category, say yes; in other words, 57 percent reject the item after trying it. Allowing for a slight "commitment" effect from having chosen the item in the earlier interview, we believe that 40 percent retention is close to what would be experienced from a promotion-assisted trial in stores to a subsequent voluntary purchase, which would represent penetration. Thus, penetration incidence ÷ 0.4 = 2.5.

   Perhaps not surprisingly, considering the increasing number of new supermarket-product entries, the NPD-estimated trial incidence for the average supermarket product has fallen—from 18 percent (of households) trial in 1979, to 15 percent in the mid-1980s, to just 13 percent for 1986–88, the most recent period for which a substantial number of cases is available. It should be noted that these are 1-year (12-month) trial figures—the usual budgeting and planning period. Also, the 1-year figures cover all seasons of the year for those products whose purchase varies during the year.

38. There is a slight refinement that can be applied rather than using the average purchase frequency for these calculations. This refinement is based on the *"double jeopardy" phenomenon,* which is quite similar to the order-of-entry effect with which we are now familiar. Basically, larger-share brands (often, earlier brands to enter) tend to achieve a slightly higher average purchase frequency among their buyers than do smaller-share brands. This is evident in the third column of Table 3.4. Thus, although the average brand is purchased 2.8 times per year by its buyers, the leading brand at the time, Maxwell House, is purchased 3.6 times and the lowest-frequency brand at the time, Brim, is purchased only 2.0 times. Therefore, sales of 12 purchases per 100 households per year would more likely be attained at an average purchase rate of *below* 2.8 (let's say 2.5), which would produce a penetration incidence of 12 ÷ 2.5 = 4.8 percent, and a trial goal of 12 percent. Similarly, 25 purchases per 100 households per year would probably be at a rate of about 2.6 and thus the penetration incidence would be 9.6 percent and the trial goal 24 percent. The double-jeopardy adjustment is a fairly slight refinement, and the overall average purchase rate is sufficient to calculate penetration and trial goals for most purposes. See A. S. C. Ehrenberg, G. J. Goodhardt, and T. P. Barwise, Double jeopardy revisited, *Journal of Marketing,* 1990, *54* (2), pp. 82–91.

39. A. S. C. Ehrenberg, same reference as note 18.

40. The "double jeopardy" phenomenon (referred to in note 38) allows the manager to make a slight refinement when setting a repeat-purchase goal for the brand. Unless massive new trial is also an action objective, the manager of a smaller-share brand could not expect to achieve a large increase in its repeat purchase rate. For instance, Maxim, with its current repeat purchase rate of 2.6, would be very optimistic to expect to equal Maxwell House's repeat purchase rate of 3.6 (a 38 percent increase in purchase rate) unless it could also increase its trial or retrial penetration to a level similar to that of the larger brand. For Maxim, a target repeat purchase rate of, for instance, 2.8 might be realistic without increased trial, but a target of, for instance, 3.3 or 3.6, matching the two leading brands, would *not* be realistic in the long run—although it might be for a short-term promotion. Many examples are provided in A. S. C. Ehrenberg, *Repeat-Buying: Theory and Applications,* Amsterdam, The Netherlands, and New York, NY: North-Holland and Elsevier, 1972; revised, London, UK: Charles Griffin & Co., 1987. A 3-year study of 44 brands of supermarket products by Information Resources Inc. (IRI) found that heavy-up advertising

sustained for a year (a 55 to 77 percent spending increase over the previous year) increased the repeat purchase rate of the average brand by 14 percent in that year, and "carried over," in that when advertising spending was reduced to normal in the second and third years, the repeat rate stayed 15 percent and 9 percent higher in those years, respectively. Note, however, that these increased repeat rates are quite modest in an absolute sense although undoubtedly profitable. See L. Lodish and B. Lubetkin, General truths? Nine key findings from IRI test data, *Admap,* February 1992, pp. 9–15.

## DISCUSSION QUESTIONS

**3.1.** You are the advertising agency account executive for Xerox copiers. Your client comes to you and asks for an advertising campaign "to target small business owners." Explain why this target audience definition is inadequate.

**3.2.** If you were the advertising manager for Dr. Pepper, which buyer group or groups would you concentrate on in your long-run sales strategy: NCUs, BLs, FBSs, OBSs, or OBLs? Rank the five groups in order of priority and explain your ranking.

**3.3.** Without looking back at the text, write out a definition of brand loyalty, then briefly describe your own loyalty status with respect to:
**a.** Beer brands
**b.** Your school or office cafeteria
**c.** Shampoo
**d.** Paper towels

**3.4.** Outline how you would go about establishing a trial goal for:
**a.** A new service that home-delivers gourmet meals from phone-in orders (by cooperation with local restaurants), for which there are no other competitors in your area.
**b.** A new brand of instant coffee that you are about to launch in the U.S. market.

**3.5.** Outline how you would go about establishing a repeat purchase goal for:
**a.** The gourmet meal home-delivery service described above
**b.** The new instant coffee brand described above

**3.6.** You are the manufacturer of a brand of tool kits sold exclusively through hardware stores. You are planning a trade promotion campaign. Describe how you would proceed with target audience selection for this campaign and what the action objectives would be.

## FURTHER READING

Jacoby, J., and Chestnut, R. W. *Brand Loyalty Measurement and Management,* New York, NY: Ronald Press, 1978.

The definitive account of brand loyalty, this book clearly explains the attitudinal and behavioral basis of this concept, which is central to sales strategy and target audience definition. Very useful to the manager who wants to pursue the subject of brand loyalty further.

McCann, J. M. Market segment response to the marketing decision variables. *Journal of Marketing Research,* 1974, *11* (4), pp. 399–412.

This is an important article describing how to select a target audience based on size and purchase level as well as response to advertising or promotion (developed as "leverage" in this chapter). Readable though in a technical journal.

Wind, Y. Brand loyalty and vulnerability. In Woodside, A. G., Sheth, J. N., and Bennett, P. D., Eds. *Consumer and Industrial Buying Behavior.* New York: Elsevier North-Holland, 1977, pp. 313–319.

This article expands on the importance of defining target audiences on the basis of behavior *and* attitude. (We also consider awareness in our definition, as will be reinforced in Part Three.)

Lilien, G. L., Kotler, P., and Moorthy, K. S. *Marketing Models,* Englewood Cliffs, NJ: Prentice-Hall, 1992.

This book is an essential shelf reference for the more quantitative-minded marketing manager. It is relevant to the present chapter and also to Chapter 18 for its comprehensive coverage of new product diffusion models.

Ehrenberg, A. S. C. *Repeat-Buying: Theory and Applications.* Amsterdam and New York: North-Holland and Elsevier, 1972; reissued, London: Charles Griffin & Co., 1987.

Professor Ehrenberg's extensive research and conclusions on buyer behavior have been overlooked in the United States (most consumer behavior texts have missed his work, although recent journal articles are now addressing it). The book's exposition is quite complex and detailed in parts, so the following reading is jointly recommended.

East, R. *Changing Consumer Behaviour.* London: Cassell, 1990, chapter 2.

This chapter provides an excellent, easy-to-read summary and review of Ehrenberg's work. East also points out many of its contentious implications for marketing and advertising. You might not like or agree with these implications but, if you're a marketing manager, you should read this chapter.

# CHAPTER 4

# Behavioral Sequence Model for Specific Targeting

At this stage of AC&P planning, the manager has selected a general target audience from one of the five buyer groups and has established general action objectives in the form of trial or repeat purchase. This chapter provides the detailed targeting focus that is necessary when planning an advertising or promotion campaign—and which assumes major importance when planning an IMC campaign. We focus here on the *decision participants* within the target audience—to decide which specific decision role(s) we want to target, and what information it would be helpful to know about the person(s) in those roles so that creative content and media placement of the campaign will be more effective. We also focus on the *decision stages and actions* preceding, accompanying, or following purchase—to decide what, specifically, the campaign should invite the target decision participant to do in order to help insure that purchase occurs. After reading this chapter, you should:

- Be able to construct a behavioral sequence model (BSM) for any product category, brand, or target audience, which identifies the decision participants and the stages in the decision process.
- Understand the alternative decision roles that target audience members can occupy and the specific action objectives that go with each role.
- Know why behavior and communication effects are the primary profile variables for describing the targeted decision participant.

- See how other personal characteristics are additionally useful in profiling the targeted decision participant.

## CONSTRUCTING A BEHAVIORAL SEQUENCE MODEL

Alternative decision participants' roles and the specifics of the decision process can most easily be identified by constructing a *behavioral sequence model*. A behavioral sequence model (BSM) uses a grid format to identify the target audience's decision: "horizontally" in terms of (1) WHAT—the major decision stages preceding, including, and following purchase; and "vertically" in terms of data inputs relating to (2) WHO—the decision participants and their decision roles, (3) WHERE—the locations of the decision stages, (4) WHEN—the time and timing of each stage, and (5) HOW—a capsule description of how each decision stage is accomplished.

A useful generic behavioral sequence model is shown in Figure 4.1. Note that this is not just a decision-stage model: it combines the stage flow with the decision roles, location, and timing, and a description of the decisions.[1] These additions are vital for advertisers because they show exactly how specific targeting can be accomplished.

A BSM can quite easily be constructed from qualitative research interviews during advertising strategy research (see Chapter 18). Alternatively, a manager al-

| Data inputs | (1) WHAT (decision stages) | | | |
|---|---|---|---|---|
| | Need arousal | Information search and evaluation | Purchase | Usage |
| (2) WHO (roles) | | | | |
| (3) WHERE (location) | | | | |
| (4) WHEN (time and timing) | | | | |
| (5) HOW (description) | | | | |

**FIGURE 4.1**

A generic behavioral sequence model (BSM). The decision stages and data inputs should be
adapted to suit the particular category (or brand) and the particular target audience.

ready knowledgeable about the decision processes in the product or service category can readily describe the decision stages and data inputs needed to construct a sufficiently useful BSM (or set of BSMs for various target audiences or competing brands). The important factor is that the BSM helps to *organize* this knowledge in the most useful form for advertising communications and promotion targeting. The five components of a BSM are explained in the sections that follow.

### (1) WHAT—Decision Stages

Our generic behavioral sequence model is shown with four stages across the top of the grid: need arousal, information search and evaluation, purchase, and usage. Some marketers label the stages differently. For example, the first stage is sometimes called problem recognition (however, we doubt that buyers are always responding to "problems," unless the term is very broadly defined[2]); the second stage may be separated into "internal" (memory) versus "external" (marketing environment) search and further into search versus evaluation (although evaluation usually occurs simultaneously during search); and so forth. The exact labels don't really matter. The important thing is to get you, the manager, thinking about *points in the buyer's decision process at which advertising communications or promotions can influence the decision outcome,* remembering that ultimately we want to stimulate purchase or usage of our particular brand of product or service.

**Stages for Various Situations.** Stages should be added, modified, or deleted to suit the *specific* target audience, product category, and even brand. Do not simply assume that the four generic stages will fit every situation. For instance, the process of buying a new home might have seven or eight stages, including those of need arousal, personal-finance review, visits to home sites, title search, valuation, and so forth. In contrast, purchase of a simple, habitually consumed product such as Chiclets chewing gum may have only two stages, need arousal and purchase—if you are a Chiclets brand loyal.

Table 4.1 shows some examples of tailor-made stages for various types of advertisers and situations.[3]

As shown in the brand loyals' BSM in the table, a brand-loyal (BL) customer will go through very little information search and evaluation, effectively deleting this stage; whereas a brand switcher (FBS or OBS) would find this stage essential. For BLs, the usage stage, as a *decision* stage, may also be deleted.

Purchase in some product categories requires retail outlet selection as well as brand selection—for instance, when buying grocery products, clothing, or other consumer durables, you have to choose which store or stores to visit. As shown in the retail purchase BSM in the table, a *store decision stage* therefore has to be added. The store-choice decision can occur before *or after* the brand purchase decision. In the table, we've shown it as occurring before brand choice, but the brand could be decided first and *then* "shopped

---
**TABLE 4.1**

### SOME SUGGESTED BSM STAGES FOR DIFFERENT AC&P SITUATIONS

**Brand loyals**

Need arousal[a] → Repeat purchase

**Direct response**

Ad exposure → Evaluate item in ad → Evaluate order mode[b] and payment method → Place order → Decide whether to retain or return item

**Retail purchase**

Need arousal → Decide which stores to visit → Browse[c] → Decide on item → Purchase item → Use item or return it for refund or credit on other purchases

**Service (business or consumer)**

Need arousal → Contact the service, evaluating answer speed, knowledgeability, and courtesy[d] → Place request → Evaluate service provided in relation to expectation → Decide whether to continue to use this brand of service → Make, accordingly, positive or negative recommendations to business colleagues or social friends

**Major industrial purchase**

Specify product requirements → Specify vendor requirements (price, delivery, service contract) → Choose list of acceptable vendors → Request proposals from vendors → Evaluate proposals → Negotiate and decide → Develop order routine → Purchase → Evaluate during usage → Reorder[e]

---
[a,b,c,d,e]Comments and references are provided in end-of-chapter note 4.

for," which is a crucial difference for retail advertising strategy.

In some instances, a particular brand may be bought differently from others in the same product category, necessitating a modified behavioral sequence model for the brand. For instance, people may buy Sears' brands more casually than they would others because of Sears' well-known liberal return policy. As in the brand loyal BSM, but for a different reason, consumers may effectively delete the information-search-and-evaluation stage for purchase of Sears' products.

We emphasize that the four decision stages shown in Figure 4.1 are only a starting framework for a *specific* behavioral sequence model for the target audience and the brand. Specific stages have to be identified for particular situations.

**Decision Stages and the Buyer Response Steps.** The stages in a BSM constitute a sequence of actions (need arousal is ultimately behavioral) that the typical target audience decision participants are likely to follow in deciding on a given product or service. It is important to understand the convergent relationship between a BSM sequence or "hierarchy" and the "hierarchy" represented by the four buyer response steps introduced in Chapter 1. The buyer response steps (exposure → processing → communication effects and brand position → target audience action) are responses to a specific *ad, adlike event, or promotion offer.* The best way to understand this relationship is with the aid of a diagram (Figure 4.2) and a metaphor. Think of the BSM stages as the roof of a building and then imagine ads, adlike events, or promotion offers being inserted as pillars to support that roof. In the example in the figure, the first pillar

**FIGURE 4.2**

The relationship between the buyer response steps and the behavioral sequence model (note that the generic BSM stages are shown and that "target audience action," step 4 of the buyer response steps, is the BSM stage itself). Two types of hierarchies of effects converge: that of the buyer response steps influenced by each ad or promotion offer, and that of the decision stages for the product or service itself.

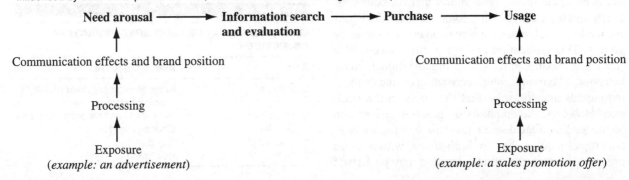

is an advertisement designed to stimulate need arousal, and the second pillar is a promotion, such as a bonus pack, intended to encourage usage. This metaphor and the diagram indicate how the two hierarchies have to be "converged" in advertising and promotion planning.

Another aspect we would like to clarify is the "postpurchase hierarchy of effects," particularly for *services. Postpurchase stages*—such as satisfaction, complaints, and return of goods or discontinuation of service patronage—are obviously important for marketers in service industries to identify (see also Chapter 12).[4] The service BSM in Table 4.1 provides examples of these stages (as do the direct-response, retail-purchase, and industrial-purchase BSMs). These are, however, additional *stages* in the behavioral sequence model, not additional buyer response steps. If advertising or promotion is introduced into these postpurchase stages, then the buyer simply *recycles* on the four basic buyer response steps. Thus, for instance, "satisfaction" is just a recycling through the communication-effects and brand position step—and specifically, is an adjustment of the *brand attitude* communication effect, as we shall see later, depending on whether the buyer's initial attitude is confirmed or disconfirmed by the postpurchase usage experience. Postpurchase events may lead to specification of new BSM *stages,* but the buyer response steps for advertising communications and for promotions (when either is employed to try to influence these stages) *remain the same.*

Review the example shown in Figure 4.2. See that the sales promotion offer's communication effects feed into the *same* communication effects that the preceding advertisement produced. It is a recycle through the buyer response steps but *not different* steps.

## (2) WHO—Individuals in Decision Roles

**Reaching Individual Decision Participants.** Much has been made of the observation that, in both consumer and industrial buying, some purchase decisions are made by individuals whereas others are made by groups. This realization has led to the concept of a "decision-making unit" or, in organizational buyer behavior, a "buying center," consisting of one *or more* individuals and the roles that they play in the decision. However, the emphasis on group decisions can be misleading. One doesn't advertise to a family or to a company but rather to *individuals* within these groups. Although the overall decision may be arrived at by the group—for example, choice of a vacation resort by a family or choice of a computer by a company—advertising communications and promotion offers have to persuade individuals separately *before* they get together to make a group decision.

This is not to say that the advertiser can ignore group decision-making processes. It has been well documented that groups vary in their implicit or explicit decision rules, and the decision rules adopted by a particular group can radically affect whether or not our brand will be chosen. For example, husband-wife decisions may follow a "democratic consensus" rule, or the decision may be delegated "autocratically" to one spouse.[5] Organizational groups, similarly, may follow a variety of decision rules, including "majority vote" or "weighted participant importance" rules.[6] But, from an advertising and promotion standpoint, differences in group decision rules *merely shift the emphasis on various individuals in the group.* Group decisions do not change the fact that advertising communications or promotion offers must persuade each person individually, beforehand. It is then the persuaded individual that enters into the group decision. Whether the individual is repersuaded in the group is beyond the direct control of advertising and promotion. What the advertiser must do is target those individuals with the most weight (the most influential roles) in the decision process.[7]

**Main Roles and Specific Action Objectives.** With the foregoing point in mind, we are now ready to list the main roles that individuals can occupy in the decision process. Each role should be regarded as producing a separate purchase-related or purchase action objective.

Many possible decision roles can be identified, but five roles occur most frequently (and hence are shown in the generic BSM). These are listed, together with the role-associated action objective, in Table 4.2.

| **TABLE 4.2** | |
| --- | --- |

**MAIN DECISION ROLES AND SPECIFIC ACTION OBJECTIVES**

| Role | Action objective |
| --- | --- |
| 1. Initiator | Propose category need (to which brand belongs) |
| 2. Influencer | Set criteria and recommend brand |
| 3. Decider | Choose brand |
| 4. Purchaser | Buy brand |
| 5. User | Use brand |

**1.** An individual in the *initiator* role gets the purchase decision started at the level of *category need*. From an advertising and promotion standpoint, the relevant specific action objective is whether or not the category of which our brand is a member is *proposed* by the initiator. (*Example:* Child saying, "Mom, we have the same old cereal all the time. Can I have something that tastes better, like Cheerios?")

**2.** An individual in the *influencer* role *sets the criteria* for the decision and *recommends* for or against particular *brands*. The relevant specific action objective is whether or not the influencer *recommends* our brand. (*Example:* Father saying, "Cheerios is pretty low in sugar; I think it would be okay.")

**3.** The individual in the *decider* role makes the overall *go / no-go* decision. The relevant specific action objective is whether or not our brand is *chosen*. (*Example:* Mother saying, "All right, I'll buy Cheerios the next time I'm at the store.")

**4.** The individual in the *purchaser* role *carries out* the decision. The relevant specific action objective is actual *purchase* of the brand—because there may still be a tendency for another brand to be considered and chosen at the point of purchase. (*Example:* Mother and child go to the supermarket. Mother is distracted by Total's on-package vitamin claims, but sees that Cheerios has only 1 gram of sugar per 1-cup serving, versus 3 grams for Total. She buys Cheerios.)

**5.** The individual in the *user* role is the actual consumer or user of the product. The relevant specific action objective is actual *use* of the brand, after purchase. (*Example:* Child nibbles at Cheerios but comments, "They're not sweet enough." Mother adds a teaspoo.n of sugar, with father's reluctant approval. . . .)

You can see the importance of these role definitions and actions for advertising and promotion. For integrated communications (IMC) campaigns, attention to decision roles is crucial because of the multiple communications delivered during the overall decision process (see Chapter 11). We advertise and promote to *individuals in role:* (1) *to initiators* to make them aware of the category need and propose our brand as a possible purchase candidate; (2) *to influencers* to communicate the reasons they should recommend our brand; (3) *to deciders* to persuade them to select our brand; (4) *to purchasers* to "lock in" the selection of our brand; and (5) *to users* to ensure that they actually use and, perhaps, more rapidly use our

brand so that, if it is satisfying to them, it will be purchased again.

We have emphasized the roles of individuals in groups so as to prevent the fallacy of defining target audiences solely on a group basis. (Of course, many purchases are decided upon totally by one individual. In such cases, one person occupies all five roles. *Example:* You buying yourself a soda. Quite evidently, when the "decision-making unit" is an individual rather than a group of individuals, the advertiser's targeting job would seem to be much easier. But the advertising communications or promotion *message* still has to address the individual in the particular mind-set or role that the message is intended to influence; for instance, the individual *as* an influencer, or *as* a user. Depending on the targeted role, media vehicle selection may also differ—for the same individual.) When the decision-making unit consists of a group, different roles may be occupied by different individuals. The advertiser must identify each individual's role, decide which role or roles are most important to target, and address the corresponding decision and action objective that accompany that role.

**Other Roles.** Initiator, influencer, decider, purchaser, and user are the most frequently encountered roles in BSMs. However, just as other stages can be usefully identified in specific situations, so too can other roles. Settle and Alreck[8] have identified a number of roles that may additionally be relevant in household consumer behavior and which may occasionally be targeted by marketers. Also, several role variations (notably, negative and positive deciders) have been identified for business behavior.[9] These other roles are listed in Table 4.3. Most of these other roles incorporate initiating, influencing, or deciding in some sense (hence our five main roles are indeed "main") but are different enough to be worth distinguishing.

Role-associated *actions* can be amazingly specific and yet of serious importance to marketers. For instance, the Coca-Cola company measures how many ice cubes (most) users put in a glass—which affects the amount of Coke added. Colgate knows that about a third of us use a toothbrush which is more than six months old—hence the new "replacement stripe" in brushes. Food marketers know that the average household spends 90 minutes a day preparing food (some more, some much less) and each of us spends 40 minutes a day, on average, munching it.[10] No wonder convenience and fast-food products are so appealing!

**TABLE 4.3**

**OTHER DECISION ROLES APPLICABLE IN VARIOUS DECISION SITUATIONS**

*(The first four are mainly for business-marketing situations although they may occur in consumer marketing. The other four were identified and defined by Settle and Alreck, 1989; see note 9.)*

| Role | Function | Action Objective |
|---|---|---|
| Gatekeeper | Screens input of information from the marketplace (such as household TV viewing, or salespersons' access to managers) | Allow access |
| Consultant | Provides expert advice to decision maker | Recommend your company as vendor |
| Negative decider | Can say "no" to marketing proposals (such as sales presentations or bids) but cannot give "yes" approval | Identify these people and avoid them, if possible. However, if you must deal with them, the action objective for them is nonrejection. |
| Positive decider | Can give "yes" approval | Approval |
| Preparer | Converts the product to a form that can be consumed | Prepare product correctly |
| Monitor | Regulates consumption by others | Advise others appropriately |
| Maintainer | Services or repairs the product or arranges for this to be done by a professional | Maintain product regularly to ensure satisfaction |
| Dispose | Discards product when it's no longer wanted or needed | Discard product properly (recyclably or safely) |

Decision stages (what) and roles (who) are the first two components of a BSM (refer to Figure 4.1 again). Along with identifying the person who plays the role, the manager should think about the typical location of the role-player when he or she is "in" a given decision stage (where); the timing of the stages (when); and their decision content (how). We now examine these last three components of a BSM, and explain their importance.

### (3) WHERE—Location

The location of each stage in the behavioral sequence model is important in media planning—specifically, in media selection (see Chapter 15). The key question is: Where is the target-audience decision participant likely to be making the decision?

The most likely locations for decision stages are fairly easily identified. Table 4.4 provides a general list, to which other locations could be added.[11] Locations may range from total in-home decisions, as in direct-mail or catalog advertising, to total in-store decisions, as may be made in response to a point-of-purchase promotion offer. The location examples in the table do not exhaust the wide varieties of possible influence and decision situations that may be relevant to one or more stages in the particular behavioral sequence model for a target audience and brand.

**Location Factors.** The theory of locations or "situations" in buyer behavior received a considerable impetus with the work of Belk.[12] More recently, Foxall has provided a comprehensive and provocative behavioral analysis of selling and consumption situations in marketing.[13] From these analyses (and some input of our own), we suggest four factors that the advertising manager should consider in each location or situation in the BSM:

**TABLE 4.4**

**SOME COMMON LOCATIONS (OR SITUATIONS) FOR THE OCCURRENCE OF DECISION STAGES IN THE BSM**

- Home—media-exposure situation
- Home—usage situation
- Commuting—private car
- Commuting—public transportation
- Shopping mall
- Public entertainment
- Office—private
- Office—business meeting or sales call
- Friend or business phone call (word of mouth)
- Social occasion (word of mouth plus possible visual influence)
- Expert contact (exposure via TV, reading, radio, lecture, professional's office, or telephone contact)
- Point-of-purchase

**1.** *Advertising communications or promotion accessibility*—varying from none, to limited, to "overaccessibility" in the sense of heavy competition for attention.

**2.** *Presence of other role-players*—whether and which other influencers or deciders are present; that is, whether the advertiser is addressing an individual or a group decision in this location.

**3.** *Time pressure*—varying from none to extreme, which could affect the role-player's opportunity to process advertising or promotion information.

**4.** *Decision participant's physical and emotional state*—various "personality states" could also affect processing (some situationally induced). We consider some personality state variables later in the chapter, in the section on additional profile variables.

Managerial attention to location factors can result in some innovative media choices. For example, in 1980, R. J. Reynolds realized that many low-tar cigarette smokers were confused by the multitude of new low-tar brands and were perhaps overloaded with media ads for them. RJR therefore shifted a sizable portion of its cigarette advertising budget to billboards, taxicabs, buses, and point-of-purchase locations in an attempt to sway confused, last-minute deciders.

On the other hand, in this era of IMC, many of us may feel that advertisers have been *overly* inventive in finding locations for advertising opportunities. In Australia, for instance, there are now sponsorships and soft-sell commercials on public TV channels. The backs of doors in public toilets carry ads in some countries. You rarely get a bill mailed to you these days without promotional material in the envelope. These intrusions are part of the price of free enterprise. Of course, advertising has some restrictions in most countries. Usually, for instance, there are limits on TV advertising per program hour (Australia experimented with no limits but reneged after widespread viewer—and advertiser—complaints) and most communities limit outdoor and poster advertising.

Locating advertising communications or promotion opportunities is serious business for marketers, value judgments aside. A carefully constructed BSM can help—especially with an IMC campaign, as we'll see in Chapter 15.

### (4) WHEN—Time and Timing

The time and timing of each behavioral sequence model stage are important in media planning—specifically, in AC&P media *scheduling*. Examples of *point in time's* importance for media scheduling in the BSM stages include publicity releases to financial analysts in the influencer role when your company adopts a new corporate advertising slogan;[14] advertising to full-time homemakers in the initiator and decider roles during the morning hours prior to when they're likely to go food shopping—for example, via morning radio, TV, or newspapers; or advertising Alka-Seltzer to users during holiday periods, when they're likely to overeat.

The *duration* of each stage will differ by target audience, and averages can be misleading. For instance, on average, the buyer of a new car will study six models and visit three showrooms before deciding.[15] However, we would expect someone buying his or her first new car (a new category user) to do a lot more search and evaluation than this. On the other hand, the Mercedes-Benz devotee (a brand loyal) may simply order the latest model from one preferred dealer.[16] Overall, NCUs will tend to take more time for the information search and evaluation stage; BLs and OBLs little or none; while brand switchers (FBSs or OBSs) would be expected to take an intermediate amount of time for search and evaluation if they are comparing prices and perhaps promotions.

More generally, *overall timing* (from start to finish of the BSM stages) reflects the buyer's *purchase cycle*. For regularly purchased products, knowledge of the target audience's average purchase cycle (the median interpurchase interval) can be of considerable help to media planners for scheduling both advertising frequency and promotion offers. In examining shopping patterns for grocery store visits in the United States, for instance, Kahn and Schmittlein[17] identified two potential segments (potential targets for the advertising and promotional timing of manufacturers as well as retailers): "Regulars," who tend to make a big trip weekly and a quick trip every two weeks, and "Quicks," who tend to make quick trips every four or five days and one big trip every two weeks. Interestingly, both types of grocery shoppers spend about the same amount on big trips ($35 to $40) and on quick trips (about $7); it is their *purchase cycles* that differ. In Chapter 16, where we analyze media strategy in detail, we will see how and when to use the purchase cycle in media planning. The behavioral sequence model is where this cycle comes from.

## (5) HOW—Decision Description

The final input to the behavioral sequence model is to specify the "how" of each decision stage. These "hows" are vitally important in aiding the formulation of the *positioning strategy* for the brand's advertising communications and promotion (see Chapter 6). The best way to illustrate the capsule descriptions of how each decision stage is achieved—and also the *overall* construction of a BSM—is with a couple of examples.

A BSM constructed for the (hypothetical) family purchase of a second TV set is shown in Figure 4.3. Notice that the brand purchase decision is made in the store, and thus we have labeled this stage "purchase decision" rather than simply "purchase." By glancing along the bottom row of the BSM, you can see the sorts of descriptions that are required for the "how" parts of the data input. The usefulness of a BSM like this for the advertiser—either a TV manufacturer or a TV retailer—should be evident. It provides the rich yet typical detail that is needed to design a well-considered and specifically targeted advertising communications and promotion campaign.

For the second BSM example, we take a slightly different approach, illustrating the use of behavioral sequence models by Johnson & Johnson, the manufacturer of Acuvue disposable contact lenses. The important thing to understand about this BSM application is that two target audiences need to be educated about this new type of contact lens: doctors and prospective patients. Thus, *two* BSMs are necessary, one for each target audience. With some disguise necessary to protect proprietary interests, the behavioral sequence model for *doctors* for the launch of Acuvue contact lenses in the United States was approximately as shown in Figure 4.4. As indicated in the figure, there were many possible sources of initiating and influencing doctors to recommend disposable contact lenses, including Johnson & Johnson's professional advertising, professional PR, and product samples.

J & J and the advertising agency, Lintas: U.S.A., also developed a parallel model for *consumers* (as pa-

**FIGURE 4.3**
Specific application of a behavioral sequence model: family purchase of a second TV set.

| Data inputs | (1) WHAT (decision stages) | | | |
|---|---|---|---|---|
| | Need arousal | Store choice | Purchase decision | Usage |
| (2) WHO (roles) | • Mother (initiator)<br>• Husbands and teenage son (influencers) | • Mother and father (influencers) | • Sales staff (influencers)<br>• Mother (decider) and father (decider and purchaser) | • Mother (main user) |
| (3) WHERE (location) | • In living room | • In home | • In store | • In master bedroom |
| (4) WHEN (time and timing) | • Beginning of baseball season | • 1 week later | • Same day (early evening or weekend) | • That evening, through next decade (approximately) |
| (5) HOW (description) | • Current set dominated by men of house to watch baseball | • Choose outlet first, and only visit one store— the nearest discount consumer-electronics store | • Look for "known" brand at $400 maximum price—buys a Magnavox | • Mother gets exclusive use of new set |

| Data inputs | (1) WHAT (decision stages) | | | |
|---|---|---|---|---|
| | Awareness and knowledge of new vision-correction options | Patient considerations | Practice-management considerations | Recommendation |
| (2) WHO (roles) | • Professional literature (initiator function) <br> • Manufacturer (initiator) <br> • Colleagues at conferences and locally (initiators and influencers) <br> • Doctor (decider) <br> • Receptionist (gatekeeper) | • Individual patient (user) | • Doctor (decider) <br> • Clinical staff (servicer) | • Doctor (decider) |
| (3) WHERE (location) | • Professional journals <br> • Direct mail <br> • Office <br> • Conferences <br> • Product samples | • Office | • Office | • Office |
| (4) WHEN (time and timing) | • 1990–91 launch and trial period | • Daily | • With trial | • Daily, for several years |
| (5) HOW (description) | • Doctor (eye specialist) hears about disposable contact lenses and learns about clinical performance. | • Eye problem– myopia, hyperopia, astigmatism, etc. <br> • Considers options– glasses, lens types, corrective surgery <br> • Patient's daily activities and (if lenses) wearing and care schedule | • Assesses frequency of follow-up visits to self or staff <br> • Patient revenue from disposables versus regular lenses | • J & J Acuvue recommended |

**FIGURE 4.4**
Specific application of a behavioral sequence model: recommendation of Acuvue disposable contact lenses by doctors.

tients). The patient BSM incorporated the finding that patient "pull-through" can be a significant factor in influencing doctors' recommendations toward the advertiser's brand.

Behavioral sequence models (BSMs) therefore provide a detailed and dynamic picture of the target audience from the standpoint of the overall decision process. The BSM pinpoints opportunities for AC&P messages to be delivered to one or more decision participants (in role) so as to favorably influence their decisions toward the advertised brand.

Having looked at the process dynamically via the BSM, we now turn to a detailed static consideration of the individual decision participants. We call this procedure "profiling the decision participant."

## PROFILING THE DECISION PARTICIPANT

It is convenient to refer to an individual in *any* of the five (or other) decision roles as a *decision participant*. Our task now is to get to know more about the targeted decision participant—so that ads, adlike events, or promotion offers can be designed appropriately to communicate with the decision participant, and so that media can be selected precisely to reach the decision participant.

### The Primacy of Behavior and Communication Effects in Profiling the Decision Participant

The first and most vital characteristic that the advertiser needs to know about the targeted decision participant is that person's *current behavior and current communication effects* with regard to the product category and especially with regard to our brand. (Note that this is consistent with our emphasis, in Chapter 3, on defining the target audience by brand-loyalty status, in terms of awareness, attitude, and behavior.[18]) By knowing the participant's *current* behavior and communication effects, the advertiser can then establish *target* behavior and communication *objectives* for the campaign to achieve.

Suppose, for example, that you are the brand manager for Magnavox TV sets and that you have decided to use the behavioral sequence model provided in Figure 4.3 to design an advertising campaign aimed at mothers who are frustrated by the men in the family hogging the family's only TV set whenever baseball games are televised. In this BSM, the mother is shown as playing four roles in the decision process: *initiator* of the need for a second TV set; *influencer* of the choice of purchase outlet; *decider,* along with the fa-

ther, of the brand at the point of purchase; and *user.* The mother's current behavior with regard to this purchase is none: at present, she does not have a TV set for her own use. The target behavior is that we want her to buy a Magnavox TV as the second set.

But before we can persuade her to move from current behavior to target behavior, we need to know her current communication-effects status and also consider some other actions that are purchase-related. For instance, we may assume that she has the overall-product-category need for a second TV set (although the advertising may remind her of this), but we cannot assume that she is aware of and favors Magnavox as a brand. Relevant purchase-related behaviors would be for her to persuade her husband of the need for a second TV set and get him to visit a store with the intention of buying one—preferably a Magnavox. Although the mother plays four roles in the decision process, the key one from the advertiser's viewpoint is the *decider* role, in that the advertising should ensure that the mother decides on the Magnavox brand.

A summary of the current and targeted behaviors and communication effects for the mother in our second–TV set example is shown in Table 4.5. In the table, we have taken the liberty of moving ahead again in the book to the topic of communication effects and communication objectives. The communication objectives (the targeted communication ef-

---

| TABLE 4.5 |
| --- |

**CURRENT AND TARGET BEHAVIORS AND COMMUNICATION EFFECTS FOR MOTHERS AS THE TARGETED DECISION PARTICIPANT IN BUYING A SECOND TV SET**

| Current behavior | Target behavior |
| --- | --- |
| • None | • Persuade husband to go to store<br>• Purchase Magnavox TV set |

| Communication effects | Communication objectives |
| --- | --- |
| *Category need*—mother has perceived the need for a second TV set | *Category need*—ads at the beginning of the baseball season must remind her of the category need for her own TV set |
| *Brand awareness*—she has heard of Magnavox but it's not at the "top of her mind" | *Brand awareness*—ads must be further designed to make her recall Magnavox ("top of mind") and recognize the Magnavox logo |
| *Brand attitude*—she has a moderately favorable attitude toward Magnavox TV sets | *Brand attitude*—ads must also induce a highly favorable, "best choice" attitude |
| *Brand purchase intention*—she has none yet for a specific brand | *Brand purchase intention*—ads must also lead her to decide to visit the store, specify, and buy a Magnavox TV set |
| *Purchase facilitation*—she does not know where Magnavox TV sets can be purchased | *Purchase facilitation*—ads must note that Magnavox is available at most consumer-electronics outlets, or provide a local dealer list. |

fects, in the right-hand column of the table) should be reasonably self-explanatory, but don't worry if they aren't entirely clear until you have read the following chapter. Our purpose in introducing the communication effects here is to emphasize the vital importance of understanding where the target decision participant is "coming from" and where the advertising must "go to" in the prospective decision maker's mind in order to achieve the target action of purchasing the brand.

To link the present discussion with the more general target audience concepts presented in Chapter 3, you may note that the mothers in the second–TV set example would be classified as favorable brand switchers (FBSs) and the doctors in the disposable-contact-lenses example as new category users (NCUs) for the new type of lens. The action objective in both cases is *trial,* where trial is probably the sole and sufficient action objective for mothers buying a second TV set but where trial would have to be followed by repeat-purchase (or repeat-recommendation) action objectives in the example of doctors and Acuvue disposable contact lenses. The present chapter has taken these concepts to the level of specific campaign-planning detail by showing (1) how to construct a behavioral sequence model and (2) how we need to understand and pinpoint the decision participant's specific behavior and communication effects to move that person from current to target status.

For a *new* brand or product category, there may as yet be no current behavior or communication effects. In such cases, the *current* status of both is zero (although note that a familiar brand name for a new product would undoubtedly produce some prior communication effects). The *target* status of behavior would be trial—and would depend on targeted com-

munication effects (such as brand awareness and a tentatively favorable pretrial attitude) first being achieved by the launch campaign.

### Current Involvement and Brand Attitude "Vulnerability"

An important issue in target audience selection—and in determining the leverage of potential target audiences, as explained in Chapter 3—is how "vulnerable" the buyer's brand attitude is to attempts to influence it. John Rice and the research firm Market Facts have popularized what has come to be known as the "conversion model," which analyzes *current* brand attitudes to yield a classification of target audiences in terms of brand attitude "vulnerability," or what they call "conversion potential."[19] Essentially, the classification examines "strength of loyalty" in target audiences based on their brand attitudes toward our brand, and toward other brands considered together. This in turn depends on *perceived risk* (low and high involvement, examined further in Chapter 5). We present our adaptation of their approach in Figure 4.5. Four classifications of a brand's buyers are useful for most brand attitude planning applications:

- "Available" (those who perceive *low* risk in switching and rate other brands as approximately *equal* to our brand): Typically, these buyers will be actual or *potential* FBSs. They are "available" now because it requires low involvement for them to switch and they see the alternative brands as equally good.
- "Comfortable" (those who perceive *low* risk in switching from our brand but rate other brands as *inferior*): These buyers are BLs but, if a competing brand could improve its attitude rating sufficiently,

**FIGURE 4.5**

Brand attitude vulnerability as a function of perceived risk (involvement) in switching to, and relative attitude toward, *other* brand(s). *Source:* adapted from Market Facts' "conversion model;" see note 19.

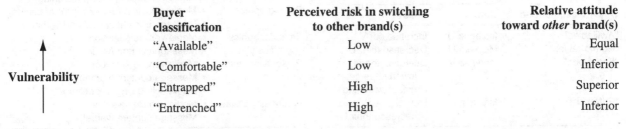

| Vulnerability ↑ | Buyer classification | Perceived risk in switching to other brand(s) | Relative attitude toward *other* brand(s) |
|---|---|---|---|
| | "Available" | Low | Equal |
| | "Comfortable" | Low | Inferior |
| | "Entrapped" | High | Superior |
| | "Entrenched" | High | Inferior |

they'd probably switch to it. They are "comfortable" now, but could become *future* "availables."

- "Entrapped" (those who perceive *high* risk in switching from our brand but rate other brands as *superior*): These buyers are pseudo-BLs—locked in to our brand by such factors as service contracts, remote availability of better brands, or just plain fear of trying what is for them a new brand (a new bank, for instance, or a new family doctor). Thus they are "entrapped" (unavailable for switching). Should another brand hope to win their patronage, it will have to reassuringly release the trap.
- "Entrenched" (those who perceive *high* risk in switching and rate another brand or brands as *inferior*): These buyers are *true* BLs—at least at present! They have the same high "switching costs" as the previous group but, unlike them, they don't see any reason to switch from our brand, rating the other brands as inferior. Another brand would find them difficult if not impossible to win.

**Brand Equity Strategies and Vulnerability.** The four groups can be usefully examined in terms of brand-equity status (described in Chapter 2, chapter appendix 2A). With regard to their current brand "availables" have high value equity but *low uniqueness* equity; "comfortables" have high value equity and high uniqueness equity but, with low involvement in switching, uniqueness equity is always under threat; "entrapped" customers have *low value* equity but high uniqueness equity; and "entrenched" customers have high value equity and high uniqueness equity—they are like "comfortables" but at a much higher level of involvement.

Brand-equity status can be applied strategically to *our* buyers or to our *target competitors'* buyers depending on the perspective the manager wants to take. The equity objectives for protecting "our" buyers and trying to win "their" buyers are summarized in Table 4.6. Current brand attitude vulnerability is a very important target audience profiling variable.

### Additional Profile Variables

In addition to the target decision participant's current behavior and communication effects, several other profile variables are useful to assist in more accurately reaching the targeted decision participant and more effectively communicating with him or her. The additional profile variables are media exposure, demographics, psychographics (or lifestyle), personality traits, and personality states. In Table 4.7, we have summarized their main applications for advertising communications. Their applications for promotion should be reasonably evident and, in integrated marketing communications (IMC) they overlap considerably. In the following sections, we explain the use of each of these decision-participant profile variables.[20]

**Media Exposure.** It is extremely useful for the manager to have a *direct* measure of target-audience decision participants' media exposure—the TV shows they watch most often, the magazines they read, and so forth. Knowledge of decision participants' media exposure will enable advertising to reach them more accurately through media (media selection) and sufficiently often (media scheduling). This is vital for step 1, exposure, in the buyer re-

---

**TABLE 4.6**

**BRAND-EQUITY OBJECTIVES RELATED TO ATTITUDINAL VULNERABILITY OF TARGET AUDIENCES**

(*V* = value equity; *U* = uniqueness equity.)

| Buyer classification | Brand-equity objectives | |
|---|---|---|
| | **Ours** | **Theirs** |
| "Availables" | Increase U | Increase our V |
| "Comfortables" | Maintain U | Decrease their U |
| "Entrapped" | Increase V | Decrease their U by lowering perceived risk of switching |
| "Entrenched" | Maintain U | Increase our V and decrease their U |

---

**TABLE 4.7**

**ADDITIONAL DECISION-PARTICIPANT PROFILE VARIABLES AND THEIR ADVERTISING APPLICATIONS**

| Profile variable | Advertising applications |
|---|---|
| Media exposure | • Media selection (direct matching)<br>• Media scheduling (direct matching) |
| Demographics | • Media selection (demographic matching)<br>• Message content (visual and verbal) |
| Psychographics (or lifestyle) | • Media vehicle selection<br>• Message content (visual) |
| Personality traits | • Media vehicle selection<br>• Message content (verbal)<br>• Media scheduling (repetition) |
| Personality states | • Media vehicle selection<br>• Message content (verbal) |

sponse steps. Direct measurement of individuals' media exposure is called *direct matching* and is explained in Chapter 17.

**Demographics.** Demographics are "societal location" characteristics of the individual. The most frequently utilized demographic variables are geographic region, age, sex, race, marital status, household size and composition, occupation, education, income, and specific area of residence, with combinations of the last four variables used to designate the individual's social class.

Demographics have two uses in advertising: for media vehicle selection by demographic matching, and for message content when a campaign is directed to a particular demographic group within one of the five brand-loyalty buyer groups.

*Media Selection (Demographic Matching).* Demographics are used to *indirectly* reach the target audience via media. Media vehicles are primarily sold to advertisers on the basis of (numerical counts of) demographic profiles of viewers, listeners, or readers. If the advertiser also knows the demographic profile of the target audience, the advertiser can then try to "match" the media vehicle's demographic profile with the target audience's demographic profile. Demographic matching, though widely practiced, usually results in less accurate media selection than if direct matching[21] is used (see Media Exposure, above).

However, we should redraw attention to the basic importance of *geographic* media selection. In Chapter 2, we saw that the budget may be set locally for established brands if Schroer's method is used. Also, in Chapter 3, we recommended that the target audience always be specified geographically, because most media campaigns have a geographic constraint. Furthermore, *some* products and services are so highly correlated with income and social class that geographic segmentation (possible in print and direct response media) makes sense. Imported luxury cars and first-class air travel would be two examples. In direct-mail print advertising, geographic or "geo-demographic" profiling is common (see Chapter 17).

We will return to the role of demographics in media selection in Part Six (Chapter 17). Here we will simply repeat that the most common use of demographics in advertising is in media (vehicle) selection, but that direct measurement of the target audience's media exposure is a better way unless there is very strong geographic concentration of the target audience.

*Message Content.* A second advertising application of demographic variables is in choosing appropriate *message content*—both visual and verbal—for advertisements. For example, if the target audience's ethnic profile shows that most are Hispanic, then, visually, the advertisement is likely to feature Hispanic models (although one could think of exceptions) and Hispanic social settings. Also, verbally the advertisement is likely to be bilingual. As mentioned in the previous chapter, demographics are often used to delineate a target audience for a particular campaign. For instance, Procter & Gamble now has six separate U.S. campaigns for Crest toothpaste, targeted at different ethnic and socioeconomic groups including Blacks, Hispanics, and white- and blue-collar Whites.[22] These separate ad campaigns use appropriate variations in the models shown and in the language and linguistic nuances of the copy.

With the declining birth rate and improved health, *age* is now becoming a relevant profile variable as the U.S. population becomes older. If your target audience includes a large proportion of older consumers, then it is very important to clearly show the brand and use larger type in print ads and in TV commercials, as eyesight tends to decline with age, and to deliver the audio more slowly and clearly in TV and radio commercials, as hearing also tends to decline.[23] The "fast-talking" Federal Express commercials, for instance, would not be appropriate for an older audience. (In this TV campaign, an on-screen announcer delivered the spoken audio at well over twice the normal speaking rate, dramatizing the need for urgency and the speed of Federal Express.)

The main demographic profile variable for fmcg (grocery and drugstore) products continues to be gender, or *sex.* Women traditionally predominate in ads for food and drug products in demographic media selection and in message content. However, everyday observation and several recent studies have attested to the increasing role of men as grocery shoppers. For instance, the trade magazine *Progressive Grocer* estimates that men are primarily responsible for grocery shopping in 17 percent of households (of course, this still leaves women predominating in 83 percent).[24] Thus, men may be the appropriate demographic target for about one in six supermarket purchases. Perhaps more importantly for advertisers, recent evidence from Nielsen's HomeScan consumer panel suggests that men account for about 30 percent of the *dollar* purchases of consumer packaged goods (although again, 70 percent of the dollar volume is purchased by women).[25] As a general rule, probably the best solution for advertisers of these products is to occasionally show men in the shopping role in one or two ad executions in an overall campaign. For instance, the tag line for Procter & Gamble's well-known campaign for Jif peanut butter is "Choosey moms choose Jif"; nevertheless, in one ad in the campaign, Dad is shown doing the shopping. Also, of course, there may be strategic reasons for emphasizing one or the other of the sexes in a campaign. For instance, Healthy Choice decided to target men in its launch campaign, probably because men may be more "heart-concerned," but then later shifted mainly to commercials directed to women as the main household food buyers.

A surprisingly neglected demographic profile variable is *social class.* Marketers frequently gather the individual demographic variables that can be used to provide a composite measure of social class—namely, occupation, education, income, and area of residence[26]—but typically do not *combine* them to calculate the social class measure. Social class is very relevant to *retailers,* as was first recognized many years ago in classic research by Martineau.[27] The contemporary relevance of social class is confirmed in a study by Dickson and MacLachlan,[28] who found the well-known positive relationship between store "quality" image and social-class patronage. Social class is also relevant as a profile variable—indeed, as a market segmentation variable—for "conspicuous consumption" products and services.

In the next section, on psychographics or lifestyle, keep in mind that social class is a well-established, quite easy-to-measure, lifestyle variable. We note its role here, rather than repeating it in the next section. However, although social class is measured by *combining demographic* variables, its function is as a *lifestyle* variable.

**Psychographics (Lifestyle).** Psychographic variables go beyond demographics by offering a picture of the typical target decision participant's "lifestyle."[29] Lifestyle reflects "the way a person lives." It reflects personal expression and affects the way in which a person spends time and money. Lifestyle measurement is based on the individual's general (not product-specific) activities, interests, and opinions[30]—known collectively as *psychographic variables* or simply "psychographics."

The value of going beyond demographics to psychographics is easy to illustrate. Two demographically identical individuals, neighbors or colleagues even, could have quite different lifestyles: One individual may lead a "postmodern" lifestyle[31] and the other a "modern" (read: traditional) one. Knowledge of the target decision participant's typical lifestyle (if it *can* be typified) is of immense help to advertisers. Lifestyle or psychographic information helps:

**1.** In selecting *media vehicles* that portray lifestyles similar to those of the target audience (although, as explained in Chapter 17, this psychographic matching method of media selection, like demographic matching, is not as accurate as direct matching).

**2.** In deciding on advertising message content—particularly *visual content* in terms of appropriate types of people, settings, and *other* products, if any, to show in the advertisement (which is particularly important for one type of advertising, which we call high-involvement/transformational advertising, as explained in Chapter 9).

For example, an automobile advertisement directed to our hypothetical postmodern man might be placed in *Rolling Stone* magazine, which presumably appeals to contemporary young men. The ad itself might portray a postmodern model (for example, a *non*celebrity but cool-looking young man) in a postmodern setting (for example, skateboarding on the steps of the Washington Monument) with other postmodern products around him (for example, a backpack and a tube-bottle of energy drink). Alternatively, an ad for the same automobile directed to our hypothetical traditional man might be placed in *Fortune,* which presumably appeals to traditionalists. The ad itself might portray a traditionally dressed man (for example, William F. Buckley) in a traditional setting (for example, at the Yale Club) with other traditional products around him (for example, an American-eagle wall plaque). It is easy to see why media planners appreciate—and copywriters love—psychographics.

**Personality Traits.** Personality traits are relatively enduring, often largely inherited, individual predispositions that produce a characteristic tendency to respond in a consistent way across situations.[32] Because some personality traits are reflected in lifestyle, they can be considered as psychographic variables and would be applied as in the previous section, particularly in media vehicle selection. However, personality traits can be important profile variables in their own right because certain traits affect the way an individual processes information—especially *verbal content in,* and *repetition of,* advertising messages.

Personality traits relevant to advertising include innovativeness and opinion leadership, intelligence, trait anxiety, introversion-extraversion, public self-consciousness, and visual imaging ability.

*Innovativeness and Opinion Leadership.* For new product category introductions, two important profiling variables are innovativeness and opinion leadership. Innovators tend to be the first to adopt (or reject) new products; about 60 percent of innovators then go on to become opinion leaders and influence the diffusion (or nondiffusion) of the product through society (or through the industry, in the case of a new industrial product or service). Midgley and Dowling[33] were among the first to argue that consumer innovativeness should be conceptualized as an innate personality trait. One potential measure of this personality trait is the Kirton Adaption-Innovation Inventory, or KAI.[34] Foxall found in a recent study that early triers of very new food products were consumers who scored high on the KAI index.[35]

Marketers introducing new product *categories* should use a screening survey to select a sample of innovators and opinion leaders,[36] rather than using a random sample, when conducting "concept testing" to gauge acceptance of the new product. They should then aim for these individuals (via direct-matching media vehicle selection) in the new product's introductory advertising communications and promotions.

*Intelligence.* Intelligence is usually measured indirectly and imprecisely in advertising through the demographic variable of education level instead of using a more valid IQ test. Intelligence is relevant to message complexity and the use of technical terminology in advertising. Intelligent individuals are better able to understand complex messages and also seem to be more impressed, and persuaded, by technical wording in advertising.[37]

Also, for intelligent individuals, somewhat fewer repetitions should be needed to learn advertising messages, whereas the opposite should be true for less-intelligent individuals.[38]

Global or multinational campaigns *in English* that reach people whose first language is *not* English should also heed these recommendations about intelligence.[39] A nonnative English speaker is functionally like a less-intelligent native speaker, and simplification of English ad copy must be insisted upon.

*Trait Anxiety.* Trait anxiety refers to a relatively persistent or *chronic* level of anxiety (autonomic nervous system arousal) as opposed to temporary states of anxiety that we all experience occasionally. Trait anxiety needs to be interpreted carefully but is relevant to advertising messages incorporating scare tactics or fear appeals, such as for many public service campaigns and for product categories such as aspirin and insurance.[40]

A "normal" fear appeal could be rejected as too frightening if the target audience contains a majority of individuals with high trait anxiety; likewise, it could be ineffectively tame if most of the individuals have low trait anxiety.

*Introversion-Extraversion.* Introverts exhibit a chronically high level of brain activity (central nervous system or cortical arousal, but unrelated to intelligence), and hence tend to seek solitude. Extraverts exhibit a chronically low level of CNS arousal and hence tend to seek extra stimulation from the sensory or social environment and are therefore more outgoing. Approximately 45 percent of people are on the introvert side of the population distribution of this trait, and 55 percent on the extravert side. British research on introversion-extraversion as a personality trait[41] suggests many intriguing implications for advertising. The main implications are for verbal message content and repetition.

Introverts should be more affected by negative appeals, such as fear or problem-solution appeals, whereas extraverts should be more affected by positive appeals, especially prestige or social-reward appeals.[42]

Introverts should learn advertising messages more rapidly than extraverts, thus requiring fewer repetitions of the ad, but should also be less brand loyal, as, with their higher cortical arousal, they are more easily distracted by new messages for competing brands.

Extraverts actually prefer loud commercials, it would seem, in keeping with their need for extra cortical stimulation. In an interesting experiment, Cetola and Prinkey played a radio commercial for a new brand of chewing gum at either same-as-program loudness or louder-than-program. Extraverts developed a markedly more favorable attitude toward the brand when exposed to the loud commercial (30 percent more favorable, on average).[43] No difference was found for introverts. This finding, if generalizable, would tend to justify loud commercials on TV and radio since they may be more effective with the extraverted half of the audience while not being detrimental to the introverted remainder.

*Public Self-Consciousness.* Public self-consciousness is a personality trait which is distinct from introversion-extraversion and reflects sensitivity to being evaluated by others in social situations.[44] Actually, since personality traits are transsituational, this is technically a personality state variable, but social situations are so prevalent that it functions as a trait. Public self-consciousness seems somewhat related to the personality trait known as "self-monitoring"[45] but is more straightforward to interpret and more directly applicable to advertising. Publicly self-conscious individuals are more likely to prefer national name brands to bargain brands.[46] Also, in terms of message content, publicly self-conscious individuals should be even more responsive than extraverts to prestige appeals.

*Visual Imaging Ability.* Visual imaging ability is a personality trait that relates to verbal message content and also visual content. Vivid visual imagers respond more strongly to concrete words in copy and also to pictorial advertising content that evokes imagery.[47]

Women, on average, have slightly greater visual imaging ability than men. For this and other reasons,[48] women may be *slightly* easier to persuade than men.

According to neurolinguistic-programming (NLP) theorists, visual processing (sight) is the mode of processing favored by about 70 percent of people; 15 percent favor auditory processing (sound); and 15 percent favor kinesthetic processing (body sensation or feeling). Orr and Murphy, in a fascinating experiment, showed that radio ads emphasizing either the sights, sounds, or feelings of a beach vacation resort produced markedly greater purchase intentions in the appropriate NLP trait groups.[49] Although it may not be practical to measure NLP types, advertisers could simply assume their presence and design multiple ads to fit them.

**Personality States.** Personality states are, paradoxically, a contradiction in terms. Personality consists of *enduring* predisposition whereas states, obviously, are *temporary*.[50] Personality states refer to the fact that, at some times and in some situations, we all experience physical or mental conditions that simulate the corresponding personality trait. Examples: a severe hangover may render the best of us functionally unintelligent; transient events, such as a TV documentary on the threat of nuclear war, can make most of us anxious; at particular times of the day we may feel mentally alert, whereas at other times we may feel tired and unwilling to think deeply; similarly, our visual imagery, an extreme form of which is daydreaming, may fluctuate with the time and situation.

Personality states are a relevant consideration in media vehicle selection and, in this sense, can be regarded as specific refinements to our first profile variable, media exposure. For example, a person watching the early-evening TV news may be in quite a different physiological and mental state than when watching a late-night movie in bed. A morning newspaper may be read in a different state than an evening one, and so forth. Many media planners take these audience states into account when selecting media vehicles (often to an exaggerated extent, though, as we shall see in Chapter 17). Personality state variables allow advertisers to predict how the audience might respond differently to ads placed in different media vehicles.

Since personality *states* are functionally equivalent in the short run to personality *traits,* personality states, like traits, should also be relevant to *verbal content* selection in advertisements. This realization suggests, for example, the use of simpler messages when the audience is likely to be tired, emphasis on audio rather than video when the audience is likely to be inattentive, and other corresponding modifications of verbal message content to suit temporary personality states experienced during media exposure.

### Applying Profile Variables

The main target audience profile variables of brand behavior and communication effects must be taken into account when designing an advertising communications or promotion campaign. This is because the purpose of advertising and promotion is to influence communication effects, and thus behavior, from their current status to the target status. If, as we recommend, the target audience is *defined* using the brand loyalty approach, which is *based on* awareness, attitude, and behavior, then the target audience will be quite homogeneous on these variables—that is, most individuals in the target audience will have the same initial communication effects and behavior. It is then easier to design one message (one campaign) capable of moving these effects to their target status.

The first of the additional profile variables, media exposure, *should* be taken into account. As we have stated, direct measurement of the target audience's media exposure means that the target audience can be reached by the advertising communications or promotion campaign more accurately than is possible with indirect methods of media selection. The media exposure of individuals in the target audience may be quite diverse; but this is reality, and the campaign must try to reach as many of them as can be afforded, presuming that to do so will result in a profitable return as estimated previously by the target audience leverage calculation. Usually, media vehicles are selected based on the number of target audience individuals reached, and a mix of 10 to 20 of the highest-reach vehicles gives majority coverage.

The remaining profile variables are *optional.* Their use depends on whether the target audience can be *majority-described* by that profile variable. Consider the demographic variable of sex, for example. We saw that women are a clear majority of decision makers for the typical grocery or drugstore product, and women would be the majority no matter whether the brand loyalty target audience is NCUs, OBLs, OBSs, BSs, or BLs. For the typical such product, the advertiser would favor media vehicles skewed toward women, if using traditional demographic media selection, and the message content of the ad or promotion offer also would be designed to appeal to women.

However, a difficult decision arises when a profile variable does *not* describe a clear majority of the target audience. For instance, we saw that the personality trait of introversion-extraversion is divided 45 percent versus 55 percent across the population; in a particular target audience, such as OBLs for our brand, we may find a 50-50 division, that is, no clear majority.[51] There are three alternative application possibilities available in such cases. One is to *ignore* that profile variable altogether. This is the correct approach if the variable is only weakly related to media habits or to persuasion in the first place. But if it is *strongly* related, then ignoring it could result in a "compromise" media selection or an "average" message that is effective in reaching or persuading neither

group—in our example, neither introverts nor extraverts. Therefore, the second possibility is to design *separate* campaigns for each group. This is the best solution if reasonably different media vehicles can be found to keep the two companies separate (possible in direct mail, but difficult in other media) or if it can be shown that cross-exposure to the campaigns does not dilute the targeted campaigns' separate effects. A third possibility is to design one campaign that is differentially effective with one trait-level group and *neutral* with the other, as was found in the Cetola and Prinkey study concerning loud commercials for extraverts. Note that the net gain in this approach is greater than using a neutral campaign for both groups. However, if pretesting of the one campaign (alternative three) indicates that the effect on the other substantial half is *negative,* turning them off the brand, then the advertiser has to keep trying to find a suitable alternative campaign while putting up with an unsuitable compromise campaign.

In summary, caution must be exercised in considering other profile variables beyond awareness-attitude-behavior and media exposure—namely, demographics, psychographics (or lifestyle), personality traits, and personality states. As interesting and powerful as these variables may be, they are only applicable if they characterize a clear majority of the brand-loyalty–defined target audience or, in "split" cases, if the split implementation—in media or in message content—can be shown to produce a net gain in effectiveness.[52]

## SUMMARY

To prepare an advertising, promotion, or IMC campaign, the manager has to have specific knowledge about the decision process and the key decision participants within whichever of the five brand loyalty groups is selected as the target audience.

Identification of the stages in the decision process leading to purchase and usage, and of the decision participant or participants who should be targeted, can best be achieved by constructing a behavioral sequence model (BSM). Such a model, generated through qualitative research (focus-group or individual depth interviews) with prospective buyers, breaks the overall purchase decision process into stages, identifies the decision-making roles and role-players in each stage, specifies the location and timing of the decision stages as they evolve from initial need arousal through to purchase and usage, and briefly describes how each decision stage is typically accomplished. The BSM shows which decision participants to target and where and when they can be reached.

There are five (main) roles that individual buyers or consumers who contribute to the purchase decision can play. Each has a specific action objective. The *initiator* proposes the category for consideration, of which the brand is a member. The *influencer* sets the choice criteria and recommends the brand. The *decider* makes the final go / no-go decision. The *purchaser* actually buys the brand. The *user* is then the actual user or consumer of the brand. Advertising communications and promotions may be directed to individuals in one or more of these roles, with the respective action objectives as described.

Many family and industrial (or business) purchases are made by group decision. However, since ads and promotion offers can't be "in" the group when the decision is made, advertising and promotion must attempt to influence the main individuals, in role, *before* they participate in the group decision. Personal purchases are simpler: The individual plays all five roles, and there is only one decision participant to reach.

The most important information the manager needs to know in profiling the target audience decision participant is the participant's current behavior and communication-effects status (notably, brand awareness and brand attitude) with regard to the brand. Once the *current* behavior and communication-effects status of the typical target audience member are known, the manager can then set objectives to reflect the *target* communication effects and action that the advertising communications or promotion seeks in the target audience.

Several additional profile variables (secondary to behavior and communication effects) help the advertiser to reach the target audience decision participant more effectively and efficiently. The most useful additional variable is *media exposure,* which increases the accuracy of media selection and scheduling.

The other profile variables are optional. These include *demographics,* a less accurate but commonly employed way of matching target audiences with media audiences, and useful also for selecting appropriate visual and verbal message content; *psychographics* or lifestyle measures, which help in selecting suitable media vehicles and in selecting appropriate visual message content; *personality traits*, which affect verbal message content and also media scheduling via repetition; and *personality states,* which may affect the decision participant during media exposure and thus may also affect the choice of media vehicle and verbal message content. As explained at the end of the chapter, these variables must either be majority descriptors or be implementable on a one-sided or split basis with an overall net gain. A strong relationship with media or message effectiveness, or both, has to be expected before it is worth applying a particular profile variable.

So, we have selected the target audience, set action objectives, prescribed a specific model of the overall decision sequence, and gained a detailed understanding of prospective buyers as decision participants within the target audience to whom the advertising communications, promotion, or IMC campaign is directed. Advertising communications and promotion work through *communication,* and it is to communication effects and communication objectives (which, with brand position, are step 3 in the buyer response steps, preceding target audience action) that we turn in the next part of the book.

## NOTES

1. Decision-stage models are prevalent in marketing and advertising textbooks, usually presenting a generic "hierarchy of effects" for marketing inputs such as advertising or personal selling. Ours differs in that the stages are *not* generic but are identified for each product category and perhaps brand—*and* the stages are combined with the data inputs of who, where, when, and how in grid form. We explain hierarchy-of-effects relationships between the buyer response steps and the decision stages later in this chapter (see Figure 4.2).

2. For instance, in a study of new car buying, Brookes and Punj, as is usual, labeled the first stage "Problem Recognition." However, their analysis showed that only about half of the new-car seekers actually had a "problem" (product depletion or dissatisfaction with current car); the other half were more "positive" in that they had a new need for a car (first car or additional car for household) or simply were excited about the prospects of a new car. Thus "Need Arousal" is a more encompassing and accurate term. See R. Brookes and G. Punj, The influence of problem recognition and prior decision in new automobile purchases, Working paper, Department of Marketing and International Business, University of Auckland, NZ, 1992.

3. This footnote provides comments and references for the notes in Table 4.1.

   [a]Note that our BLs are probably someone else's OBLs. If our competitor wanted to break this cycle, it could be attempted at the need arousal stage with advertising inserting new communication effects at this stage (particularly competitor brand awareness, such as "Gee, I could have had a V-8!") or during the repeat purchase stage (with a point-of-purchase promotion for the competitor's brand).

   [b]For evidence that the direct response BSM order mode—such as toll-free telephone number, reader-reply card, or reply coupon—affects response rate, see A. G. Woodside and P. K. Soni, Assessing the quality of advertising enquiries by mode of response, *Journal of Advertising Research,* 1988, *28* (4), pp. 31–37.

   [c]Browsing behavior is worth investigating as a stage in a retail-purchase BSM. See P. H. Bloch, N. M. Ridgway, and D. L. Sherrell, Extending the concept of shopping: An investigation of browsing activity, *Journal of the Academy of Marketing Science,* 1989, *17* (1), pp. 13–21. Donovan and Rossiter provide some evidence that time spent in stores is correlated with impulse purchasing. See R. J. Donovan and J. R. Rossiter, Store atmosphere: An environmental psychology approach, *Journal of Retailing,* 1982, *58* (1), pp. 34–57; and R. J. Donovan, J. R. Rossiter, G. Marcoolyn, and A. Nesdale, Store atmosphere and purchasing behavior, *Journal of Retailing,* 1994, *70* (3), pp. 283–294.

   [d]The items in this stage of the service BSM are suggested from a very useful discussion in H. Kasper and J. Lemmink, After sales service quality: Views between industrial customers and service managers, *Industrial Marketing Management,* 1989, *18* (3), pp. 199–208.

   [e]Industrial BSM stages or "buy phases" depend on whether the decision is a new task buy (as shown), a modified rebuy, or a straight rebuy. See F. E. Webster and Y. Wind, *Organizational Buyer Behavior,* Englewood Cliffs, NJ: Prentice-Hall, 1972.

4. See, for example, C. Dröge and D. Halstead, Post purchase hierarchies of effects: The antecedents and consequences of satisfaction for complainers versus noncomplainers, *International Journal of Research in Marketing,* 1991, *8* (4), pp. 315–328; and M. J. Bittner, The service encounter: Diagnosing favorable and unfavorable incidents, *Journal of Marketing,* 1990, *54* (1), pp. 68–81. Rich Oliver has conducted extensive theoretical and empirical research on customer satisfaction; see, for instance, R. C. Oliver, A cognitive model of the antecedents and consequences of satisfaction, *Journal of Marketing Research,* 1980, *17* (4), pp. 460–469; and J. E. Swan and R. L. Oliver, Post-purchase communications by consumers, *Journal of Retailing,* 1989, *65* (4), pp. 516–533.

5. K. P. Corfman and D. R. Lehmann, Models of cooperative group decision-making and relative influence: An experimental investigation of family purchase decisions, *Journal of Consumer Research,* 1987, *14* (1), pp. 1–13. In their study of husband-wife purchase decisions for consumer durables, they found that if one spouse has a more intense preference, his or her preferred item is chosen; but if the couple's preferences are equally intense, an alternating pattern ("your turn") tends to be followed—which makes it difficult for the advertiser!

6. See especially E. J. Wilson, G. L. Lilien, and D. T. Wilson, Developing and testing a contingency paradigm of group choice in organizational buying, *Journal of Marketing Research,* 1991, *27* (4), pp. 452–466; and J. H. Steckel, K. P. Corfman, D. J. Curry, S. Gupta, and J. Shanteau, Prospects and problems in modeling group decisions, *Marketing Letters,* 1991, *2* (3), pp. 231–240.

7. For theory and evidence in organizational behavior that individual's abilities or expertise may be more important in determining outcomes than the group process itself, see P. C. Bottger and P. W. Yetton, An integration of process and decision scheme explanations of group problem-solving performances, *Organizational Behavior and Human Decision Process,* 1988, *42* (2), pp. 234–249.

8. R. B. Settle and P. L. Alreck, *Why They Buy: American Consumers Inside and Out,* New York: Wiley, 1989.

9. Business decision roles are discussed with case-history examples in T. V. Bonoma, Major sales: Who *really* does the buying? *Harvard Business Review,* 1982, *60* (3), pp. 111–119. In organizations, the gatekeeper role may be importantly expanded to include "boundary riders" who bring in, or attempt to bring in, radically new information, as examined in S. MacDonald and C. Williams, Beyond the boundary: An information perspective on the role of the gatekeeper in the organization, *Journal of Product and Innovation Management,* 1993, *10* (5), pp. 417–427.

10. J. Koten, You aren't paranoid if you feel someone eyes you constantly, *The Wall Street Journal,* March 29, 1985, pp. 1, 26.

11. For a thoughtful model of locations that are possibilities for advertising or promotion, see J. D. Johnson, *Advertising Today,* Chicago, IL: Science Research Associates, 1978, p. 129.

12. R. W. Belk, Situational variables and consumer behavior, *Journal of Consumer Research,* 1975, *2* (3), pp. 157–164.

13. G. R. Foxall, The consumer situation: An integrative model for research in marketing, *Journal of Marketing Management,* 1992, *8* (4), pp. 383–404.

14. Firms that announce new corporate-advertising slogans to the financial press (example: Campbell Soup Company changed its 67-year-old slogan "M'm! M'm! Good!" in 1993 to "Never underestimate the power of soup") typically show almost a 1 percent increase in their stock price (statistically significant and, in this example, adding about $100 million to the firm's value) shortly afterward. See L. K. Mathur and I. Mathur, The effect of advertising slogan changes on the market values of firms, *Journal of Advertising Research,* 1995, *35* (1), pp. 59–65.

15. J. D. Power and Associates' research, cited in *Research Alert,* September 20, 1991, p. 1.

16. For instance, in a French survey of recent buyers of new cars, about one in six (17 percent) said they had considered only one brand. See E. Lapersonne, G. Laurent, and J-J. Le Goff, Consideration sets of size one: An empirical investigation of automobile purchases, *International Journal of Research in Marketing,* 1995, *12* (1), pp. 55–66.

17. B. E. Kahn and D. C. Schmittlein, Shopping trip behavior: An empirical investigation, *Marketing Letters,* 1989, *1* (1), pp. 55–69.

18. The reason for the primacy of behavior and communication-effects status in target audience definition is straightforward: The effects of more "distant" variables such as demographics (age, sex, etc.) are *already represented* in current awareness, attitudes, and behaviors toward the category and brand. This point is well discussed in M. Fishbein, A theory of reasoned action, in H. E. Howe, ed., *Nebraska Symposium on Motivation,* Lincoln, NE: University of Nebraska Press, 1980, pp. 65–116.

19. J. Rice, Ever try converting a staunch Catholic to Buddhism? *Marketing News,* September 2, 1991; Market Facts, Inc., *The Conversion Model,* Chicago: Market Facts, Inc., 1991. We have renamed their "Brittle" classification as "Entrapped."

20. Further discussion of "forward segmentation" by behavior and communication effects and the subsequent uses of decision participant profile variables can be found in J. R. Rossiter, Market segmentation: A review and proposed resolution, *Australian Marketing Researcher,* 1987, *11* (1), pp. 38–58.

21. The match is rarely perfect because to reach every member of the target audience, you'd have to advertise in at least one media vehicle that reaches each peson. If target audience individuals have diverse media exposure, this could be prohibitively expensive. Thus, marketers choose vehicles that a *majority* of target audience individuals are exposed to. See Chapters 17 and 18 for further explanation of the direct matching method of media selection.

22. Z. Schiller, Stalking the new consumer, *Business Week,* August 28, 1989, pp. 54–62.

23. For various studies of the special needs of older consumers in relation to advertising, see D. Jones, The 40+ market: In need of reassessment? *Ad News,* February 13, 1987, p. 32 (this study found an 18 percent reduction in advertisement recognition and a 37 percent reduction in correct brand recognition among consumers 35 and older compared with those under 35); C. A. Cole, G. J. Gaeth, and M. J. Houston, Encoding and media effects on consumer learning deficiencies in the elderly, *Journal of Marketing Research,* 1987, *24* (1), pp. 55–63; G. J. Gorn, M. E. Goldberg, A. Chattopadhyay, and D. Litvack, Music and information in commercials: Their effects with an elderly sample, *Journal of Advertising Research,* October-November, 1991, pp. 23–32; S. C. Lonial and P. S. Raju, The decision process and media-related interactions of the elderly: A synthesis of findings, in C. R. Martin, Jr., and J. H. Leigh, eds., *Current Issues and Research in Advertising,* 1991, *13* (2), pp. 277–311; and A. A. Ward, Marketers slow to catch age wave, *Advertising Age,* May 22, 1989, pp. S-1 to S-7.

24. Survey by *Progressive Grocer* cited in J. Lipman, Mr. Mom may be a force to reckon with, *The Wall Street Journal,* October 3, 1991, p. B4.

25. J. Mandese, HomeScan: Men are active shoppers, *Advertising Age,* November 11, 1991, p. 44.

26. See the excellent review of social class applied to marketing in R. P. Coleman, The continuing significance of social class to marketing, *Journal of Consumer Research,* 1983, *10* (3), pp. 265–280.

27. P. Martineau, Social classes and spending behavior, *Journal of Marketing,* 1958, *23* (3), pp. 121–130; and The personality of the retail store, *Harvard Business Review,* 1958, January-February, p. 47.

28. J. P. Dickson and D. L. MacLachlan, Social distance and shopping behavior, *Journal of the Academy of Marketing Science,* 1990, *18* (2), pp. 153–161.

29. The term "lifestyle" is attributed to the famous psychoanalyst Alfred Adler. See, for example, A. Adler, *Understanding Human Nature,* London, UK: George Allen & Unwin, 1962. Adler referred to "style of life" as the characteristic behavior patterns and attitudes that differentiate one person from another. Psychoanalytically, he regarded each person as "striving for superiority expressed in an individual way." Measurement of lifestyle is through psychographic questionnaire items.

30. Often abbreviated "AIO." When the measurement is based on *product category* activities, interests, and opinions, the result technically is "benefit segments" rather than lifestyle groups, although this distinction is not always observed by marketers.

31. "Postmodern" refers to consumers born after 1950, roughly post-WWII, who presumably are members of a "global" lifestyle segment. "Modern" refers to the living generations born in the period up to 1950, who presumably are more locally traditional. See T. J. Domzal and J. B. Kernan, Mirror, mirror: Some postmodern reflections on global advertising, *Journal of Advertising,* 1993, *22* (4), pp. 1–20.

32. See, for example, R. B. Cattell, *The Scientific Analysis of Personality,* Baltimore, MD: Penguin Books, 1965; and H. J. Eysenck, ed., *A Model for Personality,* Berlin, Germany: Springer, 1981.

33. D. F. Midgley and G. R. Dowling, Innovativeness: The concept and its measurement, *Journal of Consumer Research,* 1978, *4* (2), pp. 229–242; and A longitudinal study of product form innovation: The interaction between predispositions and social messages, *Journal of Consumer Research,* 1993, *19* (4), pp. 611–625.

34. M. J. Kirton, Adaptors and innovators: A description and measure, *Journal of Applied Psychology,* 1976, *61* (5), pp. 622–629.

35. G. R. Foxall, Consumer innovativeness: Novelty-seeking, creativity and cognitive style, in E. Hirschman and J. Sheth, eds., *Research in Consumer Behavior,* vol. 3, Greenwich, Conn.: JAI Press, 1988, pp. 79–113.

36. Or in industrial application, "lead user" companies; see E. von Hippel, Lead users: A source of novel product concepts, *Management Science,* 1986, *32* (7), pp. 791–805; and P. D. Morrison, A study of the relationship of leading edge users to opinion leaders. Working paper, Australian Graduate School of Management, Kensington, NSW, 1994.

37. Two interesting experiments on technical wording in ads are those by M. R. Lautman and L. Percy, Consumer-oriented versus advertiser-oriented language: Comprehensibility and salience of the advertising message, in H. K. Hunt, ed., *Advances in Consumer Research,* vol. 5, Ann Arbor, MI: Association for Consumer Research, 1978, pp. 52–56; and R. E. Anderson and M. A. Jolson, Technical wording in advertising: Implications for market segmentation, *Journal of Marketing, 44* (1), pp. 57–66.

38. For example, Burke Related Recall norms, a rough measure of learning, indicate 20 percent lower scores, on average, for individuals who did not finish high school. See Burke Marketing Research, Inc., *Day-After Recall Television Commercial Norms,* Cincinnati, OH: Burke Marketing Research, Inc., 1979.

39. Here we are talking about the international use of English (or potentially any foreign-to-the-audience) language as *copy,* audio or print, in ads—not the use of a foreign word or phrase to convey "image." For the latter, see T. J. Domzal, J. M. Hunt, and J. B. Kernan, *Achtung?* The information processing of foreign words in advertising, *International Journal of Advertising,* 1995, *14* (2), pp. 95–114.

40. B. Sternthal and C. S. Craig, Fear appeals: Revisited and revised, *Journal of Consumer Research,* 1974, *1* (3), pp. 22–34. In their excellent review of fear appeals, Sternthal and Craig conclude that a relationship between fear level and trait anxiety has not been proven. However, a more recent, real-world study indicated that a high-fear promotion of a health maintenance organization (HMO) was differentially effective with older people, who may have more chronic anxiety about their health. See J. J. Burnett and R. E. Wilkes, Fear appeals to segments only, *Journal of Advertising Research,* 1980, *20* (5), pp. 21–24. Also see J. Tanner, J. Hunt, and D. Eppright, The protection motivation model: A normative model of fear appeals, *Journal of Marketing,* 1995, *55* (2), pp. 36–45.

41. H. J. Eysenck, ed., same reference as in note 32. The trait was identified by the famous psychoanalyst Carl Jung. It appears also in the Myers-Briggs Type Indicator, which is widely used in personnel selection. A more recently identified trait, "self-monitoring," appears to be related to extraversion via concern with self-presentation in social settings; see M. Snyder, Self-monitoring of expressive behavior, *Journal of Personality and Social Psychology,* 1974, *30* (4), pp. 526–537, and D. M. Stayman and F. R. Kardes, Spontaneous inference processes in advertising: Effects of need for cognition and self-monitoring on inference generation and utilization, *Journal of Consumer Psychology,* 1992, *1* (2), pp. 125–142. The distribution of introverts versus extraverts is given in M. A. Matoun, *Jungian Psychology in Perspective,* New York: The Free Press, 1981; see also M. R. Hyman and R. Tansey, A rapprochement between the advertising community and the Jungians, in C. R. Martin, Jr., and J. H. Leigh, eds., *Current Issues and Research in Advertising,* 1991, *13* (1), pp. 105–123.

42. The extensive work of H. J. Eysenck and his colleagues shows many examples of introverts responding faster to aversive conditioning and extraverts to reward conditioning. See, for instance, H. J. Eysenck, ed., same reference as in note 32. In an advertising study, extraverts (high social self-monitors) were shown to respond more favorably to social-reward

appeals; see K. G. DeBono and M. Packer, The effects of advertising appeal on perceptions of product quality, *Personality and Social Psychology Bulletin,* 1991, *17* (2), pp. 194–200.

43. H. Cetola and K. Prinkey, Introversion-extraversion and loud commercials, *Psychology & Marketing,* 1986, *3* (2), pp. 123–132.

44. Public self-consciousness as a personality trait (or, more correctly, a prevalently occurring state) was identified by A. Fenigstein, M. F. Schier, and A. H. Buss, Public and private self-consciousness: Assessment and theory, *Journal of Consulting Psychology,* 1975, *43* (4), pp. 522–527. It is not correlated with social anxiety but seems to reflect the feeling of being "on display" socially. The authors provide a reliable seven-item scale to measure this trait, which was used in the study by Bushman (see note 46). For a sophisticated account of its importance in consumer behavior, see T. J. Domzal and J. B. Kernan, Variations on the pursuit of beauty: Toward a corporal theory of the body, *Psychology & Marketing,* 1993, *10* (6), pp. 496–511.

45. M. Snyder, *Public Appearances / Private Realities: The Psychology of Self-Monitoring,* New York, NY: W. H. Freeman and Company, 1987.

46. B. J. Bushman, What's in a name? The moderating role of public self-consciousness on the relation between brand label and brand preference, *Journal of Applied Psychology,* 1993, *78* (5), pp. 857–861.

47. J. R. Rossiter and L. Percy, Attitude change through visual imagery in advertising, *Journal of Advertising,* 1980, *9* (2), pp. 10–16; and J. R. Rossiter and L. Percy, Visual communication in advertising, in R. J. Harris, ed., *Information Processing Research in Advertising,* Hillsdale, NJ: Lawrence Erlbaum Associates, 1983, pp. 83–125.

48. W. J. McGuire discusses sex differences in persuasibility in his chapter, The nature of attitudes and attitude change, in G. Lindzey and E. Aronson, eds., *The Handbook of Social Psychology,* 2nd ed., vol. 3, Reading, MA: Addison-Wesley, 1969, pp. 136–314. A meta-analysis of this research shows a small but statistically reliable tendency for women to be more easily persuaded; another way of interpreting the results is that 55 to 60 percent of men are less influenceable than the average woman. See A. H. Eagly and L. L. Carli, Sex of researchers and sex-typed communications as determinants of sex differences in influenceability: A meta-analysis of social influence studies, *Psychological Bulletin,* 1981, *90* (1), pp. 1–20.

49. B. H. Orr and J. H. Murphy, Neuro-Linguistic Programming: Implications for advertising copy strategy?, in P. A. Stout, ed., *Proceedings of the 1990 Conference of the American Academy of Advertising,* Austin, TX: University of Texas, 1990, pp. RC-111 to RC-116. NLP theory was proposed by R. Bandler and J. Grinder, *The Structure of Magic and I and II: A Book About Language and Theory,* Palo Alto, CA: Science and Behavior Books, 1975.

50. The term "mood" is vaguely in vogue among consumer researchers to refer to a similar phenomenon. However, we prefer the term "personality states," which imply short-term variations in the corresponding personality *trait*. Personality states thus have the same properties as the trait itself.

51. This type of split, but into multiple categories, plagued the once-popular VALS (Values and Lifestyles) typology. There was a mix of several VALS types in almost every product-user target audience in which the advertiser was interested.

52. This is a common problem with academic studies. Whereas some variables, notably personality traits such as "self-monitoring" or "need for cognition," may show large mediating or moderating effects in the separate audiences (usually low-versus-high), never have we seen consideration given to the practicality of implementing two possibly contradictory campaigns. Also, the cross-effects in academic studies are often negative, resulting in no apparent net gain even if the split campaigns were implemented. We must say, however, that the NLP results obtained by Orr and Murphy (see note 49) are worth exploring further because the cross-effects were differentially positive rather than negative. Visual, auditory, and kinesthetic versions of ad copy may well pick up all three audience types.

## DISCUSSION QUESTIONS

**4.1.** You are the marketing manager for Bic Disposable razors. Based on the decision roles and specific action objectives identified in Table 4.2, prepare a more thorough account of the likely importance of men and women as target audiences for the brand's advertising communications *and* promotion.

**4.2.** Advertising to group decision makers, as is common in industrial buying, requires targeting decision participants in their individual roles. Imagine IBM is planning an advertising campaign for its personal computers for company, in-office use. Construct and discuss a likely behavioral sequence model that might assist IBM in its advertising plan.

**4.3.** What do we mean by "profiling" the targeted decision participant? Why are behavior and communication effects the primary profiling variables, and for what purpose(s) are they necessary? Why is current brand attitude vulnerability also worth special attention?

**4.4.** Summarize, with examples, the major advertising applications of the following profile variables: (a) television programs watched, (b) occupation, (c) liberated woman's lifestyle, (d) extraversion, (e) situational tiredness, and (f) innovativeness.

## FURTHER READING

Johnson, J. D. *Advertising Today.* Chicago, IL: Science Research Associates, 1978.

This is an interesting, practitioner-oriented text that was way ahead of its time (and is still very useful) in identifying IMC media opportunities for behavioral sequence models.

Percy, L. How market segmentation guides advertising strategy. *Journal of Advertising Research,* 1976, *16* (5), pp. 11–22.

This is a fairly technical article (by one of the present authors) that emphasizes the primacy of attitudes in target audience definition and specifies what ideally needs to be known about the targeted decision participant (we now emphasize behavior and other communication effects, notably awareness, as well, but this article presents a strong case for the attitude-alone viewpoint). Includes measurement details that may be of interest to technically sophisticated readers.

Wells, W. D. Psychographics: A critical review. *Journal of Marketing Research,* 1975, *12* (2), pp. 196–213.

This and the earlier and less detailed Wells and Tigert article (see our Chapter 18) should be studied by everyone who has used or is planning to use psychographic measures to profile a target audience. Also contains many practical pointers on validity, reliability, and interpretations of "high-powered" statistical results.

## PART THREE

# COMMUNICATION OBJECTIVES AND POSITIONING

**CHAPTER 5: COMMUNICATION OBJECTIVES**

**CHAPTER 6: POSITIONING**

# Communication Objectives

Advertisements, adlike events, and promotion offers create the brand's position and cause action through the process of communication: they establish relatively enduring mental associations in the prospective buyer's mind, connected to the brand, called communication effects. There are five communication effects, and they must all be at full strength before the buyer will take action. Communication *objectives* must be selected by the manager—from the five communication effects—when planning a specific advertising communications or promotion campaign. After reading this chapter, you should:

- Become familiar with the five communication effects.
- Understand the priority function of the brand awareness communication effect.
- Understand the benefit belief and emotional components of the brand attitude communication effect.
- Know how to select specific options, from among the five communication effects, which become the communication *objectives* for the campaign.

## THE FIVE COMMUNICATION EFFECTS

*Communication effects* are relatively enduring mental associations, connected to the brand, in the prospective buyer's mind, that are necessary to create the brand's position and predispose action. There are five communication effects.[1] They can be caused, in whole or in part, by *any* form of marketing communication—advertisements, adlike events, promotion offers, and personal-selling presentations (although we don't cover face-to-face selling in this book). The five communication effects are:

1. Category need
2. Brand awareness
3. Brand attitude
4. Brand purchase intention
5. Purchase facilitation

Definitions of the communication effects are provided in Table 5.1.

All potential buyers experience these effects "in their head" prior to purchase decisions. Decision participants in *other roles beside the purchaser role* also experience the communication effects; however, there is some modification in the brand-purchase-intention communication effect, and sometimes in the purchase-facilitation communication effect, because the other decision roles do not focus on purchase but rather on proposing, recommending, choosing, or using the brand (see Chapter 4). For convenience, we will focus on the *purchaser role* in this chapter.

### The "Mental Bins" Analogy

It is helpful to regard the five communication effects as a series of five "mental bins," as depicted in Figure 5.1, which must all be filled before the buyer will take action.[2] The buyer carries these bins into the stages of

## TABLE 5.1

### THE FIVE COMMUNICATION EFFECTS DEFINED

| Communication effect | Definition |
| --- | --- |
| 1. Category need | Buyer's acceptance that the category (a product or service) is necessary to remove or satisfy a perceived discrepancy between the current motivational state and the desired motivational state. |
| 2. Brand awareness | Buyer's ability to identify (recognize or recall) the brand, within the category, in sufficient detail to make a purchase. |
| 3. Brand attitude | Buyer's evaluation of the brand with respect to its perceived ability to meet a currently relevant motivation (this evaluation is based on brand benefit beliefs and the motivation-related emotional weights of the benefits and of possible freestanding emotions). |
| 4. Brand purchase intention | Buyer's self-instruction to purchase the brand or to take purchase-related action. |
| 5. Purchase facilitation | Buyer's assurance that other marketing factors (the 4Ps) will not hinder purchase. |

the behavioral sequence model (see Chapter 4). He or she carries one bin for the category need and four bins that are brand-specific. To be considered, the brand must have a share of the category need bin—it must be one of the brands "in" the category. Thus, in effect, there are five mental bins for every brand that is potentially available for purchase.

We will now examine each of the communication effects in turn, discussing the options available to the

**FIGURE 5.1**
Communication effects.[a] There are five "mental bins" to be filled for the brand.

| ① | ② | ③ | ④ | ⑤ |
| --- | --- | --- | --- | --- |
| Category need | Brand awareness | Brand attitude | Brand purchase intention | Purchase facilitation |

[a]Communication objectives = those communication effects targeted in a particular campaign, with their response objective specified.

manager in considering each communication effect for possible inclusion in the set of *communication objectives* for an advertising communications or promotion campaign. First, though, here is an important definition which is the key to understanding how communication effects are *transformed* into communication objectives: Communication *objectives* are those communication effects targeted *in a particular campaign,* with the *response objective specified.*

### 1. CATEGORY NEED

#### Category Need Defined

Category need refers to the buyer's acceptance that the category (a product or service) is necessary to remove or satisfy a perceived discrepancy between the current motivational state and the desired motivational state. Category need therefore requires a *perceived connection*—which can be established by the advertiser—between the product or service and a buyer motivation.

**Buyer Motivation.** Prospective buyers are activated to buy products or services when the buyer is experiencing any one of eight basic purchase motivations or motives. As these purchase motives are also possible motives to which *brands* can be connected (via the brand attitude communication effect), we will defer detailed consideration of them until the section on brand attitude. The eight motives, briefly, are problem removal, problem avoidance, incomplete satisfaction, mixed approach-avoidance, and normal depletion (all negatively originated motives for action); and sensory gratification, intellectual stimulation or mastery, and social approval (all positively originated motives for action). A category need occurs when one of these motives is aroused *and* the general product or service category is accepted by the buyer as a way of meeting the motive.

**Primary Demand.** By successfully establishing an accepted connection (a belief) between the product or service category and a relevant motivation, the advertiser can stimulate *primary demand,* that is, demand for the product or service category as a whole. Category need is the communication effect that causes primary demand. But note that category need—with its marketplace result, primary demand—applies to *all brands* in the category. To stimulate secondary or selective demand, the advertiser must also influence the brand-level communication effects:

brand awareness, brand attitude, and brand purchase intention.

**What is the Category?** The "category" that forms the category need is most likely to be defined or expressed by the buyer as the "basic" level of a product or service.[3] The basic level is the level that a child usually acquires first in learning the name of a group or set of objects; it's also the level at which adults spontaneously name objects. Thus, for example, "computers," "airlines," and "soda" would be basic categories.[4] These basic categories are *superordinated* by rarely referred-to, more general categories, such as, in the examples we just gave, "electronics," "modes of travel," and "beverages." In the downward direction, the basic category can be *subordinated* into more specific categories as the buyer learns more about the basic category (assisted often by advertising's "educational" function)—such as, in the above examples, "PCs," "jumbo jets," and "colas." It is virtually impossible for the buyer to prevent the basic category from emerging mentally when the category need arises. For example, even though you may be looking for a subordinate type of drink such as a diet cola, it is almost impossible to prevent all types of soft drinks (members of the *basic* category, soft drinks) from coming to mind.[5] You are almost certain to recall Coke in addition to Diet Coke, for instance. However, it is most unlikely that you will recall other types of beverages in the superordinate category, such as beer or coffee.

The "category" in category need is therefore the *basic* category—the spontaneous naming level for the product or service category when it's needed. You should also see how there can be a *category* purchase motive, at the basic level (for example, the thirst problem-removal need for a soda) and a *brand* purchase motive, at the subordinate level (for example, the fattening problem-avoidance need for a diet cola, which will narrow the buyer's choice to Diet Coke, Diet Pepsi, and other diet cola brands). But more on this later.

### Managerial Options with Regard to Category Need

Category need has to be present at full strength before purchase of a brand within that category can occur. That is, the prospect has to be "in the market" for that category of product or service. However, category need is *not always* a communication *objective.*

| TABLE 5.2 | |
|---|---|
| **MANAGERIAL OPTIONS WITH REGARD TO CATEGORY NEED AS A COMMUNICATION OBJECTIVE** | |
| **Buyer state** | **Communication objective** |
| 1. Category need already present | Category need can be *omitted* as an objective of the advertising or promotion. |
| 2. Latent category need | Category need has only to be *mentioned* to *remind* the buyer of a previously established need. |
| 3. No or weak category need | Category need must be *"sold"* using *category* communication effects. |

There are three options for the manager (Table 5.2): to omit category need—that is, to assume that it is already present, that *this* mental bin is full; to remind the buyer of category need; or to "sell" category need.

**Omit Category Need.** With frequently purchased products or services—and a category user (BL, FBS, OBS, or OBL) target audience—category need is *not* a communication objective and can be *omitted.* Category need can be assumed to be present for regular buyers of the category and does not have to be addressed in advertising communications or promotion.

Therefore, an ad, adlike event, or promotion offer for any brand of a *frequently* purchased product—providing that the ad, adlike event, or promotion offer is aimed at category users (that is, *not* the NCUs)—can assume category need to be present and can therefore omit this communication effect from its set of communication objectives. Retail newspaper ads by supermarkets and drugstores are a good example. They *assume* that category need is present and simply promote various brands to current category users.

Also, an advertising, adlike campaign, or promotion offer for an *infrequently* purchased product can omit category need *if* the manager is sure that the prospect already *has* the category need *when exposure* to the ad, adlike event, or promotion offer *occurs.* Yellow Pages or directory ads are a good example of this. Although the product or service—truck rental or emergency plumbing, for instance—is purchased infrequently, the prospect who is looking up directory ads can be assumed to have the category need.

**Remind Buyer of Category Need.** A second option, in which category need *is* an objective, is to remind the prospective buyer of a latent or forgotten (but previously established) category need.

The reminder option applies mostly to product categories that are *infrequently purchased,* like pain remedies. The classic Alka-Seltzer ad campaign, "Will it be there when you need it," is a perfect example of reminding prospective buyers of the category need. Another example, this time from the *service* sector, would be dental checkups. Most people forget to have their teeth checked regularly enough—at least in the opinion of dentists! Ads for dental services typically remind customers that frequent checkups are necessary (the category need) and then suggest that the advertiser's *particular* dental service is an appropriate choice (thereby utilizing brand-level communication effects). At the level of category need for a dental *product,* the "replacement stripe" in some brands of toothbrushes shows how product packaging or design can be used to communicate a category need reminder.

The reminder option also applies to one-time-purchase products that are *infrequently* used. Ogilvy & Mather's well-known campaign theme for the American Express Card, "Don't leave home without it," is a good example of the reminder objective for category need for infrequent users.

Category need *reminder* campaigns usually can be achieved without detailed advertising content having to be devoted to category need. This is because the prospect has already been sold on the category. The purpose is merely to *reestablish* a previously learned connection between the product or service category and the original purchase motivation for that category. More specifically, with a category need reminder objective, the advertiser wants the buyer to recognize or recall the category need. Thus, the communication content in category need reminder campaigns is directed primarily toward *category awareness* (actually, reawareness), which should also have the automatic effect of reminding the prospective buyer of the favorable category attitude that he or she can be assumed to have. With a successful reminder, category purchase intention can be expected to follow.

**"Sell" Category Need.** When the category need is not yet established in the prospective buyer's mind—as is the case with new category users—the advertising communications campaign, often with promotional support, has to "sell" the category need.

Therefore, *selling* category need is a communication objective for all *new products* and also for *established products aimed at new users of the category* (NCUs). If the target audience has not bought within the category before, advertising communications or promotion must include selling the category need as a communication objective.

"Selling the category need" is a special case because *two levels or sets of communication effects* are required—one set for the category and a second set for the brand. Selling the category need requires creating, in the prospective buyer's mind, *category communication effects.*[6] Thus, when selling the category need, it is meaningful to speak of category awareness, category attitude, and category purchase intention: for these category-level communication effects must be addressed *in addition to* brand-level communication effects. An example would be home fax machines. At the time of this writing, only about 2 percent of U.S. homes had home fax machines. However, by the year 2000, household penetration of home fax machines is expected to be about 50 percent.[7] Marketers of fax machines intended for home use will, in their advertising, first have to "sell" the category need for home fax machines, and then sell the brand. The "educational" task of advertising should be made easier by considerable word-of-mouth communication as early adopters of home fax machines influence their acquaintances to buy them.

There are also situations in which a marketer (government or social marketers in particular) would want to *unsell* a category need. An example is water conservation. A majority of American households report that they are now more likely to adjust the water level of their washing machines to the size of the load, take quicker showers, wash their cars less often, and turn off the faucet while shaving or brushing their teeth.[8] Many public health campaigns, too, are aimed at unselling the category need, such as the need to smoke. Of course, unselling one category need is usually accompanied by the selling of a *complementary* category need, such as selling the broad category need for a healthy lifestyle.

Having decided whether category need has to be addressed in the campaign, and choosing from one of the three options for addressing it—omit it, remind the buyer of it, or sell it (of which the latter two are possible communication *objectives*)—the manager must next decide how to communicate about the *brand.* The remaining four communication effects are all at the brand level.

## 2. BRAND AWARENESS

### Brand Awareness Defined

Brand awareness is defined as the buyer's ability to identify (recognize or recall) the brand, within the category, in sufficient detail to make a purchase. (In decision participants' roles *other than* the purchaser role, this definition is easily adapted to refer to the ability to identify the brand in sufficient detail to propose, recommend, choose, or use the brand, respectively.)

There is a tendency in marketing and advertising research to equate brand awareness with "brand name recall." However, as the definition states, brand awareness may be achieved by brand *recognition* rather than brand name recall. When a package (for example, Healthy Choice) is recognized in a supermarket, or a logo (for example, Master Card) is recognized when shopping or traveling, brand awareness has been achieved, not through recall, but rather through *recognition.*

The "sufficient detail" aspect of our definition also should alert the manager to possibilities *other than* identification of the brand name, awareness of which may not be necessary. For a child, or even for an adult, brand awareness may consist of a simple visual response to an identifying feature such as package color (for example, "the green one" for Healthy Choice) or a gross verbal response to an even more general identifying feature such as location (for example, "the restaurant on the corner"). Awareness of these identifying features enables brand choice to proceed even though no brand name is in the brand awareness response.

Brand awareness as a *communication objective* depends, therefore, on how the purchase decision is "entered into." What the buyer has to be aware of depends on whether the purchase decision requires brand recognition or brand recall. (The decision type can best be found by using a behavioral sequence model, as explained in Chapter 4, and note that this could be a usage decision if the campaign is designed to stimulate use of the product or service.) The distinction between brand recognition and brand recall is very, very important for the brand's advertising communications strategy, and provides the two main options for brand awareness as a communication objective.

Before we summarize these options, we must discuss several theoretical considerations that are important for managers with regard to brand awareness as a communication objective: the *universality* of brand awareness as a communication objective; its role as a necessary *precursor* to brand attitude; further understanding of the *distinction* between brand recognition and brand recall; and the realization that brand awareness is an *association* between the brand's identifying feature such as its logo or name and category need.

### Brand Awareness Is a Universal Communication Objective

We saw that the first communication effect, category need, is an *optional* communication objective in that it can be omitted if the target audience already has the category need at full strength. However, the second communication effect, brand awareness, is *not* optional. Brand awareness (either brand recognition or brand recall) must be regarded as a *universal* communication objective—that is, as a communication objective for *all* campaigns.

Whereas it might be argued that some target audiences are so fully aware of the brand that brand awareness could be omitted as a communication objective, this is not so, for two reasons. In the first place, it is impossible and indeed illegal to have an "unbranded" ad or promotion offer (although it's sometimes hard to tell who the advertiser is with some forms of "silent" sponsorship and with "advertorials"). So as long as you're showing or mentioning the brand, you may as well do it in a way that maintains brand awareness. A second and crucial reason is the relative vulnerability of brand awareness. A brand can all too easily slip out of the buyer's "recall set" or "recognition set" of brands if it is not given sufficient exposure. Therefore, it is best to regard brand awareness as a universal communication objective.[9]

### Brand Awareness Is a Necessary Precursor to Brand Attitude

At the product category level, a person won't buy unless he or she has the category need. At the brand level, a person *cannot* buy unless he or she is first made aware of the brand. For instance, almost 40 percent of the population of mainland China has never seen and thus could not recognize the Coca-Cola

(Coke) logo.[10] Presumably, they would walk right by Coke if they saw it in the store!

Brand awareness takes precedence over the remaining brand-level communication effects. This means that the *universal* communication objective of brand awareness takes precedence over the *other universal* communication objective, brand attitude (in fact, brand attitude is *inoperable* without prior brand awareness).[11] Brand awareness makes the brand a *candidate* for purchase. Indeed, brand choice (in the target audience action step) can be increased or decreased by manipulating brand awareness *without* changing brand attitude.[12] For instance, as shown in Table 5.3, two brands of imported beer, such as Heineken and Beck's, may be equally well regarded in an attitudinal sense by the target audience—but relative choice of the two brands will differ based on which brand has the higher brand awareness. In a brand recall situation, such as in a restaurant, the brand awareness difference is likely to favor the more heavily advertised Heineken brand, with consequently a greater proportion of choices going to this brand. Beer drinkers simply don't remember Beck's as often, even though they may like it as much as Heineken, so Beck's gets fewer purchases.

Consistent with brand awareness precedence, a number of theorists have proposed that brand awareness carries its own equity.[13] One of the characteristics of a "strong" brand is that it is noticed quickly in brand recognition situations and recalled quickly (usually first) in brand recall situations. Given its necessary precursor status, it is meaningful to speak of "brand awareness equity," as distinct from equity based on brand *attitude* (and, specifically, attitudinal value and uniqueness equities as introduced in Chapter 2).

## The Distinction Between Brand Recognition and Brand Recall

The distinction in brand awareness objectives between brand recognition and brand recall arises because there are two main types of choice situations in buyer behavior:[14]

- *At* the point of purchase—requiring brand *recognition*
- *Prior to* the point of purchase—requiring brand *recall*

The manager must not assume that because the brand has achieved brand recognition by the prospective buyer it will also have achieved brand recall; neither can it be assumed that because the brand is recalled it can also be recognized. For the typical individual buyer, it is estimated that the correlation between brands recognized and brands recalled in a given product or service category will be only about .5; typically, the buyer will be able to recognize many brands but recall only a small number.[15] It is also very possible to recall a brand, especially from a radio commercial, but not be able to visually recognize it when you go to buy it.

Brand *recognition*–based choice occurs in many consumer and some industrial purchase situations. Examples would include shopping at the supermarkets without a complete list of product categories and brands that you intend to purchase (most shoppers take only a partial list or no list at all); looking through company names in the *Yellow Pages;* noticing the advertiser's name in a *direct response* ad; or noticing the package of a product at home or in the office, which may stimulate usage.

Brand *recall*–based choice occurs in many consumer service and industrial purchase situations. Examples would include thinking about which shopping malls or stores to visit when planning a shopping trip; thinking of several airlines to call for a price quotation prior to flying to New York; or an industrial manager thinking of which suppliers to call for a quotation.[16]

Additionally, there are some "sequential awareness" choice situations whereby the brand must first be recalled and *then* recognized. An example would be recalling that you want to try that new type of "heart-healthy" frozen meal that you've heard about, Healthy Choice, and then having to recognize the package in the supermarket freezer. Because prior brand recall (plus a favorable attitude) leads to a "ded-

### TABLE 5.3

**BRAND CHOICE CAN BE INFLUENCED BY BRAND AWARENESS WITHOUT CHANGING BRAND ATTITUDE**

(*Hypothetical example. Brand awareness and brand attitude measured on 0 → 1.0 scales.*)

|          | Brand awareness | Brand attitude | Probability of brand being chosen |
|----------|-----------------|----------------|-----------------------------------|
| Heineken | .7              | .8             | .56                               |
| Beck's   | .2              | .8             | .16                               |

icated search" for the brand, we call this situation by the rather long name of *brand recall–boosted brand recognition.*

Research for the behavioral sequence model for the brand (see Chapter 4) should tell you which type of choice situation your brand is most likely to encounter for a particular target audience.

## Brand Awareness Associates the Brand with the Category Need

Brand recognition and brand recall—as the definition of brand awareness indicates—both require a learned association in the buyer's mind with *category need, that is, with the first, category-level communication effect.* This is best shown with the aid of a diagram (Figure 5.2).

- In the case of *brand recognition*—paths 1a and 1b—either the buyer has the category need in mind but has only a category purchase intention and must now recognize a brand (path 1a) *or* the brand is noticed first and then the buyer asks himself or herself whether he or she has a need for the category at present (path 1b). The sequence is either CN → CPI → BRGN, or BRGN → CN. *Examples:* most fmcg choices in supermarkets (1a); or when considering an ad for space-efficient air-travel luggage in a business magazine (1b).
- In the case of *brand recall*—path 2—the category need occurs first and then the brands are recalled in

response to it. The sequence is CN → BRCL. *Examples:* retail stores (when deciding from home or office which ones to visit for a particular product or service category); consultancy firms, if your organization is about to hire one.
- Also shown is *brand recall–boosted brand recognition*—path 3—where the category need occurs first, followed by brand recall, and then brand recognition. The sequence is CN → BRCL → BRGN. *Examples:* a restaurant whose name you recall but whose exact location you may have to recognize when driving to it; a new cologne that you want to try but have to find in a department or drugstore.

These three paths (or four if you count brand recognition as two paths, though recognition is the key outcome) correspond with the managerial options for brand awareness as a communication objective, reviewed next.

## Managerial Options with Regard to Brand Awareness

Technically speaking, the objective for the brand awareness communication effect in any advertising communications or promotion campaign would be to create, increase, or maintain brand awareness—depending on the initial state of brand awareness in the prospect's mind. Therefore, technically speaking, brand recognition and brand recall could be regarded as two distinct "strategies" for achieving the brand awareness "objective." However, because we can never omit brand awareness, and because a brand can never have too much brand awareness, *and* because brand recognition and brand recall are not really managerial alternatives but rather are dictated by the *buyer's* decision process, it is better to conceptualize brand recognition and brand recall not as the alternative strategies but rather as the *objectives themselves.* The understanding is that each brand awareness communication effect, brand recognition or brand recall, implies an *increase or at least maintenance* when it is nominated as an objective.

Always, the manager should be trying to maximize or, for extreme brand loyals, maintain, brand recognition, brand recall, or—under conditions specified below—*both* brand recall and brand recognition. The brand awareness objective is vitally important to get right because its occurrence initiates choice of the brand.

**FIGURE 5.2**

A schematic representation of the relationship of brand awareness to category need—showing brand recognition (path 1), brand recall (path 2), and brand recall–boosted brand recognition (path 3).

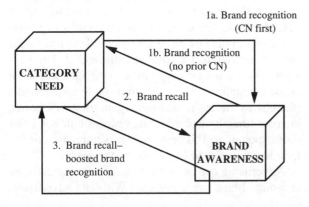

**Brand Recognition.** When buyers choose the brand *at* the point of purchase, advertisements and promotional material should ensure that the buyer will be able to *recognize* the brand.

The purest case of brand recognition occurs with so-called impulse purchases. With an impulse purchase, there is no thought of buying the brand, nor even the product category, before the brand is encountered. (This is path 1*b* in Figure 5.2.) Displays near the checkout counter for candy, chewing gum, magazines, and so forth are obvious examples of marketers attempting to stimulate impulse purchases via brand recognition. But not so obvious is the incidence of brand recognition for products not normally thought of as impulse purchases. For supermarket products, as Table 5.4 indicates, an amazingly high *47 percent* of *all* supermarket (fmcg) brand choices are actually made this way—that is, neither the category nor the brand was intended to be bought. This doesn't mean that the buyer bought something he or she didn't want; rather, we must assume in these cases that the brand display reminded shoppers of category need or sold category need at the point of purchase.[17]

We note also that most *direct response* offers follow the above brand recognition sequence in that the buyer looks at the brand first and then considers whether or not the category is needed.

The other decision sequence in which brand recognition is the single objective is where the buyer experiences the category need first, but this leads only to a *category* purchase intention—with the brand itself undecided. (This is path 1*a* in Figure 5.2.) For supermarket products, as also shown in Table 5.4, the incidence of choices via brand recognition at the point of purchase, following only a general intention to purchase in the *category,* is about 15 percent. Notice that for the foregoing impulse sequence and for this "category decided but brand undecided" sequence, the brand awareness *objective* is the same: brand recognition.

Brand recognition can be a difficult task in today's cluttered point-of-purchase displays. Figure 5.3 shows an example for a supermarket display for breakfast cereals. Look at the clutter! Observational studies[18] indicate that, on average, the buyer takes only *9.4 seconds* from first sighting the category display in the supermarket through to putting the chosen brand in the supermarket cart and moving on—which means that only about *5 or 6 seconds* are used to visually scan the category display. It is therefore vitally important that the brand be able to achieve brand recognition when choices are made at the point of purchase.

In the great majority of cases, brand recognition is a *visual* process, requiring only "iconic rote learning" if the brand's category is evident, but also verbal "paired-associates" learning if the category need is not evident.[19] Accordingly, brand recognition requires showing the product package or service logo in the advertising, in the category context, and (for a new brand especially) using exact color. Close-ups of the package or logo in TV commercials, and also in magazine ads, are the best type of advertising content for brand recognition. These ads must be in visual media (thereby excluding radio) and, again for a new brand, in color (thereby excluding newpapers unless a color insert such as an FSI or pamphlet is purchased or unless the ad is placed in a color newspaper).

Advertising can be instrumental in dramatically increasing brand recognition. Without advertising,

---

**TABLE 5.4**

**INCIDENCE OF POINT-OF-PURCHASE BRAND CHOICES FOR SUPERMARKET PRODUCTS**

| Type of choice | Percentage incidence |
| --- | --- |
| OVERALL RESULTS | |
| Specifically planned brand choice | 35 |
| Point-of-purchase brand choice | 65 |
| Total | 100 |
| TYPES OF POINT-OF-PURCHASE BRAND CHOICES | |
| Generally planned (category but not brand) | 15 |
| Substitute (switched from intended brand) | 3 |
| Impulse (neither category nor brand intended) | 47 |
| Total | 65 |
| SPECIFIC PRODUCTS: POINT-OF-PURCHASE BRAND CHOICE | |
| Snack foods | 78 |
| Cosmetics | 69 |
| Soft drinks | 67 |
| Drugs/medicines (nonprescription) | 49 |
| Cigarettes | 33 |
| Alcoholic beverages | 20 |
| Prescription drugs | 0 |

*Source:* POPAI/DuPont studies (see note 17), by permission.

cally in the buyer's mind, print media are a reasonable alternative choice. In this one situation, the brand recognition response is verbal, whereas in the great majority of cases the brand recognition response is visual.

**Brand Recall.** When the buyer must think of one or more brands to choose from *prior* to the point of purchase, having experienced only the category need, the appropriate communication objective is brand *recall*. Here, the category need *must* occur first, and there is a one-step link to brand recall (see path 2 in Figure 5.2).

For a particular brand, brand recall can be a very difficult communication objective to attain (and this refers not only to increasing but also to *maintaining* brand recall). This is because a *number* of brands are likely to come to mind in response to the category need. For example, Figure 5.4 shows *one student's* brand recall of soft drinks, illustrating the number of brands the student could recall in a time period of 2 minutes.[21] Suppose you were the advertiser of Diet Coke. In this case, Diet Coke was not recalled at all. Suppose you were the advertiser of Sprite. In this case, the consumer took more than a minute to recall Sprite—which would usually be far too long a time during a real decision. Thus, a brand may or may not

**FIGURE 5.3**
Typical supermarket display of breakfast cereals (see text discussion of brand recognition). Photo courtesy of Frank Tapia.

Heeler[20] estimates that the level of brand recognition that a new brand of fmcg product will achieve over a 3-month period *by distribution alone* is about 18 percent. With the typical level of introductory advertising for a new product, however, brand recognition can be increased to about 60 percent.

*Auditory Brand-Name Recognition.* A slightly different case—readily detectable from the buyer's behavioral sequence model for the brand—is brand *name* recognition when the brand name is *heard*. For instance, when you ask a waiter in a restaurant "What beers (brands) do you have?" (path 1a in Figure 5.2, because you have the category need), you have to *recognize* one of the spoken brand *names* the waiter tells you. Here we are dealing with *auditory recognition*. For auditory recognition, auditory media (TV or radio) are best; although, because names when read in print ads are usually "echoed" acousti-

**FIGURE 5.4**
Brand recall of soft drinks by one student in response to the category-need cue "carbonated beverages." (● = purchased in past year; ○ = not purchased in past year.) *Source:* Alba, Hutchinson, and Lynch, 1991, Figure 1.2; see note 15.

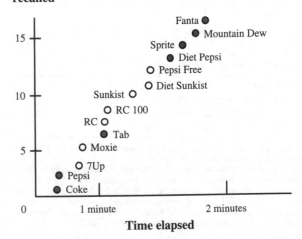

be included in the prospective buyer's "brand recall set," let alone be among the first one or two to come to mind. To give a business example, a dispatch manager thinking of which courier service to use (the category need) is likely to recall just three or four alternatives—and the advertiser's service may or may not be one of them.

Brand recall is almost always a *verbal* process, requiring verbal name recall of the brand in response to the verbal cue (occurring mentally or "subvocally") of the category need. Brand recall requires "paired-associates" learning in which, in ads and promotions, the category need *is paired with* the advertiser's brand name. The key advertising tactic for brand recall, therefore, is not simply to repeat the brand name—but rather *to repeat the association* between the category need and the brand name. For brand recall, this is where many advertising slogans or jingles fall down. They mention the brand name but do not link it to the category need. Table 5.5 provides some examples. It should be noted that the examples of incorrect brand recall may nevertheless be correct for brand benefit positioning, as explained in the next chapter. Here we are focusing solely on their suitability for generating brand recall.

---

**TABLE 5.5**

**ADVERTISING SLOGANS THAT CORRECTLY OR INCORRECTLY LINK THE BRAND NAME (BN) TO THE CATEGORY NEED (CN)**

**Correct CN–BN slogans[a]**

- "The most famous piano [CN] is Steinway [BN]."
- "The American Express Card [BN]. Don't leave home without it [CN]."
- "You deserve a break today [CN] . . . at McDonald's [BN] . . ."
- "Taster's Choice [BN] Coffee [CN]."

**Incorrect slogans for brand recall[b]**

- "Avis. We try harder."
- "Like a good neighbor, State Farm is there."
- "GE. We bring good things to life."
- "Just for the taste of it, Diet Coke."

[a] The better ones probably are those that place the category need first and the brand name last, that is CN → BN.
[b] All of these slogans are, however, correct for another essential positioning link: brand → benefit (see Chapter 6). They assume that the buyer will *automatically supply* the category need, to form the first positioning link, between CN and BN, to create brand awareness. However, this is not always a safe assumption. It may be for Avis and Diet Coke, two highly recalled brands, but not, we suspect, for State Farm or GE.

Brand recall, by associating the category need with the brand name, can be achieved in all media of advertising communications and promotion. This is because brand recall is essentially a verbal phenomenon and all media have the capacity to transmit words (either heard or read). However, we will see in Chapter 15 that some media are more suitable than others for brand recall in that they can deliver a higher frequency of exposure. Frequent repetition of the category need–brand name *association* is what is needed to generate brand recall.

**Brand Recall–Boosted Brand Recognition.** The third option for brand awareness as a communication objective is to increase *both* brand recall and brand recognition. This option is an alternative to the first option for *brand recognition* situations. Here, instead of hoping that the buyer will happen to *notice* and recognize the brand at the point of purchase, the object is to encourage the buyer to *recall* the brand name first, then *look for* and recognize the brand at the point of purchase.

However, this "double" brand-awareness objective is the *most difficult* to attain. It is also the *costliest,* because it requires extra communication content in ads or promotion offers to achieve *both* brand awareness objectives. The manager should therefore be sure that the dual objective is necessary or advisable for the brand before choosing it.

Brand recall–boosted brand recognition is, despite its difficulty and cost, an increasingly attractive option for brands that require recognition from among multiple brands displayed at the point of purchase. It's attractive because, if it can be achieved, prior recall is likely to increase the incidence of brand recognition at the point of purchase above that attained by a pure recognition strategy (hence the "boost").[22] It is increasingly attractive because today's supermarkets (and many other types of stores) are characterized by extremely large and cluttered brand displays in most product categories. (See Figure 5.3 for an example of just one product category. Try, for instance, to locate Kellogg's Complete.) The typical large supermarket now stocks 18,000 items.[23] If we make the reasonable assumption that the typical supermarket shopper is going to choose from 60 product categories in the 45 minutes that he or she averages in the store on the major weekly or biweekly shopping trip, then a "pure recognition" procedure, if all 18,000 items were looked at, would require the shopper to scan the displays at the rate of 6.7 items per second! This is physically impractical (even at 1 item per second, it would take five hours rather than 45 minutes to complete each shopping trip). To escape from this task, it is likely that, in many product categories, shoppers use a *guided search* based on brand loyalty, or what Sutherland and Davies describe as "simple locating behavior."[24] Simple locating behavior requires brand recall first, in response to the category need, followed by brand recognition (path 3 in Figure 5.2).

The overall incidence of simple locating behavior for supermarket products is about *35 percent,* as shown previously in Table 5.4. By subtraction from the percentages in the bottom section of that table, alcoholic beverages and cigarettes show the highest incidence of simple locating behavior, with 80 percent and 67 percent of shoppers, respectively, having a particular brand in mind before entering the store. At the other extreme, only 22 percent of snack-food buyers buy brands this way. Of course, it is possible that *more than* 35 percent of supermarket brand choices are *intended* to be made by simple locating behavior but that some of these intended choices get derailed at the point of purchase by, for instance, failure to recognize the brand or the store's being temporarily out of stock of it, or—more often—by promotional price discounts offered on acceptance *competing* brands. However, the POPAI/DuPont study that provides the basis for Table 5.4 puts the incidence of derailing at only 3 percent.

*Retailers* in multistore *shopping malls* are another type of marketer who would benefit from brand recall–boosted brand recognition. For instance, the new Levi Strauss clothing stores would benefit from having shoppers recall that there are now specialized Levi's stores and then looking for one in the mall.

As we said in the outset of our discussion of this option, brand recall–boosted brand recognition is a difficult brand awareness objective to achieve in advertising. This difficulty is due to the fact that *two* sets of executional tactics have to be included in the ad, namely, brand recall tactics and brand recognition tactics. The two sets of tactics can be time-consuming to execute in a broadcast ad or space-consuming to execute in a print ad, leaving less time or space for the *attitudinal* message about the brand. It is best to add time or space for the attitudinal message in this case—that is, use a longer ad—and encourage a very strong brand *attitude*. An advertisement that generates

a highly favorable brand attitude will virtually force the prospective buyer to make a mental note of the brand name (and thus rehearse it for subsequent recall) or perhaps even to write it down (thus aiding in its recognition).[25] In the ideal case, an advertisement that creates a highly favorable brand attitude acts very much like a direct response ad, such that awareness is pushed to the "top of the mind" until the brand is located and bought.

The "double" brand awareness objective is worth pursuing in two specific situations (both assuming a multiple-brand display at the point of purchase):

- For a new brand or for an established brand aimed at a *new trier* target audience (usually NCUs or OBSs), where the advertiser would like to force a deliberate choice. Longer or larger ads are recommended for this purpose.
- For a new or established brand where an *entrenched competing brand* has its own loyal buyers (OBLs) and we wish to "break them out" of simple locating behavior for *that* brand and divert them to *our* brand.

**Summary of Brand Awareness Objectives.** A summary of the three options for brand awareness as a communication objective, together with the conditions in which they should be used, is provided in Table 5.6. The conditions can be identified quite readily from the behavioral sequence model during research conducted in developing the advertising strategy.

Brand awareness is strictly a rote-learned connection between the brand and the category need. You don't have to be motivated to be *aware* of a brand, but you do have to be motivated to *buy* it. This is where

---

**TABLE 5.6**

**MANAGERIAL OPTIONS WITH REGARD TO BRAND AWARENESS AS A COMMUNICATION OBJECTIVE**

(*Note that an "increase" objective is assumed for each option.*)

| Brand choice made | Communication objective |
|---|---|
| 1. *At* point of purchase | Brand *recognition* |
| 2. *Prior* to purchase | Brand *recall* |
| 3. *Intended* brand choice made prior to purchase but *then* brand must be identified at point of purchase | *Both* brand recall and brand recognition (brand recall–boosted brand recognition) |

brand attitude, the next communication effect, comes in.

## 3. BRAND ATTITUDE

### Brand Attitude Defined

Brand attitude is defined as the buyer's evaluation of the brand with respect to its perceived ability to meet a currently relevant motivation. The buyer's brand attitude can be considerably complex, consisting of a mental structure with a number of components, which we will describe in this section.

### Brand Attitude Is the Second Universal Communication Objective

Like brand awareness, which must precede it, brand attitude is a universal communication objective. Whereas some advertising researchers have pointed to successful cases of apparently "pure brand awareness" advertising, closer analysis suggests that this type of advertising works only because one of the following two processes is operating: buyers infer *from* the awareness advertising that the brand must be "popular," "safe," or "reputable"—that is, they form a favorable attitude; or else the awareness advertising elicits a *previously* well-learned attitude in the buyer's mind.[26] Repetitive presentation of a product's brand name or package *alone,* without an attitudinal message, will increase brand awareness but will *not* increase brand attitude.[27] Therefore, it is best to assume that a favorable brand attitude (or a relatively favorable one, if all the choice options are not that attractive but the buyer must purchase anyway) is *always* an objective and is necessary for purchase.

In most choice situations, too, potential buyers become aware of *more than one brand* in a given product category. Consequently, they must choose a particular brand based on brand attitude. On average, about *40 percent*[28] of brands of which the buyer is aware will be judged acceptable, but usually the buyer must choose just one on a particular purchase occasion.

### Components of Brand Attitude

Brand attitude is the most complex of the five communication effects—and it must be fully understood. All advertising communications have to address brand attitude, usually directly, or else indirectly by reminder. Some promotions, especially customer franchise-building promotions, also address brand attitude, although price promotions more often address short-term brand purchase intention.

Brand attitude comprises four main components, the second of which has two subcomponents: (1) the superbelief, which *is* the attitude; (2) specific benefit beliefs, each with its own emotional or evaluative weight; (3) possible freestanding emotions, each weighted, that also contribute to the superbelief about the brand's ability to meet the purchase or usage motive; and (4) a "choice rule," by which the buyer combines the benefit beliefs and emotions to form the superbelief. Figure 5.5 shows these various components of brand attitude. They are explained under the next four numbered headings.

**(1) The Superbelief that Connects the Brand (in the Buyer's Mind) to a Purchase or Usage Motive.**

This superbelief—or overall summary judgment—*is* the brand attitude. When a brand attitude is created in the buyer's mind, the superbelief connects the brand to a purchase or usage motive. There are eight fundamental motives for purchase or usage. Therefore, it is possible for a buyer to hold up to eight separate superbeliefs (attitudes) toward the *one* brand. For instance, an organizational buyer may judge IBM computers as a "safe" choice for the company (an example of the problem avoidance motive) but also separately judge IBM computers as a poor choice for children's recreational use (an example of the sensory gratification motive if children's games are the major use at home). The eight motives are discussed shortly. It is important to realize, however, that the buyer usu-

**FIGURE 5.5**

The main components of brand attitude. The typical choice rule (component 4, not shown in this diagram) is simple summation of components 2 and 3—though other choice rules are also possible.

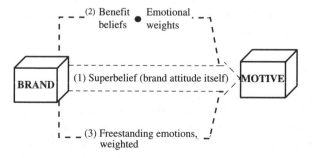

ally will have only one purchase or usage occasion in mind at a particular time. Accordingly, only one brand attitude will be relevant for a given purchase or use (at which a particular advertising communications or promotion campaign is targeted). So although there are eight potential attitudes, in most cases, only one is the brand attitude communication objective.

The eight motives (for purchase or using a brand) are listed in Table 5.7.[29] As the table indicates, buyer's motives may be negatively originated (called "informational" motivations) or positively originated (called "transformational" motivations). We will explain the negatively originated motives first, followed by the positively originated ones.

*Negatively Originated (Informational) Motives.* The negatively originated motives are actually the most prevalent energizers of buyer behavior. Think of yourself as a prospective buyer. For a given product category or category need, if you are in a typical state of "equilibrium" then you need not buy anything—you are not motivated. At some time, however, the product you are using now will break down, or you will become dissatisfied with it, or you'll be satisfied but simply run out of stock. Any of these events will put you into a negative mental state that you will seek to "relieve" by purchasing a new or replacement product. This is known in behavioral learning theory terms as "drive reduction due to negative reinforcement." Notice that the effect was to first *increase* your drive or motivation level, thus energizing you to investigate or search for the product. Drive or motivation is then reduced upon purchase of (and satisfactory experience with) the product (the chosen brand).

As shown in the table, there are five negatively originated purchase and usage motives: problem re-moval, problem avoidance, incomplete satisfaction, mixed approach-avoidance, and normal depletion. These are called "informational" motives because the buyer seeks information to reduce the negative state. They can also be called "relief" motives because they work by relieving the negative state.

*Positively Originated (Transformational) Motives.* The second set of motives listed in the table are the positively originated motives. These are relevant when you want to rise above equilibrium and "reward" yourself, as we all do from time to time, by purchasing a particular product or brand that promises a reward. With each of the positively originated motives, a positive stimulus (or reward) is promised, rather than an aversive stimulus (or punishment) being removed or reduced as in the negative motivations. The process with positively originated motivation is known as "drive increase through positive reinforcement" (see Figure 5.6). Drive or motivation increase is necessary to energize investigation of or search for the product. Eventually there *will* be drive reduction—for instance, you can eat only so many candy bars in succession!—but the essential motivating mechanism is a drive *increase* through the promise of a reward.

As shown in the table, there are three positively originated purchase and usage motives: sensory gratification, intellectual stimulation or mastery, and social approval.[30] These are called "transformational" motives because the buyer seeks to be positively transformed, in either a sensory, intellectual, or social sense. They can also be called "reward" motives because the transformation is a rewarding state.

Purchase of the *same product* can be based on a negatively originated motive for some people and on a positively originated motive for others. For instance, an advertiser of dress clothes (formal wear) would have to find out, through research, whether the potential customer is negatively motivated or positively motivated. Widrick[31] found that one in four customers does *not* like the process of shopping for dress clothes and does so under considerable discomfort (thus operating on negative reinforcement). On the other hand, three in four *do* generally enjoy the process (thus operating on positive reinforcement). For the advertiser, the distinction between negatively originated and positively originated motivations is not just theoretically important but is of real practical importance.[32] For instance, in his study, Widrick found that

---

**TABLE 5.7**

**THE EIGHT FUNDAMENTAL PURCHASE AND USAGE MOTIVES**

| Negatively originated (informational) motives | Positively originated (transformational) motives |
|---|---|
| 1. Problem removal | 6. Sensory gratification |
| 2. Problem avoidance | 7. Intellectual stimulation or mastery |
| 3. Incomplete satisfaction | 8. Social approval |
| 4. Mixed approach-avoidance | |
| 5. Normal depletion | |

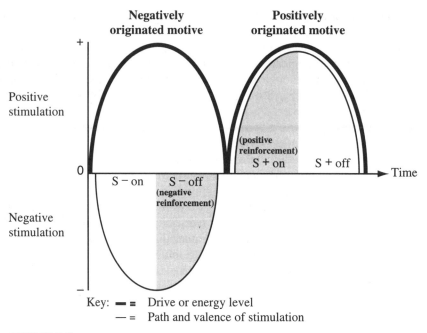

**FIGURE 5.6**

How negatively and positively originated motives *both* energize behavior (leading to negative and positive reinforcement, respectively).

negatively motivated purchasers of dress clothes spent a much shorter time shopping, traveled less distance to the store, and had a much shorter purchase horizon (one week for negatively motivated customers versus several months for positively motivated customers). For this highly involving product, two purchaser segments are clearly present, and the advertising communications to each segment should be different.

That purchase or usage motives for the same product may differ across buyer segments bears a further example. Take a simple product such as toilet paper. Some people want strength in toilet paper (problem avoidance). Others want softness (sensory gratification or, if hemorrhoidal, problem avoidance again). But in Australia by the early 1990s, one-third of all households were buying unbleached toilet paper, not for softness or strength, but because of ecological concern (problem avoidance) or because it was trendy (social approval)—even though the unbleached product is frequently priced higher than the regular version!

We will meet the eight purchase and usage motives again when we examine brand positioning in Chapter 6 and brand attitude executional tactics in Chapters 8

and 9—where they will be linked with "informational" and "transformational" advertising.

**(2) Specific Benefit Beliefs and Emotional Weights.** The second component of brand attitude (refer to Figure 5.5) is—usually—one or more beliefs about the *specific benefits* the brand offers *in support of* the overall superbelief. For instance, in support of the superbelief that IBM computers are a safe choice for corporate use, the buyer may hold specific beliefs that IBM computers are a well-known name, that they are widely used, that they are as technically advanced as most other brands of computers and so forth. These specific benefit beliefs stem from the "rational" content of marketing communications.

But specific benefit beliefs also have an "emotional" side—indeed, this is the way that benefit beliefs "hook into" the purchase or usage motive. For instance, the specific benefit beliefs about IBM computers presumably are all favorable contributors (they have a positive emotional weight) toward their being a safe choice: they are well known, widely used, technically comparable to other brands, and so forth. Thus, they help to meet the negatively originated (problem avoidance) motive by offsetting it (reducing it) with their positive weights.

**Multiattribute Model.** The combined influence of the dual subcomponents of benefit beliefs and emotional weights has been represented by attitude theorists such as Fishbein,[33] in the following type of mathematical formulation, known as a *multiattribute model:*

$$BATT_{b(m)} = \sum_{i=1}^{n} (B_{bi(m)}E_{i(m)})$$

where $BATT_{b(m)}$ is brand attitude toward brand b (for motive m); $B_{bi(m)}$ signifies a specific benefit belief, B, about brand b with regard to benefit i (or attribute i), again with regard to motive m; $E_{i(m)}$ denotes the emotional weight, E, that the buyer places on benefit i with regard to motive m; and the equation says that there are 1 up to n benefits, including i, hence 1 . . . i . . . n, for which the *weighted* benefit beliefs ($B_{bi(m)}$ multiplied by $E_{i(m)}$ for each benefit) are summed, $\Sigma$, to obtain the overall attitude. We will give an example of how this model works shortly.

**(3) Freestanding Emotions.** Not all advertising communications are entirely rational; many ad campaigns, especially for transformationally motivated products or services, attempt to imbue the brand with specific emotional associations that are not obviously tied to specific brand benefit beliefs (even though these emotions can be rationalized into beliefs if the buyer is prompted to state them). For instance, the buyer may feel that IBM is a somewhat cold company, suggested perhaps by its blue and white corporate colors and its nickname, "Big Blue," and perhaps also by its well-publicized staff reductions and elimination of permanent offices for its sales force. The buyer could probably state this rationalization of the cold feeling about IBM if prompted, but the emotional response is much more likely to operate as an unvoiced feeling. Hence we call these types of emotional responses "freestanding" because they are not connected to a belief. However, they *do* contribute to the purchase or usage motive. In this case, "cold" might actually *help* the superbelief of IBM as being safe (a positive emotional weight). For children's home use, however, the same emotion, cold, is likely to detract from the superbelief that IBM computers are appropriate for children (a negative emotional weight). Freestanding emotions are inherently emotionally weighted.

Freestanding emotions therefore need to be added to the multiattribute model, which can now be written in full as:

$$BATT_{b(m)} = \sum_{i=1}^{n} (B_{bi(m)}E_{i(m)}) + E_{o(m)}$$

where $E_{o(m)}$ refers to freestanding emotions ("E subscript o" denotes "other" emotional weights), which nevertheless contribute to the purchase or usage motive.

The multiattribute approach to brand attitude is a very useful conceptual tool for advertisers. We will put this model into operation in the positioning chapter (Chapter 6, where it will be used in the I-D-U model). It may help your understanding of it to give one more example here, and for this we'll return to Healthy Choice dinners.

How might brand attitude (BATT) toward Healthy Choice be formed? As the potential buyer begins to see or hear advertisements for the brand, he or she would begin to learn specific benefit beliefs ($B_{bi}$) about it—that it's low in fat and low in sodium. If the buyer is appropriately motivated (m), as he or she might be if concerned about possible heart trouble, then these beliefs would take on emotional weights ($E_i$) relevant to the motive. For instance, the fact that Healthy Choice is a frozen food might be *negatively* weighted, but the other two benefits, low fat and low sodium, may each be *very positively* weighted in relation to the heart-healthy motive, such that the sum ($\Sigma$) of the emotionally weighted benefit beliefs suggests a favorable superbelief toward the brand. As well, the name "Healthy" and perhaps the nutritious-looking green package may additionally contribute positive freestanding emotions ($E_o$) to further increase the buyer's brand attitude.

**(4) The Choice Rule.** So far, we have assumed that the prospective buyer *sums* (that is, "adds up") the emotionally weighted benefit beliefs, plus any freestanding emotions, to form the overall superbelief or brand attitude. Indeed, the "$\Sigma$" in the multiattribute model formula is a summation operator. This is the most usual choice rule.

However, it is possible that buyers may learn or develop a *different* choice rule, such as: "*First* consider only those brands in a given price range and *then* choose on overall attitude," which might apply to Healthy Choice dinners or "Choose the fastest-service brand *regardless* of any other attributes," which might apply to IBM computers. There are various forms of sequential (the first example) or "noncompensatory" (the second example) decision or choice rules that buyers may use. We will meet these in Chapter 6 but, for now, we'll assume the typical summative choice rule for brand attitude.

These, then, are the main components of the brand-attitude communication effect: the superbelief; specific benefit beliefs, which are emotionally weighted; freestanding emotions; and the choice rule. For convenience, when stating the options for brand attitude as a communication *objective,* we will refer only to *overall* brand attitude (the superbelief component). In Chapter 6, on positioning, and also in Chapters 8 and 9, on creative strategy, we will return to the operational components of benefit beliefs and emotions.

Chapter appendix 5A, Further Considerations for Brand Attitude, provides additional theory about brand attitude, for the advanced reader.

### Managerial Options with Regard to Brand Attitude

The managerial options when considering brand attitude as a communication *objective* are reasonably straightforward. In advertising communications and promotion campaigns, the options are to create, improve, increase, maintain, modify, or change the target audience's brand attitude. Which of these options is selected depends necessarily on the target audience's prior brand attitude (that is, prior to the campaign). The prior attitude conditions and the appropriate brand-attitude communication objectives are listed in Table 5.8 and are reviewed next.

**Create Brand Attitude.** The brand attitude objective is to *create* brand attitude when the target audience does not yet have an attitude toward the brand, that is, when they have *no prior attitude.*

---

**TABLE 5.8**

**MANAGERIAL OPTIONS WITH REGARD TO BRAND ATTITUDE AS A COMMUNICATION OBJECTIVE**

| Buyer's prior attitude | Communication objective |
|---|---|
| 1. No brand attitude (unaware) | *Create* attitude |
| 2. Moderately favorable brand attitude | Increase attitude |
| 3. Maximally favorable brand attitude | *Maintain* attitude |
| 4. Any buyer (but usually with a moderately favorable brand attitude) | *Modify* attitude ("reposition" the brand by linking it to a different motivation) |
| 5. Negative brand attitude | *Change* attitude |

Brand attitude creation is often the brand attitude objective for new category users. This is automatically true if the brand is a *new brand in a new product category.* Philips' interactive compact disk (CD-I) player is an example.

However, we must remember that NCUs could be new users for a brand in an *existing* product category that they don't want to try or have tried and rejected. In this case, the target audience could have developed prior *negative* attitudes toward all brands in the product category. Here, an attitude *change* objective, rather than an attitude creation objective, would be applicable. An example would be Yoplait yogurt if it were to design a campaign aimed at getting noneaters of yogurt to try the product category via this brand, as most NCUs for yogurt have tried the category previously and rejected it.

**Increase Brand Attitude.** The brand attitude objective is to increase brand attitude when the target audience has only a *moderately favorable prior attitude* toward the brand. Notice that we use the term "increase" to refer specifically to an attitude change that occurs from the prior level of *moderately favorable* to the target level of *highly favorable.* Although there are various other types of "increases" represented in the other brand attitude communication objectives, this special usage seems justified because the particular increase from moderate to highly favorable is such a prevalent objective in advertising campaigns.

The reason that the majority of advertising campaigns have brand attitude increase as their objective is that the largest target audience leverage can often be obtained by aiming the advertising at people who are already favorably disposed toward the brand (typically favorable brand switchers) and trying to improve their brand attitude so that they will switch in to the brand more often or perhaps, ideally, become loyal to the brand. Examples of attempted brand attitude increases aimed at FBSs (and secondarily at the brand's own BLs) can be seen in almost any TV advertising campaign for an established brand.

**Maintain Brand Attitude.** The brand attitude objective is to *maintain* brand attitude when the target audience *already has a maximally favorable brand attitude* (or, strictly speaking, when their prior attitude level is sufficient to maintain a rank order *first preference* for the brand). The "maintain" objective therefore applies to *brand loyals* only.

However, as the threat from competitors can always increase in the future, a maximum *absolute* brand attitude is a worthwhile if sometimes idealistic objective. Note that this would require an increase objective even though the target audience is BLs, unless their attitudes are already at an absolute maximum. For example, when the U.S. long-distance telephone industry was deregulated, AT&T, as the previous monopolist, undoubtedly tried to increase the brand attitude of their current customers to prevent them from defecting to the new competing brands.

**Modify Brand Attitude.** We use the term "modify" to refer to the process of connecting the brand to a different purchase motivation. The process is commonly known as "repositioning" the brand, about which we will have more to say in the next chapter. For example, American Express card over the years has been repositioned from a utility (problem avoidance) card to a prestige (social approval) card.

The benefit selected for the modification of brand attitude may be a new one for a new target audience, yet an old one for the brand. For example, Johnson's Baby Shampoo has been repositioned using the same benefit (actually, an attribute), that of a mild shampoo for children, to a mild shampoo for adults. Adults are a new target audience, being NCUs as far as baby shampoo for their own use is concerned. Notice, however, that the purchase motivation is different. Adults would buy baby shampoo for babies because it doesn't sting the baby's eyes (problem avoidance). They would buy it for themselves, on the other hand, because it allows them to have clean, shampooed hair without being too harsh on their scalp (mixed approach-avoidance) and is thus usable every day.

Any target audience could potentially be the target for brand attitude modification. However, brand attitude modification is most likely to be tried on those groups with a moderately favorable attitude *when an objective of brand attitude increase objective seems infeasible using the present attitudinal positioning* of the brand. Advertisers have learned that if you can't increase an attitude, try to generate a different attitude (a new motivation) for the brand.

**Change Brand Attitude.** Brand attitude *change* is the objective when the target audience holds a *negative* prior attitude toward the brand. Brand attitude change requires breaking a negative link between the brand and the motivation and replacing it with a positive one.

The shift from negative perceived delivery across the neutral point to positive perceived delivery is generally the hardest brand attitude objective for advertising to attain. Usually, target audiences with a negative brand attitude have extremely low leverage and are therefore bypassed by advertisers. However, in some cases attitude change is necessary for the brand to survive, so negative audiences *have* to be targeted. A recent example is the advertising campaign by New York City's Metropolitan Transit Authority: "We know what some of you think of us, and boy, do we want to change your minds."

The most difficult advertising situation is where the target audience has a negative attitude toward the brand based on *experience,* that is, based on previous trial and rejection.[34] Here, almost certainly, some repositioning of the brand—the *modification* objective—will be needed along with an attitude change. Imagine, for instance, trying to significantly increase the market share of large cars in the United States or, for that matter, anywhere in the world other than perhaps some less-developed countries where large cars are seen as a status symbol. The way to do this might be to reposition large cars from luxury (social approval) to safety (problem avoidance). Recent survey statistics have shown that large cars are much safer than small cars in terms of driver and passenger protection in accidents.[35] Back this up with the statistic that, each year, 7 percent of U.S. drivers have a reportable driving accident[36] and, with the increasing traffic density in many cities, this might be a plausible repositioning (modification) of brand attitude that could cause many prospective buyers to undergo an attitude *change* toward large cars. Of course, here we are really referring to a category need change but particular brands could take advantage of this.

In summary, we have seen that the brand attitude communication effect can be complex to achieve because of its multiple components. This acknowledged, however, the brand attitude *objective* is quite straightforward in each case. The manager must determine the initial or prior brand attitude level (or rating) of the target audience and then determine a feasible target brand attitude level (or rating) toward which the campaign will be directed.

## 4. BRAND PURCHASE INTENTION

### Brand Purchase Intention Defined

Brand purchase intention is defined as the buyer's *self-instruction* to purchase the brand (or take other relevant purchase-related action). It is, in fact, an anticipated, conscious planning of the *action* step, the final buyer response step (target audience action). Depending on which decision-participant role is targeted by the advertising communications or promotion campaign, the intention could be to propose (initiator), recommend (influencer), choose (decider), buy (purchaser), or use the brand more often (user).

### Intention: Always Desirable but Only Necessary Following High-Involvement Brand Attitude

Brand purchase intention is always a desirable communication objective for the advertiser to achieve. All advertisers would like to think that their target prospects, upon seeing, reading, or hearing the ad, will say, "I'll buy that." This "self-instruction to act" is a defining characteristic of intentions.[37] Every advertiser would welcome this deliberate intentional response to advertising or promotion offers.

However, if the advertising has already induced a favorable brand *attitude* in the buyer's mind, can we not then assume that the buyer will act on that favorable attitude when the category need next arises? In other words, wouldn't it be redundant to also induce purchase intention? The answer depends on whether the buyer is expected to act on a low-involvement brand attitude or a high-involvement brand attitude, as we now explain. The concept of purchase-risk involvement was introduced in Chapter 4 (current brand attitude "vulnerability") and is further elaborated in Chapters 8 and 9 but the concept should be evident here.

**Intention Following Low-Involvement Brand Attitude.** When the buyer is being asked to make a low-involvement (low perceived risk) brand choice, it is reasonable to suppose that a very favorable brand attitude is sufficient to *automatically* stimulate brand purchase intention when the purchase opportunity next arises. Evidence for this automatic effect comes from the rapid upshoot in purchase intention as soon as brand attitude increases beyond a "moderately favorable" threshold level. This is shown, for instance, in a study of beer brand choice, by Laroche and Brisoux,[38] illustrated in Figure 5.7. As can be seen, as

soon as brand attitude reaches +2 on the −4 to +4 attitude scale employed in the study, brand purchase intention begins to increase sharply toward the maximum feasible for the average brand considered by the buyer.

For products like beer, too much "hard sell" (urging of consumers to "buy it now") would seem to be unnecessary and may detract from the brand attitude appeal of the ad. The alternative is a "soft sell" approach in advertising, whereby the emphasis is on a very favorable brand attitude, with intention assumed to follow *at the point of purchase.*

The soft-sell approach is especially applicable with low-involvement/transformational brand choice (see Chapter 8). It is difficult to imagine, for instance, that advertising for beer or soft drinks would need to urge people to rush out and buy the product right now (here we exclude the retailer's ads and price promotions).

**FIGURE 5.7**

Low-involvement brand attitude seems to automatically and sharply increase brand choice once a "moderately favorable" brand attitude is achieved. The example is for beer brands. Note that the average brand, upon achieving a maximally favorable attitude, can expect to get about 40 percent of the buyer's choices, which places it firmly in the buyer's acceptance set of brands. *Source:* Laroche and Brisoux, 1989, see note 39, data from their Figure 1, averaged over brands.

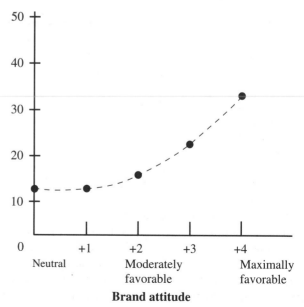

**Brand choice (number of choices of brand in next 100 intended units bought)**

Advertising for these low-risk, positively motivated products is typically of a "transformational" or "image" style which could be rendered ineffective by the addition of a hard-sell tag at the end of the ad.

Low-involvement/*informational* brand choice represents a more debatable situation as far as taking a hard-sell approach to purchase intention is concerned. However, again we do not believe that urging the buyer to act now is *necessary* for ads to be effective in this situation. Ads for pain relievers or detergents, for instance, could assume that intention will occur automatically if the brand attitude is made sufficiently favorable.

The situation changes, however, if low-involvement ads also include a *promotion* offer. This is hard sell, requiring generation of an intention, and is covered below.

**Intention Following High-Involvement Brand Attitude.** When the buyer is facing a high-involvement (high perceived risk) purchase decision, it seems that a conscious decision to act—an explicit brand purchase intention—*is* necessary for purchase to occur. In studies by Bagozzi[39] of action based on high-involvement brand attitudes, such as going on a diet or initiating conversation with an attractive stranger, which is high-risk for most of us, analysis of the "causal path" has shown that intention is a *necessary* mediating response between attitude and behavior. In these high-involvement situations, very favorable attitudes do not lead to behavior unless a definite intention is generated following the attitude.

Consider also the situation of a promotion offer. Promotion offers (in ads or alone) necessarily ask the buyer to "act now." An intention, one way or the other, must be formed immediately. The perceived risk in the promotion offer may be low *or* high; that is, this is not always a situation of high involvement.

Thus we have two different brand purchase intention possibilities: one where very favorable but low-involvement brand attitudes are sufficient to assume that a purchase intention will be formed, perhaps later at the point of purchase, even though it would be *desirable* to have the buyer form an immediate definite intention; and another where brand choice is based on high-involvement brand attitude *or* a promotion offer, such that, if no intention is formed immediately, the buyer will not take action, thereby making brand purchase intention a *necessary* communication objective.

## Managerial Options with Regard to Brand Purchase Intention

The best way to describe the options for brand purchase intention as a communication objective, given the above discussion, is to employ the labels "assume" versus "generate." These options are summarized in Table 5.9, and we will recap them briefly based on the foregoing discussion.

**Assume Brand Purchase Intention.** When the purchase decision is based on a low-involvement brand attitude, the manager can *assume* that brand purchase intention will follow automatically—provided that the brand attitude is made very favorable.

The exception to this assumption of brand purchase intention—and thus to its omission as a communication objective—is when the advertisement for the low-involvement brand *also* includes a promotion offer or indeed *is* a promotion offer rather than an advertisement. When a promotion offer is made, the buyer must decide immediately whether to take advantage of the promotion offer. An affirmative decision would constitute a generated purchase intention, and the correct option specified by the manager in this case would be "generate."

**Generate Brand Purchase Intention.** When a promotion offer is made, or when the buyer's purchase decision is based on a *high*-involvement brand attitude, then a definite purchase intention must be *generated* if the offer or ad is to work.

Note that the "generate" option for brand purchase intention presumes the occurrence of all the other communication effects at full strength. In particular, of course, in order to form an immediate intention such as "I must try that" or "I'll buy that" or other self-instructions to this effect, the buyer must have the

---

**TABLE 5.9**

**MANAGERIAL OPTIONS WITH REGARD TO BRAND PURCHASE INTENTION AS A COMMUNICATION OBJECTIVE**

| Brand attitude strategy | Communication objective |
|---|---|
| 1. Low-involvement (and no promotion offer) | *Assume* brand purchase intention |
| 2. Low-involvement *with* promotion offer; or *high*-involvement | *Generate* brand purchase intention |

*category need.* Many advertisements and promotion offers are designed to remind or sell category need while simultaneously generating brand purchase intention. This is not surprising when we realize just how small a proportion of consumers are "in the market" for a particular product during advertising exposure. For example, in any given week, only about 20 percent of adults will be planning to buy detergent; only 2 percent will be planning to buy carpet cleaning products; and a very small proportion, 0.25 percent, will be planning to buy a new car.[40] Thus, most advertisements and promotion offers do *not* produce immediate purchase intentions, because they cannot if category need isn't there.

To review, the options for brand purchase intention as a communication objective are (1) to *assume* it, for low-involvement purchase decisions where no promotion offer is incorporated; or (2) to *generate* it, for high-involvement purchase decisions and promotion offers.

## 5. PURCHASE FACILITATION

### Purchase Facilitation Defined

The fifth and final communication effect that the manager has to consider as a communication objective is purchase facilitation. Purchase facilitation can be defined as the buyer's assurance that other marketing factors, such as availability and ease of payment, will not hinder or inhibit purchase of the brand.[41] The other marketing factors that can hinder purchase come from the "4Ps" of the brand's marketing mix: product, price, place (distribution), and personal selling.

### A Proactive Approach

Our viewpoint is that advertising communications and promotion planning is incomplete if it fails to take into account these other marketing factors *in advance*. The traditional approach is to cry about marketing problems after the fact (see chapter appendix 5B, Purchase Inhibitors Must Be Facilitated). With modern market research input, however, there is little excuse for not anticipating most of the marketing factors that can inhibit an otherwise successful advertising campaign. Today's marketing manager has to take a proactive (not reactive) stance. The advertising agency, for its part, must do its homework before undertaking the campaign. The advertising manager

must work with full input from the marketing manager, manufacturing manager, sales manager, and other involved parties in preparing the campaign.

**Buyer-Perceived Problems Only.** Note, further, that we have located purchase facilitation as a communication effect in the *buyer's* mind and not in the manager's mind. What this means is that even though the company may anticipate (for instance) a distribution problem, it really isn't a problem *unless and until* it is experienced by potential buyers. This realization can result in some creative advertising and promotion solutions that prevent (for instance) distribution problems from ever becoming salient to the buyer.

However, if the problem already is perceived by the buyer or is *likely* to be, then the campaign must *adapt* to the problem (see chapter appendix 5B for examples of adaptation). The campaign adapts via the communication effect of purchase facilitation.

### Managerial Options with Regard to Purchase Facilitation

The manager has two broad options (see Table 5.10) in considering whether or not purchase facilitation should be a communication objective in a particular campaign.

**Be Assured that the Rest of the Marketing Mix is Coordinated.** (Omit purchase facilitation as an objective of the campaign.) If the advertising communications and promotion campaigns were planned from the beginning as an integrated aspect of the marketing mix, then there should be no purchase facilitation problem. In this case, the manager can *omit* purchase facilitation from the set of communication objectives.

---

**TABLE 5.10**

**MANAGERIAL OPTIONS WITH REGARD TO PURCHASE FACILITATION AS A COMMUNICATION OBJECTIVE**

| Buyer state | Communication objective |
| --- | --- |
| 1. No perceived problems with other marketing factors (and none anticipated by the manager) | *Omit* purchase facilitation as an objective; it has already been taken care of in the marketing plan |
| 2. Perceived problem(s) with other marketing factors | *Incorporate* purchase facilitation in the campaign (adapt the advertising and promotion to minimize the problem) |

**If a Problem is Present, Adapt the Advertising Communications and Promotion to Minimize It.** (Incorporate purchase facilitation in the campaign.) Problems with the other 4Ps shouldn't occur but frequently do. Buyer or consumer research prior to a campaign will often uncover marketing problems. Similarly, for new products, the marketing manager is usually aware of marketing factors that could become problems. As we have described, the advertising communications and promotion should be actively adapted to address the problems through communication. The manager thereby *incorporates* purchase facilitation into the campaign as a communication objective.

## SUMMARY

Communication effects and brand position are the focal purpose of advertising communications and promotion (the ultimate purpose is purchase action and thus sales and profit—but these ends are achieved, in advertising communications and promotions, through *communication*). Communication effects are mental associations or responses, connected to the brand, that are left "in the buyer's head" through advertising communications and promotion. They are subject to modification through experience with the product, word of mouth, personal selling, distribution, and also price` policy—as well as through further advertising communications and promotion. They also determine the brand's position in the buyer's mind.

Five communication effects (either preestablished or built by the campaign) are necessary for brand purchase to occur:

1. Category need
2. Brand awareness
3. Brand attitude
4. Brand purchase intention
5. Purchase facilitation

If these five communication effects do not already exist at full strength in the prospective buyer's mind, then advertising communications or promotion, or both, can be designed to "communicate to" these effects (aiming to fill the prospect's "mental bins of communication effects" for the brand) and thereby produce purchase action.

The purpose of AC&P campaigns is to generate or maintain communication effects that as strongly as possible favor the advertiser's brand. To accomplish this, the manager selects communication *objectives* (which are those communication effects targeted in a *particular campaign,* with the *response objective specified*) from options within the five communication effects. For convenience of reference, these options are summarized in Table 5.11.

Not all campaigns have to address all five communication effects. Rather, the manager has to decide, from prior research with the target audience, which communication effects need to be brought up to full or sufficient strength to cause purchase action (that is, which "mental bins" need to be filled or topped up more). It could be all five, for a new brand in a new product category, but more often only selected effects are relevant. In fact, there are only two communication effects that are *always* objectives, if only at a

**TABLE 5.11**

**SUMMARY OF MANAGERIAL OPTIONS FOR THE FIVE COMMUNICATION EFFECTS WHEN SETTING COMMUNICATION OBJECTIVES**

| Communication effect | Communication objective options |
|---|---|
| 1. Category need | • *Omit* if assumed to be present<br>• *Remind* if latent<br>• *Sell* if new category users are targeted |
| 2. Brand awareness | • *Brand recognition* if choice made at point of purchase<br>• *Brand recall* if choice made prior to purchase<br>• *Both* if justified |
| 3. Brand attitude | • *Create* if unaware<br>• *Increase* if moderately favorable<br>• *Maintain* if maximally favorable<br>• *Modify* if moderate with no increase possible<br>• *Change* if negative |
| 4. Brand purchase intention | • *Assume* in advertising for low-risk brand<br>• *Generate* in all other advertising and in promotion |
| 5. Purchase facilitation | • *Omit* if no problems with other 4Ps<br>• *Incorporate* in campaign if problem |

maintenance level: *brand awareness* and *brand attitude*. Other campaigns may omit particular communication effects.

We took considerable space in the chapter to explain the workings of brand awareness and brand attitude, since every campaign must address these two communication effects. The main decision for brand awareness is whether to address brand recognition or brand recall, or both, which depends on how the prospective buyer chooses the brand. Communication planning for brand attitude is much more difficult: The manager has to identify the purchase or usage motive on which the brand attitude depends; further identify benefit beliefs and their emotional weights with regard to the motive, as well as possible free-standing emotions; and anticipate the buyer's choice rule. This planning pays off, however, in that effective advertising communications campaigns are mostly dependent on correctly reading and addressing the brand attitude objective.

Up to this point in the six-step effects sequence, we have concentrated on *objectives* (the effects desired). The manager has set (in reverse order) communication objectives, target audience action objectives, and marketing objectives in the form of sales, or market share, brand equity, and profit objectives. Now, in our expansion of the focal communicative purpose of advertising communications and promotion, we turn to the final objective: *brand position,* based on the core communication effects.

## APPENDIX

# 5A. Further Considerations for Brand Attitude

**Computed and Summary Attitude.** In some brand choice situations, brand attitude must be formed or "computed" *on the spot* by the buyer—such as when responding to a direct response ad. The buyer calculates an overall brand attitude, $BATT_{b(m)}$, by forming benefit beliefs, $B_{bi(m)}$, evaluating those beliefs, $E_{i(m)}$, and applying a choice rule to arrive at the summary attitude. This computation, of course, has to be done for all brands *initially*—and it is also *final* if the choice must be made there and then.

In other brand choice situations, choice is delayed and an attitude has *previously* been computed, which is elicited in summary form following brand awareness. For instance, in recalling airline brand names when contemplating a trip to Australia, your summary attitude toward each of the air-

lines will come to mind automatically.[42] Here, the buyer will recall only the summary computation itself, $BATT_{b(m)}$, rather than try to (even if he or she were able to) reconstruct the entire computation from memory. The summary attitude situation also must occur in the supermarket on most purchases. As noted earlier, brand choice in supermarkets is made, on average, in about 10 seconds; further, only one or two brands, on average, are seriously considered. What probably happens here is that brand recognition causes elicitation of the summary attitude toward each of the recognized brands.[43] The buyer quickly makes a choice based on those attitudes, perhaps corrected for price or promotion (reflecting the difference between personal attitude and impersonal attitude, as explained shortly). There is rarely sufficient time, in 10 seconds, for the buyer to compute or recompute an entire attitude.

Some situations are a mixture of the first two in that there is some *additional* attitude computation or updating in the presence of the summary attitude. If you are buying a suit, for instance, you will probably have an immediate overall attitudinal reaction to the suit itself, but you will probably then modify this overall attitude as you inspect the suit closely, by adding in some benefit beliefs or freestanding emotions, such as to the brand name, or to the material's texture when you touch it.

Another such "mixed" situation is where the buyer knows that he or she may have to *justify* the choice to peers or other consumers. In proprietary research by the authors, we found that beer brand choice often works like this: The decision maker chooses a brand of beer from the awareness set based on relative summary attitude and *also* based on a "supportive cognition"—a benefit belief—that can be used to justify the choice socially, such as "That's the one I always drink" or "It's brewed naturally."

The advertising strategist has to know (from the behavioral sequence model) in which form the brand attitude communication effect will enter into the decision. Is the prospect going to have the time and motivation to calculate an attitude based on the benefits you would like to put in the ad? Or will there be time for only a summary judgment? Or will there be some mixture of the two? Knowledge of these brand attitude mechanisms vitally affects creative tactics—particularly as to how many and what type of benefits to include in the brand attitude message.

**Absolute and Relative Brand Attitude.** Brand attitude is important in both an absolute sense and a relative sense. In most product categories, the prospective buyer's attitude toward the brand has to be favorable enough in an absolute sense for the buyer to consider buying the brand in the first place. (We say "most" because some choices may be virtually forced, such as purchasing insurance or paying taxes.) But if the prospective buyer has found *several* brands that exceed his or her personal cutoff or threshold for acceptability, then the choice will be made between the *relative* brand attitudes, in a rank-order manner (this also applies to the forced choice situation, where you take the "least bad" insurance offer or the lesser tax option if available). Marketers have to consider both absolute and relative brand attitudes. Relative attitudes, too, were implied in Chapter 4's analysis of current brand attitude vulnerability.

**Personal Attitude and Impersonal Attitude.** A further distinction for brand attitude is important because it can affect *brand purchase intention*. This distinction is between the buyer's "personal attitude" ($PA_{b(m)}$) toward the brand, which is its long-term evaluative rating, and "impersonal attitude" ($IA_{b(m)}$), which is a short-term *adjustment* to this rating. (Thus: $BATT_{b(m)} = PA_{b(m)} + IA_{b(m)}$.) Suppose, in the Healthy Choice example, that the buyer rates Healthy Choice dinners as 70 on a personal attitude scale of $-100$ to 100, where 100 is the maximum favorable attitude. Further suppose that Healthy Choice is promoted with a half-price "two for one" offer. The promotion deal may be valued (impersonal attitude) at, say, $+20$. This combination would raise the consumer's point-of-purchase attitude rating of Healthy Choice to 90, which may be high enough to induce purchase. It is not that the consumer really feels any different about Healthy Choice in a long-term or intrinsic sense but rather that its short-term *immediate* value is too good to resist, and brand purchase intention follows. On the other hand, recent experience with a disliked item in the Healthy Choice dinner line could temporarily subtract from the consumer's personal attitude toward the brand, perhaps by enough to prevent purchase of it on the next occasion.

Impersonal attitude ($IA_{b(m)}$) is therefore a "correction factor" that may apply at the point of purchase (or point of decision). Impersonal attitude is often a response to *sales promotion activities* and is the way that the buyer accommodates the short-term brand attitude communication effect produced by sales promotion offers. (In a general sense, advertising communications can be regarded as trying to build personal attitude, whereas sales promotion tries to temporarily increase impersonal attitude—although we will see later that the best sales promotions attempt to build personal attitude *as well*.) Impersonal attitude can be increased to stimulate *brand purchase intention* (the next communication effect) by bringing the total immediate absolute brand attitude to a sufficiently high level to cause the buyer to "act now."

**Brand Equity and Brand Attitude.** Brand equity can be regarded as the contribution to absolute brand attitude made by the brand name itself—beyond the brand attitude that would result from the brand's objective benefit ratings. (Actually, it is the reputation or goodwill *represented by* the brand name rather than the brand name itself. However, the brand name itself can contribute as well, emotionally—witness "Healthy Choice.") The brand's objective benefit ratings (objective benefit beliefs) can be obtained by asking consumers to rate the product or service itself on various benefits without telling them the name of the brand, that is, by rating it unlabeled or with a neutral, "dummy" name. The rating procedure is then repeated after identifying the brand name. The difference in "no-name" versus brand-named attitude ratings provides an estimate of the brand name's equity contribution.[44]

Lavenka[45] conducted the necessary comparisons in a study of students' attitudes toward candy bars. The second column of Table 5.12 shows the initially conducted "blind" ratings of the candy bars when they were presented unwrapped, unlabeled, for the student to taste. The second column of the table shows the ratings of the candy bars with the brand names supplied, typed on 3 × 5 cards. The third column shows the ratings of the candy bars in their normal packages. The table reveals how real the brand equity effects of brand name and packaging can be. It can be seen, for instance, that Snickers received an objective rating of 72—which increased to 83 when its brand name was identified; there was then only a small improvement, to 85, when the full packaging was used, as at the point of purchase. Thus, there is a considerable equity effect, of $+11$ points, attributable to (the reputation of) the brand name "Snickers." On the other hand, 3 Musketeers exhibits brand equity effects due to *both* the name ( $+8$ points) *and* the package (a further $+11$ points), for a very large total equity effect of $+19$ points. The table also shows that some brand names, for candy bars, apparently have very little equity. Among this student sample, Bounty actually *lost* brand attitude points when its name and package were identified, thus indicating negative brand equity due to the name and package.

Brand equity is the *multiplicative* contribution that the brand's name, package, or logo makes to the brand's objective benefit beliefs. It therefore follows that brand equity

---

**TABLE 5.12**

**STUDENTS' ATTITUDES TOWARD CANDY BARS: THE BRAND EQUITY CONTRIBUTIONS OF BRAND NAME AND PACKAGING**

| Candy bar | "Blind"-taste-test rating | Name-only rating | Full-package rating |
|---|---|---|---|
| Snickers | 72 | 83 | 85 |
| 3 Musketeers | 46 | 54 | 65 |
| Milky Way | 56 | 60 | 61 |
| (Average) | 50 | 50 | 50 |
| Almond Joy | 44 | 48 | 49 |
| Clark | 36 | 36 | 40 |
| Bounty | 37 | 33 | 31 |

*Source:* Lavenka, 1991; see note 45.

cannot be measured simply by inferring it from price differences between competing brands.[46] While a high-equity brand name can command a premium price, some of this extra willingness to pay could be due to superior *objective* characteristics of the brand.

Brand equity due to the brand name should be measured rather than guessed at. For instance, do well-known brand names such as Sony and Philips *really* have brand equity in consumer electronics? A careful study by Holbrook[47] indicates that they may not, at least not in the U.S. market. The brand-name effect in consumer electronics is in most cases negligible and certainly much less than the manufacturers believe. Using *Consumer Reports,* Holbrook took objective ratings of various brands in eight consumer-electronics categories—such as TV sets, CD players, and VCRs. For these items, costing hundreds of dollars up to more than $1,000 each, he found that, on average, brand name contributed only about 2 percent to the price paid. Gratifyingly for consumers, price was very highly correlated with objective product quality ratings ($R^2 = .79$). This correlation increased only slightly when the brand name was factored in ($R^2 = .81$). The interesting aspect is that only one brand name, of the 13 investigated, contributed substantially positively to brand equity. This was Panasonic, which apparently has been able to achieve a price premium of $132 due to its brand name. The Sony name contributed a relatively minor $50 and the Philips name an even smaller $34. Interestingly, some brand names apparently had *negative* equity in consumer electronics. For instance, the RCA name effectively *subtracted* $89 from the purchase price based on objective quality alone. The JVC name subtracted $81, and the Fischer name, $56. On an item worth $500 at retail, these latter negative effects effectively present discounts of more than 10 percent! The results indicate the difficulty of successfully building brand equity for a brand name.

Of course, consumer electronics are usually carefully considered purchases with quite objectively determinable performance attributes. As Holbrook notes, we should *not generalize* these results to other product categories where attribute performance is more subjective or where social approval has an obvious influence. With fashion clothing and automobiles, for instance, one would expect a large brand equity effect attributable to the brand name. Nevertheless, it *is* interesting that such a large brand-name effect was present for candy bars, which you would think would be mostly an objective judgment. *Best advice:* Measure the equity of your brand name; don't assume it.

## 5B. Purchase Inhibitors Must be Facilitated

The traditional viewpoint is expressed rather theatrically in the following comments by the late, great advertising expert, Rosser Reeves:

You can run a brilliant advertising campaign, and sales go down. Why?
(a) your product may not be right
(b) your price may not be right
(c) your distribution may not be right
(d) your sales force may be bad
(e) your competitor may be outspending you five to one
(f) your competitor may be dealing you to death with one-cent sales and premiums and contests and special discounts to retailers[48]

With the exception of point (a) in Reeves' comments, the agency is obligated to do its best to communicate "over or around" any inherent marketing problems. (And if the product *really* isn't right, the agency shouldn't take on the account in the first place.) If (b) the *price* isn't right, the agency should find out why, then try to create an adaptive campaign—for example, a "value" campaign if the price is too high. If (c) *distribution* isn't right, the agency should adapt its media location and timing to fit the available distribution. Either that, or the agency could suggest converting distribution of the brand to mail order, via direct response advertising, as has been done for several New England clothing manufacturers such as L.L. Bean or Talbot's, who sell their products nationally this way. Or customers could be offered an incentive to come to the store, or even be brought to the store, as Atlantic City casinos have done with special buses for New York City and Philadelphia patrons. There is usually a way to adapt. If (d) the *sales force* is bad, the agency should try to lessen or bypass the problem (although this marketing problem should be corrected). For example, a campaign using reverse psychology—such as "Our salespeople are such snobs" or "It's the product, not the seller"—might help to overcome a sales-force problem. Better still is to make the brand's value so good that it is "pulled through" the sales personnel regardless. And if (e) a competitor is *outspending* you five to one, or (f) out-promoting you, this merely increases the agency's challenge to come up with a better AC&P campaign. Of course, the budget has to be adequate to justify advertising in the first place: the expected return has to be higher than for alternative use of the funds. Given this, it is the agency's mission to do the best job possible for the brand based on an understanding of the problems it may face.

## NOTES

1. This footnote is for the theoretically advanced reader. The five communication effects come from our integration of two diverse sources: (1) a content analysis of the "hierarchy of effects" literature in advertising, and (2) Hull-Spence theory. The latter provides a dynamic model which demonstrates the necessity of

communication effects being at full strength in the buyer's mind before he or she will purchase the brand. The Hull-Spence equation is:

$$E = VH (D + K) - I$$

or with correct subscripts for the stimulus-response (S-R) connections:

$$_sE_R = {_sV_R} \, {_sH_R} (D + {_sK_R}) - {_sI_R}$$

which corresponds with:

$$BPI_b = BA_b \, PA_b (CN + IA_b) - (PF_b)^{-1}$$

The analogs are: brand purchase intention = response potential ($_sE_R$); brand awareness = stimulus intensity dynamism ($_sV_R$); category need = generalized drive (D, which can also be added to by specific drive stimuli, $S_D$); impersonal brand attitude = incentive motivation ($_sK_R$); personal brand attitude = habit strength ($_sH_R$); and purchase facilitation, the inverse of which is purchase inhibition = conditioned inhibition ($_sI_R$). Brand attitude, originally described as one communication effect in the text, is later (in chapter appendix 5A) divided into personal and impersonal brand attitude; thus six variables are shown for the five communication effects. Note that intention, and thus behavior, will not occur if brand awareness is zero, brand attitude is zero or negative, or if category need and impersonal attitude do not have a positive sum. On the other hand, purchase facilitation can block purchase only if its inverse magnitude, inhibition, is greater than the resultant of the effects that precede it. See C. L. Hull, *A Behavior System,* New Haven: Yale University Press, 1953; K. W. Spence, *Behavior Theory and Learning,* Englewood Cliffs, NJ: Prentice-Hall, 1960; E. R. Hilgard and G. H. Bower, *Theories of Learning,* New York: Appleton Century Crofts, 1966, chapter 6; and R. F. Weiss, An extension of Hullian theory to persuasive communications, in A. G. Greenwald, T. C. Brock, and T. M. Ostrom, eds., *Psychological Foundations of Attitudes,* New York: Academic Press, chapter 5; and for applications in marketing, see J. A. Howard, *Marketing: Executive and Buyer Behavior,* New York: Columbia University Press, 1963, pp. 98–115; and, less compatible with our view, M. L. Ray, Psychological theories and interpretations of learning, in S. Ward and T. S. Robertson, eds., *Consumer Behavior: Theoretical Sources,* Englewood Cliffs, NJ: Prentice-Hall, 1973, chapter 2.

2. J. R. Rossiter, *Buyer Behavior: A Marketing Management Perspective,* textbook manuscript, Sydney: Australian Graduate School of Management, 1996.

3. E. Rosch, C. B. Mervis, D. M. Johnson, and P. Boyes-Braem, Basic objects in natural categories, *Cognitive Psychology,* 1976, *8* (3), pp. 382–439.

4. M. E. Eysenck, *A Handbook of Cognitive Psychology,* Hillsdale, NJ: Erlbaum, 1984, pp. 317–318.

5. J. W. Hutchinson, K. Raman, and M. K. Mantrala, Finding choice alternatives in memory: Probability models of brand name recall, *Journal of Marketing Research,* 1994, *16* (4), pp. 441–461.

6. See J. A. Howard, *Consumer Behavior: Application of Theory,* New York: McGraw-Hill, 1977, for a discussion of category communication effects. Potential new users, to whom category need must be "sold," are characterized as being in a state of "extensive problem solving," with two problems to solve: (1) should I buy this category of product? and (2) if so, which brand should I buy? For these prospects, a campaign must establish category communication effects as well as brand communication effects.

7. S. E. Nance, A facsimile of the future: Forecasts of fax markets and technologies, Technology Future, Inc., Austin, TX, report summarized in *Research Alert,* June 21, 1991, pp. 4–5.

8. P. R. Demko, Home appliances and the environment, report summarized in *Research Alert,* July 19, 1991, pp. 2, 3.

9. As we shall see in discussing creative tactics and, later, media strategy, a brand is much more likely to slip out of the *brand recall* set due to lack of exposure frequency than it is to slip out of the *brand recognition* set. Some readers may notice, also, that we avoid the popular term "evoked set" when referring to brand awareness. For definitions of evoked set, see J. G. March and H. A. Simon, *Organization,* New York: Wiley, 1958; and, later, J. A. Howard and J. N. Sheth, *The Theory of Buyer Behaviors,* New York: Wiley, 1969. The "evoked set" concept has an apparent bias toward brand recall and also refers to brands that are actively considered for purchase, thus invoking brand attitude and not simply brand awareness. Also see J. R. Rossiter, Brand awareness and acceptance: A seven-set classification, *Journal of Brand Management,* 1993, *1* (1), pp. 33–40.

10. According to an early 1995 Gallup survey conducted in China, presumably with a nationally representative sample, Coke had only 62 percent brand recognition, and Pepsi had less than 40 percent. See: For the Record, *Advertising Age,* February 20, 1995, p. 33.

11. The "brand awareness must precede brand attitude" principle is often overlooked by managers when conducting marketing or advertising research. Although this may seem like a technical measurement point better left to the chapters on advertising research, it is a vital point to emphasize here as well. In marketing and advertising research, interviewers generally ask potential buyers about their brand awareness—then make *all* interview respondents aware, so as to ask all

of them about their brand attitude. This is okay as long as the two measures are analyzed properly, but usually they are not. What usually happens is that a count is made of the "percent aware" and a *separate* count is made of the "percent with a favorable (or neutral or negative) attitude." Unless the two measures are compiled *together,* at the individual buyer level, the figures are meaningless. The manager needs to know the percent of individuals who have brand awareness *plus* a favorable brand attitude. Without prior brand awareness, a favorable brand attitude is useless, as we'll see in the following example for Beck's beer, because the individual could not purchase the brand.

12. P. Nedungadi, Recall and consumer consideration sets: Influencing choice without altering brand evaluations, *Journal of Consumer Research,* 1990, *17* (3), pp. 263–276.

13. See C. McDonald, Measuring advertising response, *Admap,* March 1980, pp. 128–135. In the days before the concept of brand equity became popularized, McDonald referred to the "mental presence" of a brand as being a necessary if not sufficient condition for buying it, with this presence, in turn, consisting of two elements: salience (the ease with which the brand comes to mind) and value (that the image of the brand should be in the brand's favor). Later, Moran conceptualized "brand presence" as pertaining only to the brand awareness function (like McDonald's concept of salience) and distinguished "brand value" as the other component of the brand's equity; see W. T. Moran, Brand presence and the perceptual frame, *Journal of Advertising Research,* 1990, *30* (5), pp. 9–16. Also see P. H. Farquhar, Managing brand equity, *Marketing Research,* 1989, *1* (3), pp. 24–33; A. L. Biel, Strong brand, high spend, *Admap,* November 1990, pp. 35–40; and S. J. S. Holden, Brand equity via brand awareness, Proposal submitted for the *Marketing Science Institute* doctoral dissertation proposal competition, Cambridge, MA, 1991.

14. See J. R. Bettman, *An Information Processing Theory of Consumer Choice,* Reading, MA: Addison-Wesley, 1979; J. G. Lynch, Jr., and T. K. Srull, Memory and attentional factors in consumer choice: Concepts and research methods, *Journal of Consumer Research,* 1982, *9* (1), pp. 18–37; and an excellent review by J. W. Alba, J. W. Hutchinson, and J. G. Lynch, Jr., Memory and decision making, in T. S. Robertson and H. H. Kassarjian, eds., *Handbook of Consumer Behavior,* Englewood Cliffs, NJ: Prentice-Hall, 1991, chapter 1. Brand recognition situations are sometimes referred to as "stimulus-based" choice situations and brand recall situations are sometimes referred to as "memory-based" choice situations. However, we don't favor the "memory" paradigm in this book.

15. Within-respondent evidence is hard to find. In one study, there was a correlation of .5, averaged across respondents, between brands recognized (by name) and brands recalled (from the product category). In our experience with many ad tests and tracking studies, the .5 correlation is a good average estimate. See D. T. A. Hefflin and R. C. Haygood, Effects of scheduling on retention of advertising messages, *Journal of Advertising,* 1985, *14* (2), pp. 41–47, 64.

16. A. G. Woodside, Measuring customer awareness and share-of-requirements awarded to competing industrial distributors, in J. G. Saegert, ed., *Proceedings of the Division of Consumer Psychology,* Northridge, CA: American Psychological Association, 1987, pp. 17–26.

17. The data in Table 5.4 come from pre- and postshopping interviews with 2,000 consumers buying supermarket products, and from a similarly large sample of consumers interviewed as mass merchandiser chains and drugstores. They are from a series of studies conducted by the Point-of-Purchase Advertising Institute (POPAI) conducted in conjunction with the DuPont Company. The data in the top two panels of the table are from a 1977 study. See L. J. Haugh, Buying-habits study update: Average purchases up 121%, *Advertising Age,* June 27, 1977, pp. 56–58. The product-category—specific data in the bottom panel of the table are taken from a study conducted in 1982. As this later study was conducted in mass-merchandiser chains and drugstores rather than supermarkets, the figures should not be precisely translated to supermarkets. It is of interest to note in relation to brand loyalty that the more physiological types of products seem less open to point-of-purchase changes of brand choice. The 1982 study was reported in *Marketing News,* August 6, 1982, p. 5. Overall, the estimate of 65 percent point-of-purchase brand choice corresponds very closely with the findings of a later *Marketing Science* study indicating that, on average, about 70 percent of households engage in "zero-order stochastic" brand choice behavior for supermarket products, which means that they exhibit no loyalty to the brand bought last. The other 30 percent are loyal to the brand they bought previously. See F. M. Bass, M. M. Givon, M. U. Kalwani, D. Reibstein, and G. P. Wright, An investigation into the order of the brand choice process, *Marketing Science,* 1984, *3* (4), pp. 267–287.

18. See J. Le Boutillier, S. Le Boutillier, and S. A. Neslin, A replication and extension of the Dickson and Sawyer price-awareness study, *Marketing Letters,* 1994, *5* (1), pp. 31–42, who studied purchasing behavior in the coffee and soda categories in a store with clear price signs; and the earlier study by P. Dickson and A. G. Sawyer, The price knowledge and search of supermarket shop-

pers, *Journal of Marketing,* 1990, *54* (3), pp. 42–53, who studied the coffee category in a store with less clearly marked price signs and observed a search duration of 12 seconds.

19. See J. R. Rossiter and L. Percy, Visual communication in advertising, in R. J. Harris, ed., *Information Processing Research in Advertising,* Hillsdale, NJ: Erlbaum, 1983, chapter 3; and also the present book's Chapters 8 and 9 for more on the two learning processes.

20. R. M. Heeler, Comment: On the awareness effects of mere distribution, *Marketing Science,* 1986, *5* (3), p. 273.

21. These data are reported in J. W. Alba et al., same reference as in note 14, adapted from their Figure 1.2.

22. See for instance, N. G. Hanawalt and A. G. Tarr, The effect of recall upon recognition, *Journal of Experimental Psychology,* 1961, *62* (4). pp. 361–367; and S. K. Wenger, C. P. Thompson, and C. A. Bartling, Recall facilitates subsequent recognition, *Journal of Experimental Psychology: Human Learning and Memory,* 1980, *6* (2), pp. 135–144.

23. Estimate by *Progressive Grocer Magazine* reported in D. Wascoe, Jr., Choices, choices, choices! *Star Tribune,* October 6, 1991, pp. 1D, 5D.

24. M. Sutherland and T. Davies, *Supermarket Shopping Behavior: An Observational Study,* Report No. 1, Melbourne, Australia: Caulfield Institute of Technology, August 1978.

25. See P. M. Herr and R. H. Fazio, On the effectiveness of repeated positive expressions as an advertising strategy, in R. H. Holman and M. R. Solomon, eds., *Advances in Consumer Research,* vol. 18, Provo, UT: Association for Consumer Research, 1991, pp. 30–32.

26. An example of a claimed brand awareness effect that fails to rule out the first process is Ehrenberg's well-known "awareness-trial-reinforcement" model. Awareness, in this model, is defined to include "interest" in the brand—an evaluative effect that is beyond mere awareness. Check our definition of brand awareness, earlier: it refers only to "identification," not interest or evaluation. See A. S. C. Ehrenberg, Repetitive advertising and the consumer, *Journal of Advertising Research,* 1974, *14* (2), pp. 25–34; and also the comment by J. R. Rossiter, Comments on "Consumer beliefs and brand usage" and on Ehrenberg's ATR model, *Journal of the Market Research Society,* 1987, *29* (1), pp. 82–88. A more recent example is the study by Hoyer and Brown which also purports to observe a pure brand awareness effect. However, in their study, they defined brand awareness as "a rudimentary level of brand knowledge," which could include evaluation. It is probable that these investigators studied "brand name familiarity" rather than pure brand awareness. Further, they claimed that brand awareness is mainly relevant for "low-interest" or "low-involvement" products when, as should be obvious from our previous discussion, brand awareness is crucial for *all* types of products. See W. D. Hoyer and S. P. Brown, Effects of brand awareness on choice for a common, repeat-purchase product, *Journal of Consumer Research,* 1990, *17* (2), pp. 141–148.

An example of brand awareness advertising that fails to rule out the second process, that of an automatically elicited positive attitude, is the study by C. Fraser Hite, R. E. Hite, and T. Minor, Quality uncertainty, brand reliance, and dissipative advertising, *Journal of the Academy of Marketing Science,* 1991, *19* (2), pp. 115–121. The advertising in question is advertising by retailers, who typically "re-advertise" well-known manufacturers' brands, or else their own store brands, which carry a built-in attitude generalized from the store's reputation. For further discussion on the awareness-inferred positive-attitude phenomenon, see M. Sutherland and J. Galloway, Role of advertising: Persuasion or agenda setting?, *Journal of Advertising Research,* 1981, *21* (5), pp. 25–29; and also Millward Brown International PLC, *How Advertising Affects the Sales of Packaged Goods Brands,* Warwick, UK: Millward Brown International, 1991.

27. Those who believe that "mere exposure" increases liking (the original Zajonc hypothesis) should read the meta-analysis by Bornstein. The mere-exposure effect mainly occurs with stimuli exposed for less than 1 second (far shorter than in most ads, especially broadcast ads). The effect is very small to nonexistent with exposures lasting 10 to 60 seconds (the normal length range of broadcast ads). Moreover, recognition of the stimulus (as would occur with a repeated ad) *inhibits* the mere-exposure effect. See R. B. Zajonc, Attitudinal effects of mere exposure, *Journal of Personality and Social Psychology Monographs,* 1968, *9* (2, part 2), pp. 1–27; R. F. Bornstein, Exposure and affect: Overview and meta-analysis of research, 1968–1987, *Psychological Bulletin,* 1989, *106* (2), pp. 265–289. The situation in advertising that might meet mere-exposure conditions is a single skimming of print ads or of passing billboards, often for less than 1 second (see Chapter 10). Indeed, small apparent mere-exposure changes were found, independent of recognition, in an experiment using naturalistic exposure to ads in newspapers: +5 percent absolute for ad liking, +3 percent for name liking, but unfortunately −2 percent for liking of the brand or company logo; see T. Perfect and S. Heatherley, Implicit memory in print ads, *Admap,* January 1996, pp. 41–42. However, creating "missable" ads to encourage mere exposure is not a reliable way to produce effective advertising!

28. Calculated from Crowley and Williams's data (1991) rather than from the Narayana and Markin study (see

J. R. Rossiter, same reference as in note 9) as the latter used extremely motivated recall. The availability → awareness proportion and the awareness → acceptance proportion are both about 40 percent. Perhaps a 100/40/16 rule would be clearer since it indicates that 40 percent of available brands reach awareness and only 16 percent then become acceptable to the typical buyer.

29. See J. R. Rossiter, L. Percy, and R. J. Donovan, The advertising plan and advertising communication models, *Australian Marketing Researcher,* 1984, *8* (2), pp. 7–44; J. R. Rossiter and L. Percy, Emotions and motivations in advertising, in R. H. Holman and M. R. Solomon, eds. (reference in note 25), pp. 100–110; J. R. Rossiter and L. Percy, The role of emotion in processing advertising, in M. Lynn and J. M. Jackson, eds., *Proceedings of the Society for Consumer Psychology,* Madison, WI: Omnipress, 1991, pp. 54–58; and J. R. Rossiter, L. Percy, and R. J. Donovan, The place of motivation in Rossiter and Percy's theory of advertising, in M. Lynn and J. M. Jackson, eds., pp. 59–62. For more detailed discussion of the origin and theoretical aspects of our motivational typology.

30. Our distinction between motivations in terms of learning and behavior theory—particularly drive reduction and negative reinforcement, versus drive increase and positive reinforcement—differs fundamentally from other superficially similar classifications. Most importantly, it differs from Katz's "functional theory" of motivation and later derivations of it such as proposed, for instance, by Locander and Spivey, 1978; by Batra and Ahtola, 1990; and later by Shavitt, 1990, 1992. These Katz-type classifications typically divide motivations into "utilitarian" versus "hedonic" or "value expressive" motives, a division that is basically flawed. For instance, Katz and Shavitt define the "utilitarian" class of motives as being concerned with "maximizing rewards and minimizing punishments," which, far from being broad, is a narrow mixture of positive and negative reinforcement that describes just *one* motive in our system: mixed approach-avoidance (a negatively originated motive because it pertains to conflict resolution and thus drive reduction). See D. Katz, The functional approach to the study of attitudes, *Public Opinion Quarterly,* 1960, *24* (2), pp. 163–204; W. Locander and W. A. Spivey, A functional approach to attitude measurement, *Journal of Marketing Research,* 1978, *15* (4), pp. 576–587; R. Batra and O. T. Ahtola, Measuring the hedonic and utilitarian sources of consumer attitudes, *Marketing Letters,* 1990, *2* (2), pp. 159–170; and S. Shavitt, The role of attitude objects in attitude functions, *Journal of Experimental Social Psychology,* 1990, *26* (2), pp. 124–148, and Evidence for predicting the effectiveness of

value-expressive versus utilitarian appeals: A reply to Johar and Sirgy, *Journal of Advertising,* 1992, *21* (2), pp. 47–51.

Early theories of motivation emphasized drive reduction as the governing principle. Modern theories emphasize both drive reduction (negatively originated motivations) and drive increase (positively originated motivations). Sole emphasis on drive reduction would imply that people prefer to exist in a state of boring neutrality, whereas the dual emphasis recognizes that while people may want to minimize pain, they want to maximize pleasure at other times, to make life interesting and stimulating. For a discussion of drive-reduction and drive-increase principles of motivation, see W. A. Wickelgren, *Learning and Memory,* Englewood Cliffs, NJ: Prentice-Hall, 1977, chapters 5 and 6 and P. J. Lang, The emotion probe: Studies of motivation and attention, *American Psychologist, 1995,* 50 *(5), pp. 372–385.* For further evidence that both negatively and positively originated motivations are needed to account for human behavior, see P. Warr, J. Barter, and G. Brownbride, On the independence of positive and negative affect, *Journal of Personality and Social Psychology,* 1983, *44* (3), pp. 644–651; J. A. Russell, A. Weiss, and G. A. Mendelsohn, Affect grid: A single-item scale of pleasure and arousal, *Journal of Personality and Social Psychology,* 1989, *57* (3), pp. 493–502; and D. Watson and L. A. Clark, Affects separable and inseparable: on the hierarchical arrangement of the negative affects, *Journal of Personality and Social Psychology,* 1992, *62* (3), pp. 489–505; which are all developments of the distinction between negative and positive affect developed by the German psychologist Wilhelm Wundt about a hundred years ago. The negative-versus-positive distinction has always been fundamental in learning theory and has recently been recognized as fundamental in attitude theory as well. Recent references for the negative-positive distinction in attitude theory applied to marketing can be found in R. P. Bagozzi, The rebirth of attitude research in marketing, *Journal of Market Research Society,* 1988, *30* (2), pp. 163–195; and for the marketing of services in R. L. Oliver, A cognitive model of the antecedents and consequences of satisfaction decisions, *Journal of Marketing Research,* 1980, *17* (3), pp. 460–469; R. A. Westbrook, Product/ consumption-based affective responses and postpurchase processes, *Journal of Marketing Research,* 1987, *24* (3), pp. 258–270; and M. L. Richins and P. H. Bloch, Post-purchase product satisfaction: Incorporating the effects of involvement and time, *Journal of Business Research,* 1991, *23* (2), pp. 145–158. In the latter study, the authors found a relatively low correlation of approximately .3 between problems' disconfirmation and benefits' disconfirmation experienced by new-car buyers. Problems' disconfirmation would be an example of "positive punishment" and benefits' disconfirmation would be an example of "negative punishment" or what is sometimes called "frustrative nonreward." The essential practical point is that the problems and benefits exerted independent influences on the overall satisfaction (post-purchase brand attitude) of new-car buyers.

31. S. M. Widrick, Concept of negative reinforcement has place in marketing classroom, *Marketing News,* July 18, 1986, pp. 48, 49.

32. The distinction between negatively originated and positively originated motivations has vital social consequences as well. For instance, Grossarth-Maticek and Eysenck found that drinkers who drink for "relief" reasons (problem removal or problem avoidance) are much more likely to contract fatal cancer or coronary heart disease than drinkers who drink for "reward" reasons (sensory gratification or social approval) even when other factors such as stress and smoking are equivalent. See R. Grossarth-Maticek and H. J. Eysenck, Personality, stress, and motivational factors in drinking as determinants of risk for cancer and coronary heart disease, *Psychological Reports,* 1991, *69* (3, Part 1), pp. 1027–1043. Also, lifelong mental well-being has been shown to depend critically on how people handle negative versus positive affect, which are the accompaniments of negative and positive motivation. See, for example, P. T. Costa, Jr. and R. R. McRae, Concurrent validation after 20 years: Implications of personality stability for its assessment, in J. N. Butcher and C. D. Spielberger, eds., *Advances in Personality Assessment,* vol. 4, Hillsdale, NJ: Erlbaum, 1985, pp. 31–54.

33. This type of model is generally known in marketing research as a "Fishbein Model," after its major promoter, the social psychologist Martin Fishbein; see, for example, M. Fishbein and I. Ajzen, *Beliefs, Attitude, Intention, and Behavior,* Reading, MA: Addison-Wesley, 1975. However, it was earlier called an "expectancy-value" model, following Rosenberg, or by economists, a "subjective expected utility" model, following Edwards. Marketing science academics also call it a "choice utility" model or simply a "choice" model. See M. J. Rosenberg, Cognitive structure and attitudinal affect, *Journal of Abnormal and Social Psychology,* 1956, *53* (3), pp. 367–372; W. Edwards, The theory of decision making, *Psychological Bulletin,* 1954, *51* (4), pp. 380–417; and D. McFadden, The choice theory approach to market research, *Marketing Science,* 1986, *5* (4), pp. 275–297.

34. See J. Deighton and R. M. Schindler, Can advertising influence experience? *Psychology & Marketing,* 1988, *5* (2), pp. 103–115; and R. E. Smith, Integrating information from advertising and trial: Processes and effects on consumer response to product information, *Journal of Marketing Research,* 1993, *30* (2), pp. 204–219.

35. Doubt cast on car safety, *The Australian,* April 23, 1992, p. 11.

36. Statistic from 1990 published by the U.S. Department of Transportation, summarized in Driving—a risky business, *Research Alert,* September 4, 1992, p. 10. The probability of an accident depends, of course, on distance driven per year and also on road and traffic conditions where most of the driving occurs.

37. Our definition was suggested originally by H. C. Triandis, in his chapter, Values, attitudes, and interpersonal behavior, in H. E. Howe and M. M. Page (eds.), *Nebraska Symposium on Motivation: 1979,* Lincoln, NE: University of Nebraska Press, 1980, pp. 195–259. The characteristic of deliberateness in intentions is further supported in R. P. Bagozzi, J. Baumgartner, and Y. Yi, An investigation into the role of intentions as mediators of the attitude-behavior relationship, *Journal of Economic Psychology,* 1989, *10* (1), pp. 35–62.

38. M. Laroche and J. E. Brisoux, Development of a nonlinear model of attitudes, intentions, and competition, *International Journal of Research in Marketing,* 1989, *6* (3), pp. 159–173. The graph in Figure 5.7 is adapted from their Figure 1 on p. 163.

39. See R. P. Bagozzi et al., same reference as in note 37.

40. These figures, and the point about how few people are usually in the market for a product on any given ad exposure, can be found in L. Bogart, *Strategy in Advertising,* New York, NY: Harcourt Brace Jovanovich, 1967.

41. The concept of purchase facilitation was developed from our experience with many advertising assignments in which the agency was, in effect, being asked to solve marketing mix problems for the client's product. Theoretically, it relates to Triandis's concept of "facilitating conditions" in allowing behavior to occur. See H. C. Triandis, same reference as in note 37. In turn, this comes from Hull's concept of conditioned inhibition; see note 1.

42. See R. Hastie and B. Park, The relationship between memory and judgment depends on whether the judgment task is memory-based or on-line, *Psychological Review,* 1986, *93* (3), pp. 258–268; F. R. Kardes, Effects of initial product judgments on subsequent memory-based judgments, *Journal of Consumer Research,* 1986, *13* (1), pp. 1–13; A. Chattopadhyay and J. W. Alba, The situational importance of recall and inference in consumer decision making, *Journal of Consumer Research,* 1988, *15* (1), pp. 1–12; J. G. Lynch, Jr., H. Marmorstein, and M. F. Weigold, Choices from sets including remembered brands: Use of recalled attributes and prior overall evaluations, *Journal of Consumer Research,* 1988, *15* (2), pp. 169–184; D. M.

Sanbonmatsu and R. H. Fazio, The role of attitudes in memory-based decision making, *Journal of Personality and Social Psychology,* 1990, *59* (4), pp. 614–662; and D. Mazursky, Temporal instability in the salience of behavioral intention predictors, *Journal of Economic Psychology,* 1990, *11* (3), pp. 383–402.

43. Consistent with learning theory, the attitude is *automatically elicited* upon encountering the attitude object. The overly cognitive term "retrieval," used, for example, in many of the references in the previous footnote, implies that there is some effort required here when in fact there usually is not. See J. A. Bargh, S. Chaiken, R. Govender, and F. Pratto, The generality of the automatic attitude activation effect, *Journal of Personality and Social Psychology,* 1992, *62* (6), pp. 893–912; and L. Berkowitz and P. G. Devine, Has social psychology always been cognitive? What is "cognitive" anyhow? *Personality and Social Psychology Bulletin,* 1995, *21* (7), pp. 696–703.

44. This is best done using a procedure such as conjoint measurement or multiple regression. See, for instance, M. B. Holbrook, Product quality, attributes, and brand name as determinants of price: The case of consumer electronics, *Marketing Letters,* 1993, *3* (1), pp. 71–83. Also see K. L. Keller, Conceptualizing, measuring, and managing customer-based brand equity, *Journal of Marketing,* 1993, *57* (1), pp. 1–22; and H. J. Riezebos, *Brand-Added Value,* Delft, The Netherlands: Eburon, 1994.

45. N. M. Lavenka, Measurement of consumers' perceptions of product quality, brand name, and packaging: Candy bar comparisons by magnitude estimation, *Marketing Research,* 1991, *3* (2), pp. 38–46.

46. For instance, Crimmins recently reported a survey in which market share leaders in various supermarket product categories commanded, on average, a price premium of 10 percent over the number two brand and 40 percent over the store brand. However, in this survey, no measurement was made of differences in *objective* attribute ratings of the brands. Therefore, the price premium is not necessarily attributable to the "name" alone. See J. C. Crimmins, Better measurement and management of brand value, *Journal of Marketing Research,* 1992, *32* (4), pp. 11–19.

47. See M. B. Holbrook, same reference as in note 44.

48. Reeves's quotation is cited in M. Mayer, *Madison Avenue U.S.A.,* Harmondsworth, UK: Penguin Books, 1961, p. 57. First published in hardcover in 1958, this book is a classic that should be read by everyone interested in advertising. Mayer's analysis of the issues facing managers and researchers in advertising provides a necessary historical perspective, yet it reads like an up-to-date account of the agency business today. His more recent book, *Whatever Happened to Madison Avenue?,* Boston: Little, Brown, 1991, is a rather discursive retrospective account and should be read only after reading his earlier book.

## DISCUSSION QUESTIONS

**5.1.** You are the marketing manager for Fisher-Price preschoolers' toys.

   **a.** You are planning an advertising communications campaign aimed at mothers (as NCU decision makers). Which of the five communication effects should your campaign address as communication objectives, and why?

   **b.** If your Fisher-Price campaign is a TV campaign, children probably will be exposed to it too. What modifications would you make to the communication effects you've described for mothers? That is, what communication objectives would you like children to acquire for Fisher-Price toys?

**5.2.** Can you think of any effect of advertising communications or promotion that meets the definition of a communication effect but does not fit well into one of the basic five? Which of the five is it closest to, and how does it relate to purchase action?

**5.3.** Category need is obviously a communication objective whenever a new product category is advertised or promoted. But "selling the category" also may be an objective for established products. Under what circumstances is this true?

**5.4.** Brand awareness responses can take the form of brand recognition or brand recall, and sometimes brand recall–boosted brand recognition. Which form of brand awareness response do you think would be most relevant for brands in the following product categories, and why?

   **a.** Airlines that fly to Florida

   **b.** TV dinners

   **c.** Fast-food restaurants located on major highways

   **d.** Elegant restaurants

**5.5.** The American Society for Quality Control and the University of Michigan Business School cosponsor a quarterly survey of customer satisfaction across various service industries, using a 100-point scale of overall satisfaction, called the ASCI. The ASCI score for hotels and motels (that category's average) is 75. Suppose you are the manager of an "average" hotel chain. How might you seek to improve brand attitude (the overall satisfaction score) toward your hotel chain?

**5.6.** Pick a category (such as men's cologne or women's perfume) and look through a magazine that advertises the category heavily (such as *Esquire* or *Cosmopolitan*). As you look at each ad, jot down your reaction toward the brand in a sentence or two. Now reread the chapter's definition of brand purchase intention. Discuss the correspondence or lack of correspondence of your brand reactions with the definition of brand purchase intention and with the options for it as a communication objective.

**5.7.** Interview an industrial marketing executive about how problems with the 4Ps are addressed, if at all, in the product or service's advertising communications and sales promotion. Write up a short report that indicates how problems with the 4Ps are addressed or might be addressed effectively by incorporating purchase facilitation as a communication objective.

## FURTHER READING

Alba, J. W., and Hutchinson, J. W. Dimensions of consumer expertise. *Journal of Consumer Research,* 1987, *13* (4), pp. 411–454.

This is the only reference that we have seen to really get into the *specifics* of brand recognition and brand recall in consumer behavior.

Alba, J. W., Hutchinson, J. W., and Lynch, J. G., Jr. Memory and decision making. In T. S. Robertson and H. J. Kassarjian, Eds., *Handbook of Consumer Behavior.* Englewood Cliffs, NJ: Prentice-Hall, 1991, chapter 1.

This is a comprehensive and contemporary review that updates and extends the Bettman article below.

Bettman, J. R. Memory factors in consumer choice: A review. *Journal of Marketing,* 1979, *43* (2), pp. 37–53.

One of the first marketing theorists to realize the difference between recognition and recall in brand choice, Bettman describes concrete marketing and advertising implications of this overlooked but essential distinction. Brand recognition and brand recall are alternative objectives when targeting brand awareness.

Fennell, G. Perceptions of the product-use situation. *Journal of Marketing,* 1978, *42* (2), pp. 38–47.

This article can be considered a forerunner to our typology of purchase and usage motivations underlying category need and brand attitude. A breakthrough article, it helps to clarify a perennial question: How do you motivate buyers? It should be noted, however, that Fennell's is a drive-reduction theory whereas we postulate both drive reduction *and* drive increase as the two motivating mechanisms.

Fishbein, M., and Ajzen, I. *Belief, Attitude, Intention and Behavior,* Reading, MA: Addison-Wesley, 1975.

This book contains a good discussion of how benefit beliefs relate to (overall) brand attitudes. However, motives are not taken into account.

Rossiter, J. R., Percy, L., and Donovan, R. J. A better advertising planning grid. *Journal of Advertising Research,* 1991, *31* (5), pp. 11–21.

This article summarizes the importance for advertising of the division between brand recognition and brand recall, and the four quadrants of brand attitude strategy. Compares our approach with the well-known FCB Grid, showing why a more advanced approach is advisable. (Also recommended as further reading for Chapters 8 and 9.)

# CHAPTER 6

# Positioning

Having identified the brand's communication objectives for the campaign, the manager must next choose (or confirm) its brand position. Using what we will refer to as the core communication effects, the brand now has to be "positioned in the prospective buyer's mind" via advertising communications. After reading this chapter, you should:

- Be able to define "brand position" and see how it relates to the core communication effects.
- At the "macro" level, know when to use a central or differentiated positioning strategy and when to concentrate on the user or on the product (the X-YZ model of positioning location).
- A the "meso" level, understand how to choose which benefit or benefits to emphasize in positioning (the I-D-U model of benefit emphasis).
- At the "micro" level, see how to choose between attribute focus, benefit focus, and emotion focus (the a-b-e model of benefit focus).
- And thereby be able to construct a positioning statement for the brand.

The positioning decision provides an important link between the broad communication objectives of the previous chapter and the specific creative tactics employed in the brand's advertising (see Part Four). Positioning gives a more focused answer to the "*what* to say" question: communication objectives indicate the *structure* of what to say whereas positioning provides the main *content*. Positioning says what the brand is, who it's for, and what it offers. However, positioning stops short of spelling out "*how* to say it or show it *best*," which is the task of creative strategy (the brand's positioning statement serves as a brief for generating the ads). Many consider the positioning decision as the most important decision in advertising (and perhaps in marketing). We agree, although, as we will see in the next chapter, the creative idea and creative tactics can either make or break a positioning strategy in its implementation.

## POSITIONING AND BRAND POSITION

"Positioning," and thus "brand position," means different things at different times.[1] Sometimes it refers to locating the brand within the product category with respect to competing brands; sometimes it refers to aiming the brand at a particular group of buyers; sometimes it refers to giving the brand an overall image; and yet at other times it refers to deciding which specific benefits of the brand to emphasize. We will consider these meanings—and more—in terms of different *options* for positioning the brand.

The key decision is *when* to use *which* of the respective positioning options. We will recommend answers by organizing the positioning decision into a series of considerations from broad to specific. These we call the X-YZ macromodel, the I-D-U mesomodel, and the a-b-e micromodel of positioning.

### Overview of the Chapter

We first examine the X-YZ model of positioning, which concerns the "macro" decision of how to position the brand in the product category (the X option) and then how to position the brand vis-à-vis other brands in terms of either the user of the product or the product itself (the Y or Z options). Two other models then follow sequentially. Since all ads have brand benefits in them, and Y is just a special case of Z, we then examine—at the "meso" (or middle) level—the Z decision of positioning by recommending which benefit or benefits to emphasize based on their importance, delivery, and uniqueness for the brand (the I-D-U model). Lastly, we move down to the "micro" level decision as to whether the positioning focus should be on attributes, benefits, or emotional consequences (the a-b-e model). The final task, then, is to write the brand's positioning statement incorporating the foregoing positioning decisions. Managers will see that the X-YZ/I-D-U/a-b-e framework provides a comprehensive overall model for positioning the brand via advertising communications.

### Definition of Positioning and Brand Position

The *macro* (general) definition of positioning that we favor is one we have adapted from those used by several large advertising agencies, Ogilvy & Mather among them, which is actually the format for a *positioning statement:*

1. To (the target audience) /
2. _____ is the brand of (category need) /
3. that offers (brand benefit or benefits).

The same positioning-statement ingredients have been neatly summarized by Stefflre[2] (in slightly different order) as: "An X product to help Y people Z." Here, the product category or category need is X, the target audience is Y, and the brand's benefits are Z. These form our first positioning model: the X-YZ macromodel of positioning location.

From this positioning definition, we define *brand position*. Brand position is a "supercommunication effect" that mentally tells the prospective buyer what the brand is, who it's for, and what it offers.

The positioning statement is agreed on and completed *after* the specific positioning decisions (outlined in this chapter) have been made. We introduce it first only so that you can see where we are headed in determining the brand's position. The

*full* positioning-statement format is given in Table 6.8, at the end of the chapter.

### THE X-YZ MACROMODEL OF POSITIONING LOCATION

Notice in the X, Y, and Z format for the positioning statement that there are *three* links that must be communicated for the brand. One link connects the brand to the category need and says that it is an "X" product (or service). This corresponds to one common meaning of positioning, known as *brand-market* positioning, such as "We'll position Diet Coke in the diet-cola market." A second link connects the brand with the chosen target audience, "Y people." This corresponds to the second common meaning of positioning, known as *brand-user* positioning, as in "We'll position Diet Coke to adults who are weight-conscious." The third link connects the brand to a relevant purchase or usage motivation (via its benefit or benefits) and "helps people Z." This corresponds to the third common meaning of positioning, known as *brand-benefit* (or sometimes *brand-brand* positioning although no other brand may be explicitly named), as in "We'll position Diet Coke as the best-tasting diet-cola brand."

In this example, Diet Coke's early advertising theme ("Only one calorie") and the *name,* Diet Coke, clearly achieved the linkage between the category need and the brand. Diet Coke's subsequent advertising ("Just for the taste of it") attempted to achieve the third linkage of connecting the brand to a relevant usage motivation via the "good-tasting" benefit.[3] Unlike the advertising for Coca-Cola's other diet-cola brand, Tab, Diet Coke has *not* emphasized the target-audience (user) link. Indeed, we will see that links Y and Z can be *options* in the X-YZ model of positioning.

These three communication linkages in positioning incorporate three of our five communication effects, which we will call the *core communication effects,* since they form the core or basis of positioning: category need, brand awareness, and brand attitude. In Figure 6.1, we depict an "in the buyer's mind" conceptualization of positioning.[4] As the figure shows, there are four concepts or "nodes" assumed to be required in the prospect's mind: category need, the brand representation itself, the user, and a benefit or benefits. The first of these nodes is itself a

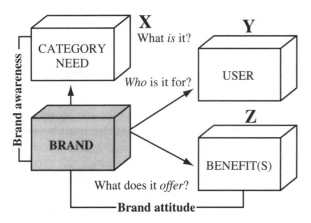

**FIGURE 6.1**
X-YZ macromodel of positioning. The roles of the core communication effects, brand awareness and brand attitude, are also shown. The result is *brand position,* a super-communication effect that tells the buyer what the brand is, who it's for, and what it offers.

communication effect (category need). The other two communication effects occur in the *linkages between* the brand and the category need, on the one hand (the brand awareness communication effect); and the brand and the user *or* the benefit(s), on the other (the brand attitude communication effect). The first linkage, between the brand and the category need, establishes what the brand *is.* This is the brand awareness linkage. The second and third linkages, between the brand and the user or benefit(s), establish *who* the brand is for or what the brand *offers* (has or does). These are the brand attitude linkages. The second and third linkages are really one linkage in terms of brand attitude because the positioning path of "for Y users" can be regarded as just another type of *benefit* (that is, a Z) that the brand can offer. For positioning strategy, however, even though Y and Z both relate to brand attitude, it is useful to keep them separate—as positioning options.

The macromodel of positioning reduces to just two decisions about "location": how the brand should be positioned with regard to the product class or category need (the X decision) and whether our brand's positioning with regard to other brands should be in terms of the product user or the product itself (the YZ decision). We describe the options for each of the two decisions below and then specify the conditions in which a given option seems best for positioning the brand.

## The X Decision: Central or Differentiated?

How should the brand be positioned with regard to the product category or category need (X)? The two main options are either to position the brand *centrally* as a prototypic or generic member of the product category, or to position it *differentially* within the product category. As mentioned in Chapter 5 in connection with the "heart-healthy" frozen-dinner positioning of Healthy Choice, in the extreme, a brand's differential positioning forms a new product category or subcategory by "partitioning" the original category need. In its less extreme form, differential positioning simply means that the brand offers different delivery of benefits than does the typical brand in the category.

Central or differentiated: how does the manager make this important initial positioning decision? In most product categories, the first brand to enter the category—the "pioneer" or, more precisely, the first *successful* pioneer[5]—occupies the "central" position in the product category because the first brand largely *defines* the product category itself. Examples include Xerox in copiers, Federal Express in overnight couriers, Levi's in jeans, Kleenex in tissues, and Jell-O in gelatin desserts. As we saw in Chapter 2, the first brand to successfully enter the category usually gains a lasting market share advantage due to its order of entry.

A brilliant analysis by Carpenter and Nakamoto[6] demonstrates that the pioneer's advantage is not simply due to industry factors such as entry barriers or switching costs, but is indeed a true positioning advantage in that the pioneer brand automatically *defines* the product category itself. In terms of the multiattribute attitude model introduced in the previous chapter, we can be specific about what "defining the category" means. Omitting the motive subscript (m) for convenience, the model is $BATT_b = \sum_{i=n}^{n} (B_{bi} \times E_i)$. The pioneer brand defines the attributes of the product category (the i's themselves and the total number of attributes, n), the importance weights that buyers place on those attributes ($E_i$), ideal belief levels for those attributes (which we will denote by $B_{ideal.i}$, where "ideal" is the ideal brand), and the way that the attributes are combined by the prospective buyer (the $\sum$ or choice rule in the multiattribute equation). Quite evidently, the pioneer brand has a determining influence on the positioning of the other brands that follow.[7]

**Central Location.** A centrally positioned brand has to deliver all the main benefits that are characteristic of the product category. In doing so, a central brand may be summarily positioned as "the best in its category." For instance, in the category of prestige cars, Rolls-Royce may be positioned as *the* most prestigious car."

When a category-leader brand adopts a central positioning in the category in this summary manner, notice that the X (the category need) is the *same* as the Z (the main benefit); that is, the brand is "the brand of X that is Z = the best X." This is a perfectly legitimate positioning for the category leader. The resulting positioning statement is not thereby "redundant" or "double-counting," though it may at first appear so.[8]

However, from time to time, a central brand should reemphasize its *category-defining* Y or Z benefits, so these should be in the brand's "longer" positioning statement. In our view, "Z = the best X" is a summary positioning statement that should be replaced and governed by the longer version whenever the brand starts to slip from its central position.

Brands in either of the two following circumstances should choose the central position:

- The successful pioneer brand (market leader).
- An attempted "me-too" brand *if* the category is one in which: (a) equal benefit delivery can be determined by the buyer reasonably objectively; and (b) the market leader's price is high and the me-too brand can deliver the same benefits at a lower price.[9]

*Market Leader.* The pioneer or market leader's choice is automatic; as noted, such a brand defines the central position in the product category (for instance, "IBM *is* computers"; "Coke is *it* [colas]"). Most market leaders then fight to protect this central positioning. Indeed, many market leader brands become generically synonymous with the product category itself (for instance, jeans are often called "Levi's," tissues are often called "Kleenex," and gelatin is often called "Jello-O"). Thus, the choice for the pioneer or market leader is automatic, unless, for some reason—such as radically changing consumer tastes or values—the market leader would wish to abandon the central position. Such cases are rare.

Market leaders sometimes abandon the central position to their apparent detriment. For example, Miller Lite, the market leader in light beers, which entered the category almost 20 years ago with its central positioning theme of "Tastes great, less filling," changed its advertising theme in 1990 to the still-central but rather faddish and vague theme of "It's it, and that's that" and subsequently "C'mon, let me show you where it's at." Miller Lite's market share of the overall beer category began to slide from 10 percent before the campaign to 8.5 percent by mid-1992. With Coors Light and Bud Light both climbing, both at about 7 percent in mid-1992, Miller decided it had better reinforce its original central positioning. Miller Lite's new advertising includes the line "One great tasting beer that's less filling,"[10] thus reinstating the category-defining benefits which gave it the central positioning in the first place (see our previous comment regarding the longer positioning statement for a central brand). McDonald's, too, is not immune from straying from the central position. In 1992, McDonald's flirted with the line "What you want is what you get," which would seem to be a weak copy of the positioning of one of its differentiated followers, Burger King: "Have it your way."[11] In March 1995, McDonald's returned to its classic category-based theme of the 1970s, "You deserve a break today," modifying it slightly to "Have you had your break today?"[12]

*Objective-Value "Me-Too" Brand.* The other situation in which a central positioning strategy should be adopted—by a "me-too" follower brand—is suggested by Carpenter and Nakamoto through analysis and experimentation. Let us consider first the circumstance in which a potential me-too brand should *not* try for the central position. Carpenter and Nakamoto argue that a me-too brand that tries to imitate the pioneer is likely to fail if the benefits in the category cannot be easily and objectively determined by the buyer. This is because the pioneer will "overshadow" the imitator in the minds of prospective buyers—an overshadowing that cannot be offset by offering a lower price. They cite the case of Purolator courier service trying to imitate Federal Express (the pioneer) where, since most courier services deliver reasonably on time, it is not easy to objectively distinguish between them.[13] Another example was the unsuccessful launch of New Coke (now Coke II) alongside the original Coke (now Coca-Cola Classic). Although New Coke was actually preferred by a majority of Coke drinkers in blindfold taste tests, it was subjectively overshadowed by the original Coke in that the new version was apparently *not* "the real thing."

However, a me-too imitator can succeed with a central positioning strategy if (a) equal benefit delivery can be reasonably objectively determined by the buyer and (b) a lower price offered by the imitator represents considerable economic value. The paramount example of this is the IBM clones in the personal computer market. Performance is reasonably easy to ascertain—the clones run IBM programs, after all—and the price savings with clones is substantial for virtually the same benefit delivery. Notably, when IBM itself introduced a line of low-priced PCs in Europe in 1992, it took its name off the product![14] A cursory analysis of fmcg categories also suggests that private-label store brands succeed as me-too imitators against the market leader in those categories where objective performance can be reasonably ascertained and where a considerable price saving is perceived by the buyer. Examples may include heavily discounted paper towels and family-pack frozen french fries.

**Differentiated Location.** All other brands should choose a *differentiated*-positioning location. Extensive simulations by marketing scientists at M.I.T. have shown that, in general, copying the market leader's central position will not maximize a follower brand's profitability. (This assumes that the market leader *has* adopted the central position—which is likely if it was the pioneer; and that the market leader's market penetration is highest—again likely; see Chapter 3.) As further evidence, a five-year-long analysis of sales-successful TV commercials by Rosenberg and Blair[15] showed that the majority employed a clearly brand-differentiating message. Only a few of these campaigns would be for market leaders; most would be for followers. In most cases, it is better for follower brands to differentiate.[16]

"Differentiated" location means either to select one of the most important *existing* attributes of the category and specialize on that attribute or, better still, if technically feasible, offer a *new* important attribute that effectively partitions the category into one or more subcategories.

Which brands should choose a differentiated position?

- Any brand that is not the centrally-positioned market leader and for which a central me-too strategy is not viable (that is, as explained above, where the brand cannot offer objectively acknowledged attribute performance equal to the market leader's at a considerable price savings).
- This means that *later* me-too brands should *also* take a differentiated position. By *imitating a differentiated brand,* later me-too's are more likely to be successful than if they imitate the leader.[17]

How does a brand "differentiate"? If the market leader has defined the central position in terms of *only one attribute,* then the follower must try to find a new attribute (other than price). One-attribute categories are quite usual at the pioneer stage. Second and subsequent attributes usually emerge *because* follower brands try to differentiate. Figure 6.2 shows some examples.[18] Originally, toothpaste was positioned for taste (Colgate); later, Crest differentiated on a new attribute, cavity prevention; still later, Aim offered both attributes in the new gel form. The same pattern holds for mouthwash, originally positioned to fight bad breath (Listerine); Scope then differentiated on pleasant taste; then Listermint offered both attributes. On the other hand, Palmolive dishwashing liquid seems always to have occupied a *two-attribute* central position, with Ivory and Ajax later going for differentiated positions on the respective attributes. Thus there are opportunities for a differentiated position along any *one* of the important attributes or along more than one if the *combination* itself is differentiated.[19]

**Locating in Another Product Category.** Another option for the X decision (not included in our model) is for the brand to attempt to locate *in another product category.* Most product categories are *themselves* located in a "hierarchy" of product categories. An example of hierarchical category structure is shown in Figure 6.3, for beverages. A brand of one of these beverages may find it advantageous to "take on" (relocate in) another product category for greater sales growth. It may try to relocate upward—for example, Coke or Pepsi taking on coffee as a morning beverage; downward—for example, Coca-Cola's early move into the diet-cola category with Tab and later with Diet Coke; or most often "sideways"—for example, colas' share of the U.S. soft drink market has slipped from a peak of 64 percent in 1984 to 60 percent now, so it might be time for Coke or Pepsi to start thinking about a sideways attack on the noncola beverages like Perrier and 7Up, perhaps with a concept such as "DCT," Diet Coke with a twist.[20] Another example of sideways relocation is General Foods' (now

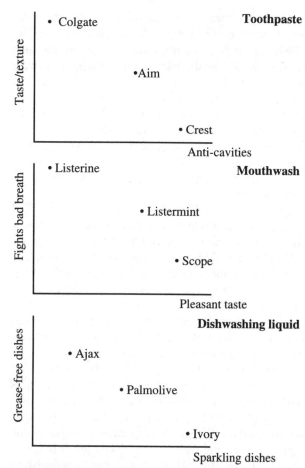

**FIGURE 6.2**

Examples of central and differentiated positions (on the two most important attributes) for several categories. Note that, in these "maps," price has been *removed* as a differentiating attribute by defining the other attributes in terms of "attribute delivery per dollar," as in the "Defender" model.
*Source:* Adapted from Shugan; see note 18.

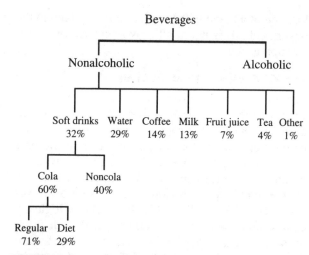

**FIGURE 6.3**

Hierarchical category structure for nonalcoholic beverages. Figures (which are percentages) indicate 1989 U.S. consumption shares of nonalcoholic beverages.
*Source of shares:* Impact Market Watch, U.S.A.

tion in the "other" category. For instance, "DCT" would not be perceived simply as a central me-too imitator of Perrier. Therefore, this third option (category relocation) is really just a differentiated positioning for a central brand *should it choose to locate in another category*. It fits within the central-versus-differentiated positioning options that are already in the model.

The options for the X decision—central or differentiated—are summarized in Table 6.1. The four options can be considered in their numerical order in the table. This is the first and probably the most important positioning decision that the advertising (or really marketing) strategist will make since the

Kraft's) positioning strategy: "Stove Top Stuffing—instead of potatoes."

The reason for not including the category-relocation strategy as an option *in* the X-YZ model is that it is already covered, in effect, by the central-versus-differentiated positioning option. Note, first, that the category-relocation strategy would be most effective for the market leader (the central brand). For instance, if RC Cola were to try a category-relocation strategy, the leaders, Coke and Pepsi, would benefit most. Second, the leader would be taking a *differentiated* posi-

**TABLE 6.1**

**THE X OPTIONS IN THE X-YZ MACROMODEL OF POSITIONING LOCATION**

(*X = product category; options for brand = central or differentiated position within the product category.*)

| Central position | Differentiated position |
|---|---|
| 1. Pioneer or market leader | 3. All other brands |
| 2. Me-too brand *if* product category is such that attributes can be *objectively* matched by follower, with a *large* price savings | 4. Including later me-too brands |

location of a brand in the product category (and in the buyer's mind!) is not at all easy to change once that location is chosen.

### The YZ Decision: Product or User?

In the three-part, X-YZ, model for macropositioning, we have now made the X decision. The second major decision concerns the choice of one of the other two parts—namely, whether to position toward the user (represented by the target audience, Y) or toward the product's benefits themselves (the Z). The easiest way of describing the YZ option is "user-as-hero" versus "product-as-hero."[21] We note that this choice logically comes after the central or differentiated X decision because a central positioning can then steer toward the product *or* the user, and a differentiated positioning can do likewise.

**User-As-Hero Positioning.** A *user* positioning (Y) should be adopted in three situations:

1. Market specialist (company or product line).
2. Technical product aimed at a novice target audience (the naive user target is a Y factor).
3. Or, with any audience, if the purchase motivation is *social approval* (a Z factor that is really a Y factor in that it's approval of the *user* that matters).

*Market Specialist.* The company (or a particular business unit or product line) may choose to be a market specialist or a product specialist.[22] A market specialist serves a particular segment of customers with any product or service the segment desires; whereas a product specialist offers a particular product or service that may meet the needs of one or more markets. Market specialists should, as is evident, employ user-as-hero positioning—for example, Hewlett-Packard calculators for the "professional" user, or Talbot's women's clothes for "up-market" women.

Notice that the benefits advertised *to* the user may emphasize product attributes, such as advanced calculator functions for H-P or the conservative dress styles for Talbot's. This is covered in the a-b-e model of benefit focus, later. However, the advertiser must always remember to keep the user as the *hero* to whom the advertising is addressed, otherwise the brand's distinctive positioning to that user group may be lost.

*Novices (Technical Product).* With a novice target audience, the attributes of the product category are not likely to be well understood.[23] This would suggest skimming over the product attributes in the advertis-ing and concentrating instead on the *user* of the product. One of the best examples of this was the late 1960s campaign featuring James Garner, at that time starring on TV as the likable but often inept private detective, Jim Rockford, as the spokesperson for Polaroid 1-Step cameras. This campaign was subsequently copied by Canon for its AE-1 camera with its "So advanced—it's simple" campaign, using tennis stars John Newcombe and, later, Andre Agassi. Most recently, Fuji has taken the extreme naive-user approach with its "Even a child can do it" campaign for Fuji cameras.

Novice target audiences can really only be called novices if the product is technological in nature—such as a camera, or, to give an example of a service, an insurance policy. While many novices are new category users, the converse is not necessarily true. Many new product categories are not technical (such as heart-healthy frozen foods) and so the term "novices" doesn't really apply. We emphasize this point in case readers infer that user-as-hero should always be the positioning for NCUs. Not so.

*Social Approval Product.* The other situation in which a user-as-hero positioning should be adopted is with product categories in which the primary purchase motivation for the majority of buyers is *social approval*. (Recall that social approval is one of the eight purchase motivations introduced in the previous chapter. Later, we will see that a brand may wish to position *away* from this motive if most brands in the category are already using it. Nevertheless, the initially correct decision at the macro stage of positioning is to make the user the "location" of the brand's positioning if social approval is the main purchase motive.) Product categories such as (regular) beer, fashion clothes, and luxury cars would be well-known examples of products for which the major purchase motivation is social approval and a user-as-hero positioning would be chosen.

Particular *brands* that decide to employ social approval as the purchase motivation, even if the rest of the category does not, will be electing user-as-hero positioning. For instance, most brands of peanut butter use a sensory gratification appeal to children. However, one brand, Jif, uses social approval: "Choosy mothers choose Jif." In this classic campaign from Grey Advertising, the mother is the hero.

**Product-As-Hero Positioning.** In all other situations—which means for the majority of brand—the *product* is the hero in the positioning strategy. The brand's positioning will be "located" on one or more product benefits (Z). These benefits relate to the product, not the user. Even though "used by group or person Y" can, as noted, be conceptualized as a benefit, the difference is that, in product-as-hero positioning, the *product's* characteristics are the message; whereas in user-as-hero positioning, the *user's* characteristics are the message, with one of these characteristics being that he or she or they use or recommend this brand. The long-running (pun intended) campaigns for Energizer and Duracell batteries are good examples: the products are clearly the heroes. Even though the Energizer campaign features users, "Whacko" Jackson in some ads and the "Energizer Bunny" in others, neither of these presenters is like a typical or ideal user; the focus is clearly on the *product's* performance.

The options for the YZ decision—user-as-hero or product-as-hero—are summarized in Table 6.2. Altogether, then, we have now made the very broad or macro decision as to where to *locate* the brand within the overall positioning framework of the product category (X), the user (Y), and the brand benefit or benefits (Z), allowing the locations Y and Z themselves to be options.

Choosing user-as-hero or product-as-hero positioning as the YZ option is only an initial positioning decision. This is where the two remaining models take over. With *either* the product or the user as the location of positioning, we still need to decide which benefit or benefits to emphasize (the I-D-U model), and we also have to decide which aspect or aspects of those benefits to focus on (the a-b-e model). We consider these models in the remainder of the chapter. The I-D-U model is the "meso" or middle-level model of positioning. The a-b-e model is the "micro" model.

## THE I-D-U MESOMODEL OF BENEFIT EMPHASIS

All brands achieve their brand attitude rating by emphasizing one or more benefits. For a centrally positioned brand, this decision is rather easy—the brand simply continues to emphasize the "generic" benefits of the category in which it is centrally positioned. But most brands will have chosen a *differentiated* positioning. For these brands, the decision becomes: On what benefit(s) should we differentiate?

### Consider the Purchase Motivation First

Our recommendation is to begin with the *underlying* basis of benefits—purchase motivations. Purchase motivations are, after all, the fundamental "energizers" of buyer behavior, and it is logical that we should start with them. These motives also energize *usage* of products and services. For convenience, however, we will refer simply to "purchase" motives.

Of the eight purchase motives, *seven* are nominated in Table 6.3. (For positioning, we *omit the normal depletion motive* because this is a motive that applies only to repeat purchase for *brand loyals;* normal depletion is not a reason for choosing the brand in the first place and thus cannot be used for positioning.)

**TABLE 6.2**

**THE YZ OPTIONS IN THE X-YZ MACROMODEL OF POSITIONING LOCATION**

(*Y* = target audience; *Z* = brand benefits; options for brand = user-as-hero (*Y*) or product-as-hero (*Z*) positioning.)

| User-as-hero (Y) | Product-as-hero (Z) |
|---|---|
| 1. Technical product with novice target audience | 3. All other situations |
| 2. Social approval product (social approval is the primary purchase motivation) | |

**TABLE 6.3**

**POSITIONING IN THE I-D-U MESOMODEL BASED ON SEVEN OF THE PURCHASE MOTIVATIONS**

(*Decision Rule: Position the brand on the primary (strongest) motive unless most brands are already positioned there; in which case, go to the secondary (next strongest) motive.*)

| Negatively originated (informational) motivations | Positively originated (transformational) motivations |
|---|---|
| 1. Problem removal | 6. Sensory gratification |
| 2. Problem avoidance | 7. Intellectual stimulation or mastery |
| 3. Incomplete satisfaction | 8. Social approval |
| 4. Mixed approach-avoidance | |
| 5. Normal depletion: omitted for positioning | |

**General Rule.** The general rule for positioning by motives is as follows: *Position the brand on the primary (strongest) motive unless most brands are already positioned there; in which case, go to the secondary (next strongest) motive.*

Motive-based positioning is extremely difficult to accomplish correctly because purchase motives are extremely difficult to detect correctly. Correct motivational classification requires good knowledge of psychology, which most managers lack. This is where qualitative researchers (the original name was "motivation researchers") come to the fore and why this type of research is so important in formulating advertising strategy.

Motive-based positioning requires a *correct* answer to the question of why buyers in the product category are *really* buying particular brands. Let's see why this is such a difficult question to answer correctly (and why most "perceptual maps" are inadequate in this respect). Consider the example for toothpaste given in Figure 6.2, from the study by Shugan. The two attributes (or benefits, in broader terminology) making up the toothpaste's positioning are "taste/texture" and "anti-cavities." But most benefits are *motivationally ambiguous.* For instance, "taste/texture" could be an instance of *sensory gratification* motivation (the obvious interpretation) or it could be an instance of *problem removal* motivation (to get food or beverage aftertaste out of the mouth) or *problem avoidance* motivation (the toothpaste's taste acting as a breath freshener for anticipated interpersonal proximity). Of course, the other benefit, "anti-cavities," is much less motivationally ambiguous. For most people, this benefit is sought for problem avoidance motivation, either preventing cavities themselves or perhaps preventing the discomfort and expense of dental work (both examples of problem avoidance).

The solution to the motivational ambiguity of benefits is to qualitatively probe *why* people buy the particular *brand.* For instance, why do most people who buy Close-up toothpaste choose that particular brand? It's very likely that most are following a problem avoidance motivation (breath freshening in this instance) rather than the purchase being motivated by a simple matter of sensory gratification via taste/texture, as implied by the positioning map. On the other hand, gel toothpastes, represented by Aim toothpaste in the map, *are* probably bought mostly for sensory

gratification from the *child's* usage perspective but—again—for problem avoidance from the *parent's* perspective, who want to encourage their children to brush their teeth, especially if the gel form also includes fluoride.

The procedure required for motive-based positioning is to have a psychologically skillful qualitative researcher identify the *primary* motivation for purchasing each of the major brands in the product category. "Primary" means that a majority of the brand's buyers appear to be purchasing it for the satisfaction of that motive. Usually, based on the percentages of the brand's buyers, there will be another one or two *secondary* motives that are quite substantial. For example, although most people who buy Crest toothpaste do so for problem avoidance, some buy it simply because it is the most popular brand (social approval).

In reality, most brands "hedge their bets" by positioning on more than one motive in an attempt to appeal to people with different primary purchase motives or to primary and secondary purchase motives sought by the same buyer. An attempt to appeal to multiple motives is especially understandable for brands that are marketed multinationally because of the likely diversity of purchase motives for a given product worldwide. However, an interesting study by Roth[24] found that the most successful multinational brands in 213 cases from the three product categories that he studied (jeans, athletic shoes, and beer), were those that concentrated at least 67 percent (two-thirds or more) of the positioning on one motive as primary and mentioned only one other motive as secondary. Although those who followed this approach were in the minority, with 88 cases versus 125, the concentrated strategy was significantly more highly associated with sales volume, market share, and profit margin than was the broad, multimotive approach. Certainly within a culture, too, we would recommend single-motive concentration, as reflected in the general rule.

As the general rule states, a brand should position itself on the *strongest* purchase motive in the product category—meaning the purchase motivation which (across all major brands) attracts or energizes the largest number of buyers. Quite evidently in the toothpaste example, the strongest motive is problem avoidance in some form or other, and most brands would be unwise to position away from the strongest purchase motivation. However, this is also where *true* niche opportunities exist, as explained in the next section.

**Niche Brands.** If most brands are positioned on the strongest purchase motive (not necessarily the same benefit but the same *underlying* purchase motive, as in the example of taste and cavity prevention both meeting a problem avoidance motive), then a follower brand could find it advantageous to position away from the strongest motive. It would then become a "niche" brand—positioned, instead, on a strong *secondary* purchase motive. In the toothpaste example, this could be, for instance, social approval. Tom's of Maine toothpaste has adopted a secondary-motive positioning with its benefit claim of all-natural ingredients, with no saccharin or formaldehyde as found in most national brands. Social approval is not exactly a strong secondary motive, but it could be a viable position despite a relatively small number of buyers because Tom's also commands a premium price for this niche brand.

Beer—regular beer, not low-calorie beer—is another product category where niche positioning based on secondary purchase motives can pay off. For regular beer brands, social approval and sensory gratification—definitely in that order—would be the strongest and next strongest purchase motives in the category. Therefore, there might be room for a niche brand to adopt the weaker but unoccupied purchase motive of intellectual stimulation or mastery by taking a "connoisseur" approach as has been done by some brands of wine. An interesting example of the niche approach in the regular beer category was the old campaign for Stroh's beer based on a minor but unoccupied purchase motive—incomplete satisfaction. One of our all-time favorite beer commercials depicted a starving, parched consumer crawling through the desert—bypassing oases—just to get to a desert cafe that sold Stroh's.

**New or Repositioned Brands.** We have found that use of the seven motives as a "what if" checklist for exploring potential new positioning opportunities for *new* brands (especially later entrants hoping to position in an existing category) or repositioning opportunities (brand attitude modification objective) for *established* brands can often be insightful and produce some "lateral thinking" positioning strategies. Tylenol is a good example of a (then) new brand that positioned itself on a new purchase motive. Prior to its entry, most aspirin products were positioned on a problem removal motivation (getting rid of headaches). Tylenol turned getting rid of headaches into virtually an "approach" motive while offering the "avoidance" of irritation to the stomach—thus utilizing the mixed approach-avoidance motive. As Haley wryly notes, stomach irritation was a problem that most people did not know they had—until Tylenol came along![25] Apparently, many people buy Tylenol in case they *might* get an upset stomach or suffer hidden internal damage by using a regular aspirin brand.

Whereas the purchase-motive checklist can be used in this "what if" manner, we should reiterate that most brands should position themselves on the strongest purchase motive unless it is already "over-occupied" by competing brands. The reason: each purchase motive is very broad—so that *within* a purchase motive there will be *differential benefit* opportunities that allow the brand to differentiate while still serving the purchase motivation that energizes the largest number of buyers.

Moreover, it must be realized that many new or established brands are *already constituted* with particular attributes—and they often have "locked themselves in" on particular benefits related to those attributes. (We consider the attribute *versus* benefit *versus* emotional consequence distinction in the a-b-e micropositioning model in the final part of this chapter.) These benefits may not necessarily fit neatly with a *single* primary or niche purchase motive, and it's too late to change. Given this virtual commitment to particular benefits, what should the brand do? Indeed, even if the potential benefits *do* fit a single motive, what should the brand do to differentiate itself from other brands appealing to the same motive? This is where the multiattribute model introduced in the previous chapter, specifically the I-D-U *implementation* of that model, comes in.

### The I-D-U Model

Benefits to be *emphasized* in an advertising or promotion campaign should be selected according to three major considerations:

1. Importance
2. Delivery
3. Uniqueness

These considerations enter into the I-D-U model of benefit emphasis (Table 6.4). The abbreviation should

---

**TABLE 6.4**

**I-D-U POSITIONING RULE (APPLIED FOR THE *HIGH-IMPORTANCE* BENEFITS)**

1. *Emphasize* the brand's *unique* benefits
2. *Mention* its *equal* benefits
3. And *trade off* or *omit* its *inferior* benefits

---

remind the manager that the benefits you select must "identify (I.D.) *you* (U.)" among other brands in the category. We will explain this model first and then return to the emphasis decision.

**1.** *Importance.* Importance refers to the *relevance of the benefit* to the *motivation* that prompts the buyer to buy the brand. In the multiattribute formulation, importance is the benefit's emotional weight, $E_i$, in energizing the purchase motivation, denoted in full by the symbol $E_{i(m)}$. A benefit assumes importance *only if* it is instrumental in meeting the buyer's purchase motivation. For example, think about an expensive-looking label on a brand of coffee. An expensive-looking label probably has no importance when selecting a brand of coffee for everyday use (sensory gratification). But it may be very important when selecting a brand of coffee to serve to guests (social approval).

Importance of the benefit applies across *all* brands that could meet the motivation. Importance is general to the category or market partition (set of perceived competing brands) and not specific to any one brand. Thus, in the premium or "social occasion" coffee category, an expensive-looking label is important to Moccona, Andronicus, Robert Timms, and all other brands competing in that category.

**2.** *Delivery.* Delivery refers to *the brand's perceived ability to provide the benefit.* Delivery is brand-specific. Hence, in the multiattribute formulation, benefit beliefs carry the brand subscript, b, thus $B_{bi(m)}$. To continue the coffee example, benefit delivery reflects the extent to which the *particular* brand—Moccona, Andronicus, or Robert Timms—is perceived as having an expensive-looking label.

Brand benefit delivery is always *perceptual.* It is based on the buyer's *belief* and not necessarily on objective fact. This is evident in the coffee label example, where the property of being "expensive-looking" is quite subjective—it depends on the consumer's perception. Delivery, therefore, is the brand's *perceived* ability to provide (deliver on) the benefit.

**3.** *Uniqueness.* Uniqueness refers to the brand's perceived ability to deliver on the benefit *relatively better than* other brands. In other words, it is not just delivery but, rather, perceived *superior delivery.* In the multiattribute formulation, uniqueness can be represented by $B_{bi(m)} - B_{ci(m)}$, where b is our brand and c is a competitor's brand (and specifically the next-best-delivering competitor on that benefit for that motive). For example, Moccona may be perceived as having the *most* expensive-looking label, even though other competing brands, notably Robert Timms, rate quite well on this benefit. Moccona would be perceived as having "expensive-looking label" as a relatively unique benefit.

Uniqueness embodies what Myers and Alpert[26] call *determinant attributes* (in our terminology, determinant *benefits*). A benefit can be important—and indeed necessary to mention in the brand's advertising communications and promotions—yet not be determinant. Specifically, if two or more competing brands are seen as delivering equally well on a particular benefit, then this benefit cannot determine preference. An equally delivered or "parity" benefit provides no basis for discrimination or choice because the brands are tied on this benefit.

Therefore, one or more benefits that produce perceived *differences* between brands—that is, allow "relative uniqueness"—must be *emphasized* in the brand's delivery. For example, if the several brands of premium or social occasion coffees are perceived as being equal on taste appeal and price, then a relatively more expensive-looking label may well be the differentiating benefit that determines choice.

Uniqueness, in summary, is *differential* delivery. Uniqueness is considered third in benefit selection. A brand has to deliver (second consideration) on the important benefits (first consideration). But it also must deliver relatively uniquely *on at least one* of the important benefits (third consideration).[27]

### I-D-U for Each Prospective Target Audience

An I-D-U analysis of benefits must be conducted for *each* prospective target audience. The benefits that appeal to a brand's brand-loyal customers (BLs), for instance, usually will *not* be the benefits needed to attract other customers—for instance, other-brand loyals (OBLs). The importance, delivery, and uniqueness of benefits usually will differ for each prospective target audience.

Chapter appendix 6A, Target Audience I-D-U Analysis, provides a detailed example of I-D-U analysis for two target audiences for Healthy Choice. It's well worth referring to this example if your brand has more than one target audience.

## I-D-U Positioning Rule

Once the manager has identified the brand's benefits in terms of their importance, delivery, and uniqueness, the following I-D-U positioning rule should be applied for the *high-importance* benefits:

1. *Emphasize* the brand's unique benefit(s).
2. *Mention* its equal benefits (that is, high delivery but not unique—usually "entry ticket" benefits necessary to compete in the product category).
3. *Trade off* or *omit* its inferior benefits (that is, important but low-delivery benefits).

The rule applies to advertising, obviously, but it should also be used to position the brand in *all* its forms of marketing communications—personal selling, PR, and so forth.

Three questions may arise in the reader's mind in applying this rule. First, what does "emphasize" mean, in concrete terms? We would suggest a "minimum two-thirds rule" from the Roth study cited above:

- *Emphasize* means that two-thirds or more of the message content in the ad should focus on the brand's unique benefit(s).

Second, what if the brand has *no* important benefits that it delivers on uniquely? The obvious answer is "Find one!" But, more practically, the answer is: Emphasize a unique benefit even if it has *low* importance (in the terminology of Figure 6.13, discussed in chapter appendix 6A, this would be a "bells and whistles" benefit). Haley, citing case histories such as Tylenol, and Carpenter, Glazer, and Nakamoto, citing case histories such as Folger's "flaked crystals" for its instant coffee, and through several intriguing experiments on apparently "meaningless differentiation," demonstrate that *uniqueness can always be found* in some form or other.[28]

We note again that a centrally positioned brand's uniqueness is *in* its centrality (a concise example is the current U.K. campaign: "Perrier. Everything else isn't"). On the other hand, a differentiated brand's uniqueness is *in* its differentiation.

The third question concerns the recommendation to trade off or omit the brand's inferior (important but low-delivery) benefits. "Trading off" is the option to take (a) if disclosure of the benefit is legally required (because of unethical ways of hiding the disclosure executionally), or (b) if the low delivery of the important benefit will be found out quickly after trial of the brand (again, usually this will be an "entry ticket" benefit).[29] Otherwise use the "omit" option.

- *Trade off* means to find a compensating benefit and relate the two by offsetting the deficit against an apparent gain (for example, limited distribution but worth the trip for the discerning buyer, or not-so-great taste but definitely the lowest in calories, and so forth).
- *Omit* means just that. You are not required to disclose everything, and it would be silly to point out that your brand is inferior on a benefit that buyers see as important but *not essential* and thereby steer them to the competition.[30] Presumably, your brand clearly offers its *unique* benefit(s), and buyers can decide for themselves which brand's "uniqueness" they want to pay for.

The I-D-U benefit positioning rule is therefore a very useful way to make the second positioning decision (the first was the X-YZ of location): that of which benefit or benefits (Z) to emphasize in the brand position. But how can this emphasis be achieved? To answer this question, the multiattribute formulation that we introduced rather mathematically in Chapter 5 now takes the spotlight.

There are five multiattribute strategies that can be applied (Table 6.5).[31] The five strategies are in order of easiest to most difficult. Most strategies in advertising are of type 1 (increase benefit delivery) or type

---

**TABLE 6.5**

### MULTIATTRIBUTE STRATEGIES FOR BRAND ATTITUDE

1. Increase the brand's perceived delivery on a benefit ($B_{bi}$).
2. Increase the importance of a benefit on which the brand delivers uniquely ($E_i$).
3. Weaken a competitor's perceived delivery on a benefit ($B_{ci}$ for competitor).
4. Add a new benefit which is important and on which the brand delivers uniquely (new $B_{bi}E_i$, with now $n + 1$ benefits).
5. Alter the choice rule to favor the brand ($\Sigma$).

2 (increase importance of the benefit) or a combination of the two; but the other three are possibilities in some circumstances.

Chapter appendix 6B, I-D-U and Multiattribute Strategies, provides a quantitative illustration of how the effect of each strategy can be estimated and thus a suitable (and deliverable) I-D-U strategy implemented for the brand.

## THE A-B-E MICROMODEL OF BENEFIT FOCUS

To review so far: We have chosen a *location* for the brand in the buyer's mind (the X-YZ model) and decided which benefits (Z) to *emphasize,* or mention, or play down (the I-D-U model). The final decision in positioning, according to our comprehensive approach, is to decide what aspect or aspects of the "benefit" to concentrate on at the micro level. For this, we use the a-b-e model of benefit *focus.*

### Attributes, Benefits, and Emotions

Up to this point, we have used the term "benefit" in a rather general way. Generally, a benefit is any potential negative or positive reinforcer—in line with our definition of brand attitude as representing overall (superbelief) delivery on a negatively originated or positively originated purchase motivation. A reinforcer is any stimulus that tends to increase a response—in this case, brand attitude. Occasionally, the advertiser may wish to decrease an attitude and may include "disbenefits" or punishers, as in public service campaigns.

Now, however, we will distinguish more sharply between attributes, benefits, and emotions. As we saw earlier, manufacturers may offer product attributes that may or may not be perceived as benefits by the buyer. Benefits, in turn, taken one step further, may have various emotional consequences or emotional *antecedents* depending on the particular purchase motivation with which they are intended to connect (or they may be freestanding emotions associated with the brand, as explained in Chapter 5). Table 6.6 provides definitions of these terms in the way that we will use them. As the table shows, an attribute is *what the product has*—physical features, for a product, or objective characteristics, for a service, such as delivery time; a benefit is *what the buyer wants*—subjective relief or subjective reward; and an emotion is *what the buyer feels*—sometimes before or after a benefit, and at other times independently. In this

framework, if a benefit is what the buyer wants, then a motive is *why* the buyer wants it—namely, to satisfy a currently relevant motivation.

All ads display or imply benefits in one form or another—as attributes, benefits, or emotions.[32] At the micropositioning level, the advertiser has to decide whether to focus primarily on attributes, or on benefits, or on emotions. As well, the focus may be on certain combinations of these elements.

The a-b-e micromodel of the alternative points of focus in an ad is shown in Figure 6.4. The basic graphic model is adapted from the work of consultant Gayle Moberg[33] but we have added extra paths and supplied its functional properties. In the a-b-e framework shown in the figure, there are no less than three focal points and three focal "paths" that can be used in advertising:

1. Attribute focus (for example, a thick potato chip): **a**
2. Benefit focus from an attribute (for example, better chip taste *because* it's thick): $a \rightarrow b$
3. Benefit focus (for example, better tasting, no reason given): **b**
4. Benefit focus from an emotion (for example, dissatisfied with taste of thin chips; solution is better taste of thick chips): $e^- \rightarrow b$
5. Emotion focus from a benefit (for example, fun because of better taste): $b \rightarrow e^+$
6. Pure emotion focus (for example, simply fun): $e^+$

**FIGURE 6.4**

The a-b-e model of benefit focus. Focus may be on the level itself (1, 3, 6) or on a sequential path ending at the level (2, 4, 5). *Source:* From a model suggested by Moberg, 1988; see note 33.

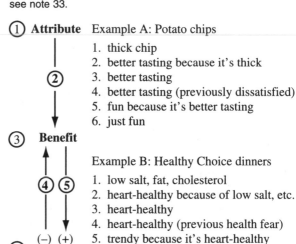

Example A: Potato chips
1. thick chip
2. better tasting because it's thick
3. better tasting
4. better tasting (previously dissatisfied)
5. fun because it's better tasting
6. just fun

Example B: Healthy Choice dinners
1. low salt, fat, cholesterol
2. heart-healthy because of low salt, etc.
3. heart-healthy
4. heart-healthy (previous health fear)
5. trendy because it's heart-healthy
6. just trendy

**TABLE 6.6**

**THE a-b-e MICROMODEL: DEFINITIONS OF TERMS[a]**

| Term | Colloquial definition | Technical definition |
|------|----------------------|---------------------|
| Attribute | What the product *has* | Physical features of product (e.g., caffeine content) or objective characteristics of service (e.g., waiting time). |
| Benefit | What the buyer *wants* | Negative ("relief") or positive ("reward") reinforcer, subjectively experienced by buyer or user. |
| Emotion | What the buyer *feels* | Affective experience of the reinforcer itself (e.g., anxiety $\rightarrow$ peace of mind; joy). |
| Motive | *Why* the buyer wants it | Fundamental drive-reinforcement energizing mechanisms, namely: problem removal, problem avoidance, incomplete satisfaction, mixed approach-avoidance, normal depletion (negatively originated or "informational" motives); sensory gratification, intellectual stimulation or mastery, and social approval (positively originated or "transformational" motives). |

[a]Also defined is motivation.

Whereas other paths are possible, such as a $\rightarrow$ b $\rightarrow$ e, these are the main ones. A second example—for Healthy Choice—is shown in the figure to further illustrate how the alternative focal points and paths operate.

The purpose of the a-b-e model is to help the advertiser decide whether the primary focus to achieve the desired brand position should be on attributes, or on benefits, or on emotions.[34] (In the model in Figure 6.5, these are either the *points* 1, 3, or 6, respectively, or the associated *paths* 2, 4, or 5.[35]) In the sections that follow, we review the principal situations in which either attribute focus, benefit focus, or emotion focus should be adopted in the brand's positioning.

### Attribute Focus

The standard recommendation in marketing and advertising texts is to emphasize the "benefit" to the customer; by this is meant that the emphasis should be on the subjective reinforcement from the (actual or perceived) attribute rather than on the attribute itself. However, the a-b-e model posits that there are positioning situations in which the *attribute itself* (point 1 in Figure 6.5) should be the focus. The main situations are:

- Expert target audience
- Intangible service
- As an alternative to emotion focus for homogeneous-benefit brands

We next explain each of these situations for which attribute focus is recommended.

**Expert Target Audience.** Attribute focus is appropriate when positioning the brand to an expert target audience because experts *know* the benefits that derive from the attribute. Indeed, it can be argued that it is *more* effective to present *only* attributes to experts because their perceptions of the benefits of these attributes probably will vary (experts often differ), and thus experts are more likely to "self-persuade" based on the attributes presented.[36,37,38]

An example of an advertisement with an extreme attribute focus is the Audi 90 automobile ad shown in Figure 6.5. This ad may have been too extreme in terms of "information overload," recognizing that not all car buyers are experts on technical features, and it is interesting that, 2 months later, the company ran a simplified ad with still considerable attribute focus but more benefit focus.

**Intangible Service.** A second situation in which attribute focus is recommended is when positioning a product that is not a product in the concrete sense but rather an intangible service. Financial services, insurance, and auto servicing are typical examples of "intangible services." Of course, the end result of these services *is* quite tangible; for instance, at a bank, you may actually experience polite or rude service, or accurate or inaccurate service; you'll abruptly experience precisely what home-and-contents insurance covers if your home is robbed; and poor or good car servicing is evident fairly concretely as well.

**FIGURE 6.5**
Audi 90 automobile ad with extreme focus on attributes.
*Courtesy:* Foster Nunn Loveder Pty Ltd. and Audi Australia.

However, the point is that when you first make the decision to purchase one of these services, the benefits are *not yet* forthcoming and thus are "intangible."

An innovative hypothesis proposed by Lynn Shostack, the market-research director at Citibank, New York, is that the more intangible the product or service, the more it requires tangible attributes in its promotion.[39] This is because the tangible attributes serve as "surrogate indicators" of the yet-to-be-experienced benefits. This hypothesis has not, to our knowledge, been put to a formal experimental test, but real-world observations suggest that it is valid. For instance, consumers are more likely to initiate and maintain a relationship with a bank whose facilities are modern and whose employees are neatly dressed and polite—even though these attributes may have little to do objectively with the ultimate service that is provided. Insurance companies which

are perceived as large are probably more successful than those which are not. Car-service shops that are tidy and where the employees are not dishevelled and grubby are more likely to get your business than places which look like "backyard operations," and so forth.

It seems a reasonable conclusion that companies which offer intangible services have more need to "demonstrate" that their services are worth patronizing—by focusing on *attributes* as "evidence" of good service.

**As An Alternative to Emotion Focus for Homogeneous-Benefit Brands.** When brands in a product category are virtually identical in terms of benefits, one well-known strategy (covered below) is to attempt to differentiate the brand on emotional associations. What is not widely recognized is an alternative strategy: If most brands in the category are advertising the same benefits, then it may be effective for our brand to *"go back" to attributes* as a means of differentiation.

The theory is that a distinctive attribute can serve as a parity-breaker even if the attribute is fairly trivial in terms of delivering the benefit to the consumer. This strategy has been used for many years in advertising. Classic campaigns include Budweiser's "beechwood-aged," Shell gasoline's "X-100," Procter & Gamble's Folger's coffee, with "mountain-grown" beans in its regular coffee and "flaked coffee crystals" in its instant coffee, and Ivory soap's "99 $\frac{44}{100}$% pure," a claim it still uses. In the service area, AT&T's "True voice" campaign also seems to be a relatively trivial parity-breaker.

Carpenter and his colleagues recently provided proof of the effectiveness of the trivial-attribute-as-parity-breaker strategy under controlled experimental conditions.[40] In the Carpenter experiment, consumers were much more likely to prefer a brand that, among otherwise identical brands, added a trivial attribute. The effect was shown for all three product categories studied: for a brand of ski jacket that advertised "alpine-class down fill"; a pasta brand described as "authentic Milanese style"; and a compact-disc player that advertised a "studio-designed signal processing system." We note that deception or consumer misunderstanding is not the explanation. Half the consumers in the experiment were *told* that the added attribute was irrelevant or meaningless, yet most of these consumers *still* strongly preferred the brand that offered it.

Thus, attribute focus, like emotion focus as described later, is worth considering as a micropositioning strategy when competitive brands are emphasizing much the same benefit or benefits.

Altogether, then, we have seen that there are at least three advertising situations in which the attribute point in the a-b-e model is the recommended focus: when advertising to an expert target audience, when advertising an intangible service, and as an alternative to emotion focus for homogeneous-benefit brands. We now consider the next level, benefit focus.

### Benefit (or Attribute-to-Benefit or Emotion-to-Benefit) Focus

Benefits, in the specific sense that we are using the term here, are subjective reinforcements that are perceived to be provided by the brand. These subjective benefits may or may not derive from the objective attributes that the brand possesses;[41,42] indeed, attributes that the product's engineers or designers see as important often turn out to be perceived by the buyer as offering no subjective benefit whatsoever.

Benefit focus can be either sole focus on a benefit (point 3 in Figure 6.5) or end-focus on a benefit which results from an underlying attribute (attribute-to-benefit, path 2). Alternatively, as we shall see, a benefit may be linked to a prior *emotion*. Usually this is a negative emotion, with the benefit providing relief (emotion-to-benefit, path 4). The common element is that the ad "ends up" by stating or portraying a benefit.

There are three situations in which benefit focus is recommended as a micropositioning strategy:

- Brand with hard-to-imitate benefit
- Negatively motivated (informational) brand
- "Logical" attack on entrenched emotion-based attitude

The first situation is fairly obvious, perhaps, but the second and third are not so obvious. All three are discussed in the sections that follow.

**Brand with Hard-to-Imitate Benefit.** Clearly, if a brand has one or more differential advantages over competitors which are hard to imitate, then those benefits should be focused upon (point 3 in the model). This is in keeping with I-D-U positioning as described above and is the "normal" marketing recommendation. However, the *hard-to-imitate* aspect is

crucial.[43] As we have stated before, price, and also price promotions, usually don't qualify, as they are easy to imitate—unless the company has a low-cost advantage and is prepared to sustain a predatory price position.

We should emphasize that for a brand with a *superior* benefit or benefits, the advertising focus should be *on* the benefit (the subjective value for the buyer) and not on the attribute or the emotion. This is because differential attributes are not necessarily differential benefits from the customer's standpoint and, at the other extreme, differential emotions are, by and large, a less sustainable means of differentiation than if the brand has a differential benefit or benefits.

**Brand Choice Based on Negative (Informational) Motives.** As we will see in Part Four, where we examine creative executional tactics based on the Rossiter and Percy "grid," informational advertising based on negatively originated ("relief") purchase motivations should "hype" the negative emotion first (the problem) and *then* demonstrate the benefit (the solution). In terms of the a-b-e model, the sequence (path 4) is therefore as follows:

$$e^- \rightarrow b$$

That is, the negative emotional state caused by the problem is sequentially relieved by the benefit. It is optional, *not* necessary, that the benefit be further accompanied by a positive emotional state after its delivery.

To illustrate the effective $e^- \rightarrow b$ sequence, two ads for detergent are compared in Figures 6.6 and 6.7. The first ad, for Wisk, hypes the negative emotion but does *not clearly* provide a benefit as the solution. The other ad, for Tide, which we think would be more effective, is better balanced: it shows the negative, though perhaps the problem could be hyped a bit more, and then associates the brand clearly with the solution. Notice that the tag line for Tide is also benefit-focused: "If it's got to be clean, it's got to be Tide."

**"Logical" Attack on Entrenched Emotion-Based Attitude.** In Chapters 4 and 5, we saw that those buyers who have an "entrenched" brand attitude are particularly resistant to approaches by competing brands. This is because they perceive high risk in switching from their current brand and also rate alternative brands as inferior. If their entrenchment is based on heavily emotional consequences of

**FIGURE 6.6**
Wisk detergent ad that focuses on negative emotions: e⁻.
*Courtesy:* Lever Brothers Company.

**FIGURE 6.7**
Tide detergent ad that focuses on the (negative) emotion-to-benefit *path:* e⁻ → b.
*Courtesy:* Procter & Gamble Australia Pty Ltd.

using the brand, then it could be argued that the only way to shift the entrenched attitude is to mount a "logical" (or "rational") rather than an "emotional" attack. An emotional attack would stimulate the ready supply of emotion that the buyer has *for* using the brand and would thus be easily rejected. A logical attack, on the other hand, might catch the buyer less prepared to defend his or her attitude.[44] This would be an attribute-to-benefit approach (path 2 in the model):

$$a \rightarrow b$$

Social problems such as teenage smoking, drugs, and AIDS are examples of buyer behavior that is reinforced by strongly emotion-based attitudes. To change these behaviors, a logical (benefit-based) approach by social agencies may offer the only hope. In the case of AIDS, for example, the revelations by public figures such as Rock Hudson, Anthony Perkins, Arthur Ashe, and Magic Johnson that they had contracted the disease would be regarded as "rational benefits" *in that* they dramatically changed many people's personal estimate (subjective probability) of their chances of contracting AIDS. Most people already know the negative emotional consequences of the disease, and preventive campaigns based simply on negative emotion seem less likely to be effective.

Overall, the benefit level in the a-b-e model is the most frequent focus for advertising. A major reason for its frequent use is that it fits informationally motivated products, which are the most prevalent category in buyer behavior. However, we identified two other advertising situations where benefit focus is recommended. One is where the brand has one or more hard-to-imitate benefits (be they informational or transformational). Another is when mounting a logical attack on an entrenched emotion-based attitude. We look now at emotion.

### Emotion (or Benefit-to-Emotion or Heavily Negative Emotion-to-Benefit) Focus

The final option to be considered in the a-b-e model of micropositioning is emotion focus. This can take one of two forms, as shown in Figure 6.5: a benefit-to-emotion path (path 5) or a "pure emotion" focus (point 6). However, we also distinguish a third form, which is the same path as $e^- \to b$ in benefit focus (path 4) but where the initial emotional emphasis is very heavy and pronounced.

The situations in which emotion focus seems most appropriate are:

- Brand with easy-to-imitate benefits
- Positively motivated (transformational) brand
- "Emotional" attack on entrenched attribute-based attitude

The three situations are discussed in the sections that follow.

**Brand with Easy-to-Imitate Benefits.** A large number of brands compete in basically "homogeneous" product categories where the benefits delivered by competing brands are essentially identical. One positioning option in this situation is to "go back" to attributes, as we explained in the attribute focus section. The other is to "go forward" to emotions or emotional consequences of benefits. The latter is sometimes skeptically referred to as the "If you've got nothing to say, sing it" school of advertising, but it works!

A well-known benefit-to-emotion (with emotion focus) example that has apparently been successful for many years is the "Fly the friendly skies of United" campaign for United Airlines.[45] Another example that is quite touchy with Australians is the practice of auto manufacturers selling identical cars under different manufacturers' "badges." Amply demonstrating that there is differential equity in a brand name alone, the same car can command a $1,000 or so price difference depending on which manufacturer's name it carries!

More generally, for a brand that has an attribute or benefit that is easy to imitate and *is* likely to be imitated quickly by a competitor, emotional positioning provides differentiation which may help preserve its

uniqueness.[46] For this purpose, the benefit-to-emotion sequence (path 5) would be used but with focus on the emotional consequence of the benefit, which the brand should try to make unique. An excellent example of this is Toyota's "Oh what a feeling" (euphoric jumping) creative device used at the end of its benefit-oriented car ads.

*"Pure Emotion" Focus.* The interesting option of "pure emotion" focus (the single point 6 in the model) is an approach that has been perfected by the German marketing professor and psychologist Werner Kroeber-Riel.[47] In case the reader had expected that the pure-emotion-focus approach might apply only to low-priced products such as soft drinks, beer, and cosmetics, Kroeber-Riel has applied the approach successfully to higher-priced products such as kitchenware and to services such as banks and insurance companies.[48] Figure 6.8 shows an ad for a German insurance company developed with the help of Kroeber-Riel's advertising expert system. The headline says "We're opening the horizon." There is no explicit benefit—only an attention-getting and emotionally arousing illustration. Benetton, too, has used the pure-emotion-focus approach with great success everywhere *except* in the United States.[49] The "social controversy" theme of Benetton's ads is so well known that we don't need to illustrate it here.

Whether pure-emotion-focus ads actually are processed purely emotionally is a debatable point. It is, however, *possible* to achieve purely emotional processing, as demonstrated in chapter appendix 6C, Subliminal Sexual Imagery in Ads.

**Brand-Choice Based on Positive (Transformational) Motives.** The positive motivations, it will be remembered, are sensory gratification, intellectual stimulation or mastery, and social approval. An important line of research by Deighton[50] has suggested that advertising which focuses on the emotional consequence *of a benefit* can actually affect the buyer's experience of that benefit when the brand is subsequently purchased and used. Thus, if the advertising has portrayed the positive benefit in an "emotionally authentic" way (see Chapter 8), then those exposed to the advertising are more likely to rate the brand's benefit delivery as better, later, when they experience it, than those not previously exposed to its advertising. Perhaps this is why Coca-Cola works so hard to achieve emotional authenticity in its TV commercials (the company tests *only* finished TV

**FIGURE 6.8**
Pure-emotion-focus ad for R&V Insurance (neither the illustration nor the headline refers to an insurance-related benefit, although the tiny body copy does). The ad was generated from Kroeber-Riel's expert system.
*Courtesy:* Prof. Dr. W. Kroeber-Riel, Dr. F. R. Esch, and Volksbanken Raiffeisenbanken.

commercials, not rough versions, because the company believes that roughs do not have sufficient emotional authenticity).

More generally, positive motivations for purchase, for which we recommend the "transformational" style of advertising, depend vitally on a positive emotional "end-state." The sequence (path 5) is usually:

$$b \rightarrow e^+$$

or simply:

$$e^+$$

In Chapter 8, we present an emotional-dynamics theory that demonstrates this point. For the negatively originated (informational) motivations, the end-state can be emotionally neutral ("relief" or "relaxation"). For the positively originated (transformational) motivations, on the other hand, the end-state *must* be a positive emotion.

**"Emotional" Attack on Entrenched Attribute-Based Attitude.** Again let us consider the "entrenched" buyer of a particular brand, where the "brand" could be some form of personal or social behavior rather than necessarily a brand in the sense of a commercial product or service. If the buyer's brand attitude is "rationally" based on an attribute, and we want to weaken or change that attitude, then positioning via an emotional attack is worth considering. This is the following sequence (path 4):

$$e^- \rightarrow b$$

Although technically this should be labeled as a benefit path, as it ends in a benefit, the key is its heavily negative emotional beginning (the underscored $e^-$ ), hence we classify it as emotion focus.

Fear appeals in advertising (or in personal selling) are the best-known application of this approach. The effect of fear (a negative emotion) is to distract the person from mounting rational counterarguments—of which, if the attitude is attribute-based and entrenched, there will probably be plenty—while he or she concentrates on getting rid of the fear.[51] Well-known examples of fear appeals in advertising include American Express Travelers Checks TV commercials ("What kind were they?") in which overseas travelers are robbed, and Prudential Insurance TV commercials of the early 1980s in which a father dies on the operating table, a mother drowns, and so forth, thus emphasizing the need for life insurance.[52] The overall conclusion from many years of research on fear appeals is that the *higher* the fear level, the more effective the attack on brand attitude will be—*provided* that the recommended behavior change is perceived as "doable" by the individual. If the behavior change is not doable, then the focus should be on finding an alternatively doable, if less effective, behavior—*not* on reducing the level of fear. The doability proviso is important. Perhaps the best examples are not in the areas of addictive habits such as smoking and drinking, whose consequences are largely *emotionally* reinforcing, but rather in the example of voting behavior. Voting is easily doable. Whereas one would think that the public's political choices in state and national elections should be based on rational appraisal of the issues (attributes), many recent elections seem to have been strongly influenced by opposing parties' emotional attacks on the personal background of the candidates. Pratkanis and Aronson[53] provide an interesting discussion of how emotional positioning can be effective in otherwise attribute-based arenas.

Summarizing the advertising situations in which emotion is the recommended focus, we see that there are at least three: when the brand has only easy-to-imitate benefits (remembering that attribute focus is also an alternative), when the brand choice is positively motivated (the $b \rightarrow e^+$ sequence), or for an "emotional" attack ($e^- \rightarrow b$) on an entrenched attribute-based attitude. These quite diverse but conditionally specific situations go beyond simplistic generalizations about "emotional" advertising.

To review, we have seen that this third or micro level of positioning—which we call the a-b-e micromodel of benefit focus—can have large effects on the success of the brand's advertising communication efforts. The a-b-e model provides a useful set of conditions or contingencies for choosing a microposition in terms of benefit focus—where the term "benefit" is now expanded into its attribute-benefit-emotion components. Table 6.7 summarizes the a-b-e model's applications.

---

**TABLE 6.7**

**SUMMARY OF THE CONDITIONS IN THE a-b-e MICROMODEL OF BENEFIT FOCUS**

**Attribute (a) focus**

- Expert target audience
- Intangible service
- As an alternative to emotion focus for homogeneous-benefit brands

**Benefit (b) focus**

- Brand with hard-to-imitate benefit
- Negatively motivated (informational) brand: $e^- \rightarrow b$
- "Logical" attack on entrenched emotion-based attitude: $a \rightarrow b$

**Emotion (e) focus**

- Brand with easy-to-imitate benefits
- Positively motivated (transformational) brand: $b \rightarrow e^+$, or $e^+$
- "Emotional" attack on entrenched attribute- or benefit-based attitude: $e^- \rightarrow b$

---

## POSITIONING STATEMENT

Now, the manager can write the *positioning statement* for the brand. To do this, we use the positioning statement format introduced at the beginning of the chapter, but elaborate on the critical third part to produce the full "long" positioning statement format shown in Table 6.8. If the manager does not wish to "spell out" to the agency how to construct the advertising, the phrase at the end of 3a, "with (a, b, or e) focus," referring to the a-b-e micromodel, can be omitted. However, we believe that the a-b-e decision may be crucial for many brands—for instance, for parity brands, or for brands planning to attack an entrenched incumbent brand, as in many social campaigns—and therefore should not usually be omitted. We leave this option for the manager.

It is always risky to give an example of the targeted brand position for a real brand, as its management may have something different in mind. However, it is fairly clear from publicly available evidence what a brand such as Volvo cars is trying to do in its positioning, so we will use it as an example. Applying the X-YZ/I-D-U/a-b-e positioning framework, we generate the following positioning statement:

1. To UPPER-INCOME, OTHER-BRAND-SWITCHER CAR BUYERS /
2. *VOLVO* is a *differentiated* brand of PRESTIGE AUTOMOBILE /
3. that offers the benefits of SAFETY (problem avoidance) and PERFORMANCE (problem removal) as well as PRESTIGE (social approval). The advertising for VOLVO:
   a. should *emphasize* SAFETY and PERFORMANCE, with a *negative-emotion-to-benefit focus,*
   b. must *mention* PRESTIGE as an entry ticket to the category,
   c. and will *downplay* its previous FAMILY-CAR orientation in the interest of appealing to a broader range of users.

From the deliberately overhighlighted example above, it should be fairly easy to see how the X-YZ, I-D-U, and a-b-e decisions are incorporated in the brand's long positioning statement. (A couple of possible additions to note with regard to the Volvo example are that the benefit mentioned in 3b should be executed with an emotion focus and that the nature of the "downplaying" in 3c should be specified—or the

**POSITIONING STATEMENT FORMAT: "LONG" VERSION**

*(The a-b-e micropositioning (italicized) can be omitted should the manager so desire.)*

1. To (the target audience, Y)/
2. _____ is the (central or differentiated) brand of (category need, X)/
3. that offers (brand benefit or benefits, Z). The advertising for this brand:
   a. should emphasize (benefit or benefits, U, uniquely delivered) *with (a, b, or e) focus,*
   b. must mention (benefit or benefits, I, important "entry tickets"),
   c. and will omit or trade off (benefit or benefits, D −, inferior-delivery benefits).

a-b-e micromodel can be omitted altogether if the manager so desires.)

When the brand's position is well established, a "benefit" positioning statement may thereafter be used to stimulate further creative ideas for advertising. The benefit positioning statement lists only the *emphasized* (3a) benefit or benefits.

## SUMMARY

The brand's positioning strategy is essentially a summary of why a particular target audience, buying in a particular category or for a particular category need, should buy this particular brand. The format for a brand's positioning statement is: "To the (target audience) / _____ is the brand of (category need) / that offers (brand benefit or benefits)." Positioning incorporates the three core communication effects of category need, brand awareness, and brand attitude. Brand awareness links the brand to the category or category need. Brand attitude links the brand to one or more benefits. The result is *brand position,* a supercommunication effect which mentally tells the buyer what the brand is, who it's for, and what it offers.

The positioning strategy for a brand can be systematically accomplished by using what we call the X-YZ/I-D-U/a-b-e model of positioning. This model actually consists of three submodels, proceeding from the macro level to the micro level of positioning.

Positioning begins with the X-YZ macromodel of positioning location. The X-YZ model is named after Stefflre's condensed form of the positioning statement: "An X product to help Y people Z."

In the macromodel, X is the product category, and the manager first has to decide whether to position the brand centrally within the category or to give it a differentiated location. The central position will be taken automatically by the brand that is the successful pioneer in the category, and it is usually the position occupied by the market leader even if the market leader was not the original pioneer. A later imitator (me-too) brand should also take central positioning if it can provide the same objectively measured benefit delivery at a substantial price saving to the buyer. All other brands should adopt a differentiated positioning, including subsequent me-too brands.

The YZ part of the X-YZ macromodel refers to the choice between user-as-hero positioning (Y) or product-as-hero positioning (Z). Locating the brand "mentally" toward the user (Y) is recommended if the brand is a market specialist brand, or a technical product aimed at a novice target audience, or a social approval brand. Otherwise (which is the majority of cases), the brand should locate on the product itself and specifically on the product's benefits (Z).

The next positioning decision concerns which benefit or benefits the brand should emphasize. (Note that user-as-hero positioning also employs benefits—the main one being that the brand is recommended for a particular type of user. Product-as-hero positioning obviously employs benefits.) This is the meso or middle level of positioning and, for this, the manager can use the I-D-U mesomodel of benefit emphasis.

The I-D-U model is first applied at the broad level of purchase motivation. Generally, a brand should position itself on the strongest purchase motivation operating in the product category—unless most of the other brands are also positioned on the same motivation. In that case, the brand should consider positioning itself on a secondary purchase motive as a means of unique differentiation. Purchase motivations are also useful, too, when repositioning an existing brand. Seven of the eight purchase motivations can be considered in a "what if" manner for the brand: four of the five negatively originated (informational) motivations, excluding normal depletion, which is not a reason for purchasing a brand in the first place; and the three positively originated (transformational) motivations. We note that there are numerous benefit positionings that can be adopted *within* a single purchase motive, and this is the usual strategy if a single purchase motive is dominant in the category.

The I-D-U model is then applied more specifically by conducting a multiattribute analysis of all the competing brands in the product category. Multiattribute analysis reveals which benefits are important, how well various brands deliver on the benefits, and which brands deliver uniquely on particular benefits. (Importance, delivery, and uniqueness provide the acronym for the I-D-U model.) From a positioning standpoint, the decision rule for the I-D-U model is that a brand should (1) emphasize its unique benefit or benefits, (2) mention its equal benefits, and (3) trade off or omit its inferior benefits.

Benefit-emphasis positioning can be achieved more precisely by employing one or more of the following multiattribute strategies: (1) increase perceived delivery on a benefit, (2) increase importance for a benefit that you deliver well on, (3) attack a competitor's delivery, (4) add a new benefit, or (5) attempt to change the buyer's choice rule for combining benefits in a way that favors your brand. Generally, these strategies are in decreasing order of feasibility. The effect of various alternative benefit-emphasis strategies can be estimated by using the multiattribute model to predict the new brand attitude for the brand.

The third positioning decision is at the micro level. For this decision, the manager can use the a-b-e micromodel of benefit focus. The generic term "benefits" is now broken down into three specific aspects: attributes (what the product has), benefits (what the buyer wants), and emotions (what the buyer feels before or after the benefit, or independently). In marketing communications for the brand's positioning, the focus can be on attributes, benefits, or emotions, or on particular sequential combinations of these aspects.

Attribute focus should be used when the brand is positioned for an expert target audience, or if the brand is an intangible service, or as an alternative to emotion-focus for a brand competing in a category where other brands offer virtually identical benefits.

Benefit focus should always be used if the brand has a hard-to-imitate benefit or several such benefits. Also, benefit focus is the normal recommendation for a negatively motivated (informational) brand; more specifically, a sequential path of *negative* emotion-to-benefit delivery is recommended. Third, benefit focus is worth trying if the brand wishes to attack an entrenched emotion-based attitude; specifically, an attribute-to-benefit path is used to attack a benefit-to-emotion path.

Emotion focus is a typically recommended option for a brand which has only easy-to-imitate benefits. If most brands in the category offer the same benefits, our brand can either go "back to" attributes (attribute focus) or "go forward" to *positive* emotions (emotion focus). The attribute focus or the emotion focus may provide differentiation that could not be provided by benefits alone. Emotion focus is also the normal recommendation for a positively motivated (transformational) brand; this could be represented by a benefit-to-positive-emotion path or simply by a pure (positive) emotion focus. Third, emotion focus can be used by a brand that is trying to attack an entrenched attribute-based attitude; specifically, the *negative*-emotion-to-benefit path is used to attack an attribute-to-benefit path.

The brand's full (long) positioning statement is then written from the X-YZ/I-D-U/a-b-e decisions made at the macro, meso, and micro levels.

Altogether, the three submodels represented in the X-YZ/I-D-U/a-b-e model represent a systematic and insightful way of choosing a positioning strategy. The next advertising planning decision is: How can the brand's positioning strategy best be translated into an actual advertising campaign to achieve and then maintain its brand position? We address this vital topic in the next chapter.

## APPENDIX

# 6A. Target-Audience I-D-U Analysis

If there's more than one target audience for the brand's campaign, *each* must undergo an I-D-U analysis before benefit emphasis can be correctly decided. This can be illustrated with the simple (and hypothetical) example of Healthy Choice entrees trying to attract customers from Lean Cuisine. Let's assume, quite realistically, that the decision between Healthy Choice and Lean Cuisine is based on two common benefits, taste and price, and a major benefit that the two target audiences perceive slightly differently: Healthy Choice loyals want "heart-healthy" meals (low fat, low sodium, and low calories) whereas Lean Cuisine loyals want "diet" meals (low calories and low fat).

Figure 6.9, panels A and B, shows how Healthy Choice BLs might perceive the two competing brands' benefits. On "heart-healthy," which is the most important benefit, Healthy Choice BLs perceive Healthy Choice as uniquely superior to Lean Cuisine. On the second most important

**A. Healthy Choice brand loyals**

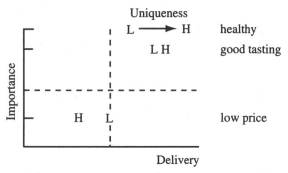

**B. Lean Cuisine brand loyals**
(i.e., Healthy Choice's other-brand loyals)

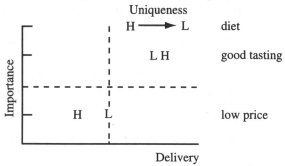

**FIGURE 6.9**
I-D-U analysis for Healthy Choice brand loyals (panel A) and Lean Cuisine brand loyals, that is, Healthy Choice's other-brand loyal prospects (panel B). (H = Healthy Choice, L = Lean Cuisine)

benefit, taste, Lean Cuisine and Healthy Choice are seen as equally good. On low price, which is less important overall to these premium-category buyers, Stouffer's price-cutting has given Lean Cuisine a slight advantage. Overall, it is the heart-healthy benefit that should be *emphasized* to Healthy Choice's own BLs; taste should be mentioned (or secondarily emphasized); with price traded off.

Now contrast a different target audience: Healthy Choice's *other-brand loyals* (presumed in this simplified example to all be loyal to Lean Cuisine). In the figure's panel B it can be seen that OBLs attach highest importance to the "diet" benefit, with Lean Cuisine perceived as delivering uniquely on this benefit. Taste is a little less important for Lean Cuisine's loyal buyers and the two brands are perceived as offering equal delivery on taste. Price perceptions are the same as for the above target audience. To attract Lean Cuisine's BLs, that is, Healthy Choice's OBLs, Healthy Choice has to make up its deficit on the "diet" benefit. Taste would be *mentioned,* but "diet" must be *emphasized* if Healthy Choice is to win over Lean Cuisine customers. This is what Healthy Choice is doing: pointing out that it has equally low calories with only " 1/2 the fat of Lean Cuisine"—low fat being the second most important *attribute* concern of dieters, after low calories.

Thus, the I-D-U model must be constructed separately for each audience that the brand elects to target. I-D-U analysis of benefit selection must be conducted for each prospective target audience because differential emphases on particular benefits, as illustrated in the example of Healthy Choice *versus* Lean Cuisine, are required to attract alternative groups of buyers to the brand. (There are other

benefit strategies that Healthy Choice could adopt, as explained shortly, but these perceived *delivery* strategies are the most obvious ones.)

The manager has to decide which potential target audience—and thus which benefit strategy for brand attitude—provides the best *leverage*. It could well be, for example, that the diet-emphasis campaign by Healthy Choice directed to its OBLs would win more new sales than might be lost by "slighting" the heart-healthy appeal desired by its own BLs. Unless Healthy Choice can split media to the two target audiences (difficult in TV but possible in magazines), it cannot aim successfully at both target audiences. Its manager will have to decide which I-D-U positioning offers the best leverage.

**Related Approaches.** A generic version of the Importance-by-Delivery matrices shown in Figure 6.9 for Healthy Choice has been widely publicized.[54] A typical application of this matrices is shown in Figure 6.10. The matrix is, for our purposes, oversimplified because first, it collapses all prospective target audiences into one (you must construct a matrix for *each* prospective target audience, separately); and second, it ignores uniqueness[55] (we have seen how the brand must strive for one or more *differentially superior* benefits). The latter criticism has been addressed in a subsequently publicized matrix[56] which essentially takes the brand's *high-delivery* benefits (the two right-hand boxes of Figure 6.10) and then plots Importance-by-Uniqueness (Figure 6.11). As might be anticipated, an I-D-U "cube" (three-dimensional) matrix has even been proposed.[57] However, we believe that our I-D-U model, which shows I, D, and U in *one* diagram, is easier to follow and more precise.

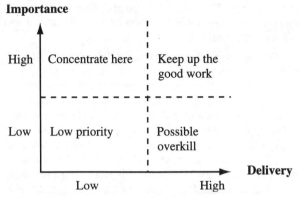

**FIGURE 6.10**
Simplified matrix showing "I-D" benefit strategy only. However, uniqueness, "U," should also be considered, and a matrix should be constructed for each target audience.

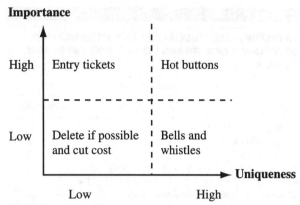

**FIGURE 6.11**
Simplified matrix showing "I-U" benefit strategy for the brand's high-delivery benefits. Again, this matrix should be constructed for each target audience.

## 6B. I-D-U and Multiattribute Strategies

First, it may help to look back at Figure 5.5 in the previous chapter. The *full* multimotive multiattribute formulation of brand attitude[58] is:

$$BATT_b = \sum_{m=1}^{8} \sum_{i=1}^{n} (B_{bi(m)} \times E_{i(m)})$$

where $BATT_b$ = attitude toward the brand b

$b$ = brands 1, 2, ... b, ... etc.

$m$ = purchase motives 1, 2, ... m, ... up to 8 (possible motives)

$i$ = benefits 1, 2, ... i, ... up to n benefits

$\sum_{m=1}^{8}$ = sum over motives

$\sum_{i=1}^{n}$ = sum over benefits

$B_{bi(m)}$ = belief that brand b delivers benefit i for motive m

$E_{i(m)}$ = emotional weight (importance) of benefit i for motive m

Next, let's construct a concrete example to illustrate how the formula is applied. Let's look at the situation of Coke II's relaunch campaign targeted at young Pepsi drinkers. (It may be remembered that Coke II, originally New Coke, is a sweeter version of Coke that compares well with Pepsi in blindfold tests. Young drinkers, in particular, prefer the sweeter-tasting colas.) Let's assume that the primary purchase motive—for the target audience—is social approval and that the secondary motive is sensory gratification represented by sweet taste. However, for clarity of presentation, let's drop the "m" part and instead reflect its influence via benefit importance, $E_i$. The simplified formula now becomes:

$$BATT_b = \sum_{i=1}^{n} (B_{bi} \times E_i)$$

Suppose that we've interviewed a large random sample of under-25 Pepsi loyals to rate both brands' benefit delivery ($B_{bi}$s) and that we have inferred the importance weights ($E_i$s) of the benefits. $B_{bi}$s are shown on a scale from 0 to 5, and $E_i$s on a scale from $-3$ to $+3$, in Table 6.9.[59] It can be seen that, as might be expected, Coke II lags behind Pepsi, with the average Pepsi brand-loyal buyer preferring Pepsi by a 2:1 margin. (This is an average, so it could mean—and you'd want to check—that the typical buyer in this target audience buys Pepsi two out of every three times and Coke II once; or that *all* buy Pepsi every time since it has the greater *relative* brand attitude, so that Coke II has to catch up by approximately *double* its present attitude, 14 up to 27, to win over Pepsi-loyal buyers. The "stochastic" first

**TABLE 6.9**

**HYPOTHETICAL MULTIATTRIBUTE FORMULATION BY YOUNG PEPSI BRAND LOYALS FOR PEPSI AND COKE II**

| Benefit | $B_{bi}s$ (Delivery) | | $E_i$ |
| | Pepsi | Coke II | (Importance) |
| --- | --- | --- | --- |
| 1. Peer acceptance | 5 | 2 | ( + 3) |
| 2. Good tasting | 5 | 3 | ( + 2) |
| 3. Low price | 2 | 2 | ( + 1) |

$BATT_{Pepsi} = 5 ( + 3) + 5 ( + 2) + 2 ( + 1) = 27$
$BATT_{Coke\ II} = 2 ( + 3) + 3 ( + 2) + 2 ( + 1) = 14$
Delivery ($B_{bi}s$) on a scale from 0 to 5
Importance ($E_i$) on a scale from $- 3$ to $+ 3$
Relative BATTs are 27:14 or roughly 2:1 (or 66% to 34%) for the *average* Pepsi BL buyer.

interpretation is somewhat more realistic but it makes no difference to the example here.)

How might Coke II apply one or more of the five multi-attribute strategies for increasing brand attitude given in Table 6.5? Let's consider them in order.

**1.** *Increase perceived delivery* ($B_{bi}$). Coke II lags Pepsi on perceived peer acceptance and perceived good taste. If it could increase its perceived popularity to equal Pepsi's, Coke II would pick up $2 \rightarrow 5 = 3 ( + 3) = + 9$ brand attitude points. This might, however, lead to a costly "battle of the celebrities" unless Coke II can find another way of increasing perceived peer acceptance. (In Australia, a "street cred" campaign is being used for Coke, that is, the original Coke, with just this in mind. Ironically, the "street cred[ibility]" creative idea apparently was "borrowed" from Pepsi's advertising.[60]) Or Coke II could try to improve its perceived taste rating to equal Pepsi's. This would yield $3 \rightarrow 5 = 2 ( + 2) = + 4$ points, a less effective strategy, according to the numbers.

**2.** *Increase importance* ($E_i$). Coke II has no benefits on which it delivers uniquely (that is, better than Pepsi). Thus, an increased benefit-*importance* strategy *alone* would benefit *Pepsi* more than Coke II. In theory, Coke II could, however, slash its price and push the importance of price savings to this younger market. A drastic price cut would cause Coke II's Bbi on this benefit to rise to 5 and the price-oriented advertising would increase the Ei of price to $+ 2$, realistically. Coke II would gain $+ 8$ points (from [2][ + 1] to [5][ + 2]) and Pepsi would *also* gain $+ 2$ points, ([2][ + 1] to [2][ + 2]), for a net advantage to Coke II of $+ 6$ points. (In all these strategies, the *total* BATTb points would change for one or both brands, so the comparison would shift to a different ratio. But, for simplicity, let's assume that the total doesn't change and that Coke II is chas-

ing Pepsi's BATTb total of 27 points.) One problem with this price strategy is that Pepsi would quickly match it and nullify Coke's gain.

**3.** *Weaken competitor's perceived delivery* ($B_{ci}$). Though difficult to execute successfully, weakening Pepsi's perceived benefit delivery would in theory be the best strategy for Coke II. The biggest deficit fo Coke II is on popularity (peer acceptance), and if Coke II could undermine Pepsi's social appeal to the under-25 age group, many Pepsi loyals might switch to Coke II. If, for instance, Coke II could reduce Pepsi's peer acceptance rating to 3, and at the same time (using strategy 1) raise its own peer acceptance rating to 4, slightly ahead, Pepsi would lose $5 \rightarrow 3 = - 2 ( + 3)$ $= - 6$ points, and Coke II would gain $2 \rightarrow 4 = 2 ( + 3)$ $= + 6$ points, for a *net* gain of $+ 12$ points. This would place Coke II much closer to Pepsi on overall attitude, BATTb at 20 versus 21. It is likely, too, that with increased perceived popularity, Coke II's *perceived* taste rating would increase relative to Pepsi's. A 1-point increase in Coke II's taste rating would produce $3 \rightarrow 4 = 1 ( + 2) = + 2$ extra points and put Coke II ahead. A popularity appeal based on taste might achieve this and perhaps equate the two brands' perceived taste ratings at 4 each, thereby putting Coke II ahead by 22 versus 19. Though difficult, this "combined" strategy represents the best benefit emphasis for Coke II.

**4.** *Add a new benefit* ($B_{bi}\ E_i$). If Coke II could find a new benefit which it could deliver uniquely, the potential for gain is quite large even if the benefit is of relatively low importance. Coke II's rating would be potentially 5, with Pepsi's at 0, so it would gain $+ 5$ points with a new $+ 1$ importance benefit, and $+ 10$ points if it could find a new $+ 2$ importance benefit. Though it's not obvious what Coke II could add, let's suppose it added a mild and legal "euphoria" ingredient, such as extra caffeine (we note that in Europe, where some countries have a liberal attitude toward soft drugs, there is a soft-drink brand that contains amphetamine). If this new benefit had an importance weight of $+ 1$, the benefits considered by the target audience would now total n = 4, and the new attitudes would be:

$$BATT_{Pepsi} = 27 + 0 (+1) = 27$$
$$BATT_{Coke\ II} = 14 + 5 (+1) = 19$$

This strategy gets Coke II closer to Pepsi but still not ahead. It also assumes that it is technically and legally feasible for Coke II to become a high-caffeine cola.

**5.** *Alter the choice rule to favor the brand* ($\sum$). In terms of the original ratings, Coke II is losing out by the fact that buyers *sum* the benefits (as shown in the calculations in the table); that is, buyers *add* the benefits of peer acceptance, good-tasting, and low price to arrive at their overall brand attitudes. (The rule, known as the "linear compensatory" choice rule, also assumes that the benefits are independent, that is, uncorrelated. It is advisable to examine whether changes in one benefit belief may cause changes in beliefs about other benefits that are correlated in the buyer's mind.) Assuming *no other* changes, Coke II's only hope using strategy 5 would be to try to induce young Pepsi loyals to consider *low price* first and choose only on price. This would put Coke II equal with Pepsi, since they are both equivalently priced. Technically known as an "elimination-by-aspects" choice rule,[61] this strategy is the obvious one for store-brand colas.

Also, technically, note that changes in the choice rule can be calculated by regarding it as equivalent to an extreme version of strategy 2, namely, changing the importance weights. Thus, in the price example above, the importance of price would increase to $+3$ while the importance of the other two benefits would reduce to zero. In theory, the new attitudes would be:

$$\text{BATT}_{\text{Pepsi}} = 5\,(0) + 5\,(0) + 2\,(+3) = 6$$

$$\text{BATT}_{\text{Coke II}} = 2\,(0) + 3\,(0) + 2\,(+3) = 6$$

The multiattribute formulation therefore provides a powerful way of "preevaluating" potential benefit-emphasis strategies—it's another valuable "what if" tool, as was the motives checklist earlier.

However, let's not lose sight of the I-D-U model as the means of putting the multiattribute calculations into *practice*. With the original ratings, Coke II had *no* unique benefit to emphasize, one equal benefit (price) to mention, and two inferior benefits to either trade off or omit (it could omit peer acceptance but would probably have to trade off good-tasting, since this presumably is easily determinable by the buyer). This amounts to a rather hopeless position for Coke II *unless* it were to adopt one or another of the five multiattribute strategies discussed above. What Coke II did, in fact, was emphasize low price (introducing a larger size than Pepsi for the same price) and target children and teens, for whom low price is important. This is a combination of strategies 1 and 2 (or possibly 1 and 5).

The I-D-U model based on the multiattribute formulation can be used for *any* product or service. Here we have illustrated it with an everyday consumer product. Day and Wensley discuss industrial and service applications, and a specific numerical example for industrial suppliers is provided by Lehmann and O'Shaughnessy.[62]

## 6C. Subliminal Sexual Imagery in Ads

It could be argued that many cases of apparently pure-emotion focus, such as the insurance company ad in Figure 6.10 and the typical Benetton ad, are in effect *benefit*-to-emotion ads in that consumers are likely to derive a benefit belief even though none is explicitly stated. For instance, in the R&V insurance ad, consumers may infer that "We're open-ing the horizon" means that the company is promising to make your future less worrisome. Similarly, benefit beliefs feasibly inferred from the Benetton ads may be that the company is socially responsible, or simply that the brand has avant-garde advertising (a positively weighted benefit for many people). If so, then these are examples of the $B_{bi}E_i$ term in the multiattribute brand attitude formulation—not of pure $E_o$, or freestanding emotions.

Worth discussing, therefore, is the use of subliminal sexual imagery in ads. Subliminal sexual imagery is a demonstration of *pure* emotion in advertising because the persuasion process is evidently not based on conscious cognitive consideration of attributes or benefits—no benefit beliefs are formed.[63] The more sensational claims by Wilson Bryan Key[64] of subliminal sexual and also death imagery in ads (according to the Freudian theories of Eros, or sexual drive, and Thanatos, or death-wish drive) have rightfully been dismissed. However, let's not throw out the baby with the bathwater. Subsequent experiments by Freudian psychologist William J. Ruth and his colleagues suggest that the sexual arousal effect is real, that it can occur subconsciously, and that it favorably affects brand attitude.[65] Ruth and his colleagues conducted their experiments with ads for liquor, a product category where the benefits are often similar across brands and for which, it could be maintained, sexual arousal (a particular instance of the sensory gratification motive usually, although sometimes social approval) is a relevant benefit (emotion focus).

In Ruth's first experiment, consumers were shown six one-page liquor ads taken from weekly news and sports magazines. Three of these ads were judged by the experimenters to contain phallic-plus-vaginal symbols—indeed, two phallic symbols and two vaginal symbols per ad (experimental group). The other three ads contained no such symbols (control group). All of the ads depicted objects only, not people, so there was no explicit hint of sex in any of the ads. Consumers, after looking at the ads, for which they were told there would be a "recall" test, were actually administered a psychoanalytic Thematic Apperception Test (TAT). The TAT is an ambiguous-picture "projective" test (like the famous Rorschach inkblots but with people in the pictures) in which the individual is asked to "write a story" about what is going on in the TAT picture. The stories were then scored by the experimenter for presence of sexual imagery, using the standard TAT coding scheme. In a postexperimental interview, none of the consumers showed awareness of the true purpose of the experiment. As predicted, consumers who saw the liquor ads containing phallic and vaginal symbols exhibited approximately twice as much sexual content in their subsequent descriptions (of the ambiguous TAT cards, not the ads) as those who saw the nonsymbolic ads. Men and women both showed the effect. This first experiment demonstrates that sexual drive can be unconsciously aroused by normal but symbolically particular stimuli in ads.

In the second experiment, with a new sample of consumers, the effect of sexual symbolic content was taken one step further by examining *purchase intentions* for advertised liquor brands. Seven paired ads were selected—again, actual ads from consumer magazines. One ad in each pair contained copulatory (male-female intercourse) symbolism; the other, none—and again no people were shown in any of the ads. The ads used in the experiment were quite normal. For example, the Freudian symbolism ads included a Christmas stocking with a bottle protruding diagonally; the nonsexual ads included a winter snow scene glimpsed through a frosty window. The ingenious prior step was that the brands and liquor types in the pairs were matched beforehand for purchase intentions based on the *name alone,* rated by a separate but similar group of consumers. In this pretest, the brands in the pairs differed by less than 0.2 of a rating point on the 7-point (1 to 7) purchase intention measure. The experiment followed the pretest, with a new sample of consumers. Table 6.10 shows the results. Purchase intentions for brands advertised in ads that included Freudian copulatory symbolism were approximately 1.0 rating points higher on the 7-point purchase intention measure than purchase intentions for the brands advertised in nonsymbolic ads. Moreover, showing generalizability, this highly significant effect was demonstrated for men in the experiment on five of the seven ads and for women on six of the seven ads. It is unlikely that other factors such as the esthetics of the ads produced these differences since the control ads were probably more attractive than the experimental (symbolic) ads. We note that the effect was obtained with only one exposure to the ads, although the laboratory-like forced-exposure conditions of the experiment probably translate to about three real-world exposures.

---

**TABLE 6.10**

**FREUDIAN COPULATORY SYMBOLISM IN LIQUOR ADS INCREASES PURCHASE INTENTION**

(*Ratings on a scale of 1 = low intention to 7 = high intention to purchase. Mean differences for both men and women between types of ads significant at p < .001.*)

| | Purchase intention | |
| --- | --- | --- |
| | Control ads (no symbolism) | Experimental ads (copulatory symbolism) |
| Men | 3.6 | 4.5 |
| Women | 3.4 | 4.5 |

*Source:* Ruth, Mosatche, and Kramer, 1989; see note 65.

Pending replication, we accept the experiments as valid demonstrations of subliminal sexual imagery "working" in ads—and as an intriguingly successful demonstration of pure-emotion focus.

## NOTES

1. See A. Ries and J. Trout, *Positioning: The Battle for Your Mind,* New York: McGraw-Hill, 1971; and J. Trout and A. Reis, The positioning era cometh, *Advertising Age,* April 24, 1972, pp. 35–38, May 1, pp. 51–54, and May 8, pp. 114–116. These authors popularized the concept of positioning 20 years ago, but contemporary references confirm that positioning is one of the most important concepts in marketing and is often implemented by advertising. For instance, see G. S. Day, *Market Driven Strategy: Processes for Creating Value,* New York, NY: The Free Press, 1990, especially chapter 7; and G. L. Urban and S. H. Star, *Advanced Marketing Strategy,* Englewood Cliffs, NJ: Prentice-Hall, 1991, especially chapter 8.

Ries and Trout likened positioning to placing a brand on a "ladder" in the prospect's mind. The rungs of the ladder are competing brands. A brand that is impossibly low on the ladder can attempt to "bring in a new ladder" by partitioning the market. Their examples of positioning imply that the ladder itself could be a brand awareness ladder (such as order of brand recall) or a brand attitude ladder (such as order of preference). We have covered the brand awareness ladder in the previous chapter in conjunction with brand awareness objectives and the awareness set, and also the brand attitude ladder in conjunction with brand attitude objectives and relative brand attitude. The notion of a "new ladder" relates to the category need communication objective and specifically to category partitioning and category repositioning, discussed in the present chapter.

When to use which interpretation of positioning is an unanswered question in Ries and Trout. This criticism is applicable also to the work of Aaker and, more recently, Crask and Laskey. The latter authors proposed a "positioning-based decision model" which was almost entirely circular; for instance, recommending that if competitors will be explicitly named in the commercial, then use a comparative positioning. Only an early paper by Frazer has made a serious attempt to identify the conditions under which different positioning options should be adopted but, as in most articles on positioning, his definitions of positioning options are none too clear. See D. A. Aaker, Positioning your product, *Business Horizons,* 1982, *25* (2), pp. 56–62; M. R. Crask and H. A. Laskey, A positioning-based decision model for selecting advertising messages, *Journal of Advertising Research,* 1990, *30* (4), pp. 32–38; and C. F. Frazer, Creative strategy: A management perspective, *Journal of Advertising,* 1983, *12* (4), pp. 36–41.

2. V. Stefflre, *Developing and Implementing Marketing Strategies,* New York: Praeger, 1986.

3. Following the "Just for the taste of it" campaign, Diet Coke's management fiddled with the short-lived "Taste it all" and most recently "This is refreshment." In early 1995, it decided to revert to "Just for the taste of it"; see *Advertising Age,* February 6, 1995, p. 41.

4. See J. R. Anderson, *Cognitive Psychology and Its Implications,* 3rd ed., New York: W. H. Freeman, 1990, for an explanation of associative network theory.

5. Some pioneers are ahead of their time and fail. We tend to remember only the successful or *surviving* pioneers. Examples of pioneers that failed include Gablinger's, the light-beer brand from Rheingold brewery which preceded the brand now regarded as the pioneer, Miller Lite, by 15 years; and most notably Sperry Rand, which invented computers, whereas IBM is widely believed to be the pioneer. See G. S. Carpenter and K. Nakamoto, Consumer preference formation and pioneering advantage, *Journal of Marketing Research,* 1989, *26* (3), pp. 285–298. The failure rate of true pioneers is much higher than most people think— perhaps as high as 50 percent—mainly because failed pioneers are quickly forgotten. Historical (archival) analysis with cross-checking of multiple informants suggests that the failure rate of true pioneers is 67 percent for durable goods and 28 percent for nondurables. Overall, the true pioneer becomes the later market leader only 11 percent of the time—thus there is a big learn-from-the-prototype effect and remarkably fast forgetting of failed pioneers. See P. N. Golder and G. J. Tellis, Pioneer advantage: Marketing logic or marketing legend?, Paper presented at the Marketing Science Conference, London Business School, July 1992. We should therefore emphasize the term "market leader" rather than "pioneer."

6. G. S. Carpenter and K. Nakamoto, same reference as in note 5.

7. As a cogent example of how this happens, Carpenter and Nakamoto describe the case of Vaseline, which pioneered in the personal-use petroleum-jelly market in 1880. Vaseline has the two attributes of being translucent (almost clear) and quite thick. New category users who tried Vaseline for personal use and found that it worked attributed the reinforcement from the product as being due to these two attributes (thus the i's and n were defined) and particularly to the translucence attribute, since Vaseline's early advertising emphasized its purity via the "pure gel" claim (thus setting a higher importance weight, $E_i$, on translucence as compared with thickness). In terms of benefit beliefs or delivery (the $B_{bi}s$), the ideal petroleum jelly, represented by Vaseline since at that time there was no other brand to compare it with, was perceived as *moderately* transparent (that is, translucent) and *quite thick* (that is, not runny but not completely "gluey" either). This *combination* of moderate transparency and quite high thickness (the choice rule, $\sum$, for the ideal $B_{bi}$ levels) set the standard for central location in the category against which later brands would be compared.

8. This is because of the following realizations: Category membership, in the consumer's mind, is a matter of brand *awareness*—the brand either is, or is not, recalled or recognized as being in the category. Of course, to be regarded as being in the category, the brand presumably would have to meet or exceed some cutoff of delivery on the category need's general attribute; in the car example, a brand of car would have to meet or exceed a high level of "prestigiousness" to be classified as being in the prestige car category. Obviously, everybody would regard Rolls-Royce as being a prestige car. This is its brand awareness. But if Rolls-Royce wishes to adopt a central location in the prestige car category, then this becomes a matter of brand *attitude:* a consideration of "how much," rather than "is or is not." Beyond the cutoff, the brand has to deliver differentially well, that is, it has to be perceived as superior, if the category need is also to be the benefit. In the prestige car example, Rolls-Royce would have to be seen not only to be prestigious, but *the* most prestigious car (unique delivery on the benefit). This is a little difficult to grasp at first because the attribute is the same for category need as for the benefit. However, if you keep in mind that "cutoff delivery" equates to brand awareness in the category whereas "superior delivery" equates to brand attitude, then the positioning statement is appropriate.

9. The "me-too" central positioning strategy *assumes* that the market leader has indeed occupied the central (ideal) position and that the leader's market penetration is high or fastest, two likely conditions.

10. Incredibly, the company has been flirting with a second theme to be used simultaneously for Miller Lite: "Best beer for the times." This would appear to encroach on Miller High Life's "Miller time" theme, although perhaps that's the intent given that the flagship brand is flopping and has been ignored in favor of Miller Genuine Draft. See I. Teinowitz, Tastes great, less filling returns to Miller Lite ads, *Advertising Age,* September 14, 1992, p. 22.

11. B. Garfield, Nice ads, McD's, but that theme not what you want, *Advertising Age,* February 24, 1992, p. 53.

12. B. Garfield, Big Mac takes a new break with a familiar McD's twist, *Advertising Age,* March 13, 1995, p. 3.

13. G. S. Carpenter and K. Nakamoto, same reference as in note 5.

14. IBM removes logo—and support, *The Australian,* March 24, 1992, p. 42.

15. K. E. Rosenberg and M. H. Blair, Observations: The long and short of persuasive advertising, *Journal of Advertising Research,* 1994, *34* (4), pp. 63–69.

16. The M.I.T. marketing scientists' work is described straightforwardly in G. L. Urban and M. H. Star, *Advanced Marketing Strategy,* Englewood Cliffs, NJ: Prentice-Hall, 1991, especially chapter 14. For a more technical description, see J. R. Hauser and S. M. Shugan, Defensive marketing strategies, *Marketing Science,* 1983, *2* (4), pp. 319–360; and J. R. Hauser and S. P. Gaskin, Application of the "Defender" consumer model, *Marketing Science,* 1984, *3* (4), pp. 327–360. Normally, pioneers can expect another entry within the first year in 38 percent of cases, beyond the first year in another 25 percent, and *no* other entry in 37 percent of cases. Of course, it depends on where the new entries position themselves as to whether the pioneer should respond. See D. Bowman and H. Gatignon, Order of entry as a moderator of the effect of marketing mix on market share, Paper presented at the Marketing Science conference, London, July 1992. It is important to know that a differentiated entry has a much *lower* likelihood (probably less than 25 percent) of having to face a counterattack from the market leader than does a me-too brand that attacks the leader. See W. T. Robinson, Marketing mix reactions to entry, *Marketing Science,* 1988, *7* (4), pp. 368–385; and also S. P. Gaskin, Comments on "Marketing mix reactions to entry," *Marketing Science,* 1988, *7* (4), pp. 388–389. Also, the reaction, if any, to a differentiated positioning will usually be slow in coming (2 years or more), thus giving the differentiated brand a chance to establish itself.

17. G. S. Carpenter and K. Nakamoto, same reference as in note 5. These authors explain that the later me-too's may help to create a "critical mass" with the differentiated brand, which attracts share away from the leader.

18. Adapted from S. M. Shugan, Estimating brand position maps using supermarket scanning data, *Journal of Marketing Research,* 1987, *24* (1), pp. 1–18.

19. A slightly more complex example is provided by the low-calorie frozen-dinner market that we have been following throughout the book:
    - The pioneer brand was Weight Watchers. There was just one dimension really—low calories.
    - Stouffer's Lean Cuisine was the next brand to enter, but it did *not* take the low-price, me-too positioning because it wanted to charge a premium price. Lean Cuisine therefore *differentiated* by focusing on the taste attribute of the category. When Weight Watchers was the only brand in the category, the category itself was regarded as being rather bland in taste, an attribute that buyers of the category were willing to trade off against the low-calorie benefit for dieting. Lean Cuisine positioned itself as a better-tasting brand that also offered the low-calorie benefit.
    - One of the next brands to enter was Budget Gourmet. This brand differentiated, as its name suggests, on price. Interestingly, as Carpenter and Nakamoto point out, price is *not* usually a good attribute on which to differentiate because it can be easily countered, if necessary, by other brands. However, Budget Gourmet's *name* very clearly suggested that it owned the low-price-yet-good-tasting position.
    - Then, along comes Healthy Choice. Healthy Choice was able to add an important new attribute to the category and thereby partition the market further. The overall category now consists of low-calorie brands, good tasting brands, budget or low-price brands—and heart-healthy brands.

    The frozen-dinner market also illustrates the point that *later me-too's* should imitate a (growing) differentiated, not a central, brand. Recent entries such as Healthy Request and Healthy Portion have all been aimed at Healthy Choice, not at Weight Watchers or Lean Cuisine in the more central location.

20. See D. Chase and B. Garfield, Can unique selling proposition find happiness in parity world? *Advertising Age,* September 21, 1992, p. 51.

21. Please excuse the unintended sexism here but the expression "product (or user) as 'hero'" is in common usage in advertising.

22. G. S. Day, same reference as in note 1.

23. See the studies by M. Sujan and by D. Mahaswaran and B. Sternthal described later in the chapter (references in note 37). Also see J. W. Alba and J. W. Hutchinson, Dimensions of consumer expertise, *Journal of Consumer Research,* 1987, *13* (4), pp. 411–454.

24. M. S. Roth, Depth versus breadth strategies for global brand image management, *Journal of Advertising,* 1992, *21* (2), pp. 25–36. In this study, 38 managers from 11 U.S. companies which market jeans, athletic shoes, or beer to other countries (213 brands in total) allocated 100 points for each brand's positioning strategy across three categories of motives: *functional,* including problem removal and problem avoidance; *sensory,* like our sensory gratification but possibly

including intellectual stimulation; and *social,* corresponding with our social approval motive. Aggregate usage of these three motive categories was as follows: functional, 49 percent; sensory, 33 percent; and social, 18 percent. The highest usage of one motive category by a single brand was 75 percent. It should be noted that the managers' classifications would quite probably differ from ours, given the difficulty of correctly classifying motives. However, the general finding of the superiority of motive concentration would be unaffected by this.

25. R. I. Haley, Benefit segmentation—20 years later, *Journal of Consumer Marketing,* 1984, *1* (2), pp. 5–13.

26. The concept of "determinance" of attributes (benefits) was proposed by J. H. Myers and M. I. Alpert, Determinant buying attitudes: Meaning and measurement, *Journal of Marketing,* 1968, *32* (4), pp. 13–20. For an update on the concept of determinance, see M. K. Alpert, Unresolved issues in the identification of determinant attributes, in J. C. Olson, ed., *Advances in Consumer Research,* vol 7, Ann Arbor, MI: Association for Consumer Research, 1980, pp. 83–88.

27. In a scientifically bold article, the late and famous market researcher Alfred Politz suggested a formula for the three criteria of benefit selection which states that Importance is most influential in causing advertising to be effective, followed by Delivery (which he called believability), and last, Uniqueness:

$$E = I \times \sqrt[a]{D} \times \sqrt[a+b]{U}$$

This formula reflects the correct order of consideration in benefit selection, but we would amend the weights to emphasize Uniqueness, thus:

$$E = I \times D \times U^a$$

where, as in Politz's formula, a is a number larger than 1.0. See A. Politz, Politz on copy: Making the sales point stick out, *Printer's Ink,* 1955, *250* (April 1), pp. 32–34. As *Printers' Ink* is now defunct and hard to obtain, a summary of Politz's theory is available in D. B. Lucas and S. H. Britt, *Measuring Advertising Effectiveness,* New York: McGraw-Hill, 1960, p. 123.

28. R. I. Haley, same reference as note 25; G. S. Carpenter, R. Glazer, and K. Nakamoto, Meaningful brands from meaningless differentiation: The dependence on irrelevant attributes, *Journal of Marketing Research,* 1994, *31* (3), pp. 339–350.

29. Serious omission of an essential "entry ticket" benefit befell Campbell Soup Company in 1989. Probably prompted by the success of new rival Healthy Choice, Campbell in 1989 attempted to link the low-fat, low-cholesterol content of most of its soups to the "heart-healthy" benefit (reduced risk of some types of heart disease). However, Campbell omitted the third attribute of heart-healthy food: low sodium. Campbell's soups are generally high in sodium (salt). The Federal Trade Commission forced Campbell to state the sodium content, and the recommended maximum daily intake, in any future ads that referred to heart disease. Campbell subsequently brought out a line of low-sodium soups under the Healthy Request label. See Campbell to disclose salt content, *Marketing News,* September 14, 1992, p. 1.

30. The brief exposure duration for ads in some media, notably TV and "mobile" outdoor, virtually forces benefits to be omitted—there is insufficient time to communicate more than one or two main benefits. With "missing" benefits, there is an important distinction between one-time purchases and repeat-purchase products. With *one-time* purchases (by nonexpert consumers), missing values for important benefits are usually inferred favorably (a "halo" effect) if the brand mentions other unique benefits (see G. T. Ford and R. A. Smith, Inferential beliefs in consumer evaluations: an assessment of alternative processing strategies, *Journal of Consumer Research,* 1987, *14* (3), pp. 363–371; and F. R. Kardes, D. M. Sanbonmatsu, and P. M. Herr, Consumer expertise and the feature-positive effect: Implication for judgment and inference, in M. E. Goldberg, G. Gorn, and R. W. Pollay, eds., *Advances in Consumer Research,* vol. 17, 1990, pp. 351–354). With trial purchase of a *repeat-purchase* product, the same halo effect applies for the trial purchase but, after trial, values for important omitted *entry ticket* attributes are quickly supplied by the buyer from experience (the consumer is now more expert) and will influence repeat purchase. Therefore, an inferior *entry ticket* benefit for a repeat-purchase brand in most cases should be traded off rather than omitted. Inferior *optional* benefits can be omitted.

31. These are the five basic strategies. Advanced readers should be interested to see how several recently introduced strategies are really variations of the basic five. We do not provide full references here; advanced readers will know the sources. The new strategies and their relationship to the basic strategies 1 to 5 are:

   **6.** *Prime the benefit* (cf. Fazio's "accessibility" concept or "salience"): equivalent to strategy 2, increasing the importance weight, $E_i$.

   **7.** *Increase confidence* (cf. Moran, Wyer, Berger): equivalent to strategy 1, increasing benefit-belief delivery, $B_{bi}$, in that the individual's *variance* in successive $B_{bi}$ ratings is reduced, thus moving the lower limit of $B_{bi}$ upward.

   **8.** *Change the purchase motive* (cf. Katz and, more recently, Edwards and Millar): this changes the

$E_i$s for all the benefits via the full formulation $E_{i(m)}$ and is thus equivalent to strategy 2; it is referred to as "brand attitude modification" in our brand attitude objectives in Chapter 5.

9. *Change the comparison set* (cf. the IIA violation in choice theory): equivalent to strategy 2, as the new comparator changes the $E_i$s.

10. *Brand value-equity increase* (cf. Moran): adds a *"name" multipler* to $B_{bi}E_i$, thus $N_bB_{bi}E_i$, where $N_b$ = name value of brand; technically a new strategy but consistent with the model.

11. *Brand uniqueness–equity increase/substitutability decrease* (cf. Moran): equivalent to strategy 1, increasing benefit-belief delivery, $B_{bi}$, such that $B_{bi}$ versus $B_{ci}$ *uniqueness* increases.

32. It is worthwhile mentioning here the series of content analyses initiated or influenced by Resnik and Stern. Resnik and Stern define information in ads as "cues . . . to assist a typical buyer in making an intelligent choice" (1991, p. 36). From the studies cited and conducted by Resnik and Stern, it appears that the proportion of ads that contain "information" ranges from a low of approximately 51 percent in major-network TV commercials to a high of approximately 80 percent in consumer magazine ads. These analyses imply that a large proportion of ads, especially TV ads, are "informationless." However, the informational cues permitted by Resnik and Stern are, understandably, focused on physical attributes or their immediately derived benefits. The cues and their proportions in a large sample of 1986 network TV commercials, for instance, are: components or contents, 22 percent; new ideas, 15 percent; price or value, 9 percent; performance, 8.5 percent; special offers, 7 percent; nutrition, 7 percent; "overall" usage, 6 percent; packaging or shape, 4 percent; availability, 3.5 percent; quality, 3 percent; guarantees or warranties, 3 percent; taste, 1 percent; independent research findings, 1 percent; company research findings, 1 percent; and safety, 0 percent, although this last type was found in earlier content analyses.

Resnik and Stern explicitly excluded "image" ads from their analyses. However, they note that image ads may be informative for consumers seeking to satisfy psychological or social motives (1991, p. 36). Image advertisements may well contain benefits that are not directly attribute-derived or they may contain emotional cues that guide the buyer's choice. For the most recent review of this work, see B. L. Stern and A. J. Resnik, Information content in television advertising: A replication and extension, *Journal of Advertising Research,* 1991, *31* (3), pp. 36–46.

In the case of "brand-name only" ads, such as on billboards at sports events, it is likely that the benefit is already known and inferred by the buyer or that the brand name, by association with the sports event, acquires an attitude via sensory gratification or social approval.

Therefore, all ads include or imply one or more benefits in the attribute-benefit-emotion sense in which we conceptualize "benefits" here.

33. G. D. Moberg, Strategy testing: To execute or not to execute? *Marketing News,* January 4, 1988, p. 30. For an earlier, related approach, see W. H. Wallace, Persuasive communications: The underlying forces that shape them, in D. W. Stewart, ed., *APA Division 23 Proceedings,* Washington, DC: American Psychological Association, 1984, pp. 56–57. For evidence that people really do focus on attributes, benefits, and emotions before and after purchase, see S. F. Gardial, D. S. Clemons, R. B. Woodruff, D. W. Schumann, and M. J. Burns, Comparing consumers' recall of prepurchase and postpurchase product evaluation experiences, *Journal of Consumer Research,* 1994, *20* (4), pp. 548–560.

34. It has been known since Aristotle in 363 B.C. that there are fundamentally three ways to persuade people. The first is by logical argument or *logos* (the word), which is clearly toward the attribute end of the a-b-e model. The second is by appealing to the emotions or *pathos* (emotion), which is clearly toward the emotional consequences end of the a-b-e model. The third is by asking the audience to trust the persuader's *ethos* (ethics), which we will conceptualize later as the *presenter effect,* whereby source credibility is used (in conjunction with either a logical or emotional message). This is a bit of an aside, but advertising should acknowledge its roots. See L. Percy and J. R. Rossiter, *Advertising Strategy: A Communication Theory Approach,* New York, NY: Praeger, 1980, for a development of Aristotle's tripartite theory of persuasion applied to advertising.

35. The a-b-e model is superficially similar to the means-end model proposed by Gutman and Reynolds. In their model, they distinguish attributes, consequences, and values (a-c-v), which form "ladders" or benefit chains. In our view, the term "consequences" instead of "benefits" implies that a benefit is always a consequence of an attribute, which is not necessarily the case. In the widely observed placebo effect for many over-the-counter drug products, for instance, the benefit is derived without any attribute at all! Further, the third term in their model is "values," a term which we believe is far too broad. Values are engaged in some consumer choices—notably for high-involvement/transformational brand attitude—but certainly not in the majority of choices. We prefer the term *emotions* to characterize this end-state. Nevertheless, their model is similar in spirit to ours. Whereas in their earlier

work based on this model, these authors implied that the desirable position was *always* on the "value" end of the chain, this has been modified in some of their recent work to recognize that different foci may be appropriate. The main references to the means-end model are: J. Gutman, A means-end chain model based on consumer characterization processes, *Journal of Marketing,* 1982, *46* (1), pp. 60–72; T. J. Reynolds and J. Gutman, Advertising is image management, *Journal of Advertising Research,* 1984, *24* (1), pp. 27–36; and W. S. Perkins and T. J. Reynolds, The explanatory power of values in preference judgments: Validation of the means-end perspective, in M. J. Houston, ed., *Advances in Consumer Research,* vol. 15, 1988, pp. 122–126.

36. The "self-persuasion" school of attitude theory was originated by Ohio State University psychologists, notably Greenwald and Brock. "Individual cognitive response" theory was postulated as an alternative to the "uniform comprehension" theory characteristic of the earlier Yale University attitude school founded by Hovland and McGuire, among others. See, especially S. Shavitt and T. C. Brock, Self-relevant responses in commercial persuasion: Field and experimental tests, in J. C. Olson and K. Sentis, eds., *Advertising and Consumer Psychology,* vol. 3, New York, NY: Praeger, 1986, pp. 149–171, who found that self-thoughts are more likely with an expert audience. Also, for an interesting discussion of self-persuasion, see A. R. Pratkanis and E. Aronson, *Age of Propaganda,* New York, NY: W. H. Freeman & Co., 1991, chapter 17.

37. A good demonstration of the "attributes-for-experts" effect was achieved in a study by Maheswaran and Sternthal. In their study, they prepared three product descriptions for a fictitious new personal computer: attribute focus, attribute-plus-benefit focus, and benefit focus. Examples of the attribute claims and the benefit claims for the personal computer are shown in Table 6.11, along with the results. Consumers in the experiment were divided into experts and novices based on a pretest of their computer knowledge. As the results show, the novices' brand attitude ratings of the new product were highest when the benefits were pointed out to them, whereas the *experts'* brand attitude ratings were highest when only attributes were provided. D. Maheswaran and B. Sternthal, The effects of knowledge, motivation, and type of message on ad processing and product judgments, *Journal of Consumer Research,* 1990, *17* (1), pp. 66–73. See also an earlier study, with similar results, by M. Sujan, Consumer Knowledge: Effects on evaluation strategies mediating consumer judgments, *Journal of Consumer Research,* 1985, *12* (1), pp. 31–46.

---

**TABLE 6.11**

**BRAND ATTITUDE RATINGS OF A NEW PERSONAL COMPUTER BY NOVICES AND EXPERTS AS A FUNCTION OF ATTRIBUTE FOCUS, BENEFIT FOCUS, OR BOTH, IN THE NEW PRODUCT'S DESCRIPTION**

(*Brand attitude ratings on a scale of 1 (negative) to 7 (positive), with 4 as the neutral midpoint.*)

| | Product description's focus | | |
|---|---|---|---|
| | **Attributes** | **Benefits** | **Both** |
| Novices | 4.8 | 6.0 | 5.9 |
| Experts | 6.1 | 4.8 | 4.5 |

EXAMPLES OF ATTRIBUTES AND BENEFITS USED IN THE STUDY

| **Attributes** | **Benefits** |
|---|---|
| • Open architecture with technical tutorial for self-developed software | • The technical tutorial provides extensive and simple instructions to help users do their own programming |
| • Single disk drive with boot-in facility | • It uses disks to store data, which increases the amount of data that can be stored |

*Source:* Maheswaran and Sternthal; see note 37.

38. Maheswaran and Sternthal manipulated involvement (perceived risk) in the experiment, telling half the consumers that they were participants in an anonymous survey, thus making their brand choice low-involvement, and telling the other half of the consumers that their opinion would decide whether or not the new product would be introduced and that they could expect to be contacted later by the manufacturer for a demonstration of the product, thus making their brand choice high-involvement. We have selected the high-involvement results for novices because novices would probably only be looking at a personal computer ad if they were seriously planning to buy a personal computer. On the other hand, we have selected the *low*-involvement results for experts because their product category knowledge means that they would probably look at computer ads anyway in forming their future consideration sets. The high-involvement results for experts were similar to the low-involvement results in that attribute focus was still highly effective, although the combination of attributes plus benefits was equally good when experts were closer to the purchase decision, both being better than benefits alone.

39. G. L. Shostack, Breaking free from product marketing, *Journal of Marketing,* 1977, *41* (2), pp. 73–80, and How to design a service, in J. H. Donnelly and W. R. George, (eds.), *Marketing of Services,* Chicago: AMA, 1981, pp. 221–229.

40. G. S. Carpenter, R. Glazer and K. Nakomoto, same reference as in note 28.

41. Yi notes that benefits can be either caused by attributes (for instance, size of automobile → comfort benefit and also safety benefit) or be merely correlated with them (for instance, for automobiles, European, an attribute, and prestigious, a benefit, are correlated in the minds of many U.S. car buyers). See Y. Yi, An investigation of the structure of expectancy-value and its implications, *International Journal of Research in Marketing,* 1989, *6* (2), pp. 71–83.

42. An apparent example of a benefit that is only vaguely related to attributes is the ubiquitous claim, "natural," a meaningless word. Or is it? An amazing campaign in Australia substantially reversed a 40 percent per-capita decline in sugar consumption by emphasizing that sugar is "natural." Sugar does, after all, grow naturally; it occurs naturally in fruit; it is naturally present in the body via blood sugar; and so forth (however, the chemical ingredient difference between "natural" and "artificial" foods—that is, the attribute difference—is nonsense). The campaign theme, "Sugar, a natural part of life," by the SSB ad agency, was largely responsible for restoring Australia's sugar consumption levels by disinhibiting people from adding sugar to food and beverages. A continuation of the "Sugar is natural" campaign then successfully held off the threat from artificial sweeteners which had entered the market as a diet aid. Remarkable, especially considering that many products claim they are natural precisely *because* no sugar is added.

    A. C. Nielsen Company conducted a content analysis of "natural" claims in food packaging. An incredible variety of meanings for the claim "natural" was found, including: "no preservatives," "no added salt or sugar," "no cholesterol," "low in calories and low in sodium," "made with honey instead of sugar," "unprocessed cheese," and even "decaffeinated." See Natural foods—the consumers' perspective, *The Nielsen Researcher,* 1984, *1* (1), pp. 13–20.

43. Frazer was perhaps the first to make this explicit in an early article on positioning. See C. F. Frazer, same reference as in note 1.

44. This goes counter to Katz's functional theory of attitude and is another reason why our approach should not be confused with that school of thought. The "opposite function" attack theory for negative target audiences has been proposed by M. G. Millar and K. U. Millar, Attitude change as a function of attitude type and argument type, *Journal of Personality and Social Psychology,* 1990, *59* (2), pp. 217–228. Their experiment provided only marginal support for the hypothesis, but they used an essentially low-involvement product, soft drinks, and we believe that the idea is valid but for high-involvement choices only. Our view is supported more generally by Pratkanis and Aronson's review of the "latitude of rejection" research wherein a high-credibility presenter may be able to override the narrow lattitude of acceptance that is held by an entrenched target audience. The effectiveness of the high-credibility presenter attack is due to blocking of counterarguments. We expect, also, that the "opposing function" attack would be successful because of lack of counterarguments. See A. Pratkanis and E. Aronson, same reference as in note 36, chapter 21. For the original reference on Katz's "same function" theory, see I. Sarnoff and D. Katz, The motivational basis of attitude change, *Journal of Abnormal and Social Psychology,* 1954, *49* (1), pp. 115–124.

45. J. McQueen, The different ways ads work, *Journal of Advertising Research,* 1990, *30* (5), pp. RC-13 to RC-16.

46. Whereas we may question the ethics of the "emotional differentiation" approach, it could be answered that if buyers are subjectively happy with their emotional choices, then the approach is justifiable. This is particularly cogent in the case of many prescription and over-the-counter drugs which are known by medical experts to work, for many consumers, only in terms of having a placebo effect. Subjective happiness is the basis of several schools of moral philosophy, such as Bentham's utilitarianism, and can be well justified on ethical grounds.

47. W. Kroeber-Riel, Nonverbal measurement of emotional advertising effects, in J. Olson and K. Sentis, eds., *Advertising and Consumer Psychology,* vol. 3, New York: Praeger, 1986, chapter 3; and Advertising on saturated markets, Working paper, Saarbrucken, Germany: Institute for Consumer and Behavioral Research, University of the Saarland, 1988.

48. K. Kroeber-Riel, Personal communication with the authors, 1992.

49. In 1991, the first year of its controversial campaign, Benetton's profits grew by 24 percent worldwide but fell to near breakeven in the United States; see Shrinkage of stores and customers in U.S. causes Italy's Benetton to alter its tactics, *The Wall Street Journal,* June 24, 1992, pp. B1, B10.

50. J. Deighton and R. M. Schindler, (see Chapter 5, note 34). These investigators found that consumers' exposure to prior advertising about an attribute (that a local radio station plays "a lot of new music") increased belief in this "fact" compared with those who hadn't heard it advertised (both exposed and unexposed consumers were asked to listen to the *same* radio station, so it was the perceptions that differed, not reality). Unfortunately, this increased belief based on ad-influenced "experience" did not cause consumers to alter

their radio-listening behavior, perhaps because the attribute was not important to enough consumers.

51. In terms of Leventhal's theory of fear communication and Rogers's protection motivation theory, this is known as concentrating on fear control rather than on danger control. See H. Leventhal, Findings and theory in the study of fear communications, in L. Berkowitz, ed., *Advances in Experimental Social Psychology,* vol. 5, New York, NY: Academic Press, 1970; and R. W. Rogers, A protection motivation theory of fear appeals and attitude change, *Journal of Psychology,* 1975, *91* (first half), pp. 93–114. Rogers later importantly modified his theory by suggesting that people add (rather than multiply) severity of danger, probability of occurrence, and difficulty of coping when facing *potential* threats, and will take avoidance action accordingly. But, if the threat *materializes,* panic or denial are the usual responses. See R. W. Rogers, Attitude change and information integration in fear appeals, *Psychological Reports,* 1983, *56* (1), pp. 179–182. Also see M. L. Ray and W. L. Wilkie, Fear: The potential of an appeal neglected by marketing, *Journal of Marketing,* 1970, *31* (1), pp. 54–62. Also see J. T. Strong and K. M. Dubas, The optimal level of fear arousal in advertising: An empirical study, *Journal of Current Issues and Research in Advertising,* 1993, *15* (2), pp. 93–99.

52. M. S. LaTour and S. A. Zahra, Fear appeals as advertising strategy: Should they be used? *Journal of Consumer Marketing,* 1989, *6* (2), pp. 61–70.

53. A. Pratkanis and E. Aronson, same reference as in note 36.

54. The simple matrix has appeared in many trade journals and also appears in J. A. Martilla and J. C. James, Importance-performance analysis, *Journal of Marketing,* 1977, *41* (1), pp. 77–79.

55. See especially the article by C. Obermiller, Generating product ideas: A modification of the dual questioning technique, in J. C. Olson, ed., same reference as in note 26, pp. 767–771.

56. J. C. Webster, Technique surpasses standard quadrant analysis, *Marketing News,* September 2, 1991, pp. 8, 9. We have changed Webster's labels slightly. This grid has been picked up by research companies such as Chilton Research Services, who call it "competitive leverage analysis"; see *Marketing News,* January 4, 1992, p. 5.

57. K. J. Clancy and R. S. Shulman, *The Marketing Revolution,* New York: Harper Business, 1991, pp. 109–115.

58. We note that academic marketing researchers usually use the symbol $A_b$ to denote attitude toward the brand. In order to distinguish brand awareness from brand attitude, both of which begin with A, we use BA for brand awareness and BATT for brand attitude.

59. The reader may notice that we use various measurement-scale numerics throughout the book. All such scales are arbitrary (chosen by the researcher) but they should, as far as possible, reflect psychological reality for the consumer or customer in that he or she seems typically to discriminate this many points when evaluating in the category.

60. P. Warneford, Pepsi ups the ante, *Ad News,* November 6, 1992, p. 1.

61. For an excellent review of choice rules, or "heuristics," see J. R. Bettman, E. J. Johnson, and J. W. Payne, Consumer decision making, in T. S. Robertson and H. H. Kassarjian, eds., *Handbook of Consumer Behavior,* Englewood Cliffs, NJ: Prentice-Hall, 1991, chapter 2.

62. See G. S. Day and R. Wensley, Assessing advantage: A framework for diagnosing competitive superiority, *Journal of Marketing,* 1988 (2), pp. 1–20; and D. R. Lehmann and J. O'Shaughnessy, Difference in attribute importance for different industrial products, *Journal of Marketing,* 1974, *38* (2), pp. 36–42.

63. Fear conditioning may provide another "subconscious" example. For instance, when exposed to pictures of fear-relevant stimuli such as snakes and spiders, most people do not consciously report fear but *will* show a reaction on a subconscious measure such as the galvanic skin response (GSR). See E. J. Mazurski, N. W. Bond, D. A. T. Siddle, and P. F. Lovibond, Classical conditioning of autonomic and affective responses to fear-relevant and fear-irrelevant stimuli, *Australian Journal of Psychology,* 1993, *45* (2), pp. 69–73. Indeed the most basic emotions of anger ("fight"), fear ("flight"), and *also* sexual arousal ("lust") may be most amenable to subconscious classical conditioning to stimuli present just prior to or during the emotion's onset. For an intriguing analysis of this, see D. Zillman, Coition as emotion, in D. Byrne and K. Kelly, eds., *Alternative Approaches to the Study of Sexual Behavior,* Hillsdale, NJ: Erlbaum, 1986, chapter 7. For an even earlier analysis, see J. B. Watson, *Behaviorism,* New York: The People's Institute, 1924, chapters 7 and 8 (reprinted New York: W. W. Norton, 1970).

64. W. B. Key, *Subliminal Seduction,* Englewood Cliffs, NJ: Prentice-Hall, 1974. For sophisticated discussion of unconscious (or subconscious) phenomena, see E. F. Loftus and M. R. Klinger, Is the unconscious smart or dumb? *American Psychologist,* 1992, *47* (6), pp. 761–765, and the following articles in that issue.

65. W. J. Ruth and H. S. Mosatche, A projective assessment of the effects of Freudian sexual symbolism in liquor advertisements, *Psychological Reports,* 1985, *56* (1), pp. 183–188; and W. J. Ruth, H. S. Mosatche, and A. Kramer, Freudian sexual symbolism: Theoretical considerations and an empirical test in advertising,

*Psychological Reports,* 1989, *60* (2), pp. 1131–1139. Earlier, Kilbourne, Painton, and Ridley demonstrated a highly reliable effect on purchase intention for an illustration of a nude female subliminally embedded in a Chivas Regal ad, although not reliably for male genitalia embedded in a Marlboro ad; see W. E. Kilbourne, S. Painton, and D. Ridley. The effect of sexual embedding on responses to magazine advertisements, *Journal of Advertising,* 1985, *14* (2), pp. 48–56. However, note that the sexual ads in Ruth's studies used normal (not subliminal) stimuli whose symbolic arrangement apparently produced subconscious (Freudian unconscious) processing. The processing responses could have included sexual arousal as a positive emotion which became conditioned in one trial to the brand; see note 63.

## DISCUSSION QUESTIONS

**6.1.** Healthy Choice's introductory campaign featured celebrities such as Con-Agra's then-CEO Mike Harper, actress Diahann Carroll, and skater Dorothy Hamill. After three years of this introductory campaign, Healthy Choice in September 1992 dropped the celebrities and switched to the theme "Never settle for less." Discuss this positioning strategy in terms of the X-YZ macromodel of positioning location.

**6.2.** In 1991, Cadillac Seville ran an advertising campaign in the United States in which a prospective buyer says, "I looked only at European cars" and then the announcer's voice and an on-screen super says, "Until now." The ad goes on to talk about Cadillac Seville's modern high-tech styling and performance. In terms of the X-YZ macromodel, what is the apparent positioning strategy in this campaign?

**6.3.** You are the marketing director of an aerobics exercise clinic. Prepare a "what if" analysis of potential patronage motivations discussing *each* of the seven initial-purchase motives from the chapter.

**6.4.** You are the advertising manager for NEC laser printers, and you're trying to win customers from Hewlett-Packard's users. Advertising strategy research has produced the following results for the two brands as perceived by H-P laser-printer brand loyals (all ratings on a scale from 0 to 10 where 10 = highest):

| Benefit | NEC | H-P | Importance |
|---------|-----|-----|------------|
| Resolution | 6 | 10 | (10) |
| Speed | 9 | 6 | (6) |
| Low price | 7 | 2 | (4) |

Use the multiattribute formulation of the I-D-U mesopositioning model to decide on a strategy, then explain which benefit(s) you would emphasize, which you would mention, and which you might omit in advertising the NEC laser printer to H-P loyals, and why.

**6.5.** Analyze the following liquor-brand campaigns from the perspective of the a-b-e micropositioning model of benefit focus:
   **a.** Jack Daniels bourbon: "Charcoal mellowed drop by drop"
   **b.** Smirnoff vodka: "Leaves you breathless"
   **c.** Dewar's scotch: "Dewar's Profiles" (of the brand's users)

**6.6.** The *launch* positioning statement for Healthy Choice dinners was: (1) To men / (2) Healthy Choice is the brand of heart-healthy frozen dinner / (3) that is low in fat, sodium, and cholesterol. Evaluate this positioning statement.

## FURTHER READING

Ries, A., and Trout, J. *Positioning: The Battle for Your Mind.* New York: McGraw-Hill, 1971.

This book offers an oversimplified introduction to positioning but is definitely inspirational.

Urban, G. L., and Star, S. A. *Advanced Marketing Strategy.* Englewood Cliffs, NJ: Prentice-Hall, 1991, chapters 8, 10, and 14.

This text provides an overview of category- and benefit-positioning decisions and of competitive considerations. It also includes a general introduction to multiattribute analysis.

Stefflre, V. *Developing and Implementing Marketing Strategies.* New York: Praeger, 1986.

This is a valuable book on product strategy from one of the most original thinkers and researchers in marketing; includes many hands-on examples.

Carpenter, G. S., and Nakamoto, K. Consumer preference formation and pioneering advantage. *Journal of Marketing Research,* 1989, *26* (3), pp. 285–298.

This article provides an excellent analysis of macropositioning, and it is readable despite being in a technical journal.

Peter, J. P., and Olson, J. C. *Consumer Behavior and Marketing Strategy,* 2nd ed. Homewood, IL: Irwin, 1990, chapters 6 and 7 and pp. 478–479.

Reading the relevant sections of this book is probably the easiest, nontechnical way to learn about multiattribute analysis and how it works. These authors also discuss distinctions between attributes and benefits but bring in values as the third level rather than, as in our a-b-e micromodel, emotions.

## PART FOUR

# CREATIVE STRATEGY

**CHAPTER 7: THE CREATIVE IDEA**

**CHAPTER 8: CREATIVE EXECUTION TACTICS: BRAND AWARENESS AND LOW-INVOLVEMENT PERSUASION**

**CHAPTER 9: CREATIVE EXECUTION TACTICS: HIGH-INVOLVEMENT PERSUASION**

**CHAPTER 10: CREATIVE EXECUTION: ATTENTION AND THE STRUCTURE OF ADS**

# CHAPTER SEVEN

# The Creative Idea

The manager has specified the communication objectives for the brand and, using the core communication objectives of category need, brand awareness, and brand attitude, has selected a specific positioning strategy. Now, the advertising agency has to create an actual advertising campaign—that is, find a way of *effectively communicating the brand position*. The most effective way, in the great majority of cases, requires finding a winning *creative idea*. After reading this chapter, you should:

- Acquire a working definition of "creative idea."
- Understand the theory of random creativity and why it is important for both advertiser and agency.
- Learn how to "brainstorm" creative ideas (a method usable by advertising agencies or when creating your own ads).
- Consider a new theory of creative idea effectiveness that indicates "what to brainstorm about."
- Appreciate the importance of long-term management of creativity for the brand.

Most—but not all—advertising campaigns depend for their success on finding a winning creative idea. The baseline procedure would be simply to run a "straight" ad that does little more than state the brand's position: what it is, who it's for, and which benefit(s) the brand offers. A straight ad can be effective in direct mail and in classified ads. However, in most advertising situations, it is more effective to use a creative idea to convey the positioning message for the brand.

This chapter begins by defining what a creative idea is and illustrating why it is vitally important in most advertising situations. We then turn to a radical notion—the theory of random creativity—and explain why this is the economically sound way of maximizing the chance of finding a winning creative idea and thus a superior advertising campaign. We explore this theory and its implementation from the advertising manager's perspective (the client) and also from the viewpoint of the producer of the advertising (the agency). Next, we present a useful procedure for generating creative ideas. This is implemented in the context of our RAM-Conveyor model (where "RAM" stands for "Remote Associative Matching"), which shows how to identify creative *and* effective ideas for ads. Lastly, we look at the long-term management of creativity for the brand's advertising campaigns.

## CREATIVE STRATEGY SEQUENCE

It is worthwhile before we begin (and for later review) to show where this chapter's topic (the creative idea) fits within the AC&P planning process, especially considering that all of the chapters in this part of the book come under the heading of "creative strategy." Figure 7.1 shows the relevant sequence. The main input to creative strategy is the brand's positioning

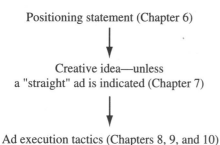

**FIGURE 7.1**
Sequence for creative strategy.

statement, as explained in Chapter 6. The creative idea, as examined in the present chapter (Chapter 7), is the agency's most important response to the positioning brief (unless a straight ad is indicated by the conditions specified later in this chapter). Next comes the actual execution of the ad or ads; and the tactics for advertising executions are the subjects of Chapters 8, 9, and 10. Thus, the basic flow is: positioning → creative idea → ad executions.

## THE CREATIVE IDEA

### Importance of Creative Ideas

**Importance for Advertisers.** The importance for advertisers (clients) in finding a great creative idea is that a brand's sales can be increased manyfold with the *same* advertising budget. We estimate "manyfold" to be *at least* by a factor of five. Since the budget is the same, the increase in sales, assuming that distribution and other marketing costs remain constant per unit, means a massive increase in profit.

Supporting evidence for the importance of the creative idea comes from a number of sources. In a landmark early study, Buzzell showed that creative quality, as measured by TV commercials' brand purchase intention pretest scores, was seven times more important in determining the brand's market share in the next 4-month period than was advertising spending, as measured by the brand's share of advertising expenditure in the category. (Buzzell made a statement in this study that has not sufficiently been heeded by researchers who claim to find only a small relationship between TV advertising *expenditure* and changes in sales or market share: "marketing models based on dollar expenditures alone cannot provide sufficient explanations of market response to advertising."[1])

Another early study consisted of an opinion survey of top management in 73 large client companies, 16 advertising agencies, and 15 other organizations, conducted by Booz Allen & Hamilton, Inc. This large, expert panel estimated that, for an identical advertising budget, "the selling power of a great idea can exceed that of an ordinary idea by a multiple of 10." The panel also pointed out that profit increase through creative ideas is much more acceptable and easily accomplished than trying to increase profit by cutting production costs or laying off employees. Thus, great creative ideas have beneficial effects beside sheer profitability.[2]

A recent study that *indirectly* supports the value of a great creative idea was reported by Margaret Henderson Blair, president of Research Systems Corporation, a leading advertising testing service in the United States. The Blair study's results are worth showing in detail because of the dramatic illustration of the importance of ad effectiveness compared with advertising expenditure levels (Figure 7.2). This study

**FIGURE 7.2**
New-product sales results (trial purchase incidence, vertical axis) as a function of advertising expenditure (in Gross Rating Points, horizontal axis) and the quality of introductory TV commercials (the four curves, representing successively better pretest "persuasion" scores). The curves suggest that higher-quality creative ideas achieve sales results at a much lower advertising cost. Compare, for instance, the sales results of the four quality levels of commercials at 3000 GRPs: approximately 1%, 3%, 6% and 13% trial for the same budget.
*Source:* Blair, 1988, see note 20. *Courtesy:* Advertising Research Foundation.

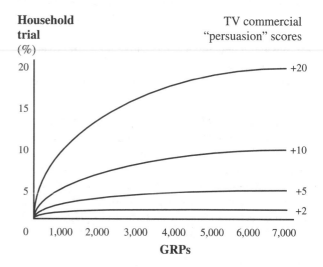

examined TV commercials for new products. Advertising campaigns for new products generally have a high success rate (about 70 percent produce a significant increase in sales), but individual success rates vary widely. The results indicate that the best commercials (again, as in the Buzzell study, as measured beforehand by a pretest "persuasion" score) produced *eight times* the level of sales (in this case, new-product trial) of the poorest commercials. (Strictly speaking, the commercials' success reflects positioning strategy as well as the creative idea, but it is probable that the highest-sales commercials had both a good positioning strategy and an outstanding creative idea.) Blair's results are also noteworthy for illustrating that it is virtually impossible to "spend your way out of" a poor commercial. The lower curve on the graph indicates that below-average commercials, even when backed with up to 7,000 GRPs (equivalent to about 90 exposures on prime time TV!), produced close to zero trial. The better the commercial, the higher the level of new product trial for the *same* advertising budget.[3] (In Chapter 19, on pretesting, we will see that better commercials are also the primary way to increase sales for an established brand.)

In perhaps the most amazing demonstration of the search for winning creative ideas, Coca-Cola Company in 1991 fired its long-standing agency for Coke (Classic), McCann-Erickson, and bypassed the traditional agencies altogether—awarding the Coke creative work to Creative Artists Agency Inc., Hollywood's leading talent agency, which uses freelancers to develop ads. Coca-Cola is pursuing a policy of using many, nontraditional ad vendors "in order to stimulate groundbreaking creative work."[4]

Overall, then, the evidence from case histories and pretesting research all supports the fact that it is extremely important for the advertiser to find a winning creative idea. We will see next that finding creative ideas—consistently—is just as important for advertising agencies.

**Importance for Advertising Agencies.** As Norman Berry, Creative Director of Ogilvy & Mather, once said when the first author was a professor in New York, creativity is the only *unique* function that an advertising agency has to offer. He made this comment over 15 years ago—but how true it has turned out to be! Three trends have made the function of creativity for the agency even *more* unique and important now: first, the emergence of media specialist companies, which have taken away a large amount of the media planning from traditional agencies; second, the growth of specialist sales promotion and public relations companies, which have kept this business away from agencies; and third, the increasing sophistication of brand managers on the client side, most of whom have MBAs, which allows them to do most of the strategic planning for advertising, with less and less being done by the agency's account management team.

The agency's ability to produce winning creative ideas is undoubtedly the major reason for clients hiring and firing their agencies. Michell[5] has conducted surveys of agency account switching both in the United States and in the United Kingdom. Consistently, the major reason for clients' switching accounts is "dissatisfaction with the standard of agency creative work." This reason was given by 62 percent of account switchers in the United States in 1983–84, and 69 percent of account switchers in the United Kingdom in 1988–89. Interestingly, although this may reflect difficulties in measuring sales effects, dismissal of the agency because of the perceived sales weakness of a campaign was only the third reason mentioned in the United States, at 47 percent, and the fourth reason mentioned in the United Kingdom, at 41 percent. Similarly, in a recent Australian survey of clients who had just switched agencies, the first-ranked reason was the "need for new creative ideas," at 74 percent importance, with "perceived sales weakness" ranked sixth, at 51 percent importance.[6] What advertisers want from the agency is creative ideas first and foremost.

A second reason for agencies' dependence on creative ideas is that awards for these ideas help them to retain the best personnel. For creative people, the winning of awards is extremely important for their self-image and career satisfaction. Creativity, after all, is what they were hired for, and awards provide a more immediate validation of their creativity than sales results do.

A final reason for the vital importance of finding winning creative ideas for the agency is the increasing trend toward remunerating agencies on the basis of creative effectiveness (as measured by advertising pretest scores or, where available, sales results). Carnation, General Mills, Campbell Soup, and Unilever are some of the companies that are known to have their agencies on incentive plans for at least some of their brands.[7] Several agencies, such as DDB Needham Worldwide—and quite a few smaller agencies—have responded positively by offering payment-by-results plans to all their clients.[8] Quite understandably, most advertising agencies have been resistant to changing the traditional media commission scheme since it provides, for them, a guaranteed income. However, it's guaranteed only for the period in which the client is satisfied with the agency's creative work. Although the dominant mode of remuneration for agencies remains the traditional percentage commission on *media* placement, the trend toward "payment by results" for *creative* performance is growing,[9] and we believe it will eventually become the predominant method of agency remuneration.

### Creative Idea Defined

The "creative idea," by its very nature, is not an easy concept to define. It is easy to identify *examples* of creative ideas but difficult to formulate a general definition. Accordingly, we will begin somewhat informally, to give the sense of the concept, and then propose a formal definition.

**How're Ya' Gonna Persuade 'Em?** This crucial question was thrown at the first author as a young man after he had presented a theoretically sound set of advertising communication objectives to a seasoned agency manager. The colloquial language has been retained because it so exactly expresses the essence of what is needed: a creative idea.

Of course, technically, the "how're ya' gonna persuade 'em" question requires an answer that incorporates more than just the creative idea. The complete components of creative strategy are the creative idea, usually, *and* the ad's message content and its executional tactics, which together (in the media schedule) must achieve the brand's communication objectives and brand position. Thus:

$$(\text{creative idea} + \text{message content} + \text{executional}$$
$$\text{tactics}) \times \text{media schedule} = \text{communication}$$
$$\text{objectives and brand position}$$

The message content (*what* to say) is largely dictated by the manager's brief to the agency stating the communication objectives and desired position for the brand. The agency is responsible for *how* to say or show it best, which consists of a creative idea, in most cases, and executional tactics (see the next three chapters). Here, however, we focus on the creative idea.

**Informal Definition.** Basically, the *creative idea* refers to *the choice of an interesting way to express the brand position in an advertising format.* The virtual necessity of a creative idea comes from the realization that rarely can we simply print the brand's positioning statement on a page (or film the words for TV, or record them for radio) and thereby produce an effective ad. Take, for instance, Volvo's presumed positioning statement from the previous chapter, and try it as an ad: "Up-market car buyers: Volvo is the brand of prestige car that provides safety and performance." This might get by—just barely—as a print ad or poster. But these 15 words alone would hardly constitute an effective TV commercial, radio commercial, or newspaper ad. What is lacking is a creative idea to translate the positioning statement into an effective ad. Whereas it must be admitted that some ads are little more than a straightforward elaboration of the positioning statement (and that there are situations, as we shall see, in which a straight ad is recommended), usually a creative idea is needed to breathe life into the positioning statement and thereby turn it into a compelling ad. A good example of a creative idea is shown in Figure 7.3, which summarizes a TV commercial for Simmons Beautyrest mattress.[10] The positioning benefit is "the independent action of the pocketed coils" and the "cat-and-bird" creative idea nicely dramatizes this benefit.

As noted in the informal definition, a creative idea is one *choice* from a virtually infinite number of ways of expressing the positioning statement and thus the intended brand position. Of course, what the advertiser is looking for is a highly effective choice—to provide a "real winner" campaign. Such winners are usually based on what advertising agencies call a "big idea."

**Big Idea: Arresting and Immediate Communication.** John O'Toole, President of the American Association of Advertising Agencies, describes the *big idea* as a "flash of insight that synthesizes the purpose of the strategy, joins the product benefit with desire in a fresh, involving way, brings the subject to life, and makes the reader or the audience stop, look, and listen."[11] This description has some of the elements that will be reflected in our definition of a creative idea although it is not quite satisfactory. For instance, the "flash of insight" presumably refers to the creative person's experience in generating the idea—but we will see that the most effective creative ideas

**FIGURE 7.3**
Creative idea of "cat and bird" for Simmons' Beautyrest mattress dramatizes the brand-positioning benefit which, according to the advertiser, is "the independent action of the pocketed coil allows two to sleep as comfortably as one."
*Courtesy:* Simmons' Canada Inc.

are those that also give the *consumer* a flash of insight. Similarly, "joins the product benefit with desire" is pretty close to linking the benefit with a relevant purchase motivation, which is the Z of positioning—but makes no reference to the Y option or to the X aspect in the fundamental positioning statement format of "an X product to help Y people Z." We do, however, agree with the last part of O'Toole's description. Making "the reader or the audience stop, look, and listen" clearly refers to the *processing* step in the buyer response steps. Here, O'Toole's description is valuable in that it points out that the creative idea refers to *processing* and not just to communication effects.

**The Power of Simplicity.** It is also the belief of many creative experts that "amazing simplicity" is the hallmark of a great creative idea. Says Edward A. McCabe, senior creative manager with the Scali, McCabe, Sloves agency in New York: "It means putting your proposition forward with such simplicity that people are both astonished and moved by it. . . . the truly great ads have a certain simplicity and directness of purpose that makes them incredibly powerful." The creative idea *must,* however, represent the brand's positioning statement. Shirley Polykoff, also a leading creative expert and president of her own agency in New York, calls this "thinking it out square, then saying it with flair."[12]

**Formal Definition.** Having, we hope, given the sense of what a creative idea—or, more precisely, an *effective* creative idea—entails, we are now ready to propose a formal definition. Again, we presume that the advertiser wants an *effective* creative idea.

The creative idea can be defined as:

1. An attention-getting and catalytically relevant representation of the brand position
2. Generated in a form that is detailed enough to be executed and tested
3. And (necessary in most cases) amenable to multiple executions.

We almost added a fourth component to the definition, which is "subject to media and legal constraints." However, we prefer to leave such constraints as an afterthought—which they should be, because we want nothing to inhibit the generation of the creative idea.

Let us now explain the components of the definition.

**1.** *An attention-getting and catalytically relevant representation of the brand position.* The creative idea must be attention-getting, first of all. We will see just what this means when we later present what we call our RAM-Conveyor theory of creativity. For now, let's just take it as obvious that the creative idea should be attention-getting.

Second, the creative idea must be catalytically relevant. We chose the term "catalytically" carefully: a catalyst is something that increases the rate of a chemical reaction. In this case, the chemical reaction is between the brand's positioning strategy and the consumer's understanding of it (the result is the brand position). The creative idea is playing the rôle of the catalyst by helping to initiate and speed up this reaction. However, while the positioning strategy is being communicated more effectively by the creative idea, the creative idea *must not change the positioning strategy itself.*

Adherence to the positioning strategy turns the creative idea into an *effective* ad, rather than just a *creative* ad. Therefore, we exclude as irrelevant creative ideas that are "simply creative" without being capable of selling the brand. Everyone can point to examples of highly creative campaigns in which the creative people seemed to be entertaining themselves rather than helping to position the product (although, of course, the blame could equally be placed on the client for approving apparently strategy-less ads). For instance, a beautiful magazine ad campaign several years ago for Johnny Walker Red Label Whiskey, featuring gorgeous photography of red Irish setters, red lobsters, red tartan, and, seasonally, a red Christmas theme, was widely acclaimed but failed to shift the brand's market share. The well-known saying in advertising that "It ain't creative unless it sells" warns against "purely creative" ideas. The idea has to be creative *and* it has to be relevant to the brand's position—*then* it will sell.

The creative idea must represent the positioning strategy and, most fundamentally, it must represent the X-YZ macropositioning model as described in the previous chapter. This is crucial because most people tend to think of a creative idea—and indeed a positioning strategy—as referring exclusively to the brand benefit or benefits (Z). However, as we have seen in the previous chapter, positioning also requires a product category location decision (X) and a *choice* between user-as-hero (Y) and product-as-hero (Z) focus. For instance, the famous "Uncola" creative idea for 7UP, which recently has been successfully revived, focuses on the category linkage aspect (X) in its positioning strategy—positioning the brand *away* from the cola beverage category. The "Uncola" creative idea also chose a product-as-hero focus (Z). On the other hand, the equally famous "Marlboro Man" creative idea for Marlboro cigarettes, which many regard as the greatest creative idea ever invented, assumes a central X location in the category and positions the brand toward the user (Y)—or, more exactly, toward an idealized macho image that the target audience consumer presumably would like to have. Many other creative ideas do, of course, focus on the brand's benefit or benefits (Z). To mention a couple of highly successful creative ideas with central X positioning and product-as-hero focus on Z: "We try harder" for

Avis rental-car service, and "Melts in your mouth, not in your hands" for M&M's candy.

What if the creative idea does change the positioning strategy? The notion of "catalytically relevant" implies that the creative idea must *dramatize* the positioning strategy without *changing* it. However, in more cases than clients care to admit (20 percent of cases or more, in our estimation), the creative idea produced by the agency is so good, or the original positioning strategy so vague—or both—that the creative idea, in a reversal of the normal process, *redefines* or *becomes* the positioning strategy (this "tactic-first" approach[13]—which must be acknowledged as a variant of normal advertising planning—is best used *iteratively,* as shown in Figure 7.4). Whereas most creative ideas are guided or at least initially suggested by the positioning-strategy statement, nearly every advertiser has had the experience of the reverse process and has had to acknowledge the power of a great creative idea. As John Eighmey, an experienced advertising professional and now a professor at the University of Alabama, has said: "Remember, consumers see the advertising, not the strategy statement." This leaves the door open for the reverse process, whereby a great creative idea can lead to a better positioning-strategy statement than the advertiser had previously been able to formulate.[14] This is almost certainly what happened with the Benetton campaign—a series of wild, attention-getting visuals that were later rationalized as expressing the company's concern with social issues (the af-

**FIGURE 7.4**
Iterative-process model that usefully combines the conventional and tactic-first approaches to advertising planning.

* The advertising agency generates multiple creative tactics (creative ideas, in the present context). Some of these may be different from those suggested by the original strategy provided by the client. If one of these tactical approaches appears to be, or tests out to be, better than the tactical approach suggested by the original strategy, then the original strategy and, if necessary, the objectives, can be revised to accommodate the winning tactical direction.

**FIGURE 7.5**
Some ad executions of Absolut's "bottle variations" creative idea.
*Courtesy:* ©1996 V&S Vin & Spirit AB.

ter-the-fact positioning strategy). Similarly, the brand manager of Absolut vodka has admitted that he did not have a strategy before the "bottle variations" creative idea (some executions of which are shown in Figure 7.5) was proposed to him by U.S. agency TBWA.[15] Following an annual growth rate in sales of 30 percent per year since the campaign began in 1985, he says that his strategy now is to "make the brand a category." Indeed, it would seem that the advertising has virtually partitioned the market such that there are other vodkas—and there is Absolut. Of course, Absolut's "superior-sounding" (and centrally X-positioned) name has not been a disadvantage, either!

Therefore, despite our definition's stipulation that the positioning strategy remain unchanged by the creative idea, we have to allow for the possibility of a change *for the better*—that is, the creative idea might actually provide a better positioning strategy than was initially devised for the brand. (This is possible because, as we saw in Chapter 6, there is a considerable

degree of judgment involved in generating a positioning strategy.) The manager should therefore be alert to the possibility that a creative idea presented by the agency will imply or suggest an improved positioning strategy. If the manager suspects an improvement, the new-strategy creative idea should be tested in comparison with another creative idea that *does* represent the original strategy, as this is too important a change to leave to judgment alone.

**2.** *Generated in a form that is detailed enough to be executed and tested.* The creative idea must be sufficiently detailed to allow it to be executed as an ad. For instance, "Let's use Tommy Lasorda as a presenter" is not a creative idea although using him *and* having him talk about how he lost 30 pounds by dieting with Ultra Slim-Fast diet drink *is* a creative idea.[16]

More generally, for ad testing purposes, it is a truism that you cannot test an "idea" but only an *execution* of that idea. As we shall see in a later section of this chapter, where we present the theory of random creativity, you can only *indirectly* test a creative idea—by "sampling" it in the form of several executions (see Chapter 19, which discusses concept development research and pretesting). A creative idea is not an ad. Rather, it is a "prescription" *for* an ad or for a series of advertising executions. As such, the creative idea must be expressed in sufficient detail to serve as a rough script for its execution.

**3.** *And (necessary in most cases) amenable to multiple executions.* In most cases, a creative idea has to be "campaignable." We say "in most cases" because sometimes a creative idea only has to be used once. (The Australian commercial for Oral-B toothbrush, code-named "Rob, the Dentist," which is now being shown in the United States, ran for 15 years as the *total* campaign in Australia and took the brand from a minor share to market leader.) But, in most cases, the creative idea has to provide the "creative platform" for a *pool* or *series* of ads that will be needed in the advertising campaign for the brand. The Absolut vodka ads, illustrated previously, are an example. Moreover, we recommend that all creative ideas be *planned* this way even if only one execution is subsequently used. (After 15 years, Oral-B eventually added a second execution, "The Dentist's Son.") Thus, it should be regarded as necessary that the creative idea be amenable to multiple executions or "variations on a theme." In this sense, the Tommy Lasorda creative idea above should be more accurately described as "testimonials from *famous celebrities* who have lost weight by using Ultra Slim-Fast," rather than referring to Tommy Lasorda specifically, although he was the source of what became the campaign's creative idea.

In theory, every creative idea is amenable to multiple executions—but some are more amenable than others. For instance, the "Famous celebrities" idea is easily extendible whereas other creative ideas, such as the remarkable Apple Computer commercial, shown once only, during the 1984 Super Bowl, and based on the novel *1984* by George Orwell, probably are more limited. In practice, the need for "pool-outs" in most campaigns—to keep the positioning strategy going even though executions of it "wear out"—means that the creative idea must be amenable to multiple executions so that it is "campaignable" if required.

For review purposes, we have summarized the informal and formal definitions of the "creative idea" in Table 7.1. For classic examples of creative ideas, see chapter appendix 7A, Examples of Great Creative Ideas.

**Forms of Creative Ideas.** Many of the early creative ideas were based on particularly effective slogans, such as are illustrated in some of the examples in chapter appendix 7A. However, with television later becoming the major medium for consumer products, creative ideas became increasingly visual. The Levi's "Launderette strip" campaign is one example.

---

**TABLE 7.1**

**THE CREATIVE IDEA: INFORMAL AND FORMAL DEFINITIONS**

**Informal definitions**

| | |
|---|---|
| Creative idea | The choice of an interesting way to express the brand position in an advertising format. |
| Big idea | A creative idea that is arresting, simple, and powerful, and communicates immediately. |

**Formal definition**

| | |
|---|---|
| Creative idea | 1. An attention-getting and catalytically relevant representation of the brand position |
| | 2. Generated in a form that is detailed enough to be executed and tested |
| | 3. And (necessary in most cases) amenable to multiple executions. |

---

More recently, the late and famous Italian film director Federico Fellini made some highly unusual commercials for Banca di Roma. These commercials are really little movies, being over two minutes long (130 seconds) and using Fellini's typical, dreamlike style. In one of the commercials, "Psychiatrist," a man dreams of a runaway train and then relates his dream to a psychiatrist. The psychiatrist interprets the dream in terms of the man's need to take control of his life, and by implication to take control of his finances—via Banca di Roma. A subsequent commercial in the series, "Bank robbers," spoofs Fellini in that the bank robbers successfully penetrate the bank's vault only to find that the money has gone—to Fellini, to pay for the advertising![17]

The creative idea, as we emphasized in the formal definition, must be detailed enough to serve as a generic script for the production of ads. But usually there are just one or two aspects of the creative idea that seem to provide its key and which help to make the creative idea "amazingly simple." To review our examples so far (including those in chapter appendix 7A), the key aspect may be one (or two—hence the numbers 1 and 2) of the following:

- A slogan—7UP, Shake 'N Bake, Cadillac, VW (1), Miller Lite (1), Clairol, M&M's, Dial
- A picture or visual device—VW (2), Miller Lite (2), Levi's (1)
- A song or jingle—Levi's (2)
- A style of advertising—Taster's Choice, Banca di Roma
- A brand symbol—Marlboro

The variety of creative ideas that we have illustrated suggests that finding a winning creative idea for a brand may well be a "chance" process. Next, we will introduce the theory of "random creativity" as a means of finding a winning creative idea.

## THEORY OF RANDOM CREATIVITY

After having worked as consultants to advertising agencies and their clients for a considerable number of years, we are now convinced that the generation of "winning" creative ideas can be regarded as a random process. By "random" we do not mean pure luck; obviously, some advertising agencies are more skilled at producing winners than others, as are individual copywriters or art directors. However, there is undoubtedly *a large element of chance* in coming up with a winning creative idea—and, if so, the more times you try to do so, by and large, the greater your odds of finding a winner. This theory is not new. It was first proposed by Gross in 1967.[18] The theory did not receive widespread acceptance, for various reasons that we note later. However, with increased pressure on advertising agencies for better creative performance, we believe it is a theory that is very appropriate for the modern advertising business.[19]

Although the creative idea may be a random choice, this does not mean that the whole process of advertising and promotion planning is random. Far from it, as this would undermine the entire premise of this book! Rather, after careful and systematic planning of marketing objectives, target audience selection and action objectives, and communication objectives and positioning, it is the *agency's main input that is random—the creative idea.* And, as depicted in Figure 7.4, we do acknowledge that sometimes the creative idea can lead to a revision of some or all of the plan. However, it is very risky indeed for the plan not to be there in the first place. In particular, you'd have no objectives against which to evaluate the potential of the independently suggested creative idea.

### Example of "Randomness" of Creative Ideas

Advertisers who put their brands' advertising accounts up for competitive "pitches" from different agencies would have a good grasp of just how varied the creative ideas can be for the same positioning strategy. However, outsiders rarely get to see this variation. A valuable opportunity to observe the typical variety of creative ideas occurred in Australia in early 1992. The Dalai Lama, the famous Tibetan spokesperson for world peace and winner of the 1989 Nobel Peace Prize, was planning a tour of Australia in April and May. Beforehand, his representatives contacted a leading Australian advertising trade paper, *Ad News,* and asked for recommendations for an advertising agency to promote the tour. *Ad News* decided to contact a number of advertising agencies and put the account up for bids (even though, as a public service account, no fee would be paid). The response was very gratifying: creative ideas were submitted by many agencies, large and small. Five different agencies' creative ideas were chosen by the newspaper for consideration by the Dalai Lama's representatives. These creative ideas are reproduced in Figure 7.6 (panels A to E).

Not only are the creative ideas extremely varied, but it is difficult to tell which ideas might have come from large agencies and which from small ones. In fact, the ad

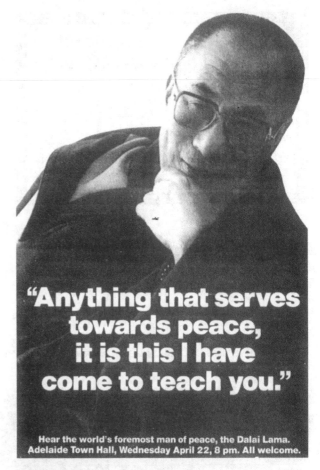

**FIGURE 7.6 A**
Creative idea for Dalai Lama tour: "Anything that serves towards peace . . ."
*Courtesy:* Ad News Magazine (Australia) and Andrew Killey and Peter Withy, Killey & Withy and Punshon Advertising (South Australia).

in panel A, "Anything that serves towards peace . . . ," came from a small agency, Killey & Withy. The two ads in panel B, "He never married . . . " and "Compassion," actually came from *two different creative teams within the same agency,* Young & Rubicam. The left-hand ad in this panel is aimed at those Australians who have not heard of the Dalai Lama and employs the pseudoendorsement of a controversial Australian religious figure, the Reverend Fred Nile, as a drawing card. The right-hand ad in this panel is designed for those who *have* heard of the Dalai Lama and adopts a more straightforward approach. The dramatic ads in panel C, "Bomber dropping hearts" and "Hitler with flowers," are from the *same creative person in one agency,* in

**FIGURE 7.6 B1 & B2**

Related creative ideas for Dalai Lama tour: "He never married . . . " (for an unaware target audience) and "Compassion . . . " (for an aware target audience).

*Courtesy:* Ad News Magazine (Australia) and Malcolm McDonough and Katrina Allen, Young & Rubicam (Melbourne, Australia).

**FIGURE 7.6 C1 & C2**

Related creative ideas for Dalai Lama tour: "Bomber dropping hearts" and "Hitler with flowers."

*Courtesy:* Ad News Magazine (Australia) and Richard Denham, Ian Morton, and Mick Hunter, FCB (Sydney, Australia).

See the Dalai Lama and change your perspective on life.

**FIGURE 7.6 C2**

THE 14TH DELAI LAMA OF TIBET
AUSTRALIAN TOUR APRIL - MAY 1992

**FIGURE 7.6 D**
Creative idea for Dalai Lama tour: "The 14th Dalai Lama of Tibet."
*Courtesy:* Ad News Magazine (Australia) and Richard Denham, Ian Morton, and Mick Hunter, FCB (Sydney, Australia).

this case Richard Denham of Foote Cone & Belding, and represent executional variations of the same creative idea. The next ad, the abstract but starkly simple "The 14th Dalai Lama of Tibet," shown in panel D, is by the *same person again*—Richard Denham of FCB. The final ad, shown in panel E, and beginning with the headline "He's got less hair than the Pope," was submitted by another smaller Australian agency, John Singleton Advertising.

These various creative ideas for the same advertising task are very different. Which one would you pick? In fact, the Dalai Lama's staff selected the dual-audience ads from Young & Rubicam (panel B) and awarded this agency the account. However, no formal test of the ads was conducted, and this selection—as happens in so many cases—was a subjective one. Our choice would have been the highly attention-getting and, we think, catalytically relevant FCB creative idea represented by "Bomber dropping hearts" and "Hitler with flowers," which are the same idea, but our choice is equally subjective. The ads should be tested with consumers, a point to which we will return shortly in showing how to apply the theory of random creativity.

The main point we wish to illustrate, to recap, is the extreme variety of creative ideas that can be generated even when the advertising purpose is quite clear and narrow. An important supplementary point illustrated in this example, which also relates vitally to the theory of random creativity, is that there are three *sources* of varied creative ideas: (1) across agencies—the five represented, (2) across creative teams within a single agency—the two Y & R ads, and (3) within a single person—the three ads by Richard Denham of FCB. The three sources of variation will become important later in applying the theory.

Other examples abound of different creative ideas for the same positioning strategy, especially in multinational campaigns. For instance, American Express Card in the mid-1980s simultaneously used

# HE'S GOT LESS HAIR THAN THE POPE. AND HE'S SHORTER THAN DANNY DEVITO.

# SO WHY'S HE SMILING?

Well, he's
the Dalai Lama.
Head of the
Tibetan Buddhists.
Nobel Peace Prize
Winner.
And a good mate
of Richard Gere.
See him,
the Dalai Lama not
Richard Gere,
on his Australian Tour.

Tour Dates and Locations TBA.

**FIGURE 7.6 E**
Creative idea for Dalai Lama tour: "He's got less hair than the Pope."
*Courtesy:* Ad News Magazine (Australia) and Harry Ledowsky, John Singleton, Jodie-Maree Read, and John Singleton Advertising (Sydney, Australia).

"Membership has its privileges" in the United States, "Do you know me?" in Australia, and a celebrity endorser campaign featuring Tina Turner and others in Singapore! The number of *potential* creative ideas for a given positioning strategy is virtually infinite.

In the next section, we explain the theory of random creativity. Following that, we show how the theory can be applied in practice.

## How It Works in Theory

The theory of random creativity is based on one major theoretical principle and four supplementary principles. The major theoretical principle is that the more creative ideas that are generated and tested, the more likely you are to come up with an "extreme positive" idea that is a "real winner."

**Multiple Tries.** Based on the experience of advertising testing and tracking companies,[20] we estimate that only about one in six campaigns is likely to prove to be a "real winner." This suggests that, generally speaking, we would have to generate and test six creative ideas in order to identify one that will be a winner. However, would six tries *guarantee* us a winner? Imagine a normal six-sided die, and let's suppose that we wanted to throw a six (the winner). In the long run, with a fair die, we would throw a six once in every six tries—on average. But suppose we had just six tries in total. Could we be guaranteed of throwing a six? Obviously, not too many people would trust this guarantee; they would rather have the opportunity of rolling the die a *larger* number of times so as to be more certain that at least one six will eventuate. We will return later to what this number of tries might be.

**Average Hit Rate.** The second principle depends on the *source or sources* of the creative ideas. Ideally, if we could go to an advertising agency that had a 100 percent track record in producing winning creative ideas, then we would only have to ask the agency to generate one ad. However, no agency has a perfect record of generating winning creative ideas. Indeed, we know that the average across *all* agencies is only one in six, so even the very best agencies are probably hitting no more than three in six, or 50 percent. Therefore, even if we went to one of the best agencies, it would still pay to ask the agency to generate and test more than one creative idea. The same average-hit-rate principle holds if, instead of an agency, the source of the creative ideas is a particular creative team or an individual creative person.

**Variability of Hit Rate.** Not only is the track record of the agency important but so also is its variability around that track record. This is the third principle. For instance, a good agency might produce two winning campaigns in every six—but also produce two real losers. Some "creative boutiques" fit this scenario. On the other hand, an agency may come up with only one winner in six but hardly ever produce real losers. Some of the larger, more conservative agencies fit this scenario.

Which of the two agencies would you patronize? The answer depends. As long as you commission and test *multiple* creative ideas, you will be more likely to locate winners by using the agency with the more *variable* performance—the first agency—regardless of the fact that it is equally likely to produce real losers. This illustrates the value of the theory of random creativity. However, if you only commission and test *one* creative idea, as is the common practice, then you would be safer going with the second agency because, although it is less likely for that one idea to be a real winner, there is also less chance that it will be a real loser. Normal practice therefore leads to *lower* long-run success rates due to selecting only one creative idea from "safer" agencies.

**Cost Limit.** The fourth principle of random creativity is that there is a limit to the number of creative ideas that can be generated and tested, due to cost. In the extreme case, you could spend a lot of money having your agency generate and test a large number of creative ideas—to the point where you have nothing left over in your media budget to spend on the winning idea! However, we will see that this theoretical limit, where the cost of generating and testing creative ideas exceeds the profitability of the winning idea, is a very large number that is nowhere near reached in practice, even for relatively small-budget campaigns. We will show, with some real-world examples, that it always pays to generate and test several creative ideas and usually many more of them than that.

Quite evidently, costs could be kept lower if, instead of approaching a number of different advertising agencies to submit creative ideas, the manager were to ask one agency (the incumbent agency, which already has the manager's account if it is an existing brand rather than a new brand, or one new agency for a new brand) to generate all of them. To increase the odds of the agency coming up with a winner, the manager could specify that independent creative teams be used to generate the ideas. However, because of the likelihood of an agency "house style,"[21] we would expect that the variation in the creative ideas produced by the same agency, even with different creative teams, would not be as wide as if different agencies had been commissioned. Thus, there is less chance of coming up with a real winner—or, to look at it another way, more creative ideas will be needed to have the same chance of coming up with a real winner—when only one advertising agency is used.

Taking this line of reasoning one step further, it would probably be less expensive still to have a single creative team or even a single copywriter generate all the creative ideas. However, the performance earlier of Richard Denham of FCB for the Dalai Lama campaign notwithstanding, observations of the performance of individual copywriters suggest that a single copywriter is likely to get "locked in" on minor variations of the same creative idea rather than producing different ones that offer a wide range of effective possibilities.

You can see the trade-off here: the more restricted the source of creative ideas, the less likely they are to differ, and thus the less likely to include a winner—unless, of course, the source of the ideas has an extremely successful (high mean) and consistent (low variance) track record.

**Accuracy of Idea-Screening Test.** The fifth principle of random creativity is that the number of creative ideas to be generated and tested depends on the predictive accuracy of the test the manager uses to screen the ideas. Paradoxically, the higher the predictive relationship between test results and ultimate sales performance, the *more* creative ideas you should generate and test. This paradox is explained when we realize that the manager who relies on intuition to select a creative idea for the campaign, rather than using a valid pretest, is just as likely to pick a loser as to pick a winner.[22] Commissioning more ideas is not going to solve the problem, because the manager is still guessing. Multiple ideas would be a waste of money if the manager is just as likely to throw away winners as losers.

On the other hand, the manager who has a reasonably accurate test for "preidentifying" a winning ad is much more likely to find one by commissioning multiple creative ideas. The more valid the pretest, the more confident the search will be for a winning ad and thus the more money should be invested in generating and testing alternative creative ideas as candidates for the winning ad. Therefore, we are going to *assume* that the manager is willing to use a reasonably valid pretest, as this is vital for the theory to work in practice. (These tests are reviewed in Chapter 19.)

The theory of random creativity is stated in more formal and precise quantitative terms in chapter appendix 7B, Mathematical Basis of the Theory of Random Creativity.

### Practical Considerations

There are two major practical considerations in applying the theory of random creativity: (1) who the source or sources of the creative ideas should be; and (2) the cost of generating, producing, and testing the creative ideas in order to select a winner. As the source decision is mostly managerial, we discuss it here. The cost considerations are included in chapter appendix 7B, on the mathematical basis of the theory.

**Source(s) of Creative Ideas.** The manager has three options for the sources of the creative ideas: different agencies, independent teams within an agency, or an individual copywriter or copywriting team. Regarding the latter option, it is usual for a copywriter and an art director to work together as a team rather than for copywriters to work alone; however, to sharpen the distinction between sources, we will refer to this third option as the "individual copywriter."

Let us assume that the manager would go only to good agencies or good copywriters. In other words, let us assume that the *mean* level (historical average) of creative performance is equal between the three alternatives of agencies, teams, or individual copywriter. According to the theory, the question then becomes one of maximizing the variance across creative ideas. Experience would suggest that the variance will be maximized by going to *different agencies.* However, not only will this cost more in terms of management time (see below) but also it is only ethically appropriate when the manager has publicly announced the willingness to change agencies or is hiring one for the first time. The most realistic option according to the circumstance is given below.

*New Product: Different Agencies.* For a new product launch, it is quite normal to put the account "up for grabs" and ask different agencies to pitch for the business. As long as they are paid for their creative ideas, there is no ethical problem in telling the agencies that the best creative idea will be selected and used, whether or not the agency with the best idea is awarded the account. The "different agencies" approach was the option chosen for the Dalai Lama campaign, although only prestige rather than payment was the reward. As was evident, this approach produced a very wide variety of creative ideas.

*Established Product: Different Teams, Same Agency.* On the other hand, for an established product with an incumbent agency, it is highly unusual, if not unethical, to ask *other* agencies to present creative ideas for the campaign. Many other agencies would do this, but the incumbent agency would be quite likely to resign the account.[23] Thus, commissioning *independent* creative teams within the same agency is

the most realistic option for an established brand. There is likely to be some reduction of variability by using the same-agency option—but, in our experience, *not that much* as long as independent teams are used.

Independence can be increased by setting up the assignment as an internal competition. Recently, Backer Spielvogel Bates adopted an internal "creative team challenge" system in its agency. Each client has the benefit of two full teams—composed of account, media, research, and creative personnel—working on the brand. The two teams are mainly in competition for a "big idea." The dual-team plan is accomplished by having everyone in the agency spend 25 percent of his or her time working as a "shadow agency" for another account.[24]

A further way in which the variability in creative ideas from different teams within an agency can be maximized is to specify that the creative teams be drawn from a *wide range of accounts,* especially those that are very different from the client's account. Thus, the manager of a consumer packaged goods brand might request that creative teams from consumer durables, industrial products, retail stores, and financial services (presuming that the agency has these types of accounts) work on the task of generating the creative idea.

*Last Resort: Individual Copywriter or Team.* The third option, having an individual creative team or even just one individual copywriter act as the source for the multiple creative ideas, would very likely produce the lowest variety. The variation can be increased by requesting a larger number of ideas from this team or person, as the formula suggests, but still there is the likelihood that the variation will be too small. The individual team or copywriter is therefore the least-effective option in most cases—unless that team or person has creative genius in the form of a very high average level of performance.

However, requesting multiple creative ideas from one person is still better than requesting just one idea. The theory of random creativity will still work in this circumstance as long as the other factors are respected. If possible, more time between idea generation sessions should be allowed, to lessen the tendency for the one team or copywriter to get blocked in a single session.

**Capitalizing on Current Practice.** Evidence from two case studies and a survey indicates that, for all but the smallest accounts, advertising agencies already practice "random creativity" in rough form.[25] That is, initial creative ideas are usually sought from two or three creative teams internally, and about 10 or 12 ideas are proposed. The agency's creative director then convenes a "creative shoot-out" to eliminate all but about four ideas for serious consideration by the account and creative personnel working on the account. These four ideas are then whittled down to one or two (often a main idea and a backup idea) to present to the client. The client is likely to approve just these one or two ideas for pretesting.

According to the theory of random creativity, current practice could be improved and capitalized on by the advertiser by (a) encouraging the agency to seek initial ideas from twice as many internal creative teams (four to six), drawn from diverse accounts and working independently, (b) asking for all the apparently *different* creative ideas (of which there would probably be at least 10) to be developed into rough-ad form for concept screening research and management judgment testing (see Chapter 19), and (c) quantitatively ad testing all those that showed reasonable promise of being effective (preferably three or more). Whereas the advertiser would have to pay the agency for the extra time, this relatively straightforward expansion of current agency practice would allow random creativity principles to be easily implemented.

The new practice—applying the theory of random creativity—will benefit not only the advertiser but also the *agency*. The benefits of random creativity, with two further case histories, are spelled out in chapter appendix 7C, Random Creativity Benefits Everyone.

We now examine the agency's contribution—the brainstorming of creative ideas—in more detail. Then we will return to the manager's perspective at the end of the chapter.

## I-G-I METHOD OF BRAINSTORMING

Recent research in the generation of creative ideas suggests that the I-G-I method of brainstorming is the best procedure.[26] Whereas this may seem like a methodological consideration best left to the research chapters, it is worth outlining the procedure here. A good reason for placing the procedure in the chapter itself is to encourage its use for student projects based on this text. However, we'd recommend it for professional advertising agencies, too.

The I-G-I method of brainstorming refers to the sequence: Individual, then Group, then Individual.[27] Its three steps can be summarized as follows:

**1.** Individuals (I) are asked to generate the initial creative ideas. About four to seven individuals are required. Under the guidance of a chairperson, who introduces the positioning strategy on which the creative ideas will be based and then merely acts as a recorder, individuals are brought together in the same room (a nominal group) but are not allowed to talk to one another during the initial brainstorming phase. In this initial brainstorming phase, the individuals are given two instructions: (a) "Go for quantity of ideas, not quality;" and (b) "The target is 10 ideas,[28] each, in a time limit of 15 minutes." The individuals then write down or type on a personal computer as many ideas as they can generate in 15 minutes.

**2.** The chairperson collects the ideas—one idea per person at a time, rotating among the individuals in random order—and displays the ideas on a central screen or flip chart. Now the group (G) is allowed to *interact* and is encouraged to develop the ideas as follows: (a) the author of each idea quickly explains it to the other individuals; (b) the other individuals, in random order, are then asked to comment on the idea and, after the first idea, to "hitchhike" the current idea onto previous ideas, if they can do so and if appropriate.

**3.** The group then goes back to the individual mode (the final I phase) to vote on the best ideas. Every individual has an equal vote. Note that the best *set of ideas,* rather than the single best idea, is to be selected. This can be determined by allowing each individual to rank all the ideas 1, 2, 3, and so on, down to the least-promising idea, and then selecting those ideas with the best (lowest) group scores. These are the creative ideas that will go forward into the advertisement executions phase, for concept development, if that route is used, and ad testing.

The entire I-G-I procedure should require only 1.5 to 2 hours. If a large number of creative ideas are required according to the random creativity formula, it is best to repeat the I-G-I procedure with a new set of individuals, second best to repeat the procedure with the same individuals, and not satisfactory to accept poorer ideas from the original session. To avoid the latter situation, the ideas, after ranking, can be *rated* on a scale from 1 to 10 of expected effectiveness, and a cutoff such as 7+ can be applied.

## RAM-CONVEYOR THEORY OF CREATIVE IDEAS

What should the I-G-I team brainstorm "on"? Here we present another new theory, developed by Rossiter and Ang at the Australian Graduate School of Management,[29] which looks very promising. We call this theory the RAM-Conveyor theory of creative ideas, where "RAM" stands for "Remote Associative Matching" and the "conveyor's" function is explained below.

The thinking behind RAM-Conveyor theory is that, in most cases, it is more effective to present the brand's key benefit "indirectly" rather than to state it or show it directly. (The exceptions are direct mail and classified ads because, in these two high-involvement choice situations, the target recipient *will* pay initial attention and is seeking an efficient, direct statement or depiction of benefits.) The RAM-Conveyor model, showing its indirect route to the key benefit claim, is shown in the theoretical model in Figure 7.7. The conveyor chosen via the indirect route must be *attention-getting* and *catalytically relevant,* in keeping with our definition of an effective creative idea.

We are going to illustrate two examples of the RAM-Conveyor theory in action. Although the theory applies to all types of advertising, including television advertising, it is simpler to illustrate it with print ads.

We will use two examples to demonstrate two different formats of the one theory.

### Example 1: Visual Conveyor

The ad for Fortis financial services group of companies in Figure 7.8 depicts excellent use of a visual conveyor. In this ad, the *conveyor* is a group of dragonflies who have combined to form a net to catch a predatory fish; the *product representation* is the company's name, Fortis; and the *attribute prompt* is the headline, "The combined strengths of Fortis." As the copy further explains, separate individuals (dragonflies = companies) can work together in the right way

**FIGURE 7.7**
RAM-Conveyor model of the creative idea's function.

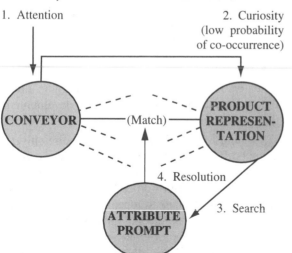

**FIGURE 7.8**
RAM-Conveyor theory: Example of visual conveyor. Conveyor = dragonflies forming net. Product representation = Fortis company name. Attribute prompt = headline, "The combined strengths of Fortis."
*Courtesy:* Fortis AG and Fortis AMEV.

THE COMBINED STRENGTHS OF FORTIS

(group of dragonflies = group of companies) to form a new entity that is very strong (net[work] = Fortis). The pool-out ads in Fortis's campaign utilize similar "combined strength" conveyors, such as many small animals combining their paw-prints into large-looking footprints that deter a threatening leopard, and a group of butterflies combining to form a pair of scissors to defend against the threatening tongue of a large lizard. In each, the attribute prompt is the corporate line, "The combined strengths of Fortis." Perhaps somewhat coincidentally, Fortis's profits rose by 29 percent in the quarter following the launch of the campaign. In an upcoming campaign for Fortis, the "predators" will be phased out and "group cooperation" becomes the dominantly conveyed benefit.

### Example 2: Verbal Conveyor

An alternative advertising format that employs the same three elements of conveyor, product representation, and attribute prompt is shown in the ad for Glad Bake nonstick baking and cooking paper in Figure 7.9. The verbal conveyor, "Grease and oil change," attempts to dramatize the benefit of avoiding grease and oil, associated with cholesterol and calories, when you use Glad Bake. In this ad, the headline is the conveyor (verbal), the product representation is both visual and verbal, and the attribute prompt is in the body copy itself. In a variation of this format, the attribute prompt is shown in a picture—not a conveyor picture, but an attribute picture.

The best verbal conveyors, though, are *positive verbal metaphors*—rather than puns, such as the one above, which associate the product with a negative attribute while trying to demonstrate the opposite. Hitchon and Churchill[30] show that metaphor headlines, such as "Prio sportswatch is a dolphin" or "Prio sportswatch is a shark," produce a more favorable brand attitude than straight headlines, such as "Prio sportswatch is waterproof." Notice that verbal-metaphor conveyors could be executed visually, and indeed a visual conveyor is a pictorial metaphor (with special properties as detailed shortly). In a further controlled experiment, Dingena[31] found that visual metaphors are usually more effective than verbal ones. We also favor visual conveyors over verbal conveyors, although both can be more effective than straight versions of the brand's main benefit claim.

**FIGURE 7.9**
RAM-Conveyor theory: Example of verbal conveyor (headline) in ad for Glad Bake nonstick baking and cooking paper.
*Courtesy:* Glad Products, Australia.

### Properties of the Conveyor

We now elaborate on the main functional aspects of RAM-Conveyor theory. Summarized in Table 7.2, these pertain to properties of the conveyor.

**1. Attention-Getting.** There are three ways of getting people's attention to ads, of which only the first two are practical.[32] The first way is to use a conveyor that gains *reflexive* attention (using the principles of stimulus change) in that the conveyor first appears incongruous or unusual in association with the product. This was the device used in the Fortis and Glad Bake ads. This method of gaining attention is particularly effective for an "unmotivated" target audience—more precisely, for those who do not have the *category need* salient at the time of advertising exposure.

The second way to gain attention is to use a conveyor that gains *selective* attention in that it is a stimulus that represents an absolute or a specific motivation. *Absolute* motivators make use of the fact that certain stimuli are relevant to everyday-life motivations, both negative and positive. For instance, stimuli that refer to disasters, such as AIDS, are—these days—an absolute motivator based on negative motivation (the universal desire to avoid AIDS). On the other hand, stimuli that directly or indirectly suggest sex are an absolute positive motivator. The "girl in a bikini" or, these days, the male "hunk in jeans" style of advertising, are good examples of motivators based on sex.

*Specific* motivators can be used *if* the target audience has the category need. For instance, if you are in the market for home repairs, then an ad that shows or mentions stimuli related to home repairs will be much more likely to catch your attention. A picture of a home being repaired, or the simple words "home repairs" in the headline, will almost certainly catch your attention—if you happen to have that particular category need motivating you at present.

The third way to ensure attention is to *instruct* people to pay attention. This happens, of course, in most academic experiments—"laboratory" experiments—on advertising. That is why we said that this third method was impractical in the real world. It has undoubtedly led to a number of unrealistic and even misleading conclusions about what works in advertising since the results are generalized from "forced attention" laboratory experiments to situations of more natural attention in advertising exposure conditions as they occur in the real world.[33] Reflexive attention or selective attention are the more natural options.

**2. Correctly Labeled by the Consumer.** To be effective, a visual conveyor used in an ad must be immediately and correctly identified—labeled—by the target audience. For example, the Fortis ad would not work with readers who could not recognize that the net is composed of butterflies. This is a common problem with ads that attempt to be "too cute" or "too creative" visually. The visual conveyor must be correctly labeled mentally, and immediately, by the target audience.

Similarly, the verbal conveyor must result in correct comprehension of the *words* used as the conveyor. Whereas many verbal conveyors rely on dramatic use of the language, they should not obscure communication. After prompting (see 4 below), the consumer's correct identification of the benefit dramatized by the verbal conveyor is essential for the ad to work.

**3. Perceived As Remote.** The third property of an effective conveyor is that it must be perceived as "remote"—initially—from the product or service being advertised. That is, the conveyor must initially be perceived as having a *low probability of co-occurrence* with the advertised product. In the Fortis ad, for example, it is rather unlikely that a fishing scene would be associated with a financial institution. Similarly, the words "Grease and oil change" in the verbal-conveyor headline of the Glad Bake ad, which usually refer to automobile servicing, are quite remote from the product category of nonstick cooking paper.

However, there are two important exceptions to the "remote conveyor" requirement when using a *visual* conveyor. A remote visual conveyor should not be used when the purchase motivation for the brand consists either of basic sensory gratification—hunger, thirst, sex—or of social approval with user-as-hero positioning. In a food ad, for instance, you want to show the food literally or describe it directly, rather than going the indirect conveyor route. Also, in social approval ads, such as a user-positioning ad for a luxury car, you should not show a *remote* user—in fact, to the contrary. You want to show a more typical user or, more precisely, as explained in Chapter 9 where we examine choice of in-ad presenters, you want to show a *typical or slightly-better-than-typical user* in the ad. Under these two conditions, extreme remoteness of the visual conveyor is not recommended.

**4. High Association of the Target Attribute When Prompted.** This is the most difficult property of an effective conveyor to achieve. It is relatively easy to find conveyors that are attention-getting and remote from the product. The whole key to RAM-Conveyor theory, however, is in finding not only a remote stimulus but also one that—usually when prompted—causes the target audience to recognize the target attribute that you want to strengthen in the product (the brand) being advertised. In the Fortis ad, for instance, the key was to find not just an attention-getting object, but an object which, when you think of it, has the attribute of combined strength. The small animal formation versus big animal has this attribute.

Usually, the attribute prompt will be necessary to elicit the target attribute from the conveyor so that it "matches" the target attribute in the brand's positioning strategy. (Hence, the full name of RAM-Conveyor theory is "Remote Associative *Matching*" Conveyor theory.) However, some ads have to work very quickly—such as mobile outdoor ads. By "mobile," we mean outdoor ads in which either the target audience is mobile, such as is the case with highway billboards, or in which the ad itself is mobile relative to the target audience, such as posters on the sides of buses. With these types of ads, there is only a very limited time to get the message across. Accordingly, it is desirable that the conveyor used in these ads be virtually "self-resolving," without the need for an attribute prompt—or, at least, requiring only a very brief attribute prompt.

An important extension of the "target attribute" notion is that the association might be "emotional" rather than focusing on a specific attribute or benefit as such. Here it is worth reviewing our distinction between attributes, benefits, and emotions from the previous chapter. In emotional positioning, the purpose is often to locate the brand in an "emotion space" defined by the three universal dimensions of emotionality: evaluation, potency, and activity (E-P-A).[34] All emotions can be located in this three-dimensional space. For instance, suppose that you wanted to position a new sports car emotionally as being "aggressive." "Aggressive" is an emotion that is high on the potency and activity dimensions, while being moderately positively evaluated. Figure 7.10 shows where the emotion "aggressive" would be located in this three-dimensional space.

What you would do in this case would be to try to find a conveyor that is also aggressive in that it is located at the same point in the three-dimensional space.[35] Examples of such conveyors might be an eagle, or an aggressive but moderately liked personality such as Arnold Schwarzenegger (well-known as the "Terminator"). We have picked "aggressive" as a very obvious example that could *also* be handled by the association process. More subtle emotional positioning can be used, such as in ads for liquor. The well-known J&B scotch ads—the "Soft" campaign—are notable examples.

**5. And Have No Strong Contradictory Attribute Associations.** The final requirement of an effective conveyor is that it must have no strong contradictory attribute associations that could "undermine" the target attribute. For instance, the Fortis conveyor executions are meant to be very clever *without* being humorous, an attribute (an emotion) that could trivialize the new company (weakening its brand attitude or image). Lack of competing attribute associations is an important constraint when selecting an appropriate conveyor.

**FIGURE 7.10**

Example of emotional matching of "aggressive" (for a sports car) with remote but suitable conveyors (eagle; Schwarzenegger as the "Terminator").

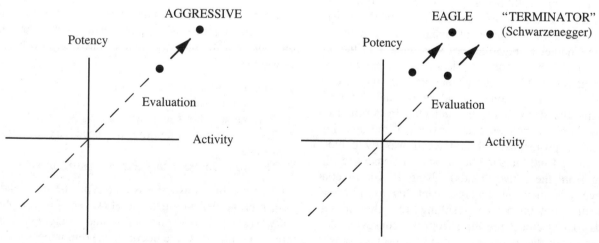

These five properties are *necessary* conditions for an effective conveyor, in our theory. That is, a potential conveyor must jump all five "hurdles" posed by the five properties. In pilot tests of the RAM-Conveyor model, we have found that a majority of otherwise "creative" ads fail on at least one of these hurdles. This reinforces our view that the five properties may *jointly* hold the key to "effective creativity" in advertisements.

**Brand Awareness Effects of Conveyors.** Conveyors operate, usually, on the brand attitude communication effect (by boosting the brand benefit belief on the target attribute). However, we know from Chapter 5 that *brand awareness* is a necessary prior communication effect. A possible concern is that an attitude conveyor may "distract" the buyer from processing the link between category need and the brand's name or package, which is needed for brand awareness learning. We now address this concern, and show how to solve it, for brand recognition and brand recall.

*Brand Recognition.* For *brand recognition,* there should be no problem in conveyor ads as long as a clear product representation (a clear brand name or package) is used in the ad. Indeed, as the ad for Balenciaga's Talisman perfume in Figure 7.11 indicates, it is possible to use a *brand awareness conveyor* that is *also,* presumably, a brand *attitude* conveyor.

*Brand Recall.* For *brand recall,* the potential problem of distraction by the conveyor is somewhat greater because the buyer definitely must associate the category need with the brand. For instance, in the Fortis ad, the buyer must associate the brand name, Fortis, with the category need for corporate financial consulting. However, this is mainly dependent on good execution of brand awareness tactics (see Chapter 8) regardless of what else is in the ad. Further, there is some evidence that conveyors do not affect brand recall and may actually increase it. Using 10 visual conveyor ads, Gray and Snyder[36] found brand recall to be unaffected in comparison with straight, nonconveyor versions of the ads (immediate postexposure brand recall was 69 percent resulting from the straight ads and 71 percent resulting from the conveyor ads). Using 10 *verbal* conveyor ads, they found a significant *increase* in brand recall (from 65 percent resulting from the straight ads to 75 percent resulting from the conveyor ads). It is likely that conveyors—good ones—lead buyers

**FIGURE 7.11**
A brand-awareness (brand-recognition) conveyor that also may work on brand attitude, for Balenciaga's Talisman perfume. *Courtesy:* Balenciaga Enterprises, New York, Paris, Milan.

to process the ad more intensively, thereby providing them with a greater opportunity to learn brand awareness.

**Brand Awareness Conveyors.** If a conveyor is employed with the primary purpose of boosting brand *awareness,* it should meet the five conveyor properties as follows:

1. Attention-getting
2. Correctly labeled
3. Remoteness: not necessary
4. Target-attribute elicitation: not necessary, but desirable
5. No strong contradictory attribute associations

Thus, for a brand awareness conveyor, the third and fourth properties are different. However, if a "double duty" conveyor (boosting both brand awareness *and* brand attitude) is intended, then remoteness and target-attribute elicitation *are* necessary; that is, the original brand *attitude* conveyor properties have to be met, as listed in Table 7.2.

## RAM-Conveyor Methodology

How does the creative person (perhaps you, doing an advertising project based on this book) go about finding an effective conveyor for use in the advertising campaign? One way is to use open-ended brainstorming. For this, you can use the I-G-I method of brainstorming with an unspecified, that is, open-ended, procedure in that the goal is to come up with a creative idea based on the positioning strategy, with no further guidelines.

Alternatively, you could try the RAM-Conveyor procedure as a structured form of the I-G-I method of brainstorming, as outlined next. The procedure consists of seven steps, as follows:

**1.** Begin with the target benefit (or attribute or emotion) and ask the brainstormers to generate, in successive brainstorming tasks, the following types of associates to it: (a) objects, (b) people, and (c) situations (or vignettes if a TV campaign is envisioned). These associations will be the potential conveyors. Thus, denoting the target attribute as $A_t$ and the potential conveyors as $C_1, C_2, C_3$, and so on, the process is:

$$A_t \rightarrow C_1, C_2, C_3, \text{ etc.}$$

Technically, this associative direction is known as "typicality" in that you want to find conveyors that typify the target attribute.

**2.** Choose as candidates the most *remote* (low probability of co-occurrence with the brand) conveyors. (The exception is if you are looking for a visual conveyor and the target attribute is based on hunger, thirst, or sex as a sensory gratification motivation for the brand, or is based on social approval motivation with user-as-hero positioning, as explained earlier—in which cases you would choose a conveyor that is highly typical of the target benefit and *least* remote from the brand. In the limiting case, this would simply be an ad in which there is no conveyor—just the brand itself, depicting its target attribute. Most often, however, such ads will use a conveyor, but not a remote one.) Let us assume the more common case of a remote conveyor.

**3.** "Back-test" each remote conveyor from step 2 for high association to the target attribute. By "high asso-

ciation," we mean, as a working rule, that two-thirds of the respondents in the test should respond with the attribute when given the conveyor as the cue. (This test should be done with a larger sample—say 30 target audience consumers—than the sample of individuals used for the initial brainstorming task.) The procedure is:

$$C \rightarrow A_t$$

Technically, this associative direction is known as "dominance" in that you want the target benefit to be a dominant associate of the conveyor. Although the conveyor was chosen initially because of its typicality (see step 1), it must work, in the ad, by dominance in suggesting the target attribute, that is, by the reverse associative process.[37]

At this point, also check for the presence of strong contradictory attribute associations and eliminate conveyors that have them. Choose the conveyor (from those of similarly significant remoteness) that has the *strongest* target-attribute association. By strongest, we mean the one with the most people (above the two-thirds cutoff) making the correct association.

**4.** If the conveyor is going to be visual, as would usually be necessary in a TV commercial and would be the main option, instead of a verbal conveyor, for print advertising, then a *picture* of the conveyor selected from step 3 must be developed. (We note that visual conveyors are usable in all media except radio, which obviously must employ a verbal or auditory conveyor.) This requires that the picture and the word for the conveyor correspond. This was referred to previously when we said that the conveyor must be immediately and correctly labeled by the target audience.

**5.** The conveyor—either visual or verbal—may then need to be "adjusted" to increase[38] (a) its attention-getting capacity (*without* distorting the accuracy of the label), (b) its *uniqueness* in comparison with conveyors used by other brands in the category in their advertising, and especially (c) its capacity to elicit the target attribute.

**6.** Brainstorm an attribute *prompt*, if necessary, for the ad. This is not difficult, as the main content of the prompt is the target attribute itself, but its execution may require some thought to make it fit the ad. The attribute prompt helps to achieve the desired associative "match" between the conveyor and the product by naming or verbally hinting at the target attribute, for a visual conveyor; or showing or describing the target attribute, for a verbal conveyor.

There are a couple of important considerations here. One is that the lower the associative strength of the target attribute in response to the *conveyor* (see step 3, above), the more direct the attribute prompt will need to be.

The second consideration arises when using emotional positioning. A good emotional-positioning ad—using an emotional conveyor rather than a direct associative conveyor—should not really need an attribute prompt. That is, the emotional properties of the conveyor should "transfer automatically" to the product. (This is similar to the process of "classical conditioning" as described in most consumer behavior textbooks, without getting too technical here.) If necessary, it is preferable to adjust the conveyor (on the E-P-A dimensions) rather than to use an attribute prompt in a purely emotional ad.

**7.** Place the conveyor, the product representation, and the attribute prompt (if used) into an advertising format (at least two executions should be produced) and test the ad(s).

The RAM-Conveyor procedure for the development of creative ideas *appears* to mimic the process that agency creative people go through when they think up an ad (presuming they decide that it is not going to be a "straight" ad but rather that some "creative oomph" is needed to communicate the brand position). However, it is much more rigorous in its conveyor evaluation (Table 7.2) than the usual "gut reaction" evaluation given conveyors in ad agencies—which is the main reason, we think, why many otherwise creative ads fail. The RAM-Conveyor procedure is a useful procedure for those who have to develop their own ads, such as students or smaller advertisers; and perhaps agency professionals might like to try it as a more formalized procedure than they use at present.

## LONG-TERM MANAGEMENT OF CREATIVITY FOR THE BRAND

Creative ideas for the brand's advertising should be *proactively* managed over time. There are two reasons for this:

**1.** Most (but not all) creative ideas in advertising campaigns will eventually "wear out" and need to be replaced. We discuss the specific causes of and remedies for advertising wearout in the final chapter of the book, Chapter 20.

**2.** There is always the possibility that a *better* creative idea may be found, resulting in increased profitability for the brand.

For long-term management of the brand's advertising, the theory of random creativity can again be usefully applied. Chow and Silk have developed a valuable extension of the theory of random creativity which we can call *sequential* random creativity.[39] In the normal theory of random creativity described in this chapter, we have assumed that the manager is searching *simultaneously* for a number of creative ideas in order to come up with a winner immediately. This is the circumstance that applies with the launch of a new brand, or when a *new campaign* is needed in a hurry for an established brand.

However, for an established brand that has a successful *ongoing* campaign, there is less of a rush to develop a new creative idea. Chow and Silk therefore have very usefully suggested that the theory of random creativity can be applied sequentially. That is, from time to time—let's say at 6 month intervals—the manager should commission *one* new creative idea and test it against the incumbent creative idea, that is, against the present campaign.

---

**TABLE 7.2**

### PROPERTIES OF THE CONVEYOR IN RAM-CONVEYOR THEORY

**1. Attention-getting**
   a. Reflexive, or
   b. Selective (absolute or specific motivator)
**2. Correctly labeled by the consumer**
   This applies to a visual conveyor. A verbal conveyor must result in correct comprehension of the words.
**3. Perceived as remote**
   That is, low probability of co-occurence with product. *Exceptions:* basic sensory gratification (hunger, thirst, sex) and social approval.
**4. High association of the target attribute when prompted**
   Where "attribute" = attribute, benefit, *or* emotion, depending on the a-b-e focus in the brand's positioning strategy.
**5. And have no strong contradictory attribute associations**
   For instance, the conveyor must not otherwise convey low quality when the target attribute is high quality.

The sequential application of random creativity has a very low cost. Instead of generating and testing multiple creative alternatives, the manager is generating and testing one at a time, at reasonably wide and affordable intervals.

For the next creative idea generated, the theory of random creativity suggests that it could be better—or worse—than the current campaign. If it is worse, obviously, the new idea should be discarded. However, if it is better, then the manager will have to make a big decision as to whether to drop the present campaign and go with the new, more promising one. A decision in favor of the better campaign will be easy to make if the established brand is supported by a so-so campaign at present. If, however, the present campaign is an outstanding one, then the decision will naturally be more difficult. In the latter case, more money should be spent developing the promising new idea into a representative sample of executions and *thoroughly* testing them. This is necessary in order to be sure of what would otherwise be a risky decision in abandoning a highly successful present campaign.

We close this chapter—which we hope has been stimulating and creative—with a realistic comment on this last point about sequentially applied random creativity. What usually happens with long-running campaigns is that, either because of real consumer wearout or, much more likely, because of wearout within the client's or the agency's mind, "new executions" of the campaign are requested. "New executions" (the buzzword is "fresh") mean that there is a considerable danger of drifting away from the original creative idea—and, worse, from the brand's positioning strategy and brand position. (As we said earlier in the chapter, creative ideas *themselves* cannot be tested; only *executions* of the idea, in the form of at least rough ads, can be tested. This was the reason for recommending that at least two executions of each creative idea be developed in order to give the idea a fair representation in the testing phase.) In our experience, established campaigns that suddenly seem to go off the rails usually do so because what management or the agency sees as being "merely" new executions are, in fact, tapping into a *new creative idea.* This is a particular danger that the theory of random creativity, with its emphasis on creative ideas and the clustering of executions under those creative ideas, can help to guard against.

In Chapter 19, we show how creative ideas can be related to their executions—and distinguished from separate creative ideas—by employing a procedure known as multidimensional scaling. That is, target audience consumers or customers, not the client or the advertising agency, should decide whether the new campaign is indeed new or simply, as may be intended, executional variations on the same creative idea that motivated the previous campaign.

## SUMMARY

The creative idea is the key to great advertising. However, you have to "hold" this key with a firm positioning strategy. The "lock" is the mind of the consumer. Most keys won't fit at all. Some keys will fit approximately but will need to be forced (with extra media expenditure). The right key, however, will open the lock immediately. Moreover, a key can have various external shapes (like various advertising executions) but the main bit that fits the lock must be the same.

Defined more formally, a "creative idea" is an attention-getting and catalytically relevant way of presenting the brand position to the consumer. A creative idea is a prescription *for* an ad, not the ad itself. In most cases, the prescription can be executed in several ways.

The functions of the creative idea are to command attention and then to dramatize the brand's positioning strategy. The best creative ideas derive their power from a catalytic reaction with the positioning strategy: there's a "chemical reaction" of immediate communication—but, at the end of it, the brand position remains unchanged. (In an occasional but certainly allowable reversal of the normal planning process, the agency's creative idea may actually suggest a *better* positioning strategy. If so, the creative idea must dramatize *that* strategy effectively.) Because of this chemical reaction, great creative ideas, or what are known as "big ideas," give the impression of being astonishingly simple—once you've thought up the idea!

Generating great creative ideas is, we believe, largely a random process. The fact that only about half of all advertising campaigns produce a significant sales increase, and the further fact that only about one in six campaigns is a "real winner," are proof that advertising agencies cannot come up with great ideas every time. We therefore recommend that the manager (the advertiser) understand and apply the theory of random creativity in order to increase the likelihood that a winning creative idea will be found. The theory of random creativity, which we have adapted from the original theory proposed by Gross, helps the manager decide how many creative ideas should be requested for a given campaign (see chapter appendix 7B). This number of creative ideas that should be requested can be very large (in theory, as many as 94 ideas) when the manager has an established brand, wants a real-winner campaign, and has an advertising agency with a below-average and hardly variable track record. In contrast, the number is small (as low as three ideas) when the manager is about to launch a new brand, is satisfied with a significant sales increase rather than necessarily a real winner campaign, and has chosen an agency with an outstanding and highly reliable track record. Whereas the ideal application of the theory of random creativity says that a large number of creative ideas should be generated and tested, it can also be applied with far fewer (only one-quarter the number of) creative ideas if the manager has faith in "concept development" research prior to ad testing. Either as input to concept development or employed directly, the theory of random creativity has practical benefits for everyone (see chapter appendix 7C): it increases the advertiser's chances of coming up with a successful campaign; it also increases the agency's creative reputation; and consumers will tend to see more creative ads.

Agencies (or smaller advertisers who create their own ads) can employ the I-G-I method of brainstorming to generate creative ideas. This method consists of an individual brainstorming phase (I), followed by a group interaction phase (G) to amalgamate and refine the initial creative ideas, and concludes with individuals (I) voting for the ideas that should proceed further for testing. The I-G-I method has been shown to be the most effective for brainstorming.

What, exactly, should creative people brainstorm about? Here we suggest that creative experts *implicitly* follow—and that you can *explicitly* follow—a new theory of creativity in advertising which we call RAM (Remote Associative Matching)-Conveyor theory. RAM-Conveyor theory regards the creative idea as being the "conveyor" of the positioning of the brand (usually of the brand's target attribute, benefit, or emotion). In the ad, the conveyor at first appears very unusual in relation to the product (less so for sensory gratification or social approval products), and for this reason is highly attention-getting. Then, often aided by what we call an attribute prompt in the ad, the match between the conveyor and the brand's target attribute becomes suddenly apparent. This process of remote associative matching is, we believe, the essence of many of the great creative ideas.

Most ads should use a conveyor approach. (The exceptions are direct mail and classified ads.) RAM-Conveyor theory is new, and tests of it are preliminary—but it promises to add some science to the art of creativity. We show how to brainstorm using RAM-Conveyor theory in the chapter.

Creative ideas for the brand's advertising should be managed over time. From a negative perspective, this is because most creative ideas eventually "wear out." More positively, there is always a chance that the manager will find a better creative idea for the brand. To manage creativity over time, we apply the theory of random creativity *sequentially*. That is, instead of generating and testing a number of creative ideas all at once, the manager should request and test a new creative idea every 6 months or so. If the new creative idea clearly "beats" the incumbent creative idea in testing, then it should be seriously considered as the genesis for a replacement campaign.

Another important aspect of creativity management for the brand over time is to ensure that successive executions of the creative idea, employed to extend the life of a campaign, continue to embody the original creative idea and to accurately represent the brand position. It is all too easy for progressive variations to begin to lose the essence of the creative idea and drift "off strategy." A continuous program of ad testing and tracking is the only sure answer to this frequent cause of eventual campaign failure (we revisit campaign management in the final chapter of the book). For now, we have the creative idea or a series of creative ideas, but how do we turn them into actual, effective ads? This is the topic of the next three chapters.

**APPENDIX**

# 7A. Examples of Great Creative Ideas

We will now look at some examples of creative ideas that most experts would regard as "big ideas" in successful campaigns. We will see that the creative idea itself may take the form of one of, or combinations of, the following: (1) a particularly effective slogan, (2) a particularly effective picture or visual device, (3) a song or jingle, (4) a distinctive style of advertising, or (5) a brand symbol that is featured in advertising. There are many forms of creative ideas (which adds to the difficulty of providing a general definition) but *all* of them share the ability to represent the brand's positioning strategy in an attention-getting and catalytically relevant manner.

To reinforce our conceptualization of positioning strategy as taking into account the X-YZ macro positioning framework, we will organize the examples approximately in terms of creative ideas that focus on X (category location), Y (user as hero), or Z (product as hero), respectively. At this point, we will *not* point out the specific use in these examples of the I-D-U model of benefit emphasis or the a-b-e model of benefit focus, although we could do this and readers may wish to try to do so. In the examples, we have acknowledged the advertising agencies who created the ideas. Sales results are given where available, but some of the creative ideas rely on hearsay evidence of their success.

**Category Location Creative Ideas**. We have already mentioned the famous 7UP "Uncola" campaign based on the idea of positioning 7UP as an alternative to colas in the overall soft-drink category. This creative idea was invented by J. Walter Thompson in 1968 and used more or less continuously until 1983 when the 7UP account was switched to NW Ayer. In 1983, 7UP and Diet 7UP had 6.3 percent share of the U.S. soft-drink market. After the "Uncola" campaign was discontinued, sales dropped by 40 percent (relatively) to a market share of only 3.8 percent in 1990. In 1992, Leo Burnett, who had won the account, revived the "Uncola" theme. Since then, 7UP's share has grown 11 percent (relatively) to a share of 4.2 percent, a healthy revival. The 7UP company has even gone as far as to add the words "The Uncola" to 7UP's and Diet 7UP's package logos, and thinks of itself in a corporate sense as "The Uncola Company."[40]

Another category-positioning success story has been Kraft General Foods' coating mix, Shake 'N Bake. Shake 'N Bake was introduced in the mid-1960s as a way to prepare chicken without frying it. The product did well in the 1970s but began to languish, so advertising for the brand was stopped in the mid-1980s. In 1989, the KGF marketing team realized they had a benefit that was becoming more important to consumers with the trends toward eating less fried food but more chicken. Ogilvy & Mather advertising agency came up with a new creative idea, based on the original benefit, but aimed at locating Shake 'N Bake *away* from the category of fried foods. The TV campaign, with the tag line "Why fry?," was an inexpensive one, using only 15-second TV spots. Sales of Shake 'N Bake rose 11 percent the first year, 1990, reviving the product.[41]

The Cadillac campaign, "Until now," which we mentioned earlier, has also been highly successful. This campaign is based on the creative idea of positioning Cadillac Seville and Cadillac Eldorado as genuine competitors with luxury import cars (an X or category-location strategy). General Motors particularly wanted to attract younger affluent buyers to the brand. During the first 4 months of the campaign, Cadillac's Seville and Eldorado sales rose 24 percent and, demonstrating that the target audience appeal of the campaign was successful, 46 percent of Cadillac showroom visitors during the period were under age 50 with $75,000 or more household income—exactly the target audience that Cadillac wished to attract.[42] This campaign was by D'Arcy Masius Benton & Bowles.

Perhaps the best-known category-positioning campaign of all time is Doyle Dane Bernbach's "Think small" creative idea for the Volkswagen Beetle. At that time, the early 1960s, most Americans were driving large cars. The Volkswagen campaign almost single-handedly made small cars acceptable. More than this, it made small "ugly" cars acceptable, which was another creative idea by Doyle Dane Bernbach used in conjunction with the "Think small" idea. (Actually, as John Eighmey explains in a historical note, the simplified positioning statement for VW Beetle was "This is an honest car." And, in keeping with our definition of the creative idea as being sufficiently detailed to guide execution and amenable to multiple executions, the full creative idea was "To use traditional automobile advertising as a 'foil' by speaking simply when others were complex, emphasizing the basics when others were emphasizing extraneous features, and offering almost monk-like virtues in an era of materialism."[43]

**User-As-Hero Creative Ideas.** When first introduced to the market, light beer was seen as a beer for "wimps." The first light beer, Gablinger's, was unsuccessful.[44] This changed with the creative idea for a me-too brand, Miller Lite. To overcome the wimpish image of light beer, the agency, McCann-Erickson, came up with the creative idea of endorsement by persons we will call "Ex-jocks." (Currently active sports stars are not allowed to endorse alcoholic beverages. Also, ex-jocks are more likely than current athletes to have weight problems.) The copy line was, "Everything you always wanted in a beer—and less." In subsequent commercials, the famous ex-athletes argued about whether it was "less calories" or the "great taste" that led them to prefer Miller Lite. The "Ex-jocks" campaign was later continued by new agency Backer & Spielvogel. The rest is history: Miller Lite rapidly became the number-one light beer and the number-three beer overall in the U.S. market.

Another classic user-as-hero campaign was designed to gain social approval for an otherwise "hidden" product: women's hair tint (dye). The creative idea was based on the copy line "Does she or doesn't she?," which suggested that many women used hair tint but that it was so subtle that other people couldn't detect it. The tag line was "Only her hairdresser knows for sure." This campaign, for Clairol, by Foote Cone & Belding's Shirley Polykoff, reportedly influenced 50 percent of American women, at the time (the early 1950s), to tint their hair! Sales of Clairol hair tint rose a massive 413 percent in the first 6 years of the campaign.[45]

A more recent user-oriented creative idea worthy of note is demonstrated in the "Launderette strip" TV commercial thought up by Bartle Bogle Hegarty, U.K., for Levi's jeans. This campaign, introduced in 1986, was one of the first to go back to old hit songs (in this case, a Marvin Gaye Motown song, "Heard it through the grapevine," which was also used at about the same time in the United States for, appropriately, California Raisin Board advertising) as the auditory part of the creative idea. The visual part of the creative idea was the famous "launderette strip" scene in which a young man calmly removes his Levi's, puts them in the washer, sits down in his undershorts in public in the launderette waiting for his Levi's to be washed and dried, then quite conspicuously and coolly dons them and walks out.

The creative idea of a "soap opera" series of vignettes for Taster's Choice Coffee (Nescafé Gold Blend in the United Kingdom) is another user-as-hero creative idea that is innovative and reportedly very successful. Invented by McCann-Erickson in Britain in 1987, where 10 "episodes" of the soapie have been aired, the campaign was adopted for the United States in 1990 and has so far used six episodes. Viewer interest has been maintained with a new episode every 6 months or so, plus a good deal of media publicity just before each new episode. Taster's Choice's market share in the highly competitive and mature U.S. instant coffee market started at 22 percent and has risen to 27 percent during the campaign.[46]

**Product-As-Hero Creative Ideas.** Most of the great creative ideas acknowledged by experts are based on product benefits. We have already mentioned such famous examples as VW's "Think small," 7UP's "Uncola," and M&M's "Melts in your mouth, not in your hands." These creative ideas were from Doyle Dane Bernbach, J. Walter Thompson, and Ted Bates advertising agencies, respectively.

Another classic product-as-hero campaign was for one of the first deodorizing soaps. Up until this point, soap was a product that merely "cleaned" rather than deodorized. The deodorizer campaign, "Aren't you glad you used Dial? Don't you wish everybody did?," from Foote Cone & Belding, immediately partitioned the soap market and made Dial the number-one brand.[47] In the 1990s, market leadership changed again with the introduction of Lever 2000—a combination deodorant-and-complexion soap. Lever Bros had a very strong product-attribute foundation to work with, but the creative idea was brilliant, consisting of the

company name (the first time it had ever been used on a Lever Bros product) coupled with the modernistic-sounding "2000," and a great copy line, from J. Walter Thompson copywriter Jim Jordan, Jr., "For all 2000 body parts." Lever 2000 now has a 7.1 percent share of the extremely crowded U.S. soap market and has helped Lever Bros overtake Procter & Gamble in total corporate share of this market.[48]

# 7B. Mathematical Basis of the Theory of Random Creativity

**Formula for Number of Ideas.** The key question in the theory of random creativity is: How many creative ideas do you need to generate and test in order to virtually guarantee that you will find at least one real winner? The answer depends mainly on four variables: the starting number, the average performance of the creative source, the variability of performance of the creative source, and the validity of the screening test. The number of creative ideas is a function of:

**1.** The "starting number," which is the number of tries that would be needed to guarantee that a winning creative idea will be among them (calculated from the binomial theorem—see note 52). This number will vary depending on (a) whether the manager is advertising a new product or an established product, (b) the degree of confidence or "firmness of guarantee" required, and (c) whether the manager is satisfied with an idea that is "likely" to increase sales or wants a "real winner." Call the starting number $M_c$, where c denotes the degree of confidence the manager requires.

**2.** The average (mean) performance of the source of the creative ideas. If the sales effectiveness of the ideas is denoted by E, and the effectiveness of i-th idea is denoted by $E_1$, and the source is denoted by s, then the average performance of the source can be denoted by the mean, $\overline{E}_{is}$.

**3.** The variability, specifically the standard deviation (S) and thus the range (plus-or-minus 3 S) of performance of the creative ideas produced by the source. Denote the standard deviation as $S_{is}$.

**4.** The predictive validity of the test employed to screen the creative ideas and select the apparent winning idea. Denote this validity as V for test type t, thus $V_t$.

We can now write the formula for the number of creative ideas required (N) with a given level of confidence (c) as:

$$N_c = M_c \left( \frac{1}{\overline{E}_{is}} \times S_{is} \times V_t \right) + 1$$

Several mathematical implications follow from this formula.

First, the starting number ($M_c$) *multiplies* with (is modified by) the other factors to determine the *actual* number of ideas ($N_c$) that you will need to request from the creative source (or sources) in a given application of the model. Es-

---

**TABLE 7.3**

**VALUES OF THE STARTING NUMBER, $M_c$, OF CREATIVE IDEAS NEEDED TO GUARANTEE A SALES-INCREASING OR REAL-WINNER CREATIVE IDEA**

(*See note 52 for computation method.*)

| | Number of creative ideas (M) with strength of guarantee (c) at | |
|---|---|---|
| | 90% | 99% |
| **New-product campaign** | | |
| • Sales-increase idea (p = .70) | 2 | 4 |
| • Real-winner idea (p = .30) | 7 | 13 |
| **Established-product campaign** | | |
| • Sales-increase idea (p = .32) | 6 | 12 |
| • Real-winner idea (p = .12) | 19 | 37 |

sentially, the other factors merely *adjust* the starting number (this is why they are parenthesized in the formula). Table 7.3 shows the values of the starting number, $M_c$.[49] As the table shows, the number of tries (creative ideas to be commissioned) depends on three factors: (1) whether you are about to produce a new-product campaign or an established-product campaign, (2) whether you will be satisfied with a "significant sales increase" campaign or a highly profitable "real winner" campaign, and (3) how confident you want to be. $M_c$ can be as low as 2 tries for a new-product campaign, sales-increase only, with 90 percent confidence. Or it can be as high as 37 tries for the most demanding situation: an established-product campaign, insistence on a real winner, with virtual certainty (99 percent confidence) of finding such a campaign. Other values of $M_c$ lie between these extremes according to the conditions specified by the manager.

Second, the number of ideas that you will need is *inversely* proportional to the average creative ability (mean historical effectiveness performance, $\overline{E}_{is}$) of the creative source. This follows from the commonsense realization that, other things being equal, the *worse* the creative source, the more ideas you will have to request in order to be sure of having a winner among them. Conversely, the *better* the creative source, the fewer ideas need be requested to obtain a winner.

Operationally, we index $\overline{E}_{is}$ at 1.0 and allow it to range from 0.5 to 2.0. That is, if the creative source is "average," then $\overline{E}_{is} = 1.0$ and $M_c$ is unmodified. At the lower extreme, if the creative source is only half as effective as average, then $\overline{E}_{is}$ is $= 0.5$ and $\frac{1}{\overline{E}_{is}} = 2$ and you will need twice as many ($M_c \times 2$) creative ideas as from an average source. At the upper extreme, with $\overline{E}_{is} = 2.0$ and $\frac{1}{\overline{E}_{is}} = 0.5$, you will need only half as many ($M_c \times 0.5$) creative ideas.

Third, the number of creative ideas that you will need depends also on the variability (standard deviation, $S_{is}$) of the performance of the creative source in producing creative ideas. If the creative source shows small variation around the mean performance, then there is not much point in requesting a lot of creative ideas from that source because the ideas won't vary much. (Ideal would be a creative source with a very high mean and low variance, such that you need only request one or two ideas from the source in order to be sure of a winner.) A creative source with wide variance, however, will produce some very good ideas and some very bad ideas, and you will need to sample more ideas to be sure of finding a very good one.

We index the standard deviation of the source's performance, $S_{is}$, at 1.0 with a range of 0.75 to 1.25. The relatively small range is because we believe that variability within a source varies a little less than absolute performance across sources. Thus, $S_{is}$ has a relatively small, but still important, effect in modifying $M_c$.

Fourth, the number of ideas that you will need depends on the validity of the testing procedure ($V_t$) that you use to evaluate the initial ideas generated in order to select one for the campaign. The validity of the testing procedure directly affects the number of ideas requested. This can be seen by considering the lower limit of validity, where the manager is simply guessing (using "intuition"[50]). If the manager is simply guessing, then he or she should request only *one* ad (hence the +1 in the formula). This is because guesswork would be just as likely to *eliminate* a winner as to identify one. On the other hand, the higher the predictive validity of the screening procedure, the more it will pay to request a larger number of creative ideas so that the test can have a chance to find a winner.

Because of its "zeroing-out" potential (this variable is not indexed and a value of zero renders the whole procedure useless), the predictive validity of the screening test,

$V_t$, is the second-most influential factor after the average performance level of the source, $\overline{E}_{is}$.[51] We operationalize $V_t$ as varying from 0 to 1.0, where 0 represents close to sheer guesswork (especially as $M_c$ becomes a larger number) and 1.0 represents a perfect-prediction pretest. As should be evident, a low-validity pretest can undermine the entire "guarantee" of the random creativity formula because even though you'll have a winner among the $N_c$ creative ideas, you won't be able to identify it!

We solve this problem, mathematically and practically, in the following way. In reality, two courses of action are open to the manager once a number of creative ideas have been generated (according to $M_c \times \dfrac{1}{\overline{E}_{is}} \times S_{is}$ up to this point):

- Firstly, and ideally, the manager is willing to test all the creative ideas and has a valid test to do so. Here we will assume $V_t = 1.0$, and so the final number of creative ideas stays equal to $Mc \times \dfrac{1}{\overline{E}_{is}} \times S_{is}$, plus 1.

- Alternatively, and corresponding with common practice,[52] the agency may claim to be able to "develop" a smaller number of *initial* creative ideas into much-improved *final* creative ideas. (This usually is accomplished by conducting qualitative "concept development" research with a small sample of consumers; see Chapter 19.) We make a judgment call here, based on experience with concept development research,[53] and set $V_t = 0.25$. That is, we estimate that the manager (and the agency) will require only *one-quarter* the number of creative ideas if the concept development route is chosen. However, this *does* assume that the test used to screen the *final* creative ideas is highly valid, $V_t = 1.0$. Thus, strictly speaking, this means an extension of the formula to $V_{t1} \times V_{t2}$, where $V_{t1} = 0.25$ and $V_{t2} = 1.0$.

In practice, therefore, the formula gives *two* solutions for the number of creative ideas, depending on the nature of the testing procedure chosen by the manager. The "solution" of using *no test* (that is, guesswork) is no solution at all, because it leaves the manager with just one ad (the $+1$ in the formula) without using random creativity.

*Putting the Formula All Together.* We can illustrate the range or "sensitivity" of the formula for determining the number of creative ideas by inserting the extreme values. We will first assume an ideal and constant value of $V_t$ as 1.0 (that is, the "test all" route). Take the toughest situation: a manager who wants to be very sure (confidence, $c = 99$ percent) of obtaining a creative idea that will generate a real-winner campaign for an established brand. For this, the starting number, $M_{99}$, is 37. Under the most difficult and demanding conditions, this number will increase to $N_{99} = 37 \times 2 \times 1.25 \times 1.0 + 1 = 92.5 + 1 = 94$ ideas required. Under the easiest conditions, it will decrease to

$N_{99} = 37 \times 0.5 \times 0.75 \times 1.0 + 1 = 13.9 + 1 = 15$ ideas required—that is, a top agency that is also consistent in producing winners will—with a valid pretest applied—be 99 percent sure of producing a sales-increasing campaign if the agency generates 15 creative ideas for the manager. Remember, these values of $N_{99}$ are for the toughest situation and will be considerably lower in other situations.

Alternatively, if the manager chooses to take the concept development route prior to ad testing, then the above numbers are reduced by three-quarters (actually, with little difference in total research costs). In the most difficult conditions, the value of $N_{99}$ becomes $92.5 \times 0.25 \times 1.0 + 1 = 25$. In the easiest conditions, the value of $N_{99}$ becomes $13.9 \times 0.25 \times 1.0 + 1 = 5$ (rounded up, just to be sure). These are more reasonable numbers for the range of creative ideas required in the very toughest situation—if the manager has faith in the concept development of fewer ideas prior to ad testing.

**It's Better to Gamble Up Front with Random Creativity Than to Gamble Later with the Traditional Method.** A manager may look at these numbers and say, "Forget it! Commissioning multiple creative ideas is too much of a gamble. I'm going to use the traditional method of commissioning *just one* creative idea up front." But the manager who opts for the traditional approach is gambling *too*—after the fact. The manager is *gambling* that the one creative idea will be at least sales-successful (a seven in 10 chance for a new product but no guarantee, and only a one in three chance for an established product) and *hoping* that it might be a "real winner" (odds of which, we estimate, are reduced to about three in 10 for a new product and one in 10 for an established product). Theoretically, the manager's chances are improved if the concept development route is used for the one creative idea. However, since *most* one-idea campaigns are developed through this route (although far fewer are subjected to a valid ad test before being released), we would not modify the above odds at all. The manager who takes a gamble on one creative idea is likely to find out *after* the campaign is up and running that it is a loser.

It seems better to gamble *up front*, using the theory of random creativity, for a 90 or 99 percent assurance of a sales-successful ad, or of a "real winner" when needed—*before* the campaign is paid for in the media. Also, even if you don't go all the way with the numbers suggested by the theory, your chances of success increase with every additional (independent) creative idea that you are willing to commission. The theory always *improves* your chances even if caution prevents you from commissioning enough ideas for a guarantee.

**Cost of Implementation.** The cost of generating, producing, and testing multiple creative ideas is also a necessary consideration. And it is a consideration that wrongly stops many managers from adopting the random creativity procedure. Evidence such as that presented in Figure 7.2, in the study of new-product campaigns by Blair, indicates that it could be worthwhile to take as much as half of the money out of the media budget and spend it on guaranteeing the production of a winning ad. However, few managers would have the gumption to do this.

It is, though, worth spending much *more* money than is typically expended at present to find a winning ad. The economics are actually very good indeed, even for quite small advertising budgets. Table 7.4 presents some typical cost figures for applying the theory of random creativity. In this example, the number of creative ideas requested is 5. The cost for generating each creative idea is shown as $4,000, which should be adequate to compensate the agency or the creative team for its time. The cost of producing the creative idea in testable form (two executions of each creative idea) is shown as $20,000, which would allow the production of two high-quality "photomatic" or "live-action rough" TV commercials for a transformational brand such as Coke.[54] For nontransformational TV commercials, or for print or radio ads, the production cost for each execution would be very much lower. The cost of testing each execution has been estimated at $10,000 per execution, which would allow a highly valid test to be applied from a research company such as Research Systems Corporation or McCollum Spielman Worldwide. In Chapter 19, we will consider less-expensive testing procedures, including a pretest followed by a final quantitative test of the best several alternatives.

The total cost in this example of applying the theory of random creativity is $220,000. To put this cost into perspective, let us make two comparisons. First, $220,000 is little more than the cost of one national TV commercial exposure (currently about $220,000 in a top-rated, prime-time show). Second, let us suppose that the commercial is going to be shown 100 times, such as three times a week on each of the three major networks for about 11 weeks. If all of these exposures are in top-rated programs on prime-time TV, then the media budget would be approximately $20 million. Thus, putting the two comparisons together, the cost of the random creativity procedure would be a minuscule 1.2 percent of the media budget and would result in the trivial sacrifice of only one or two exposures of the commercial—for a much greater sales return. Even if the media budget were only $2 million, as occurs for a regional product or as is more typical in a smaller country such as Australia, the $220,000 cost of the random creativity procedure amounts to just 12 percent of the budget—and is well worth the investment for the increased likelihood of coming up with a winning campaign.

If you were to request and test a very large number of creative ideas—say, 20—then you'd be looking at a tougher

**TYPICAL COST FIGURES FOR APPLYING THE THEORY OF RANDOM CREATIVITY**

(*Example: 5 creative ideas requested*)

| | |
|---|---|
| Generation of creative ideas (per idea)[a] | $4,000 |
| Production of two executions[b] | $20,000 |
| Testing of two executions[c] | $20,000 |
| Subtotal | $44,000 |
| x 5 creative ideas             = | $220,000 |

[a]Survey of agencies by Rossiter and Saintilan, 1991 (see note 23).
[b]TV commercials assumed (photomatics or live-action roughs).
[c]Highly valid testing procedure assumed, such as customized ad test, or ARS[sm], or McCollum Spielman's Advantage*ACT[sm] (see Chapter 19).

decision. The cost would be about $1 million. For the $20 million budget, this would undoubtedly be worth it (look again at Blair's data in Figure 7.2). But for the smaller $2 million budget, you'd rarely get approval to spend half of it up front on the ads. Yet this should be regarded as an investment decision. You should estimate the profit return from a 90 or 99 percent guaranteed winner against the much lower *chance* of a profit from generating and testing fewer ads. Having watched many advertisers throw $2 million in media expenditure down the drain, we'd advise you to do the calculation before deciding.

Finally, we note that the route of concept development followed by ad testing will require only one-quarter the number of creative ideas to be generated and tested. This cuts the ad testing cost by 75 percent but adds $20,000 for concept development research (multiple ideas are typically evaluated side-by-side in concept development research, and we've allowed for six focus groups at $3,000 each, or $20,000 as a safe total). The 5-idea case reduces to 2 ideas, and the costs to $108,000, which is an extremely low 0.5 percent of the $20 million budget and only 5.4 percent of the $2 million budget. Similarly, the 20-idea case reduces to 5 ideas, and the costs to $240,000. Even with the smaller $2 million budget, this is only 12 percent and is certainly worth a try.

# 7C. Random Creativity Benefits Everyone

**Advertiser Benefits.** Astute advertisers have picked up on the theory of random creativity and are applying it with great success. AT&T is one company that is known to have used the procedure.[55] In 1978, AT&T approached NW Ayer, its advertising agency, with the request to generate six distinct creative ideas for a campaign designed to increase long-distance telephone usage. Six campaigns were developed for television, including music and video, with respective tag lines such as "So nice talking to you" and "Call America." The commercials were produced; then they were tested; and a winner was chosen based on pretest results. The winning creative idea has become marketing legend: "Reach out and touch someone." This creative idea was so successful for AT&T that it has been copied by other telephone companies throughout the world.

In another application of random creativity, Chevron in the mid-1980s asked its agency, J. Walter Thompson, to assign six creative teams to each come up with a TV commercial to demonstrate the oil company's concern with environmental issues.[56] All six commercials were pretested in animatic form by McCollum Spielman. As the theory of random creativity would predict, the six commercials produced widely varying results. In terms of the main criterion measure, change in attitude toward Chevron, the scores among the target audience, compared with a norm of $+16$ for oil-company corporate ads (indicating that a net of 16 percent of test respondents showed a positive attitude shift), were $-14$, $-9$, $+1$, $+11$, $+16$, and $+36$. Note the wide range of scores—a range of 50 percentage points in the percent of respondents changing their attitude about Chevron. And note that only one of the six ads was above average despite the agency's best efforts.[57] The winner (the $+36$) was a commercial from what was to become the "People do" campaign, familiar to residents of the U.S. West coast and Southern states where Chevron is distributed. In a typical commercial in this campaign, an eagle is saved from landing on high-voltage power lines by wooden platforms put there by Chevron field staff (Figure 7.12). The "People do" campaign not only improved attitudes toward Chevron among the total population and among the "inner-directed," anti–oil company target audience for whom it was intended but also caused the latter target to increase their brand purchases of Chevron by 22 percent during the first year of the campaign.

It is obvious that the advertiser must come out ahead by applying the random creativity procedure. Generating and testing more, different ideas must improve the advertiser's chances of finding a winner. Realistically, though, we very much doubt that *all* advertisers will adopt the random creativity approach. If they did, this could lead to a new equilibrium in which all ads are highly creative and competitive gains will cancel each other out. Such a scenario is unlikely. Advertisers' faith in their own intuition, as well as agencies' faith in their ability to produce the "right" campaign, will continue to reinforce the status quo. This will leave plenty of opportunity for the innovative advertiser or agency to capitalize by applying the theory of random creativity.

**Agency Benefits.** The advertising agency will also benefit by applying the random creativity procedure. If the agency comes up with winning campaigns more frequently,

**FIGURE 7.12**
Lead commercial from Chevron's "People do" campaign. The creative idea was found by the random-creativity procedure. *Courtesy:* Chevron.

which is likely with this approach, client satisfaction with the agency will increase and so too should its reputation and billings.

In a survey we conducted recently with the 150 leading advertising agencies in Australia, whose numbers included most of the major international agencies, we found that about two in three agencies would be currently willing to accept the conditions required for the theory to work in practice.[58] The main conditions are that the agency must recognize the value of independence in generating the creative ideas and must be willing to submit multiple creative ideas to a valid pretesting (ad test) procedure.

**Copywriter Benefits.** Paradoxically enough, creatives should be in favor of the random creativity approach because their biggest fear of pretesting is that a highly original idea will not "get through." By pretesting a *number* of these ideas—rather than screening them out by the creative director's intuition—the chance that the creative person's "pet idea" will survive is much increased. Furthermore, the competitive aspect is likely to bring out each copywriter's best work.

**Research Company Benefits.** Pretest companies will be beneficiaries also. There would be a large increase in the number of ads submitted for testing, a necessary step in the theory of random creativity. Also, because many managers will opt for the concept development route, qualitative research companies will benefit as well.

**Media Benefits.** On the one hand, a client who has found a winning ad would be wise to increase the media expenditure behind it. Few advertisers could resist spending *more* behind a big winner. Indeed, the advertiser should pull money out of the sales force or out of other marketing functions to do so as long as the profit return is greater than these alternative expenditures of the funds. On the other hand, a fundamental advantage of the theory of random creativity is that you can achieve the same sales results with a *reduced* budget. In fact, we advocated taking money *out of* the media budget and putting it into generating and testing more ads. Overall, then, the media companies may see little net change.

**Public Benefits.** The public (consumers and customers) almost certainly will benefit. If the correlation between creativity and sales effectiveness is valid, then people will see, hear, and read ads of a more interesting and entertaining nature.[59]

## NOTES

1. R. D. Buzzell, Predicting short-term changes in market share as a function of advertising strategy, *Journal of Marketing Research,* 1964, *1* (3), pp. 27–31. The quotation is from p. 27.
2. Booz Allen & Hamilton, Inc., *Management & Advertising Problems in the Advertiser-Agency Relationship,* New York, NY: Association of National Advertisers Inc., 1965. The quotation is from p. 33.
3. M. H. Blair, An empirical investigation of advertising wearin and wearout, *Journal of Advertising Research,* 1988, *28* (6), pp. 45–50. Blair has obviously smoothed her data, but conference presentations of the same material indicate that the curves are reasonably accurate representations of the true results.
4. T. R. King and R. Frank, Coca-Cola may move its ad account to concern partly owned by Disney, *The Wall Street Journal Europe,* October 18, 1995, p. 4.
5. P. C. N. Michell, H. Cataquet, and S. Hague, Establishing the causes of disaffection in agency-client relations, *Journal of Advertising Research,* 1992, *32* (2), pp. 41–48.
6. G. R. Dowling, Searching for a new agency: A client perspective, *International Journal of Advertising,* 1994, *13* (3), pp. 229–242. We have converted importance ratings in his Table 1 to percentages-of-maximum-possible for easier interpretation.
7. See, for instance, M. Magiera, Carnation links pay, research, *Advertising Age,* March 6, 1989, pp. 1, 74; G. Levin, DDB Needham gets "guarantee" takers, *Advertising Age,* June 18, 1990, p. 16; J. Dagnoli, Campbell cuts marketing budget, *Advertising Age,* July 23, 1990, pp. 1, 48; and L. Wentz, Unilever adopts agency incentives, *Advertising Age,* September 28, 1992, pp. 1, 46.
8. K. Reinhard, Why DDB Needham offers a guarantee, *Advertising Age,* June 11, 1990, p. 34.
9. A 1990 survey by consultant Nancy Salz, sampling details of which are not available, reported that 65 percent of advertisers and 62 percent of agencies are now in favor of performance-based agency compensation. Especially in the advertiser's interpretation, this means creative performance. The practice is growing remarkably quickly. See: Agencies agree to prove themselves, *Research Alert,* August 3, 1990, p. 3.
10. This example was shown in Global Gallery, *Advertising Age,* April 2, 1990, p. 28.
11. J. O'Toole, *The Trouble with Advertising,* 2nd ed., New York: Random House, 1985. The quotation is from p. 131.
12. Both quotations are from the article by K. Sederberg, Top agency "creatives" take a closer look at creativity, *Advertising Age,* June 4, 1979, pp. S-3, S-10, S-11, S-13.
13. C. E. Lindblom, The science of "muddling through," *Public Administration Review,* 1959, *19* (2), pp. 79–88. T. V. Bonoma, *The Marketing Edge,* New York: The Free Press, 1985. N. Piercy and W. Giles, The logic of being illogical in strategic marketing planning, *Journal of Marketing Management,* 1989, *5* (1), pp. 19–31; and A. Ries and J. Trout, *Bottom-Up Marketing,* New York: McGraw-Hill, 1989, especially pp. 2, 158, and 183.
14. J. Eighmey, The main effects of science on advertising: The good, the bad, and the ugly, *Journal of Advertising Research,* 1988, *28* (1), pp. RC-3 to RC-6. See also Ries and Trout's "find a winning tactic and develop it into a strategy" argument discussed in Chapter 2 of this book.
15. The Absolut case history is reported by G. Levin, who interviewed Michel Roux, the president and CEO of Carillon Importers, distributor of Absolut in the United States, *Advertising Age,* July 6, 1992, p. S-2.
16. This is also an interesting example of how creative ideas can sometimes walk in the door—literally! Reportedly, Lasorda, then the well-known manager of the Los Angeles Dodgers baseball team, had made a bet that he could lose 20 pounds. The stakes were $20,000. He asked his agent to contact Slim-Fast Foods company for a supply of the then-new liquid meal-replacement drink. His agent saw the opportunity to propose this as an advertising campaign, and the agency accepted the proposal. Sales of Ultra Slim-Fast, which had already been growing because of the rapidly growing diet food and beverages categories, "went vertical."

According to the company, "The stuff was flying off the shelf." Lasorda won the bet and donated his winnings to charity—picking up, of course, a nice royalty from the advertising campaign. The campaign was later extended to feature similar stories from other celebrities who had lost weight using the product. See L. Freeman, Interview with Ron Stern, president of Slim-Fast's Nutrition Division, *Advertising Age,* July 6, 1992, pp. 5–8.

17. M. McCarter, Fellini: Making ads is a "fun experience," *Advertising Age,* September 28, 1992, pp. I-3, I-24. Francis Ford Coppola, famous director of *Apocalypse Now* and *The Godfather,* has made some of the "Always Coke" commercials in the United States.

18. Irwin Gross proposed the idea in his 1967 doctoral dissertation at the Carnegie Institute of Technology and then developed it while a professor at Monash University and later at the Wharton School. The most widely available reference is I. Gross, The creative aspects of advertising, *Sloan Management Review,* 1972, *14* (1), pp. 83–109. A good review of the theory can also be found in the textbook by D. A. Aaker and J. G. Myers, *Advertising Management,* 3rd ed., Englewood Cliffs, NJ: Prentice-Hall, 1987, pp. 392–403. Incredibly, these authors dropped Gross's theory in the fourth edition of their book. We believe now is the time for its revival. For follow-up studies using or referring to Gross's model, see notes 23, 28, and 29, and the recent articles by L. D. Gibson, What can one exposure do? *Journal of Advertising Research,* 1996, *36* (2), pp. 9–18, and G. C. O'Connor, T. R. Willemain, and J. MacLachlan, The value of competition among agencies in developing ad campaigns: Revisiting Gross's model, *Journal of Advertising,* 1996, *25* (1), pp. 51–62.

19. We note that others are moving toward the same conclusion: that finding winning creative ideas is largely a random process. Academic theorists Mick, McCracken, Buchanan, and Basu, for instance, have pointed out the largely arbitrary nature of the selection of symbolic content in an ad. As McCracken states, "The [creative] director is free to deliver the desired symbolic properties in any one of a nearly infinite number of ways." Kevin Clancy, who is Professor of Marketing at Boston University and also Chairman of Yankelovich, Clancy, Shulman Inc., a leading marketing research firm, and author of *The Marketing Revolution,* also has advocated an extremely wide search among alternatives to identify the 2 percent of campaigns, in his estimate, that are "blockbusters." For a large advertiser, his research procedure would examine over a hundred "selling propositions" as candidates for a campaign.

See D. G. Mick, Consumer research and semiotics: Exploring the mythology of signs, symbols and significance, *Journal of Consumer Research,* 1986, *13* (2), pp. 196–213; G. McCracken, Culture and consumption: A theoretical account of the structure and movement of the cultural meaning of consumer goods, *Journal of Consumer Research,* 1986, *13* (1), pp. 71–84, with the quotation being from p. 75; and L. Buchanan and A. Basu, The impact of advertising copy testing: Is the advertiser getting more than he bargained for? in T. K. Srull, ed., *Advances in Consumer Research,* vol. 16, 1989, pp. 470–484; and K. J. Clancy, The coming revolution in advertising: Ten developments which will separate winners from losers, *Journal of Advertising Research,* 1990, *30* (1), pp. 47–52.

20. The one in six estimate depends on whether the new campaign is for a new product or an established product and, of course, on the definition of "real winner." For new products, about 70 percent of campaigns appear to be "sales-successful" in that they produce a statistically significant (80 percent minimum confidence level) sales increase when compared with a no-advertising control market; but only about 30 percent of (new) campaigns for *established* products are sales-successful. If, however, we raise the criterion and consider only a sales increase that is clearly profitable—a "real winner"—then the new-campaign success rate appears to be only about 32 percent for new products and 12 percent for established products. Based on these latter figures, an overall "real winner" estimate of 17 percent (one in six) seems justified. The main evidence we have relied on for the sales-successful estimates is from M. Stewart, Was STAT SCAN really an advance on AMTES? *Admap,* April 1990, pp. 32–35; and several reports on the IRI's "How advertising works" project, namely, J. Gollin, Has the sales promotion pendulum swung too far? *Proceedings of the Advertising and Promotion Effectiveness Workshop,* New York: Advertising Research Foundation, 1989, pp. 74–86; M. Abraham and L. Lodish, How advertising works, *Harvard Business Review,* 1990, *9* (3), pp. 50–60; L. M. Lodish, Key findings from the "How advertising works" study, Paper presented to the ARF workshop, New York, November 1991; and B. Lubetkin, Additional major findings from the "How advertising works" study, paper presented at the same workshop. For the "real winner" estimates, we have relied on Gollin's and Lubetkin's reports, with a small sample of new products, however, and also the results of TV commercials tested by McCollum Spielman Worldwide (MSW) and ARS (Research Systems Corporation), noting that, across very large databases of all products' commercials tested, MSW designates 19

percent as clearly "above average" and ARS 17 percent as "superior." Subsequent to, but consistent with, our estimates of 12 percent for *established* brands, an analysis of TV advertising campaigns for 12 fmcg product categories covering 78 brands in the United States, using Nielsen single-source data, indicated that, for established products mainly, only 50 percent of campaigns have a "noticeable" long-term (1-year) sales effect and 30 percent caused sales to go *down;* the estimate of "outstanding" (real winner) campaigns for established products was 10 percent. See J. P. Jones, Advertising's woes and advertising accountability, *Admap,* September 1994, pp. 24–27. ARS also recently published an estimate of 10 percent "superior" campaigns for established brands. See K. E. Rosenberg and M. H. Blair, Observations: The long and short of persuasive advertising, *Journal of Advertising Research,* 1994, *34* (4), pp. 63–69.

21. According to a recent survey of creative directors of leading advertising agencies in the United States, Canada, and the United Kingdom, about 60 percent of agencies have a formal creative philosophy (such as "unique selling proposition" or "brand personality") that they try to apply consistently. The other 40 percent do not, and some, such as Doyle Dane Bernbach, use absence of a philosophy as a selling point. See D. C. West, Gross-national creative personalities, processes, and agency philosophies, *Journal of Advertising Research,* 1993, *33* (5), pp. 53–62.

22. The correlation between managers' intuition as to which ads will be sales-successful and ads' actual sales success is virtually zero. At least, this has been found for newspaper ads and direct mail ads, and we expect that TV and radio commercials are equally difficult to judge. See L. Bogart, B. S. Tolley, and F. Orenstein, What one little ad can do, *Journal of Advertising Research,* 1970, *10* (4), pp. 3–13; and G. McCorkell, *Advertising That Pulls Response,* Maidenhead, UK: McGraw-Hill, 1990, pp. 10–13.

23. See J. R. Rossiter and P. Saintilan, Advertising agencies' attitudes toward competing for creative assignments, *Australian Journal of Market Research,* 1993, *1* (1), pp. 15–27.

24. J. Lafayette, Backer revamp: New, alternative creative unit set, *Advertising Age,* October 7, 1992, p. 14.

25. The case studies are by N. Capon and D. Scammon, Advertising agency decisions: An analytic treatment, in J. H. Leigh and C. R. Martin, Jr., eds., *Current Issues and Research in Advertising,* Ann Arbor, MI: Graduate School of Business, University of Michigan Press, 1979, pp. 35–52; and M. M. Mondroski, L. N. Reid, and J. T. Russell, Agency creative decision making: A decision systems analysis, in J. H. Leigh and C.

R. Martin, Jr., eds., *Current Issues and Research in Advertising,* Ann Arbor, MI: Graduate School of Business, University of Michigan Press, 1983, pp. 57–69. The survey is in the Australian study by J. R. Rossiter and P. Saintilan, same reference as note 23.

26. Supporting evidence for claiming this to be the best brainstorming procedure is reviewed in B. Kabanoff and J. R. Rossiter, Recent developments in applied creativity, in C. L. Cooper and I. T. Robertson, eds., *International Review of Industrial and Organizational Psychology,* vol. 9, 1994, pp. 283–324; and J. R. Rossiter and G. L. Lilien, New "brainstorming" principles, *Australian Journal of Management,* 1994, *19* (1), pp. 61–72.

27. The I-G-I method is an adaptation of the method called the "Nominal Group Technique" (NGT) developed by Van de Ven and Delbecq. See, for instance, A. H. Van de Ven and A. L. Delbecq, Nominal versus interacting group processes for committee decision-making effectiveness, *Academy of Management Journal,* 1971, *14* (2), pp. 203–212; and A. L. Delbecq, A. H. Van de Ven, and D. H. Gustafson, *Group Techniques for Program Planning,* Middleton, WI: Green Briar Press, 1986.

28. The target of 10 ideas is arbitrary but is supported by a study in which the highest target, eight, produced a constant proportion of "best" creative ideas (individually brainstormed positioning statements for a new brand of beer). See B. G. Vanden Bergh, L. N. Reid, and G. A. Schorin, How many creative alternatives to generate? *Journal of Advertising,* 1983, *12* (4), pp. 46–49.

29. The first author and his (then) doctoral student, Lawrence Ang, developed this theory together, based on Ang's original conceptualization and Rossiter's contribution of the properties of the conveyor. We wish to acknowledge the important influence, in our formulation of this theory, of our late colleague Werner Kroeber-Riel, of the Institute for Consumer and Behavioral Research, University of the Saarland, Germany, whose laboratory we visited several times. In particular, the I-G-I brainstorming application of the RAM-Conveyor model, presented later in the chapter, owes much to Professor Kroeber-Riel's advertising expert system, CAAS, which we believe to be the most innovative and useful system in the world for creative development. See F. R. Esch and W. Kroeber-Riel, eds., *Expertsysteme Für die Werbung,* Munich: Vahlen, 1994. Also see W. Kroeber-Riel, *Bild Kommunication,* Munich: Vahlen, 1993. For the initial write-up of our theory, see J. R. Rossiter, The RAM-Conveyor theory of creative strengtheners in ads, in P. Weinberg, ed., *Festschrift für Prof. Dr. Kroeber-Riel,* Munich: Vahlen, 1994, pp. 119–138; and for the initial

test, see L. Ang, Unpublished doctoral dissertation, Sydney: Australian Graduate School of Management, 1994.

30. J. C. Hitchon and G. A. Churchill, To be or what to be: An empirical investigation of metaphor's perspective effects in advertising communication, Working paper, Madison, WI: School of Journalism and Mass Communication, University of Wisconsin, 1992.

31. M. Dingena, The creation of meaning in advertising, Doctoral dissertation, Erasmus University at Rotterdam, Amsterdam: Thesis Publishers, 1994.

32. Readers may be interested in a remarkably relevant identification of the three advertising attention factors 80 years ago: H. F. Adams, *Advertising and Its Mental Laws,* New York: Garland Publishing, Inc., 1916 (reissued 1985), chapter VIII.

33. D. W. Stewart, Speculations on the future of advertising research, *Journal of Advertising,* 1992, *21* (3), pp. 1–18.

34. C. E. Osgood, G. Suci, and P. Tannenbaum, *The Measurement of Meaning,* Urbana, IL: University of Illinois Press, 1957.

35. R. Tourangeau and R. J. Sternberg, Aptness in metaphor, *Cognitive Psychology,* 1981, *13* (1), pp. 27–55.

36. S. A. Gray and R. Snyder, Metaphor in advertising: Effects on memory, in M. P. Gardner, ed., *Proceedings of the Society for Consumer Psychology,* St. Louis: P. DePaulo, University of Missouri, Another experiment, with visual conveyors, found no decrease in brand recall; however, the measure was free recall rather than (the correct) category-cued brand recall measure. See N. A. Mitchell, D. M. Badzinski, and D. R. Pawlowski, Metaphors as vivid stimuli to enhance comprehension and recall of print advertisements, in K. W. King, ed., *American Academy of Advertising Proceedings,* Athens, GA: University of Georgia, 1994, pp. 198–205.

37. The distinction between typicality (here $A_t \rightarrow C$) and dominance ($C \rightarrow A_t$) was proposed in the broader context of category-brand relationships by P. H. Farquar, P. M. Herr, and R. H. Fazio, in M. E. Goldberg, G. Gorn, and R. W. Pollay, eds., A relational model for category extension of brands, *Advances in Consumer Research,* 1990, *17,* pp. 856–860.

38. L. Ang, in his doctoral thesis (same reference as in note 29), identifies three types of remoteness: between-domain remoteness (the remoteness we have been talking about, that is, conveyor versus product); within-domain remoteness (where the conveyor itself may be manipulated within its own domain to make it more unusual, so an unusual *product* representation could serve as a conveyor); and ad-domain remoteness (where the conveyor is unusual in this category of ads,

apart from its between-domain remoteness). With visual conveyors, Kroeber-Riel often increases within-domain remoteness, to gain attention, by adding an unusual visual detail; see W. Kroeber-Riel, *Bild Kommunication,* same reference as in note 29.

39. S. Chow and A. J. Silk, Advertising copy development and optimal search, Paper presented at the ORSA/TIMS Marketing Science conference, University of Washington, Seattle, March 23–26, 1988.

40. J. Lawrence, "Uncola" spot-light: Slogan returns in new ads for Diet 7UP, *Advertising Age,* September 30, 1991, p. 4; and P. Winters, 7UP logs "un"-usual gains in market share, *Advertising Age,* November 16, 1992, p. 43.

41. J. Liesse, Interview with Andy Addis, *Advertising Age,* July 6, 1992, p. S-6.

42. R. Serafin, Interview with Peter Levin, advertising director of General Motors Corp.'s Cadillac Division, *Advertising Age,* July 6, 1992, p. S-4.

43. J. Eighmey, same reference as note 5.

44. See Chapter 6's note 5.

45. F. Danzig, The Big Idea, *Advertising Age,* November 9, 1988, pp. 18, 138, 140.

46. B. Johnson, Romance warms, *Advertising Age,* February 24, 1992, p. 4; and What's next? A brew-haha? *Advertising Age,* September 14, 1992, p. 4.

47. F. Danzig, same reference as note 45.

48. P. Sloan, Interview with David Sharp, senior-VP marketing of Lever Bros, *Advertising Age,* July 6, 1992, p. S-20.

49. $M_c$ is calculated from the binomial theorem as the probability of *failing* to observe a winner in m tries. Thus, if the probability of a success is P, and the confidence required is c, then $M_c$ is obtained by solving for M the binomial expression $(1 - P)^M < (1 - c)$. Example: If P = .33 and c = 99 percent (.99), then $M_{99} = (1 - .33)^M < (1 - .99)$, or $(.66)^M < .01$, and $M_{99} = 12$.

50. See note 22. Unaided management judgment (later we will show how to systematically aid management judgment) is so subject to whim that we may as well regard it as a purely random process.

51. I. Gross demonstrated this in his thesis, An analytical approach to the creative aspects of advertising operations, Doctoral dissertation, Cleveland, OH: Case Institute of Technology, 1967.

52. R. I. Haley, *Developing Effective Communications Strategy: A Benefit Segmentation Approach,* New York: Wiley, 1985, pp. 277–278.

53. This modifies the randomness a bit. Interestingly, there is theoretical support for the "copy development" route in an influential early paper by psychologist Donald T. Campbell. Note the second concept, "selective retention," in the title; see D. T. Campbell, Blind variation

and selective retention in creative thought as in other knowledge processes, *Psychological Bulletin,* 1960, *67* (6), pp. 380–400.

54. W. F. Greene and J. E. McCullough, Animatic, photomatic to live-action rough pre-testing predictability vs. production cost tradeoffs, in Advertising Research Foundation, *Copy Research,* NY: ARF, 1985, pp. 97–117. Their top estimate for the cost of a live-action rough in 1985 was only $10,000, and this figure is sufficient today according to inquiries made to several large agencies.

55. J. Dodson, Commentary on "Conducting advertising experiments in the real world: The Campbell Soup Company experience," *Marketing Science,* 1989, *8* (1) pp. 72–73.

56. Chevron corporation, *Harvard Business School Case #9-591-005,* Boston, MA: Harvard Business School, 1991. The research director at Chevron who implemented the random-creativity procedure is Lewis C. Winters.

57. Personal communication with Chevron revealed that these six ads were actually the *second attempt* by each creative team. The first round of ideas were all rejected by Chevron, with extensive feedback provided for the second round.

58. J. R. Rossiter and P. Saintilan, same reference as note 23.

59. The praise should really go to Irv Gross for developing the original theory of random creativity. We hope we have been able to improve it, and to sell it effectively. In the church of advertising, Irv should receive a satisfying percentage of the collection money.

## DISCUSSION QUESTIONS

**7.1.** What is the "creative idea" and where does it fit in the continuum from "strategy" to "execution"? (Bonus: Try to devise a better formal definition of this term.)

**7.2.** Coke's creative ideas have usually been linked to a slogan (though the slogan is not the complete creative idea, by any means). "The Real Thing" has been used in 1942, 1969–76, and 1989–92. In 1993, Coke changed to the slogan, "Always Coke." Discuss both slogans in relation to Coke's presumed positioning strategy, and comment on how well both slogans fit the criteria of a good creative idea.

**7.3.** Construct and discuss a "balance sheet" of the pros and cons of following the theory of random creativ-ity for (a) the advertiser and (b) the advertising agency.

**7.4.** Using the $N_c$ formula given in chapter appendix 7B, estimate how many creative ideas you would need (not executions) if you (a) wanted to be 90 percent confident of generating a "real winner" campaign for a new product, (b) with $\bar{E} = 0.8$, $S = 1.4$, and $V = 0.25$.

**7.5.** Working in teams of three classmates, try the I-G-I method of brainstorming for Healthy Choice, using RAM-Conveyor theory. $A_t$ = "heart-healthy." Write a short "lab report" on your experiment and its results.

**7.6.** For long-term management of the brand's advertising, what is the best policy as far as creative ideas are concerned?

## FURTHER READING

Eighmey, J. The main effects of science on advertising: The good, the bad, and the ugly. *Journal of Advertising Research,* 1988, *28* (1), pp. RC-3 to RC-6.

This article puts forth the case that an agency's creative idea can sometimes produce a better positioning strategy than the intended positioning strategy; that is, that creativity can lead to strategy rather than the normal, reverse order. A good discussion of the nature of creativity in advertising.

Gross, I. The creative aspects of advertising. *Sloan Management Review,* 1972, *14* (1), pp. 83–109.

All advertisers should read this article by the originator of the first version of the theory of random creativity. Clearly written and carefully argued, Professor Gross's article is a revelation. You will be able to compare the original theory with our version in this chapter.

Adams, A. J., and Blair, M. H. Persuasive advertising and sales accountability: Past experience and forward validation. *Journal of Advertising Research,* 1992, *32* (2), pp. 20–25.

This article presents evidence from several real-world studies illustrating the large differences in sales results produced by TV commercials that differ in their persuasive ability (and presumably in the effectiveness of their creative ideas). Includes a recent case history with Campbell Soup Company's commercials.

# CHAPTER 8

# Creative Execution Tactics: Brand Awareness and Low-Involvement Persuasion

At this stage in the creative process, the agency has produced one or more creative ideas. Creativity has been given a relatively free reign. Now, the manager's task is to ensure that the advertising *executions* of the creative ideas are maximally effective. The executions must contain elements or employ *tactics* that will be most likely to (1) gain the target audience's attention, (2) draw it to (the category and) the brand for brand awareness,[1] and (3) communicate the brand's positioning strategy persuasively to achieve or reinforce brand position.

In this and the next chapter, we examine creative execution tactics for the second and third of these processes—the tactics for brand awareness and persuasion. (The requirements for the first process, drawing attention to the ad, vary by different advertising media and will be taken up in Chapter 10.) This chapter covers brand awareness and *low-involvement* persuasion, which are the purposes of much mass media advertising. The next chapter covers high-involvement persuasion, which is especially important for high-risk purchases and direct response advertising. After reading this chapter you should:

- Understand the use of the Rossiter-Percy grid.
- Understand that rote learning is the processing mechanism for brand awareness and low-involvement brand attitude.
- Know which "branding" tactics work best for the two forms of brand awareness—brand recognition and brand recall.

- Know which "persuasion" tactics work best for the two types of low-involvement brand attitude—low-involvement/informational and low-involvement/ transformational.

In terms of the buyer response steps, this and the next two chapters are concerned with the causal transition between processing (of the ad) and communication effects (for the brand). This transition describes the domain of advertising communication models. In this chapter, we introduce and explain the use of the major selection framework for determining the brand's advertising communication model. The Rossiter-Percy grid identifies recommended creative executional tactics for the two universal communication objectives: brand awareness and brand attitude.

## THE ROSSITER-PERCY GRID

The Rossiter-Percy grid identifies recommended creative execution tactics for ads in all media.[2] (In Chapter 10, we will recommend some additional tactics needed for an ad to gain *attention* in the particular medium in which it will be placed.) The grid tactics have been distilled from the psychology and advertising research literature on learning and persuasion.[3]

The general format of the Rossiter-Percy grid is shown in Figure 8.1. From Chapter 5, it will be remembered that the advertising campaign for a particular brand will have two main communication objectives: (1) one of the two types of brand awareness,

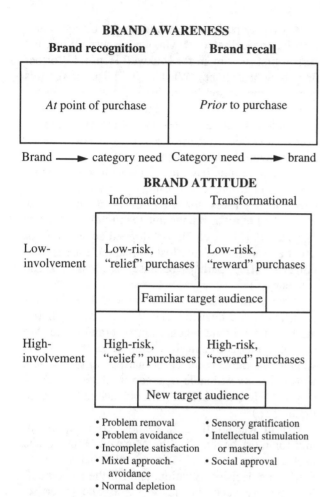

**FIGURE 8.1**

The Rossiter-Percy grid consists of six cells that differentiate creative execution tactics in ads (brand awareness processes and brand attitude motives are shown for ease of reference).

either brand recognition or brand recall—or, very occasionally, both; and (2) one of the four types of brand attitude strategies, represented by the divisions between low- and high-involvement purchase decisions and informational and transformational purchase motivations. Correspondingly, there are six "cells" in the grid: two for brand awareness, and four for brand attitude. (This means that when brand awareness and brand attitude are considered together, as they must be in every ad, there are *eight* potential communication models: 2 for BA × 4 for BATT = 8.) In the main part of the chapter, we will list and explain the creative executional tactics that fit the two brand awareness cells and the two low-involvement brand

attitude cells. To begin, however, we explain the use of the grid.

### Use of the Grid: Pre or Post?

The Rossiter-Percy grid can be used in a "pre" capacity to help guide the development of ads, and in a "post" capacity to evaluate tactics in ads produced by the agency. Based on many applications of the Rossiter-Percy grid, our recommendation is that only the classificatory dimensions of the grid should be used initially: that is, the creative brief should specify the *type* of brand awareness required and the brand attitude strategy *quadrant,* but nothing more. The grid *tactics themselves* should be applied *after* the creative team or teams have generated the creative ideas and produced *rough advertising executions* of those ideas. Postcreative use of the grid's *tactics* appears to be the best way to resolve the following typical dilemma. On the one hand, it seems only fair that the creative team should be made aware that its advertising ideas may be evaluated by the manager in terms of the appropriate grid tactics. This suggests supplying the creative team with the tactics in advance so that they can, if they wish, "write to" or incorporate the tactics upon which the ad will subsequently be evaluated. On the other hand, as we have seen in the previous chapter, creativity is an extremely elusive (we say randomly attained) phenomenon. To provide the creative team with a set of "mandatory" creative tactics up front would in most cases be dangerously restrictive. That is, it could inhibit the creative process itself—the production of unique creative ideas.

Accordingly, we believe the best overall procedure is (1) *pre-use* of the grid *classification* and (2) *post-use* of the grid *tactics.*

Regarding post-use, the brand manager should tell the creative team that he or she reserves the right to request fine-tuning of the creative executions in terms of particular tactics for visuals and copy (in the designated grid cells) that previous research has proven to work reliably. It should be stated explicitly that the grid tactics are recommendations based on past research—and that it is always possible that new or different tactics in the executions produced by the creative team might work better than the recommended tactics. This puts the creative team in the position of having to justify their particular tactics—a good policy anyway—and provides the opportunity to test two versions of an execution, if necessary: the original as produced by the creative team and a modified version with the fine-tuned tactics as recommended by the Rossiter-Percy grid. Post-use of the grid tactics allows a good deal of creative freedom up front, while the grid framework itself provides a "discipline" within which the creative work should be developed.[4] The Rossiter-Percy grid *tactics,* therefore, can be regarded as an "ad screening" procedure (see Chapter 19: especially MJT, management judgment testing) that is best performed after the agency's work is first contributed but before the final versions of the ads are decided.

The Rossiter-Percy grid tactics are covered in this and the next chapter. This chapter is concerned with brand awareness and low-involvement brand attitude tactics. These two communication effects require rote learning (hereafter mainly called just "learning") as the processing mechanism for their achievement.

## LEARNING: THE BASIS OF BRAND AWARENESS AND LOW-INVOLVEMENT BRAND ATTITUDE

By "learning," we mean learning of the very simple or *rote* type, in which the potential buyer merely has to echo or mentally repeat the content of the stimulus identically, or virtually identically, as a response.

Rote learning requires very little mental activity by the decision maker. It is basically a "passive" or "mindless" process, even though the brain certainly is engaged during learning.[5] Rote learning is passive because it goes on automatically, regardless of whether we want it to or not, and often without our conscious awareness of it occurring. Because of the passive nature of learning, repetition of the to-be-learned stimulus-stimulus association (see below) usually is required.

Learning in advertising is a necessary and sufficient form of processing for two communication effects: brand awareness and *low-involvement* brand attitude. Let us see how these two communication effects are learned.

### Brand Awareness Learning

To become aware of a brand—so as to be able to recognize or recall the brand later—the decision maker has to learn the *association* between $S_1$, the category need (for example, instant coffee), and $S_2$, the brand (for example, Maxwell House).

Most of you have already learned that Maxwell House ($S_2$) is a brand of instant coffee ($S_1$). But con-

sider a young person or a visitor to the United States who has never heard of Maxwell House. When the person first sees an ad for Maxwell House, his or her first thought will be "What *is* it?"[6] To answer this question, the person has to learn the association between the brand and the category need. The learned association is not just that Maxwell House is a brand of instant coffee. Rather, Maxwell House must be associated with the *need* for instant coffee.

All new brands have to go through this category need–brand awareness learning process. So do all new category users, for whom every brand is a new brand. And familiar brands must *maintain* the learned association. (Maxwell House stopped advertising for about a year in 1987 and lost its market leadership to Folger's coffee, perhaps because of a loss of brand awareness.[7])

What is the *response* to be learned? That depends on whether the decision maker later has to choose the brand via brand recognition or brand recall. We use the symbols $S_1$ and $S_2$ to emphasize that it is the stimulus-stimulus connection that has to be learned, with *either one* capable of emerging later as the response.[8] (Here it is helpful to look back at Chapter 5, Figure 5.2.)

**Brand Recognition.** In brand recognition learning, for most buyers, $S_2$ (the Maxwell House brand package or brand name) is the *stimulus* that will occur first in the decision situation, and $S_1$ (the instant coffee category need) is the *response*. The advertiser wants the decision maker to respond, "Ah, instant coffee—do I need some?" when he or she sees (for example, in a supermarket) or hears (for example, in a restaurant) the brand stimulus, Maxwell House. Alternatively, the buyer may have the category need already in mind (so $S_1$ occurs first), and brand recognition of Maxwell House ($S_2$) is the necessary response. Learning of the $S_1$-$S_2$ association enables either brand recognition path to be achieved.

**Brand Recall.** In brand recall learning, the same association is learned, but the functions of stimulus and response are unidirectional: In brand recall decision situations, $S_1$ (the instant coffee category need) occurs first, as the *stimulus,* and $S_2$ (the Maxwell House brand *name*) is the advertiser-desired *response.*

Coffee purchase is mainly by brand recognition, so it's a bit artificial to think of a brand recall situation. However, brand recall might be the objective for a specialized brand of instant coffee that is seeking to have the buyer make a definite choice *before* going to the store. Furthermore, the brand *loyal* buyer of Maxwell House may well be using brand recall–boosted brand recognition, as explained in Chapter 5, which requires prior recall.

Brand awareness learning—or "What *is* it?" processing—is conceptually simple. However, we shall see in this chapter that the creative tactics for brand recall, which is the more difficult to learn of the two types of brand awareness, are quite complex. The creative tactics are simpler for brand recognition.

### Low-Involvement Brand Attitude Learning

In Chapter 5, we saw that the attitude upon which brand choice is based will be either low-involvement (trial experience sufficient) or high-involvement (search and conviction required prior to purchase) depending on the nature of the product and the target audience.

The brand benefit beliefs that produce *low-involvement* brand attitude require only rote learning during processing.

In learning what benefit or benefits a brand offers, the decision maker is thinking, simply, in connection with the brand, "What *of* it?"[9] The decision maker has already learned what the brand *is* (brand awareness, connected to category need) and now is about to learn what it *has* or *does* (brand benefit beliefs, which underlie brand attitude). The two to-be-learned associations or connections are compared in Figure 8.2.

For low-involvement brand attitude learning, the stimulus roles are as follows:

$S_2$: The brand (for example, Maxwell House)
$S_3$, $S_4$, etc.: The brand's benefits (for example, good-tasting coffee, popular, reasonably priced)

The *initial stimulus* for brand attitude learning is always the brand ($S_2$). This assumes *prior* brand awareness learning. (As noted in Chapter 5, brand awareness must precede brand attitude, or the buyer cannot choose the brand.) The *responses* learned in connection with the brand are *beliefs* that the brand has the benefits ($S_3$, $S_4$, etc.) that the brand mentions in its advertising or, of course, in its other adlike communications or in its promotion offers.[10]

In rote learning of low-involvement brand attitude, the decision maker learns an *exact or close paraphrase* of the benefit claim(s) made in the ad. If the claim is made verbally, the decision maker must learn

1. "What *is* it?"

        **Brand awareness:**
        The connection between
        category need and the
        brand name or package.

2. "What *of* it?"

        **Brand attitude:**
        The connection(s) between
        the brand name or package
        and brand benefit(s).

**FIGURE 8.2**
Learning responses in the processing of brand awareness and low-involvement brand attitude.

it either verbatim or in words that preserve the same meaning. If the claim is made visually (by implication from the video of a TV commercial or the illustration of a print ad), the "paraphrase" required is that the typical buyer would describe the visual content in very much the same way as the ad's *creator* would describe it. Advertising researchers often call this the "perceived message," referring to the buyer's perception of the advertiser's *intended* message.

With low-involvement brand attitude, the degree of brand benefit learning is temporary, until the buyer actually tries the brand. The learning that the advertiser is aiming for is an *extreme if tentatively held belief sufficient to generate trial.* In the instant coffee example, the advertiser wants the decision maker to learn that Maxwell House is a "great"-tasting instant coffee or even the "best"-tasting instant coffee. Following trial, the brand has to *actually* deliver: The tentative belief has to be confirmed, to the degree promised by the brand benefit learning, for the brand to be purchased again.

### Effect of Cognitive Responses on Low-Involvement Brand Decisions

An advertisement, as we all know, is capable of provoking positive or negative reactions from the audience. This is especially true of TV commercials, because of the "captive" nature of the viewing audience, or what is often called the "intrusiveness" (reflexive attention-gaining capability) of TV. These reactions to the ad are called "cognitive responses," which are discussed extensively in Chapter 9 in conjunction with high-involvement brand attitude. However, their role in low-involvement brand attitude is important to note here.

For low-involvement brand decisions, the decision maker *does not have* to make active cognitive responses during processing in order to learn brand awareness and brand benefits relevant to low-involvement brand attitude. But what if the decision maker *does* make these responses? Their effect depends on the type of low-involvement brand attitude.

If the brand attitude to be learned is low-involvement/*informational,* cognitive responses made during processing are completely irrelevant. This is why "irritating" ads, which generate negative thoughts and comments, so often work—but only when the brand purchase decision is low-involvement/informational.

If the brand attitude to be learned is low-involvement/*transformational*—that is, based on a positive motivation, such as sensory gratification, intellectual stimulation or mastery, or social approval— then negative cognitive responses *can* hurt. This is because, for low-involvement/transformational brand purchase decisions, the target audience must *like the ad.* The ad serves as a positive stimulus that heightens the positive motivation.

Consequently, whereas rote learning is necessary and sufficient for acquiring low-involvement brand attitude, if cognitive responses do occur, their effect on brand attitude is zero in the informational case but contributory in the transformational case. Low-involvement creative tactics (this chapter) reflect this difference in processing.

### BRAND AWARENESS TACTICS (BRANDING)

It is vital that the ad be "branded" correctly by the target audience. "Branding" is a shorthand way of refer-

ring to the ad's contribution to brand awareness learning. Branding during *processing* of the ad is necessary for the first of the two universal communication objectives—brand awareness—to be achieved.

It is surprising how often ads fail to be branded correctly by consumers. For instance:

- In magazine ads, about 80 percent of consumers who notice the ad look at the advertiser's brand name or logo.[11] However, for the average magazine ad, since about half of the publication's readers fail to notice the ad in the first place, the absolute brand-noticing incidence is only about 40 percent. That is, the remaining 60 percent of readers fail to notice the brand.
- In TV commercials, on average, the incidence of branding loss is 45 percent. In other words, after seeing the average new TV commercial for the first time, only 55 percent of viewers can, a short time later, correctly name the advertised brand. The remaining 45 percent of viewers comprise 35 percent who can't remember the brand and 10 percent who mistakenly attribute the commercial to a competitor's brand.[12]

Branding failure is therefore a frequent and serious problem in advertising. If consumers miss the brand in, or misbrand, the ad, then it is obviously impossible for the ad to contribute to the communication objective of *brand awareness.*

You will remember from Chapter 5's discussion of communication objectives that there are *two types* of brand awareness: brand recognition and brand recall. These two types of brand awareness are very different from the standpoint of buyer or consumer brand choice and, accordingly, the in-ad creative tactics required to achieve them also differ substantially.

Brand recognition is a much easier response to achieve from advertising than is brand recall. Brand recognition can be achieved after only a few exposures, whereas brand recall usually requires many exposures. Chapter appendix 8A, Brand Recognition Versus Brand Recall from TV Advertising, shows typical proof of this.

Furthermore, and most importantly from the standpoint of creative tactics, the advertiser cannot assume that an ad that produces high brand recognition will also produce high brand recall (or vice versa). Studies in which individual ads have been employed as the unit of analysis[13] have shown that, for TV commercials, there is *no* correlation between the typical ad's ability to produce correct recognition of the package and its ability to generate correct recall of the brand name;[14] for print ads, the ability of the typical ad to produce both types of brand awareness is a little higher but still not strong overall.[15]

### Encoding Specificity Principle

The guiding principle for creative tactics designed to increase brand awareness, whether this be brand recognition or brand recall, is known as "encoding specificity." This principle, identified by psychologist Endell Tulving, and undoubtedly influenced by the stimulus-sampling theory developed earlier by psychologist William K. Estes, states that "successful retrieval depends on achieving a match between the information encoded at the time of learning and the information that is available at the time of retrieval."[16]

Translated to *advertising,* the encoding specificity principle implies that *the brand awareness tactics in the ad should match the stimuli most likely to be present in the brand choice situation* for the buyer. Thus, broadly speaking, if the buyer or consumer must *recognize* the brand's package from a product category display, then the ad must show the package clearly, and in the context of the same product category; on the other hand, if the buyer or consumer must *recall* the brand name, given only the category need (a mental stimulus) in the choice situation, then the ad must link the category need and the brand name so that the buyer or consumer will learn the connection and be able to retrieve the brand name mentally when the category need arises. Whereas there are other tactics, presented below, for increasing an ad's capacity to produce brand recognition and brand recall, encoding specificity is the most important principle.

The *behavioral sequence model* (see Chapter 4) is our recommended way of identifying the type of brand choice required and thereby deciding whether brand recognition or brand recall is the appropriate brand awareness communication objective for the campaign. We also remind the reader that brand recall–boosted brand recognition may be an objective under special circumstances. (It would be wise for the reader to review the three options for the overall brand awareness communication objective which were presented in Chapter 5.) The behavioral sequence model identifies the most likely *specific* stimuli that will be present in the choice situation—either physically present, such as in a brand display, for recognition; or else "in the buyer's mind," for recall.[17] The advertiser has to think carefully about the external *and internal* stimuli in the choice situation. As far as is practically possible, these stimuli must be addressed in the ad's content.

We present next the recommended creative tactics for the two major types of brand awareness— brand recognition and brand recall. Since brand recall–boosted brand recognition is a composite communication objective requiring *both* sets of tactics, we briefly summarize the tactics for it at the end of the section.

### Brand Recognition Tactics

In Chapter 5, on communication objectives, we observed that brand recognition is the main form of brand awareness in two situations: supermarket or drugstore product purchases, and direct response purchases. For supermarket and drugstore products, it was estimated that almost half (47 percent) of all brand choices are made by brand recognition—the *brand display* reminded shoppers of category need or else entirely generated and sold the category need at the point of purchase, the latter being true "impulse" purchases. So, if you are an advertiser of a product sold through supermarkets or drugstores and your target audience is not completely brand loyal, then brand recognition is probably the brand awareness communication objective you should choose. The other important situation for brand recognition is *direct response advertising,* including Yellow Pages and other directory advertising. In direct response ads, the consumer has to recognize the brand (there is no prior recall) and then decide right then and there whether or not to purchase.[18]

For brand recognition, three "branding" tactics are recommended, as summarized in Table 8.1. These pertain to the brand portrayal, its context, and exposure frequency.

**BRGN-1. Ensure Sufficient Exposure of the Brand Package and Name in the Ad.** Experiments in psychology have shown that visual recognition— such as of a package or logo—is maximized when people look at it for at least 2 seconds. Shorter viewing times result in considerably reduced recognition when the same visual stimulus is subsequently encountered.[19]

**TABLE 8.1**

**ADVERTISING TACTICS FOR BRAND RECOGNITION**

BRGN-1. Ensure sufficient exposure of the brand package and name in the ad.

BRGN-2. The category need should be mentioned or portrayed (unless it's immediately obvious).

BRGN-3. After the initial burst, less media frequency is needed for brand recognition (though check the brand attitude strategy first).

TV commercials (radio commercials are of course unable to provide *visual* brand recognition unless, as in pre-TV days, the package is elaborately described in the radio commercial) should therefore show the brand's package or logo for at least 2 seconds at a time if brand recognition is the objective. Obviously, this is extremely important for a *new* brand—which first must be recognized after having been seen *only* in TV commercials, then later must be recognized in the store. Whereas 2 seconds may seem quite brief, it should be remembered that advertising agencies generally do not like devoting video time in commercials to "simple pack shots," and therefore often make the mistake of flashing the package on the screen for *well under* 2 seconds. The manager should insist that the pack shot in TV commercials for a new brand be held for longer. We also note that several short pack shots do not seem to be able to compensate for one long pack shot.

In print ads, the package or logo (again, especially for a *new* brand of a product or service) should be large, in color, and preferably accompanied by other visual content or copy that serves to hold the reader's attention to the ad for at least 2 seconds.[20] (A good example of other visual content that draws attention to the package is the brand awareness conveyor ad for Balenciaga's Talisman perfume; see Chapter 7, Figure 7.13.) A page of a magazine or newspaper can be turned in half a second or less, so it is important that attention be held with the package or logo remaining in the reader's field of vision. As 2 seconds is a long time to hold attention to a print ad, repetition of the ad, or a variation of it, may be necessary to accumulate brand recognition.

Although it might seem that such a strong emphasis on the package or logo is excessive, it should be realized that this particular tactic doesn't have to be applied throughout the campaign. It is most im-

portant *early* in the launch of a new brand; thereafter, *occasional reemphasis* on the package or logo is sufficient (see the third tactic for brand recognition, below).

Another important aspect of this tactic is to show the *name* of the brand on the package *if* brand recall is *also* desired—such as in brand recall–boosted brand recognition.[21]

With the brand package-and-name exposure tactic, we should draw the manager's attention to an important exception to the encoding specificity principle. Since the package usually must be recognized in a brand display that consists of *competing* packages, the encoding specificity principle would suggest that competing packages also be shown in the ad.[22] However, this is definitely *not* recommended, because it would give free exposure to competitors' packages! Only the advertised brand's package should be shown. This applies also, of course, in direct response advertising where the brand has only to be recognized *in the ad* and not later in a competitive setting.

**BRGN-2. The Category Need Should Be Mentioned or Portrayed (Unless It's Immediately Obvious).** For a new brand, especially, the target audience prospective buyer has to learn that the brand is a member of a particular product category and that it is associated with a particular category need. The package should therefore be shown in a context or setting in the ad that makes it clear what the brand *is* (product category) and, generally, what it is *for* (category need). This is why a picture of the *product* is often placed on the package itself. For instance, how would a novice consumer know what "Healthy Choice" was unless the dinner itself were shown on the pack? Figure 8.3 provides a good example in a print ad for Arnott's Water Crackers. The ad clearly shows the brand logo, the product category, and *also* the *category need.*

Category *need,* in the more psychological sense, is somewhat more difficult as a tactical execution decision. Our recommendation for *new* brands is to show the product or service *in use* in the ad, as in the figure. Another example of this recommendation is for a brand of spray-on prewash, such as Spray 'n' Wash. There are two good reasons for showing this brand in use—actually being sprayed on clothes before washing—in a TV commercial or print ad. First, such products often appear in supermarket displays with lots of other products with *different* uses, such as spray-on starch or other cleaning agents. For the naive

*Quite simply,
it's the perfect biscuit for cheese.
Just perfect.*

**FIGURE 8.3**
Ad for Arnott's Water Crackers exhibiting good brand
recognition tactics by portraying the category need and
showing the package clearly.
*Courtesy:* Arnott's Australia Pty Ltd.

buyer of the brand, it is not immediately clear which specific product category the brand belongs to or for which specific category need it is intended. Therefore, the ad should show the product being used. The second reason is that, in pure brand recognition situations, the usual "mental sequence" is for the brand to be noticed first and then for the consumer to think, "Do I have the need for this category?" Unless the consumer knows what "this category" is, the mental question cannot be asked, and the brand will be ignored. Thus, it is important, in the ad, to associate the brand's package with the category need—that is, with its use or purpose.

**BRGN-3. After the Initial Burst, Less Media Frequency is Needed for Brand Recognition (Though Check the Brand Attitude Strategy First).** As chapter appendix 8A shows, brand recognition peaks after about two exposures to the ad.[23]

Thereafter, brand recognition declines very slowly, so a lighter media schedule (specifically, less frequency) is then sufficient to maintain the buyer's brand recognition response.[24] New-brand advertisements should therefore aim to attain two exposures (and here we mean *actual* exposures resulting in attention and learning) as early as possible with a heavy initial advertising "burst." The ad can then be repeated at less-frequent intervals to maintain brand recognition.

However, a strong caution here is that brand recognition awareness may not be the only communication objective of the campaign. In particular, if *transformational* brand attitude is *also* an objective, then frequent repetition of the advertisement in a heavy media schedule is necessary and would override brand recognition considerations. This is discussed later in the chapter.

As this caution illustrates, and as we will see in Part Six on media strategy, the manager must jointly consider brand awareness *and* brand attitude objectives in deciding the media plan.

### Brand Recall Tactics

Brand recall is the appropriate type of brand awareness objective when the buyer must think of brand alternatives *prior* to the point of purchase. Many industrial products and consumer services are chosen in this way. The buyer experiences the category need *first,* then must mentally *recall* a list of possible suppliers or brands that potentially can meet that need. Brand recall is the objective for all target audiences for these products and services.

For supermarket products, on the other hand, we estimated in Chapter 5 that about 35 percent of choices are made by brand recall, although these are mainly restricted to the brand's *loyal customers* (BLs) rather than to a brand switcher target audience. In the supermarket setting, brand *switchers* (BSs) are more likely to choose by brand recognition unless we have been able to induce them to make a deliberate switch to our brand by brand recall first.

The encoding specificity principle is vitally important in brand recall. Brand recall absolutely requires the buyer to have learned the *association* between the category need and the brand name. Therefore, the ad must be structured in such a way that encoding—learning—of that association is facilitated. This principle underlies most of the creative tactics for brand recall. However, there are some supplementary tactics

**TABLE 8.2**

**ADVERTISING TACTICS FOR BRAND RECALL**

BRCL-1.  Associate the category need and the brand name in the main copy line.
BRCL-2.  Repeat the association (not just the brand name).
BRCL-3.  Try to encourage a personal connection with the brand.
BRCL-4.  Consider using a special presenter.
BRCL-5.  An interactive mnemonic device or (for broadcast ads) a jingle may increase brand recall.
BRCL-6.  Use high advertising frequency, relative to the competition.

that can be employed as well. Table 8.2 summarizes the six "branding" tactics for brand recall; these are explained next.

**BRCL-1. Associate the Category Need and the Brand Name in the Main Copy Line.** Strictly speaking, the category need could be represented *visually* in a TV comercial or print ad and still be effective in producing an association with the brand name. However, because brand recall is primarily a *verbal* phenomenon, involving mental or "inner" speech for both the category need (such as "I need a dependable national or international courier") and also the brand name (such as "Federal Express"), we recommend the proactive tactic of relying not only on visual representation of the category need but also *explicit mention of* the category need, in association with the brand, in the *main copy line.* (The main copy line is the primary message about the brand stated verbally. It may appear anywhere in the ad and is usually summarized in the "headline" or "slogan" of a print ad or in the "tag line" of a TV or radio commercial.) Advertisers hope that consumers will learn and remember the main copy line literally. This is an ambitious hope, but it is important that at least the *gist* of the main copy line be remembered—and that this gist be the association between the category need and the brand name.

In Chapter 5, we gave some examples of advertising slogans that we believe to be appropriate for increasing brand recall. These included "You deserve a break today . . . at McDonald's" and also "The American Express Card. Don't leave home without it." Another slogan (or tag line) that presents the association nicely is the one for Kraft Singles cheese: "Every *single* time, it's Kraft."

However, for carefully-considered, high-involvement brand choices, the association can be learned with a "lead-in" headline (see Chapter 10) that refers to the category need, with the brand name as a "sign-off." The Ford ad in Figure 8.4 is an example. The highly-involved buyer should learn the association even though it requires a bit more effort than when the association is provided in the main copy line.

A decision made long before the brand is advertised, the choice of its *brand name,* has a big effect on its subsequent recallability (see chapter appendix 8B, Brand Name Recallability). This is something to consider if you're introducing a new brand.

**FIGURE 8.4**
Brand recall: Use of a "lead-in" headline, referring to the category need, with the expectation that consumers for whom the category need of "safety" is salient will read the copy and see the logo and thereby associate the brand name "Ford" with the category need.
*Courtesy:* Ford Motor Company.

*New Brand "Mystery" Ad Format.* For generating brand recall (and probably brand recognition) for a *new* brand, the "mystery" ad format has been shown to be very effective. In the mystery format, the product category is identified during the ad but the audience is kept guessing about the brand's identity until the end of the ad. The mystery format was employed, for example, to introduce the Nissan Infiniti automobile several years ago (in TV, radio, and magazine ads) and is now widely used. The idea is that the mystery format will stimulate a "What is it?" processing response in audience members, who will then be motivated to learn the answer (the brand name). The key to this format is that the mystery (which promises a benefit pertaining to the category need) be *interestingly executed.* Fazio, Herr, and Powell[25] found that the mystery format was effective in increasing new-brand recall by 10 to 25 percent (for four new brands and on an immediate recall test) when compared with the standard format in which the new brand was introduced early.

However, the researchers found that the mystery format was *not* effective in increasing brand recall for *familiar* brands. This could be because the audience exhibits a "Big deal! They tried to trick me into watching" response, reflecting disappointment, when the solution to the mystery is revealed to be a familiar brand. However, this ineffectiveness could also occur because the mystery format would represent a change in the initiating cue for the established brand—which would interfere with the previously learned category cue–brand name association. For established brands, the more standard early-and-late brand identification should be employed.[26]

**BRCL-2. Repeat the Association (Not Just the Brand Name).** The branding tactic here is to repeat the *association* between the category need and the brand name several times *within* the ad. This can be achieved verbally by repeating the main copy line, in all media, or it can be achieved in visual media such as TV and print ads by showing the brand *name* in the context of the category need several times. The important consideration is that the target audience buyer be encouraged to learn the *association* between the category need and the brand name.

Repetition of the brand name *alone* won't help.[27] At best, repetition of the brand name alone might establish a connection between the brand name and the *ad.* While this might help to decrease the misbranding

of ads that we mentioned earlier, it overlooks the prime purpose of brand recall—which is to establish the connection between the category need and the brand name *away* from the advertising context so that it carries over to the *choice* context. Remember, the ad will *not* be there at the point of purchase to aid the buyer.

A recommended supplementary tactic (other than when using the mystery format for new brands) is to place the category need–brand name association at the *beginning* of the ad and then again at the *end.* This supplementary tactic makes use of the well-known primacy and recency advantages or "serial position effect" in recall.[28]

We have focused here on *in-ad* repetition. Repetition of the category need–brand name association can also be achieved, of course, by *repeating the ad itself*—in the media schedule. We examine this type of repetition separately as the sixth tactic for brand recall, below.

**BRCL-3. Try to Encourage a Personal Connection with the Brand.** If the target audience buyer perceives that the ad has "personal relevance," then that person is much more likely to make an effort to remember the advertised brand. An advertising copywriter once bet a client that he could write a headline that would be *guaranteed* to make the client read the ad. The client's name was Max Hart. The headline of the ad was: "This page is all about Max Hart."[29] A similar tactic is employed by direct mail advertisers when they use "personalized" cover letters.

Personal relevance is considerably more difficult to achieve, however, in mass media ads. One tactic that can be tried is to use personal pronouns such as "I," "me," or "you." These personal pronouns signify self-referential statements. We should note that the personal pronoun may be strongly implied rather than stated directly, as in "[You should] Take Aim against cavities." Also, possessive pronouns may be used, such as "Give your cold to Contac."

U.S. advertisers seem to favor the word "you," as in "You deserve a break today . . . at McDonald's . . . we do it all for you," which has now been revised to "Have you had your break today?" However, two very successful overseas campaigns have used the even more personal words "I" and "me." The tag lines are "I feel like a Toohey's" (an Australian beer) and "Take me away, P & O" (an international cruise and holiday shipping line). Use of these first-person pronouns produces direct self-reference when the main copy line is learned—and may well have stronger subsequent motivational capacity than the second-person, "you" forms.[30]

**BRCL-4. Consider Using a Special Presenter.** A special presenter—such as a celebrity or an ad-created central character—can significantly increase brand recall. The idea is that the "visibility" of the presenter draws and holds attention to the ad, and therefore makes registration of the brand name more likely. (However, as discussed in conjunction with the VisCAP presenter model in the next chapter, presenter ads have to be carefully executed so as not to overshadow the brand; also, the category need must be clear to the audience so that the brand is properly associated with it.) For instance, a study, by Y & R advertising agency researchers Holman and Hecker, of creative elements in TV campaigns that seemed to influence brand recall (measured correctly as brand name recall in response to the product category cue) demonstrated quite strikingly that special presenters can increase brand recall.[31]

There are other considerations in whether to employ a special presenter, as we shall see later, not the least of which is cost. However, for a brand fighting for recall in a crowded product category, the use of a special presenter is worth investigating.

**BRCL-5. An Interactive Mnemonic Device or (for Broadcast Ads) a Jingle May Increase Brand Recall.** An interactive mnemonic (memory aid) device can substantially increase brand recall if it can link the category need and the brand name in the buyer's mind via either (a) visual imagery or (b) musical "tune plus lyrics" recall—especially when the musical recall is also accompanied by visual imagery.

Interactive visual imagery can be stimulated directly by *visual* stimuli in TV or print ads, or indirectly by using *concrete words* in ads in any medium (radio included). The key for brand recall is to provide interaction between the product category or category need and the brand name—visually, verbally, or both.[32] A classic high-imagery ("My shirts, too?" the viewer visualizes), concretely worded brand recall slogan that worked extremely well was "Ring around the collar? Wisk around the collar!" by James Jordan, then at BBDO ad agency, now chairman of Jordan McGrath, Case and Taylor.[33] Visual interactive imagery as a mnemonic device for linking the brand

name with the initiating category cue, therefore, is certainly worth investigating as a brand recall "branding" device.

Jingles can be employed only in broadcast ads (TV and radio commercials). A jingle can be an effective brand recall mnemonic when it links the brand name to the category need. This may be because musical tunes, like pictures, have amazingly strong memorability[34] (witness the popularity of "golden oldies" radio stations) and, in turn, because visual imagery appears to be the dominant mode of response to music.[35]

There are two aspects to be very careful about when selecting a jingle for the purpose of increasing brand recall (as distinct from influencing brand attitude, which we will consider later in this chapter). First and foremost is that the jingle must associate the category need with the brand name—the main lyric should indeed be the main copy line set to music (examples: "You deserve a break today . . . at McDonald's"; "Just for the taste of it . . . Diet Coke"). The principle is that a jingle will produce a stronger association than will straight copy in words because music is more distinctively attended to and, the advertiser hopes, because a "catchy" jingle will be rehearsed (silently or openly sung) by the audience, thus producing extra learning. Second, we do not generally recommend the use of well-known songs adapted—with new lyrics—for brand recall. As Yalch points out, it's too likely that listeners will mentally substitute the old lyrics and thereby lose the brand recall effect.[36] However, there are some carefully thought-out exceptions to this (examples: use of the Bee Gees' hit "Stayin' Alive" as the audio accompaniment to a Volvo TV commercial emphasizing the need for safety; or "Take Good Care of My Baby," for Johnson & Johnson's Baby Shampoo). Too often, though, ad agencies have jumped on the bandwagon, literally, in the past several years without thinking where the *brand*wagon was going.

**BRCL-6. Use High Advertising Frequency, Relative to the Competition.** In most product categories, a number of brands are trying to "attach themselves" to the product category or category need so that the buyer will recall them when the category need arises. Obviously, this is a competitive situation—not only in terms of media expenditure between brands but also in the buyer's mind! *Provided* that the advertiser has correctly emphasized the category need–brand name association in the ad itself, repetition of the ad will increase brand name recall (whereas sheer advertising weight, without regard to this key association in the ad, won't for an established brand, and will work only slowly for a new brand[37]). However, since other brands in the product category are probably doing the same thing, what becomes important is repetition (specifically, media frequency reaching the *same* consumers or customers) of our brand's advertisements *relative to* those for competing brands.[38] We will address this media scheduling tactic more comprehensively in Chapter 16.

Just how high a level of brand recall should the advertiser set as the objective? Again, the behavioral sequence model for the brand provides the answer. Generally, the more important—that is, *high-involvement*—the purchase decision, the more effort the buyer will put into recall and thus the "recall set" size will be quite large—say, five or six brands. However, it is obviously safer for the brand to be toward the top of this list. A much shorter list of recalled brands is applicable for *low*-involvement purchases decisions, especially when almost any brand will do, and where there is time pressure.[39] For instance, in a restaurant, when asked by a friend what brand of beer you would like to drink, you only have a few seconds to recall the brand that you want to consider. For low-involvement brand choice, first recall is definitely ideal.[40]

Therefore, whereas it is crucial to be *on* the buyer's shopping list, it is better to be as *high up* that list as possible. For this reason, later, we recommend that the brand target its advertising frequency against the leading *competitor* as a yardstick for achieving and maintaining brand recall.

### Brand Recall–Boosted Brand Recognition

As we explained in Chapter 5, brand recall–boosted brand recognition is a difficult but attractive objective for brands that must be recognized in the increasingly crowded in-store displays characterizing our supermarkets, drugstores, and department stores. The difficulty from the standpoint of creative tactics is that ads aimed at this "compound" brand awareness objective require the inclusion of *both* brand recognition and brand recall tactics. The brand has to be recalled, first of all, and then it must be recognized at the point of purchase. This means that the brand name recall tactics should be utilized in the ad and *also* that the pack-

age or logo must be shown. Given that brand recall is necessary first, and thus all six tactics—including high frequency of advertising exposure in media—should be used, it is easier here to discuss the modifications to the shorter list of three brand *recognition* tactics.

The first brand recognition tactic, to ensure sufficient exposure of the brand's package (or company's logo) and name in the ad, is now employed with joint emphasis: the package should *clearly show the name*. If the package does not clearly show the name, which is something that is difficult to change if the manufacturer has not clearly labeled the package, then a close-up shot of the name itself on the package should be considered—or else the name should be mentioned verbally every time the package is shown. This means saying it, or superimposing it in writing on the screen, in TV commercials, and writing it clearly in print ads.

The second brand recognition tactic, which is to show the brand in the context of the category need, is paralleled by the verbal brand recall tactic of associating the brand with the category need. Thus, no modification of this tactic is required for brand recall–boosted brand recognition, but rather, its use is "doubled."

Lastly—and this is very important—the recommendation of low frequency for brand recognition is overridden by the requirement for high frequency for brand recall. For brand recall–boosted brand recognition, therefore, a *high-frequency* media schedule is required.

The combined tactics for brand recall–boosted brand recognition are summarized in Table 8.3.

#### TABLE 8.3

#### ADVERTISING TACTICS FOR BRAND RECALL–BOOSTED BRAND RECOGNITION

BOTH-1. Show the package or company logo—with the brand *name* clearly visible.
BOTH-2. Associate the category need and the brand name in the main copy line.
BOTH-3. Repeat the association (not just the brand name).
BOTH-4. Try to encourage a personal connection with the brand.
BOTH-5. Consider using a special presenter.
BOTH-6. An interactive mnemonic device or (for broadcast ads) a jingle may increase brand recall.
BOTH-7. Use high advertising frequency, relative to the competition.

## BRAND ATTITUDE TACTICS (PERSUASION)

We now turn to the creative tactics in the Rossiter-Percy grid that have been shown to increase an ad's effectiveness in terms of *persuasion.*

By "persuasion," we mean that the ad will cause a *favorable attitude shift* in the target audience buyer's mind. The shift could entail creating a new brand attitude, increasing an already moderately favorable attitude, maintaining an already very favorable attitude (although the ad should still *attempt* to shift this upward even when a "ceiling" has been reached), modifying brand attitude (changing from one motivational base to a better one), or changing an unfavorable attitude to a positive one. Furthermore, as we pointed out in Chapter 5, for *high*-involvement brand choice, the ad must induce not only an attitude shift but also a definite purchase *intention.* Here, it would be very useful for the reader to review the sections on brand attitude and brand purchase intention in Chapter 5.[41]

In accordance with the definition of brand attitude presented in Chapter 5, and also the multiattribute formulation of the I-D-U model of meso*positioning* presented in Chapter 6, the creative tactics for brand attitude or persuasion operate mainly on the two main components of brand attitude:

1. Benefit beliefs ($B_{bi}$)
2. The emotional "weights" ($E_i$) attached to those beliefs or to freestanding emotions ($E_o$)

However, in presenting the tactics for each of the brand attitude strategy quadrants, we will consider the emotional tactics first (consideration A: emotional portrayal of the motivation) and the benefit belief tactics second (consideration B: benefit claim support for perceived brand delivery). This is because, as will become evident, the emotional tactics require somewhat more general considerations in planning the ad, such as whether the ad's execution needs to be "likable" or not, than the brand benefit considerations, which are very specific.

Persuasion in advertising is largely a matter of selecting, for inclusion in an ad, stimuli in the form of visual, verbal, or musical benefit *claims* that are *designed,* either by intuition or through prior research, to elicit emotional responses that will motivate the buyer and produce brand benefit beliefs evaluatively weighted by those emotional responses such that they will favorably influence the buyer's attitude toward the brand. Persuasion implements the a-b-e model of micropositioning described in Chapter 6. Note that benefit beliefs can be produced by attribute claims, as well as by benefit claims, and in some cases they may even be produced by emotional stimuli associated with the brand, with no explicit claim at all. Emotional responses, on the other hand, usually are directly induced by emotional stimuli in the ads or emerge indirectly from the buyer's evaluation of the benefit claims. These causal relationships between advertising stimuli and buyer responses will become clearer when we explain the various brand attitude tactics for persuasion.

Please look again at Figure 8.1. We will present the brand attitude strategy tactics in the following order: low-involvement/informational (top left quadrant), low-involvement/transformational (top right quadrant), high-involvement/informational (bottom left quadrant), and high-involvement/transformational (bottom right quadrant). Each set of tactics begins with emotional tactics and concludes with benefit belief tactics.[42] This chapter covers the two *low-involvement* brand attitude quadrants. The next chapter covers the two *high-involvement* brand attitude quadrants.

We should also remind the manager that the brand attitude tactics are completely separate from the earlier brand awareness tactics. "Branding" and "persuasion" are two different functions of an ad. (In Chapter 10, too, we will see that "attention" requires yet other sets of tactics which vary according to the advertising medium.) In particular, an ad may "brand" well yet not be persuasive.[43] On the other hand, even though the two functions depend on different tactics, an ad that does not "brand" well *cannot* be persuasive.

## LOW-INVOLVEMENT/INFORMATIONAL TACTICS

Low-involvement brand attitude applies when the target audience decision maker regards purchase of the brand as low-risk: either it's a "try it and see" new brand, or a familiar brand that's been bought before. Low-involvement/*informational* brand attitude applies when the low-risk purchase decision is based on a "relief" (negatively originated) purchase motivation.

The advertising tactics for low-involvement/informational (LI/I) advertisements are listed in Table 8.4. For this type of advertising, correct emotional portrayal (consideration A) is not quite as important

## TABLE 8.4

### ADVERTISING TACTICS FOR THE LOW-INVOLVEMENT/INFORMATIONAL BRAND ATTITUDE STRATEGY

**Consideration A (emotional portrayal of the motivation)**

| | |
|---|---|
| LI/I-1. | Use a simple problem-solution format. |
| LI/I-2. | It is not necessary for people to like the ad. |

**Consideration B (benefit claim support for perceived brand delivery)**

| | |
|---|---|
| LI/I-3. | Include only one or two benefits or a single group of benefits. |
| LI/I-4. | Benefit claims should be stated extremely. |
| LI/I-5. | The benefits should be easily learned in one or two exposures (repetition serves mainly as a reminder). |

as adequate benefit claim support (consideration B). Hence, more of the tactics for low-involvement/informational advertising concern benefit claim support and how it is achieved.

**LI/I-1. Use a Simple Problem-Solution Format.** The classical format for negatively originating motivations is to present the problem first (which could be any of the five negative motivations) and then the brand as the solution. This is the best format for low-involvement/informational brand attitude.

The simple problem-solution format can be illustrated with several examples of Procter & Gamble's advertising. Many of P&G's brands are based on low-involvement/informational brand attitude strategies:

- A classic example is P&G's long-running print ad for Lava soap. A simple problem-solution format is employed: "Do-it-yourselfers: Get filthy nasty ugly dirty." (problem) "We'll Lava ya clean." (solution)
- P&G's market-leading detergent, Tide, has used the following theme: "You get a lot of dirt with children." (problem) "You get a lot of clean with Tide." (solution)
- For P&G's Liquid Tide detergent (see ad in Chapter 6, Figure 6.7), the theme is: "If it's got to be clean, it's got to be Tide."

The simple problem-solution format also applies to TV commercials, where advertisers sometimes are tempted to employ more complex emotional sequences because of the extended time capacity of video relative to print. However, in a very instructive set of results from numerous TV commercial tests, researchers Schwerin and Newell[44] report that a simple

before (problem) then after (solution) sequence works best in inducing brand choice. Using an index score of 100 percent for the average of all problem-solution commercials tested, the brand choice scores for various sequences were: simultaneous before and after, −9 percent; before, then product in use, then after, −4 percent; after then before, +12 percent; and before then after, +21 percent. It seems that among the complex patterns that can emerge in TV commercials, the simple before-then-after format is best.

**LI/I-2. It Is Not Necessary for People to Like the Ad.** Low-involvement/informational advertisements are frequently annoying, especially in the "intrusive" medium of television, because they hammer away at the main selling point. Such ads do not have to be liked, and indeed they usually address disagreeable or unpleasant topics which must be portrayed with negative emotions such as anger (problem removal), fear or anxiety (problem avoidance), disappointment (incomplete satisfaction), or guilt (mixed approach-avoidance conflict). Emotions are the "executors" of motivation systems, as shown in our emotion-shift theory[45] (see Table 8.5 and, later, Table 8.7). Informational ads have to portray a negative emotion first, to dramatize the problem, then move to a more neutral emotion (such as relief) or a mildly positive emotion (such as optimism) with the solution.

The main concern of the advertiser should not be whether people like the advertisement: Ad likability is irrelevant in the low-involvement/informational brand attitude quadrant. The only thing that matters "affectively" is that the emotional portrayal gets the motivation across to the target audience.

The "Mr. Whipple" commercials for P&G's Charmin toilet tissue are a case in point. The infamous "Please don't squeeze the Charmin" executions

## TABLE 8.5

### TYPICAL EMOTION-SHIFT SEQUENCES IN INFORMATIONAL ADS (BOTH LOW- AND HIGH-INVOLVEMENT) CORRESPONDING TO THE FIVE NEGATIVE ("RELIEF") MOTIVATIONS

| Motive | Emotion sequence |
|---|---|
| Problem removal | Annoyed → Relieved |
| Problem avoidance | Fearful → Relaxed |
| Incomplete satisfaction | Disappointed → Optimistic |
| Mixed approach-avoidance | Conflicted → Reassured |
| Normal depletion | Mildly annoyed → Content |

first appeared in 1968 and ran for 14 years. They consistently topped the list of TV commercials that viewers said they couldn't stand watching.[46] However, over 80 percent of adults learned the idea that Charmin is very soft.[47] Many tried the product, and it rapidly became the leading brand in its category. In 1982 a new demonstration was introduced in the Charmin TV commercial series but the Mr. Whipple character comes in at the end to gloat, justifiably, that "The squeezing got you. The softness kept you." This is an excellent example of the low-involvement/informational strategy for brands in which trial experience is sufficient.

Moving now to benefit claim support tactics, we see that there are three main ones recommended for low-involvement/informational advertising. These are described under the next three headings.

**LI/I-3. Include Only One or Two Benefits or a Single Group of Benefits.** The low-involvement nature of brand decisions in the low-involvement/informational quadrant means that the advertisement must be kept relatively simple in terms of the number of message points or benefits that the potential buyer will be willing to process (attend to and learn) in support of brand attitude.

*Single Benefit.* Advocates of the "USP" (unique selling proposition) or the "positioning" schools of advertising basically recommend that advertisements emphasize a single point.[48] Examples would be: "7UP—the uncola"; "Always Coke"; and Count Dracula's comment to a luckless victim, "It is good. But it is not Perrier." (Astute readers will note that we took this opportunity to illustrate the importance of motivational analysis. Superficially, these soft-drink products all seem to be transformational. However, the campaigns we have listed are all *informational,* focusing on the motive of incomplete satisfaction.) The keyword here is *emphasize.* Because of the frequent need to *mention* other benefits, particularly "entry ticket" benefits, or to list one or two attributes that *support* a benefit,[49] most low-involvement/informational ads in fact contain two to four benefits.[50] But they should emphasize *one*—the unique benefit.

*Or Single Group of Benefits.* A larger number of message points or benefits in support of brand attitude can be included in low-involvement/informational advertisements *provided* that they form a single and easily construed *group* of benefits. Visine eyedrops, for

instance, used a long-running ad which asked consumers "When should *you* take the Visine test?" The ad showed four situations (after waking-up, after partying, after overtime, and after sun and swim) for which Visine promised to be beneficial; in other words, there were four benefits grouped to make the single brand attitude point that "Visine gets the red out." This is the brand attitude point to be rote-learned by the prospective buyer.

In an interesting addendum to this tactic, psychologists Petty and Cacioppo[51] have shown that "sheer number" of benefits can serve as a *single* benefit in low-involvement/informational brand choice. It is the "sheer number" perception that counts, and the actual individual benefits are not separately attended to. This tactic would appear to work best in print ads rather than in TV or radio ads where time would limit the "sheer number" execution.

**LI/I-4. Benefit Claims Should Be Stated Extremely.** An important aspect of low-involvement/informational advertising is that you can make extreme claims for the brand. Indeed, you *should* do so, provided that the claim is, in the words of famous copywriter Rosser Reeves, "FTC-able" and can be substantiated. (See chapter appendix 8C, How Do You Make Claims "Extreme"?)

The main reason for making extreme benefit claims is again low involvement. When the brand is regarded by the target audience as a low-risk decision, the decision maker is rarely motivated enough to dispute or argue with the brand's claims. Also, people have come to expect extreme or even exaggerated claims in such advertising,[52] so a quiet statement in the low-involvement arena won't get heard.

*Curious Disbelief.* The important consideration is that the prospective buyer *learns* the claim; *it doesn't have to be confidently accepted* (see our discussion of low-involvement brand attitude in Chapter 5 and the rote learning requirement at the commencement of the present chapter). Whereas outright disbelief is a danger sign, there is a middle ground of "curious disbelief" that can actually increase the consumer's intention to try the brand—to see if the claim is true.[53]

Whereas extreme benefit claims (ask more) generate a highly favorable brand attitude (get more) under low-involvement conditions,[54] this highly favorable attitude is only *tentatively held* pending the prospective buyer's trial of the brand. In low-involvement/informational brand purchase, especially, the brand then has to deliver on the promised benefit to a reasonable extent if the buyer is to *confidently* hold the positive attitude after trial.[55] Extreme claims are the best way to get trial in the first place. Thereafter, and especially with verifiable informational claims, actual satisfaction with the brand to a large extent governs repeat purchase.

*Repeat Buyers Too.* If the buyer is in the low-involvement repeat purchase phase that follows a satisfactory low-involvement or *high-* involvement trial purchase, the informational benefit claims should still be kept extreme. (Remember that high-involvement target audiences move down to low-involvement once they overcome the trial risk and are now repeat buyers, for all except infrequently purchased products.) Extreme claims for a *continuing* campaign are necessary because repeat buyers who now have a favorable brand attitude will require the same extreme claims that created the attitude initially to safely maintain it, and they certainly will require extreme claims if a further attitude increase is the objective, as when new executions of the strategy are tried in an attempt to make brand-switching repeaters switch more often or perhaps become brand loyals. Also, repeat buyers with favorable attitudes are now less likely to regard these claims as being quite as extreme as they previously might have seemed. Thus, continued extreme claims for the repeat buyer are needed to reinforce the favorable brand attitude. For example, Campbell Soup Company marketing research director Anthony Adams and advertising researcher Margaret Blair found that an unnamed Campbell's established product (possibly the flagship Campbell's Soup) could maintain market share only when extremely persuasive TV commercials were used. Mere "maintenance" commercials did not work.[56]

**LI/I-5. The Benefits Should Be Easily Learned in One or Two Exposures (Repetition Serves Mainly As a Reminder.** Low-involvement/informational ads achieve their attitudinal effect in one or two exposures. With negative reinforcement, as in problem removal and the other negatively originated motivations, the *amount* of reinforcement plays a greater role in learning than the *number* of reinforcements.[57] The prospective buyer either "gets the point" (that is, learns the extreme benefit claim) quickly or not at all. Attitude toward the brand and intention to try it peak after the first or second processing by the prospective buyer.[58]

Thereafter, repetition of the advertisement primarily serves a reminder function to maintain the brand attitude at this peak level.

*But You Do Have to Remind.* Because the brand attitude is low involvement–based, it may not be personally accepted by the buyer.[59] Thereafter, the attitude must be maintained by periodically reinstating the advertising message which produced the attitude in the first place.[60] (This of course assumes that the behavioral action objective is repeat purchase. Reinstatement would not be necessary for a one-time purchase.) Repetition also guards against competitive brand attitude learning from other brands' advertisements in the same product category.

And finally, although confident acceptance is not necessary for low-involvement brand attitude learning, psychologist Bacon and consumer researchers Hawkins and Hoch[61] have shown that trivial claims tend to be believed more as they are repeated and when they are recognized as repeated. Hence the admonition to not depart from the brand's original "position" unless absolutely necessary for strategic reasons.

*At Lower Frequency.* The "quick hit" nature of low-involvement/informational claims does, however, mean that the repetition frequency can be *relatively lower* than for transformational claims. (Repetition frequency is subject also to the communication objective of brand awareness. If the brand is chosen by brand *recall*, then high-frequency repetition will be needed regardless.) We will return to this point later in the chapter and also in Chapters 15 and 16, on media strategy.

## LOW-INVOLVEMENT/TRANSFORMATIONAL TACTICS

Low-involvement/*transformational* (LI/T) brand attitude applies when the low-risk purchase decision is based on a "reward" (positively originated) purchase motivation. Advertising tactics for low-involvement/transformational advertisements are listed in Table 8.6. For this type of advertising, correct emotional portrayal (consideration A) takes precedence over benefit claim support (consideration B). Thus, more of the tactics are addressed to emotional portrayal in low-involvement/transformational advertising.

**LI/T-1. Emotional Authenticity Is the Key Element and the Single Benefit.** In transformational advertising, it is absolutely essential that the

**TABLE 8.6**

**ADVERTISING TACTICS FOR THE LOW-INVOLVEMENT/TRANSFORMATIONAL BRAND ATTITUDE STRATEGY**

**Consideration A (emotional portrayal of the motivation)**

| | |
|---|---|
| LI/T-1. | Emotional authenticity is the key element and the single benefit. |
| LI/T-2. | The execution of the emotion must be unique to the brand. |
| LI/T-3. | The target audience must like the ad. |

**Consideration B (benefit claim support for perceived brand delivery)**

| | |
|---|---|
| LI/T-4. | Brand delivery is by association and is often implicit. |
| LI/T-5. | Repetition serves a buildup function and a reinforcement function. |

**TABLE 8.7**

**TYPICAL EMOTION-SHIFT SEQUENCES IN TRANSFORMATIONAL ADS (BOTH LOW- AND HIGH-INVOLVEMENT) CORRESPONDING TO THE THREE POSITIVE ("REWARD") MOTIVATIONS**

| Motive | Emotion sequence |
|---|---|
| Sensory gratification | Dull (or neutral) → Joyful |
| Intellectual stimulation or mastery | Bored (or neutral) → Excited |
| | Naive (or neutral) → Competent |
| Social approval | Apprehensive (or neutral) → Flattered |
| | Apathetic (or neutral) → Proud |

emotional portrayal be perceived by the target audience as authentic. As advertising expert William D. Wells[62] puts it, the advertisement must "ring true." The whole idea of transformational advertising is to get the members of the target audience to put themselves emotionally into the role of using the advertised brand.

When coupled with the low-involvement nature of the brand choice, the fact that the advertised brand elicits (through classical conditioning) the correct emotion *better* than other brands do is sufficient to favor that brand when the purchase decision is made.

An example of low-involvement/transformational advertising is the ad for Häagen-Dazs ice cream shown in Figure 8.5, from the British agency Bartle Bogle Hegarty. Appealing to the sensory gratification motivation, this campaign for Häagen-Dazs increased sales by 60 percent in the U.K. markets where it was used, and increased the brand's market share from 2.3 percent to 26.1 percent. Econometric analysis indicated that about a quarter of the sales increase was caused by increased retailer distribution as retailers recognized the success of the campaign, with three-quarters being due to increased consumer demand for the brand.[63]

Emotion-shift theory applies to transformational advertising just as it does to informational advertising, except that now the emphasis is on the positive emotional end-state of the sequence.[64] Indeed, as indicated by the "or neutral" in parentheses in Table 8.7, the "before" emotion is often presumed (in the viewer or reader) rather than actually shown or described. The respective transformational "reward" motives can commence from a mild negative *or neutral* emotional state.

*Single Benefit.* Correct execution is crucial in transformational advertising. While the brand's benefit must be important to the target audience, this is not enough. The benefit in the ad must be perceived as *authentically portrayed.* Because of the difficulty and necessity of achieving this, it is highly inadvisable to attempt to portray multiple benefits in a low-involvement/transformational advertisement. Rather, the advertisement should concentrate on excellent portrayal of the single, main benefit to the would-be user.

**LI/T-2. The Execution of the Emotion Must Be Unique to the Brand.** This recommendation is a direct corollary of the first. The most common error in low-involvement/transformational advertisements is

**FIGURE 8.5**
Häagen-Dazs ice cream ad portraying "authentic" sensory gratification.
*Courtesy:* Häagen-Dazs UK Ltd.

to fail to link an otherwise effective and authentic emotional portrayal to the specific brand. How many times have you heard people say in conversation, "That's a great ad" (usually a transformational one), but then they can't remember the brand?

There is far too much "me-too" advertising in transformational product categories (soft-drink ads and new-car ads seem prone to imitation, for instance). Imitative advertisements run a real risk that they will cancel each other out in the consumer's mind. A unique execution guards against this. In William D. Wells's words again, the brand and the execution must be "tightly connected." Good examples in low-involvement/transformational categories would be Absolut vodka ads and Marlboro cigarette ads.

A "branding device" can be of great assistance in the LI/T quadrant. Usually employed as a creative technique to aid brand awareness, in the low-involvement/transformational application the device can also assist brand attitude learning and help to distinguish the brand in the consumer's mind. Perhaps the best example of such a branding device is the "Marlboro Cowboy," which extends to the "Marlboro Country" transformational executions. Absolut vodka uses an outline bottle as its branding device. Jingles, too, can serve as branding devices in transformational advertising, but these are less durable than visual stimuli. Coke and Pepsi, for instance, have tried to distinguish themselves with various transformational jingles over the years. Presenters (see the next chapter) are another possibility, if one can be sure of a long-term presenter association. Invented presenters, such as Green Giant's "Giant" and "Sprout," or of course Marlboro's cowboy, are the most durable.

**LI/T-3. The Target Audience Must Like the Ad.** Low-involvement/transformational advertising is the one quadrant of brand attitude strategy where it is essential that the target audience like the ad. There are two reasons for this:

1. The *low-involvement* aspect dictates this because the advertisement carries relatively more weight than it does with high-involvement brand choice, where the product is more important.[65]
2. The *transformational* aspect also dictates ad likability because the target audience, during the learning process, has to undergo positive conditioning[66] by a positive emotional message.

Consistent with the foregoing two points, the several experiments demonstrating that liking the *execution* increases the brand attitude have all been for low-involvement/transformational products, such as soft drinks, corn chips, and ice cream.[67] Humor and likable music are two ways of increasing executional likability that seem to work well in this quadrant.[68]

*Production Values.* The manager commissioning or evaluating low-involvement/transformational advertisements should make sure that the target audience *likes everything about the ad*—the visuals, the people, the settings, the words, the music, or whatever other elements are included in the ad. These "production values" all add to positive conditioning.

Benefit claim support for brand delivery on the motivation is a much more subtle component in low-involvement/transformational advertising, and we need mention only two tactical points regarding it.

**LI/T-4. Brand Delivery Is by Association and Is Often Implicit.** There really is no formal selling proposition in low-involvement/transformational advertising. The advertisement does not have to "argue" that the brand delivers on the sensory gratification, intellectual stimulation or mastery, or social approval motivation so much as to *show it or imply it by association.* For example, there is no "logical argument" or "explicit claim" that Coke delivers on sensory gratification, nor that Fisher-Price toys deliver on intellectual stimulation, nor that Calvin Klein jeans deliver on social appeal. The benefit claims are implied by association.

Not surprisingly, therefore, visual content, and visual imagery generated by pictures and words, play a major role in supporting brand attitude "claims" in low-involvement/transformational advertisements (see, for instance, the Häagen-Dazs ad in Figure 8.5). In fact, consumers cannot easily verbalize claims made in these advertisements.

**LI/T-5. Repetition Serves a Buildup Function and a Reinforcement Function.** Repetition of low-involvement/transformational advertisements serves dual functions instrumental to their effectiveness: buildup and reinforcement.

*Buildup Function Before Trial.* The first function can be described as "buildup." With positive reinforcement, as is characteristic of transformational appeals, the main factor in learning is the *number of exposures* rather than the amount of reinforcement per exposure.[69] Thus, there is a cumulative effect of repetition of the ad on brand attitude formation from low-involvement/transformational advertising, leading to trial.

*Reinforcement Function After Trial.* Whereas repetition builds positive attitude gradually to a peak in the mind of the individual audience member who has not tried the brand, repetition *after* trial serves a crucial second function. It reinforces the brand user's self-image.[70]

It is dangerous for a transformationally supported brand to stop advertising for any substantial period, because a hiatus in advertising removes the "image" basis for brand loyalty.[71] This has been shown for Budweiser beer in the United States[72] and the leading-selling brand of liquor in the United States, Bacardi Rum, when in 1982 it stopped advertising for almost a year in the Australian market and lost sales rapidly until a new campaign was launched.

It is generally true that you have to have a large budget to effectively compete when using low-involvement/transformational advertising.[73] This is necessary to ensure a high frequency of advertising to the target audience (see Chapter 16 where we discuss media scheduling). In Wells's words, transformational advertising must have enough "presence" so that the brand becomes "part of the consumer's mental life."

## SUMMARY

In this chapter, we identified creative execution tactics that should increase the ad's ability, beyond its central creative idea, to produce brand awareness (a necessity for all ads) and brand attitude (persuasion) and, specifically, low-involvement brand attitude.

These tactics are organized according to the Rossiter-Percy grid, which separates brand awareness into brand recognition and brand recall, and also separates brand attitude strategies into four quadrants: low-involvement/informational, low-involvement/transformational, high-involvement/informational, and high-involvement/transformational. Use of the grid is recommended *dimensionally* as a pre–creative planning framework and then *tactically* as a post–creative evaluation procedure for checking and fine-tuning ads. No matter how creative an ad appears to be, it will not work unless its stimuli are aligned properly with the communication objectives for the brand,

of which brand awareness and brand attitude are the two essential objectives.

For brand awareness and *low-involvement* brand attitude, the essential processing mechanism is rote learning, or simply "learning." The prospective buyer learns the category need–brand name or package association, for brand awareness; and learns associations between the brand name, or package, and benefits, for brand attitude. This rote learning proceeds passively, with no effort required of the buyer—although a lot is required of the advertiser!

For brand awareness, the guiding tactical principle is "encoding specificity," which, when applied to advertising, postulates that brand awareness will be maximized if there is a *match* between the stimuli encoded from the ad and the stimuli (external or internal) most likely to be present in the brand choice situation. The two brand awareness situations are brand recognition and brand recall.

*Brand recognition* requires identification of the brand at the point of purchase. Brand recognition advertising employs visual exposure of the package and name, associated with the category need, to maximize subsequent recognition of the brand and identification of "what it is," that is, what category need it meets. Brand recognition via advertising can be achieved at much lower media frequency than brand recall.

*Brand recall* requires verbal paired-associates learning in which the brand name is attached to the category need. The category need later serves as the initiating cue for the buyer's choice of a brand—thus, the brand has to come to mind reliably, otherwise it cannot be one of the candidates for brand choice. The main tactic for brand recall is to frequently mention the brand name *with* the category need in the ad. Supplementary tactics include personal reference in the main copy line, use of a special presenter, employment of an interactive mnemonic device, and brand name jingles for broadcast ads. Brand recall–boosted brand recognition, when an objective, has to employ a combined set of brand recognition *and* brand recall tactics.

For brand attitude, four sets of tactics must be considered, depending on the brand attitude strategy quadrant in which the brand is positioned. This chapter covered the tactics for the two low-involvement brand attitude quadrants.

For *low-involvement/informational* brand attitude, the recommended tactics include a simple problem-solution format, mentioning one or two benefits only, and making extreme benefit claims. It is *not* necessary for the target audience to like the ad, in this quadrant.

For *low-involvement/transformational* brand attitude, a likable ad *is* necessary. Additionally, the ad must strive for emotional authenticity and a unique execution for the brand, and may make an implicit rather than an explicit benefit claim.

## APPENDIX

## 8A. Brand Recognition Versus Brand Recall from TV Advertising

To emphasize just how different—and differentially difficult—are brand recognition and brand recall, consider the results graphed in Figure 8.6, which are from a study by Singh and Rothschild[74] in which students were shown three new TV commercials embedded in a half-hour news program. The commercials were for new brands in three product categories: trash bags, frozen pie, and salad dressing. Students in different groups in the experiment were shown either 10-second or 30-second versions of the commercials and saw each commercial one, two, or four times during the half-hour program. Two weeks later, the students were invited back to the test setting and asked, first, to recall the brand name from each of the three commercials shown to

them 2 weeks earlier; and, second, to recognize the *package* of the advertised brand from a set of pictures of five packages of brands from each product category.[75] The results in the graph show two important findings:

1. Brand (package) recognition is a much *easier* communication effect to achieve: It peaks at an incidence of over 80 percent, measured 2 weeks afterward, after only *two exposures.*

2. Brand (name) recall is a much more difficult communication effect to achieve: After *four exposures,* only about 20 percent of consumers can recall the brand correctly from the average commercial 2 weeks afterward. (This may seem like a long delay but, given that the students would remember being in the experiment, we estimate it would be approximately equivalent to 1-week brand recall after normal advertising exposure. The incidence of brand name recall is, of course, much lower than the 55 percent brand recall *soon after* exposure given in the TV commercial branding statistics earlier.) And, unlike brand recognition, brand recall *continues to increase with the number of exposures.* To achieve a brand recall incidence of 80 percent could require as many as *12 exposures.*[76]

## 8B. Brand Name Recallability

Although the advertiser does not have control over this factor except when naming a new brand, we should point out that some brand names have a built-in advantage in that they directly refer to the category need. Examples include Ultra Slim-Fast, Ultra Brite Toothpaste (the category need being *white* teeth), Healthy Choice (applicable across a lot of food product categories and hence a reason why the brand has been so easily amenable to brand extensions), and "Diet" as a prefix to well-known brands of cola. Contrast these with brand names such as Tide, Bold, Hyundai, or Cinzano, where there is no hint as to the product category or category need, so that this association must be instituted by advertising.[77] Zaichkowsky and Vipat[78] found that (new) brand names that *referred to the category need* within the broader product category (such as Bright 'n' White laundry detergent or Blondes Shampoo) were much more likely to be recalled in response to the product category cue—about 33 percent more likely, on average—than noninformative brand names (such as Omo laundry detergent or Lakme shampoo).

Robertson[79] found that *high-imagery* brand names (such as Apple, Mustang, Dove and, we note, Ultra Slim-Fast) have a tremendous brand name recall advantage—about 50 percent higher, on average—than low-imagery brand names (such as Pledge, Exxon, Evian, or Bold).

When naming a new brand, especially in a typically "brand recall category" such as cars, liquor, or other considered purchases, thought should be given to its reference

**FIGURE 8.6**
Brand recognition versus brand recall as a function of advertising exposures for 10-second and 30-second commercials.
*Source:* Singh and Rothschild, 1983; see note 74.

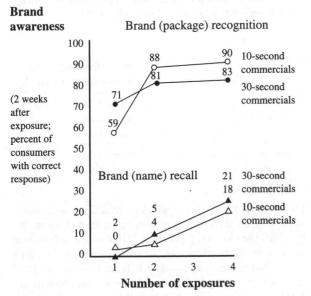

to the category need (thus: Apple *Computers,* or Dove *Beauty Soap*) and to the clarity of the mental image that the name suggests.

## 8C. How Do You Make Claims "Extreme"?

The achievement of claim extremity is a fascinating science in itself (as may be apparent from Chapter 6 in conjunction with the a-b-e model, the real action in advertising is in benefit *claims,* not in benefits per se; the former remains a much underresearched area by academics). There are at least four ways in which benefit claims can be made more extreme: direct verbal, implied verbal, implied visual, and by "paralogic."

*Direct verbal* claims are the most obvious way to increase benefit claim extremity. Increasing extremity by direct verbal claims is exemplified in an experiment by Goldberg and Hartwick[80] in which a new soft drink was described to consumers progressively more extremely as ranking either twentieth, fifth, third, or first in a taste test against the world's 100 leading brands. In the general case, a low-involvement/informational brand must be able to state or show in its advertising that it is "very effective," rather than merely "effective," in delivering a functional benefit to the consumer.

*Implied verbal* claims make use of psycholinguistics (people's interpretations of words in phrases, clauses, or sentences) to increase the perceived extremity of the claim. A strong example, even though the latter would never be used in practice, is in the experiment by Levin and Gaeth[81] in which the same hamburger meat was presented on a plate and described as either "75% lean ground beef" or "25% fat ground beef" to two groups of consumers. On a 1 (lowest) to 7 (highest) scale of expected quality, consumers who saw the "75% lean" description rated the meat as 5.3, whereas those who saw the "25% fat" description rated the same meat as only 3.7 on expected quality. Interestingly, after tasting the identical (now cooked) meat, the perceived *quality* difference persisted, 4.7 versus 3.9, although the two groups' ratings of the meat's taste did not significantly differ. Presumably, the quality difference induced by the "better" claim would influence repeat buying. The problem is that the "25% fat" claim would never be used in the real world, of course. In a much more realistic experiment, researchers Moscowitz and Rabino[82] tested two alternative claims for a brand of yogurt: "99% fat free" and "low fat." Which claim do you think would have a stronger effect on brand purchase intention? The answer, somewhat unexpectedly, is the second claim; it was twice as powerful in inducing intention to purchase the yogurt. As a final example, why does Raid Bug-Spray use the redundantly extreme claim that Raid "kills bugs *dead*" when a simple "kills bugs" has the same literal meaning? The reason, apparently,

is that most users of bug sprays like to be *sure* that their spraying has worked—by seeing the critters' dead bodies! The extreme wording implies this result.[83]

So powerful is the implied effect of words in advertising (and in packaging) that the U.S. Food and Drug Administration and the Agriculture Department have had to specify the legal meaning of descriptive terms such as "light" (or "lite"), "healthy," "low fat," and "fat free." For instance, "light" is proposed to apply only to foods or beverages containing at least one-third fewer calories than the "regular" product.[84] Because of compliance requirements, implied verbal claims are a hornets' nest for marketers as well as consumers!

*Implied visual* claims are perhaps the most powerful of all creative tactics for conveying extreme claims. "Visual exaggerations" can be used in all media of advertising except radio (and also can be employed in *any* of the four brand attitude quadrants, although they are more appropriate in the low-involvement quadrants). Best-known in the low-involvement/informational quadrant would be "product demonstration" claims such as for detergents, paper towels, or headache remedies, which are often animated for extra effect or filmed under ideal—though legal—performance conditions. Best-known in the low-involvement/ *transformational* quadrant would be "beauty shots" for food products. Individual corn flakes are chosen for wholeness, cherry syrup is painted on ham for appetite appeal, and cookies are photographed and rephotographed until they crumble just right.

*"Paralogic"* is another way of conveying extreme claims. Variously called "probabilogic," "abduction," "transduction," or the "confirmation relation,"[85] paralogic relates one or more arguments (premises) to a conclusion. For instance, consider an example suggested by Mick[86] (read down column A, then down column B):

| **A** | **B** |
|---|---|
| 1. All healthy meals are nutritionally balanced. | 1. All healthy meals are nutritionally balanced. |
| 2. Smith's frozen dinners are healthy. | 2. Smith's frozen dinners are nutritionally balanced. |
| 3. Smith's frozen dinners are nutritionally balanced. | 3. Smith's frozen dinners are healthy. |

The first argument, A, is logically correct: if statements 1 and 2 are true, then so is 3. However, the second argument, B, which uses a claim (statement 2) that could well be true and is very likely to be used in advertising, that "Smith's frozen dinners are nutritionally balanced," does *not* logically justify the conclusion that "Smith's frozen dinners are healthy." This is because while "All healthy meals are nutritionally balanced" is true and given in statement 1, the converse, "All nutritionally balanced meals are healthy" may *not* be true. However, it is, in most consumers' minds, *probably* true if not *definitely* true. Thus, by paralogic, extreme claims such as "Smith's frozen dinners are healthy" are learned even though they were never stated!

So we see that there are various ways to convey extreme claims in advertising about benefit delivery for the brand. The advertiser must not state a factually false claim. But there are other ways to enhance consumers' brand beliefs—particularly in low-involvement choice situations. Although the Federal Trade Commission prohibits "misleading" claims, they are often extremely difficult to detect, even by experts. Further, in the industry self-regulation codes that govern U.S. advertising, the buyer must prove that an affirmation of fact (as opposed to puffery) was made by the seller. For instance, how would you prove that BMW is making a factual claim in calling its cars "the ultimate driving machine" and that this claim is false or even misleading? Such extreme claims are accepted by most people as puffery. In most cases, we are "fair game" for the creative people who target us.

## NOTES

1. As explained in Chapter 5, brand awareness is the *association* between category need and the brand name or the brand's visual identifier, such as a package or store sign.

2. The creative tactics were introduced in the first edition of this book, J. R. Rossiter and L. Percy, *Advertising and Promotion Management,* New York: McGraw-Hill, 1987, chapters 9, 10, and 11. In a subsequent summary article, the sets of tactics from chapters 9 and 10 were named "The Rossiter-Percy Grid," partly to differentiate them from the popular but less specific FCB grid, which has been widely cited in the literature. See J. R. Rossiter, L. Percy, and R. J. Donovan, A better advertising planning grid, *Journal of Advertising Research,* 1991, *31* (5), pp. 11–21. (In the present edition of the book, several of the Rossiter-Percy grid tactics have been updated from those in the above references.)

3. Academic readers may note that we use the traditional term "learning" rather than "memory." Modern memory theory is becoming ridiculously overloaded with conveniently "plugged in" explanatory constructs which are reminiscent of the *homunculus* explanation (a homunculus is a little man in the brain) criticized by Skinner and more recently by Watkins (as Watkins wryly adds, the little man now almost certainly has a laptop computer!). See B. F. Skinner, *Science and Human Behavior,* New York: Appleton Century Crofts, 1995; and M. J. Watkins, Mediation and the obfuscation of memory, *American Psychologist,* 1990, *45* (3), pp. 328–335. People learn responses to stimuli, and to

say they are exhibiting "memory" when they make these responses or that memory is the "cause" of these responses is superfluous.

4. In our experience, most creative personnel are *not* familiar with the extensive research findings on learning and persuasion. And it could be argued that they shouldn't be burdened with this knowledge, given that their main role is to come up with *creative ideas* rather than tactics as such. However, the high failure rate of ads, even from the best agencies, means that creative people's "from experience" or "from intuition" tactics aren't always right. Creative people should be able to justify any obvious departures from the recommended tactics.

5. E. Langer, A. Blank, and B. Chanowitz, The mindlessness of ostensibly thoughtful action: The role of "placebic" information in interpersonal interaction, *Journal of Personality and Social Psychology,* 1978, *36* (6), pp. 635–642. For evidence that attitudinal (semantic) learning can occur from stimuli which the person cannot detect (subliminal perception), see J. A. Grueger, Evidence of unconscious semantic processing from a forced error situation, *British Journal of Psychology,* 1984, *75* (3), pp. 305–314 and K. Edwards, The interplay of affect and cognition in attitude formation and change, *Journal of Personality and Social Psychology,* 1990, *59* (2), pp. 202–216. Also see Chapter 6, note 65.

6. H. E. Krugman, Why three exposures may be enough, *Journal of Advertising Research,* 1972, *12* (6), pp. 11–14.

7. Since resuming advertising, Maxwell House has regained market share but has not achieved the dominant leadership it once had, being now coleader with Folger's. See R. Alsop, Brand loyalty is rarely blind loyalty, *The Wall Street Journal,* October 19, 1989, p. B8.

8. The learning model described here is closest to that of B. R. Bugelski, Learning and imagery, *Journal of Mental Imagery,* 1982, *6* (2), pp. 1–22. Also see in note 10.

9. H. E. Krugman, Same reference as note 6. More radically, Lastovicka and Bonfield have questioned whether buyers of brands of many supermarket products actually have attitudes toward them in the sense of rational personal reasons to support brand choice. When asked why they buy a given brand, consumers typically repeat rote-learned advertising points or rather empty platitudes such as "I just like it" or "It's the best brand." From our perspective, these buyers do have brand attitudes, but they are closely dependent on simple points or overall impressions learned from advertising. See J. L. Lastovicka and E. H. Bonfield, Do consumers have brand attitudes? *Journal of Economic Psychology,* 1982, *2* (1), pp. 57–75. Also see similar findings in W. D. Hoyer, An examination of consumer

decision making for a common repeat-purchase product, *Journal of Consumer Research,* 1984, *11* (3), pp. 822–829; and S. M. Leong, Consumer decision making for a common, repeat-purchase product: A dual replication, *Journal of Consumer Psychology,* 1993, *2* (2), pp. 193–208.

10. Readers familiar with learning principles may see that this is S-S contiguity theory, although an S-R "chain" is involved, with response-produced stimuli. For example, in evaluating a *recognized* brand, the chain is: $S_1$ (brand) $\rightarrow R_1$ (category need) $\rightarrow S_2$ (brand again) $\rightarrow R_2$ (benefits). In evaluating a *recalled* brand, the sequence is: $S_1$ (category need) $\rightarrow S_2$ (brand) $\rightarrow R_2$ (benefits). $R_2$ may also be a *chain* of learned benefits, simplified to one response here. More technically, we assume that $S_1$-$S_2$ relations are acquired by verbal paired-associates learning, just like "dog-cat," "bat-ball," (thus, for example, "IBM-computers" or "Healthy Choice–frozen dinners") which does not require reinforcement. However, virtually all ads promise a reinforcer in the form of a brand benefit, as an $S_2$-$S_3$ (for example, "IBM-reliable" or "Healthy Choice–good for my heart"). Therefore, $S_2$-$S_3$ becomes a *compound discriminative stimulus* in an operant learning paradigm for the mental operant response "If I buy brand b of category X, I will obtain Z benefit(s)," an $R_3$ which is reinforced by expected receipt of $S_3$ (see also the X-YZ positioning model in Chapter 6). The Z benefits are negative reinforcers in the case of informational motives and positive reinforcers in the case of transformational motives. For *low-involvement/* transformational advertising, the benefit or benefits may be "emotional" and the brand-benefit relationship not so consciously spelled out as in the operant paradigm. If so, Pavlovian or classical conditioning also fits such that the transformational benefits ($S_3$) are US$^+$ reinforcers, predicted by the brand as CS ($S_2$), without the buyer necessarily being aware of the connection other than experiencing a positive emotion in the presence of the brand. For a good explanation of S-S contiguity learning, see B. R. Bugelski, *Principles of Learning and Memory*, New York: Praeger, 1979. For a good account of classical conditioning and operant learning in buyer behavior, see W. R. Nord and J. P. Peter, A behavior modification perspective on marketing, *Journal of Marketing*, 1980, *44* (2), ••• pp. 36–47; for a very good examination of classical conditioning in advertising, see E. W. Stuart, T. A. Shimp, and R. W. Engle, Classical conditioning of consumer attitudes: Four experiments in an advertising context, *Journal of Consumer Research*, 1987, *14* (3), pp. 334–349, who show that backward conditioning works, though more slowly than forward conditioning, and that awareness of the CS-US contingency helps but is not necessary for conditioning; and for more detail on our interpreta-

tion of learning processes in advertising, see J. R. Rossiter and L. Percy, Visual imagery in advertising, in R. J. Harris, ed., *Information Processing Research in Advertising*, New York: Erlbaum, 1983, chapter 4.

11. This finding is based on thousands of magazine ads, in consumer and business publications, analyzed by the Starch/INRA Hooper (now Roper Starch) research service. The norms for 1-page, color consumer magazine ads, for instance, are 49 percent for noticing the ad in the first place and 42 percent for noticing the advertiser's brand name or logo. See J. R. Rossiter, The increase in magazine ad readership, *Journal of Advertising Research,* 1988, *28* (5), pp. 35–39.

12. These normative findings come from tests with over 22,000 TV commercials conducted by McCollum Spielman Worldwide, a research company in Great Neck, NY. The test ad is embedded in a half-hour program with six other ads for noncompeting products. At the end of the program, viewers, who have watched the program in an invited central-location setting, are asked "What brands were advertised in the program you just saw?"

13. Studies which use ads as the unit of analysis should be carefully distinguished from studies that use people as the unit of analysis. An excellent discussion of the importance of this distinction is provided in V. Srinivasan, P. Vanden Abeele, and I. Butaye, The factor structure of multidimensional response to marketing stimuli: A comparison of two approaches, *Marketing Science,* 1989, *8* (1), pp. 78–88; and P. Vanden Abeele and D. MacLachlan, Process tracing of emotional responses to TV ads: Revisiting the Warmth Monitor, *Journal of Consumer Research,* 1994, *20* (4), pp. 586–600. Using *people* as the unit of analysis, that is, each individual being exposed to *multiple ads,* high correlations are usually observed between brand package or name recognition and brand name recall. For instance, see the Singh and Rothschild study cited in note 74, below, and also G. M. Zinkhan, W. B. Locander, and J. H. Leigh, Dimensional relationships of aided recall and recognition, *Journal of Advertising,* 1986, *15* (1), pp. 38–46. This high correlation is to be expected when it is realized that individuals differ in their interest in the advertised product categories, or may be better at all types of memory tests, than other individuals. Of much more importance to advertisers, however, is whether a particular *ad* can produce a high proportion of individuals recognizing the package and recalling the brand name. This is an entirely different focus for the analysis and requires that each ad be assigned a proportion-recognizing score for brand recognition and a proportion-recalling score for brand recall, with the correlation between the two scores then being computed *across ads* (people ignored, so to speak). For these correlations, see next two notes. When ads

are the unit of analysis, the correlations between the ads' brand recognition and brand recall scores are much lower.

14. E. Thorson and M. L. Rothschild, Recognition and recall of commercials: Prediction from a text comprehension analysis of commercial scripts, in L. Percy and A. G. Woodside, eds., *Advertising and Consumer Psychology,* Lexington, MA: Lexington Books, 1983, pp. 287–302. Their study employed 18 TV commercials for new brands of frequently purchased consumer products not available in the test area. The brand recall measure was "free recall" from the test situation, not product category–cued recall, although this would appear to be a reasonably valid measure given that respondents could *only* have learned about the new brands from the ads. The brand recognition measure was brand *name* recognition from a list of written names provided as cues. Brand name recognition and brand name recall were measured a half-hour after exposure for one group of subjects, and 2 weeks later for another group of subjects. At both intervals, across the ads as the unit of analysis, the correlations between brand name recognition and brand name recall were not significantly different from zero.

15. R. P. Bagozzi and A. J. Silk, Recall, recognition, and the measurement of memory for print advertisements, *Marketing Science,* 1983, 2 (2), pp. 95–134. Their study was based on a large database of 95 consumer magazine ads collected much earlier, in the Advertising Research Foundation's PARM project. The measures were not really valid for our purposes here, since the database included many ads for familiar brands (for which brand recognition and brand recall could have been established long before exposure to the ads) and employed measures of *ad* recognition and *ad* recall given the brand name as a cue. However, let us assume that ad recognition and recall of an ad for the brand are at least rough proxy measures for *brand* recognition and *brand* recall. For these print ads, the correlation between ad recognition and brand-prompted ad recall was .6, suggesting an overlap (shared variance) between the two responses of only 36 percent. We estimated in Chapter 5 that the correlation between brand recognition and brand recall across all brands in a product or service category is about .5, so this doesn't suggest much extra contribution by the current ads given prior brand familiarity for many of the advertised brands. When these investigators controlled for "reader interest" in the ads, which could possibly be interpreted as a measure of category need or target audience selection, the correlation increased considerably. Specifically, a causal equation model in which the two measures of memory were treated as the same could not be rejected. Nevertheless, "reader interest" could have spuriously picked up *prior* brand recognition and brand recall

among those interested in the product category or, more spuriously, the particular brand advertised in that product category. If so, this would say nothing about the ability of a *single ad* to produce both brand recognition and brand recall. We report this study because it is the only study of its type focusing on print ads. However, given the zero relationship demonstrated for TV commercials (see previous note), we doubt that the average print ad can do much better in producing both types of brand awareness.

16. The quoted statement of Tulving's encoding specificity principle is taken from an excellent review of theories of memory by F. Haist, A. P. Shimamura, and L. R. Squire, On the relationship between recall and recognition memory, *Journal of Experimental Psychology: Learning, Memory and Cognition,* 1992, *18* (4), pp. 691–702. The principle is explained in E. Tulving, *Elements of Episodic Memory,* Cambridge, UK: Oxford University Press, 1983. To us, the origin of encoding specificity in Estes's stimulus-sampling theory (a learning theory, by the way, rather than a memory theory) is obvious. Estes's theory, in turn, was derived from Guthrie's theory. See W. K. Estes, Toward a statistical theory of learning, *Psychological Review,* 1950, *57* (2), pp. 94–107; E. R. Guthrie, *The Psychology of Learning,* New York: Harper & Row, 1935; and E. R. Hilgard and G. H. Bower, *Theories of Learning,* 3rd ed., New York: Appleton Century Crofts, 1966.

17. The importance of identifying the correct "triggering cue" (category need) for brand recall—for example, "meal substitute" versus "watching TV" for brands of snack foods, or "business lunch" versus "romantic dinner" for restaurants—is shown by the finding that the brands recalled usually *differ* according to the category need cue. See S. Ratneshwar and A. D. Shocker, Substitution in use and the role of usage context in product category structures, *Journal of Marketing Research,* 1991, *28* (3), pp. 281–295; and S. J. S. Holden, Understanding brand awareness: Let me give you a c(l)ue! in L. McAlister and M. L. Rothschild, eds., *Advances in Consumer Research,* 1993, *20,* pp. 383–388.

18. It is worth pointing out that one of the most extensively validated syndicated advertising pretest services, Research Systems Corporation's ARS[SM], employs *brand recognition* (package recognition from a simulated shelf display) as an automatic aspect of its "Persuasion" measure. Thus, what is actually being measured is purchase intention (persuasion) *given* that the consumer has recognized the brand. ARS is used primarily to test ads for supermarket products, and its incorporation of brand recognition—although not explicitly acknowledged as a feature of the procedure by the company—is probably a major reason for its very high demonstrated validity. See also Chapter 19.

19. J. R. Rossiter and L. Percy, same reference as at end of note 10. The key studies, referenced in this paper, are by Potter and Levy, 1969; Fleming and Sheikhian, 1972; and Loftus and Kallman, 1979. In Potter and Levy's study, in which the stimuli were magazine illustrations, it was found on a subsequent recognition test that only 50 percent could be recognized at a half-second exposure whereas 93 percent were recognized at a 2-second exposure. Fleming and Sheikhian found that the more complex the picture, the longer the exposure duration required for subsequent recognition. However, we would expect that most packages or logos are no more than moderately complex and that the 2-second exposure duration is sufficient to ensure recognition.

20. Supporting evidence comes from an experiment in which the recognition rate when encoding occurred during semantic processing of the target stimulus was 77 percent, compared with 48 percent for encoding during a simpler graphemic processing task; see K. Murnane and M. P. Phelps, Effects of changes in relative cue strength on context-dependent recognition, *Journal of Experimental Psychology: Learning, Memory, and Cognition*, 1995, *21* (1), pp. 158–172.

21. However, this is not so important for pure brand recognition, which appears to be largely visual. The visual nature of brand recognition was demonstrated rather dramatically some years ago in an experiment by Campbell Soup Company in which they changed the distinctive red-and-white Campbell's Soup label to green and white. Shoppers avoided the soup like the plague, even though the green-and-white package clearly said "Campbell's Soup." Imagine the amount of advertising that a soup with a green-and-white label would have to do to become as recognizable as Campbell's! In another condition of this experiment, the familiar Campbell's red lettering on white background was retained but the spelling was changed from Campbell's to the nonsense word "Gongdote," which has the same superficial visual form as the word "Campbell's" but, of course, means nothing. In this condition of the experiment, most regular buyers of Campbell's Soup simply picked up the package with the nonsense word on it without even looking at what they were buying. The experiment was suggested by the Leo Burnett agency and reported in L. Burnett, *Communications of an Advertising Man*, Chicago, IL: Leo Burnett Company Inc., 1961.

    More recently, in England, the food retailer Sainsbury was required to withdraw the packaging for its own-label Classic Cola, which was an obvious "lookalike" attempt to imitate Coke Classic's container. See: Classic Cola—a famous victory? Editorial in *Admap*, June 1994, p. 5; and I. Davies, The great Coca-Cola dispute: Look-alikes, *Journal of Brand Management*, 1994, *2* (1), pp. 59–64.

    Young children, too, commonly indicate their favorite brands of cereal and candy by pointing to them in supermarkets even when they are too young to read the brand name. See J. R. Rossiter, Visual and verbal memory in children's product information utilization, in B. B. Anderson, ed., *Advances in Consumer Research*, vol. 4, Chicago: Association for Consumer Research, 1976, pp. 523–527.

22. D. M. Thompson, paper presented at the International Conference of Applied Psychology, Sydney, Australia, August 1988. Thompson found that a target stimulus presented in a recognition test in the same context as during the learning trial produced almost perfect recognition of 95 percent. In a new context, recognition of the target stimulus dropped to 40 percent. In a different context, but a context that had itself been seen before, recognition of the target stimulus also suffered but not quite as much, falling to 52 percent. Supermarket displays would be "a context seen before," and the fall in recognition in Thompson's experiment suggests that recognition, especially for a new brand, can by no means be taken for granted. For similar evidence on the effect of context during recognition learning, see K. Murnane and M. P. Phelps, same reference as note 20.

23. This was shown in the Singh and Rothschild experiment, note 74. Also, field evidence from Bruzzone Research Corporation (BRC) shows that TV commercial recognition (which is not the same as brand recognition but does relate to recognition of a visual stimulus, just like a package) also peaks at two to three exposures. Other impressive evidence that several exposures are sufficient for visual recognition learning, with retention for periods as long as one year, is reviewed in J. R. Rossiter and L. Percy, same reference as in note 10.

24. Visual recognition (unlike verbal recall) is not subject to interference from competing ads and, once the recognition response is learned, it is extremely long-lasting. See Howe, 1967, in note 19's (10's) reference; Shepard, 1967, in note 19's (10's) reference; Bagozzi and Silk, 1983, same reference as note 15; and, more recently, R. J. Kent and C. T. Allen, Does competitive clutter in television advertising "interfere" with the recognition and recall of brand names and ad claims? *Marketing Letters*, 1993, *4* (2), pp. 175–184.

25. R. H. Fazio, P. M. Herr, and M. C. Powell, On the development and strength of category-brand associations in memory: The case of mystery ads, *Journal of Consumer Psychology*, 1992, *1* (1), pp. 1–13. The dependent variable was correct identification of the brand as a member of the product category, indicating that a product category–brand name association had been formed. In an earlier study, Fazio showed that this measure was highly correlated with category-cued brand name recall (the correct measure of brand re-

call). The fact that the brand name had to be *recognized* as a member of the category in their measure suggests that brand recognition (name rather than package) *also* was increased by the mystery format. Note: new brands only.

26. This is shown for TV commercials in Chapter 10 of this book, where the mystery format is suggested for new brands and the early-and-late format is recommended otherwise.

27. For evidence that brand recall is increased by repetition of the main copy line but *not* by the sheer number of brand name mentions, see R. H. Coulter and M. A. Sewall, A test of prescriptive advice from the Rossiter-Percy advertising planning grid using radio commercials, in C. T. Allen and D. Roedder John, eds., *Advances in Consumer Research,* vol. *21,* 1994, pp. 276–281. We expect this finding would hold also for TV commercials, as their audio is similar to that of a radio commercial.

28. The primacy and recency effect (actually, two separate effects) refers to the fact that, other things being equal, items placed toward the beginning and the end of a to-be-learned list will be best recalled, with items in the middle of the list being recalled less well. This produces a U-shaped curve when recall is graphed against the items' serial positions.

Brand recall usually is *delayed* recall, because the decision maker has to recall the brand well after the advertising exposure; and for delayed recall, the *primacy* effect is far stronger than the recency effect. In *TV and radio* ads, a list of elements is presented to the audience, and therefore early presentation of the category need–brand name association is vital. In *print* ads, however, readers may glance at the bottom of the ad quickly, to see what the brand is, so for print we would advocate beginning-and-end presentation of the association. Perhaps the safest recommendation, however, is beginning-and-end presentation. These are the two best learning positions under any circumstances.

For a review of factors affecting primacy and recency effects in recall, see G. R. Loftus and E. F. Loftus, *Human Memory: The Processing of Information,* Hillsdale, NJ: Lawrence Erlbaum Associates, 1976, particularly chapters 3 and 4.

29. David Ogilvy told this story (about another copywriter) in his book, *Confessions of an Advertising Man,* New York: Dell, 1963, pp. 136–137.

30. American advertising slogans use the second-person, possessive form "your" considerably more often than the first-person, possessive form "my," according to a content analysis by M. Carr, Key words in America's advertising slogans and in other popular expressions, *Special Report #2,* Dallas: The Salinon Corporation, 1988. Australian creative expert John Bevins, author of the P & O slogan, is perhaps the world's most suc-

cessful user of the personal approach. His campaigns are extremely memorable and very motivating according to sales results. It is important to note that the first-person effect will not work in a testimonial format, where the reference is to the presenter, not to oneself; see the study by K. Debevec and J. R. Romeo, Self-referent processing in perception of visual and verbal information, *Journal of Consumer Psychology,* 1992, *1* (1), pp. 83–102. More recently, the term "autobiographical referencing" has emerged. We avoid it because it confounds self-referencing with instructions to form a visual image.

31. R. H. Holman and S. Hecker, Advertising impact: Creative elements affecting brand recall, in J. H. Leigh and C. R. Martin, Jr., eds., *Current Issues and Research in Advertising,* Ann Arbor, MI: Graduate School of Business, University of Michigan, 1983, pp. 157–172. The weighted brand recall figures (where a weight of 7 was given for first recall, 6 for second, 5 for third, and so on) for pairs of brands with similar advertising budgets were as follows: Memorex (Ella Fitzgerald), 84, versus TDK, 15; Charlie perfume (the Charlie girl, originally Sheryl Ladd), 83, versus Enjoli, 17; Sanka decaffeinated coffee (Robert Young), 72, versus Brim, 28; and Raid bug spray (cartoon bugs, technically not celebrities and perhaps therefore showing a weaker effect), 60, versus Black Flag, 40. We should comment that most of the products in this study would seem to be more likely to be chosen by brand recognition than by brand recall, although brand recall would be appropriate if the advertiser were trying to "force" a deliberate choice via brand recall–boosted brand recognition (likely for Memorex tapes and Charlie perfume, which require a dedicated search in the store). In any event, the effect of special presenters should hold for other product or service categories that *do* rely primarily on brand recall.

32. Using pictures in Yellow Pages–type ads, Lutz and Lutz (1977) found an average increase in brand name recall from 21 percent for noninteractive executions to 37 percent for interactive executions. The correct measure of product category–cued brand name recall was employed. Using words, Kroll, Schepeler, and Angin found that sentences with high interactive imagery (for example, "A tiny red ROSE is placed in the lapel of the elegant white TUXEDO") produced superior recall of the capitalized noun when the other noun was used as the recall cue (for example: TUXEDO? → [ROSE]) than sentences with low interactive imagery (for example, "A tiny red ROSE lies on the dresser next to the elegant white TUXEDO"). See K. A. Lutz and R. Lutz, The effects of interactive imagery on learning, *Journal of Applied Psychology,* 1977, *62* (4), pp. 493–498; and K. Lutz Alesandri, Strategies that influence memory for advertising communications, in R. J. Harris, ed.,

*Information Processing Research in Advertising,* Hillsdale, NJ: Lawrence Erlbaum Associates, 1983, chapter 3. Also see N. E. A. Kroll, E. M. Schepeler, and K. T. Angin, Bizzare imagery: The misremembered mnemonic, *Journal of Experimental Psychology: Learning, Memory, and Cognition,* 1986, *12* (1), pp. 42–53.

In our previous assessment of brand recall tactics (see Rossiter and Percy, 1987, and Rossiter, Percy, and Donovan, 1991), we had advocated the use of a "bizzare" execution to increase brand recall. However, bizarreness works mainly for "free recall" (which is why bizarre ads may seem to be remembered better) but *not* for "*cued* recall," as in the category need → brand name link needed for brand recall. We therefore now withdraw this previously recommended tactic. See N. E. A. Kroll et al., same reference as above, and also K. A. Wollen and S. Cox, Sentence cuing and the effectiveness of bizarre imagery, *Journal of Experimental Psychology: Human Learning and Memory,* 1981, *7* (5), pp. 386–392; A. Pra Baldi, R. de Beni, C. Cornoldi, and A. Cavedon, Some conditions for the occurrence of the bizarreness effect in free recall, *British Journal of Psychology,* 1985, *76,* pp. 427–436, experiment 4; and G. O. Einstein, M. A. McDaniel, and S. Lackey, Bizarre imagery, interference, and distinctiveness, *Journal of Experimental Psychology: Learning, Memory, and Cognition,* 1989, *15* (1), pp. 137–146.

33. J. Lipman, Jordan McGrath drops the name of the game that made its fame, *The Wall Street Journal,* July 20, 1989, p. 84.

34. See the Rossiter and Percy chapter in the Harris volume, same reference as in note 10. In the present chapter, we refer sometimes to "memory" or "memorability," in common parlance. We emphasize from a conceptual perspective that the words "learning" or "tendency to be learned" could be substituted. See note 3.

35. J. W. Osborne, The mapping of thoughts, emotions, sensations, and images as responses to music, *Journal of Mental Imagery,* 1981, *5* (1), pp. 133–136.

36. R. F. Yalch, Memory in a jingle jungle: Music as a mnemonic device in communicating advertising slogans, *Journal of Applied Psychology,* 1991, *76* (2), pp. 268–275. For example, Levi's in the United Kingdom recently changed from cult rock and blues tunes to original music in its TV commercials because it wanted "to put the brand back at the center." See C. Beale, Levi's changes its tune with new ads, *Marketing* (UK), May 27, 1993, p. 5.

37. For evidence that amount of advertising ("weight") alone is unrelated to brand recall for *established* brands, see L. Bogart and C. Lehmann, What makes a brand name familiar? *Journal of Marketing Research,* 1973, *10* (1), pp. 17–22; and R. H. Holman and S.

Hecker, same reference as note 31. For a *new* brand launch, advertising weight will obviously have a positive effect on brand recall—but a faster effect, we would argue, if the ad contains the right association.

38. There is a further reason for a new brand, when entering an established category, to really push hard for high frequency of advertising relevative to the competition. This is due to the phenomenon known in psychology as the "part-list cuing" effect, whereby recall of the first few brands in a product category (usually those that are well-established and popular brands) can actually *supress* recall of new or minor brands. In a demonstration of part-list cuing in advertising, students were asked to recall brands of toothpaste after seeing an ad for either Crest (a leading, highly recalled brand) or for a fictitious new brand called Shane (which would be expected to have very low brand name recall since students were seeing the brand name for the first time). The number of brands recalled after seeing the Crest ad averaged only 1.4—a recall inhibition effect—and in nearly all cases the "1" in the 1.4 was Crest. In contrast, the average number of brands recalled after seeing the minor-brand Shane ad was 2.3; this latter figure compares with a control group of students asked to recall toothpaste brands without having seen a prior advertisement in the experiment, who recalled an average of 2.5 brands.

Part-list cuing is the modern name, coined by N. J. Slamecka, for a long-established phenomenon in the psychology of learning known as retroactive inhibition. Part-list cuing, however, has been given a more specific explanation, namely, that part-list cuing involves "sampling with replacement" such that early items that are recalled will *continue* to interfere with attempts to recall other items and, also, repeated reinstatement of these early-recalled items strengthens their association with the originating cue still further! See N. J. Slamecka, An examination of trace storage in free recall, *Journal of Experimental Psychology,* 1968, *76* (4), pp. 504–513; and H. L. Roediger III and S. R. Schmidt, Output interference in the recall of categorized and paired-associate lists, *Journal of Experimental Psychology: Human Learning and Memory,* 1980, *6* (1), pp. 91–105.

Also see P. W. Miniard, H. R. Unnava, and S. Bhatla, Investigating the recall inhibition effect: A test of practical considerations, *Marketing Letters,* 1990, *2* (1), pp. 27–34. This study qualifies previous important research by showing that popular—that is, highly recalled—brands inhibit the recall of minor brands whereas the opposite does not seem to occur. For the previous research, see J. W. Alba and A. Chattopadhyay, The effects of context and part-category cues on the recall of competing brands, *Journal of Marketing Research,* 1985, *22* (3), pp. 340–349, and Salience effects in brand recall, *Journal of Marketing Research,* 1986, *23* (4), pp. 363–369.

39. J. R. Hauser and B. Wernerfelt, An evaluation cost model of consideration sets, *Journal of Consumer Research,* 1990, *16* (4), pp. 393–409.

40. F. R. Kardes, G. Kalyanarum, M. Chandrashakaran, and R. J. Dornoff, Brand retrieval, consideration set composition, consumer choice, and the pioneering advantage, *Journal of Consumer Research,* 1993, *20* (1), pp. 62–75.

41. The brand attitude part of the Rossiter-Percy grid, shown in Figure 8.1, divides brand attitude strategies into four *quadrants* based on the brand purchase risk *for* the target audience (low- versus high-involvement) and on whether the purchase motivation is negatively or positively originated (informational versus transformational motivation). The origin of the Rossiter-Percy grid has been explained in detail in earlier publications (see in particular Rossiter and Percy, 1987, Chapter 7; and Rossiter, Percy, and Donovan, 1991, same reference as in Chapter 5, note 29). The key influences for the *involvement* dimension were the perceived risk theorizing of Bauer and Cox (1967); the economic search theory of Nelson (1970); the advertising theory proposed by Ehrenberg (1974); the empirical work on perceived risk by Lawrence and Tarpey (1975); and, later, the model of peripheral versus central processing, the ELM, developed by Petty and Cacioppo (1981). The creative tactics for involvement, however, are our own contribution. The *motivation* dimension (informational versus transformational) was developed from learning theory, particularly drive theory in conjunction with negative and positive reinforcement, respectively; see Rossiter and Percy, 1987, Chapter 7, and this edition, Chapter 5, notes 29 and 30. The creative tactics for motivation were initially suggested by Wells (1981) and then extended by us. Although there are several other involvement models and grids available in the literature, ours has the following advantages:
    - It is the only grid model that begins with brand awareness.
    - It is the only grid model that allows the manager to easily and clearly operationalize involvement and, a somewhat more difficult task, motivation. (Involvement and motivation are operationalized through qualitative research with the target audience during which [1] it will become clear whether most regard purchase of this brand on the next purchase occasion as either low-risk or high-risk; and [2] their primary purchase motivation, informational or transformational, from the set of eight motives, can be inferred. The brand usually can be quite clearly classified, based on the majority of *target audience* buyers, into one of the four quadrants. In rare mixed cases, classification should conservatively lean toward *high*-in-

volvement, and *informational* motivation, respectively.) Most products and brands have both functional (informational) and symbolic (transformational) benefits, and the key is to find the main motivational "trigger." This will be either an informational or a transformational benefit.
    - The grid specifies detailed creative tactics for the two types of brand awareness and the respective brand attitude quadrants.

    Petty and Cacioppo's ELM is a *unidimensional* model in which no account is taken of the second dimension, motivation. The best-known two-dimensional grid, the FCB grid (Vaughan, 1980), is superficially similar to ours but has major conceptual and operational problems (see Rossiter, Percy, and Donovan, 1991). All previous unidimensional (involvement) models and grid models fail to operationally specify the division between low- and high-involvement and, in the case of grid models, the distinctions between different types of motives. Furthermore, none of the other models has attempted to identify specific creative tactics to the extent that we have done in the Rossiter-Percy model.

42. We have numbered the brand attitude tactics 1, 2, 3, and so on, for each quadrant, but have preceded each number with letters to indicate the quadrant. Thus LI/I = low-involvement/informational, LI/T = low-involvement/transformational, HI/I = high-involvement/informational, and HI/T = high-involvement/transformational.

43. The McCollum Spielman Worldwide ad testing service has shown that there is no correlation between an ad's ability to produce brand *recall* (as measured by "Clutter Awareness") and its ability to produce a favorable attitude change (as measured by "Persuasion/Attitude Shift"). This lack of relationship is shown in the major validation study by P. R. Klein and M. Tainiter, Copy research validation: The advertiser's perspective, *Journal of Advertising Research,* 1983, *23* (5), pp. 9–17, and in subsequent proprietary reports issued by MSW. Brand *recognition,* however, has to be more carefully interpreted. In the persuasion measures used by leading testing services such as MSW and Research Systems Corporation (the ARS system), the persuasion measure *requires* that the consumer recognize the brand, because the consumer must choose it from either a written list of brands (in the MSW procedure) or from a simulated display of in-store packages (ARS). Obviously, though, people could recognize a brand name or its package and still not choose it if not persuaded. Thus, brand recognition is independent of persuasion except for the chosen brand. Moreover, brand awareness and brand attitude shift or persuasion require different types of tactics, and *both* types of tactics are vital for an ad to work. As noted, the "minihierarchy" of processing and communication effects (attention → branding →

persuasion) means that attention tactics must also be added. These are covered in Chapter 10, where it is seen that attention tactics differ by media, especially between broadcast and print media.

44. H. S. Schwerin and H. H. Newell, *Persuasion in Marketing,* New York: Wiley, 1981, pp. 165–167.

45. Emotion-shift theory was postulated in the first edition of our book and stems from theories developed by Mowrer and Hammond. Historically, see O. H. Mowrer in his two books *Learning Theory and Behavior,* and *Learning Theory and the Symbolic Processes,* both New York: Wiley, 1960, and L. J. Hammond, Conditioned emotional states, in P. Black, ed., *Physiological Correlates of Emotion,* New York: Academic Press, 1970, Chapter 12. Also see our references in Chapter 5, note 29. For a recent appraisal, see J. H. Hansell, Theories of emotion and motivation: A historical and conceptual review, *Genetic, Social, and General Psychology Monographs,* 1989, *115* (4), pp. 429–448. The individual emotions (although not the crucial shift aspect) were shown to have a good fit with informational and transformational advertising, respectively; see A. J. Kover and J. Abruzzo, The Rossiter-Percy Grid and emotional response to advertising: An initial evaluation, *Journal of Advertising Research,* 1993, *33* (6), pp. 21–27. We also see support for (a low-level version of) our shift theory in the study by E. Kamp and D. J. MacInnis, Characteristics of portrayed emotions in commercials: When does what is shown in ads affect viewers? *Journal of Advertising Research,* 1995, *35* (6), pp. 19–28.

46. The Marschalk Company, Inc., *A Study to Evaluate Consumer Attitudes Toward Television Commercials,* New York, NY: The Marschalk Company, Inc., 1981.

47. R. H. Bruskin Associates, *National AIM Study of 2,500 Adults,* New York, NY: R. H. Bruskin Associates, 1977.

48. Rosser Reeves, then at Ted Bates advertising agency, originated the USP approach. David Ogilvy, founder of the Ogilvy & Mather advertising agency, is forever urging his proteges to be "single-minded" in advertising executions. Ogilvy, it is said, coined the term "positioning," which was later made a buzzword following publication of the book by A. Ries and J. Trout, *Positioning: The Battle for Your Mind,* New York: McGraw-Hill, 1981. See our Chapter 6 for a more thorough definition of positioning.

49. In TV commercials and, we suspect, other types of advertising, judges cannot reliably identify how many different "sales points" are in a typical ad. In particular, supporting evidence for *one* benefit (a → b in our terms) is confused with *different benefits* (multiple b's). See D. W. Stewart and D. H. Furse, *Effective Television Advertising: A Study of 1000 Commercials,* Lexington, MA: Lexington Books, 1986.

50. H. H. Kassarjian and W. M. Kassarjian, The impact of regulation on advertising: A content analysis, *Journal of Consumer Policy,* 1988, *11* (3), pp. 269–285.

51. R. E. Petty and J. T. Cacioppo, The effects of involvement on responses to argument quantity and quality, *Journal of Personality and Social Psychology,* 1984, *46* (1), pp. 69–81.

52. A graphic demonstration of the claim-discounting phenomenon occurred in an experiment by Goldberg and Hartwick. They introduced a fictitious new soft drink with the claim that, in a taste test against the world's top 100 brands, the new brand ranked (according to the experimental condition) either twentieth, fifth, third, or first. Despite the fact that the company introducing the product was rather unflatteringly described, increasingly extreme claims produced increasingly high believed ranking of the brand (increasing up to the "third best" claim, since the claim of "first" boomeranged except when the company was also described as a highly reputable one). However, even with the most persuasive "third best" claim, the expected ranking was only *thirtieth* best, thus indicating a healthy discounting by consumers. See M. E. Goldberg and J. Hartwick, The effects of advertiser reputation and extremity of advertising claim on advertising effectiveness, *Journal of Consumer Research,* 1990, *17* (2), pp. 172–179.

53. J. C. Maloney, Curiosity versus disbelief in advertising, *Journal of Advertising Research,* 1962, *2* (2), pp. 2–8. However, claims shouldn't be exaggerated to the extent of inviting total disbelief or even ridicule, as in an experiment by L. J. Marks and M. A. Kamins, The use of product sampling and advertising: Effects of sequence of exposure and degree of advertising claim exaggeration on consumers' belief strengths, belief confidence, and attitudes, *Journal of Marketing Research,* 1988, *25* (3), pp. 266–281.

54. W. J. McGuire, The nature of attitudes and attitude change, in G. Lindzey and E. Aronson, eds., *The Handbook of Social Psychology,* vol. 3, Reading, MA: Addison-Wesley, 1969, pp. 136–314.

55. J. R. Rossiter, same reference as in Chapter 5, note 26.

56. By "extremely persuasive" we mean commercials that, in a pretest, caused at least a +10 percent increase in purchase intention. Several commercials that tested at below this level failed to prevent share erosion, and indeed Campbell's will accept only commercials with a persuasion score of +6 percent or better from its advertising agencies for established brands. See A. J. Adams and M. H. Blair, same reference as in Chapter 7, Further Reading.

57. See, for example, S. H. Hulse, J. Deese, and J. Egeth, *The Psychology of Learning,* 4th ed., New York: McGraw-Hill, 1975; and W. A. Wickelgren, *Learning and Memory,* Englewood Cliffs, NJ: Prentice-Hall, 1977.

58. Experimental evidence showing that low-involvement/ informational brand attitude and intention to try peak after one or two (actual) exposures comes from studies by A. G. Sawyer, A laboratory experimental investigation of the effects of repetition of advertising, Doctoral dissertation, Graduate School of Business, Stanford University, 1971 (see also M. L. Ray, A. G. Sawyer, M. L. Rothschild, R. M. Heeler, E. C. Strong, and J. B. Reed, Marketing communication and the hierarchy-of-effects, in P. Clarke, ed., *New Models for Mass Communication Research,* Beverly Hills, CA: Sage, 1973, pp. 147–176); A. J. Silk and T. Vavra, The influence of advertising's affective qualities on consumer response, in G. D. Hughes and M. L. Ray, eds., *Buyer/Consumer Information Processing,* Chapel Hill, NC: University of North Carolina Press, 1974, pp. 157–186; and G. E. Belch, The effect of television commercial repetition on cognitive response and message acceptance, *Journal of Consumer Research,* 1982, *9* (1), pp. 56–65.

59. T. S. Robertson, Low-commitment consumer behavior, *Journal of Advertising Research,* 1976, *16* (2), pp. 19–24.

60. R. E. Petty, The role of cognitive responses in attitude change processes, in R. E. Petty, T. C. Brock, and T. M. Ostrom, eds. *Cognitive Responses in Persuasion,* Hillsdale, NJ: Lawrence Erlbaum Associates, 1981, pp. 135–139.

61. See F. T. Bacon, Credibility of repeated statements: Memory for trivia, *Journal of Experimental Psychology: Human Learning and Memory,* 1979, *5* (3), pp. 241–252; and S. A. Hawkins and S. J. Hoch, Low involvement learning: Memory without evaluation, *Journal of Consumer Research,* 1992, *19* (2), pp. 212–239.

62. W. D. Wells, How advertising works, Mimeo, Chicago, IL: Needham, Harper & Steers Advertising, Inc., 1981.

63. Summary of IPA Effectiveness Awards for 1992, *Marketing* (UK), July 1, 1993, p. 19.

64. See J. R. Rossiter and L. Percy, same references as in note 41. Also R. P. Bagozzi, Further thoughts on the validity of measures of elation, gladness and joy, *Journal of Personality and Social Psychology,* 1991, *61* (1), pp. 98–104.

65. The greater weight of the ad in influencing low-involvement behavioral choice reflects what Petty and Cacioppo call the "peripheral route" to persuasion. In high-involvement behavioral choice, the product carries greater weight, reflecting the "central route" to persuasion. See R. E. Petty and J. T. Cacioppo, Central and peripheral routes to persuasion: Application to advertising, in L. Percy and A. G. Woodside, eds., *Advertising and Consumer Psychology,* Lexington, MA: Heath, 1983, pp. 3–23.

66. This conditioning, generally known as "classical conditioning" in honor of the classic research of Russian psychologist I. P. Pavlov earlier this century, may occur with the consumer's awareness and indeed may be most successful when the consumer is aware of the contingency between the to-be-conditioned stimulus, called the CS (the brand), and the unconditioned stimulus, which is the positive reinforcer, called the US$^+$ (the positive emotional stimulus or stimuli in the ad). The use of popular songs for transformational brands is a good example of advertisers attempting above-awareness conditioning. However, there is no doubt that conditioning can occur without awareness, too, although its effect may be weaker, as in the Ruth et al. experiments on subliminal sexual stimuli in liquor ads mentioned in Chapter 6 with the a-b-e model of positioning. For a good discussion of contingency awareness, see C. T. Allen and C. A. Janiszewski, Assessing the role of contingency awareness in attitudinal conditioning with implications for advertising research, *Journal of Marketing Research,* 1989, *26* (1), pp. 30–43, although the investigators were not quite correct in stating that the brand (CS) must precede the emotional stimulus (US$^+$) in ads for conditioning to occur. Backward, or "trace," conditioning can occur although it usually takes more exposures, as in the careful experiments by E. W. Stuart, T. A. Shimp, and R. W. Engle, same reference as in note 10. An example of trace conditioning is the "mystery" format in ads where the brand is revealed at the end; after *several exposures,* consumers are likely to mentally insert the brand as soon as the now-familiar ad is attended to, thus converting prior backward conditioning into subsequent forward conditioning (CS $\rightarrow$ US$^+$). For an excellent, broader discussion of how positive emotional stimuli in ads might work, see J. B. Cohen and C. S. Areni, Affect and consumer behavior, in T. S. Robertson and H. H. Kassarjian, eds., *Handbook of Consumer Behavior,* Englewood Cliffs, NJ: Prentice-Hall, 1991, chapter 6.

67. These studies, all based on humorous versus nonhumorous TV or radio commercials, where executional liking was clearly the main manipulated variable, were by B. D. Gelb and G. M. Zinkhan, Humor and advertising effectiveness after repeated exposures to a radio commercial, *Journal of Advertising,* 1986, *14* (4), pp. 15–20; Y. Zhang and G. M Zinkhan, Humor in television advertising: The effects of repetition and social setting, in R. H. Holman and M. R. Solomon, eds., *Advances in Consumer Research,* vol. 18, Provo, UT: Association for Consumer Research, 1991, pp. 813–818; and B. Stern and J. L. Zaichkowsky, The impact of "entertaining" advertising on consumer responses, *Australian Marketing Researcher,* 1991, *14* (1), pp. 68–80.

68. The effects of humor and music are reviewed in J. R. Rossiter, The limited effect of likable ads, Working

paper, Sydney: Australian Graduate School of Management, September 1993. Most advertising experts advocate that humor employed in advertising should be "product relevant." Creative director Sam Levenson, creator of the famous VW Beetle campaign when at Doyle Dane Bernbach, applies the following test: If you take the product out of a humorous ad, the ad should no longer be funny. If it is still funny without the product, then, in his view, the humor is misapplied and irrelevant.

However, the product-relevant humor principle applies only to *informational* advertising. In informational advertising, every detail in the ad should support the main selling point and must not distract from the processing of it. This is what is meant by product-relevant humor. Particularly to be avoided in informational advertising is the humorous punch line or "klinker" that many copywriters cannot seem to resist adding to an otherwise serious ad. Klinkers are irrelevant to the message and detract from message processing in the critical recency effect zone at the conclusion of the advertisement. It's okay, though, to use a "klitchik." This is Levenson's term for a *product-relevant* twist used only at the end of a *humorous* ad, such as, "Volkswagen—it doesn't go in one year and out the other." A good klitchik makes you pause and think about what the ad has just shown you or said. Klitchiks therefore make effective use of the recency effect in processing at the conclusion of a humorous advertisement.

For *transformational* advertising, unlike informational advertising, it is *not* essential that humor be product-relevant. Irrelevant humor in transformational advertising can contribute to one's liking of the ad, creating a positive emotional response that can transfer to the advertised brand via classical conditioning. However, transformational advertisements cannot rely on humor alone since humor is not in itself a motivation. Transformational advertisements must inevitably have as their foundation one of the positive motivations: sensory gratification, intellectual stimulation or mastery, or social approval.

69. S. H. Hulse et al., same reference as in note 57.
70. See especially A. S. C. Ehrenberg, Repetitive advertising and the consumer, *Journal of Advertising Research*, 1974, *14* (2), pp. 25–34.
71. S. P. Raj, The effect of advertising on high and low loyalty consumer segments, *Journal of Consumer Research*, 1982, *9* (1), pp. 77–89.
72. R. L. Ackoff and J. R. Emshoff, Advertising research at Anheuser-Busch, Inc. (1963–68), *Sloan Management Review*, 1975, *16* (4), pp. 1–15.
73. Of course, as we made clear in Chapter 7, the 1 or 2 percent of brilliant campaigns can work with a low budget. Generally, however, for low-involvement/transformational campaigns, the large budget rule holds.
74. S. N. Singh and M. L. Rothschild, Recognition as a measure of learning from television commercials, *Journal of Marketing Research*, 1983, *20* (3), pp. 235–248. We note that their measure of brand recall was cued by the commercials consumers could recall from the test situation, rather than by the product category cue. Strictly speaking, the product category cue is required for our definition of brand recall. However, we are reasonably sure that the results for brand recall would have followed the same linear increase, though probably at a lower absolute level, had the product category cue been employed.
75. We have selected the experimental conditions and response measures that are closest to real-world brand recall and brand recognition, although Singh and Rothschild also examined other conditions and measures.
76. S. N. Singh and C. A. Cole, The effects of length, content, and repetition on television commercial effectiveness, *Journal of Marketing Research*, 1993, *30* (1), pp. 91–104. The correct measure of brand recall, product category–cued brand name recall, was employed, but the delay interval was only a few minutes to 24 hours (average 12 hours) rather than a week or two. The 80 percent average brand recall result is for 30-second commercials. Also, the experimenters tested one, four, or eight exposures, so the peak at specifically four exposures is inferred. Given that the four exposures were massed and in laboratory conditions, we estimated that this would translate to about 12 *real-world* exposures. We will supply other findings supporting this result of few repetitions being necessary for brand recognition and many repetitions being necessary for brand recall. This topic is treated extensively in Part Six of the book, where we examine media strategy.
77. K. Robertson, Strategically desirable brand name characteristics, *Journal of Consumer Marketing*, 1989, *6* (4), pp. 61–71.
78. J. L. Zaichkowsky and P. Vipat, Inferences from brand names, in G. J. Bamossy and W. F. van Raaij, eds., *European Advances in Consumer Research*, vol. 1, 1993, pp. 534–540.
79. K. Robertson, Recall and recognition effects of brand name imagery, *Psychology & Marketing*, 1987, *4* (1), pp. 3–15. Robertson also found a slight *name recognition* advantage for high-imagery brand names. This name recognition effect might partly assist package recognition.
80. M. E. Goldberg and J. Hartwick, same reference as note 52.
81. I. P. Levin and G. J. Gaeth, How consumers are affected by the framing of attribute information before

and after consuming the product, *Journal of Consumer Research,* 1988, *15* (3), pp. 374–378.

82. H. Moscowitz and D. Rabino reported these results in an article that, unfortunately, we have been unable to locate for reference. In regression equations using benefit claims for several attributes such as fat content, flavor, and family member appeal to predict purchase intention, the claim "low fat" had a standardized weight of .45 whereas "99% fat free" had a weight of only .21 (about half as effective).

83. Example provided by J. F. Durgee, Rensselaer Polytechnic Institute, 1991; see also J. F. Durgee, Product drama, *Journal of Advertising Research,* 1988, *28* (1), pp. 42–49.

84. K. Deveny and R. Givson, Food marketers express relief at label plan, *The Wall Street Journal,* November 7, 1991, p. B4.

85. These terms are due, respectively, to W. J. McGuire (probabilogic); C. S. Peirce (abduction); D. E. Kanouse (transduction); and see D. N. Osherson, E. E. Smith, O. Wilkie, A. Lopez, and E. Shafit, Category-based induction, *Psychological Review,* 1990, *97* (2), pp. 185–200. See also L. Percy and J. R. Rossiter, *Advertising Strategy: A Communication Theory Approach,* New York: Praeger, 1980, Chapter 4.

86. D. G. Mick, Consumer research and semiotics: Exploring the morphology of signs, symbols, and significance, *Journal of Consumer Research,* 1986, *13* (2), pp. 196–213. We have adapted his example.

## DISCUSSION QUESTIONS

**8.1.** Discuss how the encoding specificity principle might apply in selecting brand awareness tactics in advertisements for:
    **a.** Birdseye frozen peas
    **b.** The aperitif Pernod
    **c.** USS (U.S. Steel) company

**8.2.** To stimulate brand recall, what is right and what is wrong with the following main copy lines?
    **a.** "Only your dentist can give your teeth a better fluoride treatment than Colgate."
    **b.** "LaCoste." (As in signs at tennis tournaments.)
    **c.** "I dreamt I was Cleopatra in my Maidenform bra."

**8.3.** Write a short script for a radio commercial for Lifesavers designed to maximize brand recall–boosted brand recognition. Type the script sentence by sentence, double-spaced, on the right-hand half of the page. On the left, explain the tactics you have employed.

**8.4.** An important principle of persuasion for low-involvement brand attitude is to make an extreme benefit claim. What does this principle mean in terms of creative tactics for the *two* low-involvement brand attitude quadrants? Answer with examples.

**8.5.** Advertising testing services routinely include a measure of whether consumers like or dislike the ad. For a new TV commercial about to go on air, the testing service finds that 80 percent of *all* people tested dislike the ad. How would you interpret this finding?

## FURTHER READING

Rossiter, J. R., and, Percy, L. A better advertising planning grid. *Journal of Advertising Research,* 1991, *31* (5), 11–21.

Compares the Rossiter-Percy grid with the well-known FCB grid, emphasizing the prior importance of brand awareness and brand attitude tactics. *Note:* the tactics have been updated in this text.

Do *not* read books by famous advertising copywriters.

Books by Leo Burnett, Fairfax Cone, Claude Hopkins, David Ogilvy, and others, are interesting and entertaining reading. But they won't help you to be a better advertising manager. First, these books take no account of advertising communication models (particularly the two types of brand awareness and the four brand attitude strategy quadrants); rather they promote (their own) singular view of how advertising works, and no single view can cover all types of advertising. Second, because each writer tends to have had most of his or her experience with particular product categories—again, different communication models—the recommended creative tactics frequently are conflicting and contradictory. Third, while it can be contended that the views of these famous copywriters have been "tested by experience," in fact their views too often do not withstand more controlled testing by advertising testing services. Finally, apart from too-rarely cited sales results, the criteria by which these authors judge "effective" advertising (e.g., advertising recall) are hopelessly mixed and off-base and serve to reinforce the confusion which our book, in systematizing advertising objectives, has tried to prevent.

Whereas these are strongly worded criticisms, they seem necessary in light of the fact that the biggest problem in understanding how advertising works is to get managers (and students) to stop falling back on popular and often erroneous general conceptions and to think, instead, specifically about what the advertising is trying to do, and how, specifically, it might best be done.

# CHAPTER 9

# Creative Execution Tactics: High-Involvement Persuasion

In the previous chapter, we examined creative execution tactics for brand awareness and low-involvement brand attitude. When the purchase decision is perceived by the prospective buyer as high-risk, the ad needs to employ brand awareness tactics (as before) but *high-involvement* brand attitude tactics. The main situations where high-involvement persuasion is needed are the following: major consumer and business purchases (other than for highly loyal buyers), when trying to attract trier-rejecters back to your brand (any product or service), or when trying to make the sale in one attempt (one-step direct response advertising). After reading this chapter, you should:

- Know the tactics that work best for high-involvement/*informational* brand attitude strategy.
- Additionally, know the tactics to try with negative target audiences, namely, refutational and perhaps comparative advertising.
- Know the tactics that work best for high-involvement/*transformational* brand attitude strategy.
- Know when and how to use a presenter in the ad.

The tactics in this chapter cover the third and fourth brand attitude quadrants from the Rossiter-Percy grid: high involvement/informational and high involvement/transformational.

Additionally in this chapter, we introduce the Vis-CAP model for selecting a presenter, should a presenter be tactically indicated. The presenter model applies to the entire grid (and is thus relevant to the *previous chapter* as well). Also, as we will see later, the presenter model is very important for high-involvement persuasion in direct response advertising, where the *company* is the presenter.

As in the previous chapter, we look first at the nature of *processing* of the advertisement required for high-involvement persuasion. High-involvement persuasion requires *acceptance,* not just learning, of the ad-proposed benefits. (We remind the reader that learning is still necessary, and sufficient, for the ad's brand awareness objective, as explained in the previous chapter.)

## ACCEPTANCE AND THE ALEA MODEL OF PROCESSING: THE BASIS OF HIGH-INVOLVEMENT BRAND ATTITUDE

Acceptance can be defined as the decision maker's *personal agreement* with benefit claims, in the advertisement, that are perceived to be made for the brand. The opposite response, rejection, reflects personal *disagreement* with benefit claims. These acceptance and rejection responses represent the *received* message as distinct from a low-involvement *perceived* message (see the previous chapter) and are also called "cognitive responses" (see chapter appendix 9A, Cognitive Response Theory). This is not really an appropriate name for them as they are clearly "emotional," too, as we'll now see.

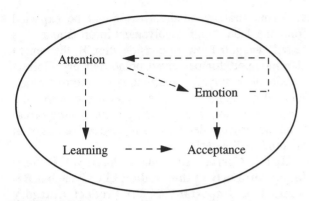

**FIGURE 9.1**
The "ALEA" (or "scrambled egg") model of short-term processing responses *potentially* made to an ad, adlike event, or promotion offer. Attention responses will continue to be made as long as there's further emotional stimulation, hence the loop at the top; learning and acceptance (or rejection) responses *may* be made while the looping is occurring.

Acceptance is essentially a combination of two of the other processing responses: learning and emotional response. The relationships among all four short-term processing responses to an ad, adlike event, or promotion offer are depicted in Figure 9.1. We call this the ALEA model of processing although, in effect, it is more like a "scrambled egg" because the prospective buyer usually makes what we call a "heterarchy" (diverse sequence), not a hierarchy (strictly-ordered sequence), of processing responses to the ad. Processing is punctuated by attention responses to various elements of the ad, following each of which learning and emotional responses, and perhaps acceptance or rejection responses, *may* be made. However, as we will see, the learning of a particular benefit claim may be quite transient, and it is the emotional response *to it* and to subsequent claims that contributes to acceptance (or rejection).

What *is* learned more permanently, and is accepted (or rejected), is the *superbelief*—the "net result" of the various benefit claim acceptances and rejections. This superbelief is the high-involvement brand attitude.

**Acceptance and the Other Communication Effects**

Acceptance is necessary for successful processing of all communication effects except brand awareness and low-involvement brand attitude.

- *Category Need.* The decision maker has to *accept* that a category need exists, based on the ad's selling the category need or reminding the decision maker of a latent category need.
- *High-Involvement Brand Attitude.* The decision maker has to *accept* the ad-proposed brand benefits before he or she will try or buy the brand. (Overall, there is only about a .4 correlation between high-involvement brand attitude and subsequent behavior;[1] so, as explained in Chapter 5, in high-involvement choice situations, an *intention* to take action is additionally necessary—the next communication effect.)
- *Brand Purchase Intention.* The decision maker has to *accept* an ad's "hard sell" invitation to purchase (note also that a hard sell invitation is made when a promotion offer is included). However, "soft sell" purchase intention inferred from *low-involvement* brand attitude does *not* require an acceptance response.
- *Purchase Facilitation.* The decision maker has to *accept* the ad's reassurance that the product, price, place, or personal selling problem(s) have been facilitated.

Acceptance responses for these communication effects are exemplified in Figure 9.2 for a high-involvement ad for the Audi A8 Sportscar. Our hypothetical buyer is processing the ad in the way the advertiser intended—though prospective buyers aren't always this obliging!

Because the elements in advertisements that refer to category need, high-involvement brand attitude, brand purchase intention, and purchase facilitation each link the brand to a motivation, they can all be thought of as advertising-induced high-involvement *attitudes* toward, respectively, the category or brand. Unlike low-involvement brand attitude, high-involvement attitudes have to be *confidently held* before the decision maker will take action.

How best to instill this confidence is what high-involvement creative tactics must address. We examine first the creative tactics for the high-involvement/ informational brand attitude quadrant, then those for the high involvement/transformational brand attitude quadrant. These are the final two cells of the Rossiter-Percy grid (see Figure 8.1 in the previous chapter), which guides creative tactics.

"I do need a new car." — **Category need**

"My best friend has an A8." — **Brand attitude** (benefit belief)

"It looks terrific." — **Brand attitude** (benefit belief)

"And it gets reasonable mileage, too." — **Brand attitude** (benefit belief)

"I think I'll go visit an Audi dealer this weekend." — **Brand purchase** (related) **intention**

"Ah, there's a dealer just a couple of miles from here." — **Purchase facilitation**

**FIGURE 9.2**
Examples of cognitive responses during processing by a consumer who is "in the market" for a new car.
*Courtesy:* Foster Nunn Loveder and Audi Australia.

## HIGH-INVOLVEMENT/INFORMATIONAL TACTICS

High-involvement/informational brand choices are high-risk purchase decisions, requiring attitudinal conviction before purchase, where the appeal is mainly to one of the negatively originated motivations: problem removal, problem avoidance, incomplete satisfaction, or mixed approach-avoidance (normal depletion is not applicable to high-involvement since it pertains only to brand loyals). Also, usually, the target audience is negatively or at best mildly positively disposed toward the brand.

The recommended tactics for high-involvement/ informational (HI/I) advertising are listed in Table

9.1. This strategy quadrant, as might be expected from the label "high-involvement/informational," is heavily weighted toward consideration B, the benefit claim support for perceived brand delivery. Correct emotional portrayal of the motivation (consideration A) is also important, but, as we shall see in the first tactic, its importance in high-involvement/informational advertising declines with progressive stages in the product life cycle.

**HI/I-1. Correct Emotional Portrayal Is Very Important Early in the Product Life Cycle but Becomes Less Important As the Product Category Reaches Maturity.** Correct emotional portrayal of the motivation is very important early in a product category's life cycle because, during the introductory and growth stages, most prospective buyers have to be *"sold" on the category need* as well as on the brand. Advertisements for products when they are new, such as microwave ovens or, more recently, interactive compact discs (CD-Is), have to motivate people to

| TABLE 9.1 |
|---|
| **ADVERTISING TACTICS FOR THE HIGH-INVOLVEMENT/INFORMATIONAL BRAND ATTITUDE STRATEGY** |

**Consideration A (emotional portrayal of the motivation)**

| | |
|---|---|
| HI/I-1. | Correct emotional portrayal is very important early in the product life cycle but becomes less important as the product category reaches maturity. |
| HI/I-2. | The target audience has to accept the ad's main benefit claims but does not have to like the ad itself. |

**Consideration B (benefit claim support for perceived brand delivery)**

| | |
|---|---|
| HI/I-3. | The target audience's "initial attitude" toward the brand is the overriding consideration. |
| HI/I-4. | Benefit claims must be pitched at an acceptable upper level of brand attitude (don't overclaim). |
| HI/I-5. | Benefit claims must be convincing (don't inadvertently underclaim). |
| HI/I-6. | Consider the addition of an expert, objective presenter. |
| HI/I-7. | For target audiences who have objections to the brand, consider a refutational approach. |
| HI/I-8. | A small brand taking on a well-entrenched competitor should try an explicit comparative approach. |
| HI/I-9. | Use a "summary" benefit claim; put your strongest benefits first; and limit the ad to about seven total benefits. |

want the category before they will seriously consider the particular brand advertised. Later in the product life cycle, most prospective buyers will already know about the category and be favorably disposed toward it, so correct emotional portrayal of the motivation is less important as the product category reaches maturity.

However, advertisers would do well to note that product life cycles are really consumer or customer life cycles;[2] that is, an established product for early adopters will still be a new product for later adopters. For example, to sell microwave ovens to the 50 percent or so of consumers who have never bought one, selling the category is still important; whereas advertising aimed at the 50 percent of consumers who already have one, intended to get them to trade up or buy another microwave oven, would not have to sell the category. Thus, the status of the *category need* communication effect in the *target audience* is the determinant of whether correct portrayal of the motivation is required.

**HI/I-2. The Target Audience Has to Accept the Ad's Main Benefit Claims but Does Not Have to Like the Ad Itself.** This recommendation is similar to the one made earlier for low-involvement/informational advertising: When the basis of the brand attitude is information, whether people like the way the information is presented is a very minor consideration.[3] Perhaps the best examples of this would be direct response ads that promise personal improvement—for example, weight reduction, bodybuilding, or breast development. Such ads are often "schlocky" in overall appearance. They concentrate on loading the copy with convincing claims, often with a "money back if not satisfied" guarantee, to reduce the typically high perceived risk.

Not having to like the ad should not be interpreted as a recommendation to deliberately create disliked ads. This sometimes is done in *low*-involvement/ informational advertising as a tactic to increase attention to and *learning of* the message point, as in the Mr. Whipple commercials for Charmin. However, in attitudinal presentations in high-involvement/informational ads, learning is only transient, and *acceptance,* the high-involvement processing response, is what counts. In high-involvement/informational advertising it doesn't matter whether the message points are presented in a likable or unlikable manner as long as the points are accepted by the target audience.

*"Engineering" Acceptance.* The message points in high-involvement/informational advertising must be very carefully engineered to gain target audience acceptance. This engineering requires the manager to understand the rationale behind a number of fairly complex tactics relating to high-involvement brand attitude. These benefit claim support tactics (consideration B) are presented next. Why are there so many of them? Because high-involvement/informational attitude strategy is the most difficult persuasion task in all of advertising. That's why traditionally it was left to personal selling, the most powerful form of marketing communications. However, the two fastest-growing types of advertising—direct response advertising (including interactive advertising) and telemarketing— are essentially personal selling translated to ads. Let's see how to engineer acceptance via advertising.

**HI/I-3. The Target Audience's "Initial Attitude" Toward the Brand Is the Overriding Consideration.** In Chapter 5, we saw that a high-involvement attitude is held by prospective buyers who perceive considerable risk in buying the brand— either because they are new category users or because they are entrenched with another brand. The buyer's initial attitude toward the brand (before the persuasion attempt) must therefore be reckoned with if a new attitude is to be achieved.

For instance, if the target audience has a *negative* brand attitude, the manager (or researcher) must find benefits that will change this attitude to a sufficiently positive attitude to motivate purchase; likewise, a *moderately favorable* brand attitude must be increased (unless the brand is to be made additionally attractive to a moderately favorable target audience by sales promotion, which normally operates on brand purchase intention, not on brand attitude); a *strongly favorable* brand attitude must be maintained; or a *new* brand attitude must be created—with the particular set of benefits thought to be important, deliverable, and unique to the new-trier target audience.

In creative terms, the *claim* made for the benefit must be tailored to the target audience. Benefit claims, like the benefits they represent, must take the target audience's initial attitude into account. In everyday terminology, this means that the claim should be worded or depicted in a way that reflects "where the audience is coming from." The following examples show how this can be achieved by copywriters who know how to write "to" an audience (high-involvement) rather than "at" an audience (low-involvement).

**1.** In addressing a target audience with a *negative* attitude toward the brand, such as other-brand loyals who have rejected your brand, or new category users with negative attitudes toward all brands in the category, the benefit claim should acknowledge the negative attitude and try to "shake" the target audience out of it with a convincing counterclaim (see also the refutational approach described later in this section). An example of "shaking" a would-be negative target audience buyer is the Apple Macintosh ad shown in Figure 9.3. The headline in the ad, " . . . for people who thought they could never have a Macintosh," as well as copy such as "Check your preconceptions at the door," indicate that the copywriter knows that the target audience is likely to be negative toward this and other Apple-brand personal computers. The detailed

copy is sympathetic to this negative attitude. Of course, the sympathetic copy then attempts to convince negatively disposed decision makers to reconsider (" . . . find out about the power that will change the way you think about Macintosh") and make their final attitude more positive.

Negative initial attitude is the most difficult for advertising to change. A large increase is usually necessary: from negative through the neutral point and into a sufficiently high positive position to produce a definite trial or retrial intention. (It is *necessary* to generate brand purchase intention in high-involvement choice situations, as explained in Chapter 5.) Usually, new benefits will have to be found to make such a large change possible. However, it is also worth revisiting the a-b-e model of *micropositioning* presented in Chapter 6. If the negative initial attitude is emotionally based, try a logical (attribute-focused) attack.

**FIGURE 9.3**

A two-page advertisement for Apple Macintosh personal computers with benefit claims worded to acknowledge a largely *negative* target audience and "shake" them out of this negativity.
*Courtesy:* ©Apple Computer, Inc. Used with permission. All Rights Reserved. Apple and Apple logo are registered trademarks of Apple Computer, Inc.

Conversely, if it is attribute-based, try an emotion-focused attack. (Actually, these strategies would have been worked out beforehand, and here we are concentrating on creative execution tactics, but the reminder is appropriate.)

**2.** In addressing a target audience with a *moderately favorable* brand attitude, such as brand switchers early in the product life cycle who are still trying to settle on a favorite brand to use regularly, or such as "interested" new category users, the benefit claims should have more of a "reassuring" or reinforcing tone. A good example of this is the direct response newspaper ad reproduced in Figure 9.4, written by John Bevins for Bankers Trust, a funds management service. This ad was the first in a series of advertisements by Bankers Trust for what is clearly a high-involvement/informational purchase decision. The copy is designed to bolster the moderately favorable initial attitude of prospective customers who may wonder whether it's worthwhile to take money out of their bank or other savings and put it into a money management account.

(However, if the moderately favorable attitude is firmly based on experience, such as for other-brand switchers who have tried our brand and found it short of the top group, then forget the reassurance! Instead, you should be attempting *attitude modification*, as explained in Chapter 5, by repositioning the brand to a new purchase motive. Technically, this is a *new attitude*, and should be executed as in 3, below.)

**FIGURE 9.4**
An advertisement for Bankers Trust investment funds where the target audience may have *only a moderately favorable* initial attitude toward this service.
*Courtesy:* John Bevins Pty Ltd.

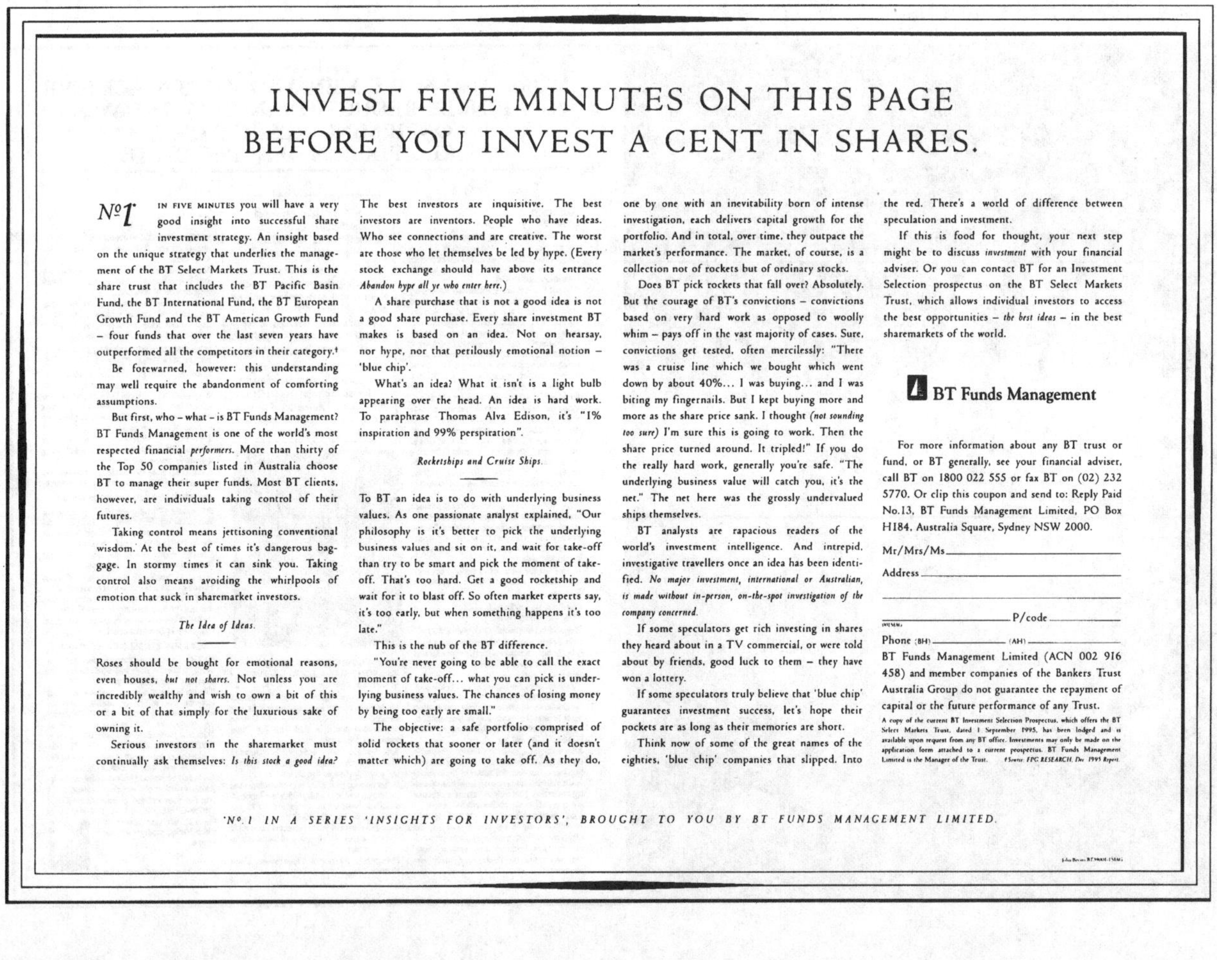

INVEST FIVE MINUTES ON THIS PAGE
BEFORE YOU INVEST A CENT IN SHARES.

Nº1* IN FIVE MINUTES you will have a very good insight into successful share investment strategy. An insight based on the unique strategy that underlies the management of the BT Select Markets Trust. This is the share trust that includes the BT Pacific Basin Fund, the BT International Fund, the BT European Growth Fund and the BT American Growth Fund – four funds that over the last seven years have outperformed all the competitors in their category.†

Be forewarned, however: this understanding may well require the abandonment of comforting assumptions.

But first, who – what – is BT Funds Management? BT Funds Management is one of the world's most respected financial *performers*. More than thirty of the Top 50 companies listed in Australia choose BT to manage their super funds. Most BT clients, however, are individuals taking control of their futures.

Taking control means jettisoning conventional wisdom. At the best of times it's dangerous baggage. In stormy times it can sink you. Taking control also means avoiding the whirlpools of emotion that suck in sharemarket investors.

*The Idea of Ideas.*

Roses should be bought for emotional reasons, even houses, *but not shares*. Not unless you are incredibly wealthy and wish to own a bit of this or a bit of that simply for the luxurious sake of owning it.

Serious investors in the sharemarket must continually ask themselves: *Is this stock a good idea?* The best investors are inquisitive. The best investors are inventors. People who have ideas. Who see connections and are creative. The worst are those who let themselves be led by hype. (Every stock exchange should have above its entrance *Abandon hype all ye who enter here.*)

A share purchase that is not a good idea is not a good share purchase. Every share investment BT makes is based on an idea. Not on hearsay, nor hype, nor that perilously emotional notion – 'blue chip'.

What's an idea? What it isn't is a light bulb appearing over the head. An idea is hard work. To paraphrase Thomas Alva Edison, it's "1% inspiration and 99% perspiration".

*Rocketships and Cruise Ships.*

To BT an idea is to do with underlying business values. As one passionate analyst explained, "Our philosophy is it's better to pick the underlying business values and sit on it, and wait for take-off than try to be smart and pick the moment of take-off. That's too hard. Get a good rocketship and wait for it to blast off. So often market experts say, it's too early, but when something happens it's too late."

This is the nub of the BT difference.

"You're never going to be able to call the exact moment of take-off... what you can pick is underlying business values. The chances of losing money by being too early are small."

The objective: a safe portfolio comprised of solid rockets that sooner or later (and it doesn't matter which) are going to take off. As they do, one by one with an inevitability born of intense investigation, each delivers capital growth for the portfolio. And in total, over time, they outpace the market's performance. The market, of course, is a collection not of rockets but of ordinary stocks.

Does BT pick rockets that fall over? Absolutely. But the courage of BT's convictions – convictions based on very hard work as opposed to woolly whim – pays off in the vast majority of cases. Sure, convictions get tested, often mercilessly: "There was a cruise line which we bought which went down by about 40%... I was buying... and I was biting my fingernails. But I kept buying more and more as the share price sank. I thought *(not sounding too sure)* I'm sure this is going to work. Then the share price turned around. It tripled!" If you do the really hard work, generally you're safe. "The underlying business value will catch you, it's the net." The net here was the grossly undervalued ships themselves.

BT analysts are rapacious readers of the world's investment intelligence. And intrepid, investigative travellers once an idea has been identified. *No major investment, international or Australian, is made without in-person, on-the-spot investigation of the company concerned.*

If some speculators get rich investing in shares they heard about in a TV commercial, or were told about by friends, good luck to them – they have won a lottery.

If some speculators truly believe that 'blue chip' guarantees investment success, let's hope their pockets are as long as their memories are short.

Think now of some of the great names of the eighties, 'blue chip' companies that slipped. Into the red. There's a world of difference between speculation and investment.

If this is food for thought, your next step might be to discuss *investment* with your financial adviser. Or you can contact BT for an Investment Selection prospectus on the BT Select Markets Trust, which allows individual investors to access the best opportunities – *the best ideas* – in the best sharemarkets of the world.

BT Funds Management

For more information about any BT trust or fund, or BT generally, see your financial adviser, call BT on 1800 022 555 or fax BT on (02) 232 5770. Or clip this coupon and send to: Reply Paid No.13, BT Funds Management Limited, PO Box H184, Australia Square, Sydney NSW 2000.

Mr/Mrs/Ms __________

Address __________

__________ P/code __________

Phone (BH) __________ (AH) __________

BT Funds Management Limited (ACN 002 916 458) and member companies of the Bankers Trust Australia Group do not guarantee the repayment of capital or the future performance of any Trust.

A copy of the current BT Investment Selection Prospectus, which offers the BT Select Markets Trust, dated 1 September 1995, has been lodged and is available upon request from any BT office. Investments may only be made on the application form attached to a current prospectus. BT Funds Management Limited is the Manager of the Trust. †Source: FPC RESEARCH, Dec 1995 Report.

*'Nº.1 IN A SERIES 'INSIGHTS FOR INVESTORS', BROUGHT TO YOU BY BT FUNDS MANAGEMENT LIMITED.*

**3.** In addressing a target audience with *no firm prior brand attitude*, and perhaps a negative or "hesitant" initial attitude toward the category, such as reluctant new category users, the wording of the benefit claims should be adjusted to take account of this indecisiveness. Figure 9.5 shows how NARHEX company has used this approach for a new wrinkle-reduction product line called Cross-Linked Elastin. The opening two paragraphs of copy are aimed at the indecisive reader. For instance, the second paragraph begins: "Even in this high tech era customers demand evidence substantiating our claims, and rightly so." In our opinion, the copywriter has done an excellent job of turning the hesitant initial attitude of the prospective buyer into a more confident and positive attitude sufficient to stimulate trial purchase.

In all the foregoing examples, the benefit claims are stated in a way that resonates with the target audience's initial attitude while attempting to change, increase, or create a positive final (postprocessing) attitude toward the advertised brand.

*Theory of Initial Attitude.* It is worthwhile at this point to emphasize the reason initial attitude is so much more crucial in high-involvement purchase decisions than in low-involvement ones. The very notion of low risk in purchasing a brand means that the buyer's initial attitude is likely to be weakly held. With high-involvement decisions, in contrast, the prospective buyer's initial attitude reflects the higher risk and is likely to be strongly held.[4]

A strongly held initial attitude is almost sure to stimulate cognitive responses during processing (see

**FIGURE 9.5**
Ad for NARHEX Cross-Linked Elastin wrinkle-reduction products with copy well addressed to the "hesitant" reader with no firm prior brand attitude.
*Courtesy:* NARHEX OPERATIONS—*Genius of Discovery.*

chapter appendix 9A).[5] These cognitive responses will be negative, moderately favorable, and so forth, depending on the target audience's initial attitude. High-involvement/informational advertising has to provide benefit claims that sympathetically anticipate these reactions and either counter them or build on them accordingly. Unless cognitive responses are addressed effectively, the benefit claims will not be accepted, and no change or improvement in *final* brand attitude will result.

**HI/I-4. Benefit Claims Must Be Pitched at an Acceptable Upper Level of Brand Attitude (Don't Overclaim).** Benefit claims in high-involvement/informational advertising not only must take the target audience's initial attitude into account but also must be tempered by how far "up" they can go in proposing a new and more favorable attitude position. This is known in the classical attitude literature as the (upper limit of) "latitude of acceptance."[6] Obviously, the manager would like as favorable a final attitude as

possible for the brand. "As possible"—that's the key operational concept for this tactic.

*How Much of an Attitude Increase Is Feasible?* Early in the product life cycle—again, actually the *consumer or customer* life cycle—it should be possible to obtain large positive shifts in brand attitude among new category users who have neutral initial attitudes and among experimental brand switchers who are still sampling the category and have neutral but "available" attitudes toward the brands they have yet to try (see Chapter 4). The ad for NARHEX wrinkle-reduction products in Figure 9.5, for example, has the potential for a large positive shift in creating brand attitude.

Later in the consumer or customer life cycle, when the brand is better known and brand attitudes toward it and toward competing, rejected brands are more strongly held (called "entrenched" attitudes in Chapter 4), smaller shifts of about one attitude "box" or "rung" (see Figure 9.6) are the most the advertiser can

**FIGURE 9.6**

The likely upper limits (of latitudes of acceptance) for brand attitude change in high-involvement/informational advertising.

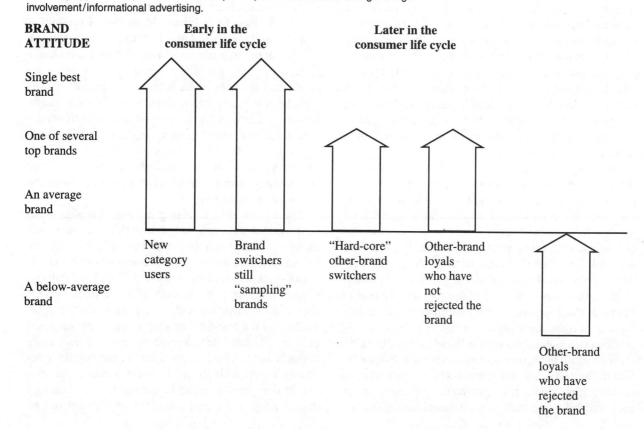

hope for—unless some hitherto unrealized benefits for the brand are discovered or unless there is a radical creative breakthrough in finding a more effective statement of current benefits.[7] For example, now that microwave ovens are well known, it's very difficult for any *brand's* advertising to change the attitude of people who are dead set against using one.

The likely upper limits of latitudes of acceptance are summarized in Figure 9.6. As indicated in the figure, *early* in the consumer or customer life cycle, it is often possible to attain positive attitude shifts of *up to two* "boxes" or "rungs" on our general-purpose brand attitude scale (this scale is discussed further in Chapter 19). New category users entering the category and brand switchers who are shopping around may be induced via advertising to rate the brand as one of the better brands or even the single best brand.

However, the figure also indicates that, *later* in the life cycle, the most feasible positive shifts are reduced to *one* "box" or "rung." Hard-core other-brand switchers who are not currently including the brand may be induced to do so, but would hardly rate it single best. Similarly, other-brand loyals who have not rejected the brand may be induced to now include it as one of several top brands, but not as a replacement for their single-best-brand loyalty. If their preferred brand is unavailable, our brand at least has a chance to be chosen as an alternative. For other-brand loyals who have tried and rejected the brand, the shift from below-average to average hardly seems worth aiming for unless the now average brand can be made additionally attractive to this target audience through promotional incentives.

*How to Find and Address the Latitude of Acceptance.* Latitudes of acceptance can be estimated for a given target audience through overall attitude measurement and pretesting of benefit claims (see Chapter 19). It is relatively easy to discover "how far you can go" before progressively more extreme claims are rejected. If the benefit claims stated in the pretest versions of the ads do not move a significant proportion of the target audience "up" to the required favorable brand attitude position, then alternative statements must be sought and tested.

(If better statements of the brand's benefits sufficient to attain the required attitude increase *cannot* be found, the tactic for that target audience will have to be abandoned. The manager could, however, try a more radical tactic such as refutational advertising or comparative advertising—as explained in tactics HI/I-7 and HI/I-8, below—if these have not already been tried.)

In finding the upper limit of the latitude of acceptance for the target audience, the manager must be wary of trying to overclaim in the final version of the ad once a version acceptable to the target audience has been found. The manager must resist the temptation to subjectively "make a few improvements," unless he or she is willing to pay to have these tested as well. For example, during its *introduction* some years ago, the main benefit claim for Stouffer's Lean Cuisine line of low-calorie entrees, "Good tasting entrees at less than 300 calories," was found to be eminently acceptable (believable) to the target audiences of new category users and other-brand loyal (Weight Watchers) users. To have said *"Great* tasting entrees at less than 300 calories" would have been overclaiming to these high-involved target audiences (although now that the brand is well established, the advertising *does* correctly use the extreme claim of "great taste" for the now low-involved target audience). Overclaiming which produces a reversion to the initial premessage attitude is called the "boomerang effect."

**HI/I-5. Benefit Claims Must Be Convincing (Don't Inadvertently Underclaim).** After all we've said about the importance of benefit claim acceptance in high-involvement/informational advertising, it almost sounds superfluous to say that benefit claims must be convincing and not inadvertently *under*claim. However, this is not a trivially obvious recommendation. As Bauer and Cox have suggested, underclaiming is just as much an error as overclaiming.[8] Indeed, we may think of an underhand throw of the "boomerang" (underclaiming) as well as the overhand throw of overclaiming.

The danger is in selecting the right benefits—that is, those that are important, deliverable, and as unique to the brand as possible—and then failing to execute the *statements* of them convincingly enough. An instructive experiment by Petty and Cacioppo[9] demonstrated that weak arguments (for important points known to be effective with strong arguments) can actually *hurt* the brand by making a negatively disposed audience's initial attitude even more negative or more strongly held.[10] This again is due to the cognitive response aspect of high-involvement message processing. If the target audience's spontaneously occurring doubts about the brand's benefits aren't removed by sufficiently convincing statements of the benefits, then these doubts will actually be *reinforced* by the ad, making the brand attitude more negative than before! An example of apparent underclaiming is the Coca-Cola claim of a few years ago, "Have a Coke and a smile." This claim apparently was not sufficiently convincing to Pepsi Cola brand loyals, a possibly *high*-involvement target audience, whom Coca-Cola was trying to win over.[11] Coca-Cola then moved to stronger and presumably more convincing claims such as "The real thing" and, more recently, "Coca-Cola is *it*" and "Always Coke." Although this change may not be the only cause, Coke has widened its market leadership over Pepsi since then.

**HI/I-6. Consider the Addition of an Expert, Objective Presenter.** A general finding in the social psychology of persuasion is that the latitude of acceptance can be extended (upward, to a more favorable final attitude) if a highly credible presenter is employed to deliver the message.[12] "Highly credible" means a presenter who is perceived as expert and objective (truthful).

Presenter characteristics are covered more fully in our VisCAP model of presenter selection later in this chapter. Suffice it to note here that for high-involvement/informational attitude change, being an expert is not enough; the presenter must be seen as an "objective expert." For instance, the launch commercial for Healthy Choice frozen entrees (see Chapter 2) undoubtedly persuaded many previous nonbuyers of frozen dinners to make an exception and try this brand (for NCUs this would be a high-involvement, definitely, and informational decision). Why? Because ConAgra's then-CEO Mike Harper, the presenter, was obviously an expert on food but had a very personal reason to be objective about the brand's "heart-healthy" benefit claims, because he'd just suffered his first heart attack. As the brand became established and moved to low-involvement for repeat buyers, a switch was made to male and female "lifestyle" presenters and, most recently, to no special presenter at all.

**HI/I-7. For Target Audiences Who Have Objections to the Brand, Consider a Refutational Approach.** The advertiser whose brand is perceived as posing a high-involvement/informational decision often will be faced with negatively disposed audiences from whom sales *must* come if the brand is to succeed. If the typical "supportive" advertising approach hasn't worked, then a "refutational" approach is worth trying. *Refutational* approaches acknowledge the negative reactions head-on and then try to refute or counter them. The refutational approach is like the selling tactic known as "Yes, but . . . " Frequently used in personal selling, the refutational approach is underused in advertising.[13]

Here's an example of its use. In the early 1970s, a large number of American adults had developed a negative attitude toward potatoes. The national farmers' cooperative, represented by the National Potato Promotion Board, commissioned the authors of this book to conduct some research and recommend an advertising strategy designed to reverse the declining trend in U.S. per capita potato consumption. Our research in 1973, prior to the campaign, indicated that although people still loved the taste of potatoes, this positive belief was being overtaken by a strong negative belief: that potatoes are fattening. This strong negative belief had to be countered if potato consumption was to increase again.

The advertiser had refutational ammunition to work with. Potatoes are actually lower in calories (per ounce) than other popular carbohydrate side dishes such as rice, bread, or noodles. And while it is true that people often add butter or sour cream to potatoes, these ingredients constitute a relatively small addition to the total calories consumed in the meal. Also, many people were already switching to margarine and low-calorie preparation and serving methods. The first ad in the campaign used the headline: "Don't blame potatoes." The refutation was then stated in the ad's copy: " . . . automatically you assume the culprit was that delicious baked potato . . . Not likely." Follow-up ads continued the refutational message and added a positive message—that potatoes are an excellent source of vitamins.

The campaign was highly successful. Consumer surveys taken in 1973, before the campaign started, and again in 1975, after it had been running for 2 years, showed a substantial reduction in the number of people believing that potatoes are fattening and a dramatic increase in the number believing that potatoes are nutritious. During the campaign, with no noticeable change in price or other market factors, consumption of potatoes by the average U.S. household not only stopped declining—it went up by over 17 percent. This major turnaround was attributable largely to successful refutational advertising.

**HI/I-8. A Small Brand Taking on a Well-Entrenched Competitor Should Try an Explicit Comparative Approach.** A specialized tactic for high-involvement/*informational* advertising is the (explicit) comparative approach. Like refutational advertising, comparative advertising is a rather radical tactic, to be used only if circumstances suggest it would be more effective than conventional supportive advertising. The *main* circumstance is a *small brand trying to challenge a larger, well-entrenched competitor* in the category. (For evidence supporting this recommendation, see chapter appendix 9B, Explicit Comparative Advertising—Research Results.) Note that because the large brand has many loyal customers, the small brand's target audience is therefore other-brand loyals (OBLs), and the decision to switch to the smaller brand is definitely *high*-involvement.

*Comparative* advertising either names competitors openly or else clearly implies who the competitors are without actually mentioning them by name. It then claims parity or, more often, superiority for the advertised brand on one or more benefits, to try to sway the target audience's attitude in the advertised brand's favor. Naming a competitor openly is called *explicit* comparative advertising, and that is the format we are advocating here. For example, American Express, in its launch ad for Optima True Grace Card, openly showed the logo for Visa, the main competitive card, and took a swipe at Visa's slogan, "It's everywhere you want," by saying, "It's everywhere you want to pay more interest charges."[14] The milder alternative, *implicit* comparative ads (in which the main competitor is suggested or implied but not directly identified by name, logo, or slogan), usually do *not* result in spontaneous identification by consumers of the compared-to brand or brands. Thus, if you're taking on an entrenched competitor, say so—by using an explicit comparative ad.[15]

Because of the adversary and possibly disparaging nature of comparative advertising, it is not a tactic to be adopted without fully considering the likelihood of costs that may result. It can result in price wars (for example, when Datril was launched against Tylenol); complaints to self-regulatory commissions such as the National Advertising Division of the Council of Better Business Bureaus, and even lawsuits (for example, McDonald's against Burger King); and also *counter*-comparative advertising (for example, Coke's Bill Cosby commercials some years ago—"You know

what *you* want to be when you grow up . . . Number one!"—which attempted to defuse Pepsi's taste-test challenge commercials). Comparative advertising can be a very costly tactic indeed.

But it can also be enormously successful. For example, Tylenol itself became established by comparative advertising against pain reliever brands containing aspirin. Burger King's comparative campaign helped to gain market share and profit against McDonald's and Wendy's. Pepsi-Cola contends that its taste-test challenge campaign has worked in markets where it lagged behind Coke's sales; in international markets, where Pepsi often trails the earlier-established Coke, it typically uses humorous but nonetheless hard-sell comparative ads.[16] Campaigns for Avis against Hertz, Savin copiers against Xerox, and Scope against Listerine are historically regarded as successful applications of the comparative approach.

*Factors in Successful Comparative Advertising.* Almost 40 percent of TV commercials now employ a comparative approach. However, only about a quarter of these commercials (11 percent) name competing brands explicitly.[17] In business magazine ads, where we might expect to see more, the figures are actually lower, with about 24 percent comparative, and only 7 percent explicitly so.[18] The majority of comparative ads are implicit comparatives, which we do not recommend.

There seem to be three main characteristics of successful comparative campaigns.

**1.** The competitor(s) the brand is advertising against should be well-entrenched in the target audience's mind, otherwise there's no sense in pursuing a comparative approach. (The presence of an entrenched competitor is why we regard comparative advertising as a high-involvement/informational tactic—it attempts to persuade people away from the entrenched brand to our brand.) There may be several entrenched competitors—for example, in the U.S. market, Lufthansa versus American, Delta, and United; or Audi versus BMW, Lexus, Mazda, Volvo, Acura, and Mercedes-Benz.[19]

**2.** The advertised brand should dominate the presentation of the comparison both visually and verbally. However, the competitor brand(s) should be named and shown, too (making the ad explicitly comparative).

**3.** The advertised brand must be able to demonstrate advantage[20] (or equality at a lower price) on one or more important benefits sufficient to increase its overall attitude rating.

Comparative advertising also can include the refutational approach if circumstances suggest it. The National Potato Promotion Board ads, for instance, refuted the fattening claim by also comparing potatoes with other side dishes. *Refutational comparative* advertising should be tried when *two* conditions apply: (1) the target audience has objections to your brand, *and* (2) the target audience prefers a well-entrenched competitor over whom you could demonstrate superiority or at least parity.

**HI/I-9. Use a "Summary" Benefit Claim; Put Your Strongest Benefits First; and Limit the Ad to About Seven Total Benefits.** The final tactic for high-involvement/informational ads is a related set of tactics pertaining to the order and number of benefit claims. High-involvement/informational ads usually (but not always) employ multiple benefits, and the advertiser needs to decide the priority of these benefits in the creative execution of the ad.

First, a *"summary" benefit claim* should be selected as the overall conclusion to be drawn from the ad. Usually, this benefit claim will address the *emphasized* unique benefit from the I-D-U analysis of the brand's positioning (review the I-D-U model in Chapter 6). The main reason for the summary benefit claim is that, even though consumers may process the multiple benefit claims, they will usually only remember their more general, summary judgment (the brand attitude: a superbelief pertaining to their purchase or usage motive, as explained in Chapter 5).[21] The summary benefit claim is not the same as a standard slogan or tag line for the brand. Rather, it is the main copy line for *this ad's* message. It can be given prominence by repetition in broadcast commercials, or by bolder placement, such as in the headline or subheadline, in print ads.

The second related tactic is to place the brand's *strongest* benefits—that is, their benefit claims—*first* in the overall ordering of benefits. (*Exception:* direct response ads, for which a first-and-last emphasis should be employed.) If brand choice is delayed, there is a strong "primacy effect" of benefit claims on choice.[22] (With direct response, there's a strong primacy *and* a strong recency effect, since choice is immediate.) For high-involvement/informational ads,

therefore, put your best benefits first (or, in direct response ads, both first and last).

The third related tactic concerns the *number* of benefits to be mentioned in the ad—assuming that a fairly large number is needed. (This may not necessarily be the case for every high-involvement/informational brand. Attempting to switch loyal Pepsi drinkers to Coke II would be an example of just two benefits being required: cola authenticity and sweet taste.) Keller and Staelin[23] have shown that the first seven *high-importance* benefits are what mainly influence high-involvement choices; beyond this number, choice actually becomes more confusing and may lead the consumer to consider another, more concisely described brand. This recommendation is in line with the classic "magical number 7" memory chunks identified by psychologist George Miller, subsequently revised to 5 plus or minus 2.[24] Seven important benefits should be sufficient to sell almost any product, and we therefore recommend this as a practically appropriate ceiling for the number of benefit claims in high-involvement/informational ads. Note that this is an upper-limit: If you can achieve the target attitude with fewer than seven benefit claims, use the lower number.

Altogether, we have seen that the persuasion tactics for the high-involvement/informational quadrant are complex and difficult to achieve. Perhaps it's just as well that the advertiser has to work harder, because the buyer does, too: these are carefully considered purchase decisions.

## HIGH-INVOLVEMENT/TRANSFORMATIONAL TACTICS

The last of the four brand attitude strategy quadrants is high-involvement/transformational advertising. This is where the brand purchase decision is perceived as relatively high-risk, requiring attitudinal conviction before purchase, and where the appeal is *primarily* to one of the positive motivations: sensory gratification, intellectual stimulation or mastery, or social approval. We say "primarily" with some emphasis in this case because, as we shall see, high-involvement/transformational advertisements frequently have to provide *information as well.* High-involvement/transformational brand choices often are *dually motivated* in that a secondary informational motivation must be met in order to attain the primary transformational motivation.

There are many high-risk products and services that primarily meet positive motivations. These include vacations (sensory gratification), corporate "images" which influence investors' perceptions (intellectual stimulation or mastery), as well as new cars, fashion clothing, and other personal luxuries subject to reference-group influence (social approval). The high-involvement/transformational quadrant pertains to considered-purchase products where positive consumption experiences are the primary factor in brand choice.[25]

Recommended tactics for high-involvement/transformational advertising are listed in Table 9.2. Correct emotional portrayal of the motivation (consideration A) assumes more importance, as we would expect, than with informational advertising. However, because of the high-involvement aspect, there are also some important brand benefit/claim support delivery aspects (consideration B)—though not, of course, as detailed as for the high-involvement/informational strategy.

**HI/T-1. Emotional Authenticity Is Paramount and Should Be Tailored to Lifestyle Groups Within the Target Audience.** Transformational advertising puts a premium on emotional authenticity in portraying the brand's usage motivation—the emotional consequences of using the brand are the main causes of purchase. In the high-involvement version of transformational advertising, the target audience's judgment of authenticity is likely to be very personal (varying across individuals) as well as very important to the person. This is because the high risk "amplifies" the emotional consequences of a correct or incorrect brand choice. A straightforward demonstration of this for common, conspicuously consumed product categories is shown in an Australian survey[26] summarized in Table 9.3: "You can tell something about a person by the brand of _____ he or she buys." And Australians are supposed to be egalitarian!

*Individual Differences.* As Myers and Shocker[27] have observed, "user-referent" benefits are unlike other benefits, in that major individual differences in desirability are present. The high-involvement, personal nature of the choice amplifies these differences. Some examples in relation to our three positive motivations would be as follows:

- *Sensory Gratification.* Some people want gourmet taste, some want delicious taste, and others just want a filling taste in a restaurant meal.
- *Intellectual Stimulation or Mastery.* Some people want highbrow entertainment, some want middlebrow entertainment, and others want decidedly lowbrow entertainment in a movie or play.
- *Social Approval.* Most notably, people have different reference groups to whom they look as a guide

---

**TABLE 9.2**

**ADVERTISING TACTICS FOR THE HIGH-INVOLVEMENT/TRANSFORMATIONAL BRAND ATTITUDE STRATEGY**

**Consideration A (emotional portrayal of the motivation)**

| | |
|---|---|
| HI/T-1. | Emotional authenticity is paramount and should be tailored to lifestyle groups within the target audience. |
| HI/T-2. | People must identify personally with the product as portrayed in the ad and not merely like the ad. |

**Consideration B (benefit claim support for perceived brand delivery)**

| | |
|---|---|
| HI/T-3. | Many high-involvement/transformational advertisements also have to provide information. |
| HI/T-4. | Overclaiming is recommended but don't underclaim. |
| HI/T-5. | Repetition serves a buildup function (often for subsequent informational ads) and a reinforcement function. |

---

**TABLE 9.3**

**PERCENTAGE OF AUSTRALIANS AGREEING WITH THE STATEMENT "YOU CAN TELL SOMETHING ABOUT A PERSON BY THE BRAND OF _____ HE OR SHE BUYS"**

(Base = 1,300 adults)

| Product category | Percentage of respondents agreeing |
|---|---|
| Perfume (women respondents only) | 78 |
| Department store[a] | 69 |
| Wine | 68 |
| Aftershave (men respondents only) | 62 |
| Instant coffee[b] | 47 |
| Beer | 46 |
| Cigarettes | 40 |
| Toilet paper | 30 |
| Toothpaste | 27 |

[a]"Buys" was changed to "buys from" for this item.
[b]Academics will recall the classic "shopping list" study by Mason Haire done in the 1950s.

for their purchases and consumption, particularly when psychosocial risk's contribution to involvement with the brand choice decision is high.[28] For instance, in casual clothing, some people want a "preppie" look, others a "Western" look, others a "grunge" look, and so forth.

Thus, with high-involvement/transformational advertising, there are likely to be substantial individual variations *within* a given target audience (that is, within new category users, or within brand loyals, or within favorable or other-brand switchers, or within other-brand loyals) in precisely what constitutes emotional authenticity in a motivation's portrayal. Notice that we include favorable brand switchers and brand loyals even though they are already buying the brand and are now in low-involvement. For high-involvement/transformational brands, current buyers are a very important *secondary* target audience.

High-involvement/transformational advertising is therefore the only brand attitude strategy quadrant in which we would recommend segmentation *within* whichever of the prospect groups (NCU, OBS, OBL) or current customer groups (FBS or BL) constitutes the target audience. In all other quadrants, once the main benefits have been found for the target audience, it is rarely worth further segmentation because the benefits usually have quite universal appeal to that audience. However, the highly individual nature of the brand-user image benefits in high-involvement/transformational advertising makes a justifiable exception.

*Lifestyle Segmentation Within the Target Audience.* The most relevant candidate for segmentation within the target audience for high-involvement/transformational advertising is *lifestyle*. Portraying the brand user's lifestyle by showing *people* in the ad (user-as-hero, from Chapter 6) is probably the most effective tactic in high-involvement/transformational advertising because the portrayed users serve as *presenters* with inherent source effects (as will be explained later in this chapter). Lifestyle portrayals show a particular type of person experiencing positive reinforcement from using the brand.

Only larger advertisers can afford ads that appeal to different lifestyle groups in a single campaign (although the smaller advertiser can sometimes do this through the judicious use of different print media with slightly different visuals). For example, P&O cruise vacation advertising (as well as its product line) is carefully segmented to appeal to younger adults, usually singles, and older adults, usually retired, with different media and creative appeals for each of their two main demographic target audiences.

If the lifestyle groups in the advertiser's target audience are many or extremely diverse, then the advertiser should use a "straight" focus on the brand's image benefits without showing people in the ad (product-as-hero rather than user-as-hero positioning, from Chapter 6). A clever solution to the problem of multiple lifestyles *within* the overall target group is shown in the three outdoor billboard ads for Volkswagen automobiles in Italy (Figure 9.7). Here, the products are the heroes but the headlines clearly indicate the lifestyle target-user for each

**FIGURE 9.7**
A clever, culturally-appropriate, Italian ad for VW's Golf automobile models illustrating high-involvement/transformational lifestyle segmentation (three separate poster ads). This campaign appeals to the diverse target audiences in Italy; however, it was not considered for the U.S. market as its treatment of divorce is too light-hearted.
*Courtesy:* VW Audi Inc. and DDB Needham, Milan.

**Bachelor.**
New Golf GTD.

**Married.**
New Golf Variant.

**Divorced.**
New Golf Cabrio.

product. More generally, not showing people in an ad can allow possibly varying lifestyle groups to "project" themselves into the ad. This can be a good tactic if the brand happens to appeal to "discrepant" (widely varying) lifestyle groups (examples might be Cadillac automobiles and Chivas Regal scotch). Here it would seem that showing discrepant lifestyle users in ads could confuse the brand's image and perhaps alienate all lifestyle groups.

**HI/T-2. People Must Identify Personally with the Product As Portrayed in the Ad and Not Merely Like the Ad.** Regardless of whether the multiple lifestyle approach is used, everyone to whom high-involvement/transformational ads are directed should identify with the brand as portrayed in the ad. In the acceptance phase of processing the ad, the target audience decision maker must experience a "That's for me" reaction. Processing for this type of advertising is highly dependent on personal "consumption imagery"—that is, people seeing themselves driving the new car shown, or taking the vacation to the resort shown, or otherwise "putting themselves in the picture."[29]

*More Than Ad Likability.* Identification with the brand portrayal goes well beyond mere liking of the ad, which was an essential feature of low-involvement/transformational advertising. In the high-involvement version, the liking must be product (brand) focused because "peripheral" liking of the ad itself is not sufficient to influence brand attitude.[30] Of course, as with all transformational (positive motivation) advertising, the advertiser should strive to make the ad likable too. But with the high-involvement nature of the brand decision, liking of, and further than this— identification with—the *brand portrayal* is the essential factor.

In addition to the tailored emotional authenticity and brand portrayal identification tactics producing the correct emotional content, there are perceived brand delivery factors to be considered. These are examined next.

**HI/T-3. Many High-Involvement/Transformational Advertisements Also Have to Provide Information.** When we analyzed brand delivery for low-involvement/transformational advertising in Chapter 8, we commented that brand delivery is by association and often implicit. In the *high*-involvement version of transformational advertising, the benefit

claims for brand delivery are usually more explicit, in keeping with the necessary *acceptance* response in processing. The desired overall processing response is: "If I buy and use this brand, I will get these positive benefits."

The high-involvement aspect of purchasing the brand often means that there are *some* obstacles to be overcome, in the audience's mind, on the way to getting the positive benefits. For instance, vacation resorts may have hidden costs; a new car costs a lot of money, and you'd want to find out something about its

**FIGURE 9.8**
A high-involvement/transformational advertisement for Kingfisher Bay Resort that also provides information (see ad copy).
*Courtesy:* Kingfisher Bay Resort.

Fraser Island is a Garden of Eden. And Kingfisher Bay Resort is pure temptation.

## It's where Adam & Eve would holiday.

You can stay for $68 a night, per person, twin share, including transfers, between Oct 24 and Dec 17.

Call 008 072 555 or see your travel agent.

**Kingfisher Bay**
Fraser Island

technical features and service availability before you purchase one; and so on. Figure 9.8 shows an example. The ad is for Kingfisher Bay, a vacation resort, where the primary motivation is almost certainly sensory gratification. However, the ad also provides information to answer the high-involvement question raised in the prospective buyer's mind regarding how much this "paradise" vacation might cost.

Many high-involvement/transformational advertisements are therefore obliged to provide information to allay the perceived risk in purchasing the brand. Although the provision of information may be seen as meeting a negative motivation, particularly problem removal or avoidance in the reduction of purchase obstacles, it is essential to realize that the ads are not thereby informational rather than transformational. Their primary appeal remains transformational: the primary energizer of purchase is the expectation of satisfying a positive "reward" motivation. That some negative motivations may have to be removed in order to get to the reward is incidental—though of course not unimportant. Such ads should be handled tactically from a high-involvement/transformational perspective although their informational *supporting* elements would do well to take note of the high-involvement/ *informational* tactics described previously.

**HI/T-4. Overclaiming Is Recommended but Don't Underclaim.** One departure from the overclaiming and underclaiming cautions that apply to high-involvement/informational advertising is that, with high-involvement/*transformational* advertising, it is permissible—even recommended—to overclaim. Indeed, the advertiser should try to "hyperclaim" the brand's delivery on the positive motivation as much as possible. The upper limit for overclaiming will extend to all but the most outrageously exaggerated claims.

The reason for overclaiming (perhaps a more accurate term would be "peak experience" claiming) is that the benefits from high-involvement/transformational products are almost entirely subjective. Who can really say whether the advertiser is "really" overclaiming about, say, the fun of a vacation resort or the experience of driving a new car? "Proof" is subjective and is for the individual buyer or user to determine. And if you don't make strong positive claims, you may not get the purchase in the first place.

*Credence Products and Public Inflation of the Brand User's Image.* Many if not most of the benefits of high-involvement/transformational products are

difficult for the user to judge objectively, even after purchase. Economists Darby and Karni[31] call these "credence goods," forming a third category from Nelson's earlier analysis of experience goods (where trial is sufficient) and search goods (where the prospective buyer must be convinced before trying). For example, most people buy life insurance based on "faith" placed in friends or in the agent.[32] Similarly, the envy of your friends when you say you've taken a Club Med vacation or have just bought a new Mercedes SEL sports car is as much part of the product benefit as the product itself.

"Hyperclaimed" advertising for these high-involvement/transformational types of products (and services) is therefore effective in large part because it influences the public image of the product *among those who may never experience it* and thereby not have an opportunity to discount the hyperclaims. This inflated yet accepted public image then raises the buyer's own attitude to a level above its "reality" level.[33]

With high-involvement/transformational advertising, then, the recommended tactic is to overclaim (hyperclaim), even to quite an exaggerated extent, and certainly to the peak-experience level. The advertiser who *doesn't* overclaim runs the risk of not inducing purchase. And quite obviously it follows that underclaiming is usually fatal in this type of advertising.

**HI/T-5. Repetition Serves a Buildup Function (Often for Subsequent Informational Ads) and a Reinforcement Function.** Repetition is essential for transformational advertising. This final tactic duplicates the tactic for low-involvement/transformational advertising with one difference. During the buildup phase, transformational advertising alone is sufficient to induce purchase of low-involvement brands. However, for high-involvement brands, transformational advertising (on the primary motivation) is often employed to pave the way for subsequent information advertising (on the secondary motivation) or other informationally based selling methods that are necessary to finalize purchase. One of the most common examples of the transformational-followed-by-informational sequence would be new-car advertisements on television employed to interest prospective buyers in a high-involvement purchase that will be consummated only after the prospect has sought out more detailed information, either from more detailed ads (usually long-copy print ads) or from friends, auto sales staff, or auto rating publications.

*More Than Awareness Building.* The *brief* transformational ads for these *high-risk* products do not just "build awareness." They build brand awareness, certainly, but they also build *transformational brand attitude.* This largely informationless transformational "pre" advertising can be very effective in its own right. For many new-car buyers, for instance, the subsequent search for "informational" advertising, or more objective information from other sources, is frequently just to confirm a decision *already made* in favor of the brand from the transformational advertising.

*Postpurchase Reinforcement.* The second reason for repetition of transformational advertising, especially high-involvement/transformational advertising, is to provide reinforcement to those who have already purchased the brand. (This is why we included FBSs and BLs as *secondary* target audiences for high-involvement/transformational advertising; it is rarely worthwhile to have a second, low-involvement campaign especially for them even though this would be technically correct.) Confirming this second phase of the decision process, Richins and Bloch[34] found that *careful* attention to auto ads, readership of auto magazines, and asking others about cars persist for about 2 months after purchase of a car (possibly to resolve postpurchase cognitive dissonance). Transformational advertising has a vital role to play *after* purchase, in reinforcing the buyer's attitude for having made the correct choice.

High-involvement/transformational purchases are typically infrequent—such as new cars and vacations. Nevertheless, advertising's postpurchase reinforcement contributes strongly to a favorably initial attitude for buying the same brand *next* time.

## THE VisCAP MODEL OF PRESENTER SELECTION

Now that we have reviewed the creative tactics for various types of advertisements, it is time to consider one further creative decision—namely, when should you use a presenter and how should you select one? Our analysis begins with a general consideration of the presenter (or "source") effect in advertising. We next consider the situations in which an *in-ad* presenter should be used, that is, as a deliberate and explicit component of the advertising message. The VisCAP model of presenter characteristics is then introduced to show how an appropriate presenter can be selected to assist branding and persuasion.[35]

## The Presenter As the Perceived Source of the Message

Advertisements are, by definition, sponsored messages. From a processing perspective, in watching or listening to an advertising message, the presenter can be thought of as the audience's answer to the question "Who says so?"[36] This is an important question for the manager to anticipate because the audience's attitude toward the perceived source or sponsor of the advertising message can contribute strongly to the audience's attitude toward the advertised brand.

As explained by Percy and Rossiter,[37] the entities that can be processed as the perceived presenters of the message are wide-ranging. They include:

- *The industry:* For example, oil companies, and the ad industry per se
- *The product category:* Feminine-hygiene products, liquor, cigarettes, candy
- *The company:* Dow Chemical, Benetton
- *The brand name:* Apple computers, Ralph Lauren
- *The media vehicle:* Violent TV programs, *Good Housekeeping* magazine's "Seal of Approval"[38]
- *Any persons or characters or even settings shown in the ad:* The "ex-jocks" for Miller Lite, the California Raisin Board's "raisin" characters, the New York City (Manhattan) skyline

Any or all of these "sources" can produce predisposing attitudes that affect attitude toward the brand. Presenter effects are present, to a greater or lesser degree, in *all* advertising messages.

However, most of these factors are considered *elsewhere* in advertising planning. Industry and product category effects are best thought of as category attitudes (under the selling-the-category option of the category need communication effect). Brand name, used as such, is really a brand benefit claim (brand attitude) or a booster of brand benefit claims (brand equity). And media vehicle effects (if there *are* any) will be examined with media vehicle selection in Chapter 17. Settings are usually not considered as presenters, when used, but rather as brand benefits (by association). Company-as-presenter effects will be considered in the next chapter in conjunction with direct response advertising. This leaves persons and characters, and they will be our focus here.

## In-Ad Presenters

In the context of creative tactics, our concern is with in-ad presenters, that is, *people or characters included in the ad to present the brand's benefit claims.* Accordingly, whereas presenter effects are always present to some degree, in-ad presenters are present to a *large* degree. That is, their characteristics are chosen purposefully and are intended to be processed along with the brand's advertising message. The decision is a major one, creatively. Two in every three TV commercials (and virtually all infomercials) show an on-camera spokesperson for the brand, with one in every three (35 percent) emphasizing the spokesperson *as* a presenter. The latter consist of only 5 percent who are celebrities and about 30 percent who are noncelebrities in the categories listed below.[39]

People or characters in the ad may be:

- Celebrities
- Experts
- Specially created product characters (human or animated)
- People representing lifestyle groups
- An anonymous presenter shown in the ad or employed as a voice-over in TV and radio commercials

The central concern is how these in-ad presenters' characteristics affect processing of the ad and thus influence the resulting communication effects (specifically, the communication objectives and brand position) for the brand.

Hereafter, we will use the word *presenter* to refer to an in-ad presenter.

## When to Use a Presenter

There are two advertising situations in which a presenter should be considered (Table 9.4): for "boosting" communication effects and to forestall "information overload."

**WHEN TO USE A PRESENTER**

1. When one or more communication effects need "boosting" above the level attainable by standard advertising.
2. When the target audience is known to suffer "information overload" in the product category when making a brand choice (applies to high-involvement choice situations).

**When One or More Communication Effects Need "Boosting."** The principal way in which presenters work in advertising is by "boosting" (or amplifying, just like an amplifier in a stereo system does) particular communication effects.[40] Personal characteristics of the presenter can "amplify" communication effects such as brand awareness (both types) and brand attitude (all four types) and also brand purchase intention. In their boosting capacity, presenters are functioning essentially as a *conveyor* (see Chapter 7 regarding RAM-Conveyor theory)—and indeed the "creative idea" itself can be a presenter.

*Brand Awareness.* The choice of a well-known celebrity presenter, for example, often is made with the purpose of increasing brand awareness. The basic idea is that a presenter, especially a well-known celebrity, will draw attention to the ad[41]—and thus to the brand (for instance, see the Naomi Campbell[42] ad for milk in Figure 9.9). While this is generally true, the advertiser has to be very careful in the execution of presenter ads that the presenter does not attract *most* of the attention and actually *reduce* attention to the brand. This is known popularly as the "vampire effect" and can be detected by appropriate pretesting of the ad (see Chapter 19). In TV commercials, this is called the "video vampire effect" because the presenter (usually a celebrity) dominates the video part of the commercial and viewers pay insufficient attention to the brand's package, logo, or name.

Moreover—and this is essential—the presenter ad still has to adhere to the specific brand recognition or brand recall *tactics,* as detailed earlier in Chapter 8. The presenter does not "create" brand recognition or brand recall; rather, the presenter merely makes the fundamental process of *learning the association* between the category need and the brand package or name *more probable* by increasing attention to the ad's execution. Only if the presenter's likeness is used on the package (example: Reggie candy bars created by Standard Brands for baseball star Reggie Jackson) would there be a direct effect of the presenter on brand awareness—and then only on brand recognition.[43] For brand recall, in particular, there is no *direct* process linking the presenter with the brand's category-cued awareness.[44]

That celebrity presenters can increase brand recall, correctly measured as category-cued brand name recall, was shown in the analysis by Holman and Hecker (see Chapter 8, note 31), where Memorex

**FIGURE 9.9**
Celebrity presenter: Supermodel Naomi Campbell featured in the campaign for milk.
*Courtesy:* International Dairy Food Association.

tapes (Ella Fitzgerald) had far greater brand recall than TDK (no presenter), Charlie perfume (Charlie girls) than Enjoli (no presenter), and Sanka decaffeinated instant coffee (Robert Young) than Brim (no presenter). Remember that in all these cases, advertising expenditure was unrelated to brand recall.[45] We assume therefore in all these cases that the celebrity increased attention to the association between the product category cue and the brand name. Hence our inclusion, earlier, of a celebrity presenter as a tactic to be considered for brand recall.

*Brand Attitude.* The addition of a presenter to boost brand attitude (via benefit beliefs) is the most widely used application of presenter tactics. There are two main ways in which such boosting can occur:

1. By making the benefit claim appear more *extreme.* This is especially relevant for *low-*involvement (both informational and transformational) brand attitude, when extreme claims are recommended. For example, if Michael Jordan, the basketball megastar, implies to kids that Wheaties helps his performance, a much more favorable benefit belief (than from a standard claim) is likely to result.

2. By reducing counterarguing in *high-*involvement/ informational persuasion situations when the target audience is *negatively* disposed toward the brand. This relies on the "expert" role of the presenter. For instance, if heart surgeon Michael de Bakey were to tell you that garlic is good for you (he hasn't, by the way), you're much less likely to counterargue than if a mere "ad" told you.

Brand attitude boosting by a presenter requires careful selection of presenter characteristics,[46] as explained shortly in conjunction with the VisCAP model.

*Brand Purchase Intention.* Occasionally, though not often, a presenter can increase the consumer's brand purchase intention via the use of "coercive power." When Karl Malden, a powerful figure, tells you "Don't leave home without it," for American Express, the message is more likely to sink in and be obeyed. Indirect evidence of this is the fact that this slogan, developed originally for American Express traveler's checks, has been adopted as the tag line for its credit card ads too. More recently, it appears that the actor James Earl Jones was selected as a presenter for Bell Atlantic ads due to his powerful personality.

**To Forestall Information Overload.** The other advertising situation in which a presenter should be considered is for complex products or services being advertised to a nonexpert target audience. In *high-*involvement/informational situations, an expert and trustworthy presenter can save "information overloaded" consumers from having to process the benefit claims, making it easier for them to opt for global acceptance of the total attitude.[47] For instance, Art Linkletter, a trusted celebrity of bygone years, sold a lot of insurance this way in direct response ads.[48] Jake Steinfeld uses the same principle today in infomercials to sell the Body by Jake Hip & Thigh Machine.

### How to Select a Presenter Using the VisCAP Model of Presenter Characteristics

Presenters should be selected in terms of personal characteristics that are aligned with the particular communication effects to be boosted in the campaign. The communication effects to be boosted will be one or more of the brand's communication *objectives,* especially the universal communication objectives of brand awareness and brand attitude with its accompanying brand attitude strategy as analyzed in the four quadrants of the Rossiter-Percy grid.

The VisCAP model of presenter selection is shown in Table 9.5. The model consists of four major presenter characteristics: *Vis*ibility, *C*redibility, *A*ttraction, and *P*ower. The second and third characteristics each comprise two subfactors, resulting in six presenter characteristics in all. These are now discussed in turn, with examples.

### Visibility

The presenter's *visibility* refers to how well-known or recognizable he or she is from previous public exposure.

Visibility is, of course, the *celebrity* presenter's immediate edge. In contrast, noncelebrity presenters (for example, Madge for Palmolive, "Old Lonely" for Maytag washers, and Shari Belafonte for Ultra Slim-Fast) and also animated presenters (for example, the Green Giant, Charlie the Tuna, and the Pillsbury Doughboy[49]) acquire visibility only slowly from cumulative advertising exposure.

---

**TABLE 9.5**

### THE VisCAP MODEL OF PRESENTER CHARACTERISTICS ALIGNED WITH COMMUNICATION OBJECTIVES

| Presenter characteristic | Communication objective |
| --- | --- |
| 1. *Visibility* (how well-known the presenter is) | Brand awareness |
| 2. *Credibility* | |
|   a. *Expertise* (knowledgeability regarding product category) | Informational brand attitude strategy: low- *and* high-involvement |
|   b. *Objectivity* (reputation for honesty and sincerity) | Informational brand attitude strategy: high-involvement |
| 3. *Attraction* | |
|   a. *Likability* (attractive appearance and personality) | Transformational brand attitude strategy: low-involvement |
|   b. *Similarity* (to target user) | Transformational brand attitude strategy: high-involvement |
| 4. *Power* (authoritative occupation or personality) | Brand purchase intention |

---

The immediately usable visibility of celebrity presenters comes at a hefty price, however. The record is probably held by Sony Corporation, which in 1992 signed Michael Jackson for $1 billion in potential endorsement fees and royalties (for PR as well as advertising).[50] In 1989, American Express paid a rumored $5 million to sign actress Meryl Streep, then at the peak of her career, and a similar amount to sign Paul Newman, in the twilight of his career,[51] and has since added a large number of specialized celebrities at what must be an enormous total price, in what has come to be known as the "Portraits" campaign. Indeed, a U.S. company, Marketing Evaluations/TVQ, conducts regular surveys of the public's familiarity with, and liking of, various stars, and their signing fees are fairly well correlated with familiarity. In 1989, Ms. Streep's familiarity rating with 18-and-over adults was 85 percent; Mr. Newman's, 93 percent. Visibility can wane, however, and in the same year Texaco dropped long-time celebrity presenter Bob Hope, now over 90 years old, from his famous presenter role.[52]

Celebrities can also become more visible for the wrong reasons, such as failing performance (for example, John McEnroe at times toward the end of his career and, even more sadly, Bjorn Borg with his numerous ill-fated comebacks, though he's now doing quite well on the seniors' tennis circuit) or moral turpitude (basketball star Magic Johnson's case is well known, as are those of Mike Tyson and O. J. Simpson; in addition, Bruce Willis and Ringo Starr both had well-publicized drinking problems while under contract to alcoholic beverage companies). In fact, advertisers in the United States and Australia can now take out "death and disgrace" insurance policies to cover themselves against celebrity presenters who die or "morally stray."[53] There is no insurance against reduced visibility caused by simple loss of fame, however!

Perhaps for these reasons—cost and risk—celebrity presenters are used in only about 5 percent of regular noninfomercial TV commercials in the United States[54] (another 30 percent use *non*celebrity presenters or animated characters as presenters). And, speaking of death, deceased celebrities (such as James Dean, Humphrey Bogart, Louis Armstrong, and Elvis Presley) are in vogue with creatives at present, perhaps because they have well-established visibility, tend to be available at a lower fee (to the deceased's estate) and, barring posthumous revelations, don't get into trouble.[55]

Also, as mentioned, there is the "vampire effect." Although this is an executional problem which should be correctable, it has led to celebrities being removed from ads, notably Catherine Deneuve from a Lincoln Mercury ad and Linda Day George from an RCA Colortrack TV-set ad when eye-tracking research discovered them to be too attractive, drawing attention *away* from the product.[56]

An alleged visibility problem with celebrity presenters is "overexposure" for those who endorse "too many" products. Ed McMahon, Arnold Palmer and Bill Cosby are among the celebrities thought to suffer this phenomenon.[57] However, we do *not* believe this to be a problem—as long as the product categories are diverse. A celebrity draws attention to an ad—any ad—and as long as he or she does not signal a competing brand *in that category,* there's no reason to avoid an "overexposed" celebrity.[58]

**Visibility Hook.** Going back to our recommendations on brand awareness tactics earlier in this chapter, it helps to use a mnemonic device to link the brand to the category. In the presenter situation, it helps if the presenter has a visibility "hook" to the product category (for brand recall) or to the brand (for brand recognition). An amusing example of this (for brand recall) is company president Mr. Frank Perdue as a presenter for Perdue chicken. In the words of one commentator, Mr. Perdue is "scrawny and baldish, with an egg-shaped head and a nose like a beak."[59] He looks like a chicken! Not too many advertisers have such luck. In the Naomi Campbell ad for milk, for instance, *the reader* has to make the association between the category need (dieting, or more specifically, attaining a figure like Naomi Campbell's) and the brand name (milk).

Presenters can sometimes be *created* to have a visibility hook to the brand or the package (for brand recognition). Examples are Betty Crocker for the Betty Crocker brand of cake mix and other cooking ingredients, Tony the Tiger for Kellogg's cereals, and numerous characters from children's cartoon programs. In these examples, there is a visual tie-in between the characters in the ads and package recognition in the store.[60]

### Credibility: (a) Expertise

Presenter credibility consists of two characteristics, expertise and objectivity. A spokesperson can be perceived as expert but not objective, for example,

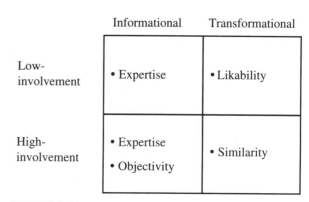

|  | Informational | Transformational |
|---|---|---|
| Low-involvement | • Expertise | • Likability |
| High-involvement | • Expertise<br>• Objectivity | • Similarity |

**FIGURE 9.10**
The *essential* presenter characteristics by brand attitude quadrant.

Richard Nixon; or vice versa—for example, Jimmy Carter may have had the opposite problem of being perceived as very honest but not overly expert. The advertiser generally seeks *both* expertise and objectivity in a presenter, but the two characteristics can vary independently and have specialized relevance to the brand attitude quadrants (see Figure 9.10). Let's first consider expertise.

**Expertise and Informational Brand Attitude.** Expertise (the perceived knowledgeability of the presenter regarding the product category) is most relevant when the advertisement is based on an *informational* brand attitude strategy—either low- or high-involvement.

- In *low*-involvement/informational advertisements, the presenter's perceived expertise may be the solely effective benefit claim booster and the basis of the learned brand attitude.
- In *high*-involvement/informational advertising, where acceptance of the brand attitude proposition is essential, the presenter's expertise helps to prevent counterarguing and thereby to increase the likelihood of acceptance of claims supporting brand attitude. Also, in "information overload" situations, the presenter's expertise seems necessary for the presenter-fallback acceptance process to operate.

**Expertise Hook.** An immediately evident expertise "hook" is what the advertiser seeks. The Robert Young campaign which launched Sanka decaffeinated coffee, a presumably "healthier" form of coffee, provided an interesting example of the credibility hook. Sanka's advertising capitalized on Robert Young's

**FIGURE 9.11**
Jimmy Connors has an obvious expertise "hook" for the low-involvement/informational pain reliever Nuprin.
*Courtesy:* Bristol-Myers Squibb.

then well-known TV-program role as "Dr. Marcus Welby," and although real doctors cannot endorse products, make-believe doctors can. More recently, tennis veteran Jimmy Connors, presumably an expert on dealing with pain, just happened to reach the semi-finals of the 1991 U.S. Open while appearing in a new campaign for Bristol-Myers Squibb company's Nuprin brand of pain reliever (the slogan: "Nupe it"; see Figure 9.11). This increased his presentership *visibility,* adding to his expertise. Sales rose 23 percent in one month, introducing many new triers to the brand.[61]

Some notable failures who apparently did not have an expertise hook for the respective products include John Houseman for McDonald's (low-involvement/informational, probably, since most people have previously tried McDonald's as a solution to the "quick meal" category need) and Bill Cosby for E.F. Hutton investment services (high-involvement/informational, probably, or perhaps transformational with an informational underlay). Misra and Beatty[62] demonstrated, in a well-controlled experiment using fictitious new products, that Clint Eastwood had the right "hook" for Unitough jeans, Carol Burnett for a board game called "Funnybone," and gymnast Mary Lou Retton for a milk-additive energy drink, whereas these same celebrities failed when (in the experiment) these products were swapped around.

The advertiser must be sure that the presenter's expertise will be *immediately perceived* by the target audience in processing the ad. This can be assured by inserting an "expertise prompt"—extra copy telling people what the presenter is expert in.[63] For instance, the "dog breeder" campaign for PAL dog food does this.

As an alternative to individual presenters as experts, an ad may refer to entire *occupational categories* for endorsement. A classic campaign was "Four out of five doctors recommend Bayer [aspirin]." More recently, there is "Tylenol. Recommended the most by people who know the most," a claim which is followed by a list of expert categories—general practitioners, gastroenterologists, and so forth.

### Credibility: (b) Objectivity

The other component of credibility is objectivity (the presenter's reputation for truthfulness or sincerity). Some theorists refer to objectivity as trustworthiness. However, trustworthiness would seem to imply a degree of expertise (as in "trustworthy source") so objectivity is the preferred and more separable characteristic.

**Objectivity and High-Involvement/Informational Brand Attitude.** Objectivity, as indicated in Figure 9.10, is most relevant for the *high*-involvement/informational brand attitude strategy quadrant because the brand attitude benefits must be *convincingly* presented.

Objectivity is much less relevant for the *low*-involvement/informational quadrant because, here, the brand attitude merely has to be rote-learned, not fully accepted prior to trial of the brand. This does *not* mean that low-involvement/informational presenters should look dishonest (although some do), but rather simply that they don't have to be highly positive on the objectivity characteristic. In a wonderful illustration of this point, Dreyer's Grand Light Ice Cream (a low-fat product and clearly low-involvement/informational) experienced "phenomenal sales" when the company employed convicted liar John Ehrlichman, famous for his part in the Watergate scandal that led to President Nixon's demise, as a spokesperson in a very creative spoof on believability.[64] So many people complained about Mr. Ehrlichman's moral character that the campaign was discontinued after only a month, despite its success.

**Objectivity Hook: Natural or Stage-Managed.** Some celebrity presenters have a "hooklike" reputation for honesty and sincerity. The signing of James

Stewart for Firestone tires some years ago was regarded in advertising circles as a contract coup. Also, TV news announcers such as Linda Ellerbee are frequently sought as presenters because of their perceived objectivity. Apparently to preserve their status and reputation (in a word, their objectivity) in the United States as "serious" actors, many well-known Hollywood stars will *not* do commercials in America but have done them in Japan, where they are extremely highly paid. The list is lengthy and includes Harrison Ford for Kirin beer, Jodie Foster for Caffee Latte, Demi Moore for Lux shampoo, Charlie Sheen for Modelo shoes, Pierce Brosnan (the new James Bond) for Lark cigarettes, and Madonna for Shochu liquor.[65] (The key characteristic for most of these products actually is likability, not objectivity, as they are mostly low-involvement/transformational products—see shortly—but the movie stars' fear of doing U.S. ads is about objectivity.)

However, objectivity is a personality characteristic that can easily be found in noncelebrity presenters and can fairly easily be *stage-managed* during commercial production. Objectivity is partly a function of eye movements and facial cues and very strongly a function of *voice* and speech cues.[66]

*Facial Cues.* The folk wisdom that some individuals just seem to have "an honest face" is good enough for advertising: perceived objectivity is what counts. However, facial cues can to some extent be stage-managed—for older men, no "5 o'clock shadow," for example; but for younger men, filming ads after his 2-day beard's growth is quite the thing! Eyeglasses (but not sunglasses) are another well-known but nevertheless effective ruse. With glasses added, the same individuals, both men and women, are perceived as more intelligent, reliable, and honest.[67]

*Voice Cues.* Voice cues are one reason male voices are used as voice-overs in nearly 80 percent of TV commercials, even when the other characters are women.[68] Highly paid male voice-over artists on TV and radio (unnamed, of course) have included Michael Douglas for Infiniti, Gene Hackman for United, and Lloyd Bridges for Hertz and Paine Webber.[69] Not only do male voices tend to attract greater attention than female voices, male voices are also, in general, perceived as less nervous, less emotional, and more logical—all traits that should increase perceived objectivity.[70] Clearly, for broadcast commercials, managers not only must evaluate the

presenter visually but also must test the voice. Exemplifying the importance of voice, a British postproduction house, Tape Gallery, offers a database of 127 voice-over artists who have recorded 920 voice clips, which can be sampled by advertisers for $16 per clip or an annual fee of $92.[71] In speech itself, cues to *perceived* deception (actual deception is almost impossible to detect) are slow speech rate, hesitations, and (on TV only) "nervous" postural shifts.[72]

Stage-managing, therefore, is an important creative (production) tactic for presenter objectivity. Another important consideration is the legal aspect: see chapter appendix 9C, Legal Requirements and Objectivity.

### Attraction: (a) Likability

Presenter attractiveness or, to use a more suitably general word, presenter *attraction,* consists of two characteristics: likability and similarity. These can be independent characteristics.[73] For instance, Popeye, for Quaker Oats, is likable but not similar to the target audience; whereas "Mrs. Olson," for Folgers' coffee, may be similar but not necessarily likable. The two characteristics can be selected independently.

**Likability and Low-Involvement/Transformational Brand Attitude.** Likability (an attractive physical appearance and personality) is most relevant to *transformational* brand attitude, particularly in the *low*-involvement/transformational quadrant (see Figure 9.10). This is because the presenter's likability serves as a positive stimulus that contributes to the positive motivation's portrayal, as explained previously in the tactics for low-involvement/transformational advertising.

Likability is a general personality trait, so it is not really appropriate to speak of a likability "hook" to a specific product or brand. (However, the physical attractiveness aspect of likability can function as a perceived *expertise* "hook" when used to advertise physical-enhancement products;[74] for example, Cindy Crawford for Revlon cosmetics.) In the general case, however, likability refers in an uncomplicated way to the use of attractive and popular people as presenters in ads.

Several celebrities rate very highly on the likability factor. For TV personalities, Marketing Evaluations, Inc., of Port Washington, New York, conducts a "Performer Q" survey of performers' popularity amongst viewers.[75] Among the high scorers in past years have been: Michael Landon for Kodak, Bill Cosby for Jell-O and Coca-Cola, James Garner for Polaroid, and Bob Hope for Texaco. More recently, seven of the 10 most popular presenters are women, with Cindy Crawford for Revlon and Pepsi, Candice Bergen for Sprint, Bill Cosby for Jell-O (still!), and Elizabeth Taylor for White Diamonds perfume heading the list.[76]

A feature of Performer Q, although we don't mean to advocate any particular rating service, is that the likability score is based simultaneously on the visibility factor. The quotient, Q, reflects the performer's popularity among those viewers who *recognize* the performer. Accordingly, past performers such as Gilda Radner and Helen Hayes achieved high Q scores because, although they were not very widely recognized, those viewers who did recognize them really like them. This knowledge can be very useful when appealing to particular target audiences and can save on the cost of a bigger-name celebrity. Bob Hope and Elizabeth Taylor, for instance, still have tremendous appeal to the older generation, and that's the growth segment.[77]

### Attraction: (b) Similarity

The other component of attraction is similarity (of the presenter, to the target user). This similarity relates to the *user* role: the presenter as user of the product or service compared with the typical target audience member as user.

**Similarity and Low-Involvement/Transformational Brand Attitude.** In *low*-involvement/transformational advertising, *likability,* not similarity, is paramount. In fact, "positive dissimilarity" should be used to make a more *extreme claim of endorsement.* Positive dissimilarity means that you should choose a presenter who represents the target user's *ideal* self-image. For instance, there is hardly a child or teenager who can slam-dunk a basketball like Shaquille O'Neal or skate like Nancy Kerrigan—but most would *like* to be able to emulate these feats. Advertising for athletic shoes, jeans, and for drugstore beauty products allows consumers to vicariously attain the presenter's image and thereby at least temporarily enhance their own self image, at a fairly low cost.

**Similarity and High-Involvement/Transformational Brand Attitude.** Similarity to the target user is most relevant in *high*-involvement/transformational advertising. The reason is again as stated in the creative tactics for this brand attitude strategy quadrant earlier: The target audience must *identify* with the emotional portrayal in the ad, and this is enhanced by showing people in the ad whose lifestyles are similar to those of target audience members.[78] However, the purpose is still to *transform* the target user's self-image. Thus, an "aspirational" increase toward a *somewhat* more ideal self-image must be attempted. The recommendation for high-involvement/transformational presenters would therefore be to make them *equal to or slightly better than* the typical target audience individual's *real* self-image (equality is the starting point because individuals typically exaggerate slightly their real self-image).[79] This means that market specialist companies employing user-as-hero advertising for products or services such as new homes, new automobiles, hotels, packaged tours, or catering services must closely study the sort of customers they are likely to attract and then, to be sure, must take the presenter or models in the advertising *"up" just a little.* As we said previously, lifestyle segmentation makes sense in this quadrant (see tactic HI/T-1). *These* presenters can then "hyperclaim" on the transformational benefits of the product or service; but hyperclaims won't work if the target audience cannot identify with the presenter to begin with.

### Power

Power, in the sense of an authoritative occupation or personality, is the sixth and final presenter characteristic in the VisCAP model. Power can increase brand purchase intention, though not attitude, by appearing to command the audience to act. It is only occasionally relevant in advertising.

**Power and Problem Avoidance Motivation.** Power is relevant for products or services sold via an element of "fear appeal" (a type of problem avoidance motivation). These *may* include pharmaceutical or medicinal products, insurance, some financial services, and, of course, public safety campaigns.

The occupational "hook" to power in a presenter may be seen in Robert Young's campaign for Sanka (doctor), and Karl Malden's campaign for American Express Traveler's Checks (policeman-detective from *The Streets of San Francisco*), which was later extended to American Express Green Card advertising.

The personality "hook" to power may also be present with Karl Malden, as well as in the late David Janssen's campaign for Excedrin (harrassed as "The

Fugitive"), and Arnold Schwarzenegger's campaigns for his "Terminator" movies. These actors have an authoritative appearance and voice. Public safety campaigns, too, typically select authoritative personalities as presenters or voice-over artists.

If the motivation for action has some basis in fear, then a powerful presenter is appropriate.

### Use of the VisCAP Model and Evaluation of the Presenter's Profile

The VisCAP model can be used in two ways:

1. As a qualitative checklist, for managers to evaluate potential presenters.
2. In a more precise quantitative rating format, to measure the *target audience's* perceptions of presenters.

Qualitative[80] use of the VisCAP model by managers has considerable face validity in the sense that the presenter, ideally, should have an obvious and quickly perceived "hook" to the product via the to-be-boosted communication effect or effects. Without this hook, quite frankly, it may not be worth testing the presenter further.

Quantitative ratings of potential presenters by a sample of target audience prospects can further improve presenter selection. The VisCAP model of presenter characteristics provides a *profile* of six characteristics—in terms of which a potential presenter may be negative, neutral, or positive. (Rating scales for the VisCAP characteristics are provided in the advertising research section in Chapter 19.) In terms of the overall profile, the presenter must be *positive* on those characteristics relevant to the to-be-boosted communication effects and *not negative* on the other communication effects. By "not negative," we mean that neutral is satisfactory and that positive is fine too, even though these other effects don't need boosting. But it is fatal for a presenter to be negative on a communication objective that attained its target level satisfactorily before using the presenter. For instance, it has been commented that Bill Cosby is not a helpful presenter for Kodak, because Kodak's "quality image" is apparently *higher* than Mr. Cosby's, high as that may be.[81]

**Testing Presenters and the Alternatives.** The manager should test a nonpresenter version of the advertisement first. Then, if boosting communication effects is required, a noncelebrity presenter (with the correct characteristics) should be tested next. If the noncelebrity presenter is insufficient to attain the communication objectives, then a celebrity presenter may be considered. Alternatively, boosting can be pursued by strengthening the advertisement's brand awareness stimuli or brand attitude benefit claims visually or verbally, without using a presenter. In a notable example of this, Kentucky Fried Chicken (KFC) in 1995 dropped the Colonel Sanders character as its longtime spokesman when Y&R developed the new nonpresenter campaign "Everybody needs a little KFC."[82]

### SUMMARY

Creative tactics for achieving high-involvement brand attitude objectives (create, increase, modify, or change) are different and more detailed than those for low-involvement brand attitude objectives. High-involvement with the brand purchase decision means that advertising claims—whether stated verbally or implied visually—are *carefully considered* and must be *accepted* by the target audience if purchase of the brand is to result.

For *high-involvement/informational* brand attitude, the target audience must be convinced by careful reasoning; the tactics in this quadrant are closer to the "textbook" tactics for attitude creation and change. Early in the product category life cycle, the ad has to emotionally sell the category need, and the target audience has to accept the ad's main points (however, they don't have to like the ad's execution as such). Acceptance of the ad's benefit claims requires "engineering" them to the target audience's *prior* attitude, without overclaiming or underclaiming for the *target* attitude. Additional tactics to consider are using an expert, objective presenter; trying a refutational approach if the target audience is negatively predisposed; and employing an explicit comparative approach if you're a small brand taking on a larger entrenched competitor. Multiple benefit claims can be (and usually are) used; however, use a "summary" benefit claim; put your strongest claims first; and limit the total number of benefit claims to about seven, as more than this will overload the prospective buyer.

For *high-involvement/transformational* brand attitude strategy, the primary purchase motive is transformational but information may have to be provided as well. For the transformational main claim or claims, emotional authenticity is paramount but may have to be differentially tailored to lifestyle groups within the target audience; and it *is* recommended to overclaim for transformational benefits, although any informational benefits should, as in the previous quadrant, not be overclaimed.

A *presenter* with special characteristics should be considered in advertising when particular communication effects require a "boost," depending on the communication objectives of the campaign. If any of the brand's communication effects—brand awareness, brand attitude, and brand purchase intention—are suspected to be below the maximum attainable for the target audience using a "straight" ad, then the manager should try a presenter with the aim of amplifying these effects.

Including a presenter is one creative technique for making low-involvement brand attitude benefit claims more extreme. Sometimes, the presenter's endorsement is the *sole* benefit. This approach can be used in low-involvement brand choice, and also in high-involvement brand choice in product categories where a majority of decision makers suffer "information overload."

Presenters must be chosen very carefully so that their characteristics are aligned with the particular communication effects to be boosted. A useful model to help managers in making this selection is our Vis-CAP model. Although we discussed the six presenter characteristics in this model as separate presenter dimensions, the manager should seek a presenter who offers a *profile* of characteristics that have positive "hooks" to the targeted (to-be-boosted) communication objectives and is not negative on the others.

## APPENDIX

## 9A. Cognitive Response Theory

Acceptance responses were first identified in a classic series of studies of persuasion by Hovland, Janis, and their colleagues at Yale University in the 1950s.[83] However, the full importance of acceptance as a processing response was realized only later, with the emergence of *cognitive response theory*.[84] Cognitive response theory enlightens our understanding of high-involvement persuasion and, in ad testing, helps to diagnose a high-involvement ad's effectiveness (see Chapter 19).

The phenomenon of cognitive response can be explained as follows. When an individual is exposed to an advertising message, he or she often attempts to relate the expected and actual information in the message to his or her existing knowledge about the product or brand (exemplified

in the chapter in Figure 9.2). In seeking a relationship between new information and existing knowledge, the individual usually will generate a number of message-relevant thoughts or images that may support or oppose the new information. The thoughts or images—cognitive responses—originate from a prior attitude toward the brand (for a familiar brand), from a prior attitude toward the product category (for a new brand in a familiar product category), or from the advertisement itself when there is no prior attitude (for a completely new product from the potential buyer's standpoint). If the individual's thoughts or images are primarily favorable, a positive shift in brand attitude will occur; if these thoughts or images are primarily unfavorable, a negative shift in brand attitude will occur.

Cognitive response theory assumes that the potential buyer is *motivated to try to make sense of* incoming information from the advertisement in order to formulate or adjust his or her brand attitude. However, this is likely to occur only if the buyer is *highly involved* with the purchase decision. If the potential buyer is highly involved with the purchase decision, cognitive (acceptance or, contrary to the advertiser's usual intent, rejection) responses are *necessary* in processing if the advertisement is to have an effect on brand attitude.

Acceptance responses during processing—in other words, positive cognitive responses—are also necessary if the advertisement is to have an effect on category need, hard-sell induced brand purchase intention, and purchase facilitation. This is because, as previously explained, these communication effects function as (high-involvement) attitudes when the individual is processing the ad.

## 9B. Explicit Comparative Advertising—Research Results

We base our recommendation of explicit comparative advertising on a valuable study by Pechmann and Stewart.[85] All previous studies had shown no advantage of direct comparative advertising—but these null results had been obtained under "laboratory" conditions in which attention to the ads was virtually assured or "forced." Pechmann and Stewart were able to use ad testing data from Response Systems Corporation in which consumers were shown the comparative ads in a "clutter" context along with other commercials in a TV program; thus, attention in this test occurred more similarly to natural, on-air exposure conditions. The database for their study consisted of 234 explicit comparative ads, 315 implicit comparative ads, and 467 standard (noncomparative) ads. Pechmann and Stewart categorized the advertised brands in terms of relative market share from small (brands that had attained less than or equal to half the market share that would be expected if shares were distributed equally according to the number of brands in the category) through to large (brands that had relative shares of greater than 2.5 times their expected share, that is, virtual monopolists). The main dependent variable we are interested in is the category-adjusted "persuasion" score (ARS Persuasion[sm]) which is calculated as the percentage of consumers choosing the brand, from a number of competing alternatives, after exposure to the advertising, minus the percentage who choose it before exposure.

The advantageous results for explicit comparative advertising in the Pechmann and Stewart study occurred *only* for small brands and large brands (Table 9.6). Most interestingly, standard ads and implicit comparisons actually *hurt* the (very) small brands severely, in that they lost virtually all of their preexposure customers after exposure! However, explicit comparative advertising for these low share brands increased persuasion by + 10 percent (relative to zero persuasion), which is not much (but it is better than a loss). Thus, direct comparative advertising *should* be used by very small (including late-entrant new) brands *instead of* standard ads.

For medium-share brands, standard advertising was best. Implicit comparative advertising (against an unnamed competitor) tended to hurt the brand, and explicit comparative advertising was not as effective as standard advertising. Medium-share brands should therefore not bother with comparative ads.

At the other extreme, (very) high share brands showed a massive increase in preexposure-to-postexposure purchase intention when using explicit comparative advertising. Whereas standard advertising and implicit comparative advertising *also* worked well for dominant brands, explicit comparative advertising produced approximately double the persuasion effect of the other types of ads. Why, then, do we not recommend explicit comparative advertising for very high share brands? If the dominant brand is a virtual monopolist (for instance, AT&T in the U.S. long-distance telephone market with over 60 percent market share), then our value judgment is that its explicit comparative advertising is predatory; the leader can do very well with normal advertising and should "stand on its own two feet" (explicit comparative advertising may prove irresistible for a market leader under threat, however, and we have to say that it works, in television ads). If market leadership is shared by two dominant brands (for instance, Coke and Pepsi in the U.S. market, but not elsewhere, where Coke is a virtual monopolist), then we believe explicit comparative advertising is a "no win" game because the other dominant brand can easily, and equally effectively, retaliate.[86]

For *print* ads, and again using realistic exposure conditions, Pechmann and Stewart[87] found initial attention and subsequent persuasion advantages *only* for small brands taking on large brands. Explicit comparative ads did *not* help large brands in print advertising (perhaps because there is too much opportunity for the reader to regard large brands' comparative advertising as unfair). Nor did they help medium brands. This reinforces our recommendation that explicit comparative advertising should be used by small brands against an entrenched larger competitor.[88]

# 9C. Legal Requirements and Objectivity

A question often occurring in the public's mind relating to objectivity is the issue of whether presenters must, in fact, be *users* of the products they endorse. Legal-marketing expert Dorothy Cohen[89] provides a good summary of the Federal Trade Commission's guidelines in this regard. The two most frequent concerns are product usage and financial gain.

---

**TABLE 9.6**

**PERSUASIVENESS OF DEGREES OF COMPARATIVE ADVERTISING FOR LARGE, MEDIUM, AND SMALL BRANDS**

(*Entries in parentheses are numbers of commercials. Entries in table are percentage changes in purchase intention from pre- to postexposure and have been adjusted according to product category norms.*)

| | Standard commercials (%) | Implicit comparative commercials (%) | Explicit comparative commercials (%) |
|---|---|---|---|
| Large brands[a] (185) | + 74 | + 117 | + 186 |
| Medium brands (609) | + 28 | − 26 | + 8 |
| Small brands[b] (222) | − 109 | − 100 | + 10 |
| Average of all brands (1,016) | + 4 | − 12 | + 40 |

[a]Large means very large: brands with market share over 2.5 times the share that would obtain if all brands in the category were equal. For instance, if there were five brands in the category, a "large" brand had over 50 percent market share; if 10 brands, over 25 percent market share; and so on.
[b]Small means very small: brands with market share less than or equal to 0.5 times the share that would obtain if all brands in the category were equal. For instance, if there were five brands in the category, a "small" brand had 10 percent or less market share; if 10 brands, 5 percent or less market share; and so on. Although these were brands already on the market, we generalize the results to new brands, which of course must start small *when* there is already an entrenched large brand or brands in the category.

*Source:* Adapted from Pechmann and Stewart, 1991; see note 85.

Generally, if a *special-presenter* advertisement implies that the presenter uses the brand, then he or she must in fact use it. For example, in Ogilvy & Mather's "Do you know me" campaign and later the "Portraits" campaign, both for American Express, the agency would only sign personalities who had been cardholders for a year or more. Moreover, the advertiser may be required to check "at reasonable intervals" to ensure that the spokesperson continues to be a user if the campaign is continued.

The legal situation is more ambiguous with *consumers-as-presenters*. Consumers who deliver testimonials implying that they are *experienced* users must have a factual usage history. However, consumers interviewed as unwitting and random participants in "hidden camera" tests need not be bona fide users other than in the test. Advertisers can be selective about which interview test results to use in the advertising, although they must be able to substantiate that the average consumer can expect comparable performance from the brand.

Further, advertisers are required to disclose any financial connection that a presenter may have with the brand or company if this is not evident, other than the fee paid for presenting. For Healthy Choice presenter Mike Harper, who was then the CEO of ConAgra company, for instance, the financial connection would be evident. However, if an outside presenter is a stockholder in the company, this must be disclosed.

There are many other legal issues surrounding the use of presenters, and these aren't always as rule-bound as the above cases. For example, the use of "lookalikes" for living celebrities is sometimes fought by suit and won (for example, Princess Diana, Barbra Streisand), as are "soundalikes" (singer Patti Page lodged a suit on this score[90]). Deceased celebrity characters are also a legal quagmire. For example, the estate of Groucho Marx has successfully prevented unauthorized use of the "Groucho" character, whereas Bela Lugosi's estate lost entitlement to the "Dracula" character because Lugosi himself had not exploited this persona outside films.[91]

In general, it seems that consumers are reasonably well protected against unobjective presenter testimonials in ads. In fact, the self-regulatory and FTC guidelines are probably stricter than most members of the public realize. And, even allowing for a normal degree of consumer skepticism about endorsements in ads, the critical factor is probably the perceived *emotional* sincerity of the presentation itself, underlining the importance of correct emotional portrayal in advertising.

## NOTES

1. This average correlation between attitude and subsequently measured behavior comes from a meta-analysis of social psychology studies dealing with high-involvement issues. See S. J. Kraus, Attitudes and the prediction of behavior: A meta-analysis of the empirical literature, *Personality and Social Psychology Bulletin,* 1995, *21* (1), pp. 59–75. Actually, our estimate from his data, weighted to reflect nonstudent respondents, would be .42.

2. John A. Howard deserves full credit for emphasizing the essential dependence of product life cycles on consumer life cycles, which entail different stages of decision making: from extended problem solving (introduction) to limited problem solving (growth) to routinized response behavior (maturity and decline). See J. A. Howard, *Consumer Behavior: Application of Theory,* New York: McGraw-Hill, 1977, especially chapter 1.

3. For an excellent explanation and demonstration of the irrelevance of ad likability in mediating high-involvement/informational brand purchase decisions, see L. Percy and M. R. Lautman, Creative strategy, consumer decision goals, and attitudes toward the ad and advertised brand, Paper presented at the 3rd Annual Advertising and Consumer Psychology Conference, Ted Bates Advertising, New York, June 14–15, 1984.

4. It should be realized that brand loyals in high-risk product categories *also* have a strongly held (loyal) attitude, even though the decision to repeat purchase is, for them, now low-involvement.

5. The relationship of cognitive responses to *initial attitude* in *high*-involvement choices is discussed in L. Percy and J. R. Rossiter, *Advertising Strategy: A Communication Theory Approach,* New York: Praeger, 1980. Also see J. R. Rossiter and L. Percy, *Advertising and Promotion Management,* New York: McGraw-Hill, 1987, chapter 8.

6. See C. W. Sherif, M. Sherif, and R. E. Nebergall, *Attitude and Attitude Change,* Philadelphia: Saunders, 1965; also W. J. McGuire, The nature of attitudes and attitude change, in G. Lindzey and E. Aronson, eds., *The Handbook of Social Psychology,* vol. 3, Reading, MA: Addison-Wesley, 1969, pp. 135–314; and L. Percy and J. R. Rossiter, same reference as in note 5.

7. Although almost certainly in a low-involvement product category unless aimed at cola-loyals, 7UP would have to win a prize for the most original restatement of an existing benefit: "7UP . . . the *uncola*."

8. R. A. Bauer and D. F. Cox, Rational vs. emotional communications: A new approach, in D. F. Cox, ed., *Risk Taking and Information Handling in Consumer Behavior,* Cambridge, MA: Harvard University Press, 1967, pp. 469–486. This paper was first published in L. Arons and M. May, eds., *Television and Human Behavior,* New York: Appleton-Century-Crofts, 1963, but business school libraries are more likely to have the later reference.

9. R. E. Petty and J. T. Cacioppo, Issue involvement can increase or decrease persuasion by enhancing message-relevant cognitive responses, *Journal of Personality and Social Psychology,* 1979, *37* (10), pp. 1915–1926.

10. An interesting but largely academic phenomenon is when the target audience already has a *positive* attitude and a favorable but weak argument is presented. This can result in a more positive final attitude due to "bolstering" by the favorable audience. For instance, if you are a New York Yankees "brand" loyal and a friend says the Yankees are just an "okay" team, your retort would probably be "Whaddaya mean, *just* an okay team!" The weak argument of your friend would cause you to defend your loyalty and, in doing so, develop an even stronger favorable attitude. However, we would not recommend the use of this tactic in advertising. For one, it's too risky when the ad may be seen or heard by many not-so-loyal customers; the weak claim will backfire. Second, a positive prior attitude means a *low-*involvement brand choice, and we have already demonstrated that an extreme claim should be used in this situation.

11. This was a strong rumor in the advertising industry during the "Smile" slogan's use in the early 1980's.

12. For a review of this literature and some interesting examples, see A. R. Pratkanis and E. Aronson, *Age of Propaganda,* New York: W. H. Freeman & Co., 1991, chapter 17.

13. A test of the refutational approach by Sawyer is very instructive because it is one of the few studies in the advertising research literature to examine the effects of advertising strategies on *different* target audiences. Table 9.7 shows an example of conventional supportive ad copy used by Sawyer, together with the refutational version. Note that the refutational version mentions the likely objection, "Why pay $1.98 for a ballpoint pen?" and then attempts to refute it with, "You pay $1.98 for a Parker, but you never have to buy another." Five pairs of supportive and refutational ads for five brands were employed in the experiment, so the results do not depend on just this one ad. The refutational approach was more successful than the supportive approach against a negative audience (users of other brands). However, even the refutational approach, in this experiment, could not improve negatively disposed consumers' attitudes sufficiently to get them to buy the brand. This overall failure represents an average across all negative consumers, and the results really should have been analyzed further to see how many *individuals* were favorably moved enough to purchase the brand; however, the average result suggests that the proportion of individuals moved to purchase would be disappointingly small. Remember, we

| TABLE 9.7 |
|---|

**AN EXAMPLE OF THE REFUTATIONAL APPROACH USED IN ADVERTISING PARKER PENS**

**Supportive ad copy**

Just one could be all you ever need. At $1.98 it's the best pen value in the world . . . .

**Refutational ad copy**

Why pay $1.98 for a ballpoint pen? You can get them for 49¢, 69¢, or for free. . . . The kind that skip, stutter, and run out of ink.

You pay $1.98 for a Parker, but you never have to buy another.

*Source:* A. G. Sawyer, see note 13, *Journal of Marketing Research.* Adapted from Table 1, p. 25. Used by permission of American Marketing Association.

said that negatively disposed audiences with strongly held attitudes may not be worth trying to win over. See A. G. Sawyer, The effects of repetition of refutational and supportive advertising appeals, *Journal of Marketing Research,* 1973, *10* (1), pp. 23–33.

14. Objection, your honor, *Advertising Age,* December 19, 1994, p. 19.

15. C. Pechmann and S. Ratneshwar, The use of comparative advertising for brand positioning: Association versus differentiation, *Journal of Consumer Research,* 1991, *18* (3), pp. 145–160.

16. PepsiCo decides to play hard ball in soft drinks ad wars, *The Australian,* January 20, 1995, p. 30.

17. These are 1986 figures for *pretested* TV commercials, which would be *more likely* to include comparative ones because of the risks of using this format. However, observation suggests a rising trend, and we believe these figures would be close to accurate today. See D. W. Stewart and D. H. Furse, *Effective Television Advertising: A Test of 1000 Commercials,* Lexington, MA: Lexington Books, 1986.

18. L. E. Swayne and T. H. Stevenson, Comparative advertising in horizontal business publications, *Industrial Marketing Management,* 1987, *16* (1), pp. 71–76.

19. T. E. Barry, Comparative advertising: What have we learned in the past two decades? *Journal of Advertising Research,* 1993, *33* (2), pp. 19–29.

20. We should note that the "Nobody beats . . . " or "No one beats . . . " benefit claim (which is a parity claim that most consumers perceive as a superiority claim) seems to be just as effective as explicitly claimed superiority. For a test of the "No one beats . . . " approach, see R. Snyder, Multiple misleading effects of implied superiority claims, in M. P. Gardner, ed., *Proceedings of the Society for Consumer Psychology,* St. Louis, MO: P. De Paulo, University of Missouri, 1989, pp. 88–91.

21. A. Chattopadhyay and J. W. Alba, The situational importance of recall and inference in consumer decision making, *Journal of Consumer Research,* 1988, *15*(1), pp. 1–12. Remember that we define brand attitude as delivery on a purchase motivation (an "abstract belief," in their study) not as global evaluation.

22. Kardes and Herr cleverly demonstrated that they could lead consumers to prefer a slightly inferior model of color TV set when its positive attributes were presented in primary positions, compared with a slightly better model whose positive attributes were spread throughout the list describing the TV set. When the choice was delayed, as it normally would be in reality, the primacy effect was very strong: 80 percent chose the slightly inferior TV set against a chance level of 50 percent. F. R. Kardes and P. M. Herr, Order effects in consumer judgment, choice, and memory: The role of initial processing goals, in M. E. Goldberg, G. Gorn, and R. W. Pollay, eds., *Advances in Consumer Research,* vol. 17, 1990, pp. 541–546.

23. K. L. Keller and R. Staelin. Effects of quality and quantity of information on decision effectiveness, *Journal of Consumer Research,* 1987, *14* (2), pp. 200–213. We are generalizing pretty heavily from their results, but it seems sensible to do so. Also, never add low-importance benefits. Low-importance benefits will *pull down* the brand attitude that would have resulted from using only high-importance benefits, due to an "averaging" effect. For recent studies of this, see J. Friedrich, D. Fetherstonaugh, S. Casey, and D. Gallagher, Argument integration and attitude change: Suppression effects in the integration of one-sided arguments that vary in persuasiveness, *Personality and Social Psychology Bulletin,* 1996, *22* (2), pp. 179–191.

24. In a famous review (1956), George Miller concluded that "working memory" capacity is seven "chunks" of information, plus or minus two. George Mandler (in 1967) later concluded that the number is more often seven minus two, that is, five. Simon Broadbent (in 1971) suggested it is three major chunks, each able to hold three additional chunks, that is, nine. A safe upper limit for benefit claims, which can be quite detailed, is seven. See G. A. Miller, The magical number seven, plus or minus two: some limits on our capacity for processing information, *Psychological Review,* 1956, *63* (1), pp. 81–97; G. Mandler, Organization in memory, in K. W. Spence and J. T. Spence, Eds., *The Psychology of Learning and Motivation: Volume 1,* San Diego, CA: Academic Press, 1967, pp. 327–372; D. E. Broadbent, The magic number seven after fifteen years, in A. Kennedy and A. Wilkes, Eds., *Studies in Long-Term Memory,* New York: Wiley, pp. 2–18; and A. Baddeley, The magical number seven: Still magic after all these years? *Psychological Review,* 1994, *101* (2), pp. 353–356.

25. For many years, the esteemed Sidney J. Levy has drawn attention to the fact that most products have positive symbolic value to their users. And, more recently, Holbrook and Hirschman have correctly criticized consumer researchers for not fully recognizing the obviously powerfully motivating "experiential" consequences of consumption. See S. J. Levy, Symbols for sale, *Harvard Business Review,* 1959, *37* (4), pp. 117–124; M. B. Holbrook and E. C. Hirschman, The experiential aspects of consumption: Consumer fantasies, feelings, and fun, *Journal of Consumer Research,* 1982, *9* (2), pp. 132–140; and M. B. Holbrook and J. O'Shaughnessy, The role of emotion in advertising, *Psychology and Marketing,* 1984, *1* (2), pp. 45–64, especially figure 1.

26. Survey of 1,300 adults in Australia by Frank Small & Associates, reported in *Ad News,* June 17, 1988, p. 29.

27. J. H. Myers and A. D. Shocker, The nature of product-related attributes, in J. N. Sheth, ed., *Research in Marketing,* vol. 5, Greenwich, CT: JAI Press, 1981, pp. 211–236.

28. W. O. Bearden and M. J. Etzel, Reference group influence on product and brand choice, *Journal of Consumer Research,* 1982, *9* (2), pp. 183–194.

29. In Chapter 19, where we discuss ad testing, the visual imagery version of the acceptance response is explained in more detail.

30. R. E. Petty and J. T. Cacioppo, 1983, same reference as in Chapter 8, note 65.

31. M. R. Darby and E. Karni, Free competition and the optimal amount of fraud, *Journal of Law and Economics,* 1973, *16* (1), pp. 67–88.

32. R. A. Formisano, R. W. Olshavsky, and S. Tapp, Choice strategy in a difficult task environment, *Journal of Consumer Research,* 1982, *8* (4), pp. 474–479. In this survey, the authors found that 75 percent of people buying life insurance (median policy amount: $25,000) sought a quotation from only *one* insurance company. Forty-eight percent bought from the first salesperson who contacted them (thus showing considerable "faith"), and 27 percent bought from the first company recommended to them by an acquaintance.

33. Although described as public inflation of image, more technically the process is social reinforcement of the individual's brand attitude.

34. M. L. Ritchins and P. H. Bloch, After the new wears off: The temporal context of product involvement, *Journal of Consumer Research,* 1986, *13* (2), pp. 280–287. We have interpreted the nonrecent buyer group in their study as being like future buyers.

35. The VisCAP presenter model was first proposed by L. Percy and J. R. Rossiter in *Advertising Strategy: A*

*Communication Theory Approach,* New York: Praeger, 1980, chapter 3. It is based on the earlier work of H. C. Kelman, Compliance, identification, and internalization: Three processes of opinion change, *Journal of Conflict Resolution,* 1958, *2,* pp. 51–60, and W. J. McGuire, The nature of attitude and attitude change, in G. Lindzey and E. Aronson, eds., *The Handbook of Social Psychology,* vol. 3, Reading, MA: Addison-Wesley, 1969, pp. 136–314. We added the visibility factor and adapted the model to advertising. In the first edition of the present book (1987, chapter 11), we refined the model further by fitting it more precisely to the Rossiter-Percy grid. It should be noted that the VisCAP model goes much further than the "match-up" model proposed, for example, by Baker and Churchill (1977) and the "adaptive significance" model proposed by Kahle and Homer (1985). See M. J. Baker and G. A. Churchill, Jr., The impact of physically attractive models on advertising evaluations, *Journal of Marketing Research,* 1977, *14* (4), pp. 538–555; L. R. Kahle and P. M. Homer, Physical attractiveness of the celebrity endorser: A social adaptation perspective, *Journal of Consumer Research,* 1985, *11* (4), pp. 954–961; and J. R. Rossiter, A. Smidts, and M. McOmish, Rossiter and Percy's VisCAP in-ad presenter model; an experimental test, in J. Beracs, A. Bauer, and J. Simon, (Eds.), *Proceedings of the 25th Annual Conference of the European Marketing Academy*, Budapest, Hungary: Budapest University of Economic Sciences, 1996, pp. 2043-2052.

36. R. G. Haas, Effects of source characteristics on cognitive responses and persuasion, in R. E. Petty, T. C. Brock, and T. M. Ostrom, eds., *Cognitive Responses in Persuasion,* Hillsdale, NJ: Lawrence Erlbaum Associates, 1981, pp. 141–172.

37. L. Percy and J. R. Rossiter, same reference as in note 35, chapter 3.

38. About 50 percent of women shoppers recently rated the *Good Housekeeping* "Seal of Approval" as very important (a rating of 8 + on a 1-to-10 scale of importance); see Warwick Baker & Fiore, Inc., *Common Advertising Language: The Consumer's Takeaway,* New York: Warwick Baker & Fiore, Inc., 1990. However, using the unobtrusive method of preparing ads with and without the seal, a recent experimental study with continuing-education students suggested that this and other well-known seals of approval such as the USDA, American Dental Association, and American Heart Association cause only a small and nonsignificant increase in the believability of ads using these seals; see R. F. Beltramini and E. R. Stafford, Comprehension and perceived believability of seals of approval information in advertising, *Journal of Advertising,* 1993, *22* (3), pp. 3–13. On balance, seals are probably effective as a presenter device, though the effect is probably small.

39. An incidence of 36 percent of TV commercials using an on-camera spokesperson in a *major* role was reported in a 1974 survey by A. Bellaire, *Advertising Age,* December 30, 1974, pp. 17–18. Everyday observation suggests that a figure of about one in three is still currently correct. About two in three TV commercials *use* an on-camera spokesperson, but only half of these *emphasize* the spokesperson; see D. M. Stewart and D. H. Furse, same reference as note 17. Probably because of the lack of literal visibility, only 2 percent of radio commercials employ celebrity presenters (see A. M. Abernethy et al., 1993, reference in Chapter 10, note 30). However, voice-over radio commercials use carefully chosen presenters and also, radio announcers are likely to have near-celebrity status with their listeners. Newspaper ads seem to use presenters less often because most are retail store ads. Consumer magazine ads, however, show people as presenters in 43 percent of ads: celebrities, 22 percent; typical consumers, 10 percent; CEOs, 6 percent; and noncelebrity experts, 5 percent; see P. A. Stout and Y. S. Moon, Use of endorsers in magazine advertisements, *Journalism Quarterly,* 1990, *67* (3), pp. 536–546.

40. The boosting process is similar to that identified in the RAM-Conveyor model of creativity in Chapter 7, and indeed presenters are a special case of a conveyor.

41. This has been documented for magazine ads with women readers (see Chapter 10) but is less clear for TV commercials in that neither of the two main testing services, MSW and ARS, show an advantage in ad recall for celebrities. However, we maintain in Chapter 10 that TV commercials are automatically given attention.

42. According to the advertiser, celebrities such as Ms. Campbell and actress Lauren Bacall were chosen because they are "contemporary, cutting edge, and popular in the mass culture," so as to reverse the beliefs that milk is "old-fashioned, just for kids, and bad for your health." Thus the communication objectives for milk as a brand were to increase brand awareness of milk and also to convey the brand attitude benefits of low fat, high in nutrients, and good for adults. The ad is one of a series in the Fluid Milk Processors Education Program (MilkPEP).

43. Some laboratory evidence that celebrity–brand name pairings may directly increase recognition speed of the brand *name* was obtained in an experiment by W. J. Burroughs and R. A. Feinberg, Using response latency to assess spokesperson effectiveness, *Journal of Consumer Research,* 1987, *14* (2), pp. 295–299. Although the effect was statistically significant, it was not large in a practical sense, averaging less than 5/100th of a second. Whether recognition speed would increase over multiple exposures is speculative and not encouraged by the realization that subjects had probably received multiple exposures to the pair-

ings in real-life advertising exposures prior to the experiment.

44. Evidence of avoiding the "vampire effect" can be obtained by asking whether consumers can correctly remember which brand or brands a given celebrity endorses. However, this does not ensure brand awareness, since the celebrity is not the initiating cue for brand choice in the real world.

45. R. H. Holman and S. Hecker, same reference as in Chapter 8's note 31.

46. We caution against the finding of one experiment that suggests you should use *multiple* presenters in an ad. Such a step is helpful only in the long run to maintain *attention* to the advertising when the strategy and creative idea stay the *same* (for instance, American Express's "Do You Know Me" and, later, "Portraits" campaigns). In the experiment in question, the investigators apparently did not realize that they had positioned the product, a fictitious new pizza restaurant, as "a favorite of thousands of pizza lovers." Thus it was not surprising that ads showing four such people worked better than ads showing only one! This is a benefit claim effect, not a presenter effect. See D. J. Moore and R. Reardon, Source magnification: The role of multiple sources in the processing of advertising appeals, *Journal of Marketing Research*, 1987, *24* (4), pp. 412–417. In a subsequent experiment, these investigators showed that multiple presenters in a single ad can *detract* from brand attitude if the presenters are perceived as being paid for their endorsement (a possible "overkill" effect). We ignore the results from their single-presenter condition  because again this manipulation was confounded with a "thousands of people" main product claim. See D. J. Moore, J. C. Mowen, and R. Reardon, Multiple sources in advertising appeals: When product endorsers are paid by the advertising sponsor, *Journal of the Academy of Marketing Science*, 1994, *22* (3), pp. 234–243.

47. The concept of "information overload" was introduced in marketing by Jacob (Jack) Jacoby who, with colleagues, conducted a long series of investigations of the phenomenon. See J. Jacoby, Perspectives on information overload, *Journal of Consumer Research*, 1984, *10* (4), pp. 432–435.

48. Some high-risk product categories are perceived (especially by new category users) as so complicated, either by virtue of having a very large number of important attributes, or attributes that are technically specialized and thus difficult to evaluate, that the decision maker trying to make a brand choice experiences "information overload." Examples include life insurance (for almost 75 percent of consumers) and major appliances (for about 40 percent of consumers). See R. A. Formisano, R. W. Olshavsky, and S. Tapp, Choice

strategy in a difficult task environment, *Journal of Consumer Research*, 1982, *8* (4), pp. 474–479; and R. W. Olshavsky and D. H. Granbois, Consumer decision making—fact or fiction?, *Journal of Consumer Research*, 1979, *6* (2), pp. 93–100.

49. A remarkable proportion of animated presenters in advertising are the creations of the Leo Burnett agency. Known affectionately as "the critters," Burnett's creations include the Keebler Elves, Morris the Cat (not animated!), the Green Giant, the Pillsbury Doughboy, and Tony the Tiger.

50. Sony in red after Dangerous deal, *The Australian* (excerpted from *The Times*), February 25, 1992, p. 19.

51. J. Graham, Amex lands Paul Newman, *Advertising Age,* December 11, 1989, pp. 1, 52.

52. B. Garfield, Texaco star shines in Hope-less effort, *Advertising Age,* June 19, 1989, p. 78.

53. Presenter problems? No worries, *Ad News,* July 29, 1988, p. 4.

54. D. W. Stewart and D. M. Furse; see note 17. Celebrity presenters are, however, much more prevalent in Asian TV commercials, particularly in Japan.

55. M. Sutherland, Macabre marketing sees dead celebs live, *Ad News,* May 21, 1993, pp. 16–17.

56. B. Whalen, Eye-tracking technology to replace day-after recall, *Marketing News,* November 27, 1981, pp. 18, 20. The eye-tracking research company was Telcom.

57. J. G. Kaikati, Celebrity advertising: A review and synthesis, *International Journal of Advertising,* 1987, *6* (2), pp. 93–105.

58. A controlled lab study supports our contention. Celebrities Dustin Hoffman and Matthew Broderick were presented in the experiment as endorsing one, two, or four products (Visa charge card, Kodak film, Colgate toothpaste, and Certs breath mints). Multiple endorsements of other products had no effect on brand attitude or intention to buy the originally endorsed products (Broderick for Visa and Hoffman for Kodak). See C. Tripp, T. D. Jensen, and L. Carlson, The effects of multiple product endorsements by celebrities on consumers' attitudes and intentions, *Journal of Consumer Research,* 1994, *20* (4), pp. 535–547.

59. D. Kowet, It helps if you look like a chicken, *TV Guide,* February 21, 1981, pp. 20–23. The quote is from p. 20.

60. K. L. Keller, Cue compatibility and framing in advertising, *Journal of Marketing Research,* 1991, *28* (1), pp. 42–57.

61. Although the coendorsement of young tennis star Michael Chang may have helped, Jimmy Connors's fortuitous success was undoubtedly the major factor. See B. Garfield, Nuprin scores a smash with Connors' "Nupe it" ad, *Advertising Age,* September 16, 1991,

p. 50; and P. Sloan, Nuprin's smash hit, *Advertising Age,* October 14, 1991, pp. 3, 62.

62. S. Misra and S. E. Beatty, Celebrity spokesperson and brand congruence: An assessment of recall and affect, *Journal of Business Research,* 1990, *21* (2), pp. 159–173.

63. This fits RAM-Conveyer Theory (see Chapter 7).

64. The ad's copy *is* amusing. Mr. Ehrlichman appears on the TV screen with a carton of the ice cream, saying, "When I said I never knew a thing about the Watergate break-in, you probably didn't believe me, did you? To show you what a good guy I am, I will give you another chance. Dreyer's Grand Light Ice Cream is 93 percent fat-free and tastes great. So even if you didn't believe me last time, you'd better try this stuff." Reported in D. Gram, Nixon aide "too hot" for ice-cream ad, *The Australian* (reprinted from *The Sunday Times*), May 25, 1987, p. 5. Note that Mr. Erlichman is some sort of an expert in that he was overweight at the time, lending an expertise hook to the product.

65. N. Wasson, Japan's ads go Hollywood, *USA Today,* October 13, 1995, p. 5A.

66. See M. Zuckerman, M. D. Amidon, S. E. Bishop, and S. D. Pomerantz, Face and tone of voice in the communication of deception, *Journal of Personality and Social Psychology,* 1982, *43* (2), pp. 347–357; and P. J. De Paulo and B. M. DePaulo, Can deception by salespersons and customers be detected through nonverbal cues?, *Journal of Applied Social Psychology,* 1989, *19* (18), pp. 1552–1577.

67. T. Bartolini, J. Kresge, M. McLennan, B. Windham, T. A. Buhr, and B. Pryor, Perceptions of men and women under three conditions of eyewear, *Perceptual and Motor Skills,* 1988, *67* (3), pp. 779–782. The opposite was found for men in sunglasses ("shades" imply shady). Those who wear normal glasses may be pleased to know that glasses have no effect on perceived overall attractiveness, friendliness, or sexiness. Nor do they increase perceived wealth.

68. *TV Guide,* June 20, 1981, p. A-21, citing statistics provided by the American Federation of Television and Radio Artists and Screen Actors Guild.

69. See R. Alsop, Listen closely: These TV ads might have a familiar ring, *The Wall Street Journal,* October 22, 1987, p. 34; and W. Brandes, Star power leaves some voice-over artists speechless, *The Wall Street Journal,* June 2, 1995, p. B-6. Female voice-overs tend to be used for "softer" products, such as Glenn Close for Hallmark cards and Kathleen Turner for Dove chocolate and Diet Dr. Pepper.

70. J. Robinson and L. Z. McArthur, Impact of salient vocal qualities on causal attribution for a speaker's behavior, *Journal of Personality and Social Psychology,* 1982, *43* (2), pp. 236–247.

71. D. Daley, British shops craft voice-over database, *Advertising Age,* February 27, 1995, p. 24.

72. P. J. De Paulo and B. M. De Paulo, same reference as in note 66. They cite previous studies showing that professionals—such as detectives, police officers, and customs officials—*cannot* reliably detect lying.

73. In forming *first impressions* of people, physical attractiveness is also positively correlated with the VisCAP dimensions of credibility, namely expertise and objectivity. See, for example, G. L. Patzer, Source credibility and physical attractiveness, *Journal of Business Research,* 1983, *11* (2), pp. 229–241; and K. Debevec, T. J. Madden, and J. B. Kernan, Physical attractiveness, message evaluation, and compliance: A structural examination, *Psychological Reports,* 1986, *58* (2), pp. 503–508. However, with presenters in *ads,* it is easy to manipulate these dimensions separately.

74. In various experiments referenced below, high physical attractiveness worked for perfume, aftershave, and cologne (all physical-enhancement products and mostly high-involvement, so *similarity* between the ideal and the actual self could well have been causal) but did *not* work for disposable razors, religious books, home computers, or a luxury car (none of which is directly physically enhancing). There is no theoretical reason why physical attractiveness should be relevant for these latter products. See Baker and Churchill, same reference as in note 35; R. E. Petty, J. T. Cacioppo, and D. Schumann, Central and peripheral routes to advertising effectiveness: The moderating role of involvement, *Journal of Consumer Research,* 1983, *10* (2), pp. 135–146; M. J. Caballero and W. M. Pride, Selected effects of salesperson sex and attractiveness in direct mail advertisements, *Journal of Marketing,* 1984, *48* (3), pp. 94–100; and M. A. Kamins, An investigation into the "match-up" hypothesis in celebrity advertising: When beauty may be only skin deep, *Journal of Advertising,* 1990, *19* (12), pp. 4–13.

75. See K. Stabiner, Willie Stargell, you're hot; Shelley Hack, you're not, *TV Guide,* March 1, 1980, pp. 14–18; and *TV Guide,* July 15, 1978, p. A-14.

76. These examples are from Video Storyboard Tests, Inc., which uses a methodology similar to Performer Q. For those interested, the other favorites are Jerry Seinfeld for American Express, Whitney Houston for AT&T, Shari Belafonte for Ultra Slim-Fast, June Allyson for Depend, Chevy Chase for Doritos, and Cybill Shepherd for L'Oreal. Sports stars were apparently excluded from the survey. See D. Enrico, Celebrity endorsements: Women take the lead, *USA Today,* October 20, 1994, p. 2A.

77. H. Schlossberg, Expert on aging warns against "stupid marketing," *Marketing News,* September 28, 1992, p. 2.

78. This is especially true for services that are quite personal, such as interior decorators, restaurants, and hair salons, where similarity may be more important than expertise. See L. Feick and R. Higie, The effect of preference heterogeneity and source characteristics on ad processing and judgments about endorsers, *Journal of Advertising,* 1992, *21* (2), pp. 9–23.

79. Although we are not necessarily referring to celebrity presenters here, Michael J. Fox and Jay Leno produced a very strong effect on luxury cruise choice (high-involvement/transformational) in a recent realistic experiment. It could be suggested that these two celebrities are "guy next door" types for the college students who participated in the experiment (equal to or slightly better than). See T. B. Heath, D. L. Mothersbaugh, and M. S. McCarthy, Spokesperson effects in high involvement markets, in L. McAlister and M. L. Rothschild, eds., *Advances in Consumer Research,* vol. 20, 1993, pp. 704–708.

80. "Qualitative" here refers to "no-yes" checklist use of the model (which is really zero-one quantitative use) or use of the model simply to aid in identifying the relevant presenter dimensions as bases for discussion.

81. See S. W. Colford, How to find the right spokesperson, *Advertising Age,* October 28, 1991, p. 17; and C. Miller, Even without HIV issue, using celebs can be risky, *Marketing News,* December 9, 1991, pp. 2, 8.

82. For the record, *Advertising Age,* March 20, 1995, p. 29.

83. C. I. Hovland, I. L. Janis, and H. H. Kelley, *Communication and Persuasion,* New Haven, CT: Yale University Press, 1953.

84. Good descriptions of the basic ideas in cognitive response theory can be found in R. M. Perloff and J. T. Brock, And thinking makes it so: Cognitive responses to persuasion, in M. E. Rolloff and G. R. Miller, eds., *Persuasion: New Directions in Theory and Research,* Beverly Hills, CA: Sage, 1980, pp. 67–99; R. B. Cialdini, R. E. Petty, and J. T. Cacioppo, Attitudes and attitude change, *Annual Review of Psychology,* 1981, *32,* pp. 357–404; and P. L. Wright, Message—evoked thoughts; persuasion research using thought verbalizations, *Journal of Consumer Research,* 1980, *7* (2), pp. 151–175.

85. C. Pechmann and D. W. Stewart, How direct comparative ads and market share affect brand choice, *Journal of Advertising Research,* 1991, *31* (6), pp. 47–55.

86. It is difficult to gauge the probability of retaliation in terms of overall incidence. However, Buchanan and Smithies (1991) reported on 119 challenges to comparative claims for food products (obviously a biased sample since it includes only claims for which challenges to the National Advertising Division of the Council of Better Business Bureaus were made), and found that 71 percent of the investigations were initiated by a competitor. Of the challenges overall, 61 percent were substantiated, and the comparing brand had to withdraw the advertising. If we apply this incidence to the 71 percent "retaliation" cases, then the chances are approximately 43 percent that an explicit comparative claim will be only temporarily successful in that subsequently it will have to be withdrawn. Of course, this assumes that there *is* a challenge. A very loose way of estimating this "ecological" probability is based on Robinson (1988) and on computations based on his data by Gaskin (1988): about 38 percent of companies will face a reaction in the first year, and about 50 percent will face a reaction by the end of the second year. Thus, in the long run, we may roughly estimate that at least one in five explicit comparative campaigns will be curtailed. Of course, a year or two of explicit comparative advertising may yield considerable profit. See B. Buchanan and B. H. Smithies, Taste claims and their substantiation, *Journal of Advertising Research*, 1991, *31* (3), pp. 19–35; W. T. Robinson, Marketing mix reactions to entry, *Marketing Science*, 1998, *7* (4), pp. 368–385; and S. P. Gaskin, Commentary on "Marketing mix reactions to entry," same journal, pp. 388–389.

87. The main measure was 24-hour delayed brand purchase intention. This measure *subsumes* attention and brand *recall.* However, higher initial attention to the ads suggests a superior brand *recognition* possibility also. See C. Pechmann and D. W. Stewart, The effects of comparative advertising on attention, memory, and purchase intentions, *Journal of Consumer Research,* 1990, *17* (2), pp. 180–191. For further evidence of the small brand advantage in print ads, see P. W. Miniard, R. L. Rose, M. J. Marone, and K. C. Manning, The need for relative measures when assessing comparative advertising effects, *Journal of Advertising,* 1993, *22* (3), pp. 41–57.

88. In our opinion, Coke II (originally the ill-fated "New Coke") took the right approach in its relaunch by using explicit comparative advertising against Pepsi. The new-formula entry from Coca-Cola, it may be remembered, was originally designed to compete with Pepsi's sweeter taste. The relaunch campaign, used only in geographic markets where Pepsi is ahead of Coke (Classic) or very close, has the main copy line: "Coke II: Real cola taste plus the sweetness of Pepsi." Coke II at the time of relaunch had less than a 1 percent share of the U.S. soft-drink market and therefore fitted the definition of a very small share brand. It has little to lose and much to gain by positioning itself directly against Pepsi. See P. Winters, Coke II enters markets without splashy fanfare, *Advertising Age,* August 24, 1992, p. 2.

89. D. Cohen, In re final guides concerning endorsements and testimonials in advertising, *Journal of Marketing* (Legal developments in marketing section), 1980, *44* (4), p. 95.

90. Associated Press, Singer sues ad agency over voice imitation, *Marketing News,* February 19, 1990, p. 9. We didn't hear the outcome.

91. S. A. Diamond, A matter of survival, *Advertising Age,* December 28, 1981, p. 20.

## DISCUSSION QUESTIONS

**9.1.** For high-level involvement/informational advertising, the target audience's initial attitude is the overriding factor that must be taken into account. Interview a friend about his or her overall attitudes and specific benefit beliefs about several makes of cars. Select a car toward which your friend appears to have a moderately favorable, but not a strongly favorable, brand attitude. Paying particular attention to wording, draft a set of benefit claims that you think would be effective in increasing this attitude to a strongly favorable one. Test the benefit claim statements with your friend. Then write a short report on this exercise.

**9.2.** The refutational approach and the (explicit) comparative approach are two creative tactics that can be used when the target audience has a negative attitude toward your brand. Which of the two approaches do you think would be more appropriate, and why, for the following brands:
   **a.** IBM personal computer
   **b.** R-C (Royal Crown) Cola
   **c.** The U.S. Internal Revenue Service

**9.3.** "Overclaiming" refers to benefit claims that exceed (the upper limit of) the target audience's high-involvement latitude of acceptance. Write a 2-page memorandum on when you should overclaim in high-involvement advertisements and when you should not.

**9.4.** What *is* a presenter, as defined in this chapter? When should an advertiser consider using one? What are the advantages and disadvantages of using a celebrity presenter? And what are the alternatives to using a presenter?

**9.5.** After first listing the likely communication objectives (including the brand attitude strategy or quadrant) for each of the brands below, conduct your own VisCAP profile ratings of their respective presenters, discussing their appropriateness in each case.
   **a.** Bill Cosby for Smith Barney Shearson investment brokers
   **b.** Sophia Loren for Oil of Ulan
   **c.** Michael J. Fox for Pepsi
   **d.** George Foreman for Mieneke mufflers

## FURTHER READING

Percy L., and Rossiter J.R., *Advertising Strategy: A Communication Theory Approach.* New York: Praeger, 1980.

Our earlier book, prepared before low-involvement theory was fully recognized in advertising, provides an excellent review of high-involvement communication tactics in advertising. Much more detail appears there —detail which has been condensed and adapted in the tactics presented in the present book. As well, there are other topics not treated in depth in the present book, such as creative applications of visual imagery and psycholinguistics to produce more effective advertising.

Whereas in the present book we focus on in-ad presenters, this earlier book discusses presenter characteristics from the broader perspective of the perceived sender of the advertising communication. It provides more detail on the processes underlying credibility, attraction, and power; it also includes an application of the VisCAP model.

We wish there were more outside readings on presenter effects with direct application to advertising. However, most previous research on presenters has a narrow focus (usually on credibility, sometimes on attraction) and fails to consider the particular communication objectives for which the presenter is sought.

# CHAPTER 10

# Creative Execution: Attention and the Structure of Ads

**A**s we noted at the beginning of Chapter 8, advertising executions attempt to accomplish three things: attention, brand awareness, and persuasion. The previous two chapters considered tactics for brand awareness and persuasion. The present chapter takes a specialized look at the construction of ads in each of the respective advertising media—particularly structural tactics designed to maximize *attention* to the ad. These attention factors are well supported by large-scale research. However, we then venture boldly into new, mostly uncharted territory by offering a structural formula for each major type of advertising that *also* bears on *brand awareness and persuasion*. These structural formulas accommodate (and indeed presume) the grid-based creative tactics from the previous two chapters. Readers should be warned that the formulas may need to be changed or modified as new research findings emerge; however, the formulas employ the best currently available findings. After reading this chapter, you should know how to design creative executions for:

1. TV commercials
2. Radio commercials
3. Newspaper ads
4. Consumer and general business magazine ads
5. Industrial magazine ads
6. *Yellow Pages* and directory display ads
7. Outdoor and poster ads
8. Direct response ads

## ATTENTION: ITS FUNCTION AND IMPORTANCE

The function of attention in advertising is to increase the reach ("exposure") of the creative message. For instance, an ad whose attention value or rating is 0.5, when 1.0 is the standard level of attention, will reach only half of its potential prospects. Alternatively, it will have to be run twice as often, roughly speaking, to achieve the attention level of a standard ad or ad placement. Later, in Chapter 17, these attention values are interpreted as contributions to "minimum effective frequency" (MEF) so that they can be used in media planning. (For example, if 15-second commercials usually elicit less attention than 30-second commercials, then the media plan will have to run them more often to achieve the same "effective" level of frequency to the target audience. The minimum number of times the ads have to be shown to the target audience in order to be effective in an advertising cycle is known as the minimum effective frequency, or MEF.) It will be convenient to refer to the attention adjustments in terms of MEF here so that this chapter can be consulted meaningfully when devising the media plan. Also note that we adjust only when the attention difference is 20 percent (0.2 MEF) or greater.

Our primary concern here is with *initial attention* paid to the ad. Once initial attention is achieved, the ad's creative idea and executional tactics have to take over to achieve further attention, necessary for brand awareness and persuasion.

Initial attention to an ad is mainly dependent on three factors:

1. The media vehicle in which the ad is placed
2. The ad unit (mainly length for broadcast commercials, and size and color for print ads)
3. The structural execution of the ad

In considering these three factors, it is evident that there is an overlap of media strategy with creative strategy. The first factor, the media vehicle, is largely a media strategy decision and will be examined in Chapter 17. The second factor, the advertising unit, is partly a creative decision and partly a media decision; but the ad unit selected for the advertisement has such a large effect on attention that we will examine it first, in this chapter, as a creative strategy decision. The third factor, the structural execution of the ad, is clearly a creative strategy decision and will therefore also be examined in this chapter.

The chapter proceeds as follows. The eight media-based types of advertising will be discussed in turn: TV commercials, radio commercials, print ads (encompassing newspaper, magazine, directory, and outdoor and poster ads), and direct response ads. For each type of advertising, we will first look at the effects of ad unit selection on attention. Second, we will look at how structural execution factors can further influence the level of attention paid to the ad. (These sections on attention are detailed and will therefore be somewhat difficult to absorb. You may wish to skim them now, and return to them in detail when planning an actual campaign.) At the end of each section, we will offer a structural execution "formula" for that type of ad which also considers branding and persuasion. These formulas are certainly not supposed to preempt professional creativity—they are intended more for the do-it-yourself advertiser or as guidelines that managers can use as a basis for appraising the creative approach taken by the advertising agency.

## TV COMMERCIALS

### Attention: Ad Unit Factors

**Overall Attention.** About 88 percent of the TV program's audience is in the room within sight or hearing of the average TV commercial.[1] However, only about 60 percent will have watched enough of the video to be able to recognize it when tested later with visual excerpts from the commercial.[2] This compares with 49 percent recognition for magazine ads, 43 percent for newspaper ads, and 30 percent auditory recognition for radio commercials (see later sections).

**Length of Commercial.** Attention to a TV commercial[3] is directly related to its length. Table 10.1 shows estimated attention levels for TV commercials of various lengths, taking the most frequent length (30 seconds) as the standard. Notice that these numbers are indexed against the standard length, which receives an attention value of 1.0.

In the United States at present, about 65 percent of (network) TV commercials are the standard 30-second length, and about 31 percent are 15-second commercials. The remaining 4 percent consist of longer commercials—60 seconds, usually, but occasionally 45, 90, or 120 seconds—or shorter, 20-second or 10-second, commercials.[4] The longer commercials are more prevalent in cable TV programs. Taking the 30-second commercial as the standard, it can be seen that doubling the length to 60 seconds increases attention by 20 percent (contribution[5] to MEF = 1.2), whereas halving the length to 15 seconds reduces attention by 20 percent (MEF = 0.8). Longer commercials, 90 seconds or two minutes, which are usually used only to introduce complex new products, for radical repositioning campaigns for established products, or for direct response TV advertising, are so distinctive on television that we have made a judgment adjustment and indexed these at twice the attention value (MEF = 2.0) of a standard 30-second commercial. At the other extreme, for the shorter, 10-second commercials, we have estimated the attention value (MEF = 0.7) by extrapolation.

| TABLE 10.1 |  |
| --- | --- |

**ATTENTION ADJUSTMENTS (CONTRIBUTIONS TO MEF) FOR TELEVISION COMMERCIALS**

| Length of commercial (in seconds) | Index |
| --- | --- |
| Infomercials | 2.0[a] |
| 120 | 2.0[a] |
| 90 | 2.0[a] |
| 60 | 1.2 |
| 30 (standard) | 1.0 |
| 15 | 0.8 |
| 10 | 0.7[b] |

[a]Judgment
[b]Extrapolation

The 15-second length is now so frequent in TV advertising that it deserves comment. The shorter length is rarely used to launch new products, unless the product is extremely simple; primarily, 15-second commercials are employed to advertise established products.[6] When 15-second commercials first began to be used in the mid-1980s, most of them were "lifts," that is, edited versions of "parent" 30-second commercials (also called "boosters" because their purpose is to remind people of the message in the previous, longer ad[7]). Nowadays, the great majority of 15-second commercials are "originals," that is, they are specially created in the shorter length originally and are not direct derivatives of a longer commercial (they are also called "solos," or "stand-alone":15s[8]). It may be noted that *both* original :15s and lift :15s have the same attention value (0.8) relative to 30-second commercials. Also, 15-second lifts have the same attention value (0.8) relative to their 30-second *parent* commercials.[9]

"Infomercials" are included in the attention (MEF) table. Infomercials are more like miniprograms rather than commercials and, indeed, many are a half-hour long. It is therefore impossible to estimate an attention value for these very long commercials, other than to rate their MEF value as at least 2.0. Infomercials are shown mainly on cable television; some cable TV stations run as many as 6 hours a day of infomercials. Mostly, the infomercials are for self-help or self-improvement programs, appliances and gadgets, or musical collections on compact disc. About nine in 10 infomercials are for previously unknown brands; about one in 10 are for well-known brands.[10] Celebrities are often engaged to increase attention to infomercials. Recent infomercial presenters include Fran Tarkenton, Joe Namath, Victoria Principal, and Cher. Although many infomercials are programlike, they nearly always carry clear disclaimers stating that they are paid advertisements.[11] Infomercials influence more people than you might think: a recent survey on this new form of TV advertising found that two in 10 U.S. adults had purchased items from stores as a result of an infomercial, and just under one in 10 had ordered an item direct.[12] However, a leading producer of infomercials estimates that only 15 percent are sales-effective[13] (plug in 0.15 as their p value in the random creativity formula in Chapter 7, chapter appendix 7A).

**Other In-Media Factors.** Although this takes us ahead to media scheduling, several little-known facts about media factors' effects (or noneffects) on attention to TV commercials are worth mentioning here. First, attention to TV commercials is *not* affected by "clutter," that is, by the number of other commercials in the commercial break or "pod."[14] Second, the position of the TV commercial in the commercial break is not worth adjusting for in terms of attention. Contrary to popular opinion, position in the pod does not make a substantial difference to initial attention. Whereas the first and last commercials in a break get a slight advantage, the difference in advertising recall is less than 5 percent (0.05 MEF) and is not worth adjusting for. Third, position in in-program versus between-program breaks makes little difference.[15] The vast majority of TV commercials are placed by time of day (daypart) or by program and only *rarely* by specific positions in a break (where the cost premium is prohibitively high for most advertisers). Consequently, position in general is not worth adjusting for. Finally, attention to the commercial certainly *is* affected by attention paid to the TV program in which it appears. However, we will adjust for this factor in the media plan (see the VA, or vehicle attention, factor in Chapter 16's MEF formula).

### Attention: Structural Factors

**Video Factors and Attention.** Recent research has begun to identify some of the video factors that influence attention to TV commercials. The first of these, the video's "rhythm" or "pattern," will be incorporated in our recommended formula for TV commercials presented later.

A second factor is the *pace* of the video. There has been a trend in recent years toward "fast cut" commercials. For instance, in the early 1980s, the average "shot" or "scene" in a 30-second TV commercial lasted 3.9 seconds; by 1991, that average was down to 2.3 seconds—which is 40 percent faster, on average. (To put these figures in perspective, a movie nowadays averages about 11 seconds per shot; a prime-time TV program about 5 seconds; and, at the other extreme, an MTV video averages less than 2 seconds a shot.) Looked at another way, the average 30-second commercial nowadays has about 13 separate camera shots during its 30-second video sequence. A very interesting experiment by MacLachlan and Logan, in conjunction with the research firm of Mapes and Ross, Inc., found that TV commercials with more than 13 shots in 30 seconds suffer a decrement in attention (and accordingly also in persuasion). At the rate of 20 or more shots per commercial, the "MTV type" of commercial has an attention loss of 17 percent, which would represent an adjusted MEF value of only 0.8. The interesting corollary of the attention disadvantage of "fast cut" commercials is that the attention loss is *greatest* among the *youngest* age group studied, 18-to-34-year-olds, who are often the target of this modern advertising style. Among this age group, the attention value of MTV-type commercials suffers by 25 percent and persuasion by even more.[16]

We note that these findings about the pace of commercials exclude the even more recent technique of "morphing," which is accomplished by continuous video transfusion rather than choppy cutting. Those who saw the movie *Terminator 2* will know what we mean. For instance, in a U.K. TV commercial for Castrol GTX Motor Oil, a car metamorphoses into other cars and then into a pool of oil. It is not known how morphing affects attention, but we speculate that there is *no* loss, unlike for fast cuts.

Several other video techniques are better examined as part of media scheduling, such as "impact scheduling" and "top and tailing," and we will return to these in Chapter 17. However, one interesting new technique which attempts to increase attention is "interrupts." In the first commercial of this type, shown in the United States in 1989, the Energizer Bunny interrupted a Ralston Purina Cat Chow TV commercial and then later interrupted a commercial for Alarm bath soap, and other products. Energizer, an Ever-Ready product, is owned by Ralston, which also has among its brands Purina and Alarm.[17] Again, we do not know whether "interrupts" actually do increase attention. Initial attention would not be increased because the to-be-interrupted commercial starts out normally. Attention during the commercial may be increased but, we suspect, only once or twice until the novelty wears off. Meanwhile, the message for both products may be confused. We think "interrupts" are risky and we therefore don't recommend them.

**Audio Factors and Attention.** The audio track in TV commercials consists usually of words, music, or both. Many viewers have the distinct impression that TV commercials operate at peak volume on the audio track in order to increase attention. This is partly true: the peak allowable level of the audio volume (in decibels) is the same for TV commercials as it is for programs, but the difference is that programs only *occasionally* hit the peak level whereas TV commercials

tend to stay near or at the peak *throughout* their duration. Thus, commercials *seem* louder. Also, modern audio techniques allow voices to be filtered in terms of frequency or pitch (not loudness per se) to within a band of 2–6 kilohertz, which is the speaking level that commands greatest attention.[18]

Musical accompaniment is used, in some form, in about one in every two TV commercials. Interestingly, music in general may have the effect of *slightly detracting* from attention to the commercial as a whole. An analysis by advertising researchers Walker and von Gonten[19] found that TV commercials with no music or just light background music tended to be better recognized from a subsequent *verbal* description than did commercials with medium or heavy use of music (a finding that is relevant for campaign tracking research, discussed in Chapter 20). However, conventional measures of advertisement recall show *no effect* of music on attention.[20] "Golden oldies" hit songs on the audio track may be a separate case (discussed in the previous chapter in connection with brand recall); with old hit songs, attention to the *ad* may be increased but attention to the *brand* may suffer. A study by Tom[21] found that unadapted hit songs used as TV commercial soundtracks were much less likely to initiate correct brand recall (24 percent) than were lyric-adapted hits that sang the brand name (44 percent). Best of all was originally written music (78 percent). This finding is relevant to TV commercial exposure in programs which viewers use as "background" listening, when only the audio is attended to.

### Suggested Structural Formula for TV Commercials

As discussed extensively in Chapter 7, the first and foremost requirement of a TV commercial (and indeed all types of advertisements except, perhaps, direct response) is that it be based on a good *creative idea*. In Chapters 8 and 9, we also saw that there are important executional tactics to be incorporated depending on the communication objectives for brand awareness (brand recognition and brand recall) and brand attitude (persuasion). With these considerations in mind, we now turn to a suggested structural formula for the TV commercial itself, summarized in Table 10.2.

**(1) Choose the Type of Video Story Script.** There are five basic types of TV commercial video story scripts from which to choose.[22] In actuality, the type of script will be dictated largely by the creative

**TABLE 10.2**

**SUGGESTED STRUCTURAL FORMULA FOR TELEVISION COMMERCIALS**

1. Choose the type of video story script (see Table 10.3).
2. Write the audio script—the copy or lyrics of the commercial—to fit the video script.
3. Consider the "rhythm" or "pattern" of the video and audio together (see Figure 10.1).
4. Go back through the script—both video and audio—and check that the brand name or logo is clearly connected to the product category (for brand awareness) and that the brand's main benefit claim is clearly shown and stated (informational persuasion) or authentically portrayed (transformational persuasion).
5. Check that the video alone (in storyboard form or on videotape) does a reasonably good job of conveying the message.

idea, but the choice is also correlated with whether the commercial is to be informational or transformational, as shown in Table 10.3.

* *Informational* commercials generally will use a "demonstration" script or one of the scripts that can go either way, such as "straight list of benefits," "slice of life," or "testimonial."
* *Transformational* commercials generally will use one of the three "either way" scripts or, exclusive to transformational, a "lifestyle" script.

Again, we emphasize that the creative idea is the main deciding factor, and indeed there is no strong evidence that script type, as such, can override a very good creative idea.[23] If the creative idea requires a "crossover" or different script than we have suggested, go with it regardless.

**(2) Write the Audio Script—the Copy or Lyrics of the Commercial—to Fit the Video Script.** The speaking rate in TV commercials is about 1.5 words

per second. Thus, if you are planning a 30-second commercial, you must use no more than about 45 words in the audio script. The audio length is easily tested by reading the script aloud, allowing pauses for any "video alone" sequences.

**(3) Consider the "Rhythm" or "Pattern" of the Video and Audio Together.** Speculation from two studies by advertising researchers Young and Robinson, as well as earlier theorizing by Rossiter and Percy, suggests that two patterns are generally most effective for informational and transformational TV commercials, respectively.[24] These patterns—and their basic content—are detailed in Figure 10.1. For want of a better description, we have called the target response (the vertical axis in the "pattern" diagrams) "viewer interest" but it may as well be described as the "rhythm" to be achieved.[25] Our speculation here is based on sound learning theory principles for negative reinforcement (informational) and positive reinforcement (transformational), respectively.

* *For informational* TV commercials, the rising pattern of viewer interest is punctuated by two "pauses" in the video action—to facilitate brand awareness learning and to allow the problem message and the solution message, sequentially, to "sink in." The video pauses consist of nonessential visual "filler," short breaks in the action or, more precisely, in visual delivery of the benefit(s). In these video pauses, put the corresponding *audio* claim(s): the "promise" and, later, the "reinforcement."

* For *transformational* TV commercials, the pattern is one of rising viewer interest throughout (positive reinforcement building to a "crescendo"), preceded and followed by brand identification (the to-be-conditioned stimulus in classical conditioning terms).

The one possible exception to the pattern of early brand identification (see first brand i.d. in each graph)

**TABLE 10.3**

**FIVE MAIN TYPES OF TV COMMERCIAL VIDEO STORY SCRIPTS**

**Informational scripts**

1. Demonstration
   a. Straight performance
   b. Before-after
   c. Side-by-side comparative
   d. New use

**Informational or transformational scripts**

2. Straight list of benefits
3. Slice of life (minidrama)
4. Testimonial (by an in-ad presenter: celebrity or user)

**Transformational scripts**

5. Lifestyle (user-as-hero)

*Source:* Adapted from Klein, 1990; see note 22.

**Informational**

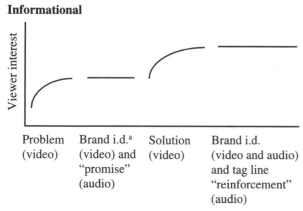

Problem (video)

Brand i.d.[a] (video) and "promise" (audio)

Solution (video)

Brand i.d. (video and audio) and tag line "reinforcement" (audio)

**Transformational**

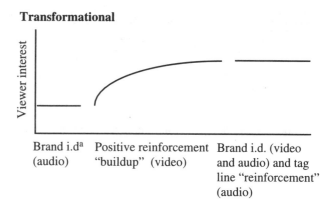

Brand i.d[a] (audio)

Positive reinforcement "buildup" (video)

Brand i.d. (video and audio) and tag line "reinforcement" (audio)

[a]For a new brand, the initial brand i.d. is omitted if a "mystery ad" format is chosen (see text).

**FIGURE 10.1**
Suggested patterns for TV commercials.

is when the TV commercial introduces a *new brand* with a "mystery" format. For mystery commercials, of course, the brand is not identified until the end of the commercial. As discussed in Chapter 8, the mystery format has been shown to be most effective in creating brand awareness when introducing a new brand, by encouraging a "What is it?" response during processing,[26] but not for a familiar brand, where early-and-late brand identification is superior.

**(4) Go Back Through the Script—Both Video and Audio—and Check That the Brand Name or Logo Is Clearly Connected to the Product Category (for Branding) and That the Brand's Main Benefit Claim Is Clearly Shown and Stated (Informational Persuasion) or Authentically Portrayed (Transformational Persuasion).** Be ruthless about removing any extraneous video or audio material. Actually, this is the point at which it is worthwhile to apply the post–creative execution check using the Rossiter-Percy grid tactics described in the preceding two chapters.

**(5) Check That the Video Alone (in Storyboard Form or on Videotape) Does a Reasonably Good Job of Conveying the Message.** This final recommendation—to ensure that the TV commercial is reasonably understandable from the video alone—is based on three considerations. The first and main consideration is that very carefully controlled research by Bryce and Yalch[27] has demonstrated that video-transmitted content is considerably better learned than the *same* content transmitted in the audio. The second consideration is that many TV commercials are nowadays intended for multicountry or even global use. Because of language differences, it is obviously advantageous to produce such commercials to be reasonably comprehensible from the video alone. The third consideration, though a lesser one in terms of incidence, is the increasing prevalence of remote-control TV instruments, leading to fast-forwarding ("zipping") and channel switching ("zapping") during ads. For brand recognition brands, in particular, it is crucial that pack shots be clearly visible at the beginning of the commercial at the faster pace; it is better still if the basic message can be extracted under these conditions.

All this is not to neglect the audio. Another trend, as with morning news programs, is for the TV set to be on longer but to be more often used as a "background" medium, much like radio often is. (Hence later, in Chapter 16, we distinguish low-attention and high-attention TV vehicles.) Therefore, the brand name and the main benefit claim should certainly also be given in the audio—as indicated in the recommended patterns in the figure.

## RADIO COMMERCIALS

### Attention: Ad Unit Factors

**Overall Attention.** We estimate that the average radio commercial engages the attention of only about 30 percent of the listening audience (about half that of TV's visual attention).

The recommended ad unit adjustments for radio commercials, according to their length, are shown in Table 10.4.[28] In the table, we have shown the most common lengths employed on radio: 60 seconds, 30 seconds, and 10 seconds. Many radio commercials are read "live" by announcers so their lengths obviously vary, although they usually adhere to a 30-second or 60-second target.

**Length of Commercial.** Attention to a radio commercial is a fairly direct function of its length.[29] Taking a 30-second length as the standard, there is a 40 percent increase (MEF = 1.4) in attention to :60s and a 30 percent decrease for :10s (MEF = 0.7). When using :10s, for instance, you would need three exposures of the :10s to equal the MEF of two exposures of the :30s (MEF = 2.1 versus 2.0).

**Audience's Sex and Age.** Radio stations and their programs, much more so than TV programs, are often quite segmented by listenership "skew" in terms of sex and age. Accordingly, the MEF adjustments in the table can be used when such differences sharply apply. Overall, women are more attentive than men (especially to :60s), and teenagers are more attentive than adults.

**Radio Commercial Format.** Format or type is not really an ad unit decision but it *does* affect initial attention to radio commercials. Using announcer-read commercials as the base, it appears that the most attention-getting format for radio commercials is "slice of life" (defined, as for TV commercials, as a "minidrama"); it is not surprising that a "story" on the radio is considerably more likely to draw in the listener (MEF = 1.4 for :30s and 1.7 for :60s). The interview or testimonial format also attracts greater than average attention (1.3 and 1.5, respectively). Jingles, on the other hand, make little if any difference to attention—although their use as a structural creative factor deserves separate consideration, given in the formula section.

### Attention: Structural Factors

Interestingly, the two most frequently used audio elements in radio commercials—music (used in about 80 percent of radio commercials, but in 53 percent only as background),[30] and humor (used in 23 percent of radio commercials in the United States; more in the United Kingdom)—do not play any reliable role in increasing attention to the commercial.[31] However, we will consider some special uses of music and humor, next, in our recommended formula for increasing the effectiveness of radio commercials.

### Suggested Structural Formula for Radio Commercials

Radio is in many ways a limiting medium in which to advertise. The main limitation is that it cannot, of course, show pictures. The lack of visual stimuli virtually *eliminates* radio advertising as a medium for advertising products whose brand awareness depends on *brand recognition*. However, it is perfectly suitable

---

| TABLE 10.4 | | |
|---|---|---|
| **ATTENTION ADJUSTMENTS (CONTRIBUTIONS TO MEF) FOR RADIO COMMERCIALS** | | |
| **ADJUSTMENT FACTOR** | **INDEX** | |
| **Length of commercial (in seconds)** | | |
| 60 | 1.4 | |
| 30 (standard) | 1.0 | |
| 10 | 0.7[a] | |
| **Audience's sex and age** | **:30** | **:60** |
| Men (all ages) | 0.9 ≈ 1.0 | 1.2 |
| Women (all ages) | 1.1 ≈ 1.0 | 1.5 |
| Adults | 0.9 ≈ 1.0 | 1.3 |
| Teenagers | 1.2 | 1.6 |
| **Commercial format or type** | **:30** | **:60** |
| Slice of life (minidrama) | 1.4 | 1.7 |
| Interview or testimonial | 1.3 | 1.5 |
| Sing and sell (jingle) | 1.0 | 1.2 |
| Announcer-read (live) | 1.0 | 1.2 |

[a]Extrapolation

for products whose brand awareness relies on brand recall. Also, the lack of visual stimuli means that visual "conveyors" cannot be employed (see Chapter 7) although verbal conveyors—such as verbal metaphors—are perfectly possible. A second limitation of radio is its relatively low attention-getting capacity. With some exceptions, such as regularly timed or clearly signalled news and weather reports, radio is very much a "background" medium to which people listen while doing something else; they "prick up their ears" only when something really interesting comes on. We will try to get around both these limitations in the creative recommendations that follow.

A structural formula (more a set of recommendations) for radio commercials is provided in Table 10.5. The recommendations are organized in terms of the opening, middle, and ending of the commercial.

**1. Find a Very High Interest Opening Device.** Because of the typically lower attention paid to radio, it is important to find an opening device that will "grab" the listener's attention. There appear to be two main possibilities. Informational commercials, especially, can use words[32] or sounds of "absolute interest." Absolute-interest words (or themes) include sex, danger, money (lots of it) and, for specific target audiences, descriptions of problems such as AIDS or hemorrhoids. Absolute-interest sounds include, due to long conditioning in our culture, a telephone ringing, a police siren, and a fire alarm.

For musical radio commercials, which are often used for transformational products, using the favorite music style of the target audience is recommended as an opening device. Presumably, people listen to

music-radio stations that play their preferred style of music, so that matching this style should maintain interest leading into the commercial. Overall, in the United States, about 18 percent of radio commercials use music that fits the station's music format.[33] This "segmented" production of radio commercials, of course, can be expensive unless the campaign is designed to run on a group of radio stations that adhere to a single style, such as country and western; but large advertisers such as Budweiser have designed their radio commercials in four or five different styles to cover the major musical tastes.

**2. Use High-Imagery Sentences or Lyrics Throughout.** Radio advertising, as we noted, is suitable for brand recall (but not for brand recognition). One of the creative tactics that we recommended for brand recall in Chapter 8 was an interactive mnemonic device. The interaction has to be between the product category or category need and the brand name. This can be executed in radio commercials by using an *interactive sentence* in the copy or in a jingle's lyrics if a musical style of radio commercial is selected.[34] Several examples will illustrate this point. Let's pretend we're writing a radio commercial script for British Airways' flights to Paris. A low-imagery, low-interactive copy line for brand recall might be: "Going to Paris? Go British Airways." A better, high-imagery, high-interactive copy line might be: "The experienced traveler going to Paris telephones British Airways." In this second sentence, the "action story" perspective with the use of the active verb "telephones" creates an interaction between the category need (going to Paris) and the brand name (British Airways). The addition of the adjective "experienced" adds to the vividness of the mental image that this sentence is likely to create in the listener's mind. Here's another example: "The large, reddish-brown cockroach crawls slowly over the top of your stove. . . . Then, zap! Raid to the rescue." The use of concrete nouns, active verbs, and colorful adjectives can help to increase the imagery of the copy. It can be difficult to fit these types of sentences into lyrics for jingles, but that is what should be done. A classic example would be: "Shaeffer's is the one beer to have when you're having more than one" (this campaign was a jingle).

RAM-Conveyor theory can be applied to increase the effectiveness of the brand attitude benefit claim or claims. (The exception is if the product or service being advertised via the radio commercial is

---

**TABLE 10.5**

**SUGGESTED STRUCTURAL FORMULA FOR RADIO COMMERCIALS**

1. Find a very high interest opening device:
   - Words or sounds of absolute interest
   - Favorite music style of target audience
2. Use high-imagery sentences or lyrics throughout:
   - Interactive sentences (or jingle lyrics) for brand recall
   - Verbal conveyor (metaphor or joke in copy or lyrics) for the brand attitude benefit claim, unless the ad is for a "serious" product or service
3. End with a relevant punch:
   - Straight ads—rhetorical-doubt question
   - Humorous ads—"klitchik"
   - Musical (jingle) ads—upbeat finish on brand name

"serious"—a high-involvement/informational, multi-attribute-based brand choice.[35]) With any style of radio ad, a metaphor can be used as a conveyor. With a humorous ad, a metaphorical joke can be employed. With a musical ad, metaphorical lyrics can be employed. Hitchon and Churchill provide examples of effective metaphors of the type that can be used in radio commercial scripts. For instance, the metaphorical claim, "Prio sportswatch is like a kaleidoscope on your wrist," was found to produce a significantly more favorable attitude toward the watch than the literal claim, "Prio sportswatch is very colorful on your wrist."[36]

Note that in our earlier discussion of RAM-Conveyor theory, we recommended avoiding the conveyor approach for ads in which the purchase motive is sensory gratification or social approval—because in those cases authentic, literal visual portrayals are paramount. This was because we were talking about *visual* conveyors. However, in radio ads, *verbal* conveyors can be used for sensory gratification and social approval. Thus, for instance, the sensory gratification that comes from eating Häagen-Dazs ice cream might be conveyed with this statement: "Send a chill down your spine—and his, too." A notorious verbal conveyor, also, is Brooke Shields's line, "Nothing comes between me and my Calvins," in her famous ad for Calvin Klein jeans. Note the suggestive imagery here in the use of a double entendre to express the literal claim that she and her favorite brand of jeans can't be parted. For those with a more vivid imagination, the double entendre also suggests that Ms. Shields doesn't wear underpants.

The use of high-imagery sentences or lyrics is further enhanced if the radio commercial has been preceded by a television campaign in which the same or a similar sound track has been employed. This is an application of what is known as *imagery transfer*. Researchers Coffin and Tuchman conducted an imagery transfer experiment in which the audio tracks from 12 previously aired TV commercials were used as radio commercials. (Table 10.6 shows a recent example—a Coca-Cola radio commercial jingle which is the sound track of a previous TV commercial.) Respondents were played the radio commercials and were asked to describe "what was happening on the TV screen." On average, 72 percent of respondents were able to give an acceptable description of the visuals of the TV commercial upon subsequently hearing the radio commercial.[37] Imagery transfer is discussed further in conjunction with media scheduling.

---

**TABLE 10.6**

**COCA-COLA RADIO COMMERCIAL JINGLE TAKEN DIRECTLY FROM THE TV COMMERCIAL SOUND TRACK—POSSIBLY TO ENCOURAGE IMAGERY TRANSFER**

Whenever there's a pool there's always a flirt,
Whenever there's school there's always homework,
Whenever there's stars birds always sing,
As long as there's a thirst there's always the real thing . . .
 Coca-Cola Classic is always the One.
Whenever there's a beat there's always a drum,
Whenever there's fun there's Always Coca-Cola.
*Courtesy:* The Coca-Cola Company, by permission.

---

Remember, again, that you only have time for about 45 words in a 30-second radio commercial. Thus, it should not be too difficult to go back through the script and check for high-imagery, interactive, and metaphorical wording.

**3. End with a Relevant Punch.** Radio is a verbal medium and, in verbal learning, the recency effect is quite strong. The radio commercial should therefore end with a "relevant punch." This, however, will vary with the style or form of radio commercial selected—a straight ad, a humorous ad, or a musical ad.

For *straight* ads, some intriguing research by Howard and Burnkrant[38] investigated the use of radio ad scripts that ask the audience a question. Whereas questions are used in about one-third of radio commercials, the researchers found that the most effective type of question is a "rhetorical doubt" question placed at the *end* of the commercial, that is, in the relevant-punch position. An example would be "Are you sure your diet is giving you the vitamins you need?" asked at the end of a commercial for the hypothetical brand Multi-Vite. This rhetorical-doubt type of question at the end of the ad is effective because it catches people either way. For those who *haven't* listened closely to the ad, it provides a provocative reinsertion of the "problem," assuming they've at least heard the brand name, Multi-Vite, which is the recommended "solution." For those who *have* listened closely to the arguments in the ad, the closing question is likely to prompt them to review those arguments in a favorable manner. Although their experiment needs replication with a larger sample of ads, the investigators found that the rhetorical-doubt question placed at the end of the radio commercial produced a significantly more positive attitude toward the advertised brand than the same question placed at the beginning (the usual location for these types of questions). The closing question was also more effective than a literal statement substituting for the question at either the beginning or the end, or questions or statements in *both* positions.

The relevant-punch ending for *humorous* ads should be a "klitchik," not a "klinker." Humorous ads—and especially humorous radio commercials—often employ a throwaway line at the end simply to be funny, called a "klinker." These throwaway lines are rampant in British radio commercials, where humor has become almost an art form. But a klinker—an irrelevant joke at the end of a commercial—is likely to erase short-term memory and thus interfere with the main message of the ad. On the other hand, an ending line that *is* product-relevant—a "klitchik"—*reinforces* the main message of the ad. We discussed this, in the broader text of humorous advertising, in note 68 of Chapter 8. The example we gave there of a good klitchik was DDB's Sam Levenson's ending line for the VW Beetle: "Volkswagen—it doesn't go in one year and out the other." Another example, from a New Zealand beer poster in London but which could be used on radio and is quite funny if you know the context, is: "Steinlager. Not just another Australian in Britain."[39] Like a rhetorical-doubt closing question, a good klitchik makes you pause and think about what the ad has just said.

*Musical jingle* radio commercials are a somewhat different case; it is difficult to put a closing question or a klitchik at the end of a jingle. The relevant-punch ending for jingle radio commercials should therefore be an *upbeat finish on the brand name.* Examples (sung): "*Coca-Cola* is it!" or (for an Australian beer now being exported worldwide) "I feel like a *Toohey's*—or two!"

It may be noted that, throughout the suggested formula for radio commercials, we have allowed for three flexible styles: the "straight words" ad, the humorous ad, and the musical jingle ad. Again, there is no one particular style that is universally superior,[40] although a recent review suggests that humorous and musical ads are more likely to be effective (for brand attitude as the measure of persuasion) in the low-involvement/transformational quadrant.[41] Overall, a high-interest opening, a strong-imagery middle, and a relevant-punch finish seems to constitute an effective general formula for radio commercials.

## PRINT ADS: AN OVERVIEW

Print advertising is the largest advertising medium in the world. Traditionally, print advertising includes ads in newspapers, consumer magazines, business magazines, industrial magazines and trade journals, and *Yellow Pages* and other directories. Considering just these categories, print advertising accounts for 93 percent of all advertising expenditures in Sweden, 83 percent in the Netherlands, 75 percent in Germany, 64 percent in the United Kingdom (although TV advertising is growing rapidly in Europe with the advent of cable and pan-European satellite stations[42]), and 53 percent in the United States. Only in several countries—such as Australia, 48 percent, and Italy, 43 percent—does print advertising account for less than a majority of all advertising expenditures.[43] If we were to include direct mail advertising—now the single largest medium in the United States and growing rapidly in most countries—then the dominance of print advertising would be even greater.

In this chapter, we are going to treat direct response advertising, which is mostly direct mail *print* advertising, in a separate section (since it concerns exclusively high-involvement choices). However, we are going to include outdoor and poster advertising in the present section on print advertising because, whereas outdoor and poster advertising usually is considered to be a separate medium, it shares most of the characteristics of print ads and conceptually should be regarded as the same. We will further distinguish "mobile" outdoor and poster advertising (which leaves time for only a brief message) from "stationary" outdoor and poster advertising (in which a longer message is possible). This distinction is similar, as we shall see, to that between low-involvement and high-involvement print ads.

Attention is a crucial initial response to print advertising. Indeed, approximately 50 percent of print ads fail to get past this initial step of processing. Ads that are not processed (attention) have no chance to influence the brand's communication objectives (brand awareness and persuasion). Therefore, we will devote a considerable amount of analysis to factors which increase the ability of print ads to gain attention.

All print ads—no matter which print medium is being used—tend to employ the same four structural factors: picture, headline, body copy, and brand name or logo. By "body copy," we mean the text of the ad other than the headline and logo. By "logo," we refer to the brand's unique identification in addition to its literal brand name, be it in pictorial form (such as Borden's "Elsie the cow" or Shell Oil's "shell") or purely verbal form (such as the lettering used by IBM or the signature used by Coca-Cola). Although these four structural factors are standard, the brand's name or logo is the only universal element. Many newspaper and directory ads, for instance, do not have a picture. Other ads consist of just a picture and the brand name or logo, omitting the headline and copy (these are usually low-involvement/transformational print ads). And many ads consist of a picture, a headline, and the brand name or logo without any body copy (mobile outdoor and poster ads often use this format). Finally, some print ads—such as sponsor identifications at sporting events—consist *only* of the brand name or logo. Nevertheless, all print ads draw *potentially* from these four basic elements.

Print ads are discussed in the following order:

- Newspaper ads
- Consumer and general business magazine ads
- Industrial magazine ads
- *Yellow Pages* and similar directory ads
- Outdoor and poster ads

We look first at the physical characteristics of the ad unit and its placement that affect attention. Next, we examine structural factors in the ad itself that influence attention. Finally, we offer a suggested formula, one for each major print medium, for constructing effective print ads.

## NEWSPAPER ADS

### Attention: Ad Unit Factors

**Overall Attention.** The average newspaper ad has the *opportunity* to be seen by 87 percent of readers, which is the normative figure for page openings in newspapers. However, the typical newspaper ad is *actually* noticed by half this many—43 percent of readers. The brand name or logo is noticed by 34 percent of readers, which means that 79 percent, or about four in five, of those readers who notice the ad also notice the brand name or logo; this is the "branding ratio" for newspaper ads. About one in five readers, 19 percent, reads half or more of the body copy[44] (which means that 44 percent of those who *notice* the ad then

proceed to read most of the copy). Compared with consumer magazine ads, discussed shortly, newspaper ads receive somewhat lower attention, have slightly lower branding effectiveness, but receive almost twice the level of body copy readership.

The recommended ad unit attention indices (contributions to MEF) for newspaper ads are shown in Table 10.7. As mentioned earlier, the attention norms for print ads are based on advertisement recognition

**TABLE 10.7**

**ATTENTION ADJUSTMENTS (CONTRIBUTIONS TO MEF) FOR NEWSPAPER ADS**

| Adjustment factor | Index | |
|---|---|---|
| **Size of ad** | | |
| 2 pages | 1.2 | |
| 1 page (standard) | 1.0 | |
| 1/2 page | 0.7 | |
| 1/4 page | 0.5 | |
| **Color of ad** | | |
| 4-color | 1.8[a] | |
| 2-color | 1.5[a,b] | |
| Black and white (standard) | 1.0 | |
| **Position in paper** | Men | Women |
| General news | 1.0 | 1.0 |
| Sports | 1.0 | 0.5 |
| Women's | 0.6 | 1.0 |
| **Opposite-page effects (1-page ads)** | | |
| Other ads | $1.1 \approx 1.0$ | |
| Nonrelated editorial (standard) | 1.0 | |
| Related editorial | 0.8 | |
| **Same-page effects (smaller-than-1-page ads)** | | |
| Nonrelated editorial (standard) | 1.0 | |
| Related editorial | 0.6 | |
| Other ads | 0.4[b] | |
| **Position on page (smaller-than-1-page ads)** | | |
| Top (standard) | 1.0 | |
| Bottom | 1.2 | |
| Outer (edge) | 1.3 | |
| Inner (fold) | $0.9 \approx 1.0$ | |
| **Factors not worth adjusting for** | | |
| Right-hand page | 1.0 | |
| Left-hand page | 1.0 | |

[a]These figures precede the popularity of color newspapers. In color newspapers, the advantage of color ads would undoubtedly be reduced: we'd estimate 2-color ads at 1.3 and 4-color ads at 1.5.
[b]Judgment

—specifically, the Starch advertisement recognition measure.[45]

There are two main adjustment dimensions for newspaper advertisements: size and color. In terms of *size,* taking a 1-page ad as standard, we see that doubling the size, to a 2-page ad, produces a 20 percent higher probability of initial attention (1.2 contribution to MEF), not double the attention or a 100 percent increase. Further, we see that attention is reduced by 30 percent for half-page ads (MEF = 0.7) and by 50 percent for quarter-page ads (MEF = 0.5). This higher-than-size-proportional attention for less-than-1-page ads is probably due to the tendency of newspaper readers to scan everything on the page, including smaller items, a habit reinforced by finding smaller news items of interest.

In terms of *color,* taking black and white newspaper ads as standard, we see that the addition of *any* color increases attention: by 50 percent for 2-color ads (black and white plus one color) and by 80 percent for 4-color ads (full-color), which produces MEF values of 1.5 and 1.8, respectively. However, we would estimate that the use of color ads in predominantly full-color newspapers, such as *USA Today,* would show a *reduced* attention effect. We would recommend setting the MEF value for color ads in these papers at 1.3 for 2-color and 1.5 for 4-color ads. There is still a color advantage over black and white ads, even in full-color newspapers, but it is unlikely to be as large as in regular newspapers.

To estimate the *combined* effect, on attention, of size and color, the indices are *multiplied.* Thus, for instance, the MEF value of a 2-page black and white newspaper ad would be 1.2 × 1.0 = 1.2; whereas the MEF for a 2-page, 4-color ad would be 1.2 × 1.8 = 2.2. Combinations of any of the factors in the table can be estimated by multiplying their index scores.

A third set of adjustment factors that have to be applied for newspaper ads is placement within the paper. Placement comprises several considerations. If the ad is placed in the sports section of the paper, its attention among women is reduced by 50 percent (MEF = 0.5). If it is placed in the women's section, which still exists in most papers as fashion news and special stories directed to women, its attention among men is reduced by 40 percent (MEF = 0.6).

For full-page ads, editorial text on the opposite page that is related to the ad's content, such as an ad for a stockbroker firm placed opposite the stock reports, actually *detracts* from attention to the ad, contrary to popular belief (MEF = 0.8). (The same applies to ads in "special supplements" which some newspapers carry, such as a weekly supplement on computers. A company advertising computers in the computer supplement would have to be sure that the "editorially relevant" supplement attracts at least 20 percent *additional readers* to the newspaper itself. Otherwise, the computer ad would gain more readers' attention elsewhere in the paper, where it wouldn't suffer the 20 percent attention loss.)

The final two position factors pertain to *smaller-than-full-page* ads. The surrounding content has a large effect on attention to smaller ads. "Editorially relevant" text on the same page really hurts: a 40 percent reduction in attention to the ad is the result (MEF = 0.6). The presence of other ads on the page is even more damaging (MEF = 0.4). Overall, placing smaller ads near *unrelated* editorial text is best. We admire the innovative media choice by Armani, for instance, of a very small ad for its aftershave lotion placed right in the middle of the employment ads in the U.K. newspaper *The Times* (Figure 10.2). The keys to the Armani ad placement are two forms of contrast: a pictorial ad in the middle of all-copy ads, and color (a yellow bottle) on an otherwise monotone page. Finally, where on the page smaller ads are placed makes a difference. The bottom of the page offers an attention advantage (1.2) as does outer-edge placement (1.3).

Among the factors that do *not* make a difference in initial attention to newspaper advertisements is placement on a left-hand page versus a right-hand page. The actual figures are 1.00 and 1.03 (for left and right, respectively), a negligible 3 percent gain (shown as 1.0 in the table). Many advertisers believe that right-hand pages gain much more attention and many newspapers (and magazines—see next sections) charge a premium for this position; if so, cost savings can be obtained by using left-hand pages, as attention will be unaffected.

### Attention: Structural Factors

We will now consider the four main structural factors in newspaper ads: the picture, the headline, the body copy, and the brand name or logo.

**The Picture.** The picture is the most important structural element in newspaper ads for gaining attention. Newspaper ads (all sizes) are looked at for just 0.84 seconds, on average, and pictures are more likely

**FIGURE 10.2**
Small-size, two-color ad for Armani aftershave that almost
certainly gains attention well above its normative MEF value.
Note that the bottle, in the actual ad, was shown in *yellow*.
*Courtesy:* Armani Fragrances, Prestige et Collections
International, Paris.

to be seen than other elements.[46] Thereafter, in ads for
low-involvement brand choice, the picture plays a
major role in persuasion. For high-involvement brand
choice, as might be expected, the verbal text of the ad
becomes relatively more important.

In newspaper ads specifically, the inclusion of even
a small picture increases initial attention by 30 percent (MEF = 1.3).[47] If the picture takes up half or
more of the ad, initial attention increases by 80 percent (MEF = 1.8). Therefore, in most cases, the use

of a large picture or illustration is advisable in newspaper ads.

**The Headline.** In print ads, the headline is the
second most important structural element, after the
picture, in creating initial attention and subsequent
readership. The headline is a crucial element for low-
involvement brand choice ads and can provide a
provocative lead-in to the copy for high-involvement
brand choice ads.[48]

Headlines in newspaper ads perform quite differently from headlines in magazine ads. In a newspaper
ad, there is almost total freedom in the creative choice
of the physical format of the headline. Readership of
newspaper ads is unaffected, surprisingly enough, by
the length of the headline; thus, the headline can be as
long as you like. Nor does it matter where the headline is placed; if there is a picture in the ad, the headline can be placed above, below, or to either side of
the picture without affecting readership. Also, headlines in newspaper ads perform no differently in either
all capitals or upper- and lowercase letters (although
the type case used in body copy is a different matter,
as we shall see).[49]

However, it seems worthwhile to apply some theory to the choice of the *type* of headline that is employed in newspaper ads.

- If the ad is aimed at *low*-involvement brand choice,
then it seems logical that a "complete" headline be
used. Complete headlines can take one of three typical forms: announcement (new benefit or new focus on major benefit), testimonial, or command.
- If the ad is aimed at *high*-involvement brand choice,
the advertiser will almost certainly want the reader
to continue from the headline and read the body
copy of the ad. For this purpose, a "lead-in" headline should be used. There are four main types of
lead-in headlines: how to . . . , reason(s) why . . . ,
a question (without an answer in the headline),
and a curiosity headline.

An example of a curiosity headline is the famous
one-word headline "Lemon," used in the 1960s by
Doyle Dane Bernbach for the VW Beetle. Another
example of a curiosity headline is in David Ogilvy's
famous print ad for Rolls-Royce: "At 60 miles an hour
the loudest noise in this new Rolls-Royce comes from
the electric clock." As a newspaper ad, it would work
fine even though the headline is 18 words long! These
two examples indicate the freedom the copywriter has
with headlines in newspaper ads.

**The Body Copy.** Long copy works very well in newspaper ads. Compared with ads of less than 50 words, the portion of readers who read half or more of the ad actually increases by 40 percent when the copy is 50 words or longer, and there is no falloff even with copy of longer than 150 words.[50] But we now qualify this recommendation:

- For newspaper ads aimed at *low*-involvement brand choice, there is no point in including long copy— somewhere up to 49 words should suffice (notice that this is about the same number of words that would appear in the audio of a 30-second TV or radio commercial).
- For newspaper ads aimed at *high*-involvement brand choice, where the body copy is intended to be read, we recommend that the advertiser use long copy—50 words up to 200 or so words.

Here are several other recommendations for the body copy of newspaper ads: use lowercase lettering, which greatly improves speed of reading; avoid "reverse" type, light-colored type on a dark background, which is more difficult to read; and use a "serif" typeface, the kind with serifs or "little feet," on the ends of letters (as is used in the general text of this book) rather than a sans-serif typeface, as is used in the chapter titles and display heads in this book. Of these well-known guidelines for the style of type used in body copy, the lowercase rule is the most important. Many studies have shown that lowercase letters are far easier to distinguish than are all caps (although the research evidence on newspaper ads shows that the proscription *against* all caps does *not* apply to *headlines*). In any event, it is quite easy to determine subjectively how readable the text of the body copy *looks* to be. If it's difficult to read quickly, then apply the above guidelines.

**The Brand Name or Logo.** Given the above-stated finding that about one in five readers who notice a newspaper ad *fails* to notice the brand name or logo, our recommendation would be to give the brand name or logo *more prominence* in the ad. The brand name will automatically be given prominence if it appears in the headline (which it should for the three types of low-involvement "complete" headlines listed earlier). However, high-involvement "lead-in" headlines may not necessarily include the brand name and, in such cases, the brand name or logo should be in a prominent position somewhere below the headline and either below or to the side of the body copy.

## Suggested Structural Formula for Newspaper Ads

Summarizing the foregoing considerations, we present in Table 10.8 a suggested formula for constructing newspaper ads. The first recommendation really relates to media strategy, but we have put it in the formula because it pertains to the *size* of the newspaper ad. The remaining recommendations summarize the theoretical points made above.

## CONSUMER AND GENERAL BUSINESS MAGAZINE ADS

### Attention: Ad Unit Factors

**Overall Attention.** Ads in *general* business magazines such as *Fortune* and *Business Week* perform similarly to ads in consumer magazines. For convenience, we will refer to both these types of magazines as "consumer magazines" (and will contrast them later with *industrial* magazines aimed exclusively at a

---

**TABLE 10.8**

**SUGGESTED STRUCTURAL FORMULA FOR NEWSPAPER ADS**

1. *Size:* For a new campaign, launch with 2-page newspaper ads; for the continuation of an established campaign, use a 1-page ad if reach is the main objective and several half-page ads if frequency is the objective.

2. *Color:* Use color, even in full-color newspapers. Color in the picture is most important; also, use color for the logo if your logo is normally in color.

3. *Picture:* Devote as much space as you can in the ad to the picture; however, for high-involvement/informational brand choice newspaper ads, write the copy first then leave the rest of the ad for the picture.

4. *Headline:* For low-involvement brand choice newspaper ads, write a "complete" headline; for high-involvement brand choice newspaper ads, write a "lead-in" headline.

5. *Body copy:* For low-involvement brand choice newspaper ads, keep the body copy to less than 50 words. For high-involvement brand choice newspaper ads, use long copy (50 to 200 words) and list the benefits in multiple block paragraphs. Use lowercase letters for body copy.

6. *Brand name (including logo):* For low-involvement brand choice newspaper ads, include the brand name in the headline and repeat the brand name or logo at the bottom right of the ad. For high-involvement brand choice newspaper ads, place the brand name or logo anywhere below the lead-in headline. In all cases, make the brand name or logo prominent.

technical business audience). Consumer magazines are a relatively low-reach medium compared with TV, newspapers, and radio. In Western countries such as the United States, the United Kingdom, and Australia, only about 50 percent of the population reads magazines with any degree of regularity. Among the typical magazine's readers, however, magazine ads have the *opportunity* to be seen by 84 percent of them (the normative figure for average page opening). The percentage of readers who *actually* notice the typical consumer magazine ad is 49 percent. Branding is relatively good: 42 percent of readers notice the brand (a "branding ratio" of 86 percent). However, for the average ad, very few readers—only 11 percent—read most (half or more) of the body copy,[51] which is 22 percent of those who noticed the ad.

The recommended ad unit adjustments (contributions to MEF) for consumer magazines[52] are shown in Table 10.9. Again, the two main adjustment dimensions are size and color.

In terms of *size,* and taking a 1-page consumer magazine ad as standard, we see that doubling the size (a 2-page "spread") increases attention by about 30 percent (1.3 exposures contributed to MEF). Interestingly, multipage spreads (MEF = 1.3) are no more attention-getting than 2-page spreads—unless they are placed as a special insert, in which case they gain 60 percent in attention (MEF = 1.6). Halving the standard size loses about 30 percent of attention; a half -page ad contributes about 0.7 of an exposure to MEF. Note also the various combinations that are possible (relevant for media planning). In round figures, an MEF value of 4 can be achieved by four 1-page ads or three 2-page ads. Likewise, an MEF value of 2 can be achieved by two 1-page ads or three half-page ads. Of course, the simplifying assumption here is that the same people are exposed and pay attention to the ads in the series making up the total MEF value, which is quite likely if all the ads appear in the *same* issue of the magazine but less likely if they are in *successive* issues. However, the same-issue summation effect does *not* work if the ads are on the same page or facing pages. The fact is that "checkerboard" formats, such as two adjacent half-page ads or two quarter-page ads placed diagonally opposite on the same page, have exactly the same attention value as their sum total *size* rather than their sum total MEF value, that is, 1.0 and 0.7, respectively.[53]

The ad-size effect works *within* magazines. For example, a full-page ad in *Time* magazine, which has a "normal" page size, does not gain greater attention than a full-page ad in *Reader's Digest,* which has a smaller page size.[54] This is because readers tend to adapt automatically to the context of the magazine's size, so that a full-page ad gets full-page attention regardless of its absolute size.

In terms of *color,* full-color (4-color) ads have become standard in consumer magazines. Black and white ads lose 30 percent attention (MEF = 0.7) relative to full-color ads. While this fall off could be because less creative advertisers use black and white ads, it also argues against the belief that black and white ads will "stand out" in an all-color advertising environment. Black and white plus one color (called 2-color) ads are intermediate, with 20 percent lower attention (MEF = 0.8) than 4-color ads.

Position in the magazine is another ad unit dimension long believed to be important by consumer

### TABLE 10.9

**ATTENTION ADJUSTMENTS (CONTRIBUTIONS TO MEF) FOR CONSUMER AND GENERAL BUSINESS MAGAZINE ADS**

| Adjustment factor | Index |
|---|---|
| **Size of ad** | |
| Multipage insert | 1.6 |
| Multipage spread | 1.3 |
| 2-page spread | 1.3 |
| 1-page (standard) | 1.0 |
| 1/2 page | 0.7 |
| **Color of ad** | |
| 4-color (standard) | 1.0 |
| 2-color | 0.8 |
| Black and white | 0.7 |
| **Position in magazine**[a] | |
| Inside front cover | 1.2 |
| First third of magazine | 1.0 |
| Second third of magazine | 1.0 |
| Third third of magazine | 1.0 |
| Inside back cover | 1.2 |
| Outside back cover | 1.3 |
| **Factors not worth adjusting for** | |
| Right-hand page[a] | 1.0 |
| Left-hand page[a] | 1.0 |
| Bleed | 1.0 |
| No bleed | 1.0 |
| Ad(s) on opposite page | 1.0 ≈ 1.1 |
| Editorial material on opposite page | 1.0 |

[a]If primarily a direct response ad, see Table 10.10.

advertisers. It turns out that only cover positions (inside as well as outside) gain an advantage in attention, and then only to a maximum increase of 30 percent (MEF = 1.3) on the outside back cover, with the two inside covers gaining 20 percent (MEF = 1.2). Position *within* the magazine makes a negligible difference (1.05 for the first third, 1.00 for the second third, and 1.01 for the final third: all shown as 1.0 in the table) and is *not* worth either seeking or adjusting for *unless the magazine ad is primarily intended to be a direct response ad* (discussed separately below).

Another factor that does *not* make a difference in consumer magazines is left-hand page versus right-hand page position (just as in newspapers). With magazines, the belief that reading habits cause right-hand pages to gain "fuller" attention as pages are turned or flipped is not justified by relative attention scores. Similarly, the "bleed" ad format, for which the advertiser pays extra because the ad runs to the edges of the page rather than being enclosed in the magazine page's normal white border, makes no difference to attention in consumer magazines.

Finally, a common myth in consumer magazine advertising is that placing the ad opposite a normal page of text or "editorial" material, especially if the editorial material is "compatible" with the theme of the ad,

is a big advantage. About 95 percent of consumer magazine ads are placed opposite *some* editorial material, and 79 percent are placed opposite a full page of editorial material. The common—but false—concern is to keep your ad away from another ad on the opposite page. In fact, it makes only 10 percent difference (1.1 or less and therefore not worth adjusting for) whether there is editorial material plus ads opposite or only ads opposite, and the difference goes *the other way* (in favor of only ads opposite). Nor does it matter whether the editorial material is compatible with the theme of the ad. The only such placement that makes a slight but significant difference (1.2) is to place the ad opposite the magazine's table of contents; however, this is usually a costly or unavailable placement.[55]

**Direct Response Magazine Ads.** Several very important exceptions to the findings regarding position and page side apply if the magazine ad is *primarily* intended as a *direct response* ad—that is, if its main purpose is to generate inquiries or sell the advertised product directly. In presenting these changes, we now "override" attention and focus on response rate (inquiries) as the criterion measure. Based on an analysis of over 1,400 direct response magazine ads, Phillips[56] has shown that response rates vary substantially with position in the magazine, page side, and

---

### TABLE 10.10

**RESPONSE RATE ADJUSTMENTS FOR DIRECT RESPONSE MAGAZINE ADS**

**Adjustment factor**

| Position in magazine | Index[a] |
| --- | --- |
| First quarter | 1.4 |
| Second quarter | 1.5 |
| Third quarter | 1.0 |
| Fourth quarter | 1.7 |

**Page side**

| | |
| --- | --- |
| Left-hand page | 1.4 |
| Right-hand page | 1.0 |

**Reply-coupon position on page[b]**

| | Left-hand page | | | Right-hand page | | |
| --- | --- | --- | --- | --- | --- | --- |
| | Left | Middle | Right | Left | Middle | Right |
| Top | 2.8 | 3.7 | 2.0 | 1.0 | 13.3 | 1.3 |
| Middle | 2.5 | 5.2 | 4.7 | 2.1 | 1.7 | 5.3 |
| Bottom | 1.0 | 9.8 | 6.0 | 2.4 | 8.2 | 1.7 |

[a]Index based on *inquiries* rather than attention.
[b]"Reply coupon" refers to a *clearly boxed* reply device for cutting and mailing or faxing, or a toll-free telephone number to call. Reply-coupon indexes *include* page side and can be compared across both pages. See also note 5b.

position of the reply coupon on the page (Table 10.10). For position in the magazine, the third quarter is the "deadest" position, here indexed at 1.0, and the first half (1.4 and 1.5) or fourth quarter (1.7), especially, are much stronger. Page side, quite surprisingly, favors the *left-hand* page by 40 percent (1.4 MEF). Position of the reply coupon on the page, in turn, *interacts with* page side to produce the complex pattern of results given at the bottom of the table. This study's sample size of direct response magazine ads is large enough to make these findings quite reliable, and the differences are very large. The reply coupon results include page-side effects (inquiries indexes are comparable across both pages).

### Attention: Structural Factors

As explained in the overall attention figures for consumer magazine ads, only about 11 percent of the magazine's readers will read half or more of the text (body copy) of the ad. This represents 22 percent of those who paid initial attention to the ad.

To explain the low incidence of reading most of the body copy in consumer magazine ads, it must be realized that consumer magazine ads are clearly of *two types:* those aimed at low-involvement brand choice and those aimed at high-involvement brand choice. In fact, the first author of the present book has long advocated that the Starch (now Roper Starch) Readership Service's "Noted" and "Seen Associated" scores are the two key measures of readership performance for low-involvement brand choice magazine ads; whereas Noted, Seen Associated, *and* "Read Most" scores are the important measures of readership performance for high-involvement brand choice.[57] The correlation between Noting the ad and Seen Associated for the brand name or logo is about .9; but Noting is correlated only .7 ($r^2$ of 50 percent) with Read Most.[58]

**The Picture.** The picture is the most important structural element in magazine ads, for both consumer and business audiences. The time spent looking at the average magazine ad is only 1.65 seconds! Most of this brief time (70 percent, or 1.15 seconds) is spent looking at the picture, and thus only about half a second is spent glancing at the headline or logo. Without a picture to "pull the reader in," the ad is unlikely to work.[59]

The size of the picture and several *mechanical* features of the headline—regardless of the content or "meaning" of the picture or headline—account for just over 40 percent of the variation in attention to consumer magazine ads.[60] The straightforward rule for magazine ads, therefore, is: the bigger the picture, the better. In most cases, the omission of a large picture will severely reduce attention to the ad—after which little else matters. If we *do* consider the "after which," a large picture may have little effect on persuasion (brand attitude) for informational brand choice, but it greatly affects persuasion for transformational brand choice.[61]

Pictures with one dominant focal point work best.[62] Compare the two ads for Vivitar cameras shown in Figure 10.3. The multiple-illustration ad on the left was noticed by only 37 percent of readers, was correctly branded by only 30 percent, and only 5 percent read most of the ad. Corresponding scores for the single-picture ad at the right were 45 percent, 39 percent, and 12 percent.[63] This result is quite typical. A single dominant focal point is more effective considering the brief initial attention given to magazine ads.

What should be in the picture? Starch research generally shows that pictures of products *or* people, or people using products, gain equal attention. This result very nicely fits the positioning options discussed in Chapter 6—"product-as-hero" versus "user-as-hero"—and also allows a mixed option. Whatever the content, the picture should have either one of the following two qualities:

**1.** "Inherent visual power," as in a highly unusual visual conveyor (see Chapter 7)
**2.** Quickly apparent "meaning" in its own right, as in most product or people illustrations[64]

Abstract pictures, in conveyor ads and straight ads, should be avoided.

With women readers—but not with men readers—a picture of a *woman* celebrity (acting as an in-ad presenter) is also very effective. With women readers, the celebrity testimonial style of ad increases attention by 26 percent on average and *also* increases the incidence of reading most of the body copy by 20 percent. Confirming the Visibility factor in our VisCAP model, the more well-known the celebrity, the bigger the effect.[65] Also, the more of the celebrity that is shown, the greater the effect on both attention and the incidence of reading most of the copy; a full-figure celebrity illustration works best, followed by a waist-up illustration; and least effective is a head-only illustration. Also, just to make sure, the woman celebrity's

**FIGURE 10.3**
Two ads for a Vivitar camera using multiple illustrations (left) and a single illustration (right).
*Courtesy:* Vivitar Corporation.

*name* should be shown prominently—and separately from the headline in the ad. Note that these advantages for celebrities apply only to female celebrities advertising what are traditionally "women's" products. For some reason, however, male celebrities show no significant advantage for attention and the incidence of reading most of the copy in print ads when advertising men's products.[66]

**The Headline.** In most cases, the headline is the second most important structural element in a magazine ad. Keeping in mind that 49 percent of the magazine's readers (the average Noted score) see the picture, 30 percent will read the headline.[67] However, for *low-involvement/transformational* magazine ads, the brand name or logo is the second most important element after the picture.

The headline in a consumer magazine ad should be short—one to eight words for consumer ads aimed at low-involvement brand choice and one to *five* words when the headline is aimed at high-involvement brand choice. Also, the headline should occupy no more than two lines.

- For *low*-involvement brand choice consumer magazine ads, the initial attention score declines significantly for headlines that go beyond eight words or occupy more than two lines. Anywhere from one to eight words can be used to get the low-involvement benefit claim across.
- For *high*-involvement brand choice consumer magazine ads, the critical factor is that, for headlines of six or more words, the incidence of reading most of the *body copy* falls off dramatically (by 29 percent for headlines of six to nine words and proportionately more thereafter).[68] For high-involvement brand choice, you want the body copy to be read. You don't want to tell the whole story in the headline, and therefore a short headline works best.

Studies of how consumer magazine ads are read suggest that the position of the headline, above or below the picture, does not affect the incidence of reading. However, we are going to make a theoretical recommendation from the RAM-Conveyor model here.

If the headline itself is a *verbal* conveyor, then it should appear *above* the picture, because the picture then serves as a prompt to resolve the message. However, if the ad employs a *visual* conveyor, then it is obviously better for the headline to appear *below* the picture, to serve as a verbal prompt (see Chapter 7). For all other consumer magazine ads with "straight" headlines and pictures, headline placement can be anywhere around, or even in, the picture.

People can read the key words in a magazine ad headline very quickly (at the rate of three or four words in a second).[69] Importantly, the *types* of words included in the headline of consumer magazine ads can increase *initial attention* to the ad.[70] Two types of key words have a strong positive effect on initial attention: nouns (which would be used to describe the brand name and, sometimes together with adjectives, its benefits) and personal reference words (personal pronouns such as "I," or "you"). Another type of key word, verbs, actually have a *negative* effect on attention but may be unavoidable except in short, cryptic headlines, such as the "Lemon" headline for the VW Beetle. For brand noticeability, placing the brand name at the end of the headline (which would be recommended for low-involvement ads) is most effective. An example is the headline in the left-hand ad for Vivitar shown in Figure 10.5: "Picture yourself with a Vivitar." This headline uses an imperative verb that could also be a noun ("picture") and a reflexive pronoun that provides a personal reference ("yourself"), and puts the proper noun that is the brand name ("Vivitar") at the end of the headline for prominence.

Positive and negative headlines can also influence attention to, and the incidence of reading of, consumer magazine ads.[71] Positive headlines cause normal "noting" of the ad (50 percent) and significantly improve the incidence of reading most of the body copy (16 percent). Negative headlines, containing words like "stop," "reject," or "not," considerably depress noting of the ad (down to 37 percent), which again indicates that people can skim and get the gist of a headline very quickly, and *severely* depress the incidence of reading most of the body copy (down to 4 percent). Negative headlines should be avoided in all cases except one. The one exception is where the target audience predominantly believes that the *opposite* of the headline's claim is true. For instance, "Orange juice—not just for breakfast any more," is an effective negative headline because most people believe

that orange juice *is* strictly a breakfast drink. Contrast this with a more typical negative headline: "Pierre's Restaurant is not as expensive as you think." This wording is likely to put the apprehension in readers' minds that Pierre's Restaurant *may* be very expensive whereas they may not have thought of this previously. So as a general rule with one exception, avoid negative headlines.[72]

By the way, updated research on consumer magazine ads shows that the valid admonition against "reverse type" in newspaper ads (light words on dark background) does not apply here. Reverse type in either the headline or body copy of a consumer magazine ad affects neither attention nor the incidence of reading.[73] Similarly, the use of sans-serif type in consumer magazine ads (as long as it is reasonably spaced and, in body copy, not bold) does not affect the incidence of reading.[74] But please note carefully that these "easings of bans" apply to consumer magazine ads only. It is still prudent to retain these bans for newspaper ads, especially, and probably for industrial magazine ads as well.

**The Body Copy.** There is a clear dichotomy in the length of body copy that is effective for consumer magazine ads. As might be expected, copy that is very short (less than 50 words) has about a 40 percent greater incidence of people "reading most" of it than copy that is 50 words or longer.[75] On the other hand, once the copy has reached 50 words, lengthening it to 250 words produces no further decline in readership. This undoubtedly reflects the difference between magazine ads for low-involvement brand choice, which should use short copy, and magazine ads for high-involvement brand choice, which can use quite long copy, of up to about 250 words. For long-copy ads, we recommend listing the benefit claims in bulleted paragraphs or using subheads to delineate and summarize them.

Here is an interesting finding that we're instantly going to back away from: within surprisingly broad limits, the "readability" (word length and sentence structure) of the copy itself has *no effect* on comprehension or understanding of the copy. Nor does readability appear to affect persuasion.[76] As reading experts J. R. Miller and W. Kintsch explain, the use of uncommon words and longer sentences—the two typical indices of poor readability—may slow the reader down, but, once they are read, there is no effect on the reader's understanding of the text.[77] What is retained is the general theme of paragraphs and the gist of sentences, rather than literal memory of sentence length or wording.[78] This is heartening news for writers of textbooks, such as ourselves. But in *ads,* there *is* a good reason for attempting to keep the body copy readable by using shorter sentences and shorter (one- or two-syllable) words. This has nothing to do with comprehension but rather with visual perception. Readability of the body copy has the effect of increasing *initial attention* to the ad.[79] Because initial attention is such a critical factor in print ads, *making copy more readable* is the right recommendation. (Note that the formatting and design of the type can influence this perception of readability as well as word and sentence length.)

Further, we recommend making the copy itself as concrete (high-imagery words and phrases) as possible, because this has a significant positive effect on persuasion.[80]

**The Brand Name or Logo.** As previously mentioned, if the consumer magazine ad is aimed at low-involvement brand choice, the brand name should be in the headline, *or* placed so it is read as a continuation of the headline or as a combination headline. For high-involvement brand choice, it doesn't matter where the brand name is placed, although the usual position is at the end of the body copy. If the reader is interested in the ad's message, on account of the picture or the headline or both, he or she will search for the brand. For nonheadline placement, where a logo rather than necessarily the brand name can be used, it matters little whether the brand identification consists of a picture, a picture plus words, a symbol plus words, or words alone.[81] Confirming the willingness of readers to quickly search for the brand name or logo, attention to the brand name or logo differs little no matter where it is placed on the page.[82] A logo placed in the traditional lower-right corner achieves a "branding ratio" ("Seen Associated" as a percentage of "Noted") of 86 percent. The best position, by only a small amount, is to place the logo in the middle of the page (the dominant focal point), which achieves a branding ratio of 92 percent. But this is only slightly better than other positions. Similarly, a "prominent" logo achieves a branding ratio of 88 percent with a surprisingly slight loss for a "nonprominent" logo, which achieves a branding ratio of 82 percent.[83] These findings indicate that readers will search for the brand if they are interested in the ad.

Rather than proposing a recommended formula for consumer magazine ads here, we will first review the important (but several only) differences for *industrial* magazine ads. Then we will offer a *combined* formula for consumer magazine ads and industrial magazine ads at the end of the next section.

## INDUSTRIAL MAGAZINE ADS

### Attention: Ad Unit Factors

**Overall Attention.** Perhaps because of specialized readership, initial attention to industrial magazine ads is high: estimated at about 64 percent for 4-color ads.[84] Also, the ad unit findings (below) show that size and color make a big difference in industrial magazine ads. There is a 70 percent advantage for 2-page ads over 1-page ads in initial attention; and a 40 percent advantage for 4-color, and a 20 percent advantage for 2-color, over black and white ads. These findings are probably due to the tendency in industrial magazines to run smaller ads and to use many more black and white ads. Therefore, larger ads and color ads stand out.

Some changes from consumer magazines in terms of attention adjustments occur when advertising in industrial magazines.[85] The recommended ad unit adjustments (contributions to MEF) for industrial magazines are shown in Table 10.11, beginning with the two main print ad dimensions of size and color.

The notable feature of the *size* adjustments is that double-page spreads in industrial magazines have a considerably greater effect on attention (a 70 percent increase, representing 1.7 exposures contributed to MEF) than in consumer magazines (1.3). This occurs possibly because larger ads are more unusual in an industrial setting or because readers attribute more importance to advertisers who use larger ads. The attention loss with half-page ads (30 percent, resulting in MEF = 0.7) is, however, identical in industrial and consumer magazines.

In terms of *color* in industrial magazine ads, we set black and white ads as the standard. Addition of one color (called 2-color) increases attention by 20 percent (MEF = 1.2) and addition of full-color (called 4-color) increases attention by 40 percent (MEF = 1.4).

The combined effect of size and color on attention to industrial ads can be estimated by multiplying the separate indices. As might be expected from the

TABLE 10.11

**ATTENTION ADJUSTMENTS (CONTRIBUTIONS TO MEF) FOR INDUSTRIAL MAGAZINE ADS**

| Adjustment factor | Index[a] |
|---|---|
| **Size of ad** | |
| 2-page | 1.7 |
| 1-page (standard) | 1.0 |
| 2/3-page | 0.8 |
| 1/2-page | 0.7 |
| 1/3-page | 0.5 |
| 1/4-page | 0.4 |
| **Color of ad** | |
| 4-color | 1.4 |
| 2-color | 1.2 |
| Black and white (standard) | 1.0 |
| **Position in magazine[b]** | |
| Cover (average of all three cover positions) | 1.3 |
| Inside pages of magazine | 1.0 |
| **Bleed** | |
| Bleed | 1.2 |
| Non bleed | 1.0 |
| **Insert** | |
| Ad with insert | 1.3 |
| No insert (run-of-press ad) | 1.0 |
| **Factors not worth adjusting for** | |
| Right-hand page[b] | 1.0 |
| Left-hand page[b] | 1.0 |
| In-ad coupon | 1.0 |

[a]Multiply indices for multiple adjustment.
[b]If primarily a direct response ad, see Table 10.10. Page side here is based on judgment.

preceding individual factors, 2-page, full-color ads are estimated to provide a very large increase in attention—2.4 exposures contributed to MEF.

Other dimensions worth adjusting for in industrial magazines advertisements include, first, position in the magazine. Although individual cover position data are not available, cover positions, on average, contribute 1.3 to MEF. Also, in industrial magazines, but not consumer magazines, the bleed format adds a small but significant increment to attention (1.2). An in-ad coupon makes no significant difference to attention and hence is shown as 1.0 in the table. However, a freestanding insert ad (FSI), or ads that incorporate

such an insert, increase attention by 30 percent (MEF = 1.3), as would be expected due to the physical tendency of the magazine to open at the insert.

No data are available on left-hand versus right-hand pages for industrial magazine ads. However, given the negligible effect of page side for newspapers and consumer magazines, our best estimate is that *no* adjustment should be made for page side in industrial publications. (The exceptions for position and page side may apply to *direct response* ads as shown in Table 10.10, although there are no specific data for these ads in industrial magazines.)

**Ads in Special Supplements or Special Feature Sections.** Industrial magazines or trade journals—and here we include *all* types of industries such as farming and production, services and maintenance, and engineering and durables—often receive very "uneven" incidence of reading *within* the publication. (The reading pattern is very different from daily newspapers and consumer magazines, which typically are read, or at least skimmed, from cover to cover by all readers, allowing ads within them a very similar opportunity to be seen [OTS] regardless of placement.) The uneven attention pattern for industrial or farm publications means that ads placed in the dullest or "most-skipped" sections will suffer an attention deficit. Ads placed near the most widely read sections, notably near the social news but also in special supplements or special features of seasonal or topical interest, will be the only ones to warrant a 1.0 MEF rating. If the special feature or, especially, special supplement attracts *additional readers* to the publication *issue* itself, then the situation is more complicated: the ad (let's say a standard 1-page ad) would receive its normal attention value of 1.0, but there would be more readers seeing it. This can be handled in media planning *either* by multiplying the ad's attention value by the known proportion of increased readership that the issue of the publication has attracted because of the special section (for example, 1.0 times 1.4 if there are 40 percent additional readers) or by knowing or estimating the additional readership and directly changing the MEF value of an ad in the section to (for example) 1.4. (The publication's editors should be able to provide data, but often, they just make estimates too!) The "base" for these adjustments—the standard MEF of 1.0—is ad placement in those sections of the publication that are *regularly looked at* by the publication's *regular readers*.

## Attention: Structural Factors

The research findings for ads in industrial magazines have to be interpreted carefully, because some studies are based on ads placed in general business magazines, such as *Forbes* or *Business Week*, whereas others are based strictly on ads placed in industrial and trade publications, which have a much narrower and more technical readership. The results for ads in business magazines are very similar to the results for consumer magazines, and thus were categorized with consumer magazine ads. However, the results for ads in *industrial* publications are slightly different.

**The Picture.** In a study of industrial magazine ads using the visual and psycholinguistic variables of Rossiter's earlier study with consumer magazine ads, Soley and Reid found picture size to be by far the largest determinant of attention to industrial ads.[86] Picture size and two headline psycholinguistic variables (see below) account for almost 50 percent of the variation in initial attention to industrial magazine ads.

**The Headline.** The two headline variables that increase attention to industrial ads are personal reference words (as in Rossiter's study of consumer magazine ads) and the number of phrase units (that is, "multiple sentence" headlines). The effects are not so large, however, as to make these recommendations mandatory.

The same two investigators, Soley and Reid, found slight—but we think practically significant—evidence that "lead-in" headlines increase the incidence of reading most of the *body copy* in industrial magazine ads. This incidence is quite low, perhaps because only technical readers and occasional general management readers who are in the market for the product or service category at that time will actually read the ad. In any case, although the results are based on a small sample, the "question," "how to," and "news" types of headlines received "read most" scores of 14, 14, and 13 percent, respectively (meaning that that percentage of readers "read most" of the body copy), compared with all other types of headlines, for which "read most" scores averaged 12 percent (in their study; see note).[87] This is not a large difference, but it is consistent with our recommendation that lead-in headlines should be used if the brand choice is high-involvement/informational, which it may often be for industrial magazine ads.

**The Body Copy.** As with long-copy consumer magazine ads, for body copy of 50 words or more, the length of industrial magazine ads has no further effect on the incidence of reading. Industrial ads with more than 200 words of copy gain about the same readership as those with just 50 words; for the average industrial ad, about 11 percent of readers read most of the copy (which, allowing for 64 percent initial noting of the ad, is 17 percent of the *ad's* readers).[88] The 11 percent almost certainly reflects the average industrial ad's incidence of technically interested and category need–relevant readers.

The readability of industrial ad body copy is generally not a factor to be concerned with, because copywriters tend to automatically adapt the difficulty level of their copy to suit the audience of the industrial publication in which the ad is to appear.[89]

**The Brand Name or Logo.** Our recommendations here would be exactly the same as for consumer magazine ads.

## Suggested Structural Formula for Magazine Ads

Our combined recommendations for constructing magazine ads—*both consumer and industrial*—are summarized in Table 10.12. This formula is comprehensive and allows for the main contingencies that affect the performance of magazine ads.

# YELLOW PAGES AND DIRECTORY DISPLAY ADS

## Attention: Ad Unit Factors

**Overall Attention.** Overall (initial) attention to ads in *Yellow Pages* and similar directories (including electronically supplied directories) is potentially 100 percent, because readers *actively* consult this medium. However, on-page ad units show tremendous variation in actual attention.

Ads in *Yellow Pages* and directories can range from regular listings of one or more lines in normal type size (listings are, after all, a form of advertising) to "display" ads as large as a full page, although the typical largest unit is one-quarter or three-tenths of a page.[90] As well, for display ads, a choice of black-only, 2-color (red or, where available, blue or green, with black), or multicolor (combination of any three of the previous colors with black) can be purchased. Table 10.13 shows the estimated adjustments for attention value (MEF) for size and color in directory display ads.

The table indicates that size and color have a major influence on attention to directory display ads.

---

**TABLE 10.12**

**SUGGESTED STRUCTURAL FORMULA FOR (ALL) MAGAZINE ADS**

1. *Picture*
   a. The larger the picture relative to the rest of the ad, the better.
   b. The picture should have a single dominant focal point.
   c. Pictures of products or people, or both, work equally well.
   d. For women's products, a picture of a named celebrity presenter works exceptionally well.

2. *Headline*
   a. For low-involvement brand choice, the headline should be one to eight words and should be a "complete" headline that includes or immediately directs attention to the brand name. For high-involvement brand choice, the headline should be one to five words and should be a "lead-in" headline to the body copy.
   b. Use a positive headline always—unless most of the target audience believes the opposite of your claim, in which single case a negative headline is appropriate.
   c. Try to include personal reference words (such as "I," "you") and nouns (brand name, benefits) in the headline.
   d. For straight ads, the headline can be placed anywhere around, or even in, the picture. But for visual conveyor ads, the headline should be placed below the picture. And if the headline itself is a (verbal) conveyor, it should be placed above the picture.

3. *Body copy*
   a. For low-involvement brand choice, keep the body copy to less than 50 words. For high-involvement brand choice, the body copy should be 50 to 250 words.
   b. Short sentences and short one- or two-syllable words increase initial attention to the ad and should therefore be used even though subsequent incidence of reading is unaffected by the "readability" of the text.
   c. Use concrete (high-imagery) words and phrases as much as possible throughout the body copy.

4. *Brand name (including logo)*
   a. For low-involvement brand choice, the brand name should be in the headline or placed so that it is "read" as a combination headline. The logo can be placed anywhere. For high-involvement brand choice, the brand name can be placed either in the headline or at the end of the copy.
   b. If a (pictorial) logo is used, it does not have to be prominent.

---

A 1-unit display ad is 1 column wide by $1/4$-column deep. A 4-unit display ad, which is four times the

---

**TABLE 10.13**

**ATTENTION ADJUSTMENTS (CONTRIBUTIONS TO MEF) FOR *YELLOW PAGES* AND DIRECTORY DISPLAY ADS**

| Adjustment factor | Index |
|---|---|
| **Size of ad** | |
| 6-unit | 17.0 |
| 4-unit | 10.5 |
| 3-unit | 7.0 |
| 2-unit | 3.5 |
| 1-unit[a] (standard) | 1.0 |
| **Color of ad** | |
| Multicolor | 6.7 |
| 2-color | 4.5 |
| Black and white (standard) | 1.0 |

[a]A 1-unit size ad is 1 column wide by 1/4-column deep. Other units are multiples of this, and the 5-unit size is not available. A 4-unit ad in a 4-column directory is one-quarter of the page. A 6-unit ad in a 5-column directory is three-tenths of the page. We do not have data for larger units, which are not available in many directories.

---

size of a 1-unit ad, draws 10.5 times greater attention. The addition of a color (usually red, and called a 2-color ad) draws 4.5 times greater attention, and a multicolor ad draws 6.7 times greater attention, than a black-only display ad. (The table provides no estimate for the required normal *in-column* listings, whether regular, boldfaced, or with a logo. However, Australian research indicates that for the average product or service category searched, almost nine in 10 directory searchers make a choice from the *display* ads.[91])

The attention value of size and color *combinations* should perhaps best be conservatively estimated for directories by *adding* the indices rather than multiplying them as in other media. Our reasons for recommending this conservative approach, in the absence of direct measurement results, are twofold. First, the studies on the effects of size on attention were conducted with a mix of black-only and color ads; thus there is already some color multiplication, inevitably, in the size indices—and vice versa. Second, directory ads' attention depends on what *else* is on the page. For example, a multicolor ad in a whole page of multicolor ads would gain less attention, obviously, than if it were the only multicolor ad among a page of black-only ads. As the advertiser cannot predict or control this placement, we recommend conservative estimates. Display ads in directories are placed by the directory owner using the sequential criteria of size (largest first), seniority (how many years you've been advertising in the directory) and, if necessary, alphabetic order of company names. If you've been lucky vis-à-vis size or color, or both, relative to the competition on the page on which your ad is placed, then you can judgmentally adjust the MEF upward, though there is no exact formula for doing so.

### Attention: Structural Factors

*Yellow Pages* and other consumer and business directories are a very influential medium for companies that sell "non-fmcg" products—that is, products and services other than those found in your local supermarket or drugstore. The *Yellow Pages* is the most-researched directory, as it is the most widely used. For instance, a recent U.S. survey estimated that 47 percent of airline choices, 32 percent of auto repair choices, 31 percent of florist choices, 24 percent of beauty salon choices, 24 percent of banks' financial service choices, and 9 percent of restaurant choices are made via the *Yellow Pages*.[92]

The incidence of consumers who decide on a supplier or brand from the *Yellow Pages,* versus those who merely use the *Yellow Pages* to check an address or phone number for a choice already made, varies widely by category. For instance, restaurants and physicians are by far the most frequently looked-up categories in the *Yellow Pages* (each being looked up about 10 times a year in the average household[93]), but most of these are just address checks; note that only 9 percent of restaurant *choices* are made from the *Yellow Pages,* and probably a similar low incidence of actual choices applies to physicians. On the other hand, auto repair shops, plumbers, and florists are looked up only when they are needed, and most people researching these businesses do not have a particular brand in mind or are certainly open to persuasion even if they do. Once they look up the advertiser, for either an address or to make a choice, consumers telephone the company in about 90 percent of cases and make a purchase about 65 percent of the time.[94]

**Communication Objectives for *Yellow Pages* and Directory Display Ads.** The communication objectives for display ads in the *Yellow Pages* and other directories (presuming that the target audience buyer is looking to make a choice rather than merely checking an address or phone number for a previously made choice) should be carefully considered.

**1.** *Category need* is not, of course, a communication objective in this situation. The prospective buyer already *has* the category need, otherwise he or she would not be looking in the directory in the first place. However, the advertiser must carefully consider precisely how the prospective buyer is liable to *label* this category need. This critically affects the heading or headings, in the directory, under which the advertiser should be listed. For instance, an advertising agency might be listed under "Advertising Agencies" but might *also* place a listing under "Market Research Services" if that is a service that is also an important part of the agency's business. Similarly, a plumbing company may wisely choose to be listed under "Home Maintenance and Repairs" as well as under "Plumbers and Gas Fitters," which would be the conventional listing. It all depends on how the category need is "labeled" in the buyer's mind.

**2.** *Brand awareness* in directory ads is by *brand recognition*. The initial decision may have been made by brand recall–boosted brand recognition, but the directory ad *itself* has as its communication objective brand recognition, whether or not the buyer has recalled the brand beforehand.

**3.** *The brand attitude* objective in directory ads is to *create or increase* brand attitude, depending on whether the prospective buyer is making the choice solely from the ads in the directory or from a wider "consideration set." The brand attitude strategy for directory ads is almost always high-involvement/informational.

**4.** *The brand purchase intention* objective is to *generate* a definite intention to call or visit the company *immediately.*

**5.** *Brand purchase facilitation* is also an objective for directory ads: it must be *incorporated into* the ad by including an address and phone number.

The creative tactics from Chapter 8 (for brand recognition) and Chapter 9 (for high-involvement/informational brand attitude strategy) are therefore well worth reviewing if you are planning a *Yellow Pages* or other directory display ad.

The structural elements available to the advertiser in directories consist of requirements and options (for display ads):

- *Basic requirements:* headline, company name, and phone number

• *Optional elements:* picture, body copy, logo, and address

Figure 10.4 shows an ad for a scuba-diving school, Anderson's, from the *Yellow Pages* that employs the requirements and all the optional elements including (necessary for this service) an address.

### Suggested Structural Formula for *Yellow Pages* and Directory Display Ads

A *Yellow Pages* or other directory display ad is just like a *high-involvement* magazine ad. Accordingly, for general guidelines, we begin with the formula recommended for high-involvement magazine ads in Table 10.12. The two major amendments here are the prominence requirement for brand recognition—people should not have to search for your brand name and logo; and the fact that a directory ad is usually like a *small* magazine ad—and thus the number of words in the body copy will necessarily be restricted. Also, there has to be room for the brand's purchase facilitation copy—phone number, address, and location (if it's the sort of place that the prospect is expected to visit), and credit card payment option. A summary of our main recommendations for *Yellow Pages* and directory display ads is given in Table 10.14. The range of alternative creative elements for directory display ads is so wide, and this type of advertising is so specialized, that we also refer the reader to the excellent book by U.S. directory expert Barry Maher, especially his chapter 10.[95]

### FIGURE 10.4

A *Yellow Pages* ad for Anderson's Scuba School showing the correct elements of a directory display ad.
*Courtesy:* Anderson's Scuba School.

## OUTDOOR AND POSTER ADS

We have used the terminology "outdoor and poster ads" because it suggests to most people that outdoor ads are large billboards, usually on exterior sites, whereas posters are smaller and are usually placed on indoor sites. The reader should note that the terminology varies in different countries.[96]

| TABLE 10.14 |
|---|

**SUGGESTED STRUCTURAL FORMULA FOR *YELLOW PAGES* AND DIRECTORY DISPLAY ADS**

1. *Picture:* It is best to include a picture or sketch, even a small one. (The exception might be for industrial directories where specialist buyers are seeking strictly attribute and price information.) If the ad is for a high-involvement/transformational product or service, make sure the picture portrays the "image" you want to project for the company.
2. *Headline:* Use a short (one- to five-word) "lead-in" headline, since it is a high-involvement brand choice situation. (See also headline tactics 2b–2d in Table 10.12.)
3. *Body copy:* Use bulleted points for your benefit claims, as body copy has to be detailed enough to cover high-involvement benefits but must be short due to the space constraint. (See also body copy tactics 3b and 3c in Table 10.12.)
4. *Brand name (including logo):* The brand name is most important; the logo, if you have one, is optional. Right next to the logo should be the company's phone number, address, and location (if visits are intended), and credit card options.

### Attention: Ad Unit Factors

**Overall Attention.** Valuable research on outdoor and poster ads has been published recently in Britain; we could find no comparable research for the United States or other countries.[97] Based on "street intercept" interviews, and covering 400 campaigns, the British researchers established that the average outdoor or poster campaign gains the attention of 40 percent of this ambulatory population. (The measure used is procedurally equivalent to the Starch Noted recognition score for magazine and newspaper ads but without the control of incidence of reading most of the *vehicle*.) However, allowing for the fact that only the ambulatory population was interviewed, with about, we would estimate, 20 percent who are *not* frequent commuters or shoppers (and would therefore *not* ordinarily notice such campaigns), attention by the *total* population to outdoor and poster campaigns is probably on the order of 32 percent (80 percent of the 40 percent cited above).

The branding ratio is probably very similar to magazine ads (about 85 percent) resulting in an *estimated* 27 percent branding level for the total population.[98] The incidence of "read most" is almost certainly very high on a relative basis for outdoor and poster ads, though this depends on whether the copy is short or long, as discussed in the suggested structural formula for the type of ad.

Only a small amount of research is available on the factors affecting attention to outdoor and poster ads. Therefore, we have had to employ judgment, plus some logical reasoning, to arrive at our MEF estimates. These are shown in Table 10.15.

### TABLE 10.15

**ATTENTION ADJUSTMENTS (CONTRIBUTIONS TO MEF) FOR OUTDOOR AND POSTER ADS**

| Adjustment factor | Index[a] |
| --- | --- |
| **Size of ad** | |
| Stand-alone (all sizes) | 2.5 |
| Adjacent to other ads (standard) | 1.0 |
| **Color of ad (not worth adjusting for)** | |
| 4-color (standard) | 1.0 |
| 2-color | 1.0 |
| Black and white | 1.0 |

[a] All judgments

The biggest factor affecting attention for outdoor and poster ads is whether they are adjacent to other ads (as with most outdoor ads in high-traffic locations[99] and most indoor posters in shopping centers, train stations, airline terminals, and similar high-pedestrian-traffic sites) or are stand-alone ads (as in some outdoor and a few indoor sites). In an adjacent context, it could be argued that the situation is like a competitive multi-ad newspaper or directory page. In multi-ad outdoor and poster sites, almost invariably the ads are of the same size. Just as with magazines of different page sizes, the viewer or reader will automatically adjust for size such that it does not become an attention-determining factor. What determines attention, we contend, is the typical "scanning capacity" of the viewer or reader. Based on judgment supported by recent research, we have given the typical outdoor or poster ad in a competitive setting the *standard* attention value of 1.0. But if the outdoor ad or poster is on a *stand-alone* site, we assign it an attention value of 2.5 *regardless* of its size, because it should get 100 percent attention compared with 40 percent attention for the standard outdoor ad or poster.[100]

The other factor that might affect attention to outdoor and poster ads, as with all print ads, is color. Most outdoor and poster ads tend to be 4-color. However, we have assigned *no* attention adjustment to those that use black and white or add only one color (2-color). With the lack of hard data, we conclude that "a billboard is a billboard," and likewise for posters, *regardless* of color or its absence.[101] Color in billboards or posters, we estimate, is not worth adjusting for.

**Miscellaneous and POP Ads.** Almost no information is available on advertising units' attention in miscellaneous media, including point-of-purchase displays. The overwhelming miscellany of options available suggests, again, that judgment in the exposure context is the only reasonable resort. Accordingly, we cannot provide any useful adjustment dimensions for miscellaneous and POP ads.

### Attention: Structural Factors

An outdoor or poster ad, structurally, is just like a print ad. The structural elements are the picture, the headline, the body copy, and the brand name or logo. There is a total lack of published research on how these elements affect attention to the incidence of reading outdoor and poster ads. Thus in arriving at a suggested formula, we use some theory and common sense.

### Suggested Structural Formula for Outdoor and Poster Ads

Our recommendations for outdoor and poster ads are summarized in Table 10.16. The important distinction in outdoor and poster ads is whether the ad is "mobile" or "stationary."

With a *mobile* outdoor or poster ad, either the audience passes it quickly, as in a car on a highway or in a train, or the ad passes the audience quickly, as in transit ads on the sides of buses. Here, the exposure time is very short, and the audience response is similar to the quick scan given to magazine ads—about 1.6 seconds. Thus, only a low-involvement brand choice message can be achieved with mobile outdoor

and poster ads. (Indeed, there may not be *any* body copy, as in the truly mobile monorail train ad for Fuji film shown in Figure 10.5.) With these mobile ads, because of the very short exposure time, we would generally *not* recommend the use of complex conveyors. Conveyor ads may require up to 4 seconds to "decode," and this is too long for most mobile outdoor and poster ads.

With a *stationary* outdoor or poster ad, the situation is entirely different. These exposure situations occur when the ad is stationary relative to the audience, as with ads in railway or bus stations or *inside* trains and buses. A long exposure time is possible and, indeed, people may stare at these ads as a means of retaining a semblance of privacy in a public setting. (Also, a conveyor can be used, as in the verbal conveyor poster for Tontine Body Pillow shown in Figure 10.6.) Therefore, for stationary and outdoor poster ads, our recommendations for high-involvement brand choice, long-copy, *newspaper* ads can safely be followed.

### DIRECT RESPONSE ADS

Direct response ads include any advertising that (a) makes an offer, (b) provides enough information for a decision, and (c) includes a response device.[102] However, only certain types of products and services, exemplified below, are suited to direct response advertising. (Marketers of fast-moving consumer goods sold in supermarkets and drugstores need read no further. Instead, read Chapter 14. Direct response ads and consequent "database building" to develop files of customers is an expensive overkill strategy for mass-marketed "fmcg" products.)

---

### TABLE 10.16

**SUGGESTED STRUCTURAL FORMULA FOR OUTDOOR AND POSTER ADS**

#### Mobile

1. *Picture:* Use a large, *non*conveyor picture.
2. *Headline:* Use a *short* (one- to five-word) but *complete* headline, since this is also the body copy.
3. *Body copy:* The body copy (which must be short) is part of, or is seen to be a continuation of, the *headline*.
4. *Brand name (or logo):* This must be prominent, and can be placed anywhere in the ad as long as it is, or is seen to be, a continuation of the headline.

#### Stationary

1. *Picture:* Write the copy first, and leave any remaining space for the picture. (A picture always helps but is less important than the headline and can be omitted if necessary for space reasons.)
2. *Headline:* Use a complete headline only if you can state the whole message in a line or two. Otherwise, for a long-copy ad, use a lead-in headline (this will be the key element of the ad) for high-involvement brand choice.
3. *Body copy:* This can be 50 to 200 words; use lowercase letters.
4. *Brand name (including logo).* For low-involvement brand choice, include the brand name *in* the headline (complete headline) and repeat the brand name or logo at the bottom right of the ad. For high-involvement brand choice, place the brand name or logo in the lower-right position. In all cases, make the brand name or logo prominent.

---

**FIGURE 10.5**
"Mobile" outdoor ad for Fuji film exemplifying a brief message (mainly branding; no body copy). The monorail train is painted in Fuji's colors of green, red, and white.
*Courtesy:* Hanimex, Australia P/L.

**FIGURE 10.6**
"Stationary" poster for Tontine Body Pillow exemplifying a relatively long processing time for the long headline and the verbal conveyor that has to be understood in relation to the picture.
*Courtesy:* Tontine Bedding, Melbourne, Australia.

Direct response ads are the fastest-growing category of advertising. Indeed, the two primary direct response media, telemarketing and direct mail, are now the two largest single media of advertising in the United States (or first and a very high fourth by some counts[103]) and a new direct response medium, the World Wide Web on the Internet, is small but growing rapidly. Telemarketing, a form of direct response advertising which overlaps with personal selling, is smaller outside the United States. Direct mail is increasing in most Western countries, though it has apparently peaked in the United Kingdom[104] and may peak soon in the United States. Interactive advertising on the Web, or on CD-ROM or diskette, is a form of direct response advertising which has somewhat flexible message content; it is like personal selling in that the recipient can select benefits of interest, and its use is global.

Direct response ads are of two types:

**1.** *One-step* direct response ads, sometimes called "off the page" ads, in which the ad alone is intended to get the order—that is, to sell the product "off" (from) the page (or off the TV or radio commercial in the analogous broadcast situations). In the case of telemarketing, one-step ads are called "outbound" telemarketing. On the Web, one-step ads are called "on-line purchase" or "home-shopping" ads.

**2.** *Two-step* direct response ads, in which the ad is intended to lead only to an *inquiry*. Two-step direct response ads can be placed in any medium. The inquiry is then followed up, as the second step, by direct mail (or further direct mail if the initiating ad was direct mail) or by the sales force either personally or by phone, the latter being known as "inbound" telemarketing, because it follows an inquiry "in" to the company.

We would estimate that fully one-third of *all* ads are now direct response in some form. This is not just print ads; about one in six TV commercials, one in three cable-TV commercials in the United States and most Web ads worldwide, include a direct response telephone number.[105] The inclusion of direct response devices (usually two-step) in *general* ads (also called "across the line" or "double duty" ads) is now commonplace as advertisers realize the value of direct measurement of sales effects and become more sophisticated in building and managing customer "databases" for follow-up sales.

There are many reasons for the growth of direct response advertising. The overall declines in television viewing and newspaper and magazine reading are one factor. Changing work styles, especially the increase in working women with less time spent in the home, is another. But the biggest reason by far is the use of computers and the availability of software for database management (see Chapter 14).

However, one-step direct response advertising has very skewed usage by both advertisers and consumers. First, in the United States, only about half of all *households* (53 percent) order items direct; these households order an average of 3.5 items per year.[106] Most of these orders come from direct mail (catalogues account for 45 percent of all direct mail purchases; and direct mail letters, 10 percent). Direct response ads in mainstream media form a substantial proportion, though, with magazine ads accounting for 14 percent of purchases; TV commercials, an amazing 9 percent (see Table 10.17[107]); newspaper ads, 4 percent; and radio ads, 1 percent. We would also estimate direct response ads on the Web to account for about 1 percent of direct response purchases, although this proportion is growing rapidly.

The *types* of products that consumers buy as a result of one-step direct response advertising fall into a limited set of categories. Notice that they are all consumer durables, not fmcg products, with the marginal exception of speciality food and wine. *Among* the 53

TABLE 10.17

**ONE-STEP DIRECT RESPONSE TELEVISION ADVERTISING: HOW IT'S DONE**

**Case history: Demtel International**

- Demtel sells its products, using its own 2-minute, hard-sell TV commercials, in 15 countries including the United States.
- Products suitable for direct response TV ads are sought by "market sniffers" in those countries, and many inventors offer products for consideration. The main criteria for TV direct response product selection are:
  1. Good value for money
  2. Unique design
  3. Likely strong category demand
  *Example:* The company's best-selling product for the past 12 years has been a "dry fry" oven convection pan.
- Most of their 2-minute TV commercials use a demonstration format. "Execution of the demonstration is vital," says CEO David Hammer, "and we spend up to three months writing a commercial." The commercials are written and directed in-house (in Sydney headquarters) then licensed to overseas partners.
- In addition to the product demonstration, the ads emphasize:
  1. Quick delivery (the product is never advertised unless stock is in the warehouse)
  2. Unlimited money-back guarantee
- Interestingly, although the company has tried to pinpoint demographic trends in responders, most products draw from "all walks of life," says Hammer.
- The company's phone system can take 1,300 calls at a time (!) so as not to lose orders.
- Demtel has had sales and profit increases every year of its 13-year history.

*Source:* S. King, Aggressive television sales beat recession, *The Australian,* June 21, 1991, p. 19.

percent of households that have ordered products by one-step direct response ads, the product categories are as follows: clothing, ordered by 93 percent; gifts, 80 percent; gardening items, 71 percent; home furnishings, 70 percent; housewares, 66 percent; speciality food and wine, 62 percent; hardware items, 61 percent; and sporting goods, 49 percent. Direct response also tends to be a rather "up-market" form of advertising, especially for catalogues, with the incidence of orders from direct response advertising being 62 percent among upper-income households, 54 percent among middle-income households, and 37 percent among lower-income households.[108]

**Direct Response Advertising Planning**

There are four main steps in direct response advertising planning. These are not inconsistent with the planning stages that form the basis of this book but are more specialized for this application. The four steps are: (1) choose target audience, (2) choose medium of direct response advertising and also medium of response, (3) design creative (see below), and (4) manage the resulting database. If television or radio is chosen as the direct response medium, then the target audiences can be quite broad. On the other hand, with telemarketing, direct mail, or interactive advertising as on the Web, the target audience can be geographically or demographically very narrow indeed.

In *direct mail,* there is a "40/40/20 rule" that is widely adhered to by experienced practitioners.[109] This refers to the belief that the quality of the *list* (the target audience definition) accounts for 40 percent of direct mail effectiveness; the quality of the primary appeal in the *ad* accounts for a further 40 percent (mainly in the headline—which can be, and is, easily and extensively tested); and the quality of the body copy of the ad itself accounting for only 20 percent of the ad's effectiveness. We would expect that the same rule holds for *telemarketing,* which is like "direct mail on the telephone," with the primary appeal being the "opening pitch"—which functions as a long headline. However, *interactive advertising* on the Internet's World Wide Web or CD-ROM or diskette is a specialized case which is discussed separately below.

There are two ways to develop a good list:

**1.** Run a *mass* audience ad in newspapers or magazines, or on television or radio. This is usually an "across the line" or "double duty" ad, serving to increase company or brand awareness and attitude *as well as* incorporating a direct response coupon or phone number. In its direct response role, it is a two-step ad aimed at generating inquiries (leads). From these inquiries, a list of prospects can then be developed for direct mailing or telemarketing.

**2.** Rent a list of companies or households that are known to have purchased in a given product category, or otherwise to be demographically suitable for a new product category, and use that as the list of prospects. With company listings, it is necessary to telephone the company to identify the key decision maker to whom the mailing or telemarketing call should be addressed.[110] (It is worth emphasizing, from the ethical perspective of privacy, that individuals or companies can request that their names be removed from lists. For instance, the Australian Direct Marketing Association circulates every month to its members the names of consumers or organizations who've requested no mail contact, no telephone contact, or both. In actuality, the incidence of self-removal, especially for direct mail, is very small.[111])

We will return in Chapter 14 to the fourth step— list or "database" management. Our main focus here is on the construction of direct response ads.

### Attention to Direct Mail and Telemarketing

**Direct Mail.** On average, recipients open 74 percent of direct mail that they receive.[112] However, the range is from as low as 50 percent up to about 90 percent. The main structural factors that determine opening of direct mail appear on the *envelope* itself. These are: (1) the company name, or a guess at the company name in the case of "blank" mailings; (2) whether the envelope has been seen before (usually a turnoff); and (3) the creativeness of the "invitation" on the envelope.

Of *all* direct mail received, 45 percent of it is read, at least to the extent of determining what the offer is about.[113] This figure compares extremely favorably with general print ads, where the "read most" scores are much lower, being 19 percent for newspaper ads and only 11 percent for consumer magazine ads. For direct mail ads, an approximate estimate is that 6 percent respond, by inquiring or ordering.[114]

**Telemarketing.** It is estimated that "attention" to telemarketing "cold calls" (outbound telemarketing) is approximately 40 percent; that is, about 60 percent of those called terminate the call once they realize it's a sales pitch.[115] However, the attention level for well-targeted category users or current customers would probably be similar to that for direct mail, with about 50 percent listening to the offer. Outbound telemarketing, of course, tries for an order since there's no inquiry. The average *order* incidence is about 7 percent.

**Interactive Ads.** Interactive ads can be placed on a CD-ROM or diskette for distribution to prospects or on the Internet. We will assume Web placement in the following analysis. Attention to interactive ads is 100 percent, as prospects activate the exposure themselves. The "hits" on the advertiser's Website can then result in "visits," whereby the prospect spends at least several minutes processing the ad's message by clicking through several pages of it.[116] Visits to various "pages" of the ad are called "page views," and are self-selected (hence interactive). The ad visitor may be seeking entertainment, information, or both. The

ad visitor may then terminate (leave the site) or decide to request further information from the advertiser by another medium (two-step ad) or place a purchase order on-screen (one-step ad).

### Communication Objectives for Direct Response Ads

After achieving initial attention, direct response ads, like all ads, are concerned with brand awareness and persuasion—the difference being that persuasion now refers to a further inquiry (for two-step direct response ads) or an outright purchase (for one-step direct response ads). Furthermore, with direct response ads of all types, *all five* communication effects are objectives. These are summarized in Table 10.18 and explained next.

**1.** *Category Need.* Direct response ads on the Web can assume category need to be present, but all others have to remind the target audience of the category need, at minimum, or more often, sell the category need. Direct response ads almost always quickly show or say what the product *is,* especially new products that have to position themselves instantly. Those that do not identify the product category quickly have a much lower response rate.[117]

**2.** *Brand Awareness.* Direct response ads have to induce immediate brand awareness—where, in this case, the most important brand is the *company* that is selling the product (there may or may not be a brand of *item*). The VisCAP model of presenter effectiveness from Chapter 9 can be applied here. The company must achieve instant visibility, expertise, and ob-

---

**TABLE 10.18**

**COMMUNICATION OBJECTIVES FOR DIRECT RESPONSE ADS**

1. *Category need:* remind or sell
2.–3. *Brand awareness and attitude:*
   a. The company making the offer is the main brand and acts as its own "presenter"; thus, it must be recognized and perceived in the ad as visible, expert, objective, and attractive (if selling a transformational product or service).
   b. The brand of item (if applicable) need only be recognized. The brand attitude objective is to create, or increase, to the maximum positive attitude.
4. *Brand purchase intention:* generate
5. *Purchase facilitation:* incorporate

jectivity—and, if it's a transformational choice situation, similarity to the target prospect's values as well. There may also be an element of power if a coercive direct response offer is being made, as by some government and public utility companies where the buyer has little option but to comply.

**3.** *Brand Attitude.* For a new item or service, the brand attitude has to be created from zero and increased to maximum positive—all in one exposure. For direct response ads, the brand attitude strategy is always high-involvement and, depending on the nature of the product or service, it can be sold by an informational motivation (such as household items) or by a transformational motivation (such as clothing or wines).

**4.** *Brand Purchase Intention.* In direct response ads, brand purchase intention is based on "hard sell": the intention to buy must be immediately and consciously generated. For this reason, direct response ads almost universally include a sales promotion incentive to urge the buyer to "act now." This is certainly the case for one-step direct response ads, although less of an incentive may be needed for two-step direct response ads since the prospect is only committing himself or herself to an inquiry rather than a purchase.

**5.** *Purchase Facilitation.* In direct response ads, brand purchase facilitation has to be incorporated into the ad: the prospect must know where to order, how to order (by phone, fax or mail, or at a local retailer), and how to pay (these days, usually by credit card). For TV direct response ads, the phone number should remain on the screen for at least 10 seconds.[118]

### Suggested Structural Formula for Direct Mail or One-Step Direct Response Print Ads

Direct mail or one-step direct response print ads usually will employ a "straight ad" format, not a conveyor. The body copy may use metaphorical verbal conveyors to some extent, but the lead-in in terms of picture and headline should be direct, rather than indirect as in the conveyor ad format (see Chapter 7).

There are five main structural elements in a direct mail or one-step direct response print ad, as shown in Table 10.19. For direct response ads, the classical AIDA formula provides the best summary of the sequence of responses to aim for: attention, interest, desire, and action.[119] (Note that AIDA is a summary communication model which concatenates processing and communication effects in the buyer response steps into a single hierarchy of effects: Attention [pro-

cessing], with the five communication objectives of Table 10.18, condensed into the Interest and Desire headings, with Action following.) Each structural element is linked to an AIDA objective by a communication strategy, as follows:

**1.** The first structural element is the *company* and how it is presented. If the company is unknown or does not appear credible, the respondent is unlikely to proceed further. Include some copy on company attributes or a "registered member" logo to enhance company credibility if you're unknown. (This should be accomplished first on the envelope of the offer, if using direct mail, and then in the offer itself. And if you're mailing repeatedly to the same respondents, *change* the envelope at least slightly each time.) The strategy is colloquially summarized as "credibility" and is mainly directed at the *attention* step in the hierarchy of effects.

**2.** The *product illustration,* or an illustration of the *service in action* if it is a service rather than a product being offered, is the next important element (more important than the headline if the offer is high-involvement/transformational). This should emphasize an "image match" between the offer and what the prospect is likely to want.[120]

**3.** The *headline* is also important (more important than the illustration if the offer is high-involvement/informational) and should also aim at attaining the image match. The best type of headline is two or three lines long, known as a "Johnson Box" headline,[121] which states the promise, but not its details, so that you want to read further ("How to

---

**TABLE 10.19**

**SUGGESTED STRUCTURAL FORMULA FOR DIRECT MAIL OR ONE-STEP DIRECT RESPONSE PRINT ADS[a]**
(Creative elements are aligned with AIDA hierarchy of effects objectives through four communication strategies.)

| Structural element | Communication strategy | Objective |
|---|---|---|
| 1. Company | "Credibility" | Attention |
| 2. Product or service illustration | "Image match" | Interest |
| 3. Headline | | |
| 4. Body copy | "Fact match" | Desire |
| 5. Response device | "Dealer match" | Action |

[a]See text for more detail.
*Source:* Adapted from KHBB advertising agency, London.

. . . ," "Find out . . . ," "You could win . . . ," and so forth). The image match strategy is aimed at the *interest* step in the hierarchy of effects.

**4.** The *body copy*, which will invariably be lengthy in direct response ads, should use the technique of "fact match," because it requires a high involvement/ informational, or an informational underlay to a high involvement/transformational, brand attitude strategy. "Fact match" is a shorthand description of selecting benefits and *benefit claims* that match up with (have high importance weights, $E_i$, with regard to) the prospect's needs (main purchase motive or motives, hence $E_{im}$). The fact match strategy is aimed at the *desire* step of the hierarchy of effects. Other tips:[122] (a) personalize or semipersonalize the addressee ("Dear Marketing Director"), (b) use testimonials from current customers, (c) add a bonus offer, and (d) specify a time limit for responding.

**5.** Finally, there is the *response device*. The strategy for the response device is known as "dealer match," and the purpose is to make it *credibly easy* for the prospect to respond. Clearly tell the reader *exactly* what he or she will get and *how* to respond. The dealer match strategy is aimed at the *action* step of the hierarchy of effects.

The ad for Berlitz Think and Talk language courses shown in Figure 10.7 quite discernibly shows the five structural elements of a direct response ad.

The product or service illustration, headline, and response device (creative elements 2, 3, and 5) are the three variables that are most often tested (by split-run) in direct response campaigns. As mentioned earlier, the body copy itself is less important[123] than the overall appeal represented by the illustration and the headline. Whereas it is well known that the illustration and headline are the two structural elements that are most often varied experimentally to find the highest-pulling version of the direct response ad, the response device itself is also an element that should be tested. In fact, response devices are often written in the form of a benefit claim.

The formula for direct response *broadcast* ads (TV or radio) would be quite similar. Again, AIDA is the response sequence to aim for and the communication strategies are the same, requiring only adaptation to the medium.

**FIGURE 10.7**
One-step direct response ad for Berlitz Think and Talk language courses, showing the five main structural elements: (1) company credibility—see the second sentence of the body copy and the photo caption at right; (2) product illustrations, clear and concrete; (3) a Johnson Box "find out how" headline with image-match content; (4) fact-match body copy, remarkably succinct; and (5) the response device, including a bonus offer.
*Courtesy:* Berlitz Publishing Co., Inc.

**Suggested Structural Formula for Telemarketing**

As mentioned previously, telemarketing is rather like "direct mail over the phone" except that, once past the (largely one-way) initial presentation, the message can be personally tailored to the customer just like personal (face-to-face) selling. However, little tailoring is usually necessary; in fact, one study suggests that a "canned" presentation is more effective than a customer-specific one.[124]

A "creative formula" for telemarketing sales pitches is given in Table 10.20, taken from an interesting and revealing article by telemarketing expert Stan Gyles.[125] The recommendations are self-explanatory.

### Suggested Structural Formula for Interactive Ads

Interactive ads are unlike other forms of ads because of the large degree of message self-selection built into their design. The "creative" in an interactive ad comprises two components: content (the message) and design (the execution). The structural elements in the message are much like a high-involvement, one-step, direct response *print* ad and, accordingly, the five-point, AIDA-aligned, direct response print ad formula (Table 10.19 and accompanying text) is recommended for the overall content in an interactive ad. The second component is the structure in the interactive ad's design that enables the prospect to click through pages by going from screen to screen; one page may occupy several consecutive screens and the prospect can select which pages to view. The banners and box-labels that guide the interested prospect through the ad function like "subheadlines." (In the pioneering Website ad entitled "Mama's Cucina" for Unilever's Van den Bergh division's Ragu sauces, a screen-page of which is shown in Figure 10.8, the subheadlines are the captions under the "plates" at the bottom of the screen-page.) These subheadlines are critical creative elements in that they must communicate quickly and interest the prospect to go to the elaborating page. Overall, interactive ads must be (1) structurally easy to use, (2) entertaining *if* prospects are likely to be less than intent on seeking information for its own sake, (3) informative, and (4) persuasive in the high-involvement manner (see Chapter 9) of exhibiting sensitivity to the buyer's initial attitude toward the brand. Interactive ads, because of their content-plus-design structure, require thorough pretesting before they are placed.

---

**TABLE 10.20**

#### SUGGESTED STRUCTURAL FORMULA FOR DIRECT RESPONSE TELEMARKETING

1. *Before placing the call:* Know the demographics of whom you're calling (so you can adapt your opening tone and ad-libbing style). If calling a repeat customer, have the customer's response history handy.

2. *Script:* The script of the prepared message should be no longer than eight short paragraphs (1 minute over the phone if it were delivered without pauses). The first 10 seconds is straight delivery; within 15–20 seconds you'll usually know whether it's worth continuing.

3. *To secretary (business calls):* Use a quick, efficient, assumptive tone.

   *To prospect (all calls):* Use short, clear sentences with active verbs and descriptive adjectives.

4. *Message points:* Deliver benefits in order of their importance, but save one or two for the close as "added" benefits; make the price clear.

5. *Objections:* Ask a clarifying question, restate the benefit, and try to close.

6. *Buyers:* Recap exactly what they've committed to (you have a legal responsibility to do this).

7. *Remember your company image:* Thank even *nonbuyers* as well as buyers.

*Source:* Gyles, 1991; see note 125.

---

**FIGURE 10.8**

A screen-page from the "Mama's Cucina" Website ad for Ragu Sauces, showing box-labels (subheadlines at bottom) to entice the viewer to process the ad further.
*Courtesy and source:* A different kind of menu, *BRANDWEEK*, April 15, 1996, pp. 42-43 and Van den Bergh Foods.

## SUMMARY

This chapter covers many different types of ads and their attention tactics and structural formulas. These are best summarized in the tables within the chapter itself. If you need more explanation, reread the text accompanying those tables.

## NOTES

1. S. Broadbent, *Spending Advertising Money,* 3rd ed. London: Business Books Ltd, 1979. This estimate is for prime-time programs and is the lower end of Broadbent's range assuming that attention has declined a little in recent years with the aging population and perhaps more distractions. The 88 percent figure for evening programs (5 PM onward) was independently confirmed in a carefully conducted in-home observational study by Clemenger advertising agency in Australia; see Clemenger Pty Ltd., *Your TV Commercial—Who's Really Watching?* Sydney, Australia: Clemenger Pty. Ltd., 1983.

2. The TV commercial ad recognition norm is about 60 percent as measured by Bruzzone Research Corporation (BRC). We use this measure to provide comparability with the Starch ad recognition measure for print ads. People are far more likely to be doing something else while watching TV, such as eating or reading, than they were several years ago, and visual attention, if not auditory attention, has declined; see Burke Marketing Research survey conducted for the Newspaper Advertising Bureau, summarized in *Research Alert,* June 7, 1991, p. 3.

3. For the ad length adjustments for TV commercials, we have to rely on advertisement recall data from syndicated services. The estimates in Table 10.1 are adapted primarily from Burke Marketing Research Inc., *The Effect of Environment and Executional Variables on Overall Memorability,* Cincinatti, OH: Burke Marketing Research Inc., 1979, which employs 24-hour or "day-after" advertisement recall, and is supplemented, for shorter commercials, by McCollum Spielman Worldwide's "Clutter Awareness" measure, with data reported in McCollum Spielman, Inc., Update: The 15-second commercial, *Topline,* 1989, *31,* whole issue. Recent TV commercial recall figures from South Africa, based on 9,430 commercials, confirm our indexes in Table 10.1 exactly; see E. DuPlessis, An advetising burst is just a lot of drips, *Admap;* July-August 1996, pp. 51–55.

4. ADWEEK, *Marketers Guide to Media,* 1994, *17* (1), p. 25.

5. As should be evident, the ad unit adjustments indicate their *contribution* to MEF, not the MEF itself. For in-stance, if the MEF for a particular brand and target audience is 2, then one 60-second commercial would contribute 1.2 toward the 2. For convenience, we will refer to "MEF =" rather than spelling out "contribution to MEF =" each time.

6. Field evidence, and our estimated attention index for 15-second commercials, would support the wisdom of avoiding them for new-product launch campaigns. For instance, McCollum Spielman Worldwide reports that only 6 percent of the hundreds of 15-second commercials it has tested over the years have been used to launch new products. See McCollum Spielman, Inc., same reference as in note 3.

7. J. Walter Thompson's Media Department report, summarized in: Small spots run, *Research Alert,* 1990, *8* (10), p. 6.

8. Same reference as in previous note.

9. McCollum Spielman, Inc., same reference as in note 3.

10. K. Haley, Expect wider brand name use of half-hours, *Advertising Age,* March 6, 1995, p. A2.

11. S. Winzenberg, Infomercials flowering on cable TV, *Advertising Age,* February 27, 1993, p. 18.

12. National Survey of 1,005 adults in 1992 conducted by Hudson Street Partners and Bruskin/Goldring Research. Reported in K. Haley, The infomercial begins a new era as a marketing tool for top brands, *Advertising Age,* January 25, 1993, pp. M-3 to M-4.

13. As reported by U.S. infomercial producer Greg Renker in *Marketing* (Australia), March 1994, p. 56. Like other direct response ads, infomercials are often tested in one or two local markets before a national media expenditure is decided. See T. Triplett, Big names crowd the infomercial airwaves, *Marketing News,* March 28, 1994, pp. 1–2.

14. M. S. Mord and E. Gilson, Shorter units: Risk—responsibility—reward, *Journal of Advertising Research,* 1985, *25* (4), pp. 9–19. Although attention is not affected by clutter, we will see in Chapter 17, that brand recall *is* affected by clutter if the clutter is specifically due to proximity of commercials for a *competing* brand.

15. Contrary to popular opinion, and somewhat surprisingly, Nielsen metered viewing data do *not* demonstrate that more channel switching takes place during commercials than during programs, which is the usual argument against between-program commercial positions. Also, with channel switching, the viewer is as likely to pick up a commercial on the new channel as to miss a commercial on the old one given that the switch is virtually instantaneous.

These results are confirmed by an independent study using meters, which found *less* switching of channels in between-program breaks (2 percent) than in during-program breaks (4 percent in daytime, 6 percent in prime time). The author of the latter study suggests that people switch to check other programs and avoid switching when they know commercials will be on the other channel. See G. J. Eskin, Tracking advertising and promotion performance with single-source data, *Journal of Advertising Research,* 1985, *25* (1), pp. 31, 33–39. On the other hand, channel switching could be less during between-program breaks because people are more likely to leave the room or concentrate on something else than during within-program breaks; the Clemenger study (see note 1) found 25 percent lower visual attention in between-program versus within-program breaks, and a British study in 1993 found 21 percent lower visual attention (K. Jonas, Does clutter matter? *Admap,* March 1996, pp. 14–15; *and* C. McDonald, What do we know about zapping and zipping? *Admap,* January 1996, pp. 13–14). However, ad recognition and ad recall data do *not* indicate any difference, so we continue to advocate no adjustment.

16. J. MacLachlan and M. Logan, Camera shot length in TV commercials and their memorability and persuasiveness, *Journal of Advertising Research,* 1993, *33* (2), pp. 7–61. These investigators studied over 600 30-second commercials that had a pace of one to 19 shots, and over 500 additional 30-second commercials that employed the "fast cut" rate of 20 or more shots in a 30-second interval.

17. J. L. Erickson, Energizer Bunny will plug Purina, *Advertising Age,* December 4, 1989, pp. 1, 54. The "interrupt" creative technique is spreading, as do most creative fads. For instance, in the United Kingdom recently, viewers were treated to a very sexy commercial, apparently for Häagen-Dazs, in which a guy, while "making out" with his girlfriend, opens the refrigerator, ostensibly to get Häagen-Dazs ice cream—but reaches instead for a Foster's beer! Even more bizarre, in Belgium, a local detergent manufacturer "recycled" a Unilever detergent commercial by blanking out the Unilever product and substituting it with the new brand! Whereas these attention-getting video techniques for TV commercials are undoubtedly creative, they are as yet too infrequently used to establish their effectiveness. Recycling, though, is becoming a business in itself. AdvantEdge Television Advertising, in New York, has inventoried award-winning retail commercials that are not used any more and is selling them to other retailers, in the same retail category but in a different region of the country or surviving the earlier retailer, whose logos can be easily dubbed in. Examples: commercials for the now defunct Alexander's department store chain, and for Delsym cough medicine. The original stores get a percentage of the royalties of the recycled commercials, though the original agency gets no further compensation. Recycled TV commercials are very low cost: $15,000–25,000 versus $200,000 for production of the original campaign in the case of Delsym, bought by True Quality Pharmacies in Texas. See M. Wells, Old ads get recycled by different retailers, *Advertising Age,* February 15, 1993, p. 12.

18. J. Koten, To grab viewers' attention, TV ads aim for the eardrum, *The Wall Street Journal,* January 26, 1984, p. 35.

19. D. Walker and M. F. von Gonten, Explaining related recall: New answers from a better model, *Journal of Advertising Research,* 1989, *29* (3), pp. 11–21. Interestingly, Stewart, Farmer, and Stannard found that musical commercials, as might be expected, were much better recognized when a *musical* cue was used during tracking. However, this is not always practical, requiring a video recorder to be used during personal interviews or an audio recorder during telephone interviews. See D. W. Stewart, K. M. Farmer, and C. I. Stannard, Music as a recognition cue in advertising tracking studies, *Journal of Advertising Research,* 1990, *30* (4), pp. 39–48.

20. D. W. Stewart and D. H. Furse, *Effective Television Advertising: A Study of 1000 Commercials,* Lexington, MA: Lexington Books, 1986.

21. G. Tom, Marketing with music, *Journal of Consumer Marketing,* 1990, *7* (2), pp. 49–53. Three commercials per music condition were tested for brand recall from their music tracks with the brand name deleted. The music tracks all had similar familiarity.

22. The five types of scripts are adapted from E. L. Klein, *Write Great Ads: A Step-by-Step Approach,* New York: Wiley, 1990. A further and sophisticated typology consisting of theme, plot, character, tone, and language has been identified by Stern and Gallagher, 1991; however, this is less conventional and remains more a framework for future research than a prescription for action. See B. B. Stern and K. Gallagher, Advertising form, content, and values: Lyric, ballad, and epic, in J. H. Leigh and C. R. Martin, Jr., eds., *Current Issues and Research in Advertising,* Graduate School of Business, University of Michigan, 1991, *13* (1), pp. 79–103.

23. McCollum Spielman Worldwide has shown that "hard sell" (types 1–3) and "celebrity testimonial" (type 4) TV commercials tend to do somewhat better in persuasion tests than "mood" or "humor" commercials, which parallels our informational-versus-transformational distinction. However, low-involvement/transformational ads should be tested with brand attitude rather than brand purchase intention as the measure of persuasion, so we didn't place much importance on this finding. See P. Klein, Image/mood television

advertising and the multiple exposure of test stimuli; Working paper, Great Neck, NY: McCollum Spielman Worldwide, Inc., 1991. Also, the other major testing service, ARS (Research Systems Corporation) finds no significant relationships between script type and persuasion; see D. W. Stewart and D. H. Furse, same reference as note 20.

24. See C. E. Young and M. Robinson, Video rhythms and recall, *Journal of Advertising Research*, 1989, *29* (3), pp. 22–25, and Visual connectedness and persuasion, *Journal of Advertising Research*, 1992, *32* (2), pp. 51–59; J. R. Rossiter, Visual imagery applications to advertising, in A. A. Mitchell, ed., *Advances in Consumer Research*, vol. 9, Ann Arbor MI: Association for Consumer Research, 1982, pp. 396–401; and J. R. Rossiter and L. Percy, *Advertising and Promotion Management*, New York: McGraw-Hill, 1987.

25. "Viewer interest" could be measured using "moment-to-moment" recording of target audience response to the ad on an interest scale. See especially G. D. Hughes, Realtime response measures redefine advertising wearout, *Journal of Advertising Research*, 1992, *32* (3), pp. 61–77.

26. See Chapter 8's discussion of brand recall tactics and also the study by Fazio, Herr, and Powell, cited in note 25 in that chapter.

27. W. J. Bryce and R. F. Yalch, Hearing versus seeing: A comparison of learning of spoken and pictorial information in television advertising, *Journal of Current Issues and Research in Advertising*, 1993, *15* (1), pp. 1–20. Using three carefully prepared and matched pairs of video-only or audio-only TV commercials, shown in a fairly natural "incidental learning" context, the study found an 8-to-1 advantage in learning of the ad's content (recall test) after one exposure and a 3-to-1 advantage even after four exposures.

28. These norms are based on over 2,000 tests by Radio Recall Research, Inc., using incidental listening and day-after recall (similar to the method described earlier for TV commercials). The norms are reported in R. Galen, I saw it on the radio: An overview of radio copy testing approaches, in Advertising Research Foundation, *Copy Research*, New York: ARF, 1985, pp. 227–236.

29. M. A. Sewall and D. Sarel, Characteristics of radio commercials and their recall effectiveness, *Journal of Marketing*, 1986, *50* (1), pp. 52–60.

30. The statistics for music and humor are from a large-scale content analysis of U.S. radio commercials by A. M. Abernethy, J. I. Gray, and H. J. Rotfeld, Combinations of creative elements in radio advertising, *Journal of Current Issues and Research in Advertising*, 1993, *15* (1), pp. 87–99.

31. M. A. Sewall and D. Sarel, same reference as note 29. For radio commercials, executional recall as a measure of overall attention is unaffected by humor; see cells with sufficient sample size in M. G. Weinberger and L. Campbell, The use and impact of humor in radio advertising, *Journal of Advertising Research*, 1991, *30* (6), pp. 44–51.

32. "Absolute interests" were identified formally by psychologist Roger Schank, but have been recognized informally for a long time in advertising. See R. C. Schank, Interestingness: Controlling inferences, *Artificial Intelligence*, 1979, *12* (3), pp. 273–297; and H. F. Adams, *Advertising and Its Mental Laws*, New York: Macmillan, 1916, pp. 129–146, especially Hollingworth's study described therein.

33. A. M. Abernethy et al., same reference as note 30.

34. This recommendation was suggested by the research of N. E. A. Kroll, E. M. Schepeler, and K. T. Angin, Bizzare imagery: The misremembered mnemonic, *Journal of Experimental Psychology: Learning, Memory, and Cognition*, 1986, *12* (1), pp. 42–53. See also our discussion of interactive mnemonic devices in Chapter 8 under brand recall tactics.

35. High-imagery or "vivid" copy used in a conveyor role in radio messages for serious, complex topics can actually result in *less* persuasion than "straight" copy because its imagery may distract the listener from listening closely to the content of the message arguments. See K. P. Frey and A. H. Eagly, Vividness can undermine the persuasiveness of messages, *Journal of Personality and Social Psychology*, 1993, *65* (1), pp. 32–52.

36. J. M. Hitchon and G. A. Churchill, Jr. (see Chapter 7, note 30).

37. Note that consumers in the experiment were prompted: the experiment did not estimate the proportion of radio listeners who would *spontaneously* experience visual imagery transfer. Also, the extent to which the "secondhand" radio-stimulated image is sufficiently detailed and vivid to provide an effective substitute for a TV commercial exposure is not known. Last, the audio tracks of most TV commercials would not be suitable or complete enough to serve as radio commercials—TV commercials whose audio tracks can double as radio commercials would have to be specially produced. See T. Coffin and S. Tuchman, TV without pix, *Media/Scope*, 1968, 12 (February), pp. 46–53.

38. D. J. Howard and R. E. Burnkrant, Question effects on information processing in advertising, *Psychology & Marketing,* 1990, *7* (1), pp. 27–46.

39. At the time, mid-1993, the U.K. beer market was being invaded by a number of Australian lagers, notably

Foster's and XXXX (Four-Ex). Australians visiting the "mother country" are regarded as a bit loud or loutish and, according to the ad's intent, these loutish Australian beers should not be confused with this sophisticated New Zealand entry.

40. A recent study suggests that tactical variables in radio commercials may explain only about 10 percent of the variance in persuasion—a figure very similar to that suggested by Stewart and Furse for TV commercials (see note 20). See R. H. Coulter and M. A. Sewall, A test of prescriptive advice from the Rossiter-Percy Advertising Planning Grid using radio commercials, in C. T. Allen and D. Roedder John, eds., *Advances in Consumer Research*, vol. 21, 1994, pp. 276–281. For broadcast commercials, the *creative idea* is probably the main factor. For print ads, however, the "mechanical" tactics explain much more variance.

41. J. R. Rossiter, The limited effect of likable ads, Working paper, Sydney: Australian Graduate School of Management, 1993. Also, the humor finding is basically supported by the Weinberger and Campbell study; see note 31.

42. The European television landscape, *Admap*, February 1994, pp. 96–97.

43. Survey by Starch/INRA Hooper (now Roper Starch), Mamaroneck, NY, 1991.

44. The norms for newspaper advertisements were obtained from the most recent source available, a study of 763 newspaper ads in Australia in 1990 by Quadrant Research and the Newspaper Advertising Bureau, using Starch methodology. Newspaper readers were interviewed within 25 hours of receiving the daily paper. See G. Kelly, How to advertise in print media, Melbourne, Australia: Quadrant Research, 1991. The men's and women's position-in-paper norms, however (see Table 10.7), were taken from older Starch norms in the United States and confirmed by a recent British study by G. Wicken, What newspapers' readers like best, *Admap*, April 1994, pp. 27–32.

45. Australian newspaper ad study, same reference as in note 44.

46. Eye-tracking study of 36 randomly selected newspaper ads with 70 readers per ad; see J. Chisolm, Does color make a difference? *Admap*, December 1995, pp. 17–21.

47. Australian newspaper ad study, same reference as in note 44.

48. J. R. Rossiter, Predicting Starch scores, *Journal of Advertising Research*, 1981, *21* (5), pp. 63–68; and The increase in magazine ad readership, *Journal of Advertising Research*, 1988, *28* (5), pp. 35–39.

49. Australian newspaper ad study, same reference as in note 44.

50. Australian newspaper ad study, same reference as in note 44.

51. J. R. Rossiter, 1988, same reference as in note 48.

52. For the consumer magazine ad norms, we have used new data from a 1992–93 Australian study of over 2,500 ads using the Starch procedure. The consumer sample is from readers of the major *women*'s magazine in Australia and consists of primary shoppers only. The main reason we favor this data set over others is that, after ad size norms were calculated, we were able to evaluate all other norms while holding ad size constant. Acknowledgement: Chris Gibson and Australian Consolidated Press, Ltd.

53. The data on "checkerboard" ads come from Starch/INRA Hooper, Inc., *Starch Tested Copy*, 1989, *1* (11), p. 2.

54. Starch/INRA Hooper, Inc., *Starch Tested Copy*, 1990, *1* (12), pp. 1–2.

55. Starch/INRA Hooper, Inc., *Starch Tested Copy*, 1990, *2* (8), pp. 1–2. The editorial- and ad-opposite noneffects were also confirmed in the Australian database.

56. A. Phillips, Lessons from response advertising, *Journal of Targeting Measurement and Analysis for Marketing*, 1993, *1* (3), pp. 273–279. The coupon position findings probably also hold for response devices in which a toll-free telephone number, rather than a "cut out" coupon, is used. In primarily direct response ads, the phone number is usually "boxed" anyway, often with an option to reply by cutting and mailing or faxing. As bottom right or bottom middle is the *usual* reply coupon position, and these positions draw better on left-hand pages, this seems to explain most of the left-page advantage for direct response ads. Note that if other positions became more frequent, the page-side advantage indexed in the table could disappear, as for non-DR print ads.

57. J. R. Rossiter, 1981 and 1988, same references as in note 48.

58. A. Finn, Print ad recognition readership scores: An information processing perspective, *Journal of Marketing Research*, 1988, *25* (2), pp. 168–177.

59. Although consumer magazine ads without a picture are rare, the Australian database results suggest over 40 percent lower attention if a picture is *not* included in the ad.

60. J. R. Rossiter, 1981, same reference as in note 48.

61. A direct effect of picture size on brand attitude was obtained in two studies for transformational products (beer and a soft drink). See J. R. Rossiter and L. Percy, Mediating effects of visual and verbal elements in print advertising upon belief, attitude, and intention responses, in L. Percy and A. G. Woodside, eds.,

*Advertising and Consumer Psychology*, Lexington, MA: Lexington Books, 1983, Chapter 9.

62. A single dominant focal point for the picture has been recommended by Starch testers for many years; see, for instance, What makes people look at advertisements and read them through—part I, *Starch Tested Copy*, early series, no date, *2* (17), whole issue. We ignore a later analysis that showed very little difference in attention for single dominant focal point versus one dominant with one subordinate, as this undoubtedly was confounded by including a small (and usually necessary) additional product illustration rather than a multiple-focal point single illustration. See With focal points, the fewer the better, *Starch Tested Copy*, 1990, *2* (6), pp. 1, 2, 4.

63. The Vivitar ads and their Starch scores are from Which ad pulled better? *Starch Tested Copy*, 1990, *2* (3), p. 3.

64. Which ad pulled better? *Starch Tested Copy*, 1991, *3* (8), p. 5.

65. The Starch organization has actually published two studies of celebrities in consumer magazine ads. The first, conducted in 1979 and 1980, was a carefully matched study among women readers using celebrity and noncelebrity ads for the same product categories. The second study, reported in 1990, did not apply as precise controls and found, as we might expect, a somewhat weaker overall effect, celebrity ads averaging only 15 percent gain in attention in women's magazines and 10 percent gain in men's magazines. Also, the sample of celebrity ads was small. The earlier, better controlled study is emphasized here. Also note that women paid greater attention only to female celebrities, not to male celebrities who are sometimes used to advertise products suitable for both sexes in women's magazines. See Celebrity testimonials still effective, *Starch Tested Copy*, early series (ca. 1980), *1* (10), whole issue; and When celebrities play roles in advertisements, *Starch Tested Copy*, 1990, *2* (5), pp. 1–2.

66. See the later study cited in note 65. The relative gain in attention was only 10 percent, and the sample of celebrity ads was very small, making this result not very reliable.

67. About (type) face, *Starch Tested Copy*, December 1992, *4* (11), p. 2.

68. Canadian Starch studies summarized in Reader's Digest Australia's *Research Digest*, 1985, October, pp. 1–2.

69. M. A. Just and P. A. Carpenter, *The Psychology of Reading and Language Comprehension*, Boston: Allyn and Bacon, 1987.

70. J. R. Rossiter, 1981, same reference as in note 48.

71. Canadian Starch studies, same reference as note 68.

72. See L. Percy and J. R. Rossiter, *Advertising Strategy: A Communication Theory Approach*, New York: Praeger, 1980, pp. 159–161, and also L. Hickey, Being positive about the negative in advertising, *International Journal of Advertising*, 1984, *3* (4), pp. 369–372.

73. Reverse print revisited, *Starch Tested Copy*, 1992, *4* (1), pp. 1–3.

74. Reverse print revisited, same reference as note 73, pp. 1–3, 6.

75. It's not how long you make your copy; it's how you make it long, *Starch Tested Copy*, 1990, *2* (11), whole issue. Significantly, the 750 ads included in this study were for high-involvement product categories: financial, automotive, and travel.

76. M. C. Macklin, N. T. Bruvold, and C. L. Sheay, Is it always as simple as "keep it simple"? *Journal of Advertising*, 1985, *14* (4), pp. 28–35. In this experiment, the investigators used three versions of copy difficulty using the Coleman formula, which counts the number of syllables per 100 words and which has been found to be a very good predictor of the more precise Cloze procedure ($r = .83$). The investigators took an original ad for a cold remedy with a Coleman index of 170 (1.7 syllables per word) and prepared three test versions with Coleman indices of 147, 165, and 176. Admittedly, these are not large variations. Nevertheless, the investigators found no effect of copy readability on purchase intention for the advertised brand. See also W. L. Taylor, Cloze Procedure: A new tool for measuring readability, *Journalism Quarterly*, 1953, *30* (3), pp. 415–433; G. M. Zinkhan, B. D. Gelb, and C. R. Martin, The Cloze Procedure, *Journal of Advertising Research*, 1983, *23* (3), pp. 15–20; E. B. Coleman, Improving comprehension by shortening sentences, *Journal of Applied Psychology*, 1962, *46* (2), pp. 131–134; and J. Sushan and U. O. Boya, Readability formulas and print ads: Problems and a new approach, T. A. Shimp, ed., *American Marketing Association Educators Conference Proceedings*, Chicago: American Marketing Association, 1986, pp. 201–205.

77. J. R. Miller and W. Kintsch, Readability and recall of short prose passages: A theoretical analysis, *Journal of Experimental Psychology: Human Learning and Memory*, 1980, *6* (4), pp. 335–355. In a very interesting but unreplicated experiment (one ad only), Lowrey found that syntactically complex copy containing negative, passive, and left-branching sentences ("For colds, take Contac" is left-branching whereas "Take Contac for colds" is right-branching) may help to overcome weak benefits, perhaps by reducing counterarguing. For the fictional breakfast cereal ad used in the study, strong benefits were taste, low fat, and crispy; weak benefits were lightweight package, small box for easy storage, and widely available. Brand attitude was significantly lower for the weak claims with

simple copy but equalled the strong claims when complex copy was used. See T. M. Lowrey, The relationship between syntactic complexity and advertising persuasiveness, in J. F. Sherry and B. Sternthal, eds., *Advances in Consumer Research*, 1992, vol. 19, pp. 270–274.

78. R. E. Christiansen, Prose memory: Forgetting rates for memory codes, *Journal of Experimental Psychology: Human Learning and Memory*, 1980, *6* (5), pp. 611–619.

79. R. J. Donovan, A. Oshinsky, and J. R. Rossiter, High involvement print ads and copy readability, Unpublished paper, Sydney: Australian Graduate School of Management, 1989.

80. J. R. Rossiter and L. Percy, Attitude change through visual imagery in advertising, *Journal of Advertising,* 1980, *9* (2), pp. 10–16.

81. Logotypes, the sequel, *Starch Tested Copy*, 1990, *2* (7), pp. 1–2.

82. The place of the logotype in advertising effectiveness, *Starch Tested Copy*, 1990, *2* (1), pp. 1–2, 4.

83. Logotypes, the sequel, same reference as note 81. The Australian database (see note 52) confirms this by finding a branding ratio of 72 percent for difficult-to-detect brand names or sponsors, compared with 79 percent for brands or sponsors judged easy to detect.

84. Ad Chart "Noticed" average from *Iron Age* magazine, 1-page, 3- and 4-color ads, as reported in L. C. Soley and L. N. Reid, Industrial ad readership as a function of headline type, *Journal of Advertising*, 1983, *12* (1), pp. 34–38.

85. The industrial and business magazine attention data are 1978 results taken from Carr Reports, published by Cahners Publishing Company, Boston (ca. 1983). The exact advertising recognition method used was not reported, although industrial and business magazines usually use a mail sample version of Starch scores. Thus, the adjustments should be internally applicable to advertising in this medium if not exactly comparable across media. The sample of magazines is skewed toward truly industrial publications such as trade and technical journals and is thus more truly applicable to industrial ads than data from more general-interest business magazine such as Business Week.

86. L. C. Soley and L. N. Reid, Predicting industrial ad readership, *Industrial Marketing Management*, 1983, *12* (3), pp. 201–206.

87. L. C. Soley and L. N. Reid, same reference as note 84. The 12 percent "read most" figure for other ads is 1 point higher than the 11 percent average for all industrial ads, possibly because the investigators excluded ads with headlines that were difficult to identify or classify and also restricted the sample to 1-page, 3- and 4-color ads.

88. L. C. Soley, Copy length and industrial advertising readership, *Industrial Marketing Management*, 1986, *15* (3), pp. 245–251.

89. G. L. Clark, P. F. Kaminsky, and G. Brown, The readability of advertisements and articles in trade journals, *Industrial Marketing Management*, 1990, *19* (3), pp. 251–260.

90. Directories such as the *Yellow Pages* appear in 2, 3, 4 and 5-column formats in various countries and regions. Most common in the United States is the 4-column format. The largest display ads permitted are 2 or 3 columns wide and half a page long—occupying about a quarter of the total page for a 4-column directory. Display ads can use an illustration in addition to the company logo (the company must *also* be listed in the regular in-column alphabetic listings). However, up to 3-inch long in-column listings can be bought, with a company logo, so these are displaylike also. For simplicity, the size indexes in Table 10.13 are based on display ads, not in-column listings ads.

91. Special acknowledgement is due to William Burlace and John Chalmers of Yellow Pages Australia for these statistics. The size indexes are estimated from studies commissioned by YPA in 1988 and 1991 in which large samples of adult shoppers were shown randomly selected pages containing display ads (5-column) of various sizes and asked, "Which one would you ring [call]?" This is a very good measure of attention since it averages over creative content. The color indexes are estimated from further YPA-commissioned studies in 1991, conducted similarly, in which shoppers were asked, "Which ad did you notice first?," a measure which should be comparable to the (averaged) "would call" measure in registering, approximately, competitive attention. In another recent YPA-commissioned survey, 87 percent of category shoppers claimed to make their choice from the display ads rather than the in-column listings. The survey's results are summarized in the booklet, *Yellow Pages™ Customer Information*, Burwood, Victoria, Australia, Yellow Pages Australia, 1993.

92. This survey was conducted in 1986–87 by Statistical Research, Inc., for the American Association of Yellow Pages Publishers and reported in B. Maher, *Getting the Most from Your Yellow Pages Advertising*, New York: Amacom Press, 1988, appendix C. The sample size was very large, consisting of over 14,000 adults, so the figures should be highly reliable. However, the sample for this survey included only those who had purchased at least one of 24 different types of products or services in the preceding 30 days, so the figures may be *slightly* biased upward in that the survey presumably excluded about 20 percent of adults who had *not* looked in the *Yellow Pages* in the

past month. In any given month, about 80 percent of adults consult the *Yellow Pages* for one or more products or services.

93. See B. Maher, same reference as previous note, referring to a 1985–86 survey by the same company in which a large sample of the general population of adults reported the number of *Yellow Pages* references per year for various product and service categories. The data are reported in Maher's table 1.1, on pp. 29–30, and have been adjusted here to a per capita basis.

94. B. Maher, same reference as note 92, figures from the 1986–87 survey representing the average incidence across 24 product and service categories.

95. B. Maher, same reference as note 92.

96. In the United States outdoor ads are technically "posters" for media-buying purposes, with effective ad sizes of 10′ × 22′ (8-sheet) and 5′ × 11′ (30 sheet). Larger outdoor ads, such as UniRoyal's tire in Detroit or the Marlboro sign in Chicago, are called "bulletins." See ADWEEK, *Marketer's Guide to Media*, 1994, *17* (1), pp. 88–91.

97. A. Hodges, How poster campaigns perform, *Admap*, 1993, April, pp. 32–33, 35, 36.

98. The Hodges Study, by RSL-signpost, attempted to measure branding by the "masked recognition" procedure. Technically, this is a *recall procedure* in which the cue is the ad and the brand name has to be recalled, though probably from visual memory. The branding level achieved by this procedure was only 21 percent. Dividing this by the noting level of 40 percent, we get a "branding ratio" of only 53 percent—which is very poor. However, we are reasonably sure that had the investigators used a conventional recognition procedure for measuring branding, similar to the "seen associated" score used by Starch, the branding level would be the same as for magazine ads.

99. In a typical city, 15 percent of roads account for 85 percent of vehicular traffic; same reference as note 97.

100. In the most relevant available study, though with a small sample of ads (see the following note) it was found that unaided recall of the average outdoor ad (billboard) in a competitive setting by regular commuters past the ad's site was about 40 percent, consistent with our estimate. See N. Donthu, J. Cherian, and M. Bhargava, Factors influencing recall of outdoor advertising, *Journal of Advertising Research*, 1993, *33* (3), pp. 64–72. An even more recent study by this team reported a Starch-type ad recognition average of 33 percent but did *not*, apparently, control for opportunity to see the ad as in the previous study, and so this is probably an underestimate of attention. Also, this study seems to have mixed billboards and posters in the ad sample. See M. Bhargava, N. Donthu, and R.

Caron, Improving the effectiveness of outdoor advertising, *Journal of Advertising Research*, 1994, *34* (2), pp. 46–55. Note that for stand-alone ads, the attention value of 2.5 is the ratio of 100 percent attention to 40 percent for ads in competitive settings

101. A limited set of billboards (7 color, 3 black and white) was studied in the 1993 article by N. Donthu et al, who actually found a 43 percent advantage in attention (unaided and recall) for *black and white* billboards. However, as ad content was not controlled, we hesitate to use this finding.

102. B. Stone, *Successful Direct Marketing Methods*, 5th ed., Lincolnwood, IL: NTC Publishing Group, 1994.

103. Estimates of the expenditure on direct mail varies, with some commentators putting it ahead of newspapers and TV advertising and others just behind them. In any event, following telemarketing, direct mail is one of the next three largest media.

104. J. Howard-Brown, How targeting reduces resistance to direct mail, *Journal of Targeting, Measurement and Analysis for Marketing*, 1993, *1* (4), pp. 403–413.

105. A. J. Bush and R. P. Bush, A content analysis of direct response television advertising, *Journal of Direct Marketing*, 1990, *4* (1), pp. 6–12.

106. Simmons Market Research Bureau's 1990 and 1991 Study of Media and Markets, cited in *Research Alert*, December 18, 1992, pp. 1,2.

107. S. King, Aggressive television sales beat recession, *The Australian*, June 21, 1991, p. 19.

108. SMRB 1990 and 1991 Study of Media and Markets, same reference as note 106.

109. B. Lamons, Creativity is important to direct marketers, too, *Marketing News*, December 7, 1992, p. 10.

110. B. Sharp, Direct marketing—the database, *Marketing Intelligence & Planning*, 1989, *7* (1,2), pp. 19–21.

111. G. Baker, Taking sellers' case direct to the consumer, *The Australian*, July 19, 1991, p. 19.

112. U.S. Postal Service Household Diary Study, 1990, reported in J. R. Wargo and J. L. Rogers, USPS: A marketing and sales partner, *Advertising Age*, August 31, 1992, p. M-6. The statistics cited here are a little higher in the United Kingdom: 80 percent open, 59 percent read, and 7 percent respond; see J. Howard-Brown, same reference as note 104. Notice that these response rates are for ordering *or inquiring* and are therefore higher than the "1.2 percent" *order* norm widely used some years ago for direct mail. Also, targeting has presumably improved, leading to a higher response rate for direct mail.

113. J. R. Wargo and J. L. Rogers, same reference as previous note.

114. Translated to U.S. figures from J. Howard-Brown, same reference as note 104.

115. Factoids, *Research Alert*, February 19, 1993, p. 6.

116. P. Berthon, L. F. Pitt, and R. T. Watson, The World Wide Web as an advertising medium: toward an understanding of conversion efficiency, *Journal of Advertising Research*, 1996, *36* (1), pp. 43–54.

117. A. Phillips, same reference as note 56.

118. S. Andrews, Direct response on the small screen, *Admap*, June 1994, pp. 38–40. Andrews actually recommends "rather longer than three seconds," and we translate this British understatement to "at least 10 seconds."

119. First publicized in E. K. Strong, *The Psychology of Selling*, New York: McGraw-Hill, 1925, but apparently invented by St. Elmo Lewis.

120. Adopted from the "KHBB Bucket" formula developed by the KHBB advertising agency, London, and discussed in G. McCorkell, *Advertising That Pulls Response*, London: McGraw-Hill, 1990, chapter 2.

121. See M. L. Roberts and P. D. Berger, *Direct Marketing Management*, Englewood Cliff, NJ: Prentice-Hall 1989, pp. 224–225.

122. M. Pavlish, Great direct mail [pieces] generate great results, *Marketing News*, February 19, 1990, p. 8.

123. In a field experiment reported recently, the readability (mainly the vocabulary level) of the body copy was varied significantly in a mailing to professional and nonprofessional audiences. No difference in response rates, in either segment, was found. See D. L. Williams, J. D. Beard, and J. P. Kelly, The readability of direct-mail copy, *Journal of Direct Marketing*, 1991, *5* (1), pp. 27–34. Similarly, it seems to make little difference even if the body copy is "disorganized." One experiment (with forced exposure, although we doubt whether this would have affected the results) scrambled the paragraph order and found no difference in purchase intentions compared with the original version! The illustration and the headline (the "appeal") seem to be far more important. See W. H. Motes, C. B. Hilton, and J. S. Fielden, Reactions to creative variations of a direct response ad, *Journal of Direct Marketing*, 1989, *3* (3), pp. 16–26.

124. M. A. Jolson, The underestimated potential of the canned sales presentation, *Journal of Marketing*, 1975, *39* (1), pp. 75–78.

125. S. Gyles, Threading your way through a minefield, *The Australian*, June 21, 1991, p. 18. Stan Gyles is managing director of Action Direct Marketing, Melbourne, Australia.

## DISCUSSION QUESTIONS

**10.1. to 10.8.:** For each of the eight types of ads discussed in this chapter, find three ads that you think are effective and three ineffective (48 ads total), then analyze them in terms of the attention characteristics and the recommended structural formula for each. (This will be a lengthy project, or it can be done for selected ad types only.)

## FURTHER READING

Roberts, M. L., and Berger, P. D. *Direct Marketing Management.* Englewood Cliffs, NJ: Prentice-Hall, 1989.

This is an excellent academic text on direct marketing. It is comprehensive and combines excellent knowledge of the academic perspective with broad knowledge of the practitioner perspective. The book covers all forms of direct marketing, including direct response advertising , although it predates interactive advertising.

The *Journal of Direct Marketing* (U.S.) and the *Journal of Targeting, Measurement and Analysis for Marketing* (U.K.).

These are the two best journals for those interested in direct response advertising and database marketing. The U.S. journal is somewhat more academic and experimental, but much experimentation is needed in this growing field of advertising. The U.K. journal tends to be dominated by practitioners and contains many managerially useful articles.

## PART FIVE

# INTEGRATED COMMUNICATIONS STRATEGY

**CHAPTER 11: CORPORATE ADVERTISING COMMUNICATIONS**

**CHAPTER 12: MANUFACTURER'S PROMOTIONS**

**CHAPTER 13: RETAILER'S PROMOTIONS**

**CHAPTER 14: DIRECT MARKETING PROMOTIONS**

# Corporate Advertising Communications

$\mathbf{P}$art Five is about integrated marketing communications (IMC) and integrated communications strategy.[1] This chapter explains what an integrated communications strategy requires and then shows how corporate advertising communications (the corporation being any company or organization, government or private, manufacturer or retailer) can achieve such a strategy. The second chapter in Part Five shows how manufacturers can achieve an integrated communications strategy with promotions. The third chapter shows how retailers can achieve an integrated communications strategy with retail promotions. The final chapter examines integrated communications strategy for direct marketing promotions.

In this chapter, after explaining integrated communications strategy, we look at corporate advertising communications activities, defined as advertising-related means of contributing to the company's (and, indirectly or directly, its brand's or brands') communication objectives and position. The principal corporate advertising communications activities are *general advertising* (covered previously in Chapters 8 through 10); *corporate identity and PR; corporate image advertising;* and *sponsorships, event marketing, and publicity.* After reading this chapter, you should:

- Understand what integrated communications strategy requires in terms of positioning and timing.
- Know how to allocate the overall AC&P budget to the IMC activities selected for the campaign.

- Appreciate the value of a corporate identity program and public relations activities.
- Understand when to employ corporate image advertising.
- See how corporate sponsorhips, event marketing, and publicity can be used as complements to—and, in some cases, as substitutes for—general advertising.

## INTEGRATED COMMUNICATIONS STRATEGY

### The Essence of IMC: Three Principles of Integration

To *integrate* (from the Latin verb *integrare*) means to "make whole or complete by adding or bringing together parts."[2] Integrated marketing communications (IMC), therefore, adds or brings together various techniques (see Figure 11.1) for advertising and promoting the product or service to the buyer. The "bringing together" part of the definition we interpret as referring to the need for *centrally* integrating the various advertising communications and promotion activities to reinforce the brand's positioning—as well as, before that, media *selection* integration of the activities themselves. The "adding" part of the definition we interpret as referring to the successive addition of advertising communications and promotion activities along the customer *timeline* of the marketing channel.

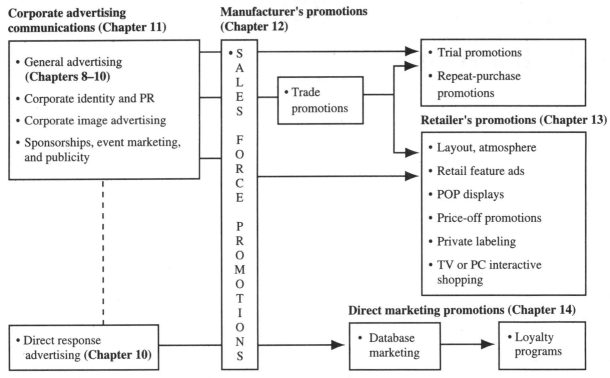

**FIGURE 11.1**
IMC activities and the customer timeline (chapter locations shown).

Essentially, the three main questions (and, in parentheses, the three principles of integration) in IMC strategy are as follows:

**1.** Which are the best and most efficient advertising communications and promotions *media* to use in combination to achieve the brand's communication objectives? (*selection* integration)

**2.** How can each advertising communications activity and promotion activity's *message* be made synergistically consistent with the brand's positioning? (*positioning* integration)

**3.** At what points in the marketing channel should advertising communications or promotions reach *buyers* and perhaps speed up the decision in favor of our brand? (*customer timeline* integration)

### IMC Activities and Media (Selection Integration)

IMC activities work on the same five communication effects as advertising. This realization enables *selection integration* of IMC activities as *media*.

(Here we will provide an introduction sufficient to explain the principle. IMC media selection is presented operationally in Chapter 15.) The manager should think of the prospective buyer in the target audience as needing to have the five basic communication effects "filled as mental bins" in his or her head—and then decide which forms of advertising communications and promotion would be the best means of doing so.

The relative communication strengths of advertising communications and promotions are depicted graphically in Figure 11.2. Advertising communications generally make their strongest contributions to brand awareness and brand attitude (as emphasized in Part Four of this book). Promotions generally make their strongest contributions to brand awareness and brand purchase intention. However, a point we wish to make early and then continually emphasize is that the best promotions are those which *also* work on brand attitude. These are called customer franchise building (CFB) promotions.[3]

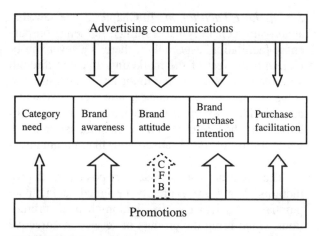

**FIGURE 11.2**
The relative strengths of advertising communications and promotions in contributing to the five basic communication effects are indicated in the diagram by the relative thickness of the arrows.

The relative strengths and weaknesses of advertising communications and promotions in contributing to the five communication effects are as follows.

**1.** *Category Need.* Category need, in most product or service categories, originates mainly from cultural changes (for new categories) and becomes motivating due to the individual's overall or temporary circumstances (for new and existing categories). Advertising communications activities can have some effect on category need by "selling the category" (see Chapter 5's category need options). However, selling the category is more a matter of *suggesting* the category—for example, heart-healthy foods—as a solution to an already reasonably strong buyer motivation, such as avoiding the problem of heart attacks in adult years. Only rarely can advertising create a motivation as such. Rather, advertising communications *position* the category as a better way of meeting an *existing* motivation.

Promotions can accelerate category need—can make it occur earlier—although usually only to a fairly minor degree. For example, car manufacturers usually offer substantial rebates whenever the economy is in a slump, but these have only a relatively minor effect. "Accelerate" rather than "sell" is the operative term here: promotions don't really "sell" the category need so much as attempt to "speed up" the sales process somewhat.

In the figure, advertising communications and promotions are shown as having—in general—a relatively *minor* influence on category need. Again, although this is their general effect, many specific instances of successfully selling or accelerating category need do occur, particularly with one-step direct response ads, as explained in Chapter 10.

**2.** *Brand Awareness.* Brand awareness is a traditional strength of advertising communications—and of promotions as well. You may remember from Chapter 1 that new product introductions, where brand awareness is a major objective, are typically launched with equally heavy expenditures on advertising communications (including publicity) *and* promotion.

Some of the advertising-like communications activities—particularly sponsorships, event marketing, and publicity, since they work in a similar manner to media advertising—can increase *brand recall* as long they associate the brand with the category need. Similarly, loyalty programs can make you more likely to recall the brand when the category need arises (for example, frequent-flier programs tend to increase members' recall of the airline).

Promotion offers help prospective buyers to consider new brands and to reconsider existing, familiar ones. Promotions achieve this by drawing reflexive attention to the brand (for example, via a display or sample pack) and also by producing selective attention (for example, by offering a coupon promising extra value). More specifically, as these examples suggest, most promotions work via *brand recognition*. Cash-register issued coupons, for instance, can make you smartly *recognize* and *reconsider* the couponed brand for your next purchase.

It is very important, therefore, that the executional tactics of advertising-related communications and promotional activities adhere to the same tactics recommended for brand recognition and brand recall in general advertising, as outlined in Chapter 8.

**3.** *Brand Attitude.* Brand attitude achievement is traditionally the province of advertising communications. However, the best promotions *also* work on brand attitude (and here we mean the buyer's *personal* attitude toward the brand, $PA_b$, not merely impersonal attitude, $IA_b$, which promotions obviously affect, a distinction we made in Chapter 5, chapter appendix 5B). Whereas this is quite evident for advertising-like communications activities such as sponsorships and publicity, it is much less evident for *price-based* promotions. Whereas most price-based promotions are aimed simply at causing a short-term increase in sales, there are ways of executing them such that they are more likely to make a longer-term contribution to the brand's "image" in the form of brand attitude (the more permanent $PA_b$ component, in the more advanced conceptualization of brand attitude given in Chapter 5, appendix 5A). The ideal promotion should create a longer-term brand attitude effect and thereby *maximize full-value purchases when the promotion is withdrawn.*

In fact, the evidence is now considerable that promotions of any type should not be used unless they *do* have a longer-term effect in favor of the brand. This can occur in two ways: (a) by bringing new triers into the brand's franchise, or (b) by increasing brand awareness and, our focus here, brand attitude, among the brand's current buyers. Thus, CFB (customer franchise building) promotions mean just that—they either bring in new customers or strengthen the patronage of current customers. In Chapters 12 through 14, we will show how most promotions, if thoughtfully implemented, can produce more permanent brand attitude effects—and thus continue to positively influence sales after the promotion period has ended.

**4.** *Brand Purchase Intention.* Brand purchase intention is the second communication strength of promotions, along with brand awareness. All promotions are aimed at "moving sales forward" immediately (regardless of their longer-term consequences), and *most* of them achieve this by stimulating immediate brand purchase intention (usually through impersonal attitude, $IA_b$, again as explained in Chapter 5's appendix 5A). The intentions that promotions aim at with regard to *purchase* are the following:

- To buy the brand in the first place (rather than not buy it)
- To buy it now (rather than later)
- To buy multiple units or a larger amount of it (rather than the normal amount)
- To continue to buy the brand (repeat-purchase or customer retention)

As well, promotions are responsible for many *purchase-related* intentions for consumer durables and industrial products—such as to visit showrooms, to call for a sales demonstration, or to remain as a customer in the future.

**5.** *Purchase Facilitation.* In Chapter 5, we saw that advertising generally has a limited influence on purchase facilitation, especially if there is a severe problem with the rest of the marketing mix that through poor planning has been left to the advertising to try to solve. In some circumstances, however, advertising can provide a short-term alleviation of these problems. This short-term circumstantial alleviation is not a capability of other advertising-like communications, however.

The situation is somewhat more positive with promotions. Many are expressly designed to facilitate purchase, particularly distribution-channel promotions which bring the product or service in attractive form right to the customer, and special introductory price promotions. However, *real problems* with the 4Ps of product, price, place, and personal selling (the main purchase inhibitors) should be corrected at the source rather than patched over with promotions. Promotions, at best, are only a temporary solution and can become very costly if used persistently to facilitate sales. Overall, we attribute a moderate influence to promotions in achieving purchase facilitation.

Although we have compared advertising communications and promotions, it must be realized that promotions *alone* can create all five necessary communication effects. Advertising, in the conventional sense of general advertising, may not be part of the marketing communications mix for some products and services. An industrial marketer may use only trade shows, for instance; a consumer marketer may use only trade promotions and in-store consumer promotions; and a retailer may rely exclusively on point-of-purchase promotions and perhaps also use database and loyalty marketing to the store's regular customers. Each of the nonadvertising promotions can be constructed to create or remind prospective customers of category need, increase brand awareness, increase brand attitude, stimulate brand purchase intention, and facilitate purchase when necessary.

With advertising communications and promotion activities, it's a matter of deciding which avenue to communicating with the target audience will work best at the lowest cost. Chapter appendix 11A, Avon's New IMC Strategy, provides a prominent example of this decision. However, the mechanics of selection integration are essentially a media selection decision (see Chapter 15) and then a *budgeting allocation* decision. We will continue with the integration principles of IMC, then address IMC budgeting in the next section.

### IMC Activities and Messages (Positioning Integration)

IMC activities' *messages* should be integrated centrally with regard to the brand's positioning. (Positioning, you will remember from Chapter 6, refers to the *message content of the core communication objectives* of category need, brand awareness, and brand attitude, this content defining *brand position.*) However, integrated positioning can—and should—be taken only so far. The popularly expressed "one voice" objective of IMC is an oversimplification, as we now explain.

The advertising communications and promotion activities' message content should be integrated at the *X-YZ macro level* of the brand's positioning—reinforcing the brand's position within the category or category need (X) and in terms of its general target audience (Y) and main benefit or benefits (Z). There is no necessity to integrate it at the meso (middle) or micro levels. Here it may be useful to refer to Chapter 6 to remind yourself of the macro, meso, and micro levels of positioning.

At the *meso* level of positioning—the I-D-U model—benefits are emphasized with regard to a *particular* target audience which, by implication, will be in a particular decision stage. However, IMC activities frequently have *multiple* target audiences: some may be aimed at attracting new triers (NCUs, OBLs, or OBSs) and others may be designed to retain and perhaps increase the patronage of current customers (FBSs and BLs). Accordingly, it is simplistic to insist that positioning at this meso level be identical for each and every IMC activity. Also, *different* benefit positioning may be optimal *between* advertising and promotions. For instance, American Express may emphasize prestige as a benefit in its advertising, but card membership benefits in its promotions. Similarly, L.L. Bean's catalog advertising may emphasize the user-as-hero benefits of rugged but stylish outdoor clothing, whereas its loyal-customer club may emphasize substantial price discounts.

I-D-U positioning, therefore, does *not* necessarily have to be consistent across advertising communications and promotion activities. Rather, the opera-

tive rule, as with different advertising campaigns, is that differentiated I-D-U positioning should *not be inconsistent* with the brand's *macro X-YZ* positioning.

The same rule applies to the most specific level of positioning—the attribute-benefit-emotion (a-b-e) *micro* level. Advertising communications and promotion activities, just like advertising, should incorporate in their message content whichever forms of "benefits" are *most suited to the persuasion task at hand.* For instance, industrial marketers may use attribute focus for their products at trade shows, while their ongoing corporate image advertising and public relations activities may employ benefit focus or emotion focus. Different micro level foci can thus be used without departing from the brand's macro-positioning.

Therefore, whereas the "one voice" idea sounds sensible, it is oversimplified and is usually not correct. Perhaps a more precise analogy might be "one speaker," who may say different things to different people, or to the same people at different times, while remaining consistently recognizable as the same speaker.

### IMC Activities and Buyers (Customer Timeline Integration)

Beside positioning integration of IMC activities to an appropriate degree, we must also consider *timeline* integration for the brand's buyers. IMC activities must be timed to follow a logical decision-influencing sequence from the *consumer or customer's viewpoint.* (Note that the marketer may be implementing multiple IMC activities simultaneously and only follows a timeline from the *company's* viewpoint when launching a new product or service.[4])

The arrows in Figure 11.1 indicate the customer timeline of IMC activities. To the *prospective buyer,* the product or service is introduced via advertising or an advertising-like communications activity, through either "mass" media or "direct" (which may become databased) media. Trade promotions are then used if the product or service is distributed through retailers. Trial promotions may accompany this introduction. Repeat-purchase (and, in the direct marketing case, loyalty) then becomes the major objective, with various advertising communications activities *continued* and repeat-purchase promotions (or loyalty incentives) taking over the promotional emphasis. Thus, the consumer or customer receives or experiences, ideally, from his or her perspective, a "flow" of advertising communications and promotions for the brand, integrated over time in conjunction with his or her trial and repeat-purchase decisions.

## BUDGET ALLOCATION FOR IMC ACTIVITIES

As you will recall from Chapter 2, the manager will have decided on an overall AC&P budget for the planning year. That budget—if the manager followed our advice—was arrived at by "thinking in terms of general advertising" as the standard means of achieving the total marketing communications task for the brand. If the manager decides to use *solely* general advertising, then the total budget will be allocated across various main media of advertising (as explained in Chapter 15), with a portion of the budget held out for advertising research and the production of ads. It may be perfectly satisfactory to use general advertising for the entire brand communications task, although this choice is increasingly *less* common as managers consider the wide variety of IMC activities available to them as complements or alternatives to general advertising (see the rest of Part Five and also Chapter 15 in Part Six). Relative effectiveness and cost (hence the activities' budget allocations) are the major considerations.

The decision of whether to pursue one or more advertising-like activities or promotions as *alternatives* to general advertising is not easy. One complication is the wide variety of such activities, some of which can be very tempting if competitors aren't yet using them. Further complicating this decision is the fact, albeit the usually positive fact, that if more than one activity is used, or if promotions are used *with* advertising, there is the likelihood of interactions or "synergistic" effects, which are the main intended outcome of selection integration. These too must be estimated in planning the total communications mix.

Considering just the first decision, that of "trade-offs" between general advertising and alternative IMC activities, the following scenarios are typical.[5] Is it more effective to have:

- One mention by Bryant Gumbel on the *Today Show,* or three TV commercials during breaks in the *Today Show?*

- A sample home-delivered to two million households, or one TV commercial seen by six million households?
- A direct mail letter sent to 5,000 people, or a magazine ad seen by 500,000 readers?

Considering additionally the second complicating scenario, these may be complementary activities rather than alternatives. For instance, what would be the effectiveness of three commercials shown during breaks in the *Today Show and* one mention by Bryant Gumbel? Or what would be the effect of a mass magazine ad *followed by* a direct mail letter, perhaps to those who have made an inquiry if the magazine ad were to include a direct response coupon or toll-free response number?

### Task Matrix Method

There is only one *correct* way for the manager to make these complex choices and allocate the budget across various IMC activities, which may or may not include general advertising: The manager must apply the *task method* on an "integrated" basis, or what can be called the *task matrix method*. This method requires a work plan of the following sort (an example is shown in Table 11.1):

**1.** Write across the page the sequence of *stages* to be achieved by the overall marketing communications program. These will be indicated by the *behavioral sequence model* for the brand (see Chapter 4). Note that if the program is to include direct response advertising or database marketing, the BSM's stages may be preceded by an initial stage designed to generate a list of potential customers, unless a rented list or previously compiled company database is employed in the program.

**2.** Down the left-hand side of the page, write a list of the types of advertising communications and particular promotions that are *most likely* to be suitable for achieving the total program—for example, general advertising, publicity, an introductory price-off promotion, direct mail advertising, and telemarketing.

**3.** Working backward from the target audience action goal in the final stage of the behavioral sequence model, estimate the *column totals* in terms of the number of people required to "get through the gates" of each of the stages to attain the target audience action goal. (Gate or stage probabilities, you will re-

**TABLE 11.1**

**EXAMPLE OF A TASK MATRIX METHOD WORK PLAN FOR AN IMC CAMPAIGN**
(*Estimated conversion ratios are in parentheses.*)

| Advertising and IMC activities | BSM Stages | | | |
| --- | --- | --- | --- | --- |
| | **Exposure** (reach of advertising and IMC activities) | **Awareness** (brand's full communication objectives attained) | **Trial** (promotion-assisted) | **Customers** (stable repeat purchasers) |
| General advertising | 15 million → 9 million (.5) = 4.5 million | | | |
| Publicity | 8 million → 2 million (.3) = 0.6 million | | | |
| | (Overlap) → 6 million (.8) = 4.8 million | | | |
| Introductory price-off | | 9.9 million (.1) = 1 million | | |
| Direct mail | Congratulatory letter to the 1 million trial purchasers | | 1 million (.5) = 500,000 | |
| Telemarketing | Two calls in the first year to the 1 million trial purchasers | | | |
| Column totals | 17,000,000 | 10,000,000 | 1,000,000 | 500,000 |
| Global conversion ratios | (E → A ≈ .6) | (A → T ≈ .1) | (T → C ≈ .5) | |

member from Chapters 1 and 2, are the essence of the task method.) Be advised that these column-total figures will probably be "trial balance" figures because they were made using "global" conversion ratios from each stage to the next, that is, without accounting for the specific conversion capabilities of each IMC activity.

**4.** Now review the advertising communications and promotion options listed down the left-hand side of the page. For each stage, decide which one or several of the advertising communications and promotion options will be best (most cost-effective *given* that they can carry the communication objectives—see Chapter 15) for delivering the required number of individuals for this stage. Note very carefully here that:

a. The individual prospects arriving at the final target audience action stage will be drawn from the original pool of individuals that began in the first stage (exposure). That is, if you began with 17 million exposed individuals, and the target is 500,000 repeat customers, then these repeat customers will be individuals who have gone through all of the stages successively, not different individuals.

b. This means that when more than one advertising communications or promotion activity is used to achieve a given stage, you must estimate the *overlap* between audiences.[6] For instance, in the first stage (exposure), a TV campaign might be used to reach 15 million people, and coinciding publicity in newspapers might be used to reach 8 million people. But the "overlap" between these two groups might be 6 million people. Out of this combined total of 17 million people (*not* 23 million, because of the overlap) you now need to convert 10 million people to the second stage (awareness). Some will get there by TV alone, some by publicity alone, and some by the combination of the two—and these three different "exposure" groups may have different probabilities of conversion.

**5.** Progressively, you will probably need to *revise* the column totals for each of the stages leading into the last target audience action stage (described as stable repeat purchasers, or "customers," in Table 11.1). The reason is that these column totals, as noted previously, were estimated with *global* conversion ratios whereas now the manager has more closely considered the *specific* conversion ratios of individual and combined advertising communications and promotion activities. For example, the specific exposure-to-awareness conversion ratios may be estimated as .5 for TV alone, .3 for publicity alone, and .8 for those exposed to both (the overlapping audience). These ratios provide a total of 9.9 million "aware" prospects, which is slightly short of the intended 10 million. The manager can then decide whether to (a) increase the reach of advertising or publicity, (b) sweeten the price-off trial offer to get a few more triers; (c) wait and increase the intensity of telemarketing to triers to increase the repeat rate; or (d) stay with the original plan and hope it was conservative.

**6.** Finally, the *cost* of these marketing communications inputs has to be estimated, and the total cost of the program calculated.

Does this seem complicated? It is! Far too many IMC programs have simply thrown multiple activities "out there" with a wild hope that they will be hitting the same individuals, and enough of these individuals, to get through the stages and achieve the campaign's ultimate action goal. Integrated campaigns are *not* easy to plan and should only be embarked upon if the manager is willing to do the hard work required to make the sorts of estimates that we have outlined above.

The IMC budget allocation usually will be finalized by a senior manager—the marketing director or marketing vice-president. This is because other managers tend to have vested interests favoring general advertising (the agency's account manager), trade promotions (the sales manager), or consumer promotions (the product or brand manager looking for an immediate sales increase). A senior manager is needed to mediate the budgeting conflicts that are likely to arise when a multi-input IMC program is proposed.[7]

The same senior manager's supervision is also necessary to control the *timing* of the IMC activities and oversee their *implementation*. With the vested interests described above, which are typical of most except very small companies, it is all too easy for the IMC program to "dis-integrate."[8] As IMC expert Don Schultz emphasizes, IMC has to be driven from the top, not the bottom.

## Budgeting for a Specific IMC Activity

In the IMC "activities mix" budgeting decision described above, the manager will have used the task matrix method to estimate the main and interactive effects of each of the activities. Having decided on each particular activity, there are now *implementation costs* to be considered. With nontraditional advertising and promotions activities especially, but also with advertising campaigns, there is a likelihood that the manager will have misestimated the numbers in the stages of effects, or that the communication activity or promotion, once implemented, does not work as well as planned and may have to be terminated—usually to be replaced by another activity for achieving the same stage of effects.

The budgeting formula developed by Thomas L. Powers[9] is very useful for identifying implementation costs. The formula is an elaboration of the "leverage" principle of target audience selection referred to in Chapter 3. Powers's formula is as follows:

$$P = S (L) (M) - (UF + OF + V [S] [L] + T [E])$$

where

P = expected profit

S = sales increase (expressed as a fraction of the base level of sales)

L = base level of sales in dollars

M = product margin (unit profit expressed as a fraction of unit selling price)

UF = up-front costs

OF = ongoing fixed costs

V = variable costs

T = termination probability

E = termination expense

Most of the terms in this formula should be self-explanatory; however, examples of the less familiar terms will help. Suppose the manager is considering a telemarketing campaign as an IMC activity. Up-front costs (UF) for telemarketing would include fees paid to an agency or specialized telemarketing contractor for developing the telemarketing "script" to be used in the campaign. Ongoing fixed costs (OF) would include rental of the telephone lines for the campaign as well as salary and expenses for a supervisor. Variable costs (V) for the telemarketing would be the hourly rates paid to the telemarketing operators, perhaps with bonuses or commissions paid as well. Termination expense (E) for the telemarketing campaign would include the cost of canceling the supervisor before the contract has expired and canceling the rental agreement for the telephone lines. Whereas these costs are by no means complete and are only indicative, they cover the main factors that should be taken into account in estimating the contribution of a particular IMC activity.

One point to clarify about Powers's formula is that the sales increase—S in the formula—has to be interpreted as the sales increase that would result from the inclusion of that activity in the *overall* IMC program, not as a solo activity—unless, of course, it *is* the only activity for the brand. For instance, if publicity is to be added to the overall IMC program, the manager has to estimate what the sales increase would be, above and beyond that generated by the other components of the program, that is added by the publicity component alone. Clearly this is not an easy estimate to make, because publicity will probably not simply add to but rather will *interact* with other activities in the program, such as general advertising. Therefore, the best way to make this sales increase estimate is simply to forecast the sales expected *with* the activity in place, *taking into account the interaction,* and then subtract the sales forecast *in the absence of* that activity. Then express this sales difference as a decimal fraction of the latter sales forecast. For example, if the sales estimate *with* the activity in place is $110 million, and the sales estimate *without* the activity is $100 million, then the sales difference would become S = 0.10 in the formula.

### The Total IMC Program Decision

We have introduced the marketing communications budgeting "mix" decision very early in Part Five of our book to alert the manager to the necessity of having to make this decision before plunging blindly into an "integrated marketing communications" program. In fact, there is a lot more to consider before finally deciding on the program. In particular, we have referred to advertising in general and to various other IMC activities without carefully considering their suitability and *capability* of delivering the required communication effects. To make an informed decision here, the manager has to understand the capabilities—not just the costs—of alternative advertising communications and promotions media. The IMC activities as *media options* are reviewed in Chapter 15 of Part Six, on media strategy.

Perhaps another realization has occurred, too. With IMC programs, the media planning decision is moved considerably *earlier* in the manager's planning stages than when using general advertising alone. With IMC, the manager is essentially considering media options before thinking about creative strategy, in many cases. Although this book places creative strategy *before* media strategy, in reality there is a good deal of simultaneous planning; and we therefore recommend an iterative "propose and revise" procedure in practice.

### CORPORATION'S PERSPECTIVE

For the rest of this chapter, we consider *corporate* advertising communications activities (in particular, when reading the next two chapters, be aware that manufacturers *and distributors* such as retailers can undertake corporate image advertising and the other advertising communications activities covered in the present chapter). The corporate advertising communications perspective is indicated by the activities boxes shaded in the overall advertising communications and promotions diagram; see Figure 11.3. We first examine the broadest forms of corporate communications: corporate identity and PR. Then we examine corporate image advertising—which may complement or replace general product or service advertising (discussed in Chapters 8 through 10) or complement direct response advertising (discussed in Chapter 10) for the company—or complement personal selling.[10] With direct response advertising, of course, the company's image is of major importance in that the company is the presenter of the message. Finally, we examine the narrower forms of corporate communications, namely, sponsorships, event marketing, and company-initiated publicity. (Academic instructors and practitioners may be surprised by our organization of these topics. Most notably, corporate identity

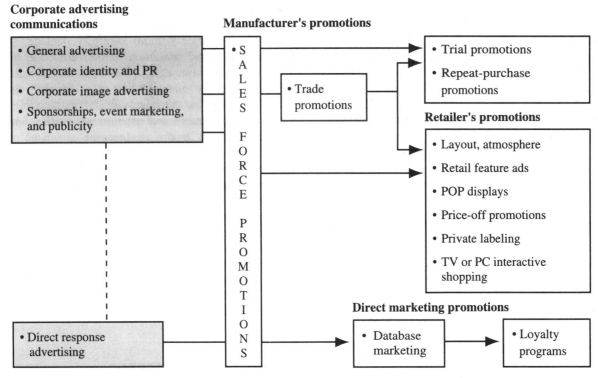

**FIGURE 11.3**
Corporate advertising communications (shaded boxes).

is often linked with corporate image advertising, and PR is often linked with publicity—in practice. However, we recommend the *conceptual* ordering here: from the broadest to the narrowest choices of corporate advertising communications.)

### Corporate Target Audiences and Action Objectives

Corporate advertising communications in the total activities sense are potentially aimed at *any* audience that has some stake in the company's well-being. As Figure 11.4 shows, the company must look *backward* down the channel toward its inputs: to product and material suppliers, to funds suppliers, and to its supply of prospective employees. Second, the company must look *laterally* in two directions: at regulators, such as government and industry bodies, and at competitors. Third, the company must look *internally* at its own employees, both management and staff. And fourth, it must look *forward* to its customers, be they distributors or final consumers.

The *action objectives* for these potential target audiences are as follows:

1. *Suppliers:* to maintain constant supply and favorable terms
2. *Regulators:* not to hinder the company's operations
3. *Competitors:* to be (signaled as to the company's actions) deterred, or even misled
4. *Employees:* to support the company's mission and perform more effectively
5. *Customers:* to buy the company's products and patronize its services

To achieve these diverse "stakeholder" action objectives, the company will usually choose a corporate identity program and public relations (PR) activities, and perhaps also corporate image advertising. We discuss corporate image advertising afterward because it is less widely used and less broadly applicable than corporate identity and PR, which are activities that *all* companies undertake, whether in a planned way or not.

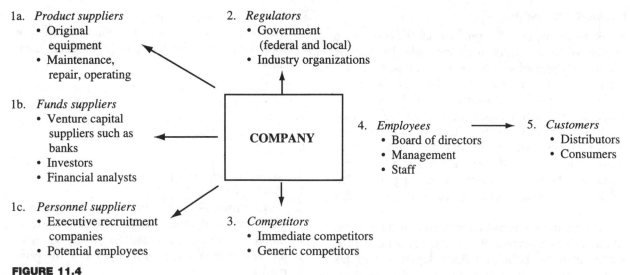

**FIGURE 11.4**
Potential audiences for a company's corporate advertising communications.

## CORPORATE IDENTITY AND PR

Most companies, as Figure 11.4 shows, have an array of diverse "publics" or "stakeholders" to which their corporate identity is presented and their PR (social events as well as publicity in nonpaid media) directed. The communication function of *both* these activities is either to communicate about the company or brand in a positive manner or to defend against likely or actual negative publicity from external sources. A corporation's identity and its public relations should obviously be consistent, and thus an integrated communications perspective is appropriate.

### Corporate Identity

Corporate *identity* refers to how the company presents itself *visually*—through its name, logo, signage, annual reports, stationery, uniforms, vehicles, packaging, and other visible symbols.[11] Corporate identity (CI) should be a planned process. Conceptually, it is the use of consistent visual stimuli to enhance the two universal communication effects (where the "brand" in this case is the company): (1) *company awareness,* especially company recognition but also company recall with regard to the industry or category; and (2) *company attitude* via corporate image. Company attitude is also referred to as *corporate reputation,*[12] which is the overall evaluation of the company that stakeholders derive from the various beliefs about it

that constitute its corporate image. In other words, CI is the company's set of visual stimuli, and company awareness and company attitude are the communication effects as responses.

**Corporate Design.** Corporate *design* programs are a powerful means for a company to portray its desired identity. Corporate design as a professional field (usually offered by PR companies or, more recently, by specialist design houses) has attained an impressive level of sophistication.[13] Corporate design programs are largely implemented through the choice of company names and logos—and then the new design is extended to all other visual manifestations of the company, including signage, company reports, stationery, uniforms, vehicles, and packaging. Chapter appendix 11B, Corporate Design—Examples, provides some notable case histories.

For every company, CI is a very important form of corporate advertising communications. The recommended procedure is a complete situation audit (see Chapter 18), and then a design audit, with the engagement of a professional and therefore objective PR company. An essential further step is pretesting (see Chapter 19) the visual CI stimuli before making a final commitment to them, to insure that they can accomplish the goals that the company is seeking in terms of company awareness and company attitude via corporate image.

## Public Relations (PR)

Public relations, or "PR," refers to all the company's efforts to foster better relations with its various publics or stakeholders, beyond relationships necessitated by sales transactions. (The narrower term, *publicity,* refers to *media reportage* of PR activities. Media reportage about the company may be initiated from any source. Publicity initiated *by the company itself* is essentially a form of *advertising* and is specifically either a form of corporate image advertising, discussed shortly, or support advertising for sponsorships and event marketing, covered later in this chapter.)

Public relations, broadly considered, is the responsibility of all employees. When asked how many people were in the public relations department of his firm, an Australian CEO answered, "Sixteen thousand," which happened to be the total number of employees in his company.[14] Companies for whom PR is a large part of the marketing communications mix, such as, one might expect, oil companies and tobacco companies, tend to have their own in-house PR department, whereas many others hire specialist PR companies and, these days, even paid political lobbyists. PR specialists, companies or individuals, are usually hired on a per-project basis only, and are paid at an hourly rate.

**PR Message Content.** The main "message" areas of public relations, whether these are conveyed via media or personal communications (see below), fall into three long-term or ongoing areas and two short-term areas.[15]

The three ongoing PR message areas are as follows:

1. *Company activities:* the company's overall business performance, goodwill deeds for the community or a charity
2. *Product publicity:* new product announcements, R&D expenditure
3. *Employee publicity:* new appointments, promotions, emp3loyees' achievements

And the two short-term PR message areas are as follows:

4. *Issues management:* attempts to proactively influence issues that affect the company, or to react to unforeseen issues that arise (known as "crisis management")

5. *IMC project support:* public relations associated with event sponsorships, new product launches, or other significant advertising or promotional campaigns

**PR Activities.** Public relations managers have a wide range of activities or "media" through which to transmit the company's messages to the various and diverse target audiences. The nine principal PR activities are as follows:

1. Annual or quarterly reports
2. Newsletters
3. News releases—for national, local, or trade media (increasingly, these are in the form of 3- to 4-minute videotapes for broadcast media, but there are also conventional written releases for print media)[16]
4. Signed articles—ranging from advertorials to individually signed articles in technical journals
5. Press conferences (or interviews)
6. Company speakers who make presentations to schools and other organizations
7. Open-house days
8. Invitations to sponsored events
9. Informal get-togethers
10. A company "homepage" on the Internet

A considerable amount of planning should go into even the most "social" or informal of the PR activities, with the company remembering that these activities will affect the company's image whether or not an explicit message is planned. Ruud provides excellent tactical details, which are much too specific to include here, for the planning of most of these PR activities.[17]

PR is most particularly intended to influence *company attitude* in the minds of the target audience to which the PR is directed. Usually, the objective is to create, increase, or maintain a *positive* company attitude. However, PR may also be employed in the *defense* of company attitude, as practiced in the PR area known as "crisis management." Chapter appendix 11C, Crisis and Rumor Management, covers this area of corporate communications.

## CORPORATE IMAGE ADVERTISING

Corporate image advertising, classically defined, refers to advertising that promotes the company rather than its specific products or services.[18] However, a "hybrid" form of advertising is common in which corporate image and product advertising are combined.[19] As well, the company may choose to use a more recent form of corporate image advertising known as "advocacy" or "issue advocacy" advertising, in which the company does not promote itself *directly* but rather promotes an issue or cause that has an indirect bearing on its operations.[20] Environmental concern[21] and personal health are two broad issues for which some companies may choose to take a public stance.

Only about 50 percent of U.S. companies engage in corporate image advertising, and it constitutes only about 1 percent of total advertising expenditure, though the company-plus-product hybrid type of corporate image advertising makes these figures somewhat hard to pin down.[22] The 50 percent figure also fluctuates, with many companies eliminating corporate image advertising during economic recessions and adding it during economic recoveries. Moreover, there is no relationship between companies' corporate image advertising spending and their spending on product advertising.[23] These statistics raise the questions of which companies should engage in corporate image advertising, and to what extent it should be used with product advertising.

As to which companies should use corporate image advertising, the two most important factors are as follows:

**1.** *The length of the purchase cycle.* Companies selling products or services with a long purchase cycle, such that buyers are "in the market less often" and thus don't have relatively continuous company or brand name reinforcement, should use corporate image advertising. This recommendation is supported by the fact that corporate image advertising is used more often by service companies (65 percent) and industrial companies (61 percent) and less often by consumer product manufacturers (41 percent).[24]

**2.** *The degree of company name–brand name overlap.* Companies for whom the company name is the sole or major part of the brand name of their products or services have little need for corporate image advertising (considered independently of factor 1). Those with partial or no overlap face a more complex decision about corporate image advertising, as discussed shortly.

The first factor, concerning the purchase cycle, is rather obvious. Companies such as Philips and Westinghouse, whose products are purchased (by final customers) on relatively long purchase cycles, would have more need to keep the company name before the public through corporate image advertising than would companies such as Coca-Cola and Wrigley's, whose products are purchased on very short purchase cycles.

The second factor, the degree to which the company name is prominent in the brand name of the products or services it sells, is more complicated. *Case 1:* At one extreme are companies whose company name is *almost invisible* on the product or services the company sells—from the consumer's perspective. (*Examples:* Procter & Gamble, which makes products such as Pert shampoo and Oil of Ulan; or Unilever, which makes Omo detergent and Lipton tea.) *Case 2:* Then there are companies who put the corporate name on *some* products but not on others. (*Examples:* PepsiCo, which makes Pepsi-Cola, but also 7Up and Mountain Dew; or Colgate-Palmolive, which makes Colgate toothpaste and Palmolive soap but also UV sunscreen products and Cold Power detergent.) *Case 3:* Next there are companies whose corporate name always appears *jointly* with the product name. (*Examples:* Ford Falcon or Ford Laser cars; or Kellogg's Corn Flakes or Kellogg's All-Bran cereals.) *Case 4:* Finally, at the other extreme, there are companies whose corporate name *is* the product or service name. (*Examples:* Century 21 real estate; or Diners Card.)

Assume that every company has both a product or service image *and* a corporate image to consider—which they all do for target audiences *other than consumers* (refer to Figure 11.4). The decision is easy for companies at the two extremes. At the first extreme, where company name and brand names are *separate* (case 1), the company will have to engage in corporate image advertising (or corporate identity and PR) to project a corporate image, but *only* to nonconsumer audiences. At the other extreme, where the company and brand names are *one and the same* (case 4), product or service advertising *simultaneously* projects the corporate image to all audiences, so corporate image advertising is *not* needed (though PR may be advisable). Note that most very small manufacturers and most retailers fall into this category.

Probably more than half of all companies, however, are in the two *mixed* categories in between (case

2, the partial-overlap category, and case 3, the dual-name category). For them, it is a major decision whether corporate image advertising should be undertaken in addition to product or service advertising. There are three main options for these case 2 and case 3 companies to consider:

**1.** Conduct only product or service advertising, with the expectation that the "summation" of ads for corporately compound-named products or services will contribute sufficiently to a favorable corporate image.

**2.** Conduct "mixed" advertising, in which the corporate message is a reasonably salient part of every product or service ad (such as Toyota's "Oh what a feeling—Toyota" tag line prominent in all its TV commercials for individual Toyota cars and trucks).

**3.** Conduct "umbrella" corporate ads *in place of* product and service advertising, with the expectation that the corporate image advertising will not only serve its own purpose of maintaining corporate image but will also add, by a carryover process, to the image of particular products and services.

The question of which option is best for the case 2 and case 3 companies is one that we, as consultants, are asked frequently. There is no general answer. The recommendation we make is that the company should try all three options on a test basis and then track the effects on both product or service image *and* corporate image (where here we are using the term "image" in a shorthand way to refer to *all* the communication objectives, particularly to brand awareness and brand attitude and also company awareness and company attitude). In practice, in perhaps our hardest-learned conclusion, we have found that it is very difficult to assess the relative merits of these three options using pretests of ads alone. Advertising pretests measure *immediate* responses, and are thus of too short a duration to assess image effects. A program of continuous tracking, usually with the three options tried in different regional markets, is the only practical way to produce a reliable choice of the best option. As we will see in Chapter 20, where we discuss campaign tracking, the assessment itself is relatively straightforward.

## Communication Objectives for Corporate Image Advertising

Corporate image advertising—as we have already indicated—always has two main communication ob-

jectives, the universal communication objectives of brand awareness and brand attitude; and it may have a third, brand purchase intention, if the brand attitude strategy is high-involvement. (Here, the company *is* the brand, so we will substitute the word "company" as appropriate.) The three specific communication objectives of corporate image advertising are described in the following paragraphs.

**1.** *Company Name Recognition.* For the business customer, the main company awareness objective of corporate image advertising is to get the company's name *recognized* when the sales force calls on prospects; likewise, other target audiences must recognize the company name when considering it for stock purchase investments, employment, regulation, or special interest action.

**2.** *Company Attitude.* The *objective* for the communication effect of company attitude could be any of the five options, depending on the purpose of the campaign: to create, increase, maintain, modify, or change the target audience's attitude toward the company. The "create" option, as we saw, is very important for direct response advertising when the company making the offer is unknown. Increase or maintenance, and sometimes modification and change, are the more likely options for better-known companies in their ongoing corporate image advertising.

The company attitude *strategy* could be based on any of the four brand (here company) attitude quadrants, depending on the target audience *action* that the campaign is expected to achieve. Where the target audience action is relatively indirect and delayed, such as to buy the company's stocks or take a job with the company, then the low-involvement/transformational quadrant (intellectual stimulation as a "wise" stock choice, or social approval as a company to work for) is most appropriate. However, "issue advocacy advertising," aimed at regulators to discourage restrictive lawmaking, or at consumers in times of trouble to forestall boycotting of the company's products or services, is more likely to be high-involvement/ informational (problem avoidance in the regulatory instance, and problem removal when trouble with consumers arises). The other two quadrants' strategies are also possibilities, but low-involvement/ transformational and high-involvement/informational are the two most usual strategies.

For example, Cathay Pacific, a mostly British-owned airline based in Hong Kong, undertook a corporate image repositioning campaign in 1995 leading up to the transfer of this once-British colony to Chinese rule in 1997. The campaign reflects the realization that Asian travelers, who already constitute 80 percent of Cathay's passengers, are likely to continue to be the airline's core market in the future. The new style of Cathay Pacific's advertising (Figure 11.5) and the slogan, "The Heart of Asia," present the airline as essentially Asian.[25] The company attitude *objective* for Cathay Pacific's campaign is attitude modification (an attempted increase by repositioning the airline from British to Asian). The *strategy* is low-involvement/transformational (seeking social approval by Asian travelers who choose to fly with an Asian airline, which is a low-risk choice).

**3.** (*If High-Involvement Attitude*) *Company Purchase or Purchase-Related Intention.* If the company atti-

## FIGURE 11.5
Cathay Pacific's corporate image campaign (typical ad shown) designed to reposition the mostly British-owned airline as more Asian.
*Courtesy:* Cathay Pacific and McCann-Erickson.

THE BEST WAY TO THE BIG NOODLE

Discover the real Hong Kong. Fly there non-stop from Los Angeles on the airline that calls it home. Cathay Pacific. The Heart of Asia.

tude message is low-involvement, then the target audience will infer the appropriate action to be taken when the time arises. Thus, for instance, a company which has maintained a strong social approval image with low-involvement/transformational advertising has no need to "hard sell" on specific action to be taken such as applying for a job with the company. With high-involvement/informational corporate image advertising, on the other hand, as may be used for a specific stock offer or when an immediate issue is at stake, the *generation* of a purchase intention (as in a stock purchase) or purchase-related intention (as in not boycotting the company) would be the relevant intention objective.

Figure 11.6 shows a corporate image magazine advertisement for Bank of America, where company name recognition is the brand awareness objective, and where an improvement in company attitude is the brand attitude objective, using a low-involvement/transformational strategy. This particular corporate ad performed well above the norm on attention (67 percent), branding (62 percent noticed the company name), and incidence of reading most of the corporate message (18 percent, which is over double the norm for corporate image advertising). A second corporate image ad, shown in Figure 11.7, indicates just how easy it is to do a poor communication job in corporate image advertising; this British Aerospace ad scored a very low 26 percent on attention and 24 percent on branding—and only 4 percent read most of the copy.[26]

Corporate image advertising usually provides an excellent "return on investment" in the long run.[27] A landmark study by Niefeld across 460 major U.S. companies estimated that corporate image advertising produced an average 4 percent increase in the company's stock price compared with the projected stock price if it had not advertised.[28] At the average value of the stock prices, a return of 33 to 1 was observed; for instance, a company that spent $1 million a year on corporate image advertising would receive, on average, a $33 million increment in total stock value at the end of the year.

Interestingly, in the Niefeld study, the *content* of the corporate image advertising appeared to make a difference in that new product announcements and employee productivity were among the most successful themes—but so also was straight "puffery" about the company. Less successful ads focused on financial

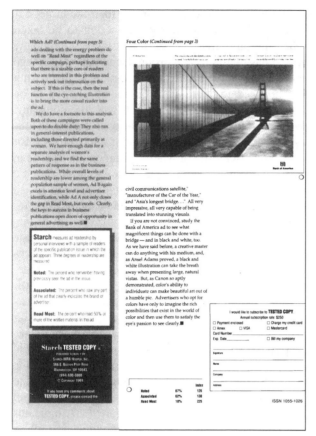

**FIGURE 11.6**
High-scoring corporate Image ad for Bank of America: 67 percent of readers noticed the ad, 62 percent noticed the company name, and 18 percent read most of the copy.
*Courtesy: Starch Tested Copy*, September 1991, Starch INRA Hooper, Inc.

**FIGURE 11.7**
Low-scoring corporate image ad for British Aerospace: 26 percent of readers noticed the ad, 24 percent noticed the company name, and 4 percent read most of the copy.
*Courtesy: Starch Tested Copy*, September 1991, Starch INRA Hooper, Inc.

details or technological points, or mixed a number of topics during the campaign. In another study, it was found that company CEOs as presenters in ads (a fairly typical creative tactic) showed wide variation in their perceived expertise, objectivity, and likability (see the VisCAP presenter model described in Chapter 9), which would affect the performance of corporate image advertisements.[29]

### Political Advertising

Some corporate image advertising by companies, and particularly by government organizations, can be classified as political speech rather than commercial speech, in legal terms. Companies that run ads for issues such as the justifiability of profits and the capi-talist system, women's rights, health and safety, or the environment may not be directly promoting the company or its products, and they thereby enjoy the unusual rights of political speech. In U.S. law, political speech is *not* regulated for deceptiveness and false-hoods, unlike commercial speech in regular advertising. TV stations are reluctant to carry issue-advocacy ads, however, because they must also grant a *free* right of reply to other interested parties.[30] Print media, such as newspapers, are more likely to carry such ads even though they, too, are bound by the free right of reply provision.

Obviously, there is a very fine line for companies between what constitutes political speech as distinct from what constitutes commercial speech,[31] but readers may be interested to know that governments and politicians can say anything they like in the media without fear of sanctions for untruthfulness. By law, their utterances are political speech and therefore protected.

## SPONSORSHIPS (INCLUDING EVENT MARKETING AND PUBLICITY)

The company's general advertising for its products or services may be complemented or replaced by advertising-like activities in the form of sponsorships, event marketing, or company-initiated positive publicity.

*Sponsorship* refers to the company's financial support of a media, social, sporting, or cultural activity in return for exposure of its brand or brands. Media activities include TV programs, radio programs, or special editions or supplements in print media. Social activities include support for hobbyist or outdoor interest clubs, or charitable support for organizations for the disabled, children, or the elderly. Sporting activities include the support of sports organizations, sports teams, and sports venues. Cultural activities include support of the visual or performing arts.

*Event marketing* is distinguished from sponsorship only in that it refers to financial support of a particular *short-duration* activity, such as the Super Bowl, the Olympic Games, or a specific art exhibition or concert performance.

*Publicity* refers to news media reportage about the company and its products or services, and is here used to refer to *company-initiated, positive* media reportage.[32] Coverage of the activity or event in the news media is usually part and parcel of sponsorship or event marketing.

Sponsorships, event marketing, and publicity are related here as a single advertising-like communications activity. They are related because event marketing is simply a short-term form of sponsorship; and sponsorship, in turn, can be defined as payment in cash or kind, such as free products or services, to an organizational activity in return for publicity. This publicity takes the form of *intermediaries'* advertising, such as by retailers, or "free" publicity in news media (in actuality, publicity rarely is free because a good deal of management time is devoted to it, making it a cost for the company). (*Note:* in the following analysis, we will use the term *sponsorship* generically to cover all three activities, although event marketing and publicity will be identified specifically when appropriate.)

Sponsorship is an alternative to general advertising. The approximately estimated $3 billion annual expenditure on sponsorship in the United States places it at about 3 percent of total advertising expenditures—making it larger than the smallest general advertising medium, outdoor (and poster) advertising. In most countries, there has been a growth in sponsorship as a complement to, or a substitute for, general advertising. The highest proportional expenditure is in Italy, where marketers spend the equivalent of about 8 percent of their advertising expenditure on sponsorship, most of it on soccer.

For some companies, sponsorship is used as almost a complete substitute for general advertising. For instance, the British auto maker Jaguar, after its merger with another auto maker, British Leyland, began to suffer an image problem because the latter company was not associated with the sportiness of auto racing as Jaguar was. General advertising did not seem able to reverse this problem. In the mid-1980s, Jaguar began entering its cars in world sports car championships, and by 1989 had won the Le Mans 24 hours endurance race twice, the Daytona 500 once, and the World Sportscar Championship twice. During this period, Jaguar diverted the majority of its advertising budget to sponsorship of endurance rallies and motor races, using the rest of its advertising budget in an IMC manner to advertise its wins. Jaguar's emphasis on sponsorship was most evidently successful. Worldwide sales of Jaguar increased from 25,000 cars in 1985 to 55,000 by 1989. Endurance racing and speed racing were good choices of events to sponsor given that durability and speed were two of the positioning benefits that Jaguar most wanted to regain and reinforce for the brand.[33]

Another example of almost complete reliance on sponsorship is Cornhill Insurance Company in the United Kingdom. Cornhill, a virtually unknown competitor in the insurance category, spent £2 million (perhaps £4 million if entertainment costs are included) over 5 years to sponsor test-match cricket, which is enormously popular in England. By careful tracking, the company estimated that brand recall of Cornhill as an insurance company rose from 2 percent to 21 percent over the 5-year period, and that the return in terms of insurance sales by the company was on the order of £15 to £20 million. To have achieved these results with advertising may have cost approximately £50 million over the 5 years.[34] Most tellingly,

Cornhill "merchandised" the sponsorship very thoroughly by obtaining exclusive rights to the televised coverage of the cricket matches; by placing its logo on the sports grounds where the matches were played (indeed, on the actual grass of the grounds, which no other companies were allowed to do); and by printing its name very prominently (and tastefully) on the tickets for the games.

For most companies, however, sponsorship is a *complementary* activity alongside general advertising and other forms of promotion. For example, although U.S. companies spent $23 billion on sports marketing in 1990, only 15 percent of this went to sponsorship payments to the sports organizations themselves, compared with 30 percent that went to *advertising,* mainly on TV sports programs and in sports-related print media. Interestingly, most of the remaining 55 percent was spent on the often-overlooked "invisible costs" of sponsorship—which are corporate entertainment, corporate overhead and travel, and public relations activities.[35] (Including management planning time, it has been estimated that these PR-related "invisible costs" add a further 70 to 100 percent to the base cost of a sponsorship, that is, to the direct payments made to the sponsored organization and to the media.[36])

If the marketer undertaking the sponsorship is also distributing the product through retailers, it has been estimated that approximately 70 percent of sponsorships are followed by *retail* promotions, such as retail advertising, special displays, or promotional pricing by the retailer.[37] These tie-in activities illustrate the necessity for customer timeline integration when using the IMC approach.

Local follow-through is very important. For instance, when Borden sponsored a 75-city tour by the perennial soft-rock band The Beach Boys in 1991 to promote the company's line of snack products, major trade customers were given backstage tours at the concerts; local stores who stocked the products were provided with tickets to give away; and local radio stations were given a special Beach Boys anthology which the company hoped would be given air time, and it was.[38] Sponsorships are undertaken not just to increase awareness or create goodwill but to produce a measurable result in terms of sales, and local trade follow-through is instrumental in achieving this goal.

Just like advertising campaigns, sponsorships have to be carefully selected and planned rather than op-portunistically rushed into, because they have approximately a 50 percent failure rate. Among the successes have been Volvo's sponsorship of tennis and later golf, and also the Jaguar and Cornhill examples mentioned earlier. But there have been some notable apparent failures of sponsorship. For instance, Ford spent £2.5 million a year to sponsor English national soccer and £300,000 a year to sponsor European soccer, with no apparent effect. At the end of the 5-year sponsorship, only 1 percent of the public could link the Ford name with soccer.[39] Similarly, sponsors of the 1988 Olympic Games in Los Angeles found themselves frequently losing in "awareness" to competing brands which had not been sponsors, partly due to so-called "ambush marketing" (event-adjacent advertising) by competitors.[40] (We criticize here the typically incorrect approach taken in these surveys, which gets the causal process backward. Typically, the survey uses the *event,* such as the Olympics, as the cue, and then asks which companies sponsored it. From a brand attitude perspective, the correct measurement procedure is to use the *company* as the cue and ask which events *it* is associated with—a connection which would thereby enhance the company's "image" if the event were appropriately selected. The first measure means little, so we should not strictly use this as proof of sponsorship failure.)

Sponsorship is more likely to succeed if it is planned and evaluated just like an advertising campaign. For details, see chapter appendix 11D, Planning and Evaluating Sponsorships.

Sponsorships also provide excellent opportunities for public relations contacts through corporate entertainment at sponsored events.[41]

### Advertorials

A form of sponsorship that does not receive much attention but is growing in use is "advertorials" in broadcast and print media. Stout, Wilcox, and Greer define advertorials as "those advertiser-paid blocks that combine clearly identifiable advertising with simulated editorial text."[42] The advertorial content is usually some form of *positive publicity* capitalizing on recent favorable news stories, such as oat bran cereal makers talking about cholesterol reduction, following the publication of Kowalski's book on the subject in 1987; or wine makers pointing out the apparent health benefits of moderate wine consumption, following *60 Minutes'* 1991 program to this effect.[43]

However, advertorials are suitable for only *some* advertisers. The main users tend to be those companies whose products or services would make a logical story in the program or publication itself, such as travel advertisers, health and fitness advertisers, and occasionally pharmaceutical advertisers. Also, as is well known, there is the potential ethical problem of deceptive presentation[44] with advertorials with which we, the authors, are not entirely comfortable.

## SUMMARY

Implementing an integrated marketing communications (IMC) program requires an integrated communications strategy. This includes (1) selection integration, (2) positioning integration, and (3) customer timeline integration.

Selection of the best mix of IMC activities—selection integration—is a complicated procedure and is essentially a *media selection* and then *budget allocation* decision. We recommend the *task matrix method* (an extension of the task method presented in Chapter 2). The key buyer decision stages are identified across the top of the matrix, and the most likely alternative IMC activities are listed down the left side of the matrix. The manager then has to make estimates, using task method steps, of the number of prospects who would be converted through the buyer decision stages with various combinations of activities. We then recommended *Powers's formula* for estimating the expected profit from budgetary expenditure on a particular activity. (The specifics of IMC media selection are presented in Chapter 15.)

The message contents of the IMC campaign should also be integrated "centrally" with regard to the brand's positioning (where the brand may be the corporation itself). By positioning integration, we mean that the content of the advertising communications and promotion activities and their manner of implementation should be consistent with the overall *macropositioning* of the brand (see Chapter 6). However, particular benefits emphasized (the I-D-U model) and the message focus on attributes, benefits, or emotions (the a-b-e model) will vary with the nature of the target audience and the stage of the buyer's decision process. These meso and micro levels of positioning do *not* have to be the same as—but *should not be inconsistent with*—the brand's macropositioning. The analogy: There should be clearly "one

speaker" but not necessarily saying the same thing to different audiences or at different times.

Also, the components of the IMC campaign should be integrated sequentially with regard to the "customer timeline" of the distribution channel. Figure 11.1 provides an overall plan for this.

The three guiding principles of IMC integration and their key details are summarized for review in Table 11.2.

Corporate advertising communications comprise five main activities, here listed in terms of breadth of use: (1) general advertising (discussed in the chapter only as an alternative to corporate image advertising but extensively covered elsewhere in the book); (2) corporate identity and PR; (3) corporate image advertising; (4) the more narrowly used alternatives of sponsorships, event marketing, and company-initiated positive publicity; and (5) direct response advertising, which may be via general or corporate image advertising (also covered elsewhere in the book).

*Corporate identity* (CI) is an aspect of marketing operations that all companies should monitor. CI refers to how the company presents itself visually to its various audiences—so as to increase company awareness and change or increase company image or attitude. Professional PR fims can advise on a *corporate design* program, an emerging field of corporate market research and advertising-like implementation that has demonstrated recent notable successes.

*Public relations* (PR) should be practiced by all the company's employees, all the time. In its more

---

### TABLE 11.2

**THE THREE PRINCIPLES OF INTEGRATION FOR IMC CAMPAIGNS.**

1. *Selection integration of media*
   - communication-effects capacity
   - task matrix method of budget allocation
2. *Positioning integration of messages*
   - macro (X-YZ) level consistency only
   - meso (I-D-U) and micro (a-b-e) messages can differ by target audience, though should "not be inconsistent with" the brand's macropositioning
3. *Timeline integration for customers*
   - behavioral sequence model (BSM) to pinpoint advertising communication and promotion opportunities
   - database marketing, loyalty program (when appropriate)

formal sense, PR consists of ongoing company activities designed to foster relationships with various publics or "stakeholders" beyond the relationships necessitated by sales transactions. Ongoing PR includes company, product, and employee publicity; and short-term PR is necessitated by IMC projects or emerging issues. Negative publicity in the form of crises or rumors is the most threatening and difficult area of short-term PR, for which psychologically based strategies (within the bounds of truth) provide some insights.

The customer timeline of IMC activities usually begins with general advertising or its alternatives. Corporate image advertising, sponsorships, event marketing, and company-initiated positive publicity are activities that can be used to complement the company's specific product or service advertising. In fact, if they are more cost-effective, one or more of these activities can replace general advertising.

*Corporate image advertising* is not an automatic choice for all companies. Companies that most need to use corporate image advertising are those with a long purchase cycle or those where there is little overlap between the company name and the names of the products or services that it offers. However, *nonconsumer* target audiences also have to be considered: suppliers, regulators, competitors, employees, and distributors. Some or all of these target audiences may respond well to corporate image advertising even if it is not necessary for consumers or final customers.

*Sponsorships, event marketing, and (company-initiated positive) publicity* are regarded as a related set of alternatives that may be used in place of—or as complements to—general media advertising. In effect, they have become media of advertising and therefore must be considered in terms of their target audience reach, message carrying capacity, and cost in relation to the target audience. The most important decision prior to their media considerations, however, concerns the suitability of the sponsored organization or event in relation to the company's image. Because the sponsored entity can become a "brand attribute" of the company, its effect on company attitude must be carefully estimated beforehand.

In this chapter, we examined corporate advertising communications activities, where the corporation may be a company or organization, government or private, manufacturer or retailer. Chapter 12 examines manufacturers' promotion activities, Chapter 13 looks at retailers' promotion activities, and Chapter 14 discusses direct marketing promotions.

## APPENDIX

# 11A. Avon's New IMC Strategy

The IMC strategy decision requires total consideration of the best means for the job of communicating with the target audience. Avon cosmetics provides an interesting example of this total consideration decision.[45]

Avon cosmetics have traditionally been sold door-to-door by the famous "Avon ladies" sales representatives. In 1992, Avon's profit slipped for the first time in many years: with more women working, fewer potential customers were at home when the Avon lady called, and the company was also experiencing higher turnover in its sales staff, which was not a good sign for a product sold largely on the basis of relationship marketing. To this point, Avon had used only magazine advertising to supplement its personal selling channel of distribution.

In February 1993, Avon decided to use TV advertising for the first time in its history, allocating $34 million for this purpose. Avon also produced a catalog in late 1992 which was distributed by direct mail. Both the TV ads and the catalog included a toll-free telephone number with the slogan, "Call us," instead of the traditional personal selling greeting, "Avon calling." The benefits of these additional *prepurchase* modes of advertising communications were, via *TV:*

- Brand awareness of the name, "Avon," was boosted, thus helping the sales force's brand recognition.
- Brand attitude improved (being on TV gave Avon's cosmetics more "legitimacy" in the customers' minds).

And via the *catalog:*

- Prospective customers could see the full range of Avon products in the catalog *first,* before deciding whether or not to buy (it was not possible to show the entire range of products in magazine or TV ads). Variety of choice, meaning more opportunities for personalization, is very important in cosmetics marketing.
- Interested customers could phone the company direct from the catalog (actually, from any of the three types of advertising). The company then redirected the calls to the local sales representative, and an appointment was arranged at the customer's convenience with an already-qualified prospect.

The Avon ladies, nationwide, were receiving 9,000 calls a month from the magazine advertising. With the additional TV and catalog advertising, the inquiry rate rose *tenfold* to 90,000 calls a month. This "integrated reconsideration" by Avon neatly helped to solve the home-access problem, made personal selling and relationship marketing slightly less crucial by preselling Avon's products, and undoubtedly returned the company to strong profitability.

## 11B. Corporate Design—Examples

The choice of a name logotype (a scripted name) or logo (pictorial symbol) can be a major CI contributor to *company awareness*. Coca-Cola, for instance, has hardly changed its "handwritten signature" logotype at all since it was first designed by company bookkeeper Frank Robinson in 1887.[46] Here's what the original looked like:

On the other hand, McGraw-Hill, the publisher of this book, recently changed its logo (see p. iv) and its corporate name (to The McGraw-Hill Companies) to reflect, in the CEO's words, "the increasingly global and diverse nature" of the company's services and products.

A CI program created by the corporate image consultancy and design firm of Landor Associates for GM's Saturn automobile is shown in Figure 11.8. Saturn's design program emphasizes the multiple opportunities to reinforce brand recognition and, thereby, brand awareness equity for this company brand.[47]

Corporate identity programs are also intended to influence *company attitude,* more popularly known as corporate image.[48] In a well-known negative case, the world's largest advertiser, Procter & Gamble, decided in 1985 to abandon its classic corporate logo which it had used since the 1870s (admittedly in gradually reduced form on its various brand's packages but prominently on company stationery). The logo, a crescent moon with 13 stars patriotically representing the 13 original American states, was unable to sur-

vive the rumor that it stood for devil worship and was thereby offensive to America's religiously conservative heartland.

## 11C. Crisis and Rumor Management

Crises (negative events) or rumors (associations with a negative attribute) can affect almost any company at any time. The nature of the crisis is fairly predictable in some industries, such as oil spills for the oil industry (for example, the Exxon-Valdez grounding off Alaska in 1989) or airplane crashes for the airlines (for example, USAir's Pittsburgh crash of 1994, in which all 132 passengers and crew were killed); whereas in other industries the crises are completely unpredictable (for example, the syringes found in Pepsi-Cola cans or the rumor that McDonald's was using worms in its hamburger meat). Companies in industries with somewhat predictable crises have the advantage that well-orchestrated responses can be practiced in advance to limit the damage, both to the company's reputation and, more important, to those affected by substantial negative events. Interestingly, companies should *not* try to "inoculate" themselves against the effects of predictable disasters, such as by pointing out in advance that the occasional oil spill or air crash is bound to happen. Rather, the response should always be made *afterward,* and as immediately as possible.[49]

Negative publicity about a company can be extremely damaging, even when the media reporters are careful to use apparently neutral innuendo rather then making a direct allegation. This is because the public tends to accept implications as assertions and to discount any qualifiers that may be offered. In a prototype experiment, Wenger, Wenzlaff, Kerker, and Beattie[50] found that innuendo headlines were virtually as damaging as direct allegation headlines. Compared with a truly neutral control headline, such as "P is arriving in town," which resulted in a neutral attitude toward P, the direct allegation "P is a criminal" resulted in a 21 percent negative shift in attitude toward P; the innuendo

**FIGURE 11.8**
Corporate design program for GM's Saturn automobile.
*Courtesy:* Saturn Corporation.

question "Is P a criminal?" resulted in a 22 percent negative shift; and even the innuendo's *denial,* known as an "incriminating denial," "P is not a criminal," resulted in a 12 percent negative shift. Moreover, the two innuendo headlines—the innuendo question and the incriminating denial—were unaffected by the credibility of the *source* of the innuendo (the *New York Times* or the *National Enquirer*); that is, innuendo from a "scandalmonger" source was just as readily believed as innuendo from a more objective source. This experiment shows why companies should be concerned about negative publicity, even "mere innuendo." It suggests that they should prepare formally for crisis or rumor management.

As Jorgensen[51] explains, a crisis is, by definition, an unexpected, highly negative, and salient event. Such an event inevitably prompts people—the public—to seek an explanation. Rarely is there direct information with which to form an explanation, so people rely on news media coverage and on word-of-mouth from their acquaintances. The affected company, in a responsible way, should try to influence the news media coverage by issuing its own explanation and response, although one strategy is to ignore the crisis and its salient negative publicity altogether, as discussed shortly.

Ethically, the company may not have very much choice over the explanation, because the truth should be told no matter whether it is in the company's interest or not; but it does have a choice as to the *strategy* that can be adopted as the response.

Consider the model shown diagramatically at the top of Figure 11.9. It represents a company with a belief connection (in the public's mind) to a negative event (a crisis) or a negative attribute (a rumor). There are five main PR response strategies that the company could adopt. The first two—direct refutation, as one strategy, and ignoring the situation, as another—are the obvious strategies that are most widely used. However, Tybout, Calder, and Sternthal,[52] using information processing theory and an experimental approach, have identified three other strategies that are effective depending on certain conditions. The five strategies are explained next and are summarized in the figure.

**1.** *Attack the negative publicity head-on by trying to refute the connection between the company and the negative event or attribute.* This is probably the most common strategy and is usually the worst. The "incriminating denial" result offers one explanation, but why won't a direct refutation work? Obviously, if the refutation is weak or disbelieved, the company's attack increases awareness of the situation and strengthens belief in the allegation. But public perception is *also* likely to worsen *even if* the refutation is strong and logically correct. Tybout and her colleagues explain this as occurring because the mere "association" between the company and the negative entity is rehearsed each time

| Strategy | Considerations |
|---|---|
| 1. Attack head-on; try to directly refute the connection. 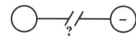 | Likely to *worsen* the situation because affective association is rehearsed even if logical connection is broken. |
| 2. Ignore and hope it will dissipate.  | Best strategy if awareness is limited or word-of-mouth trend is declining (do daily surveys). |
| 3. Externalize or decontrol the *connection.*  | Good strategy if based on truthful explanation. Actual decontrol necessary with repeated negative events. |
| 4. Neutralize or positivize the *attribute* itself.  | Good strategy *if* attribute can be reperceived less negatively. |
| 5. Outflank with *company's positive* attributes. 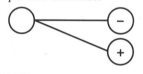 | Best strategy if awareness is widespread. However, won't work with repeated negative events. |

**FIGURE 11.9**
PR response strategies for crises and rumors.

the situation is mentioned, and thus the *affective* connection remains (and is strengthened) even if the *logical* connection appears to be broken.

To demonstrate this, the researchers used the rumor that McDonald's was using red worms in its hamburger meat (an actual rumor which, although not substantiated by fact, caused McDonald's sales to decline by as much as 30 percent in areas where the rumor circulated). The researchers tested the actual direct refutation used by McDonald's in the rumor-affected areas; McDonald's instituted TV and print ads emphasizing that its hamburgers were "100 percent pure beef" (strategy 1) and also issued a semihumorous statement to the effect that the company wouldn't use worms anyway because red worms are more than five times as expensive as hamburger meat! (strategy 4; see shortly). McDonald's refutational response did not work in the real world, nor did it work in the experiment. In the experimental test of strategy 1, translated to a percentage scale, the average consumer's attitude toward eating at McDonald's was 57 percent in the group of subjects unaware of the rumor. It declined to 44 percent among the group exposed to the rumor. Then came the refutation attempt. McDonald's refutation had virtually no effect, because after the refutation, the average consumer's attitude toward eating at McDonald's was 46 percent, which represents no significant improvement from the rumor-depressed attitude.

A more recent instance of direct refutation failing badly was seen in Europe in 1994 when Unilever's newly launched Power brand of laundry detergent (Omo Power or Persil Power in different countries) was attacked with negative publicity by rival detergent-maker Procter & Gamble, the latter claiming that the stain-fighting ingredient in Power, manganese, rotted clothes. Unilever traded press releases with P&G, issuing scientific claims and counterclaims. The clothes-rotting rumor worsened and, in early 1995, Unilever withdrew the brand, suffering a $90 million write-off. Unilever may have been better served *not* trying to refute P&G's attack—either withdrawing the product (at much lower cost than with the refutational publicity) or simply waiting. P&G later eased off its attack and launched its own stain-fighting brand, under the Ariel label, containing a different main ingredient.[53]

As Tybout and her colleagues comment regarding the direct refutation strategy, "Consumers are affected because they *process* the rumor, not because they necessarily believe it."[54] Negative affect, and often negative imagery, remains when the consumer thinks of the company—even if the rational belief connection is weakened or removed.

**2.** *Ignore the negative publicity and hope it will dissipate.* Commissioning an immediate survey should be the first response whenever a crisis or negative rumor arises (many research companies will do these surveys overnight). If awareness of the crisis or rumor is limited to a small minority of stakeholders and, perhaps more important, if public discussion of the crisis or rumor seems to be declining (several daily surveys are necessary to ascertain this trend), then the best strategy is to ignore the crisis or rumor: to make no response and allow the negative publicity to dissipate.

For instance, a long-running rumor is that jockey shorts cause male insterility. Jockey International, Inc., has always ignored this rumor and has seen sales increase over the years.[55] This could be because the rumor is believed by only a very small proportion of consumers, or it could be because of fashion cycles. Recently, the famous Levi's commercials seem to have restored the popularity of boxer

shorts, and fashion cycles are surely a larger determinant of underwear sales than this particular rumor about jockey shorts.

Of course, in the case of a crisis originating from a genuine disaster or a rumor emanating from a real problem, the company has an ethical responsibility to issue an explanation. However, the company can say as little as is legally required and "lay low" as far as any other public communications are concerned. There is no need to feed the negative publicity if it is limited or declining.

**3.** *Externalize or decontrol the connection between the company and the negative attribute or event.* The externalization or decontrol strategy (actually two related strategies) attempts to break the belief connection while not being as blunt as direct refutation (strategy 1, above). Externalization or decontrol is ethically defensible if the company indeed had little control originally, or had control and has corrected the problem.

If the cause of the event or attribute connection can be factually attributed to external factors or factors over which the company has *little control,* then *externalizing* the connection would be a good strategy for the company to investigate. For instance, some air crashes are due entirely to unpredicted weather conditions, such as "wind shears." If the negative event or attribute can be truthfully attributed to an external cause, then externalization is an ethical and usually effective option.

A *decontrol* strategy, of course, is necessary when the company *is* to blame for the negative event. The requires correcting the cause of the problem as far as is technically and humanly possible, no matter what the expense, and then publicizing the correction. For example, USAir will have to follow this route if it is to survive as an airline. Johnson & Johnson's Tylenol, as a brand, managed to do this successfully following its fatal cyanide tampering incidents, at great expense, after first improving the safety of the product's container.

**4.** *Neutralize or "positivize" the negative attribute or event itself.* This is a good strategy if indeed the attribute (or the event) can be repositioned as not so negative, or even positive. In the McDonald's experiment, an attribute positivization strategy was implemented by replying to the worm rumor with this statement: "That may sound funny to you, but last week my mother-in-law was in town and we took her to Chez Paul and had a really good sauce that was made out of worms."[56] This is a variation of McDonald's actual neutralizing strategy which, as described earlier, referred in a humorous way to the high price of worms. In the experiment this strategy restored consumers' average attitude toward McDonald's to 61 percent, slightly above the prerumor attitude!

Neutralization, rather than positivization, might be a realistic aim if the negative event is not truly a crisis. For instance, not all oil spills are major, and in a minor case it could be pointed out that the oil spill is limited to a remote area, and that the chance of it causing extensive damage to sea life and shore life is small. Major crises, however, such as air crashes in which members of the public die, are hardly amenable to event neutralization.

**5.** *Outflank the negative publicity with the company's positive attributes.* As indicated in the subdiagram accompanying this strategy in the figure, the outflanking strategy attempts to offset the negative publicity surrounding the negative event or attribute by reminding people of the company's *positive* achievements or attributes. (Or the *brand's* positive attributes if a brand name rather than the company name is implicated.) This would appear to be the best strategy if awareness of the negative event or attribute is widespread and daily surveys suggest that it is likely to spread further. The outflanking strategy will work provided that the negative event or attribute is a one-time occurrence or is at least relatively isolated in the public's mind from any similar occurrences in the past.

In the McDonald's experiment, the researchers, in the "outflanking" experimental condition, asked consumers exposed to the rumor to think of the location of the McDonald's they visit most often, how often they visit it each year, and whether or not it has indoor seating. They assumed that this task would cause consumers to remember positive characteristics about McDonald's that would offset the worm meat rumor. It did. Consumers in this experimental condition showed a restored average attitude toward eating at McDonald's of 58 percent, which is almost identical to the prerumor attitude of 57 percent.

The "positive" outflanking strategy is probably the best all-around strategy. It may help, after acknowledging responsibility and accepting blame, even in the case of a major disaster. For instance, when a Pan Am jet crashed at Lockerbie in 1988 after a bomb had been planted on board, the company could have pointed to its excellent safety record over the years in relation to the number of passenger-miles flown. This would not have alleviated the suffering of the relatives of the victims, to which the company should devote separate attention, but it might cause others to put the disaster in a perspective more favorable to the company.

The positive outflanking strategy does have limits if the event is not perceived as a one-time or isolated incident. Negative events may be perceived as recurrent, such as USAir's five fatal crashes in five years including the September 1994 crash in Pittsburgh, or Tylenol's tampered containers disaster in which a series of people were poisoned by a maniac. Here the only possibility would be a decontrol response (see strategy 3, above) in which the company decontrols the connection with the negative event *after* fully correcting the problem.

The theoretical crisis management strategies suggested by Tybout, Calder, and Sternthal make an important contribution to PR management. The key is to "test out" alternative strategies that the company might take when a crisis or negative rumor arises. Specifically, as indicated, the company should conduct an *immediate survey* among the public or target audience groups who are potentially affected by the situation (with open-ended, not direct questions, so as not to feed the negative publicity). This survey should be *repeated daily,* or even several times a day in the early stage, until the situation is accurately assessed. At the same time, the alternative strategies can be operationalized by preparing responses that are ethically responsible choices for crisis management or rumor alleviation. These should be quickly *pretested* with survey respondents before release because, as we have seen, an ill-chosen response can worsen the negative publicity.

The company has a week to 10 days[57] to prepare a detailed response based on the selected strategy. Recent thinking on negative publicity has advocated an "apologize anyway" immediate response,[58] but we believe this dangerously oversimplifies crisis or rumor management. In the case of a *crisis*—a negative event that has already been publicly reported—the company is obliged to say *something* immediately, but the immediate response should be a noncommittal "we're investigating it thoroughly" news release. In the case of a *rumor*—a negative attribute association that may not be true—the company should make *no* immediate response in that "ignore and hope it goes away" may ultimately be the chosen strategy.

## 11D. Planning and Evaluating Sponsorships

As we have emphasized throughout, most advertising-like communications can be planned in exactly the same way as advertising. Sponsorships, event marketing, and (company-initiated positive) publicity should be regarded as alternative media to carry the company's or brand's message, just like advertising media. In considering a potential sponsorship, the manager has to evaluate the following factors:

**1.** *Target Audience Reach.* For instance, Pepsi wants to reach younger cola drinkers, so it tends to sponsor rock concerts and MTV programs, which appeal to younger members of the public. Volvo, as mentioned, wants to reach "upscale" car buyers, so it sponsors upper class (technically upper-middle and upper-class) sports such as tennis and especially golf. The audiences for sports and for particular events such as the Miami International Boat & Sailboat Show or the Indianapolis 500 are carefully studied for their demographic characteristics as well as the number of people reached, just like media vehicles in advertising campaigns.[59]

**2.** *Compatibility with the Company's or Brand's Positioning.* Some sponsorship selections are very logical because the event *uses* the product; for example, Mobil 1's sponsorship of motor racing, or Adidas's sponsorship of soccer. But others are chosen more indirectly for their "image" compatibility with the product. Thus beer companies tend to sponsor working-class sports such as baseball and football, as beer consumption is highest among working-class males; although Heineken, an upmarket beer in the United States, now sponsors ATP tennis tournaments.[60] Gillette sponsored cricket in the United Kingdom for a number of years to try to reduce the brand's American image. Also in the United Kingdom, Yardley, which had rather a feminine image due to the company's original focus on women's cosmetics, began sponsoring Formula One motor racing in order to convey a more "macho" positioning for its men's line of products.[61]

**3.** *Message Capacity.* The message capacity of sponsorships ranges from the brand name only, such as field-surrounding billboards at sporting events, to full capacity, such as television commercials on large screens at the game and, of course, on TV coverage of the game. An interesting study by European researchers of TV exposure of sports-field billboards suggested almost zero attention and consequently minimal effect.[62] An ingenious solution to this problem is emerging in the form of electronic changeable field billboards in which an advertiser can buy a strip of consecutive billboards for blocks of four minutes, which enables quite a long message to be printed and also allows the message executions to be varied during the game. For example, changeable billboards are offered by Dorna AdTime for British soccer, and Sega uses this new medium[63] to advertise its new video games, together with the launch date of the game.

How can the company make an evaluation of the effects of sponsorship? The answer is to conduct a tracking study (see Chapter 20). Suppose that Mobil 1 wanted to evaluate its sponsorship of Formula One Grand Prix auto racing for the season. The evaluation steps would be as follows:

**1.** Conduct a *preseason* survey of a random sample of the population, and measure their motor oil brand awareness, preferences, and purchase behavior.

**2.** Continue the surveys *during* the season, but add a question on reported *viewing* (versus nonviewing) of the Formula One Grand Prix races on television. This would give an estimate of the "reach" achieved by the sponsorship.

**3.** In the surveys during the racing season, processing and communication effects measures could be taken, just as in normal campaign evaluation or tracking. For instance, self-reports of noticing Mobil 1 (and competitors') logos and signage could be obtained as a measure of attention to the sponsorship stimuli. Less obtrusively, analysis of videotapes of the events could measure the *opportunity* for attention in terms of the length of time the respective stimuli were on-screen.

**4.** If the sponsorship is successful, brand awareness and preference for Mobil 1 motor oil should increase during and after the racing season among those television viewers who had been exposed to one or more Grand Prix races sponsored by Mobil 1. Sales, of course, should also differentially increase as a direct function of frequency of exposure to the sponsored event.

As with advertising, it is most important to track the results of sponsorships and associated publicity, both for ongoing sponsorships (many are contracted for 3 to 5 years at a time) and for short-term event marketing. Using tracking studies over the years, Volvo has estimated that its return is $8 in *profit* per sponsorship dollar. This means that the $25 million Volvo spent over a 5-year period up until 1993 sponsoring tennis tournaments returned an estimated $200 million in profit on sales of Volvo automobiles.[64]

## NOTES

1. The authors are greatly indebted to Professor Don Schultz of Northwestern University for valuable input to Part Five of this book.
2. *Webster's Ninth New Collegiate Dictionary;* Merriam-Webster, Inc., 1988.
3. Adapted from the "consumer franchise building" concept introduced by Prentice. The term "customer" recognizes the extension to business and industrial customers. R. M. Prentice, How to split your marketing funds between advertising and promotion, *Advertising Age,* January 10, 1977, p. 41.
4. Again we thank Don Schultz for emphasizing the important distinction between seller and buyer perspectives on the timeline of IMC activities.
5. P. Wang and L. Petrison, Integrated marketing communications and its potential effects on media planning, *Journal of Media Planning,* 1991, 6 (1) pp. 11–18. This journal is not held in all libraries; it can be obtained from the Medill School of Journalism, Northwestern University, Evanston, IL.
6. Cross-media or so-called "mixed media" mathematical models are helpful for this purpose. These are discussed in Chapter 17.
7. G. Low, Marketing communications budget allocation decision, in *Marketing Communications Strategies Today and Tomorrow: Integration, Allocation, and Interaction Technologies,* MSI Report Number 94-109, Cambridge, MA: Marketing Science Institute, 1994, pp. 22–25.

8. D. E. Schultz, How communications dis-integrate, *Marketing News,* June 20, 1994, p. 12.

9. T. L. Powers, Should you increase your sales promotions or add salespeople? *Industrial Marketing Management,* 1989, *18* (4), pp. 259–263.

10. From an IMC perspective, the sales force's personal selling has a strong analogy with advertising. Like all forms of marketing communications, the sales force has to be effective at producing all four buyer response steps: exposure, processing, communication effects, and target audience action. From an integrated communications standpoint, it is worth emphasizing this analogy, which operates as follows.

   a. In terms of personal selling's *exposure,* each salesperson can be thought of as a "media vehicle," with varying capacity across salespeople for effectively carrying the company's or brand's message. The two main sales management tasks—assigning the salespeople to territories and deciding the number of calls to customers in a territory—are directly analogous to reach and effective frequency in the advertising media plan.

   b. In terms of *processing,* the sales message is just like an advertising message (indeed, the early description of advertising by copywriting pioneers such as Claude Hopkins, before the advent of broadcast advertising, was "salesmanship in print"). Sales training, often with scripted openings and answers to potential objections, is an important way of facilitating prospective customers' processing of the sales message, as are presentation aids and leave-behind brochures.

   c. In terms of *communication effects,* these are the same for personal selling as for advertising. As we emphasized earlier (Chapter 5), the five communication effects are *marketing* communication effects, not just advertising communication effects. For products and services that are heavily dependent on personal selling, a frequent reason for the failure of *advertising* to work is that the positioning adopted in advertising is not first developed in conjunction with, nor supported by, the sales force. It is vital that personal selling and advertising be promoting the same macropositioning for the brand, using an integrated communications strategy. Again, however, remember that the benefit emphasis may vary with the target audience and that the sales force will frequently have a distributor target audience rather than a final-user target audience as is the case with most advertising.

   d. In terms of the *action* step, the sales force is often specialized according to salespeople who are proficient in gaining new business (trial) and those who

perform best when servicing existing customers (repeat purchase).

Chapter 12 provides further coverage of personal selling in conjunction with sales-force promotions.

11. For a review of definitions of corporate identity, which mainly converge on our definition, see C. B. M. van Riel, *Principles of Corporate Communication,* London: Prentice-Hall, 1995, especially chapters 2 and 4. His definition of CI refers to the use of "symbols, communication and behavior" (p. 28) but we, like most others, restrict CI to *visual symbols,* leaving "communication" to corporate image advertising, and "behavior" to PR. All, of course, communicate about the company in an advertising-like way.

12. W. Olins, *Corporate Identity,* Boston: Harvard Business School Press, 1989; G. R. Dowling, *Corporate Reputations: Strategies for Developing the Corporate Brand,* Melbourne, Australia: Longman Professional, 1994, p. xiii.

13. Trade journals and everyday observation.

14. G. R. Dowling, same reference as in note 12.

15. Some of this material is drawn from J.-E. Ruud, *Strategic Marketing Plan,* Selangor Darul Ehsan, Malaysia: Pelanduk Publications, 1987, chapter 11.

16. *Marketing* (UK), July 1, 1993, p. 23.

17. J.-E. Ruud, same reference as note 15.

18. M. Davids, 16th Annual review of corporate advertising expenditures: Tough stuff, *Public Relations Journal,* 1987, *43* (9), pp. 28–31, 63–64.

19. B. J. Coe, Corporate advertising: Target audiences and primary objectives: 1980–1988, in P. Stout, ed., *American Academy of Advertising Proceedings,* 1990, pp. RC-99 to RC-104; and D. W. Schumann, J. M. Hathcote, and S. West, Corporate advertising in America: A review of published studies on use, measurement, and effectiveness, *Journal of Advertising,* 1991, *20* (3), pp. 35–56.

20. Advocacy advertising should be distinguished from crisis management, which is an emergency *publicity* activity. See chapter appendix 11C.

21. J. J. Davis, Consumer response to corporate environmental advertising, *Journal of Consumer Marketing,* 1994, *11* (2), pp. 25–37.

22. D. W. Schumann et al., same reference as in note 19.

23. The finding of no significant relationship between corporate advertising spending and product advertising spending comes from a recent analysis of expenditures by the top 200 U.S. advertisers conducted by J. S. Raju and S. K. Dahr, Firm diversification and corporate advertising expenditures, Abstract, Marketing Science conference, Sydney, Australia, July 2–5, 1995.

24. W. S. Sachs, Corporate advertising: Ends, means, problems, *Public Relations Journal,* 1981, *37* (11), pp.

14–17. Although this is now a fairly dated survey, we use its figures because we believe they are typical. Corporate image advertising expenditures have not changed much over the long term but rather have tended to fluctuate in the short term with the state of the economy.

25. P. Dhar, Cathay Pacific seeks to make itself more Asian, *Advertising Age International,* January 16, 1995, pp. 1–4.

26. How to get the most from 4-color advertising, *Starch Tested Copy,* 1991, *3* (8), pp. 1–4, 6. See Chapter 10 of the present book for further explanation of attention (Noting), branding (Seen Associated), and incidence of reading (Read Most) measures in the Starch (now Roper Starch) Readership service from which these examples were taken.

27. Two excellent case histories documenting the effects of corporate image advertising campaigns are available in the *Journal of Advertising Research:* for the DuPont company, by Grass and his colleagues, and in a series of extremely well detailed cases conducted over the years for Chevron oil company by Winters. See R. C. Grass, D. W. Bartges, and J. L. Piech, Measuring corporate image ad effects, *Journal of Advertising Research,* 1972, *12* (6), pp. 15–22; and four studies by L. C. Winters, as follows: Should you advertise to hostile audiences? *Journal of Advertising Research,* 1977, *17* (6), pp. 7–15; Comparing pretesting and posttesting of corporate advertising, *Journal of Advertising Research,* 1983, *23* (1), pp. 25–32; The effect of brand advertising on company image: Implications for corporate image, *Journal of Advertising Research,* 1986, *26* (2), pp. 54–59; and Does it pay to advertise to hostile audiences with corporate advertising? *Journal of Advertising Research,* 1988, *28* (3), pp. 11–18.

28. J. S. Niefeld, How stockholders profit from corporate advertising, unpublished report, Bozell & Jacobs Advertising, New York, 1984. This report provides an extended and far more specific appraisal of preliminary results that were reported in a more widely available article by E. P. Schonfeld and J. H. Boyd, The financial payoff in corporate advertising, *Journal of Advertising Research,* 1982, *22* (1), pp. 45–55. A recent and careful study of corporate image advertising in *The Wall Street Journal* aimed at the financial community showed no effect on stock price in the following 20 days; however, long-term effects were *not* measured. See G. S. Bobinski, Jr., and G. G. Ramirez, Advertising to investors: The effect of financial-relations advertising on stock volume and price, *Journal of Advertising,* 1994, *23* (4), pp. 13–28.

Also, whether the company's total advertising (corporate or not) would have had the same stock-price increase effect is answered in the affirmative by Cooil and Devinney's study; see Chapter 2, and Chapter 2's note 7.

29. R. E. Reidenbach and R. E. Pitts, Not all CEOs are created equal as advertising spokespersons: Evaluating the effective CEO spokesperson, *Journal of Advertising,* 1986, *15* (1), pp. 30–36, 46.

30. D. Kowet, When is an ad an editorial? *TV Guide,* February 4, 1978, pp. 21, 22, 24, 26.

31. K. R. Middleton, Advocacy advertising, the First Amendment, and competitive advantage: A comment on Cutler & Muehling, *Journal of Advertising,* 1991, *20* (2), pp. 77–81.

32. J. D. Williams, Industrial publicity: One of the best promotional tools, *Industrial Marketing Management,* 1983, *12* (3), pp. 207–211.

33. D. Marshall, Opportunities for brands through sports sponsorship, *Journal of Brand Management,* 1994, *1* (5), pp. 303–308.

34. This case was originally written up by F. Dinsmore, Cricket sponsorship, *The Business Graduate* (UK), Autumn, 1980, pp. 68–72; and further reported in T. Meenaghan, The role of sponsorship in the marketing communications mix, *International Journal of Advertising,* 1991, *10* (1) pp. 35–47; and B. Witcher, J. G. Craigen, D. Culligan, and A. Harvey. The links between objectives and function in organizational sponsorship, *International Journal of Advertising,* 1991, *10* (1), pp. 13–33.

35. Sports marketing: A high-rollers game, *Advertising Age,* September 9, 1991, p. 16.

36. D. W. Marshall and G. Cook, The corporate (sports) sponsor, *International Journal of Advertising,* 1992, *11* (4), pp. 307–324.

37. M. P. Gardner and P. J. Shuman, Sponsorship: An important component of the promotions mix, *Journal of Advertising,* 1987, *16* (1), pp. 11–17.

38. Big sponsorships double as local happenings, *The Wall Street Journal,* October 30, 1991, p. B1.

39. Sponsorship fails for Ford, *Marketing* (Australia), March 1994, p. 9.

40. For an excellent analysis of the various ploys of ambush marketing, and preventive or counterresponses to them, see T. Meenaghan, Ambush marketing: Immoral or imaginative practice? *Journal of Advertising Research,* 1994, *34* (5), pp. 77–88.

41. D. R. Scott and H. T. Suchard, Motivations for Australian expenditure on sponsorship—an analysis, *International Journal of Advertising,* 1992, *11* (4), pp. 325–332.

42. P. A. Stout, G. B. Wilcox, and L. S. Greer, Trends in magazine advertorial use, *Journalism Quarterly,* 1989, *66* (4), pp. 957–960.

43. T. H. Dodd and S. Morse, The impact of media stories concerning healthiness on food product sales: Management planning and responses, *Journal of Consumer Marketing*, 1994, *11* (2), pp. 17–24.

44. Some ethically contentious instances of major companies engaging in deceptive publicity promotion practices are given in S. K. Balasubramanian, Beyond advertising and publicity: Hybrid messages and public policy issues, *Journal of Advertising*, 1994, *23* (4), pp. 29–46.

45. J. A. Trachtenberg, Avon's new TV campaign says, "Call us," *The Wall Street Journal*, December 28, 1992, pp. B1, B4.

46. R. DeNeve, What ever happened to corporate identity? *Print*, May-June, 1989, pp. 92–98, 157–164.

47. R. DeNeve, same reference as previous note.

48. As explained in Chapter 5, corporate image is the set of beliefs associated with, and freestanding emotional responses to, the company. When weighted in the multiattribute model sense into an overall evaluation, this image becomes company attitude.

49. B. Yandell, Those who protest too much are seen as guilty, *Personality and Social Psychology Bulletin*, 1979, *5* (1), pp. 44–47.

50. D. M. Wenger, R. Wenzlaff, R. M. Kerker, and A. E. Beattie, Incrimination through innuendo: Can media questions become public answers? *Journal of Personality and Social Psychology*, 1981, *40* (5), pp. 822–832.

51. B. K. Jorgensen, Consumer reaction to company-related disasters: The effect of multiple versus simple explanations, in C. T. Allen and D. Roedder John, eds., *Advances in Consumer Research*, vol. 21, 1994, pp. 348–352.

52. A. M. Tybout, B. J. Calder, and B. Sternthal, Using information processing theory to design marketing strategies, *Journal of Marketing Research*, 1981, *18* (1), pp. 73–79.

53. See C. Silver, Unilever drains Power, *Advertising Age*, January 16, p. 8; and L. Wentz, Unilever's power failure, a wasteful use of haste, *Advertising Age*, March 6, 1995, p. 42. Reportedly, P&G's CEO had warned Unilever's Vice Chairman that P&G would raise the manganese issue if Power was launched, but didn't let on that P&G had its own stainfighting brand in its laboratory. Unilever was so enthusiastic about the new product that it skipped formal test-marketing and went straight to a national rollout in its home country, Holland, and then distributed tens of millions of samples to European consumers' mailboxes. The clothes-rotting rumor had some truth to it in that delicate clothing could be affected if too much detergent or very hot water was used (as P&G's negative-publicity TV commercials showed!).

54. A. M. Tybout et al., same reference as note 54, p. 74.

55. J. Montgomery, Rumor-plagued firms use various strategies to keep damage low, *The Wall Street Journal*, February 6, 1979, pp. 1, 22.

56. A. M. Tybout et al., same reference as note 54, p. 76.

57. B. K. Jorgensen, Components of consumer reaction to company-related mishaps: A structural equations model approach, in K. P. Corfman and J. G. Lynch, Jr., eds., *Advances in Consumer Research*, vol. 23, 1996, Provo, UT: Association for Consumer Research, pp. 346–351.

58. S. Roslow, J. A. F. Nicholls, and H. A. Laskey, Hallmark events and measures of reach and audience characteristics, *Journal of Advertising Research*, 1992, *32* (4), pp. 53–59.

59. Since about 1993, by our observation.

60. Briefs, *Advertising Age*, March 13, 1995, p. 26.

61. T. Meenaghan, same reference as in note 34.

62. G. d'Ydewalle, P. Vanden Abeele, J. Van Rensbergen, and P. Coucke, Incidental processing of advertisements while watching soccer games broadcast, in M. M. Gruneberg, P. E. Morris, and R. N. Sykes, eds., *Practical Aspects of Memory: Current Research and Issues, Vol. I: Memory in Everyday Life*, Chichester, UK: Wiley, 1988, pp. 478–483; and G. d'Ydewalle and F. Tamsin, On the visual processing and memory of incidental information: Advertising panels in soccer games, Working paper, Department of Psychology, University of Leuven, Belgium, no date.

63. D. W. Marshall and G. Cook, same reference as note 36.

64. T. Ramsay, European sponsor drives past tennis: Company makes $8 for every dollar spent on promotion, *The Australian*, February 10, 1993, p. 25.

## DISCUSSION QUESTIONS

**11.1.** In terms of the five communication effects, what are the relative strengths of advertising communications (in general) versus promotions (in general)?

**11.2.** BMW automobiles are positioned to upscale car buyers as "the ultimate driving machine." But would this positioning suffice in BMW's communications to retail distributors? Outline how BMW as a brand might be presented to retail distributors in a way that will appeal to them while reinforcing the brand's central position.

**11.3.** Using the task matrix method, outline a corporate identity program *and* a fully integrated corporate image advertising program aimed at *retailers* for NEC computers. The total budget to be allocated across this IMC effort is $30 million.

**11.4.** You are the communications manager of a large medical clinic. An HIV-infected former patient has just called a reporter claiming that the infection was acquired in your clinic. The reporter has called you for a response. Outline the steps you would take in this crisis management situation.

**11.5.** What types of sports, social, or cultural events would be most worth investigating for event-marketing sponsorships by the following brands? In making your recommendations, consider the events' target audience reach, compatibility with the company's or brand's position, as appropriate, and message capacity.
   **a.** Midas mufflers
   **b.** Nabisco cookies
   **c.** John Deere tractors
   **d.** Videomate dating service (a fictional brand)

**11.6.** What are your personal views on advertorials? What sort of pretest could be conducted for advertorials to minimize the ethical problem of potential deception?

**11.7.** You are a cereal manufacturer and you decide to sponsor the state champion junior woman swimmer, hoping she will make it to the next Olympic Games. You expect that your sponsorship association with her progress will increase sales of the designated cereal brand by 5 percent in the first year on a base level of sales of $10 million. The product's unit profit margin is 30 percent. Up-front costs for the sponsorship are $500,000, ongoing fixed costs are $20,000 per month, and variable costs are zero. You estimate the termination probability at the end of the first year to be .2 and the termination expense, in the form of a straight donation to her program in the event of your termination of the sponsorship, as $50,000. Using Powers's formula, calculate the expected profit on this sponsorship for the first year.

## FURTHER READING

Schultz, D. E., Tannenbaum, S. I., and Lauterborn, R. F. *Integrated Marketing Communications.* Lincolnwood, IL: NTC Publishing Group, 1992.

This book was also recommended for further reading in Chapter 1 as offering the first comprehensive coverage of the new field of integrated marketing communications (IMC).

van Riel, C. B. M. *Principles of Corporate Communication.* London: Prentice-Hall, 1995.

This book is an eclectic compendium of theoretical frameworks and research findings on corporate identity and corporate image communications. It includes European contributions not cited elsewhere.

Dowling, G. R. *Corporate Reputations.* Melbourne, Australia: Longman Professional, 1994.

This is a systematic, conceptual, but very practical book on how to measure and manage corporate image and thus company attitude or reputation.

Irwin, H., and More, E. *Managing Corporate Communications.* St. Leonards, Australia: Allen & Unwin, 1994.

This is a valuable book for marketers because it is written from an organizational-behavior rather than a marketing perspective. It ranges comprehensively from international corporate communications right down to personal communications within the company.

# Manufacturer's Promotions

**P**romotions consist of a repertoire of activities designed to "move sales forward" more rapidly than would occur with advertising alone. To apply IMC strategy to promotions, the content of the brand's promotions should be integrated *centrally* (mostly with but sometimes without advertising) with regard to the positioning of the brand. Also, promotion activities should be integrated systematically *over time* with regard to the buyer's decision process.

This chapter covers promotions employed by the manufacturer: sales-force promotions, trade promotions, customer or consumer trial promotions, and repeat-purchase promotions. The next chapter covers retailer's promotions. After reading this chapter, you should:

- Understand the IMC "over time" sequence of the main promotion activities available to the manufacturer.
- Learn the main methods of sales-force promotions.
- See how to manage trade promotions.
- Understand the various forms of trial promotions and how to implement them most effectively.
- Know when to use the various forms of repeat-purchase promotions.

The *timeline* of manufacturer's promotions from the customer's perspective is indicated in Figure 12.1 and provides the topic order for this chapter. It should be evident, of course, that the manufacturer is likely to be employing all four major forms of pro-

motions simultaneously—but to different prospective or current customers. The first and second forms of promotions—sales-force promotions and trade promotions—occur in the manufacturer's distribution channel to *distributor-customers*. The third and fourth forms—trial promotions and repeat-purchase promotions—are for *end-customers or consumers*.

## SALES-FORCE PROMOTIONS

Manufacturers either have their own sales force or a commissioned external sales force to motivate. Sales-force promotions most importantly include the way in which the sales people are compensated in terms of commissions or bonuses, either added to or in some cases totally replacing salary, as well as nonmonetary encouragement and incentives in the form of motivational meetings, sales contests, training programs, and selling aids.

Although this necessarily takes us into sales-force management, full coverage of which is beyond the scope of this book, we outline below an important analysis by Newton[1] of management recommendations for different types of personal selling. These may be regarded as promotional strategies as they speed up the rate of sales. Newton's analysis essentially regards the sales force as "campaigners" to be chosen, assigned, and compensated in much the same way that creative campaigns are used for advertising. Newton identifies four main types of sales forces or

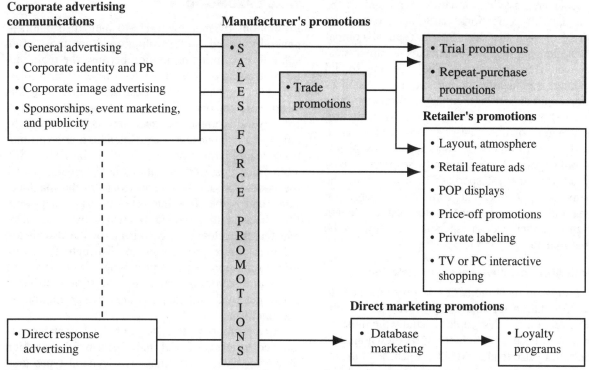

**Corporate advertising communications**

**Manufacturer's promotions**

**Retailer's promotions**

**Direct marketing promotions**

**FIGURE 12.1**
Manufacturer's promotions (shaded boxes).

personal-selling functions: new business selling, technical selling, missionary selling, and trade selling. The recommended policies for each are in some cases quite surprising and very sensible.[2] The reader is reminded that age discrimination (which varies both ways in the policies) is illegal in some countries. It is recent education or long experience (as the case may be) that are required rather than age per se.

**New Business Selling (Cold Calling)**

Older, more experienced salespeople should be hired or employed temporarily based on their track record in new business sales success. Territorial assignments do not matter, as new business selling is basically a shotgun activity. Because of the frequent misses (rejections) in new business selling, it is recommended, paradoxically, that new business salespeople be paid a fixed salary, to minimize their anxiety,[3] but dismissed quickly if they are not performing to target sales levels. Frequent in-house "update" meetings are also recommended to counter the often lonely role characteristic of this type of selling.

**Technical Selling**

The main requirement for technical salespeople is the ability to absorb specialized training provided in-house by the company. Accordingly, recent college graduates in engineering or the sciences are naturally favored as having the aptitude for this type of selling. It is recommended that territories be kept reasonably constant because of the opportunity to build a relationship with customers; therefore, territories (or, more correctly, customers) are transferred only when the relationship is proving unsuccessful in terms of a continued or increased rate of sales. Compensation should be approximately 80 percent fixed salary, so that the technical salesperson feels that he or she is truly a member of the company,[4] with 20 percent commission based on *sales* results.

**Missionary Selling**

Missionary selling is practiced by salespeople who sell to professionals such as doctors and dentists, and is sometimes given the rather derogatory description of "animated direct mail." The idea is that these salespeople are just "missionaries" who spread the word and, with professional customers, cannot be certain of closing the sale. Pharmaceutical companies' detailers calling on physicians as their customers would be an example. The company should hire young, enthusiastic people as the missionary sales force and expect high employee turnover. Sales territories should be rotated often, because of the impersonal nature of this type of selling, and so as to add variety to an otherwise routine job. Compensation should again be approximately 80 percent fixed salary so that the salesperson identifies with the company, with 20 percent commission based on meeting the *call quota,* since sales results are not sufficiently under the salesperson's control to be commissionable.

### Trade Selling (to Wholesalers or Retailers)

Trade selling, in most industries, is very much an instance of "relationship marketing." Accordingly, hiring relatively older salespeople is usually the most effective policy because the chief buyers on whom they will be calling also tend to be older. Because of the relationship nature of this selling, territories should be transferred only at the salesperson's request, unless it is obvious that the relationship is not working. The compensation recommendation is 60 percent fixed salary and a very high proportion, 40 percent, in commission. The reason for the high proportion of commission—on actual *sales*—is to offset the tendency of trade salespeople to spend too much time during sales calls in "maintaining the relationship" rather than focusing on the task at hand, which is to sell the product or service.

*Nonmonetary* forms of sales-force promotion—such as motivational meetings, attendance at training programs, and sales contests—are an extremely mixed bag in terms of promotional effectiveness. We will not discuss them further here as no general recommendations are possible.

The IMC approach views the sales force and personal selling not just as a form of marketing communications but also as a *promotional* medium to be chosen and managed in ways that will improve the rate of sales. Research using sales rate as the outcome measure strongly favors *hiring policy* and *salary structure* (as described above) as the manufacturers' *principal* promotion activities for the sales force.

## TRADE PROMOTIONS

Promotions by manufacturers to their distributors—generally called trade promotions—are most often some form of price promotion because the main factor motivating distributors is their reseller profit margin. For companies who distribute through agents (who work for one company) or brokers (who work for several companies) paid on commission, the amount of *commission* is equivalent to a price promotion because it increases the agent's or broker's profit. With other types of distribution, the distributor "buys" the goods (products or services) from the manufacturer[5] and is therefore interested in *price-off* promotions because they reduce the distributor's cost price and thereby allow a larger profit for the distributor. Whereas some promotions to distributors are *not* price promotions, such as providing sales materials or sponsoring an occasional sales contest for distributor personnel, by far the majority are price promotions in various forms.

Price promotions to distributors are somewhat specialized in terms of trial and repeat-purchase action objectives.[6] We review these two general types first, and later consider the particular situations of trade advertising and trade promotions to packaged goods retailers.

Manufacturers are ultimately interested in the end-customer and, accordingly, usually want extra *performance* from the distributor to those customers in return for price promotions—particularly better display, more effort put into selling the manufacturer's brand, and cooperative advertising. This "price-off for performance" objective is reflected in the promotions reviewed below.

### Trade Trial Promotions

Price promotions most often used to gain trial—that is, an initial stocking of the product or offering of the service by the distributor—are mainly of three types:

**1.** *New line fees,* or slotting allowances, which are cash payments or sometimes a proportion of the shipment donated free, which amounts to a price inducement, in return for stocking a new product or offering a new service for a specified time period.

**2.** *Price-offs,* which are a straight reduction in the selling price to the distributor and are sometimes called "off invoice" promotions.

**3.** *Returns,* by which the manufacturer agrees to buy back unsold quantities of the product, the extreme form of which is distributing "on consignment," meaning that the distributor pays nothing to the manufacturer until the product is sold.

### Trade Repeat-Purchase Promotions

Price promotions most often used to encourage repeat purchase by the distributor—continued stocking of the product or offering of the service—are of the following four types:

**1.** *Price-offs* as described above, but usually with the understanding that at least part of the discount will be passed through to the consumer or end-customer, or that the distributor will provide extra display, advertising, or both, in return for the extra margin that the distributor is gaining.

**2.** *Cooperative advertising allowances,* which are agreements by which the manufacturer and distributor both contribute funds toward *retail* advertising of the product or service; the proportions may vary, and a ratio of at least 70:30 in favor of the manufacturer is needed to give the manufacturer control over the content of the advertising. (A more elaborate form of co-op advertising is "comarketing," in which the manufacturer offers an integrated communications program to attract the distributor to participate, with the distributor's financial contribution being lowered according to how much retail advertising the distributor delivers. For example, Kimberly-Clark created an ad that was mainly an ad for Pathmark stores— which happened to be featuring Kimberly-Clark's Kleenex tissues on special. This new type of double-barreled ad promotes the retailer throughout rather than merely appending the retailer as a tag at the end.[7]) The manufacturer's percentage contribution is called the *participation rate* (ranging from 25 to 100 percent but most often 70 to 90 percent); this is usually accompanied by an *accrual rate*, which sets a limit on what the manufacturer agrees to pay, as a percentage of product or service purchases by the distributor (ranging from 2 to 6 percent of dollar sales).[8]

**3.** *Sales contests,* which are applicable in any industry.

**4.** *Sales education,* which is applicable mainly to industrial products and services or to the more technical types of consumer durables.

### Trade Advertising

Price promotions to distributors for new products or services are quite often accompanied by *trade advertising,* usually as part of a "sales kit." The main distinction here is between personal-selling distributors and self-service distributors.

Distributors who have to *personally sell* the product or service to further customers or final buyers are interested in advertising information that helps their sales staff sell the product. Trade ads to these distributors should contain more than the average buyer would need to know, arranged in a sales-education-kit format to facilitate the distributor's training of sales staff.

*Self-service* distributors, on the other hand, such as supermarkets and mass merchandisers, do not want the sort of information about product benefits that appears in consumer advertising (although samples of consumer ads should be appended in the trade advertising package). Trade ads to self-service distributors should emphasize *acceptance* details such as margin, expected turnover, shelf space required, and manufacturer support services.

### Trade Promotions to Packaged Goods Retailers

Retailers in many Western countries, through the formation of large chain or cooperative buying groups, have in the past decade or so come to wield virtual oligopoly power over manufacturers and have been able to extract very large trade promotion allowances from them. In the United States, for instance, it is estimated that the larger packaged goods marketers now pay approximately 50 percent of their advertising communications and promotion budget in the form of trade promotions to retailers, a proportion that is up from about 34 percent a decade earlier.[9] What keeps these payments so high is the competitive threat: if one manufacturer refuses to pay, the retailer will simply substitute the products of another manufacturer who *is* willing to pay, and so most go along with the "going price" for trade promotions.

Trade promotions are by and large not profitable and most manufacturers wish they could avoid them. (This perspective is remarkably different from the *retailer's* perspective, as we will see in the next chapter.) The evidence that trade promotions are unprofitable for manufacturers is now overwhelming. A 1990 study of trade promotions (case allowances and other forms of price-off inducements to retailers, about half of which are passed through as *consumer* promotions) by Information Resources Inc. reported that only 17 percent were profitable for the manufacturer.[10]

A major problem with trade promotions is that the retailers have become so powerful that there is no guarantee that any extra services will be performed in return. Consequently, the larger manufacturers whose brands have high equity with consumers are attempting to exercise countervailing power by allocating trade promotion dollars on a "pay for performance" basis. For instance, a division of Information Resources Inc., called Customer Marketing Resources, uses analysis of the manufacturer's sales on a store-by-store basis to help the manufacturer use trade promotion dollars to reward performance. Performance, in the retail application, takes the form of increased advertising space in retail newspaper and TV ads (called "feature ads" or simply "features"), in-store merchandising, and honoring of the manufacturer's intended price positioning of the brand. A further aim is to reduce the retailers' practice of "forward buying" during price discount periods. The manufacturer's objective is to reward the retailer for *selling* more, not simply buying more.[11]

The "pay" (the reward) may be partly in the form of giving retailers access to the brand's mass media advertising and sponsorships, usually as a "dealer tag" added to the message. This "let's work together" idea is inherent in *comarketing,* which we referred to above as a form of cooperative advertising.

Manufacturers are interested not only in having the retailer stock their products but also in obtaining favorable *shelf space.* Shelf space, in most retail outlets, means as many *facings* of the brand as possible (horizontally) and the best shelf *height* to catch the shopper's eye (vertically). The advantage of broad horizontal facings is the increased (longer) attention gained as the shopper walks past the display. The advantage of eye-level positioning was shown in an extensive experiment conducted by *Progressive Grocer* magazine in conjunction with A & P Supermarkets (Figure 12.2).[12] In the extreme situation, shifting a brand from the top (eye-level) to the bottom shelf results, on average, in approximately an 80 percent decrease in sales. It should be noted that these results apply to adult shoppers. Children's eye-level position (for example, for children's cereals and snacks) would be on lower shelves.

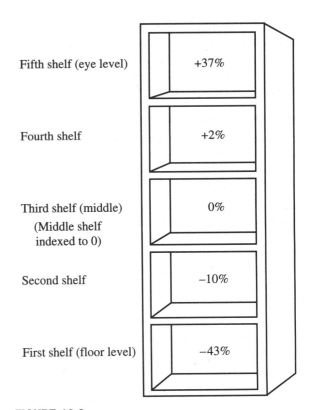

**FIGURE 12.2**
Sales effects of shelf height in supermarkets.
*Source:* Adapted from a privately conducted study by *Progressive Grocer* magazine and A & P Supermarkets, ca. 1982, by permission.

### Trade Promotion Timing

Promotions to distributors are most effective when timed to accompany promotions to end-customers or consumers. This is an application of timing integration in IMC: the manufacturer should push the product (through the trade channel) and pull it (via end-customer demand creation) at the same time for best results.[13] If the distributor knows that the product or service is being simultaneously promoted to final buyers or consumers, the distributor is more likely to give the product favorable shelf space and display, or more selling time in the case of a service.

### CUSTOMER OR CONSUMER TRIAL PROMOTIONS

The next promotion activity in the customer timeline available to the manufacturer is trial promotions to the end-customer or consumer. The action objective of these promotions is *trial* of the product or service. To backtrack, it is worth restating that trial by *distributors* is the first necessary step (for all brands except those that are sold direct) prior to trial by consumers or final buyers. We mentioned previously the importance of "distribution trial" and its exponentially increasing (positively accelerating) relationship with market share.[14]

The importance of trial by *end-customers or consumers* was emphasized in Chapter 3 where we discussed action objectives for advertising communications and promotions. There we saw that the British marketing theorist Ehrenberg[15] and his colleagues have provided voluminous evidence, for industrial as well as consumer products and services, demonstrating that a brand's *penetration* is the major determinant of sales level and thus market share. This follows from the equation that sales = penetration (the number of people who buy the brand) × buying rate (the number of times they buy it in a given period)—and also from the finding that although penetration varies widely across brands, the variation in buying rate across brands in a given product category is small. Therefore, penetration is the main determinant of sales (and, on a relative basis, market share). And although penetration represents the *final* number of people who buy the brand, unless the brand is really inferior, penetration obviously is a close correlate of the *initial* number of people who *try* the brand.

There are four main types of trial promotions:

1. Product or service sampling
2. Price-off techniques
3. Premiums
4. Coupons (offered by manufacturers of fast-moving consumer products and services)

Product or service sampling is usually the most effective and profitable trial promotion activity. Price-offs, which include serveral different implementation techniques, are usually the second best. Premiums have to be very carefully chosen if they are to attract triers. Coupons, primarily an fmcg promotional activity, are effective if they can be targeted at new triers rather than the brand's regular buyers. These four trial activities are examined in the above-listed order.

## Product or Service Sampling

Product or service sampling promotions can be used by all types of marketers. However, because of the na-ture of the products or services, in each case the trial promotions are likely to be *different forms* of sampling, as follows:

- Industrial marketers—trade shows, feasibility studies, demonstrations
- Consumer durables marketers—demonstrations, home-trial offers
- Consumer packaged goods marketers—free or low-cost samples

Trial promotion by sampling is initially expensive but is the strongest known trial-generating technique. Its high initial cost is "amortized" over repeat purchase, assuming you have a reasonably good product or service to be tried in the first place. The reason sampling is such a strong trial-generating technique for major products and services is that, by agreeing to try the product or service, the prospective buyer is likely to commit himself or herself to a further purchase in order to maintain self-consistency.[16] This commitment process is especially likely in sampling promotions for *high-involvement* purchases. For instance, once a company or organization has allowed a supplier company to perform a feasibility study, there is already considerable commitment to continue. Once you have agreed to test-drive a new car, you usually feel more commitment toward that particular model, and toward the salesperson, than if you had not agreed to take the trial. After you have tried on an item of clothing at a clothing store, or several items, you feel somewhat more committed to buying one of the items.

However, commitment is *unlikely* to be felt for sampling of *low-involvement,* frequently purchased consumer packaged goods. Much more basically for fmcg products, the product *has to work immediately*—that is, be favorably evaluated from the sample of it. About 75 percent of consumers who receive a sample will try it, and about 15 to 20 percent will then proceed to make a subsequent full-priced purchase.[17] These eventual trial rates are considerably higher, though, than can be obtained with other consumer promotions such as coupons.

The two most widely used trial-sampling techniques—trade shows for industrial marketers, and product or service sampling for consumer marketers—require considerable planning and are discussed in more detail next.[18]

**Trade Shows.** For industrial marketers, trade shows are typically the second largest marketing expenditure after industrial magazine advertising—averaging about 20 to 25 percent of the industrial marketer's advertising communications and promotion budget.[19] The average industrial firm exhibits at six trade shows a year. The great attraction of trade shows for industrial marketers is the efficient generation of high-quality *leads* for trial of the industrial product or service. Prospects (with the category need) come to the marketer rather than the marketer having to go look for them. By way of comparison, it is estimated that the average industrial sales call costs $292 (a 1992 figure) and that the number of calls required to close a sale, averaging 3.7, brings the total cost of making that sale to $1,080. In contrast, the average inquiry at a trade show costs only $185 per contact and requires an average of just under one (0.8) follow-up sales call to close the sale, for a total cost of only $419.[20] This lower "frequency" means that the target audience "reach" of trade shows is the major consideration in deciding whether and in which shows to exhibit.

As to the trade show exhibition itself, the quality of booth personnel and their active rate of making contacts are the most important factors in trade show effectiveness (see chapter appendix 12A, Factors in Trade Show Promotion). Looking ahead, *advertising* your exhibit on "virtual reality" interactive TV or PC so that prospective visitors can "preshop" will also be an important factor.[21]

**Consumer Product or Service Sampling.** Consumer marketers have a wide variety of means to enable prospective triers to experience a free or low-cost sample of their product or service.

For larger products (durables), *shopping center or in-store demonstrations* are the most efficient method. These have largely replaced door-to-door demonstrations and sampling, such as used to be practiced by the Fuller Brush men and still is practiced on a somewhat reduced basis by the Avon ladies. Consumer *shows* are another alternative for larger products such as home furnishings and household items (example: the Atlanta Home Show), boats and boating equipment (example: the New York Boat Show), and other products related to lifestyle activities such as camping, cooking, and pet ownership. It has been estimated that approximately 35 percent of the U.S. population attends one or more of these shows annually, and the attraction for marketers is that most of those who do attend are "in the market" for the broad product category and thus are likely to have the category need communication effect active at the time. *Home-trial offers* may follow demonstrations or be used independently as a trial-generating promotion. For instance, Apple ran an over-the-weekend home-trial promotion when it launched the Macintosh PC.

Smaller products (fmcg) can be sampled in shopping centers or in stores (examples: food samples, fragrance "testers"). *In-store* "trial size" packages of products, priced at a discount, are another common method for sampling consumer packaged goods. Small products that are divisible into "sample-able" units can be distributed via direct marketing media, such as shampoos and cereals distributed door-to-door or in doorknob hang-bags, samples sent by direct mail, and the tear-out or "scratch and sniff" type of sample for fragrances that is placed in magazines. Other means include cooperative sample packs (such as distributed on many college campuses at the beginning of the school year) and also "cross-product" coupons which are distributed on the package or product that you've already bought, with the coupon good for trial purchase of a *different* product offered by the same, or a cooperating, manufacturer.

Consumer *services* can, of course, be sampled but services are much more likely to be introduced to triers with a low-price trial offer. How often, for example, have you been offered a free car wash (without having to buy gas) or a free haircut? Although there is no reason why sampling cannot be used for services, perhaps their less tangible nature means that the tangible payment of money seems more appropriate to both the seller and the buyer.

The cost-effectiveness of sampling has to be estimated beforehand. The task method in conjunction with Powers's specific-cost formula can be used (see Chapter 11). Note that the initial focus should be on the first *full-priced* trial purchase. Thereafter, the repeat-purchase rate by triers following a sample will tend to be the same as that for regular buyers, a fact which may help in your estimate.

*CFB Presentation of Samples.* Sampling is the one promotion technique that is automatically customer franchise building. Receipt of the sample generates immediate brand awareness, and trial of the sample establishes brand attitude (the key communication effect in the CFB approach) and brand purchase intention.[22] A further CFB bonus is that favorable trial of a sample seems more likely than other trial offers to generate favorable word-of-mouth communication to other prospective triers. Of course, *unfavorable* trial experience can generate *negative* word of mouth—though usually, fortunately, at a lower level than the positive effect.[23]

*When to Use Sampling.* There are five main marketing situations in which the manager should use sampling. (If none of these situations applies, then the manager should use another, less-expensive, trial-generating promotion, or simply rely on advertising alone to create trial). The five marketing situations are as follows:

**1.** *New Product Category Introduction.* When a new product *category* is being introduced to the market, *speed* of trial is usually of the essence for the initial brands launched in the category. This is because of the order-of-entry effect described in Chapter 2: consumers will often settle on the first "good" brand tried. Note that this situation goes against the usual admonition that only demonstrably superior brands should use sampling. A parity brand, if tried first, could gain the advantage (see also our earlier discussion on the importance of the initial number of triers).

**2.** *Superior Brand Introduction in an Established Category.* The second situation is the traditional one for sampling. When a new, improved brand enters an established product category, sampling is an excellent way to gain trial. With an established product category, the new, improved brand has to be perceived as superior, otherwise the sampled triers will revert to their previous brand or brands. With the routinization or "inertia" of buyers in established product categories, sampling is perhaps the *only* technique that will successfully produce trial among *routinized other-brand switchers* and *other-brand loyals* who, as we have seen, are two of the hardest target audiences for advertising alone to convert.

**3.** *Where Advertising Is Inadequate to Demonstrate the Brand's Benefit or Benefits.* Advertising is most successful for the many brands whose benefits can be shown visually or described verbally (tantalizingly, for low-involvement decisions, or convincingly, for high-involvement decisions—see Chapters 8 and 9). However, some brands are in product categories where the benefits are best *experienced directly or by continued usage.* Direct-experience products are those that depend on the various sensory modes of consumption: taste (for example, foods, beverages); smell (perfumes, aftershaves); touch (hand lotions,

fabrics); and hearing (records, CD players). Continued-usage products include those whose performance is difficult to gauge from just one application or use, such as shampoo or cosmetics, and also services, such as couriers or consultants. Sampling, through free or low-priced trial offers, is an excellent means of demonstrating that the product or service will in fact deliver the often subtle benefits promised. If the benefits are not subtle, or are easy to gauge immediately, then sampling is not warranted, because of the high cost (unless situation 1 or 2 holds).

**4.** *To Precede Seasonal Purchasing.* A lesser-known use of sampling applies in seasonal product categories. This is the use of preseason sampling to induce brand switching which may carry over into seasonal purchases.[24] The reason sampling is more effective than other trial-inducing techniques in this application is that it places the brand with the prospective buyer when the preseason "near-zero" category need would not be strong enough to motivate a full-price purchase. The brand placed in this manner therefore has an edge in being more likely to receive initial trial when seasonal purchasing begins.

**5.** *To Force Retail Distribution.* Distributors like sampling because it generates fast action at the retail level at little or no cost to the retailer. Sampling therefore can be used by manufacturers to "force" distribution, either for new brands or for older brands in areas where their distribution is weak. However, this is a dangerous game. The retailer has to agree to carry the brand *before* the sampling takes place; sampling without the brand being available in stores is not only a waste of money, but it may also engender a negative brand attitude among resentful consumers whose expectations were raised by the sample. As we have seen, manufacturers must do their homework on distributors as *target audiences* before undertaking this or any other type of promotion designed to gain trial by distributors.

### Price-Off Techniques

Price-offs, as trial promotions, can be implemented tactically in four different ways:

**1.** Refunds or rebates
**2.** Bonus packs
**3.** Direct price-offs
**4.** Warranties

The four variations are ordered on the basis of general to narrow applicability as trial promotions.

**Refunds or Rebate Offers.** Refunds or rebates are *partial* money-back offers. They are not used in the old sense of a refund, which implied all your money back if not fully satisfied (this is a money-back *guarantee,* discussed later under warranties). Rather, modern refunds—or the equivalent name, rebates—function much like a coupon. For convenience, we'll use the single term *refunds.*

To induce trial, a refund offer, like a coupon, must be processed by the would-be trier as representing *immediate* value, even though the trier does *not* in fact receive the money back until *after* the product is purchased and the refund offer redeemed. In support of the idea that refunds represent immediate value, it is estimated that as many as half of all purchasers never claim the refund. Redemption is typically about 1 to 2 percent, but purchase is estimated at about 3 to 4 percent[25]—similar to the rate achieved by coupons.

Indeed, although most refunds are paid in cash or, for larger amounts, by check, it has become increasingly common to offer coupons back ("bounce-back" coupons) in place of money, thus emphasizing the similarity between the two techniques. Bounce-back coupons, offered as the refund, can stimulate repeat purchases of the brand.

*When to Use Refunds for Trial.* For trial, refund offers should require only *one proof of purchase.* With only a single purchase required, the prospective buyer will be less hesitant to buy than when multiple purchases are required.

Refunds rarely seem to be appealing in amounts less than $1.00. This means *trial* refunds should be considered only *for new products that are priced at $5.00 or more at retail.* A discount of $1.00 on products selling for less than $5.00 would be too expensive for the manufacturer to bear, and would be overdoing the consumer incentive needed to induce trial. For discounts smaller than $1.00, and thus for low-priced product categories, a coupon is more appropriate.

Refunds can be used for very expensive products to induce trial. In 1981, Chrysler's president, Lee Iacocca, offered a $500 rebate on the purchase of any Chrysler model, and $1,000 on some models, to boost sinking sales. This was a pioneering use of refunds or rebates for such expensive products. In the recession-racked economy of the early 1980's, these massive offers seemed to work, although many other factors, not the least of which was Iacocca himself, contributed to Chrysler's successful turnaround.

*CFB Presentation of Refund Offers.* Refund offers are clipped from ads like coupons and thus represent message delivery opportunities. They are perhaps not quite as good as coupons in getting extra exposure, in that refund offers are typically mailed immediately rather than being saved and then taken to the store.

Managers, however, often miss the opportunity to include brand awareness and especially brand attitude elements with the refund offer. Depending on the brand awareness objective, the refund offer should reproduce a picture of the package or of the service's logo to increase the likelihood of brand recognition at the point of purchase, and should also include the brand name prominently to increase brand recall for subsequent purchases. To assist brand attitude, the main message—the main benefit claim or claims—should be featured on the refund certificate.

A further CFB tactic with refund offers prevents them from being perceived as "just" price-offs which, for a new brand, can undermine brand attitude. The accompanying copy in the refund offer's advertisement—such as "We're so confident you'll like this product . . ." or "We'll send you $1.00 to prove it to yourself"—should be worded in a way that minimizes the idea that this is just another discount and emphasizes the manufacturer's faith in the product.

**Bonus Packs.** Bonus packs offer more product in (a) a larger container or (b) multiple units, which also applies to services for the same or a reduced price. Thus, there is effectively a price-off per unit for bonus packs, and the buyer ends up with more product or more service opportunities than he or she would normally buy. Bonus packs have obvious implications for increased usage (as discussed for repeat-purchase promotions later in this chapter) because of the extra product or services received. But they can also be used to induce trial.

*When to Use Bonus Packs for Trial.* The conditions in which bonus packs can be used as a trial offer are somewhat restricted. First of all, the product or service has to be one that is *"divisible" into units* for packaging into bonus packs. Coffee, for example, would qualify, but computers would not. For food products to be bonus-packed in a larger container, the product must be able to retain its freshness after the larger container is opened. Again, coffee would qualify, but milk would not. Not all services are divisible, either. For instance, dry cleaning (laundry service) would qualify, but a personal tax-return completion service couldn't.

Second, bonus packs seem most appropriate as a trial device when the brand choice is *low-involvement.* Contrast the trier of a high-involvement product or service, who would not want more but rather less—a sample—of the product or service to try. However, this consideration is relaxed for low-involvement products and services. The low-involvement trier has not lost much if the bonus pack brand is not as satisfactory as expected. The buyer lost no extra money, and is simply stuck with a little extra of a low-risk item. Thus the initial "immediate value" of the bonus pack may have sufficient appeal for low-involvement brand trial.

Third, bonus packs (for products) can only be used when the manufacturer's relationships with retailers are good. Bonus packs require more shelf space than normal packs or more time than normal services and are therefore not as easily accepted by retailers. When used to increase retail distribution, bonus packs will not penetrate unless the retailer regards the manufacturer as a favored client.

Bonus packs therefore are a limited-application trial technique. If the product or service is divisible, if it is also relatively low-risk, and if the retail relationships are strong, then bonus packs are worth considering.

*CFB Presentation of Bonus Packs.* Bonus packs part ways on customer franchise-building potential in the difference between the larger containers and multiple units. Bonus packs do not increase brand awareness prior to the trial purchase (unlike a sample, coupon, or refund offer) because they are not encountered until the consumer is in the store. However, larger containers provide an opportunity to catch and recapture attention when they are purchased and used, thus facilitating brand recognition and brand recall for *subsequent* purchases. Furthermore, the increase in the size of the package and label provides an opportunity to portray the brand's advertising message, thus increasing brand attitude—although, again, not prior to the point of purchase for trial but rather for *subsequent* purchases.

Multiple-unit bonus packs (which applies also to services) are a different matter. The wrappers or service packages in which they are presented work only at the point of purchase, where they may facilitate brand recognition. But then, the wrappers or packages, even if carrying a message, are usually discarded immediately and thus lose the ability to communicate further about the brand. To provide a CFB advantage beyond the point of purchase, multiple-unit bonus packs therefore have to contain individually wrapped units or, for services, individually labeled service unit vouchers.

**Direct Price-Offs.** Direct price-offs are a reduction in the "normal" price of the brand. The discount is offered directly, rather than indirectly through a coupon or refund. The word "normal" is in quotes because, as we will see, the normal price against which the discount is compared is often subject to managerial influence when designing the offer. Here we are talking about the *manufacturer's* introductory price-offs offered directly to the consumer or end-customer (not the *retailer's* price-offs, which are discussed in the next chapter). The discount comes out of the manufacturer's margin, not the retailer's margin. The retailer's margin must be maintained to keep the brand attractive to retailers.

*Two Forms of Direct Price-Offs: Both Limited.* Direct price-offs can be offered either (a) in advertisements or (b) through the use of specially labeled "price packs" sent by manufacturers for display by retailers (price-offs marked on signs in stores are almost invariably retailer's price-offs, not manufacturer's price-offs). Both methods have their limitations.

*In-ad price-offs* instituted by manufacturers for a new brand are problematic in that the advertised price may not coincide with the price individual retailers would like to charge; thus, strict control over retailers is required, which is increasingly difficult to achieve.

*Price packs* also have limitations. Many retailers—about half of all retailers, on average—won't accept price packs.[26] The reason is the same: price packs circumvent the retailer's desire to set prices.

*Moreover, manufacturers'* use of price-offs to the *consumer,* as distinguished from price-offs to distributors in the form of trade promotions, is restricted in the United States by the Federal Trade Commission to a limit of three price-off promotions per year on a given size of the brand, with no more than 50 percent of the brand's total distributed volume being price-off *by the manufacturer* within a year. The FTC's intent is to ensure that price-offs are not used as a promotional substitute for what would effectively be a permanent price reduction if the brand were always discounted.

*When to Use Direct Price-Offs As a Trial Promotion.* The use of introductory price-offs to induce trial is appropriate in only one circumstance: for attracting trial among *new users for a familiar brand in an established category.* Why? Because price-offs work only when the prospective buyer knows beforehand what the "normal" price of the brand would be and can equate this price with the brand's received quality or "value." In Monroe's terms, there must be a reference price in the prospective buyer's mind against which the discounted price can be compared.[27] An Apple computer offered with a price-off, for example, will only attract new triers if the triers have a firm idea of the quality of the Apple computer and know its normal price.

Accordingly, price-offs cannot be used to introduce a new brand that represents an entirely new product category—such as Apple computers when they *first* appeared on the market and introduced the personal computer *category.* A new product category has no reference price and so there is nothing to compare a discount against. Hence the first brand in a new product category is usually priced at the highest price that the manufacturer believes prospective buyers will be willing to pay, because a high price in the absence of other information implies high quality. For new *product* category introductions, as we saw earlier, *sampling* is the appropriate trial promotion technique. (Note that small computers can be "sampled" in retail stores and larger computers sampled via home- or office-trial offers.)

Additionally, price-offs should *not* be used to introduce a new (unfamiliar) brand into an established category—unless the price-off is preceded or accompanied by advertising that makes the brand familiar and establishes its value.

*CFB Presentation of Direct Price-Offs.* Manufacturers' direct price-offs can be trial generators as well as customer franchise building if they are presented correctly. The first CFB communication effect, brand awareness, can be heightened by flagging the price-off offer in ads or on price-packs. Note the advantage of using in-ad price-offs to generate brand awareness: ads reach more prospective triers in the mass audience than price packs can reach at the point of purchase.

Brand attitude, also, can be increased via thoughtful price-off presentation. Four presentation tactics appear to increase purchase by operating on brand at-

titude and thence brand purchase intention: (1) showing the regular price and the savings clearly, (2) describing the "value" of the offer effectively in words, (3) including the brand's main benefit in price-off signs or ads, and (4) if appropriate, using the retailer's store image as an endorsement. These are explained further in chapter appendix 12B, Direct Price-Off Presentation Tactics.

**Warranties.** A warranty is a contract offered by a manufacturer to a customer to provide restitution in some form (such as money back, replacement, or free service or repairs) should the product prove deficient within a given time period. Warranties are actually a form of price-off offer, although not usually thought of as such. Although it is really a *future conditional* price-off, to the extent that the warranty serves as an *immediate* incentive to buy—by reducing perceived risk—it is functioning subjectively like an immediate price-off promotion. For example, American Motors (now part of Chrysler corporation) some years ago spurred car sales by offering a 2-year/24,000-mile service warranty when the standard for the industry was 1 year or 12,000 miles. (Of course, car warranties have since escalated, but this was a bold promotion at the time.)

Warranties have the most limited application of all price-off techniques. They are suitable mainly for *high-involvement* products. This usually means high-priced products such as cars, appliances, or industrial equipment. Although several stores, such as Sears, have made 100 percent money-back or store credit guarantees a purchase incentive for almost any item, such guarantees (warranties) should be most effective on high-risk products offered by the store.

*CFB Presentation of Warranties.* Warranties have only a minor effect on brand awareness—however, they don't really need to influence this communication objective if they're offered on high-involvement products for which prospective buyers engage in deliberate search.

Warranties can have a much larger effect on brand attitude. In fact, an attractive warranty can completely create a favorable brand attitude leading to purchase. *High-quality* warranties—those that cover every component, for full repair, for a substantially long usage period—reduce perceived purchase risk significantly.[28]

Another significant aspect from the standpoint of brand attitude is that high-quality warranties work regardless of the introductory price or the manufacturer's reputation. If they functioned *simply* as a price-off, high-quality warranties would work best with better-reputation brands, via a brand purchase intention effect. However, they seem just as likely to reduce risk for unknown brands,[29] which means that warranties are capable of creating brand attitude, a true CFB effect.

### Premiums

Premiums are articles of merchandise offered free or at price less than their retail value as an incentive to buy one or more units of the brand. There are two types of premium offers:

**1.** *Free premiums* are simply a giveaway just like a free sample, coupon, or refund offer. They are usually inexpensive merchandise.

**2.** *"Self-liquidating" premiums,* on the other hand, can be very expensive merchandise (for instance, Kool's sailboats) because the customer sends money with the proof(s) of purchase—enough money to cover the marketer's purchase and delivery costs (hence the self-liquidating aspect) while still representing a price to the customer that is well below the normal retail price of the item.

Premiums tend to be *quite limited* trial generators because of the almost inevitable selective appeal of the merchandise offered. The well-cited figure is that less than 10 percent of households have ever sent in for a free or self-liquidating premium. And the average send-for premium redemption rate is only about 1 percent.[30]

The selective appeal of a premium can be used to tactical advantage by *helping to skew purchase toward a particular subgroup of users.* For instance, a women's premium could be used to increase purchase by women of a unisex brand, such as Head & Shoulders shampoo. Or a "classy" self-liquidator, such as a Perrier umbrella, could be employed to try to increase "upmarket" usage of an otherwise nebulous brand.

Perhaps one exception should be noted here. Banks and S&Ls, which incidentally are the largest users of premiums, do seem to be successful in gaining triers. One bank's premium offers, studied by Preston, Dwyer, and Rodelius,[31] increased new account openings by 43 percent. Although these new customers tended to keep lower deposit balances and to terminate sooner, the promotions were still profitable. Premiums may be effective for trial when the brands are at parity in a "commodity" category.

**CFB Choice of Premiums.** Premiums should be chosen not just to be attractive in their own right as a trial generator but also as a communication vehicle that is customer franchise building for the brand. Herein lies the potential disadvantage of premiums. An ill-chosen premium can hurt the brand image (brand attitude) of the product and actually lose sales. Simonson, Carmon, and O'Curry[32] found that an ill-considered premium may hurt even market-leading brands. When a Pillsbury Doughboy Collector's Plate was offered for $6.19 as a premium with purchase of Pillsbury Brownie Cake Mix at $2.59, choice of the cake mix brand declined by over half compared with its no-premium choice incidence! So you just can't tell: you have to pretest the *appeal* of the product-plus-premium package among targeted triers.

On the other hand, a premium offer may be *too* attractive, emphasizing that you should also forecast from the pretest the likely *take-up* rate among triers. Whereas an unanticipated high take-up rate may be just what you want because it means more triers, it may also leave the company unprepared to deliver on the premium offer and can thus badly backfire. Such a fate befell Hoover in England in December 1992 when the company offered "Two Free Flights to the U.S.A.," airline tickets worth about £400, as a premium for buying a Hoover vacuum cleaner for £119.[33] Consumers obviously "reframed" this offer as "two plane tickets to the United States for £119, plus a new vacuum cleaner." Over 200,000 people attempted to take Hoover up on the offer, at once! One man whose plane tickets didn't arrive as promised phoned Hoover for an ostensible service call—and then impounded the repair technician's van in his garage until the tickets were delivered! It cost Hoover an estimated £20 million (at its wholesale ticket-buying price) to honor the offer and another £30 million in advertising to try to restore the loss of goodwill occasioned by the inevitable delays. Of course, Hoover got 200,000 triers, but at a much greater cost than the marketing manager (now ex-manager) had anticipated. Also, this premium was totally unrelated to the product. Perhaps an IMC perspective in the selection of the premium would have prevented this marketing fiasco.

Several excellent examples of trial premiums that reinforce the brand user's image for *transformationally* motivated brand purchase include:

- Western gear for Marlboro
- Racing decals for Cam-2 high-performance motor oil
- Perrier umbrellas for Perrier mineral water

Appropriately selected trial premiums can reinforce *informationally* motivated brand choices as well. For example:

- Summer t-shirts (with the brand logo) offered by Cheseborough-Pond's in trying to extend trial of Vaseline Intensive Care Lotion as an after-sun remedy.
- A lightweight indoor stepladder for Hoover vacuum cleaners (Hoover's corporate slogan is: "Hoover—one step ahead of the rest").

Premiums therefore should be centrally integrated with the brand's macropositioning. This applies not only for trial but also for repeat-purchase premiums as well (see the next section of this chapter).

### Coupons

A final trial-generating technique is manufacturer's coupons. We consider coupons last because their use is limited to marketers of fast-moving consumer products and services. Coupons may be defined as vouchers or certificates that entitle the buyer to a price reduction on the couponed item. Coupons—especially manufacturer's coupons—are somewhat more than a simple price reduction or price-off offer. A coupon is a tangible object that typically is regarded with appreciation by consumers as a small gift from the manufacturer.

In this section, "coupons," following common usage, refer to *manufacturer's* coupons—not trade coupons, which are distributed by the retailer. Manufacturer's coupons are designed and priced solely by the manufacturer. Consumers can redeem them by sending them directly to the manufacturer or, more commonly, they can be redeemed indirectly by turning them into a discount on the brand at *any* retail outlet that sells the brand. Trade coupons, in contrast, are designed and distributed by the distributor (retailer), although they are usually paid for by the manufacturer and the retailer *jointly,* out of co-op funds; they are redeemable only at the outlet or outlets of the *particular* retailer who offers them (one store or chain of stores). Retailer's trade coupons are considered in Chapter 13.

For fmcg products and services, couponing is generally acknowledged to be less effective than sampling as a promotional technique for generating trial. Fewer prospective buyers will redeem a coupon than will try a sample. This is because there are various "response costs" associated with redeeming a coupon.[34] Responses may include most or all of the following 10 stages, depending on the type of coupon and where it is redeemed: (1) cutting, (2) trimming, (3) saving, (4) filing, (5) storing, (6) remembering to take it to the store, (7) finding the product, (8) checking the product size, (9) juggling the coupon among others at the checkout counter, and (10) possibly receiving intolerant treatment by the checkout clerk.

Nevertheless, about 80 percent of the nation's households use coupons at least occasionally.[35] And there are only minor differences in usage across socioeconomic groups. The large observational study by POPAI/DuPont indicates that on any given day, 24 percent of customers entering supermarkets are carrying coupons, with about 19 percent able to use them in the store that day.[36] Recent studies—conducted in years in which the recession caused coupon usage to peak—suggest there is a "heavy user" phenomenon with coupons, in that one-third of all shoppers who redeem them carry five or more coupons per store visit and account for two-thirds of total redemptions.[37] Heavy coupon users may be skewed toward homemakers, who presumably have more time than working men and women to clip and redeem coupons, even though both types of shoppers are equally price-sensitive.[38] The implication of the homemaker skew will be considered shortly.

Managers can expect about 3 to 5 percent of couponed households to buy the brand, as compared with about 15 to 20 percent of households who will make a purchase following sampling. It should be noted that *direct mail* distribution often produces up to 40 percent response for sampling, but these are higher-than-average figures caused by the selective targeting of direct mailing to higher-buying-potential households.

Because couponing is considerably less expensive than sampling—on an immediate basis, although the long-run profit comparison might be quite different—it is the most prevalent promotional technique used by manufacturers. We note at the time of writing that P&G is cutting back on coupon offers because they are insufficiently profitable. However, this refers to coupons' general use rather than their role as a trial promotion.

**When to Use Couponing for Trial.** There are four main marketing situations in which the manager should use couponing as a brand *trial* technique:

**1.** *New Brand or New Users in Established Category.* In an *established* product category, speed of trial of a new brand, or speed of extending an existing brand to new users, is generally *not* a critical factor. This suits couponing because the average (median) time taken for consumers to redeem coupons is, depending on the medium of delivery, about 2 to 6 *months.* Consumers typically wait until they are low in product supply before they use a coupon.

**2.** *For Trial: Never Without Prior Advertising (or Sampling).* Coupons work best in prompting trial when the would-be trier has a favorable (if tentative) prior attitude toward the brand. The "recognized" brand with a coupon represents good value, whereas an unknown brand does not. Establishing a favorable attitude requires advertising or sampling prior to the couponing (if justified by the situations for sampling discussed earlier), or both.

**3.** *When Repeat Purchase Is an Acceptable Secondary Target Behavior.* Sampling, for completely new brands, is the only situation in which the response to the promotion offer consists entirely of new triers. With couponing, the response usually consists of a *mix* of new triers and current users, with the latter making a repeat purchase rather than a trial purchase. For a *new* brand, current users become part of this mix because, with the delay in redeeming coupons, they may already have tried the brand without one; or with the distribution of coupons through magazines and newspapers, they may receive and redeem *more than one* coupon and thus go beyond trial into repeat purchase. For an *existing* brand that is trying to attract new triers with coupons, it is virtually impossible to prevent the coupons from being received and redeemed by current users.[39]

The manager can raise the proportion of triers by using the more expensive consumer-direct methods of coupon distribution rather than "mass" media distribution, which tends to duplicate coverage to the same household. The media of coupon distribution will be considered shortly.

**4.** *When the Target Audience Is Skewed Toward Full-Time Homemakers.* Triers, of course, will come from the potential target audiences of new category users, other-brand switchers, or other-brand loyals who have not (recently) tried the brand. If the demographic *profile* of the target audience (see Chapter 4) shows that a majority are homemakers, then coupons would seem to have a higher probability of being redeemed. As indicated earlier, full-time homemakers are presumed to have somewhat more time available to collect and use coupons.

On the other hand, if the target audience's demographic profile is skewed toward working men and women, then a price-off promotion, which involves no response cost, would generate higher trial.

The manager must indeed have the research data on the *brand's* target audience and not *assume* that certain "demographic segments" will be better targets. For example, despite the alleged greater time pressures facing working men and women, they are *not* more likely than full-time homemakers to use "convenience" foods or appliances. However, for various "family life cycle" products, such as baby food, there is naturally a skew toward homemakers, and coupons should be differentially effective for these products.

**The Media of Couponing.** The six basic "media" available for the distribution of coupons have particular applications regarding trial (Table 12.1). The recommendations are our interpretations from various sources, including Aniero; Aycrigg; Haugh; and Schultz and Robinson.[40] The applications should be self-explanatory to the manager concerned with these finer tactical aspects of coupon implementation. The variations by media are in (1) the proportion of triers versus users, (2) redemption rate, (3) cost, and (4) reproduction quality, with the latter relevant to the CFB effectiveness of coupons. Included for completeness (in Table 12.1) as the sixth medium of distribution are in-pack or on-pack coupons. This medium is *not* discussed here because in/on-packs are primarily a *repeat-purchase* medium: they are good only for the next purchase and thus reward mainly current users who have previously tried the brand, rather than new triers. In/on-packs will be examined later in the chapter, when we cover repeat-purchase promotions.

**CFB Presentation of Trial Coupons.** Coupons can be an excellent technique for instilling communication effects during trial that are consumer franchise building for the brand and assist full-price purchase of the brand. Coupons can increase brand awareness as well as brand attitude.

**TABLE 12.1**

**SIX BASIC COUPONING MEDIA FOR GENERATING TRIAL**

| Medium | Uses | Limitations |
|---|---|---|
| 1. *Consumer-direct* (direct mail, door-to-door, central location, in-store take-one's) | • Best method for maximizing proportion of triers versus users since each household gets only one coupon<br>• High-quality reproduction (CFB)<br>• High redemption rate (average: 11%) | • Expensive unless co-oped with other coupons—which doesn't affect redemption rate<br>• Slow redemption (median: 5 months) |
| 2. *Freestanding card inserts in newspapers* | • Second best method of maximizing proportion of triers<br>• Less expensive than consumer-direct if not misredeemed<br>• High-quality reproduction (CFB)<br>• Moderate redemption rate (average: 5%) | • Very open to theft and misredemption—perhaps 20% of redemptions<br>• Moderately slow redemption (median: 3 months) |
| 3. *In-ad in Sunday newspaper magazines* (supplements) | • Probably third best method overall<br>• Fair- to high-quality reproduction (CFB)<br>• Low redemption rate (average: 3%) | • Somewhat open to theft and misredemption through gang-cutting<br>• Moderately slow redemption (median: 3 months) |
| 4. *In-ad in magazines* | • Best for special interest products that appeal to the magazine's readers<br>• High-quality reproduction (CFB)<br>• Low redemption rate (average: 3%, though more expensive "pop-ups" redeem at 5%) | • Broad target would mean multiple magazines are needed to reach enough triers<br>• High competition for attention unless pop-ups<br>• Very slow redemption rate (median: 6 months) |
| 5. *In-ad in newspapers* (but in manufacturer's ad, not retailer's ad) | • Cheapest method<br>• Low duplication if offer not repeated too often<br>• Low redemption rate (average: 3%) | • Low-quality reproduction so not advisable for new brands<br>• Moderately slow redemption (median: 3 months) |
| 6. *In/on-packs* (see usage promotions) | • Mainly for stimulating usage | • In/on-pack coupon is good for next purchase, not trial purchase |

The processes of paying attention to a coupon, clipping it, saving it, taking it to the store, and so forth—the very limitations that were mentioned earlier—are assets in that the prospective trier is getting extra exposure to the brand name on the coupon, which increases *brand awareness*. If the brand is typically chosen by brand recognition, then the coupon should include a picture of the brand—preferably a color picture. If the brand is typically chosen by brand recall, a salient brand name on the coupon is sufficient, as long as the category need to which the new brand is to be connected is evident.

The other necessary communication effect for CFB creation is *brand attitude*. To increase brand attitude, the brand benefits or the main selling message should be reproduced on the coupon. (The use of ad-like FSIs to distribute coupons has facilitated inclusion of the brand's selling message.) This reinforces the prior advertising by serving as an extra exposure to the message. Several extra exposures may be attained if the prospective buyer reads the coupon not only when clipping it but also when filing it and retrieving it to take it to the store.

Independently contributing to brand attitude is the "good feeling" that occurs because a coupon is seen as a gift (an $E_o$ for the *brand* in multiattribute attitude model terms, as explained in Chapter 5). Evidence that coupons are perceived as a gift beyond their (price-off) face value (currently about 70 cents) comes from Nielsen data indicating that the average face value of coupons over the years has risen far more slowly than have prices themselves. Moreover, an 80¢ coupon will *not* produce twice the response of a 40¢ coupon, indicating that the coupon *itself* has extra value.[41]

A further advantage with coupons is that the CFB effects on brand awareness and brand attitude can occur even if the coupon is not ultimately redeemed. Many consumers clip coupons, save them, but forget to take them to the store—yet still buy the brand.[42] Thus communication effects can be established without the manufacturer bearing the cost of redemption.

For convenient reference, the recommendations for manufacturer's trial promotions are summarized in Table 12.2. We next consider manufacturer's repeat-purchase promotions.

## REPEAT-PURCHASE PROMOTIONS

Repeat-purchase promotions refer to those promotions that are intended or expected to increase the incidence of *repeat purchase,* by those who have already tried the product or service, *beyond* the level that would have resulted from intrinsic satisfaction with the product or service alone. These promotions take a relatively short-term view of repeat purchase rather than necessarily being concerned with the long-term patronage of the buyer.

We consider *tangible* repeat-purchase promotions (whether for products or services) first; then we consider the intangible, somewhat amorphous attribute of *"service" itself* as a repeat-purchase promotion.

### Tangible Repeat-Purchase Promotions

The five most widely used *tangible* repeat-purchase promotions—which mostly apply to products but also occasionally to services—are as follows:

1. Packaging
2. Next-purchase coupons
3. Multiunit coupons, refunds, or rebates
4. Multipurchase contests and instant-win sweepstakes
5. Multipurchase premiums

Stamps (such as S & H Green Stamps or Raleigh cigarette stamps) are repeat-purchase promotions that are used rarely these days, possibly due to legal problems.

**Packaging.** The manager has to think: What happens to my product after the buyer has bought it? Are there opportunities to increase the chance of repeat purchase through take-away or leave-behind communication vehicles? Carry bags, service stickers, and product containers provide such packaging communication opportunities.

In implementing packaging promotion opportunities, the manager should consider the first three or "core" communication effects in the following ways:

1. *Try to be where the category need is strongest.* Thus, installation or repair personnel should place a company sticker *on* the machine that has just been installed or repaired, such as a piece of industrial equipment or a home appliance, so that the buyer will notice it whenever the category need arises, that is, when using the machine. Products that are consumed in multiple units, such as coffee or tea bags, or in successive uses, such as sprays, lend themselves to the use of containers that are seen each time the category need arises. A thoughtful example is the provision of a plastic container for holding prewash laundry spray that attaches to the laundry wall or to the side of the washing machine. This makes it less likely that the prewash product, once purchased, will be put in a

---

### TABLE 12.2

**PRINCIPAL CONDITIONS FAVORING THE FOUR MAIN TRIAL PROMOTION TECHNIQUES**[a]

| | |
|---|---|
| Sampling<br>• New product category introduction<br>• Superior brand introduced in an established category | Refunds or rebates<br>• Alternative to coupons for products priced at $5.00 or more at retail |
| Premiums<br>• New demographic or lifestyle target audience | Bonus packs<br>• Low-involvement products only (and must be quantity-divisible, with good shelf life) |
| Coupons<br>• New brand in an established category<br>• Especially if target audience is skewed toward homemakers | Direct price-offs<br>• New users for familiar brand in an established category<br>• Especially for consumer durables and other expensive products |
| | Warranties<br>• High-involvement (high perceived risk) products |

[a]The right-hand column consists of four *price-off* techniques (see text), hence our reference to only four *main* trial techniques in total, where price-offs are the fourth.

cupboard and sometimes overlooked. Indeed, almost any product or product-related service other than single-unit, entirely consumed products or services present opportunities for placement of reminders in category need locations.

**2.** *Remember the brand awareness objective.* Products are most often repeat-purchased by *brand recognition;* therefore, it is important to display the package itself or, at minimum, the brand name and logo, on reusable containers and other in-home or in-office communication materials, such as recipe books or calendars, since this is the brand stimulus that will have to be rerecognized when the next purchase opportunity arises. Product-related services, also, are mainly purchased by brand recognition and, accordingly, it is most important that the leave-behind material(s) prominently display the brand name and the service's phone number.

**3.** *Make sure the packaging is compatible with the desired brand attitude.* Carry bags from upmarket stores or for premium brands should be expensive and classy, whereas those from middle-quality or lower-priced retailers can be more functional, in keeping with the store's or brand's image. Similarly, multiunit or reusable containers should reflect the image or, better still, some distinctive attribute, that the brand is projecting in its overall *brand position.* Examples might be a McDonald's pencil box for children[43] or a sporty logo-embossed key ring for Alfa Romeo drivers. Consider the industrial packaging innovation shown in Figure 12.3. It's placed right where the category need occurs; it maintains brand recognition for ICI company; it reinforces the company's innovative reputation and ecological responsiveness—and it encourages repeat purchase.[44]

The principle here is that by "tapping into" the first three communication effects whenever possible, the *fourth* communication effect, brand purchase intention—for *repurchase*—will be maximized. In the case of product-related *services,* stickers with phone numbers or fax numbers can also assist purchase facilitation, the fifth communication effect, for repeat purchase.

**Next-Purchase Coupons.** Next-purchase coupons can be delivered in or on the pack, at the cash register, or by direct mail to known purchasers. Here we are distinguishing sharply between *trial*-purchase coupons and *next*-purchase coupons. Redemption

**FIGURE 12.3**
Packaging as repeat-purchase promotion. Industrial chemical drum with replaceable polyliner inner drum (at right) allows reuse of previously single-use drums. Customer calls ICI for drum collection and liner replacement, thus facilitating repeat purchase of ICI chemicals.
*Courtesy:* ICI and Southcorp Packaging.

rates for in/on-pack coupons are quite high: about 20 percent compared with only 2.1 percent for FSI coupons (freestanding inserts in newspapers or magazines) and 1.4 percent for newspaper-ad coupons.[45] Redemption rates for so-called "instant on-pack coupons" are even higher, at 27.1 percent, but it is questionable whether these can be considered repeat-purchase coupons as they are typically used to buy another unit of the product on the spot, thus boosting the number of units purchased but not necessarily the future repeat-purchase incidence.

Next-purchase coupon promotions are rarely profitable for manfacturers, and one must question why they are so widely used, as P&G has apparently done. Bawa and Shoemaker[46] found that a direct mail coupon increased brand choice but that most consumers reverted to their precoupon choice behavior immediately after their redemption purchase. In a careful study in the instant coffee category, Neslin[47] found that FSI coupon promotions were not profitable for any of the seven brands in the study; for the average brand, over 50 percent of the coupon redeemers were loyal brand buyers who would have bought anyway, and the 44 percent incremental sales caused by the coupon fell short of the 85 percent increase that he calculated would have been needed to break even.

Nevertheless, FSI coupons, as illustrated in Figure 12.4 for Healthy Choice Ice Cream, are by far the largest form of consumer promotion.

With next-purchase coupons, as with all the repeat-purchase promotions considered in this section, the manager has to estimate the incidence of repeat purchase that *would have occurred anyway* without the promotion. This is most easily ascertained by a point-of-purchase survey of shoppers who are making a repeat-purchase with a coupon by asking them whether they would have purchased this brand regardless of the inducement. Only if the next-purchase coupon significantly increases the repeat-purchase rate among those who would have switched to another brand, such that the profit gained from the repeat sales exceeds the cost of the coupon promotion, should the manager engage in this type of promotion.

*CFB Presentation of Next-Purchase Coupons.* Next-purchase coupons, just like trial coupons, should be designed with their CFB properties in mind. The coupon should include a picture of the brand or feature the name prominently, depending on whether the brand choice is by brand recognition or brand recall, respectively, and should also reinforce the main selling message.

**Multiunit Coupons, Refunds, or Rebates.** Multiunit promotions require *proof of purchase of two or more units* of the product or service in order to qualify for a reward. The multiple units may be purchased together or sequentially, the latter being a true repeat purchase. The reward can be a coupon for a further purchase, or a partial refund (rebate) of money for the original purchases. Coupons are usually used for grocery and drug products. Refunds can be used for these, too, and are also suitable for higher-priced consumer and industrial products and services.

A multiunit coupon promotion for Sun-Maid Raisins is shown in Figure 12.5. Here, two purchases of Sun-Maid Raisins Six-Packs (which may be bought simultaneously) are required, and the coupon (offering a 100 percent discount, that is, a free Six-Pack) strongly encourages a further choice of this brand.

The number of purchases required to qualify for the coupon or refund can be stretched, in theory, to any number, although consumers seem to resist making more than three purchases to qualify for a refund.[48]

**FIGURE 12.4**
Newspaper FSI (freestanding insert) coupon promotion for Heathy Choice Ice Cream.
*Courtesy:* ConAgra Frozen Foods and Mayer-Douglas, Inc.

**FIGURE 12.5**
Multiunit coupon promotion for Sun-Maid Raisins designed to encourage repeat purchase.
*Courtesy:* Sun-Maid Growers of California.

Still, three purchases can stall switching to a competing brand for quite a long time. Moreover, many multipurchase refund offers are offered on a sliding scale such that a greater number of purchases brings a larger refund but at a lower per-unit savings—for example, 50¢ for one, $1 for three, and $1.50 for six.

On- or in-package refunds are typically redeemed at a lower rate (about 4 percent) than on/in-package coupons. This is probably because people must send in for refunds whereas coupons usually are store-redeemable. However, the redemption rate understates the actual effectiveness of on/in-package refund offers because of the "slippage" factor—meaning that people buy because of the refund offer then fail to claim it. This is quite likely to occur with multiple-purchase refunds when people intend to buy, for example, three units but carry out their intentions for only one or two units.

*CFB Presentation of Multiunit Coupons or Refunds.* CFB presentation of multiunit coupon or refund offers is accomplished by regarding the proof of purchase that the buyer saves just like a coupon and ensuring that it contains brand awareness stimuli as well as the brand's main selling message. The Sun-Maid Raisins proof-of-purchase certificate to be used with the coupon shown in Figure 12.5, for example, contains brand recognition stimuli (pictures of the Six-Pack); and the selling message, "sun-dried," is reinforced on the pack via the name (Sun-Maid implies sun-made) and as an on-pack claim.

Quantitative models are now available for calculating the optimal amount of refund (percentage discount) for products with different purchase cycles and which differ in their intrinsic quality rating or personal attitude value.[49]

**Multipurchase Contests and Instant-Win Sweepstakes.** Contests and sweepstakes are similar promotional techniques overall but have some technical differences. *Contests* are supposed to require a degree of *skill* (often not very much) to enter and are judged on the basis of the best entry or the first winning entry drawn; they can (and should) require *proof of purchase* to enter. *Sweepstakes,* on the other hand, are based purely on *chance,* with the first series of randomly drawn entries winning prizes. With instant-win sweepstakes, such as instant scratch-ticket lotteries, you know immediately whether you have won rather than having to wait for a draw to be conducted. Sweepstakes can't require proof of purchase *unless* they are a government-run lottery, in which case entry

in the lottery is, of course, the purchase. With normal products and services, however, sweepstakes can *suggest* a proof of purchase be sent with the entry, but the organizer must accept a handwritten facsimile if the entrant so decides. About 75 percent of entries are facsimile entries, so the higher participation rate for sweepstakes over contests is largely offset by widespread avoidance of purchase.[50]

The challenge is to design contests or sweepstakes such that they will encourage repeat purchase of the brand. With contests, this can be achieved by offering a series of clues in advertising or in successive production runs of the product that require time (and thus the opportunity for repeat purchases) to accumulate. With sweepstakes, the best format for repeat purchase is the "lucky number" type of *instant-win* sweepstakes such as has been offered by Coca-Cola or Pepsi-Cola, from time to time, in soft-drink cans. The chance to win a lucky number tends to encourage multiple purchases of the brand.

Promotions can also be *combined* to increase the incentive for repeat purchase. Figure 12.6 shows an Ajax instant-win "game" promotion in which entrants can win a Black & Decker Dustbuster as a prize. As the game is a sweepstakes, it cannot require proof of purchase to enter. However, purchase is encouraged by combining the game promotion with a $2.00 refund offer (see top left of figure) that *does* require proof of purchase of two Ajax products.

**Multiple-Purchase Premiums.** To encourage repeat purchase, premiums should include a multiple-purchase requirement in the proof of purchase. The Hershey's promotion in Figure 12.7, for instance, requires three proofs of purchase plus $9.95 (a self-liquidator) to get a pair of NFL sweatpants. Or the premium itself might be a series of "collectibles," such as a dinner set, the individual items of which are obtainable with each visit to the retail outlet. For obvious reasons, premiums are best used when the target audience has homogeneous demographic or lifestyle characteristics, to which the premium can be selected to appeal.

As suggested in the previous section of the chapter, premiums can also serve as a packaging promotion—this time for repeat purchase. For instance, if you are carrying a Perrier umbrella, you would look a bit silly ordering another brand of soft drink in public. Once accepted, a well-chosen premium (a CFB premium) can favorably influence the buyer's attitude toward the brand and thus encourage repeat purchase.

**FIGURE 12.6**
Sweepstakes promotion for Ajax that also includes a refund offer so as to encourage repeat purchase.
*Courtesy:* Colgate-Palmolive.

### Service Itself As a Repeat-Purchase Promotion

When we talk about products and services, we use the word "service" to refer to any intangible action that we pay a person or company to perform for us. Many examples come to mind: shampoo is a product, a haircut is a service; a car is a product, a tune-up is a service (in fact, in this case we usually pay separately for parts and labor—products and service, respectively).

However, there is another very important sense in which we use the word "service." We define "service" from a *promotional* perspective as seller activities performed during or after the purchase transaction that are intended or expected to enhance the

# INTRODUCING HERSHEY'S KING SIZE LINE.

**Save 20¢** on HERSHEY'S King Size products and get top-quality NFL sweat pants for only $9.95 each!

Now, there's more reason than ever to enjoy HERSHEY'S King Size or Big Block products. A 20¢ savings, plus an offer on high-quality sweat pants in your favorite NFL team colors with official team logos, OR choose sweat pants with the official Super Bowl XXVI logo. These premium weight (50% cotton/50% polyester) fleece sweat pants have an elasticized waistband and elasticized ankles. They're an officially licensed NFL product and they're made in the U.S.A.

A $21 retail value, these great sweats are available for only $9.95 each, plus shipping and handling, with 3 proofs of purchase from any HERSHEY'S King Size or Big Block product. Available in S, M, L, and XL. MADE IN U.S.A.

The Team names and nicknames are registered trademarks of the Teams indicated. NFL is a registered trademark of the National Football League.

**FIGURE 12.7**
Premium offer (self-liquidating) for Hershey chocolates requiring three proofs of purchase.
*Courtesy:* Hershey Chocolate U.S.A.

incidence of repeat purchase *beyond* the level that would have been attained by instrinsic satisfaction with the product (the car) or the "core service" (the tune-up or other car repairs) alone, *excluding* the provision of any repeat-purchase incentive. (This last part clearly distinguishes service, in the promotional sense, from loyalty programs, discussed in Chapter 14, which *do* provide an explicit incentive for repeat purchase.)

Service, in this promotional sense, refers to the *manner* in which salespersons or other representatives of the company interact with us on a *personal* level—which affects our *attitude* toward that company or brand. For example, was the new-car salesperson—or, later, the same dealership's service-department manager—friendly, helpful, and courteous in responding to our questions and in handling the specific details of the sale? If so, we would probably be more

likely to want to buy another car, or get another tune-up, from that same dealer.

Service is relevant to all products and services where there is a degree of personal contact—either face-to-face, over the phone, or by mail or fax—between the seller and the buyer. The applicability of service therefore extends to virtually all purchases except those transacted impersonally in large self-service stores or with vending machines, although even these can now flash "Thank you" or print it on the receipt.

Service is an effective promotional activity because, in this increasingly impersonal world, most people like to feel "wanted" (social approval motivation). A little service, especially when it is perceived as "extra service" rather than part of the core service necessary to accomplish the purchase transaction itself, goes a long way. Even in the "objective" situation of industrial purchasing, this "extra service" is a surprisingly strong factor in retaining customers—or, when the service is poor or otherwise unacceptable, in causing them to switch to a competitor. Tom Peters, well known for the best-selling book *In Search of Excellence,* which he coauthored, recently cited survey results showing that, of customers who switched, 15 percent cited a better product as the reason, another 15 percent said it was because a competitor's product was cheaper, and *70 percent* said it was because "they weren't getting good service."[51] Similarly, Kaspar and Lemmink,[52] in a study conducted for an office equipment supplier, found that managers—indeed, after-sales service managers—consistently underestimated the importance placed by customers on personal factors in after-sales service. When customers themselves were asked to rate the importance of various factors, the "general attitude and behavior" of technicians, a subjective service factor, was rated highest, ahead of such objective factors as availability, price-performance ratio, and response time.

Consumer transactions, too, are highly sensitive to social reinforcement—and to the lack of it. Bank patronage provides a good example. Whereas about 80 percent of bank customers retain their account with the bank for at least 5 years, about 20 percent do switch within this time. Of these switchers, apart from a small percentage who are moving house or job to a location where there's not a convenient branch of the bank, almost half switch because of "poor service," and by this they mean primarily "lack of friendliness and personal recognition."[53] In fact, among the well-known three main factors in choosing a bank—convenience of location, financial charges for transactions and loan interest, and personal service—it is evident that the first two factors will equalize across institutions in the longer term, leaving personal service as the main differentiating factor. With banks, other than for ATM transactions, smart tellers should find it easy to recognize your face and can flatter you by knowing your name even if they have just refamiliarized themselves with it by reading it off your check or deposit slip. And even during telephone contacts (for a variety of product and service categories), the current capabilities of computers makes it easy for the sales or customer-service representative to quickly pull up the customer's record and—to exhibit personal interest in the customer's patronage.

For further examples of these dynamics, see chapter appendix 12C, Social Reinforcement in Service Transactions.

It is important to point out that the promotion activities of with-sales and after-sales service do not require database marketing as such. With-sales service requires the customer's name if the contact is by telephone but not if the contact is in person. Similarly, after-sales service, such as the "Nice to have you as a customer" type of reinforcement, requires customer receipts or a customer list but does not constitute database marketing in the advanced sense. We examine database marketing, proper, in Chapter 14.

**Additional Service for High-Involvement Purchases.** *Additional* service, in this promotional sense, is especially important to maintaining brand loyalty and increasing the likelihood of repeat purchase following the purchase of a high-involvement product with a substantial service or servicing component, or any purchase of a high-involvement service itself. This is because the recent buyer is likely to feel "locked in" to the purchase and to experience a considerable degree of *cognitive dissonance* (approach-avoidance motivation, in our terminology) as to whether this major choice was correct. Consumer examples would include the purchase of a new car or personal computer, or the choice of a new doctor, dentist, or hairdresser where it does not seem easy to reverse your decision once it has been made.[54] From the service provider's standpoint, the customer may *appear* loyal but then suddenly switch suppliers or discontinue visits (see chapter appendix 12D, The Cusp-Catastrophe Model of High-Involvement Repeat Purchases).

Altogether, then, we have seen that with-sales and after-sales service, or simply "service," is—or can be—an important form of (or opportunity for) promotion for all products and services where there is some degree of personal contact and also for high-involvement purchases of service-laden products or of services themselves, for which there should be "additional" service provided if the provider wants to retain the customer. Again, the provider can sell a product or deliver a service and rely on the customer's intrinsic satisfaction with that product or service to lead to repeat purchase. However, the likelihood of repeat purchase can be increased above this level by applying service itself as a promotional activity. (Not only that, but if the exceptional service leads to positive word-of-mouth communications to new prospective customers, then it could increase the likelihood of *trial* purchase as well.)

## SUMMARY

Manufacturer's promotions in the customer timeline of IMC strategy include sales-force promotions, trade promotions, customer or consumer trial promotions, and repeat-purchase promotions.

*Sales-force promotions* most vitally center on monetary incentives for increasing the rate of sales, through the selective application of commissions added to salary. We identified four main selling situations—new business selling (cold calling), technical selling, missionary selling, and trade selling (to wholesalers or retailers)—in which not only the commission structure but also the preferred age and experience of hired employees, the nature of sales territory assignments, and the time of tenure should be varied for optimal performance. Sales-force promotions also include nonmonetary stimulation such as motivational meetings, sales training, and selling aids, but the evidence on their effectiveness is so mixed as to prohibit generalization.

*Trade promotions* are used by all marketers other than those who sell direct. An especially major expenditure for consumer packaged goods marketers is trade promotions to *retailers*. We emphasized the need for manufacturers to try to tie the provision of trade promotion monies to the sales-stimulating performance activities of retailers—such as featuring the product in retail advertising, giving it more and better (closer to eye-level) shelf space, and (important for long-run sales) keeping its retail price consistent with the price positioning of the product that the manufacturer intends.

Following sales-force promotions and trade promotions, the manufacturer next has to consider *trial promotions* to end-customers or consumers. Trial is the most important action objective for virtually every brand because of the importance, to sales, of penetration. Penetration is the main determinant of sales and market share because usage rates tend to be quite constant across brands once trial is achieved (presuming satisfaction). Trial promotions can be used with new brands and also to attract new buyers to established brands.

There are four main types of trial promotions: product or service sampling, price-off techniques, premiums, and coupons.

*Sampling* is a trial-promotion technique available to all marketers and is overall the best trial generator. Sampling is a very powerful means of inducing trial for high-involvement purchases because of the commitment a buyer makes in accepting a sample. Industrial marketers use trade shows and feasibility studies for this purpose. Retailers use demonstrations and free home-trial offers. Consumer packaged goods marketers use actual product sampling to increase the number of people who try their brand, a technique that is usually successful for a parity brand early in the product category life cycle or for a superior brand that enters later, even though there is no buyer commitment with these relatively low-involvement purchases.

*Price-offs,* in four main forms, require careful consideration when used to generate trial. More than any other trial technique, price-off techniques (except warranties) tend to attract current users rather than triers. But by thoughtful implementation, such as limiting refund or rebate purchase requirements to one unit of the brand, these techniques can be steered more effectively toward triers.

*Premiums* and *coupons* are limited-application trial promotions. Premiums too often have narrow appeal, although this can be used deliberately to skew trial toward a new (for the brand) demographic or lifestyle target market if that is the objective. Coupons, for fmcg products and services, are best used with sampling; used alone, it is too difficult to confine redemption to triers.

With all four types of trial promotions, the manager must plan the promotion offer's presentation so that it stimulates brand awareness and brand attitude (we call this customer franchise-building, or CFB, presentation) and thereby operates beyond short-term purchase intentions to maximize full-price purchases when the promotion offer is withdrawn. Whereas sampling does this automatically, the other trial promotion techniques have to be designed specifically to generate CFB effects along the respective tactical lines suggested in this chapter.

After trial of the brand is accomplished, the manufacturer finally must consider *repeat-purchase promotions*. Here we focus on short-term repeat purchase rather than long-term loyalty promotions, which are better used with direct marketing, as explained in Chapter 14.

*Tangible repeat-purchase promotions* include packaging; next-purchase coupons; multiunit coupons, refunds, or rebates; multipurchase contests and instant-win sweepstakes; and multipurchase premiums. Apart from packaging, which is a low-cost medium of encouraging repeat purchase, the other types of repeat-purchase promotions are rarely profitable and should be used sparingly if at all. The most important implementation tactic is to require multiple purchases.

From a promotional perspective, *service* is defined as those seller activities performed during or after the purchase transaction that are intended or expected to enhance the incidence of repeat purchase *beyond* the level that would have been attained by instrinsic satisfaction with the product or "core service" alone, *excluding* the provision of any repeat-purchase incentive. The key here is personal recognition and reinforcement. When it's an integral part of the purchase transaction or applied as a follow-up, this social reinforcement is the most important factor in encouraging repeat purchase in service-oriented industries. For high-involvement purchases of services, or of products with a substantial service component, service in this promotional sense should be perceived by the customer as *extra* service. This perceived extra service is an additional contributor to brand or supplier attitude in these situations, and tends to keep the customer attached to the brand or supplier by making the psychological cost of switching very high. Therefore, extra service is clearly a repeat-purchase promotion.

In the next chapter, we look at the promotions available to the retailer.

APPENDIX

## 12A. Factors in Trade Show Promotion

Gopalakrishna and Williams[55] have conducted a valuable analysis of the effective factors in trade show promotion, based on results from 28 industrial trade shows.

As the results criterion in their study, they used a measure of "lead efficiency," which is the proportion of leads (names) generated from people with definite plans to buy from the company in the next 12 months, in relation to the total number of attendees at the trade show who are interested in the product category. (Not all those interested will have time to visit your exhibit; of those who do visit, about three in 10 are planning to buy and the rest are just "lookers."[56]) They found, contrary to conventional wisdom (no pun intended), that merely attracting category-interested prospects to the company's exhibit is not important in itself—nor, notably, is the relative attraction power of exhibits by competing firms in the product category.

Rather, the main effectiveness variable is "booth personnel efficiency," which is the proportion of personal contacts made among those interested prospects who visited the booth. (On average, only 63 percent of visitors are talked to; the average contact lasts 3 to 5 minutes, which means about 12 to 20 contacts per sales person per hour.) The second most important variable is the prospect's (after-the-fact) rating of the competence of the booth personnel relative to those at other booths at the show. (The main complaints from prospects about booth personnel are insufficient product knowledge and inability to answer questions.) Thus, your best and most active salespeople should be "invested" in trade shows because there is a very strong return in terms of the quality of leads generated.

Other factors found to be important in the analysis were that "vertical" trade shows, which are specialized by industry, are considerably more effective in generating high-quality leads than "horizontal" trade shows, where different industries are exhibited in the one show. Further, there is a small but significant relationship between expenditure per attendee (for preshow trade magazine advertising and direct mail advertising as well as for the exhibit and personnel[57]) and the generation of high-quality leads, indicating that the budget should not be stinted.

## 12B. Direct Price-Off Presentation Tactics

**Show the Regular Price and the Savings Clearly.** This first tactic is the most important of the direct price-off presentation tactics—showing the regular price and the savings clearly. The Federal Trade Commission has enforced this in a way that aids the marketer by aiding communications. Price-off offers must show (1) the regular price, (2) the cash savings, and then (3) the new price. The regular or "normal" price is subject sometimes to collusive and possibly misleading manipulation by marketers, and especially by retailers.[58] This, however, is an ethical issue separate from the undoubted effectiveness of the format. The importance of communicating the regular price is that the buyer probably will remember it and thus keep the brand's "image" where the manufacturer wants it to be.

Interestingly, consumers tend to attribute a 10 percent savings to *any* advertised price, even if it is not a price-off offer.[59] For a new brand, even the seemingly innocuous wording of "reasonably priced" implies to consumers a price that is lower than average for the category.[60]

This raises the important question of *how much* of a discount to offer in a direct price-off. Blair and Landon[61] tested price-off amounts for a Texas Instruments calculator, which at that time was retailing for about $50. (This fits our recommendation of using price-offs for a familiar brand in an established product category.) They found that while prospective buyers were skeptical of very large discounts, nevertheless, the larger the discount, the stronger the intention to buy. However, a 40 percent discount was needed before purchase intention increased significantly over a 10 percent discount (which would be attributed to a nondiscounted price mentioned in an ad anyway). We suspect that if the study had been confined to people who were "in the market" for a calculator (that is, who had the category need), then a much smaller discount would have been effective. This considered, we'd recommend that at least 15 to 20 percent off the "normal" price must be offered in order to stimulate trial. The exact amount can be pretested by measuring purchase intentions, among category prospects, at increasing price-off discounts (see the promotion testing section of Chapter 19).

**Describe the "Value" of the Offer in Words.** The second direct price-off presentation tactic relies on the fact that the words (semantic cues) chosen to accompany price-offs can have powerful effects on perceptions of value and thus, we presume, purchase intention. Table 12.3 shows the ratings of four commonly used semantic cues in terms of perceived value for money.[62] The words "Sale Price" appear to be most effective, and considerably more effective in suggesting value than the words "Now Only." Presentation of price-offs in words, and not just numerically, is well worth the manager's consideration.

**Include the Brand's Main Benefit.** The third tactic is to include the brand's main *benefits* in a direct price-off ad or a POP sign (instituted by the manufacturer, which may require retailer acceptance). This can significantly increase

**TABLE 12.3**

**TABLE 12.3**

**FOUR COMMONLY USED PRICE-OFF SEMANTIC CUES IN TERMS OF PERCEIVED VALUE FOR MONEY**

| Semantic cue | Rating:[a] |
|---|---|
| "Total Value _____; Sale Price _____" | 5.04 |
| "Regular Price _____; Sale Price _____" | 4.96 |
| "Compare at _____; Our Price _____" | 4.54 |
| "Percent Off _____. Now Only _____" | 3.82 |

[a]Seven-point scale where 7 = strongly agree, 4 = neither agree nor disagree, and 1 = strongly disagree with the statement that the given semantic cue usually means a good buy for the money.

*Source:* J. R. Walton and E. Berkowitz, Information needs for comparative pricing decisions, in P. E. Murphy et al., eds., *Proceedings: AMA Educators Conference,* Chicago: American Marketing Association, 1983, pp. 241–245. By permission.

sales of the item. McKinnon, Kelly, and Robinson[63] conducted an experiment in a major national department store chain in which six products' sales were tracked for 54 observation days under three rotated conditions: normal price-off ticket (regular price, sale price); price-off standing sign; and the same price-off standing sign with two or three benefits included (for example, a women's slacks product included the benefits "dressy or causal," "elastic waist," and "see our coordinated top"). Compared with the normal price-off ticket, while the price-off standing sign increased average sales of the products by 24 percent, the price-off standing sign *with benefits mentioned* increased sales by 50 percent. Clearly, there is much to be gained by this direct CFB presentation of price-off promotions.

**Consider Retailer Endorsement.** As a final tactic to consider, the store image of the retailer through which the brand is offered can also affect brand attitude. A direct price-off offered for the brand in a discount retailer's ad or in a discount store might be very effective because of a "double discount" attribution. However, a direct price-off offered through a higher-image store that doesn't discount regularly may imply good value and may also be effective. Given that direct price-offs to attract new buyers should be used only with *familiar* brands, the brand's already established attitude in the prospective trier's mind may tend to lessen the retailer effect. The retailer endorsement effect is by no means clear-cut and should be tested for the brand.[64]

## 12C. Social Reinforcement in Service Transactions

Social reinforcement, with the sale or after it, doesn't cost much and can be very profitable. For instance, one study found that the degree to which a waitress smiled (yes, the intensity of the smile) was positively correlated with the size of tips received (from men *and* women customers).[65]

In another study of social reinforcement, a small-town jeweller, participating in a controlled experiment designed by Skinnerian academics, found that a simple "thank you" phone call increased sales by 27 percent the following month. The majority of the additional purchases were from dormant (inactive) customers; and although there was a slight dip the following month, suggesting some degree of purchase acceleration, sales stayed above average for the next several months. Most interestingly, and for marketers who may wish to try this positive reinforcement tactic, the most effective phone call message was simple reinforcement rather than telemarketing in the usual sense. One randomly selected group received just the following call: "Hi, I'm [caller's name] from M & M jewellers and I would like to thank you for being one of our customers." A second randomly selected group received the following call, with a sales promotion: "Hi, I'm [caller's name] from M & M jewellers. I would like to thank you for being one of our customers, and tell you about our big diamond sale. During the next two months we will offer twenty percent off all diamonds in stock." Although the groups were of equal size, 70 percent of the increase in sales came from the first (simple reinforcement) group, and only 30 percent from the second (promotion added) group. A control group who did not receive a telephone call showed no change in purchase frequency.[66] Of course, this personal reinforcement technique could not be used too often but, with a slightly varied message, a couple of calls a year could bring very profitable results as well as happier customers.

Larger businesses can also profit from social reinforcement of customers simply by conveying the messages that "you're important, and we're listening." British Telecom, for its small business customers, has installed district telephone account managers for those accounts that are too small to be visited personally. The accounts are contacted entirely by telephone four times a year with little more than a "How are you?" message. BT reported a "fantastic" increase in revenue accompanied by a 50 percent improvement in attitude toward the telephone company.[67]

## 12D. The Cusp-Catastrophe Model of High-Involvement Repeat Purchases

High-involvement repeat purchases are those where the buyer never really goes into a low-involvement mode because the decision to buy again is carefully considered each time (examples: a big reorder from a supplier, or a visit to your dentist). The marketer of such products or services will in many cases observe a period of steady behavioral loyalty which is in fact attitudinally "brittle" and can suddenly blow up with the loss of a customer. This is well explained by target audience vulnerability analysis and the "cusp-catastrophe" model.[68] Figure 12.8 shows our adapta-

**Involvement
in switching
brands
or suppliers**

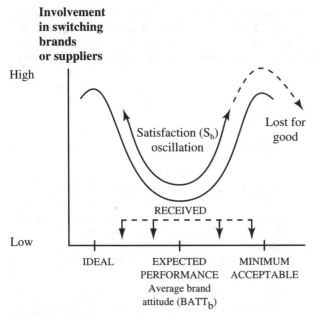

**FIGURE 12.8**

Cusp-catastrophe representation of fluctuating customer satisfaction (oscillation in brand attitude) with a high-involvement product or service where the perceived risk of switching is high, showing loss over the right (negative) cusp if oscillations become too negative or service clearly falls below minimum acceptable levels.

tion of the cusp-catastrophe model as it applies to high-involvement repeat-purchase products and services. In astronomy, the "points" on a crescent moon are referred to as its cusps, and this provides a good analogy with a buyer "caught in the crescent" of a high-involvement product or service relationship. In the middle of the crescent is the buyer's relatively permanent or average attitude toward the brand, which represents the *expected* level of performance.[69] Actual experiences in using the product or service provide doses of "received" attitude which, in everyday terms, can be described as satisfaction with product usage or service transactions. Satisfaction ($S_b$) therefore refers to short-term fluctuations in brand attitude (brand attitude being $BATT_b$). These fluctuations cause the buyer to oscillate mentally between being assured that he or she has made a good choice (toward the left cusp) and experiencing severe doubts about the choice (toward the right cusp). Note that oscillations which fall short of reaching the cusp on *either* side tend to keep the buyer "caught in the crescent." On the left cusp this is because higher satisfaction leads to greater attraction to the current choice and makes it appear increasingly risky to change to another brand or supplier. Toward the right cusp, the risk of switching *also* increases because the buyer is now thinking about actually having to

terminate the relationship and having to go to the trouble of establishing a new relationship with a new brand or supplier. If these oscillations begin to tip toward the right-hand negative cusp, such as several poor service experiences successively, or become outright unacceptable, such as one decidedly major negative service experience, then the customer will flip over the right-hand negative cusp and be "lost for good."[70]

From the service provider's standpoint, the effort to provide "extra" service with all or nearly all encounters, or to follow up with occasional customer contact in the case of products such as personal computers that don't require regular service visits, is very important because of the likely effect on short-term satisfaction and thus on the long-run maintenance of brand attitude. For each service encounter or contact, it is likely that:

Received > Expected service leads to $S_b$ + +
Received = Expected service leads to $S_b$ +
Received < Expected service leads to $S_b$ −
Received < Minimum acceptable service leads to $S_b$ − −

Cumulative $S_b$ − 's or one or two $S_b$ − − 's result in rejection of the brand or supplier.

It should also be understood that positive and negative deviations from expected service do not exactly offset one another in that negatives nearly always carry greater weight.[71] Therefore, it is relatively more important to avoid negatives than to garner positives. The optimal practice is for the service provider to avoid negatives, apart from the occasional slip, but also to build a history of service encounters that are clearly equal to or above expectations so as to contribute to positive satisfaction and a stronger brand attitude.

With the concept of satisfaction, $S_b$, a distinction should be made between $S_b$ and the impersonal attitude component, $IA_b$, discussed in Chapter 5 (chapter appendix 5B) for temporary fluctuations due to price and availability. $S_b$ certainly is a *personal* attitude but it represents fluctuations around the *average* personal attitude, $PA_b$, that the buyer holds toward the product or service. It is only applicable in high-involvement choice situations in which product performance and service delivery do indeed vary over purchases or transactions. Such variations are rarely experienced with consumer packaged goods. For low-involvement purchases, the concepts of personal attitude, $PA_b$, and impersonal attitude, $IA_b$, do *not* need to be supplemented by the $S_b$ concept.

**NOTES**

1. D. A. Newton, Get the most out of your sales force, *Harvard Business Review,* 1969, *47* (5), pp. 130–143.

2. More recent studies of sales-force management have *not* distinguished the major different types of selling and have tended to focus on technical selling and on compensation alone. See G. John and B. A. Weitz, Salesforce compensation: An empirical investigation of factors affecting the use of salary versus incentive compensation, *Journal of Marketing Research,* 1989, *26* (1), pp. 1–14; and R. Lal, D. Outland, and R. Staelin, Salesforce compensation plans: An individual-level analysis, *Marketing Letters,* 1994, *5* (2), pp. 117-130.

3. A recent study of two technical firms' sales-force compensation policies found sales environment uncertainty to be generally handled by a higher fixed salary component. See R. Lal, D. Outland, and R. Staelin, same reference as in note 2.

4. R. Lal et al., same reference as in note 2.

5. We put "buys" in quotes because there are various arrangements other than outright 100 percent purchase of the manufacturer's product, as discussed shortly.

6. J. P. Guiltinan and G. W. Paul, *Marketing Management: Strategies and Programs,* 4th ed., New York: McGraw-Hill, 1991.

7. Brands fight back as private labels make big inroads, *The Australian,* March 7, 1995, p. 75. The term "co-marketing," and the example, are attributed to Chris Hoyt, president of Hoyt & Co. marketing consultants.

8. S. Dutta, M. Bergen, G. John, and A. Rao, Variations in the contractual terms of cooperative advertising contracts: An empirical investigation, *Marketing Letters,* 1995, *6* (1), pp. 15–22. These investigators analyzed over 2,000 co-op advertising plans, across industrial, consumer durable, and consumer fmcg industries, finding average participation rates of 69 percent, 69 percent, and 88 percent, respectively, and average accrual rates of 3.1, 3.6, and 5.8 percent, respectively.

9. Donnelley Marketing publishes annual surveys of advertising and promotion spending conducted among the 60 or so *largest* U.S. marketing spenders, which tend to be almost all consumer packaged goods companies. Called the *Annual Survey of Promotional Practices,* Donnelley's reports are published by Dun & Bradstreet, New York.

10. M. H. Abraham and L. M. Lodish, Getting the most out of advertising and promotion, *Harvard Business Review,* 1990, *68* (3), pp. 50–60.

11. New IRI division targets trade promotions, *Advertising Age,* February 22, 1993, p. 43.

12. Adapted from a privately conducted study by *Progressive Grocer* magazine and A & P Supermarkets, ca. 1982.

13. E. Gerstner and J. D. Hess, Pull promotions and channel coordination, *Marketing Science,* 1995, *14* (1), pp. 43–60.

14. P. W. Farris, et al., see reference in Chapter 3, note 22.

15. For a brief description of Ehrenberg's empirically based theory of the importance of penetration, see Chapter 3 of this book and A. S. C. Ehrenberg, Predicting the performance of new brands, *Journal of Advertising Research,* 1971, *11* (6), pp. 3–10. For more detail, see A. S. C. Ehrenberg, *Repeat-Buying: Theory and Applications,* Amsterdam: North-Holland Press, 1988.

16. R. B. Cialdini discusses numerous illustrations of the commitment principle in his book *Influence,* New York: Quill, 1984.

17. Based on estimates by H. Aniero, an expert promotion consultant, in a privately circulated document.

18. G. J. Barczak, D. C. Bellow, and E. S. Wallace, The role of consumer shows in new product adoption, *Journal of Consumer Marketing,* 1992, *9* (2), pp. 55–67.

19. S. Gopalakrishna and J. D. Williams, Planning and performance assessment of industrial trade shows: An exploratory study, *International Journal of Research in Marketing,* 1992, *9* (19), pp. 207–224. The U.S. expenditure is closer to 20 percent and the European expenditure closer to 25 percent according to sources cited in S. Gopalakrishna and G. L. Lilien, A three-stage model of industrial trade show performance, *Marketing Science,* 1995, *14* (1), pp. 22–42.

20. Estimates from Cahners Advertising Research Report #542.1F, 1992, as interpreted by S. Gopalakrishna and G. L. Lilien, same reference as in the previous note.

21. M. Snell, Now for the "virtual" trade fair, *The Australian,* October 4, 1994, p. 26. A computer software company, Ubique Ltd., offers "Virtual Places" software which allows trade shows to be exhibited over the Internet.

22. A conceptual note is appropriate here. Sampling is described by many marketing writers as an example of behavior change leading to attitude change, which apparently reverses the normal sequence—in advertising —of attitude change leading to behavior change. However, this description is not correct. Before a person would try a sample, he or she must at least have a tentatively favorable attitude toward the brand. Would you, for example, try a new shampoo or a new aspirin that you did not at least tentatively trust? Some degree of attitude change (actually, positive attitude creation—see Chapter 5) therefore *precedes* the trial behavior. It is true that a *confirmed* attitude follows the trial behavior but this happens, too, in low-involvement brand trial induced by advertising (see Chapter 8).

Thus, the contention in many textbooks that promotion, and especially sampling, somehow works differently than advertising is not true. Both work through *communication effects.* Furthermore, the behavioral action step in the six-step sequence still occurs after the communication effects, in that the behavior of interest is *purchase* behavior, not trial sample behavior.

23. J. H. Holmes and J. D. Lett, Jr., Product sampling and word of mouth, *Journal of Advertising Research,* 1977, *17* (5), pp. 35–40.

24. This strategy is described in D. E. Schultz and W. A. Robinson, *Sales Promotion Essentials,* Chicago: Crain Books, 1982, chapter 13.

25. D. E. Schultz and W. A. Robinson, same reference as previous note.

26. H. Aniero, same reference as note 17.

27. K. B. Monroe, *Pricing: Making Profitable Decisions,* New York: McGraw-Hill, 1979; also K. B. Monroe, The influence of price differences and brand familiarity on brand preferences, *Journal of Consumer Research,* 1976, *3* (1), pp. 42–49.

28. T. A. Shimp and W. O. Bearden, Warranties and other extrinsic cue effects on consumers' risk perceptions, *Journal of Consumer Research,* 1982, *9* (1), pp. 38–46. Shimp and Bearden examined the effect of warranties on the trial purchase of three high-risk, innovative products: a multiscreen TV set, a plastic auto tire, and a computerized indoor jogging device.

29. T. A. Shimp and W. O. Bearden, same reference as previous note.

30. D. E. Schultz and W. A. Robinson, same reference as note 24, chapters 8 and 9.

31. Two separate premium offers were studied: cookware (a free premium) and a discount on purchase of a calculator (the calculator thus being a self-liquidating premium). Both premiums were quite similarly effective. See R. H. Preston, F. R. Dwyer, and W. Rodelius, The effectiveness of bank premiums, *Journal of Marketing,* 1978, *42* (3), pp. 96–101.

32. I. Simonson, Z. Carmon, and S. O'Curry, Experimental evidence on the negative effect of product features and sales promotions on brand choice, *Marketing Science,* 1994, *13* (1), pp. 23–40.

33. See Hoover and its publicity stunt dive, *Marketing* (UK), April 8, 1993, p. 18; Hoover is sued over flights deal, *The Sunday Times,* June 6, 1993, p. 5; and K. Newman, Editorial, *International Journal of Advertising,* 1993, *12* (2), p. 94.

34. L. J. Haugh, Women cool to promotions, "LHJ" tells premium executives, *Advertising Age,* October 10, 1977, pp. 10, 102.

35. R. H. Aycrigg, *Current Couponing Trends,* Northbrook, IL: A. C. Nielsen Company, 1977.

36. To be able to use a store-redeemable coupon, the brand has to be in stock, and the coupon must still be valid (not expired). The 1977 POPAI/DuPont study is summarized in L. J. Haugh, Buying-habits study update, *Advertising Age,* June 27, 1977, pp. 56–58.

37. John Blair Marketing and Donnelley Marketing, *Cents-Off Couponing and Consumer Purchasing Behavior,* Stamford, CT: Donnelley Marketing, 1982.

38. Opinion Research Corporation study, 1981, summarized in Cost effectiveness of sales promotion efforts, *Marketing Review,* New York Chapter, American Marketing Association, 1981, *37* (3), p. 12.

39. On a gross basis, and this includes the use of coupons to "load" users as well as to generate trial, only about one in three coupon redemptions represents brand trial; two in three redemptions are by users. As an obvious qualification to these figures, the newer the brand, in the market, the higher the ratio of triers to users. Same reference as previous note.

40. References cited previously (see notes 17, 24, and 35), plus L. J. Haugh, How coupons measure up, *Advertising Age,* June 8, 1981, pp. 58, 63.

41. Schindler and Rothaus have coined the term "the coupon effect" to refer to the widely observed ability of cents-off coupons to cause a greater short-run sales increase than the equivalent reduction in price. (Of course, coupons also *cost* more to implement as a promotional program than simple price-off offers or straight price reductions, and cost must be considered against increased sales in calculating profitability.) In a laboratory experiment in which leading brands from 12 frequently purchased supermarket product categories were offered at either a low price or at the equivalent low price via a coupon, the coupon form of the price reduction caused almost double the brand choice incidence than the straight price reduction (45 percent versus 26 percent, in relation to the chance level of 20 percent for the five brands in each category). These figures are indicative but are not generalizable and hence not emphasized in the main text because this was a laboratory experiment with student subjects. See R. M. Schindler and S. E. Rothaus, An experimental technique for exploring the psychological mechanisms of the effects of price promotions, in E. C. Hirschman and M. B. Holbrook, eds., *Advances in Consumer Research,* vol. 12, 1985, Provo, UT: Association for Consumer Research, pp. 133–137.

42. John Blair Marketing study, cited in *The Wall Street Journal,* September 25, 1980, p. 1.

43. Promotions to children under a quasi-educational guise are controversial but becoming increasingly widespread with the financial problems in U.S. schools (and in other countries' schools such as England's and Australia's). For instance, ads can be placed on children's schoolbook covers via Cover Concepts Marketing Concepts, Inc., and about 70 percent of first through fifth graders use these covers; the company will not accept ads for alcohol, tobacco, condoms, or R-rated movies. Also, about 40 percent of the nation's

middle and high schools have accepted Whittle Communications' Channel One, a TV news program shown in class that includes ads for children's products; by signing on, schools receive about $50,000 worth of free video equipment that can be used for educational purposes. In another venture, Reebok sponsors a weekly exercise video for school gym classes that features some of its advertising celebrities. See C. Miller, Marketers find a seat in the classroom, *Marketing News,* June 20, 1994, p. 2.

44. The industrial chemical drum shown in the figure, called the Rheem P200, was a packaging collaboration between ICI Surfactants and Southcorp Packaging and won the 1996 award for innovative packaging from the Packaging Council of Australia. See D. Ribaux, Packing a Punch, *Marketing Magazine,* August 1996, p. 23, 24, 26–29.

45. *Research Alert,* June 4, 1993, pp. 1–2.

46. K. Bawa and R. W. Shoemaker, The effects of a direct mail coupon on brand choice behavior, *Journal of Marketing Research,* 1987, *24* (3), pp. 370–376.

47. S. A. Neslin, A market response model for coupon promotions, *Marketing Science,* 1990, *9* (2), pp. 125–145. Also see K. J. Cheong, Are cents-off coupons effective? *Journal of Advertising Research,* 1993, *33* (2), pp. 73–78. The latter study found that use of a coupon had no effect on the repeat-purchase rate of the brand, although larger face value coupons tended to slightly undermine the repeat-purchase rate; also, shoppers who used more coupons did not spend more money at the store.

48. L. J. Haugh, Cash refunds multiply, *Advertising Age,* May 5, 1980, p. 48.

49. A. Ali, M. A. Jolson, and R. Y. Darmon, A model for optimizing the refund value in rebate promotions, *Journal of Business Research,* 1994, *29* (3), pp. 239–245.

50. D. E. Schultz and W. A. Robinson, same reference as note 24.

51. Business section, *The Sun-Herald,* July 31, 1994, p. 48.

52. H. Kaspar and J. Lemmink, After sales service quality: Views between industrial customers and service managers, *Industrial Marketing Management,* 1989, *18* (3), pp. 199–208.

53. C. Shoemaker, Higher bank fees don't equal value, *Marketing News,* June 20, 1994, pp. 4, 5. His statistics are based on a 1993 survey of customers of Midwestern Bank.

54. The difficulty of withdrawing from service relationships where there is a high personal intangible component, such as with doctors, dentists, and hairdressers, is documented in a study of "final service visits" conducted by R. A. Higie, L. L. Price, and J. Fitzmaurice,

Leaving it all behind: Service loyalties in transition, in L. McAlister and M. L. Rothschild, eds., *Advances in Consumer Research,* vol. 20, 1993, Provo, UT: Association for Consumer Research, pp. 656–661.

55. Same reference as in note 19.

56. The parenthesized comments in this and the following paragraph are based on J. D. Williams, S. Gopalakrishna, and J. M. Cox, Trade show guidelines for smaller firms, *Industrial Marketing Management,* 1993, *22* (4), pp. 265–275.

57. For further details on expenditure effectiveness, see S. Gopalakrishna and G. L. Lilien, same reference as in note 19.

58. For evidence of deceptive reference prices used as a sales tactic, see M. A. Sewall and M. H. Goldstein, The comparative price advertising controversy: Consumer perceptions of catalog showroom reference prices, *Journal of Marketing,* 1979, *43* (3), pp. 85–92; E. A. Blair and E. L. Landon, Jr., The effects of reference prices in retail advertisements, *Journal of Marketing,* 1981, *45* (2), pp. 61–69; and S. A. Ahmed and G. M. Gulas, Consumers' perceptions of manufacturers' suggested list price, *Psychological Reports,* 1982, *50* (1), pp. 507–518.

59. E. H. Blair and E. L. Landon, Jr., The effects of reference prices in retail advertisements, Working paper, College of Business Administration, University of Houston, 1979. Despite the same title, this is a different study than the 1981 study cited in the previous note.

60. J. Faberman and A. Tarlow, Point-of-view; price—the forgotten marketing variable, *Journal of Advertising Research,* 1981, *22* (5), pp. 49–51.

61. The 1979 study, same reference as note 59.

62. J. R. Walton and E. Berkowitz, Information needs for comparative pricing decisions, in P. E. Murphy, G. R. Laczniak, P. F. Anderson, R. W. Belk, O. C. Ferrell, R. F. Lusch, T. A. Shimp, and C. B. Weinberg, eds., *Proceedings: AMA Educators Conference,* Chicago: American Marketing Association, 1983, pp. 241–245. The sample in this study consisted of 562 consumers with a broad range of demographics; value-for-money ratings did not differ across respondent demographic characteristics.

63. G. F. McKinnon, J. P. Kelly, and E. D. Robinson, Sales effects of point-of-purchase in-store signing, *Journal of Retailing,* 1981, *57* (2), pp. 49–63.

64. E. N. Berkowitz, Contextual influences on consumer price responses: An experimental analysis, *Journal of Marketing Research,* 1980, *17* (3), pp. 349–358.

65. K. L. Tidd and J. S. Lockard, Monetary significance of the affiliative smile: A case for reciprocal altruism, *Bulletin of the Psychonomic Society,* 1978, *11* (6), pp. 344–346. Two conditions were used: Minimal smile

(mouth corners turned up but teeth not showing) and maximal smile (broad smile with teeth showing). The setting was a cocktail lounge, and patrons were alone. The waitress was a 23-year-old college student. Men tipped almost $10 more after the maximal smile ($14.15 versus $4.75, on average) and women $4.40 more ($9.05 versus $4.65).

66. J. R. Carey, S. H. Clicque, B. A. Leighton, and F. Milton, A test of positive reinforcement of customers, *Journal of Marketing,* 1976, *40* (4), pp. 98–100.

67. Cited in K. Fletcher, C. Wheeler, and J. Wright, Database marketing: A channel, a medium or a strategic approach? *International Journal of Advertising,* 1991, *10* (2), pp. 117–127.

68. The vulnerability analysis stems from the work of Market Facts and J. Rice; see our Chapter 4 regarding "attitudinal vulnerability." The cusp-catastrophe model has been most clearly applied to marketing by T. A. Oliva, R. L. Oliver, and I. C. MacMillan, A catastrophe model for developing service satisfaction strategies, *Journal of Marketing,* 1992, *56* (July), pp. 83–95; and T. A. Oliva, R. L. Oliver, and W. O. Bearden, The relationships among consumer satisfaction, involvement, and product performance: A catastrophe theory application, *Behavioral Science,* 1995, *40* (2), pp. 104–132.

69. Our analysis here draws on the service quality literature and especially on the formulation by Berry, Zeithaml, and Parasuraman; see especially V. Zeithaml, L. Berry, and S. Parasuraman, The nature and determinants of customer expectations of service, *Journal of the Academy of Marketing Science,* 1993, *21* (1), pp. 1–12.

70. B. B. Jackson, Build customer relationships that last, *Harvard Business Review,* 1995, *85* (6), pp. 120–128.

71. R. N. Bolton and J. H. Drew, Mitigating the effect of service encounters, *Marketing Letters,* 1992, *3* (1), pp. 57–70.

## DISCUSSION QUESTIONS

**12.1.** In the chapter, we commented that "the sales force has a direct analogy with advertising." For each of Newton's four types of selling, discussed in the chapter, extend this analogy further. Specifically, write a 1-page script for an *ad,* corresponding to each of the four sales situations, that would mirror what each type of salesperson does.

**12.2.** In what ways can manufacturers attempt to make trade promotions really stimulate the company's sales rather than being merely "a cost of doing business" with the trade?

**12.3.** International Harvester is about to introduce a radically new type of tractor. Explain how the following trial promotion techniques might be used, and justify which one you think would be best:
 **a.** Sampling
 **b.** Rebate
 **c.** Direct price-off
 **d.** Warranty

**12.4.** Outline a 1-page strategy for exhibiting at trade shows.

**12.5.** You are the manufacturer of a small market-share brand of men's hair spray. You have the plant and production capacity to "go national" with the product. Outline an integrated marketing communications program which includes advertising and sampling. You may also use other IMC activities discussed so far, provided that you justify their inclusion.

**12.6.** Briefly outline a program for using service itself as a repeat-purchase promotion for:
 **a.** A hairdresser
 **b.** An office-cleaning company

**12.7.** Select a service relationship in which you are involved as a customer that appears to correspond to the "cusp-catastrophe" model. Describe how the model operates in this case, and outline a program that the service marketer might implement to prevent losing you as a customer.

## FURTHER READING

Ruud, J.-E. *Strategic Marketing Plan.* Selangor Darul Ehsan, Malaysia: Pelanduk Publications, 1987.

In our book we have not had the space to go into technical detail about how to implement the manufacturer's in-channel promotions. The book by Ruud is very practically oriented and includes many useful implementation checklists for personal-selling incentives, trade shows, customer service, and public relations. In fact, it covers all areas of marketing planning with useful "this is what to do" checklists.

Totten, J. C., and Block, M. P. *Analyzing Sales Promotion: Text and Cases,* 2nd edition. Chicago, IL: Dartnell, 1994.

Here is another very practical book, this one on the implementation of sales promotion techniques. It covers trade promotions and consumer promotions from the perspectives of manufacturers and retailers. Extensive worked examples and cases show how sales promotions are actually implemented.

Bateson, J. E. G. *Managing Services Marketing: Text and Readings,* 2nd edition. Fort Worth, TX: Dryden, 1992.

This is a stimulating collection of chapters and articles on all aspects of services marketing. The various readings provide many ideas for designing and promoting services. This book is highly recommended for service marketing managers.

# CHAPTER 13

# Retailer's Promotions

Retailers are the front line of the distribution channel for many products and services and, often acting quite independently of the manufacturers whose products and services they distribute, retailers are very active marketers. This chapter examines the six main promotion activities available to the retailer: retail layout and atmosphere, retail feature ads, point-of-purchase displays, price-off promotions, private labeling, and TV or PC interactive shopping. These promotions should be planned as integrated communications. After reading this chapter, you should:

- Understand the retailer's marketing perspective.
- See how the retailer can employ retail layout and atmosphere to advantage.
- See how the retailer constructs feature ads.
- See how the retailer uses POP displays.
- See how the retailer can implement price-off promotions most effectively.
- See how the retailer can use private labeling as a means of promotion.
- See whether the retailer should offer TV or PC interactive shopping.

## THE RETAILER'S MARKETING PERSPECTIVE

As a marketer, the retailer can use *almost* all the IMC activities shown in the IMC activities diagram (Figure 13.1): all forms of corporate advertising communica-

tions including direct response advertising, as well as direct marketing promotions, sales-force promotions, and retailer's promotions. Note that because the former three categories of AC&P activities are covered elsewhere, only the box for this chapter's subject is shaded—retailer's promotions.

To provide the necessary background to retailer's promotions, we first describe the characteristics of retail shopping behavior. We must then see what happens with manufacturer's trade promotions, which produce a vital interplay between manufacturers, as suppliers, and retailers, as buyers and marketers.

### The Realities of Retail Shopping Behavior

Considering the store as the "brand," the retailer's sales are dependent on two types of customers: *store loyals,* who will buy at that store anyway and are not price-sensitive (about 35 percent of customers, on average[1]), and *store switchers* (about 65 percent of the store's customers), on whom the retailer is dependent for the rest of the store's sales volume and who are distinctly price-sensitive.[2] Of course, the store loyals can take advantage of price discounts, too, and it is difficult for the retailer to decide how often and how widely to offer switcher-attracting price promotions to achieve a profitable balance between the two target audiences' patronage.

Store-loyalty and store-switching statistics from supermarket shopping behavior are the most widely available because grocery stores are the most inten-

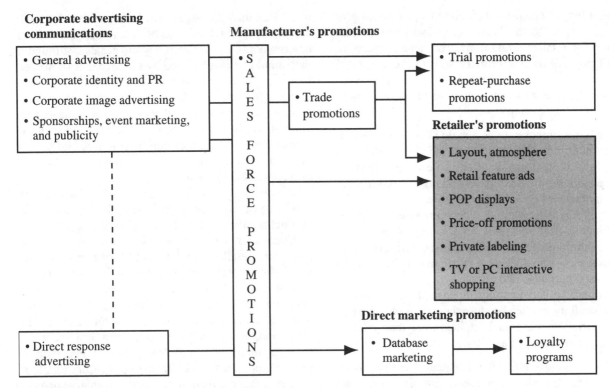

**FIGURE 13.1**
Retailer's promotions (shaded box).

sively studied category of retailing, although other types of retailers would undoubtedly show a similar pattern. These are provided in chapter appendix 13A, Grocery Store Shopping Statistics.

The importance of attracting store switchers responsive to price is emphasized by the earlier finding, presented in Chapter 5, that approximately 65 percent of brand and item choices are not decided until the point of purchase. On the other hand, the importance of brand loyalty (which may or may not reflect store loyalty and undoubtedly varies by product category) is reinforced by the related finding that approximately 35 percent of shoppers have a brand clearly in mind beforehand when making a purchase.[3]

### Retailers' Use of Trade Promotions

Retailers make about 35 percent of their profit margin from trade promotions received from manufacturers.[4] Upon receiving these discounts, retailers can either pocket the savings (which happens about half the time) or pass through some of the discount in the form of a point-of-purchase (POP) price discount to con-

sumers.[5] From the trade-discounted items, retailers decide which ones *they* will promote during any given week or on any particular day.

**Inventory Transfer: The Overriding Objective for Retailers.** Blattberg, Eppen, and Lieberman[6] have shown, through a detailed analysis of consumer panel purchases in relation to retail promotions, that the overriding promotional goal or objective for retailers is not simply to attract customers from other stores (which, if overdone, could lead to price wars to the detriment of all retailers) nor even to satisfy manufacturers' plans for promotion through retail outlets (about which more below). Rather, the goal or objective that accounts for over half of retail promotions is to *transfer inventory holding costs to the consumer.* When consumers are induced to stockpile products, this keeps shelf space available for new products, increases turnover, and maximizes the retailer's profit. To move stock from their inventory to the consumer's home inventory, retailers will tend to select any brand for promotion, at times which suit the retailer's stock-clearing needs.

Blattberg, Eppen, and Lieberman's panel data give strong support to this "inventory adjustment" explanation for retailer promotions. The actual effects of retail price deals (the primary and quickest form of retailer-initiated promotion) differ from the "textbook" effects of retail promotion as planned by manufacturers. For example:

- Deals are supposed to be a main avenue for launching new brands; yet, in fact, existing brands are bought on deal just as often as new ones, through deals offered by the retailer and not necessarily the manufacturer.
- Deals are also supposed to be a prime technique for inducing trial that will lead to repeat purchase; yet the majority of deal purchases cut into future purchases—an inventory effect rather than an increased purchase-rate effect.
- Similarly, it is commonly supposed that small sizes are dealt more often because they are more likely to gain trial; yet the actual findings show that retailers deal large sizes just as often as small ones.

Retailers' promotional strategies also depend in many cases on what *competitors* are promoting and are far more complexly determined than they appear on the surface.[7] As we shall see when we discuss retail advertising, it is not surprising that computerized expert systems are finding ready acceptance by retailers, and by multiline retailers especially.

With this introduction to the realities of retail marketing, we now turn to the six main IMC promotion activities available to the retailer: retail layout and atmosphere, retail feature ads, POP displays, price-off promotions, private labeling, and TV or PC interactive shopping.

## RETAIL LAYOUT AND ATMOSPHERE

The retailer's selling environment can be favorably designed to promote sales through the use of retail layout, color, music, and olfactory (based on the sense of smell) cues.

### Retail Layout

The physical layout of the store or selling environment can have quite a dramatic effect on purchase propensity. (Store or retail layout overlaps with corporate identity communication—for the retailer; see Chapter 11. However, here we are focusing on promotional effects, that is, immediate purchase stimula-

tion.) Certainly the suggestive findings from the small amount of research that has been conducted on selling environments make retail layout a sales stimulator that should be investigated by the manager (however, there may be ethical concerns with some of the techniques which we feel obliged to point out). With computer simulation so easily available now, research on alternative layouts can easily be conducted to measure customer preference and its emotional underpinnings, as well as cognitive beliefs relevant to the type of business being conducted.

We briefly review below some indications of how retail layout research might be applied by consumer product retailers and professional services.

**Consumer Product Retailers.** Of all types of marketers, retailers are the most likely to have recognized the importance of layout and to have investigated it on a trial-and-error basis if not in a more systematically experimental manner. Store image–forming items should be placed at the front of the store (and, as we shall see later, given prominent position in retail ads); and "must buy" items, such as milk and other staples in the case of grocery retailers, or replacement parts in the case of automotive or electronic retailers, should be placed at the back of the store in order to draw customers through the aisles past other product displays.

Product category layouts (brand and item allocations) have become a science in themselves with the emergence of computer programs such as A. C. Neilsen's SPACEMAN, which is used by many supermarket and drugstore retailers to allocate shelf space. Many retailers have appointed "category managers" whose purpose is to increase sales of the entire product category rather than playing off one manufacturer against another in a "zero sum" game. Indeed, the results of the shelf allocation analyses are shared with every manufacturer, and a plan is worked out for the greatest gain for all. For instance, one retailer's application of SPACEMAN turned around a 10 percent below-industry average in shampoo sales to 10 percent above the industry average within 6 months, and all brands showed a profit increase, across all stores.[8] Hoch,[9] a marketing academic advising a chain of supermarkets in the Chicago area, found that alternative arrangements within product categories produced increases in sales for the store. For instance, arranging cereals by brand produced more sales than arranging them by cereal type, and arranging soft drinks by manufacturer produced more sales than arranging them by bottle size. Opportunities for complementary product layouts were also found; for instance, sales of toothbrushes increased by 8 percent when they were placed in the middle of the toothpaste section rather than in an adjacent section.

*Retail Atmosphere.* A pair of studies by Donovan and Rossiter[10] demonstrated that the retail store's internal environment or "atmosphere" is perceived by consumers in terms of two basic dimensions— pleasantness and arousal—which significantly affect consumers' willingness to spend time in the store and also to purchase more than they would in a less attractive store. The two dimensions interact in an interesting manner. In *pleasant* retail environments, increasing the arousal level, via stimuli such as colors or popular music (see below), is the most effective policy. In contrast, in *unpleasant* retail environments, such as doctors' or dentists' offices, toning *down* the arousal level, via softer colors or soothing music or no music at all, appears to be the more effective approach.

An experimental study by Kerin, Jain, and Howard[11] suggests that for supermarket customers, the pleasantness of the store environment is relatively more important than price and quality in affecting customers' overall judgment of value for money. This finding is the more remarkable because it was based on telephone interviews, and thus on the recall of these three factors, rather than on in-store interviews where the environmental influence would presumably be at its strongest. Pleasantness of the store environment, in turn, was found to be a function of store cleanliness, overall variety and selection, the store's check-cashing policy, the friendliness of its personnel, and a brief waiting time at the checkout counter.

Finally, we should mention the remarkably strong—though perhaps ethically questionable— effect of the presence of credit card stickers on purchase propensity. The prominent display of pictorial logos of credit cards, to signify that these cards are accepted by the retailer, has been shown, in both simulated store settings and in retailers' catalogs, to make consumers more willing to buy (versus not buy) the item as well as to pay a higher price for it. For willing customers, credit card payment is a convenience, albeit an expensive one. However, there is also an implication of unwitting overspending for some.[12]

**Professional Services.** The professional's *office* is the primary "selling area." A long-known recommendation for the professional's office is to include "credibility stimuli" such as academic credentials and awards, in a semidiscreet manner, within the prospects' or clients' view. Furthermore, the professional is probably more effective if he or she adopts a more authoritative office layout. Figure 13.2, adapted from Molloy,[13] shows that an authoritative setting can be achieved by placing somewhat greater distance— by using a larger desk, for example—between the professional and the prospect or client. Another well-known authority induction technique is to ensure that the professional's eye height is slightly above that of the person or people to whom he or she is talking, usually achieved by differential heights of seating. Whereas this might be regarded as deception, professionals might justify the greater authority as assisting compliance with their recommendations.

For medical and health care professionals, in particular, but really for all types of professionals, it is also sound advice to try to provide as much privacy for patients or customers so that they don't have to undergo the scrutiny of other people who may be

**FIGURE 13.2**
Authoritative office layout for professional service providers. *Source:* Molloy, 1981; see note 15. By permission.

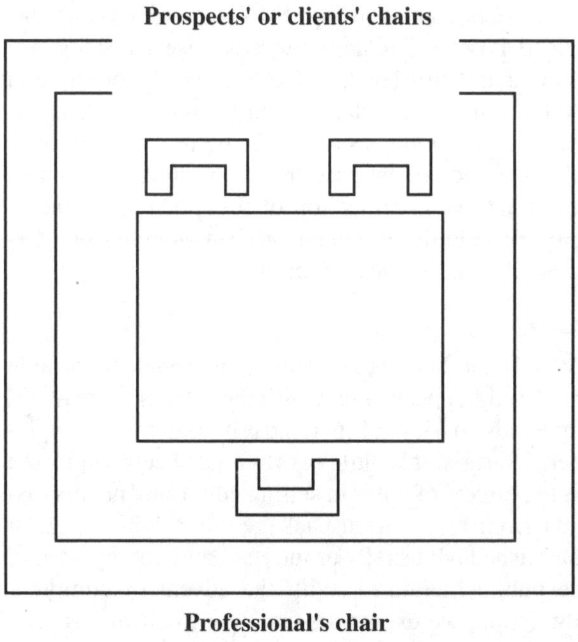

**Prospects' or clients' chairs**

**Professional's chair**

waiting. Many professional's offices are poorly laid out in this respect, allowing waiting customers to see or hear the personal problems of others, to eavesdrop on private financial conversations, and so forth. Privacy is of the utmost important for professional services, and the layout should ensure this.

For "retailers" of professional services, such as doctors, dentists, and accountants, the *reception area* is likely to be a contact point in which the customer can expect to spend a considerable amount of time. This has led to the phenomenon of place-based media in waiting rooms (usually television and special magazines). These are not strictly POP media since they are also usually used by *other* advertisers rather than just by the professional service provider. For instance, Whittle Communications in 1988 launched its Special Report Network (SRN), which provided media to 32,000 doctors' offices in the United States, consisting of a 1-hour repeating TV program, a related magazine, a poster, and a take-away booklet. The cost for an advertiser to be featured in all four media was approximately $3 million per year. The "customer traffic" to these doctors' offices is quite considerable: approximately 532 million visits per year, with a good many repeat visitors, of course. Surveys conducted by the company indicated that over half the visitors watched the TV show (or part of it), about one-third looked at the booklets, but very few looked into the magazine or noticed the poster. Companies using SRN for advertising included Procter & Gamble to advertise its Safeguard soap, and Chrysler to advertise its Plymouth and Dodge minivans.[14] Place-based media in professionals' waiting rooms seem to still be in an experimental stage and we suppose that cost-effectiveness will determine the continuation of this practice. Incidentally, Whittle discontinued SRN in March 1994, because it couldn't make a profit.[15]

### Color

Color is another store or selling environment variable that would appear to be worth the retailer's attention, especially in view of its relatively low cost to implement. Surprisingly little research has been conducted on the effects of color in selling environments (as distinct from research on package color, which is well established but usually proprietary and not reported in the public literature). With the advent of computer simulation, we expect the situation to change so that color will become a primary consideration in selling-environment design.

*Retail store* environments can quite easily make use of color, although which color depends on the type of retail products or services. Some speculative but interesting research on color *preferences,* using the Luscher color chips, which are a set of standard colors used in research on personality, rather than color applied to actual retail environments, suggests wide variation among types of shoppers. For instance, brand-switching shoppers showed a preference for green, as did those shoppers who preferred to shop in the suburbs rather than in the city; careful shoppers and users of promotion offers showed an aversion to yellow although, interestingly, shoppers who prefer to use credit showed a slight preference for this color; and all-around bargain shoppers showed a neutral response to most colors, perhaps because they focus strictly on the merchandise and price![16]

*Professional services* can draw directly on the literature in environmental psychology when considering color choice for reception areas and offices. With an "unpleasant" service, such as medicine or dentistry, the reception or waiting area should probably be a cheerful color, but the actual patient areas might be better in muted colors which help to lower the arousal level.[17] There are also, of course, cognitive associations to take into account. One can imagine the effect of a doctor's operating room painted in livid red or a sickly green. Whereas inappropriate choices like this may be rare, the point is that there is a wide range of colors from which a more appropriate and more "effective" color may be chosen with apparent ease.

### Music

Music is a promotional stimulus that can be used in most selling environments. It is also inexpensive to manipulate—and, in the several experiments that have been conducted to date, has shown remarkable effects on sales. Professional music providers such as MUZAK undoubtedly conduct careful research for specific companies.

The main two variables in the effectiveness of music are tempo (which seems to operate emotionally) and type (which seems to operate through a more cognitive associative process). In terms of tempo, *slow* music appears to have a positive effect on sales. In the pioneering experiment on music tempo, Milliman[18] found that slower instrumental music, averaging 60 beats per minute, caused shoppers to spend 17 percent more time in the store and to spend a remarkable 38 percent more money on their purchases when compared with fast instrumental music, at 108 beats per minute. Milliman then followed this study with an experiment on music tempo in an upper-middle-class restaurant. Using a controlled design on alternating days, he found that slow-tempo background music produced an increase of over $7 in gross margin (profit) per table compared with fast-tempo background music. This was almost entirely due to patrons drinking an extra $9 worth of alcoholic beverages per table in the presence of slow background music.[19] Another less scientifically reported study conducted in Minnesota confirmed this finding by showing that patrons in bars drink at a faster rate to slow music than to fast music.[20]

The *type* of music is the second variable to consider. Milliman was careful to use purely instrumental music for his experiments on tempo and thus did not investigate the effects of music type. But there are differences in sales effectiveness by type. For instance, Areni and Kim[21] found that classical music played as background in a wine store caused an average purchase of $7.43, compared with Top 40 background music, which produced an average purchase of only $2.18. Unfortunately, the average expenditure without music was not measured, leaving open the possibility that *both* kinds of music may have suppressed wine sales—but let us assume that the classical music *increased* sales. The probable explanation for this result is cognitive in that the classical music may have suggested a more sophisticated type of store in which patrons would feel uncomfortable if they were to buy the lower-priced wine selections.

A third variable is *how* music is presented. Yalch and Spangenberg[22] found in a clothing store experiment that 25-to-49-year-old patrons tended to buy more with music in the *foreground* of the shopping setting (presented by a tape player), whereas those 50 and older tended to buy more with *background* music (presented by the store's audio system). The effects were remarkably large. For young men's sportswear, foreground music produced an average purchase of $34.18 whereas background music produced an average of only $18.13. The reverse occurred with older women's dresses and coats, where foreground music produced an average purchase of $8.91 whereas background music produced an average of $22.22. The in-

vestigators took supplementary ratings of people's moods and also their liking of the music, factors which did *not* explain the results. They therefore suggested a cognitive interpretation, that the foreground versus background presentation of music affected perceptions of the store (lower prices versus more sophisticated, respectively), which in turn suited younger versus older shoppers and buyers of sportswear versus dresses.

All of these studies suggest that music is well worth investigating as a means of speeding up or maximizing sales (measured in dollars) in retail settings. However, some managers might regard the manipulation of music as an unethical practice and choose to refrain from the use of this retail promotion technique.

### Olfactory Cues

The olfactory or smell sense is one of the most primitive in humans; its effectiveness in selling environments seems quite powerful although very few publicly reported studies have been conducted. In one small-scale study, Hirsch[23] placed an identical pair of Nike tennis shoes in two experimental rooms, one containing purified, odor-free air and the other containing a pleasant floral scent. It was found that 26 of the 31 respondents, well above the chance level of 16, preferred the Nike shoes that were presented in the scented room. Also, the expected price of the Nike shoes in the scented room was over $10 higher than those in the odor-free room. Preference for the shoes in the scented room was found to be relatively independent of whether participants could detect the scent. Women were somewhat more strongly affected by the influence of scent than were men. Hirsch comments that younger men seem to prefer a spicy scent whereas older women prefer a floral scent as used in the experiment. It should be noted that the scent was administered at a fairly low concentration, hardly enough to be annoying in a retail setting. Nevertheless, managers may regard the use of nonproduct scents as an unethical retail technique.

Grocery retailers have also reportedly used artificial scent, such as the simulated smell of baked goods near that department, which they have found to increase sales quite dramatically. There is clearly an ethical issue of deception here in that shoppers may believe that the smell is an actual attribute of the product.

In summary, store layout and atmosphere variables can have a remarkably strong effect on the propensity to purchase the product or service. Indeed, the effects are sufficiently large to recommend these variables as retail promotion activities. However, the modulation of such environmental variables as store layout, color, music, and also lighting (a variable which we have not discussed because of the absence of systematic research) could be regarded as manipulative if not outright deceptive. We choose to recommend them in a pragmatic sense while pointing to some ethical concerns about their use.

## RETAIL FEATURE ADS

Retail ads, placed mostly in city and suburban newspapers and occasionally on local television or in local editions of magazines, are a very big business. It has been estimated that retailers spend $20 billion[24] per year on retail advertising, a figure that is larger than the total expenditure on consumer promotions by manufacturers, at $18 billion. Retail ads typically feature a number of products which are usually (but not always) offered at a discount price. Hence, they are also called "feature ads" or simply "features."

Examples of feature ads by a supermarket retailer —two strategies tried by the same store—are shown in Figure 13.3. Ads like there were used in a field experiment conducted under the supervision of Mulhern and Leone[25] designed to test the effects on total store

**FIGURE 13.3**
Alternative retail ad formats: several items featured at large discounts (panel A) versus a large number of items featured at small discounts (panel B). See text for discussion of the experiment by Mulhern and Leone, 1990, examining the effectiveness of these two formats.
*Courtesy:* Ralphs Grocery Company.

**A. Few items, large discounts**

sales of featuring a few items at deep discounts (left panel) or many items at small discounts (right panel). It was found that the few-items-at-deep-discounts strategy led to significantly more sales for the store as a whole (except in the rare situation of the store having no competitors nearby, where either strategy worked equally well). A possible explanation is that the few-items strategy results in clearer, "less cluttered" advertising of the promotions. Furthermore, the featuring of few items at deep discounts, as the investigators point out, would probably be more profitable in the long run because such ads are simpler to construct, require fewer items to be discounted in total, and fewer items for which to prepare in-store price-off signs and displays.

Two other details are worthy of note in these ads. The produce items in the left panel simply state the price without showing the amount of savings, a tactic we will review shortly in conjunction with retailer's price-off promotions. However, regular buyers in the category would probably realize that these prices are substantially discounted. In contrast, the ad in the right panel *does* state the amount of savings on each product. The second aspect to note in both panels is the retailer's attempt to limit the number of units purchased per customer when using the store's Smart Coupons. As we emphasized, the retailer's objective is to use price specials to draw in additional customers *who are then likely to buy other items in the store,* thus achieving greater total inventory transfer, rather than to allow a smaller number of customers to stock up on multiple units of the discounted items.

In retail ads, the choice of which items to include, and at what amount of discount, are the two critical and continual decisions. The typical supermarket retailer has to decide among 1,000 to 3,000 items (mainly those on trade promotion deals from the manufacturer) per *week!* From these, only about 15 items will be included in the typical weekly or twice-weekly retail ad, either in a cluttered 1-page format or in a less-cluttered 3-page format. Complex but repeated decisions such as this lend themselves well to an expert system approach. McCann, Tadlaoui, and Gallagher show how this could be achieved for a

**B. More items, smaller discounts**

supermarket retailer.[26] Their expert system was developed with input from managers and indeed tries to "model" what experienced retail managers do when making retail advertising decisions. For instance, using a 3-page retail ad format, the expert system was designed to feature four "hot items" on the first page—top brands deeply discounted due to manufacturers' case allowances; five "good deals" on the second page—top brands with medium turnover offered at not quite as deep a discount (but still those permitting a discount from the case allowance); and six items of "good margins" for the retailer on the final page—which could be any brands, from low turnover categories, which are actually offered at *no discount* but represent a profit to the retailer because they were bought on deal from the manufacturer. Supplementary decision rules include not repeating any item in the product category during its purchase cycle; and the constraint, for the "hot items," that one must be from each of the four departments of the store, namely, edible grocery, nonedible grocery, produce, and meat. As well, this retailer tries to maintain an average price cut of 33 percent on the page 1 items, and an average profit margin of 45 percent on the page 3 items. These decision rules are quite easily entered into the expert system, and it will quickly recommend which items to promote in the required ad format.

A similar academic contribution has been made by Rao and Simon[27] to those retailers, such as Sears or L.L. Bean, whose advertising is via catalogs. These investigators found that profit for the catalog retailer would be maximized by adjusting the ad space devoted to each product such that the profit per square inch (or square centimeter) is equal across products. For instance, an item generating $2,000 profit per week should get twice as much ad space as an item generating $1,000 profit per week.

Lastly, we would like to point out a very interesting analysis of retail "bait and switch" advertising by Gerstner and Hess.[28] Bait and switch is the practice whereby retailers advertise items that they know will be attractive to consumers with a low price (to get them into the store) but then deliberately stock only a limited number of the discounted items so that they can try to persuade interested customers to switch to a higher-priced or higher-margin substitute once they are in the store. Although bait and switch is *illegal,* it continues to be practiced by many re-

tailers because it is very difficult to police. Gerstner and Hess, implying an ethical view that the end justifies the illegal means, show that consumers are likely to *benefit* from bait and switch advertising in that they are usually *more satisfied* with the items that they *do* purchase, given they might not know exactly what they want before going to the store. (We note the satisfaction could stem from dissonance reduction, too.) Gerstner and Hess claim that the retailer, in any event, is unlikely to overuse bait and switch ads because there is too much risk to the retailer's reputation.

## POP DISPLAYS

Displays at the point of purchase (POP) are a widely used retailing device for drawing customers' attention to a promotion. Because of the attention enhancement effect, displays are considered to be a form of "merchandising" rather than a form of sales promotion per se. Meyer[29] states the distinction as follows: promotions (such as price-offs, coupons, and premiums) move the product, whereas merchandising *sells the idea* that moves the product (such as displays, package flags or "shelf talkers,"[30] and sales brochures). Thus, since displays are a contrasting stimulus, one way in which displays work is by eliciting *reflexive* attention to the promotional message and thus to the brand.

However, it is clear that most displays are not simply merchandising but are perceived by consumers *inherently* as price-off promotions. They also work through the process of *selective* attention. Because consumers in the past have been rewarded or reinforced by purchasing promoted brands from displays, the mere presence of a display causes them to believe that the brand on display is also "on special" when in reality it may not be, or when in reality the "deal" might be very minor. An illusory price cut, of course, is another ethically questionable retail promotion technique. The "on special" effect was hypothesized long ago for special displays by Engel and Blackwell[31] and the sales effect of displays *without* a price cut has been confirmed in at least two studies[32] and also by Information Resource Inc.'s (IRI) research.

It should be emphasized that displays are not always profitable for *manufacturers* (most in-store sales promotions are not). An exception was the special displays used by Borden to launch Doodle O's cheese snacks in 1992. Borden used in-store displays only, with no other advertising. The displays were quite expensive for the manufacturer to set up. However, the displays were so attractive that they were readily accepted by retailers. Each display featured a cartoon-like mascot, dubbed Fox Z. Doodle, with 200 sample-size packages of Doodle O's. The displays were so successful that they had to be restocked daily instead of on a weekly basis as had been originally expected.[33]

Displays are very effective for *retailers* in their quest to move products and achieve inventory transfer. An analysis of the three main forms of retailer's promotions—retail feature ads, displays, and price-offs—demonstrates that displays are relatively the most effective. Figure 13.4 shows an analysis conducted by IRI[34] based on 780 brands in 116 product categories over the course of a year. It can be seen that the simplest type of promotion, a 10 percent price-off,

increases sales by 20 percent. When this price-off is featured in a prior retail ad, sales increase a further 78 percent. Alternatively, if the price-off is part of an in-store display, sales increase 105 percent. The effect of all three promotional devices used together is a massive (short-term) 203 percent increase in sales—with the display being the single largest factor, coupled with the considerable interactive effect of the display following feature advertising. However, the risk of cluttering aisles places a physical limit on the number of displays that can be accommodated on any shopping day.[35]

For the manufacturer, we emphasize again, the sales effects of POP displays have to be traded off against the trade promotion cost of the display: the display will only be a profitable promotional technique if the revenue from the increased volume sold offsets that cost. For instance, in 1992, PepsiCo's Pepsi-Cola was able to persuade retailers to put the brand frequently on display and sold 62 percent of its supermarket volume from displays. Coca-Cola, in contrast, sold only 25 percent of its volume through displays. But it is by no means clear which of the two brands had the more profitable strategy (for the manufacturer). The only cost for retailers is the labor in setting up and dismantling displays, most of which is paid for by the manufacturer's trade promotion.

## PRICE-OFF PROMOTIONS

A price-off is a temporary reduction in the "normal" price of the brand. It was noted in Chapter 12 that manufacturers are restricted in the United States by FTC law as to the frequency and volume-applicability of price-offs that they can offer per brand. *Retailers,* however, face no such restrictions: they are free, within manufacturers' varying and, it appears, lessening degrees of control, to use price-offs as often as they like. For supermarket and drugstore retailers, the large number of items competing for the retailer's price-off promotions as well as the natural competitive pressures to rotate price-off promotions among manufacturers means, in effect, that the FTC's rule is reasonably well honored by retailers. This is not the case for retailers of consumer durables, however, many of whom depart from the FTC's intent by using a tactic known as high-low pricing, which we discuss later in conjunction with implementing price-offs (see chapter appendix 13C).

**FIGURE 13.4**

Sales results for 10 percent price-offs, retail feature ads, and POP displays (and their combinations). Unit sales increases, indexed to no-promotion base sales, are here averaged over 780 brands in 116 retail grocery product categories.
*Source:* IRI results reported by Fulgoni, 1987; see note 34. By permission.

**Percent incremental response (over base)**

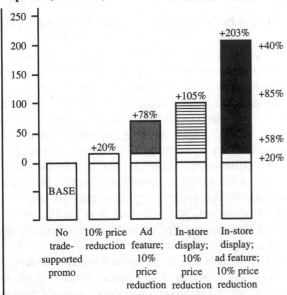

Retailers can implement price-offs in a number of ways: through feature ads in newspapers or other media, including store flyers, which announce the price-off available at the point of purchase; through price-off coupons included in these ads or available at the shelf or at the cash register; by using a display *with* a price reduction; by having a price reduction, clearly designated as such, at the shelf; or by reducing the price with no explicit mention of the reduction. (We could also include "private labeling" as a price-off technique available to the retailer; see the next section of this chapter.) Henderson[36] has found some evidence that these various "media" of price-offs tend to attract different consumers, and it is probably in the retailer's interest to use a variety of means of implementation in order to attract a larger number of different individuals to the store.

The retailer's price-offs may well attract store switchers, as they certainly attract habitual brand switchers (demonstrated in chapter appendix 13B, Who Responds to the Retail Price-Off?). Of course, the retailer's primary concern is that *category* sales increase.

The sales volume effect of price-offs depends on the amount of price-off (percent-off), *assuming* average-brand price elasticity. This is also shown in chapter appendix 13B in an important table for both retailers *and* manufacturers to consider (see Table 13.3).

### The Reference Price Effect

In order for a price-off to be effective, there must be a "normal" or *reference* price against which the buyer or consumer can evaluate the amount of savings.[37] This reference price may be established in the buyer's mind in two ways: by experience over time, or through the competitive context. For *frequently purchased* products and services, and excepting new category users buying for the first time, there will be a *temporal* reference price perceived by the buyer, which is the average (actually the geometric mean) of past prices of the item. This is how a straightforward price reduction, without any announced discount, can be effective. Also, for any product or service sold in a competitive context, and all types of buyers, there is an immediate *context* reference price; and Rajendran and Tellis[38] have shown that shoppers usually make the context comparison against the *lowest* price among the competing items on offer.

For industrial or consumer durable products (or services) purchased *infrequently,* and for new cate-

gory users buying *any* product for the first time, the *context* reference price will dominate because buyers do not have "memory" of a temporal reference price. An NCU being offered a price in isolation, with no context to compare it against—as happens to all of us from time to time—is at the mercy of the seller. Note that the seller may attempt to establish an "immediate" temporal reference price by announcing a discount, for example, "Previously $100, now $89," or simply "15% off."

For *frequently purchased* products or services, only NCUs or those who buy very infrequently in the category would *not* have a mentally established reference price. Thus, for most shoppers of these products and services, the temporal reference price and the context reference price are *both* important determinants of the effectiveness of a price-off. This is why, by the way, everyday low pricing (EDLP) seems likely to fail. Retailers want the flexibility to alternate prices between a normal price, to establish the temporal reference price, and a discounted price "on the day" which will be *seen as good value* in comparison with the temporal reference price.[39] A relatively constant price, as intended by EDLP, would be less likely to attract brand switchers.

For interesting details on how retailers can make price-offs more effective, see chapter appendix 13C, Implementing Retailer's Price-Offs.

### PRIVATE LABELING

Private labeling refers to the practice whereby retailers ask manufacturers to pack or label products with the retailer's "own" label. Usually, this is the name of the store, so private labels are also known as "store brands." The practice of private labeling has largely replaced the earlier practice of "generic" labeling, which is somewhat different in that generic or "no name" brands were typically put on the market by groups of smaller manufacturers who could not afford to advertise and therefore banded together to offer a clearly unadvertised, low-priced "brand." Private label brands, and generic brands where they still exist, are typically sold at a price that is at least 20 percent lower than the average price for national brands and often up to 80 percent lower.

The success of private labeling varies widely by category and retailer. It is estimated that in the *average* supermarket product category, about 18 percent of that category's sales go to the private label brand.[40]

For instance, in 1994, private labels led ice cream sales with 27 percent market share, but were well down in other dessert categories.[41] For supermarkets in the United Kingdom, the market share of private labels or "own brands," as the retail brands are called in England and the other U.K. countries, is considerably higher. Among leading supermarket retailers, ASDA sells about 32 percent of its total turnover through its own label; and the highest incidence of own label sales is observed at Sainsbury's, where 54 percent of its products are sold under the Sainsbury label. Up-market clothing retailers in the United States, such as Brooks Brothers, and in the United Kingdom, such as Marks & Spencer, probably have an even higher percentage of own label sales. And private labels together (combining retail brands such as The Gap) now lead U.S. jeans sales with 28 percent market share.[42]

The incidence of private label sales in a given product category is, interestingly, *not* proportional to the degree of price differential in comparison with the national brands. Rather, the incidence of private label sales is positively related to the degree to which the product is perceived to be "commodity-like," with brands differing little in quality, such as milk in supermarkets or aspirin in chain drugstores, and to a lesser extent, inversely related to total advertising in the product category. For instance, Buck[43] found that the highest 10 supermarket product categories for own-label sales had an average advertising-to-sales ratio of only 1.4 percent (see Chapter 2 for examples of A/S ratios), whereas the lowest 10 categories had an average A/S ratio of 7.3 percent. Even with the product category variations, Buck found that there *tends* to be a segment of shoppers who prefer "store brands" in every store in which they shop. Thus, private labeling is an effective device for attracting brand switchers and explains why most retailers now offer their own private label merchandise.

For the retailer, the private label brand serves as a point-of-purchase promotion because most shoppers perceive the private label brand to be similar in quality to the national brands (although this varies by product category) yet it is always offered at a substantial discount. Also note that the private label brand, being usually the lowest-priced brand, is likely to serve as the anchor price for the entire product category for the contextual price effect.

## TV OR PC INTERACTIVE SHOPPING

In-home or, more precisely, online shopping has been made possible by *interactive* TV or PC advertising. Offered mainly by retailers, TV or PC interactive shopping can also be offered by manufacturers as a bypass-the-retailer form of direct marketing (see Chapter 14). Necessary components for the consumer or customer are access to cable (or satellite or microwave dish) TV connected to the Internet, or simply a personal computer (which has a TV screen) with a modem connection to the Internet, or with a CD-ROM drive for playing interactive CDs. For the latter, ordering is done by telephone, or by fax or mail or in person. Or you can access an interactive TV presentation at a kiosk in a shopping mall or at a trade or consumer show. The process is as diagrammed in Figure 13.5. As you can see, for the consumer or customer it's as "easy as 1-2-3"—although there are actually five steps in the process overall.

Preceding and now coexisting with interactive advertising, of course, is home shopping from *non*interactive direct response advertising, as on TV shopping channels, in catalogs, or indeed from direct response ads in any medium, with the order made by mail, fax, or phone. At the time of this writing, only 1 percent of total retail sales were made through *any* form of "home shopping," but this percentage is expected to

**FIGURE 13.5**
TV or PC interactive shopping.

1. Consumer/customer accesses ad via Internet TV, Internet PC, or CD-ROM PC and "walks through" ad (interactive) using TV remote control or computer mouse. → 2. Consumer/customer enters order directly, or, from CD-ROM, indirectly by phone or mail or fax or in person. → 3. Consumer/customer receives products at home or at office.

2a. Order goes to manufacturer or retailer and is filled. - - - - → 2b. Delivery by courier or mail.

grow quite rapidly.[44] However, it appears to be the *interactive* form of advertising and shopping that is proving to be the successful retail promotion.

The evolution of shopping options is depicted in Figure 13.6.[45] This diagram, from a presentation by the Young & Rubicam advertising agency, suggests a supermarket shopping context, but of course, TV or PC interactive shopping is possible for any product or service category. For instance, among U.S. retailers using the Internet's World Wide Web are J.C. Penney and Marshall Fields.[46] There is also the Internet Shopping Network, which is linked to numerous retailers. It is important to realize, when contemplating this "evolution," that it is more a progression of *adding on* new forms of shopping rather than new forms replacing old ones. In fact, all of the previous forms of retail shopping, going back to street vendors, are still very much around.

For marketers planning to use TV or PC interactive shopping as a promotional vehicle, a forecast of whether and when interactive shopping will represent a substantial "medium" for selling their type of product or service is required.[47] We expect that there will be four main factors determining the diffusion of TV or PC interactive shopping for a particular type of product or service, which may be summarized as the "four Ss": supply, search, and sensory and social factors.

**1.** *Supply.* From the marketer's standpoint, supply covers a host of technical factors such as the availability of cable (or satellite or microwave dish) TV channels in an area, purchase by consumers of a TV/home computer capable of playing interactive programs, and the establishment of a fast and reliable ordering and delivery system. From the *consumer's or customer's* standpoint, supply undoubtedly means the "coverage" of the market, in terms of the number and nature of participating *suppliers* that can be accessed in the product category via interactive shopping. The shopper looking for maximum variety will want to be assured that his or her preferred manufacturers or retailers are available on the system; and the shopper looking for savings will want to be assured that the lowest price is available for a particular item. This will be a chicken-and-egg game for a while as potential suppliers wait to become convinced of shopper demand, and shoppers, in turn, wait to be assured of adequate supply. The complex supply factor, alone, makes the penetration of interactive shopping very difficult to predict.

**2.** *Search.* TV or PC interactive shopping would appear to be most appealing for so-called "specialty" or "shopping" goods by massively saving on search costs for the home shopper. However, there will also be segments of "convenience goods" shoppers who would prefer home shopping via TV, such as older people, those in big cities with high crime rates, or simply those who have an aversion to visiting stores. The reduction in the time and effort of searching is clearly the main appeal of interactive home shopping.

**3.** *Sensory Factors.* Even with the high-definition TV reception predicted to become standard in the future, it will still not be possible to see the to-be-considered products as well as you might like—and, of course, you won't be able to touch them before you

**FIGURE 13.6**
The evolution of shopping modes from the peddler through to TV or PC interactive shopping. Note that all previous modes currently coexist.
*Source:* Y & R presentation reported in Cummins, 1994; see note 45, by permission.

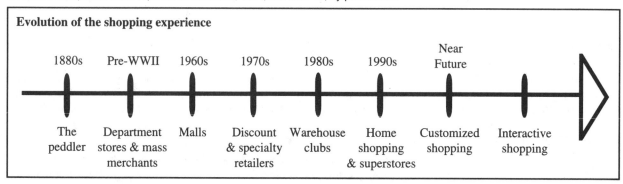

buy. For example, would you buy a Lexus SC Coupe based *only* on what you can see and read on Lexus's World Wide Website, an Internet access point (Figure 13.7)? Virtual reality simulation could change this, but the expensive equipment needed to make virtual shopping technically possible is unlikely to be available for home use until well into the future. The lack of sensory contact will be limiting for products such as cars and furniture, where there is a substantial experiential "sampling" component. Nevertheless, free home trial and liberal return policies may go a long way toward overcoming this limitation. Most suited to interactive shopping will be products such as consumer packaged goods which, apart from fresh meat and produce, require little sensory contact in the purchase decision.

**FIGURE 13.7**
Advertising information for Toyota's Lexus line available interactively on the Internet.
*Source:* L. Freeman, From salesman's web to online web.
*Advertising Age,* April 3, 1995, pp. 5–30, by permission.
*Courtesy:* Toyota Lexus.

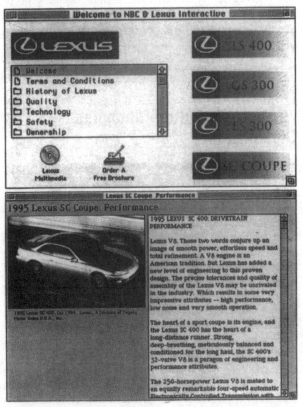

**4.** *Social Factors.* Then there are the social factors to consider. For a large segment of consumers, shopping is a social experience—witness the gigantic Mall of America in Minneapolis, where people go not only to shop but also to take their children to its indoor fun park, or to visit the variety of restaurants, bars, and sports and dancing facilities located within the mall. Also, a good deal of shopping is done in pairs: people often like to take a spouse or friend along when they go shopping, to advise on their choices of furnishings, clothing, and other expressive products and services. The counterimage of a hermitlike consumer shopping at home alone, or even inducing another household member or friend to "watch TV to shop with me," is none too appealing to many consumers.

Overall, therefore, it is clear that TV or PC interactive home shopping will be attractive only for certain types of products and services, sold to particular market segments, and will be only a partial solution to most people's shopping needs. Like other shopping innovations before it, TV or PC interactive shopping will take its place among the many options currently available. The foregoing "four Ss" may help the individual marketer (retailers especially but also manufacturers) decide whether interactive shopping is a promotion that should be actively pursued, or whether to remain with more conventional forms of marketing.

## SUMMARY

The retailer can employ six principal means of promotions: retail layout and atmosphere, retail feature ads, point-of-purchase displays, price-off promotions, private labeling of their own brand of products, and TV or PC interactive shopping. We offer the following summary without commenting on ethical considerations (which we did in the chapter itself). Those summarized here are legal promotion techniques.

How you design the layout and atmosphere of the *place of sale* itself is a promotional activity. Retail store environments and professional services offices should be thought of as promotional media for the company. Using the selling environment as a promotion medium, marketers can select four main stimulus factors for maximum effect: layout, color, music, and olfaction (scent). These four stimulus factors can create a selling "atmosphere" that favorably influences the buyer's disposition to purchase by temporarily altering the buyer's emotional state—or by subtly inducing cognitive beliefs about the seller's attributes that increase brand attitude and intention to buy. These place-based stimuli are not just speculative pop psychology: they can produce remarkably large increases in sales. Moreover, they lend themselves relatively easily to experimentation and are quite inexpensive to implement.

*Retail feature ads,* in newspapers, catalogs, or flyers, can be improved scientifically with the aid of expert systems that are now emerging for the retailer's use. Which items to promote, how much space to devote to each, what sort of discount (if any) to offer, and how often to promote each item are complex, continual challenges that are most accurately solved with the aid of an expert system.

*POP displays* are extremely effective for retailers, helping them to meet their inventory transfer objective. Displays work spectacularly well—even when no price-off is given on the displayed items.

*Price-offs* are the most widely employed retail promotion technique. For frequently purchased products, retailers prefer to alternate prices between a normal price and an occasional price-off; the normal price establishes a temporal reference price in the buyer's mind, against which the price-off is thereby rendered more effective by offering clearly perceived value for money. There is also a context reference price operating when competing brands are sold together; the lowest-priced brand is perceived as the anchor against which other prices are compared.

How the price-off is presented makes a considerable difference, as shown in chapter Appendix 3C. For infrequently purchased products, retailers can create an "immediate" temporal reference price by using wording in price signage such as "regular price/sale price." For single items, showing the *dollar amount* of savings seems to be the most effective way of implementing a price-off offer. However, for a whole range of items, or for a storewide sale, *maximum percentage* wording is most effective. "Price-endings" can also make a difference. Across the board, 99-cent endings are probably most effective because they suggest a deal and yet may require only a minimum discount. For an upmarket retailer, however, even-dollar pricing may help to preserve a prestigious image.

*Private labeling* is another promotional activity used by many retailers to appeal to store-switching price shoppers. Private labeling (usually) uses the store name as the brand name, thus trading on the retailer's corporate image, and is consistent with the IMC approach applied at the retail level.

A new retail promotion technique is *TV or PC interactive shopping*—either in-home, in-office, or at a trade show or shopping center—for which the shopper uses an Internet TV/computer or a CD-ROM computer. Interactive shopping is taking its place as yet another of the many forms of shopping. Whether a *particular marketer* (manufacturer or retailer) should pursue TV or PC interactive shopping as a distribution channel, however, depends on what we termed the "four Ss." *Supply*—of technology, and of other manufacturers or retailers on the system—has to be adequate. The reduction in the time and effort required to *search* for a product is clearly the main appeal overall. However, the lack of direct *sensory* contact is a limiting factor for certain types of products and services. Finally, *social* assistance and *social* reinforcement are basically missing from the home shopping method, and for many purchases their importance should not be underestimated. All we can say with certainty at this time is that for some products and services, for some market segments, some of the time, interactive shopping is a viable promotion activity.

## APPENDIX

# 13A. Grocery Store Shopping Statistics

To illustrate the grocery store shopping pattern, we first go back to ground coffee—a product category that we examined in detail in Chapter 3, chapter appendix 3B, in conjunction with target audience purchase behavior and brand loyalty—and consider now the same category with regard to retail shopping behavior. Take a typical supermarket chain such as Safeway. Safeway's *average* ground coffee purchaser makes only about one-third of his or her ground coffee purchases at Safeway—and two-thirds at other stores. However, there is a heavy skew toward the small group of *relatively* store-loyal Safeway customers. For instance, and this depends on where we make the cutoff for "store loyalty," the 12 percent of shoppers who buy more than half their ground coffee at Safeway will account for 49 percent of all ground coffee volume sales at Safeway; if we loosen the cutoff for store loyalty, the 54 percent of Safeway shoppers who buy their ground coffee at Safeway two or more times a year will account for 86 percent of Safeway's ground coffee sales.[48] Moreover, each of the supermarket chains has approximately the same *proportion* of store-loyal and store-switching shoppers—although again there is a "double jeopardy" effect for smaller stores, illustrating the importance of distribution for *stores,* in that larger chains with more retail outlets not only have a higher penetration in terms of people who shop there but also a higher repeat-shopping rate than smaller chains.

Store loyalty, as we would expect, diminishes as the analyzed time period lengthens: the longer the time period, the more likely it is that shoppers will have visited other stores. This is shown clearly in a study of 10,000 households' grocery (supermarket and small stores) shopping behavior by the research firm of Information Resources Inc.[49] To allow for the occasional "emergency" or "side trip," store loyals were defined by IRI as those who made 85 percent or more of their shopping trips to the one store. As shown in Table 13.1, the proportion of store loyals, by the realistic "85 percent-plus" criterion, is quite high over the short period of 1 week (58 percent) but declines to only about one in three shoppers who are loyal to a single store over a 6-month period (34 percent). Also shown in the table is the distribution of stores shopped over a middle-length time interval of 3 months (12 weeks): the average shopper visits three to four grocery stores over a 3-month period. Because of store switching and because of emergency or side trips, only 8 percent of consumers shop exclusively at a single store over a 3-month period. Most important, and consistent with the importance to retailers of store switchers who take advantage of price deals, the more stores visited, the more the shopper is likely to be purchasing on deal.[50]

The average grocery shopping trip lasts just 22 minutes (in the store).[51] However, this represents an average of major trips every 2 weeks (about 44 minutes) and quick trips every 2 to 4 days (about 10 minutes each).[52] Approximately half of the shoppers at a supermarket will buy 10 or fewer items on that trip—those shoppers we see in the express checkout lanes. The other half will buy perhaps 50 to 60 items in the 40 to 50 minutes they are in the store. Whereas this seems like an item chosen every 50 seconds or so, the rate is actually much faster after subtracting the walking time and the checkout time.[53] As pointed out in Chapter 5, observational studies of supermarket shopping behavior indicate that, for the average product category, the time from first sighting the display to putting the item in the shopping cart is only 9.4 seconds, with 48 percent of purchases requiring less than 5 seconds![54]

## 13B. Who Responds to the Retail Price-Off?

From the consumer's perspective, the two main reasons for brand-switching behavior are "variety seeking," which occurs even with constant prices for each brand,[55] and saving money because of a "deal." That price-off deals attract brand switchers (and not other-brand loyals or, to much extent, the brand's own loyals) is shown in Table 13.2 for what IRI describes as a "typical" brand of supermarket product. The second column in the table shows the target audience composition of the brand's buyers when the brand is offered at its normal price. You can see that 52 percent of the brand's sales are to its own brand loyals (BLs are

---

**TABLE 13.1**

### SHOPPER LOYALTY TO RETAIL GROCERY STORES[a] DECLINES WITH TIME

(*In a 3-month [12-week] period, most shop at three or four stores. The more stores visited, the more likely purchases are on deal.*)

| Store loyalty | Time period | | | |
|---|---|---|---|---|
| | **1 week** | **4 weeks** | **12 weeks** | **24 weeks** |
| Percent doing 85% + of their grocery shopping at *one* store | 58 | 44 | 36 | 34 |

**Actual number of stores shopped (by *all* shoppers) in a 12-week period**

| | **Percent** | **Index of on-deal purchases** |
|---|---|---|
| 1 store only | 8 ⎫ | 100 |
| 2 stores | 18 ⎭ | |
| 3–4 stores | 48 | 116 |
| 5 or more stores | 26 | 133 |
| | 100 | |

[a]Retail *grocery* stores (supermarkets and small stores). Sample = 10,000 households in 1984.

*Source:* IRI data reported in Totten and Block, 1987; see note 49.

**TABLE 13.2**

**TARGET AUDIENCE RESPONSES TO A TYPICAL BRAND OF SUPERMARKET PRODUCT AT ITS NORMAL PRICE AND WHEN OFFERED ON A PRICE-OFF DEAL, MEASURED IN SALES UNITS**

| Type of buyer | Percent (and index) of brand's buyers at normal price | Indexed purchases during deal | Increase | Percent of brand's buyers for the *additional* sales |
|---|---|---|---|---|
| Brand loyals (80–100% loyal) | 52% | 68 | +16 | 11% |
| Brand switchers (less than 80% loyal to any brand) | 43% | 156 | +113 | 83% |
| Other-brand loyals (80–98% loyal to *another* brand) | 2% | 6 | +4 | 3% |
| New category users (first purchase in category) | 3% | 6 | +3 | 2% |
| | 100% | 236 | +136 | 99% |
| | (index also) | (index) | | (with rounding, the total is 99%) |

*Source:* Adapted from IRI data reported in Totten and Block, 1987; see note 49.

defined here as those who buy that particular brand at its normal price on 80 percent or more of their purchase occasions); 43 percent are to favorable brand switchers (FBSs are those who are less than 80 percent loyal to any particular brand but already include the brand in their repertoire); and only 2 percent are to other-brand loyals (OBLs) and 3 percent to new category users (NCUs) making their first purchase in the category. The third column shows what happens when the brand is offered on a price-off deal. First of all, notice that the brand's sales that week increase by a total of 136 percent (so that total sales in the deal week are indexed at 236) and that most of this increase comes from habitual brand switchers. The final column in the table shows the percentages of the *additional* sales that come from each of the target audiences. You can see that 83 percent of the additional sales are to habitual brand switchers.[56]

We must emphasize that the 136 percent sales increase is an average for the "typical" brand studied by IRI and that the actual increase may be anywhere from zero percent to several hundred percent, depending on the price sensitivity of the brand, the price reduction amount, the relative prices of *other* brands, and the number of brand switchers in the store. However, although a 136 percent sales increase looks "good," you must remember that while this is nearly always profitable for the *retailer,* whose profit margin is preserved even at the discounted price because the *cost* has been lowered in most cases due to a trade promotion price reduction

by the manufacturer, it is not necessarily profitable for the *manufacturer.* Whether the manufacturer would make a profit on the 136 percent sales increase depends on the manufacturer's profit *goal* for the product and also the amount of the price reduction in the trade promotion to the retailer. Table 13.3 shows this calculation assuming "typical" upside price elasticity. Look at the fifth column of the table. Let us suppose that the manufacturer's original profit margin from (or "markup" to) the retailer is 40 percent. Only if the price reduction to the retailer in the trade promotion were about 20 percent or less would the *manufacturer* make a profit by observing a 136 percent increase in sales (and, strictly speaking, these sales would have to be sales *to* the retailer, regardless of how much product the retailer eventually sells). If the trade promotion price reduction is about 25 percent (the exact figure is 23 percent) or more, the manufacturer would experience a loss. For instance, at a 25 percent price-reduced trade promotion, an *additional 167 percent of units* of the product would have to be sold to the retailer in order for the manufacturer to make a profit.

The same table could be interpreted from the *retailer's* perspective. Look again at the last column of the table. This column is realistic because a retailer normally wants to make at least 40 percent profit per unit. Here it can be seen that the 136 percent sales increase (sales to consumers) would be profitable all the way up to and including a 20 percent price-off offered to consumers *by the retailer*

**TABLE 13.3**

**VOLUME INCREASE (V, IN PERCENT) NEEDED TO MAINTAIN GROSS PROFIT FROM THE PRICE-OFF PROMOTION AT VARIOUS LEVELS OF PRICE-OFF**

| Price-off | Profit margin (before the price-off) | | | | | | |
|---|---|---|---|---|---|---|---|
| | 5% | 10% | 15% | 20% | 25% | 30% | 40% |
| 1% | + 25% | + 12% | + 8% | + 6% | + 5% | + 4% | + 3% |
| 5% | (loss) | + 100% | + 50% | + 34% | + 25% | + 20% | + 15% |
| 10% | (loss) | (loss) | + 200% | + 100% | + 67% | + 50% | + 34% |
| 15% | (loss) | (loss) | (loss) | + 300% | + 150% | + 100% | + 60% |
| 20% | (loss) | (loss) | (loss) | (loss) | + 400% | + 200% | + 100% |
| 25% | (loss) | (loss) | (loss) | (loss) | (loss) | + 500% | + 167% |

[a]Calculated by comparing 100 percent sold at the original profit margin with (100 + V) percent sold at the discounted profit margin so that the volume increase (V percent) produces the same gross profit as would have been obtained at the original price. Example for the first entry in the table: 100% × 5% = (100 + V)% × (5 − 4)%, which yields V = 25%. V is therefore the percentage volume increase needed to "break even" on the expected profit at the original selling price. For volume sold beyond V, the price-off promotion would be *profitable*, that is, bring additional profit that would not have accrued without it.

*Source:* Reprinted courtesy of Miller Publishing Company, by permission.

and would only start to lose money at about a 25 percent price-off.

# 13C. Implementing Retailer's Price-Offs

Price-offs are implemented so frequently by retailers that, through a process of experimentation, they quickly develop an idea of which type of implementation works best. Nevertheless, it is worthwhile to examine retailer's price-off tactics, if only for our education as consumers! There are three interesting variables to consider: the wording of the price-off offer, whether the savings is stated in monetary or percentage terms, and the effects of "price endings."

**Price-Off Wording.** The retailer's *wording* of the price-off offer, in feature ads or in point-of-purchase signage, seems to exert quite a strong effect. For instance, Walton and Berkowitz[57] found that a comparison which includes the magic words "Sale price," either in the format "Total value/Sale price" or "Regular price/Sale price," is perceived as better value for the money than other wordings such as "Now only" or "Our price."[58] This type of wording (which you may recognize as using a temporal reference price) is implicated in the controversial issue of *high-low pricing* whereby retailers set the original price at an artificially high level for a brief period and then discount the item for a *long* period against the original price.[59] It is estimated that some 60 to 75 percent of the volume of consumer durables is sold via low prices offered against an artificially high prior price. The FTC's guidelines are too loose to prevent this, and so some U.S. states have introduced their own legislation. For instance, Massachusetts law now requires that 30 percent or more of the item's sales

must occur at the normal (original) price, *or* that this price must be in use for at least 15 continuous days prior to the sale, and that the sale price can then be offered for no more than 45 percent of the next 180 days.[60] Price wording may also imply an unfair *competitive* claim (a between-store context effect). In an example of industry self-regulation, Wal-Mart stores was forced in 1994 by the National Advertising Review Board to stop using its 5-year running slogan, "Always the low price. Always." Wal-Mart has since amended its slogan to "Always low prices. Always. Wal-Mart."[61] Wal-Mart can no longer imply *the* low price, that is, the low*est* price available.

**Monetary or Percentage Savings.** The second consideration for the retailer is whether to show the price-offs savings in terms of *monetary* savings, in dollars or cents, or whether to show the savings in *percentage* terms.[62] For a single item, indicating the monetary savings would appear to be more effective than indicating the percentage savings in that, in practice, retailers more often use the monetary savings format (consistent with the FTC's recommended practice, as noted in chapter appendix 12B). However, for a retailer who is trying to attract customers to the store by offering savings on *many* items, percentages are more appropriate and several choices are available. For all the items in the store, or for a category of promoted items, the retailer could calculate the average percentage savings and use what is known as an "objective" claim of, say, "Save 25 percent." However, the savings on different items would vary unless all items were priced at exactly 25 percent off, and the objective claim would then be misleading unless stated as "Average savings: 25 percent." Alternatively, and perhaps more realistically, the retailer could use what is known as a "tensile" price claim in which a vaguer reference is made to the amount of savings. The most common forms of tensile claims are *maximum,* such as "Save up to 40 percent"; *range,* "Save 10 to 40 percent"; and *minimum,* "Save 10 percent or more." In an experiment using retail price claims for color TV sets, where the measure of interest was intention to shop for color TVs at that *store,* Biswas and Burton[63] found that the objective claim ("Save 25 percent") and the maximum claim ("Save up to 40 percent") produced about 10 percent higher store-shopping intention than either the range claim or the minimum claim. The most realistic all-purpose tensile claim would therefore be "Save up to 40 percent," because the "Save 25 percent" claim would only be truthful if *all* the color TVs were discounted by *at least* that amount. Further investigation by these authors indicated that consumers mostly seem to assume a minimum discount of 10 percent and then mentally compute the average of 10 and 40 percent (the maximum claimed), which would be equivalent to the 25 percent objective discount claim. However, when asked to state what they thought the *maximum* discount would be for a claim of "Save up to 40 percent," most interestingly, 80 percent of consumers thought that the maximum would be 40 to 49 percent, being optimistic about the maximum possible deal. There is a considerable "caveat emptor" implication in retailers' use of percentage price claims across products.

**Price Endings.** The third implementation tactic for retailer's price-offs (which also applies to pricing in general) is the use of particular *price endings.* It has long been known that various price endings have subjective or "psychological" connotations. Schindler points out that a price ending of 95 or 99 cents, such as $49.99, may connote a discount; an unusual ending such as 63 cents, as in $7.63, may suggest a carefully determined price where the retailer has perhaps offered the maximum savings down to some fixed margin; and a 00 or rounded ending, such as $200, may connote a high-quality product (or store).[64]

Price endings can make significant differences to the purchase rate of the product. In one experiment, Schindler[65] varied the prices of items in the winter sale catalog of a direct mail women's clothing retailer. Three versions of the catalog were prepared, in which the prices all had 88-cent endings, all 99-cent endings, or all even-dollar endings (such as $33.88, $33.99, or $34.00). Measurement of sales 3 months after the catalogs were distributed showed that both the 88- and 99-cent endings produced about 10 percent greater volume of sales than the even-dollar endings. The 99-cent ending would maximize profit because the 88-cent ending is 12 cents below the even-dollar price revenue per unit, whereas the 99-cent ending is only 1 cent below. Schindler quite rightly is hesitant to generalize this finding across all types of products and especially across all types of retailers, since retailers vary in terms of whether they adopt a *very* upmarket positioning (such as Brooks Brothers) or a lower-priced

positioning (such as Radio Shack). Thus, pricing is part of IMC. However, the main implication is that price endings *can* make a difference to sales and are worth being varied in an experimental manner by retailers.

## NOTES

1. R. E. Bucklin and J. M. Lattin, A two-stage model of purchase incidence and brand choice, *Marketing Science,* 1991, *10* (1), pp. 24–39.
2. R. C. Blattberg, G. D. Eppen, and J. Lieberman, A theoretical and empirical evaluation of price deals for consumer nondurables, *Journal of Marketing,* 1981, *45* (1), pp. 116–129; K. Helsen and D. C. Schmittlein, How does a product market's typical price-promotion pattern affect the timing of households' purchases? An empirical study using UPC scanner data, *Journal of Retailing,* 1992, *68* (3), pp. 316–338.
3. See Chapter 5, Table 5.4.
4. S. Hume, Marketers question lower pricing, *Advertising Age,* March 16, 1992, p. 38.
5. Other retailer deviations from manufacturers' promotional plans are common. One is failure to provide merchandising support. Even when trade allowances require this, one survey found that in 67 percent of instances merchandising was not provided. Another is failure to pass deal allowances through to the consumer as intended by the manufacturer. For supermarket items, only about 45 percent of products on allowance result in a price reduction to consumers. In new car sales, only about a quarter of the dealer's allowance (a rebate to the dealer) gets passed on as a reduction in the negotiated selling price. For the supermarket survey, see M. Chevalier and R. C. Curhan, Retail promotion as a function of trade promotion: A descriptive analysis, *Sloan Management Review,* 1976, *17* (1), pp. 19–32. For the car dealer survey, see S. M. Crafton and G. E. Hoffer, Do consumers benefit from auto manufacturer rebates to dealers? *Journal of Consumer Research,* 1980, *7* (2), pp. 211–214.
6. R. C. Blattberg, G. D. Eppen, and J. Lieberman, Same reference as in note 2. Their results have recently been replicated by K. Helsen and D. C. Schmittlein, same reference as in note 2.
7. For theory and some experimental results on supermarket retailers' responses to price changes by competitors, see P. R. Dickson and J. E. Urbany, Retailer reactions to competitive price changes, *Journal of Retailing,* 1994, *70* (1), pp. 1–21.
8. See A. Mitchell, Category captains, *Marketing* (UK), April 8, 1993, p. 24; and C. Buckingham, Onset of the category management phenomenon, *Admap,* August 1993, pp. 12–16.

9. R. Gibson, The fine art of stocking a supermarket's shelves, *The Wall Street Journal,* October 15, 1992, pp. B1, B10.

10. R. J. Donovan and J. R. Rossiter, Store atmosphere: An environmental psychology approach, *Journal of Retailing,* 1982, *58* (1), pp. 34–57; R. J. Donovan, J. R. Rossiter, G. Marcoolyn, and A. Nesdale, Store atmosphere and purchasing behavior, *Journal of Retailing,* 1994, *70* (3), pp. 283–294.

11. R. A. Kerin, A. Jain, and D. J. Howard, Store shopping experience and consumer price-quality-value perceptions, *Journal of Retailing,* 1992, *68* (4), pp. 376–397.

12. R. A. Feinberg, Credit cards as spending facilitating stimuli: A conditioning interpretation, *Journal of Consumer Research,* 1986, *13* (3), pp. 348–356. With reference to the ethical question we raised, Feinberg also found that donations to charity (United Way) were higher in the presence of credit card stimuli—student donations averaged $4.01 in the credit card condition and only $1.66 in the absence of credit card cues. Does the end (social good) justify the means (possible unfair persuasion technique)?

13. Marketers showing more interest in waiting-room media network, *Marketing News,* April 12, 1993, p. 5.

14. Waiting room TV suspended, *Marketing News,* March 28, 1994, p. 1.

15. J. T. Molloy, *Live for Success,* New York: Morrow, 1981. Also see J. D. Wineman, *Behavioral Issues in Office Design,* New York: Van Nostrand Reinhold, 1986.

16. J. C. Rogers, M. Slama, and T. G. Williams, An exploratory study of Luscher Color Test–predicted personality types and psychographic shopping profiles, in P. E. Murphy et al., eds., *AMA Educators' Conference Proceedings,* Chicago: American Marketing Association, 1983, pp. 30–34.

17. R. J. Donovan et al., same references as in note 10.

18. R. E. Milliman, Using background music to affect the behavior of supermarket shoppers, *Journal of Marketing,* 1982, *46* (3), pp. 86–91.

19. R. E. Milliman, The influence of background music on the behavior of restaurant patrons, *Journal of Consumer Research,* 1986, *13* (2), pp. 286–289. The slow music, however, also slowed "turnover" of tables, so there is some doubt as to whether it would be more profitable than fast music on a *per-hour* basis, rather than the per-table basis analyzed in the study.

20. Faster drinking to slow music, *The West Australian,* December 1, 1988, p. 76.

21. C. S. Areni and D. Kim, The influence of background music on shopping behavior: Classical versus top-forty music in a wine store, in L. McAlister and M. L. Rothschild, eds., *Advances in Consumer Research,* vol. 20, 1993, Provo, UT: Association for Consumer Research, pp. 336–340; also see R. Yalch and E. Spangenberg, The effects of store music on shopping behavior, *Journal of Services Marketing,* 1990, *4* (1) pp. 31–39.

22. R. F. Yalch and E. Spangenberg, Using store music for retail zoning: A field experiment, in L. McAlister and M. L. Rothschild, eds., *Advances in Consumer Research,* vol. 20, 1993, Provo, UT: Association for Consumer Research, pp. 632–636. Indeed, foreground music is now the "go" and is offered to retailers by companies such as AEI Music Networks Inc., in competition with MUZAK's background music; see C. Rubel, Marketing with music, *Marketing News,* August 12, 1996, pp. 1, 21. Retailers Eddie Bauer, Banana Republic, and Bath & Body Works, for instance, use AEI's foreground music service.

23. A. Hirsch, Study reported in C. Miller, Research reveals how marketers can win by a nose, *Marketing News,* February 4, 1991, pp. 1–2.

24. A. D. Cox and D. Cox, Competing on price: The role of retailer price advertisements in shaping store-price image, *Journal of Retailing,* 1993, *66* (4), pp. 428–445.

25. F. J. Mulhern and R. P. Leone, Retail promotional advertising: Do the number of deal items and size of deal discounts affect store performance? *Journal of Business Research,* 1990, *21* (3), pp. 179–194.

26. J. McCann, A. Tadlaoui, and J. Gallagher, Knowledge systems in merchandising: Advertising design, *Journal of Retailing,* 1990, *66* (3), pp. 257–277.

27. V. Rao and J. L. Simon, Optimal allocation of space in retail advertisements and mail-order catalogues: Theory and a first approximation decision rule, *International Journal of Advertising,* 1983, *2* (2), pp. 123–129.

28. E. Gerstner and J. D. Hess, Can bait and switch benefit consumers? *Marketing Science,* 1990, *9* (2), pp. 114–124.

29. E. Meyer, Promotion: 29 things to remember about it, *Advertising Age,* December 21, 1981, p. 35.

30. "Shelf talkers" traditionally refer to signs on the shelf which direct attention to the price-off on a package. However, they now can literally talk! Using an infrared beam activated by shoppers within a 12-foot (4-meter) radius, an audio device issues a taped promotion for the brand. Experiments in the United Kingdom and Belgium for Purfect cat food showed dramatic sales increases, though we should suspect a novelty effect here.

31. J. F. Engel and R. D. Blackwell, *Consumer Behavior,* 4th ed., Hinsdale, IL: Dryden, 1982, pp. 554–556.

32. P. M. Guadagni and J. D. C. Little, A logit model of brand choice calibrated on scanner data, *Marketing Science,* 1983, *2* (3), pp. 203–238; J. J. Inman and

L. McAlister, A retailer promotion policy model considering promotion signal sensitivity, *Marketing Science,* 1993, *12* (4), pp. 339–356.

33. *The Wall Street Journal,* October 15, 1992, pp. B1–B6.

34. G. M. Fulgoni, The role of advertising—is there one? *Admap,* 1987, *23* (4), pp. 54–57.

35. Same reference as note 33.

36. C. M. Henderson, Promotion heterogeneity and consumer learning: Refining the dual-proneness construct, in C. T. Allen and D. Roedder John, eds., *Advances in Consumer Research,* vol. 21, 1994, Provo, UT: Association for Consumer Research, pp. 86–94.

37. K. B. Monroe, *Pricing: Making Profitable Decisions,* New York: McGraw-Hill, 1979; also K. B. Monroe, The influences of price differences and brand familiarity on brand preferences, *Journal of Consumer Research,* 1976, *3* (1), pp. 42–49.

38. K. N. Rajendran and G. J. Tellis, Contextual and temporal components of reference price, *Journal of Marketing,* 1994, *58* (1), pp. 22–34.

39. In an important large-scale field experiment for a major supermarket chain, Hoch and his colleagues found that the occasional price-off policy as described here produced a 15 percent increase in profit compared with constant full prices whereas the EDLP produced an 18 percent *decrease* in the retailer's profit. See S. J. Hoch and M. E. Purk, EDLP, hi-lo, and margin arithmetic, *Journal of Marketing,* 1994, *58* (4), pp. 16–27.

40. *Marketing* (Australia), March 1994, p. 8.

41. Brand scorecard, *Advertising Age,* December 19, 1994, p. 26.

42. Second is VF (the Girbaud brand) with 27 percent, and third Levi's with 26 percent. Levi's, after failing to form reliable alliances with major jeans retailers such as The Gap stores, is pursuing vertical integration by owning its own stores. See A. Z. Cuneo, Levi's Strauss sizes the retail scene, *Advertising Age,* January 23, 1995, p. 4.

43. S. Buck, Own label and branded goods in fmcg markets: An assessment of the facts, the trends and the future, *Journal of Brand Management,* 1993, *1* (1), pp. 1–8.

44. Home shopping: The last good buy, Reprinted from *The Economist,* in *The Australian,* August 23, 1994, p. 59; M. Williams, Test driving on the superhighway, *Marketing* (Australia), August 1994, pp. 50–52.

45. E. R. Cummins, TV shopping gives plenty of food for thought, *The Australian,* June 2, 1994, p. 26; reproducing a chart from a presentation in Sydney by Young & Rubicam advertising agency.

46. Making moves on the Internet, *Advertising Age,* January 9, 1995, pp. 22, 24.

47. General factors to keep an eye on include announcements of investments in the infrastructure technology, and household penetration of PCs, CD-ROMS, and digital TV sets; see S. Myerson, Beyond the hype: Taking the pulse of the information revolution, *Admap,* July 1994, pp. 25–27. In our discussion, we focus on specific factors.

48. M. D. Uncles and A. S. C. Ehrenberg, The buying of packaged goods at U.S. retail chains, *Journal of Retailing,* 1990, *66* (3), pp. 278–296.

49. 1984 IRI study of 10,000 households' shopping behavior, reported in J. C. Totten and M. P. Block, *Analyzing Sales Promotion: Texts and Cases,* Chicago, Il: Commerce Communications, Inc., 1987.

50. IRI study, same reference as previous note.

51. K. Deveny, Displays pay off for grocery marketers, *The Wall Street Journal,* October 15, 1992, pp. B1, B5.

52. B. E. Kahn and D. C. Schmittlein, Shopping trip behavior: An empirical investigation, *Marketing Letters,* 1989, *1* (1), pp. 55–69; L. Rickard, Shopping lists tell just half the real story, *Advertising Age,* January 9, 1995, p. 20.

53. K. Deveny, same reference as note 51.

54. See Chapter 5, note 19.

55. A recent article by H. C. M. van Trijp, W. D. Heyer, and J. J. Inman, Why switch? Product-category level explanations for true variety-seeking behavior, *Journal of Marketing Research,* 1996, *33* (3), pp. 281–292, provides the theory of brand switching in relation to variety and other causes; and a quantitative model which predicts variety-seeking brand switching is offered by F. L. Winter and J. R. Rossiter, Pattern-matching purchase behavior and stochastic brand choice: A low-involvement model, *Journal of Economic Psychology,* 1989, *10* (4), pp. 559–585.

56. IRI data reported in Totten and Block, same reference as note 49.

57. J. A. Walton and E. Berkowitz, Information needs for comparative pricing decisions, in P. E. Murphy et al., eds., *AMA Educators' Conference Proceedings,* Chicago: American Marketing Association, 1983, pp. 241–245.

58. A study by Friedmann and Hains confirms the attraction of the word "sale" in retail newspaper ads and also the word "wholesale." They note that the word "sale" can be used in compliance with FTC guidelines only if the reduced price is indeed for a "limited" selling period. As we shall see shortly in conjunction with "high-low" pricing, the FTC's vague prescription allows wide latitude. See R. Friedmann and P. Hains, An investigation of comparative price advertising and newspapers, *Journal of Current Issues and Research in Advertising,* 1991, *13* (1), pp. 155–173.

59. P. J. Kaufmann, G. Ortmeyer, and N. C. Smith, Deception in retail sale pricing, in G. Bamossy and W. F.

van Raaij, eds., *European Advances in Consumer Research,* 1993, *1,* pp. 345–351.

60. P. J. Kaufmann et al., same reference as previous note.

61. Always a slogan, *Marketing News,* June 20, 1994, p. 1.

62. From a content analysis of retail newspaper ads, Friedman and Hains found that about two-thirds of retailers stated price-offs in monetary terms whereas one-third used percentage statements. See R. Friedman and P. Hains, same reference as note 58.

63. A. Biswas and S. Burton, An experimental assessment of effects associated with alternative tensile price claims, *Journal of Business Research,* 1994, *29* (1), pp. 65–73. Biswas and Burton were careful not to overgeneralize the results of their study, and in an earlier study provide some evidence, and a very good discussion, of situations in which using a range of savings or even the minimum level of savings may be more effective for the retailer: a range of savings could be perceived as more honest if in fact very few items are offered at the maximum savings, and a minimum savings might be effective if the retailer were offering a very narrow range of savings with a low maximum. See A. Biswas and S. Burton, Consumer perceptions of tensile price claims in advertisements: An assessment of claim types across different discount levels, *Journal of the Academy of Marketing Science,* 1993, *21* (3), pp. 217–229.

64. R. M. Schindler, Symbolic meanings of a price ending, in R. H. Holman and M. R. Solomon, eds., *Advances in Consumer Research,* vol. 18, 1991, Provo, UT: Association for Consumer Research, pp. 794–801.

65. R. M. Schindler, A field test of the effects of price ending on sales, Working paper, School of Business, Rutgers University, Camden, NJ, 1989.

## DISCUSSION QUESTIONS

**13.1.** What career are you pursuing or going to pursue? For this career, design your ideal office. Use the four retail layout and atmosphere promotion factors discussed in the chapter, with any others you believe might be appropriate.

**13.2.** Summarize the pros and cons of price-off promotions from the manufacturer's and retailer's perspectives, respectively.

**13.1.** Consider the supermarket retailer's feature ad shown in the left panel of Figure 13.3. Based on the price-off implementation techniques discussed in the chapter, how might you improve the effectiveness of this ad?

**13.4.** Review and discuss the ethical implications of bait-and-switch advertising and high-low pricing.

**13.5.** What is your personal experience with TV or PC interactive shopping? For the industry that you are working in or expect to join in the future, do you believe interactive shopping will be a substantial distribution channel? Why or why not?

**13.6.** (This question is probably best done as a team project but could be completed individually with sufficient time.) Interview six or so different retailers competing in the same product category, such as supermarkets, with regard to their stocking policy and beliefs about the proportion of "loyal shoppers" and "price shoppers" in their drawing area. How have the retailers you interviewed tried to meet and balance these two segments' needs?

## FURTHER READING

Donovan, R. J., and Rossiter, J. R. Store atmosphere: An environmental psychology approach. *Journal of Retailing,* 1982, *58* (1), pp. 34–57; and Donovan, R. J., Rossiter, J. R., Marcoolyn, G., and Nesdale, A. Store atmosphere and purchasing behavior. *Journal of Retailing,* 1994, *70* (3), pp. 283–294.

The former article outlines the psychology of store (or place) atmosphere, showing how it can emotionally influence disposition to buy. The latter article documents effects in terms of extra sales.

Davis, J. The perils and pitfalls of the multimedia revolution. *Admap,* November 1994, pp. 27–29.

This article provides a caustic overview of TV and PC interactive services and their future outlook. Its author argues that the consumer has largely been ignored in the rush to develop technology, that countries' differences in required technical standards are going to be a big hindrance, and that most interactive services have so far underdelivered on expectations. With regard to the first point, critics are probably underestimating the bulge of computer literati coming through in the younger generations.

The *Journal of Retailing,* published by JAI Press Inc., Greenwich, CT. Retail marketing managers should find a subscription to this journal worthwhile. It presents current developments in retail marketing theory and research, and each article concludes with a management summary highlighting its practical implications.

# CHAPTER 14

# Direct Marketing Promotions

The ultimate promotion strategy that the manager can consider in the customer timeline of IMC activities is to "go direct" using database marketing and perhaps a loyalty program. Direct marketing is an appropriate channel for many companies (manufacturers *and* retailers). However, *database marketing* and *loyalty programs* are appropriate only under certain conditions that we identify in this chapter. Both are powerful, highly segmented, customer-oriented forms of promotion in the right circumstances. After reading this chapter, you should be able to:

- Ascertain whether database marketing is likely to be appropriate and profitable—for customer retention or purchase activation.
- Understand how to use the database most effectively.
- Decide whether to add a loyalty program.

Database marketing is a logical promotional extension of direct response advertising (see Figure 14.1) or direct (personal) selling. Database marketing can be used in its own right, without adding a loyalty program. Both database marketing and loyalty programs are activities designed to speed up sales in the direct marketing channel, and thus we refer to them as direct marketing *promotions.*

## DATABASE MARKETING

*Database marketing* can be defined as the practice of (1) compiling individual prospects' and customers' names and contact details (address, phone number, fax number, electronic mail address—depending on the planned method of future contact); (2) together with their individual purchase records (timing, monetary amount and, where appropriate, type of purchase or usage); and (3) using this information to retain the customer or activate the individual's purchase behavior.

Several operational comments are necessary regarding the three parts of this definition of database marketing.

First, the compilation of individual names and contact details is greatly aided by computerized recording. Although databases have existed successfully for years on file cards and other more primitive systems, computers make database usage much more efficient and effective. *Direct response advertising for new prospects* (see Chapter 10) and a *survey of current customers* (see below) are necessary prerequisites for establishing a database.

Second, for those marketers commencing a database for the first time, past purchase records of current customers, in terms of what they have purchased and when, can be compiled fairly accurately by conducting a customer-addressed *survey;* that is, you don't have to wait until the customer develops a *future* purchase record—unless, of course, you are launching a totally new product or service.[1]

Third, database information on individual prospects and customers and their purchase records can be used for retention *or* for activation. The distinction

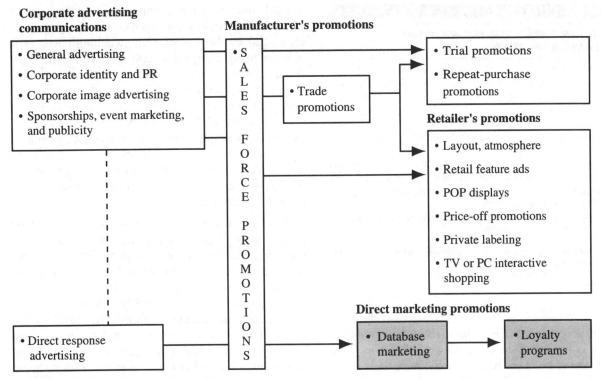

**FIGURE 14.1**
Direct marketing promotions (shaded boxes).

between retention and activation corresponds with whether the product or service is a "lost for good" (LFG) or "always a share" (AAS) type.[2]

- LFG products and services are those with a *long purchase cycle* and which the customer usually purchases from only *one* vendor when buying. Purchase and *renewal* of purchase are the main considerations, such that if a customer does not renew, he or she is essentially "lost for good." (*Examples:* insurance, magazine subscriptions, and purchases of automobiles and other consumer durables.)
- AAS products and services, on the other hand, are those that have the actuality or possibility of *frequent purchase transactions* for which the customer has a *number* of vendors to choose between when buying. Therefore, renewal of purchase is not so much a consideration as obtaining a good share of those transactions for your brand among competing brands or suppliers. (*Examples:* retail stores, airlines, hotels, restaurants, and other service establishments.)

As we shall see, database marketing can be used effectively in either application, although its implementation through *database usage* is very different in the two cases.

### When to Use Database Marketing

The cost of establishing and operating a database is substantial, and four essential conditions should be met before a marketer undertakes database marketing as a promotional activity. These conditions are summarized in Table 14.1 and explained next.

**1.** *Substantial Number.* There has to be a substantial number of actual or potential customers who are or could be made brand loyal (for LFG products and services) or whose activity rates could be increased (for AAS products and services). The quantification of "substantial number" will enter into the profitability estimation in condition 3, below. This first condition means that it could be worth operating a database program even in product categories characterized *overall* by a lack of brand loyalty or low activity rates. The

---

**TABLE 14.1**

**CONDITIONS ESSENTIAL FOR PROFITABLE
DATABASE MARKETING**

---

1. A *substantial number* of actual or potential brand loyal customers (for LFG products and services) or customers whose activity rates could be increased (for AAS products and services).
2. A *realistic chance* of reducing switching (for LFG products and services) or increasing activity (for AAS products and services).
3. The *expected profit* from database concentration on existing customers is higher than the profit expected from acquiring new customers without using a database, with normal customer turnover.
4. It will be *difficult for competitor(s)* to duplicate the program with *your* customers.

---

LFG = "lost for good" products and services, such as life insurance, consumer durables, and business contracts.
AAS = "always a share" products and services, such as airlines, hotels, and restaurants.

essential requirement is to have enough potential or active customers *from the total available pool* who are or could be brand loyal or could have their activity rates increased. Database marketing is then applied to this "preferred" or "high activity" subset of all buyers of your product or service.

An LFG category characterized by high rates of brand switching is, for example, athletic shoes. Yet Saucony has been able to find enough loyal users of the brand to put their information in a database and begin loyalty clubs—for walking shoes and running shoes, respectively—which saw Saucony's sales rise 50 percent in 1992 and a further 50 percent in the first part of 1993.[3]

An AAS category characterized by frequent transactions and weak loyalty is catalog buying through department stores. Yet Nieman-Marcus realized that there were *enough* highly loyal Nieman-Marcus catalog shoppers—or, at least, those who used the catalog often enough even if they were also loyal to one or two other department store catalogs (hence "always a share")—to offer its "In Circle" gift program in which chocolates and caviar are sent to its best customers. Reportedly, this databased loyalty program has increased the level of spending per customer and also improved long-term retention of customers.[4]

For LFG products and services, it should be noted (as suggested by the cusp-catastrophe model discussed in Chapter 12, chapter appendix 12D) that

brand loyalty, where the brand could be the supplier or a brand offered by the supplier, may be *negatively* reinforced by the fear of high switching costs, as is true for many consumers with their personal GP or physician—or *positively* reinforced by a beneficial "relationship," as is preached by most business marketing consultants nowadays. For AAS products and services, however, brand loyalty is usually motivated by relatively simple positive reinforcement, as in mail order or credit card buying of products and services that the customer wants. No matter what the source of loyalty, database marketing is still appropriate if there are enough loyal customers.

**2.** *Realistic Chance.* There has to be a realistic chance (a good probability) of reducing customers' switching activity, in the case of LFG products and services, or increasing their purchase activity, in the case of AAS products and services.

For instance, consider an LFG category such as home loans (mortgages). You might be "loyal" to the financial institution to which you have your home mortgaged. But would it be worthwhile for the financial institution to use database marketing for its home loan customers? Realistically, in this LFG category, most customers will stay with the financial institution because of inertia or the fear of penalty fees for switching. And even if some customers switched when a significantly lower interest rate was offered by a competing financial institution, there is very little that the original institution could do, or could have done, about this through database marketing. (However, given our earlier illustrations of the power of after-sales service, perhaps we shouldn't underestimate the value of even an occasional "Thank you for being a customer" phone call, which would be a simple and inexpensive use of database marketing and may deter some would-be price switchers.)

Similarly, in many AAS categories, there would appear to be little chance of increasing repeat-purchase activity by using database marketing. For instance, freight shippers typically and deliberately maintain a "portfolio" of freight forwarders among whom they distribute their freight business. It is unlikely that any one freight forwarder could realize a significant increase in business from a shipper by using database marketing.

Most frequently purchased consumer packaged goods fall into this category as well: there seems little sense in setting up elaborate databases for marketing purposes. For instance, Pepsi-Cola has reportedly established a database of 30 million cola drinkers in the United States, but what are the chances of the company being able to increase these individuals' purchase rates of Pepsi-Cola in the long term through database marketing? Very slim, we would predict, other than by bribing brand switchers with an endless and costly series of short-term promotions. And for loyal Pepsi buyers, there is little chance that they could be induced to become even more loyal by drinking more Pepsi per capita per day! A database marketing excercise for this type of product seems misguided.

However, *retailers* of fmcg products may well meet the realistic-chance condition for the *store's* customers—that is, across all manufacturers' products that they offer.

**3.** *Expected Profit.* Before engaging in database marketing, the marketer has to make a careful calculation to be reasonably sure that the expected profit from concentrating on existing customers (the normal database application despite its occasional use for "conquest" strategies to attract new customers) will be greater than the profit received from the "status quo" strategy—which, for most companies, is the strategy of acquiring new customers through market penetration without using a database and with normal customer turnover. Much touted in the popular marketing literature these days is the axiom that it costs five or ten or more (we have even seen the words "infinitely more") times as much to acquire a new customer as it does to retain a current one. The five-times-more figure may be true for many industrial products and consumer durables. But it is patently *untrue* for most consumer packaged goods. How much does it cost to acquire a Pepsi customer, for instance? Almost nothing, we would venture. The "cost per thousand" for advertising that may have induced the customer's initial trial of Pepsi would be about $45 for five prime-time TV exposures, so the cost per individual customer would be less than 5 cents. Also, we saw in Chapter 5 in conjunction with Ehrenberg's work that, for packaged goods, market penetration, not repeat purchase, is the most important objective.

Later in this chapter, we will present some mathematical formulas for calculating the expected profit from concentrating on the future or "lifetime" value of existing customers as compared with acquiring new customers. This calculation *must* be made. It can-

not simply be assumed that a concentration on repeat purchase is more profitable than a concentration on trial purchase with normal repeat rates. Database marketing, which mainly concentrates on repeat purchase, is suited to particular types of products and services only.

**4.** *Difficult for Competitors.* A database marketing program, if it is to be profitable in the long run, must be difficult for competitors to duplicate with *your* customers. The predicted failure of airline's frequent-flier programs, for example, is almost entirely due to the fact that it is very easy for competitors to duplicate them on the same customer base. Competing frequent-flier programs cannibalize each other's customers to every airline's detriment. On the other hand, a quiet and concentrated database marketing program for your own customers, such as those practiced by Saucony and Nieman-Marcus, is unlikely to attract competitive duplication.

However, even when duplication is present, most database marketing programs are executed so haphazardly that there is room for an astute database marketer to "do it better" than the competitors. For instance, in the authors' experience, several catalog marketers are much better than others in that they obviously *use* their database to the fullest by knowing which styles of products in their lines their customers are most interested in and when they are most likely to be "in the market" for repeat purchasing. Moreover, their database marketing efforts are usually accompanied by superior *advertising* in conjunction with better use of database marketing.

**Privacy Concerns.** The future of database marketing as a promotional activity is difficult to predict. There are two countervailing forces. On the positive side, there is the ever-increasing sophistication of technology, including analysis programs, which makes it much easier and more economical to practice database marketing.[5] On the negative side, there are increasing concerns about the invasion or loss of *privacy* in companies' acquisition and use of personal information about us.

As to these privacy concerns, one person's *Brave New World* is another's *1984*. Consider the following statement from Kevin Randolph, a marketing manager for the US WEST chain of hotels: "In [US WEST] hotels in San Francisco, when you turn on your TV to watch a movie, you now have the opportunity to 'walk through' San Francisco with your remote control. And we track every button press that you do, every instance that you do it throughout the time that you are on that television. So we know exactly where you came from, how long you did whatever you did or watched an ad, or selected a piece of information, and exactly where you went afterwards. We can monitor the transactions that occurred. Soon, we'll add transaction capabilities to that as well, so consumers will be able to buy products from their hotel."[6] To many, this is a horrifying scenario: Big Brother does exist, and he is watching us. Others, however, will welcome the utopian opportunity to do their shopping without leaving the hotel room. The future of database marketing will probably depend on the relative proportions of these two opposed consumer segments.

A similar scenario, offered somewhat tongue-in-cheek, is described by Barry Cook, a senior VP and chief research officer of Nielsen Media Research: "After a hard day at work, where your income is tracked and fed into the hypertargeting database, you drive home. The route you take, including the stores you pass, is captured from the homing signals of your car phone. Home at last, you have a great dinner, prepared with food that has been scanned at the checkout counter (along with the coupons your husband used when he bought them), and linked to your infoaccount because he charged the groceries on a credit card. . . . Your TV has everything you could possibly want to see, when you want to see it, and it is absolutely free as long as you answer the simple questions at the end of each commercial. The commercials aren't that bad; actually they're all pretty interesting because they are selected especially for you. The hypertargeting database takes the information about how much money you have left, what you purchase, and what you watch. Each time you watch, no matter what it is, the commercials that fit your needs and abilities to pay are custom-fed into the programs you select."[7] As Cook adds, the technology to accomplish this scenario exists right now.

Advocates of database marketing point out the self-selection "safeguard": if you don't want to participate, you don't have to. As we mentioned earlier, most industry bodies have mechanisms whereby you can remove your name from mail or telephone databases. You can, of course, also contact the company directly and ask that your name (and address) be removed from its list—or that it not be sold to other

companies. Through these procedures, consumers should be able to receive only what they want to receive. However, the "spying" aspect or capability of databases bothers a lot of people and is worrisome to governments in many countries. Petrison and her colleagues,[8] for instance, observe that many European countries have already enacted highly restrictive laws that limit the ability of direct marketers, and particularly database marketers, to do business there. A related privacy concern is the sale of the personal information you have provided to one company (or government organization), to another. In response to this concern, a number of U.S. states have begun to consider laws restricting the dissemination of information about credit, auto registrations, and other financial data.

**Within-Company Use of Data Is Okay.** There is, however, nothing unethical about companies collecting and monitoring data that customers would expect the company to have—notably, their name, contact details, and purchase record *with that company*. There is much that can be effectively done by way of database marketing with this relatively straightforward information, as we shall see in the next section.

### Database Usage

As suggested by the condition of expected profitability, in order for database marketing to be successful, the database must be *used* effectively rather than simply being compiled. Mathematical calculations are necessary here: there is one formula for the case of LFG products and services, and another for the case of AAS products and services.

**"Lifetime Value" Calculation for LFG Products and Services.** Lifetime value (LTV) calculations are basically of the form:

$$\text{LTV} = (\text{yearly revenue} - \text{yearly expenses} \\ \text{and service costs}) \times \text{number of years} \\ \text{retained} - \text{acquisition cost}$$

Whereas particular industries can devise more specific formulas to reflect the particular nature of revenue and costs in their industry—such as revenue increases over the years due to premium pricing and referrals, and cost decreases due to reduced operating costs or other economies of scale—most are variations on this basic formula.[9] The manager has to make LTV calculations specifically for his or her company and individual products or services.

Some indicative LTV figures have been published. Clancy and Shulman,[10] in an analysis of a U.S. bank's credit card customers, calculated that the acquisition cost for obtaining a new credit card customer was approximately $100. By the time the credit card customer had remained with the bank for 5 years, the average yearly profit from that customer was $100. After 10 years, the average yearly profit was $300, because longer-term customers tended to be stable, high-spending customers with lower operating costs to service each year. Given that LFG product and service marketers are concerned with customer retention, Reichheld and Sasser[11] estimate that just a 5 percent reduction in customer defection produces, over the average customer life of the retained customer for various industries, LTV increments (that is, profit increases) as follows: credit insurance, 25 percent; auto-service establishments, 30 percent; computer software, 35 percent; office building management, 40 percent; industrial distribution, 45 percent; insurance brokerage, 50 percent; credit card companies, 75 percent; and bank branch deposits, 85 percent. These are impressive figures, and a 5 percent reduction in defection (equivalent to a 5 percent increase in customer retention) seems a reasonable target for database marketing as a promotion activity. Once more, however, the manager must do these calculations for his or her particular company and be assured that the cost and revenue-flow estimates are accurate.

**Defection Prevention.** Careful analysis of the database can reveal when customers are most likely to defect. For annually renewable contracts, of course, the critical defection time is just prior to renewal, although this may be too late for a last-minute effort to retain the customer. Household insurance and industrial contracts would be examples, although more and more of these contracts are breakable before the annual renewal date with only a slight penalty. For other products and services, such as auto-repair services or banks, the customer can defect at any time, but analysis of defection times may still reveal a pattern. For instance, the U.S. company Weight Watchers knows from its database records that new customers are most likely to leave the program during the third, fifth, and eighth weeks after signing on. Accordingly, the company sends mailings (a loyalty program) timed to arrive in those weeks with relevant gifts such as sweatshirts and beach towels, and discount coupons for the next few visits.[12]

Note also that database marketing can be used as a promotional activity without necessarily offering a loyalty program; for instance, a reassuring phone call at the critical defection times may be quite effective in retaining customers at lower cost.[13]

**"Reach-Frequency-Monetary Value" Calculation for AAS Products and Services.** A somewhat different formula for calculating financial profitability is appropriate for AAS or "customer activity" products and services such as retail store patronage and catalog and direct mail purchases. This is the reach-frequency-monetary value (RFM) formula, the first version of which was developed in the 1920s by Alden Catalog Company and is still used by many companies today.[14] The basic version of the formula is as follows:

$$\text{Total profit} = \text{reach (the number of customers)} \times \\ \text{average frequency of purchases in a given period} \times \\ \text{average monetary value of purchases in the period} - \\ \text{promotion costs}$$

(By subtracting customer acquisition costs, for those industries where acquisition costs are substantial, this formula can be easily combined with the LTV formula. In many AAS businesses, however, such as mail order and retail stores, the acquisition cost is minimal.)

*The Importance of Purchase Timing.* Sophisticated versions of the RFM formula have been introduced by Schmittlein and Morrison,[15] which take into account the *timing* of purchases as well as the frequency of purchases in a given period. Their formulas can accommodate a range of monetary values, when expenditures differ greatly, or can assume monetary value to have a constant average level per purchase. The focus of their formulas is on estimating the *probability* that the customer will *repeat purchase* from the company, that is, the probability that the customer is still "active" and will make purchases in the future. Their formula is extremely simple:

$$p(\text{Active}) = t^n$$

where $p(\text{Active})$ is the probability that the customer will make another purchase and is still indeed a customer, $t$ is the time interval between the beginning of the analysis period and the time of the most recent purchase (expressed as a decimal fraction of the total analysis period), and $n$ is the number of purchases made in the analysis period. The analysis period is usually the calendar or fiscal year, although a longer period should be used for AAS categories that involve less frequent purchases.

This simple but very valuable formula leads to some important nonintuitive results, as shown in Figure 14.2. The upper panel of the figure shows two hypothetical customers, A and B, each of whom has made four purchases, but the time of the most recent purchase varies. The value of t for customer A is .9, indicating that this customer made his or her most recent purchase approximately 10.8 months into the year, that is, $.9 \times 12 = 10.8$ months. Customer B, on the other hand, made his or her last purchase 3.6 months into the year, for a t value of .3. Although they have both made an equal number of purchases over the year, customer A turns out to be the far more active customer and much more likely to make a further purchase from the company. This can be seen by calculating the value of p(Active) which is .656 for customer A and only .008 for customer B. The likelihood is, of course, that customer B has for some reason met his or her requirements or become dissatisfied with the company, not having made a purchase for over 8 months, and has probably defected. The lower panel of the figure shows two other hypothetical customers for whom the time interval is equal but the number of purchases, n, varies. Customers C and D have both made their most recent purchase 6 months ago, or 6 months af-

ter the start of the year. However, customer C made six purchases in the first 6 months whereas customer D made only two purchases in the first 6 months. Who is likely to be the more active customer? Intuition suggests that customer C would have a higher probability of being active because of the larger number of purchases made. However, the formula predicts that customer D is more likely to still be an active customer. The p(Active) for customer C is $.5^6 = .016$, whereas the p(Active) for customer D is $.5^2 = .250$. The likely explanation is that customer D is simply a slower, but nevertheless more regular, customer whereas customer C is likely to have defected after a burst of activity.

When the *monetary value* of purchases varies substantially, as with catalog purchases and credit card purchases, a useful version[16] of the RFM formula is:

$$p(\text{Repeat}) = (F + 1)\,(R^{-1})\,[(M + 1)^r]$$

where F is the number (frequency) of purchases made in the past 12 months, with 1 added in case the first purchase occurred more than 12 months ago, to keep the result from zeroing out; R is the time in months since the most recent purchase and thus $R^{-1}$ or 1/R indicates recency; M is monetary value in terms of the total *net* dollars from the customer *ever*, with 1 added to allow for the fact that a customer who buys then returns an item still has an above-zero probability of repeating; and r is a power parameter to be estimated

**FIGURE 14.2**

Illustrations of the basic Schmittlein-Morrison active customer formula: p(Active) = $t^n$. (See text and note 15.) Purchases denoted by asterisks (∗).

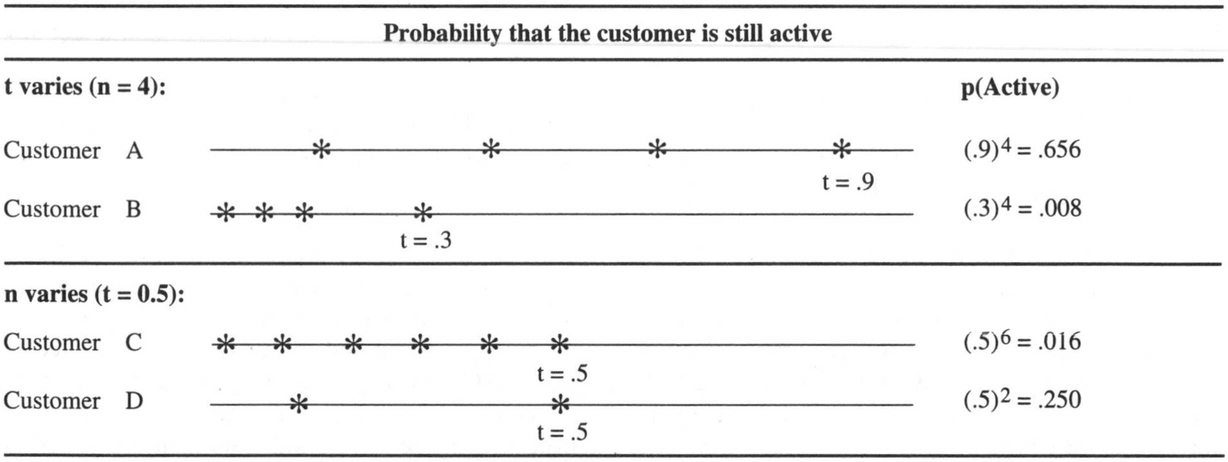

| Probability that the customer is still active | | |
|---|---|---|
| **t varies (n = 4):** | | **p(Active)** |
| Customer  A  —————∗—————∗—————∗—————∗———  t = .9 | | $(.9)^4 = .656$ |
| Customer  B  ∗–∗–∗————∗————————  t = .3 | | $(.3)^4 = .008$ |
| **n varies (t = 0.5):** | | |
| Customer  C  ∗—∗—∗—∗—∗—∗——————  t = .5 | | $(.5)^6 = .016$ |
| Customer  D  ————∗————————∗————  t = .5 | | $(.5)^2 = .250$ |

from previous data, which varies between zero and 1 such that r = 1 means that a large recent purchase usually results in a long delay before the next purchase. For instance, a book or CD club would usually have a *low* r value due to the small size of the purchase and short interval to the next one, whereas auto servicing would have a fairly high r value as the service usually lasts a while.

*Customer Migration Objective.* Using the "reach" variable of the RFM formula, customers can be segmented into "migration cells" for database marketing action. Direct marketing consultant Graeme McCorkell[17] provides a useful sequence of classifications for the list of respondents, which we have modified slightly. These are shown in Table 14.2. Going from the least to the most important, first there are "suspects"—from whom no response has been obtained, yet their names still appear on the list. After several abortive mailings or one or two unsuccessful telephone sales attempts over the course of a year, these names should be deleted from the list. Second, there are "prospects"—those who have made an inquiry only. Third, there are "trialists"—those who have bought once from the company, recently. Fourth, there are "lapsed buyers"—those who have bought more than once but not for a long time. Fifth, there are "regular buyers"—those who have bought several times or at least more than once, including recently. Finally, there are "advocates"—regular buyers who introduce other trialists to the company. The objective is to try to move as many people from the first classification through to the sixth.

Expected profit values can be calculated for trialists, lapsed buyers, regular buyers, and advocates. The objective is to try to "migrate" customers forward into the last two, most profitable classifications—which then suggest the type of marketing effort that is required. For example, customers B and C from Figure 14.2, who appear to be "lapsed" customers, could be sent an especially attractive promotion to try to bring them back into active status. To save money, only lapsed customers would receive the mailing (this illustrates the selectivity enabled by the database). Customers A and D, on the other hand, who appear to be reasonably active, could continue to receive regular marketing efforts.

Segmentation of the databased customer list can be accomplished to a very fine degree using regression analysis, particularly log-linear (Logit or Probit) re-

### TABLE 14.2

**CLASSIFICATION OF DIRECT RESPONSE PROSPECTS IN DATABASE**

1. Suspects (no response)
2. Prospects (inquiry only)
3. Trialists (one purchase, recently)
4. Lapsed buyers
5. Regular buyers
6. Advocates (regular buyers who introduce trialists)

gression.[18] For instance, OBSs or OBLs can be identified (if you have competitive purchase data) for "conquest" marketing, or FBSs or BLs can be identified for loyalty programs—to which we now turn our attention.

## LOYALTY PROGRAMS

*Loyalty programs* refer to *incentive-based* promotion activities intended to increase *long-term* repeat-purchase behavior *above* the level that would occur with intrinsic product or service satisfaction. Loyalty programs are distinguished from repeat-purchase promotions, as defined in Chapter 12, in that the focus of the former is long term whereas the focus of the latter is on just the next purchase or two. They are further distinguished from "extra service" used as a repeat-purchase promotion, also defined in Chapter 12, in that extra service does not require or entail an incentive (a reward), whereas loyalty programs invariably do.

### When to Add a Loyalty Program

The classification drawn from the bargaining and negotiation literature by Dabholkar, Johnston, and Cathey[19] shows the two main situations in which it is appropriate to use a loyalty program in addition to database marketing. They classify seller-buyer interactions into four categories based on time perspective and gain perspective (Figure 14.3).

Two situations are short term from both the buyer's and the seller's perspective and would therefore *not* be appropriate for a loyalty program. The first of these, *competitive* behavior, characterizes *short-term* buying situations in which the seller and the buyer are each trying to maximize their *individual* gains. The great majority of retail shopping, as at supermarkets or self-service department stores, falls into this

| Gain perspective | Time perspective | |
|---|---|---|
| | Short term | Long term |
| Individual | **Competitive** | **Command** |
| Joint | **Cooperative** | **Coordinative** |

**FIGURE 14.3**
Classification of seller-buyer interactions by time perspective and gain perspective (see Dabholkar, Johnston and Cathey, 1994, note 19). Loyalty programs are best used in the two long-term situations.

category; both the seller and the buyer are out to get the best price at the time. Hence we do not in general recommend (either database marketing or) loyalty programs for fast-moving consumer goods or for self-service retailers. The second short-term classification, *cooperative* behavior, which occurs less often, characterizes *short-term* buying situations in which the seller and the buyer wish to maximize their *joint* gain. Obviously, the card game of bridge from the partners' perspective offers an exact analogy, but occurrences in industrial or consumer behavior are relatively infrequent. Selling a house would perhaps be an example. A good deal of other "cooperative" behavior, such as price fixing *between sellers,* is illegal. Because of the short-term perspective, loyalty programs are not appropriate for cooperative marketing situations, noting here that "cooperative" does not mean "coordinative," a classification discussed as long-term, next.

The two *long-term* categories identified by Dabholkar, Johnston, and Cathey (again, see Figure 14.3) represent the best possibilities for loyalty programs. And, as we will explain, the appropriate loyalty programs themselves clearly fall into two categories, price-oriented and relationship-oriented loyalty programs.

**Command Behavior: Price-Oriented Loyalty Programs.** *Command* behavior characterizes *long-term* buying situations in which the seller and the buyer are each trying to maximize their *individual* gains. The long-term perspective is usually forced on these situations by moderate to high switching costs

for the customer, such as in the businesses of banking and insurance, and in consumer choices of professionals such as doctors, dentists, and accountants. Although switching is possible, it is unlikely to occur unless the negative deviations from expected product delivery or service performance become extreme (see Chapter 12's cusp-catastrophe model in chapter appendix 12D). The seller, within these limits, is clearly in command—hence the name.

In command situations, the type of loyalty program that is most likely to be successful is almost certainly *price-oriented.* Thus, for instance, bank customers with high average balances typically receive a waiver of transaction fees or other monetary rewards; insurance company customers with no claims for a given period are typically rewarded with a reduction in their premiums; and service professionals may offer a quantity discount for customers who agree to undertake a long or substantial program of treatment or consultancy. In this sense, loyalty programs in command situations are simply *an extension of repeat-purchase price promotions* with the difference being that the focus is long term.

One of the largest price-oriented loyalty programs is offered through General Motors' GM Card, introduced in 1992 in the United States and now available in the United Kingdom and Australia as well. The GM card enables cardholders, and members of their families, to earn discounts (refunds or rebates) of up to $3,000 on a new GM car over a 5-year period by crediting them with 5 percent of the value of all retail purchases made using the card. About 10 million car buyers have signed up for the GM card in the United States, which is about one in 10 households! As cardholders enter GM's database, the prospective scenario is that the manufacturer will be able to sell cars to program members direct, thus bypassing the dealer and saving on the dealer's margin.[20] There is also, as explained next, an opportunity for GM to move from a command situation to a coordinative situation by anticipating the future car-buying needs of its data-based customers.

**Coordinative Behavior: Personal Relationship Maintenance and Evolutionary Database Loyalty Programs.** The other long-term classification, *coordinative* behavior, characterizes *long-term* buying situations in which the seller and the buyer wish to maximize their *joint* gain. Maximization of long-term joint gain is, of course, the ideal referred to in the concept of "relationship marketing." A good deal of lip service is paid to this concept (it *sounds* ideal, for everybody), but how can it be accomplished? If we exclude the practice of continually "buying" your way into a long-term relationship, as in the command situation, what other types of marketing techniques might be applicable? We have been able to identify just two: personal relationship maintenance (applicable only in long-term buying situations with a high personal service component) and evolutionary database marketing (applicable where customers' needs change according to the customer's product category–related lifecycle). These relationship activities may be implemented separately or, in appropriate industries, together.

*Personal relationship maintenance* is the technique of making an extraordinary effort to retain and reward those *employees* who are the preferred contacts of target customers. This has long been the practice in the advertising agency business, for instance, but it is profitably applicable in other industries where most customers prefer to deal with someone they know. A good example is the personal relationship maintenance strategy implemented by State Farm Insurance Company, as described by Reichheld.[21] In the first place, State Farm recognizes the lifetime value of insurance customers by paying its agents the *same* commission on *renewals* (even though these are supposed to be "easy") as it does for obtaining new business (which is supposed to be "difficult"). State Farm's agents are very loyal employees, with a 13-year average tenure compared with the 7 or 8 years that is average for the life insurance industry. This means that customers are more likely to be able to deal with their preferred agent for a longer period. In turn, this is reflected in State Farm's extremely high customer retention rate of 90 percent, which is far above the industry average. With more customers retained for longer periods, State Farm's service costs are about 10 percent lower than the industry average, and it is reportedly the most profitable insurance company in the United States.

*Evolutionary database marketing* is a technique applicable in those industries where the customer's product category needs change over life stages or over a learning cycle. These changes are quite easily signaled via the database, so astute companies can anticipate them and alter their product and service offerings to fit the evolution as it occurs. For instance, State Farm agents, as their customers get older, are alert to the typical sequence of insurance needs evolving from needing car insurance to needing homeowner's insurance to needing term life insurance to cover a family during critical early- and middle-life stages, to needing retirement investment products. According to another example provided by Reichheld,[22] Honda Motor Company is a successful practitioner of evolutionary database marketing. By being alert to customer life stages from its database of initial buyers, Honda judiciously suggests trading up from, for example, the subcompact Civic, to the compact Accord, to the Accord wagon as the customer's family needs mature. Honda has been rewarded with a repeat-purchase rate of 65 percent compared with the industry average for automobile companies of only 40 percent.

In other industries, the evolutionary stages may reflect a learning cycle rather than an aging cycle. Computers and software would be evident examples, as might customers' use of market research techniques. With long-term customers who are keen to learn, coordinative—that is, loyal—behavior can be fostered through the use of evolutionary database marketing.

## SUMMARY

Direct marketing promotions, by definition, require direct marketing to have been selected as a distribution channel by the manufacturer or retailer—meaning that direct marketing promotions follow direct response advertising or direct (personal) selling. The two main direct marketing promotional activities are database marketing and loyalty programs.

Database marketing and loyalty programs are promotion activities that take a *long-term* view of repeat purchase. It is important to realize that they can be used separately or together.

*Database marketing* requires four conditions to be met before it is worth using: (1) there has to be a substantial number of customers whose loyalty to the supplier or brand could be increased, or whose purchase activity rates could be increased for frequently purchased products and services; (2) there has to be a realistic chance of reducing these customers' switching activity or increasing their purchase activity; (3) the expected profit from concentrating on these existing customers, rather than on acquiring new ones with normal repeat-purchase and turnover rates, has to be demonstrated to be higher; and (4) it has to be difficult for competitors to duplicate the program with *your* customers. These four conditions eliminate most consumer packaged goods manufacturers from using database marketing (however, fmcg *retailers* might use it for the *store's* customers). Also, in some states and in some countries, privacy concerns regarding the use and dissemination of information obtained on databases severely restrict this form of marketing.

For database marketing to be used effectively, the manager must be prepared to calculate *customer lifetime value* for so-called "lost for good" products or services, and *reach-frequency-monetary value* for so-called "always a share" products and services. With the latter type of product or service, which relies on customer activity, the marketer's objective is to "migrate" customers, via database marketing, from nonresponse to frequent response, by using different incentives at each stage and very carefully monitoring the timing and progression of contacts.

*Loyalty* marketing is aimed at increasing the *long-term* repeat-purchase rate and is essentially an extension of repeat-purchase promotions (see Chapter 12). It is a suitable promotional activity only when the customer is prepared to take a long-term perspective, which can happen in command buying situations and in coordinative buying situations.

In *command* situations, both the buyer and the seller take a long-term view, but each is out to maximize their *individual* gains. In command situations, *price incentives* form the basis of the loyalty program.

In *coordinative* situations, both the buyer and the seller take a long-term view, but they can benefit from trying to maximize their *joint* gain. In coordinative situations, loyalty marketing is best implemented by *personal relationship maintenance* (in which the seller retains its own employees longer and rewards them for maintaining their customers) or, when customers' needs change over life stages or over a learning cycle, *evolutionary database marketing* (where the database is used to upgrade customers "when they are ready" and thereby increase their long-term loyalty). In the latter type of buying situation, the two relationship activities can be implemented together.

## NOTES

1. F. R. Dwyer, Customer lifetime valuation to support marketing decision making, *Journal of Direct Marketing,* 1989, *3* (4), pp. 8–15.

2. B. B. Jackson, *Winning and Keeping Industrial Customers,* Lexington, MA: D.C. Heath and Company, 1985; also B. B. Jackson, Build customer relationships that last, *Harvard Business Review,* 1985, *85* (6), pp. 120–128.

3. S. Rapp, Define the market and win, *Marketing* (UK), July 8, 1993, p. 16.

4. B. Carroll, Developments in the technology and practice of target marketing consumers in North America, *Journal of Targeting, Measurement and Analysis for Marketing,* 1992, *1* (1), pp. 107–112.

5. The technological advancements in database marketing over the last 50 years or so are very well documented in L. A. Petrison, R. C. Blattberg, and P. Wang, Database marketing: Past, present, and future, *Journal of Direct Marketing,* 1993, *7* (3), pp. 27–43.

6. K. Randolph, US WEST, in *Marketing Communication Strategies Today and Tomorrow: Integration, Allocation, and Interactive Technologies,* MSI Report No. 94-109, Cambridge, MA: Marketing Science Institute, 1994, pp. 49–50.

7. Cited in J. Honomichl, "Hypertargeting" scenario not as farfetched as it seems, *Marketing News,* November 9, 1992, pp. 11–12.

8. L. A. Petrison et al., same reference as note 5.

9. See M. L. Roberts and P. D. Burger, 1989, same reference as in Chapter 10's Further Reading, for further details of revenue and cost components in LTV formulas.

10. K. J. Clancy and R. S. Shulman, *The Marketing Revolution: A Radical Manifesto for Dominating the Marketplace,* New York: Harper Business, 1991.

11. F. F. Reichheld and W. E. Sasser, Jr., Zero defections: Quality comes to services, *Harvard Business Review,* 1990, *68* (5), pp. 105–111.

12. International dm roundup, excerpted from *Marketing Globe's Newsletter, Marketing* (Australia), March 1994, p. 56.

13. A Markov chain model has been developed for predicting the profitability of the best retail customers at Merrill Lynch stockbrokerage company, for instance. The Markov chain shows how customers "migrate" into various states of activity and calculates the probability with which they will do so. See D. G. Morrison, R. D. H. Chen, S. L. Karpis, and K. E. A. Britney, Modeling retail customer behavior at Merrill Lynch, *Marketing Science,* 1982, *1* (2), pp. 123–141.

14. L. A. Petrison et al., same reference as note 5.

15. The t$^n$ formula comes from D. C. Schmittlein and D. G. Morrison, Is the customer still active? *The*

*American Statistician,* 1985, *39* (4, part 1), pp. 291–295. Statistically advanced readers are also advised to consult the most recent developments in the "active customer" model, using an NBD (Negative Binomial Distribution) approach, described in D. C. Schmittlein and R.A. Peterson, Customer base analysis: An industrial purchase process application, *Marketing Science,* 1994, *13* (1), pp. 41–67.

16. We obtained this version of the formula from an anonymous paper reviewed for a journal and would like to thank the authors.
17. G. McCorkell, *Advertising That Pulls Response,* London: McGraw-Hill, 1990.
18. Regression techniques for database marketing are well introduced by E. L. Nash, *Database Marketing: The Ultimate Marketing Tool,* New York: McGraw-Hill, 1993, chapters 12 and 13.
19. P. A. Dabholkar, W. J. Johnston, and A.S. Cathey, The dynamics of long-term business-to-business exchange relationships, *Journal of the Academy of Marketing Science,* 1994, *22* (2), pp. 130–145.
20. M. Kable, GM card sets scene for car retail shake-up, *The Australian,* July 10, 1995, p. 19.
21. F. F. Reichheld, Loyalty-based management, *Harvard Business Review,* 1993, *71* (2), pp. 64–73.
22. F. F. Reichheld, same reference as previous note.

## DISCUSSION QUESTIONS

**14.1.** What is database marketing, and for what types of businesses is it appropriate? What does the manager have to do to make it successful? What potential ethical problems exist with its use?

**14.2.** What is the basic difference between a postpurchase promotion and a loyalty program? For what types of products or services are loyalty programs most appropriate, and what types of loyalty programs should be used?

## FURTHER READING

Petrison, L. A., Blattberg, R. C., and Wang, P. Database marketing: Past, present, and future. *Journal of Direct Marketing,* 1993, *7* (3), pp. 27–43.

This article provides an assiduously researched and highly informative review of the history of direct marketing and database marketing. It traces the evolution of direct mail into modern-day database marketing, as well as the technological innovations that accompanied that evolution. It also offers thoughtful speculations about ethical issues and the future acceptance of database marketing in other countries with strong concerns about privacy.

Nash, E. L. *Database Marketing: The Ultimate Marketing Tool.* New York: McGraw-Hill, 1993.

This is a recommended how-to book for would-be database marketers. It provides an excellent introduction to mathematical calculations for using the database.

Jackson, B. B. Build customer relationships that last. *Harvard Business Review,* November/December, 1985, *85* (6), pp. 120–128.

Despite its advocacy-sounding title, Jackson's article is actually an objective analysis of the types of businesses for which relationship marketing is likely to work. It introduces the valuable distinction between lost-for-good (LFG) products and services and always-a-share (AAS) products and services which, we have seen, require different database marketing approaches.

Uncles, M. Do you or your customers need a loyalty scheme? *Journal of Targeting, Measurement and Analysis for Marketing,* 1994, *2* (4), pp. 335–350.

This article argues that loyalty programs are by no means universally suitable for all marketers. It also identifies some of the conditions that favor the implementation of a loyalty program.

Deighton, J. The future of the marketing communications industry: Implications of integration and interactivity. In *Marketing Communications Strategies Today and Tomorrow: Integration, Allocation, and Interactive Technologies.* MSI Report No. 94-109. Cambridge, MA: Marketing Science Institute, 1994, pp. 40–43.

This article provides an insightful view of where IMC is headed from the supplier standpoint of advertising agencies, clients, the media, and promotion specialists. It predicts that access to, and computerized control of, customer databases will be the key factor; that the dominance of advertising agencies and the media, and to some extent manufacturers themselves, will be diminished; and that IMC control will move toward new organizations of two types: information intermediaries and affinity marketers. This author assumes no or minimal privacy legislation.

# MEDIA STRATEGY

**CHAPTER 15: ADVERTISING AND IMC MEDIA SELECTION**

**CHAPTER 16: MEDIA STRATEGY: THE REACH PATTERN AND EFFECTIVE FREQUENCY**

**CHAPTER 17: MEDIA PLAN IMPLEMENTATION**

# Advertising and IMC Media Selection

The chapters in Part Six examine media planning for advertising and for IMC media when using promotion. On average, over 90 percent of the total advertising budget is spent in media, with the balance going to advertising research and the production of the ads and promotions themselves. So, monetarily at least, media planning is the most important part of advertising and promotion.

Media *strategy* comprises two main decisions: "where," or in which media, to advertise (media selection); and "how often" to expose the advertising to the target audience (media scheduling). In this chapter, we examine the manager's broad options for media selection—the question being: Which media *types* have the capacity to deliver the communication objectives for the brand? Having narrowed down the media types to those suitable for a particular campaign, we then consider media strategy *proper* in Chapter 16. We will see that media strategy is essentially a matter of deciding on the reach pattern for the campaign and estimating the effective frequency level to be delivered during it. In Chapter 17, we will show how to *implement* the media plan, which includes the selection of particular vehicles and advertising units that make up an actual media schedule. After reading this chapter, you should:

- See how media selection must be based on the communication objectives of the campaign.

- Understand the concepts of primary and secondary media for a campaign.
- Know which primary and secondary (often IMC) media are most suitable for different types of advertising communications and promotions.

The reader may need to consult a media planning workbook or other specialized sources if his or her interest is in *buying* media. Here, we'll concentrate on the more *strategic* aspects of media selection.

## MEDIA SELECTION BASED ON COMMUNICATION OBJECTIVES

Media are the means of delivering the creative message (to the target audience) to thereby achieve the communication objectives of the campaign. The basic requirement of media selection is *capacity:* the medium or media selected must be able to convey the creative content of the campaign in a way that meets the communication objectives. As we have seen in Part Three, there are two universal communication objectives: brand awareness and brand attitude. We will see that the creative content and also the frequency tactics for these two communication objectives (discussed in Part Four, on creative strategy) largely dictate media selection. Like creative strategy, media strategy must fit the brand's communication objectives.

First, we will consider *advertising* media selection—that is, the media used for mass media advertising, also known as mainstream advertising. Second, we will consider *IMC* media selection—that is, the media used for adlike communications and for promotions. The IMC media typically have a narrower reach in terms of the target audience and many are focused on direct-response action, but they still must be selected by their capacity to deliver the communication objectives for the brand.

### Advertising Media Selection Based on Brand Awareness and Brand Attitude

Table 15.1 is an advertising media selection table based on the creative content and frequency tactics for the two types of brand awareness (brand recognition and brand recall) and the four types of brand attitude strategy (low-involvement/informational, low-involvement/transformational, high-involvement/informational, and high-involvement/transformational). These communication objectives largely dictate media selection.

**Brand Recognition.** If the campaign's brand awareness communication objective is brand recognition, the creative content and frequency tactics are usually as follows:

1. *Visual* content to show the brand's package, store logo, or name for subsequent recognition.[1]
2. *Color* content to further aid recognition of the brand.
3. Relatively *brief processing time* is sufficient.
4. Relatively *low frequency* is sufficient.

Working down the column for brand recognition in the advertising media selection table, we see that television is a suitable medium; cable television is a suitable medium (as is *cinema,* which is not shown in the table but has been revived in the United States as a medium of advertising for 60-second up to 120-second *TV commercials* and is available in most other countries for TV commercials and printlike, voice-over *slide* ads); radio is not a suitable medium (for it cannot show visual content[2]); newspapers are limited (full 4-color advertising capacity is not always available); magazines are suitable; stationary outdoor advertisements and posters are suitable; and mobile outdoor advertisements and posters (where either the advertising vehicle or the target audience is moving relative to the other) are suitable.

Brand recognition requires visual, color media. Therefore, radio (definitely) and newspapers (probably, but it depends) are eliminated from consideration when brand recognition is the objective. Full

---

**TABLE 15.1**

**ADVERTISING MEDIA SELECTION BASED ON BRAND AWARENESS AND BRAND ATTITUDE**

| Mainstream advertising medium | Brand awareness | | Brand attitude | | | |
| --- | --- | --- | --- | --- | --- | --- |
| | Brand recognition | Brand recall | Low-involvement/ informational | Low-involvement/ transformational | High-involvement/ informational | High-involvement/ transformational |
| Television | YES | YES | YES | YES | No | YES |
| Cable television | YES | YES | YES | YES | YES | YES |
| Radio | No | YES | YES | Lim (vis) | No | Lim (vis) |
| Newspapers | Lim (c) | YES | YES | Lim (c) | YES | Lim (c) |
| Magazines | YES | Lim (f) | YES | Lim (f) | YES | YES |
| Outdoor (stationary) | YES | Lim (tf) | YES | Lim (tf) | Lim (tf) | YES |
| Outdoor (mobile) | YES | Lim (tf) | YES | Lim (tf) | Lim (pt) | YES |

YES = the medium is appropriate for the given objective or strategy
No = the medium is not appropriate
Lim = the medium may be appropriate but entails certain limitations
c = color limitation
f = frequency limitation
pt = processing time limitation
tf = travel frequency limitation
vis = visual limitation

color (4-color) ad reproduction in newspapers *can* now be very good, and newspapers *are* an option for brand recognition *if* good, reliable full color is available. One limitation is that not all newspapers, particularly suburban papers, offer 4-color ads other than as expensive special inserts. Another limitation is the variable quality of color *reproduction* in print runs in papers that do offer 4-color ads. Not only may color quality vary across ads in an issue but also from issue to issue (we have seen many instances of these variations since newspaper color ads became available). To use newspapers for color ads, the advertiser must be assured of good, reliable color.

**Brand Recall.** When the campaign's brand awareness communication objective is brand recall, the creative content and frequency tactics are usually as follows:

1. *Verbal* content (written or spoken words) to convey the brand name.
2. There is *no color* requirement.
3. Relatively *brief processing time* is sufficient.
4. *High frequency* within the purchase cycle is usually necessary to allow frequent repetition of the brand name–category need association.

Working down the column for brand recall in the advertising media selection table, we see that television is suitable; cable television is suitable; radio is suitable; newspapers are suitable; magazines are limited (they cannot provide sufficiently high frequency for short purchase cycles[3]); stationary outdoor advertisements and posters are limited (insufficient travel frequency); and mobile outdoor advertisements and posters are similarly limited (insufficient travel frequency). Note that for regular travelers (commuters or shoppers), outdoor ads and posters are an option as they can provide a high frequency of exposure to this subgroup of the target audience. However, outdoor ads and posters are very slow to deliver frequency to the rest of the population.

Brand recall requires verbal, high-frequency media that permit frequent repetition. Repetition for brand recall is necessary for new products, where a new brand name is being learned, and for established products, to protect against competitive brand recall. Unless the purchase cycle is very long, thus allowing the lower frequency media of magazines and outdoor

advertising to provide sufficient repetition, the main media for brand recall are television, cable television, radio, and (daily) newspapers.

**Both Types of Brand Awareness.** In the occasional event that *both* brand recognition *and* brand recall are required—such as for a new, planned- or considered-purchase brand that will be sold in a cluttered, multibrand retail display—the media selection table provides a "double knockout" function.

Because the campaign has to meet *both* brand recognition *and* brand recall media requirements—in other words, that there must be a "YES" in *both* of the brand awareness columns—we can see that the only suitable medium under normal circumstances will be *television,* including cable television.

Brand awareness is the first universal communication objective upon which media selection must be based. Brand *attitude* is the second universal communication objective; and its four *strategy* options further govern media selection, as indicated by the remaining four columns of the media selection table.

**Low-Involvement/Informational.** When the campaign's brand attitude objective is to be attained via a low-involvement/informational brand attitude strategy, the creative content and frequency tactics are usually as follows:

1. *Verbal* content to convey the informational benefit claim or claims.
2. There is *no color* requirement.
3. Relatively *brief processing time* is sufficient because with low involvement the focus is on just one or two benefit claims.
4. Relatively *low frequency* is sufficient because informational benefits must be learned in one or two exposures.

Looking at the media selection table for brand attitude and working down the low-involvement/informational column, we see that *all media* are suitable. The brief, verbal claims characterizing most low-involvement/informational campaigns can be conveyed in any mainstream advertising medium.

The one exception here would be when the informational benefit claim requires *demonstration*. Television, including cable television, is the only medium that allows *moving* visual content, and would therefore be the best selection in this case. Newspapers and magazines may be suitable if the demonstration can be depicted easily in an illustration or two, such as for "before and after" product claims.

**Low-Involvement/Transformational.** When the campaign's brand attitude objective is to be attained via a low-involvement/transformational brand attitude strategy, the creative content and frequency tactics are usually as follows:

1. *Visual* content if the transformational motive is sensory gratification or social approval (only with the intellectual stimulation or mastery motive is visual content *not* an advantage).
2. *Color* likewise enhances sensory gratification and social approval.
3. Relatively *brief processing time* is sufficient.
4. *High frequency* within the purchase cycle is usually necessary because of the slower buildup of transformational brand attitude and the typically short purchase cycle for low-involvement/transformational products.

Working down the low-involvement/transformational brand attitude column of the advertising media selection table, we see that television, including cable television, is really the only suitable medium; radio is limited (because of the lack of visual content; however, it is suitable if the motive is intellectual stimulation or mastery); newspapers are limited (they cannot always provide good color, except with expensive color inserts, but are suitable if the motive is intellectual stimulation or mastery); magazines are limited (they cannot provide sufficiently high frequency for short purchase cycles); and both types of outdoor and poster media are limited (they cannot provide sufficiently high frequency except to regular travelers).

For low-involvement/transformational brand attitude, television, including cable television, is the only advertising medium that reliably meets all requirements. Color newspapers are an option *if* good color is guaranteed. If, however, intellectual stimulation or mastery is the transformational motive, rather than sensory gratification or social approval, then the high-frequency media of radio and (daily) newspapers are also suitable.

**High-Involvement/Informational.** When the campaign's brand attitude objective is to be attained via a high-involvement/informational brand attitude strategy, the creative content and frequency tactics are usually as follows:

1. *Verbal* content to convey the informational benefit claims.
2. There is *no color* requirement.
3. *Long processing time* is usually required so that the target audience can process multiple benefits and longer, more carefully reasoned benefit claims.
4. Relatively *low frequency* is sufficient because informational benefits must be accepted in one or two exposures.

Working down the high-involvement/informational column in the advertising media selection table, we see that television is not suitable (there is insufficient processing time with normal-length TV commercials); however, *cable* television (using longer commercials or infomercials) is suitable; radio is not suitable (insufficient processing time); newspapers are suitable; magazines are suitable; stationary outdoor advertisements and posters are limited (they cannot provide sufficiently high frequency except to regular travelers); and mobile outdoor advertisements and posters are also limited but for a different reason (insufficient processing time).

Print media are the best choice for high-involvement/informational advertising—unless the brand happens to be a high-risk purchase that depends on one major benefit that can be conveyed convincingly with short copy. It is noteworthy that high-involvement/informational brand attitude is the *only* universal communication objective for which television, using *regular* TV commercials (read across the table), is unsuitable. Cable television, however, is suitable if longer commercials or infomercials are used.

**High-Involvement/Transformational.** When the campaign's brand attitude objective is to be attained via a high-involvement/transformational brand attitude strategy, the creative content and frequency tactics are usually as follows:

1. *Visual* content if the transformational motive is sensory gratification or social approval (only with the intellectual stimulation or mastery motive is visual content *not* an advantage).
2. *Color* likewise enhances sensory gratification and social approval.
3. Relatively *brief processing time* is sufficient *unless* the high-involvement/transformational strategy also has to provide *information*.

4. Relatively *low frequency* is usually sufficient because, although transformational attitude builds slowly, the purchase cycle for high-involvement/transformational products is generally quite long, thus allowing a relatively low *rate* of frequency to be sufficient.

Working down the final column of the advertising media selection table, for high-involvement/transformational advertising, we see that television is suitable (see the next paragraph); cable television is suitable; radio is limited (because of the lack of visual content; however, it is suitable if the motive is intellectual stimulation or mastery); newspapers are limited (they cannot always provide good color, except with expensive color inserts, but are suitable if the motive is intellectual stimulation or mastery); magazines are suitable; and outdoor advertisements and posters may be suitable (see the next two paragraphs).

There are, however, limits to the foregoing selections when the high-involvement/transformational strategy also has to provide *information*. When the primary purchase motivation is transformational but a secondary informational purchase motivation *also* must be addressed (for example, with new cars or luxury vacations), television, using *regular* TV commercials, and *mobile* outdoor ads and posters become limited. However, TV *can* be used, as follows: TV tends to have very good target audience reach for high-involvement/transformational products. Also, television's transformational capacity really cannot be ignored; but now an *additional* medium will be needed to handle the informational component. This may be a print medium or, in many cases, the information function may be left for the "nonadvertising" medium of personal selling. New car sales and luxury vacation sales are typical examples where personal selling is often used to "close" a high-involvement/transformational sale. Note that with cable television infomercials, there is already a fair amount of personal selling *in* the commercial. However, the selling is not strictly personal, and the prospective customer may require more personalized selling via telemarketing (inbound, from an infomercial-prompted inquiry) to close the sale.

We must distinguish between stationary and mobile outdoor and poster media for high-involvement/transformational products when information has to be provided. As we saw earlier, if the outdoor or poster media vehicle offers a stationary display to a stationary consumer, thus allowing a relatively long processing time, then such *stationary* outdoor and poster media vehicles are suitable for high-involvement/transformational advertising with information. In this capacity, stationary outdoor ads and posters function similarly to magazine ads. Also, if no information is necessary, or if outdoor or poster ads are used as a first-stage medium for further information, then *mobile* outdoor ads and posters remain an option. An example would be airlines' schedule-convenience ads or price ads on billboards near airports.

### Other Communication Objectives

So far, we have concentrated on the two universal communication objectives of brand awareness and brand attitude. Many campaigns have other communication objectives as well. For example, all campaigns except those for low-involvement/transformational products have immediate brand purchase intention as an objective. Category need and purchase facilitation are also objectives for some campaigns.

As discussed in Chapter 9, these other communication objectives require *acceptance* of their content by the target audience. Because of this, these other communication objectives operate essentially like high-involvement *attitudes* and may therefore require *print media* or cable television *infomercials* to allow the target audience sufficient time to process their content and accept their claims. In particular, print media or infomercials should be considered for the following communication objectives:

- *Category Need.* When the objective is to *sell* category need, more space is usually required to present category benefits, so print media are usually required, or cable television infomercials.
- *Brand Purchase Intention.* When the tactics suggest *hard sell*—especially in the form of a promotion offer—again, print media or longer commercials are usually required.

Longer TV commercials—usually available only by using *cable television*—have emerged as an alternative to print media for these other communication objectives. However, print media remain the easiest and least expensive way of transmitting high-involvement messages when these other communication objectives are necessary for the brand.

## IMC Media Selection Based on Brand Awareness and Brand Attitude

We now assess the additional media employed in integrated marketing communications (IMC) campaigns. These are the delivery media for corporate advertising communications, manufacturers' promotions, retailer's promotions, and direct marketing promotions (see Part Five, on integrated communications strategy). The IMC media, just like mainstream advertising media, have varying capacities for achieving the communication objectives of brand awareness and brand attitude. When we consider the functions of primary and secondary media, shortly, we will see that most of the IMC media are *secondary* media in that they are considerably limited in their capacity to achieve the *brand awareness* objective. This is why—with some exceptions—mainstream "mass media" advertising is usually an essential part of an integrated marketing communications program.

Tables 15.2 and 15.3 are IMC media selection tables based on the creative content and frequency tactics for the two types of brand awareness and the four types of brand attitude strategy. (These tables' structure exactly parallels Table 15.1 for mainstream advertising media.) The IMC media options are so numerous that we have placed them in two tables:

*prepurchase* IMC media are shown in Table 15.2, and *point-of-decision* IMC media are shown in Table 15.3.

Note that we have classified PR as a *prepurchase* IMC medium, or set of media, in the first table (Table 15.2). Even though PR is an ongoing function for most companies, it can be used to help launch new products or to relaunch and reposition existing products, and is therefore better classified as a prepurchase IMC media alternative. Publicity, too, is referred to as a "medium": it is implemented through any news-carrying medium virtually equally well. The same perspective is applied to sampling: it's condensed as one "medium" here (for sampling's "submedia," see Chapter 12).

Also note that we have classified direct response (DR, in Table 15.3) advertising *delivery* media as *point-of-decision* IMC media. This classification is certainly appropriate for one-step direct response ads, which seek an immediate purchase (see Chapter 10). It is less appropriate for "double duty" or two-step direct response ads, which seek an inquiry rather than the final sale and so also may serve as mass media ads even if they don't produce a direct response. However, the brand awareness and brand attitude communication objective capacities of the respective direct response *media* are the same regardless of whether it is a one- or two-step direct re-

---

**TABLE 15.2**

**PREPURCHASE IMC MEDIA SELECTION BASED ON BRAND AWARENESS AND BRAND ATTITUDE**

| Prepurchase IMC medium | Brand awareness | | Brand attitude | | | |
|---|---|---|---|---|---|---|
| | Brand recognition | Brand recall | Low-involvement/ informational | Low-involvement/ transformational | High-involvement/ informational | High-involvement/ transformational |
| PR | Lim (f) | Lim (f) | YES | YES | YES | YES |
| Distribution outlet (external) | Lim (rp) | Lim (f) | YES | YES | No | YES |
| Sponsorship | YES | YES | YES | YES | Lim (pt) | YES |
| Event marketing | Lim (rp) | Lim (f) | YES | YES | Lim (pt) | YES |
| Publicity | Lim (vis) | Lim (f) | YES | Lim (vis) | YES | Lim (vis) |
| Sampling | Lim (rp) | Lim (f) | YES | YES | YES | YES |

YES = the medium is appropriate for the given objective or strategy
No = the medium is not appropriate
Lim = the medium may be appropriate but entails certain limitations
f = frequency limitation
pt = processing time limitation
rp = requires previous exposure
vis = visual limitation

sponse ad; hence it is convenient to classify these media in the one table.

### Prepurchase IMC Media

The prepurchase IMC media options are shown in Table 15.2. With the exception of sponsorship, their capacity for achieving brand awareness is limited or nonexistent. However, their capacity for achieving brand attitude is in many cases very good, and this is where their integration is best used: to help speed up sales among those already "pre-aware" of the brand.

**Brand Recognition.** Of the six prepurchase IMC media, only one—sponsorship—is suitable for achieving brand recognition. Most of the others are limited because they require *previous exposure of the brand*— usually through mass media advertising—before the brand can be recognized in the IMC medium. The prepurchase IMC media that are unsuitable for brand recognition for this reason are external signage at distribution outlets, event marketing (since it is tempo-

rary), and sampling. PR is limited because it cannot be relied on alone to provide enough frequency, even for brand recognition. PR activities are usually spread out over time and in terms of stakeholder audiences and would therefore not be a likely choice. Finally, publicity is limited because there is no guarantee that it will provide visual exposure of the product, especially in print media publicity.

**Brand Recall.** Most of the prepurchase IMC media have severe limitations in terms of the frequency required to generate brand recall. The media that are unsuitable for brand recall for this reason are PR, external signage on distribution outlets, event marketing, publicity, and sampling. Once again, the only prepurchase IMC medium suitable for generating brand recall is sponsorship.

As we saw in Chapter 12, sponsorship is the one IMC activity that some companies employ as a *substitute* for mass media advertising. Cornhill Insurance Company in the United Kingdom sponsoring British

---

**TABLE 15.3**

**POINT-OF-DECISION IMC MEDIA SELECTION BASED ON BRAND AWARENESS AND BRAND ATTITUDE**

| Point-of-decision IMC medium | Brand awareness objective | | Brand attitude strategy | | | |
|---|---|---|---|---|---|---|
| | Brand recognition | Brand recall | Low-involvement/ informational | Low-involvement/ transformational | High-involvement/ informational | High-involvement/ transformational |
| Place-based (internal) | Lim (rp) | No | YES | YES | Lim (pt) | YES |
| FSIs | Lim (rp) | Lim (f) | YES | YES | YES | YES |
| POP promotions | Lim (rp) | No | YES | YES | Lim (pt) | YES |
| Telemarketing | No | No | YES | Lim (vis) | YES | Lim (vis) |
| Direct mail | Lim (dm) | Lim (f) | YES | YES | YES | YES |
| DR television | Lim (dm) | Lim (f) | YES | YES | YES | YES |
| DR newspaper | Lim (dm) | Lim (f) | YES | Lim (c) | YES | Lim (c) |
| DR magazine | Lim (dm) | Lim (f) | YES | YES | YES | YES |
| DR radio | No | Lim (f) | YES | Lim (vis) | YES | Lim (vis) |
| Interactive TV or PC advertising | Lim (dm) | Lim (f) | YES | YES | YES | YES |
| Postpackaging | Lim (pc) | Lim (pc) | YES | YES | Lim (pt) | YES |

YES = the medium is appropriate for the given objective or strategy
No = the medium is not appropriate
Lim = the medium may be appropriate but entails certain limitations
c = color limitation
dm = direct-marketed products only
f = frequency limitation
pc = purchase cycle limitation
pt = processing time limitation
rp = requires previous exposure
vis = visual limitation

test cricket is a prime example. Both types of brand awareness would probably be objectives of the sponsorship: insurance can be sold through personal selling (brand recognition) or from the prospective customer calling for a quotation (brand recall). Sponsorship is the only IMC medium capable of delivering both brand recognition and brand recall.

**Low-Involvement/Informational.** Almost every medium—IMC media included—is capable of delivering the simple informative message typically used in a low-involvement/informational ad or promotion offer. When the brand attitude strategy is low-involvement/informational, *all* prepurchase IMC media are suitable.

**Low-Involvement/Transformational.** When the brand attitude strategy is low-involvement/transformational, all of the prepurchase IMC media are suitable *except* publicity, where again there is no guarantee that the product will be visibly shown, which is usually necessary to convey transformational benefits.

Now for an important observation: for low-involvement/transformational messages, all of these prepurchase IMC media (except sponsorship) would normally be eliminated because of their inability to provide the *high frequency* necessary for this type of advertising (compare Table 15.1 for mainstream advertising media). However, because they are already eliminated as primary media due to *brand awareness limitations,* we have not double-penalized them by ruling them out as options for *secondary* media to *support* advertising. This is, after all, what most IMC activities in their prepurchase role do: they support (and speed up) the communication effects of advertising rather than replacing advertising.

**High-Involvement/Informational.** The detailed message that usually accompanies a high-involvement/informational brand attitude strategy causes many of the prepurchase IMC media to be unsuitable or limited. Distribution outlets' exterior signage is eliminated for high-involvement/informational messages because the brief exposure duration does not allow sufficient processing time for most prospects to attend to and accept the message. Processing time is also a limitation for sponsorship and event marketing, unless the message is restricted to one or two main informational benefits.

The remaining prepurchase IMC media—PR, publicity, and sampling—are all suitable for delivering relatively detailed high-involvement/informational messages when this is the applicable brand attitude strategy.

**High-Involvement/Transformational.** All of the prepurchase IMC media are suitable for high-involvement/transformational messages with the single exception of publicity, where again its inability to guarantee visual representation is a limitation. We add the caution that, if the high-involvement/transformational message incorporates a considerable *informational underlay,* then three of these IMC media can become problematic: distribution outlets' exterior signage, sponsorship, and event marketing.

### Point-of-Decision IMC Media

The point-of-decision IMC media options are shown in Table 15.3. Point-of-decision promotional activities include those employed at decision points prior to the actual point of purchase, such as FSI coupon ads or direct response ads, where the prospective buyer has to decide whether to take purchase-related action immediately; as well as normal point-of-purchase promotions; and also *post*purchase media, such as point-of-*use* media, where the prospect may make a further decision regarding purchase-related action. The common characteristic is that these IMC messages demand an immediate decision to act now.

**Brand Recognition.** As should be evident, the point of decision is too late to *establish* brand recognition (unless the product or service is being offered *only* by direct marketing, in which case the ad in *direct response* media *has* to establish brand recognition in one exposure). Hence, most of the point-of-decision IMC media are limited in their brand recognition capacity to situations in which there has been prior advertising for the product or service. New products requiring brand recognition could not be launched using these IMC media alone. But *established* products could use some of these media to capitalize on recognition from previous exposure: place-based (internal) media, FSIs, POP promotions, direct mail, all direct response media (except radio), interactive TV or PC advertising, and postpackaging (carry bags, reusable containers, service stickers, billing letters, and the like).

Two of the point-of-decision IMC media, however, are eliminated for brand recognition altogether—unless the brand recognition requires only *verbal* recognition of the brand or company name. These usually eliminated IMC media are telemarketing and direct response radio, because they cannot show the package or logo for visual recognition.

**Brand Recall.** Point-of-decision IMC media are also unsuitable or severely limited when the communication objective is to generate brand recall. Place-based (internal) media, POP promotions, and telemarketing are unsuitable for generating brand recall because they occur right at the point of decision and therefore cannot be used to generate *prior* brand recall. Seven other IMC media—FSIs, direct mail, direct response TV, direct response newspaper, direct response magazine, direct response radio ads, and interactive TV or PC advertising—may seem to be possibilities for generating brand recall because of the "double duty" nature of direct response ads in these media. However, the low frequency with which these ads would be seen or heard prior to the *decision-making* exposure may make them too limited to use for this purpose. The brand recall limitation is especially true of direct mail, which is typically received only once or twice before the purchase or inquiry decision is made. The final IMC medium in the table, postpackaging, can contribute to brand recall, but its effectiveness depends on the usage frequency of the product or service as exposures are limited to usage occasions.

If *both* brand recognition and brand recall are brand awareness communication objectives for the brand, then we can see from the table that *none* of the point-of-decision IMC media is suitable, with the possible exception of postpackaging. Again, many of these IMC media can capitalize on previous brand recognition or brand recall but cannot in themselves effectively generate either type of brand awareness.

**Low-Involvement/Informational.** All 11 of the point-of-decision IMC media are suitable for delivering brief informational messages characteristic of low-involvement/informational brand attitude strategy.

**Low-Involvement/Transformational.** When the brand attitude strategy is low-involvement/transformational, three of the point-of-decision IMC media are limited: telemarketing and direct response radio both lack visual capacity, which is important when the transformational purchase motive is sensory gratification or social approval, and direct response newspaper often has a color limitation, important for the same motives. If the transformational motive is in-

tellectual stimulation or mastery, on the other hand, then these media are suitable options.

The other eight point-of-decision IMC media are all suitable for low-involvement/transformational *support.* However, none of these IMC media alone could provide for this type of advertising.

**High-Involvement/Informational.** The more detailed message typical of high-involvement/informational brand attitude strategy means that three of the point-of-decision IMC media are limited because of insufficient processing time: place-based (internal) media, POP promotions, and postpackaging. This still leaves eight of these media as suitable options (see below), even for relatively complex messages.

From our discussion in Chapter 9 of other communication objectives—that is, category need, brand purchase intention, and purchase facilitation—you should remember that these can be treated as high-involvement/informational *attitudes,* because their message content has to be *accepted* by the buyer. All eight of the point-of-decision IMC media designated as suitable for high-involvement/informational brand attitude strategy are also suitable for achieving these other communication objectives. These "high involvement" point-of-decision media are FSIs, telemarketing, direct mail, direct response TV, direct response newspaper, direct response magazine, direct response radio, and interactive TV or PC advertising.

**High-Involvement/Transformational.** The three point-of-decision IMC media that are unsuitable when the brand attitude strategy is high-involvement/transformational are the same as for *low-*involvement/transformational: telemarketing and direct response radio, due to their lack of visual capacity, and direct response newspaper if good color is unavailable, for sensory gratification and social approval.

Note that we have included postpackaging as a suitable option for high-involvement/transformational purposes. There is no doubt that, for example, shopping bags from Tiffany's, Ralph Lauren's Polo labels, and Alfa-Romeo key rings serve to reinforce these high-involvement purchases and make it more likely that repeat purchase will occur. Note that these repeat purchases would be high-involvement *and* transformational, given the cost of these types of products and the prestige attached to them.

Altogether, then, we have seen that the IMC media, whether these be prepurchase or point-of-decision media, *are weak as brand awareness generators in their own right* but can capitalize on brand awareness from previous *mainstream advertising* exposures. Also, many of these IMC media are powerful contributors to brand attitude. Because they do not have the capacity to deliver well on *both* brand awareness and brand attitude, however, they are most properly employed as *secondary* rather than primary media in the campaign—a media selection distinction we examine next.

## THE CONCEPTS OF PRIMARY AND SECONDARY MEDIA

Almost every advertising campaign makes use of a *primary* medium, in which half or more of the media budget will be spent, and one or more *secondary* media. In this section of the chapter, we will examine which medium should be designated as primary and which media should be used as secondary media.

### The Primary Medium

The *primary* medium is selected because it is the single most *effective* medium for achieving all of the brand's communication objectives and causing buyer behavior. Although cost is a factor, effectiveness is initially more important. The advertiser should identify one medium that could alone do a *sufficient* job of communication if enough money were spent in that medium. (Usually, there will be only one such primary medium when target audience reach is also taken into account; see Chapter 17.) Then the advertiser should investigate whether the partial substitution of other media in secondary capacities (see below) could do the same job more *efficiently,* that is, at less cost. The task matrix method of IMC budget allocation described in Chapter 11 is used for this investigation and decision.

**Combined Brand Awareness and Brand Attitude Objectives.** The primary medium must be capable of achieving *all* of the brand's communication objectives. The most important communication objectives are the universal objectives of brand awareness and brand attitude; also, one or more of the other three communication objectives may have to be addressed. In selecting a primary medium from the advertising media and IMC media selection tables

(Tables 15.1 to 15.3), brand awareness requirements must now be *combined* with brand attitude requirements.

Beginning from the left in the tables, and going across to the right, a *primary* medium that is "knocked out" by brand awareness requirements "stays out" when brand attitude is considered. This is seen more easily by constructing a "positive" selection table (Table 15.4) showing the media that remain for consideration after brand awareness and brand attitude constraints have been jointly applied. One "No" entry in either of the two columns being considered eliminates that medium as an option. One "Limitation" entry *usually* eliminates that medium as an option; we note exceptions in the table footnotes and below.

We see that in most of the "cells" in the table (which are the eight Rossiter-Percy grid cells), the options for *primary* media are quite limited. This is especially true when you realize that there were 24 media options (listed in Tables 15.1 to 15.3) to select from initially! Primary media selection by communication objectives makes the media planner's choice a lot easier.

We have included *direct response* media, including interactive TV or PC advertising, as *primary* media possibilities for just two of the classifications in the table: brand recognition plus high-involvement/informational *or* high-involvement/transformational brand attitude strategy. As a primary medium, direct response advertising for otherwise unadvertised products and services *tries* to establish brand recognition—in *one exposure* (see the company credibility tactics for direct response ads detailed in Chapter 10). Moreover, direct response ads, in their *direct response role* rather than their "double duty" role if they are also intended for the latter, necessarily require a *high-involvement* decision, either informational or transformational depending on the main purchase motive for the product or service. Thus, for these two grid classifications, direct response media are a primary medium option.

If more than one medium survives the primary medium selection process, a single primary medium can be selected on the basis of superior target audience reach by using direct matching (described in Chapter 17). The "losing" primary medium or media may still be strong candidates for secondary media, whose functions are explained next.

**TABLE 15.4**

**PRIMARY MEDIA FOR ACHIEVING COMBINED BRAND AWARENESS AND BRAND ATTITUDE COMMUNICATION OBJECTIVES**

| Brand recognition and the following brand attitude strategy | | | |
| --- | --- | --- | --- |
| Low-involvement/ informational | Low-involvement/ transformational | High-involvement/ informational | High-involvement/ transformational |
| • Television<br>• Cable television<br>• Newspapers[a]<br>• Magazines<br>• Stationary outdoor<br>• Mobile outdoor<br>• Sponsorship | • Television<br>• Cable television<br>• Newspapers[a]<br>• Sponsorship | • Cable television<br>• Newspapers[a]<br>• Magazines<br>• Direct response[d]<br>  (mail, TV, newspaper,<br>  magazine, and interactive<br>  TV or PC advertising,<br>  but rarely radio) | • Television<br>• Cable television<br>• Newspapers[a]<br>• Magazines<br>• Stationary outdoor<br>• Mobile outdoor[b]<br>• Sponsorship[b]<br>• Direct response[d] (mail, TV,<br>  newspaper, magazine, and<br>  interactive TV or PC<br>  advertising, but rarely radio) |
| **Brand recall and the following brand attitude strategy** | | | |
| Low-involvement/ informational | Low-involvement/ transformational | High-involvement/ informational | High-involvement/ transformational |
| • Television<br>• Cable television<br>• Radio<br>• Newspapers<br>• Sponsorship | • Television<br>• Cable television<br>• Radio[c]<br>• Newspapers[a]<br>• Sponsorship | • Cable television<br>• Newspapers | • Television<br>• Cable television<br>• Radio[c]<br>• Newspapers[a]<br>• Sponsorship[b] |

[a] Newspapers are included in these categories *only if 4-color* advertising is available.
[b] These media are not suitable *if information also* has to be provided.
[c] Radio is suitable in transformational categories *only if* the transformational motive is intellectual stimulation or mastery.
[d] Primary medium for direct-marketed products only.

### Secondary Media

*Secondary* media are used for three reasons:

**1.** There may be some *significant proportion of the target audience* that the primary medium does not reach or cannot reach at an effective frequency level; for example, very light television viewers, or non-readers of newspapers. Thus, a secondary medium is "imperative" in the plan to reach these people.

**2.** There may be *one or two communication objectives* that can be attained equally effectively, but at a lower cost, with a medium other than the primary one. Secondary media may be used in the role of boosting *particular* communication objectives (such as increased brand awareness, maintained brand attitude, or reminded purchase intentions) either (a) *simultaneously* with the primary medium during the early phases of the media plan, to contribute to the overall communication effects, or (b) *later* in the media plan after the main shifts in communication effects have been attained and the communication objectives become maintenance or "reinforcement" objectives,[4] which may be attainable with lower-cost media.

**3.** There may be a *timing advantage near or at the point of purchase or usage,* that is, close to the target audience's decision, offered by a secondary medium.

*IMC media*—to deliver the corporate advertising communications and the various promotions—are most often used for the second and third reasons. As we have seen, IMC media can opportunely trigger *previous* brand awareness; they can also contribute to brand attitude; and they are very often employed to stimulate immediate brand purchase intention and sometimes purchase facilitation. The timing advantage reason is reflected in the *timeline* integration aspect of IMC (the third meaning of "integrated," the first being selection integration and the second being consistency across IMC activities of macropositioning for the brand—see Chapter 11).

Recommended primary and secondary media selections are examined next for five main categories of advertising—national consumer advertising, retail advertising, industrial advertising, corporate image advertising, and direct response advertising. (Respective sections can be skipped if you are not interested in all these types of advertising.) We refer to these as categories of "advertising" because of our advocated view that advertising should lead the media plan—with ad-like communications, and promotions, as complementary, in most cases.

## NATIONAL CONSUMER ADVERTISING

National consumer advertising refers to advertising for consumer products or services that are available nationwide. Advertising campaigns for national brands are usually standard across the nation, although sometimes the media strategy and occasionally the creative strategy (more likely its creative executions) may vary regionally or locally. Most national media provide geographic options if the advertising plan requires them.

### Primary Medium Is Almost Always Television

For national advertisers of consumer products and services, the best primary medium is almost always *television*. We say "almost always" because the exception is high-involvement/informational products that require long copy. Even here, for the national advertiser, television may be used as a secondary medium for the brand awareness communication objective.

Notice that we are not including *cable* television when we refer to television for national consumer advertising. Cable television is available to about 66 percent[5] of homes in the United States (that is, it misses about a third of the consumer target audience), and the multitude of cable channels makes a national consumer media buy very difficult. Only for an unusually high involvement/informational new product, with an upmarket demographic skew, would cable TV be worth the trouble as the primary medium for the national consumer advertiser.

We do, however, include *sponsored* television programs. American Express, for example, has successfully sponsored the *Seinfeld* TV program in its national consumer advertising.

Why is television the primary advertising medium of choice for most national consumer advertisers? The explanation lies in the fact that television is undeniably the single most effective medium for achieving overall communication objectives and producing sales.[6] The reasons for television advertising's persuasive superiority are fairly easy to discern in terms of the first two steps of our six-step approach. No other medium can match television for exposure and processing.

1. *Exposure.* TV offers very high reach in a relatively short period and can also deliver high effective frequency levels, if needed, to most target audiences.

2. *Processing.* Whereas most media provide *initial* attention to the ad at the same level as TV, none can equal the "intrusive" nature of television for *sustaining* attention to the entire message. (When a commercial comes on TV, it is easier to watch and listen than to do anything else unless TV is being used for background sound, like radio, as happens for some daytime programs). The attention-sustaining characteristic as well as TV's unique ability to carry multiple advertising stimuli (pictures, color, movement, seen words, and heard words) also make it the superior medium for rote learning, needed for brand awareness of either the brand recognition or brand recall type, and for low-involvement brand attitude registration. With multiple exposures, or longer commercials, TV *may* also provide the opportunity for acceptance responses, needed for high-involvement brand attitude shifts. (However, TV can do this for only a limited number of benefits. It is not suitable for processing multiple or detailed logical support benefit claims where the target audience has to consider each claim carefully.)

Our recommendation is that the media planner for nationally advertised consumer products should consider television as the first choice against which all other choices should be compared. The national consumer advertiser should only move to another medium as primary if the brand choice is high-involvement and television advertising cannot handle the informational message requirements.[7] This "other" medium would usually be cable TV, newspapers, or magazines.

## Secondary Media and Substitutes for Television

Many national consumer advertisers have little need for a secondary medium beyond television advertising. Coke and Pepsi, for example, spend only 10 percent of their (consumer) advertising budget outside TV. These non-TV expenditures are most likely to be for the third use of secondary media listed earlier: *point-of-purchase reminders.*

Point-of-purchase (really point-of-decision) reminder ads are relatively easy to experiment with to see if they contribute to sales because POP ads can be easily installed or removed to observe their effect on sales. POP reminder ads can be powerful communication devices. Think about a Coke ad in a restaurant: it can remind you of category need, cause brand recognition, and, given a favorable prior attitude, create an immediate intention to buy.

Other national consumer advertisers seek secondary media to *support TV* as the primary medium because particular secondary media may be very effective in contributing to *one* of the brand's communication objectives of either brand awareness or brand attitude. Here, we can go back to the advertising media and IMC media tables for suitable choices and construct a new table (Table 15.5) for *secondary* media based on the communication effect to be "boosted." Notice the many IMC options which are suitable for boosting brand attitude.

The remaining use of secondary media is to reach those *hard-to-reach target audience members* for whom the primary medium, TV, cannot deliver enough frequency to achieve the effective frequency level for the brand. However, even light viewers of TV—as long as they have a fairly regular pattern of light viewing, such as one or two favorite programs or the late news on most weeknights—can be reached at high frequency by using *impact scheduling,* that is, by running the commercial several times during the one program. The advantages and disadvantages of impact scheduling are discussed in Chapter 17.

The media planner must ensure that these "extra reach" secondary media, selected on their ability to provide target audience reach at additional frequency, are capable of delivering the required communication effects. As we saw in Tables 15.1 to 15.3, most media either have limitations or are unsuitable when *joint* communication objectives are required. There *are* creative ways of getting around most of the negatives and limitations listed in the tables, but most of these

creative alternatives are expensive and are not practical unless that medium represents the only way of reaching the target audience, or unless that medium has some other distinct advantage that makes it worth using. These alternatives are discussed next as *substitutes* for television for hard-to-reach target audience members.

**Radio.** Radio is normally eliminated if brand *recognition* is a communication objective. Radio, of course, is unable to show packages or logos. Brands that later have to be recognized at the point of purchase cannot be advertised effectively on radio.

The creative way around this limitation involves describing the package or logo in the radio commercial. This was often done in the old days of radio before TV emerged as a major advertising medium (for example, Pepsodent's "Look for the yellow tube at the grocer's"). However, package descriptions are rather imprecise, especially considering today's typically crowded shelf displays, and descriptions take away time from the copy needed for the benefit claims.

Radio has limited effectiveness if the brand attitude strategy is *transformational,* in either the low- or high-involvement quadrants. Of the three positive motivations, radio is most handicapped for sensory gratification (for example, it cannot show appetizing "beauty shots," as they are called, for food products) and for social approval (for example, it cannot show people as brand users). Radio is less handicapped for intellectual stimulation or mastery as a motivation (although the handicap applies if the brand requires a demonstration).

The creative way around transformational brand attitude limitations on radio is for the copywriter to select words and sentences that stimulate imagery in the listener's mind (see Chapter 10 for the recommended structural formula for radio ads). For example, gustatory (taste) imagery can be stimulated by kitchen sounds, drinks pouring over cracking ice, and so forth. Similarly, visual imagery of brand user types can often be generated through voice cues, particularly for social class perceptions. However, these imagery effects can be difficult to generate reliably and consistently across all listeners.

A second creative solution to the transformational brand attitude limitation of radio is to attempt to generate *imagery transfer* from TV advertising to radio advertising. (Creative tactics for imagery transfer were discussed in Chapter 10.) Aside from radio,

---

**TABLE 15.5**

---

**SECONDARY MEDIA TO "BOOST" SINGLE COMMUNICATION EFFECTS FOR NATIONAL CONSUMER ADVERTISING**

(*The primary medium is television.*)

| Communication effect to be boosted | Recommended secondary media |
|---|---|
| **Brand awareness** | |
| Brand recognition | • Newspapers (if 4-color) |
| | • Magazines |
| | • Outdoor |
| | • FSIs |
| | • POP |
| Brand recall | • Radio |
| | • Newspapers |
| **Brand attitude** | |
| Low-involvement/informational | • Radio |
| | • Newspapers |
| | • Magazines |
| | • Outdoor |
| | • FSIs |
| | • POP |
| Low-involvement/transformational | • Radio (with image transfer) |
| | • Newspapers (if 4-color) |
| | • Magazines |
| | • Outdoor |
| | • FSIs |
| | • Event marketing |
| | • POP |
| High-involvement/informational | • Cable TV |
| | • Newspapers |
| | • Magazines |
| | • Stationary outdoor |
| | • FSIs |
| | • Telemarketing |
| | • Direct response (all DR media) |
| | • Interactive TV or PC advertising |
| High-involvement/transformational | • Cable TV |
| | • Newspapers |
| | • Magazines |
| | • Outdoor |
| | • Sponsorship |
| | • Event marketing |
| | • FSIs |
| | • POP |
| | • Direct response (all DR media except radio) |
| | • Interactive TV or PC advertising |
| | • Postpackaging |

other *visual* media could also be used for imagery transfer, where the illustration duplicates a key scene from a previously viewed TV commercial.[8]

**Newspapers.** Practically considered, newspapers lack color as a creative content element. Although color ads can be purchased at a 20 to 30 percent price premium, normal or run-of-paper (ROP) color can be unreliable from market to market and from paper to paper within press runs, as we pointed out earlier.

The color limitation of newspapers poses a problem when *brand recognition* is an objective. (Note that later, when we assess retail advertising, lack of color in newspaper ads is less of a problem for those retail *readvertisers* who show brands whose color recognition has been achieved in the manufacturer's advertising in other media. The ability to recognize a black-and-white version of a colored package could be regarded as an instance of imagery transfer.) Furthermore, many *transformational* campaigns rely on color to provide full positive reinforcing stimulation.

The creative way to overcome the color limitation of newspapers is to buy high-quality color inserts or to place ads in FSI (freestanding insert) or newspaper "magazine" supplements. However, since many newspapers will take these on weekends only, the color insert or supplement route can negate the high-frequency advantage of newspapers. On the other hand, the *daily* availability of *high-quality color* gives newspapers a very considerable high-frequency advantage over magazines.

**Magazines.** The main limitation of magazines is their relatively poor ability to deliver the *high frequency* needed for the many nationally advertised consumer products which have brand recall or low-involvement/transformational brand attitude communication objectives. Weekly magazines, of course, have an advantage over monthly magazines in this respect. But apart from their publication frequency, the frequency with which magazines are *read* is often patchy or delayed. Magazines also have relatively narrow audiences. To achieve high frequency for most target audiences, the advertiser would therefore have to buy space in a variety of magazines because each target audience member may read only one or two, and these one or two magazines may differ widely from individual to individual.

A reasonably good creative solution to the high-frequency problem with magazines is *impact scheduling,* which we mentioned previously for television. In the magazine application of impact scheduling, multiple ads (which should be executionally a little different, to renew attention) for the one brand are placed in the *same issue* of the magazine. The main weakness of impact scheduling, as discussed in Chapter 17, is that the piling up of exposures into one reading time slot leaves a subsequent delay period during which competitive brand advertising can interfere. However, this may average out if competing brands are also confined to magazines.

More generally, for new brands, where the brand awareness and brand attitude communication effects have a long way up to go from zero, the frequency limitation of magazines can be a substantial problem. Later in the brand's life cycle, when targeting brand switchers or brand loyals who have well-established communication effects, which require less frequency to top up or maintain, magazines are a more attractive secondary medium, and may become the primary medium if they can now achieve the brand's communication objectives at a lower cost than TV.

**Outdoor Ads and Posters.** One limitation of outdoor ads and posters occurs when *high frequency* is required. Nevertheless, careful examination of target audience exposure to outdoor (or indoor transit) sites can often provide opportunities to deliver high frequency. The extra cost is in conducting detailed audience research to detect commuting or shopping patterns that allow frequent exposure. British market researchers have introduced the measurement of audience "journey days" for outdoor ad and poster sites to estimate their reach and frequency potential.[9]

The other limitation of outdoor ads and posters is for *high-involvement brand attitude* strategies, because the multiple benefit or detailed benefit claim capacity of outdoor ads is typically limited. However, *stationary* outdoor or poster vehicles, such as subway or train posters, often allow substantial processing time, so these are *not* limited for high-involvement messages. Also, not all high-involvement brand decisions require multiple message points or detailed benefit claims. If a high-involvement campaign requires a strong but relatively short message, then outdoor and poster advertising can be an effective medium.

**Direct Mail.** The main limitation of direct mail for the national consumer advertiser is its inability to deliver *high frequency.* In fact, most direct mail campaigns are designed to effectively close the sale in a single exposure, not repeated exposures. Hence, direct mail is hardly ever used alone as an advertising medium for frequently purchased consumer products. However, it can be used to deliver *promotion offers* (which attempt to close the sale) when consumers are aware of the brand from other media and when a good target audience mailing list is available. Stouffer's, for instance, periodically uses direct mail coupons which are sent to a list of prime Stouffer's brand loyals.

**Point-of-Purchase (POP).** The main limitation of point-of-purchase advertising is that the exposure comes too late to affect *brand recall.* Brand recall must occur *prior* to the point of purchase. There is no creative solution to this problem, because of the timing of POP in the purchase decision sequence.

Point-of-purchase is, in contrast, an excellent secondary medium in *brand recognition* situations, when the decision is made at the point of purchase. A good POP display can serve as a near-perfect recognition cue if it duplicates visual and verbal elements shown previously in the brand's advertising, such as on TV.[10]

Point-of-purchase has a second limitation: it is of limited effectiveness for *high-involvement* brand attitude objectives. The prospective buyer of *frequently purchased* consumer products, trying a new high-risk brand, cannot be expected to process detailed information at the last minute.

However, for *consumer durables,* POP advertising can be an effective *secondary* medium for the national advertiser because the customer is likely to deliberate carefully before making a final decision. Examples include brand purchase decisions for expensive calculators and cameras, or complex home appliances. Manufacturers' brochures or detailed display cards at the point of purchase are often consulted to find out more about risk-laden brands that are only superficially familiar from mass media advertising. These POP materials nevertheless need to be easily understandable from skimming as the shopper is usually processing information under relatively high pressure.

A final limitation of point-of-purchase advertising is that it cannot provide *high frequency,* if needed, *between* purchases—that is, during the purchase cycle. The prospective purchaser is only likely to attend to POP advertising at the beginning of each purchase cycle when "in the market" for the product. However, point-of-*use* and postpackaging, when feasible, *can* deliver high frequency during the purchase cycle if the product is frequently used.

Thus, although POP can be a very effective secondary medium for products purchased via brand recognition, it is rarely sufficient *alone* as a *primary* medium for national consumer products.

**Summary.** The national consumer advertiser should use TV as the primary medium unless the brand attitude strategy requires long copy, where cable television or a print medium will be primary. Secondary media for the national consumer advertiser depend on the purpose for which they are needed; most often, the need is for a secondary medium to boost a particular communication objective at relatively low cost, and very often this will be an IMC medium. A wide range of choices for secondary media is available, but these are quickly narrowed down based on communication objectives. An "unsuitable" medium that otherwise has excellent target audience reach can be used in some instances by creatively getting around the communication limitation, but such substitutions are usually expensive and less effective than using suitable media and impact-scheduling the ads to reach the "lighter" viewing, reading, or listening target audience members.

## RETAIL ADVERTISING

Retail advertising fundamentally is *local* advertising because each retail store draws customers from only a limited geographic area (most of the target audience lives or works within several miles of the store). Furthermore, nearly all retailers have two "brands" to advertise:

1. The products sold by the store (product advertising)
2. The store itself (store image advertising)

These two types of retail advertising have different communication objectives. Accordingly, the best selection of media for retail product advertising and store image advertising usually differ, as we will see next.

### Retail Product Advertising

Many local advertisers, such as supermarkets or department stores, have a wide range of products that they wish to expose to prospective buyers. There are too many products to be shown on TV—although there is no doubt that local advertisers would use (local) TV if they could afford detailed and lengthy commercials, as TV is the most effective selling medium. (With the emergence of shop-at-home cable TV, or interactive "electronic newspapers or catalogs" available on TV screens on CD-ROM home computers, there is an increasing movement of retail advertisers to TV.)

For the local, multiproduct retailer, the product advertising options depend on whether they are a "readvertiser" of national brands or an "original advertiser" of local brands.

**Retail Readvertisers: Newspapers.** Many retailers —notably, supermarkets—sell products that already have been advertised by the manufacturer. These retailers are therefore *readvertisers.* Retail ads in this case are functionally "point-of-purchase" media that work primarily on brand purchase intention (that is, by telling the prospective buyer that a known brand is available, at an intention-inducing price, at that store). For this purpose, *newspapers* are the best medium.

Because brand awareness and brand attitude have already been established and are addressed only in a reminder role in the newspaper ad, newspapers for the retail readvertiser do not pose any of the limitations that they pose for the national advertiser. In particular, lack of full color, which normally would hinder brands seeking brand recognition or those using a transformational brand attitude strategy, or both, is not a problem for the retail readvertiser.

The choice of newspapers as the primary medium for local advertisers is further encouraged by newspapers' practice of giving local advertisers very attractive low rates. Local advertisers provide the main financial support for newspapers. Thus local newspapers (both city and suburban) are vitally concerned with maintaining for local advertisers an attractive price compared with other local media alternatives, notably local TV and local radio. But only retail *readvertisers* should automatically use newspapers.

**Original Retail Advertisers: TV, Sunday Newspaper Supplements, Catalogs, or Handbills.** Other retail stores are *original advertisers;* that is, they sell their own products rather than national brands advertised by national manufacturers. These retailers include banks, department stores which sell mainly their own-brand merchandise, and various specialty and smaller stores.

Original advertisers at the local level have the same product advertising communication objectives as the national consumer advertiser does at the national level. However, media choices for the original retail advertisers are contingent on three additional factors: (1) product versus service retailing, (2) breadth of product mix, and (3) number and geographic dispersion of customers.

*Television* is the best choice for the original retail advertiser who sells *products or services* with a *limited* product mix that can be typified by a small number of leading items, and draws a *large* number of customers to one store or a chain of stores. Examples include furniture stores, banks, and local chain restaurants.

*Sunday newspaper supplements* (color brochure inserts[11] or FSI ads in color) are the best choice when the original retail advertiser has a *wide product* mix and draws a *large* number of customers to one store or a chain of stores. Examples may include discount department stores and chain hardware stores.

*Direct mail* is the best choice for the original advertiser who sells a *wide* mix of *products,* and also has geographically *dispersed* customers in *large* enough numbers to make the printing of direct mail (which can range from fairly inexpensive color brochures to costly multipage color catalogs) worthwhile. Some examples are the more "exclusive" department stores, specialty clothing stores, and sports stores. *Interactive TV or PC advertising* (electronic catalogs) is emerging as an alternative for these advertisers. However, direct mail is a better *initiating* medium because it prompts the consumer to action—such as to *access* the electronic catalog.

Direct mail is also the best choice for a *single product-line* retailer with geographically *dispersed* customers. A direct mail letter with a small brochure would be used in this case.

*Handbills* (distributed in mailboxes where it's legal to do so, or centrally distributed at high-traffic locations) are the best choice for original retail advertisers who sell *services* and have a *small* number of very *localized* customers. Examples include dry cleaners, plumbers, and lawn and garden care services. These types of advertisers don't need to use color and can't afford expensive advertising media. Alternatives are small-space ads in *suburban* newspapers, or *miscellaneous* media such as calendars.

*Small* stores that sell *products* but also have very *localized* customers should also use handbills. Although color would be an advantage, it's too expensive. Some examples are corner grocery stores, local hardware stores, and local independent restaurants whose special menu items change regularly.

**Retail Promotional Media.** All retailers, of course, are likely to use retail IMC media—particularly place-based (internal) media and POP promotions. These media either function like direct response media (for example, special displays or on-pack promotions), or as reminder media, reinforcing previous brand awareness and brand attitude, at the point of purchase (for example, in-store signage). Retail promotions were extensively discussed in Chapter 13.

## Store Image Advertising

Retailers not only sell the products in their stores but first must get people attracted to the store itself. This is the purpose of store image advertising. While we might think of retailers' product advertising media as primary and their store image advertising media as secondary, for many retailers the ability to constantly reattract store traffic is vital for success, and the primary and secondary roles for the two types of retail advertising may therefore be reversed.

Store image advertising typically has the following communication objectives (with the *store* now serving as the *brand*):

1. *Brand recall:* so that prospective customers will include the store in their evoked set (the exception is stores in high-traffic areas that rely on walk-in traffic, but many of these stores would do better to predispose customers through brand recall).

2. *Brand attitude:* but *only if* the store's "image" is not well known to the target audience.

3. *Brand purchase intention:* that is, *intention to visit* the store when the category need arises, which is usually hard-sell.

The focus on brand *recall* and short-term brand purchase intention means that all high-frequency media (see Table 15.1) are possibilities: TV, including cable TV, radio, and newspapers. We have reincluded TV here because for shorter, store-reminder ads, TV may now become cost-effective for the local advertiser. If not, radio or newspaper advertising certainly would be cost-effective. Radio or newspaper ads can be used just prior to, or on, major shopping days.

Some retailers do not require high frequency, even for brand recall, because the *visit* cycle is very long. A furniture store, for example, does not require high effective frequency because the visit (and purchase) cycle is probably up to a decade long. A Kentucky Fried Chicken (KFC) outlet, on the other hand, has a short purchase cycle and requires high frequency. If low frequency is adequate, several more possibilities for store image advertising open up: outdoor ads and posters, radio, city magazines (when available), and direct mail. Indeed, these media are preferred for the low-frequency store image advertiser because they allow a high-quality store image to be maintained through good color-reproduction graphics.

If the retailer is trying to create or increase a brand *attitude* (store image) that is largely transformational,

there are many possibilities. Suitable advertising media are local TV, cable TV, newspapers, city magazines, and outdoor ads and posters (and note that a national retailer could, for *store image* advertising, use *national* TV and print media). For store image boosting alone, the following IMC media are *secondary* media possibilities: PR, distribution outlets (external), sponsorships, event marketing, and publicity (all pre-purchase IMC media); and place-based (internal), POP, interactive TV or PC advertising, and postpackaging (all point-of-decision IMC media).

These complex considerations for retail advertisers' media selections are summarized in Table 15.6.

## INDUSTRIAL ADVERTISING

Media selection for the industrial or business-to-business advertiser depends mainly on two factors: (1) the size of the target audience and (2) the decision makers (in their respective roles) to whom the advertising is directed. In the following discussion, we assume that the target audience has *already* been identified as either new category users, other-brand loyals, other-brand switchers, favorable brand switchers, or brand loyals. Target audience size and roles therefore apply *within* these groups. Industrial decision roles, discussed in Chapter 4, are gatekeeper, initiator, influencer (perhaps consultant), decider (various levels), purchaser, and user.

### Small Target Audience

Some businesses have a relatively small target audience—say, less than 100 individual decision makers, in total—to reach. Many small local businesses have small target audiences but so, too, do many large businesses selling to only several large customers.

When the target audience is small, *no advertising* is recommended, at least not in major media. Personal sales calls can achieve the communication objectives more effectively and produce orders and sales at much lower cost. The media used, if any, would consist of pamphlets or brochures intended as *sales aids* carried by the sales force.

### Moderate-Sized Target Audience

If the target audience size is moderate, then *trade publications* and *direct mail* are the best media choices. Moderate-sized target audiences of, say, 100 to 1,000 decision makers are too small to justify use

| TABLE 15.6 | |
|---|---|
| **MEDIA SELECTION FOR RETAIL ADVERTISERS** | |
| **Retail advertising situation** | **Recommended media** |
| **Retail product advertising** | |
| Retail readvertisers (e.g., supermarkets) | • Newspapers |
| Original retail advertisers (e.g., furniture stores) | • Local TV (narrow product mix, large audience)<br>• Direct mail (smaller or dispersed audience) and interactive TV or PC advertising<br>• Handbills, suburban newspapers, calendars (local service retailers) |
| **Store image advertising** | |
| Store recall and store purchase intention (store image known) | • Local TV<br>• Radio<br>• Newspapers |
| Above, plus transformational store attitude (store image to be created, improved, modified, or changed) | • Local TV<br>• Newspapers (if good 4-color)<br>• Outdoor (long visit cycle)<br>• City magazines (long visit cycle)<br>• Direct mail (long visit cycle) |
| Transformational store attitude (store image) to be boosted by secondary (IMC) media | • PR<br>• Distribution outlets<br>• Sponsorships<br>• Event marketing<br>• Publicity<br>• Place-based<br>• Interactive TV or PC advertising<br>• Postpackaging |

of a mass medium but are large enough to justify advertising in narrower-reach media as a cost-effective means of paving the way for sales calls.

Target audience size includes multiple decision makers (across all the decision-making roles) in the same prospect- or customer-firm. The industrial or business-to-business advertiser should always conduct a careful analysis of decision roles within the typical buying center. The major division in nearly all cases is between important but lower-level decision makers (especially initiators and users) and top management upper-level decision makers (deciders). Most lower-level decision makers read *trade publications,* but upper level decision makers don't. Hence, another medium, *direct mail,* is needed to reach top management when the target audience size is moderate.

### Large Target Audience

Of course, the same division in decision-making roles by organizational levels applies for the large industrial or business-to-business advertiser as well. To reach lower-level decision makers, *trade publications* are again the obvious choice because they reach initiators and product or service users, by industry, with very little target audience waste.

However, for the now numerous upper-level decision makers who are the top management deciders, the use of *business magazines* is recommended. The target audience size justifies the use of a more "mass" medium than direct mail. And, possibly, the perceived prestige of advertising in business magazines ("they must be a large and successful company," the management thinks) gives this medium an effectiveness advantage over direct mail. In the future, a corporate "home page" on the Internet may also reach enough upper-level decision makers to recommend this medium.

Because of the technical nature of most industrial products or services, print media are required that reach specialized target audiences (users or top managers) with minimal waste. The greater cost of using a vehicle capable of reaching a broader audience rules out mass print media such as newspapers and general magazines.

Only occasionally, with a *simple* product or service and a *very large* target audience, should a mass medium be considered—for example, Federal Express's use of television.

Most firms' industrial or business-to-business *product* or *service* advertising will therefore be placed in the specialized print media of trade publications or business magazines (Table 15.7). For *corporate image* advertising, however, the advertiser may make a wider choice, as we discuss next.

### CORPORATE IMAGE ADVERTISING

Just as the retail advertiser has a store image to project and remind people about, industrial *and* consumer advertisers have a corporate image to project to certain "stakeholder" target audiences. Which companies should use corporate image advertising, and to whom, was extensively discussed in Chapter 11. Here we focus on corporate image advertising media selection.

Media selection for corporate image advertising depends fundamentally on the size of the company: small, or medium to large.

### Small Companies

For the small company with a small or very localized target audience, corporate image advertising, in the

conventional sense, is too costly to be used *in addition to* product or service advertising. However, small companies advertising products or services in handbills, suburban newspapers, calendars, or sales aids should plan to include a corporate image component—such as a tested company slogan or logo.

As well, small companies have much to gain from *local sponsorships* and *local PR* activities. Financial assistance to community organizations, local athletic programs, and for concerts and social events, for example, is almost always worthwhile; the company's name (brand recognition) will reach all local target audiences through the use of concert programs or other printed materials.

### Medium to Large Companies

For the medium to large company, corporate image advertising can create and maintain brand (company) recognition and then transmit messages fitting any of the four brand attitude strategies (see Chapter 11). Brand recognition dominates (Table 15.4) and the usual choices are between television, cable television, newspapers (if 4-color), magazines, outdoor ads and posters, sponsorships, and direct mail.

*Television,* including cable television, is the most persuasive corporate image advertising medium, and can be used for corporate image advertising even when the company's product or service advertising is placed primarily in other media. The omnipresent nature of TV, especially its ability to catch executives "off the job" in a relaxed mood, and its ability to dynamically depict company achievements, make television the most effective corporate image advertising medium.

If the cost of television is prohibitive despite its known or estimated sales effectiveness, because of a small or extremely low TV-watching target audience, then *newspaper* (4-color ads), business or consumer *magazines,* or *direct mail,* in this order based on diminishing target audience size, would be the alternative choices.

*Outdoor and poster* advertising is an appropriate media choice when the corporate image advertising message is *short.* Outdoor and poster corporate image advertising is also a good choice when the target audience has a reasonably consistent commuting or shopping pattern, especially in relation to the company's products or services. Billboards on main roads

---

**TABLE 15.7**

**MEDIA SELECTION FOR INDUSTRIAL (BUSINESS-TO-BUSINESS) ADVERTISERS**

| Size of target audience (number of individual decision makers) | Recommended media |
|---|---|
| Small ( < 100) | • None (use personal selling, perhaps with pamphlets or brochures as sales aids) |
| Moderate (100–1,000) | • Trade publications (lower-level decision makers)<br>• Direct mail (upper-level decision makers) |
| Large ( > 1,000) | • Trade publications (lower-level decision makers)<br>• Business magazines (upper-level decision makers) |

to office areas or airports (industrial) or shopping centers (consumer) provide excellent target audience reach for short corporate image advertising messages.

Medium to large companies should also consider sponsorships and PR "media" for impressing government, employee, and special interest group target audiences. However, whereas small companies are well known in local areas, medium to large companies may not be, unless they have a local plant or office. Accordingly, medium to large companies should seek *advertised sponsorships* for events that are advertised in broader media such as television or magazines. *Event marketing* is included here as a short-term sponsorship.

### All Companies

Corporate *identity* stimuli should be proactively managed as contributors to corporate image by every company, small or larger. The key avenues for such stimuli are the following IMC media: head offices and distribution outlets (external), place-based (internal), and all customer-contact materials (annual reports, direct mail, billing, and postpackaging, if applicable). It is incredible to see companies trying to improve their corporate image in the general media while neglecting the image-transmitting aspects of direct-contact media to which customers (not just end-customers but also suppliers and employees) are exposed. The analogy in product advertising is a great campaign offset by terrible packaging at the point of purchase. Corporate identity activities should be done *whether or not* corporate image advertising is subsequently added.

All companies—small or larger—should also seek favorable *publicity* when they have news that is worth publicizing. For small companies, the media will usually be local newspapers or local radio. For medium to large companies, TV and newspapers are the usual choices.

Corporate image media selection is summarized in Table 15.8.

## DIRECT RESPONSE ADVERTISING

Direct response advertising is at the opposite end of the spectrum from corporate image advertising: it calls for behavioral action immediately rather than later and is usually directed at a relatively narrow target audience rather than broad or multiple target audiences. As discussed in Chapter 10, direct response

### TABLE 15.8

**MEDIA SELECTION FOR CORPORATE IMAGE ADVERTISING**

| Corporate advertising situation | Recommended media |
| --- | --- |
| **Small companies** | |
| | • Corporate slogan or logo in handbills, suburban newspaper, calendars, or sales aids<br>• Local sponsorships and PR<br>• Local publicity |
| **Medium to large companies** | |
| a. Large target audience | • Television<br>• Cable television<br>• Newspapers (if 4-color)<br>• Outdoor (short message only)<br>• Advertised sponsorships, event marketing, and PR |
| b. Smaller target audience | • Business or consumer magazines<br>• Direct mail |
| **All companies** | |
| | • Head offices and distribution outlets (external)<br>• Place-based (internal)<br>• All customer-contact materials<br>• Publicity |

advertising is used primarily to do one of the following things:

**1.** Sell merchandise outright (called one-step direct response advertising)

**2.** Produce sales inquiries (to "qualify leads") for personal selling (called two-step because a second action is required for the sale)

Also:

**3.** *Mass media* direct response ads are often intended to do "double duty" by serving as mass media ads for those prospects exposed to the ad who don't necessarily respond directly (called double-duty or "across the line" ads)[12]

Direct response advertisers have a choice of five mass media—television, cable television, newspapers, magazines, and radio; and three IMC media—telemarketing, direct mail, and interactive TV or PC advertising. Choices among these media are discussed next. Remember, though, that direct response advertising (in its first two roles) is for *high-involvement* purchases, either of an informational or a transformational nature, the latter usually requiring an informational underlay.

**Television, Cable Television, and Interactive TV or PC advertising.** The limitation of mainstream television for high-involvement/informational advertising is circumvented, in direct response advertising, by employing 60-second, 90-second, or 2-minute commercials to allow for long copy. Often these appear in off-peak time slots when advertising is cheaper. But even with longer commercials, television doesn't really give the target audience decision maker as much time to pause and consider multiple benefit claims as does a print medium, or the next two TV alternatives.

An alternative is *cable* television infomercials, which can be up to a half-hour long, for more complex products or services. Most programs on regular television do not offer precise targeting. However, particular cable channels can provide quite precise demographic targeting because the demographics of the channel's subscribers are known.[13]

Another alternative for TV direct response advertisers is *interactive* (two-way) TV or PC advertising for those few but growing numbers of consumers who have CD-ROM-equipped PCs or TV sets. Targeting is self-selective, so interactive advertising is *very* precise but still very *limited,* for most products and services, in reaching the total target audience (interactive

TV and PC use skews heavily toward high-income households). An advantage of interactivity is that the decision maker can process the benefit claims at his or her own speed.

Television is an obvious choice for direct response when the benefit claim or claims depend on *demonstration.* Kitchen and workshop appliances, and also record collections with audio sequences, are among the most frequently advertised direct response products on TV. Products appearing in infomercials, too, tend to be demonstration-dependent, such as do-it-yourself kits, home exercise equipment, and "experiential" travel offers. Products and services advertised on interactive TV or PCs often include demonstrations, and these are easily accommodated there.

**Newspapers.** Over 95 percent of the direct response advertising in newspapers is in the form of freestanding, preprinted color inserts (FSIs). Newspapers, then, mainly are a medium for carrying what would otherwise be more direct mail. The advantage of newspaper distribution, of course, is that the advertiser doesn't have to address the mailing pieces. The corresponding *disadvantage* is that the advertising reaches everyone who subscribes to the newspaper, without the targeting provided when mailing or telephoning from a list. Accordingly, only for products with demographically *broad* appeal are newspapers a suitable direct response medium.

**Magazines.** Magazines, although identified in Table 15.3 as suitable for direct response advertising, have some practical problems. First, magazine *on-page* direct response ads are more restricted in format than preprinted newspaper inserts (in effect, newspapers are distributing "unique little magazines"). Second, long copy advertisements in magazines usually require a full-page ad plus, often, a special insert for the reply form—which is expensive compared with the cost of simply mailing the material or distributing it in newspapers.

Magazines, however, have a place in direct response advertising because their coverage falls somewhere between the broad coverage of newspapers and the specific coverage of addressed direct mail. Magazines, whether business or consumer, reach fairly well-defined occupational groups (business) and demographic groups by sex, age, and income—or psychological groups by interests or lifestyles (consumer). Magazines should be considered by advertisers whose target audience corresponds well with one of these defined groups.

**Radio.** The least-used conventional medium for direct response advertising is radio; its usage is much less than 1 percent. There are communication limitations in using radio for direct response ads. Brand recognition, obviously, is limited to verbal description on radio, as it is for telephone. High-involvement/informational brand attitude messages are also limited, although this limitation can be overcome, as in television, by buying longer radio commercials.

However, the main problem with radio as a direct response medium has to do with the communication objective of *purchase facilitation* together with radio's typical use as a "background" medium. It would be ridiculous to expect a radio listener in the shower or driving to work to be able to write down an address or telephone number for direct response! Radio direct response advertising is mainly suitable only in the somewhat rare instances of daytime or evening radio programs that reach a high proportion of a particular demographically defined or psychographic-interest defined target audience *known* to be listening in a setting that permits the response to be made, such as "alternative music" radio programs reaching teens and under-30s on weekday nights, and then only if the advertiser's target audience fits such a group.

If you *do* use radio for direct response, first obtain an easily remembered phone number, such as KLM airline's 747-747 used internationally and in some countries with preceding digits, or the famous 1-800-FLOWERS. An easily remembered number helps overcome the problem of the prospect forgetting the number before he or she can get to a telephone (or not even trying to remember it, because of the delay involved). Of course, cellular phones and car phones help if your target audience is likely to have these, for anytime ads and drive-time ads, respectively.

**Telephone (Telemarketing).** The leading position of the telephone as an "advertising medium," accounting for about 50 percent of direct response advertising, is misleading. The large majority of telephone expenditures is for *order taking,* on toll-free numbers, rather than for advertising (or selling) in the conventional sense. The telephone, rather than return mail, is the preferred *response* mechanism for *direct mail* advertising.[14] Although a large amount of business is conducted by telephone, only a fraction of this

is direct response advertising or, as it is usually referred to, direct response selling (telemarketing). The telephone *is* a direct response advertising medium, but it is not the largest.

As an advertising medium, the telephone would be closest in creative content characteristics to radio, with the advantages that, as in personal selling, the message can be tailored to the individual target audience prospect, and that the prospect is likely to have pen and paper handy when answering the telephone at his or her home or office.

The nonvisual nature of the telephone medium makes it suitable only for selling services (for example, insurance) or for selling products that are so well known to the prospect that the product doesn't have to be seen (for example, subscriptions to well-known magazines). Attention tactics for telemarketing were presented in Chapter 10. It is not possible to achieve visual brand recognition by telephone, although verbal brand recognition, including company name recognition, can be attained. The limitation that applies to radio for high-involvement/informational messages does *not* apply to telephone. Telephone as a medium provides the capacity to personally tailor the message (thus taking into account initial attitude and allowing the use of refutation and comparative tactics for this quadrant) and to extend the message as long as necessary (long copy format).

Telephone is thus a good high-involvement/informational direct response medium as long as visual information is not required.

**Direct Mail.** Direct mail is the best direct response medium for accomplishing all five communication objectives. Direct mail can carry advertising as brief as postcards or as extensive as catalogs, and can even deliver products for sampling or trial offers. Over the years, postal charges have risen less than the costs of other media, and this has helped direct mail to retain its attractiveness to advertisers. The growing appeal of direct mail to marketers has been aided by the increasing sophistication of mailing lists, computerized addressing and letter-writing, 800-number telephone ordering, and credit card payment. There is now no product or service that cannot be advertised by direct mail.

Direct response advertising media selection is summarized in Table 15.9. We have assumed that one primary medium will be used for direct response. However, we should note the occasional use

**TABLE 15.9**

**MEDIA SELECTION FOR DIRECT RESPONSE ADVERTISING**

| Nature of product and target audience | Recommended media |
|---|---|
| Any product or service sold to a broad or narrow target audience | • Direct mail |
| Product or service that is well known and doesn't have to be seen | • Telephone |
| Products or services with broad target audience (no mailing list available) | • Newspaper<br>• Television (demonstration products) |
| Products or services whose target audience is well defined by an occupational or other demographic or psychographic readership or listenership group | • Magazine<br>• Radio (daytime or evening)<br>• Interactive TV or PC advertising (upper income) |

of television or radio as "support media" whereby commercials are run telling viewers or listeners to look for a particular direct response offer in a *particular* TV program, or at an interactive TV or PC site, or in newspapers, magazines, or in the mail. Also, when direct response advertising is employed to produce sales leads rather than to sell merchandise outright, it is itself serving as a secondary medium for the primary "medium" of personal selling.

## SUMMARY

Media selection (selection of general media types) is based on the brand's communication objectives. More specifically, the medium or media selected must be capable of transmitting the creative content required of a given communication objective, with sufficient frequency to achieve the objective.

Most advertisers will employ a primary medium, in which the majority of the advertising budget is spent, and one or more secondary media. The primary medium must be capable of conveying all the brand's communication objectives, and it is selected by jointly considering whether the brand requires brand recognition or brand recall (the brand awareness objective) *and* whether the brand choice is low- or high-involvement and informational or transformational (the brand attitude strategy). From this joint consideration, one primary medium will usually emerge or one can easily be selected, from the options remaining, based on target audience reach.

Secondary media are employed to reach target audience members who are not reached sufficiently frequently by the primary medium, or to boost (raise the frequency delivery of) *particular* communication objectives, or because of a special timing advantage near or at the point of purchase. The latter two reasons—boosting and timing advantages—are the strengths of most *IMC media* and are why IMC activities are becoming frequent additions to AC&P programs.

*National consumer advertising* generally will use television as the primary medium unless the brand attitude is high-involvement/informational with a long copy format that requires cable television or print media. *Secondary* media for national consumer advertisers, depending on the brand's communication objectives, are as follows: newspapers (if 4-color), magazines, outdoor, FSIs, and POP to boost brand recognition; radio and newspapers to boost brand recall; radio, newspapers, magazines, outdoor and posters, FSIs, and POP to boost low-involvement/informational brand attitude; radio with imagery transfer, newspapers (if 4-color), magazines, outdoor, FSIs, event marketing, and POP to boost low-involvement/transformational brand attitude; cable TV, newspapers, or magazines (if these aren't primary), stationary outdoor and posters, FSIs, telemarketing, direct response (all DR media), and interactive TV or PC advertising to boost high-involvement/informational brand attitude; and cable TV, newspapers (if 4-color), magazines, outdoor and posters, sponsorship, event marketing, FSIs, POP, postpackaging (though not the last four if there is a large informational support requirement), direct response (all DR media except radio), and interactive TV or PC advertising to boost high-involvement/transformational brand attitude. Again, these are *options,* and are narrowed down when target audience reach is considered.

*Retail advertising* consists of retail product advertising and store image advertising. Retail readvertisers of nationally advertised products (such as supermarkets) generally will use newspapers for their product advertising. Original retail advertisers, on the other hand, will use local TV, if the product mix is narrow; Sunday newspaper supplements, if the mix is wide and the retail drawing area large; direct mail and perhaps interactive TV or PC advertising, for a dispersed target audience; or locally distributed print media if they are a local service retailer or a very small retailer. Nearly all retailers also use POP media.

Retail store image advertising is different from retail product advertising. If the store image is well known, the retail store's brand recall and immediate intentions to visit can be stimulated by store image advertising in local TV, radio, or newspapers. Alternatively, retailers with a store image to promote (visually) will use local TV, newspapers (4-color) or, if the visit cycle is longer, outdoor and poster advertising, city magazines, or direct mail. They can also use IMC media for store image advertising: PR, distribution outlets (external), place-based (internal), publicity, postpackaging and, if they can afford them, sponsorships, event marketing, and interactive TV or PC advertising.

*Industrial or business-to-business advertising* occurs largely in print media, for two reasons: (1) the technical nature of most industrial products and services (high-involvement/informational), and (2) particular print media can be channeled to business audience decision makers with little target audience waste. Industrial advertisers with a small target audience will use personal selling rather than advertising, although pamphlets or brochures may be prepared for the sales force to use as sales aids. Industrial advertisers with a moderate-sized target audience will use trade publications to reach lower-level decision makers (initiators and users) and direct mail to reach top management decision makers (deciders), who rarely read trade publications in detail. Industrial advertisers with a large audience will also use trade publications to reach lower-level decision makers, but to reach top management deciders, business magazines now become cost-effective and possibly more effective due to their prestige value.

*Corporate image advertising* sells the company to customers, investors, prospective and current employees, government regulators, and special interest groups—all of whose actions, positive or negative, affect the company's profits. Corporate image can be projected by small local companies through in-ad attention to the company slogan or logo, and by local sponsorships, local PR, and local publicity. Companies with a large target audience should use television, the most persuasive medium, including cable television advertising, or newspapers (if 4-color). Companies with a target audience too small or narrow for television or newspapers should use magazines (business or consumer, as appropriate), direct mail, point-of-purchase sales literature or, for short corporate messages, thoughtfully placed outdoor ads or posters. Medium to large companies can also communicate corporate image advertising messages with advertised sponsorships, event marketing, and PR. All companies should first ensure that their corporate identity delivers the image they wish to project—with or without corporate image advertising. Corporate identity is projected through head offices and distribution outlets (external), place-based (internal) atmosphere, all customer-contact materials, and publicity.

*Direct response advertising* is the fastest-growing form of advertising. With credit card ordering, any product or service can be sold direct. Direct mail is the largest direct response medium. Telephone direct response (telemarketing) is suitable for advertising well-known products or services that don't have to be seen. Television is the best choice for products that require demonstration, and will compete strongly with direct mail when two-way interactive TV or PC shopping facilities become widely available. For direct response advertisers with a demographically *broad* audience, newspaper inserts are worthwhile; whereas advertisers with a demographically or psychographically *narrow* target audience should use magazines, or possibly radio, steering clear of times when listeners cannot write down a direct response address or phone number.

Having explained and reviewed media *type* selection, we are now ready to move on in the next chapter to the most important decision in media planning—that of *media strategy.* Then, in the final chapter of

Part Six, we conclude with a discussion of media vehicles and advertising unit selection for implementation of the media schedule.

## NOTES

1. As discussed in Chapter 5, the exception is when the brand recognition objective is *auditory recognition*—for example, recognizing a brand name when a salesperson tells you what brands are in stock.

   Auditory recognition is only occasionally an objective, so it is not incorporated in the media selection table. For auditory recognition, media which convey spoken words, allowing consumers to hear and learn to pronounce the brand name, are superior. TV and radio convey spoken words and are therefore best for auditory recognition. Note the suitability of radio here, although it is eliminated for visual recognition.

2. In the section on primary and secondary media selection for consumer advertising, later in the chapter, we will make use of this table again, this time from the perspective of individual media. We will see that there are creative ways around most of the unsuitable and limited media selections. However, the creative solutions are usually expensive, requiring extra time or space, and are rarely as effective as selecting another medium that can meet the communication objectives directly.

3. A possible creative solution for overcoming low frequency in magazines is "impact scheduling," discussed later in the chapter and in Chapter 17.

4. If the advertising campaign has been successful, initial high-involvement target audiences (new category users, other-brand loyals, or other-brand switchers) would now have become repeat buyers (brand loyals or favorable brand switchers) who are now, in most product and service categories, making *low*-involvement (re)purchase decisions. As explained further in Chapter 16, the required frequency is lower for these low-involved "inner" target audiences. Therefore, not only in secondary media but also in primary media, the options widen for continuing campaigns as opposed to new campaigns directed toward high-involvement target audiences.

5. Estimate of cable TV access in TV households (98.3 percent of all households) for 1993 by Nielsen, reported in ADWEEK's *Marketer's Guide to Media*, 1994, *17* (1), p. 54 (New York: ADWEEK).

6. In sales or sales-related tests with a broad variety of nationally advertised supermarket brands, for *every* brand tested, TV has been shown to generate more sales than radio, and more sales than magazine ads.

These studies employed only a single exposure to TV commercials, radio commercials, or magazine ads, respectively, and it is sometimes argued that the results are misleading because one could buy several radio commercials or several magazine ads for the price of one TV commercial. However, this "lower cost" argument is not convincing. First of all, the sales results for TV are two or three times as high as for other media, and there is little likelihood that these sales levels could be achieved just by repeating ads in non-TV media. Secondly, for most consumer products, the advertising has to work quickly. There is no doubt that for short-term sales effectiveness, sought by most nationally advertised consumer products, TV is the most effective medium.

The media experiments are from privately published studies by CBS 1960–61, and 1970–71; and Teleresearch 1968–69, 1970–71, and 1980. The first four experiments are abstracted in W. E. Barlow and E. Papazian, eds., *The Media Book 1979*, pp. 566–568, and *The Media Book 1980*, p. 41; New York: The Media Book, Inc., 1979, 1980. The fifth experiment is abstracted in the Radio Advertising Bureau, Inc., *Radio Facts*, New York: Radio Advertising Bureau, Inc., 1980, p. 37.

7. Legal restrictions may also prevent or limit the use of television; for example, for cigarette or liquor advertising.

8. R. C. Grass and W. H. Wallace, Advertising communication: Print vs. TV, *Journal of Advertising Research*, 1974, *14* (5), pp. 19–23.

9. J. Klue, Tracking down the poster audience, *Admap*, December 1994, pp. 35–37.

10. K. L. Keller, Memory factors in advertising: The effect of advertising retrieval cues on brand evaluation, *Journal of Consumer Research*, 1987, *14* (3), pp. 316–333.

11. Color brochures can be alternatively distributed by hand, in mailboxes. This method of distribution should be used when the retailer's circumstances meet the criteria for handbills (see three paragraphs later).

12. For an excellent model for double-duty direct response ad planning, see A. G. Woodside, Modeling linkage advertising: Going beyond better media comparisons, *Journal of Advertising Research*, 1994, *34* (1), pp. 22–31.

13. B. Stone, *Successful Direct Marketing Methods*, 5th ed., Chicago: Crain Books, 1994.

14. Industry wisdom has it that the response rate with toll-free telephone numbers is three times greater than with return mail, and that telephone orders tend to be larger in dollar amounts.

## DISCUSSION QUESTIONS

**15.1.** Select and explain the most likely primary media type and one likely secondary media type for each of the following advertising situations:
  **a.** A corporate image campaign for DuPont
  **b.** A retail "store specials" advertisement for the Safeway supermarket in White Plains, New York
  **c.** The national introduction of Silkience shampoo

**15.2.** You are the advertising manager for unrecorded blank cassette tapes made under license for Capitol Records. Your advertising claims that Capitol cassettes are the best technical recording tapes to buy, and you want prospective buyers to recognize Capitol tapes at the point of purchase. Radio is your primary media choice because of its high reach against the target audience. Are there any problems with employing radio in this situation, and if so, how would you solve those problems?

**15.3.** You are an advertising consultant to the manager of a new chain of luxury decorating stores. At present you have outlets in only 10 states, scattered throughout the United States. You wish to run a store image campaign. Which primary medium would you recommend for this campaign and why? Discuss alternatives before making your recommendation.

**15.4.** You are the advertising manager for Hewlett-Packard's consumer products division, which sells computers, calculators, and other equipment for personal home or office use. Discuss the media that you would most likely be using throughout the year.

## FURTHER READING

ADWEEK's *Marketer's Guide to Media* (New York: ADWEEK).

Facts-and-figures publication by ADWEEK magazine on all media, including most IMC media. Updated every 6 months.

Sissors, J. A., and Bumba, L. J. *Advertising Media Planning,* 5th edition. Lincolnwood, IL: Crain Books, 1991.

This book provides detailed coverage of basic media options. However, the strategic approach is limited and follows conventional media wisdom. The topic of media buying, mentioned only in passing in our chapter, is covered more fully here.

Lancaster, K., and Katz, H. *Strategic Media Planning.* Lincolnwood, IL: NTC Business Books, 1990.

Like the Sissors and Bumba book, this book takes a conventional approach to media planning. If you want to buy and implement a conventional media plan, this book and its accessory computer disk provide the best technical assistance.

The references listed above are good for identifying the strengths and weaknesses of various advertising media, but there are no references that discuss the concepts of primary and secondary media selection in any detail. Also, none of the references adopts a true communication objectives approach, and none considers advertising media *and* IMC media in terms of communication objectives as we have done in this chapter. And absolutely no media textbook covers the strategic and implementation topics of our next two chapters.

# CHAPTER 16

# Media Strategy: The Reach Pattern and Effective Frequency

The manager has now accomplished the broad media selection decision by selecting the primary and secondary media—from the mainstream advertising media and IMC media alternatives—for the campaign. Next comes the most important part of media planning: determining the *media strategy*. Media strategy fundamentally comprises the joint decisions of *who* (or whom) to reach (loosely called "reach") and *how often* to reach them in terms of number of exposures (loosely called "frequency"). But media strategy is much more than this. In this chapter, we introduce the more advanced concepts of a *reach pattern* in making the reach decision, and *effective frequency* in making the frequency decision. Other concepts, and particularly the "parameters" of the media plan, are also necessary for choosing an appropriate media strategy. After reading this chapter, you should:

- Appreciate the importance of media strategy or "preplanning" the media plan.
- Understand the parameters of the media plan and the trade-offs associated with them.
- Be able to select an appropriate reach pattern for the campaign.
- Be able to calculate the effective frequency for the advertising cycle or cycles in the plan.
- See how to incorporate short-term scheduling and timing into the plan.

In this chapter, we focus on media strategy: planning the plan. In the next chapter, we show how to implement the plan.

## THE IMPORTANCE OF MEDIA STRATEGY AND ITS PARAMETERS

Media strategy is sometimes called "preplanning" by the most knowledgeable media planners.[1] The redundancy of the term "preplanning" is deliberate (you can't or shouldn't "postplan"!) and serves to emphasize that there is a vitally important stage of planning before you launch into the media plan itself. The essential tasks of media strategy or preplanning are to decide on the reach pattern for the campaign and to calculate the required effective frequency levels throughout the campaign.

However, before you can appreciate the importance of media strategy, you have to be armed with definitions of its components. These are provided in Table 16.1 and are known as the *parameters* of the media plan. A parameter is a quantity that is constant in a particular case, such as in a particular media plan, but which varies in different cases, such as in alternative media plans being considered.

### The Planner's Basic Trade-Offs

In essence, the manager or planner faced with the overall decision about how best to spend the media

**TABLE 16.1**

**MEDIA PLAN PARAMETERS: DEFINITIONS**

| Term | Definition |
|---|---|
| Reach | The number of target audience individuals exposed to the advertising or promotion, in an advertising cycle. Reach and effective reach (see below) can also be expressed as *percentages* of the target audience, *provided* that the base number of target audience individuals is clearly specified. |
| Effective reach | The number of target audience individuals reached at the effective frequency level in an advertising cycle. |
| Individual continuity | The time-distribution of exposures, over successive advertising cycles in the planning period, for the *typical target audience individual.* |
| Reach pattern | Distribution of individual continuity over target audience individuals so as to maximize effective reach during the planning period. |
| Timing | Short-term individual continuity tactic whereby *media vehicles* are selected to deliver the advertising or promotion as close as possible to the target audience individual's experience of category need or to the point of decision. |
| Frequency | The number of exposures per individual target audience member, in an advertising cycle |
| Effective frequency | The number of exposures, in an advertising cycle, believed or known to be able to maximize the target audience individual's disposition to act. Effective frequency is always expressed as a minimum effective frequency (MEF) and sometimes additionally with a maximum effective frequency beyond which additional exposures *decrease* disposition to act (MaxEF). |
| Exposure | Placement of the advertisement in a media vehicle that the target audience is *known or expected* to see, hear, or read; same as an OTS (see below). Exposure is an *opportunity* for the target audience to pay attention to the ad but does not refer to actual attention. |
| Exposure distribution | Frequency distribution of exposures in an advertising cycle, expressed as reach percentages; thus the percentage reached 0 times (that is, *not* reached), the percentage reached 1 time, the percentage reached 2 times, and so forth. Because the zero (unreached) cell is included, the percentage frequencies add up to 100 percent of the target audience. Reach (see first definition in table) is 100 minus the zero-cell percentage. |
| Dominance | Frequency tactic whereby the MEF is set higher than the frequency used by the largest or leading competitor (called LC + 1 in the MEF formula) for one or more advertising cycles. |
| Advertising cycle | A flight of advertising (or promotion) within the advertising period. The extremes are a continuous schedule, in which there is one long advertising cycle equal to the entire period; and a discontinuous schedule, in which the advertising cycles may be as short as 1 day or even 1 hour. |
| Purchase cycle | The average length of time, for the average target audience member, between purchases in the *category* (also known as the IPT or interpurchase time, or IPI or interpurchase interval). |
| GRPs | Gross Rating Points, also referred to as "weight." The GRPs of a media schedule are the sum of the percentage reach of each advertising (or promotion) insertion in an advertising cycle. One GRP means that the insertion reaches 1 percent of the target audience; 10 GRPs means that that the insertion reaches 10 percent; and so on. The target audience on which the GRPs are based should be clearly specified. GRPs are usually calculated as the *sum* of the target audience ratings of every vehicle used in the advertising cycle, with multiple insertions in a vehicle receiving the vehicle's rating each time. Thus 3 insertions in a vehicle with a 10 rating is 30 GRPs, as is 3 insertions in three *different* vehicles each with a 10 rating. (Note that actual reach and frequency are lost in this gross sum. GRPs are an estimate of the total number of exposure opportunities, or OTS, per 100 target audience members, in an advertising cycle, without regard to whether the individuals receiving these OTS were the same people or different people.) GRPs apply to any and *all* advertising and promotional media and have the same definition universally. |
| ERPs | Effective Rating Points. Based on the exposure distribution, the ERP measure counts only the percentages reached at the effective frequency level. It is therefore an estimate of "effective GRPs" and, also, of effective reach in *percentage* terms. |
| Insertion | Placement of the ad or promotion offer in a media vehicle. The insertion represents an OTS (see below) *only* to those people who are reached by the vehicle. |
| OTS | Opportunity(ies) to See (or Hear) the ad or promotion offer. Can be used as a singular or plural term. In a singular usage, OTS is the same as an "exposure." In a plural usage, OTS is the same as frequency. |

budget has to grapple with three basic parameters: reach, frequency, and the number of advertising cycles affordable for the year. These trade-offs are shown diagrammatically in Figure 16.1 with the aid of a metaphor that we call the "media balloon."

If the balloon is "tied off" (meaning that there is a fixed media budget), the manager cannot make one sphere larger without squeezing at least one of the other two. However, if the manager is allowed to "inflate" the balloon to any necessary size (meaning that there is no ceiling on the media budget), then all three spheres will enlarge and a more comprehensive media plan will result. Inflating from a flat balloon, so to speak, represents the *task method* of media budget estimation, and this is the method we advocate most generally as the primary method of budgeting (see Chapter 2). We should emphasize that in most management situations, the media balloon *will* have a maximum size. The balloon's size will be constrained by the media budget, set either by one of the budgeting methods described in Chapter 2 or by some higher level corporate decision. The budget constraint forces trade-offs between and among the spheres—that is, between reach and frequency, reach and the number of advertising cycles, and frequency within each advertising cycle.

The principle that governs these trade-offs is a simple but vital one: *It is better to sell some people completely than many people not at all.* As we shall see, this principle is based on effective frequency in the media plan.

**Reach Versus Frequency.** A media plan with a fixed budget can be designed to reach either a lot of people a few times, or a few people a lot of times. This is the trade-off between reach and frequency. For example, by scattering the budget—and hence the advertising or promotion exposures—across a lot of different media types (such as TV, radio, newspapers, magazines, outdoor ads, and various IMC media) and across many different media vehicles (such as different TV programs, radio stations, sponsored events, and POP devices), a large number of different people will be exposed to the advertising or promotion campaign—but they won't be exposed very often.

In contrast, by spending the same budget in only one media type, such as magazines, and in very few vehicles, such as *Time* and *Newsweek* magazines only, a much smaller number of people will be exposed to the advertising—but they will be exposed very frequently. The same goes for promotion: if you use only in-pack coupons, for instance, you'll be reaching only those who've already decided to buy the brand—but you'll do so with very high frequency.

*Geographic Reach Versus Frequency.* A similar trade-off operates geographically. The advertiser could try to reach either every prospect in the nation, at low frequency, or every prospect in a more limited geographic region, at high frequency.

For new products, the geographic trade-off is often automatically made in favor of geographic reach, following the strategy of a *national rollout* of the new product, with the frequency being adjusted as the manager observes what has happened in the initial market or markets. (With a new product rollout, the total AC&P budget usually is—and should be—changeable, ready to be cut if the product looks like it's failing, or increased should it show indications of being a winner.)

For established products, Schroer's method of budget allocation (see Chapter 2) comes to the fore. In Schroer's method, frequency is deliberately set low in some areas and high in others, depending on the brand's *competitive* strengths and weaknesses in those areas.

Reach versus frequency represents the most common trade-off in the media plan (apart from an already decided upon national rollout). As we will

**FIGURE 16.1**

The "media balloon" metaphor for the trade-offs involved in the basic parameters of the media plan.

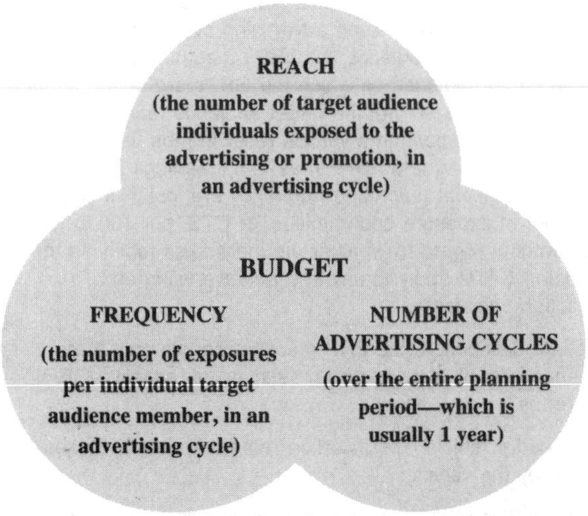

**REACH**

(the number of target audience individuals exposed to the advertising or promotion, in an advertising cycle)

**BUDGET**

**FREQUENCY**

(the number of exposures per individual target audience member, in an advertising cycle)

**NUMBER OF ADVERTISING CYCLES**

(over the entire planning period—which is usually 1 year)

see shortly, frequency, properly conceptualized as effective frequency within the advertising cycle, should always govern this trade-off. Reach at too low a frequency is wasted advertising (this applies to a national rollout, too!).

**Reach Versus Number of Advertising Cycles.** A second trade-off is between reach and the number of advertising cycles in the planning period (usually 1 year). It is usually impossible—and indeed in many cases unnecessary, as we will see in the reach patterns to follow—to reach everyone in the target audience continuously throughout the year. Rather, the year is judgmentally divided into a number of advertising (or promotion) *cycles* which may be advertised in continuously *or* periodically.

If it is advantageous to advertise in continuous or nearly continuous cycles, as with a frequently purchased product or service, then reach should be sacrificed. For instance, a marketer employing a direct response, databased program for low-cost products or services that are frequently bought would return to the same "proven prospects" relatively continuously rather than always trying to extend the reach to new "suspects" (see Chapter 14). Loyalty marketing programs to databased "club" members can fit the extreme of this trade-off: low reach but many advertising cycles.

In contrast, the marketer of an *infrequently* purchased product or service may be advised to adopt a broad reach media plan and to advertise only occasionally, with just several advertising cycles a year. This may be sufficient to keep long-term target audience individuals "interested" (brand aware and favorably disposed in terms of brand attitude) without having to reach them continuously. Indeed, continuous advertising might be overkill and a waste of the budget. Advertising for consumer durables, many industrial products, and also corporate image advertising and PR (see Chapter 11) would be likely situations in which to favor reach over the number of advertising cycles.

**Frequency Versus Number of Advertising Cycles.** The remaining trade-off is between frequency *per* advertising cycle and the number of cycles in which to advertise (or promote). Holding reach constant, you could either advertise at "thin" frequency in many advertising cycles or at *effective frequency* in fewer cycles. This is easiest to appreciate when the advertising cycle is based on the *purchase*

cycle for the product, such as every 21 days for instant coffee. For instant coffee, at least two exposures per purchase cycle seems to be an effective frequency level when brand switchers are the target audience (see Chapter 17). Thus a "thin" schedule—fewer than two exposures for most of the target audience for most or all of the 17 advertising and purchase cycles in the year (365 days divided by 21 days = 17 cycles)—would be poor use of the budget. So-called "maintenance" media plans usually fall into this trap and delude the client into wasted spending.

The solution is to "flight" the advertising over fewer advertising cycles (that is, to place your advertisements in only some of the cycles that are potentially available, concentrating its frequency in the selected cycles). Remember, you "can't win 'em all," unless you have an unlimited budget, and it is better to win some than none. We show how to design flighted schedules later in this chapter.

Reach, frequency, and number of advertising cycles are, therefore, the basic parameters whose numerical values must be set in the media plan by working out the best trade-offs between and among them within the allocated budget. The best trade-offs obviously depend on the media strategy for the target audience and the brand. To decide on the best strategy, you also need to know about the other, more advanced parameters that you can work with in the media plan.

### Advanced Media Plan Parameters

Table 16.1 provides definitions of the basic as well as the advanced parameters of the media plan. We have also provided some other useful definitions, such as GRPs and OTS, which are typical measurement units in an advertising plan.

The advanced parameters are extensions of the two basic parameters, reach and frequency.

**Reach → Individual Continuity → Timing.** Advanced media planning requires that the concept of *reach* be taken further in the form of *individual continuity*, which in turn can be considered in terms of the precise *timing* of the ads or promotion offers as they are delivered to the target audience. *Reach,* as we have seen, refers to the number of target audience individuals exposed to the advertising or promotion in an advertising cycle. Reach can be expressed alternatively in terms of proportions or percentages of the target audience rather than in gross numbers, but it is much clearer to plan in terms of numbers (especially when using the task method of budgeting).

*Individual continuity* is the time-distribution of exposures, over successive advertising cycles in the planning period, for the typical target audience individual. It is something like frequency over the entire planning period, taking the time or temporal "distance" between exposures into account. Suppose you want to reach 1 million target audience individuals. Do you want to reach them just once during the entire year? You may, if you are selling a product or service that they will purchase only once. Or do you want to reach the typical target audience individual at least several times throughout the year? If so, you will have to choose particular advertising cycles in which to insert ads (or promotions) aimed at that individual. It is easiest to think of individual continuity as a media plan parameter from the *prospect's* perspective. The prospect would ask, if he or she were in the advertiser's role: "How many times during the year would this advertiser have to reach me to (1) get me interested in the product and (2) keep me persuaded to buy it?"

Reach and individual continuity can be taken still further with the media plan parameter of *timing*. Here, the prospect would ask not only how many times he or she would need to be reached but also: "And (3) when are the best times to reach me?" Timing is a short-term individual continuity tactic whereby *media vehicles* are selected to deliver the advertising, adlike event, or promotion as close as possible to the target audience individual's experience of category need[2] or to his or her point of decision. For IMC activities especially, the behavioral sequence model for the target audience (see Chapter 4) is instrumental in helping to decide the best timing of media vehicles with regard to the decision process.

The evolution of reach into individual continuity and timing will be most evident when we show how to determine the *reach pattern* for the media plan, in the next major section of this chapter.

**Frequency → Effective Frequency → Dominance.** Frequency, at the individual level, is not of much use unless it is "effective frequency." *Effective frequency* is the number of exposures, in an advertising cycle, believed or known to be able to maximize the target audience individual's disposition to act. The most important number relating to effective frequency is

*minimum effective frequency* (*MEF*) at which the advertising or promotion offer will "start working" and below which it won't work at all.[3] Exposures beyond the MEF level are still effective but could represent "overadvertising" and—in some particular cells of the Rossiter-Percy grid—could actually cause a *decrease* in the disposition to act. If so, the number of exposures just before disposition starts to decrease is known as *maximum effective frequency* (*MaxEF*).

Effective frequency can be taken further in another advanced parameter of the media plan called *dominance*. Dominance is a frequency tactic whereby the MEF is set higher than the frequency used by the *leading competitor*. This dominance is then sustained for one or more advertising cycles, but typically for every other or every third or fourth *potential* cycle, depending on what the advertiser can afford. In our MEF formula described later in this chapter, dominance enters in the "LC + 1" component. We are explicit about when to use dominance, again in accordance with Rossiter-Percy grid theory.

**Effective Reach.** The parameters of reach and effective frequency are *combined* in the parameter of *effective reach,* which is the number of target audience individuals reached at the effective frequency level (MEF or higher) in an advertising cycle. When expressed in numbers rather than percentages, effective reach is the most important number for evaluating a media plan as it evolves cycle by cycle.

**Advertising Cycle.** An *advertising cycle* refers to a flight of advertising (or promotion) within the advertising period. The entire period (usually 1 year) may be divided up into one or a number of discrete periods in which advertising or promotional insertions *could* be made in the media plan. The *actual* insertion periods, the advertising cycles, are often referred to as "flights" of advertising or promotion. The intervals *between* flights or advertising cycles are often known as *hiatus* periods.

The cycles advertised in, and their durations, depend on the reach patterns (as we'll see). There is no fixed time for an advertising cycle: it may be as long as 1 year in the case of a continuous advertising schedule, or it may be as short as 1 day or even 1 hour in the case of, for example, retail sales promotions. However, note that the definition refers to a *flight* rather than to a particular duration because, in the case of some media such as magazines and direct mail, the timing of the advertising insertion and when it is actually *seen or read* by the target audience individual may be very far apart in time.

From the media planner's perspective, the notion of a *flight of insertions* captures the advertising cycle concept most clearly.

A *purchase cycle,* on the other hand, is buyer-based rather than advertising-based and refers to the average length of time, for the average target audience member, between purchases in the product or service *category.* The purchase cycle is also known as the IPT, interpurchase time, or IPI, interpurchase interval. Advertising cycles in media plans may be geared to purchase cycles if the product or service is one that is purchased frequently and at reasonably regular intervals.

Armed with these concepts and parameter definitions, we are now ready to examine the two major aspects of media strategy: the reach pattern and effective frequency.

## THE REACH PATTERN

Determination of the *reach pattern*[4] for the media plan is the first of the two major decisions in media strategy. It is vitally important not only for advertising media plans but also for integrated marketing communications plans.

To determine the appropriate reach pattern, the manager or media planner has to conceptualize the entire advertising communications and promotion schedule from the *individual* target prospect's viewpoint.[5] The individual prospect with whom we are concerned is the *typical member of the target audience.* The target audience, you will recall from Chapter 3, can be new category users, other-brand loyals, other-brand switchers, favorable brand switchers, or brand loyals.

We offer a "menu" of eight fundamental reach patterns from which the manager can choose. There are four reach patterns for new product media plans and four reach patterns for established product media plans. You should be able to find a reasonably good fit of *one* of these reach patterns to your present advertising communications or promotion situation—and can then implement minor adaptations as necessary (see the final section of this chapter, on short-term

scheduling and timing). The eight reach patterns are presented and discussed next.

### Reach Patterns for New Product Introductions

Reach patterns for *new product introductions* are shown in Figures 16.2 through 16.5; these are called the blitz pattern, the wedge pattern, the reverse-wedge/PI pattern, and the short fad pattern. In showing the reach patterns diagrammatically, we have depicted reach by the vertical height of the blocks in the bar charts, and the relative frequency, per flight, by the *width* or thickness of the bars. The vertical axis is reach *of* the target audience, and the horizontal axis is time over the advertising planning period, which marks advertising cycles.

**Blitz Pattern.** It is virtually impossible to overadvertise a new product or service during its introduction.[6] The ideal pattern, then, if you can afford it, consists of a "blitz" of continuous advertising for the first year. The blitz pattern (Figure 16.2) is shown for advertising. The blitz pattern for *introductory promotions,* to gain trial, would usually occur only for the first 6 months because that is the length of time for which a product or service can legally use the description "new."

In the blitz pattern, you go for 100 percent reach of the target audience—regarding the advertising cycle as the full year—and pile on as much frequency as you can afford, to the *same individuals* for the entire cycle.[7] This blitz pattern will not only maximize the rate of trial (and remember from Chapter 3 that with new product trial, it can take up to 2 years before maximum penetration is attained) but will also tend to suppress the effects of any competitors' advertising by use of sustained dominance.

**FIGURE 16.2**
"Blitz" reach pattern (new products).

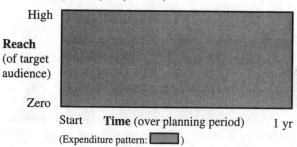

For a really new product—because of the difficulty of defining a precise target audience, with virtually everyone being a potential new category user—the blitz pattern can be *very* expensive. It has been estimated that the typical advertising cost for a national launch of a new consumer product with a new brand name is about $35 million, whereas for a line extension of a national brand the cost is about $20 million. To launch with a blitz (say, 80 percent reach via prime-time TV with two exposures per week for an entire year) would cost about $105 million![8] However, remember from Chapters 2 and 6 the rewards of pioneer advantage. Although this is jumping ahead to Chapter 20, you probably would also need a fairly large pool of advertising executions, built around the same positioning strategy, to prevent advertising wearout, which is likely to be rapid with such a heavy schedule.

**Wedge Pattern.** The wedge pattern—rather than the blitz pattern—is probably the most common pattern for new product launches. The "wedge" actually refers to the pattern of *expenditure,* which begins like a blitz and then tapers off throughout the continuous introductory advertising cycle. Thus, for a new product launched by the wedge pattern, 400 GRPs a month may be bought for the first several months, tapering down to 50 or so by the end of the year. Note carefully, however, that the wedge pattern for the typical target audience *individual* is *not* wedge-shaped (Figure 16.3) but instead is received as a succession of advertising flights—each with the *same high reach* but successively *declining frequency.*

The wedge pattern makes a lot of sense as an introductory media strategy for *low-involvement*

products and services where the trial risk is minor. High frequency is needed initially to create brand awareness for the new product and to enable prospective triers to learn the new product's benefits (informational) or learn its intended image (transformational). Thereafter, most of those who try, if all goes well, will become favorable brand switchers (FBSs) or brand loyals (BLs) who will require less frequency in later cycles to maintain their communication effects' status (see the MEF formula later in this chapter).

In fact, if you could achieve very precise media placement, the ideal reach pattern would be to combine a blitz with a wedge, such that a blitz is continued against those who have not yet tried the brand (NCUs, OBLs, and OBSs), with trier-rejectors avoided, and a wedge used against those who have tried the brand and have responded favorably (FBSs and BLs). Direct matching in media vehicle selection (see Chapter 17) can enable this composite reach pattern to be attempted.

**Reverse-Wedge/PI Pattern.** As in the wedge pattern, the "reverse-wedge" refers to media *expenditures* over the planning period rather than to exposures as received by the typical target audience individual (Figure 16.4). The target audience individual receives *increasing* frequency with each flight, and reach is held constant at 100 percent of the target audience. The personal influence (PI) component is explained below.

When should a reverse-wedge/PI pattern be used? Its usage is most appropriate for the introduction of a product or service that has a purchase motive of so-

**FIGURE 16.3**

"Wedge" reach pattern (new products). Width of bars indicates frequency.

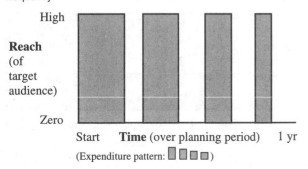

**FIGURE 16.4**

"Reverse-wedge/PI" reach pattern (new products with social approval motive). Width of bars indicates frequency. Asterisks denote an emphasis on innovators within the target audience.

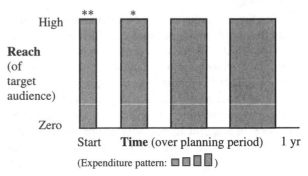

cial approval, when the advertiser is willing to bet on *personal influence* (word of mouth, or visual influence in the case of products or services that are socially consumed) as a *complement* to the advertising. The idea is that the *low* initial advertising frequency will make the product or service appear to be somewhat "exclusive" (this works better still if the low frequency is accompanied by low reach targeted particularly to *innovators,* many of whom will act as opinion leaders). Then, as the hoped-for personal influence begins to spread, the advertising frequency is stepped up to help persuade the growing number of prospective adopters (in the innovator version of this pattern, the *reach* is also stepped up).

To our knowledge, the reverse-wedge/PI pattern was first used by Toohey's Brewery (now Lion Nathan) in Australia for the introduction of its Toohey's Red and, later, Toohey's Blue bitter beers. The reverse-wedge/PI strategy was very successful and has since been imitated, certainly in Australia, by almost all other new beer launches, especially the "boutique" beers whose positioning is almost exclusively based on social approval.

**Short Fad Pattern.** Well discussed in the marketing and consumer behavior literature is the fact that some products are strictly "fad" products with a short product life cycle.[9] Some of these products, such as inexpensive fashion wear or new toys, may be purchased more than once while the fad lasts.

The short fad pattern (Figure 16.5) is like a short blitz pattern with an important difference: you want to get in early, during the *introduction* stage of the fad life cycle, and this calls for broad reach (unless you know who the innovators are likely to be) and high frequency; the broad reach and high frequency need to be sustained during the *growth stage* of the product life cycle (though this won't last long with most fads) in order to catch the large "middle majority" as they become ready to adopt the fad. (Note that we have *not* assumed here that there is a large personal influence (PI) effect, as in the previous pattern. But even if there is, we would not advise the reverse-wedge/PI pattern, because with fads you have to blitz for only a relatively short time, and you may as well do so.)

New movies are an interesting example of a product that follows the short fad pattern. Weinberg[10] has shown that the amount of introductory advertising is similarly influential to newspaper critics' reviews,

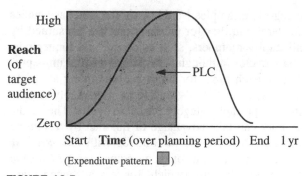

**FIGURE 16.5**
"Short fad" reach pattern (fad products).

with both more influential than word of mouth, in determining the size of new films' first-run theater audiences. (Perhaps this is why we have to sit through so many previews for other new releases when we go to see a new movie!)

### Reach Patterns for Established Products

Most media plans are for *established* products and services. Even new products, after their first year or so, become "established" and are no longer introductory unless a new target audience is being sought. There is a choice of four fundamental reach patterns for established products, and these demand considerable thought if you are serious about saving money in the media plan rather than just throwing GRPs "out there" and hoping for the best. The alternative reach patterns for established products (and services) are shown in Figures 16.6 through 16.9; these are called the regular purchase cycle pattern, the awareness pattern, the shifting reach pattern, and the seasonal priming pattern.

**Regular Purchase Cycle Pattern.** Most consumer packaged goods (fmcg products) and some services, such as visits to the barber or hairdresser, are purchased by individuals on a regular and relatively short purchase cycle—"short" meaning that there are a number of purchase cycles during the year. For instance, U.S. data from Nielsen show that the average household purchases margarine every 19 days, toilet tissue every 20 days, tuna fish every 31 days, peanut butter every 48 days, and ketchup every 50 days.[11] Of course, these are only averages, and more precise surveys may show that particular demographic subgroups within the target audience follow shorter or longer purchase cycles for a particular product category. Examples would be shorter purchase cycles for large families for products that are consumed by all family members, such as cereal, and longer purchase cycles (although perhaps just smaller units purchased each time) for single persons living alone. In any event, individuals tend to be remarkably regular in their product category purchase cycles. The media planner can take advantage of this fact by designing the *advertising* cycle to coincide with the *purchase* cycle. Thus, instead of using some *standard period* for media planning (which, for less advanced planners, is usually 4 weeks), it makes much better sense to gear the advertising to the purchase cycle, because this is the true time interval that the advertising (or promotion) has to induce the consumer to switch brands.

The regular purchase cycle pattern (Figure 16.6) divides the year into a number of advertising cycles of equal duration, corresponding with the target audience's product category purchase cycles. The graph actually shows a regular purchase cycle *flighting* pattern (a strategy discussed below) for which, in this particular illustration, the purchase cycle is 50 days. In this illustration, there are seven possible advertising cycles, in which the advertiser has placed advertising in four of them. Of course, these purchase cycles are averages—not every individual consumer starts at the same time and finishes at the same time even if his or her purchase cycle is exactly equal in duration to other consumers' purchase cycles. However, setting *frequency* on the basis of the *average* purchase cycle will tend to produce the right *rate* of

advertising frequency for everyone, no matter when their *individual* purchase cycle starts and finishes.

The strategic question for the regular purchase cycle reach pattern is mostly a matter of budget. The ideal pattern, with an unlimited budget, would be to reach *every* target audience individual in *every* purchase cycle successively (that is, continuously throughout the year). Why? Because, on every purchase cycle, the buyer of a frequently purchased product or service essentially *becomes a new prospect again* and is functionally a new individual to be reached even though he or she may have been reached before. Thus, the potential reach is 100 percent of prospects on *each* purchase cycle. If there are, for example, 12 purchase cycles on average during the year, the yearly potential reach is 1,200 percent! Fortunately, many of these prospects would be, or should become, favorable brand switchers or loyal buyers— so they would not require more than minimal frequency on each purchase cycle. Nevertheless, few advertisers could afford to advertise at this rate.

The trade-off to save budget is twofold: (1) sometimes, depending on marketing strategy and ability to measure delivery of media vehicles, to cut down on reach, eliminating OBL and OBS rejectors and negative NCUs; and (2) usually, to advertise in alternate or occasional purchase cycles rather than in every successive purchase cycle (flighting).

A *flighting* pattern within the regular purchase cycle reach pattern is actually more effective than continuous advertising[12] unless you have a large pool of equally persuasive ads that you can change on each purchase cycle. The advantage of flighting is due to the well-documented phenomenon known as "hysteresis" whereby a particular ad has its greatest purchase effect immediately, which then begins to fade even though the ad is continued.[13] The idea is that by stopping an ad while it is still working and before it has faded too much, and then running it again one or two purchase cycles later so it appears "new" again, you can achieve a gradual upward trend in purchase effectiveness.[14]

Flighting applies to *retail promotions* as well. Since retailers rarely promote a particular brand continuously, they achieve a *de facto* flighted reach pattern for promotions for the brand such that its promotions usually occur several purchase cycles apart. Retailers' promotion patterns were discussed in Chapter 13, and it is important to realize that these,

**FIGURE 16.6**
"Regular purchase cycle" reach pattern (established products with a short, regular purchase cycle). Width of bars indicates frequency *and* equals one purchase cycle (pc). (With a bigger budget, the bars would be closer together: in other words, there would be more *advertising* cycles.)

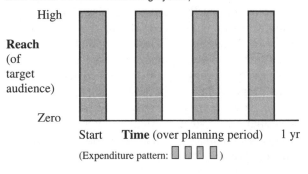

too, are media patterns in the same sense as are advertising patterns practiced by the manufacturer for the brand.

The flighting pattern within a regular purchase cycle reach pattern can be greatly aided by the use of continuous tracking (see Chapter 20), which allows you to try different flighting patterns and observe their effects in terms of sales and profit.

**Awareness Pattern.** The "awareness" reach pattern applies to consumer and industrial products and services that have a *long purchase cycle* and a *long decision time*. These products or services are purchased infrequently—perhaps only once every several years—and are typically "pondered" for a long interval before the purchase decision is made. Long-haul holiday travel, new cars, and other luxury items would be consumer examples. New cars, for instance, have an average purchase cycle of 5 years in the United States.[15] Installing a new computer system in a company, adopting TQM (total quality management), or hiring a consultant to help set up a customer database would be typical industrial examples. Virtually everyone in the target audience is "interested" or semi-interested in buying but, at any one time, only a few of these people actually decide to buy.

This situation is well handled by the awareness reach pattern shown in Figure 16.7. This reach pattern is called the "awareness" pattern[16] because the strategy is to keep all prospects "aware" of the brand, while the marketer realizes that the timing of the decision to buy is unpredictable for any particular individual prospect. "Aware" is a loosely employed term in advertising, and in *our* terms, it means that the prospect has brand awareness *and* a favorable brand attitude.

The awareness pattern consists of very high reach, to virtually all prospects, but relatively *low* frequency per advertising cycle, with the advertising cycles occurring at quite widely spread intervals. Each of the advertising cycles, though, has to contain an MEF level of insertions sufficient to sustain the "awareness" (again, actually brand awareness and favorable brand attitude). If this "awareness" includes brand recall *or* transformational brand attitude as a communication objective, then it will be highly sensitive to competitive advertising, that is, to our brand's "share of voice." This means that continuous tracking (see Chapter 20) will be needed to properly implement this particular reach pattern—in terms of frequency, pre-

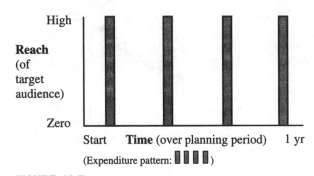

**FIGURE 16.7**
"Awareness" reach pattern (established products with long purchase cycle, long decision time). Width of bars indicates frequency.

cisely, rather than in terms of reach, which always aims to be as high as affordable.

The awareness reach pattern for products or services with a long purchase cycle and a long decision time is ideally accomplished in an *IMC* manner by combining mass media advertising with direct response ads. In fact, the main application of "double duty" direct response ads, which serve a general communication effect purpose as well as a direct response function, is for the types of products and services that exhibit both a long purchase cycle and a long decision time. Thus, for instance, the famous Paul Hogan "Throw another shrimp on the barbie" TV commercials run in the United States by the Australian Tourist Commission always included an 800-number "super" on the screen at the end of the commercial which people could call to obtain further information; after providing information on the phone, the ATC then mailed to prospects an Aussie travel booklet. Industrial or business-to-business ads run on an awareness reach pattern also typically include a toll-free direct response number, a reply coupon, or online information and ordering location.

**Shifting Reach Pattern.** The shifting reach pattern applies to products and services with a long purchase cycle and a *short* decision time. The shifting reach pattern is a rather unconventional one that regularly moves its focus, rather like a searchlight. It is shown graphically in Figure 16.8.

The logic behind this pattern—consumer durables would be an appropriate example to keep in mind—depends on the realization that although the product or service may have a long purchase cycle, the

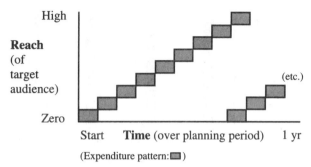

**FIGURE 16.8**
"Shifting reach" reach pattern (established products with a long purchase cycle and a *short* decision time). Width of bars indicates frequency.

*decision* to buy it is made very rapidly—such as when your present durable suddenly dies on you. Most of us have had this experience with refrigerators, washing machines, and the other necessities of domestic life. Let's consider such purchases from an advertising perspective: On the one hand, you want the advertising to be "out there" whenever a prospect's category need occurs and he or she is thrust into the market; but, on the other hand, you cannot afford to be out there all the time for everybody. Add to this the further realization that once an individual has bought, that individual will be out of the market (a non-prospect) for a very long time afterward.

The solution is to adopt a *shifting* reach pattern of advertising. Like a searchlight, you successively scan 100 percent of prospects, hoping to catch *some* of those who are in the market at that time. The reach *eventually* accumulates to 100 percent of prospects, but on any one advertising cycle it might be only—say—10 percent. Why this pattern? The blitz pattern would be theoretically correct in this situation but hardly affordable year in and year out over the long purchase cycle of durables. The awareness pattern is inappropriate because, first, there is not a long decision time involved here and, second, the wide spacing of the advertising cycles in the awareness pattern (refer to Figure 16.7 again) means that you would miss many particular days on which certain prospects are ready to buy. Thus, the shifting reach pattern is the appropriate compromise.

The shifting reach pattern is quite an easy media strategy to implement in practice. Although this is really a topic for Chapter 17, you may be intrigued as to how it is accomplished. You simply concentrate your advertising on one or two particular media vehicles for one advertising cycle, then change to another small set of particular vehicles for the next advertising cycle, and so forth. The overlap between media vehicles—even in a relatively "mass" medium like network television—is so small as to virtually ensure that you will achieve a shifting reach of new prospects on each advertising cycle. (Any overlap overlays an *awareness* reach pattern on the shifting reach pattern, which is fine. But remember the selling purpose of the advertising and don't be tempted to *try* for overlap.) This shifting reach pattern also has advantages for the manufacturer and the retailer by *evening out* sales over the year and thus simplifying production and inventory management.

**Seasonal Priming Pattern.** The seasonal priming reach pattern, as the name suggests, is appropriate for products and services whose sales are characterized by one, and sometimes two or three, large seasonal peaks (Figure 16.9). Low-involvement products exhibiting major seasonality include cold and flu medicines, Scotch whisky, and some grocery products such as turkeys at Thanksgiving. High-involvement seasonal purchases would include ski equipment, exterior house paint, and tax consultancy services.

It is naturally advantageous for a seasonal brand's advertising to reach people near (either just prior to or early into) the seasonal peak, because it will reach people when their category need is strong and thus when they are ready to learn or be reminded about brand differences. However—and this is where the "priming" comes in—most other competitors will

**FIGURE 16.9**
"Seasonal priming" reach pattern (established products with one or several seasonal sales peaks—two are shown here to illustrate the concept). Width of bars indicates frequency; the thinner bars represent preseasonal primes.

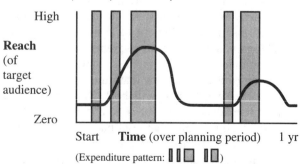

usually be following the same media strategy, so there will be a lot of competitive advertising around the peak. An effective strategy is to put in a couple of short flights of advertising a month or two *before* the seasonal peak develops. Simulations conducted by Strong[17] suggest that such "preseasonal" advertising can "prime" seasonal advertising, probably because it starts to move consumers toward the effective frequency level that will be needed for the brand *during* the peak. This early priming, of course, reaches people in a low state of category need, but can create brand awareness and teach the brand's message without competitive interference.

**Summary.** If you think about what you are trying to do with your advertising and promotions at the *individual* level (a good method is by imagining *yourself* in the role of the typical prospective customer), then you will be on the right path to identifying an appropriate reach pattern for the media plan. The second consideration is that there are a lot of individual prospects to be reached (besides yourself, if you are imagining this through), and you usually cannot afford to reach all of them all of the time. These two composite considerations—within an individual and across individuals—indicate the correct reach pattern for the media plan.

After you have decided on the reach pattern, the second major aspect of media strategy is to estimate effective frequency levels for those people reached during the advertising cycles *in* the particular pattern chosen.

## EFFECTIVE FREQUENCY

The concept of *effective frequency* is based on the idea that an individual prospective customer has to be exposed to a brand's advertising a certain minimum number of times, within an advertising cycle, in order for the advertising to influence purchase.[18] Effective frequency actually consists of a range of exposures between the minimum effective frequency level and a possible maximum effective frequency level. Exposures within this range raise to a practical maximum the individual's *disposition* to purchase the brand, or to engage in other appropriate purchase-related behavior.

The concept of effective frequency is also applicable to *promotion,* as we shall see, although its main use is in planning the media schedule for advertising.

In this section of the chapter, we examine the concept of effective frequency in detail, along with its component concepts of insertion, exposure, and disposition to purchase, and the derivative concepts of minimum effective frequency, maximum effective frequency, and effective reach.

### Insertion

An *insertion* is simply the placement of an ad in a media vehicle. A media "schedule" comprises all the insertions that are placed in all the media vehicles used in the plan.

There is a fundamental difference between insertions in a media schedule and the exposures that result from that media schedule:

- Insertions are the gross or aggregate input.
- Exposures are the individual-level result (see also below for a more precise definition).

The difference is easily understood with an example. Suppose an ad is inserted four times in a media schedule. If the four insertions are in the *same* media vehicle, it is quite likely that everyone reached by the vehicle will get four exposures to the ad. However, if the four insertions are in *different* media vehicles, hardly anyone will get four exposures—most of the individuals reached will get only one exposure. There have been four insertions in both cases, but the exposures to individuals that these insertions produce are very different. Insertions go in, and a *distribution* of exposures across individuals comes out. The distribution differs depending on where the insertions are placed.

### Exposure

Effective frequency is based on *exposures* to the advertising. By "exposure" we mean *placement of the advertisement in a media vehicle* that the target audience is *known or expected to see, hear, or read.* The British term for exposures, OTS, or opportunities to see (hear or read) the advertisement, nicely expresses what we mean by exposure.

Whether target audience individuals *do in fact* see, hear, or read the advertisement—that is, in our terminology, whether they begin to *process* the advertisement by at least paying initial attention to it—is jointly a function of three things: (1) the attention-getting characteristics of the media vehicle itself, (2) the size (time or space) of the advertising unit, and (3) the creative content of the advertisement.

There is, you will realize, a "gray area" between *exposure,* in the sense of an "opportunity to see," based on insertions, and exposure in the everyday sense of "being exposed to the ad," which implies attention to the ad and is where *processing* begins. Here's how we bridge this gap from a media standpoint. In estimating effective frequency, we begin with exposures (insertions in vehicles that *reach* the target audience) and then adjust for *media-caused* attention—that is, for attention elicited by the media vehicle (the subject of this chapter) *and* attention elicited by the duration or size of the advertising unit (the subject of Chapter 10). Whereas the creative director undoubtedly will advise on the latter, we will treat the advertising units used in the plan as a factor that the *media planner* must consider. This takes the audience right to the point at which the creative content takes over. A reasonably clear division is thereby drawn between where media strategy ends and where creative strategy begins—both, of course, being necessary to attain the brand's communication objectives.

### Disposition to Purchase

The other component of the concept of effective frequency which requires clarification is the notion of "influencing" the next purchase. Whereas any degree of processing that occurs on any of the five communication effects can be said to influence purchase to some extent, we focus here on *disposition to purchase* and the role of effective frequency in raising this disposition to an actionable threshold.

As we shall see in Part Seven in conjunction with advertising research, disposition to purchase (or to take other purchase-related action) is reflected best by:

- *Brand awareness* (a necessary prerequisite to purchase) *plus*
- *Brand attitude* for low-involvement/transformational advertising, *or*
- *Brand purchase intention* for the other three types of advertising, namely, low-involvement/ informational, high-involvement/informational, and high-involvement/transformational advertising.

Effective frequency is the frequency of exposure to the individual that raises, to threshold, disposition to purchase as reflected in the criterion measures of brand awareness *plus,* depending on the advertising communication model, either brand attitude or brand purchase intention.[19]

**The Meaning of "Threshold."** "Threshold" refers in this context to the level of stimulation (joint communication effects, or dispositions, caused by advertising exposure or promotion exposure) below which there is no action (purchase or purchase-related action). It is the minimum level of stimulation necessary for action to occur.

The idea of effective frequency is to bring the *individual* target audience prospect up to threshold—to cause him or her to enter the brand choice situation predisposed to buy the advertised brand (which may also be a promoted brand if promotion exposure has taken place) and no other brand. Now, whereas this threshold disposition is obviously dependent on the communication effectiveness of the creative content of the advertising, in media scheduling the concern is to give the creative content sufficient exposure(s) to work. An illustration of this, using the singular concept of disposition to purchase to represent the multiple communication effects that in fact must occur, is shown in Figure 16.10.

For example, we may know that the creative content can produce brand recall, if that is the brand awareness objective, but it may take multiple exposures or repetitions to bring the individual's recall of the brand up to a level where the brand will be in the individual's "evoked set" of two or three brands the next time he or she makes a purchase decision in that category. Similarly, with the *concurrent requirement* of brand attitude or brand purchase intention, we may know that

**FIGURE 16.10**

Individual threshold of disposition to purchase as a function of frequency of exposures.

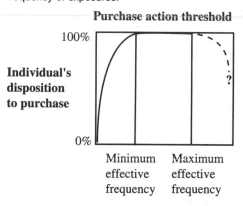

the advertisement—given a sufficient number of exposures, as in the forced or "hypered" exposure of an ad test—is capable of, for example, converting an other-brand loyal to try the advertised brand. The media planner's responsibility is to give the advertisement this "sufficient" threshold number of exposures. "Sufficient" applies to *both* communication objectives: brand awareness *plus* either brand attitude or brand purchase intention, as the case may be.

Note here the importance of collaboration between the creative director and the media planner. If the ad doesn't work, no amount of repetition is going to save it. But an ad that is *known* to work must not be limited by the media schedule through a repetition rate too low to *allow* it to work.

### Minimum Effective Frequency (MEF)

In estimating the effective frequency level for a campaign, we are interested primarily in the *minimum* effective frequency level necessary to raise disposition to purchase to the action threshold (again see Figure 16.10). This is because we want to reach threshold disposition to purchase with the fewest insertions—that is, at lowest cost.

In the easiest-to-grasp case, the minimum effective frequency needed to cause disposition to purchase would be 1 exposure in the advertising cycle. This may occur, for example, with direct response advertising, such as a direct mail offer—or with a promotion offer—where the target audience has only one chance to go through the buyer response sequence of exposure to action. However, as we shall see, an MEF of 1 may also be sufficient in some situations when advertising to a brand-loyal target audience.

With an extremely brand-loyal target audience (single-brand loyals) the minimum effective frequency may even fall below 1, that is to 0 or no advertising, at least for one or two *purchase* cycles. That is, the communication effects constituting disposition to purchase may be strong enough from previous advertising cycles' advertising to "carry over" for one or more subsequent purchase cycles without continued advertising exposure. Word of mouth or personal influence is another factor that could reduce the required MEF of advertising to 0, at least temporarily.

In most cases when targeting less loyal audiences —for example, brand switchers—the minimum effective frequency per advertising cycle will be greater than 1. The nature of the brand's communication objectives or the presence of competing brands' communication effects will also increase the required MEF to a number above one exposure.

Shortly, we will examine the factors that determine minimum effective frequency, and also show how to estimate minimum effective frequency for any advertising situation. Hereafter, as we began to do above, we will usually abbreviate minimum effective frequency as MEF. And to emphasize that MEF must *always* be considered over a fixed time period (namely, MEF per advertising cycle), we will also usually use the terminology k/c or k+/c, where k is the number of exposures (MEF value) and c is the duration of the advertising cycle.

### Maximum Effective Frequency (MaxEF)

In Figure 16.10, disposition to purchase becomes a horizontal line when the exposure frequency goes above the minimum effective frequency needed for purchase. Although it may be hard to imagine "too much" effective frequency, this can happen when the individual has been "oversold," after 100 percent disposition to purchase has already been attained. For example, you may be on your way to an IBM computer retailer fully resolved to buy an IBM PC when you hear another advertisement for the IBM PC on your car radio or see a window poster for the IBM PC as you're entering the store. If you were indeed fully resolved to buy, these extra exposures would be unnecessary, because they wouldn't affect your decision.

Indeed, at some point, further exposures *might* turn your disposition in a negative direction, that is, downward below threshold. As we shall see in Chapter 20 when we discuss "wearout," this downturn is fortunately a rare event (hence the question mark in Figure 16.10). If wearout does occur, the frequency of exposure at which disposition to purchase would decline *below* threshold if there were 1 *more* advertising exposure is called *maximum effective frequency*.

Exposures above minimum effective frequency (MEF) *up to* maximum effective frequency (MaxEF) are wasted exposures from a cost standpoint even though they do *not* affect sales. The less-than-perfect accuracy of media plans and their insertion schedules is such that the key is to advertise at *at least* MEF when in fact you may be above that.

## Effective Reach

*Effective frequency* is inherently an individual phenomenon: during an advertising cycle, an individual target audience member is either exposed at MEF level or not. *Effective reach,* in an advertising cycle (R/c), is simply the *number of individuals reached at at least MEF.* For example, if the MEF is 2 exposures in an advertising cycle, then the effective reach of the media schedule is given by the number of individuals who receive 2 *or more* exposures in that cycle (2+/c). (For now, we will assume no maximum effective frequency upper limit.) The effective reach can then be referred to as "R2+/c"; or "Rk+/c" for an MEF of k exposures over cycle duration c in the general case.

The conventional definition of reach is not useful for advanced media planning. The conventional definition of "reach" is the number or, more often, the percentage of a particular audience reached at least once in some standard period (usually 1 week for broadcast media and 4 weeks for print media). Similarly naive is the concept of "cumulative reach," the number or percentage reached at least once over some longer period (such as 4 weeks for broadcast media and 3 months for print media). Neither of these traditional concepts bears any relationship to a media plan's effectiveness. "Reach" in this sense would coincide with effective reach only in the rare event that the MEF equaled 1 and the advertising cycle equaled the standard period used in conventional reach measurement; and "cumulative reach" would coincide with effective reach only if the MEF equaled 1 and the advertising cycle equaled the *longer* period. Not only media planners but managers, too, should forget the conventional approach and concentrate on *effective reach.*

To look ahead, the idea of media plan *implementation* (Chapter 17) is to maximize effective reach per advertising cycle at the lowest cost. Effective reach depends on what the minimum effective frequency (MEF) is, for the advertising cycle.

## Average Frequency Doesn't Help

The problem with "average frequency"—another conventional term best forgotten—is that it ignores effective frequency. This can be illustrated easily with several diagrams (Figure 16.11) showing hypothetical *frequency distributions* for alternative media plans. All have an average frequency of exactly 2 (total ex-

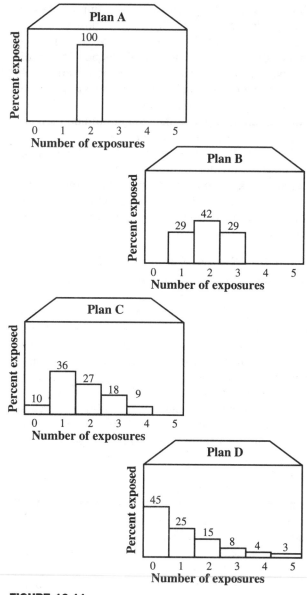

**FIGURE 16.11**

Hypothetical frequency distributions of exposures, all with average frequency = 2. Now compare them for increasing levels of MEF.

posures divided by reach equals average frequency). But in terms of effective reach, if the MEF is 1, then plans A and B are best; if MEF = 2, then Plan A is best; if MEF = 3, Plan B is best; if MEF = 4, Plan C is best; and if MEF = 5, Plan D is best. Obviously, average frequency tells us nothing about a media plan's effectiveness.

Also, as most frequency distributions (exposure distributions) are right-skewed (peak to the left at low frequency and *tail* to the right at high frequency), average frequency will almost always exaggerate the frequency at which the *typical* target audience individual is reached. The typical person gets the *mode* (the most frequent value in a set of data), and the mode of a regular right-skewed distribution is always less than the mean.

A related and very common mistake caused by the average frequency concept is to forget that it is a *mean* and interpret it as a minimum. For instance, a media plan with a "reach of 80 percent and an average frequency of 2" does *not* mean that 80 percent of people received two exposures. Only in the unusual case of Plan A in the figure would this be true. In most cases, *far fewer* than 80 percent of people would receive two (or more) exposures.

Effective frequency is the only type of frequency that matters, and it is a measure of *individual-level exposures*. In no way can average frequency be equated with effective frequency.

## ESTIMATING MINIMUM EFFECTIVE FREQUENCY

The advertiser's objective in the media plan is to *maximize the number of target audience individuals reached,* during each advertising cycle, at *at least the minimum effective frequency level,* within the budget constraint. In other words, the objective is to maximize *effective reach* per advertising cycle (Rk+/c), for as many cycles as possible, subject to budget.

Determining the *minimum effective frequency* is our concern in the remainder of this chapter. The question of whether there is a *maximum effective frequency* level, beyond which exposures are negatively effective, will be left to Chapter 20's discussion of campaign evaluation.

Strictly speaking, the only exact way to determine the minimum effective frequency level in a particular advertising situation is by trial and error—that is, by experimentation.[20] However, precise experiments are prohibitively expensive for most advertisers. For a new product, such experimentation would require multiple test markets to cover the frequency levels, an expensive undertaking. For an established product,

there is legitimate managerial concern about "playing around with the brand," especially at advertising frequencies that are feared to be destructively low. And in no way is there a single "magic number" (such as "3+," which is blindly popular or, more recently, Jones's "single exposure" theory[21]) that can possibly be correct in all circumstances.[22]

Hence an approach based on *logic* rather than experimentation must generally be used. This is true even *if* an experiment is conducted, because the experimental frequency levels would still have to be chosen on some reasonable a priori basis. Indeed, the best policy toward MEF is: estimate it, then track it (see Chapter 20).

Our approach to effective frequency *estimation* makes use of the theory and concepts described in the previous chapters relating to target audiences and communication objectives. We assume that 1 exposure in the advertising cycle (1/c) is the beginning or "building block" level. We then add or subtract exposures according to four strategic factors:

1. Vehicle attention
2. Target audience
3. Communication objectives
4. Personal influence

These four factors for estimating effective frequency are explained next.

### Factor 1: Vehicle Attention

Media vehicles differ in the level of attention given them by the typical audience member. Vehicle attention constrains exposure, that is, it places limits on the opportunity for the ad to achieve attention. There have been many studies of attention to various media types and media vehicles using observational methods or, more often, self-report measures. However, detailed perusal of these studies suggests that the media planner can achieve a reasonably accurate frequency weighting factor by dividing media vehicles into just two classes: high-attention vehicles and low-attention vehicles.

For *high*-attention vehicles—prime-time TV and daytime serials, primary-reader newspapers, primary-reader magazines (where "primary reader" in both cases refers to individuals who subscribe to or buy the publication, as contrasted with other, "pass-along" readers of it), direct mail, and *stationary* outdoor ads and posters—the effective frequency stays at 1 exposure (prior to the other three correction factors being applied.)[23]

For *low*-attention vehicles—all other TV time periods, radio, pass-along-reader newspapers, pass-along-reader magazines, and *mobile* outdoor ads and posters—the effective frequency should be *doubled*. This means doubling the effective frequency calculated from the remaining three correction factors. The reason for the doubled frequency is that the individual's probability of attention to these three media vehicles is about half that of high-attention vehicles, so that double the frequency is needed to give the ad an equal chance of being attended to.[24]

### Factor 2: Target Audience

The rationale for a target audience correction factor is that some target audiences have more to learn about the brand than other target audiences.

Brand loyals (BLs) have little or nothing extra to learn, so that no adjustment is needed when advertising to this audience (however, see factor 3, which may modify this judgment). Favorable brand switchers (FBSs) seem to need at least 2 exposures in the advertising cycle (2/c) before switching is induced,[25] so 1 more exposure to the building block level of 1 exposure. Other-brand switchers (OBSs) and other-brand loyals (OBLs)—assuming that a message strategy has been found that promises to be effective with these typically more negative target audiences, such as refutational advertising or comparative advertising (see Chapter 9)—have substantial new learning to undergo, so add 2 more exposures (3/c total) when advertising to this group.

New category users (NCUs), on the other hand, are a more variable target audience for which to estimate effective frequency, as some may be positively disposed toward the category and others not (see Chapters 3 and 18). Essentially we recommend a competitive approach. Most NCU target audience situations will occur with new brands early in the product category life cycle in a growing market—hence market share is the major objective. Following the argument developed in Chapter 2, the only way to increase market share (assuming equivalent message effectiveness) is to advertise *more* than the leading competitor. This means trying to reach more potential new category users than competitors are reaching (greater penetra-tion) and reaching each potential new category user with higher frequency than the leading competitor.

The *insertions rate* of the largest competitor can be obtained from Broadcast Advertisers' Reports or Leading National Advertisers syndicated report services, or from Monitor Plus if TV advertising is the only concern; the insertions can be run through a reach and frequency program (see Chapter 17) to estimate the largest competitor's frequency distribution. However, you will still need to estimate the *largest competitor's MEF;* this can be done by running the largest competitor through our MEF formula, using +2 instead of LC (see below) and remembering to nominate the competitor's target audience. Then advertise to exceed this frequency by at least 1 exposure (LC+1) per advertising cycle, that is, (LC+1)/c. Exceeding the largest competitor's overall frequency by more than 1 would be even better, remembering that it is almost impossible to overadvertise a new brand. However, a margin of 1 exposure per advertising cycle, if carefully checked at the individual level by thorough vehicle reach and frequency analysis, should be sufficient frequency to wage an effective market share battle if the advertising message is comparably good.

A special situation occurs when advertising to NCUs when your brand *already* is the largest competitor. For the first-in brand, or for the leading brand when others are also in the market, the advertiser has to set effective frequency according to the other factors, since there is no larger competitor to overtake. However, we would recommend a minimum level of at least +2 exposures above the building block level (equal to that for OBSs and OBLs) because the amount of new learning, even for a monopolizing brand, is substantial. A fast-gaining competitor using heavy advertising would, however, indicate a competitive posture and the use of LC+1 *as if* the fast-gaining brand were the largest competitor.

### Factor 3: Communication Objectives

To a considerable extent, the foregoing target audience correction factor has already allowed for the initial level of communication effects within target audience individuals by using a higher frequency when the effects are at or near zero (new category users) down to no adjustment when the effects are at or near a maximum (brand loyals). However, further adjustments are necessary depending on particular communication objectives.

The two communication effects whose objectives require the most variation in effective frequency are brand awareness and brand attitude. The reasoning underlying the brand awareness and brand attitude adjustments is presented in detail in Chapters 8 and 9 and will be recapped here.

The first decision concerns the type of brand awareness. If brand *recognition* is the objective, then the effective frequency needed will be relatively low, and no correction is necessary (subject, of course, to the other correction factors and notably introductory advertising to NCUs). In contrast, if brand *recall* is the communication objective, then the effective frequency needed will be relatively high. It is virtually impossible to make the frequency for brand recall too high.[26] The maximum level for brand recall would be everyone in the target audience recalling the brand first, which happens for only a very few heavily advertised brands. More realistic would be to use the LC+1 guideline for brand recall; that is, to set the minimum effective frequency level at least 1 exposure higher than the frequency used by the largest competitor, or to use +2 if your brand already is the largest competitor in the category.

Brand attitude strategy also has implications for effective frequency in the media plan, as discussed in Chapters 8 and 9. The involvement component of brand attitude strategy is already allowed for in the target audience correction factor, whereby involvement increases as we move from brand loyals to new category users; to correct again would be redundant. However, we do apply a correction for the purchase motivation component. An *informational* brand attitude strategy should be effective within the first 1 or 2 exposures—the brand is either perceived immediately as solving a problem or as irrelevant to the consumer's current motivation or need. Hence no adjustment is recommended for informational advertising. A *transformational* brand attitude strategy, by contrast, requires heavy repetition—for buildup *and* for reinforcement of the brand image or attitude.

Brand awareness and brand attitude correction factors for effective frequency are additive. A brand recognition/informational attitude campaign would require no additional frequency (subject again to the other correction factors). A brand recognition/

transformational attitude campaign, or a brand recall/informational attitude campaign, would require +2 or LC+1 exposures. And, highest of all, a brand recall/transformational attitude campaign would require +4 or LC+2 exposures (note that only the +1's are added when adding LC+1's). Examples of brand recall/transformational attitude campaigns would be the main campaigns for Coca-Cola and McDonald's, who are among the most frequent of the nation's advertisers.

### Factor 4: Personal Influence

The final correction factor for estimating effective frequency is personal influence (PI). This refers to social diffusion of the advertising message, usually via word of mouth but also by visual influence, as when brands are seen by others in a reference-group or reference-individual context.[27] You may remember that PI was assumed in the reverse-wedge/PI reach pattern described earlier in the chapter. Now we see how it affects advertising frequency.

Every advertiser would like his or her brand's campaign talked about, or displayed visually on T-shirts and whatnot, because this publicity serves as free advertising. At the very least, personal communication provides brand awareness, and if favorable comments are made about the features of the advertised brand (for informational advertising) or about the ad campaign itself (for transformational advertising) then brand attitude can be influenced as well. For example, there is no doubt that the Miller Lite "ex jock" ads benefited considerably from frequent favorable comments among beer drinkers; beer is one product where peer-group influence stemming from the advertising has now been recognized as a major factor in advertising's success.[28] Some TV commercials over the years, such as Life Cereal's Mikey commercial, the infamous Brooke Shields commercials for Calvin Klein jeans (and recently the outdoor campaign featuring rapper Marky Mark and model Kate Moss in a suggestive embrace), as well as the equally infamous "Mr. Whipple" commercials for Charmin, Wendy's comparative "Where's the beef?" commercials, and of course the much talked-about Benetton print and poster campaign (in Europe rather than in the United States, where a milder campaign is used) would seem to have generated plenty of opportunities for personal influence as an augmenter of advertising frequency.

Personal influence, providing it is favorable (which the advertiser would check during the advertising strategy and ad testing stages of research and then double-check during campaign evaluation once the campaign is launched), has a number of advantages over advertising per se. First, it is free, which means that the advertiser saves on advertising costs. Second, one word-of-mouth contact appears to be about twice as effective[29] as one advertising exposure, probably because a favorable brand or advertising *attitude* is nearly always conveyed rather than just awareness.[30] Third, personal influence can operate at any stage of the life cycle for any type of product, not just new, high-risk products as was commonly believed.[31] In particular, a new *advertising* campaign, even for an old brand, can trigger word of mouth.

Some years ago, Ozga[32] proposed that social diffusion serves as a substitute for part of the total amount of advertising that would otherwise be required. He introduced the notion of a *contact coefficient,* which indicates the average number of other people told about the advertising by the average individual exposed to it (this could of course be extended to include visual contact). More recently, the word-of-mouth contact coefficient has been included with advertising in models of new product diffusion.[33]

Based on the synthesis of the available studies of interpersonal influence, we would estimate that a contact coefficient of at least .25 is necessary to justify reducing the effective frequency estimate by 1 exposure. This means that for every four people reached by the advertising, at least one person contacts as least one other person during the advertising cycle. Because this contact should be doubly effective, and because it may spread, it in effect replaces an exposure. Thus, a contact coefficient of at least .25 seems a reasonable figure to justify a reduction of 1 exposure (that is, $-1$) in the minimum effective frequency calculation. For a personal contact coefficient of less than .25, no adjustment is made.

With the 1 exposure reduction in effective frequency under conditions of frequent personal influence, it should be noted that there is no recommended reduction in the *reach* of the media plan. This is because the interpersonal influence phenomenon works best when the "other" person contacted has also seen the campaign (discussing an ad with someone who has *not* seen it is somewhat frustrating, whereas discussing it with someone who *has* seen it is usually

mutually reinforcing). Thus, the idea is to maintain the reach while reducing the required number of exposures because of the bonus exposure created by interpersonal influence.

### MEF Calculation Summary Formula

A summary of minimum effective frequency estimation using the four correction factors is given in Table 16.2. A summary formula can now be stated to allow combined application of the correction factors and produce a minimum effective frequency estimate for any advertising situation. The formula is as follows:

$$MEF/c = 1 + VA(TA + BA + BATT + PI)$$

where

MEF/c = minimum effective frequency (per advertising cycle, c)

1 = the building block or starting level of 1 exposure

VA = the media vehicle attention correction factor: a multiplier which is 1 for high-attention vehicles and 2 (doubled) for low-attention vehicles

TA = the target audience correction factor

BA = the brand awareness correction factor

BATT = the brand attitude correction factor

PI = the personal influence correction factor

Several examples will illustrate how the formula can be applied.

The very lowest effective frequency would be no advertising (0 exposures) in the advertising cycle. However, this would only occur in one particular circumstance, and not indefinitely but rather between flights. This circumstance would be following a high-attention vehicle campaign (for example, prime-time TV) aimed at brand loyals, for a brand purchased via brand recognition and sold via an informational brand attitude strategy, that *also* generated strong personal influence. It would be quite rare for a campaign to meet all these criteria simultaneously. In particuar, campaigns likely to generate strong word of mouth would be new campaigns rather than campaigns directed with low frequency at brand loyals (for example, the Brooke Shields campaign for Calvin Klein jeans would have generated word of mouth only while

**TABLE 16.2**

**MINIMUM EFFECTIVE FREQUENCY (MEF) ESTIMATION FACTORS AND THEIR NUMERICAL CORRECTION VALUES. THE FORMULA IS MEF/C = 1 + VA(TA + BA + BATT + PI)**

| Factor | Correction value (starting from 1 exposure in advertising cycle) | | | | |
|---|---|---|---|---|---|
| | −1 | 0 | +1 | +2 | LC + 1[a] |
| 1. Vehicle attention | | | high attention | low attention | |
| 2. Target audience | | brand loyals | brand switchers | other-brand switchers; other-brand loyals | new category users |
| 3. Communication objectives (two factors) | | brand recognition | | | brand recall |
| | | informational brand attitude | | | transformational brand attitude |
| 4. Personal influence | high (average contact ≥ .25) | low (average contact < .25) | | | |

[a]If market share leader, use +2 exposures; if not leader, set equal to largest competitor's average frequency +1 (called LC + 1). LC + 1 is additive on the 1 only; e.g., a campaign aimed at new category users, with brand recall and transformational brand attitude objectives, would use LC + 3 exposures.

the ads were new). Also, with the apparent trend toward "safe" ad testing in recent years, it is fair to say that American campaigns in general have become more conservative and therefore less likely to spark the strong public reaction that is needed to meet the high personal influence criterion.

Most estimates of minimum effective frequency will be between 1 and 13 exposures per advertising cycle. Some hypothetical examples of MEFs calculated from the formula (and here we have *assumed* a regular *purchase* cycle reach pattern, that is, the length of an advertising cycle = c = 1 purchase cycle) include the following:

- Hellmann's mayonnaise (1), advertising in primary-reader magazines (1×), to brand switchers (+1), via a brand recognition (0) and a taste-based transformational brand attitude strategy (assume Kraft, the largest competitor is using +2 and then add 1) = 5 exposures per purchase cycle, which is probably about 2 weeks for mayonnaise. Thus, 5/2.
- Bold detergent (1), advertising on daytime TV serials (1×), to other-brand loyals (+2), via a brand recognition (0) and an informational brand attitude strategy (0) = 3 exposures per purchase cycle,

which is probably about 3 weeks for detergent. Thus, 3/3.
- Blue Nun Wine (1), advertising on radio (double the following, that is, 2×), to new category users as the market leader (+2), via a brand recall (+2) and informational brand attitude strategy (0) = 9 exposures per purchase cycle, which is probably about monthly for dinner wines. Thus, 9/4.

We may note that the highest MEF would occur with a late entry trying to break into a new category, with communication objectives that require brand recall and a transformational brand attitude, by using a low-attention medium, such as radio, pass-along-reader newspapers or magazines, or daytime TV other than serials. Such media would normally not be chosen for a new product campaign, but if they were, we can see that an MEF of at least 13 exposures per advertising cycle would be needed. For frequently purchased consumer products, this could be a very expensive campaign; however, for consumer durables or industrial products, this would be feasible because of the longer purchase cycle, with the budget spread by using either the awareness" reach pattern or the "shifting" reach pattern explained earlier in the chapter.

**MEF If You Can't Determine LC.** In situations where you can't determine or even make a good "guesstimate" of the largest competitor's advertising frequency to the target audience, such as by analyzing the competitor's *insertion* schedule, the MEF you need can be *approximated* by the procedure described earlier. Run the largest competitor through the formula, using +2 to reflect market leader status, to calculate the LC value. Then substitute the LC value in the formula and calculate your own MEF. For example, consider 7Up against Coke, assuming a high-attention vehicle, brand recognition, and a transformational brand attitude strategy. Coke would probably be using MEF/c = 1 + 1 (0 + 0 + 2 − 0 = 3/c for its BLs. For 7Up, this target audience would be OBLs, and 7Up's MEF/c would be 1 + 1 (+2 + 0 + [3 + 1] − 0) = 7/c. Note that Coke's 3 exposures are substituted for the LC term in 7Up's MEF calculation.

**LC in Low-Attention Vehicles.** Another caution when using the MEF formula has to do with an LC value with a low-attention vehicle (VA = 2). In this case, *halve the LC value* before inserting it. The reason is that the largest competitor presumably has *already* doubled its frequency to reflect the low-attention vehicle, so you don't want to "double double."[34]

**MEF Across High- and Low-Attention Vehicles.** Media strategies may arise which call for a mixture of high- and low-attention media vehicles—such as prime-time TV (high) and early-morning daytime TV (low), or newspapers (high) plus radio ads (low). In these situations, it is best to (1) calculate the MEF as if for all high-attention vehicles, (2) estimate how many of the MEF exposures are likely to be contributed by the low-attention vehicle, then (3) double *that* number and add it to the high-attention number. For example, supposed we calculate the high-attention MEF to be 6, and that we expect newspaper ads to contribute 4 and radio 2. We would then set the MEF *for newspaper* at 4, and the MEF *for radio* at 2 × 2 = 4. Note that this is *not* an "MEF of 8" but rather the respective MEFs to aim for *when* using the two media together.

### MEF for Direct Response Ads and Promotions

For direct response (DR) ads, where the purpose is to generate an inquiry or make an outright sale, we estimate the MEF/c as follows:

- Broadcast DR ads (TV, cable TV, radio) = 4/c (4 *OTS*/c; see below)

- Print DR ads (newspaper, magazine, direct mail) = 2/c
- Interactive TV or PC DR ads = 2/c

The broadcast MEF estimate comes from a large-scale analysis of infomercials: the modal response—an inquiry or direct purchase—occurred at 2 exposures.[35] Because DR commercials are longer (contributing 2 to MEF; see Chapter 10), this represents an MEF of 4/c *achieved with 2 exposures—that is, 2 OTS*—in the advertising cycle. However, because the viewer or listener does not have *control* over broadcast advertising exposure (being a "passive" recipient), a safe exposure frequency of *4 OTS*/c is recommended, which technically would be MEF = 8. We would expect 90-second and 2-minute TV *DR* and radio *DR* commercials to be similar to infomercials; because of the longer commercials for DR, radio does not need to be doubled.

The print (including direct mail) DR estimate of 2/c is lower than that for broadcast DR because the recipient has plenty of time to consider the offer. Actually, 1 exposure should suffice but, for safety's sake, we've made it 2.

The same applies to interactive TV or PC DR advertisements: for these, the viewer is definitely "active." It seems likely that an exploratory contact (page visits) will be followed by a second "confirmation" contact after checking other brands, hence 2/c. Note that the "c" is important for interactive TV or PC advertisers: it tells them how long they can go before changing the ad.

Promotions, on the other hand, have to work immediately or they won't work at all. Thus, the MEF for promotion offers is:

- Promotion offers = 1/c

An interesting (but limited) exception to the MEF of 1 for promotion offers would be a *postpackaging* promotion for *people who have just bought the brand* (primarily BLs) and where the product or service has *multiple usage occasions* within the purchase cycle. *Examples:* washing powder, soft drinks bought by the six-pack or by the case, cosmetics, bank checks, and credit cards. In these situations, multiple exposure to the package would substitute for advertising exposures[36] and would make the MEF *during* the purchase cycle for those who've just bought = 0/c. These package exposures could easily attain the otherwise-advertised MEF and are one reason why these types of products and services can endure long hiatus periods of no advertising *for* brand loyals.

The MEF/c estimation procedures can therefore be summarized as follows:

Follow formula for mass media advertising

4 (OTS) for DR broadcast advertising

2 for DR print advertising

2 for DR interactive TV or PC advertising

1 for a promotion offer

0 for a postpackaging promotion, involving multiple usage occasions, to BLs

### MEF and "Outer" Target Audience Change

Clearly, the usual purpose of advertising to a particular target audience is to have that target audience *change*—in awareness, attitude, and behavior status—to an audience that is more favorable toward the brand.

There are only two *exceptions* to this: *favorable brand switchers* and *brand loyals*. These two groups, which already comprise the fringe and the core, respectively, of the brand's sales, would, if targeted, not be expected to change their status over the course of the campaign. Favorable brand switchers—for regularly purchased products—are not expected to become brand loyals (but rather just to "switch in" a little more often) because their purchasing patterns are *routinized*. Brand loyals are expected to stay loyal and to use the brand a little more often, but again not to change.

All other target audiences are expected to *change* as the campaign works on them—and to change to groups requiring *less frequency*. The target audience requiring the highest MEF, new category users, in most campaigns is expected to become brand loyals, with a dramatic reduction in MEF from $LC+1$ per advertising cycle, c, to 0 (on the target audience correction factor). Similarly, other-brand loyals in most campaigns are expected to convert to loyalty to our brand, with a consequent reduction (on the target audience factor) of 2/c exposures. And although we did not differentiate them from other-brand loyals in the target audience correction factor, we might judge that other-brand switchers could be reduced by about 1/c exposure should they become routinized favorable

brand switchers and definitely if they become brand loyals.

In fact, when you think about it, it is not very likely that you would want to continue to advertise to these "outer" target audiences—NCUs, OBLs, or OBSs—for more than a few advertising cycles or purchase cycles (the shifting reach pattern, note, moves to other subsets of NCUs). If the campaign hasn't worked after several purchase cycles in which the target audience has been reached at MEF each time and now has had several purchase opportunities, chances are the campaign will not work at all and it is time to reconsider the advertising strategy and perhaps even the marketing objectives.

If, on the other hand, the campaign aimed at one or more of these "outer" target audiences *has* been successful, they then will have moved to a more favorable, lower MEF group. Accordingly, the media planner's task regarding *individual continuity* over multiple advertising cycles in the advertising period is to estimate when the shift to lower required MEF should be made. (It is noteworthy that one of the best new product tracking models for fmcg products, BBDO's NEWS, based on case history experience, allows only two purchase cycles' worth of advertising for trial purchase to occur.[37])

"Outer" targeting therefore tends to produce a "sliding scale" of frequency whereby a high MEF burst is used in the first few advertising cycles to try to persuade the outer target audience to try or retry the brand; a moderate MEF burst then follows for several more advertising cycles as the outer audience goes through the brand trial or retrial phase and functionally becomes brand switchers; and finally, a reduced MEF continuation is aimed at the now-favorable buyers captured by the campaign.

Thus, only with "inner" targeting, to favorable brand switchers or brand loyals, would a constant MEF level be used.

### "Maintenance" MEF and "Inner" Target Audiences

Media planners sometimes advocate running "maintenance weight" during the media plan (a low *rate* of GRPs, such as about 30 GRPs a week). The low weight is employed during what would otherwise, in a *flighted* pattern, be *hiatus* periods of no advertising. This produces a GRP or *spending* pattern called "pulsing." (Its *reach* pattern could be anything, and note that we were careful to show reach patterns and expenditure patterns separately in Figures 16.2 through 16.9.)

Maintenance weights make sense only if they are delivered with enough frequency (actually a high enough *rate,* MEF/c) to at least provide MEF to the "inner" target audiences of favorable brand switchers and brand loyals. If this maintenance MEF effect can't be demonstrated, then you're better off stopping advertising altogether from flight to flight (which would be *true* flighting as opposed to pulsing) and spending the money in the flights themselves where it will increase *effective* reach.

### Retailer Support

It could make sense to advertise at below MEF in a particular advertising cycle when the *retailer also is advertising the brand.* In this case, the manufacturer's extra advertising, even at low frequency, may help to achieve total MEF.

More practically, too, some continued advertising, even in a weak area, can help to convince retailers that the brand is being supported in the area and thus is still deserving of shelf space and perhaps special display. Because of the undeniable importance of display to the sales of products sold through retailers, this continued advertising can be vital.

Note, however, that "retailer conviction" advertising differs from the previous situation of "MEF top-up" advertising. Because retailer conviction advertising will be *below* MEF for consumers, it is advisable to place it in media or media vehicles to which *the retailer will be exposed* while occupying his or her out-of-store role as a private consumer. Retail attention to the brand could then maintain sales even though the advertising is not, except by its influence on retailers.

### SCHEDULING OVER TIME: SHORT-TERM TACTICAL ADJUSTMENTS

The final media strategy decision concerns short-term scheduling (which is essentially a tactical matter). Generally, the media planner should work out an overall reach pattern for the planning period, then make already-known short-term adjustments in *frequency* for special events (discussed shortly) and, still further, hold some of the budget (and thus frequency) for very short term contingencies such as actions or reactions to competitors' plans.

### Short-Term Adjustments in Frequency

"Short-term" here is used to mean less than a year. The overall reach pattern for the year may need to be adjusted to accommodate *known* events throughout the budgeting year. (We exclude seasonality here, which has already been discussed as a reach pattern in terms of balancing low competitive interference before the seasonal peak or peaks against increased category need during the peak or peaks.) Most often these known events consist of:

1. Promotion dates to consumers
2. Special promotions to the trade

In the case of promotion dates to consumers, the important tactic is to shift the *timing* of advertising exposures so that they *precede* the promotion date and create the "ratchet effect" (Figure 16.12) by priming the brand's brand attitude going into the promotion.[38] This should cause the brand's *value equity* to temporarily increase (see Chapter 2) and the promotion to thereby produce more sales.

Note that the MEF requirement remains the same, so more frequency is not needed, but rather frequency that *precedes* the promotion date. Because the promotion itself—if customer franchise building (CFB)—contributes to MEF, advertising can accordingly be *reduced* by at least 1 exposure during the advertising cycle in which the promotion occurs, and by more than 1 exposure if the promotion is an *advertised* promotion that incorporates multiple exposures.

With special promotions to the trade, advertising to consumers is used in many cases to impress distributors that the brand is being given strong consumer support at the same time as the trade drive. As in the foregoing case, some concentration of exposures within the *consumer* advertising cycle leading up to the *trade* promotion can add to this impression. Where possible, use of media that the retailer is also exposed to is desirable because of the dual (trade and consumer) target audience.

### Very Short Term Scheduling

On top of the overall scheduling pattern and the short-term adjustments for known events, the advertiser will want to keep some reserve frequency, and thus part of the budget, for very short term actions and reactions.

The most obvious of these very short term contingencies is *response to a leading competitor.* Unanticipated competitive actions, such as the surprise launch

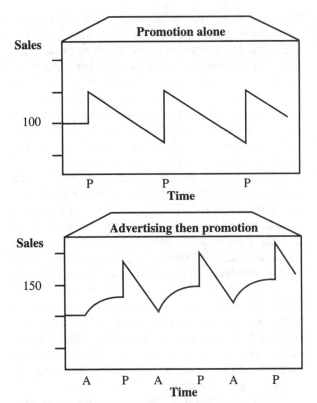

**FIGURE 16.12**
The "ratchet effect" of effective advertising (A) prior to promotion (P).
*Source:* W. T. Moran; see note 38.

of a new campaign or even a new brand, have the effect of raising our brand's MEF under three circumstances (see Table 16.2): (1) when the target audience is new category users (for example, for personal computers); (2) when brand recall is the brand awareness objective (for example, for airlines, especially with "outer" target audiences); or (3) when the brand attitude strategy is transformational (for example, for soft drinks or liquor). All these use the LC + 1 adjustment, so if the "LC" increases advertising, you should too.

Conversely, notice that for target audiences, other than new category users, who are being reached with brand recognition/informational communication objectives, the "LC" term doesn't enter the calculation and therefore *no reaction* would be the appropriate reaction. Many supermarket and drugstore (fmcg) products are in this classification and should *not* worry about competitive SOV (see Chapter 20 for more on this).

A second frequent very short term circumstance is caused by *variation in supply.* Just as a factory breakdown or distributor problem could cause advertising to be withdrawn that otherwise would be wasted, a factory overrun or large purchase of stock could require extra advertising to stimulate demand. For the brand that is already advertising at MEF, this extra advertising would be used to increase the number reached at MEF, or perhaps to attract an outer target audience with a higher MEF. For example, a fire-damage sale at Saks Fifth Avenue probably would attract many first-time Saks visitors.

A last very short term variable that affects a surprising number of products is *variation in demand caused by the weather.* We are not talking here about well-known seasonal patterns but rather unexpected daily or weekly variations. Unseasonable rain can cause the demand for umbrellas and raincoats to skyrocket. Unseasonable fine weather can boost sales of house-and-garden products. But among the products most affected by daily variations in weather are foods and beverages. Advertiming, a service in New York that monitors product demand in relation to weather, reports that soda consumption increases in gusty weather, and hot cereal and soup consumption increase in stormy weather. Increases of 50 to 100 percent have been demonstrated for some products. Campbell's Soup apparently sets aside $750,000 of its media budget for very short term radio commercials on days when storms threaten.[39]

What MEF should be assumed if advertisers wish to take advantage of weather variations? It depends on the target audience. The increase in category need doesn't change the frequency required to direct choice toward a particular brand. Rather, it temporarily shortens the purchase cycle, thus pushing the frequency *rate* up. Because there is usually a corresponding decrease during opposite weather patterns, the overall effect is to keep total advertising frequency constant while simply varying its timing.

## SUMMARY

Media *strategy* necessitates "preplanning" of the media plan. The two main components of media strategy are the reach pattern and effective frequency.

The *reach pattern* of a media plan requires the manager or media planner to think about *when,* over the entire year, the typical target audience individual should be reached, together with *which* of the target audience individuals should be reached with each flight of advertising or promotion. To aid this vital but difficult thought process, there are two sets of reach patterns—one set for new product introductions and another for established brands—which the manager can employ in a templatelike manner to decide on the appropriate reach pattern for his or her campaign. Adjustments can then be made to suit the particular advertising situation in finer detail.

The four new product introductory reach patterns are the blitz pattern (the best reach pattern if you can afford it and have a large pool of advertising executions that vary around the same positioning for the brand); the wedge pattern (a heavy but declining frequency pattern that is most often used in practice); the reverse-wedge/PI pattern (used for new product introductions where personal influence or word of mouth is expected to be a significant contributor and the purchase motive is based on social approval); and the short fad pattern (used for brief life cycle fad products).

The reach patterns for established brands are the regular purchase cycle pattern (most often employed for fmcg products, usually with flighting); the awareness pattern (used for products with a long purchase cycle and a long decision time); the shifting reach pattern (used for products with a long purchase cycle and a *short* decision time); and the seasonal priming pattern (used for products or services that have one or more distinct seasonal peaks throughout the year).

These reach patterns are extremely important to understand and identify, and are one of the two keys, along with effective frequency, of advanced media planning.

The second aspect of media strategy is *effective frequency*. In this chapter we have seen that effective frequency in the media plan depends primarily on the manager's ability to estimate the minimum frequency of exposures, to the average target audience member, in the advertising cycle, that will effectively achieve the communication objectives. The best estimation method would be by experimentation up front, but this is expensive and is not without problems even when it is affordable. (However, continuous tracking allows experimentation *afterward,* and is highly advisable; see Chapter 20.) Necessary for all media plans, including experimental plans, is a logical approach to minimum effective frequency estimation per purchase cycle. This estimate (MEF/c) is based on media vehicle attention, target audience, communication objectives, and the extent of personal influence.

The minimum effective frequency per advertising cycle (MEF/c) is calculated by starting with 1 exposure and adjusting upward for low-attention media vehicles, target audiences with more to learn about the brand, a brand recall communication objective, and a transformational brand attitude communication objective, and then making a downward adjustment for personal influence if the brand is fortunate enough to have this operating. Nonformula estimates are provided for direct response ads and promotions.

Although this logical approach to MEF calculation is not exact, it certainly helps the manager think about the right sorts of issues in determining how frequently the advertising should be scheduled. The manager *has* to make an estimate of MEF/c in order to choose the media schedule, and our method is a good way to start.

It is indefensible to advertise at below MEF/c to any target audience. That is, *effective reach* should govern the media plan. The one exception to below-MEF advertising in an advertising cycle is for retailer support. If the retailer is also advertising the brand, consumer advertising combined with the retailer's may reach MEF; or it may nevertheless encourage the retailer to push the brand.

The final decision is MEF scheduling over time. For "outer" target audiences—new category users, other-brand loyals, and other-brand switchers—the MEF/c requirement will diminish if the campaign is successful and these audiences change to become more favorable or "inner" customers. For "inner" target audiences—favorable brand switchers and brand loyals—advertising only at MEF, in cycles, was shown to be the best strategy.

Short-term adjustments to the schedule then need to be made for known events occurring in the planning period. Last, some of the budget has to be saved for concentrating frequency to meet unanticipated very short term contingencies.

The reach pattern coupled with effective frequency is the soundest basis for deciding advertising "weight," the objective being to maximize effective reach per advertising cycle—the number of target audience individuals reached, in each advertising cycle, at at least the minimum effective frequency level—while also staying within the budget. In the next chapter, we see how to achieve this objective.

## NOTES

1. A. B. *Priemer, Effective Media Planning*, Lexington, MA: Lexington Books, 1989. This book should be re-

quired reading for all marketing managers and advertising managers, not to mention media planners.

2. A. B. (Gus) Priemer is a highly experienced media planner who strongly advocates the "coincidence theory" of media planning, such that media vehicles whose time of delivery is very close to the target consumer's experience of category need are heavily favored in the media plan. See A. B. Priemer, New alternatives to effective frequency and media planning, *Journal of Media Planning,* 1986, *1* (1), pp. 25–28.

3. Notice that we define "start working" as the *threshold* of disposition to act (see Figure 16.10 later in this chapter). We don't actually care about the individual's response function *below* the MEF threshold, although we expect that most often it will be convex due to the concatenation of brand awareness learning (usually linear) and brand attitude learning or acceptance (usually convex, that is, positive exponential decelerating). There has been much confusion in the literature caused by trying to infer *individual-level* response functions from *aggregate* sales curves. See also J. Z. Sissors, Advice to media planners on how to use effective frequency, *Journal of Media Planning,* 1986, *1* (1), pp. 3–9.

4. The idea of a *reach pattern* was stimulated by the earlier theorizing of practitioner-researcher Ken Longman, the importance of which the present authors have not fully appreciated until now. We have elaborated on Longman's idea. See K. A. Longman, *Advertising,* New York: Harcourt Brace Jovanovich, 1971.

5. In our earlier book, we broke with tradition by defining key media terms such as "frequency" and "continuity" from the individual perspective. The wisdom of this departure was reinforced by the subsequent opinion of Priemer, whose following quotation encapsulates exactly our reason for the individual perspective: "Once we can visualize how to 'sell' one consumer, we are ready to reach out *effectively* for millions (but not before then)." The quotation is from Priemer's 1986 article, p. 28 (see note 2), which appeared after we had finished our earlier book. The individual perspective on media planning is comprehensively developed in his 1989 book; see note 1.

6. D. A. Aaker and J. M. Carman, Are you overadvertising?, *Journal of Advertising Research,* 1982, 22 (4), pp. 57–70. Their overadvertising conclusions, as they note, apply only to established products, not new products.

7. The sustained "blitz" pattern works best, according to IRI's results, for new (fmcg) product introductions. See L. M. Lodish and B. Lubetkin, General truths? Nine key findings from IRI test data, *Admap,* February 1992, pp. 9–15.

8. Estimates inferred from reported budgets in advertising industry publications such as *Advertising Age* for new product launches over the past several years.

9. See, for example, T. S. Robertson, *Innovative Behavior and Communication,* New York: Holt, Rinehart and Winston, 1971.

10. C. B. Weinberg, Seminar presented at the Australian Graduate School of Management, Sydney, July, 1994.

11. K. Helsen and D. C. Schmittlein, How does a product market's typical price promotion pattern affect timing of household's purchases? An empirical study using UPC scanner data, *Journal of Retailing,* 1992, *68* (3), pp. 316–338.

12. IRI has found that—for *established* brands of fmcg products—the same GRPs concentrated in fewer weeks are more effective than when spread over every week. See L. M. Lodish and B. Lubetkin, same reference as note 7. J. L. Simon's reanalysis of the famous Zielske data also showed that the once a month (4-week hiatus) pattern maximized "recall weeks" as compared with a continuous weekly pattern. See J. L. Simon, What do Zielske's data really show about pulsing? *Journal of Marketing Research,* 1979, *16* (3), pp. 415–420.

13. "Hysteresis" is a physics term first used in this context by John D. C. Little in his classic article, Advertising models: The state of the art, *Operations Research,* 1979, *27* (4), pp. 629–667. The phenomenon has been well documented by R. I. Haley, Sales effects of media weight, *Journal of Advertising Research,* 1978, *18* (3), pp. 9–18, and G. J. Eskin and P. H. Baron, Effects on price and advertising in test market experiments, *Journal of Marketing Research,* 1977, *14* (4), pp. 499–508.

14. See V. Mahajan and E. Muller, Advertising pulsing policies for generating awareness of new products, *Marketing Science,* 1986, *5* (2), pp. 89–111; and H. I. Mesak, An aggregate advertising pulsing model with wearout effects, *Marketing Science,* 1992, *11* (3), pp. 310–325. Also H. Simon, ADPULS: an advertising model with wearout and pulsation, *Journal of Marketing Research,* 1982, *19* (3), pp. 352–363.

15. ADWEEK, *Marketing to the Year 2000,* New York: ADWEEK, 1989.

16. K. A. Longman, same reference as note 4.

17. E. C. Strong, The spacing and timing of advertising, *Journal of Advertising Research,* 1977, *17* (6), pp. 25–31.

18. Historical appreciation of the concept of effective frequency and its importance can be gained from the following references: K. A. Longman, same reference as note 4, chapter 7; A. A. Achenbaum, Effective exposure, a new way of evaluating media, Paper presented at the Association of National Advertisers' Media Workshop, New York, NY: Association of National Advertisers, Inc., February 1977; and M. J. Naples, *Effective Frequency: The Relationship Between Frequency and Advertising Effectiveness,* New York: Association of National Advertisers, Inc., 1979.

19. The concepts of advertising communication models and the criterion measures for each are discussed in Chapter 19, on ad testing.

20. Experiments on effective frequency are feasible for *television* advertising using split-cable technology such as that offered by AdTel, IRI, or Nielsen. Different frequency levels can be programmed into randomly selected cable households, whose purchases are then recorded on UPC scanners at stores or in the home using a handheld electronic "wand." Reported cost is about $50,000 per experimental level or, say, $200,000 to test four estimates of MEF. A much cheaper but admittedly less exact method is continuous tracking—but this is usually a "post" experiment (see Chapter 20). One of the few theorists who has realized the value (necessity really) of the logical approach to MEF estimation is P. Turk, The relevance of environmental variables in setting effective frequency thresholds for television, in K. B. Rotzoll, ed., *American Academy of Advertising Proceedings,* Urbana-Champaign: University of Illinois, 1989, pp. RC-1 to RC-26.

21. John Philip Jones's (1995) book, *When Ads Work,* is likely to receive considerable attention from marketing managers and perhaps media planners and therefore warrants detailed comment. Here are the main problems with Jones's "single exposure" conclusion:

a. His data assume that the advertiser is advertising an established brand. His conclusion cannot be generalized to the launch of a new brand.

b. He assumes that the same campaign is used throughout. His conclusion cannot be generalized to the restaging of (new campaign for) an established brand.

c. He assumes, because of his data, a 1-week (7-day) purchase cycle. But, of the 12 fmcg product categories in his study, only one, diet soft drinks, could possibly be on a purchase cycle as short as 1 week. He observed the effect of 1 exposure in a 1-week period, *not* the effect of 1 exposure over the entire purchase cycle. McDonald's classic (1971) study (see note 25) in which 2 exposures per *true purchase cycle* were found to be optimal for a *brand switcher* target audience contradicts Jones's conclusion, although in discussing the McDonald study, Jones doesn't appreciate this. By not looking back further than 1 week, Jones cannot know whether there may have been 1 or more prior exposures leading up to the 1 exposure that he observed in the week before purchase. Thus, the conclusion of 1 exposure per *purchase cycle,* which is what Jones concludes, is not justified by his data and is dangerously misleading.

d. His analysis also ignores different target audiences (brand loyals, brand switchers, other-brand loyals, and new category users). It cannot possibly be true that 1 exposure would be equally effective for each of these target audiences. His data are probably a composite of favorable brand switchers, for whom 2 or 3 exposures in the purchase cycle would be necessary, and brand loyals, for whom 1 or even 0 would be effective. His average across the two target audiences therefore comes out to about 1 or 2. (Although he claims that the biggest *increase* is with 1 exposure, the effect on market share actually reaches a peak *beyond* 1 exposure; he lumps all subsequent exposures together.)

e. His analysis of short-term advertising effects, using STAS (short-term advertising strength) quintiles, is completely circular. First he defines the STAS quintiles in terms of short-term effect of advertising. Then he ranks these quintiles in terms of size of that effect. Finally, he shows that the 1-exposure effect is largest in the highest quintile, but that's how this quintile was defined in the first place! Therefore we should ignore his STAS quintiles and look only at the total effect.

f. He studied only regular purchase cycle, supermarket products (fmcg). These are, of course, the types of products suited only to the regular purchase cycle reach pattern, not any of the other seven reach patterns given in the present chapter. Even if we ignore all the above problems with Jones's analysis, his conclusion cannot in any way be generalized to other types of products and services.

In short, Jones's "1-exposure" theory is just another simplistic magic number theory, like the "3-hit theory." However, media planners won't be keen on Jones's theory because 1 hit means a two-thirds lower budget than 3 hits!

Interpreted in the very best light, Jones's analysis provides some support for the notion that 1 or 2 exposures *in the week leading up to purchase* is more effective than no exposures during that week. But the week leading up to purchase is a different week for just about everybody in the category. Accordingly, this policy suggests that the advertising should aim for 1 to 2 exposures *per week* for fmcg products. Using the conventional 4-week basis of most media plans, this would be 4 to 8 exposures per month, which is about the range that our MEF formula would estimate, anyway, for regularly purchased products with a combined brand switcher and brand loyal target audience. This is a far cry from the conclusion that "1 exposure is enough."

22. For vivid evidence against the notion of a single number, see the data provided by H. Zielske, Using effective frequency in media planning, *Journal of Media Planning*, 1986, *1* (1), pp. 53–56; and by A. Roberts, What do we know about advertising's short-term effect? *Admap*, February 1996, pp. 42–45. The latter study was similar to that of Jones (see previous note) and shows the error of Jones's overgeneralization.

23. High-attention vehicles have a probability of .8 or higher that the target audience will pay initial attention to an ad in the vehicle. Simon Broadbent, a very experienced media researcher, in his book *Spending Advertising Money* (3rd ed., London: Business Books Ltd., 1979), estimates that 85 to 88 percent of the average prime-time program's TV audience is watching or within hearing range during a commercial break (p. 90). A recent review by Abernethy estimates the in-room figure during TV commercial breaks at 85 percent; see A. M. Abernethy, Physical and mechanical avoidance of television commercials: An exploratory study of zipping, zapping and leaving, in R. Holman, ed., *American Academy of Advertising Proceedings*, Athens GA: American Academy of Advertising, 1991, pp. 223–231. Broadbent's estimate for primary-reader newspapers and, we may infer, primary-reader magazines, is similarly impressive: 90 percent of the average vehicle's readers look at the page on which an advertisement appears (p. 120). He also claims a high figure of page openings by secondary "skim readers" of magazines and newspapers, but we have chosen to assume that relative to primary readers, secondary readers pay low attention to the vehicle. Also, judgmentally, we have classified *stationary* outdoor and poster media, where the target audience has time to process the ad as in a magazine, as high-attention vehicles.

An important review of attention studies by M. R. Swenson (Attention to advertisements by prospects and nonprospects, in K. W. King, ed., *American Academy of Advertising Proceedings*, Athens GA: University of Georgia, 1994, pp. 207–212) strongly suggests that *category prospects* pay considerably higher attention than nonprospects. The difference for TV commercials is about +12 percent for prospects and −12 percent for nonprospects, and for print ads, about +20 percent and −20 percent. For *category users*, therefore, who include all target audiences except NCUs, the high-attention probability would be effectively 1.0.

24. If we take a conservative estimate of .8 as the probability of initial attention to the ad for high-attention vehicles, and a conservative estimate of .4 for low-attention vehicles, some simple simulations with the binomial theorem (exposed versus unexposed over successive insertions) indicate that you need about double the number of OTS in low-attention vehicles compared with high-attention vehicles. For example, if the MEF is 2 exposures, you need four OTS to get 90 percent 2+ "attention reach" in a high-attention vehicle, and double that, or eight OTS to get 90 percent 2+ "attention reach" in a low-attention vehicle. When the MEF is greater than 2, the difference is much more than double. However, we believe doubling is practically sufficient, with the theoretical shortfall offset by the noticeability of the resulting doubled "impact schedule."

Our classifications of high- versus low-attention media, made in our first edition of this book, were subsequently lent further confirmation in an estimation of GRP rates required to achieve the same "effective frequency" in various main media; see G. B. Murray and J. R. G. Jenkins, The concept of "effective reach" in advertising, *Journal of Advertising Research*, 1992, *32* (3), pp. 34–42.

We are grateful to Doug Hausknecht for his suggestion for improving the MEF formula on the vehicle attention factor.

25. We rely here primarily on a very carefully performed field experiment: C. McDonald, What is the short-term effect of advertising? Special Report No. 71-142, Cambridge, MA: Marketing Science Institute, 1971. A summary of his study is given in M. J. Naples, same reference as note 18, pp. 83–103. This study appeared to have brand switchers as the target audience.

McDonald's study with nine brands was subsequently replicated with 16 brands by the sponsoring agency, J. Walter Thompson, U.K., with essentially the same results: the peak of brand switching was at 2 OTS in the purchase cycle (usually about 2 weeks for these grocery products) with a second, smaller rise at 4 OTS. We believe this might reflect an informational versus transformational difference. See P. Gullen and H. Johnson, Product purchasing and TV viewing: Measuring and relating the two, *New Developments in Media Research*, Amsterdam: ESOMAR, 1986, pp. 345–363.

26. The most direct evidence on the extent of repetition needed for the two types of brand awareness comes from the laboratory experiment by S. N. Singh and M. L. Rothschild, Recognition as a measure of learning from television commercials, *Journal of Marketing Research*, 1983, *20* (3), pp. 235–248, discussed in Chapter 8 (see especially Figure 8.6). Obviously, brand recall depends not only on the number of exposures but also on the number, and degree of learning of, competing brand names in the category, especially during the exposure-to-purchase opportunity interval

(2 weeks in the above experiment). For comparison, the McCollum-Spielman ad testing norms for brand recall after 1 exposure, just half an hour later, with seven commercials shown in the program (so the chance level = 1/7 or 14 percent), is 39 percent for new brands and 56 percent for established brands.

Thus, we can see that brand recall not only increases with exposure, but also drops off very rapidly (mostly within 24 hours) the longer the delay between exposure and the purchase opportunity. This is quite unlike brand recognition, which peaks quickly and stays high for long delay periods (of at least 1 month) until purchase.

27. T. S. Robertson, same reference as note 9, pp. 174–175.

28. J. M. McCann and E. S. Ojdana, On the form of the lagged effect of advertising, in R. P. Bagozzi, K. L. Bernhardt, P. S. Busch, D. W. Cravens, J. F. Hair, Jr., and C. A. Scott, eds., *1980 Educators' Conference Proceedings,* Chicago, IL: American Marketing Association, 1980, pp. 298–301.

29. In a laboratory study comparing a simulated word-of-mouth exposure with an advertising exposure, for a new brand, the brand attitude effect was almost exactly twice as strong for word of mouth. This held, in opposite directions of course, for both a negative and a positive message. See P. M. Herr, F. R. Kardes, and J. Kim, Effects of word-of-mouth and product-attribute information on persuasion: An accessibility-diagnosticity perspective, *Journal of Consumer Research,* 1991, *17* (4), pp. 454–462.

30. In two field experiments on word-of-mouth effects, positive information was conveyed more often than negative information. See J. N. Sheth, Word-of-mouth in low risk innovations, *Journal of Advertising Research,* 1971, *11* (3), pp. 15–18; and G. S. Day, Attitude change, media and word-of-mouth, *Journal of Advertising Research,* 1971, *11* (6), pp. 31–40.

31. See notes 29 and 30 and also J. H. Holmes and J. D. Lett, Product sampling and word-of-mouth, *Journal of Advertising Research,* 1977, *17* (5), pp. 35–40.

32. S. A. Ozga, Imperfect markets through lack of knowledge, *Quarterly Journal of Economics,* 1960, *74* (1), pp. 29–52.

33. See especially J. A. Dodson and E. Muller, Models of new product diffusion through advertising and word of mouth, *Management Science,* 1978, *24* (15), pp. 1568–1578. Some theorists have pointed out that word of mouth about a new *product* should decline as knowledge about the product spreads (see, for example, V. Mahajan, J. Wind, and S. Sharma, An approach to repeat-purchase diffusion analysis, in P. E. Murphy, G. R. Laczniak, P. F. Anderson, R. W. Belk, O. C. Ferrell, R. F. Lusch, T. A. Shimp, and C. B. Weinberg, eds., *1983 Educators' Conference Proceedings,* Chicago: American Marketing Association, 1983, pp. 442–446). However, a new *advertising* campaign or a new advertisement in a pool-out campaign can regenerate word of mouth even for an established product.

34. The authors wish to thank Margaret Nash for pointing out this problem.

35. National Infomercial Marketing Association study reported in *USA Today,* October 21–23, 1994, p. 1A. The actual distribution of purchases by exposures prior to purchase was as follows: 1 exposure, 27 percent; 2 exposures, 31 percent; 3 exposures, 18 percent; then 4 exposures, 9 percent (cumulative 85 percent); 5+ exposures, 15 percent. Four exposures seems a reasonable MEF to aim for.

36. See M. Givon and D. Horsky, Untangling the effects of purchase reinforcement and advertising carryover, *Marketing Science,* 1990, *9* (2), pp. 171–187; and A. B. Priemer, same reference as note 2, who suggested this explanation with the example of one 15-minute furniture polishing usage being the equivalent of four TV commercials for the brand.

37. L. G. Pringle, R. D. Wilson, and E. I. Brody, NEWS: A decision-oriented model for new product analysis and forecasting, *Marketing Science,* 1982, *1* (1), pp. 1–29.

38. The "ratchet effect" was introduced by W. T. Moran, Insights from pricing research, in E. B. Bailey (Ed.), *Pricing Practices and Strategies,* New York: The Conference Board, 1978, pp. 7–13. A recent experiment provided clear evidence of the ratchet effect in advertising and promotion scheduling. The study used ads for the 12 leading brands of candy bars in Canada. Consumers saw either the full, 30-second TV commercial for each brand, which provided information on brand benefits; or a simple "reminder" slide ad showing the package, the product, and the brand name (no benefit claims); or no advertising. Exposure to the benefit ads, but *not* the reminder ads, increased choices of the advertised brand when it was subsequently discount-priced and *also* increased the proportion of purchases (during 16 simulated shopping trips) of the brand bought at full price. Price was varied from actual to 25 cents off. See A. Mitra, Advertising and the stability of consideration sets over multiple purchase occasions, *International Journal of Research in Marketing,* 1995, *12* (1), pp. 81–94.

For further evidence of the ratchet effect, see A. Roberts, same reference as in note 22. In his study of 11 established brands in several typical fmcg product categories, sales among those consumers who had seen advertising for the brand in the previous 4 weeks were two to seven times greater during a subsequent (price-) promotion week than during a subsequent nonpromotion week. Moreover, the ratchet effect worked for all 11 brands. Compared with sales among consumers who had not seen the prior advertising, the sales among "advertising primed" consumers during promotion weeks were 2 percent to 47 percent higher, with a median absolute increase of about 10 percent.

39. The information about the Advertiming Company, which advises clients when to run advertisements in short-term media such as television, radio, or newspapers, as well as the examples, was reported in the journal of the Association of Canadian Advertisers and reproduced in the Australian Association of National Advertisers' newsletter, *National Advertiser,* 1985, *231*, pp. 55, 57.

## DISCUSSION QUESTIONS

**16.1.** Why is exposure a difficult concept to define? Comment on how well we resolve this difficulty in the chapter, with particular reference to where the media planner's responsibility ends and the creative director's responsibility begins.

**16.2.** What is an advertising cycle? Why does the advertising cycle override any "standard" intervals (such as 4 weeks) used in conventional media planning to calculate reach and frequency?

**16.3.** In a sentence or two for each, explain the most likely reach pattern when advertising the following:
  **a.** A new but easily imitated brand in a new product category
  **b.** A fad product
  **c.** Sunburn lotion
  **d.** A home-renovation service
  **e.** A variety store

**16.4.** Estimate (calculate) the minimum effective frequency per advertising cycle, and the length of the advertising cycle, thus MEF/c, for each of the following examples:
  **a.** Digital minicomputers, advertising in industry management magazines, to brand switchers, via a brand recall, informational brand attitude strategy.
  **b.** Kraft cheese, advertising in nonserial daytime TV, to brand loyals, via a brand recognition, transformational brand attitude strategy.
  **c.** Southern Comfort bourbon, advertising on billboards, to other-brand loyals, via a brand recall, transformational brand attitude strategy, using a campaign that is known to generate favorable word of mouth from one in every three people exposed.
  **d.** Circuit City, advertising Sony Walkmans, on radio, to new category users, via a brand recall, informational brand attitude strategy.

**16.5.** How is MEF/c estimated for direct response ads, interactive TV or PC ads, and promotion offers?

**16.6.** (Advanced question that will require looking up media chapters in other advertising texts or a media text.) Below is an example of a media plan for a target audience of 10 people (this could as well be 10 million people, but smaller numbers are easier to work with). It is based on a 3-week advertising cycle. An exposure is indicated by an x.
  a. According to the definition in the chapter, what is the reach of this plan?
  b. According to the conventional definition of reach in any advertising textbook, what is the "cumulative reach" of this plan for the 9-week period? In a sentence or two, describe why the "cumulative reach" figure is misleading.
  c. Suppose the minimum effective frequency is estimated or known to be 2 exposures in an advertis-

| Individual | Advertising cycle 1 (week no.) | | | Advertising cycle 2 (week no.) | | | Advertising cycle 3 (week no.) | | |
|---|---|---|---|---|---|---|---|---|---|
| | 1 | 2 | 3 | 1 | 2 | 3 | 1 | 2 | 3 |
| 1 | | | x | x | x | | x | | x |
| 2 | | | | | | | | | |
| 3 | x | | | | | | x | x | x |
| 4 | | | | x | x | | | x | |
| 5 | | | | | | | | | |
| 6 | x | x | x | x | | | | | |
| 7 | | | | | x | x | x | x | x |
| 8 | | | x | x | x | x | | | |
| 9 | x | x | | | | | | | |
| 10 | | x | x | | | | x | | x |

ing cycle (2/c). Then, as per the conventional textbook definition, calculate the *average frequency* for each advertising cycle. Are cycles 1 and 2 equally effective for the advertiser?

**d.** Suppose that the advertiser is pursuing a *shifting reach pattern,* with MEF = 2. What is the effective reach of the plan?

**e.** Finally, suppose instead that the advertiser is pursuing a *regular purchase cycle* reach pattern, with MEF = 2. What is the effective reach of the plan?

## FURTHER READING

Longman, K. A. *Advertising.* New York: Harcourt Brace Jovanovich, 1971.

Although published some time ago, this is the only book other than Priemer's (see below) that comes close to explaining media strategy from a correct perspective. Particularly to be studied is Longman's excellent discussion of how advertising media strategy must take purchase cycles into account.

Priemer, A. B. *Effective Media Planning.* Lexington, MA: Lexington Books, 1989.

This is absolutely the best book on media *strategy* ever written. It exposes the high-sounding but empty jargon used by many media planners to cover their ignorance and "snow" clients. It emphasizes the individual perspective on media planning (as we do) and offers many valuable insights from the author's long and observant tenure as a media planner. This book is *required* reading.

Naples, M. J. *Effective Frequency: The Relationship Between Frequency and Advertising Effectiveness.* New York: Association of National Advertisers, Inc., 1979.

This book makes a good case for the centrality of effective frequency in media strategy. Unfortunately, the varying criteria of "effectiveness" limit the conclusions to be drawn from the studies reported in the book (it takes an empirical rather than a logical or theoretical perspective on identifying MEF).

Turk, P. B. The relevance of environmental variables in setting effective frequency thresholds for television. In K. B. Rotzoll, ed., *American Academy of Advertising Proceedings,* Urbana-Champaign: University of Illinois, 1989, pp. RC-1 to RC-26.

This article is a thoughtful discussion of factors affecting MEF. The careful reader will see that the earlier edition of our book, as does this one, offers solutions for all the major issues identified in Turk's article. Nevertheless, it is still well worth reading for its broader perspective on effective frequency.

# CHAPTER 17

# Media Plan Implementation

Having determined the reach pattern and calculated the minimum effective frequency for each advertising cycle in the media plan, the media planner's final task is to implement the plan. The planner has to *select specific media vehicles* (particular TV dayparts or programs, particular magazines, and so forth, depending on the primary and secondary media types previously selected) and *ad units* (see Chapter 10), then devise a schedule of *insertions* that will deliver the required level of frequency in each advertising cycle to as many target audience individuals as possible within the media budget. Insertions can be ads, adlike events, or promotions.

After reading this chapter, you should:

- Understand how to make a first-stage selection of media vehicles by direct matching, and appreciate the advantages of this method over the traditional method of demographic matching.
- Know which "qualitative" media vehicle factors to use, if any, to modify the initial list, thereby achieving the second stage of vehicle selection.
- See how and when to adjust the plan for ad units' contribution to MEF.
- Gain a basic appreciation of how to schedule insertions to attain effective reach with various reach patterns and frequency requirements.
- Learn how to evaluate media schedules by profit potential, not simply by cost.

This chapter is important for product managers[1] so they can understand how the media plan is intended to work.

## FIRST-STAGE SELECTION OF MEDIA VEHICLES BY DIRECT MATCHING

The initial or first-stage selection of media vehicles is best made by a method known as *direct matching.*[2] Direct matching is sometimes (loosely) called "single source" media vehicle selection, which is the right idea but doesn't go far enough, as we'll see.

We will describe the procedure for direct matching shortly. Before doing so, we need to demonstrate the limitations of the most widely used media vehicle selection procedure, *demographic matching.* Direct matching, as forewarned in Chapter 4 in conjunction with target audience profile variables, is to be distinguished from the traditional but less accurate vehicle selection method of demographic matching. (Figure 17.1 summarizes the two methods.)

### Demographic Matching

Demographic matching relates target audiences to media vehicles through demographics. As Figure 17.1 shows, this requires three intervening steps:

1. The advertiser has to profile the target audience in terms of its demographics.

**Direct matching**

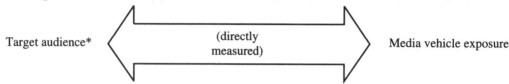

*The target audience is defined by awareness, attitude, and behavior as one of the 12 prospect subgroups or, at minimum, as one of the five main groups from which sales must come: brand loyals, favorable brand switchers, other-brand switchers, other-brand loyals, or new category users.

**Demographic matching**

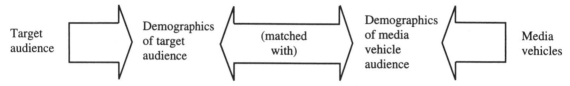

**FIGURE 17.1**
Direct matching and demographic matching in media vehicle selection.

2. The media planner has to profile each potential media vehicle's audience in terms of *its* demographics. (As most media owners sell their vehicles on the basis of head counts by demographic categories, demographic profiles of vehicle audiences are readily available, which accounts for the widespread use of demographic matching in media selection.)

3. The demographic profile of the target audience must then be compared, in some way, with alternative prospective vehicles, to find vehicles whose demographics most closely match the demographics of the target audience.

Most often, the demographic matchup is achieved by picking just one or two demographic variables that differentiate the target audience from all other consumers, such as sex and age. The media planner then searches through the alternative vehicles' profiles to find one or more vehicles that are also differentiated by, or are "skewed" toward, the sex and age groups desired.[3] For example, an advertiser might know from research that the target audience, in this case brand buyers, comprises 10 percent of the population. This brand buyer group, in our example, has the following sex and age composition:

- 60 percent women; 40 percent men
- 50 percent are aged 18–34; with 25 percent each from the under-18 and over-35 age groups

These are single demographics. Even better, though not always done, would be a cross-tabulation of sex by age among brand buyers. The cross-tabulation may show the largest proportion of brand buyers, say 40 percent, to be in the Women 18–34 cell, which would be one of six cells or categories in the cross-tab table. Women 18–34 constitute 13 percent of the population. This means that the probability that a woman aged 18–34 will be a buyer of the brand is 4/13,[4] or .31, which is considerably higher than the probability of .10 that a randomly chosen individual will be a buyer of the brand.[5] Therefore, the media planner searches for media vehicles whose audiences have a "Women 18–34 skew." Had the media planner been advertising on television in 1994, TV program audience ratings might have shown the following programs to have the highest ratings among women 18–34:

- *Roseanne*
- *Murphy Brown*
- *Married with Children*

However, whereas a random individual has a probability of .10 of being a buyer of the brand, and women 18–34 have a probability of .31, *brand buyers* have (by definition) a probability of 1.00. If the media planner can find *brand buyers* via media vehicles, this would be much better, obviously, than finding women 18–34. In this example, based on these probabilities, direct matching (media vehicles reaching only brand buyers) could provide a 69 percent gain in accuracy over demographic matching (media vehicles reaching only women aged 18–34) and a 90 percent gain over random selection (media vehicles reaching the population at large). It is the prospect of reaching large numbers of brand buyers *directly* via media vehicles (that is, reaching mainly the target audience and no one else) that makes direct matching worth investigating.

There should be no presumption to use demographic matching when you can survey the media habits of the target audience directly. The same conclusion applies to "psychographic matching." As pointed out by Wells and Tigert,[6] indirect matchups through *any* third set of variables, be they demographics or psychographics, are bound to produce lower accuracy than if a direct linkage is sought. This is especially the case if *category user* demographics are used to select media vehicles, which is common practice. As most brands in a category tend to have the same demographic user profile,[7] it is virtually impossible to apply brand loyalty targeting (Chapter 3) with this approach. This does not mean that demographic or psychographic characteristics cannot be used to *further define* a brand loyalty–based target audience. For instance, Coke may target favorable brand switchers (FBSs) who are *mothers,* for one campaign, and FBSs who are *young people* aged 10–14, for another. It simply means that we should find out *directly* what each of these two loyalty-cum-demographic target audiences' media exposure patterns are.

### Direct Matching

Direct matching is essentially an empirical "hope to improve accuracy" procedure. There is no guarantee that target audience individuals (for example, category users of personal computers, if we are IBM targeting PC users) will differ in their media habits from the "average" individual. However, surprisingly often, they do; and direct matching is certainly worth investigating to see if this is the case. For instance, Cannon[8] found that TV programs—and TV is widely regarded as being the most "mass" medium—varied in their category user reach by an *average* of plus-or-minus 11 percent, with a range of −38 percent to +93 percent for the 25 programs and five product categories studied. This is certainly enough difference to investigate.

Many case histories could be cited to demonstrate large-percentage and large-dollar improvements in accuracy of target audience reach by using direct matching. For instance, in a classic study of five consumer products (furniture, color TVs, garden tools, plays, and movies) and print media, Assael and Cannon[9] demonstrated an average 36 percent gain in reach of category users via direct matching compared with demographic matching. More recently, Wilson[10] used direct matching of TV programs to reach sparkling wine drinkers (for a client who marketed champagne) and found a 100 percent gain in accuracy over the traditional demographic TV buy of Adults 25–54; in other words, to use his example, 200 Adult 25–54 GRPs delivered only 100 GRPs to the category-user target audience, compared with 200 GRPs obtained by direct matching of the TV programs they most often watch. Of course, this is a dramatic example, but it illustrates the accuracy that you *might* gain by trying direct matching. More common are gains of 10 to 30 percent.[11]

What about large advertisers who "bulk buy" their media plans? Many large consumer fmcg marketers with many brands to advertise, such as General Foods and RJR/Nabisco, bulk buy media, especially TV.[12] However, these large advertisers can still use direct matching to assign the *programs* bought in the corporate bulk buy more effectively to their respective brand-user target audiences. The gains will be considerably less than if programs had been bought directly for each brand rather than being constrained by the bulk buy, but the gains, conservatively, are still in the 8 to 10 percent range.[13] For example, Mars Kal Kan dog and cat food brands, after bulk buying for all Mars products, were able to increase product category user-by-volume reach by 18 percent and specific brand reach by 8 percent using direct matching.[14] The 18 percent represents $180,000, and the 8 percent $80,000, per $1,000,000 of budget, and these savings accrue in addition to the bulk-buying discount.

Actually, the only case we have heard about where direct matching reportedly has *not* shown enough of an accuracy advantage to be worthwhile is for Coke (Coca-Cola) in Australia, where Coke represents a massive 50 percent of *all* soft drinks purchased. For its mainstream advertising, as distinct from its promotions, Coke basically targets "everybody," or so the company claims, and hence there is little to be gained by direct matching. However, this situation is unusual, and we believe it would change if another cola, such as Pepsi Max, aimed at teenagers, or Schweppes' Stuff cola, aimed at children, becomes a threat. Teenagers or children, respectively, would be quite accurately targeted using demographics (age), but targeting precisely those who have switched to the new cola would likely be most accurate with direct matching.

**IMC Use of Direct Matching.** Direct matching can be used to identify IMC promotion opportunities, as well, for the brand. Two general findings from direct matching research by IRI exemplify this.[15] One finding is that "coupon prone" grocery shoppers—defined as those who make 25 percent or more of their purchases with a coupon, versus 10 percent for the average household—watch 38 percent less *cable TV* than the average household. This suggests that *regular* (network) TV should be used to advertise coupon promotions in an IMC plan. Another finding is that grocery product "innovators," those who make 12 or more new-brand purchases a year versus three or fewer for "followers," are about 26 percent more likely to try *new TV programs* than are followers. This suggests that advertising trial promotions in new programs each fall, rather than returning programs, would provide a reach gain if you were trying to target innovators (as in the reverse-wedge/PI reach pattern discussed in the previous chapter). Thus, there may be general insights for the IMC plan to be gained from direct matching.

Also, of course, direct matching is the ideal way to identify *cross-media* linkages within your target audience—and these include both mass media and "narrow" media linkages. For example, how many or what proportion of your target audience are likely to read a particular magazine *and* "surf" the Internet, thus potentially being exposed to the World Wide Web of advertising sites? What proportion watches particular prime-time TV programs *and* also drives to work, passing outdoor media or one of your distribution outlets? A direct matching survey (see Chapter 18) is an excellent way of quantifying the cross-media linkages hypothesized from the behavioral sequence model that you have constructed for your target audience.

**Exceptions to the Need for Direct Matching.** Exceptions to the need to measure target audience media exposure directly might occur for local retail readvertisers, for *some* industrial advertisers, and for direct mail advertisers. The first two types of adver-

tising were discussed in Chapter 15, and direct mail was discussed in Chapters 10 and 14. Here we focus on whether these types of advertisers should use direct matching.

- *Local Retail Readvertisers.* The *product* advertising medium will usually be the local newspaper—a choice of only one vehicle, that is, no choice at all—and so direct matching is unnecessary. However, if the local retailer is also seeking a *store image* advertising medium, then direct matching would help to decide between, for example, local TV stations, local radio stations, city magazines, or direct mail.

- *Industrial Advertisers.* The *product* advertising target audience in many cases is so tightly contained within a particular industry or occupational "demographic" that a more direct measurement becomes unnecessary. However, larger industrial advertisers —and especially those using *corporate image* advertising aimed at upper-level decision makers as an umbrella for specific product advertising—have a considerably broader set of media vehicle options, and here, direct matching could be an advantage.

- *Direct Mail Advertisers.* Some direct mail advertisers mail to a previously developed database of prospects (see Chapter 14). In a database of prospects, of course, direct matching has already occurred, by definition. For the many direct mail advertisers who do *not* use a database, geographic or *geodemographic* "media selection" is a worthwhile method. (This is a sophisticated form of demographic matching, but is not direct matching.) Geodemographic profiling of the U.S. population has been taken to the extreme by research suppliers such as CACI, R.H. Donnelley, Equifax, and Claritas. Geodemographic direct mail profiling is now available to the street-block address level or even to the "ZIP + 4" level (about 10 to 15 households per subgroup)! Claritas's PRISM + 4, for instance, divides the United States into approximately 240,000 geographic subgroups.[16] Category users, regardless of demographics, can also be identified for many products and services geographically, thus lessening the need for direct matching.

The national consumer products advertiser and the larger industrial advertiser, on the other hand, nearly always can develop a more accurate media plan by employing direct matching.

**Best Use of Direct Matching: Brand Loyalty Targeting.** So far, we have been referring to direct matching of category buyer or brand buyer target audiences. The main reason for this is that category buyer and brand buyer direct matching is now widely and inexpensively available from syndicated "single source" services (see Chapter 18). However, the best use of direct matching is for target audiences that are precisely defined by their *brand loyalty* status—that is, NCUs, OBLs, OBSs, FBSs, or BLs (see Chapter 3). To accomplish this, you will need a *customized survey,* either by designing it yourself, or by paying to have additional awareness, attitude, and behavior questions added to a syndicated survey, and for the extra tabulation this entails. We discuss these data-collection options for direct matching in Chapter 18.

For review, Table 17.1 summarizes the first-stage media vehicle selection methods.

#### TABLE 17.1

**FIRST-STAGE MEDIA VEHICLE SELECTION METHODS (IN ORDER OF PREFERABILITY)**

1. *Direct matching of brand loyalty–defined target audiences.* Clearly the most accurate method for precise targeting. Note that NCUs, OBLs, OBSs, FBSs, or BLs can have a demographic or psychographic profile overlay (see Chapter 3) and still be direct-matched. This method requires a customized survey, or customized questions added to a standard service's survey, in order to identify brand loyalty groups.
2. *Direct matching of category buyers or brand buyers.* Preferable to the above because it bypasses demographic or psychographic "third variables" and seeks a direct link between category buyers or brand buyers and their media vehicle exposures. Again, if your true target is BLs and FBSs, match by your brand buyers; if OBLs or OBSs, match by its or their brand buyers; if all four, match by category buyers. If NCUs, you'll have to try demographic matching with a survey.
3. *Demographic matching by category buyer or brand buyer demographics.* Use the same demographic variables and levels (such as sex, and particular age groups) that the media vehicle owners can supply. If your true target is BLs and FBSs, match by your brand buyer demographics. If your target is another brand's buyers—that is, OBLs and OBSs—match by *its* brand buyer demographics. If your true target is all four, match by category buyer demographics. If your target is NCUs, you'll need a survey to see if they are demographically distinguishable. (The same recommendations apply to psychographic matching, but psychographic data are rarely available from media suppliers.)

### ADJUSTMENT FACTORS FOR SECOND-STAGE MEDIA VEHICLE SELECTION

Target audience reach is the most important criterion in media vehicle selection, but it might not be the only one. From the first-stage list of vehicles selected by direct matching (or by demographic matching, if this traditional method is used), we can make further adjustments based on "qualitative" considerations concerning each vehicle. There are five main factors for which adjustments can be made:

**1.** *Vehicle Environment Effects on Ads.* Certain vehicles may be more, or less, compatible with the brand's advertising and thus make it more, or less, effective—even with target audience reach held constant. (However, as we will see, vehicle environment effects are much smaller than advertisers believe, and are hardly ever worth adjusting for.)

**2.** *Competing Ads in the Vehicle.* The presence of competitors' ads in the same vehicle may inhibit our ad's effectiveness. (Competitors' ads can be a problem in certain circumstances but may be unavoidable if we want to reach our target audience.)

**3.** *Timing of Vehicle.* The time at which the vehicle reaches the typical target audience member may be either opportune or inopportune from the standpoint of the ad's effectiveness.

**4.** *Impact Scheduling.* We may be able to increase effective reach (reach at MEF) by placing more than one ad in a single vehicle.

**5.** *Ad Unit Effects.* The length (for broadcast) and size (for print) of the advertisements to be used in the media plan may produce differing attention levels *regardless* of creative content and are therefore a media consideration that can affect MEF delivery.

But before we review these adjustment factors and recommend which ones to adjust for and when, what do we mean by "adjustment"? How exactly do we allow for "qualitative" factors in media vehicle selection?

#### Qualitative Adjustments Become Quantitative

Qualitative factors become quantitative when applied to the media plan. Although the causes of hypothesized media vehicle superiority or inferiority may be qualitative, the effect on the media plan is quantitative.

Not uncommonly, media vehicles such as TV programs or magazines are added to—or more often, deleted from—a plan purely on the basis of a manager's judgment about the vehicle's compatibility or incompatibility with the brand's advertising. For example, when the nuclear disaster TV movie *The Day After* was first televised in the United States in late 1983, family advertisers such as McDonald's refused to advertise in it even though the program was watched by an estimated 46 percent of the nation's homes and would have had very high target audience reach. Coca-Cola reportedly has an ongoing policy of avoiding TV news programs because bad news is feared to conflict with Coke's upbeat positioning.[17] Alternatively, vehicles may be deleted not because they are thought to be ineffective for the advertising but because consumers boycott those companies or products that advertise in the vehicle. In 1995, the American Family Association called for a boycott of Unilever's products because the company's media plan included violent and profane TV programs such as *NYPD Blue;* Unilever ignored the boycott, presumably because the programs reached too many consumers who *weren't* concerned.[18]

Deleting or adding media vehicles on a purely qualitative judgment is equivalent, quantitatively, to applying *zero-one weights* to media vehicle selection. Zero-one weights are *radically* quantitative; and managers had best be sure that such vehicles do have the hypothesized radically negative or positive effect on their advertising, because, in deleting such vehicles, they are overriding selections that have appeared in the plan because of their high reach to the target audience; and in adding such vehicles, they are adding selections that otherwise would not have been used because of their low target audience reach.

The alternative method of allowing for qualitative factors is also quantitative, and that is to apply *indexed weights* to each media vehicle based on its expected compatibility or incompatibility with the brand's advertising. Average vehicles are given a weight or index of 1.0, then compatible vehicles may be weighted up to a maximum of, say, 2.0, with incompatible vehicles weighted down from 1.0 to as low as 0.0. Operationally, the effect of indexed weights is *to adjust the vehicle's contribution to effective frequency.* A moderately positive vehicle with

a weight of 1.5, for example, may be regarded as contributing "1.5 exposures" to MEF, whereas a moderately negative vehicle may be regarded as contributing "0.5 of an exposure." If both vehicles are used to reach the same target audience, they together would contribute 2 exposures to the MEF level. Because of the difficulty of thinking in terms of fractional exposures, and the specialized computer program required to apply the weights, such weighting schemes are not used in practice as widely as they should be. Theoretically, they are the correct way to incorporate qualitative judgments in media vehicle selection.

Under what circumstances should qualitative adjustments be made? Let us now assess the evidence for the five adjustment factors as they affect mass media vehicles; we'll then separately discuss adjustments for direct response vehicles.

### Vehicle Environment Effects on Ads

Vehicle environment effects are the most common—and the most erroneous—source of media plan adjustment. Even if there were reasons to adjust for "environment," media planners would not be able to interpret and apply them reliably. In a revealing study, Haley[19] asked 60 media professionals from 10 leading agencies to rate a large set of vehicles, from all main media, on an "impact" scale of 0 to 100 points. The ratings were shockingly inconsistent (for example, a range of 250 percent in lowest to highest ratings for a 30-second TV commercial, and a 400 percent range for a quarter-page black-and-white newspaper ad), and individual raters were just as varying in their ratings as were agencies. Subjective weights are not the answer!

Our actual recommendations are as follows:

- *Likable Vehicles.* No adjustment; likability is already reflected in vehicle exposure frequency obtained in direct matching.[20]
- *Dislikable Vehicles.* No adjustment; no *naturalistic* exposure studies have ever shown ads to be less effective in "negative" (depressing or distressing) vehicles.[21]
- *Prestigious Vehicles.* No adjustment; there is no evidence that any types of ad work better in more prestigious or high-quality vehicles.[22]
- *Design or Adapt Ads to Suit Vehicles.* No; the evidence favors the hypothesis that an ad already designed for the *target audience* will work virtually

anywhere. There is no payoff in redesigning ads for the respective *vehicle audiences.* (The one exception is musical *radio* ads, to gain attention; see Chapter 10.)

- *Print Ad Editorial Environments.* In newspapers, adjust *downward* by 0.2 (so MEF = 0.8) if the ad is opposite a text page. In magazines, do not adjust. Only if the editorial content attracts completely additional readers to the publication is it worth adjusting for, and then the adjustment is to revise *reach* upward, with frequency staying the same.

Overall, vehicle environment effects are greatly exaggerated. Almost never should vehicles be added or deleted or otherwise up- or down-weighted because of presumed environment effects. A much surer principle is: "A good ad will work anywhere."

### Competing Ads in the Vehicle

Is the presence of competing ads a serious problem in media vehicle selection in the vehicle? On an average day, the average U.S. TV viewer watches $4^1/_2$ hours of TV, and even college-educated viewers watch about 3 hours daily![23] At the current U.S. prime-time rate of about 18 commercials per hour, this amounts to about 80 potential commercial exposures per night for the average viewer, and about 54 for the college-educated viewer. Many of these commercials will be for competing brands. Similarly, leafing through a copy of *House Beautiful,* or *Redbook,* the magazine reader is likely to be exposed to 100 or so ads, many for competing brands. What should the individual advertiser do about this apparent "overload" of ads? The answer is not as straightforward as many advertisers believe, as we now explain.

Whereas all ads in a media vehicle to some extent compete with each other for the viewer's, listener's, or reader's attention, producing what is commonly known as "clutter," we have concluded (in Chapter 10) that competition for *attention* is *not* in most cases a serious problem.[24] This is because an ad demands only microseconds of an audience member's time to pay the ad reflexive attention, and only a second or two more to pay selective attention. Also, in most media, ads occur *sequentially,* so attention itself is not "cluttered." Only in retail print advertising, and notably *Yellow Pages* advertising, where there are *simultaneous demands* on the person's attention due to multiple ads *on the same page,* should

competition for attention pose any problem—and here, the ad that best elicits reflexive attention, through its mechanical elements, usually wins the attention battle.

Rather, the main problem caused by competing ads occurs in the *learning* phase of processing. This problem is known as *interference.*[25] (Attention does not get cluttered, except for the retail print ads or directory ads. Rather, it is certain *communication effects* that get cluttered.) Interference occurs for:

**1.** *Brand recall*[26] when the consumer is faced with learning two or more different responses (brand names or packages) to the same stimulus or originating cue (the category need). Learning experiments indicate an increase in *brand recall* interference, the more often two or more to-be-learned responses (such as Coke, Pepsi, RC Cola) are presented in conjunction with the same stimulus (cola beverages). The interference extends backward and forward and affects each brand's recall (but not its brand recognition).[27]

**2** *Low-involvement/transformational brand attitude* where the consumer is faced with learning which (different) brand names or packages possess which (similar) "image" benefits. Low-involvement/ *informational* brand attitude is only subject to interference during the first few exposures in which it is being learned; once learned, it becomes quite resistant to competitive interference, provided that there are at least occasional learning reminders in the form of continuing ads to maintain the attitude. Low-involvement/*transformational* brand attitude, in contrast, is continually subject to interference because of the larger frequency of exposures necessary prior to acquisition and the somewhat tentative positive-affect conditioning process which maintains the attitude. Indeed, all transformational brand attitudes are sensitive to competition (hence the LC + 1 correction factor for transformational brand attitude when estimating media frequency in the MEF formula), but the low-involvement type is interfered with by learning whereas the high-involvement type is more sensitive to the acceptance strength of the transformational benefit claims in the competing ads rather than the number of competing ads.

The cause of interference with brand recall and low-involvement/transformational brand attitude is *not the proximity* of competing brands' ads (since time is not a causal factor in verbal interference[28]) but rather their *competitive frequency,* relative to our brand, in the *advertising cycle.* That is, it is the *number* of competitors' ads that matters, not *how close* they are to ours.

The foregoing analysis leads to the conclusion that the only situations in which advertisers should worry about competing ads in the vehicle are the following:

- In *retail print advertising,* including *Yellow Pages and directory* advertising, when there is simultaneous competition for attention on the *same page.* Here, the solution is to use a reflexive attention-getting creative execution, not to avoid the vehicle.
- When *only one or two vehicles are available* to deliver MEF in the advertising cycle, and competitors face the same vehicle selection constraint (this happens mainly with newspapers and specialized consumer or trade magazines) *and* when either brand recall *or* low-involvement/transformational brand attitude is a communication objective. The advertiser cannot really avoid such vehicles, because they are likely to have the largest reach to the target audience, which is why they attract so many competitors. We would estimate that the interference effect when there is at least one other competitor in the vehicle is sufficient to *halve* an ad's contribution to MEF; that is, each exposure contributes only 0.5 to MEF. Thus, our recommended solution is to *double* the number of our ads in these unavoidable competitive vehicles.

Otherwise, the advertiser should make *no* allowance for competing ads when selecting media vehicles for normal media plans.

### Timing of Vehicle

Another potential factor in making second-stage adjustments to the initial list of media vehicles is the timing of the vehicle. Certain vehicles in various media tend to be avoided because they reach the target audience at a particularly unsuitable time; whereas certain other vehicles are widely believed to have a timing advantage in terms of when exposure occurs in relation to purchase or purchase-related action opportunities.

All media types have timing options, to some extent, that the advertiser can consider. The main timing options are as follows:

- *TV:* dayparts and specific programs within dayparts.
- *Radio:* dayparts including, notably, drive-time versus in-home listening times.

- *Newspapers:* morning versus evening newspapers.
- *Magazines:* a division might be made between office or "work" reading versus home or "leisure" reading in terms of types of magazines; otherwise, magazines provide the *least* control over timing, with readership (and thus advertising exposures and GRPs) *lagging* in a distribution of individuals' reading times that appears to average about 2 weeks afterward for weekly magazines and about 7 weeks afterward for "fat" monthly magazines.[29]
- *Outdoor ads and posters:* time of day the outdoor (or indoor) display is usually passed or encountered; also timing in the sense of proximity to retail stores when category need is likely to be strongest.
- *IMC media:* time of day the medium is encountered; also, proximity to the purchase decision or usage decision, the ultimate being point-of-purchase and point-of-use promotions.

**Vehicle Adjustments for High-Involvement Brand Choice Timing.** Whether to adjust vehicles for timing depends entirely on the type of brand attitude the advertising is trying to achieve. (Brand awareness, a rote-learned response, should *not* be affected by the time at which exposure occurs.) *Low-involvement* brand attitude, which requires only rote learning (as discussed in Chapter 8), has *no* timing implications, and the effects of "moods" during vehicle exposure are likely to be weak. However, as we saw in Chapter 9, *high-involvement* brand attitude formation or change is *facilitated* by positive thoughts or cognitive responses and is *inhibited* by negative thoughts or cognitive responses during processing. This was one of the main reasons that we advised in Chapter 4 (profiling the target audience decision maker) assessing the decision maker's likely personality state during exposure. In particular:

**1.** For *complex* (high-involvement/informational) products, media vehicles that reach the target audience when a majority of such individuals are in one or more of the following moods should be *deleted:*

- **a.** Tired
- **b.** Anxious
- **c.** "Low IQ" state, for example, experiencing a hangover

**2.** For *expensive luxury* (high-involvement/transformational) products, media vehicles that reach the target audience decision maker in a "leisure" state on weekends or just before or during typical vacation periods should probably be *up-weighted*—say, to the equivalent of 2.0 exposures.

**Vehicles to Seek for Immediate-Action Advertising.** Ads (or promotion offers) designed to stimulate immediate action, with either a purchase-related or direct purchase action objective, are very sensitive to the timing of the delivery vehicle. For immediate-action advertising, it makes obvious sense to seek vehicles whose timing (1) capitalizes on category need and (2) allows the best opportunity for brand purchase intention to be carried out in the form of purchase or purchase-related action.

The three most common immediate-action advertising situations are the following:

**1.** *Retail Shopping Opportunity Ads.* Vehicles that reach the target audience just prior to shopping trips or on the way to shopping (outdoor ads or posters, drive-time radio) should be favored by retailers. Directory ads or *interactive TV or PC ads* are perfect, of course, because the shopper exposes him- or herself to the ad when category need is at its peak.

**2.** *Usage Reminder Ads.* Ads timed to coincide with usage opportunities include, for example, serving-suggestion ads before mealtime, beer ads at ball games or during sports programs, or credit card ads in stores.

**3.** *Direct Response Ads.* Vehicles that reach the target audience when they are near a phone or pen, and are therefore likely to have the means to respond should be most advantageous for direct response advertisers.

Such vehicles, which can be identified easily with the use of a behavioral sequence model (see Chapter 4), should be up-weighted to an MEF contribution of 2.0. This will have the effect of causing ideal timing vehicles to *dominate* the media plan, which they *should* for immediate-action campaigns. Whereas communication effects can be transmitted at other times, the likelihood of maximizing all five communication effects is greatest when using the category need and brand purchase intention–maximizing vehicles. By the MEF adjustment, too, IMC *timeline* integration (see Chapter 11) is credited quantitatively.

Overall, then, we see that vehicle timing is a relevant media vehicle adjustment factor if the advertising is aimed at a high-involvement brand choice, or if immediate action is called for.

## Impact Scheduling

For brands whose minimum effective frequency requirement in the advertising cycle is high—for instance, a new brand facing an "outer" target audience of new category users or other-brand loyals, or any brand with brand recall or transformational brand attitude communication objectives—*impact scheduling* should be considered. As defined previously, impact scheduling is the practice of repeating the ad several times in the one vehicle on a single occasion, such as a commercial repeated three times in the TV program *60 Minutes* on a given Sunday, or the same ad run twice in the same issue of *Newsweek*. Ideally, the repeated commercials or ads should contain executional variations on the same easily recognizable creative idea or "theme." Figure 17.2 shows an example of impact scheduling by Bundaberg Rum in *Rolling Stone* magazine. The ads, variations on the brand's single positioning idea, appeared twice in the middle and then again late in the magazine (near the avidly read music ratings), and are directed to its young cognoscenti audience.

Most media will accept multiple insertions in the one vehicle, although there may be a practical upper limit, especially for broadcast media where time cannot be added, unlike space in a magazine or newspaper. To our knowledge, the record number of insertions in a single vehicle is 13. In the October 31, 1983, issue of *The New Yorker*, London Fog placed 13 consecutive quarter-page ads, each featuring a different London Fog clothing item, with a common corporate theme.

Impact scheduling is basically in keeping with the media strategy principle that it is better to sell some people *completely* than many people not at all. It is increasingly being employed as a solution to "media fragmentation" (described later in this chapter). However, as we discuss briefly next, its advantages have to be weighed against its disadvantages.

**Advantages of Impact Scheduling.** Impact scheduling sacrifices *overall* reach, but for the same number of insertions, it tends to maximize *effective reach* (reach at effective frequency). Let us suppose, for instance, that the minimum effective frequency for a brand is estimated to be 3 exposures over a 3-week purchase cycle. Three commercials placed in one episode of *60 Minutes* would deliver more people at the MEF level of 3 than one commercial a week for 3 weeks in a row (Figure 17.3). The average repeat viewing figure for weekly programs is about 41

**FIGURE 17.2**

Impact-scheduled ads in *Rolling Stone* magazine for Bundaberg Rum. The first insertion is a double half-page ad across pages 42 and 43 of the magazine; the second insertion is a small strip ad at the bottom of page 45; and the third a sweepstakes promotion occupying one-third of page 114 at the end of the magazine next to the music charts that regularly appear there. *Courtesy: Rolling Stone* Australia magazine and United Distillers.

percent for adults,[30] so immediately the second week's insertion has lost 59 percent of the first week's audience. The 3-week repeat viewing incidence is 41 percent of 41 percent, or only 17 percent. This compares very poorly with the close-to-100 percent (allowing for some *partial* viewing of the program) who attained the effective frequency level of 3 exposures in the first week under the impact schedule.

Note that for the *regular purchase cycle* reach pattern, if the vehicle frequency is longer than or equal to the purchase cycle (for example, a monthly magazine advertising a product with a monthly or shorter purchase cycle), impact scheduling is the *only* way for that vehicle to achieve an MEF requirement that is 2 or more exposures per purchase cycle.

**Limitations of Impact Scheduling.** As is true for most media strategy decisions, there are trade-offs to be considered with impact scheduling. One limitation *may* be the increase in the average delay

between exposure and the individual's purchase opportunity. Consider, for example, a *regular purchase cycle* reach pattern with a purchase cycle of 2 weeks. In the *60 Minutes* even schedule (see Figure 17.3), the average delay would be 3 1/2 days, whereas for the impact schedule it is 10 1/2 days—three times as long as for the separate weekly ads.[31] (With other reach patterns, the delay factor is not critical, because either the advertising cycle is continuous or the purchase cycle is so long that spacing of ads within an advertising cycle or flight makes little difference.) The *effect* of this delay depends on the amount of competitive activity in the delay period (again, for the average individual), and it affects the brand *only* if its communication objectives include brand recall *or* low-involvement/transformational brand attitude.[32] However, these are *precisely* the communication objectives that require the highest MEF (see above). For *high-frequency brands,* com-

pared with the drastic loss of reach at effective frequency, as in the *60 Minutes* example, the net outcome is very likely to *favor* impact scheduling.

A potentially more serious limitation is the *probable loss of attention* when an ad is repeated at short intervals, either in broadcast or print vehicles. The loss is somewhat less for TV because of its intrusive or captivating nature, but attentional wearout through tedium (see Chapter 20) is likely to be increased in any medium.[33] The creative solution is to use slightly different ads (variations on a theme). The Bundaberg Rum ads shown in Figure 17.2 illustrate this technique. By varying the executional content, attention loss with an impact schedule should be minimized. Although somewhat more expensive in terms of production, it is well worth producing executional variations if you are going to use a lot of impact scheduling.

**MEF Adjustment for Impact Scheduling.** What should the MEF adjustment for impact scheduling be? The first exposure in an impact sequence should contribute the normal 1.0 to MEF. If varied executions are used, the second and subsequent exposures should also come close to 1.0—perhaps even a bit above, as

the audience remembers the previous exposure, somewhat like imagery transfer—but the loss of attention still seems more likely than for a new ad. Overall, an average estimate is 0.5 for second and subsequent exposures. Safely, the advertiser should assume 3 insertions for every 2.0 exposures contributed to MEF.

However, with either brand recall or low-involvement/transformational ads, when used with a regular purchase cycle reach pattern, assume 4 insertions to get 2.0 MEF (or 2 to get 1.0 MEF) because of the likelihood of interference during the longer delay to purchase opportunity.

An increasingly used form of impact scheduling is "top and tailing," rather than simple repetition. *Top and tailing* refers to the practice of running a two-part ad, usually a normal-length or normal size ad followed *shortly* thereafter (usually one or two ads' duration afterward) by a short "tail" or reminder ad.[34] Although ad unit adjustments (see below) would suggest 1.0 + 0.5 = 1.5, we judge that the "continuity theme" of the top-and-tail style is worth 2.0 MEF. However, these ads are also more expensive to place, in either broadcast or print media, because specific positions are required.

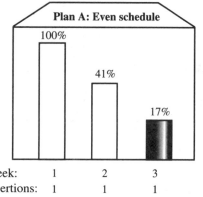

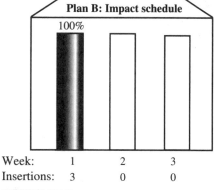

**FIGURE 17.3**
Example of how impact scheduling tends to maximize effective reach (see text for qualifications). Three-week purchase cycle with MEF = 3.

## Ad Unit Effects

The "unit" or "units" of advertising—different ad lengths or sizes, color, and several other physical characteristics apart from the creative content of the ad itself—are a fifth possible adjustment factor. (Whereas ad units are a creative factor rather than a media vehicle factor, the media planner has to *buy* the time or space in the vehicle to accommodate ad units, and *availability* may affect the final list of vehicles. Availability may even result in a forced change of ad units.) For instance, if a 30-second TV commercial contributes 1 exposure to the MEF level required, does a 60-second commercial contribute the equivalent of 2 exposures? Similarly, does a half-page magazine ad contribute 0.5 of an exposure compared with the normal one-page size? In Chapter 10 we saw which ad unit dimensions matter and how much to adjust for them. *Whether* to adjust is a question we'll consider shortly.

Notice that we adjust only for *initial* attention attributable to differing ad units—*not* for the subsequent performance of different ad units in producing *communication effects*. Different lengths or sizes of ads *do* differ in communication effectiveness. The differences are not surprising, because larger (longer) or smaller (shorter) ads are completely different in terms of:

- The sorts of target audiences they are aimed at (for example, new category users versus brand loyals).
- The products they are used for (for example, new versus established brands).
- Communication objectives (for example, all five communication effects versus the basic two of brand awareness and brand attitude).
- The length of copy or audio permitted (and thus brand awareness and brand attitude benefit mentions).
- The picture-word ratio, which varies with the size of print ads.

Therefore, it is spurious to try to compare advertising units in terms of communication effectiveness because different units are used for quite different communication purposes.

The advertising unit or units should be selected by the creative director, based on target audience type and the communication objectives. The media planner then adjusts only for the *ad unit's or units' physical ability to gain initial attention,* as this factor (just like media vehicle attention, discussed earlier) will alter the attained MEF level.

**Initial Attention Adjustment Measures.** In Chapter 10, we presented our "best estimate" adjustments for advertising units in all major media: television (including cable television), radio, newspapers, consumer magazines, business and industrial magazines, outdoor ads and posters, and directories. We assumed that advertising units have to make at least a 20 *percent* (plus or minus 0.2) difference to initial attention before they are worth adjusting for when estimating achieved MEF in a media schedule. A 20 percent increase in attention means, for instance, that 5 units of that type are equivalent in MEF to 6 standard advertising units, in terms of initial attention-gaining capability.

Here are our recommendations on when to adjust for ad units:

- For *broadcast* campaigns (TV or radio): If the schedule consists *predominantly* of either longer ads or shorter ads, adjust. (For instance, if using mainly 60-second commercials for TV, worth 1.2 each, reduce the insertions to $1.0 \div 1.2 = 83$ percent of the original MEF number; on the other hand, if using mainly 15-second commercials for TV, *increase* the insertions to $1.0 \div 0.8 = 125$ percent of the original number.) The other variation in ad-unit attention in broadcast vehicles is for direct response ads (90-second commercials through to infomercials). These longer ads contribute 2.0 to MEF, but (in Chapter 16's MEF section) we recommended that *4 OTS*/c for broadcast DR ads be aimed for, which is technically an MEF level of 8.

- For *print* campaigns (all print media): *Always* adjust. Attention to the ad is too greatly affected by ad unit factors to ignore their effects. (Again, see Chapter 10 for these adjustments.)

### Direct Response Vehicle Adjustment

Media *vehicles* for direct response ads will have been selected in the first stage according to target audience reach, just as any other media vehicle is chosen. However, the second-stage adjustment to shorten the list of direct response media vehicles is made quite differently from that of mass media advertising vehicles. It is not made subjectively or qualitatively but rather quite objectively—by *trial and error*. Two DR media vehicles, for instance, could have identical target audience reach but one may "pull" extremely well and the other hardly at all. The reasons for this could be manyfold, and it is really not worth trying to sort them out. The direct response advertiser should be a ruthless empiricist, placing the brand's DR ads wherever they will generate the highest response (actually, the highest profit per response, as explained at the end of this chapter).

The various mass *media* in which direct response ads are placed—other than direct mail—have a number of media *vehicle* options with which to experiment.

- TV programs may vary in direct response effectiveness, even those with identical target audience reach, but usually the variation can be pinned down to day of week or time of day. ("Low resistance theory" has it that late-night TV is the ideal time for direct response ads, although this time period is probably popular because the commercial time is cheaper then, producing a lower cost per response.)

- Radio has similar options between stations, day of week, and time of day.
- Newspapers will vary, in direct response effectiveness, by paper, day of week, and position in the paper (particularly in different sections of the paper if it is in a sectioned format).
- Magazines will vary, in direct response effectiveness, by magazine—again, despite highly similar or identical target audience reach—and especially by position in the magazine. The complex effects of position on direct response reply rates were presented in Chapter 10, although the individual advertiser should conduct his or her own experiment.

Direct response ads, therefore, are the one broad type of advertising where you *shouldn't* make any adjustments *up front* for the DR media vehicle. Adjustments to the list of suitable vehicles are made only *later,* after the ads have been run at least once. Furthermore, because these direct response "experiments" are rarely fully controlled experiments—controlling for seasonality, for example—it is a good policy to give each of the vehicles on the original list with high target audience reach at least two chances to demonstrate its measurable pulling power.

### SCHEDULING INSERTIONS IN THE VEHICLES

Now we come to the really complicated stage of media plan implementation. We have selected our media vehicles, but how do we schedule *insertions* in them such that these insertions in various vehicles will, in combination, produce the required effective reach (reach at MEF/c or higher) of *exposures* to the target audience? This is a much more difficult question than it sounds—and it is not well solved in practice. In most cases, rough approximations are used (but advertising agencies' clients rarely know this, because they see only the plan that's actually bought).

The complexity arises because of *duplication of exposures*. Duplication of exposures is absolutely necessary if the plan is to produce a frequency of exposures greater than 1. There are two types of duplication:

**1.** *Within-Vehicle Duplication.* For example, as we discussed previously, how many target audience individuals who saw *60 Minutes* on one particular Sunday also saw it the following week? And the week after? And how many saw one of these *60 Minutes* programs but not the other two? And two but not the other one?

We have to know the extent of audience duplication *within* the vehicle, over successive presentations, in order to calculate how many exposures various individuals might receive.

**2.** *Between-Vehicle Duplication.* For example, how many target audience individuals who saw *60 Minutes* on a particular Sunday *also* watched the movie on CBS that followed? Or watched *Seinfeld* on NBC the following Thursday? Or read *The Wall Street Journal* (cross-media between-vehicle duplication) the following Monday? If we had an ad in each of these vehicles, we would have to know the extent of duplication *between* the vehicles in order to calculate how many exposures various individuals might receive.

We recommend three main methods to implement a schedule. The first of these is rather crude but is *strategically* sound, and that's three-quarters of the battle in media planning. The second builds on the first and is for the small advertiser with a relatively simple schedule to implement (that is, a schedule restricted by a relatively small number of media vehicle options). The third also builds on the first but is for the large advertiser and represents the best of the available mathematical "search heuristic" models that advanced media planners should be able to program and use on their computers. These methods are explained in the next section and in chapter appendices 17A and 17B.

### The Crude Strategy Method

Media vehicle exposure is fragmenting rapidly in all media. This is largely due to the incredible number of choices available to the average consumer (especially in the United States but increasingly worldwide as well). For instance, just a decade ago, the average U.S. household could receive 11 TV stations; now the number is more like 33. Just a decade ago, there were 9,700 radio stations across the United States; now there are over 11,000. Just a decade ago, there were about 1,800 magazines available; now the number is more like 2,500. Daily newspapers are the only mass medium to have declined in the last decade, from 1,700 down to 1,600, but the number of local weeklies (and sometimes local weekday dailies) has increased correspondingly.[35] Add to the fragmentation of mass media the variety of *IMC media* that are now

being used in integrated marketing communications programs, and you will quickly appreciate the complexity facing today's media planners.

In the face of this complexity, a crude approach that is mathematically loose but strategically correct seems quite defensible. As the first author's Wharton colleague Len Lodish has said: "It is better to be vaguely right than precisely wrong." We therefore propose a *crude strategy* method of media schedule implementation. We will first propose several general rules, and then present some more specific rules for achieving the reach pattern identified for the plan. Before looking at these general rules, it will be very helpful to study the reach of typical media vehicles and their within-vehicle and between-vehicle duplication figures in Table 17.2.[36] These figures will give an idea of the empirical basis of the rules.

The three general rules are described below.

**Reach Rule.** For high *reach,* buy many *small, competing* vehicles. By "competing" vehicles we mean, for example, TV or radio programs in the same time slot but on different channels or stations; or magazines that are close substitutes, such as *Time, Newsweek,* and *U.S. News & World Report.* This buying strategy will tend to scatter the target audience GRPs very widely. The *small* vehicles mean that there will be less within-vehicle duplication because small media vehicles tend to suffer a "double jeopardy" effect whereby each one reaches a small audience which is also less loyal to the vehicle in terms of repeat exposures. For prime-time weekly TV programs, for instance, a program with a 9 rating (meaning that 9 percent of households watch it) will have 37 percent of the first-week audience repeat-viewing the next week; a program with a 12 rating (the prime-time average) will have 41 percent; and a program with a 16 rating will have 45 percent.[37] The small-vehicles factor will therefore maximize reach. The use of *competing* vehicles means, of course, that there is little or no opportunity for between-vehicle duplication (although there will be some in the total plan, naturally, between other vehicles that don't compete) and thus frequency will be minimized—and reach maximized—by this factor as well.

**Frequency Rule.** For high *frequency,* concentrate on buying *large, noncompeting* vehicles (particularly "strip" vehicles, that is, regularly repeated vehicles). Large-audience vehicles tend to have the highest repeat-audiences (this is the double-jeopardy effect

TABLE 17.2

**TYPICAL REACH AND REPEAT-EXPOSURE FIGURES FOR MASS MEDIA VEHICLES**

(Base = all adults 18 + unless otherwise specified.)

**Vehicle by medium**

| | Average rating (% reach) | Proportion repeating: day-to-day[a] | | | Week to next week | Any 2 weeks in 8-week period |
|---|---|---|---|---|---|---|
| **Television** | | | | | | |
| Prime-time program | 12.0[b] | .53[c] | Households | | .40[d] | .28[e] |
| | | | Adults | | .41 | |
| | | | Teens | | .27 | |
| | | | Children | | .28 | |
| Evening news program | 10.7[b] | .54[c] | | | | |
| Daytime program | 5.0[b] | .61[cf] | | | | |
| Early-morning program | 4.4[b] | .44[c] | | | | |
| Late-evening program | 4.1[b] | .37[c] | | | | |
| Any two prime-time programs, same channel | | .16[f] | | | | |
| Any two prime-time programs, different channels | | .13[f] | | | | |
| Evening news, different channels | | .12[f] | | | | |
| Daytime, different channels | | .05[f] | | | | |
| **Radio** | | | | | | |
| Same station | 0.7[f] | .47[f] | | | | |
| Different stations | | .01[f] | | | | |
| **Newspapers** | | | | | | |
| Daily paper | 46.2[f] | .82[f] | | | | |
| Between papers | | ~.00[g] | | | | |
| **Magazines** | | | | | | |
| Same magazine | 4.3[f] | .50[f] | | | | |
| Between magazines | | .07 | | | | |
| **Outdoor ads and posters** | | | | | | |
| Same site | 25.0[f] | .50[f] | | | | |
| Between sites | | ~.00[g] | | | | |
| **Interactive TV or PC** | | | | | | |
| | 3.6[h] | .56[h] | | | | |
| **Impact schedules[g] (multiple insertions in same program, issue, or site)** | | | | | | |
| TV prime-time | .83 | | | | | |
| TV non–prime-time | .40 | | | | | |
| Radio | .47 | | | | | |
| Newspapers | .90 | | | | | |
| Magazines | .90 | | | | | |
| Outdoor ads and posters | .60 | | | | | |

[a] Or issue-to-issue for magazines, or once for interactive TV or PC-accessed Web site.
[b] ADWEEK's *Marketer's Guide to Media* (see note 36).
[c] Headen, Klompmaker, and Rust (see note 36).
[d] Barwise (see note 36).
[e] Ehrenberg and Wakshlag (see note 36).
[f] Stankey (see note 36).
[g] Authors' judgment.
[h] Williamson (see note 36).

working *for* you, a "double bonus" in reality). For example, on TV, buy big serials or quasiserials such as *E.R.* or *LA Law,* although almost any large regular program will do even if it is not a serial; buy evening news on *one channel* if that has good target audience reach. With daily newspapers, buy ad space frequently in the one paper. With weekly or monthly magazines, concentrate on only a few large-audience magazines. This strategy will reduce reach—although target audience reach will already have been sought using direct matching—but will maximize frequency (individual continuity of exposures) to the same target audience.

**Reach and Frequency Rule.** For high reach *and* high frequency, buy many *small, strip* vehicles. For example, on TV, buy smaller-rating strip programs such as *Hard Copy* or *The Simpsons.* This strategy, quite evidently, is a combination of the first two strategies. The many small vehicles will tend to increase reach, while at the same time their strip (repeat-audience) characteristics will increase frequency. As you'll remember from the "media balloon" metaphor, reach and frequency have to be traded off for a given budget, and here you are trying to maximize both, within the budget.

**Strategies for the Respective Reach Patterns.** The various reach patterns described in Chapter 16 require only a few additions to the three general rules because they are, in effect, specific implementations of those rules.

*Blitz Pattern.* The blitz pattern applies the reach and frequency rule to the hilt.

*Wedge Pattern.* The wedge pattern applies the reach and frequency rule initially, then gradually evolves into the reach rule, since frequency is gradually reduced on subsequent flights.

*Reverse-Wedge/PI Pattern.* Use direct matching to target innovators within the target audience initially, and apply the reach rule. On subsequent flights, broaden beyond innovators, and gradually evolve into the reach and frequency rule.

*Fad Pattern.* This is a short blitz: use the reach and frequency rule until the peak of the fad's growth, then stop.

*Regular Purchase Cycle Pattern.* Use the frequency rule, especially if you are going for dominance in particular purchase cycles. If your primary medium is magazines, survey the distribution of target audience reading times, as the lag in reading can greatly displace intended purchase cycle exposures.

*Awareness Pattern.* This is the reach rule applied to the hilt, with the *same* set of small, competing vehicles bought consistently to produce high individual continuity. More widely spaced flights with impact scheduling are probably more effective than more frequent flights without it because, on each flight, you want to "dose" with MEF everyone reached.

*Shifting Reach Pattern.* This requires the reach and frequency rule but with the reach part achieved by buying *different* sets of vehicles each time. Frequency is needed as well because you want to "zap" those with the category need who are reached. Longer or larger ads or impact scheduling is therefore recommended.

*Seasonal Priming Pattern.* Use the reach rule for the prime or primes and then the reach and frequency rule for the seasonal growth phases.

If you apply these rules, you will find that the number of media vehicle options diminishes quite rapidly—leading to convergence on a "crudely optimal" plan (if that's not a complete oxymoron). Favor strategy over tactics. The schedule may not be precisely optimal, but fine-tuning it would be quibbling over small and relatively unimportant differences compared with getting the strategy correct.

Optimization can be pursued further using two computer programming methods detailed in the chapter appendices—for the smaller advertiser (appendix 17A) and the larger advertiser (appendix 17B).

## PROFIT AND THE MEDIA SCHEDULE

So far we have referred only indirectly to the cost of the media schedule and thereby its contribution to the brand's profit. Most advertisers (and media planners) quite wrongly focus only on cost and do not attempt to estimate profit. In evaluating alternative media schedules, most advertisers use "cost per thousand," or CPM. However, the advertising cost per thousand *people* is a virtually useless statistic, for three main reasons. (1) It is not just "people" who will buy the product but rather *target audience* people. Two vehicles could have an identical cost per thousand members of the total audience but reach very different numbers or percentages of the target audience. This is the usual case with the possible exception only of very large mass audience vehicles such as the most popular TV programs. (However, using "cost per thousand" *target audience* individuals, or CPMT, doesn't answer the next two criticisms.) (2) Cost per thousand, or even cost per anything, is meaningless without considering revenue and profit. (3) Revenue does not begin to flow until target audiences have bought the product. This usually requires multiple exposures (indeed, MEF)—a realization which is completely ignored in the statistic of CPM *any* exposures.

### CPERP and the Profitability of the Schedule

The first thing to keep in mind is that the advertiser essentially pays for the total *vehicle* audience when placing an ad in that vehicle, whereas the advertiser is interested in reaching only the *target* audience, within the total vehicle audience. Also keep in mind that only individuals in the target audience are likely to buy the product.

In choosing between similar schedules, all of which appear to meet the media *strategy,* "cost per effective reach point," or CPERP, is the determining factor. You want the lowest CPERP or, looking at it the other way around, the highest effective reach percent per dollar. Now, given the schedule, we have to go back to effective reach *numbers.*

The profitability of the media schedule can be calculated as follows:

1. The *number* of target audience individuals *effectively* reached by the vehicle, *multiplied by*
2. The probability that the average target audience individual will buy the product, once effectively reached, *multiplied by*
3. The profit contribution of one unit of the product, which is the unit selling price minus the unit cost of goods sold, other than the unit advertising cost (see Chapter 2), *minus*
4. The cost of the schedule

To give a simplified (MEF/c = 1) example, suppose a direct response ad in *Reader's Digest* reaches one million *target audience* individuals; and their probability of buying, once effectively reached, is .7; and the profit contribution per unit sold is $1.00; and the cost of the *Reader's Digest* ad is $200,000. The profit expected from this ad placement is then $1,000,000 \times .7 \times \$1.00 - \$200,000 = \$500,000.$

The tricky figure in this formula is "the probability of buying" after being effectively exposed. The idea of minimum effective frequency, of course, is to bring the target audience individual up to a *maximum predisposition* to buy. The maximum predisposition, represented here by a probability of .7, may require *multiple exposures* (MEF/c = 2 for the typical DR print ad) which in turn are the result of a larger number of

insertions, perhaps in several vehicles, before the individual receives effective frequency. This is handled in the above formula by subtracting the total advertising cost of the *multiple* insertions.[38]

**Primary and Secondary or Other Target Audiences.** A media schedule may reach several target audiences of varying response potential. For instance, the media *plan* may be directed at brand loyals, yet the *schedule* will inevitably reach not only brand loyals but also brand switchers and other-brand loyals. The ads in the schedule may influence some of these latter individuals as well—indeed, they may be secondary target audiences—but presumably not to the extent that brand loyals are influenced. This is handled in the above formula by repeating steps 1 and 2 for each target audience. For example, brand loyals may be assigned a purchase probability of .8; favorable brand switchers, .5; and other-brand switchers, .1. The products of steps 1 and 2 are added, and steps 3 and 4 are then carried through to calculate profitability.

Of course, this is only an *estimate* of profitability. In particular, the numbers of target audience individuals reached may be a little off, depending on whether direct matching is used and how accurate the media model is; and the MEF/c is *always* an estimate until after the plan can be tracked (see Chapter 20). However, it is the right procedure.

### SUMMARY

Media plan implementation—the selection of specific programs, publications, and so forth, in which the ads or promotions in the campaign will be placed—should proceed in three stages.

In *first-stage* media vehicle selection, we need to find a set of vehicles that *reach* the target audience—the target audience being one or more of the five potential buyer groups (or 12 subgroups; see Chapter 18) of new category users, other-brand loyals, other-brand switchers, favorable brand switchers, or brand loyals. These NCU, OBL, OBS, FBS, or BL groups may be additionally delineated by a particular geographic, demographic, or psychographic profile.

Direct matching is the best method of first-stage media vehicle selection. Direct matching measures which vehicles (a representative sample of) the target audience is exposed to and how often. It therefore also provides within-vehicle and between-vehicle duplication patterns directly. It is worth a separate survey to gather direct matching data, as the increased accuracy in attaining effective reach will almost always increase the profitability of the plan well above the survey cost.

By contrast, the usual method of demographic matching, except for industrial advertising, and the occasionally employed method of psychographic matching, are usually less accurate in reaching the target audience and do not provide duplication-of-exposure information for calculating exactly whether effective frequency has been attained. These "indirect but easy" methods of media vehicle selection usually result in improved accuracy compared with a random buy of media vehicles—but only by increasing the reach of the plan to category users.

Direct matching, the preferred method, can also be used strategically to select vehicles that allow different campaigns to be aimed at specific target audiences. Of course, multiple target audience campaigns presume that each target audience has sufficient leverage to make multiple campaigns worthwhile and, in practice, no more than two simultaneous campaigns are usually run except by the very largest advertisers. Direct matching can be used to improve target audience reach for brands even when the company "bulk buys" its media.

In *second-stage* media vehicle selection, the original list of vehicles from the first stage may be subjected to a series of adjustment factors for processing of advertising in the vehicle. These adjustments up-weight or down-weight the contribution of an advertising insertion in the vehicle toward the total desired minimum effective frequency (MEF) level per advertising cycle (MEF/c). An extreme down-weighting, a contribution of 0 to MEF/c, means deleting the vehicle. The adjustments are for vehicle environment effects; competing ads in the vehicle; timing of the vehicle; multiple insertions in a single vehicle, known as impact scheduling; and advertising units to be used.

Vehicle environment effects are much weaker than most advertisers believe. In general, a good ad will work anywhere. So there is no need to delete negative-mood vehicles or low-prestige vehicles from the list: if these vehicles are what the target audience chooses to watch, read, or listen to, then they should be left in the plan. Real-world studies, as opposed to forced-exposure laboratory studies, show no mood or prestige influence on advertising effectiveness. Similarly, the widespread practice of up-weighting vehicles whose program or editorial content appears to be "compatible" with the ad's content (or even including

vehicles solely on this qualitative basis) receives virtually no support in the research literature and should not be followed.

Competing ads in the vehicle are a problem in only two circumstances. First, simultaneous demands on the consumer's attention can occur when *multiple ads appear on the same page,* as often happens in retail advertising and in *Yellow Pages* or directory advertising. These vehicles cannot be avoided, and the solution is not a media one but a creative one, namely, to make sure you use attention-getting creative executions when using these vehicles. Second, interference occurs for *brand recall* and *low-involvement/transformational brand attitude* learning when competing ads occur in the same advertising cycle. This is negligible for any one vehicle when the vehicle is one of many in the plan, but if the vehicle is one that you and the competitors must rely on to deliver a *high proportion of MEF* for the advertising cycle, because of its high target audience reach, then your ad's contribution to MEF/c will be approximately halved, to 0.5. So, if possible, double the number of your ads in such vehicles for brand recall or low-involvement/transformational brand attitude. In all other media plans, make no allowance for competing ads when selecting media vehicles.

Timing of the vehicle with respect to the target audience's purchase or purchase-related action opportunity is a further potential adjustment factor. It should be used in the following circumstances. If the brand attitude strategy is high-involvement/informational (a "complex" multiattribute brand choice), delete vehicles that reach the target audience when most of these individuals are tired, anxious, or otherwise "non compos mentis." If the brand attitude strategy is high-involvement/transformational (such as for a vacation or a new car), up-weight vehicles that reach a majority of the target audience in a "leisure state" to 2.0 (contributions to MEF/c) exposures.

Additionally, for ads in which immediate action is required, up-weighting (to 2.0 exposures, that is, a contribution of 2 to the required MEF/c) is appropriate in three circumstances: (1) for retail shopping opportunity ads, up-weight vehicles that reach the target audience just prior to shopping trips or on the way to shopping; (2) for usage reminder ads, up-weight vehicles timed to coincide with the usage opportunity; and (3) for direct response ads, up-weight vehicles where the target audience has the time and opportunity (telephone or pen and paper handy) to respond immediately.

The fourth adjustment factor, when applicable, is for impact scheduling. The placement of an ad twice or more in a single vehicle on a single occasion (but preferably done with slight executional variations) is an excellent way of increasing effective reach of a brand with a high MEF/c requirement. With the regular purchase cycle reach pattern, impact scheduling has the disadvantage of increasing the average delay between exposure and purchase opportunity for brand recall or low-involvement/transformational brands, which allows competitive interference; however, since these brands typically require high frequency and high effective reach, we recommend its use anyway. Impact-scheduled ads may also suffer an attention loss, for any brand. Because of this, we estimate close repetitions of the first exposure to be worth only about 0.5 of an exposure; that is, you need 3 impact-scheduled ads to get 2 MEF/c.

Advertising units—physical characteristics of the ad or ads to be used apart from the creative content per se—constitute a fifth possible adjustment factor. The advertising unit(s) should be selected by the creative director, in line with the brand's target audience and communication objectives, then adjusted for their attention value, if nonstandard, by the media planner. The adjustments (MEF contributions) for advertising units were detailed in Chapter 10. With sustained unusual-unit broadcast campaigns, and with *all* print campaigns, it is worth making an adjustment for advertising units.

Media vehicles for *direct response* ads are second-stage selected by trial and error (experimentation) to select those that yield the highest response rates.

The *final stage* of media plan implementation requires scheduling *insertions* of the ads or promotion offers in the chosen vehicles such that, in combination, the vehicles and insertions will deliver maximum effective reach of *exposures* to the target audiences—within the budget. This is very difficult and is inaccurately done in practice. We proposed a crude but strategically correct method as a first step (and the final one if you're not adept with a computer). Building on the crude strategy method, we then recommend (see chapter appendix 17A) an easy-to-use computer program for the BBD-LD REPEAT media model for smaller advertisers, or smaller plans, which will also give reasonably optimal results even for quite large plans. For the very large advertiser, a "search heuristic" computer program is required, and (see chapter appendix 17B) we suggest VIDEAC for

general use and Craig and Ghosh's program if you have precise duplication information from direct matching as input.

The profit contribution of the media schedule should also be estimated. Per advertising cycle, the revenue expected from the insertions (*number reached at effective frequency* × probability of purchase or purchase-related action × profit contribution from that action) must exceed the cost of the insertions (totaled for the advertising cycle), and the overall cost over advertising cycles must be within the budget.

## APPENDIX

# 17A. Schedule Implementation for the Smaller Advertiser

The smaller advertiser with a relatively manageable number of media vehicles already selected (say, 2 to 50 across all media) will probably be considering several fairly similar schedules that appear to fit the media strategy. The process of finding the optimal strategy is then a matter of juggling insertions slightly between vehicles and perhaps dropping or adding a vehicle or two—again, without departing from the strategy. This trial-and-error process can be quite accurately achieved by employing a simple computer routine, easily programmable on a PC (Table 17.3). The routine shown is an *adaptation* of one of the easiest-to-use published media models, the BBD-LD model developed by Leckenby and Rice.[39] Our version is called the BBD-LD REPEAT model. A significant advantage attributable to the original BBD-LD model is that it appears to handle mixed-media schedules quite well, which is important if you are using primary and secondary media and especially important for evaluating multimedia IMC schedules. Our BBD-LD REPEAT model importantly improves the BBD-LD model by incorporating repeat-exposure estimates (from Table 17.2) when multiple insertions are placed in the same vehicle.[40] The BBD-LD REPEAT model has proven to be very accurate for broad TV advertising schedules, and considerably more accurate than the typical syndicated media models widely used by advertising agencies.[41]

To illustrate the output from the BBD-LD REPEAT model, we simulated a $1-million, 4-week media spend (Table 17.4) for, respectively, the two extremes: a reach strategy and a frequency strategy. For the reach strategy, we have assumed that the advertiser wishes to maximize reach (in other words, that the effective reach is R1+ /4). In the reach plan, we "bought" 10 small, competing TV programs in prime time, each with a rating of about 5 (for example, *Empty Nest, Fox Hollywood Theater*), and 25 small

**TABLE 17.3**

**BBD-LD REPEAT COMPUTER PROGRAM[a]**

```
DIM A(100), N(100), V(100), SI(100), E(100)
PRINT "WELCOME TO THE BBD-LD REPEAT MODEL"
PRINT "TYPE THE NUMBER OF VEHICLES IN SCHEDULE"
INPUT NUMVE
PRINT "FOR EACH VEHICLE, ENTER THE AVERAGE AUDI-
ENCE AND"
PRINT "NUMBER OF INSERTIONS IN THAT VEHICLE AND"
PRINT "VEHICLE TYPE"
PRINT "1 = TV PRIME-TIME WEEKLY PROGRAM"
PRINT "2 = TV EVENING NEWS DAILY PROGRAM"
PRINT "3 = TV LATE EVENING WEEKLY PROGRAM"
PRINT "4 = TV PRIME-TIME IMPACT SCHEDULE"
PRINT "5 = NEWSPAPER DAILY"
PRINT "6 = MAGAZINE WEEKLY"
PRINT "7 = NEWSPAPER OR MAGAZINE IMPACT SCHED-
ULE"
SUMIN = 0
S1 = 1
S2 = 1
R1 = 1
GRPS = 0
FOR I = 1 TO NUMVE
   INPUT A(I), N(I), V(I)
   SUMIN = SUMIN + N(I)
NEXT I
FOR I = 1 TO NUMVE
   IF V(I) = 1 THEN SI(I) = 1 - (1 - A(I)* 41)^N(I)
   IF V(I) = 2 THEN SI(I) = 1 - (1 - A(I)* 54)^N(I)
   IF V(I) = 3 THEN SI(I) = 1 - (1 - A(I)* 28)^N(I)
   IF V(I) = 4 THEN SI(I) = 1 - (1 - A(I)* 83)^N(I)
   IF V(I) = 5 THEN SI(I) = 1 - (1 - A(I)*.82)^N(I)
   IF V(I) = 6 THEN SI(I) = 1 - (1 - A(I)*.5)^N(I)
   IF V(I) = 7 THEN SI(I) = 1 - (1 - A(I)*.9)^N(I)
   GRPS = GRPS + A(I)* N(I)
S2 = S2* (1 - SI(I))
R1 = R1* (1 - A(I))
NEXT I

S2 = 1 - S2
R1 = 1 - R1
S3 = 1 - (2* R1* S2/(R1 + S2))
PRINT
BG = 1
FD = .5
ALPHA = 1
WHILE BG
   ALPHA = ALPHA - FD
   BETA = (ALPHA* (SUMIN - GRPS))/GRPS
   D = 1
   Y = 1
   FOR I = 1 TO SUMIN
      L = I - 1
      IF D > = 1.67D + 34 THEN D = D/1.66D + 34
      D = D* (ALPHA + BETA + L)
      IF Y > = 1.67D + 34 THEN Y = Y/1.66D + 34
      Y = Y* (BETA + L)
   NEXT I
   IF (ABS(S3 - Y/D) < FD) THEN FD - FD/50
   IF (FD < .0011) THEN BG = 0
WEND
EXPLEV = SUMIN + 1
FOR I = 1 TO 100
   E(I) = 0
NEXT I
E(1) = Y/D
FOR I = 2 TO EXPLEV
   E(I) = E(I - 1)* ((SUMIN - I + 2)/(I - 1)*
   ((ALPHA + I - 2)/(BETA + SUMIN - I + 1)))
NEXT I
PRINT "EXPLEVEL   %EXPOSED"
PRINT
FOR I = 1 TO SUMIN + 1
PRINT USING "####    ##.##"; I - 1; E(I)*100
NEXT I
```

[a] Adapted from Rice (1988); see note 39. Our most important adaptation of the BBD-LD program in the Rice article is that we have incorporated the repeat-exposure estimates for various vehicle types (the V statements in the program). Hence we call our version BBD-LD REPEAT. For conciseness, only several vehicle types are shown here (see Table 17.2 for other types). The program is in QBASIC computer language.

non–prime-time programs in widely scattered time periods, with ratings of 2 to 3 (for example, *CNN Early Morning II, Robin Hood Trilogy, Apollo Comedy Hour*), placing one 30-second commercial in each for the 4-week advertising cycle. In the frequency plan, we "bought" just two vehicles: a quite popular, 11-rating, strip TV program (for example, *Oprah Winfrey*) and a largely popular 22-rating, weekly magazine (for example, *TV Guide*), placing two 30-second commercials per week in the TV program and one 1-page, four-color ad per week in the magazine for the 4-week advertising cycle. As shown in the table, for the same budget, the reach plan delivers, relatively, 10 percent greater

reach (R1+ /4 = 44) than the frequency plan (R1+ /4 = 40). The big difference in the plans, however, is seen in the frequency plan (R4 + /4 = 19) compared with the reach plan (R4+ /4 = 10), a relative advantage in effective reach of 90 percent.

Using the program, you might be able to find combinations of vehicles and insertions that are even "more optimal" than we found here. We applied only rough trial-and-error adjustments. In trying these schedule variations in order to maximize the desired level of effective reach, the manager or media planner has to be careful not to exceed the total budget. To allow for this, you will need estimates

TABLE 17.4

**COMPARATIVE RESULTS FROM BBD-LD REPEAT FOR TWO MEDIA PLANS, ONE BASED ON REACH STRATEGY AND ONE BASED ON FREQUENCY STRATEGY, EACH REQUIRING A $1-MILLION MEDIA SPEND OVER 4 WEEKS** [a]

|  | Reach plan | Frequency plan |
|---|---|---|
| Reach 1 + /4 | 44% | 40% |
| Reach 4 + /4 | 10% | 19% |
| Insertions | 35 | 12 |
| GRPs | 112 | 196 |

[a] See text for further descriptions of the plans.

of the approximate costs of the insertions in each media vehicle. Approximate costs can be obtained from ADWEEK's *Marketer's Guide to Media*,[42] which is the source we used to estimate the costs of the schedules and limit them to approximately $1 million for the 4 weeks.

Notice in these examples that the traditional media plan descriptors (the bottom two rows in the table) are completely uninformative, consistent with our criticism of these terms. For instance, the reach plan employs far fewer GRPs (112) than the frequency plan (196) yet achieves higher reach; similarly, the frequency plan employs far fewer insertions (12) than the reach plan (35) yet achieves greater frequency. Traditional media planning parameters are just about useless for evaluating media plans.

Managers should put the BBD-LD REPEAT program into their computers and try it on current or prospective media schedules. Rice[43] provides a reasonably easy to follow explanation of how this type of model works; but even without having to understand the mathematics, the client manager will gain a greater understanding of what the media planner at the advertising agency is attempting to achieve. As we commented earlier, most clients do not know how media schedules are chosen, and using this model is a good way for them to find out.

## 17B. Schedule Implementation for the Larger Advertiser

For the larger advertiser, the number of alternative schedules that may "look" close to optimal—even after rigorously applying the strategy rules to limit their number—will be very large. The trial-and-error process employed with the BBD-LD REPEAT model, above, is far too time-consuming and, instead, a model with a search heuristic is required. A *search heuristic* uses decision rules on the computer to mathematically search hundreds of optional schedules to find the best one. The difficulty is that you will have to program these search heuristics, and this requires quite advanced mathematical and computer programming knowledge.

Recommendations for the two possible situations are given below: for when you haven't measured duplication (you have vehicle reaches only), and for when you have (you've done a direct matching survey).

**Reach Without Measured Duplication.** If you know the target audience reach of each of the vehicles but have not conducted a precise direct matching study to obtain the exact duplicated reach, a good media model to use appears to be VIDEAC, developed by Rust.[44] Like the original BBD-LD model described above, VIDEAC also uses the BBD mathematical procedure—but with a better duplication estimate. BBD stands for "Beta-Binomial Distribution," which is actually a mixing of two statistical distributions, the beta and the binomial. The beta distribution is employed to represent individuals' probabilities of exposure to a particular vehicle; thus, although the probability across the total population would on average be .10 for a 10-rated vehicle (a TV program, for instance), individuals differ in that some never watch the program yet others are highly loyal, with a very high probability of watching it. The binomial distribution is used to represent the probability that an individual is exposed 0, 1, 2, 3, 4, and so on times to insertions in the vehicles in the schedule; the more insertions in the schedule, the greater the number of exposures the typical individual who is exposed to that schedule will receive. By mixing the two distributions, insertions can be put in *multiple vehicles* as inputs, and the exposure distribution across *all individuals* is derived as output. The VIDEAC program requires vehicle ratings, only, as inputs and is computationally efficient in that it takes only about 15 minutes on a PC to pick the best of a very large number of schedules. VIDEAC appears to handle strip programs well,[45] and it is worth pointing out that most proprietary models do not handle strips well in that they overestimate reach and underestimate frequency, and frequency is what strips are intended to achieve. VIDEAC uses two heuristics, the "greedy" and the "switch" heuristic, which have to be added to the BBD routine. It can be employed for mixed-media plans by substituting the Dirichlet multinomial distribution for the BBD.[46]

**Reach with Measured Duplication.** If you have exact direct matching data that measures *duplication*—by which we mean a *matrix* of target audience individuals × vehicles × repeat exposure—then the optimal media schedule can be chosen without using any media model at all, although a search heuristic is still required. The procedure for exact direct matching data is explained by Craig and Ghosh,[47] who employ the "vertex substitution algorithm" as the search heuristic. Their applications have been to TV schedules and to magazines schedules separately, but the procedure could evidently be used just as well for mixed-media schedules. In their TV application, they used a matrix of 500 households whose TV viewing was recorded across the three major networks for the 6 main half-hour time slots for 28 days—a matrix of 500 rows and 504 columns. It is very easy to input MEF and MaxEF using their procedure, and the great advantage is that its use of precise direct matching data means that strategies such as strip programming are exactly incorporated in calculating effective reach.[48]

## NOTES

1. With the media plan consuming about 90 percent of the advertising budget, the product manager had *better* know how the plan is intended to work! Most have only a vague idea and, as we'll show in this chapter, their agencies aren't a whole lot wiser. Still, the more you spend, which is fine for the agency, the more you are likely to eventually reach the right people a sufficient number of times.

2. N. Garfinkle, A marketing approach to media selection, *Journal of Advertising Research,* 1963, *3* (4), pp. 7–15. See also F. W. Winter, Match target markets to media audiences, *Journal of Advertising Research,* 1980, *20* (1), pp. 61–66.

3. A somewhat better demographic matchup can be obtained by using *multiple demographics,* such as age, sex, income, education, occupation, and so forth, to profile both the target audience and prospective media vehicle audiences. This can be done by using *index numbers* for each classification category within each demographic variable, and then computing the sum of the absolute differences, or the squared differences ($d^2$), between the target audience index and the vehicle audience index across all the demographic categories, or simply by computing a correlation coefficient between the two sets of index numbers.

   Either $d^2$ or the conventional correlation coefficient is an improvement over the use of just one or two demographic variables, because these correlational approaches use more information and thus provide a better match. Details of the multiple demographic index numbers approach can be found in J. Z. Sissors, Matching media with markets, *Journal of Advertising Research,* 1971, *11* (5), pp. 39–43. The biggest problem with the multiple demographic index numbers approach is that, whereas detailed demographic information may be available on the target audience side, it is rarely available for media vehicle audiences other than, perhaps, for magazine audiences. Simmons Market Research Bureau (SMRB), for example, does not provide demographic data on TV programs but only on heavy-to-light viewing "quintiles" regardless of network or program.

   A second problem is the computation. Only in the occasional instance outside academic studies are $d^2$ or correlations ever computed. And the computations are tedious to set up. Finally, why go through this tedium when you can use direct matching?

4. Brand buyers are 10 percent of the population, and we know that 40 percent of brand buyers are Women 18–34, therefore 4 percent of all people are Women 18–34 who are brand buyers. Women 18–34 are 13 percent of the population, so the probability of being a brand buyer given that you are a Woman 18–34 is 4/13 or .31.

5. That is, a 10 percent incidence of brand buyers in the population at large means a randomly chosen individual has a probability of .10 of being a brand buyer.

6. W. D. Wells and D. J. Tigert, Activities, interests, and opinions, *Journal of Advertising Research,* 1971, *11* (4), pp. 27–35.

7. See, for example, the many studies of correlates of brand loyalty cited in J. F. Engel and R. D. Blackwell, *Consumer Behavior,* 4th ed., New York: Dryden, 1982; and the work of A. S. C. Ehrenberg (see Chapter 3's Further Reading). A clear example of lack of demographic discrimination in people's preferences for family restaurants can be seen in A. S. Boote, Market segmentation by personal values and salient product attributes, *Journal of Advertising Research,* 1981, *21* (1), pp. 29–35.

8. H. M. Cannon, A method for estimating target market ratings in television media selection, *Journal of Advertising,* 1986, *5* (2), pp. 21–26.

9. H. Assael and H. M. Cannon, Do demographics help in media selection? *Journal of Advertising Research,* 1979, *19* (6), pp. 7–11. Later studies by Assael's team have used confusing index numbers, and cost-indexed at that, which we don't recommend (see also F. W. Winter, same reference as in note 2). Nevertheless, direct matching has invariably emerged superior. See the two articles by H. Assael and D. F. Poltrack, Using single source data to select TV programs based on purchasing behavior, *Journal of Advertising Research,* 1991, *31* (4), pp. 9–17, and Using single source data to select TV programs: Part II, *Journal of Advertising Research,* 1993, *33* (1), pp. 48–56.

10. R. Wilson, Realities of people meters, *Marketing Landscape* (Wilson Market Research Newsletter), September 1994, p. 1.

11. R. I. Haley, Beyond benefit segmentation, *Journal of Advertising Research,* 1971, *11* (4), pp. 3–8.

    Recent evidence of the gains achieved by direct matching (more particularly losses due to other methods) is provided in the study by H. M. Cannon and B. L. Seamons, Simulating single-source data: how it fails us just when we need it most, *Journal of Advertising Research,* 1995, *35* (6), pp. 53–62. In their study, the investigators used a typical cross-section of 29 TV programs and measured the concentration (number) of product category users (the broadly-defined target audience) in each program, for 20 typical TV-advertised product categories. The highest user-concentration TV program (largest reach of the target audience) for each of the 20 product categories served as the *direct-matching method* against which other methods could be compared. They found that the target audience reach for the *demographic matching* method (which used matching by sex and age, the two standard demographics available to media planners when selecting TV media plans) was *20 percent lower* than the reach achieved by direct matching. Further, they found that the target audience reach for the *random selection* method (that is, no matching at all, but sometimes used in TV plans because of media planners' belief that TV is a "mass audience" medium) was *30 percent lower* than the reach achieved by direct matching. For national media plans, these percentages translate to very large losses in target audience reach. Had the target audiences been defined not just by category users but more sharply by brand loyalty status—NCUs, BLs, and so forth, as we recommend—we suspect that the target audience reach advantage of direct matching over demographic matching and over random selection would have been even larger.

12. "Bulk buying" refers to the practice of negotiating a discount from TV networks, for example, by offering to buy large blocks of media which are then assigned to individual brands. A large advertiser may buy for all the company's brands en masse, or smaller advertisers may band together for the buy.

13. Nielsen's CASY service claims these reasonable gains in nearly all cases. See G. Shabbabb, True winners—using single-source to allocate TV time, *Admap,* February 1992, pp. 26–31.

14. Case history from Mediamark Research, reported in H. Kamin, Why not use single source measurements now? *Journal of Media Planning,* 1988, *3* (1), pp. 27–31.

15. P. Graham, Making it work better—integrating ad research into the marketing and media plan, *Admap,* February 1992, pp. 22–25.

16. B. Morris, Marketing firm slices U.S. into 240,000 parts to spur clients' sales, *The Wall Street Journal,* November 3, 1986, pp. 1, 25.

17. Reference to an *Advertising Age* article cited by M. A. Kamins, H. Sanft, and T. Kiesler, Abstract of paper, Context-induced mood effects in advertising, in R. M. Holman and M. R. Solomon, eds., *Advances in Consumer Research,* vol. 18, 1991, Provo, UT: Association for Consumer Research, p. 624.

18. T. Rhodes, Christians condemn "Blue" TV sponsor, *The Australian,* June 1995, p. 8.

19. R. I. Haley, *Developing Effective Communications Strategy: A Benefit Segmentation Approach,* New York, NY: Wiley, 1985, pp. 358–359.

20. A. S. C. Ehrenberg and G. J. Goodhardt, Attitudes to episodes and programmes, *Journal of the Market Research Society,* 1981, *23* (4), pp. 189–208 (note especially their table 2: although a British study, these authors report virtually identical findings with U.S. TV programs; stated liking of programs closely reflects frequency of viewing, so likability data add practically nothing to exposure frequency data).

If demographic matching is used instead of direct matching to select first-stage vehicles, frequency of exposure will not be available. In this case, you could adjust by obtaining vehicle likability ratings from SMRB. We would suggest giving favorite vehicles an MEF/c value maximum of 1.5, down to least-favored vehicles at a minimum of 0.5. For example, if 10 million demographic target audience women aged 18–34 watch an episode of *Dynasty* in which the ad is placed, and *Dynasty* receives a likability weight of 1.2, then these 10 million women have received the equivalent of 1.2 exposures.

21. For example, Goldberg and Gorn placed four pairs of ads (an "informational" and an "emotional" ad in each pair) for four brands (Heinz ketchup, Tang breakfast drink, Maxwell House coffee, and Reunite wine) in a "happy" segment from *Real People* and a "sad" (actually, distressing) segment from *60 Minutes.* This was a forced (laboratory) exposure so should have produced effects. In fact, there were no significant differences in brand purchase intention for *any* of the ads in either of the programs. A careful reading of other laboratory studies shows no evidence of practically significant differences in communication effects by vehicle positivity or negativity, with just one exception. Prasad and Smith placed an ad for a new brand of children's cereal following a very violent or a mildly violent segment of an adult movie; subjects were 7-to-9-year-old boys. When measured immediately afterward, brand attitude was 13 percent lower after the very violent episode, but it was 15 percent *higher* after the mild violence. This supports other (laboratory) studies showing that the vehicle has to be really extreme before there is any negative effect. If forced exposure studies don't reliably produce an effect, we can hardly expect self-selected vehicles in the real world to do so. See M. E. Goldberg and G. J. Gorn, Happy and Sad TV programs: How they affect reactions to commercials, *Journal of Consumer Research,* 1987, *14* (3), pp. 387–403; V. K. Prasad and L. J. Smith, Television commercials in violent programming: An experimental evaluation of their effects on children, *Journal of the Academy of Marketing Science,* 1994, *22* (4), pp. 340–351.

On the other hand, when advertising high-involvement/informational products, we do recommend avoiding vehicles likely to reach target audience individuals when they are in an extreme negative mood and, when advertising high-involvement/transformational products, favoring vehicles timed for positive (particularly "leisure") moods. This is discussed under "Timing of Vehicle" heading below. And see J. D. Mayor, L. J. McCormick and S. E. Strong, Mood-congruent memory and natural mood, new evidence, *Personality and Social Psychology Bulletin,* 1995, *21* (7), pp. 736–746.

22. "Prestige" is a description usually applied to print vehicles rather than broadcast vehicles. In the best study to date, conducted under the auspices of the Advertising Research Foundation, 12 ads ranging from corporate image to aspirin were "tipped in" to two higher-prestige magazines, *McCall's* and *Reader's Digest,* and two lower-prestige magazines, *People* and *National Enquirer.* Among *regular readers* of these magazines, no differences in ad believability or rated product quality were found for any of the ads. Prestige, obviously, is in the mind of the advertiser, not in the minds of the vehicle's own audience. See V. Appel, Editorial environment and advertising effectiveness, *Journal of Advertising Research,* 1987, *27* (4), pp. 11–16.

23. Nielsen diary data reported in *TV Guide,* May 24, 1980, *28* (1), p. A-4.

24. Our conclusion is supported by extensive data on day-after advertising recall (a measure of attention to the ad) for TV and magazine advertisements. Attention loss for competing-brand TV commercials shown within 10 minutes of one another averages only 6 percent. No comparable figure is given for proximity of competing-brand ads in magazines, but the overall relationship ($R^2$) between magazine ad recall and competing ads in the magazine averages only 2 percent. On average, then, for all media in which ads appear sequentially, *attention* to ads is *not* affected by competing ads in the vehicle. We thank William F. Greene of Gallup & Robinson, Inc., for providing these data. Also, as noted in Chapter 10, *category users* tend to self-select ads in the category in which they're interested, which would remove the competing-brands effect on attention to our ad.

25. See B. R. Bugelski, *Principles of Learning and Memory,* New York: Praeger, 1979; and W. A. Wickelgren, *Learning and Memory,* Englewood Cliffs, NJ: Prentice-Hall, 1977.

26. Brand *recognition* should not be subject to interference because in nearly all cases it is a visual response (pack recognition or brand name recognition) affected only by eventual time decay (see Chapter 20). The category need, as the in-store response when the package is seen, is usually evident from the shelf placement of the brand as well as from the package itself. Verbal brand recognition, a less prevalent brand awareness objective, also would not be affected by interference.

27. We hypothesized this in our earlier book. It has recently been confirmed experimentally by R. J. Kent

and C. T. Allen, Does competitive clutter in television advertising "interfere" with recognition and recall of brand names and ad claims? *Marketing Letters,* 1993, *4* (2), pp. 175–184.

28. B. R. Bugelski, and W. A. Wickelgren, same references as in note 25.

29. G. Pincott, Investigating readership lag, Working paper, Millward Brown Plc, Leamington Spa, UK: Millward Brown, 1990.

30. T. P. Barwise, A. S. C. Ehrenberg, and G. J. Goodhardt, Watching TV at the same time on different weekdays, Working paper, London Business School, London, 1978. Their analysis is based on U.S. data from Arbitron's television rating service.

31. Assuming that purchase of the brand is going on continuously, so that any 2-week purchase cycle has an arbitrary starting point, for the even schedule, the average consumer is "topped up" to MEF every week, leaving an average of 3 1/2 days to purchase before the next exposure occurs; for the impact schedule, the average consumer and indeed all consumers reach MEF every 3 weeks only, producing an average delay of 1 1/2 weeks to purchase before MEF can be attained again.

32. Note that time, per se, is not a relevant variable if the brand is chosen by brand recall because the "forgetting" process is due to interference, not trace decay (see Chapter 20). Nor is time relevant for brand recognition except over very long periods, say, a couple of months or more. Interference is the critical factor, too, for brand attitude. As brand awareness is the "carrier" of brand attitude, an interesting divergence occurs. For brand recall, a competitive campaign has to be effective only in interfering with brand recall (even if it is ineffective attitudinally); whereas for brand recognition, as this is not subject to interference, a competitive campaign has to interfere with brand attitude to be effective. A good example of this latter theory in practice (assuming soda purchase in supermarkets is by brand recognition) is the perennial battle of Coke versus Pepsi advertising on the "image" (low-involvement/transformational brand attitude) factor.

33. In a semiforced exposure experiment, 10 exposures of the same ads in 2 1/2 hours of TV programming (2 per half-hour) were found to depress brand recognition and brand recall. The fact that both were depressed suggests a loss-of-attention explanation. See D. T. A. Heflin and R. C. Haygood, Effects of scheduling on retention of advertising messages, *Journal of Advertising,* 1985, *14* (2), pp. 41–47.

34. The Bundy ads (Bundaberg Rum) in Figure 17.2 are a complex example with a double half-page "top" and two smaller "tails." We'd estimate the four ads' contribution to MEF as 2.0, which is greater than the sum of the ad units' individual contributions to MEF.

35. The estimates for TV and magazines are from H. Katz and P. Turk, The winds of change: The outlook for media in the 1990s and beyond, *Journal of Media Planning,* 1992, *7* (1), pp. 42–49, and the estimates for radio stations and newspapers are from T. Duncan, C. Caywood, and D. Newsom, Task Force on Integrated Communications Report, Denver: University of Colorado, December 1993.

36. This footnote provides references for the notes in Table 17.2.

    [a]Self-explanatory.

    [b]Calculated from 1993 ratings reported in ADWEEK, *Marketer's Guide to Media,* New York: ADWEEK, 1994, *17* (1), p. 26

    [c]R. S. Headen, J. E. Klompmaker, and R. T. Rust, The duplication of viewing law and television media schedule evaluation, *Journal of Marketing Research,* 1979, *16* (4), pp. 333–340.

    [d]T. P. Barwise, Repeat-viewing of prime-time TV series, *Journal of Advertising Research,* 1986, *26* (4), pp. 9–14.

    [e]A. S. C. Ehrenberg, and J. Wakshlag, Repeat-viewing with people meters, *Journal of Advertising Research,* 1987, *27* (1), pp. 9–13.

    [f]M. J. Stankey, Using media more effectively, *Business,* 1988, April–June, pp. 20–27.

    [g]Self-explanatory.

    [h]Study by DoubleClick Network reported in D. A. Williamson, New ammo for click-rate debate, *Advertising Age,* August 19, 1996, p. 24. This study found that the average click-through rate for a Web ad seen the first time is 3.6 percent; the average ad banner is then accessed again by about 2 percent (that is 56 percent of the original attenders); and falls to below 1 percent for any subsequent click-throughs. A "click-through" occurs when a Website visitor clicks on a banner in the advertiser's ad, after first "hitting" the site by downloading the file. The click-through *rate* is the number of click-throughs divided by the number of hits. For a good discussion of measurement issues in Web advertising, see I. P. Murphy, On-line ads effective? Who knows for sure? *Marketing News,* September 23, 1996, pp. 1–38.

37. U.S. data from T. P. Barwise, same reference as in note 36. For the history of the double-jeopardy effect identified for TV viewing, see G. J. Goodhardt, A. S. C. Ehrenberg, and M. A. Collins, *The Television Audience: Patterns of Viewing,* 2nd ed., London: Gower, 1987.

38. When using nonstandard advertising units, such as broadcast ads shorter or longer than 30 seconds, or print ads smaller or larger than one page, the computation is a little more complicated. First, the adjusted MEF contribution to exposure has to be compared against the required MEF level, so that effective reach will change. Then, since nonstandard units cost less or more, the cost component of the profit calculation will also change. In practice, this is not very difficult because most variations from standard units are of one type—for instance, occasional 10-second amid 30-second spots in a broadcast campaign, or a leadoff of a double-page spread in a print campaign.

39. J. D. Leckenby and M. D. Rice, A beta binomial network TV exposure model using limited data, *Journal of Advertising,* 1985, *14* (3), pp. 25–31. See also M. D. Rice and J. D. Leckenby, An empirical test of a proprietary television media model, *Journal of Advertising Research,* 1986, *24* (4), pp. 17–21; and M. D. Rice, A practical method for estimating reach and frequency of mixed media, *Journal of Media Planning,* 1988, *3* (2), pp. 29–39.

40. We are grateful to Adee Athiyaman of Charles Sturt University for programming this model.

41. A recent survey (1993) of the leading U.S. advertising agencies' media planners found that whereas about 80 percent use computer models to estimate reach and the frequency distribution of the plan, about half don't trust their accuracy. Very few understand how the models work (hence the wholesale purchase of syndicated models' results such as those offered by Telmar and IMS), and they buy them mainly to be able to "show the client some numbers." This is scandalous. There are great advantages to working *directly* with models such as the BBD-LD. For the survey, see J. D. Leckenby and K. Him, How media directors view frequency estimation: Now and a decade ago, *Journal of Advertising Research,* 1994, *34* (5), pp. 9–21.

42. See our Chapter 15's Further Reading.

43. M. D. Rice, Estimating the reach and frequency of mixed media advertising schedules, *Journal of the Market Research Society,* 1988, *30* (4), pp. 439–451.

44. R. T. Rust, Selecting network television advertising schedules, *Journal of Business Research,* 1985, *13* (6), pp. 483–494. This model is also a BBD-based model.

45. This seems to be because the parameter estimates are derived by a regression estimate in which proportion of self-pairs (that is, "strips") is a predictor variable.

46. For further explanation, see R. T. Rust, *Advertising Media Models: A Practical Guide*, Lexington, MA: Lexington Books, 1986.

47. C. S. Craig and A. Ghosh, Maximizing effective reach and media planning, in R. F. Lusch, et al., eds., *AMA Educators Conference Proceedings,* Chicago: American Marketing Association, 1985, pp. 178–182, and C. S. Craig and A. Ghosh, Using household-level viewing data to maximize effective reach, *Journal of Advertising Research,* 1993, *33* (1), pp. 38–47.

48. Their procedure is exact for the calibration data (the direct matching survey) but its future accuracy, like all

models', depends on the stability of individuals' media exposure habits in the application period in which the media plan is actually run. Most probably, with large schedules, these individual variations average out, and the plan would remain very accurate.

## DISCUSSION QUESTIONS

**17.1.** In this chapter, demographic matching was described as being less accurate than direct matching as a method of media vehicle selection. Is psychographic matching better than demographic matching—in general? Under what conditions would psychographic matching be (a) inferior to and (b) superior to demographic matching? Give a likely example for (a) and (b).

**17.2.** Write a memo to your manager, a national consumer products advertiser, arguing why the company should spend $100,000 on a media exposure study after the company has recently spent a lot of money on advertising strategy research.

**17.3.** Suppose that it costs $100,000 to place a full-page, four-color advertisement in *Time* magazine. The purchase cycle for your product is 5 weeks (for example, liquor), and you estimate that the effective frequency is 2. Moreover, you know that there is virtually a perfect likelihood that *Time*'s primary readers read every issue. You therefore place the ad on a 2-week on, 3-week off flighting pattern. There are 500,000 target audience individuals among the primary readers of *Time*. Assume that the probability of purchase, at effective frequency, is .3 and that the profit contribution per unit purchased is $2.00. What profit would you expect, per purchase cycle, from advertising in *Time*?

**17.4.** You are the media director of an advertising agency, and one of your clients habitually adds and deletes vehicles from your proposed media plans for "qualitative" reasons. Write a memo, no longer than 2 double-spaced pages, that explains to the client in your own words how qualitative factors (those in second-stage vehicle selection) *should* be handled.

**17.5.** Calculate the contributions to MEF of the following advertising units and plans (use Chapter 10's tables, and show detailed calculations). Assume the target audience is exposed to every insertion.
  **a.** Three 10-second radio commercials on successive days.
  **b.** A double-page, black-and-white ad, followed by three single-page, right-hand page, black-and-white ads, all four with bleeds, in successive weeks in a consumer magazine.
  **c.** A left-hand page, first inside cover, four-color ad, with an in-ad coupon, in an engineering magazine.
  **d.** A one-eighth page, below-the-fold, two-color newspaper ad for toothpaste, in the sports section.

  **e.** Two 60-second television commercials, with slight executional variations, impact-scheduled in the NBC *Sunday Night Movie*.

**17.6.** You are addressing a conference of soft-drink marketers, from different companies, about the problem of TV advertising "clutter." What would you advise them to do? What would you advise regarding retail store cooperative newspaper advertising, where their brands are featured with other brands?

**17.7.** Using Birdseye frozen vegetables and *McCall's* magazine (a monthly with a high proportion of pass-along readers) as an example, outline the advantages and disadvantages of impact scheduling.

**17.8.** Using the BBD-LD REPEAT computer program described in chapter appendix 17A, Table 17.3, calculate the reach and frequency distribution of the following two media schedules:

  Schedule A: One insertion in each of 20 TV late-evening weekly programs, each with an average target audience rating of 10.

  Schedule B: Ten insertions in a TV prime-time movie, with a target audience rating expected to be 20.

  If the schedule is for one flight of advertising and you were applying the frequency rule with MEF/c = 5+/week, which schedule would you choose? Alternatively, which would you choose if you were applying the reach rule?

## FURTHER READING

Garfinkle, N. A marketing approach to media selection. *Journal of Advertising Research,* 1963, *3* (4), pp. 7–15.

This was the first publication, to our knowledge, to advocate direct matching of media vehicles with target audiences. Garfinkle, then president of a syndicated service called Brand Rating Index (since superseded by SMRB), shows examples of the limitations of demographics for media selection.

Eskin, G. J. Tracking advertisement and promotion performance with single-source data. *Journal of Advertising Research,* 1985, *25* (1), pp. 31, 33–39.

Eskin's article, written 20 years after Garfinkle's, reinforces the value of direct matching in media vehicle selection by using the modern technology of consumer panels linked to store purchase scanners.

Craig, C. S., and Ghosh, A. Using household-level viewing data to maximize effective reach. *Journal of Advertising Research,* 1993, *33*(1), pp. 38–47.

This article shows the general superiority of direct matching in evaluating the media schedule. Unfortunately, the authors do not provide enough detail to implement their procedure from this reference alone.

## PART SEVEN

# ADVERTISING RESEARCH AND EVALUATION

CHAPTER 18: ADVERTISING STRATEGY RESEARCH

CHAPTER 19: CONCEPT DEVELOPMENT RESEARCH, MJTs, AND AD TESTING

CHAPTER 20: CAMPAIGN TRACKING AND EVALUATION

# Advertising Strategy Research

The first and most important stage of advertising research is *advertising strategy research*. In this first stage of research, the marketing objectives and budget are established, the target audience is defined, and the general advertising (or promotion or IMC) approach is identified, leading to the development of a detailed advertising strategy statement for the brand. After reading this chapter, you should:

- Realize the importance of a thorough situation audit in setting marketing objectives and the budget.
- Understand the essential contributions of qualitative research to advertising strategy development.
- Further understand the additional contributions of quantitative advertising strategy research.
- Be able to write a summary advertising strategy.

Advertising strategy research is the single most important stage of advertising research. If the strategy is wrong, then everything that follows—the creative idea, the promotion offers, the media plan—is likely to be wrong too. In marketing, correct strategy is more important than correct execution: of course, one should aim for correct strategy *and* correct execution. But deciding on a correct strategy (there may be several possibilities) is more vital because, as we'll see in Chapters 19 and 20, execution can usually be improved to fit a good strategy, whereas it's difficult and expensive to have to retreat from a poor strategy.

Advertising strategy research ideally consists of three types of research, in this order:

1. Situation audit
2. Qualitative research
3. Quantitative research

These three types of research are the subjects of this chapter. The chapter also shows how to prepare a 1-page summary of the advertising strategy, which most managers find useful—and which can serve as the creative "brief" for the agency's creative team. Operationally, though, the manager must work with the detailed strategy statement as exemplified by the advertising communications and promotion (AC&P) plan described in the Appendix.

## SITUATION AUDIT

### Purpose of the Situation Audit

A situation audit consists of background (or "secondary") research into all factors that do, or could, affect the profit, sales, market share, and equity performance of the brand. Advertising communications is just *one* of these factors, as is promotion. Because the entire marketing mix is implicated (see Chapter 1), the main purpose of the situation audit is to set the *marketing objectives* for the campaign.

Table 18.1 lists what should be sought in the situation audit. The measures themselves are somewhat specialized.

### Profit Measures

If profit objectives are to be expressed as goals, the level of profit must be measured.

There are numerous ways to measure profit, and only two of the more important ones will be mentioned here.[1]

**1.** *Internal Rate of Return.* This measure of profit takes into account the cost of capital and the time value of money through the application of a discounted rate of return. It is advocated by leading consultants such as Booz-Allen & Hamilton. The return may be calculated on sales, on assets, or on equity, for which various accounting procedures may be applied.

**2.** *Profit Contribution.* A profit measure of more specific value to the manager's determination of the profitability of a particular product in the product line is the *contribution method.* A product's contribution (also called "gross margin") is simply the difference between its unit revenue or selling price (received by the seller) and its unit direct cost (also called "cost of goods sold"). The difference or margin is then multiplied by the number of units sold to obtain an overall contribution, that is:

$$\text{Contribution} = (\text{revenue} - \text{direct cost}) \times \text{units sold}$$

This "cash contribution" is then available to cover any fixed costs that may be allocated to the product, such as part of the cost of production equipment or fixed sales-force salaries—and also the overall advertising communications and promotion budget. A product's profit or "profit impact" is thus:

$$\text{Profit} = \text{contribution} - \text{fixed-cost allocation}$$

A new product may, of course, experience a negative profit (that is, a loss) until sales reach a level sufficient for the cumulative contribution to cover fixed costs. The sales level at which a product's contribution equals its fixed-cost allocation is known as the "breakeven" level of sales. When sales increase further such that the product becomes profitable, it still has to cover the *opportunity loss* of its own investment, that is, the amount that could have been earned had its expenditures been invested elsewhere. The time taken from initial development of a product to recovery of its own investment is known as the *payback period*—and thereafter realized profits begin.

### Sales Measures

Sales measures are needed for the brand in order to evaluate a possible sales volume objective for the campaign (which, it will be remembered from Chapter 2, is one avenue to profit along with unit cost and unit price). Sales measures will be needed if the manager is planning to set the budget by the task method, the IAF/5Q method, spending test, or statistical projection (see Chapter 2). Product *category sales* will also be needed, as a background factor for the judges to consider, if the IAF/5Q method is used.

Companies in different industries use different methods for measuring sales, and some companies use more than one measure. These can be placed in four categories:

**1.** *Exact Measures*
  **a.** *Sales Receipts.* Actual sales receipts are the most exact measure of sales. However, sales receipts can be very slow to reach the company and, since evaluation of advertising or promotion campaign effectiveness should be made as early as possible, various other methods (described below) are frequently used.

**2.** *Presales Measures*
  **a.** *Factory Shipments.* This seemingly is the fastest measure, but it has the problem of having to allow for returns, which are very hard to estimate, and may be slow for new products.
  **b.** *Warehouse Withdrawals* (monitored, for example, by the A.C. Nielsen Company or by Selling Areas Marketing, Inc., now SAMI-Burke, known as "SAMI"). This measure is a little better than factory shipments since warehouse

---

**TABLE 18.1**

**SITUATION AUDIT: MEASURES AND METHODS**

- Profit measures
- Sales measures
- Market-share measures
- Brand equity (price elasticity of demand) calculation
- Action measures (trial and repeat purchase)
- Advertising communications expenditure and content analysis
- Sales promotion content analysis
- Industry research
- Internal company research

withdrawals imply actual demand by distributors; this may not translate to consumer or end customer demand, however, as there is still the problem of "forward buying" by distributors (especially retailers) in response to trade deals by the manufacturer, and the problem of returns.

3. *Scanner-Sales Measures*
   a. *Store-Level Scanners* (for example, Erhart-Babic's National Retail Tracking Index; Nielsen's Drug Index and Mass Merchandise Index; SAMI-Burke's SamScan). Electronic cash-register scanners which read the bar codes on items purchased are as good as sales receipts but, as only about two-thirds of stores have them, they do not provide a complete record of sales and have to be supplemented by other methods of estimation. They are the most widely used sales measures for food and drug (fmcg) products.
   b. *Household-Level Scanners* (for example, IRI's BehaviorScan, Nielsen's Local Market Household Panel, SAMI-Burke's SamScan Panel). These measures use scanners, either via *household purchase cards* used at retail stores or via *in-home scanning* of purchases with an electronic, computer-connected wand. Valued because of their more specific level of recording (*household* trial and repeat purchase—see Chapter 3—as well as overall sales), these methods nevertheless pose potential problems with sample representativeness (the respondents are paid panelists) and cooperation. Still, to many marketers, household-level scanner data are worth the price of some inaccuracies because the alternative household-level or individual-level measures have greater limitations (see 4, below).

4. *Diary and Survey Sales Measures*
   a. *Purchase Diary Panels* (for example, The National Purchase Diary Group, National Family Opinion, Inc., Market Research Corporation of America). These measure sales and also *household* trial and repeat purchase. Diary panels give fairly accurate projections from sample to actual sales; however, the self-completion method used to record panel purchases suffers from some recording errors and a possible reporting bias toward national brands.

   b. *Simulation Tests* (for example, IRI's Assessor, Yankelovich Clancy Shulman, Erhart-Babic Group). These measure sales but only under "simulated store display" conditions; hence the unreliability of sales projections to actual stores may be substantial. Simulation tests are mainly used for predicting *households'* or *individual firms'* trial rates and repeat purchases on a relative or "normed" basis.[2]
   c. *Surveys* (customized by most large marketing research firms or by many industry organizations). Surveys are less accurate because of their even greater reliance on the buyer's memory than with the diary method, and again there is a possible reporting bias toward national brands. However, surveys are the *only* reasonable method of measuring *competitors'* sales for industries whose products and services are not sold through audited or scanned retail outlets or are not sold through retail outlets at all. For most industrial product and service companies, therefore, surveys are the only feasible method: they provide *individual-customer* trial and repeat-purchase results as well as overall sales.

Figure 18.1 shows where these categories or types of measures come from in the overall channel of distribution and usage for consumer fmcg products. For industrial products, the same types of measures are available but, beyond the company's own data (the first two types of measures), a *survey* is required. For some industries, such as new-automobile sales, syndicated or industry-sponsored surveys are available. Industry sales can nearly always be located with a dedicated library search (*examples* are given in Table 18.2).

### Market Share Measures

Because market share is simply relative sales, almost all of the foregoing sales measures can *also* be used to measure market share. The suitable measures are those which report competitors' sales or, at the minimum, category sales, against which to assess the brand's own sales. Market share calculation will be needed if one of the "competitive" budgeting methods is employed, namely, the Peckham's 1.5 rule/order-of-entry method (for a new brand) or Schroer's method (for an established brand).

Market share, like sales, can be measured in terms of product units sold or sales dollars received. The

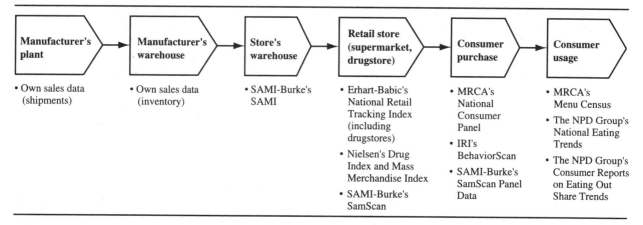

**FIGURE 18.1**
Sales information sources in the typical distribution channel for consumer fmcg products (examples only).

manager should use both measures. Market share in *units* reveals how well the brand is selling versus competing brands and is the basic measure of market share. However, market share in *dollars* is additionally informative because it reflects the effects of selling-price differentials, which are in turn (via uniqueness equity) usually related to profit. A brand pursuing the price differential avenue to profit, for instance, might be quite happy with a constant unit market share and an increasing dollar market share.

**Market Definition.** The most critical component in setting market share objectives is *correct definition*

| TABLE 18.2 | |
|---|---|
| **EXAMPLES OF INFORMATION SOURCES FOR SALES OF BUSINESS PRODUCTS, DURABLES, AND SERVICES (HYPOTHETICAL CLIENTS)[a]** | |
| **Category and brand** | **Sales information sources** |
| **Business products** | |
| Anderson windows | • National Retail Hardware Association Annual Financial Data Survey |
| DuPont nylon carpet | • Carpet Manufacturers' Marketing Association |
| | • Carpet and Rug Institute: Carpet and Rug Statistical Review |
| **Business services** | |
| U.S. Sprint long-distance telephone service | • *Telephony* |
| | • *Communication Week* |
| | • *Networking Management* |
| **Consumer durables** | |
| Kenmore washing machines | • *Dealerscope Merchandising* Annual Statistics and Marketing Report |
| | • Association of Home Appliances Manufacturers' Report |
| Chevrolet automobiles | • Ward Automotive Reports |
| | • *Automotive News* |
| **Consumer services** | |
| CitiBank | • *American Banker* Top Numbers |
| | • Report: Top 100 Holding Companies |
| American Airlines | • *Air Transport World* Annual Report |

[a]*Note:* These sources are meant to be illustrative only. Courtesy Lintas: Campbell-Ewald information library.

*of the market*—that is, the product category or "category need" in which the brand is *actually* or could be *potentially* competing. Actual competition occurs when a substantial number of customers regard certain brands or suppliers as close substitutes (purchase alternatives). Potential competition has to be considered as future actual competition if you decide to position your brand in that category. Actual competition, and thus the "true" market, is not always easy to determine. For instance:

- *Heineken beer:* Heineken has a 2 percent share of the U.S. beer market; however, it has a 40 percent share of the U.S. market for *imported* beers. But does Heineken just compete with imports, or does it also compete with quasi-imports such as Lowenbrau and superpremium U.S. beers such as Michelob? If so, Heineken's "true" market share is neither 2 percent nor 40 percent but some figure in between.
- *Xerox copiers:* Does Xerox compete with all copiers, including cheaper desktop models, or mainly against other expensive, high-speed, multiple-copy machines?
- *Sanka coffee:* Does Sanka compete with all coffees, or just instant coffees, or just instant decaffeinated coffees?
- *Digital computers:* Does Digital Equipment Corporation compete with IBM for all types of computers, or is Digital's "true" market in midsized computers?

**Market Partitioning.** As these examples indicate, market share objectives can be statistically and *strategically* misleading if they are not based on an appropriate competitive-market definition. An analytical technique of great value to managers in deciding on the "true" market or "competitive frame" for a brand is known as "partitioning" or "hierarchical market definition."[3] As far as we can determine, The Hendry Corporation deserves major credit for developing this technique, although it has been applied in many ways by others.

The basic idea of partitioning is that the overall market or *product category* (often industry-defined) can be subdivided *successively* into partitions or submarkets which increasingly approximate the true market for a *brand* or *brand-item* (as defined from the *consumer's* or *customer's* standpoint). As you go "down" the hierarchy of partitions, perceived substitutability increases, and actual brand or item switching behavior increases. This is shown in Figure 18.2.

The partitions that divide a market into submarkets (in consumers' or customers' eyes) can be based on a number of factors. Most often these are the following:

**1.** *Product forms,* where there are distinct physical differences between products (for example, large, medium, desktop, or portable computers; margarine in sticks or cups).

**2.** *Benefits sought,* where products vary in the features they emphasize (for example, cavity prevention or fresh taste in a toothpaste; status or value pricing in a pair of jeans).

**3.** *Usage situations,* where benefits sought in the "same" product may vary over usage situations (for

**FIGURE 18.2**
Total market partitioned into submarkets in which each brand or brand-item faces the most direct competition.

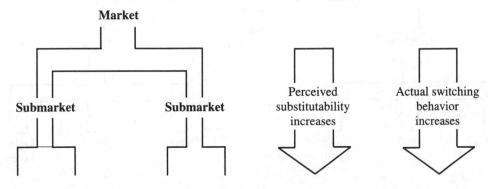

example, "special occasion" beers versus "regular" beers; family versus adult movies).

**4.** *Brand names,* where the brand name signifies a particular "image" or quality level, and various items are available under that brand name (for example, Black & Decker versus Skil power tools; Sears versus Saks Fifth Avenue own-label clothing).

**Partitioning and Positioning.** Partitioning identifies the *category need*—the X in the X-YZ macro model—in positioning and also the *main benefits* in the I-D-U meso model (see Chapter 6). A brand can be positioned, either deliberately or by consumer perception, in one subcategory or another of the total

product category. The "trick" in partitioning is in identifying the order of the partitions. For example, in choosing a yogurt (the category or category need), do consumers decide first on a brand name and then on a product benefit such as flavor? Or do they choose a flavor first and then a particular brand? In other words, the yogurt market could be partitioned in at least two different ways, as shown in Figure 18.3.

The starting level of a partitioning diagram indicates the *category need,* X (see Chapter 5's explanation of "basic level" categories as the means of identifying category need); the next level indicates *subcategories* on the most important "entry ticket" benefit for segments of the market, a Y or Z; and the

**FIGURE 18.3**

Alternative partitioning of the yogurt market. Panel A shows primary competition between brands followed by frequent switching between flavors. Panel B shows primary competition between flavors followed by frequent switching between brands.

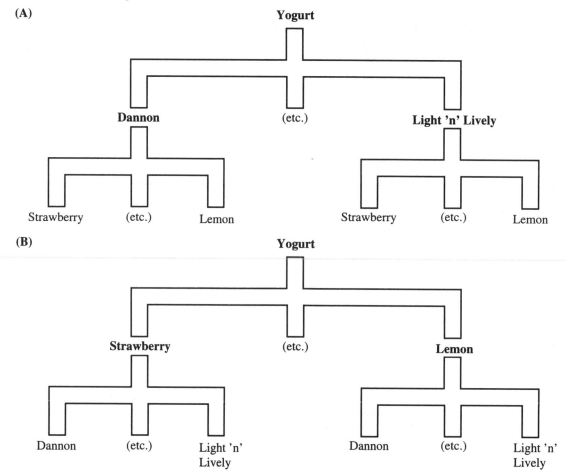

lowest level indicates the main "unique delivery" benefit, also a Y or Z, on which the brands are competing. Note the importance of the different partition orders. If the yogurt market is partitioned by consumers in the manner shown in panel A, Dannon's main advertising and promotion objective would be first to convince consumers to buy the Dannon brand (a "good brand" is the entry ticket), then to offer "flavors that suit Dannon lovers" (the unique benefit). Alternatively, if the yogurt market is partitioned by consumers in the manner shown in panel B, Dannon's main advertising and promotion objective would be first to appeal to, for example, "strawberry lovers" (the user-based entry ticket), then to convince those consumers that Dannon offers "*better* strawberry yogurt" (the unique benefit) than any other brand.

Another example of partitioning of the market for a consumer packaged good is personal deodorants (Figure 18.4). The starting level (category need) is personal deodorants or simply "deodorant." At the second level, that of subcategories, there is a fairly sharp division between spray deodorants and nonspray deodorants, with about half of all consumers preferring each of these two product forms and rarely switching between the two. At the third level are sub-subcategories of product form that have become a second entry ticket for many consumers: aerosol versus pump (within sprays) and roll-on versus stick versus powder (within nonsprays). Only at the fourth level do we see close brand competition, although even this may be relegated to a fifth level if consumers further partition the market into "regular" versus "long-acting" deodorants.

Thus, a fairly simple product may have a quite complex partitioning structure. The multiple levels of partitions in this example indicate that choice of a personal deodorant is a high-involvement process for most consumers until they've worked out their

**FIGURE 18.4**
Market structure for personal deodorants. Market share trends are shown as percentages in parentheses. The first figure in each pair is from 1973, the second from 1976, and the arrow shows the trend.

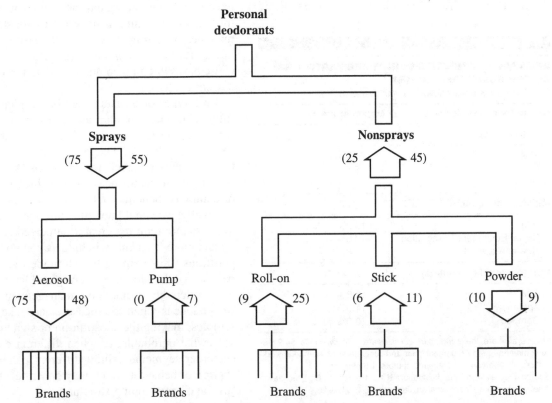

preferred branching ("down" the partition levels) and settled on one or two favorite brand-items. Note that "luxury" brands such as Polo or Armani in men's deodorants (a partition we assumed but didn't show at the category level) try to force *brand* as the second level because each only offers one product form, namely, stick for Polo and roll-on for Armani.

**Partitioning Markets for Durables.** With consumer packaged goods, consumers are frequently "in the market" and can perceive substitutes and switch brands as they wish. But for consumer durables, such as TV sets or automobiles, or for industrial durables, such as equipment and machinery, brand switching is less meaningful because of the relatively long purchase cycle—the long interval between purchases.

However, even for durables, customers do change brands or suppliers and, more pertinently, they are likely to confine their selections to a subset of similar offerings. Thus, it is still meaningful to partition markets for these less frequently purchased products so that the firm can identify where its true market is and who its real competitors are. IBM, for instance, faces *different* competitors in each of the three principal computer market partitions in which it competes (Table 18.3). IBM has no close competitors in the mainframe market, which it continues to dominate; two close competitors, Digital and Hewlett-Packard, in the midsized market; and two different close competitors, Apple and Compaq, in the desktop or PC market.

Partitioning is, therefore, a relevant means of market definition for virtually any type of product or service. The main difference with durables is that the partitioning measure is likely to focus on customer-perceived substitutability rather than, as for packaged goods, on brand-switching behavior, as we shall see next in looking at measurement.

**Market Partitioning Measures.** There are two broad types of measurement methods for partitioning markets and thereby arriving at an appropriate definition of the "true" market and a reasonably sound basis for calculating market share: (1) perceived substitutability measures and (2) actual switching measures.

Whereas actual switching measures would at first appear to be superior, since they are based on behavior, this depends on the manager's purpose.[4] Actual switching measures are best for calculating market share in existing, short purchase-cycle markets. However, a manager deciding how best to position a *new* product (perhaps even just a concept at this stage) will have to rely on perceptual measures since obviously there is no switching history yet established. Also, a manager operating in a long purchase-cycle market has to use *current perceived* (intention) measures because past switching could be outdated or irrelevant to current choices.

Both types of measures can be supplemented usefully with questions that ask consumers the *reasons* for their substitutability judgments or their brand-switching behavior. Diagnostic information of this type can help to "label" the partitions. Also, it can often suggest ideas for new products incorporating new or combined benefits.

Finally, we should note that although the partitioning structure requires greater perceived substitutability and more frequent switching as you go "down" the partitions (thus helping to determine the ordering of partitions), the ultimate ordering and lateral divisions must often be decided by management judgment. This happens when the measures are taken on small samples, making the substitution or switching figures somewhat unreliable, or when different consumer or customer segments exhibit different patterns of perception or behavior which may generate a misleading "average" partitioning structure.

---

**TABLE 18.3**

**IBM's MAIN COMPETITORS IN THREE PARTITIONS[a] OF THE COMPUTER MARKET**
(*Market shares are worldwide dollar shares for 1993.*)

| Computer market leaders | Market share |
| --- | --- |
| **Mainframe computers** | |
| IBM | 50.4% |
| Fujitsu | 7.5% |
| Unisys | 6.9% |
| **Midsized computers** | |
| IBM | 19.9% |
| Digital Equipment Corporation | 13.6% |
| Hewlett-Packard | 11.8% |
| **PCs (personal computers)** | |
| IBM | 13.6% |
| Apple | 11.0% |
| Compaq | 10.0% |

[a] In *overall* share, the market *partition sizes* are as follows: PCs, 54.9 percent; mainframes, 17.5 percent; midsized computers, 17.4 percent; workstations, 8.4 percent; and supercomputers, 1.8 percent.
*Source:* Figures from Dataquest reported in J. Robotham, Big Blue leaves others in its wake, *The Australian*, January 18, 1994, p. 25.

### Perceived Substitutability Measures

**1.** *Qualitative.* These are focus groups or individual open-ended interviews in which consumers or customers are asked about each brand's category (actually subcategory) membership.[5] An illustrative question for Scotch whisky partitioning would be: "Which brands of Scotch whisky would you place in the very top quality category?"

**2.** *Perceptual Mapping.* A set of statistical techniques known loosely as "perceptual mapping" can provide indications of perceived substitutability based on similarities or preference judgments.[6] However, perceptual mapping does not directly provide the "tree" structure characteristic of partitioning. Indeed, Urban and Hauser[7] recommend constructing the maps *within* partitions identified by some other method.

**3.** *Dollar-Metric or Price-Sensitivity Method.* Consumers or customers are presented with pairs of brands at their regular prices and then asked by how much the other's price would have to be lowered to induce them to switch from the preferred alternative.[8] Although this method provides a range of substitutability coefficients, it often requires additional diagnostic questions to arrive at a meaningful partitioning structure.

### Actual Switching Measures

**1.** *Forced Switching.* In simulated choice settings, one common method is to create "out-of-stocks" by successively removing the consumer or customer's first, second, third, and so on, choices and observing which brands are chosen instead. (This can also be done hypothetically in an interview.) Respondents can also be interviewed after the choice situation to determine the reasons for their switching behavior.

**2.** *Surveys or Panels.* Surveys or panels are often used to track brand-switching behavior. Hendry partitioning measurement is often based on telephone surveys in which individual shoppers are asked which brand of "X" they bought last and which brand they bought the time before last—a measure of *reported* switching. For consumer packaged goods, home-scanner or in-store shopping card scanner panels are used to track *actual* brand-switching behavior.[9]

**3.** *Competitive Market Structure Analysis.* Using brand purchase records from panel studies, this method of analysis (developed by Fraser and Bradford[10]) focuses on the household's *time interval* between brand purchases in the overall category. Brands bought close together in time are probably *not* competing but rather are preferred by different individuals within the household or else by the same individual for independent (situational) uses (for example, Crest and Ultra Brite). Brands bought at longer intervals, when the previous brand has had time to be used up, most likely *are* directly competing in that they are regarded as substitutes for each other (for example, Crest and Colgate). Purchase or usage interval analysis is an improvement over standard switching analysis in that the latter assumes that alternate purchase of two brands means they are competing whereas they may in fact be complementary or reflect independent preferences within the household.

## Brand Equity (Upside and Downside Price Elasticity of Demand)

Building brand equity is becoming an increasingly recognized marketing objective for advertising and advertising communications more broadly considered. Similarly, "not undermining brand equity" has become a desired objective for sales promotion. To measure brand equity as a *marketing objective or goal,* we favor the "dual" price elasticity of demand method proposed by Moran (see Chapter 2), which we will now describe for the manager's use. (In the final section of this chapter, we will also provide a "quick" method that is less accurate but is useful for identifying in which *benefits* the equity resides.)

To estimate Moran's concepts of the brand's upside and downside price elasticity of demand, the manager needs to know the brand's average price trend in the category relative to competing brands' average prices (after correcting for price-off promotions for all brands). This can only be calculated historically for established brands, of course, but the manager planning to measure brand equity effects for a new brand should begin the process during the *situation audit,* using the brand's anticipated launch price.[11]

Moran[12] provides an example of how upside and downside demand elasticity are calculated (Figure 18.5). In this example, we will use the term "price" to refer to the effective unit selling price; that is, price adjusted for any price-off promotions that may be offered. In panel A of the figure, our brand is shown with its price being exactly *equal* to the product category average price (or to the average price of the

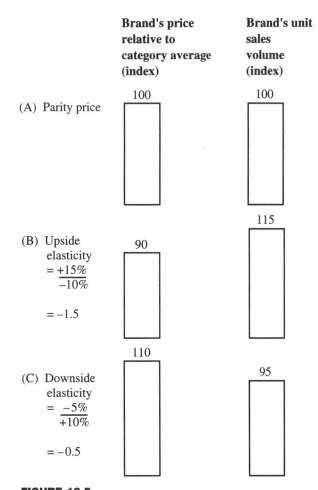

|  | Brand's price relative to category average (index) | Brand's unit sales volume (index) |
|---|---|---|
| (A) Parity price | 100 | 100 |
| (B) Upside elasticity $= \dfrac{+15\%}{-10\%}$ $= -1.5$ | 90 | 115 |
| (C) Downside elasticity $= \dfrac{-5\%}{+10\%}$ $= -0.5$ | 110 | 95 |

**FIGURE 18.5**
Example of upside and downside price elasticity calculations.
*Source:* Adapted from Moran, 1978; see note 12.

In this case, our brand has reduced its price by 10 percent below the category average, and our sales have gone up (hence, upside) by 15 percent above our parity-price sales level. Our brand's *upside elasticity of demand* at this point is therefore $+15\% \div -10\% = -1.5$. For upside elasticity, the *more negative* the number, the better. Panel C shows an example of *downside elasticity*: In this case, we have raised our price by 10 percent (or the average price of the rest of the brands is 10 percent lower), and at this higher price our sales have declined (hence, downside) by 5 percent. Our brand's *downside elasticity of demand* at this point is therefore $-5\% \div +10\% = -0.5$. For downside elasticity, the *closer to zero* the number, the better. In this set of examples, our brand is doing quite well in that it has relatively high upside elasticity—hence suggesting positive "value"; and relatively low downside elasticity—hence suggesting reasonable "uniqueness" in that buyers are less willing to substitute competing brands for it when its price goes up.[13]

Upside and downside elasticity (value and uniqueness) are calculated dynamically for the various prices over time. They could be calculated at weekly or monthly intervals, depending on how often prices are changed by brands in the category, or on whether the brand's advertising inputs or other promotional inputs are on a particular time cycle to which the manager desires to relate price elasticity of demand, such as the advertising cycles in the brand's media schedule.

It is instructive, also, to calculate upside and downside price elasticity trends for major competing brands in the category. For instance, suppose you are the manager for a brand of margarine that wishes to challenge Fleischmann's Stick margarine, a premium-quality brand in the margarine category. Allenby and Rossi[14] report some real elasticity data (although it is not precisely in the form required for brand equity analysis in that Fleischmann's price changes are shown around *its* average price rather than *the product category's* average price). In their study, Fleischmann's Stick's market share was shown to be constant in the face of large changes in store (private-label) brands' price changes (Fleischmann's Stick therefore has *low* downside elasticity, indicating strong uniqueness). Moreover, whenever Fleischmann's Stick cut *its* price below its average price of $1.02 to about 60 cents, close to store brands' upper price of 50 cents, store brands' sales fell linearly by up to two-thirds (so Fleischmann's Stick also

competing-brand set if a market share perspective is adopted). If our brand, historically, has not been priced at exactly the category average, the sales volume *at* the average can be relatively easily interpolated from its price fluctuations around the average, assuming that such price changes have been tried from time to time, or that the other brands' prices have fluctuated so that our brand's price has also fluctuated, relatively. (If our brand has not yet been launched, we have to estimate what its sales would be if it were launched with its price equal to the product category average.) Continuing with panel A, the sales volume (in units) that our brand achieved *at* the category average price, its "parity" price, is indexed at 100. Panel B shows an example of upside elasticity:

has *high* upside elasticity, indicating strong value). It would therefore be very difficult to challenge Fleischmann's unless you could develop a similarly high-equity brand. Although Fleischmann's price elasticity seems fairly symmetrical relative to store brands, "asymmetrical" price-elasticity effects do occur, and they differ for different brands.[15] Moran's dual-elasticity concept of brand equity is well supported in the marketplace and is well worth the effort to measure and track.

As noted, in the final section of this chapter, on quantitative advertising strategy research, we will present a method that allows brand equity to be traced to particular benefits (a brand attitude approach).

### Action Measures (Trial and Repeat Purchase)

Action (buyer behavior) measures in the form of trial and repeat purchase are usually obtained with particular sales measures that record purchase and the *individual-buyer* level (the firm, customer, household, or consumer). These were noted during the descriptions earlier and can be summarized as follows:

- *Industrial or consumer durable products and all services:* sales receipts (for your own company's customers' trial and repeat purchase), which can be converted to a database, and a survey for (your own and) other brands' trial and repeat-purchase rates.
- *Consumer fmcg products:* household-level scanners or individual-level purchase diaries, simulated-test-market studies, or a survey.

As we mentioned in Chapter 3, the most difficult task for the manager is not so much measuring trial and repeat purchase *after* these actions occur but rather *forecasting* the trial incidence and repeat-purchase rate for a new product introduction. Ehrenberg's method can be used for regularly purchased products, but major new *product category* introductions pose a more difficult forecasting task. For this challenge, we recommended the Bass model for major new products, and the purchase intentions method for new brands of durables.

**Bass Model for Predicting Trial of New Product Categories.** In Chapter 3, we referred to the Bass model, as it has come to be known,[16] for predicting *trial* in new product category introduction. (For really new products, trial is the critical action objective, not so much repeat purchase, which occurs after trial.) Such a method is needed because there are, of course, no sales or market shares in the category as yet and so

other methods cannot be employed. The Bass model reportedly is used for new product category predictions by companies such as AT&T, Sears, Kodak, RCA, and IBM.[17]

Because of the fear many managers have of equations, we will present the main Bass model equation as a figure, with explanatory labels (Figure 18.6). During the first period after the launch of the new category (t = 1), only innovators will have bought, since there are not yet any imitators; thus the number of adopters (triers) in the first period is $n_1 = p[M]$, which is the propensity to innovate times the number of potential buyers. For instance, if the propensity to innovate is p = .03 and there are M = 100 potential buyers, then 3 will buy in the first period. During the second period, more innovators will buy, and there will also be some imitators who buy because now there are some earlier buyers to imitate. This imitation may be pure imitation, as in clothing fashions, or it may result from personal recommendations ("word of mouth"). The number of additional *innovators* in period t = 1 will be given by $p[M - N_{t-1}] = .03[100 - 3] = 3$ more innovators. The number of *imitators,* and let us assume that the propensity to imitate is q = .38, is given by

$$q\left[\frac{N_{t-1}}{M}\right][M - N_{t-1}] = .38\left[\frac{3}{100}\right][100 - 3] = .38$$

[.03] [97] = 1. In total, by the end of the second time period, 4 buyers (approximately) will have adopted. As time goes on, the number of innovators will naturally diminish and most of the trial will come from imitators. Eventually, there will be no remainder left to buy, that is, $N_{t-1} = M$, so $M - N_{t-1} = 0$, and the peak or saturation level of trial will have been reached. The timing of the peak of trial can be estimated mathematically from the model.[18] For instance, if t is measured in months, with p = .03 and q = .38, saturation will be expected in 10.6 months.

The three "unknowns" the manager has to estimate in order to use the Bass model are p, q, and M. The total market potential, M, is a judgment call; and we recommend using the management-jury IAF/5Q method to make this estimation, especially when it's a new-to-the-world product with no immediate comparison categories (for example Philip's CD-I interactive compact disc product). Fortunately, for estimating p and q, academics have come to the rescue;[19] an important meta-analysis of 213 *actual* new product introductions found, as given in our

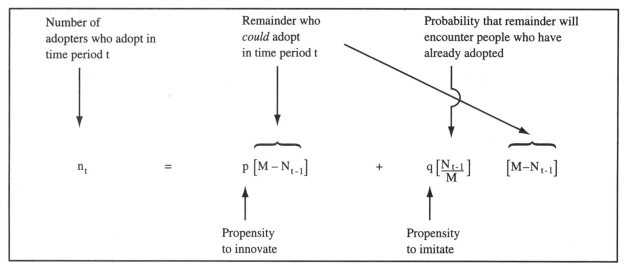

Definitions of the terms:

| | | |
|---|---|---|
| $n_t$ | = | Number (frequency) of people (or companies or other buyers) who adopt during time period t |
| t | = | 0, 1, 2, . . . weeks, months, years (as appropriate) so that t = 0 is the launch, t = 1 is the first period, t = 2 is the second period, and so forth; thus t − 1 is the previous time period |
| p, q | = | propensity to innovate (p) and propensity of the remainder to imitate those who have already adopted (q); p and q are probabilities with values ranging from 0 to 1.0 |
| M | = | total number of potential adopters in market |
| $N_{t-1}$ | = | cumulative total of people who have already adopted by the time period "going into" t, thus t − 1 |

**FIGURE 18.6**
Predicting the number of adopters (trial) at each time period using the Bass model.

example, an average value of p = .03 (range = .00 to .05) and an average value of q = .38 (range = .00 to .80). For industrial products, the suggested values are p = .04 and q = .58. For consumer durables, the suggested values are p = .03 and q = .24. If you are conducting a tracking study of the new product launch, these starting values of p and q can be used as "priors" which are then easily "updated" as the actual innovator and imitator sales data become available.[20]

**Purchase Intentions for New Brands of Durables.** If the new product is less of a radical innovation and not likely to depend on "diffusion" via personal influence, then using the Bass model is probably overkill and a straightforward measure of *purchase intentions* will suffice to predict trial. We may note that purchase intentions can be regarded as a special case of the Bass model where p = the individual's probability of purchase as *translated* from his or her intention rating; imitation, q, is zero; and the adoption decision is instantaneous once the consumer

is aware of the product, that is, t = 1. For example, Infosino[21] at AT&T used a simple 1-to-10 purchase intent scale to predict trial of a new pricing option for a residential telephone service. This "new product" could easily be adopted privately without any need for a social imitation effect. The ratings on the purchase intent scale then have to be translated (downweighted, mainly) into purchase likelihood predictions, since people's stated intentions are not always followed through to actual purchase behavior. We show how to make these translations in Chapter 19 on ad testing, rather than duplicating them here.[22]

Purchase intentions could also be (and often are) used to predict trial for a new brand in a regularly purchased (fmcg) category. Again this measure will be quite accurate as long as there is no social diffusion effect. However, we strongly recommend primary reliance on the order-of-entry "norms" method or Ehrenberg's penetration method (see Chapter 3). A purchase intentions survey can then be used as a supplementary check or backup method.

### Advertising Expenditure and Content Analysis

Another important type of information that the manager needs to compile in the situation audit is advertising information—on expenditures and content—for competitors in the product category. Expenditure and content information should be traced back at least 2 years, and longer if the statistical projection method of budgeting is being employed. We assume, unless our brand is new, that expenditure and advertising content information for *it* can be obtained internally, although this information should be requested in the external information search so that it can be checked against internal records.

**Expenditures Analysis.** Advertising expenditure figures can be obtained from several sources for the main *measured* media: TV advertising, radio advertising, newspaper advertising, and magazine advertising. LNA/Arbitron Multi-Media Service is a good general source. However, direct response and other IMC media expenditure is *virtually impossible* to obtain, other than from occasional reports in the trade press.

Advertising expenditures should be analyzed in terms of their *amounts* (needed, for example, to compute share of voice, SOV, for the Peckham's 1.5 rule/order-of-entry method and for Schroer's method of budget setting) and also in terms of the apparent *pattern* of expenditures adopted by each major competitor. The latter information will be useful, later, for determining our brand's media strategy.

If information about competitive expenditures is unavailable, then company records can at least reveal our brand's own expenditure over time in relation to sales. Our own advertising and sales data are sufficient for the IAF/5Q budgeting method and can also be used for the task method.

**Advertising Content Analysis.** It is extremely important that the manager not rely on his or her (or anyone else's) "memory" of what the competitors are doing in their brand's advertising. Much more precise external information is available, and there is no need to trust memory, which is probably distorted by the most recent campaigns.

If the category has been advertised on TV, 1-page "photoboards" of competing brands' commercials can be obtained through companies such as Radio TV Reports, Inc., VMS, or ADBANK. These 1-page summary commercials are very convenient for content analysis. If you want to see actual commercials, a company called Competitive Media Reporting can

deliver them electronically to your PC within 48 hours of their being aired, together with the markets, stations, and times. For print campaigns, either in newspapers or magazines, copies of print ads for most product categories can be obtained through Vance, Coughlan & Woodward, Inc.

In addition, it is extremely helpful to commission a *library search,* using an electronic database, from your own company library or through a university business school, of everything you can find listed under the companies' and brands' names for the past couple of years. The reason for this additional step is that articles in trade magazines, such as *Advertising Age* and *ADWEEK,* often report the companies' intended *strategy* behind the advertising. These strategies may not be apparent from inspecting the advertising itself. It is surprising how often competitors, perhaps quite proudly, let their strategies "leak" to the trade press.

The manager's analysis of advertising content should, however, be much more systematic than a simple collation of the ads and news items. The ads themselves should be closely content-analyzed and a summary prepared of the "positioning" of each of the competing brands both currently and historically. In particular, the manager must be sure to identify the apparent category or subcategory in which competing brands are attempting to position themselves and, for each, what main benefits are mentioned in the advertising. Other aspects of competing brands' advertising —such as the use of a particular presenter, theme, or logo which may have become a "property" of that brand—should also be noted since these may place a limitation on what our brand can do in its advertising.

Finally, it is necessary also to conduct a *legal* search. Managers are often not fully aware of the legal restrictions that may apply to the advertising of brands in their own product category. If the creative team is not notified of mandatory restrictions that affect benefit claims, very costly litigation can result for the advertiser. Industry associations and relevant government departments such as the FTC and FDA should be consulted. An excellent source for legal commentaries is the *Journal of Marketing*'s section of abstracts on legal developments in marketing. It is worth a "back-search" of recent to previous abstracts to check on how legal restrictions in the product category and its advertising have been interpreted in practice. This can be done as part of the library search.

The advertising content information will be useful, perhaps crucial, for devising the brand's advertising communications strategy, as will a separate promotions analysis for categories in which promotions are a substantial part of the marketing communications mix.

### Sales Promotions Content Analysis

Sales promotions employed by competitors and previously by the brand (unless it is new) must also be compiled as part of the situation audit.

If the product is sold at retail in supermarkets or drugstores, Nielsen or IRI research companies can track competitive sales promotions. However, *store or retail visits* are an essential step in compiling a competitive point-of-purchase advertising and promotions file. The manager should make store visits personally, to a cross section of stores, then commission a research company or junior staff members to revisit the stores to record and photograph details. Also, don't forget FSIs in newspapers. These "promotions" usually duplicate the *advertised* benefits of brands.

For industrial products, and for services, a physical search of retail promotions is the only way to compile the necessary information.

The manager should then conduct a content analysis of the sales promotions (to complement the competitive advertising content analysis). A summary of creative approaches taken, benefits emphasized, types of promotions offered, and price-off policies used by the major competing brands should be the outcome.

### Internal Sources of Information

**Analyze Previous Company Data and Research Reports on the Category.** Unless the category is completely new, the manager's own company will have advertising and sales records and nearly always will have previous research reports in the company's files. Sometimes the problem is that the *manager* is completely new and doesn't know what information the company already has, or is reluctant to review "old" work. This is always a mistake; the historical pattern must always be considered. We would suspect, for instance, that required reading for new Coca-Cola managers would be Pendergrast's 100-year history of the brand;[23] or for new IBM managers, the biography of founder Thomas B. Watson.[24] Historical reviews can be used to make managers remember the benefits that helped give an established brand its

*brand equity.* For instance, Coca-Cola has recently revived the benefit claim "refreshing," used now with the new creative idea as "Always refreshing," a benefit claim first made by Coke in 1929 with the famous line "The pause that refreshes."[25]

The manager should analyze, not just read, previous data and research reports. The manager should arrange the information to suit the advertising communications and promotion plan's checklist sections. Company data can be used to plot trends in brand sales and, if competing brands' sales data are available, market shares. From research reports, information can be extracted to supplement other sections of the AC&P plan, such as target audience profile characteristics, and benefits for brand attitude strategy.

**Interview Those Who Produce or Provide the Product or Service.** The manager should personally compile a "fact book" of technical details about the product or service. This will require interviews with (as appropriate) the company's physicists, engineers, chemists, nutritionists, or service managers.

Many excellent campaigns are derived from the technical characteristics of the product. (For informational buying motives—less so for transformational buying motives, where the usage consequences are more subjective—advertising's task basically is to turn product attributes into consumer benefits, and more specifically into benefit claims; see Chapters 6 through 9.) Claude Hopkins's early campaign for Budweiser—"It's beechwood aged"—is a good example. Another example is Federal Express, which technically described its "hub system" of package routing, whereby all packages go to Memphis and then out on the next plane going to the "spoke" destination city, as an advertising explanation of faster service.

Of course, primary research with potential or actual *customers* will be required to see which technical attributes can indeed be turned into benefits. This comes in the last two stages of advertising strategy research—qualitative research and quantitative research—as explained in the final section of this chapter.

**Interview the Company's Distributors.** Many advertising communications and promotion campaigns either are directed to, or depend largely for their success upon, the trade. It is always worth conducting interviews with each link in the channel of distribution to obtain distributors' opinions on what's been done in the past by way of product, price, distribution, and promotion efforts, and what distributors believe will work in the future.

While the manager should become familiar with the product's present and potential distribution, it is better to commission an independent research firm to conduct distributor interviews. This is because the company's own distributors (especially the immediate sales force) are likely to provide somewhat biased or guarded answers if they know they are talking to a senior representative of one of the companies for which they distribute.[26] The exception, as mentioned earlier, is when the sales force must be used to identify key role-players in a particular client's or prospect's company.

Distributor information fits various sections of the advertising plan. At a broad level, it might indicate a major strategy of advertising and promoting to the trade, beyond normal trade promotions, whereas this is too often an afterthought in many advertising plans (see Chapter 12). At a more specific level, it may indicate the incorporation of purchase facilitation as a communication objective (see Chapter 5).

**Interview Financial Managers to Obtain the Cost, Pricing, and Profit Basis of the Product or Service.** In Chapter 2, we discussed how advertising communications and promotions contribute to profit through price margin, cost reduction, or increased volume. The manager cannot complete the marketing objectives section of the AC&P plan unless he or she understands the financial basis of the product or service. Interviews with financial officers should be conducted personally by the manager.

**Conduct Statistical Analysis If Data Are Available and Poll Managers to Set the Overall Advertising Communications and Promotion Budget.** The final application of the situation audit is to obtain the information necessary to set the overall AC&P budget. As explained in Chapter 2 in conjunction with the statistical projection method of budgeting, if the campaign is for a continuing brand, statistical analysis—including a graphic plot—should be conducted on trend relationships between respective marketing expenditures and the decided-upon market performance criterion: brand equity (upside and downside price elasticity of demand), market share, sales, or profit.[27]

For continuing brands (usually) and for a new brand (of necessity), a management jury will additionally be needed to establish the overall AC&P budget. This involves a poll of six to 10 managers, as explained in Chapter 2. For continuing brands, a computer-interactive marketing model such as BRANDAID can assist in setting the budget.[28]

In summary, we see that the situation audit—with all its components—is an extremely important, if arduous, part of advertising strategy research. The situation audit is necessary to set sound marketing objectives. It is, basically, *secondary* research because we have not yet interviewed consumers or final customers. *Primary* advertising strategy research, involving customers, is described next. This consists of qualitative research and quantitative research.

## QUALITATIVE RESEARCH

To help select the target audience and set appropriate action objectives and communication objectives and to determine or confirm the to-be-communicated *brand position,* interviews with potential and actual customers are nearly always necessary. It is particularly risky to attempt these steps in the plan through management judgment alone, although this sometimes has to be done for very small budget or very urgent campaigns.

Qualitative research, we believe, is theoretically *essential* to developing advertising strategy. (Shortly, we will see how quantitative research can *add* to the qualitative results. But one could, in practice, simply extend the number of qualitative research interviews until they become quantitatively reliable, that is, until the inferences become based on enough respondents to be safely projectable.) Qualitative research is the only research method capable of—and we stress *capable* of, not assured of—discovering the causes of buyer behavior.[29]

### What Is Qualitative Research?

Qualitative research consists of either *focus groups,* also called *group depth interviews* or GDIs, or *individual depth interviews,* IDIs. Focus groups are the usual method, although individual interviews are used quite typically in industrial, medical, or personal product fields where purchase decisions are too sensitive to disclose in front of others. Actually, individual depth interviews are far more efficient[30] than focus groups, and we recommend their general use. If the usual decision making unit (see Chapter 4) *is* a group, however, then some group interviews should be conducted with *intact* groups as well as the individual interviews. With either the group or individual interview procedure, qualitative research uses open-ended questions focusing on a range of topics, designed to help the advertiser to arrive at an advertising strategy.

A skeleton discussion outline (from which the qualitative researcher would write actual, askable questions and probes) is provided in Table 18.4. The

---

**TABLE 18.4**

### SKELETON DISCUSSION OUTLINE FOR QUALITATIVE RESEARCH

**Introduction and purpose**

- Moderator's preamble: purpose is to ask your opinions on (category); interaction encouraged; no majority rule; recorded, to get all valuable comments

**Decision maker roles**

- Which members of household initiate, influence, decide, buy, use the general product category

**Decision sequence**

- Trace through each person's decision process from beginning to end: what, when, where, how, and why people buy in this general product category

**Category partitions**

- Awareness (recalled then recognized) of types and brands
- Which types and brands are similar, dissimilar—and why
- Probe extensively for all motivations for purchase and benefits sought in category

**Brand behaviors and attitudes**

- Which brands not tried, tried and rejected, tried and purchased again, purchased most often—and why
- Each brand in turn: strengths and weaknesses
- User images associated with each brand

**Advertising**

- (Show examples of each brand's advertising or adlike communications); which advertisements are most appealing, least appealing—and why
- Suggestions for new brand benefits to be advertised
- Suggestions for new media to be employed

**Promotion**

- (Show examples of each brand's promotions); awareness and opinion of media promotions for each brand
- Awareness and opinion of POP promotions
- Preferred types of promotion

**Summary**

- Identify client's brand, and review by asking people what the brand would have to do to get them to buy it, or buy it and

---

qualitative research interviewer elicits and probes buyers' or potential buyers' opinions about the product category, various brands, the people who use those brands, and different advertising approaches.[31]

Even the smallest advertiser usually can afford qualitative research; the cost is generally about $3,000 to $5,000 per group, depending on the product category usage incidence and hence the availability of respondents (participants), as well as the experience and skill of the moderator-analyst (see below). Three or four group discussions or about 20 individual interviews with potential and actual customers can be sufficient to supplement the smaller advertiser's own ideas and lead to a reasonably good advertising strategy.

For larger advertisers in very competitive product categories, however, the qualitative research should be more extensive and more precise. It should sample across *all potential target audience groups* and replicate with *at least three groups or about 15 individual interviews on each* to provide more reliable findings.

The *validity* of qualitative research findings is largely dependent on the psychological and marketing abilities of the interviewer—the moderator-analyst. The person who is going to analyze the results by listening to the tapes of the sessions and writing the report should *also* be the moderator, or discussion leader, of the GDIs or IDIs. Only the same person can know *why* certain questions or probes were asked and why particular avenues of thought were pursued. Indeed, a skilled and experienced *moderator-analyst* is the most important ingredient in qualitative research because the research results are so heavily based on his or her interpretations of what the participants do and say. (The results of qualitative research are about 50 percent consumer or customer input and 50 percent analyst interpretation. This contrasts sharply with quantitative survey research, where the ratio is about 90 percent data and 10 percent interpretation.) An illustration of the skill required in qualitative interpretation—on the run—is given in Table 18.5.

The *report* of qualitative research findings should be cognizant of the research's purpose: to help develop the advertising strategy. The report must *not* be a mere summary of "what participants said." The report's content should cover the areas we now discuss.

### Applying Qualitative Research Results to the Advertising Plan

Like all forms of advertising research, qualitative research is undertaken to provide information to aid the

### TABLE 18.5

**ILLUSTRATION OF QUALITATIVE RESEARCH MODERATING AND INTERPRETATION**

One of the most innovative qualitative researchers in the business, Mike Brownlee of Creative Dialogue in Sydney, Australia, listens to consumers' *verbs* to detect thoughts (cognitive) versus emotions (affective). This takes a practiced ear and brain, because most consumers have difficulty separating and explaining their thoughts and feelings, as the following excerpt from a focus group discussion indicates.

Consumer: When I bought my new Mazda, I felt, "What a bargain!"
Moderator: I hear what you *thought,* but what did you *feel?*
Consumer: Well, I felt that the price was fine.
Moderator: And what did you *feel?*
Consumer: You know, I felt a little cheap. . . .

*Source:* M. Elfverson and M. A. Brownlee, Group discussions, Pamphlet issued by Creative Dialogue Ltd., Sydney, Australia, no date, by permission.

manager in preparing the advertising communications and promotion plan (see the Appendix for a detailed description of the AC&P plan). Table 18.6 lists the main purposes for which qualitative research is used to contribute to the AC&P plan, and these purposes are explained next.

**1.** *Identify the most leverageable target audience(s) for advertising communications and promotion.* Qualitative research can *broadly* identify the most leverageable (most persuadable at least cost) target audience *for* advertising communications and *for* promotion. This broad identification is sufficient for many advertisers.

Note, however, that qualitative research usually cannot make a good estimate of the *size* and thus detailed sales potential of alternative prospect groups, especially if the manager wants to go beyond the basic five prospect groups (see Chapter 3) and into target audience subgroups (see the discussion of quantitative advertising strategy research later in this chapter). Large advertisers generally will want to do this, and therefore will need quantitative research, or a very large number of qualitative interviews, *unless* they are fortunate enough to have prospect group sizes available from secondary research (situation audit).

**2.** *Identify decision roles and action objectives.* A second purpose of qualitative research is to identify

the participants in the purchase decision. The *roles* to which advertising communications and promotion offers can most effectively be directed, and therefore the associated action objectives, can be most validly isolated through qualitative research. This is because the qualitative research can probe beyond the typically surface answers given by respondents in surveys which ask respondents directly about their relative decision influence.[32]

Identifying decision participants by role is crucial in *business-to-business* marketing. Here it may not be possible to get a target clients' role-players together in a group discussion; however, it is certainly possible to conduct a (partial) individual interview during sales calls.

Speckman and Stern[33] suggest the following questions to help identify decision participants' roles (referring to the most recent purchase decision):

**a.** Were you involved in identifying the need and getting the purchase decision started?
**b.** Did you help specify the main criteria for choosing the supplier or brand?
**c.** Did you recommend particular suppliers or brands?
**d.** Did you reject particular suppliers or brands?
**e.** Were you the final decision maker for the selection of the brand or supplier?
**f.** Were you responsible for implementing the new product or service within the organization, that is, for its usage?

Of course, the questions may not be literally as direct as these, but over the course of a prospective sales meeting or two, the salesperson should be able to gain

### TABLE 18.6

**PURPOSES OF QUALITATIVE RESEARCH IN RELATION TO THE AC&P PLAN**

1. Identify the most leverageable target audience(s) for advertising communications and promotion.
2. Identify decision roles and action objectives.
3. Construct a behavioral sequence model.
4. Determine communication objectives (including brand awareness type, brand attitude quadrant, and benefits to support brand attitude) and brand position.
5. Suggest advertising communications or promotion stimuli that might be suited to the communication objectives.

a fair idea of the various individuals' roles and importance, which can be confirmed by cross-checking among interviewees.

**3.** *Construct a behavioral sequence model.* One of the topics in the qualitative research outline has the researcher asking buyers to trace back their decision sequence. The researcher then, from a number of such "protocols" as they are known, pieces together a typical behavioral sequence model for the product category or, if different, for the particular brand. The BSM details the stages, roles, locations, time and timing, and the *how* of purchase decisions. (The procedure for BSM construction was explained in Chapter 4.)

**4.** *Determine communication objectives and brand position.* A further (essential) purpose of qualitative research is to determine the communication objectives for the advertising, promotion, or IMC campaign (see Chapter 5). The content of the first three or "core" communication objectives below will determine the brand's *position* in the target buyer's mind (see Chapter 6). Remember, too, that there will be different communication objectives, and perhaps different positions for the brand, for each target audience.

    **a.** The *category need* objective will be fairly obvious from the nature of the target audience; qualitative research also has the prior task of deciding precisely what the category *is,* from the consumer's or customer's standpoint.

    **b.** The *brand awareness* objective should be evident from the behavioral sequence model, which indicates whether most buyers decide on the brand (or should be induced to decide) prior to purchase via brand recall, or at the point of purchase via brand recognition. Note that the advertiser may attempt to "force" a different brand awareness objective, such as brand recall–boosted brand recognition (see Chapter 5).

    **c.** The *brand attitude* objective likewise should be fairly evident from the target audience selected, but the brand attitude *strategy* requires very careful analysis: qualitative research is the *best* way to determine the level of involvement with brand choice[34] as well as the real underlying motive or motives to which purchase or usage of the brand is connected or could be potentially connected—hence quadrant placement in the Rossiter-Percy Grid must be done from qualitative research. As explained in Chapter 6 on positioning using the I-D-U model, the qualitative

researcher must also identify the important, deliverable, and unique *benefits,* and the benefits' choice rule, to support the brand attitude strategy.

    **d.** The *brand purchase* (or purchase-related) *intention* objective follows from the behavioral sequence model and from the brand attitude quadrant.

    **e.** The *purchase facilitation* objective may arise in the qualitative interviews, or it may be something that customers don't yet know about (but you know about it from the situation audit). In the latter case, the advertiser has to decide whether to be preemptive and make it an objective or whether it can be safely omitted.

Accordingly, we can see that qualitative research is vital for deciding the campaign's communication objectives and the to-be-communicated position (or positions) for the brand. Of particular importance is the qualitative analyst's skill in interpretation and application.[35] In buying qualitative research, by and large, you get what you pay for in terms of the quality of the analyst and the resulting strategy.

**5.** *Suggest advertising communications or promotion stimuli that might be suited to the communication objectives.* This final purpose of qualitative research is stated cautiously: it is seen by some people as encroaching on the creative function. Nevertheless, there is no reason other than the creative team's elitism or defensiveness that should prevent a qualitative report from suggesting effective types of stimuli (visual, verbal, musical) and also tactics (see Chapters 8, 9, 10, 12, 13, and 14) for creative executions of advertisements and promotion offers. The creative *ideas,* however, as explained in Chapter 7, should best be left to the creative professionals to provide.

### Special Techniques for Uncovering Motivations

Qualitative research was originally and aptly called "motivation research." Although we have just seen that qualitative research has additional purposes besides detecting motivations, an essential purpose is to uncover the *real* motivations, and the associated benefits, that are used to influence brand attitude. If the motivational "triggers" to purchase of the brand are not found, then qualitative research has not fulfilled its most valuable function.

The understanding of motivations requires a skilled moderator-analyst using either the focus group

(GDI) method or the individual depth interview (IDI) method. The flexible questioning and deep probing of qualitative research are required for the following reasons:

1. Respondents may not easily understand what the interviewer is looking for.
2. They may not know what their motivations are.
3. They may be unable to remember them even if they do know what they are.
4. They may not be able to articulate them even if they do remember them.
5. They may not want to tell the interviewer even if they could.
6. During any telling, the interviewer must probe deeply enough to enable correct classification of the answers in terms of true underlying motivations.

Only the skilled qualitative researcher with psychological training can reasonably circumvent these ever-present barriers to identifying motivations.

In qualitative investigations, the interviewer asks actual and potential consumers or customers why they do or do not buy or use the product or service. Specific brands are also asked about because answers at the product category level, alone, are often too general or abstract. The interviewer is seeking two main types of information: (1) the nature of the *motivation* or *motivations* operating in the product category—negatively originated or positively originated, from the eight identified in Chapter 5; and (2) the particular *benefits,* described in "consumer language," that appear to be *important* (as in the I-D-U model of mesopositioning described in Chapter 6) in meeting these motivations.

**Special Techniques.** Written-answer techniques are sometimes used to supplement the usual oral questions and answers in qualitative research. For negatively originated (informational) motivations, and associated "relief" benefits, *problem-detection analysis* can be useful. Developed by the BBDO advertising agency from the Hotpoint Company's technique of "reverse brainstorming," problem-detection analysis employs the following types of questions,[36] which can be asked for the product category in general but are usually asked for each brand:

1. Does this product (brand) *solve* a problem or need? If so, please describe it.
2. Does this product (brand) *produce* any problem(s)? If so, please describe it or them.

3. (For each problem or need mentioned): How *important,* to you, is this problem or need?
Very important _____
Moderately important _____
Slightly important _____
Not important _____

For positively originated (transformational) motivations, and associated "reward" benefits, *benefit chaining,* a technique popularized by Grey Advertising from a procedure copyrighted by Hal Lee in 1970,[37] can be useful. Benefit chaining is a system of sequential probing. In the written version, the consumer begins by writing down two benefits (an arbitrary number—and the consumer may well begin with attributes rather than benefits; see the a-b-e model of micropositioning described in Chapter 6) derived from using the product. For each of the two benefits, the consumer next writes down two more *following* benefits. The resulting chain for one of the benefits may be as follows (for a hair spray product):

| Holds without sticking | $\rightarrow$ | Leaves hair easy to manage | $\rightarrow$ | Leads to compliments on natural-looking hair |
|---|---|---|---|---|

Of course, it still remains for the analyst to infer from these types of responses the actual motivation and how "surface" benefits relate to it. In the hair spray benefit chain above, for instance, it is *not* clear whether the *real* motivation (the main reason for using the hair spray) is problem avoidance, represented in the first link, or social approval, represented in the second; the analyst has to judge this. Also note that the example shows not simply a benefit chain but rather (in our terminology of Chapter 6's a-b-e micropositioning model) an attribute $\rightarrow$ benefit $\rightarrow$ emotional consequence chain.

It should be noted that despite the names of the two techniques (problem-detection analysis and benefit chaining) and the classification above, each can identify negative as well as positive motivations, although they seem likely to favor one or the other type. Both techniques can of course be used in the same qualitative study. The generic name for these sequential probing techniques is "laddering."[38]

Another useful technique, actually a set of techniques, is *projective techniques.* These are able to detect all types of motivations but are especially effective for products where deep personal motives or unadmitted or unrecognized social influence may be operating. Projective techniques include questions such as "What do your friends buy and why?"—which is perhaps the most widely used type of projective technique, the purpose being to infer why *you* buy this brand; similarly, they include the presentation of incomplete or ambiguous stimuli such as cartoons of characters in brand purchase or usage situations in which respondents are asked to fill in the words in the cartoon characters' word balloons; they also include "be-a-brand" role-playing, in which respondents try to "impersonate" various brands, thereby revealing personal and social likes and dislikes about each. Projective techniques are described in most market research texts, and they often produce valuable insights for advertising strategy in qualitative research.

By employing these special techniques, too, the qualitative researcher can identify possible a-b-e (attribute-benefit-emotion) paths that the brand could adopt in its micropositioning strategy. (The a-b-e model of benefit focus was explained in Chapter 6.)

## QUANTITATIVE RESEARCH

*Adding* quantitative research to the prior qualitative research in advertising strategy research serves a number of additional information needs in preparing the advertising communications and promotion plan. We emphasize that this is additional information. Quantitative research can in no way replace—and is not "better than"—qualitative research.[39] Rather, quantitative research *supplements* the AC&P plan in ways to be described shortly.

### What Is Quantitative Research?

In the context of advertising strategy research, quantitative research consists of a questionnaire survey with a large number of target audience customers or consumers (200 to 1,000, depending on the number of *prospective* target audience groups and the degree of precision or reliability required) followed by appropriate statistical analysis of the results.[40]

The quantitative research interviews are *not* administered by psychologically trained interviewers as in qualitative research: their suitability is for gathering objective "numbers" data rather than for obtaining the subjective psychological inferences that come from qualitative research. (This is in keeping with the 10 percent contribution of analysis, in contrast

with 50 percent for qualitative research, as mentioned earlier.)

Questionnaire content areas covered in quantitative advertising strategy research are listed in Table 18.7. Again, of course, these content areas have to be converted to actual questions for survey administration. Because of the interview length and the large sample sizes, it is not unusual for quantitative research to cost between $50,000 and $150,000. Considered in relation to a large AC&P budget, which may be over a thousand times the lower amount (that is, $50 million), this money is considered well spent.

As seen from the table, there are three main purposes of quantitative research:

1. To classify more precise target audience subgroups.
2. To align benefits more precisely with target audiences.
3. To fully profile the target audience decision maker (including media exposure).

### TABLE 18.7

**QUANTITATIVE RESEARCH: QUESTIONNAIRE CONTENT AREAS**

**Target audience classification**

Category and brand awareness, attitude, and behavior measures to classify respondents into the 12 prospective target audience subgroups

**Brand benefit ratings**

Ratings of each brand in terms of benefits (stated in consumer language) relating to *situations* (motives)

**Demographics**

Geographic: region, state, urban/suburban/rural
Individual: age, sex, race, income, education, occupation

**Psychographics**

General: various A-I-O[a] inventories, including social class values
Category-specific: A-I-O for category attitudes and behaviors

**Personality traits**

Reliable measures of intelligence, anxiety, introversion-extraversion, imaging ability, and so on, that relate functionally to persuasion

**Media exposure**

Frequency of exposure to media vehicles in each medium
Locations and personality states during exposure

These functions are explained next.

## Target Audience Subgroups Classification

For the large advertiser who may be developing advertising communications and promotion campaigns for several target audiences and is trying to decide which precise prospect subgroups are the most feasible targets, quantitative research can be of great assistance.

There are 12 prospect subgroups (see Figure 18.7), which can be quite efficiently identified by using the questions listed in Table 18.8. As you can see, the subgroups are subsets of the five brand loyalty–based groups that we introduced in Chapter 3 and have referred to throughout the book. We elaborate on the subgroups here.

**New Category Users.** New category users are actually nonusers of the product category and, as such, could be referred to as non–category users. We prefer to be optimistic. When targeting NCUs in advertising and promotion, we want them to be *new* category users, which they will be if our campaign works.

The term "new category users" includes several relevant subgroups: those with a positive attitude toward the *category* (PNCUs), those who are unaware of the category and therefore have no attitude toward it as yet (UNCUs), and those who are negatively disposed toward the category (NNCUs). Positive new category users represent better prospects than negative new category users who have decided against the category. Unaware new category users

**FIGURE 18.7**

The 12 buyer subgroups (potential target audiences) summarized: (a) franchise (buying our brand), and (b) nonfranchise (not buying our brand). See text for explanation of each subgroup. The closeness of each subgroup to single-brand loyalty (shaded circle) approximately indicates its leverage.

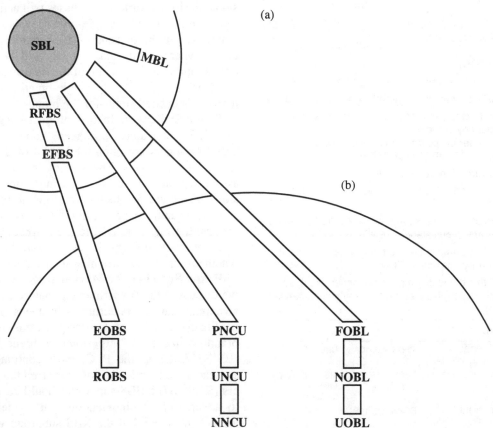

**QUESTIONS TO CLASSIFY RESPONDENTS INTO THE 12 TARGET AUDIENCE PROSPECT SUBGROUPS (SEE FIGURE 18.7)**

**Product category**

1. ❑ Not aware of this category (END)
2. ❑ Aware of, never used, but might try this category (GO TO 11)
3. ❑ Aware of, never used, and would not try this category (END)
4. ❑ Used this category in the past, no longer use it, but might retry this category (GO TO 11)
5. ❑ Used this category in the past, no longer use it, and would not use this category under any circumstances: (END)

**Client's brand**

6. ❑ Use *only* this brand (END)
7. ❑ Use *only* another brand (WRITE BRAND BELOW) _____ (GO TO 11)
8. ❑ Use this brand *and* other brands (WRITE OTHER BRANDS BELOW)
   _____ _____ _____ (GO TO 10)
9. ❑ Use other brands *but not* this brand (WRITE OTHER BRANDS BELOW)
   _____ _____ _____ (GO TO 10, NEXT QUESTION)
10. Which type of *brand buyer* are you more like?
    ❑ A. *Prefer* several brands and buy *only* those brands
    ❑ B. Buy a *variety* of brands and *don't* feel strongly about any of them
       (If a user of client's brand, END; if nonuser, GO TO 11, NEXT QUESTION)
11. ❑ Not aware of this brand (END)
12. ❑ Aware of, never used, but might try this brand (END)
13. ❑ Aware of, never used, and would not try this brand under any circumstances (END)
14. ❑ Used this brand in the past, no longer use it, but might retry this brand (END)
15. ❑ Used this brand in the past, no longer use it, and would not use this brand under any circumstances (END)

**Classification**

| | | | |
|---|---|---|---|
| UNCU = 1 | FOBL = 7, 12; or 7, 14 | RFBS = 8, 10A | SBL = 6 |
| PNCU = 2 or 4 | NOBL = 7, 11 | EFBS = 10B, 12; or 10B, 14 | MBL = 8, 10A (maximum three brands) |
| NNCU = 3 or 5 | UOBL = 7, 13; or 7, 15 | EOBS = 9, 10B | |
| | | ROBS = 9, 10A | |

fall somewhere in between, requiring "educational" advertising to make them aware of the category with the hope that their category attitude will become positive.

**Brand Loyals.** A buyer can be attitudinally and behaviorally loyal to more than one brand (though typically two or three brands at most). Multibrand loyalty, of course, reduces sales to our brand loyals, so it is worth distinguishing from single-brand loyalty.

In brand attitude measurement, it is quite common to distinguish those buyers who regard the brand as their "single preferred brand" (single-brand loyals, or SBLs) from those who regard it as "one of several preferred brands" (multibrand loyals, or MBLs). For fmcg products, about 55 percent of buyers claim to be SBL for the average category, ranging from 25 percent for canned vegetables to 71 percent for cigarettes. For consumer durables, the average claimed SBL incidence is about 30 percent, ranging from 27 percent for athletic shoes to 39 percent for gasoline.[41] Behaviorally, because of out-of-stocks or the occasional desire for variety, purchases will actually fall a little behind attitude. Single-brand loyals will be devoting about 90 percent of their purchases to the brand, whereas multibrand loyals will be buying it only about 30 to 80 percent of the time as one of their "regular" brands. Clearly, single-brand loyalty is the manager's desired status for the brand.

**Brand Switchers.** In most product categories, and especially consumer packaged goods categories, brand switchers are often the largest of the four potential buyer groups. The size of the overall brand switcher group also expands during economic recessions. There are two factors in terms of which brand switchers can be meaningfully distinguished into subgroups: the first is related to the market stage of the PLC (product *category* life cycle), and the second to whether their brand switching includes our brand.

**Brand Switchers by Market Stage.** In Chapter 3, we discussed the "experimental" nature of the brand switching that occurs during early stages of the product life cycle. It is useful to designate this subgroup of brand switchers as *experimental* brand switchers (EBSs). Later in the PLC, most continuing brand switchers are "hard-core" or *routinized* brand switchers (RBSs). The EBS subgroup should be vulnerable to advertising communications, since their choices are not yet fixed, but the RBS subgroup will be responsive to price-related promotions only.

**Brand Switchers Who Include or Exclude Our Brand.** Brand switchers, by definition, switch between a number of brands (usually many more than the multibrand loyals, who focus on two or three preferred brands). Obviously, it makes a big difference whether brand switchers include our brand in their switching repertoire, or whether they exclude it, and switch only among other brands. Thus, in Chapter 3 we distinguished between *favorable* brand switchers (FBSs), who include our brand, and *other*-brand switchers (OBSs), who exclude our brand and do their switching only among other brands.

The reader will notice a continuity between multibrand loyals (MBLs) as described previously and routinized brand switchers (RBSs) of the FBS type. Both MBLs and favorable RBSs *buy* our brand, but MBLs buy only one or two other brands *and* have very positive attitudes toward them, whereas favorable RBSs buy three or more other brands and have more "switchable" attitudes toward these and our brand.

Brand switchers therefore can be distinguished into *four* subgroups: EOBSs (experimental other-brand switchers), EFBSs (experimental favorable brand switchers), ROBSs (routinized other-brand switchers), and RFBSs (routinized favorable brand switchers). The size and importance of the overall brand-switcher group, for advertising and *also* promotion, justifies these sharper distinctions into four subgroups.

**Other-Brand Loyals.** Other-brand loyals (OBLs) are quite different from other-brand *switchers* (OBSs, both EOBSs and ROBSs). We have a good chance to win over OBSs, notably with promotion, but very little chance to convert OBLs. The chance would seem to be greater in low-risk product categories but, remember, we are fighting against satisfied purchasers who have "been through the mill" in that category and who will be content to stay with their current choice.

If the manager does decide that other-brand loyals are a worthwhile target, then it is worth making further division of OBLs into attitudinal subgroups. (An OBL target might be chosen by a small-share brand in a mature market dominated by one or two large-share brands with many loyal customers. In this situation, there's little option but to try to attract the large OBL group.) The OBLs should be distinguished in terms of their attitude toward *our* brand: favorable other-brand loyals (FOBLs), neutral other-brand loyals (NOBLs), and unfavorable other-brand loyals (UOBLs). If the neutral or unfavorable brand attitudes are based on

prior trial of our brand, then the second and especially the third subgroups will be very difficult to convert and in most cases hopeless.

### Aligning Benefits with Target Audiences

The purpose of obtaining benefit ratings is to perform an I-D-U analysis (see Chapter 6) for selecting benefits to employ in advertising communications and promotion offers to each target audience. Several methodological considerations can now be noted that were passed over in Chapter 6.

**Situational Benefit Ratings.** As explained in Chapter 5, in conjunction with brand attitude, benefits are relevant only in relation to particular purchase or usage motivations for the brand. Motivations are psychological inferences (in the analyst's mind) whereas the specific benefits are in consumer language (in the consumer's mind). To repeat an example used earlier, the "fresh taste" benefit in a toothpaste may be desired because of underlying problem removal motivation (bad taste in mouth) or sensory gratification motivation (nice taste without any "problem") or social approval motivation (for example, "sex appeal"). The questionnaire cannot, in most cases, state the benefit in relation to the motivation by referring directly to the psychological motive, such as by asking, "Do you want fresh taste in a toothpaste so as to enhance social approval?" Instead, the motivational basis of the benefit must usually be stated *indirectly*, without reference to the psychological mechanism.

This can be achieved by stating the motivation, for the consumer, in terms of a *situation*. The situation avoids direct reference to the psychological mechanism. Examples covering several possible motives in the toothpaste category might be "a toothpaste for problem tastes" versus "a refreshing toothpaste" versus "a toothpaste for intimate occasions." Situations then form the motivations against which brand benefit delivery is rated (as superbeliefs). Thus, for example, a person might have three separate brand *attitudes* for Crest, depending on three different motivations, disguised as "situations." Fortunately, most target audiences have a single overriding motivation, in which case only one brand attitude is operating.

**Preserving Benefit Statements in Consumer or Customer Language.** When placing benefits in questionnaires for brand ratings, the quantitative researcher must stay as close to the exact consumer or customer wording (from qualitative research interviews) as possible. This is where many crucial errors are made in quantitative research. Often, in an attempt to simplify benefit statements to suit questionnaires, the original consumer wording is lost. The sterile wording of rating scales in most questionnaires loses the meaning and emotionality of the actual benefit claims and produces misleading if not useless results. Ironically, sterilized ratings from questionnaires are then typically taken to the creative department with a request to "put these into consumer language." The copywriter, in effect, is being asked to recreate the original qualitative research that contained the consumer language in the first place!

The researcher must try as far as possible to preserve consumer or customer language in questionnaire rating scales. For instance, if consumers say they avoid "cheap" brands, this benefit belief *cannot* be represented on a questionnaire by the item "low price." The benefit statements must preserve the original meaning: indeed, three items may be required, such as "cheap quality," "low status," and "inexpensive." As a safeguard, it would be wise to let the qualitative researcher screen the benefit statements before they are finalized on the quantitative questionnaire.

**How Should the Benefits Be Rated?** Whereas different types of benefit rating (brand benefit delivery) scales may seem to produce similar results, in fact the communication relevance and thus managerial interpretation of the rating scale results is a vital methodological consideration. However, because benefits are again rated in the subsequent ad testing stage of advertising research (as a diagnostic measure), we will defer discussion of rating scales until Chapter 19, where measures for *all* communication effects are provided.

**Deciding Benefit Importance.** In the I-D-U analysis, selecting important (I) benefits is the first step. Quantitative benefit ratings yield brand delivery ratings (D), which can then be compared across brands for uniqueness of delivery (U).

Importance of benefits can be selected in two ways. One way is to have the *qualitative researcher infer* importance. The qualitative researcher's classification of low-importance and high-importance benefits—again, for the particular motivation—can then be used—with managers' judgment—to set up the I-D-U matrices. This is the method that we believe to be most valid.

Alternatively, many researchers prefer to *derive* importance statistically. (Note that we don't recommend asking consumers to rate importance directly.[42]) This is achieved by correlating *specific* brand benefit (delivery) ratings with *overall* ratings of the brand's suitability for various situations (that is, each overall superbelief or brand attitude). If a large number of benefits are rated, many of which will not be used in the final advertising strategy, the *simple correlation coefficients* should be used initially to screen benefits for importance.[43] Then, when a *smaller set* of final benefits is selected, a *regression* of benefit ratings on overall brand attitude should be computed and, because the benefits may interact, standardized regression weights should be used to decide benefit importance.[44] In using this procedure, however, the researcher must be careful to include only distinct benefits, *not* "support benefits" for a more general benefit, or else the inherent colinearity of the benefits will render the regression results nonsensical.[45]

Both ways of deciding benefit importance can be used and compared; however, we would not recommend using the statistically derived method alone. If only one method can be afforded, use the qualitative inference method.

**Brand Equity and Benefits.** In the quantitative phase of advertising strategy research, the manager may be interested in knowing the extent of the brand's brand equity in a specific brand attitude sense: the contribution of its "name," beyond its objective benefits, to brand attitude (see Chapter 5). Note that by using Moran's method, described earlier in the present chapter, we would know the brand's *overall* equity but we wouldn't know in which *benefits,* if any, the equity resides.

Park and Srinivasan[46] describe a reasonably straightforward method of estimating the brand-name equity contribution, as well as the "multiplier" effect that this equity has on subjective benefit belief delivery (that is, on benefit beliefs). We say "reasonably" because the method requires that objective ratings of the brand's benefits (uninfluenced by name) be obtained. In the candy bar brand-equity study in Chapter 5, chapter appendix 5A, this was done for $BATT_b$ by "blind" ratings of the products; the "blind" ratings could have been extended to produce objective ratings of the products' *benefit delivery* on the main benefits (the $B_{bi}$s) that characterize candy bars (flavor, chewiness, chocolate quality, and so forth). Alternatively, objective ratings of the brands' benefit deliveries (objective $B_{bi}$s) could be obtained from *experts,* who presumably are immune to brand-name effects. The expert approach—specifically, ratings from *Consumer Reports* magazine—was used in the electronics products brand-equity study in Chapter 5.

Assume that objective benefit delivery ratings *can* be obtained. Park and Srinivasan show how a 20-minute telephone (or face-to-face) interview survey can then be used to generate the subjective measures required to calculate brand-name equity and benefit-based equity. The key measures are given in the first three steps of their five-step procedure:

1. $BATT_b$ ratings of each brand on a scale from 1 to 10, with price ignored.

2. Dollar-metric scaling of the $BATT_b$ ratings by measuring each respondent's perceived price premium for his or her most perferred brand over his or her second most preferred brand. (Note that this is a quick and singular "static" measure, not a dual and dynamic measure as in Moran's upside and downside elasticity method described earlier.)

3. Benefit delivery ($B_{bi}$) ratings of each brand on the main benefits, also on scales from 1 to 10. Alternative benefit wordings can also be rated here, with the best of the alternatives, or an average, used for $B_{bi}$ (we recommend using the best alternative, as long as it is "FTC-able," as this gives a better indication for the best advertising benefit *claim*).

4. Importance weights ($E_i$) can be *inferred* from the regression weights of the $B_{bi}$s on $BATT_b$, or (less preferable) rated directly on scales from 1 to 10. (Do not use alternative wordings of the same benefit in a single regression, for the colinearity reason noted earlier.)

5. The $B_{bi}E_i$s are then dollar-metricized, as was $BATT_b$, so that overall brand-name equity ($= BATT_b - \Sigma$ objective $B_{bi}E_i$) and benefit-based equities ($= B_{bi}E_i -$ objective $B_{bi}E_i$) can be compared on a common scale—in fact, valued in dollars and cents!

In their study, brands of toothpaste (using dentists' ratings as the objective data) were shown to differ markedly in their brand-name equity effects. For example, the market leader, Crest, showed a 22¢ price premium overall, with 17¢ of this attributable to its brand name alone and only 5¢ attributable to the Crest name's favorable bias on benefit delivery. However, regarding the latter, the name "multiplied" every benefit belief (cavity prevention, plaque fighting, breath freshening, and teeth whitening) positively, to the

value of about 1¢ per benefit. Close-Up, a smaller brand, had an overall price deficit of 2¢ versus the average brand of toothpaste. This was found to be due mainly to negative equity of the Close-Up brand name overall, 5¢, offset by a less negative effect of its name on benefit delivery as perceived by consumers than that perceived by dentists(!), thus producing a small positive effect of 3¢; the net negative effect was therefore 2¢.

Clearly, this detailed quantitative brand equity research is very insightful for deciding a brand's future brand benefit strategy.

### Profiling the Target Audience Decision Maker

The AC&P plan also calls for the manager to develop a personal profile of the target audience decision maker—that is, of the initiator, influencer, decider, purchaser, or user, and perhaps gatekeeper and negative and positive decider in industrial marketing, to whom the advertising communications or promotion campaign is directed (see Chapter 4).

A fairly good profile of the decision maker in terms of obvious demographics and obvious psychographic characteristics may be evident from the qualitative research. However, a detailed profile that also includes personality traits and, most important, media exposure, requires quantitative research.

Table 18.6 indicates the types of profile measures, under each personal-characteristics category, that are useful to advertisers. Detailed measures and their applications are beyond the scope of this book.[47] However, some general methodological observations about profile measures are offered below, and we *do* describe methods for direct matching of media exposure.

**Demographics.** Demographic variables—covering geographic, individual, and group-membership personal characteristics of the decision maker—are useful for copywriters in developing a better idea of whom they are addressing. (Copywriters regard the "pen-picture" of the typical target audience individual as the most important contribution of advertising research.[48]) Traditionally and still commonly, demographics are also used in media vehicle selection—although, as shown in Chapter 17, demographic matching usually produces less accurate target audience reach than direct matching of media exposure.

Statistically, to develop a demographic profile of target audiences, you simply cross-tabulate each demographic variable's categories (for example, age groups) by prospect group membership (for example, single-brand loyals, multibrand loyals, and so forth). The manager then considers the percentage of individuals in each demographic category (not the mean level, which is too ambiguous and in any case means nothing for nominal-category demographic variables such as sex or race).

**Psychographics.** Psychographic measures come in two varieties, and both can be useful in gaining a more detailed picture of the target audience decision maker, as well as in deciding what background stimuli to put in advertisements.

*General* psychographic inventories cover a broad range of activities, interests, and opinions (A-I-O measures) that apply universally to all consumers. Two cautions: First, as explained in Chapter 3, you should never try to develop target audiences using psychographics as the primary basis.[49] Segmentation by awareness-attitude-behavior groups comes first, as in our five prospect buyer groups (or their respective subgroups as identified in this chapter), then psychographics can be used to describe *these* groups. Second, you should not use *shortened* inventories of psychographic typologies—either syndicated ones such as VALS or VALS II *or* custom-designed inventories.[50] In quantitative research, use the *full* set of psychographic items.

*Category-specific* psychographic inventories can be constructed from the prior qualitative research. In the discussion outline provided earlier, consumers are asked to give their opinions on what types of people do or do not use the product category and particular brands. From their opinions, and from any previous research discovered in the situation audit, category-specific items can be compiled.

Statistical analysis of psychographic profile data generally will consist of an initial factor analysis (as there may be over 200 individual measures or items) followed by cross-tabulation against target audience prospect groups. What, on the psychographic side, should be cross-tabulated? Some researchers favor using factor scores from the factor analysis, dividing these into categories such as high negative, moderate negative, neutral, moderate positive, and high positive. This is probably the most reliable method, but the practical validity to copywriters can be obscured when summary factors are used instead of individual psychographic items. More practically, but less reli-

ably, high-loading items on each factor can be cross-tabulated.[51]

**Personality Traits.** For most personality traits of interest to advertising researchers, highly reliable measures are available in the psychological literature. The essential step in using personality traits to profile target audience decision makers is not measurement, which is relatively straightforward, but rather specifying how each trait, or constellation of traits, relates *causally* to persuasion.[52] Statistically, each multi-item trait measure can be summed to a total trait score that is then divided into categories, such as low versus high, and cross-tabulated against target audience prospect groups.

### How to Gather Direct Matching Data

Direct matching data on media exposure is the best way to select media vehicles (see Chapter 17). Direct matching information can be gathered during the quantitative advertising strategy phase of research, simultaneously with the awareness, attitude, and behavior data used to define the target audience, by including a section on media exposure in the questionnaire.

Alternatively, a *separate media exposure study* can be conducted. It is worth conducting a separate media exposure study if media exposure data were not collected during the quantitative advertising strategy research. In fact, it is more efficient to conduct a separate study on media exposure *after* one or more target audiences have been identified from the strategy research because, now, awareness, attitude, and behavior "marker" variables (see Table 18.7) can be used to briefly screen target audience groups, leaving more time for detailed media exposure recording.

A separate media exposure study can be conducted for the equivalent price of about one national, prime-time TV commercial insertion—about $120,000. The resulting direct matching data almost surely will save many times that amount in increased media plan accuracy.

Data selection methods for media exposure studies comprise two good options and two others which should not be used.

**Panel Method (Diary) Is Best.** The best method for direct-matching data collection is through the use of a consumer or customer panel in which participants maintain diary records of their media exposure.[53] Continuous diary measures are more reliable than one-shot questionnaires or interview measures, because memory for media exposure, like memory for brand purchases, is not very long-lasting. Also, the advertiser may wish to investigate a very large number of media vehicle options, now including Websites. It is easy for respondents using a diary to indicate these options because the vehicles are arranged by day and time period.

Further, the media planner wishes to know *how often* each vehicle is watched, listened to, or read, so that vehicle exposure frequency can be related to effective frequency of advertising exposure. Vehicle exposure frequency is more accurately recorded in the diary panel method than by a one-shot estimate of recalled or estimated frequency of exposure. (Using Nielsen or IRI, this can be done mechanically by TV meters for TV programs and by bar code scanning for radio programs and print vehicles.) For media planning, one-shot estimates overstate diary records for TV program viewing frequency by about 20 percent (for example, 5 rather than 4 exposures) and for "educational" programs like news or documentaries by at least double (for example, 2 rather than 1 exposure).[54] An immediately updated diary minimizes the need to remember frequency (however, recalled frequency has an important function in campaign tracking, as will be explained in Chapter 20). The diary record of media vehicle exposure should be kept for at least one and preferably two or three advertising cycles (for reliability).

*MLI Method.* Best of all diary methods is Australia's Media Leverage Index service, provided by Roy Morgan Research company. In this method, 1,000 people are recruited nationwide each week, and only for a week, to complete a media diary and a purchase diary, with room for customized awareness and attitude questions to be included. The cumulative sample size is very large (4,500 a month, covering, for instance, 450 teenagers a month) and, because the service is syndicated, the price is very reasonable at about $30,000 (U.S.) per product category. As part of the service, MLI provides a media vehicle selection output which ranks vehicles according to their target audience reach (and *you* can define the target audience), and reach divided by vehicle advertising cost if desired (target audience percentage reach per dollar, or cost per target audience GRP). Similar services are likely to be initiated in other major world markets.

**One-Shot Questionnaires.** The practical alternative to panels for most advertisers is to conduct their own survey of the target audience(s) with a customized questionnaire which asks for brand communication effects and action information for all brands in the category (to classify target audiences), and at the same time asks for media exposure and frequency of exposure for all likely media types and vehicles (hence it is a "one-shot" single-source survey). Demographics, geodemographics and other potential target audience profiling information can also be requested (see Chapter 4) if this was not obtained during quantitative advertising strategy research. The sample size has to be large (500 or so) and, as mentioned previously, such a survey can be expensive but is very reasonable considering the likely increase in accuracy of target audience reach and the resulting savings in the media budget. Assuming TV is a likely media type in the media plan, it is worthwhile to repeat the survey annually after new programs have had the chance to be accepted or dropped (predictable about 12 weeks into the new season[55]). With *other* media types, people's vehicle preferences are relatively stable and so an annual survey is adequate. Because of the length of the questionnaire, a "drop off and pick up" method, with an attractive incentive, is advisable.

*Media Types.* Suppose you're designing your own direct matching questionnaire: On a questionnaire or personal interview, specific media vehicle options can be very time-consuming to go through. In an attempt to shortcut this problem, some researchers have advocated the use of broad vehicle *types*, to which similar vehicles can then be related. We caution against the use of vehicle types for the following reasons, by media.

For TV, vehicle types might be documentaries, police-detective shows, sitcoms, and so forth.[56] The use of vehicle types may be roughly indicative for broadcast media because these media are "free" to the audience and there is virtually no limit, for instance, on the number of sitcoms an individual viewer may choose to watch. But a more accurate alternative for one-shot TV exposure, we have found, is to photocopy the previous week's TV listings and have respondents check off the programs they watched and state how often they've watched them in the last 4 weeks. For movies and specials, which are one-time showings, the question has to be modified to refer to "this type of program" (thus movies and specials are the *only* programs that have to be typed). This method seems much more accurate than total reliance on TV program types.

Radio stations can be quickly narrowed down from a list to those stations the respondent listens to—usually no more than six. These can then be asked about by daypart to gauge frequency of station exposure, and by location (home, car, work) for IMC media tie-ins. Again, this is much more accurate than "station types."

For print media, the use of vehicle types is not appropriate because these vehicles are not free and there is a substitution effect. For instance, among the weekly news type of magazine, most individuals are unlikely to subscribe to both *Time* and *Newsweek*. With print media, all the individual vehicles should be listed.

**Single-Source Syndicated Services Are Too General.** Syndicated services that supply media and product data on the same sample of respondents—hence the name "single-source" data—are not, in most cases, a satisfactory substitute for a customized media exposure study. Services such as SMRB or MRI in the United States, or TGI in the United Kingdom, for example, provide cross-tabulations between brand usage (heavy, medium, light, nonusers) and media vehicle audiences. Nielsen and IRI focus on TV media vehicles but have recently added print vehicles through home-scan panels. But the problem is with the product usage side of the data. As we have seen in our discussion of target audience definition in Chapter 3, and again in this chapter with the 12 subgroups, neither category *usage* nor single-brand *usage* can provide sufficient definition of a target audience for advertising communications or for promotions. An awareness, attitude, and usage (behavior) definition must be used to identify the prospective target audience groups, as in Chapter 3 or the present chapter, which may further be delineated by a demographic or psychographic profile variables (see Chapters 3 and 4). Syndicated services (the exception is Media Leverage Index, MLI, described above) do not provide this degree of target audience definition.

However, some syndicated services may accept customized target audience identification questions if you pay for them. This is an option worth exploring—but without it, syndicated services are not much help for direct matching.

**Data Fusion Is Not Worth the Effort.** What should not in general be attempted is "data fusion" using demographics. This is an attempt to "match" respondents from two separate surveys—such as a product survey and a media survey—by their demographic similarity. Matching (actually, pairing) is possible since each survey collects the same basic demographic information. However, fusion methods have had a poor track record: the gains for direct matching are delicate enough without trying artificial matching, and especially through a third factor like demographics.[57]

In conclusion regarding media exposure measurement, single-source syndicated service data are usually too general for anything other than a rough idea of which media vehicles grossly defined target audiences are exposed to. The best alternative for the specificity of media planning advocated in this book is a customized media exposure study using either a panel, preferably, or a one-shot questionnaire survey.

In summary regarding quantitative research, we can see that quantitative research *adds* to qualitative research in preparing the advertising strategy. It buys refinements that qualitative research alone can't provide (including, most importantly, direct media measurement) and it is therefore of immense value to the large advertiser.

### ADVERTISING STRATEGY SUMMARY

The output from advertising strategy research—be it intuitive, or qualitative only, or qualitative plus quantitative—should not only be fitted into the AC&P plan but should also be prepared in the form of an *advertising strategy summary* (recognizing that the "advertising strategy" may well be implemented with advertising communications or promotions, or both in a full IMC plan). This is what managers refer to when they talk about summarizing the advertising strategy (for each target audience) in "one page." In practice, this is the document that we recommend be used as the *creative brief.*

The advertising strategy summary should briefly describe the main characteristics of the target audience at the top of the page, then summarize the essential content, only, of the four steps in the buyer response sequence, that is, exposure → processing →

communication effects and brand position → target audience action, in list form.

An example of an advertising strategy summary is shown in Table 18.9 for a campaign for American Express (Personal) Green Card. The strategy is addressed to a high-involvement target audience, new category users, to attempt to persuade them to apply for the card. Note the emphasis on acceptance of the card's brand position in processing ("business-emergency solution") and the fact that all five communication effects are objectives for this campaign.

To illustrate the point that a separate advertising strategy must be prepared for each target audience, a second summary strategy is shown in Table 18.10.

This describes a campaign for a low-involvement target audience—current loyal American Express cardholders—to stimulate increased usage. The brand position for this target audience is a *category need* positioning ("essential 'personal effects' item"). The emphasis here is on learning, for increased brand awareness (linking the brand name to the category need) and for maintaining (their low-involvement) brand attitude, with the other communication effects already being at full strength.

Note that the advertising strategy summary, while a very useful document for quick reference by managers, cannot replace the detailed advertising strategy spelled out in the AC&P plan. The AC&P plan's first

---

**TABLE 18.9**

**AN ADVERTISING STRATEGY SUMMARY FOR AMERICAN EXPRESS GREEN CARD (ACQUISITION)**

*Target audience:* Noncardholders who qualify on income requirement (new category users). Current attitude to AE Green neutral; target attitude top-box positive. Primarily men, with a wide range of occupations, lifestyles, and personalities.

1. *Exposure*
   - See and hear AE Green "Acquisition" commercial on TV
   - Attentive programs, e.g., *60 Minutes*
2. *Processing*
   - Accept category need for credit cards to avoid emergency payment problems
   - Learn to recognize card and the take-one "blue box" and typical "blue box" locations
   - Accept attitudinal message that AE Green is "for me," based on "business-emergency solution" positioning, portrayed by the benefits of having card for unexpected business lunch, extended business trip, and emergency purchases when on business trip
   - Accept intention to look for and fill out application

3. *Communication Objectives*
   - Category need: sell (problem avoidance)
   - Brand awareness: recognition
   - Brand attitude: create (high-involvement, problem avoidance)
   - Brand purchase intention: generate
   - Purchase facilitation: distribution
4. *Target Audience Action*
   - Find application box and fill out AE Green application form and mail it

---

**TABLE 18.10**

**AN ADVERTISING STRATEGY SUMMARY FOR AMERICAN EXPRESS GREEN CARD (USAGE)**

*Target audience:* AE Green cardholders who use the card less than once a month. Mostly nonexecutives and spouses of cardholders. Meet income requirement but with a wide range of other sociodemographics.

1. *Exposure*
   - Hear AE Green "Usage" commercial on radio
   - Moderately attentive programs in morning time slots
2. *Processing*
   - Learn AE Green Card as "essential 'personal effects' item" response to situational category stimulus of leaving house (recall "leaving house . . . take AE Card" from tag line "Don't leave home without it")
   - Learn (relearn) how versatile the AE Card is

3. *Communication Objectives*
   - Brand awareness: recall
   - Brand attitude: maintain (low-involvement, problem avoidance)
4. *Target Audience Action*
   - Increased frequency of carrying AE Green (assumed to increase chances of usage when usage situations naturally occur)

three sections (see Appendix) are needed in *detail* for concept development research, management judgment ad testing, and for ad testing with the target audience (see the next chapter). The advertising strategy summary can, however, serve nicely as the creative brief.

## NOTES

1. For other measures, see L. Y. S. Lin, Brand equity, profitability, price elasticity and repeat rate, *Marketing and Research Today,* 1993, *21* (2), pp. 69–74.

2. For an overview and evaluation of simulated test market procedures, see K. J. Clancy, R. S. Shulman, and M. M. Wolf, *Simulated Test Marketing,* New York: Lexington Books, 1994.

3. The term "partitioning" apparently was introduced by The Hendry Corporation in various industry presentations, some of which are compiled in a book by the company, *Speaking of Hendry,* New York: The Hendry Corporation, 1976. "Hierarchical market definition" is a more general term for the several techniques that have much the same purpose as partitioning; see G. L. Urban and J. R. Hauser, *Design and Marketing of New Products,* 2nd ed., Englewood Cliffs, NJ: Prentice-Hall, 1993, chapter 4.

4. For a discussion of conditions of application of various measures of partitioning, see G. S. Day, A. D. Shocker, and R. K. Srivastava, Customer-oriented approaches to identifying product markets, *Journal of Marketing,* 1979, *43* (4), pp. 8–19.

5. For example, see J. A. Howard, The concept of product hierarchy, Working paper, Graduate School of Business, Columbia University, New York, 1981.

6. For example, see P. E. Green and V. R. Rao, *Applied Multidimensional Scaling: Comparison of Approaches and Algorithms,* New York: Holt, Rinehart and Winston, 1972.

7. See G. L. Urban and J. R. Hauser, same reference as in note 3, especially chapter 4 but also chapter 11.

8. For example, see E. A. Pessemier, *Product Management: Strategy and Organization,* Santa Barbara, CA: Wiley/Hamilton, 1972.

9. For example, see I. S. Currim, R. J. Meyer, and N. T. Le, Disaggregate tree-structured modeling of consumer choice data, *Journal of Marketing Research,* 1988, *25* (3), pp. 253–265.

10. C. Fraser and J. W. Bradford, Competitive market structure analysis: Principal partitioning of revealed substitutabilities, *Journal of Consumer Research,* 1983, *10* (1), pp. 15–30.

11. For fmcg products, several of the retail sales services have additional services that track product category

pricing specifically, including price-off promotions. Interested readers should contact suppliers such as those listed in Figure 18.1 for further details.

12. W. T. Moran, Insights from pricing research, in E. B. Bailey, ed., *Pricing Practices and Strategies,* New York: The Conference Board, 1978, pp. 7–13.

13. Our labeling differs somewhat from Moran's here in that he sometimes refers to downside elasticity as "substitutability," whereas we have called it "uniqueness" (see our Chapter 2). Of course, uniqueness is the inverse of substitutability, but we think uniqueness is a clearer term. Note again that "low" downside elasticity indicates greater uniqueness of the brand.

14. G. M. Allenby and P. R. Rossi, Quality perceptions and asymmetric switching between brands, *Marketing Science,* 1991, *10* (3), pp. 185–204.

15. See R. C. Blattberg and K. Wisniewski, Price-induced patterns of competition, *Marketing Science,* 1989, *8* (4), pp. 291–310; W. A. Kamakura and G. J. Russell, A probabilistic choice model for market segmentation and elasticity structure, *Journal of Marketing Research,* 1989, *26* (4), pp. 379–390; and N. C. Mohn, Pricing research for decision making, *Marketing Research,* 1995, *7* (1), pp. 11–19, for clear examples in the soft-drink market worldwide.

16. Named after its originator, the esteemed professor Frank M. Bass. See F. M. Bass, A new product growth model for consumer durables, *Management Science,* 1969, *15* (1), pp. 215–227. For an update, see V. Mahajan, E. Muller, and F. M. Bass, New product diffusion models in marketing: A review and directions for research, *Journal of Marketing,* 1990, *54* (1), pp. 1–26.

17. V. Mahajan et al., same reference as in previous note.

18. Perhaps most clearly given in the Mahajan et al. reference in note 18. Readers may note that most versions of the model give the formula with $N_t$ rather than $N_{t-1}$, but we think our version is clearer because $n_t$, the number of adopters in the present period, correctly depends on the cumulative number of adopters in the *previous* period, $N_{t-1}$.

19. F. Sultan, J. U. Farley, and D. R. Lehmann, A meta-analysis of applications of diffusion models, *Journal of Marketing Research,* 1990, *27* (1), pp. 70–77.

20. F. Sultan et al., same reference as previous note. Also P. J. Lenk and A. G. Rao, New models from old: Forecasting new product adoption by Hierarchical Bayes Procedures, *Marketing Science,* 1990, *9* (1), pp. 42–53.

21. W. J. Infosino, Forecasting new product sales from likelihood of purchase ratings, *Marketing Science,* 1986, *5* (4), pp. 372–384.

22. Use the high-involvement purchase intention weights or, if available, weights based on previous new brands in your industry.

23. M. Pendergrast, *For God, Country and Coca-Cola,* London: George Weidenfeld and Nicholson, 1993. All marketers should read this fascinating and informative book.

24. T. J. Watson, Jr. and P. Petre, *Father, Son & Co.: My Life at IBM and Beyond,* New York: Bantam, 1990.

25. Penned by the great McCann-Erickson copywriter Archie Lee from his earlier 1923 line "Pause and refresh yourself," the phrase "The pause that refreshes" was used by Coke as its main copy line from 1929 until about 1950. See M. Pendergrast, same reference as note 23, pp. 164–165.

26. See J. M. Fouss and E. Solomon, Salespeople as researchers: Help or hazard? *Journal of Marketing,* 1980, *44* (3), pp. 36–39; and A. Sharma and D. M. Lambert, How accurate are salespersons' perceptions of their customers? *Industrial Marketing Management,* 1994, *23* (4), pp. 357–365.

27. In plotting trends in the relationship between advertising and sales, the manager has to be alert for the possibility of advertising "carryover" to future sales. The presence of substantial carryover, or customer "holdover" with print advertising that may not be read or acted upon immediately, can make a *current* plot look as if there is no relationship between advertising and sales when really there is a relationship. Trial-and-error plotting with some simple carryover or "lag" functions, such as $S_t = \text{base sales} + .57A_t + .29A_{t-1} + .14A_{t-2}$ wherein the coefficients of current and prior advertising add up to 1.0, with advertising having in this case about 40 percent carryover, can often reveal carryover effects.

28. See G. L. Lilien, P. Kotler, and K. S. Moorthy, *Marketing Models,* Englewood Cliffs, NJ: Prentice-Hall, 1992, chapter 11, for an overview of BRANDAID and similar models.

29. Quantitative (survey) methods are purely descriptive, not causal. The experimental or hypothetico-deductive method of hypothesis generation and painstaking testing *is* capable of yielding causal explanations, but in its usual form, it takes far too much effort and time. Qualitative researchers essentially engage in a fast (and sometimes unreliable) form of the hypothetico-deductive method. For an excellent analysis of this point, see B. J. Calder, Focus groups and the nature of qualitative research, *Journal of Marketing Research,* 1977, *14* (3), pp. 353–364.

30. A. Griffin and J. R. Hauser, The voice of the customer, *Marketing Science,* 1993, *12* (1), pp. 1–27.

31. Qualitative researchers use a variety of supplementary techniques to stimulate ideas. Some of these are described in the "special techniques" section following shortly. Also see, for example, D. N. Bellenger, K. L. Bernhardt, and J. L. Goldstucker, *Qualitative Research in Marketing,* Chicago: American Marketing Association, 1976.

32. Witness, for instance, the confused state of the family decision-making literature in consumer behavior—largely due to superficial surveys rather than a more valid investigatory method such as evaluative participation.

33. R. E. Speckman and L. W. Stern, Environmental uncertainty and buying group structure: An empirical investigation, *Journal of Marketing,* 1979, *43* (4), pp. 54–64. See also A. K. Kohli and G. Zaltman, Measuring multiple buying influences, *Industrial Marketing Management,* 1988, *17* (3), pp. 197–204.

34. In qualitative research, retrospective protocols provide a sufficiently valid indicator of whether the brand choice is low- or high-involvement. For those who want a more structured questionnaire approach, consideration of multiple alternatives, multiple attributes, and overall decision time appear to be good indicators of high-involvement choices, though note that in many cases the choice may be whether to accept or reject a single offer rather than multiple alternatives. For the questionnaire approach, see E. Cooper-Martin, Measures of cognitive effort, *Marketing Letters,* 1994, *5* (1), pp. 43–56.

35. On this score, we'd like to specifically recommend *against* the newly popular "automated content analysis" programs, most recently in "neural network" form, for analyzing GDI or IDI data; for example, see K. Moore, R. Burbach, and R. Heeler, Using neural nets to analyze qualitative data, *Marketing Research,* 1995, *7* (1), pp. 35–39. All these programs can do is *count,* and superficially at that. They cannot *interpret* the consumer data and produce the sort of advertising inputs that we require. See also our "special techniques" section, following.

36. Adapted from E. Tauber, Reduce new product failures: Measure needs as well as purchase interest, *Journal of Marketing,* 1973, *37* (3), pp. 61–70. Also see J. R. Kieff, When research does make a difference?, in D. C. Stewart, ed., *APA Division 23 Proceedings,* Washington, DC: American Psychological Association, 1984, pp. 54–55.

37. S. Young and B. Feigin, Using the benefit chain for improved strategy formulation, *Journal of Marketing,* 1975, *39* (3), pp. 70–74.

38. For the classic articles on laddering, or means-end, theory, see J. Gutman, A means-end chain model based on consumer categorization processes, *Journal of Marketing,* 1982, *46* (1), pp. 60–72; T. J. Reynolds and J. Gutman, Advertising is image management, *Journal of Advertising Research,* 1984, *24* (1), pp. 27–37; and T. J.

Reynolds and J. Gutman, Laddering theory, method, analysis and interpretation, *Journal of Advertising Research,* 1988, *28* (1), pp. 11–31. These articles and many applications of laddering are available in T. J. Reynolds and J. C. Olson, *Understanding Your Customer: Means-End Theory and Practice,* Hillsdale, NJ: Lawrence Erlbaum Associates, in press. A chapter by Rossiter and Percy in that book compares the means-end model with the a-b-e micromodel of benefit focus.

39. Again, see the article by B. J. Calder, same reference as note 29.

40. Quantitative researchers ideally should use two phases of research: a first phase, consisting of "exploratory quantitative" interviews with a sample of about 200 consumers to develop reliable target audience profile measures and also benefit or motivation segments (see Chapter 4); followed by a second phase of "quantitative probability" research interviews using the reliable measures with a national probability sample of about 1,000 consumers, which includes a media exposure inventory. See L. Percy, How market segmentation guides advertising strategy, *Journal of Advertising Research,* 1976, *16* (5), pp. 11–22, for a description of this two-phase quantitative research.

41. R. Alsop, Brand loyalty is rarely blind loyalty, *The Wall Street Journal,* October 19, 1989, p. B8.

42. The direct or "self-explicated" method, which asks consumers to *rate* importance, tends to produce nonvalid results because consumers often do not have good insight into how they actually make their brand choices (note that the qualitative researcher *infers* this and doesn't necessarily take what consumers say at face value). For damaging evidence on direct consumer measures of importance, see J. Jacard and D. Sheng, A comparison of six methods for assessing the perceived consequences of behavioral intentions, *Journal of Experimental Social Psychology,* 1984, *20* (1), pp. 1–28.

43. See, for example, P. E. Green and C. M. Shaffer, Ad copy testing, *Journal of Advertising Research,* 1983, *23* (5), pp. 73–80.

44. A division into unimportant, low-importance, and high-importance benefits is usually sufficient. The predictive validity of importance weights tends to be insensitive to small numerical differences in regression coefficients. See for example, J. M. Blin and J. A. Dodson, The relationship between attributes, brand preference, and choice, *Management Science,* 1980, *26* (6), 606–619. However, *qualitative* research inference might suggest a finer division of importance levels, and this should be examined.

45. See G. L. Urban and J. R. Hauser, same reference as in note 3, their chapter 10, p. 270, for discussion of this tricky point.

46. C. S. Park and V. Srinivasan, A survey-based method for measuring and understanding brand equity and its extendability, *Journal of Marketing Research,* 1994, *31* (2), pp. 271–288. The ratings were thoroughly normalized in their analysis, but we have omitted this from our summary description for clarity's sake.

47. The article by L. Percy (see note 40) indicates how these profile measures can be applied. The details are too numerous and complex to summarize here.

48. The most usual method of writing copy is for the copywriter to imagine a "dialogue" with his or her temporary mental "other." See A. J. Kover, Copywriters' implicit theories of communication: An exploration, *Journal of Consumer Research,* 1995, *21* (4), pp. 596–611.

49. Psychographic segmentation rarely works in practice as a primary basis for selecting target audiences, and when it does, it is generally because of relationships with, or direct inclusion of (for example, the VALS system), *demographic* measures. For a negative appraisal by a researcher who has tried psychographic segmentation many times, see S. Yuspeh, Slamming syndicated data, *Advertising Age,* May 17, 1984, magazine section.

50. A common advertising-industry practice is to use "marker items" from a previous psychographic study to classify respondents into psychographic types in later studies. Shortened measures are so unreliable as to be useless if not dangerously misleading. For an example using a carefully constructed customized inventory rather than a syndicated one, yet still failing, see S. Yuspeh and G. Fein, Can segments be born again? *Journal of Advertising Research,* 1982, *22* (3), pp. 13–22.

51. In either case, the factor analysis should be internally "cross-validated" (checked for reliability) by conducting separate analyses on split halves of the sample.

52. The functional relationship of selected personality traits to persuasion (brand attitude and brand purchase intention) is exemplified in L. Percy and J. R. Rossiter, *Advertising Strategy: A Communication Theory Approach,* New York: Praeger, 1980, pp. 31–48.

53. In a useful and less fatiguing variation of continuous panels, MLI (see below) in Australia uses monthly diaries, with a new sample of consumers drawn each month. Aggregate results are comparable across monthly "waves."

54. A. S. C. Ehrenberg and G. J. Goodhardt, Attitudes to episodes and programs, *Journal of the Market Research Society,* 1981, *23* (4), pp. 189–208.

55. P. Graham, Making it work better—integrating ad research into the marketing and media plan, *Admap,* February 1992, pp. 22–25. Failing programs have the same trial rate (penetration) as successful programs but a

lower *repeat* rate, which is quite reliably evidenced after 12 weekly episodes.

56. D. H. Gensch and B. Ranganathan, Evaluation of television program content for the purpose of promotional segmentation, *Journal of Marketing Research,* 1974, *11* (4), pp. 390–398.

57. However, one fusion method being tried in the United Kingdom is worthy of note; it fuses two *panels,* a TV-viewing panel and a purchase panel, thus acquiring the advantage of continuous panel data, by matching respondents on a one-shot TV-*viewing* questionnaire—that is, *not* through demographics. In a test of this TV viewing–fused source, an 18 percent improvement in accuracy of reaching brand buyers compared with a random program selection, and a 6 percent improvement over upmarket women grocery buyers as a demographic selection, were shown (the brand was Nestle's Gold Blend instant coffee, which is the Tasters Choice brand in the United States). But even this type of fusion may be wasted effort. With single-source panels now available through research companies such as Nielsen, IRI, Mediamark, or TN AGB, there is no need for this complex fusion procedure. However, syndicated single-source panels have the "bluntness" problem described in the text. See A. Roberts, TV exposure, brand buying and ad effects, *Admap,* June 1994, pp. 31–37.

## DISCUSSION QUESTIONS

See Discussion Questions at end of Chapter 20.

## FURTHER READING

Lucas, D. B., and Britt, S. H. *Measuring Advertising Effectiveness.* New York: McGraw-Hill, 1963.

This text, now out of print but available in libraries, is the *only* good book ever published on advertising research. Even for the modern manager, it remains a gold mine of information about what types of research to do and when, lacking only some of the newer statistical techniques.

Calder, B. J. Focus groups and the nature of qualitative research. *Journal of Marketing Research,* 1977, *14*(3), pp. 353–364.

This article provides enlightening reading (for academics) on the validity of qualitative research. Readers will note that the type of qualitative research required for developing advertising strategy is, in his terminology, "analytic" qualitative research. We will take this opportunity to emphasize that qualitative research, while virtually essential for the *development* of advertising (this chapter and first section of next chapter), should never be used to *test* advertisements (next chapter) once they have been prepared.

Walker, R. (ed.), *Applied Qualitative Research.* Hants, UK: Gower, 1985.

This book provides the best overall coverage of qualitative research theory, practice, and analysis. Essential reading for qualitative researchers.

Goldman, A. E., and Schwartz McDonald, S. *The Group Depth Interview: Principles and Practice.* Englewood Cliffs, NJ: Prentice-Hall, 1987.

This is a very good book on the practice of conducting and analyzing qualitative strategy research, written by two experienced qualitative research specialists at one of the nation's leading research firms. It offers especially good coverage (unlike most other qualitative research texts) of "analytic" qualitative research.

Percy, L. How market segmentation guides advertising strategy. *Journal of Advertising Research,* 1976, *16*(5), pp. 11–22.

This article is for advanced practitioners with statistical training. Although it favors benefit segmentation rather than the awareness-attitude-behavior segmentation we now advocate, it illustrates the sophisticated use of target audience profile research in detail unavailable from other sources.

# CHAPTER 19

# Concept Development Research, MJTs, and Ad Testing

**A**dvertising strategy must, of course, be reflected in the ads, adlike events, or promotion offers to be employed in the campaign. *Concept development research* helps in this translation process. Then *management judgment tests* (MJTs) provide a low-cost way of pretesting ads that also allows *management's* input into the ad selection process before it's too late. *Ad testing* proper provides additional assurance from the *target audience* that creative executions of advertisements are "on strategy"—that is, that they are capable of producing the communication effects that will achieve the communication objectives and positioning for the brand. All three forms of research are also called "pretesting" because they are done *before* the ads are placed in media.

After reading this chapter, you should:

- Know how and when to use concept development research.
- See the value of conducting a management judgment test prior to the target audience ad test.
- Know how to choose the overall design, methodology, and measures for an ad test.
- Know how to analyze the results and how to decide what action should be taken as a result of the test.

We begin the chapter with an example of pretesting research that illustrates all three forms of it. The chapter itself is in three sections. First we describe the methodologies of concept development research. Then we describe a preliminary method of ad testing—the MJT. Finally, we explain quantitative ad testing: we examine what ad testing actually is, what it can and cannot do, and how much it costs. Once it is decided that ad testing is worthwhile, the manager then has to select a design (overall) and measures (specifically) to fit the communication objectives; a considerable part of the chapter is devoted to how to do this. We conclude the coverage of ad testing by explaining how to analyze the results so as to select advertisements for the campaign.

## AN EXAMPLE: AT&T'S "COST OF VISIT" CAMPAIGN

From 1975 to 1980, the leading U.S. telecommunications company, AT&T, spent an estimated 1 million dollars[1] on advertising research—just to develop and test its "Cost of visit" campaign. The result: an estimated profit increase of $22 million per year. This case history, reported in detail by Kuritsky, Little, Silk, and Bassman,[2] provides a useful overview and convincing evidence of why concept development research and ad testing are a worthwhile investment for all advertisers—though on a smaller scale, of course, for smaller advertisers.

In the late 1960s, AT&T had a monopoly in the U.S. long-distance telephone service market and was advertising with its well-known and highly profitable "Reach out" campaign (developed using the theory of random creativity, as noted in Chapter 7). During the early 1970s, the Federal Communications Commission (FCC) deregulated the long-distance telephone service market; other carriers entered, and price competition became fierce. AT&T was annually tracking its advertising (see Chapter 20), and in this tracking detected a sizable segment of residential customers who had reasons to call long-distance but were limiting the number and duration of their calls due to perceived high cost. AT&T called this segment "light users"; they would be equivalent in our terminology to brand switchers, in that they switch between calling on AT&T and not calling (frequent callers, or "heavy users," would be AT&T brand loyals). As heavy users were already calling at presumably maximum frequency, AT&T's action objective was to increase the calling behavior, in terms of number and duration of calls, of light users.

AT&T's annual tracking survey included 68 benefit belief statements reflecting various beliefs about long-distance calling. Using factor analysis (a part of quantitative advertising strategy research; see previous chapter), these were reduced to 17 relatively distinct benefit beliefs. From these, the management and research team judgmentally selected five that seemed most promising as alternative positioning strategies (potential main benefits, Zs, in the X-YZ macropositioning model, and simultaneously important benefits, I, if not entirely unique benefits, U, in the I-D-U mesopositioning model; see Chapter 6). The action objective of these benefits was to increase long-distance calling by light users while not affecting heavy users. Then, with the help of three focus groups (GDIs) as *concept development research* (this chapter), the five benefit strategies were written up as five creative ideas or, more correctly, benefit "propositions" (for high-involvement/informational strategies such as this, verbal propositions can be suitable[3]) as follows, to which we've added comments on motivation and micropositioning in parentheses:

**A**. *Lifeline:* "It's easy to drift apart when you're far away from family and friends. Long-distance can help keep you together." (problem avoidance, $e^- \rightarrow b$)

**B**. *Cost of Visit:* "Many people are still depriving themselves of long-distance because they think it costs too much. If they only knew how cheap it really is!" (mixed approach-avoidance, $e^- \rightarrow b$)

**C**. *Feel Good:* "When you're feeling happy, it [long-distance calling] can make you even happier. When you're feeling down, it can cheer you up. However you feel, long-distance can make you feel better." (both sensory gratification, $b \rightarrow e^+$, and problem removal, $e^- \rightarrow b$)

**D**. *Letters:* "When you stop to think of the advantages of long-distance calling, you've got to wonder why some people still only write letters." (positioning the brand against the dominant brand in the long-distance communication category, X, using incomplete satisfaction, $e^- \rightarrow b$)

**E**. *Comfortable:* "A lot of people don't realize how easy it is to have a relaxed long-distance conversation." (probably mixed approach avoidance, $e^- \rightarrow b$)

Each of the five propositions was then produced by the advertising agency as an "animatic" rough TV commercial—drawings on slides videotaped in sequence with accompanying audio. Strictly speaking, in our terminology, this was when the strategies became *creative ideas* (see Chapter 6) and in fact became *one execution* of each creative idea (examining only one execution per creative idea is a likely and common error in concept development research—see later in this chapter). For instance, the "Cost of visit" creative idea was to show one person calling a friend or relative while depicting and mentioning at least three key elements to dramatize the main proposition (see B above): a plausible reason why the two people should keep in touch; surprise (the intended emotion shift was from apprehensiveness to surprise; see Chapter 9) at the actual low cost of long-distance calls, especially in off-peak periods (in the 1982 launch commercials, this was stated as $4.00 or less for a 20-minute call); and that the prices quoted were tax-inclusive. One *execution* of this creative idea was the TV commercial shown in Figure 19.1. We note again (see Chapter 7) that many other creative ideas could have been created to dramatize the "Cost of visit" main benefit, and indeed to dramatize the other main-benefit concepts being considered.

The five executions of the five propositions (the five advertising concepts) were then subject to *ad testing* (this chapter) using individual interviews with light users, the primary target audience, and heavy users, the loyal franchise as the secondary target audience (see Chapter 3), to select the best concept. Sample sizes of at least 100 light users and 100 heavy users were probably employed.[4] The primary measure

Figure 1. The storyboard for a typical "Cost of Visit" advertisement — 1982 execution.

**FIGURE 19.1**

Typical TV commercial in AT&T's "Cost of visit" campaign. This execution is entitled "Sister."
*Courtesy:* AT&T and *Interfaces.*

in this ad test was brand purchase intention, in the form of intention to call long-distance more frequently, using an 11-point Juster scale (this chapter). The winning concept in this ad test, where the action standard (this chapter) or criterion was to maximize light users' intentions to call more often while not reducing heavy users' intentions, was "Cost of visit."

AT&T then conducted what only larger advertisers can generally afford: a test-market ad test. Using AdTel's split-cable TV method, AT&T tested "Cost of visit" against the incumbent "Reach out" campaign in a test-market sample (16,000 households) for a period of 2 years. The test consisted of a 6-month baseline period in which all households received only the AT&T national campaign with no long-distance commercials; a 15-month test period in which a randomly selected half of the households (8,000) were switched to "Cost of visit" while the other half (8,000) received "Reach out," both at an average of 3 exposures per week; and a 5-month period where again all households were reverted to only the national campaign.

During the 15-month test period, revenue (profit) from light user households increased by 15 percent, coming from an average increase of 1.5 calls a month over the preperiod light-user baseline rate of 2.5 calls a month. Revenue from all households increased by 1 percent. Projecting from the ad-test sample, AT&T estimated that shifting $30 million of the total advertising budget from "Reach out" to "Cost of visit" would generate an additional $22 million in *profit* per year. Therefore, the budget shift was made. Interestingly, the "Cost of visit" campaign seemed to increase light users' calls only while the commercials were on air, suggesting a brand recall "reminder" effect (see Chapter 5) together with the increase in brand attitude benefit beliefs that occurred when the campaign first began. It was vastly profitable for AT&T to run the "Cost of visit" campaign continuously, and AT&T did so. To do this, more executions of the basic concept had to be generated and produced to maintain audience attention (see Chapter 20).

The AT&T example highlights several major questions, which we answer in this chapter:

- Exactly what is being, and what should be, developed and tested: a strategy? a creative idea? an ad execution?
- How should the developmental research (concept development research, or CDR) be conducted?
- When should management become involved in assessing the creative concepts?
- How should the ad test be conducted and a winner chosen?

Implicitly, too, we consider the cost-benefit decision for these types of advertising research.

## CONCEPT DEVELOPMENT RESEARCH

Concept development research (CDR) encompasses research techniques that are employed to cultivate creative ideas *and* their exemplifying executions (advertising concepts) into final or near-final ads. CDR was referred to specifically in the random creativity procedure in Chapter 7 as a means of finding winning ads.

Because there is considerable ambiguity about what constitutes an "advertising concept" and what, precisely, is being "developed" in CDR, we provide a definitional and operational guide in Figure 19.2. The guide distinguishes three levels: positioning strategies (most often summarized as the *main benefit*), creative ideas (how the main benefit will be *dramatized*), and ad executions or *concepts* (further classifiable into *specific elements* of the ad). As the arrows indicate, the objectives of CDR are, horizontally, to *evaluate and select* across strategies, creative ideas, and executional elements; and, vertically, to *improve* creative ideas and executional elements after the most promising strategy/creative idea/executions have been selected. Note that positioning strategies and creative ideas cannot be observed *except* as they are represented in rough ad executions.

A further example besides the AT&T example which opened this chapter will certainly help to clarify these very important distinctions. In Figure 19.3, we depict an (abbreviated) example of the strategies and creative idea levels examined in CDR research for the Australian Tourist Commission's recent advertising campaign promoting Australia as the destination (brand) for overseas holiday travel. We have omitted the executional details of the concepts tested, for proprietary reasons, but an idea of the *types* of executional details examined can be obtained from the generic CDR diagram in the previous figure.

Many advertisers skip concept development research and proceed directly to the preparation and testing of rough ads. However, there are several frequently occurring circumstances in which concept development research can be useful. For these applications, it is helpful to divide CDR into two phases: creative idea generation and concept screening research.

**1a.** For advertisers developing a *new* campaign, even though the overall strategy has been determined, the

**FIGURE 19.2**
Concept development research (CDR): definitions (*italics*) and purposes (CAPITALS).

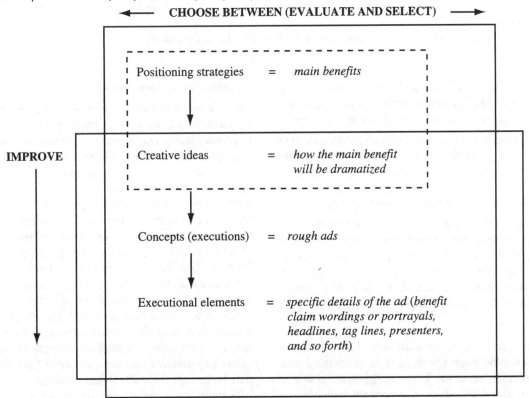

CHOOSE BETWEEN (EVALUATE AND SELECT)

IMPROVE

Positioning strategies = *main benefits*

Creative ideas = *how the main benefit will be dramatized*

Concepts (executions) = *rough ads*

Executional elements = *specific details of the ad (benefit claim wordings or portrayals, headlines, tag lines, presenters, and so forth)*

KEY: indicates that positioning strategies and creative ideas are testable only in the form of concepts (rough-ad executions) and cannot be tested directly.

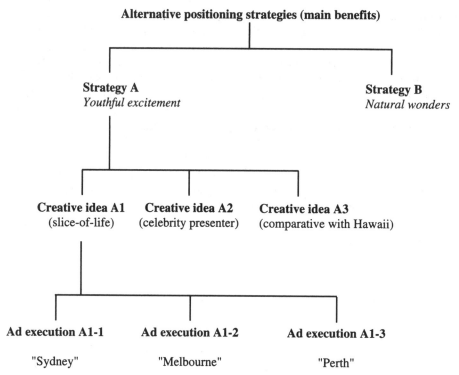

**FIGURE 19.3**
Example: CDR options (partial) for a recent campaign by the Australian Tourist Commission.

creative team may get "blocked" when generating creative ideas for the execution of the campaign. *Creative idea generation* research can often break the block.

**1b.** For advertisers seeking "fresh ideas" to spruce up a *continuing* campaign (see Chapter 20 regarding "wearout"), advertising *creative idea generation* research, similarly, can help to provide new creative ideas to dramatize the *same* positioning strategy.

**2.** Finally, for the fortunate advertiser for whom *too many* ideas have been forthcoming from advertising strategy research (or from idea generation research), *advertising concept screening* research càn help the creative team to reduce these ideas to a reasonable number for incorporation into rough ads for ad testing.

Therefore, let us proceed with describing, first, creative idea generation research, then advertising concept screening research. Then, in the next section of the chapter, we will show how concept screening research can be adapted for use by managers in conducting a management judgment test of the ads.

### Creative Idea Generation

As one of America's foremost creative directors, Stephen Baker, as well as many geniuses and some psychologists have observed, creativity can rarely rely on intuition alone. Thomas Edison said that invention is "2 percent inspiration and 98 percent perspiration." Creative idea generation can almost always benefit from various aids which serve as stimulus inputs to the "intuitive" breakthrough. Three types of idea generation aids are described here.

**Thought-Starter Lists.** Thought-starter lists are helpful when the advertiser doesn't know what benefits to emphasize or is not committed to any particular approach (this would likely be only the smallest advertisers who have not conducted advertising strategy research). A virtually costless research method is to acquire previously published thought-starter lists. Many experienced creative personnel have their own lists tacked on the wall. Baker[5] provides many useful lists covering a variety of advertising situations. To give just one example, he lists 30 possible benefits to use when advertising a service. Services don't have physical attributes like products, of course, and it can be difficult to find service benefits to advertise. If more creatives used these lists we might have fewer "me too" campaigns where the thought starter was nothing but a competitor's campaign. Thought-starter lists can be inserted in a creative person's PC for ease of use.

**Benefit Chaining.** Benefit chaining, which was described in Chapter 18 as a technique that can be incorporated in qualitative research to develop advertising strategy, can also be used in creative idea generation. Benefit chaining is very useful for the smaller advertiser who has done no strategy research and has to begin with the brand's obvious attributes. (In terms of our a-b-e micropositioning model, benefit chaining generates benefits and emotions to go with the fundamental attributes.) For example, Jolt, the high-caffeine cola, could use benefit chaining to generate situations in which high caffeine is most likely to be seen as beneficial.

Individual interviews (not focus groups) should be employed for the benefit chaining procedure. This is to ensure that logical chains of ideas can be traced at the individual consumer level. The most frequent or typical individual thought patterns are then selected for final (or to-be-tested) advertising executions.

**Brainstorming Procedures.** In Chapter 7, in conjunction with the RAM-Conveyor model of creative idea generation, we recommended the I-G-I (Individual-Group-Individual) method of brainstorming. This is a very efficient method of brainstorming and is much more effective than the typical unstructured brainstorming sessions most advertising agencies use to generate creative ideas for a campaign. Do-it-yourself advertisers, and agencies for that matter, should review its essential procedure.

More recently, computer-assisted brainstorming programs have emerged. These are of two types. One type is little more than mechanized brainstorming: the computer provides as "prompts" a series of concepts from different conceptual domains that could potentially be conveyors for the brand's attributes (the computer user decides on their suitability). Some programs, such as MacCrimmon and Wagner's GENI, further provide various combination rules, such as means-to-ends or metaphor, for combining attributes with the concepts.[6] To date, the limited evidence available suggests that these computer-prompt types of brainstorming procedures are no more effective,

for the average brainstormer, than the I-G-I procedure,[7] although further preliminary evidence suggests that such programs may be differentially effective for individuals who have above-average creativity to begin with, as may be found among creative personnel in an ad agency.[8]

The other type of computer-assisted brainstorming program is a much more elaborate system containing computer stores of visual images (for illustrations or video in ads) as well as word associations and the words' semantic ratings (a useful but primitive start to ad copy generation). By far the best system, taking over 10 years and many person-hours to develop, is the German system CAAS (Computer-Aided Advertising System) developed by the late Werner Kroeber-Riel and his colleagues[9] (notably, Franz-Rudolf Esch) at the University of Saarland. CAAS's development was supported by five major companies, among them BASF, CIBA, and Procter & Gamble, and five advertising agencies, four of which are reportedly avid users of the system—after, understandably, considerable initial professional skepticism. Originally available only to its subscribers in Germany, CAAS has now been commercialized by Allcom Advertising AG, of Basel, Switzerland, a subsidiary of CIBA, and thus should become more widely accessible. Distinctive in CAAS is the visual image subsystem, which provides a large number of pictorial conveyors for attribute words such as "ecological" (Kroeber-Riel was the world expert in visual advertising theory). Figure 19.4 shows the output of this subsystem used to transform a mundane ad for Peugeot automobiles into two executions that reposition the brand as being responsibly concerned with the environment. The copy reads: "Germany's cleanest diesel fleet." Whereas other computer stores of visual images exist, notably the Bettman Archives in New York and PHOTO-SAURUS, offered by Hulton Deutsch Collection, both worldwide, no other system has its images explicitly connected to *attributes,* as does CAAS.

Computer-assisted brainstorming systems such as CAAS are exciting new stimulators of creativity in advertising. It must be realized, however, that there is still a large human element of selection and evaluation in choosing computer-suggested concepts. A partial solution to this is to *also* incorporate a concept screening system (see shortly). CAAS has attempted to do this but, most important, its validity has yet to be formally established.

**FIGURE 19.4**
Concept development of an (actual) ad for Peugeot automobiles showing two new executions designed to better emphasize the company's (and cars') environmental responsibility. The executions were developed using Kroeber-Riel's CAAS expert system.
*Courtesy:* Dr. F-R. Esch and *Expertensysteme für die Werbung,* Appendix, 1994, Verlag Franz Vahlen, Munich.

In summary, a range of creative idea generation procedures is available for use by advertisers (and especially advertising agencies). Whether your company is small or large, there is a procedure that will help, and the days of the copywriter staring at a blank wall for inspiration are already being superseded by the copywriters' interaction with a computer.

## Advertising Concept Screening

The other circumstance in which creative guidance is sometimes needed is when the creative team has *too many* ideas, especially regarding executional elements of the ads for the campaign. The creative team, particularly when the strategy research has been extensive, may have developed several creative ideas and numerous specific elements that may or may not work in an ad. Examples of such elements include:

• Headlines (print), tag lines (broadcast), or slogans

• Illustrations (print) or story-board video illustrations (TV)
• Benefits stated in alternative wordings (benefit *claims*—actually *verbal* benefit claims, because benefit claims can also be conveyed in the *visuals* of the ad)
• Presenters
• People representing lifestyle groups
• Settings
• Situations

These elements are often too numerous and too specific to be tested in just a few overall advertising executions, so executional element screening research is indicated *before* the final or near-final ads are prepared.

Two methods are recommended for concept screening. The first is (again) qualitative research but with a quantitative refinement; this is the most widely used method for *creative idea* screening and also a little more expensive. The second is the Q-sort procedure, which employs individual interviews at moderate cost and is ideal for screening *executional elements,* especially when there is a large number of them. The methods can be employed in any order, depending on the nature of the screening to be done.

**Qualitative Research (Modified).** Qualitative research can be used as a relatively convenient way of screening a large number of *creative ideas.* (This is the method most advertising agencies refer to as "concept development research"—see Chapter 7's discussion of the random creativity model.) The sample for this research should be selected from the target audience or audiences, which will of course be known from the prior advertising strategy research or can be grossly inferred if no strategy research was done.

The main change from regular qualitative research is the introduction of quantitative measures coupled with an emphasis on individual reactions to the ideas (sometimes called "qual/quant" research). In a group setting, each participant should be asked to write down his or her private opinion or rating of each idea presented before any group discussion of the idea is allowed. In the individual depth interview setting, the same procedure is followed except that the discussion would be between the individual and the moderator rather than a group discussion.

With group qual/quant interviews, the problem of group influence is substantial—and ads themselves should *never* be tested in focus groups (see later in this chapter). The main reason for resorting to groups in concept screening research is the saving on interviewer time, since 6 to 12 respondents can be interviewed at once. A really expert group moderator is not needed, unlike in strategic qualitative research; competent interviewers who probe well are sufficient.

Preferably, concept screening research should use *individual* interviews to avoid group influence altogether. About 200 individual interviews can be obtained for the equivalent price of three or four focus groups. Central location or shopping mall interviews are appropriate (the interviews have to be face-to-face although interactive TV or PC interviews might become broadly feasible in the future). Because of the quantitative aspect of this research, a sample size of at least 200 respondents *from* the target audience is recommended, to produce reasonably reliable ratings. With a sample size of 200, an observed difference in ratings of 10 percent or greater will be a reliable (95 percent confidence) difference, as shown in Table 19.3 (below). The relatively large sample is necessary because of the extreme importance of reliably detecting a winning concept or concepts.

Researcher Martin Lautman[10] of ARBOR, Inc., a Philadelphia research firm, has developed a very useful set of ratings for screening advertising *concepts* (rough ad executions that present the strategy and the creative idea in adlike form). Rough storyboard ads are usually used as the research stimuli. The ratings are especially useful for student projects (with a smaller sample, naturally) but are highly recommended for professional creative idea screening. As modified slightly by us, the ratings are summarized in Table 19.1.

In Lautman's more quantitative application of the above procedure, similarities judgments are made (step 4) and multidimensional scaling, superimposed on a simple plot of mean scores, is used to "map" the concepts onto both the preference (step 1) and uniqueness (step 2) dimensions. We provide a *hypothetical* example of this for the Australian Tourist Commission's advertising concepts, from Figure 19.3, in Figure 19.5. Strategy A seems clearly the best, and creative idea A1 seems the best way to dramatize it. Not unusually, some executions appear to belong to other ideas or strategies, as evaluated by respondents, differently from the ways the creative department intended them. It is, of course, *respondents'*

---

**TABLE 19.1**

**ADVERTISING CONCEPT SCREENING RATINGS**

1. *Preference.* An overall rating of how much the ad "makes you want to try or buy" (informational advertising concepts) or of how much "I like this ad for the brand" (transformational advertising concepts) on a 0-to-10 scale.
2. *Uniqueness.* A rating using a 0-to-10 scale where 0 = "exactly the same as most other brands [or the leading competitor]" and 10 = "extremely different."
3. *Consistency/Appropriateness.* Use this rating *only* for an established brand *if* it is important that the creative strategy be "consistent" or reflect historical "brand values"; remember that sometimes you want just the opposite, a complete repositioning of the brand. A 0-to-10 scale of 0 = "not at all consistent" to 10 = "completely consistent" would suffice.
4. *Similarities Sorting.* The ideas or concepts should then be "grouped" by respondents by asking each respondent to classify together any concepts that he or she believes say or show "much the same thing." This final step is *very important* as it reveals, in a basic but sufficient way, whether the concepts represent the *same* positioning strategy (brand position), or—as often happens or may be deliberate for evaluative purposes—whether they represent *different* positionings of the brand (see Figures 19.2 and 19.3).

*Source:* Adapted from Lautman, 1993; see note 10.

---

*perceptions* that matter. The authors have employed Lautman's screening procedure with great success (it corresponds with our I-D-U model nicely) in consultancy and student project applications.

**Q-Sort Procedure.** A very useful method for screening a large number of advertising *executional elements* is the Q-sort procedure. Again, a representative sample of the *target audience,* or target audiences if there is more than one, must be taken, but a sample of 50 consumers per target audience is sufficient.[11]

Q-sort is a method that allows a large number of stimuli of a particular type—advertisement headlines, benefit claims, illustrations, and so on—to be rated by consumers without inducing the fatigue and errors that would result if they rated or ranked them all at once. Up to about 60 stimuli can be rated.[12]

Any desired rating criterion can be employed. Some *examples* might be:

- *Strong* (versus *weak*) for benefit claims to be used in a low-involvement/informational brand attitude strategy

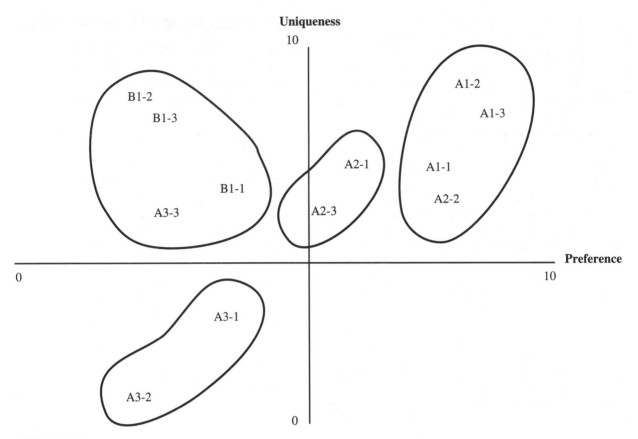

**FIGURE19.5**
Hypothetical multidimensional scaling (overlaid on the concepts' mean scores) of the Australian
Tourist Commission's advertising concepts in terms of uniqueness and preference. Each balloon
indicates perceived similar concepts.

- *Like* (versus *dislike*) for settings to be used in a low-involvement/transformational brand attitude strategy
- *Convincing* (versus *unconvincing*) for benefit claims to be used in a high-involvement/informational brand attitude strategy
- *Similar to me* (versus *not similar to me*) for presenters to be used in a high-involvement/transformational brand attitude strategy

The Q-sort procedure itself is straightforward. Beforehand, the items are typed (verbal stimuli) or photographed or pasted (visual stimuli) onto 3 × 5 inch cards for ease of sorting. The respondent is first asked to read or look through all the cards. Second, the respondent is instructed to place the cards into three general piles: − , 0, and + (for example, weak claims, moderate claims, strong claims; or dislike,

neutral, like). Then, working from each pile in turn, the respondent performs a finer sort into a fixed frequency distribution, usually of 11 categories along the criterion scale, with a specified number of cards in each category. An example for 50 stimuli might be:

| Dislike Most | | | | | | | | | | Like Most |
|---|---|---|---|---|---|---|---|---|---|---|
| −5 | −4 | −3 | −2 | −1 | 0 | +1 | +2 | +3 | +4 | +5 |
| (categories) | | | | | | | | | | |
| 1 | 2 | 4 | 6 | 7 | 10 | 7 | 6 | 4 | 2 | 1 |
| (frequencies) | | | | | | | | | | |

Each item's score is then averaged across respondents. The highest scoring stimuli are selected for incorporating in advertisements.

**Screening Potential Presenters.** Potential presenters (see Chapter 9) can be screened using the Q-sort procedure. If the advertiser has narrowed down the candidates to just two to six, however, direct ratings of each candidate separately, using the VisCAP approach, is the preferable procedure.

As the VisCAP characteristics are "bipolar" in that negatives must be avoided while selecting on theoretically appropriate positive "hooks," the rating scale format must be bipolar. Our colleague Rob Donovan designed the following format, which we recommend:

### Characteristic

| NO ❏ | no ❏ | yes ❏ | YES ❏ |
|---|---|---|---|

The characteristic above the scale is, of course, the VisCAP trait. Each trait, however, should employ two or three appropriate adjectives or adjectival phrases for reliable measurement. These adjectives are placed in random order on the questionnaire. For instance, we have used as adjectives for the VisCAP traits:

1. *Visibility:* well-known, familiar, famous
2a. *Expertise:* qualified, knowledgeable, skilled
2b. *Objectivity:* truthful, reliable, honest
3a. *Likability:* likable, attractive, appealing
3b. *Similarity:* I can relate to this person, he/she seems to have similar values to me, he/she looks to be of just a little higher social class than me
4. *Power:* authoritative, powerful, I would do what he/she says

Clearly, the particular adjectives (or phrases) chosen have to fit the advertising context (actually, the desired "hook") in which the presenter is expected to work.

Scoring of the VisCAP profile was explained in Chapter 9.

**How Many Concepts Should Be Requested from Concept Screening?** There is no simple answer to this question other than to say, in general: the more concepts, the better (the greater the likelihood of finding a real-winner campaign, consistent with the principle of random creativity as explained in Chapter 7). In a specific situation, however, the question of "how many concepts" is very important, and its answer is certainly *the* most important decision made in concept development research. It is important for several reasons. One is the creative effort and management time and money involved in generating and screening concepts. Another is the realization that if few or none of the originally generated concepts are acceptable, then more will have to be generated and screened: you should not settle on the best of a

mediocre list of concepts if it doesn't meet your absolute standards for acceptance. But the final reason is the most misunderstood or ignored fact in concept development research, and that is that the differences in effectiveness between *executions* of a creative idea can be *larger* than the difference between the effectiveness of the creative ideas *themselves*—and both differences can be larger than the differences in effectiveness between advertising *strategies* (alternative main emphasized benefits) for the brand!

Remember, you are testing advertising *concepts;* these in turn are particular executions of a particular creative idea representing a particular positioning strategy. Each concept is therefore a complex compound of three components, or a "triple variability" equation, as follows:

$$C_{ijk} = S_i I_{ij} E_{ijk}$$

where $C_{ijk}$ = the advertising concept to be evaluated

$S_i$ = the strategy, i = A, B, C, and so on

$I_{ij}$ = the creative idea j for strategy i, where j = 1, 2, 3, and so on

$E_{ijk}$ = an execution (rough ad) k of creative idea j for strategy i, where k = 1, 2, 3, and so on

For example, the AT&T "Sister" ad shown in Figure 19.1 is a *concept:* it is one execution ($E_{ijk}$) of the "People with a reason to call, surprised by low cost" creative idea ($I_{ij}$) for the "Cost of visit" positioning strategy ($S_i$) for AT&T's residential long-distance telephone service. In testing this ad as a rough-ad concept, you would be testing simultaneously all *three* components: the strategy, the creative idea, and the execution. What AT&T actually tested was five strategies (A through E, described earlier) but they gave each strategy only one chance to work, with one creative idea and one execution per strategy (in terms of the equation above, they tested $S_A I_{A1} E_{A11}$, $S_B I_{B1} E_{B11}$, and so forth). Quite evidently, different creative ideas or different executions might have made one of the "losing" strategies a winner. This probably confirms quite a few managers' suspicions about their own strategies, but the fact is that tests of such suspicions are rare because 99 percent of the time, managers and their agencies do what AT&T did, namely, they generate and test only one creative idea and one execution per strategy. (To their credit, AT&T at least tested a reasonable number of alternative *strategies*.)[13]

So now back to the question: How many concepts should be requested from (the previous) concept screening phase of research? A practical answer is that *if* you are sure of the strategy (the main benefit to be advertised), then a *minimum* is two creative ideas and two executions of each, that is, four concepts. This is a minimum. If you're *not* sure about strategy, then test at least two strategies—with two creative ideas and two executions of each, which makes a total of eight concepts. We're working in multiples of two here. The large advertiser, in a high-risk situation or in any situation where the advertiser wants to be surer of a winner, would be advised to work in multiples of three or four—the four executions of each at the end providing a better idea of a concept's "campaignability."

Obviously, the cost of testing the desirable number of concepts can escalate rapidly at about $20,000 per rough ad plus test (even four concepts is usually too many for small advertisers to produce in rough form and test, and, unadvisedly, as we argued in Chapter 7, most large advertisers *also* would hesitate to test more than one or two rough ads). A compromise recommendation is to employ a management judgment test (MJT). It is a compromise solution because, as we'll see, MJTs can inexpensively detect poor concepts, which is a considerable advantage in its own right, but cannot detect a real winner with a high degree of accuracy. Nevertheless, MJTs are strongly recommended for a wider reason, as explained shortly.

## MANAGEMENT JUDGMENT TESTS (MJTs)

By employing a management judgment test in a systematic and disciplined manner, it is possible to conduct a moderately valid ad test *without* formal consumer testing. In fact, a leading marketing consultant to whom we have referred previously, William T. Moran, foresees expert-system versions of MJTs replacing much of consumer ad testing.[14] Our viewpoint is that management judgment testing is a very useful initial step for all ads, but that the additional step of testing ads with consumers is essential when introducing a new product or a new campaign.

Experience in using MJTs in our consulting work has revealed several wider benefits which together lead us to recommend MJTs for all rough ads prior to all campaigns. Enlisting management's participation in an MJT of the prospective ads prior to their (or its)

final production accomplishes the following objectives:

**1.** It prevents the usual "gut reaction" to advertising concepts, whereby managers tend to forget the target audience and original communication objectives and brand position and react to the ad at face value.

**2.** It encourages widespread and reasonably objective commitment to the final concepts chosen (or to proceed to formal ad testing) in that managers cannot say "I had no say in that" or "That was an idiosyncratic choice" (and it simultaneously discourages the agency from being able to say "It's too late to change the concept").

**3.** It permits the product manager to present an objective case to senior management for a budget increase (or no decrease) should an outstanding concept be found.[15]

Accordingly, it is worth conducting an MJT even if extensive ad concept screening research with consumers or customers has been conducted (see the Lautman method, earlier, which screens final *concepts*). In fact, an MJT should be conducted *prior* to any final-concept screening work with consumers or customers, as the screening research tends to be quite expensive whereas an MJT can screen out "off-strategy" concepts at a relatively low cost. Certainly an MJT should be conducted if there has been *no* audience screening of final concepts or if *no ad test* is planned.

In short, MJTs are worthwhile and strongly recommended.

### Overview of the MJT Method

**The Checklist.** The management judgment test (MJT) uses a checklist approach to evaluate the ad's content. It is an "expert system" approach, although it's not computerized, and it draws on the knowledge provided in this book. Basically, the purposes of an MJT are to check that the ad is "on strategy" and that the execution "seems right."

- To check whether the ad is "on strategy," we need input from two areas—target audience action objectives, and communication objectives and positioning—which can be taken from either the advertising strategy summary (Chapter 18) or the AC&P plan (Appendix).
- To check whether the execution "seems right," we first include brand awareness and brand attitude

creative tactics with their respective communication objectives (from Chapters 8 and 9). Then, finally, we apply the *attention* execution guidelines (from Chapter 10).

Table 19.2 shows the factors we use in our MJT checklist (these are described generally, and in actual applications they are customized in detail for each brand and strategy). Compiling the checklist is a detailed exercise but worth the trouble given the fairly low cost in management time and the insights gained.

We use an 11-point rating scale for each factor (and tactic) rated, as follows:

```
0    1    2    3    4    5    6    7    8    9    10
↑                        ↑                        ↑
Totally                  Neutral,              Excellent
unacceptable             so-so
```

This scale is easy for managers to use. Moreover, the common scale for all factors and tactics avoids any arbitrary weighting of them.

### TABLE 19.2

#### MJT RATING FACTORS[a]

A. *Target Audience Action Objectives*
 1. Target audience compatibility
 2. Decision-participant correctly addressed
 3. Action objective specification (explicit for direct response ads, or clearly implied)

B. *Communication Objectives and Positioning*
 1. Category need: Correctly portrayed and adequately sold, or reminded, or omitted
 2. Brand awareness: adequacy of tactics for brand recognition (Table 8.1) or brand recall (Table 8.2) or both (Table 8.3) as appropriate
 3a. Brand attitude (benefit positioning): emphasis on unique benefit(s), mention of entry-ticket benefit(s), trade off or omission of inferior delivery benefit(s), other mandatory elements (if required)
 3b. Brand attitude: adequacy of tactics for brand attitude strategy quadrant (Table 8.4, 8.6, 9.1, 9.2, or 9.4) as appropriate
 4. Brand purchase intention: adequately generated, or assumed
 5. Purchase facilitation: adequately incorporated, or omitted

C. *Attention Tactics (Optional)*
 1–n. Adherence to formula tactics, depending on type of commercial or advertisement (Table 10.2, 10.5, 10.8, 10.12, 10.14, 10.16, 10.18 and 10.19, or 10.20) as appropriate

[a]See comments and 11-point (0-to-10) rating scale in text.

**The Judges.** In the MJT, *multiple* judges should be used, and they must make their judgments *individually,* that is, independently and without any sort of meeting or discussion until after the results have been collected and summarized.[16] Ideally, six to 10 (and at the very minimum, three) judges should be selected. In large companies, we have employed 20 randomly selected judges *per ad;* less preferable but still adequate is to have about 20 randomly selected judges rate *all* the ads (the ads should be randomly ordered across judges). Ideally, too, the client and the agency should be represented among the judges.

The judges need not be advertising experts and, indeed, diligence rather than experience (which actually could get in the way of careful analysis) is required. We have had excellent results by employing research assistants or management trainees as judges, but (for reasons given earlier) the *product's* management should be the first panelists chosen.

**Interpreting the Results.** The researcher or principal product manager should tally the scores for each ad, across judges for each rating dimension. A frequency distribution is then written down along each rating scale (we have found it convenient to do this on a blank questionnaire from the MJT rating task) and its *median* score written at the end. The judges, or a smaller panel of decision makers from the judges if many judges have been employed, then meet to discuss the results. Interpretation usually proceeds as follows:

**1.** Eliminate ads (concepts) with many "below 5" scores, either with a median less than 5 or with a bimodal distribution of scores such that many, say a third, are below 5.

**2.** Consider those left in terms of their median "upside" scores, that is, with medians between 5 and 10.

It is logical to give each surviving ad a "total" score, although this provides little more than a relative ranking of the ads and should not be interpreted as an absolute predictor of their effectiveness. To compute a total score, we suggest weighting each of the *factors* on the 0-to-10 scales if they stand alone but weighting each of the *tactics* in a multitactic factor (for example, brand recall tactics or high-involvement/informational brand attitude tactics) as 0 or 1 ("fail/pass") and then summing these and converting the sum to a 0-to-10 scale. This gives the factors equal weighting, unless management decides to weight them differently, in the total score.

The main validity of the MJT is in detecting, and preventing or correcting, *errors* in the factors and tactical executions—that is, "minimizing the downside"—rather than in predicting upside effectiveness. In this regard, the total scores are not so important, though they may help management decide which ads deserve to proceed to ad concept screening or ad testing with the target audience—or to be produced as finished ads if no further testing is planned.

There are thus three outcomes for each ad in the MJT:

- Reject it
- Return it for improvement (with its errors specified)
- Accept it

Quite clearly, the MJT can contribute substantially toward ensuring that creative executions will meet their communication objectives. The judges in this method are nonetheless managers, who, with the possible exceptions of creative managers, may not be able to intuit the target audience's responses to ads or promotion offers to the degree of accuracy required to forecast success. Testing with the target audience is therefore the next advisable stage of advertising research.

## THE PURPOSE OF AD TESTING AND THE DECISION TO TEST

### General Purpose of Ad Testing

The general purpose of ad testing[17] is to improve the chances that *finished* ads will work as planned when placed in media. As we saw in Chapter 7 in supporting the theory of random creativity, the chance of a sales-successful campaign is about 70 percent for new brands but only about 32 percent for established brands. The chance of a "real winner" campaign is about 30 percent for new brands and 12 percent for established brands.[18] Whether the ads *will* work as planned depends on three factors (assuming no changes in marketing mixes or in the market):

1. *Creative content* being able to meet the brand's communication objectives and positioning
2. *Correct media* placement and scheduling
3. *Competitive advertising* activity (if the brand's communication objectives include brand recall or transformational brand attitude)

Ad testing evaluates ads on the *first* of these factors. Campaign tracking—the final stage of advertising research—is needed to assess all three factors. In terms of our six-step effects sequence, ad testing is concerned with evaluating the causal link between step 2, processing (of creative content), and step 3, communication effects (specifically, the brand's communication objectives and brand position). Ad testing sometimes proceeds to step 4 (target audience action). However, the advertising strategy research should have specified communication objectives and a brand position that are *fully expected* to produce the desired action. Hence, ads are usually tested only against communication objectives and brand position.

### Specific Purposes of Ad Testing

There are two forms of ad testing and three specific purposes for testing. The first purpose pertains to the testing of preliminary or "rough" executions of ads, and the second and third purposes pertain to the testing of finished ads.

**Rough-Ad Testing to Select Finished Ads.** The general purpose of ad testing is to assess how well finished ads will work when they are placed in media. However, because it is expensive to produce finished ads, testing is usually conducted first with *rough* executions of the ads to decide whether each ad is indeed worth producing. (Just how "rough" these executions can or should be we will consider in the design section of this chapter.)

A comparatively large number of inexpensive rough ads can be tested to select the best executions for production. (A careful analysis of ad testing by Gross[19] suggests a guideline of producing and testing three rough ads for every intended finished ad; see the discussion of this is in our theory of random creativity in Chapter 7.) For example, an advertiser might test six rough executions with the aim of producing two finished ads.

To provide an idea of the economics behind the decision to test rough ads, let's consider television commercials, which are generally the most expensive type of advertisement. It costs about $20,000 to prepare and test a rough "storyboard" version of a TV commercial (of which about $12,000 is for the test itself). This is about one-fifth of the $100,000 cost of producing (but not testing) the average finished commercial.[20] Our hypothetical advertiser could therefore test the six rough executions for $120,000—whereas it would cost $552,000 more to test no rough versions but to produce and test six finished versions. The outlay for testing six rough versions and then producing, but not testing, two finished commercials would be about $320,000, a savings of over 50 percent compared to the cost of producing *and* testing all six finished ads.

**Testing Finished Ads Before Media Placement.** Many advertisers proceed directly to media with finished ads based on the tested rough versions, without testing the finished ads. At first this seems understandable. The media expenditure on a typical TV commercial (one commercial, and in the U.S. market nationally) is about $1.5 million.[21] Thus, there is $3 million to be spent on the two commercials in media. Our hypothetical advertiser already has spent $320,000 in testing six rough ads and producing two finished commercials, as above, for a total expenditure of $3,320,000. The cost of additionally testing the two *finished* commercials (about $24,000) would only increase the *total cost* ($3,320,000) by about three-quarters of 1 percent, which seems very reasonable.

And this is why large advertisers, and many not-so-large advertisers, test *finished* ads before accepting or rejecting them for the campaign: *it costs the same to run an ineffective ad as it does to run an effective one, but the profit difference can be enormous.*[22] You have to look at the expected *profit* and not just the costs.

Let's switch to magazine advertising to illustrate this, because magazine ads (indeed, print ads in general) are rarely ad tested beforehand. A single insertion of a full-page color ad in *Playboy* costs about $80,000. Its potential exposure is about 5 million readers. Let's suppose only 10 percent of readers actually pay attention to, and process, the ad: that's 500,000 readers. By ad testing several finished versions for about $20,000 (which *seems* exorbitant relative to the media cost of one insertion) we could probably find a final version that is processed by *20* percent of readers—1 million readers. Suppose further that (a constant) 5 percent of those who process the ad buy the brand (a travel bag, for example) and that the profit contribution per unit of product sold is $10. The comparison is then as follows:

| | Without testing | With testing |
|---|---|---|
| Exposed | 5,000,000 | 5,000,000 |
| Processed ad | 500,000 | 1,000,000 |
| Bought item | 25,000 | 50,000 |
| Profit contribution | $250,000 | $500,000 |
| Cost of ad | $80,000 | $80,000 |
| Cost of testing | 0 | $20,000 |
| Net profit | $170,000 | $400,000 |

In this example, the untested ad produced a $170,000 profit whereas the tested ad produced a $400,000 profit—a profit difference of $230,000 that easily justifies the testing of finished ads.

Large advertisers will therefore "shelve" a finished advertisement, even after paying a lot to produce it, if it fails to meet the communication objectives in its finished form. It's actually profitable for them to do so, provided they have other advertisements to use instead. This brings us to the third use of ad testing.

**Assigning Initial Relative Exposure Frequencies in a Pool of Ads.** All but the smallest of advertisers do, or should, run multiple advertisements (a "pool") in a campaign. Multiple executions of the creative idea help to prevent particular types of wearout (see Chapter 20).

Ad testing of finished versions of the ads prior to the campaign can be used to establish the initial relative exposure frequencies across the ads. It is naive to use an equal "rotation" unless all the ads performed virtually identically in the ad test, which is a rare occurrence. Rather, the best ad should receive the largest early exposure frequency, the second best the next largest, and so on.

The relative percent of individuals converted on the brand attitude or brand purchase intention criterion measure (explained later in the chapter) by each ad is the best way of assigning *initial* weights. The weights—exposure frequencies—for the pool of ads can *later* be more validly adjusted as campaign tracking results come in.

### Don't Test Ads in Focus Groups

Focus groups are highly appropriate for *advertising strategy research* and, when the focus group procedure is modified, *concept development research,* but are totally inappropriate for *ad testing.* Yet focus groups are the most common method of ad testing. There are four principal reasons for not testing ads in focus groups:[23]

**1.** *Nonvalid Exposure Conditions.* The first validity problem is that focus groups vastly overexpose ads in comparison with real-world media exposure conditions in which ads must actually operate. In focus groups, an ad is typically shown and discussed for 10 minutes or more. Overexposure leads the research participants to exaggerate both positive and negative aspects, as well as to focus on elements that would never get processed in the minute or less in which a

TV commercial has to communicate or the few seconds available to most print ads.

**2.** *Nonvalid Processing Reactions.* The second validity problem is that group settings produce group interactions that largely prevent individual reactions to the ad from occurring as they would normally. Consumers process ads as individuals, even when they are watching TV together. In real-life advertising exposure, group reactions are an extreme rarity; yet in focus groups they are inevitable unless all discussion is suppressed.

**3.** *Lack of Reliable Projection of Results.* Even if focus group test results were valid, there remains a serious reliability problem. Most ad tests with focus groups use three groups, for a "two out of three" decision if necessary, totaling about 30 consumers. The statistical projection error from a sample of 30 people can be as high as plus or minus 20 percent (see Table 19.3, panel A). In other words, a factual 50 percent approval rating could be observed in the focus group sample as 70 percent (a success) or 30 percent (a bomb). In any event, the interactive observations from group results prevent proper statistical analysis.

---

## TABLE 19.3

**TWO USEFUL REFERENCE TABLES FOR SURVEY OR TEST-RESULT INTERPRETATION BASED ON SAMPLES OF DIFFERENT SIZES (95 PERCENT CONFIDENCE LEVEL)[a]**

**A. Single percentage**

| Sample Size | Plus or minus error when the percentage is close to | | | | |
|---|---|---|---|---|---|
| | 10% or 90% | 20% or 80% | 30% or 70% | 40% or 60% | 50% |
| 1,000 | 2 | 3 | 3 | 3 | 3 |
| 500 | 3 | 4 | 4 | 4 | 4 |
| 250 | 4 | 5 | 6 | 6 | 6 |
| 200 | 4 | 6 | 6 | 7 | 7 |
| 150 | 5 | 6 | 7 | 8 | 8 |
| 100 | 6 | 8 | 9 | 10 | 10 |
| 50 | 8 | 11 | 13 | 14 | 14 |
| 25 | 12 | 16 | 18 | 19 | 20 |

*Example:* A reported percentage of 30 percent, based on a random sample of 200 consumers, has an error rate of plus or minus 6 percent. That is, we could be "95 percent confident" that the actual population percentage, had everyone been surveyed, is between 24 and 36 percent.

**B. Difference between percentages**

| Average of the two sample sizes | Difference needed when the average of the two percentages is close to | | | | |
|---|---|---|---|---|---|
| | 10% or 90% | 20% or 80% | 30% or 70% | 40% or 60% | 50% |
| 1,000 | 4 | 4 | 5 | 5 | 5 |
| 500 | 4 | 5 | 6 | 6 | 6 |
| 250 | 5 | 7 | 8 | 9 | 9 |
| 200 | 6 | 8 | 9 | 10 | 10 |
| 150 | 7 | 9 | 10 | 11 | 11 |
| 100 | 8 | 11 | 13 | 14 | 14 |
| 50 | 12 | 16 | 18 | 19 | 20 |
| 25 | 17 | 22 | 25 | 27 | 28 |

*Example:* Suppose a TV commercial day-after-recall test, based on a random sample of 200 viewers, indicates a recall score of 20 percent. You are disappointed. You decide to repeat the test with a new random sample of 100 viewers, and the commercial now obtains a recall score of 30 percent. Are these reliably different scores? The average of the two sample sizes is 150. The average of the two recall scores is 25 percent. The conservative difference needed is 10 percent (from the table at the intersection of the 150 row and the 30 percent column). Yes, you can be "95 percent confident" that the second recall score is reliably higher than the first.

---

[a]Tables compiled from more detailed tables in Newspaper Advertising Bureau, *The Audience for Newspaper Advertising,* New York: NAB, 1978, appendix.

**4.** *The Lower Cost Is Misleading.* For the price of three or four focus groups, about $10,000 to $20,000, the price depending on how widely used the product or service category is (narrow audiences being more difficult to recruit), the advertiser could conduct 100 to 200 individual interviews—for a much larger, more reliable, and more valid test.

Ad testing, therefore, should always be conducted by using individual interviews. Furthermore, the test ad presentation should be controlled, and the interviewing procedure should be quantitative (generating measurable responses from individual consumers or customers), not qualitative.

### How to Choose an Ad Test

The manager has two basic options[24] in choosing an ad test:

**1.** Choose a *proven* syndicated ad test service (we can strongly recommend only two: McCollum Spielman Worldwide's ADVANTAGE/ACT, and Research Systems Corporation's ARS ad test).

**2.** With the help of a research company, design your own *customized* ad test using the guidelines in this chapter. (MarketMind Technologies and OmniCom Research offer customized ad tests, known as ADTEST and RPM PRETEST, respectively, based on the Rossiter-Percy procedure, but these ad test services so far have a limited number of licensees outside Australia.)

The choice between the two options comes down to what we call basic versus advanced validity. The two proven syndicated systems (hereafter we will refer to them as McCollum Spielman and ARS, as they are widely referred to by these names in the United States) have demonstrated *basic* validity—by which we mean a highly reliable ability to identify successful and real-winner ads and, more important, to not *miss* identifying them and thus cause the advertiser to lose profit by running a poor ad. This is a major achievement in itself, and most advertisers would be rightly satisfied with basic validity, because at least they know they're running an ad that will work—that is, that will increase sales—assuming correct media placement and scheduling, and the absence of unpredicted heavy competitive advertising activity.

The customized ad test, as outlined in this book, goes for *advanced* validity—by which we mean the ability to predict *how much* success the ad will have

when placed in the media schedule. This ambitious goal does away with "norms," because it aims to predict the absolute, not the relative, sales effect of the ad. We hasten to comment that one of the syndicated services, ARS, may now be able to demonstrate advanced validity, although its published case histories so far do not include exact prediction.

The options for ad testing are discussed next.

### SYNDICATED AD TESTING: MSW AND ARS

Both McCollum Spielman and ARS are "theater test" procedures whose main measure is "pre-to-post" exposure "persuasion shift" (explained shortly).[25] Respondents, 100 to 150 consumers screened for *category* purchase, are invited to a central-location theater, ostensibly to preview a new TV program.[26] Before seeing the program ("pre"), they indicate choices of brands as a gift for participating, from a list or display of brands including the test brand. Embedded in the TV program is a "clutter reel" of seven or so commercials, one being the test brand's ad. After the TV program has ended ("post"), respondents are again asked to indicate their brand choices from the same brands they chose from earlier.[27] The aggregate proportion of respondents *shifting* their choice to the test brand on the post measure signifies the test ad's "persuasion" score; thus, if 10 percent chose it on the pre measure and 20 percent chose it on the post measure, the test ad's persuasion score is +10 percent.[28] Of course, the shift can be neutral (0) or sometimes negative, indicating that the ad turns consumers "off" the brand. Persuasion performance standards are discernible in both systems (they differ somewhat).

### McCollum Spielman

McCollum Spielman offers a flexible selection of "persuasion" measures, although the single-brand-choice "brand purchase intention" measure is used most. Other measures include "constant sum" choice for categories in which several brands or varieties are typically bought on one purchase occasion, such as cereals, soft drinks, or snacks; a category need—installing "if you were buying" brand purchase intention measure for infrequently purchased products or services, such as consumer appliances; and an "image" (brand benefit beliefs) measure for corporate ads.[29] All these are measured as pre-to-post changes to derive the persuasion score—which usually combines the *top two* "boxes" on the intention measure, namely, "Probably will buy" and "Definitely will buy." McCollum Spielman's procedure then adjusts the persuasion score by subtracting the norm, that is, the category-average persuasion score.

Basic validity is very good for McCollum Spielman's ad test. We assess this by the procedure's ability to reject unsuccessful ads.[30] (We'd also like to not reject an ad that would be successful, because to do so is to forego profit. However, this assumes there was a successful candidate ad available to begin with, which we can't know since all available ads are not tried out. What we *can* observe from historical data is the chance or probability of choosing an unsuccessful ad, and this is our basis for assessing an ad test's basic validity.)

- *For New Brands:* The typical manager would accept an unsuccessful ad, based on intuition, 30 percent of the time (that is, 70 percent of new brand campaigns are sales-successful but 30 percent are not). By rejecting any ad that was *below-norm* on persuasion (P−) in McCollum Spielman's ad test—or, to word this more positively, if you accepted only ads that scored at the norm or higher—you would reduce this error rate by almost half, to 17 percent.[31] That is, new-brand ads that *pass* the test will be sales-successful 83 percent of the time. Line extension "new" brands have corresponding error figures of 45 percent for intuition, and much less, 26 percent, by the "P−" rule. That is, line-extension ads that pass the test will be sales-successful 74 percent of the time.
- *For Established Brands:* The typical manager would accept an unsuccessful ad, based on intuition, 69 percent of the time (only 31 percent are successful in MSW's database, which is close to our overall 32 percent estimate given in Chapter 7 for established brands). By rejecting any ad that was below-norm on the test (P−) or, the same thing, accepting only those ads at norm or higher, you would reduce this error rate dramatically—to 15 percent. That is, established-brand ads that *pass* the test will be sales-successful 85 percent of the time.

These are impressive statistics indeed for the basic-validity track record of McCollum Spielman's ad test. Managers using intuition, as most do, could not expect to beat those odds, at least not in the long run across many ads. Priced at about $12,000 per TV commercial (rough or finished), though with price depending on category-user incidence, McCollum Spielman's ad test fits any product or service.

## ARS

ARS, at the time of this writing, had published data for only 37 campaigns,[32] all fmcg, but their track record so far is most impressive. Because these cases did not distinguish new from established brands, and is too small a sample of cases to do so anyway, we have assigned the intuitive rejection error based on the ARS data at 65 percent (that is, 35 percent successes).

The ARS average persuasion score across all product categories is +2; a safe not-miss-a-winner score is +5; and an almost certain real-winner *minimum* score is +7.[33] By rejecting any ad whose persuasion score was +5 *or lower,* that is, accepting only +6 ads or higher, the error is reduced to *probably* about 4 percent! The "probably" is because of the small number of cases; with 95 percent confidence, we can state that it is between 0 percent and 21 percent (see Table 19.3, panel A).

Although not cast in precise form, some indication of ARS persuasion scores' *advanced* validity for predicting *new product* trial penetration is given in an analysis of 28 cases by Gleason and Byers.[34] A high correlation of $r = .85$ ($r^2 = .72$) between the ad's persuasion score and subsequent trial of the new advertised brand was observed after correctly allowing for media weight (GRPs) and the extent of the new products' distribution.

On the basis of these data,[35] we are confident in recommending ARS as an fmcg syndicated ad testing service that managers should investigate. The price for an ARS TV commercial test is a little higher than McCollum Spielman's: about $15,000, which will assure a minimum of 100 category users, depending on incidence. Again, the odds are well in favor of the test.

### Multinational (or Global) Ad Testing

For a brand that is sold in more than one country—to much the same target audience and with much the same brand position—the manager may wish to investigate the multinational use of a standard creative idea with minor executional adaptation of visuals (not always necessary) and copy (translation usually necessary). If so, the manager must test the standardized campaign, using its leading one or two ads, against the "incumbent" local ad campaign, also represented by its one or two leading ads. Because of estimated cost savings from using a standardized campaign, its estimated profit in a local market may be greater even if sales are slightly reduced, assuming no change in selling price. (Profit, by the way, is the only good reason for "going global," rather than doing so because of a *subjective* impression that standardization might work better or should be done.)

The manager should be warned that the cutoff scores for rejecting or accepting ads in the MSW or ARS ad tests are likely to be culture-specific (practically speaking, country-specific). Whereas these services are only now beginning to be used outside the United States on a large scale, preliminary indications are that cultures differ quite considerably in terms of "inherent persuasibility" on the pre-post shift measure. As the number of ad tests in a particular country accumulates, a reliable "local" norm becomes available to allow a reject-accept decision for the tested ads. The alternatives are to regard the comparison of standardized and local ads without adjustment for inherent persuasibility, the dangers in this being that both campaigns may be unacceptable and that the amount of increased or reduced sales will be difficult to estimate, or to employ a custom-designed ad test, such as described next, which attempts to predict the absolute performance of an ad and does not rely on norms.

## CUSTOM-DESIGNED AD TEST (ROSSITER-PERCY METHOD)

Highly valid (advanced validity) ad testing depends on designing the ad test to fit the advertising strategy for the brand. Whereas the advertising strategy covers all four steps in the buyer response sequence, from exposure to processing to communication effects to target audience action (see the advertising strategy summary format in the previous chapter), the critical consideration that governs the customization of the ad test can be called the *advertising communication model* for the brand.[36]

Advertising communication models are based on the Rossiter-Percy grid (Chapter 8) and focus on the following two things:

**1.** *Brand Awareness Objective.* Brand recognition versus brand recall (or both if the objective is brand recall–boosted brand recognition).

**2.** *Brand Attitude Strategy.* Low-involvement versus high-involvement brand choice coupled with informational versus transformational purchase motivation—that is, the particular brand attitude strategy quadrant upon which brand choice is based.

The two types of brand awareness and the four types of brand attitude result in eight basic advertising communication models (Figure 19.6) of which *one* will fit the brand's advertising strategy best. As we will see, the differences in these models determine the *design* and the *measures* for the ad test.

Let us proceed with the actual decisions to be made in constructing the ad test and analyzing the results, and we will see how most of them depend on the advertising communication model. There are seven decisions to be made:

**1.** Interview method
**2.** Design
**3.** Sample (cell) sizes
**4.** Test ads' degree of finish
**5.** Number of exposures
**6.** Order and selection of measures
**7.** Analysis and action standards

### Decision 1. Interview Method

Because test advertisements have to be *shown* to respondents, ad testing has to be conducted via personal (face-to-face) interviews.[37] The one exception is radio commercials, which can be played over the phone and

**FIGURE 19.6**
The eight basic communication models based on the Rossiter-Percy grid.

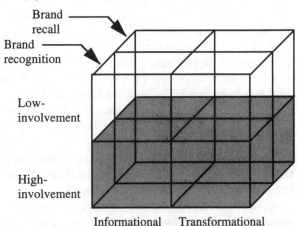

tested via telephone interviews.[38] As we shall see in the next chapter, campaign evaluation (tracking) studies can be conducted by telephone or even by mail, but ad testing cannot.

**Central Location.** For ease of administration, most ad tests are conducted in a central location—most often in shopping malls where the research company has an office, or occasionally using caravan testing facilities as a mobile office that can be placed in high-traffic locations such as shopping center parking lots or downtown areas. It is *possible* to test print ads, radio commercials, and even TV commercials by door-to-door interviews at respondents' homes, by carrying a print portfolio, audiocassette recorder, or lightweight videocassette recorder, respectively, but most testing of all types of advertisements nowadays is central-location testing.

**How the Test Ads Are Shown.** Some research methods, such as those used by McCollum Spielman and ARS described earlier, show the test ad in a competitive or "clutter" context—for example, in a portfolio or simulated magazine for print ads, or in a commercial break embedded in a TV program or radio segment for broadcast ads. However, the "clutter awareness" or "clutter ad recall" measures thus resulting have no demonstrated validity in predicting ad effectiveness[39] (even though these two systems' persuasion measures are valid, as explained earlier). The competitive exposure context *confounds* testing of the ad's capability of producing communication effects with its probability of *gaining attention in the media* (compare our extensive discussion of the structural determinants of attention to ads in Chapter 10, and also see Chapter 16 on effective frequency estimation, specifically for low- and high-attention media). Not only is it impossible, practically speaking, to sample the "real media environments" in which the ad will be exposed, but also to attempt to do so interferes with an *absolute* communication effect assessment of the ad (needed for advanced validity). Clutter-exposure testing systems work (for basic validity) not because of the clutter measure but because of the "bottom line" measure of communication effects, that is, persuasion.

Test ads should be shown *singly* to respondents, not in a competitive context with other ads (for the actual number of exposures, see decision 5).

As we will explain shortly, attention-testing only needs to be undertaken in an *ad test* as a diagnostic measure (at the end) in case the ad doesn't meet its communication objectives.[40] Attention in media, on the other hand, can only be assessed *in* the media, during campaign tracking research.

### Decision 2. Design

The design of the ad test refers to the nature and number of test "cells" (groups or subdivisions of respondents) that will be required.

**One Ad per Respondent.** The first rule is that each respondent should be shown only one test ad. It is an error to try to economize by showing two or more test ads to each respondent, in rotated order across respondents. Instead of "counterbalancing" and equating each ad's results, you in fact obtain valid results for only the *first* ad shown to each respondent, and then only if the test measures are administered immediately following the first ad. That is, if you have 100 respondents and two ads to test and you do so by showing half of the respondents ad A first and ad B second, and the other half ad B first and ad A second, you have only 50 valid respondents for each ad, *not* 100 for each ad. Accordingly, you will need at least as many cells as the number of test ads.

**Pre-Post Versus Experimental-Control Design.** The advertising communication model dictates the ad test design (the first of many such considerations in designing the test to fit the model).[41]

**1.** If the brand attitude strategy is *informational,* then the *pre-post* design can be used. In this design, each cell is given disguised pre-measures (for several brands including the test brand), then exposed to the test ad, then given postexposure measures. The total number of cells is equal to the number of test ads. The pre-post design is used by the syndicated services mentioned earlier, McCollum Spielman and ARS, although McCollum Spielman will alternatively use the experimental-control design when appropriate.

**2.** If the brand attitude strategy is *transformational,* the "ego-involving" nature of the attitude as well as, almost paradoxically, the resulting "softer" nature of the imagelike benefit beliefs, together mean that even a disguised pre-measure would sensitize respondents. More plainly, to bring the almost subconscious image of a brand such as Coke to the surface by having a respondent rate it on a pre-measure, then showing a Coke ad, then having its brand image rated again, would be too "obvious."[42] Corporate image ads are similarly feared to be too sensitive for the pre-post design. Accordingly, an *experimental-control* design is recommended in which test ad (experimental) cells receive the ad then the post-measure, and an additional (control) cell receives only the pre-measure. The pre-measure for the control cell in this design need not be disguised. This adds one cell—serving as a comparison or control for all other cells—to the number of test ad cells.

In the pre-post design for informational communication models, the communication effects produced by the test ad are assessed by measuring, for each respondent, the change from pre-scores to post-scores. In the experimental-control design for transformational communication models, the communication effects produced by the test ad are assessed by measuring the change from (actually the difference in) the proportion of individuals reaching the criterion on the pre-score in the control cell to the proportion of individuals reaching the criterion on the post-scores in the various experimental cells.

In both designs, respondents must be randomly assigned to cells to ensure that the cells do not differ in any way other than exposure to the test ads. In practice, this is achieved by having recruiters assign respondents to cells in rotation, that is, the first respondent to cell 1, the second to cell 2, and so on, which is near enough to random assignment.

### Decision 3. Sample (Cell) Sizes

Ad testing needs reliable numbers of respondents *in each cell* in order to:

**1.** Project reasonably accurately the *absolute* effects produced by a single ad.

**2.** Compare *differences* in effects pre-to-post or control-to-experimental, or between different ads, in order to conclude that differences in scores are real.

The reader can refer to Table 19.3 for determining sample size based on reliability. A normal minimum would be 100 respondents per cell, which will produce a projection error of no more than plus or minus 10 percent (panel A) and a required difference score of no more than 14 percent (panel B). A less expensive alternative (often) is to use 50 respondents per cell initially, test the results for significance, and then double the sample size and extend the test if the results are close. However, 50 respondents per cell makes the results much less projectable for advanced validity assessment of the ad.

### Decision 4. Test Ads' Degree of Finish

"Degree of finish" is the advertising term for how close the test ads are to the final quality of ads that appear in media. Black-and-white sketches for a TV storyboard or a magazine storyboard, for example, would be the lowest (visual) degree of finish.

Test ads are presented to respondents in ad testing as follows:

- *TV:* storyboard; videotaped slide series (animatic or photomatic); or videotape (stealomatic of previous footage, live-action rough, or *finished* commercial)
- *Radio:* audiotape
- *Magazines, newspapers, outdoor ads and posters, direct mail, interactive TV or PC:* storyboard or slide(s)
- *Promotion offer:* storyboard (in-ad promotion); or actual (for example, POP or premium)

The degree of finish of test ads is not a trivial question from a cost standpoint. For TV commercials, a storyboard costs about $2,000; an animatic or photomatic, on videotaped slides with a sound track, or an edited-videotape stealomatic with a sound track, about $10,000; and a finished commercial, about $50,000 up to $300,000. Evidently, it would save time and money if quite rough black-and-white sketches could be used in the initial ad test, even if finished ads will be tested later. But the decision is not this straightforward, as we now explain.

**Informational Models: Rough Ads Are Sufficient.** For ads based on *informational* communication models, black-and-white executions of the test ads—storyboard for print ads, animatic for TV ads—are sufficient. (Of course, if you can get color versions done cheaply, do so, because better finish will increase predictive validity to the finished version—but for informational ads, not by that much.) Rough ads are sufficient because the informational ("reason why") message should be apparent regardless of the executional quality of the test ad presented to consumers.[43]

**Transformational Models: Close-to-Finished Ads Required.** As explained in Chapters 8 and 9 in conjunction with creative tactics, advertisements based on the positive motivations inherent in *transformational* brand attitude strategy depend greatly on "production values." Emotional authenticity is crucial for the extreme, unique, usually single, and often implied benefit claim in low-involvement/transformational ads. Emotional authenticity is very important too, in high-involvement/transformational ads, where you should emotionally overclaim on the transformational benefits. Transformational communication models require authentic production of the test ads.

Accordingly, for transformational test ads, more money should be allocated to produce color-photograph quality visuals, and for TV and radio ads, professionally recorded audio. For TV visuals, it seems to make little difference whether the visuals are a storyboard, or are slides shot dynamically on videotape—as long as the color and finish of the storyboards are very good.

As a safeguard, it makes sense for managers using transformational advertising (especially TV commercials, which depend so much on movement) to proceed and test the *finished* commercials before committing them to media. In any event, to select which ads to produce in the first place, close-to-finished test ads are required, as described.

We wish to reassure managers that well-executed rough ads will produce almost identical ad test results as their finished counterparts (assuming no obvious changes are made between the rough version and finished version; if there are obvious changes, test the finished version!). Valuable proof of this is given in a recently reported McCollum Spielman study[44] in which 92 pairs of rough and finished TV commercials (without obvious changes in the content of the finished versions) were put through the MSW ad test procedure. The overall correlation (r-*squared,* to be conservative) was .78, and the closeness of the relationship is evident from Figure 19.7. The results for individual brands in which the rough version was an animatic (the most common form of rough TV commercial) are shown in Table 19.4. The persuasion results—even for those brands that probably used transformational commercials—are almost identical. The manager would make the *same decisions*—namely whether to accept, revise, or reject the ad (see "action standards," discussed below)—based on the test results for the rough version as he or she would have made if the finished ad had been tested.

**Equivalent Degree of Finish?** It is widely believed that to make valid comparisons *between* test ads, they should all be tested in an equivalent degree of finish. This belief applies to informational ads but especially to transformational test ads.

However, equivalent degree of finish should *not* be a concern beyond a good minimum standard. As we

**FIGURE 19.7**
Persuasion scores for 92 rough TV commercials and their finished versions; data from McCollum Spielman Worldwide (by permission). The overall relationship, r², is .78.

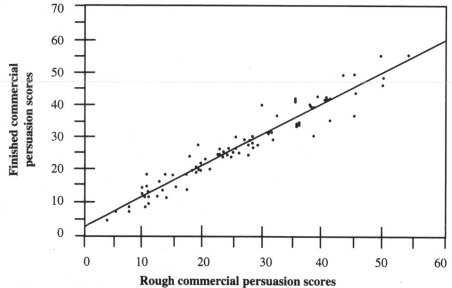

## TABLE 19.4

**COMPARISON OF PERSUASION SCORES ACHIEVED BY ANIMATIC (ROUGH) VERSUS FINISHED COMMERCIALS**[a]

| Product type | Persuasion scores | |
| --- | --- | --- |
| | Animatic version | Finished version[b] |
| Over-the-counter drug | 40 | 32 |
| Air conditioner | 36 | 38 |
| Pet food[c] | 33 | 36 |
| Lipstick[c] | 27 | 29 |
| Ready-to-eat cereal[c] | 27 | 29 |
| Condiment | 20 | 22 |
| Beverage[c] | 15 | 19 |
| Jeans[c] | 12 | 15 |
| Fast food[c] | 11 | 13 |
| Tires | 11 | 13 |
| Average scores | 23.2 | 24.6 |

[a]Animatics are the most common type of rough commercial tested; the 10 products listed here comprise all the animatics graphed in Figure 19.7.
[b]Finished versions had no obvious changes in content from the rough versions; that is, they were the same ads in the two different forms.
[c]Likely transformational commercial.
*Source:* Data from McCollum Spielman Worldwide (by permission).

have just seen, good rough ads produce almost identical test results as do their corresponding finished ads. Also, in our procedure, no respondent sees other than one ad, so differences in finish are not seen by respondents.[45] In "single cells" ad tests, use a good minimum standard of finish, but do not bother to try to equate the finish across ads.

### Decision 5. Number of Exposures

The next decision the manager or researcher has to make is how often—in the test setting—to expose the test ads to respondents. This decision is governed by three factors:

1. Broadcast and mobile exposure outdoor[46] versus print ads
2. Informational versus transformational advertising communication models
3. Test situation–produced wearout

Let's go straight to the recommendations, justifying them in terms of these three factors.

**Print Ads: One Ad-Lib Exposure.** With print ads (magazine, newspaper, direct mail, and "stationary" outdoor ads or posters), the target audience decision maker, in the real world, can control the exposure duration, spending little or much time with the ad according to interest. This should be simulated in the ad test with a single ad-lib (untimed) exposure. The usual instruction is: "Please look at this ad as you would normally."

Although transformational print ads should reach their peak effectiveness after multiple exposures (but note Chapter 20's recommended variations-on-a-theme to maintain attention, especially to print campaigns), there is no realistic way of simulating this in the test situation.[47] Thus, whether the communication model is informational or transformational, one ad-lib exposure is the best solution for print ad testing.

This also applies to the testing of *interactive* TV or PC commercials, wherein exposure can be controlled by the respondent. Test them on slides.

**Informational TV and Radio Commercials: Two Exposures.** The recommendation to show or play informational commercials twice comes from a compromise. The message in informational TV and radio commercials should be apparent quickly, thus suggesting one exposure. However, because broadcast commercial exposure duration is fleeting, the respondents should be allowed a first exposure to begin to comprehend the commercial ("What is it?"), then a *second* exposure for the ad to work ("What of it?").[48]

"Mobile" informational outdoor ads or posters (see Chapter 15) should also be given two exposures. Exposure is on slides, each exposure approximating the time for which a driver (mobile audience) or pedestrian (mobile ad) will see the ad in real conditions.

**Transformational TV and Radio Commercials: Three Exposures.** The recommendation to show or play transformational TV and radio commercials—and, as should be evident, "mobile" transformational outdoor ads or posters—three times, is based on all three factors outlined earlier. First, broadcast means at least two exposures will be necessary for respondents to process the commercial. Second, transformational commercials should continue to increase brand attitude beyond two exposures. However, third, more than three successive exposures in a single-ad setting might begin to induce either attentional wearout (unlikely for broadcast) or attitudinal wearout (likely, and counterarguing is fatal for transformational ads[49]).

A transformational commercial should, though, *still be peaking at three successive test exposures;* three exposures is our recommendation.

## Decision 6. Order and Selection of Measures

There are actually two order-of-measures decisions to be made. The first is the overall order of measures according to the design of the study. This order is summarized in Table 19.5; we will discuss it now. The second is the order of measures within the ad test questionnaire itself, discussed later in this section.

**Order for the Pre-Post Design.** In the pre-post design, the *same* respondents go through the entire procedure. After screening for target audience membership, the (disguised) pre-measures are administered, then the test ad, then the post-measures. Shortly, we will explain why there is a delayed post-test for brand awareness and why attention is measured later if required.

**Order for the Experimental-Control Design.** In the experimental-control design, *different* respondents undergo the control procedure and the test procedure. The control cell, in effect, takes the (undisguised) "pre" measures, and the experimental cell takes the "post" measures. In other words, apart from leaving out the false-brands disguise on the pre-measures, the same measures are used as for the pre-post design except that different respondents take them and both cells have to be given the screening questions.

**Why Is the Post-Measure of Brand Awareness Delayed?** Brand awareness is the "kingpin" communication effect that has to result from advertising. It forms a "gate" to the other communication effects (and thus purchase of the brand) because if the prospective buyer does not recognize or recall the brand, it can't be purchased—regardless of how well established or how favorable the other communication effects for the brand are in the prospective buyer's mind.

Brand awareness measures administered at short delay intervals within the ad testing session itself (for example, about 30 minutes for ad testing services that use "theater" tests of TV commercials) do *not* provide a reliable measure of the advertisement's ability to create or increase brand awareness.[50] Short-interval measures should never be interpreted as absolute measures of the ad's ability to create or increase brand awareness, particularly for *brand recall,* which declines drastically. For instance, recall of a single item, such as a new brand name, after a single exposure, will drop after 24 hours to about 18 percent, and after 48 hours to about 11 percent; recognition, however, stays considerably higher, at about 75 percent and 70 percent, respectively.[51]

Only in the special case of *direct response broadcast* advertising—such as the "call or write now" type

---

**TABLE 19.5**

**OVERALL ORDER OF MEASURES FOR THE TWO AD TEST DESIGNS**

*Pre-post design* **(same respondents)**

1. Target audience screening (disguised)
2. Brand awareness: pre-measure (disguised)
3. Other communication objectives: pre-measures (disguised)
**Exposure(s) of test ad**
4. Processing measures
5. Other communication objectives: post-measures
6. Brand awareness: delayed post-measure (immediate if direct response broadcast ad; omit if direct mail ad)
7. Attention diagnostics (later if required)

*Experimental-control design* **(different respondents)**

*Control cell*
1. Target audience screening
2. Brand awareness
3. Other communication objectives

*Experimental cells*
1. Target audience screening
**Exposure(s) of test ad**
2. Processing measures
3. Other communication objectives
4. Brand awareness: delayed
5. Attention diagnostics (later if required)

of ad that appears on TV or radio, or infomercials—should the brand awareness post-measure in the ad test be immediate. (Direct response ads are designed to produce immediate and blatantly obvious effects, so the pre-post design applies.) For broadcast direct response ads, there is often a short delay while the viewer or listener grabs a pencil or goes to the phone, so in this instance, a measure of very short term brand recall (about 1 minute after exposure) is the appropriate post-test measure.

For *direct response print* ads—including *direct mail* ads and *interactive* TV or PC ads—brand awareness should pose little problem because the brand name is right there in front of the reader. There is no need for a post-test of brand awareness for direct response print ads, or for interactive ads: they have to work *now*.

In all other types of advertising, there will be a *delay* between advertising exposure and the next purchase decision opportunity. This may range from an hour or so for "same day" retail advertising to a week or much longer for other products. Ideally, the advertiser should estimate the average exposure-to-decision interval for the target audience and then measure brand awareness *after that interval* from the time of the ad test. However, as we will see shortly, a *week* is usually sufficient for the reinterview delay in an ad test.

- For *brand recall,* this can be achieved by phone: an interviewer calls the test respondents back at least 48 hours later (a week later is safer) and asks them what brands in product category X (actually *category need X*) they recall.
- For *brand recognition,* the measure is more difficult because it requires a personal reinterview in which the test respondents are shown a brand display photograph and asked which brands they recognize at a glance (see brand recognition measures at the end of this chapter). Two-way TV methodologies for ad testing will greatly help for brand recognition measurement, but at present, a personal follow-up interview is essential. This reinterview can be done at any time other than immediately afterward, because brand recognition is very stable, but a delay of 48 hours to a week seems sensible.

We cannot say enough about the necessity of measuring brand awareness correctly in ad testing. Remember that an ad test "forces" brand awareness to an artificially inflated level; on an immediate post-test, brand awareness will be close to 100 percent! Brand

attitude or brand purchase intention ad test results have to be *discounted,* that is, adjusted downward, by the brand awareness level that occurs under actual exposure and purchase interval conditions.[52]

As we shall see in conjunction with action standards, only those respondents who meet the delayed brand awareness criterion should be eligible for "passing" the ad test.

**Why Measure Attention Separately, and Only As a Diagnostic Procedure If Required?** Attention (actually a series of attention responses) is necessary if an ad or promotion offer is to be processed by the target audience. So why isn't attention measured as the first post-measure (in the processing measures) during the ad test?

The reasons for not measuring attention during ad testing are practical. Crude measures of attention, such as asking respondents what they noticed in the ad, would disrupt the assessment of communication effects. Refined measures of attention (see later) are very expensive, requiring separate testing equipment and detailed recording and analysis. It is therefore advisable to go to the expense of measuring attention to the ad only if the ad fails, in the test, to meet one or more of the communication objectives. In other words, attention is measured in a *diagnostic* capacity as the final step in ad testing if this should become necessary due to communication failure.

**Order of Measures in the Ad Test Questionnaire.** The second order-of-measures decision is the order *within* processing (measured, of course, only on the post-test or for the experimental group, after exposure to the ad) and the order *within* communication effects (measured pre *and* post, or for the control *and* experimental groups) in the ad test questionnaire. This "within measures" decision must be made so as to prevent responses to earlier measures biasing responses to later ones.

Table 19.6 shows the order of measures to use. For convenience of discussion in the measurement section (later), we have numbered the measures 1 through 9. There are two things to note from this table:

- Measures 1 and 2 (processing) would not appear in the pre-measures or for the control group.
- Measures 3 to 8 (communication effects) may not all be necessary, depending on the communication *objectives* that you are testing against.

Finally, selection of *particular* measures to employ depends on the advertising communication model.

**TABLE 19.6**

**THE ORDER OF RESPONSE MEASURES IN AD TESTING**

**A. Processing responses (Post only or Experimental group only)**

Measure 1: Acceptance, . . . if *high*-involvement brand attitude is an objective
Measure 2: Learning . . . if *low*-involvement brand attitude is an objective

**B. Communication effects (Pre *and* Post or Control *and* Experimental)**

Measure 3: Category need, . . . if an objective
Measure 4: Brand purchase intention, . . . except if low-involvement/transformational brand attitude is an objective
Measure 5: Brand attitude (overall), . . . except if low-involvement/transformational brand attitude is an objective
Measure 6: Brand attitude benefit beliefs
Measure 7: Purchase facilitation, . . . if an objective
Measure 8: Brand awareness (delayed)

**C. Communication failure**

Measure 9: Attention (diagnostic)

This is more easily explained in conjunction with the measures themselves, which follow shortly.

### Decision 7. Analysis and Action Standards

**Percent of Individuals Attaining the Criterion.** In ad testing, the analysis of results must be conducted in terms of the percent of *individual respondents* attaining the criterion. (What the criterion is we will explain below.) Ads, adlike events, and promotion offers work by persuading individuals, so it is in terms of individuals that the manager must assess the results.

Group results averaged *across* individuals are misleading and should not be used. Let us illustrate this point. Suppose the criterion measure is a four-point brand purchase intention scale, conventionally scored as follows:

| | | |
|---|---|---|
| Definitely will buy | = | 3 |
| Probably will buy | = | 2 |
| Might buy | = | 1 |
| Will not buy | = | 0 |

Suppose that the mean score on the pre-measure (or control group measure) is 1.5, indicating that the "average" respondent "might or probably will" buy. Well,

it doesn't mean this at all. Perhaps 50 percent of the individuals said 2 and 50 percent said 1; or perhaps 50 percent said 3 and 50 percent said 0; these two vastly different *distributions of individual responses* will give a *mean* of 1.5. Do you see the problem?

Let's go further. Suppose that the mean on the pre-measure (or control group measure) is 1.5, and the mean on the post-measure (or experimental group measure) is also 1.5. Does this mean that the ad was ineffective? Not necessarily. In fact, using the two distributions above as examples, the ad could have moved all the 2 respondents up to 3, and all the 1 respondents down to 0. The mean shows no change but there would hardly be "no effect" as 50 percent now *definitely* intend to buy the brand whereas 0 percent did previously. (In the experimental-control design, this would be equivalent to 0 percent saying 3 in the control group, and 50 percent saying 3 in the experimental group.) The fallacy of using group-averaged results should be evident.

In ad testing, you must analyze the results in terms of the *percentage of individuals* who attain the criterion.

**What Is the Criterion?** The criterion is a designated position on the *brand attitude or brand purchase intention measure* (depending on the communication model) *given* that the individual has also attained a designated *position* on the *brand awareness measure* (which again depends on the communication model). The joint communication effects criterion is a specified "disposition" measure as used to conceptualize MEF in Chapter 16. The designated positions are known or estimated by the manager to be sufficient to lead to purchase (or purchase-related) action. For example:

- A brand recognition/high-involvement/informational model might designate as the criterion top-box brand purchase intention (definitely will buy) *given* that the respondent recognized the brand within 5 seconds (on the delayed brand recognition measure).
- A brand recall/low-involvement/transformational model might designate the top two boxes on two main brand attitude benefit belief (semantic differential) measures *given* that the respondent recalled the brand within the first two brands recalled (on the delayed brand recall measure).

This approach to defining the criterion (actually, joint criteria incorporating brand awareness and brand attitude or its resultant intention) is consistent with the disposition principle previously emphasized: The would-be buyer has to *first* be aware of the brand before he or she can buy, and *also* have a favorable attitude toward the brand.

More guidance on how to pick the criterion *position* on the brand awareness and brand attitude measures will be provided in conjunction with the measures themselves in the following sections.

**Action Standards.** The very last but very important decision that the manager has to make before actually conducting the ad test concerns "action standards." *Action standards* are the manager's *prior* considerations of what should be done with the ad depending on alternative outcomes of the results.[53]

Action standards are necessary because they force consideration of what percentage of the target audience in the ad test sample, projected to the population and then translated to the *number* of target audience people, needs to be persuaded in order to achieve enough people taking action and thus meeting the sales goal[54] for the campaign. This is the application of *advanced* validity to the ad test. It is also a judgment required in the task method of budget setting, which was described in Chapter 2, and the task matrix method of IMC budget allocation, described in Chapter 11.

Here is an example: The manager might calculate that an increase of 20 percent of the target audience (other-brand loyals, for instance) who meet the criterion (brand awareness *and* brand purchase intention) is the minimum required to meet the sales goal. Here it is helpful to look ahead in this chapter to the brand purchase intention measure, where the manager can estimate the *probability that the individual will buy* given that he or she said "definitely will buy" (or some lesser intention level) in the ad test. Unfortunately, softer brand attitude measures, when used as the criterion, do not have this relatively straightforward translation to probability of purchase, so the manager must estimate instead. Action standards might then be as follows. We emphasize that this is an *example:*

| Increase in the percentage of individuals meeting the criterion (example only) | Action |
| --- | --- |
| 20+ | Accept ad |
| 15–19 | Revise ad |
| 14 or fewer | Reject ad |

As an experienced advertising manager and researcher, Dr. Neil Holbert, has pointed out, there is no need to be completely rigid about the action standards.[55] They can never be that precise, because of the errors in the chain-of-effects estimates required to lead to sales. In the example, for instance, the observed increase might be 19 percent, which is right on the borderline, and the manager may decide to go ahead with the ad anyway.

Action standard specification, if only to within an approximate range, *is* necessary. The manager is deciding, essentially, whether to go with, revise, or reject an advertisement upon which millions of media dollars will be spent. This decision requires careful forethought, and the requirement of having to set action standards *before* the ad is tested is a good way of ensuring that the decision will not be made in haste. It also enables advanced (absolute predictive) validity to be assessed for the ad test.

In total, then, there are seven overall decisions that the manager has to make in designing an ad test: (1) interview method, (2) design, (3) sample (cell) sizes, (4) test ads' degree of finish, (5) number of exposures, (6) order and selection of measures, and (7) analysis and action standards. After that, there is yet another set of decisions to be made. These decisions concern the selection of *actual* measures (questions and response categories) to put in the ad test questionnaire.

## SCREENING QUESTIONS AND PRE-MEASURES

### Screening Questions

We will assume that target audience screening questions are fairly easy for the researcher to work out. Ad testing should always be conducted with a sample that is randomly or at least representatively chosen from the target audience for the advertising. To select a target audience sample means that potential participants in the ad test will have to be asked *screening questions* about the product category and brand.

The screening questions are disguised in a set of dummy screening questions for other product categories and brands so that respondents will not be alerted to the purpose of the test. The questions ask potential respondents:

**1.** Whether they are aware of the category (if new) and whether they are aware of (can recognize from a set of photographs, preferably, or a list of names) the relevant set of brands including the test brand.

**2.** Whether they've tried each of the brands and, if so, how often.

**3.** How each brand rates in terms of overall attitude (including *expected* attitude for those brands that are new or that the respondent is not aware of): the single best brand, one of several top brands, an average brand, or a below-average brand

With a little thought, screening questions to identify any of the target prospect subgroups can be easily constructed. A *general* set of questions for comprehensive target audience screening was provided in Chapter 18, Table 18.8.

### Pre-Measure Questions

This is where ad test questionnaire design becomes difficult. For the pre-measures (*pre-post* design only), depending on the advertising communication model, questions measuring brand recall, brand purchase intention, and (if deemed necessary) brand benefit beliefs have to be "woven in" with the screening questions. For example, brand recall should be measured *between* category awareness and brand recognition in the first series of questions. Then, brand purchase intention precedes the second question set, and brand benefit beliefs (if measured) follow the third question set. These placements are to avoid bias.

Also, the questions have to be disguised with regard to the test brand—which means that you have to ask the same questions about *other* brands as well. It's tricky, but with clear thinking and pretesting of the questionnaire itself, the pre-measures can be properly designed and inserted. Note, of course, that each pre-measure must correspond exactly with its associated post-measure.

There are, of course, no disguised pre-measures in the *experimental-control* design. After screening, the control group goes straight to the communication effects measures, and the experimental group does processing and then communication effects measures. Three main measurement selection decisions pertain to the processing measures and the communication effects measures. These are discussed in the next three sections of the chapter, using the measure order (1 to 9) from Table 19.6.

### PROCESSING MEASURES

At this point, the test ad is exposed to the respondents (in the pre-post design, or to the experimental group in the experimental-control design). The number of exposures was covered earlier. Following exposure, the processing measures are administered.

### Measure 1: Acceptance

If the advertising communication model is based on *high*-involvement brand attitude strategy (or requires selling category need, inducing a hard-sell brand purchase intention, or achieving a major purchase facilitation objective—any of which are clearly high involvement), then acceptance responses should be measured first. The astute reader may notice, following the above argument regarding measurement of attention only in a diagnostic capacity, that the next two (alternative) processing responses, learning and acceptance, are also diagnostic for communication failure and therefore could be omitted pending such failure. This is true. However, unlike attention, the responses of learning and acceptance are relatively easy to measure, so it is convenient to obtain these diagnostic measures here, in case they are needed later to interpret communication failure on the brand attitude communication effect measure. Moreover, these processing measures do not affect the subsequent measurement of communication effects.[56]

The acceptance measure is taken immediately after exposure to the ad because it must reflect *spontaneous* responses during processing. These responses are immediate and transient, so they have to be measured immediately following exposure to the test ad; to measure them during processing, when they actually occur, would of course disrupt processing.

There are two basic types of measures of acceptance: open-ended cognitive response measures and closed-ended adjective checklist measures. The most valid measure of processing is *cognitive response measurement,* where respondents are questioned as follows:

**1.** While you were watching and listening to the commercial (or reading the ad), what *thoughts, feelings,* or *mental images* did you have? What did you think about? How did you feel? What did you see in your mind?

**2.** Now, I'll read your comments back to you, and I'd like you to tell me whether you regard each comment as positive, neutral, or negative.

Using the answers of question 1, each consumer's spontaneous comments can be classified for diagnostic purposes into brand-related, ad execution–related, presenter-related (if applicable), and other comments —and even more finely within these categories by identifying comments relating to particular benefits. The positivity or negativity of each comment is best judged by the respondent personally, hence question 2. It may further be noted that the best predictor of attitude change appears to be a simple "valence" statistic which, for each *individual,* is his or her total number of positive comments *minus* negative comments. This statistic is sometimes called "net cognitive response," and the proportion of net positive, net neutral, or net negative individuals is assessed.

More about cognitive response measures can be found in a comprehensive review of the technique by Petty, Ostrom, and Brock and in a more recent evaluative review by Rossiter and Holland.[57]

The alternative *adjective checklist (ACL) measure,* while it has yet to have its validity fully established, offers a practical administrative advantage.[58] An ACL is very easy to administer and score because it only asks respondents to check off adjectives (or short adjectival descriptions) that reflect their reactions to the advertising. There is no need to use continuous rating scales for measuring reactions; the dichotomous (0, 1) checklist captures the essential diagnostic information.[59]

The important consideration in compiling an ACL measure is the selection of appropriate adjectives to match the appropriate advertising communication model. For example:

- *Attention:* interesting, held my attention, distracting (−), and so on.
- *Low-involvement/transformational:* likable ad,[60] leaves you with a good feeling, unappealing ad (−), and so on.
- *High-involvement/informational:* convincing, no better than similar brands (−), and so on.
- *High-involvement/transformational:* I could really relate to this ad, this brand is not for me (−), and so on.

However, our suspicion is that ACLs are less valid than cognitive response measures because ACLs may *overdiagnose* the ad: the adjectives included on the list may "prompt" responses that did not in fact occur during processing of the ad. For this reason we prefer the cognitive response measure, especially for high-involvement ads.[61]

With the cognitive response measure or the alternative adjective checklist measure, it is essential to check that the respondents are acquiring an attitude toward or about the right brand! This can be checked by scoring the cognitive response answers for references to the brand (strong evidence) *and* by following the adjective checklist with a question that asks the respondent to name (and, if brand recognition, to describe the appearance of) the brand that was advertised (weaker but *sufficient* evidence that the cognitive responses are related to the right brand—if the respondent can't remember the brand or gets it wrong, then he or she fails the ad test on the brand awareness criterion).

### Measure 2: Learning

Learning responses of the "rote" type are relevant to *low*-involvement brand attitude strategies. (Learning is also necessary for brand awareness, but this is measured later). In the low-involvement brand attitude strategy, what counts is the *perceived* message regarding the brand. It doesn't matter whether the target audience fully accepts, or is convinced by, the message during processing, as long as it is perceived correctly; a successfully registered low-involvement attitude shift will show up as an increase in intention to *try* the brand (for low-involvement/informational advertising), or as brand attitude benefit beliefs (for low-involvement/transformational advertising), as we will explain shortly in conjunction with measures 4 and 6, respectively.

The processing measure for low-involvement attitudinal learning is straightforward. It consists of the following type of question: "In this ad, what do you think the advertiser is trying to tell you about the brand?" The respondent's answer is recorded and then compared with the actual benefit claim itself. Answers, for example, might be: "The advertiser is trying to tell me that Visine is the best product for getting the 'red' out of your eyes," or "The ad shows you that kids who drink Dr. Pepper have a lot of fun." *Verbatim playback or accurate paraphrases* of the ad-proposed brand benefit are scored as successful learning during processing.

Once again, the interviewer should ask: "What was the brand advertised?" (if not already mentioned in the answer). This is because the association to be learned is between the brand (awareness) and the benefit (attitude) and *not* the benefit in isolation.[62] A nonanswer or wrong answer means that the respondent fails the ad test because he or she could not meet the brand awareness criterion.

**Interpretation of Processing Measures' Results.** In interpreting the results of the processing measures —learning, or learning and acceptance—remember that they are *not* ends in themselves. More plainly: If the ad achieves its action standards on the *communication effects* measures (see below), then don't worry about what may appear to be weak processing results. (The exception is the brand awareness communication effect, which could fail in processing, as specified above.) Ads can work in many ways, as we have seen, and even in different ways for different respondents. For instance, some target audience respondents may focus on one element as a benefit, and other respondents may focus on another. (In fact, in analysis of "message takeout" from processing measures, it is rare for any one message point or benefit to be registered as "the main point" by more than 40 percent of respondents, and the message-points results may bear surprisingly little relationship to persuasion. The Benetton ads are a notable example of extremely heterogeneous main message takeout yet unquestionably strong persuasiveness.[63]) However, if the ad *fails* to meet one or more communication objectives, especially a brand benefit belief or brand attitude objective, then scrutiny of the processing measures' results might diagnose the cause of the problem, such as a missed or mislearned claim or a weak presenter.

So if the ad works fine at the communications effects end, don't overreact to the processing results (the exception again: the brand awareness communication effect, which must be processed correctly). Their main role is *negative-diagnostic.* Any such diagnosis should be done at the individual (disaggregate) level, not by comparing percentages of respondents on one measure with another. Regression or at least cross-tabulation (see also the sections on analysis later in this chapter and in Chapter 20) is the appropriate procedure.[64]

## COMMUNICATION EFFECTS MEASURES

The order of communication effects measures is different from the order in which they typically occur in the buyer's mind (see again Table 19.6). The reasons for the differing order of measurement from the buyer's more typical sequence of category need, brand awareness, brand attitude, brand purchase intention, and purchase facilitation are twofold. First, as previously explained, the brand awareness measure (the real one, not the check in processing) has to be delayed because, except in the case of a direct response ad, it is pointless to measure brand awareness after the respondent has just seen or heard the ad. Not only would nearly everyone have perfect awareness with this virtually immediate measure, but also it would not validly reflect the usual postexposure interval during which brand awareness has to endure in the real world. The second reason for the altered order of measurement pertains to brand attitude and brand purchase intention. The order of these two measures is reversed to prevent respondents from forming or modifying their purchase intentions from the attitude measure rather than from the ad. We elaborate on these points in relation to the respective measures.

### Measure 3: Category Need (If an Objective)

The first communication measure taken is category need—if *reminding or selling* of the category need is a communication objective of the campaign. Let us first consider measurement when the objective is to remind the target audience of category need, then we will consider measurement for the more complicated objective of selling category need.

**Reminding of Category Need.** When the category need communication objective is to *remind* the prospective buyer of a previously existing or latent category need, the measure to be used is *category purchase intention.* For example, if the objective is to remind current owners of personal computers of the category need in order to influence them to buy a new one, ask: "How likely is it that you will buy a new personal computer for home use in the next 6 months?"

**Selling Category Need.** To measure the communication objective of *selling* the category need requires three measures at the category level: *category purchase intention, category benefit beliefs,* and *category awareness* (delayed). Category benefit beliefs are required to assess whether, indeed, the advertisement has "sold" the prospect on the need to buy this product category. Category awareness is required to ensure that the prospect "remains sold" by remembering the product category. Category awareness occurs within the context of competing purchase *categories* (for example, "What new items are you thinking of buying for your use at home within the next 6 months?"). The brand measures then follow.

The multiple measures at the category level are required by the consideration, when selling category need, to "treat the category as if it were a brand." The potential buyer must first be aware of the category, accept its (category attitude) benefits, and intend to buy within the category—before the particular brand's communication effects can come into play. Brand communication effects are then measured at this "second level."

Category communication effects, from a measurement standpoint, are conceptually identical to brand communication effects, although the respondent is rating the category in the first instance and the brand in the second. The measures themselves are therefore discussed only at the brand level in the sections to follow. All one has to do for constructing category measures is to treat the category as a brand and revise measures 4 through 8 to reflect the category as the measurement level.

### Measure 4: Brand Purchase Intention (Except Low-Involvement/Transformational Models)

There is one situation (applying *only* to ad testing) in which brand purchase intention should *not* be used as a measure. This is for *low-involvement/transformational* communication models. The reason is that the low-involvement "image" type of attitude that this advertising addresses takes "time to build"—actually, multiple exposures to build. In the ad test situation, it is not reasonable to expect an immediate effect on brand purchase intention. Indeed, the effect may be largely subconscious.

Instead, the effect of low-involvement/transformational ads should be inferred from increases on the *brand attitude benefit beliefs (measure 6)* because this is the only reasonable effect that can be expected during the ad test. In campaign evaluation after the ad has been running for a while, on the other hand, both brand purchase intention (measure 4) and overall brand attitude (measure 5) would be used because the transformational advertising has now had time—that is, a sufficient number of exposures—to work.

For all other communication models, a brand purchase intention measure is included. And it should be the first communication effect measured (other than category need when that is an objective) so that this desired result of the advertising is not "contaminated" by the brand attitude measure.

**Constructing the Purchase Intention Measure.** Measures of purchase intention involve four considerations: (1) the wording of the intention question in

terms of "try," "buy," or "use"; (2) a time frame for intention; (3) the type of rating scale; and (4) how to interpret the ratings.

The first consideration, wording, should be elementary but is not. For new product categories (and brands), consumers or potential customers are more willing to state intentions to "try" a brand, which implies less commitment, than they are to state intentions to "buy" it. (This is especially true of intentions to "request further information" or to send in a fairly noncommitting reply coupon, as in *two-step* direct response ads. This does not mean the prospect intends to *buy* the product or service.) Similarly, purchase versus usage may be relevant, depending on the specific action objective of the advertising. For example, many consumers own power tools, or dangerous chemical fertilizers, or drugs, but for a number of reasons are not really classifiable as "users," since they own them but rarely or never use them. Advertisers targeting loyal users of variable consumption products (such as pasta) or services (such as long-distance telephone calls) would also want to focus on intended usage rate.[65] The wording of the intention measure should therefore *reflect precisely the purchase or purchase-related action objective.*

The second consideration, time frame, must be included for the *category* purchase intention measure. For example, many consumers "intend" to buy a CD-ROM interactive TV set, but most of them have somewhat vague ideas as to when. The sample question about personal computers specified a time frame of 6 months. For a consumer packaged good, a more relevant time frame might be "the next time you visit the supermarket." The point is that open-ended intention measures can be misleading. The manager needs a time frame in order to make an unambiguous assessment of category purchase intention results.

Time frame for the *brand* purchase intention measure is incorporated by making the intention *conditional* on category need.[66] For example:

- *If you were going to buy a personal computer for home use, how likely would you be to buy an IBM PC?*
- The *next time* you buy yogurt, how likely is it that you will buy Dannon?

The third consideration concerns the type of rating scale to employ. We favor "unipolar" scales ranging from 0 to positive; in our view, an intention *cannot* be negative, since you cannot "unbuy" a product—either you don't buy (0) or you do (positive). The exception is when *amount* of purchase is also a consideration; for example, Healthy Choice may wish to measure category purchase intention as, "Do you intend to buy more, the same, or fewer frozen dinners in the coming year?" Apart from this, unipolar scales should be used.

The type of scale has to be combined with the fourth consideration, interpretation. At the *individual* buyer level, with which communication objectives are concerned, we believe the fractional or "box" measure is the most interpretable and meaningful to the manager.[67]

For *low-involvement* products where *trial* or a *single purchase over a long purchase cycle* is the action objective, a four-point brand purchase intention scale can be used and interpreted (within parentheses) as follows: "definitely will buy" (an estimated 90 percent of these individuals will actually buy), "probably will buy" (40 percent), "might buy" (10 percent), and "will not buy" (0 percent). For low-involvement products where *usage* of the brand *among several acceptable brands bought reasonably often* is the action objective, we need to allow for more than one brand. A good (three-point) measure results from the following questions: "If you were shopping for (the product category), which brand would you be most likely to buy? What would be your second choice?" Indications are that, on the next purchase occasion, 75 percent of consumers who nominated the brand as their first choice will buy it; 15 percent who nominated it as their second choice will buy it; and 7 percent, also, who did *not* name it will buy it (thus, the three points on the scale). The heavy weighting toward the "top box" in both the foregoing measures reflects consumers' tendencies to develop clear-cut and simplified brand purchase intentions for low-involvement products.

For *high-involvement* brand purchase intention, such as for industrial products and major consumer durables, when more discriminating judgments by consumers seem feasible, Juster's 11-point probability or percentage scale can be used. The 11 points on the scale are as follows:

Certain or practically certain (99 percent chance)
Almost sure (90 percent)
Very probable (80 percent)
Probable (70 percent)

Good possibility (60 percent)
Fairly good possibility (50 percent)
Fair possibility (40 percent)
Some possibility (30 percent)
Slight possibility (20 percent)
Very slight possibility (10 percent)
No chance or almost no chance (0 percent)

In this case, the parenthesized percentages are *in* the scale and do *not* represent the purchase-forecast weights. These may differ considerably for different high-involvement products or services, although a reasonable set would appear to be linear weights starting from 5 percent ("no chance" end of scale) and proceeding in 5 percent increments to 55 percent ("certain" end of scale).[68]

When measuring brand purchase intention for brand *recognition* communication models, the validity of the measure will be increased if a *picture of the brand* is used. We will discuss this further in conjunction with brand awareness (measure 8).

### Measure 5: Brand Attitude (Except Low-Involvement/Transformational Models)

Next comes the overall measure of brand attitude. This measure is omitted only when testing low-involvement/transformational advertisements, as explained above.

Brand attitude measurement helps to interpret the ultimate ad test criterion measure: brand purchase intention (given brand awareness). Whereas in brand purchase intention we measure how likely the respondent is to *buy* the brand, in overall brand attitude we measure how favorably the brand is *evaluated relative to other brands,* regardless of whether the respondent would buy it at the next purchase opportunity.

**Constructing the Brand Attitude Measure.** The main thing to remember in preparing the brand attitude measure is to specify the "situation" (motivation) for which the brand is to be evaluated. This is consistent with brand attitude as a "superbelief" about the brand (see Chapter 5). Note that if there's any doubt, the situation *also* should be specified in the *purchase intention* measure (for example, a personal computer *for home use*). As we have seen in Chapter 5, global evaluations, without the motivation, are meaningless.

The set of brands against which the test brand is to be rated has to be chosen. Generally, the relevant set will be apparent from advertising strategy research—for the target audience. If the relevant set is not known, which is almost inexcusable, McCollum Spielman testing service recommends including the leading competing brands accounting in total for at least 70 percent of market share. Unless the category is a product such as shampoos, where the market is atomized by an incredible number of small-share brands, this will usually provide a list of manageable length. For brand *recognition* communication models, again, *pictures of the brands* will increase the validity of the brand attitude measure.

Many researchers favor the "constant sum" measure for overall attitude rating.[69] However, we favor a four-level measure in which respondents are asked if they would rate the advertised brand, along with competitor brands, as "the single best brand," "one of several top brands," "an average brand," or a "below-average brand," for a specific situation. It is conceptually equivalent to constant sum, and much easier for the manager to interpret. Notice too that the focus is on *evaluation,* not purchase.

### Measure 6: Brand Attitude Benefit Beliefs

Having respondents rate the brand's perceived delivery on the specific benefit or benefits employed in the advertisement to influence brand attitude serves as a *diagnostic* measure for the overall brand attitude result as well as the sole measure of brand attitude when low-involvement/transformational brand attitude is an objective. This measure (a set of measures) follows the overall brand attitude rating (measure 5)—again, so as to avoid contamination. The advertiser does not want the respondent forming a spurious attitude based on benefits suggested in the *measures* rather than on benefits spontaneously processed in the *ad.* Hence, the diagnostic benefit measures follow the overall attitude measure.

The form of brand benefit belief scales should be adapted to the type of brand attitude (advertising communication model), as explained next.

**Low-Involvement/Informational Model.** In the low-involvement/informational brand attitude strategy, the brand is perceived as either having the benefit or not having it. Consumers are *not* involved enough to discriminate *degrees* of benefit delivery, and even if they do, the brand choice probably is made on a "pass-fail" basis of benefit possession anyway. Thus we recommend a *no-yes* (0, 1) set of benefit belief measures for the low-involvement/informational model.

**High-Involvement/Informational Model.** When consumers are highly involved with brand choice, degrees of benefit delivery *do* make a difference. Often researchers employ what are called Likert scales to reflect gradations of perceived delivery. For example: "How strongly do you agree that the IBM PC is expensive: Do you agree strongly, agree slightly, neither agree nor disagree, disagree slightly, or disagree strongly?" However, the gradation really should not be a part of the agreement. Rather, the gradation should be in *amount of benefit possession.* For example: "Do you believe the IBM PC is not at all expensive, somewhat expensive, moderately expensive, or very expensive?" The latter type of scale is much easier for the manager to interpret.

A refinement in measuring benefit beliefs for high-involvement/informational advertising communication models is to add a *confidence measure* (see Chapter 5). After each benefit delivery rating, a second scale asks respondents how sure they are of the rating scale *point* they chose on the benefit delivery scale, for example, "not at all sure," "somewhat sure," "moderately sure," or "very sure." Moran[70] contends that advertising can work by making consumers *more sure* of a brand's benefit delivery without necessarily making them believe that the brand delivers an *increased amount* of the benefit than they previously thought. This increased confidence fits high-involvement theory whereby consumers have to be convinced by advertising (be very sure or confident) before trial. What the advertisement is doing in this case is producing a *more strongly held* benefit belief.

**Low-Involvement/Transformational Model.** When testing low-involvement/transformational advertisements, measure 6 is the sole attitude measure and also substitutes for the purchase intention measure. The theoretical rationale for this was explained at length in Chapter 5.

Recommended for low-involvement/transformational ads is a "softer" measure of perceived benefits popularly known as "semantic differential" scales.[71] For *each* benefit, and there may be only one (for example, that a brand of Scotch is socially sophisticated), several scales are employed to improve the reliability of this softer measure. The scales consist of bipolar adjectives separated by seven-point intensity ratings. For example, to measure the brand's perceived "sophisticated" image, the advertiser may use the following three scales:

| An upscale drink | ⊔⊔⊔⊔⊔⊔⊔ | A downscale drink |
| My friends would not approve | ⊔⊔⊔⊔⊔⊔⊔ | My friends would approve |
| A discriminating choice | ⊔⊔⊔⊔⊔⊔⊔ | A choice of the masses |

The manager unfamiliar with semantic differential scales should consult a good marketing research text, or Osgood, Suci, and Tannenbaum's classic book,[72] for details of labeling, rotation of order and scale direction, and calculation of significant "image" shifts when using these measures.

**High-Involvement/Transformational Model.** Brand benefit delivery ratings for *high*-involvement/transformational brand attitudes require some thought on the part of the manager or researcher. Because of the high-involvement aspect, gradations of benefit delivery are appropriate, suggesting the same type of scales as for a high-involvement/*informational* model. However, if the product type is such that the brand attitude is "soft"—such as, for example, choice of expensive designer jeans for a first-time buyer (NCU) target audience—then semantic differential scales, which are also gradated, would be a better selection.

**Use Common Sense in Benefit-Delivery Measure Selection.** Throughout this section, we have tried to demonstrate that rating scales should be selected according to two commonsense considerations:

1. The advertising communication model, which is the model of *how the consumer or customer decides.*
2. Ease of interpretation of what the ratings mean in terms of diagnostic or corrective action.

With these two principles in mind, it shouldn't be too difficult to select appropriate measures—for brand benefits or, indeed, for any communication objective to be measured.

## Measure 7: Purchase Facilitation (if an Objective)

The last immediate communication effect measure is purchase facilitation, if this is an objective of the ad-

vertising. Usually, the measure will consist simply of a direct open-ended question (for example, for a distribution problem: "Do you think this brand will be easy to obtain in this area?"). Alternatively, purchase facilitation items can be *added to the benefit belief ratings* of measure 6 (for example, easy to obtain . . . difficult to obtain). Either measure should be capable of rating whether purchase facilitation has been successfully addressed in the advertisement.

## Measure 8: Brand Awareness (Delayed)

Because of its importance in ad testing, we gave considerable previous discussion to the delayed brand awareness measure. Here we will focus on the physical measures themselves—one for brand recognition and the other for brand recall.

**Constructing the Brand Recognition Measure.** The main consideration in constructing the measure of brand recognition is to *simulate the real-world recognition situation as closely as possible.*

Usually this will be visual recognition,[73] so a personal reinterview is required, at the average exposure-to-decision interval. However, when using the *experimental-control* design so that there is no pre-measure sensitization, it could be argued (see also Chapter 8 and Chapter 20) that because visual recognition declines relatively little over time, an *in-test* rather than a delayed measure would be satisfactory. Tomlin[74] has used the in-test (experimental versus control) brand recognition measure with, he reports, realistic results. Nevertheless, we believe that a 48-hour to 1-week delayed measure is preferable.

When visual recognition in the real world occurs singly—as in, say, choosing a motel or a fast-food restaurant when traveling on a freeway or turnpike—then the visual stimuli in the test should be administered singly. Actual logos or, better still, photographs of storefronts, should be used. The recognition response to each is no-yes.

When visual recognition in the real world occurs in a multiple-brand, competitive display—as is the case with most supermarket or drugstore products—a simulation of the display must be used. Color photographs are best for this. And if the number of competing brands, shelf spaces, or shelf positions vary widely, then several photographs, randomized across respondents, should be used. Respondents should be asked to point to the brands that they recognize, in the *order* in which they recognize them from the display. Display types, too, should be taken into account: package recognition varies markedly, for instance, in open versus closed freezers for frozen foods.[75]

What should the *cutoff* for brand recognition be, in the competitive context? There is no *general* answer to this question. (And it is a vital question, because the criterion measure for ad tests is brand purchase intention or brand attitude *given* brand awareness.) The best answer is empirical: in the advertising *strategy* research, find out how many brands the typical buyer looks at before deciding. The next best answer is theoretical: for low-involvement purchases, the maximum would be about three brands, whereas for high-involvement decisions, there probably should be no cutoff, as long as the buyer *does* recognize the test brand.

**Constructing the Brand Recall Measure.** Brand recall measures, because they are completely aural, can be conveniently administered on a delayed basis by telephone interview. The delay *is* important for accurate brand recall communication effect measurement, because brand recall declines quickly from the test situation, and is far more subject to competitive interference than brand recognition.

An example of a typical brand recall measure would be: "When you think of personal computers for home use by people like yourself, what brands come to mind?" The main thing to remember is to specify the *category need cue* or stimulus, to which recalled brands are the responses, in the brand recall question itself; for example, personal computers for *home* use, rather than personal computers for *office* use at the person's place of work, which normally would not be a personal purchase.

The brand recall *cutoff* criterion must be set to provide valid interpretation of brand recall results. Again, empirical determination of the number of brands the typical buyer usually recalls before making the purchase decision provides the best answer to the cutoff measure. For low-involvement decisions, this very often will be the first or "top-of-mind" brand recalled. But for high-involvement decisions, up to five or six brands may be recalled for purchase consideration. Specification of a realistic cutoff becomes vitally important when ad test results are analyzed because, as explained, the criterion is brand purchase intention or brand attitude *given* that the brand was recalled within the real-world cutoff number.

## COMMUNICATION FAILURE

### Measure 9: Attention (Diagnostic)

If an advertisement fails to meet its "action standard" on a criterion measure, and if the other diagnostic measures (1, 2, or 6) have not revealed the problem, then this is the time to employ a diagnostic *attention* measure.

**The "Show-and-Tell" Measure of Attention.** A basic but often adequate diagnostic measure of attention is the "show-and-tell" method. The researcher takes a sample of about 30 of the target audience respondents and re-presents the ad to them individually. To measure *visual* attention, you hand them the print ad again, or reshow the TV commercial and, by giving them a remote control device, enable them to pause and "freeze" at scenes that they noticed earlier. You then ask them to describe *what* they noticed, that is, what they noticed during the earlier exposure or exposures. To measure *auditory* attention, TV audio tracks or radio commercials can be re-presented sentence by sentence, and respondents are asked what they remembered hearing during the ad test's earlier exposure.

The weakness of this method is that it does not represent normal processing (natural attention). Nevertheless, because of its relatively low cost, it should be tried as a first resort to see whether the attentional problem or problems in the ad can be easily pinpointed.

**Physiological Measures of Attention.** More valid but considerably more expensive diagnostic attention measures require the use of physiological (for example, eye-movement, pupillometric, or EEG) apparatus, or semiphysiological (for example, CONPAAD or "moment-to-moment" button-pressing or dial-turning) apparatus.[76]

*Visual* attention problems—which include TV video and print visuals, *and* copy, since it is visually read—are most accurately traced through eye-tracking analysis. Burke's Telcom division, in Teaneck, New Jersey, can analyze TV commercials in dynamic presentation. Print ads or still video frames can be analyzed by commercial firms such as Perception Research Services (Englewood Cliffs, New Jersey), The Pretesting Co., Inc. (Fairlawn, New Jersey), or E.Y.E., Inc. (New York).

*Auditory* attention problems—which include TV audio and radio commercials—require a device like

ARBOR, Inc.'s CONPAAD, in which respondents depress a foot or hand switch to maintain audio intensity. Because you can't "see" the ear responding, auditory attention is particularly difficult to measure. However CONPAAD can detect which parts of a TV or radio commercial sound track respondents appear to tune out and which parts they find useful (informational) or attractive (transformational) to listen to. (It should be noted that more recent imitations of CONPAAD, such as PEAC or SPEEDBACK,[77] measure *visual* attention only.)

The general conclusion is that detailed diagnostic attention measures are affordable only by the very largest advertisers. The diagnostic capacity of these measures for *attention* problems seems good. But their "prognostic" or predictive capacity for developing more effective advertising in terms of *communication effects* has yet to be established. (What is needed is a validated theory of commercials' "patterns" like the speculative theory we presented in Chapter 10—along with, probably, emotion *shift* ratings for the brand attitude communication effect, as we postulated in Chapters 8 and 9.) At present, we must conclude that such measures should be employed only as a last resort in ad testing, when communication failure cannot be diagnosed by simpler and less expensive analysis.

## BUYER BEHAVIOR MEASURES

Some ad testing methods incorporate buyer behavior (target audience action) measures. These include follow-up self-report interviews of brand purchases; providing test respondents with coupons for an entire product category or all major brands within a category including the test brand, redeemable only at a nearby store; and the split-cable method for testing TV commercials, used by Burke's AdTel, IRI's BehaviorScan, and Nielsen's HomeScan, which is very much like split-run testing for print or direct mail ads.[78] All such measures are reasonably straightforward for the manager to interpret. These methods measure step 4 in the buyer response sequence (target audience action), and provide a useful but expensive addition to the measures of step 2 (processing) and step 3 (communication effects).

However, buyer behavior measures in split-cable or split-run tests cannot *alone* substitute for testing on the two prior steps unless the advertiser is willing to experimentally vary the elements in an ad across a number of possible combinations in a large-scale and costly experiment. Even then, diagnosis of *why* the ads—and, specifically, various elements *in* the ads—did or did not work is indirect. So most managers prefer to test processing and communication effects directly in the manner described in this chapter. A buyer behavior test can then be added if the testing budget is large and the manager wants a really high level of assurance before approving the ad's use in a campaign.

## TESTING PROMOTION OFFERS

Promotion offers can be just as complex as advertisements. There is every reason to test (pretest) promotion offers just as the intelligent manager would always test an advertisement. The objective is the same: to determine whether the promotion offer is being *processed* in a way that will meet its *communication objectives*.

Most often the two communication objectives for a promotion are brand awareness and brand purchase intention. However, brand attitude should always be a complementary objective (for the customer franchise-building, or CFB, aspect of offer implementations). Also, there are often two target audiences for whom communication effects are relevant: distributors, and the prospective customers themselves. We will concentrate on customer pretesting here.

### Processing of Promotion Offers

To produce communication effects, the promotion offer has to be *processed* correctly by the prospective buyer. Elements of the promotion offer pertaining to the respective communication effects have to be attended to and learned (for brand awareness and low-involvement brand attitude) or attended to and accepted (for promotion offers that attempt to stimulate category need, high-involvement brand attitude, brand purchase intention, or purchase facilitation).

As Russo[79] has reminded us, promotion offers are not automatically processed. The first processing response, attention, is far from guaranteed for point-of-purchase offers given the profusion of other stimuli, although it is more probable with media offers or direct mail offers. And, following initial attention, the prospective buyer must decide whether to further process the offer based on the expected benefit it entails as weighed against the time and effort it would take to respond.

**Attribution As a Processing Response for Promotion Offers.** Of most interest to the manager is the processing of promotion offers such that they result in acceptance of an immediate purchase intention and—via the CFB concept—an increase in brand attitude. With regard to purchase intention, it is meaningful to speak of the *attribution* the prospective buyer makes regarding the promotion offer. The attribution response can occur during or after acceptance, and in either case represents an *additional* processing response that is unique to promotion and does not occur for advertising or adlike communications.

As Raju and Hastak[80] have observed, there are many diverse attributions that prospective buyers may make in response to promotion offers. However, it is possible to organize these attributions into four main categories (Table 19.7). Our approach postulates that promotions cause attributions that reinforce purchase intention in one of four ways. Two of the attributional mechanisms are negatively reinforcing and therefore represent *informational* motivations for brand choice. Two are positively reinforcing and therefore represent *transformational* motivations for brand choice. Thus, promotion offers operate via the motivational foundations of brand attitude introduced in Chapter 5.

### TABLE 19.7

**ATTRIBUTIONS MADE IN PROCESSING PROMOTION OFFERS**

**Informational attributions**

1. Immediate value      (Problem removal)
   - Price-offs
   - Bonus packs
   - Rebates, refunds
   - Trade coupons
2. Future value: risk reduction      (Problem avoidance)
   - Samples, trial offers, free demonstrations
   - Warranties
   - Loyalty programs

**Transformational attributions**

3. Gifts      (Sensory gratification)
   - Coupons
   - Premiums
   - Stamps, continuity offers
4. Chance: risk taking      (Sensory gratification or intellectual stimulation)
   - Contests, sweepstakes

**Immediate Value.** Four types of promotion offers—price-offs, bonus packs, rebates and refunds, and trade coupons—prompt an attribution of *immediate value,* which reinforces the purchase intention "negatively" by *removing the problem* of paying a normal high price. These four types of promotion offers are perceived as immediate rewards that represent "good value" to the buyer.

**Future Value (Risk Reduction).** Two types of promotion offers—free or discounted samples (or their common industrial counterparts, trial offers or free demonstrations) and warranties—prompt an attribution of future value. By allowing the buyer to try the brand on a sample basis before committing to paying the full price, and by offering recompense or replacement if something goes wrong, these promotions operate on *problem avoidance* motivation. As such they are "negatively" reinforcing. It is important to note that they work on current purchasing behavior but by providing the *expectation of "future value"* rather than providing the buyer with immediate value. A third type of promotion offer—loyalty programs—also fits this classification because the buyer "signs on" now for the expectation of future price savings.

**Gifts.** Three types of promotion offers—coupons, premiums, and stamps or other continuity plans—prompt an attribution of gift reception.[81] In numerous interviews with shoppers, it is clear that (manufacturers') coupons are regarded as something more than the equivalent price-off. A 50¢ coupon usually will be more effective than an equivalent 50¢ price-off.[82] Coupons, premiums, and continuity offers such as stamps leave the buyer with something tangible, which consumers tend to regard as a *gift.* The gift aspect invokes the psychology of exchange whereby the buyer often feels a reciprocal obligation to continue to patronize the brand.[83] The "good feeling" generated by these types of offers is a form of *sensory gratification,* and therefore the attribution is "positively" reinforcing.

**Chance (Risk Taking).** The remaining type of promotion offer—contests and the related variant of sweepstakes—appeals to mild risk-taking motivation in the prospective buyer by offering participation in a game of chance. The motivation here is *sensory gratification* or even *intellectual stimulation,* and the attribution is "positively" reinforcing.

**Understanding How Promotion Offers Work.** All of the above categories of attribution in the processing of promotion offers suggest that there is a lot to be understood about the "psychology" of promotions. Promotion offers are not simply mechanistic economic incentives. Rather, they involve processes of adaptation level in perception;[84] response costs and reinforcement schedules;[85] social exchange;[86] and subjective probability[87] and skill versus luck, or internal versus external control.[88] Academic researchers are beginning to examine the implications of these theories for promotion.[89] Managers, while not expected to be psychologists, should at least be thinking more about how promotion offers actually work.

### Pretesting Promotion Offers Based on Processing

It is important for the manager to understand the basic differences in the way promotions are processed attributionally to produce brand purchase intentions. The managerial questions to be answered (via the pretesting of promotions) correspond with the way the promotion is processed:

- Does the offer represent enough immediate value (price-offs, bonus packs, rebates and refunds, trade coupons)?
- Does the offer sufficiently reduce perceived risk and thereby promise future value (sampling, warranties, loyalty programs)?
- Does the offer constitute an appreciated gift (coupons, premiums, continuity offers)?
- Does the offer excite through the possibility of a reward won by skill or chance (contests, sweepstakes, lotteries)?

Promotion offer pretests must be conducted with a properly screened target audience sample. For trial promotions, you want people who have not yet tried the brand, or at least not recently. For repeat-purchase or usage promotions, you want *only* triers of the brand. Further pretest sample divisions will allow precise analysis of how each prospective target audience subgroup processes the promotion offer in its alternative (pretest) executions.

**Immediate Value Promotions.** Price-offs, bonus packs, rebates and refunds, and trade coupons must suggest immediate value to prospective buyers. The most straightforward way to pretest the *amount of price-off* (in all of the above) that will be effective is to present the brand, in a survey interview format with several other closely competing brands—all at their normal prices—then progressively introduce better and better offers on the to-be-promoted brand until an acceptable percentage of the target audience sample indicates that they would switch to the promoted brand.[90]

**Future Value (Risk-Reduction) Promotions.** Samples, trial offers, demonstrations, warranties, and loyalty programs function by reducing the perceived risk of trial of the brand.

The major method of testing *samples* is by home placements. The sample is placed with several hundred target audience prospects, and a count is made of how many try the sample, prefer it to whatever product or brand they are currently using, and indicate an intention to switch to it. An introductory price or price-plus-coupon test (as above) can then be conducted with the intentional triers.

*Trial offers and demonstrations* (usually for consumer durables and industrial products) and also *loyalty programs* can be tested by trying them on a limited basis—usually with those prospects, or in geographic areas, that the manager regards as relatively expendable should the offer not work. During testing, trial offers can be sweetened by varying the time or the terms of the offer. But if a free demonstration doesn't convert prospects in the test, then the product may be in trouble!

*Warranties* contain three attributes that can be varied, which makes pretesting very important: the *parts* of the product covered by the warranty, the *extent* of replacement or repair, and the *time period* of the offer. The manager should offer a good enough warranty to induce an acceptable percentage of prospects to buy, but not so good as to lose money on subsequent servicing and repairs. A multifactor experimental design is necessary, covering combinations from within the feasible range for each attribute.

**Gift Promotions.** Coupons, premiums, and continuity offers are attributed primarily as gifts, overlayed on their price-off characteristics.

With *coupons* the testing procedure is the same as for price-offs. A coupon should stimulate trial usage, depending on its purpose, at a lower face value than a direct price-off (it has to cover the additional cost of couponing). For the CFB aspects of the coupon, immediate recognition of the package portrayed on the coupon and immediate recall of the brand and main message (following brief exposure to the coupon) should also be tested.

*Premiums* need to be tested first and foremost for their *product* appeal to the target audience, quite aside from their value appeal. The most efficient method is to test several alternative premiums side by side as gifts—without price—one of which, if possible, is a previous premium with known performance among the target audience, to be used as a "control." Second, the one or two most widely appealing premiums should then be shown with the (carrier) brand, and questions should be asked about each premium's compatibility with the brand's "image." Finally, unless it is free, the price of the premium should be tested for intention to buy, on a downward progressive price scale. Obviously, for self-liquidating premiums, the lowest price tested would be the breakeven price, allowing for distribution and handling costs.

*Continuity offers* can be tested by varying the purchase ratio (number or dollar amount of purchases required) against various types of gift merchandise. "Magnitude estimation" is a good procedure for this. Start with a standard gift at an agreeable redemption number, then ask consumers to provide numbers (as if "bidding") for other items. Human nature being what it is, the marketer could probably add slightly to the consumers' bids without reducing the offer's appeal.

**Chance (Risk-Taking) Promotions.** *Contests* and *sweepstakes* basically appeal to mild risk-taking motivation. Prizes should be tested for target audience appeal first. For cash prizes, this is straightforward. For merchandise prizes, the first two steps in premium testing are applicable here: audience appeal and compatibility with the to-be-promoted brand.

Contest *versus* sweepstakes entry requirements should then be examined. Sweepstakes entry is easy but is less preferable because it doesn't require purchase. (If re-creating brand awareness among as many "lapsed" users as possible is the communication objective, then sweepstakes would probably be the choice.) Contests should not be so difficult as to discourage entry and thus reduce entry-qualifying purchases, but they should not be so easy as to lose their "intellectual" appeal and degenerate into a sweepstakes. Test consumers, notified of the prize, should be asked to state their likelihood of entry under contest *then* sweepstakes conditions.

### Posttesting Promotion Offers

Whenever possible the final promotion offer should be "posttested" on a limited geographic basis (this isn't always possible with fast-reaction promotions). This is important for obtaining a good estimate of the promotion offer's redemption rate. Field testing provides a more reliable estimate than pretesting under laboratory conditions. Fractions of a percentage point can mean the difference between profit and loss on a promotion.

Two other types of posttesting are extremely informative for the manager who really wants to understand how promotions work. These are in-store observation and interviews, and follow-up survey interviews with responders and nonresponders to the promotion.[91]

In-store observation and intercept interviews with shoppers at the point of purchase are relevant for store-distributed promotions. Bettman[92] even had shoppers "think aloud" into a tape recorder, to see how promotion offers fit in with other brand benefits in influencing brand choice. Much can be learned from this type of investigation to improve the effectiveness of POP promotions.

Follow-up survey interviews with samples of consumers (or business prospects) who did or did not respond to the company's promotion offer are a useful research exercise for all forms of promotion. By conducting follow-up surveys (equivalent in advertising research to campaign evaluation; see Chapter 20), the manager can measure the communication effects that did or did not occur during the promotion and thus gain diagnostic insight into the promotion's causal influence on buyer behavior. In particular, follow-up surveys can determine which target audiences the promotion actually reached; whether the promotion was consumer franchise-building; and whether it resulted in trial, repeat purchase, or both, in producing sales.

### Calculating the Return on Promotions

The profit return on promotions is relatively straightforward to calculate after the fact, but obviously the return must be estimated beforehand in deciding whether to launch a promotion offer in the first place. Holbert, Golden, and Chudnoff[93] provide a general summary of the steps involved. Hypothetical figures are shown with the steps as follows:

**A.** Number of offers distributed: 500,000

**B.** Cost of promotion: $600,000

**C.** Response rate: 15 percent

**D.** Number responding (A × C): 75,000
**E.** Conversion rate to full-price purchasers: 13 percent
**F.** Number of converters (D × E): 9,750
**G.** Net profit per converter per year: $40
**H.** Total profit from converters per year (F × G): $390,000
**I.** Loss of sales from buyers who would have bought anyway: $50,000
**J.** Net profit per year (H − I): $340,000
**K.** Payback period (B ÷ J): 1.76 years

As you can see, there are a number of steps to be estimated if the financial results of the promotion are to be gauged in advance.

- The *cost* of mounting promotion offers (step B) is particular to the promotion technique. For some techniques, the cost varies with the redemption rate, such as for self-liquidating premiums. The components of cost—advertising, production, distribution, handling, and so forth—are far too specific and complicated to summarize here. Schultz and Robinson[94] provide an excellent review of the main cost components of each technique and its main "media" implementation methods.
- The *response rate* to promotions (step C) can be estimated with either and, if possible, both pretesting and field-testing procedures. The only substitute for testing is to rely on internal company experience with similar promotions, or to consult an experienced promotion house.
- The *conversion rate* to full-price purchasers (after the promotion is withdrawn) can also be estimated by pretesting, or by field-testing, or on the basis of previous or expert experience. The related step of estimating the *number of people who would have bought anyway* (without the offer) can be made in the same way. (Note that if no one is converted by the offer to making a subsequent full-price purchase —that is, if the promotion offer has only a temporary "inventorying" effect—then steps E through I are replaced by an estimate of the total number of buyers, at the reduced price, and the calculation becomes equivalent to a price-reduction calculation.)

We cannot go further into the detailed financial aspects, such as discounted rate of return, that an accountant would apply to promotion offers. However, these summary steps provide a general outline of the financial evaluation procedure.

**NOTES**

1. This is our estimate, consisting of $100,000 for a national segmentation study, $15,000 for three focus groups, $15,000 for 200 IDIs, $500,000 for a 2-year AdTel split-cable field experiment, and the balance in consultants' fees.
2. A. P. Kuritsky, J. D. C. Little, A. J. Silk, and E. S. Bassman, The development, testing, and execution of a new marketing strategy at AT&T Long Lines, *Interfaces,* 1982, *12* (6), pp. 22–37.
3. By our definition, creative ideas should be in "executable detail" (see Chapter 6). This was done only for the subsequent ad testing phase of the research, as described shortly.
4. The case report does not state the actual number of individual interviews (as they are referred to as "individual depth interviews" [IDIs], we have inferred conservative sample sizes).
5. S. Baker, *Systematic Approach to Advertising Creativity,* New York: McGraw-Hill, 1979.
6. K. R. MacCrimmon and C. Wagner, Stimulating ideas through creativity software, *Management Science,* 1994, *40* (11), pp. 1514–1532; C. Wagner and A. Hayashi, A new way to create winning product ideas, *Journal of Product Innovation Management,* 1994, *11* (2), pp. 146–155.
7. B. Kabanoff and J. R. Rossiter, Recent developments in applied creativity, in C. L. Cooper and I. T. Robertson, eds., *International Review of Industrial and Organizational Psychology,* vol. 9, London: Wiley, 1994, pp. 283–324.
8. K. R. MacCrimmon and C. Wagner, same reference as note 6.
9. For descriptions of CAAS, see F. R. Esch, Evaluating cross-cultured advertising by expert systems: The CAAS-diagnostic system, and W. Kroeber-Riel, Computer-aided globalization of advertising by expert systems, both in G. Bamossy and W. F. van Raaij, eds., *European Advances in Consumer Research,* 1994, *1,* pp. 87–98 and 110–117, respectively; and W. Kroeber-Riel and F. R. Esch, eds., *Expertsysteme, Perspektiven für die Werbung,* Munich: Vahlen, 1994.
10. M. R. Lautman, The ABCs of positioning, *Marketing Research,* Winter 1993, pp. 12–18. ARBOR, Inc., then known by its full name of Associates for Research in Behavior, was where the first author first worked in market research and where the two authors (Rossiter and Percy) met. This biographical note is mainly added because some people think we are clones! We differ, but our opinions on advertising are much the same and on beer, identical.
11. The sample of 50 presumes a homogeneous target audience: other-brand loyals, for example, might differ

considerably in being loyal to various other brands, in which case it would be advisable to take a reasonable sample, say 30, of those loyal to each of the major brands. Note that this consideration refers to Q-sort as a rating technique, *not* Q-factor analysis, which requires a small heterogeneous sample of respondents and a large but reasonably homogeneous or factorially balanced set of stimuli. See J. C. Nunnally, *Psychometric Methods*, 2nd ed., New York: McGraw-Hill, 1978, chapter 15; and also W. C. Stephenson, *The Study of Behavior*, Chicago: University of Chicago Press, 1953.

12. The best practical description of Q-sort methodology is in M. J. Schlinger, Cues on Q-technique, *Journal of Advertising Research*, 1969, *9* (3), pp. 53–60. For researchers interested in performing a quick "benefit segmentation," this article shows how to do it with a Q-sort followed by Q-factor analysis. Because this is backward segmentation, we won't promote this use of Q-sort here.

13. Two sets of data have been published recently which suggest that the "triple variability" equation describes the normal real situation in advertising concept testing.

    Chow reports one set of data which just happen to be for a long-distance telephone service. Two independent creative teams from a single advertising agency each prepared a campaign for the brand, one following an "emotional" strategy and the other following a "price" strategy. Each team was asked to provide six executions of the respective strategies. It is not clear to what extent the "executions" were based on one creative idea or several, but our suspicion about variability (in $I_{ij}$ or $E_{ijk}$ or both) is fully confirmed. Using as the effectiveness criterion the "top two boxes" of a 10-point purchase intention measure (that is, 9 and 10 on a 1-to-10 scale) as rated by a target audience sample, the percentage scores for the six executions of the "emotional" strategy were 8, 10, 15, 18, 36, and 42; and those for the six executions of the "price" strategy were 17, 21, 24, 26, 32, and 32. Had only one execution of each strategy been generated and tested (the typical case), either strategy could well have won. Our interpretation based on the "triple variability" equation is that the "price" strategy should be selected. Although the executions of "emotional" strategy had the highest-scoring ad, a 42, the mean (average) of its executions was 21.5, with much variability (standard deviation = 14.1). On the other hand, the "price" strategy had a higher mean, 25.3, and apparently was easier to execute *consistently*, as indicated by its smaller variability (s.d. = 6.0). The consistency result is important from a *campaign* perspective. In the typical case, one ad is tested, then variations of it are produced subsequently and used later in the campaign without testing

and with the expectation that they will perform equally as well as the first ad, whereas they may not. This would have happened in Chow's data had only the "emotional" 42 execution and the "price" 32 execution been generated and evaluated initially.

In another set of data, reported by Kuse of Research Systems Corporation, very low effectiveness strategies, as exemplified by one creative idea and execution tested for each, were "milked" by the creative teams, who were told to go away and generate multiple executions of the original strategies in the hope of improving them and finding an acceptable ad. Three such case histories were provided by Kuse, each for a different brand. For brand A, the original ad's pre-post shift persuasion score (see chapter 7 and later in this chapter) was 3.9; the creative team submitted 16 (!) more executions, the worst at 2.7 and the best at 5.5. For brand B, from the original ad's score of 2.0, 11 attempts produced execution scores ranging from 0.2 to 3.0. For brand C, from the original ad's score of 0.1, 14 attempts produced execution scores ranging from −0.4 to 1.3. A couple of observations can be made about these data. First, the original ads—by luck (randomness)—were pretty close to the true average score for the strategy ($S_i$ in our equation), so management had an unusually accurate appraisal of the strategies' worth from testing just one ad. It is important to realize, however, that the original ad generated in each case could almost as easily have been a very bad or a very good execution of the underlying strategy. We say "almost" because if the joint term $I_{ij}E_{ijk}$ is normally distributed, the chance of drawing an average ad approximating the true $S_i$ is higher than if the distribution is rectangular (flat). Given the diversity in creative ideas, we'd opt for a rather flat joint distribution. Second, had these strategies been for the same brand, which they could well have been when we consider they were probably for similar fmcg products, we would see that the best execution of the worst strategy (C) outperforms the worst execution of the second best strategy (B), and thus by chance, either strategy could have been chosen. The same holds for the best execution of the second best strategy (B) compared with the worst execution of the best strategy (A).

Overall, these two data sets illustrate why it is so important to realize that an advertising "concept" is merely a *sample* of what might have happened with your campaign. See S. Chow, A Bayesian hierarchical model of advertising copy development, Working paper, University of South Carolina, June 1995; and A. R. Kuse, Measurement tools for ads that sell, in *Copy Research: The New Evidence* (Proceedings, ARF 8th Annual Copy Research Workshop), New York: Advertising Research Foundation, 1991, pp. 127–139.

14. W. T. Moran, Advertising research: What is it all coming to? *Journal of Advertising Research,* 1986, *26* (1), pp. 107–111.

15. The authors wish to thank Vicki Tanner, a colleague and manager at ANZ Bank and an experienced user of our MJT procedure, for identifying these internal management benefits.

16. Management judgment (jury) methodology was described in Chapter 2 as a method for setting the advertising budget. It is worth rereading that section.

17. This chapter concentrates on ad testing. However, it should be noted that the conceptual issues discussed in conjunction with testing advertisements apply *also* to the testing of promotion offers. Promotion-offer testing is covered at the end of the chapter.

18. Our estimates are generally confirmed in a recent analysis of 78 Nielsen-tracked TV advertising campaigns by J. P. Jones, Advertising's woes and advertising accountability, *Admap,* September 1994, pp. 24–27. These were an undisclosed mix of new-brand and established-brand campaigns, hence the high figure of 50 percent sales-successful (but only 10 percent "outstanding" successes). And 30 percent actually caused sales to *decline.*

19. I. Gross, The creative aspects of advertising, *Sloan Management Review,* 1972, *14* (1), pp. 83–109. Professor Gross's analysis further suggests that it's worth spending at least 15 percent of the advertising budget on creating and testing ads—a figure that is high by actual standards yet not unrealistic if advertisers truly believe creative ideas to be important. And if you think 15 percent is too much to spend on creative, a recent analysis using Gross's model suggests it is usually *too little.* This is because Gross assumed a normal distribution of effectiveness of ads whereas in fact it is more likely to be exponential (with just a few highly effective ads in the right tail of the distribution). See G. C. O'Connor, T. R. Willemain, and J. MacLachlan, The value of competition among agencies in developing ad campaigns: Revisiting Gross's model, *Journal of Advertising,* 1996, *25* (1), pp. 51–62. We supported the importance of creative ideas in Chapter 7.

20. Obviously the costs can vary widely above or below these averages. The $20,000 figure is based on an estimate of $12,000 for the ad test, a cost that remains quite constant no matter what form the ad is tested in, rough or finished. Only $8,000 has been allowed for "storyboard" preparation, and this is where the dilemma comes in. For $2,000, the advertiser gets a series of color sketches (like a big comic strip pasted across a board) for the video, and an unprofessional recorded sound track for the audio. A better rough version, known as an "animatic" (color sketches) or a "photomatic" (color photographs), prepared as storyboards and then videotaped, with a professionally recorded audio, costs about $15,000—or about one-fourth the cost of a finished, low-budget commercial. A live-action rough videotape version of the commercial can cost about $30,000—or half the cost of the finished version of a low-budget commercial—which clearly begins to become uneconomical. This puts enormous pressure on the predictive validity of testing inexpensive storyboards, about which we will have more to say in the design section. See also E. Tauber, Editorial: Can we test storyboards?, *Journal of Advertising Research,* 1983, *23* (5), p. 1.

21. Updated estimate from B. J. Coe and J. MacLachlan, How major TV advertisers evaluate commercials, *Journal of Advertising Research,* 1980, *20* (6), pp. 51–54.

22. See E. Young, Use eye tracking technology to create clutter-breaking ads, *Marketing News,* November 27, 1981, p. 19. For the larger advertiser, the additional reassurance—in other words, the stronger expectation of profit—from testing finished TV commercials outweighs the additional cost. For example, in 1984, Burger King spent $40 million in its comparative TV campaign against McDonald's and Wendy's. Obviously, the profit implications of the success or failure of the comparative commercials are enormous. At, say, $400,000 to produce and test the commercials in both rough and finished form, the testing costs would be only 1 percent of the media budget.

23. For more detail on these criticisms, see J. R. Rossiter and R. J. Donovan, Why you shouldn't test ads in focus groups, *Australian Marketing Researcher,* 1983, *7* (2), pp. 43–48.

24. At the time of publication of the first edition of this book, as recently as 1987, there was (in our opinion) only one choice: a customized ad test. Since then, two syndicated ad testing services, named in the text, have published impressive predictive validity information, and we therefore recommend them.

25. Both are descendants of the Schwerin research company (now ASI), which pioneered persuasion shift ad testing. See H. S. Schwerin and H. H. Newell, *Persuasion in Marketing,* New York: Wiley, 1981.

26. We provide only a "joint" sketch of their methodologies here, but we do get specific shortly.

27. You may consider this preexposure-postexposure choice procedure to be transparent—but even if it is, it works! In practice, the disguise is a little more elaborate than we have described.

28. Note that this score represents an aggregate score. Individuals may have shifted up or down or not at all—but the *net* shift across the sample was 10 percent ab-

solute. We return to this point in describing our (Rossiter-Percy) ad test analysis.

29. McCollum Spielman Worldwide, Choosing the right attitude measure, insert in *Journal of Advertising Research,* 1992, *32* (6), front of issue.

30. See J. R. Rossiter and G. Eagleson, Conclusions from the ARF's Copy Research Validity Project, *Journal of Advertising Research,* 1994, *34* (3), pp. 19–32, for more on this rationale.

31. The McCollum Spielman estimates were derived by us from the large data set published by P. R. Klein and M. Tainiter, Copy research validation: The advertiser's perspective, *Journal of Advertising Research,* 1983, *23* (5), pp. 9–17.

32. M. H. Blair, An empirical investigation of advertising wearin and wearout, *Journal of Advertising Research,* 1988, *27* (6), pp. 45–50.

33. While this analysis is partly based on ARS's published data, we should emphasize that these are largely *our* interpretations. Also, it is noteworthy that ARS's recent published studies that we cite in this chapter use *raw,* not norm-adjusted, persuasion scores and these are what we have reported. McCollum Spielman's scores are somewhat higher because they usually combine the "top two boxes" ("Probably will buy" and "Definitely will buy") of a brand purchase intention measure.

34. L. Byers and M. Gleason, Using measurement for more effective advertising, *Admap*, May 1993, pp. 31–35.

35. Also case histories for Campbell's Soup and Goodyear tires; see A. J. Adams and M. H. Blair, 1992, same reference as Chapter 7's Further Reading; and R. P. Conlin, Goodyear advertising research: Past, present, and future, *Journal of Advertising Research,* 1994, *34* (3), pp. RC-7 to RC-10. The latter study is the only published ARS case history for a non-fmcg product. We have recommended ARS at present only for fmcg ad testing.

36. Because of the vital way in which brand awareness and brand attitude affect the choice of creative content, the media strategy, and the means of testing and evaluating advertising, we have promoted the term *advertising communication models* to encompass primarily these two communication effects and their strategic and tactical considerations. See J. R. Rossiter and L. Percy, Advertising communication models and their implications for advertising research, in E. C. Hirschman and M. B. Holbrook, eds., *Advances in Consumer Research,* vol. 12, Provo, UT: Association for Consumer Research, 1985, pp. 510–524. An earlier version of this article, with Australian examples, was published by J. R. Rossiter, L. Percy, and R. J. Donovan,

The advertising plan and advertising communication models, *Australian Marketing Researcher,* 1984, *8* (2), pp. 7–44.

37. The future possibilities of two-way interactive cable TV may allow testing of TV commercials, interactive TV and PC ads, radio commercials (blank screen), print ads, direct mail, and outdoor ads—as well as promotional offers—very conveniently by a combination of TV presentation of ads and questionnaires with TV response via the phone line.

38. The testing of radio commercials by phone interviews presumes that the brand awareness objective is *brand recall,* which it usually is when radio is the primary medium (see Chapter 15). If *brand recognition* is the objective for radio commercials, then personal interviews have to be used, at least for the delayed brand recognition test (see later in the present chapter), because visual brand recognition stimuli have to be administered in person.

39. Evidence on the predictive validity failure of McCollum Spielman's (now MSW's) clutter-awareness measure is presented in P. R. Klein and M. Tainiter, same reference as note 31. See also note 50.

40. Of course, creative experts should make every effort to design attention-maximizing characteristics *into* the structure of the ad (see Chapter 10). Because attention is particularly difficult in print and radio, we can see some value in a portfolio (print) or simulated program (radio) attention test in addition to or prior to the ad test proper. Such tests will give a *relative* indication of the ad's in-media attention strength but cannot be used to make an absolute prediction.

41. The best design for either informational or transformational ad testing is the Solomon four-group design. Although rarely used in practice, it should be understood by managers for use in high-risk decision situations. Four cells are needed:

**1.** Preexposure AD Postexposure
**2.** AD Postexposure
**3.** Preexposure Postexposure
**4.** Postexposure

This design enables statistical assessment of the premeasure's sensitizing effect (3 versus 4) as well as the advertising exposure effect (1 versus 3) as well as possible interaction between the pre-measure and the advertising exposure (1 versus 2 versus 3 versus 4). See D. T. Campbell and J. C. Stanley, *Experimental and Quasi-Experimental Designs for Research*, Chicago: Rand McNally, 1966. However, the Solomon fourgroup design is rarely used because it adds *at least* three cells to the test for informational ads (cells 3 and 4, plus another cell 2 for every cell 1 depending on the number of test ads) and *at least two* cells to the test for transformational ads (cell 3, plus another cell 1 for every cell 2 depending on the number of test ads). For academic theory-testing research, or in applied advertising research when the manager wants a highly accurate calculation of each ad's effects (accuracy depending also on the size of the sample), this is the design that should be used. It is hardly ever used in practice.

42. If the manager levels the same charge against pre-post ratings for an informational test (where, we argue, the benefit and thus attitude shift should be obvious), then the Solomon four-group design *should* be used to resolve the issue.

43. Detailed comparison of test results for rough (artwork storyboard) TV commercials versus finished TV commercials indicates that the rough versus finished correspondence is noticeably higher for processing measures (adjective checklist type) that are informational rather than transformational. Test results are reported in M. J. Schlinger and L. Green, Art-work storyboards versus finished commercials, *Journal of Advertising Research,* 1980, *20* (6), pp. 19–23. This can be overcome with photo-quality artwork. Also communication effects are more important than processing; see also next note.

44. McCollum Spielman Worldwide, Rough vs. finished commercials, Company report, Great Neck, NY: McCollum Spielman Worldwide, January 1994.

45. In the McCollum Spielman and ARS type of clutter-reel procedure, if the test ad is a rough, the clutter reel consists of all rough ads, too. This is to prevent the test ad appearing "unusual," which might increase attention (or give the test away) and thereby alter persuasion.

46. Also "mobile exposure" outdoor media—where either the *audience* is mobile or the *ad* is (see Chapter 15). Mobile exposure outdoor media, such as drive-by billboards and exterior bus or taxi signs, function like TV in that the audience cannot control exposure duration.

47. By using a simulated magazine (usually called a portfolio presentation but it can also be presented on slides, where the respondent "turns the pages" with the remote-control switch on the slide projector), the same print ad could be inserted more than once to produce multiple exposures for transformational ads. However, as stated earlier, the interference caused by the particular selection of competing ads and editorial material would not be generalizable to real exposure environments, so attempted multiple exposure of print ads is not worth the effort.

48. H. E. Krugman, Why three exposures may be enough, *Journal of Advertising Research,* 1972, *12* (6), pp. 11–14. In this article, Dr. Krugman theorizes that processing is essentially complete in *two exposures,* with the third and subsequent exposures serving as re-minders to maintain the communication effects already established. We believe this to be correct for *informational* commercials. However, *transformational* commercials should continue to *increase* (or improve) brand attitude *beyond* two exposures. (Note that by "exposure," Krugman means *attention.* This depends, actually, on media vehicle attention, as explained in Chapter 16.)

49. McCollum Spielman's TV commercial testing service uses two exposures to measure brand attitude effects. (They use one "clutter" exposure first, then measure brand recall, then a "solus" exposure of the commercial on its own before measuring brand attitude.) The service hypothesizes that these two exposures are equivalent to six natural "on air" exposures (again, attentions). We doubt this. Given that the first exposure is cluttered, and the second delayed somewhat, we suspect that their procedure probably brings a commercial up to sufficient exposure for informational commercials but not enough for transformational commercials. See McCollum Spielman & Company, Inc., Choosing the right attitude measure, *Topline,* 1980, *2* (2), whole issue but especially p. 1.

50. For example, the brand *recall* measure used by McCollum Spielman testing service lacks reliability *and* validity. (The ARS testing service measures *advertising* recall, not brand recall.) McCollum Spielman measures only brand recall, *not* brand *recognition,* so this service will not suit brand recognition communication models. Moreover, brand recall is not measured in relation to other brands in the *category,* but against other noncompeting brands advertised at the testing session. As a measure of brand recall as it occurs competitively in the real world, the results are meaningless. At best, attention to brand stimuli in the commercial is being measured, and in a nongeneralizable context.

51. C. W. Luh, The conditions of retention, *Psychological Monographs,* 1922, *31* (3), whole issue.

52. As an example of this, let's suppose that the advertising communication model is a brand recall model, and that McCollum Spielman's measure *is* valid and reliable. According to *ad forum,* May 1981, p. 13, the service's norm for brand recall is 39 percent (of individuals) and the norm for attitude or purchase intention change is 20 percent (of individuals). Roughly calculated, this means that only 39 percent of 20 percent, or 8 *percent,* of individuals would buy the brand.

In fact the entire brand awareness measurement issue is immensely complicated, and we have been forced to make some heroic assumptions. Brand *recognition* should be okay, because the one (print) or two or three (broadcast) test ad exposures should be enough to bring brand recognition to a peak. But for brand *recall,* it could be argued that the ad in the actual media plan will get many more exposures to build brand recall (assuming continued attention) and thus is disadvantaged by the few test exposures when recall of the test brand is assessed against the recall of competing brands that have had many more exposures in media. However, the competitive isolation of the test ad, as well as the inherent personal memorability of attending the test, plus the one to three exposures, should, we believe, reasonably simulate the number of in-media exposures necessary to put the test brand's recall on a fair basis to measure against competing brands. The relationship between number of exposures (per individual) and brand recognition or brand recall can be measured more accurately in tracking studies, but until someone suggests a better solution for measuring brand awareness on the basis of *ad tests,* we'll stay with our recommended delay measure.

53. For a good discussion of how action standards are considered beforehand at one major company, see J. Staffaroni, Copy testing—a true team effort, *Journal of Advertising Research,* 1993, *33* (4), pp. RC-2 to RC-3.

54. Strictly speaking, sales *goals* can be set only for a total campaign, not for individual ads or promotion offers where directional objectives, only, are appropriate (see Chapter 2). However, the manager will have a fair idea of how any single ad is expected to contribute to the campaign (for the small advertiser, the single ad or promotion offer may *be* the campaign). Thus, the estimate is a reasonable one to require.

55. N. B. Holbert, Before we start any research, let's look at it from ends to end, *Marketing Review* (American Marketing Association, New York Chapter), 1984, *39* (9), pp. 11–14.

56. J. T. Cacioppo, S. G. Harkins, and R. E. Petty, The nature of attitudes and cognitive responses and their relationship to behavior, in R. E. Petty, T. M. Ostrom, and T. C. Brock, eds., *Cognitive Responses in Persuasion,* Hillsdale, NJ: Lawrence Erlbaum Associates, 1981, pp. 31–54.

57. R. E. Petty, T. M. Ostrom, and T. C. Brock, eds., *Cognitive Responses in Persuasion,* Hillsdale, NJ: Lawrence Erlbaum Associates, 1981; and J. R. Rossiter and O. Holland, Cognitive response theory: Its transference from psychology to advertising research and some considerations for its application, in K. Grant and I. Walker, eds., *Proceedings of the Seventh Bi-annual World Marketing Congress,* Melbourne, Australia: Department of Marketing, Monash University, 1995, pp. 2-102 to 2-109.

58. The origin of adjective checklists to measure reactions to advertisements seems to be attributable to, independently, researchers at the Leo Burnett advertising agency in Chicago, and the research firm of ARBOR, Inc., in Philadelphia. For examples of the Burnett lists over the years, see W. D. Wells, C. Leavitt, and M. McConville, A reaction profile for TV commercials, *Journal of Advertising Research,* 1971, *11* (6), pp. 11–17; M. J. Schlinger, A profile of responses to commercials, *Journal of Advertising Research,* 1979, *19* (2), pp. 37–46. M. J. Schlinger and L. Green, Artwork storyboards versus finished commercials, *Journal of Advertising Research,* 1981, *20* (6), pp. 19–23; and D. A. Aaker and D. E. Bruzzone, Viewer perceptions of prime-time television advertising, *Journal of Advertising Research,* 1981, *21* (5), pp. 15–23. The ARBOR list is not publicly available.

59. S. L. Crites, L. R. Fabrigar, and R. E. Petty, Measuring affective and cognitive properties of attitudes: Conceptual and methodological issues, *Personality and Social Psychology Bulletin,* 1994, *20* (6), pp. 619–634.

60. Note the use of "ad liking" as a measure in the low-involvement/transformational quadrant *only.* Many practitioners have wrongly stated that *all* ads have to be liked in order to work. Overall, the correlation between ad liking and pre-post persuasion shift (the valid McCollum Spielman and ARS persuasion measure) is only $r = .16$! These data are from D. Walker and T. M. Dubitsky, in their ill-titled article, Why liking matters, *Journal of Advertising Research,* 1994, *34* (3), pp. 9–18. For reasons why the universal liking view is wrong, read the article that follows their article, by J. R. Rossiter and G. Eagleson, Conclusions from the ARF's Copy Research Validity Project, same journal, pp. 19–32. Also see our Chapters 8 and 9.

61. Open-ended measures probably more validly tap spontaneous processing; see Y. F. Niemann, L. Jennings, R. M. Rozelle, J. C. Baxter, and E. Sullivan, Use of free responses and cluster analysis to determine stereotypes of eight groups, *Personality and Social Psychology Bulletin,* 1994, *20* (4), pp. 379–390.

62. Acquisition of an attitude to an unspecified or wrong brand would, of course, signal a serious problem with the ad. Again, we emphasize the necessity of brand awareness preceding brand attitude.

63. See I. G. Evans and S. Riyait, Is the message being received? Benetton analyzed, *International Journal of Advertising,* 1993, *12* (4), pp. 291–301. Main messages taken from the famous "Umbilical cord" ad, with which Benneton first launched its controversial campaign, for instance, included "Love, the force from which life itself is born," "A baby is the most permanent form of love," and "Holding onto the security and warmth of a mother's womb." French students overwhelmingly liked the ad whereas British students overwhelmingly disliked it.

64. An example of regression in this diagnostic role is shown in A. Mehta, How advertising response

modeling (ARM) can increase ad effectiveness, *Journal of Advertising Research,* 1994, *34* (3), pp. 62–74. Cross-tabs do a clearer job.

65. B. Wansink and M. L. Ray, Estimating an advertisement's impact on one's consumption of a brand, *Journal of Advertising Research,* 1992, *32* (3), pp. 9–16.

66. P. R. Warshaw, A new model for predicting behavioral intentions: An alternative to Fishbein, *Journal of Marketing Research,* 1980, *17* (2), pp. 153–172.

67. The sources for interpretation of the measures are as follows. For the four-point intention measure, see G. L. Urban and J. R. Hauser, *Design and Marketing of New Products,* Englewood Cliffs, NJ: Prentice Hall, 1980. For the three-point intention measure, see J. MacLachlan, *Response Latency: A New Measure of Advertising,* New York: Advertising Research Federation, 1976. For the 11-point intention measure, see T. F. Juster, Consumer buying intentions and purchase probability: An experiment in survey design, *Journal of the American Statistical Association,* 1966, *61* (3), pp. 658–696; and D. G. Morrison, Purchase intentions and purchase behavior, *Journal of Marketing,* 1979, *43* (2), pp. 65–74. For evidence that low-involvement intentions are basically dichotomous and high-involvement intentions gradated, see M. U. Kalwani and A. J. Silk, On the reliability and predictive validity of purchase intention measures, *Marketing Science,* 1983, *1* (3), pp. 243–286.

68. This scale of weights is inferred from Juster's study with automobiles and is identically replicated by Morrison in a later study with automobiles and closely confirmed by Infosino's study on adoption of a (promoted) new telephone service; see T. F. Juster and D. G. Morrison, same references as in previous note, and W. J. Infosino, same reference as Chapter 18, note 21. Should Juster's 11-point scale be used with fmcg products, translations to the four-point scale are DWB = 99 percent on Juster's scale, PWB = 76 percent, MB = 40 percent, and WNB = 6 percent; see A. Gruber, Purchase intent and purchase probability, *Journal of Advertising Research,* 1970, *10* (1), pp. 23–27.

69. In the constant sum measure, the respondent is asked to allocate a total of 11 points across the brands to reflect evaluation, allocating as many or as few as appropriate to each brand. This amounts to the same thing as arranging *brands* along a scale, which is what the four-level measure does. For interpretation of point allocations in constant sum, see J. MacLachlan, same reference as in note 67, table 4.8.

70. W. T. Moran, The circuit of effects in tracking advertising profitability, *Journal of Advertising Research,*
1985, *25* (1), pp. 25–29. Related theory is in R. S. Wyer, *Cognitive Organization and Change,* Potomac, MD: Lawrence Erlbaum Associates, 1974, chapter 2. The concept of increased confidence (reduced variance) also fits Moran's contention that good advertising will reduce the price-increase elasticity of the brand and make it more resistant to competitive promotions (as explained earlier in Chapters 2, 11, and 18 on the interdependence of advertising and promotion). Reduced variance at the *individual* level is also a good way to explain the postpurchase *reinforcement* effect of *transformational* advertising. However, the transformational brand attitude measure is too fragile, in most cases, to withstand the addition of confidence scales.

71. C. E. Osgood, who invented the semantic differential, used the term to refer to the *factorial structure* obtained from ratings on these scales, not to refer to the scale format itself. However, the latter usage has become popular. See C. E. Osgood, G. Suci, and P. H. Tannenbaum, *The Measurement of Meaning,* Champaign: University of Illinois Press, 1957. This book, the most widely cited book in social psychology, is of more than historical interest. It indicates how brand attitudes, or "brand images," are learned, and also has several sections on applications of the semantic differential technique to marketing and advertising, as well as discussing measurement considerations in more detail than we can provide here.

72. C. E. Osgood et al., same reference as in the previous note.

73. The occasional occurrence of *verbal* or, more precisely, *auditory* recognition was discussed in Chapter 5 (for example, when a waiter tells you what kinds of beer brands the restaurant has). Auditory brand recognition could be measured in a telephone interview by reading a list of brands.

74. E. R. Tomlin, Pot Pourri: A miscellany of practical market research techniques, Paper presented at the Annual Conference, Market Research Society of Australia, Wrest Point, Tasmania, September 1982.

75. L. Weinblatt, New research technology for today and tomorrow in Advertising Research Foundation, *Copy Research,* New York: Advertising Research Foundation, 1985, pp. 179–192.

76. Eye-movement apparatus, known as eye-tracking, traces a dot of light reflected off the cornea as the eye scans the ad or, more recently, uses a tiny video camera that clips onto an eyeglasses frame to record the direction and duration of gaze. Pupillometric apparatus measures dilation of the eye's pupil, which can measure attention over time (for a TV commercial) but not

*where* attention is directed within the visual field (for example, within a TV commercial video scene or within a print ad). Electroencephalographic, or EEG, apparatus provides a gross measure of attention in the form of decline in alpha waves from the brain, but is notoriously unreliable and expensive. For a review of these measures, see D. W. Stewart and D. H. Furse, Applying psychophysiological measures to marketing and advertising research problems, in J. H. Leigh and C. R. Martin, eds., *Current Issues and Research in Advertising,* Ann Arbor, MI: Graduate School of Business Administration, University of Michigan, 1982, pp. 1–38. CONPAAD is a foot-pedal or button-pressing "operant-response" apparatus. For TV commercials, one foot pedal or hand button controls the brightness of the TV screen, which fades if you don't press it, thus providing a rough measure of visual attention; the other foot pedal or hand button controls the loudness of the audio track, which also fades if you don't press it, thus providing the *only known measure* of auditory attention. CONPAAD is offered by ARBOR, Inc., of Philadelphia. For a description, see P. E. Nathan and W. H. Wallace, An operant behavioral measure of TV commercial effectiveness, *Journal of Advertising Research,* 1965, *5* (4), pp. 13–20; and R. C. Grass, L. C. Winters, and W. H. Wallace, A behavioral pretest of print advertising, *Journal of Advertising Research,* 1971, *11* (5), pp. 11–14. A more modern version of (visual) CONPAAD involves pushing a button or turning a dial to indicate attention (or other moment-to-moment ratings), offered by companies such as ASI or PEAC. See G. D. Hughes, Diagnosing communications problems with continuous measures of subjects' responses: Applications, limitations, and future research, in J. H. Leigh and C. R. Martin, Jr., eds., *Current Issues and Research in Advertising,* Ann Arbor, MI: University of Michigan, 1991, *13* (1), pp. 175–196; and G. D. Hughes, Real time response measures redefine advertising wearout, *Journal of Advertising Research,* 1992, *32* (3), pp. 61–77.

77. See G. D. Hughes, same references as in the previous note.

78. AdTel or BehaviorScan (for TV) and split-run (any medium, but usually print) are methods in which different test ads are delivered to randomly selected "cells" of households, using cable TV, or "tip-ins" in print media. Purchases in each household are then recorded in a diary, or electronically in stores or at home. Direct response ads in any medium can be split-run tested by "keying" the reply to a particular ad. Results for alternative test ads are thus compared in terms of buyer behavior.

79. J. E. Russo, The decision to use product information at the point of purchase, Working paper no. 57, Chicago: Graduate School of Business, University of Chicago, 1980.

80. P. S. Raju and M. Hastak, Consumer response to deals: A discussion of theoretical perspectives, in J. C. Olson, ed., *Advances in Consumer Research,* vol. 7, Provo, UT: Association for Consumer Research, 1980, pp. 296–301. Also see R. L. Oliver, Predicting sales promotion effects: Assimilation, attribution, or risk reduction?, in the same volume, pp. 314–317.

81. C. M. Siepel, Premiums—forgotten by theory, *Journal of Marketing,* 1971, *35* (2), pp. 26–34.

82. B. C. Cotton and E. M. Babb, Consumer response to promotional deals, *Journal of Marketing,* 1978, *42* (3), pp. 109–113; R. M. Schindler and S. E. Rothaus, An experimental technique for exploring the psychological mechanisms of the effects of price promotions, in E. C. Hirschmann and M. B. Holbrook, eds., *Advances in Consumer Research,* vol. 12, Provo, UT: Association for Consumer Research, 1985, pp. 133–137.

83. R. Cialdini, *Influence,* New York: Quill, 1984.

84. H. Helson, *Adaptation-Level Theory: An Experimental and Systematic Approach to Behavior,* New York: Harper, 1964.

85. B. F. Skinner, *The Behavior of Organisms,* New York: Appleton-Century, 1938; and C. B. Ferster and B. F. Skinner, *Schedules of Reinforcement,* New York: Appleton-Century-Crofts, 1957. For marketing applications of Skinner's concepts, see W. R. Nord and J. P. Peter, A behavior modification perspective on marketing, *Journal of Marketing,* 1980, *44* (2), pp. 36–47; M. L. Rothschild and W. C. Gaidis, Behavioral learning theory: Its relevance to marketing and promotions, *Journal of Marketing,* 1981, *45* (2), pp. 70–78; and J. P. Peter and W. R. Nord, A clarification and extension of operant conditioning principles in marketing, *Journal of Marketing,* 1982, *46* (3), pp. 102–107.

86. G. C. Homans, *Social Behavior: Its Elementary Forms,* New York: Harcourt, Brace & World, 1961: R. P. Bagozzi, Marketing as exchange, *Journal of Marketing,* 1975, *39* (4), pp. 32–39; R. W. Belk, Gift-giving behavior, in J. N. Sheth, ed., *Research in Marketing,* vol. 2, Greenwich, CT: JAI Press, 1979, pp. 95–126; J. F. Sherry, Jr., Gift giving in anthropological perspective, *Journal of Consumer Research,* 1983, *10* (2), pp. 157–168.

87. F. W. Irwin, *Intentional Behavior and Motivation,* Philadelphia: Lippincott, 1971.

88. J. B. Rotter, Generalized expectancies for internal versus external control of reinforcement, *Psychological Monographs,* 1966, (80), whole issue.

89. For a summary of these efforts, see A. G. Sawyer and P. R. Dickson, Psychological perspectives on consumer response to sales promotion, Working paper, Cambridge, MA: Marketing Science Institute, 1985.

90. Some researchers, such as Chris Blamires, recommend randomized presentation of price-off amounts to prevent respondents from "rationally" waiting for progressively larger price-offs in the ordered series. This probably is a more valid procedure because price-offs are encountered randomly in actual shopping trips. However, it is more cumbersome to administer in a test and may, to the contrary, tend to confuse respondents. See C. Blamires, Pricing research: A review and a new approach, *Journal of the Market Research Society,* 1981, *23* (3), pp. 103–126.

91. N. B. Holbert, R. J. Golden, and M. M. Chudnoff, *Marketing Research for the Marketing and Advertising Executive,* New York: American Marketing Association, 1981.

92. J. R. Bettman, The structure of consumer choice processes, *Journal of Marketing Research,* 1971, *8* (4), pp. 465–471.

93. N. B. Holbert et al., same reference as note 91, p. 202.

94. D. E. Schultz and W. A. Robinson, *Sales Promotion Essentials,* Chicago: Brain Books, 1982.

## DISCUSSION QUESTIONS

See Discussion Questions at end of Chapter 20.

## FURTHER READING

The best preparation that a manager can have for designing an ad test is to call or write the major ad test services (listed in the American Marketing Association's *Green Book* or in the advertising section of the *Journal of Advertising Research*) and ask to be sent *descriptions* of their ad testing methodologies. Then, the manager should reread this chapter, make up a table of all the processing and communication effects, and try to align each service's measures appropriately. There should, however, be sufficient information in this chapter to enable the manager to custom-design an ad test.

If you decide to use a syndicated ad test service, we recommend McCollum Spielman's (now McCollum Spielman Worldwide's) ADVANTAGE/ACT (especially for corporate campaigns or where you want a more customized "persuasion" measure) or Research Systems Corporation's ARS service (for fmcg products). However, you should examine their literature first. Other services may offer similar methodology and measures to what MSW and ARS offer, but only these two services have published sufficient (basic) validation data to enable action-standard *decisions* to be made with high confidence.

# Campaign Tracking and Evaluation

The final stage of advertising research is campaign tracking and evaluation. In this chapter we will concentrate on *campaign tracking* research (which includes the posttesting of advertisements) and on the managerial action to be taken if an advertising campaign seems to be "wearing out." After reading this chapter, you should:

- Understand the purpose of campaign tracking and know which measures to use.
- Know when to use partial (aggregate) tracking methodology and when to use complete (market survey) methodology.
- Within the AC&P plan, know which problems cause various types of advertising wearout, and how to correct these problems.

As with all the stages of advertising research, campaign tracking, in the formal sense, is optional. The majority of campaigns are not tracked formally; instead, the manager observes the brand's sales trend before and during the campaign and then *infers* that the advertising (or promotion or IMC program) is working or not.[1] However, about half of all advertising campaigns produce no measurable sales increase, and about three in 10 actually cause the brand to start losing sales![2] Advertisers who do not track their campaigns may have a very nasty shock awaiting them—too late to take corrective action.

Sophisticated (and large-budget) advertisers conduct campaign evaluation or tracking research even when all signs in the marketplace imply that the advertising (or IMC or promotion program) *is* meeting its sales goals. The sophisticated manager wants to be sure that the advertising is *causally responsible* for sales—rather than other factors in the marketing mix, or in competitors' marketing mixes, or in the market itself (such as economic conditions) being the sole causes. Further, the manager also wishes to estimate the *extent* of advertising's contribution, for the next budgeting period.

Campaign tracking research is expensive. First of all, the manager will need to conduct a *precampaign* or "benchmark" survey, if this has not already been done as part of advertising strategy research. Then, one or more "waves" of surveys will be needed *during the campaign,* to compare against the benchmark and thus "track" the campaign's progress. Each survey wave could cost $20,000 at a minimum, depending on sample size, the length of the survey questionnaire, and the incidence of product category purchase.

## MEASURES USED IN TRACKING

A complete tracking study will use measures of all six steps of the advertising effects sequence: (1) exposure, (2) processing, (3) communication effects and brand position, (4) target audience action, (5) sales or market share, and perhaps brand equity, and (6) profit. In this section, we recommend and describe which measures to use.

## Exposure Measures

We define exposure (Chapter 16) as the *opportunity* for exposure—the opportunity to see (or hear) the ad (OTS). That is, exposure occurs when the advertisement is *placed* in a media vehicle that reaches the target audience so that the prospective buyer can see or hear it. Whether or not the prospect actually *does* see or hear it is a matter of attention, which is part of the second step, processing.

Exposure, then, is essentially a *media measure*—specifically, a *rate of media input*[3] which can then be related to sales rate, or to the intermediate steps of the effects sequence. The rate of media input can be measured in various ways, ranging from gross measures such as advertising dollars or, as defined in Chapter 16, gross rating points (GRPs), to measures that more closely approximate exposure, such as reach at minimum effective frequency (effective reach).

Each media measure is expressed as a rate for a particular time period. The time period can be weekly, monthly, or less often—depending on the corresponding rate at which the manager wants to measure (or has available) changes in sales or any other intermediate effect.

**Advertising Dollars.** The rate of overall expenditure on advertising is what most concerns senior management. The expenditure rate in relation to the rate of sales growth or decline provides an overall input-output evaluation. Advertising dollar-expenditure rate is an important measure *financially,* but it is a gross measure of exposure from a *causal* perspective.

**Gross Rating Points (GRPs).** The rate of GRPs achieved per time period also provides a gross measure of exposure. Total GRPs per week or month or for any other relevant time period, such as the advertising cycle duration, can be found by adding the *audience* figures (percentages reached) for all vehicles in which the ad was placed,[4] that is, the total audience—repeated or not—for the total number of placements, in the time period. As explained in Chapter 16, GRPs take no account of how many exposures an *individual* receives and are simply a count of the (often repeated) exposures that are "out there" to be attended to.

First, GRP rate can be related to dollar-expenditure rate to see whether the advertising money is being spent "efficiently" (GRPs per dollar, over time periods). A high ratio means you're getting cheap media buys; a low ratio means that you're paying more than usual for each exposure. This index stops here; there's no reason "efficiency" (a ratio) would relate to "effectiveness" in terms of sales rate.

Second, GRP rate can be related directly to sales rate or to the rate achieved on intermediate measures. This provides a crude measure of the effectiveness of the media plan—crude because GRPs can be attained from many different individual audience member exposure patterns. That is, a GRP figure can represent many alternative reach patterns (see Chapter 16) and levels of frequency.

**Reach at Minimum Effective Frequency (Effective Reach).** The rate of *target audience* reach at minimum effective frequency, called effective reach (see Chapter 16), is the most precise measure of exposure.

To measure effective reach, the manager either needs to include direct media measurement (direct matching) in the tracking study market-survey questionnaire (see later in this chapter) or, as a much less time-consuming and reasonably accurate alternative, claimed ad-recognition frequency (see Processing Measures, next) from the survey can be used. Minimum effective frequency (MEF) is calculated for each advertising cycle (MEF/c) but *reach* at MEF (effective reach) is a figure that can be translated to whatever time period has been used for the *other* tracking measures, such as 4 weeks, rather than, say, 3 weeks for an advertising cycle.

If the rate of target audience reach at minimum effective frequency (effective reach) doesn't relate to the sales rate, then there's likely to be something wrong—not with the media plan but with either the advertising strategy or with its creative execution (either of which signals a major problem with earlier planning). Fortunately, tracking, since it traces the six-step effects sequence, can usually isolate the location of the problem, as we will see with the remaining measures.

## Processing Measures

Processing consists of the prospect's *immediate* responses to the ad (attention, learning, emotional responses, and acceptance). Processing cannot be measured directly in a tracking study because interviewers can't "be there" when every exposure occurs. Instead, processing is measured *indirectly* in the tracking study in a very important way. Remember that in the "laboratory" setting of ad testing, the ad is shown in isolation, or out of its natural media context, with attention guaranteed by the test procedure. What ad testing misses out on is examining the ad's ability to be processed in the actual, competitive, real-world media environments[5] in which it is placed. In campaign tracking, we have these environments. But we can't interview people immediately after they've been exposed, and certainly not after each of their exposures if there's more than one exposure per person.

So in tracking, we measure *competitive attention indirectly* (which actually includes at least partial *processing,* because the respondent has to have *learned* in order to remember the ad when the interviewer calls). The most frequently employed competitive attention measures are ad recognition, ad recall, and advertising category "cut-through." We will now define each of these measures and explain its purpose.

**Ad Recognition Measures.** Ad recognition is (1) partly a check on the *media-plan*—whether each ad in fact reached the number of people that the plan called for; and (2) partly a check on the ad's ability to gain *attention* given that it reached those people. There are several measures of ad recognition: simple ad recognition (called "ad recognition"), "masked recognition," and, usable with either of the first two, ad recognition frequency.

*Ad Recognition.* In ad recognition, tracking study respondents are shown—or for radio, played—the ads from the campaign and asked whether they have seen or heard them before.[6] With answer categories of "Yes," "Not sure," and "No," only the "Yes" answers should be counted as signifying ad recognition. Notice that the memory cue or stimulus (the "prompt") is the *ad* itself and the response required is ad (*not* brand) recognition.

*"Masked Recognition."* In fact, ad recognition ads can be shown or played with the pack or brand name blanked out—the so-called "masked recognition" method—and then respondents asked to specify the brand. Technically, masked recognition requires the respondent to *recall* the brand, so it is somewhat of a misnomer. Masked recognition offers an additional diagnostic advantage over normal ad recognition in that it measures the extent to which respondents can remember the ad but not which brand it was advertising (a common experience among the general public). If, and only if, there is a problem with *actual* brand recognition or brand recall (see later measures), masked ad recognition may diagnose the problem as residing in the execution of the ad.

*Ad Recognition Frequency.* Those respondents who recognize the ad should also be asked about ad recognition *frequency:* how many times they have seen, read, or heard the ad, usually asked with reference to a given time period such as the last several weeks but sometimes just "recently" and "ever." This is *claimed* exposure frequency for checking on the achieved effective reach level in the media plan. We discuss its analysis in conjunction with causes of advertising wearout later in the chapter.

Our colleague Max Sutherland refers to ad recognition as "mental reach."[7] If you know that the media *vehicle* reached the number of people specified in the media plan, yet the number who recognize the ad is lower than this, then the problem most likely is with the creative idea or execution—specifically, its ability to gain attention in actual media environments. If your campaign has a "mental reach" problem and you are confident that it's had sufficient frequency of exposure, the first corrective action should be a "show-and-tell" attention test[8] (see Chapter 19).

**Brand-Prompted Ad Recall.** A measure which demonstrates that an ad has been linked to the brand correctly during in-media processing is brand-prompted ad recall (BPAR). Notice that the memory cue or stimulus (the prompt) is the *brand,* and that the response is the ad. Recall of the ad's content provides evidence on the extent to which the brand's associated benefits came from the advertising and not elsewhere. It therefore provides a check on the advertising's causality in influencing brand attitude; but note that it does *not* have anything to do with brand awareness.

Day-after recall (DAR) should *not* be used, unless the advertiser is prepared to pay for *multiple* DAR tests (see note 8). A far cheaper and more straightforward measure tied to the brand (memory cue or stimulus) rather than initially and prejudicially to the particular media vehicle (which is the initial memory cue in DAR) is the BPAR measure proposed by Colman and Brown.[9]

The Colman-Brown BPAR measure is a two-stage measure, and we have improved their first stage by making it fit the appropriate advertising communication model:

**1.** *Show a list of brands* (*if brand recall model*) *or pictures of brands* (*if brand recognition model*). Then ask: "Which of these brands have you seen or heard[10] advertised recently?[11]"

**2.** *For each brand named,* say: "Please describe the advertisement or advertisements for this brand in as much detail as you can remember, and in particular, what the advertisement showed or said about the brand." *Probe thoroughly.* Say: "Tell me more about the advertisement. What else did it show or say?"

Scoring (coding) for this measure is as follows: The respondent has to describe the advertisement, or each advertisement recalled for the brand, in *sufficient detail* to satisfy the coder that the advertisement was indeed seen or heard or read, and that the respondent is not guessing or describing some other brand's advertisement—hence the need for heavy probing during the second-stage answer. Then the recalled *content* of the advertisement of advertisements is classified into categories corresponding to the brand's benefits, to allow the manager to infer what benefit beliefs the advertising caused.[12]

Again we stress that this is not day-after advertising recall (the common measure): DAR measures recall of a particular insertion of an ad, in a particular media vehicle, at a particular time. Rather, the appropriate measures seek *general* recall of the ad resulting from the *overall* media plan (BPAR, here, or CPAR, discussed next). Day-after recall and general advertisement recall measures are *not* comparable and cannot be interchanged for interpretive purposes.

**Category-Prompted Ad Recall, or "Cut-Through."** Whereas ad recognition is proof that people attended to the ad (ad-prompted), and ad recall is proof that people processed the ad in relation to the brand (brand-prompted), the third measure, category-prompted ad recall (CPAR), or "cut-through," is the toughest test of the ad's ability to gain attention in media (to cut through the "clutter" of other ads) and be processed by the target audience.

The category-prompted ad recall (CPAR) or "cut-through" measure doesn't ask people what advertising they remember in general, because that question would be too vague. Instead, the recall task is directed by giving them the product *category* as the cue or prompt (for example, "fast-food restaurants"), and asking them what advertising they remember for this category of product or service. *Then* they are asked what *brand* was being advertised, if the brand was not mentioned spontaneously in their description of the recalled ad.

Cut-through (CPAR) should be tested for *each medium separately* (for example, first for TV adver-

tising, then for magazine advertising). This is to further direct the recall task and to curb the tendency for people to think that the question refers *only* to TV, as may happen if the question were to use the general term "advertising." Separate questions are needed for each advertising medium of interest.

The responses are then coded for adequate description of the advertisement's content *and* scored for correct or incorrect association of the brand with the advertisement. *Branded* cut-through (Branded CPAR) is what is wanted; wrongly branded cut-through (Executional CPAR minus Branded CPAR) indicates the incidence of processing failure.

**Comparing the Processing Measures.** There is much confusion, even among experienced practitioners and certainly among managers, about the foregoing "advertising awareness" measures, which technically are all measures of in-media ad processing. Many regard advertising awareness measures as equivalent and interchangeable, but they're not. In Figure 20.1, we depict exactly which links are being measured in each case. As you can see, the processing measures are measuring different learned connections in advertising and therefore have different diagnostic purposes. The distinction between ad recall (a processing measure) and brand recall (a communication effects measure) is another source of common confusion, and study of this diagram shows why.[13]

### Communication Effects Measures

The communication effects measures in the tracking study should be *exactly* the same as the communication *objectives* measures used in the ad testing stage. (If a syndicated ad test was used, this will usually not have comparable measures—a subsequent disadvantage of syndicated as opposed to customized ad tests. The same problem occurs in reverse if you use a syndicated tracking service without previously using its ad testing service.)

The advertising should be "posttested" on the same communication measures on which it was "pretested." And, once again, to be valid, these measures must fit the advertising communication model for the brand, as explained in the previous chapter.

For *low-involvement/transformational* communication models, we now include the brand attitude and brand purchase intention measures that were omitted (in favor of brand benefit beliefs) in ad testing. Brand attitude and brand purchase intention should emerge

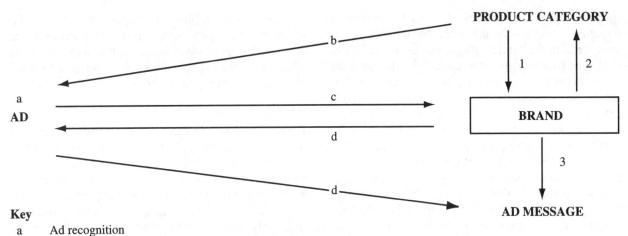

Key

| | |
|---|---|
| a | Ad recognition |
| b | Category-prompted ad recall, or cut-through (unbranded) |
| c | Category-prompted ad recall, or cut-through (branded) following b |
| d | Brand-prompted ad recall |

| | |
|---|---|
| 1 | Brand recall |
| 2 | Brand recognition |
| 3 | Brand benefit beliefs induced by an ad (brand attitude) |

**FIGURE 20.1**
Linkages between the ad, product category, brand, and ad message. This diagram shows the locations and directionality of ad-processing measures (letters) and brand communication effects (numbers).

consciously if the campaign is working, and can now be measured.

There is one difference in the *order* of the measures. Brand awareness (brand recall or brand recognition, and in this order if both) can now be measured *first,* preceded only by category communication effects if category need is an objective. There's no need for a delayed measure of brand awareness, because brand awareness has now had time to operate and must emerge first (before brand attitude) if purchase is to occur.

### Target Audience Action Measures

Target audience action at the individual buyer level is the next step measured in campaign tracking and is the final step in the exposure → processing → communication effects and brand position → target audience action sequence of buyer response. The target audience action measures are the same as those reviewed in Chapter 3 and in conjunction with the situation audit in Chapter 18. Depending on the target audience, the campaign's action objectives could be

trade or consumer (or customer) behavior; purchase or purchase-related; and would refer to, specifically, trial or repeat purchase.

At this point, we have to think carefully about what is happening during the campaign (Table 20.1). If the campaign is successful, the "inner" target audiences of brand loyals (BLs) and favorable brand switchers

---

**TABLE 20.1**

**WHAT HAPPENS TO PROSPECT GROUP MEMBERSHIP IF THE CAMPAIGN IS SUCCESSFUL?**

| Prior to campaign (that is, the target audience *for* the campaign) | Movement to final status if the campaign is successful |
|---|---|
| Brand loyals | ⟶ Brand loyals (no change) |
| Routinized favorable brand switchers | ⟶ Routinized favorable brand switchers (no change) |
| All *other* brand switchers <br> Other-brand loyals <br> New category users | Routinized favorable brand switchers *or* brand loyals |

(particularly routinized FBSs), who are the brand's franchise, should stay the same, while individuals who were in the "outer" target audiences of OBSs, OBLs, or NCUs prior to the campaign will *move out of those audiences* and into an inner audience. For example, new category users, if a target, should become category users, not stay NCUs. In fact, we want NCUs to enter our brand's franchise by becoming favorable brand switchers, or better still, brand loyals.

This realization means that one index of the campaign's performance is *the changing incidence of prospect group membership itself.*[14] For example, in a campaign aimed at new category users, the percentage of consumers who are NCUs should get smaller; and in a campaign aimed at brand loyals, the percentage of consumers who are BLs should *not* get smaller. (For simplification, Table 20.1 shows only the main potential target audiences. A table organized by subgroups—see Chapter 18's Figure 18.5—could show increases in status for all 12 subgroups *except* single-brand loyals.) A further reason for tracking changes in target audience status is that the campaign's required MEF/c in the media plan (see Chapter 16) depends on it. In particular, the manager can gradually reduce MEF/c during the campaign *only* if the tracking proves that individuals are becoming more loyal.

So, unlike in ad testing, we do *not* want to sample only the target audience. Rather, for tracking studies, we need a *random sample of the total potential audience* (for example, all adults, for an adult-purchased consumer product, or all firms in the industry, for an industrial product). Target audience classification is done later, during the analysis, so that the incidence of membership can be tracked as a percentage of the *total* base of consumers.

Similarly, the action measures—percent trial, or percent repeat, percent switching in versus switching out—must be taken on the total base. For example, if we mistakenly sampled *only* NCUs throughout the tracking study, trial would always be zero! Yet the campaign might be very successful because the base of NCUs is itself getting smaller relative to the total base. We'll add more on this in a moment in the methodology section of the chapter.

### Sales and Market Share Measures

Sales measures and market share measures (relative sales in relation to the category or market, correctly defined) were described in Chapter 18. Sales can be estimated by aggregating customer purchases, or measured directly from store audits, and so on. In Chapter 18, we explained why these alternative measures of sales may or may not give identical results.

### Brand Equity and Profit Measures

Brand equity (here referring to the brand's upside and downside price elasticity) and profit measures were also described in Chapter 18. Profit can be tracked by substituting dollar contribution for dollar sales revenue, per period, and then subtracting the advertising expenditure per period. Although it is more usual to track only sales or market share, brand equity and, ultimately, profit should be tracked as the "bottom line" measures of campaign effectiveness. The reason is that brand equity (which is influenced by advertising) produces *sustained* profit.

## METHODOLOGY FOR TRACKING STUDIES

So far we have not indicated where the various measures used in tracking (see Table 20.2) come from. By and large, the exposure (input) measures and the sales, market share, brand equity, and profit measures (output) come from audit services or from company records. However, the measures for the "middle steps"—processing, communication effects, and target audience action—must come from market surveys with consumers or customers.

| TABLE 20.2 | |
|---|---|
| **MEASUREMENT SOURCES BY STEP** | |
| 1. Exposure | Media audit (direct measurement, though, comes from the market survey) |
| 2. Processing | |
| 3. Communication effects and brand position | → Market survey |
| 4. Target audience action | |
| 5. Sales or market share | Retail audit, factory withdrawals, etc. |
| 6. Profit | Company calculation |

## Market Survey Methodology

Tracking studies can use one of three market-survey methodologies: panel, wave, or continuous. Each has advantages and disadvantages but, as we explain shortly, the continuous method is the best overall methodology.

**Panel Method.** To diagnose the causality of advertising through every step, the most valid procedure—in theory—is *panel* survey methodology. In a panel survey, the *same* consumers are interviewed in the benchmark (precampaign) wave and in each successive (during-campaign) wave, which allows causality to be established at the individual consumer or customer level. Unfortunately, panels can prove to be very expensive and difficult to maintain. Also, if the waves are too close together, the successive interviews can sensitize respondents and make them more likely to buy in the product category.[15] Finally, panels typically provide slow data and therefore slow management response.

**Wave Method.** Interviewing *separate samples* of consumers or customers each time—the wave method—allows us to relate steps in the chain of effects only on an *aggregated* basis. We can relate exposure (for example, advertising dollars) to percent processing, or percent processing to percent acquiring the communication effects, or percent acquiring the communication effects to percent acting, or exposure to sales (no survey needed). But we can't *causally* (over time) link processing to communication effects and then to action, because we have not tracked the same individual respondents over time. Also, if the survey waves are far apart—say, 3 months or 6 months, as is typical—the data are slow and, again, so is management response.

**Continuous Method.** In the continuous survey method, small random samples of consumers or customers are drawn for an interview from the potential target audience population on a *daily or weekly* basis.[16] Instead of, for example, interviewing 600 respondents nationwide every quarter in a wave survey, the continuous method would interview 50 respondents a week, interviewing a new sample of 50 every week for 12 weeks. These weekly samples of 50 would cumulate to 600 a quarter (or actually 650, since there are 13 weeks in a quarter). Thus, instead of four waves of 600 respondents measured at quarterly intervals, we would have the same number of interviews spread evenly throughout the year. This is known as "continuous tracking."

In continuous tracking, the small sample size in any one week, which could produce erroneously varying results due to small-sample error (again, see Table 19.3 in the previous chapter), is overcome by plotting the results as a *moving average.* This is called "rolling the data"; for instance, a 4-week roll[17] would plot the first data-point as weeks 1–4, the second as weeks 2–5, the third as weeks 3–6, and so forth, yielding data points based on 200 observations each. These observations are not independent, as they overlap many of the same respondents with each roll. Classical statistical analysis therefore cannot be applied to the rolled results but only to the raw data, which can of course be aggregated over longer periods, such as a quarter, if desired.

The continuous tracking method is the best method of tracking. First, there is no sensitization of respondents, as the continuous method is not a panel. Second, although continuous tracking is essentially a wave survey (a very short cycle wave survey) rather than a panel, and therefore does *not* allow causality to be inferred at the individual level, it does have the considerable advantage of allowing the manager to "read" causal factors in the market *as they occur.* The causes and effects are *inferred* from the *aggregate trends* in the results. Specifically, for instance, if an upward trend in aggregate processing, such as in "cut-through," is followed shortly afterward by an upward trend in aggregate communication effects, such as in brand awareness, the manager can infer that the former caused the latter. Although it is possible that the same individuals did not produce the two trends—which is to say, there is no causality—this is presumed unlikely. The causality can be partially checked by cross-tabulating the current state of processing with the current state of communication effects, and so forth, for successive steps in the buyer response sequence. A large proportion of respondents demonstrating cut-through at time *t and* brand awareness at time *t* would tend to rule out the "different respondents" danger though would not be proof of *sequential* causality as all were interviewed at time *t* (see turnover analysis later in this chapter).

Let's look at an example of continuous tracking results (Figure 20.2). The data are from the launch campaign for a new brand of shampoo. The upper graph, panel A, shows CPAR for the 60-second TV commercials used during the brand's launch period. Advertising awareness, we can see, rose rapidly. At this point,

### A. CPAR advertising awareness

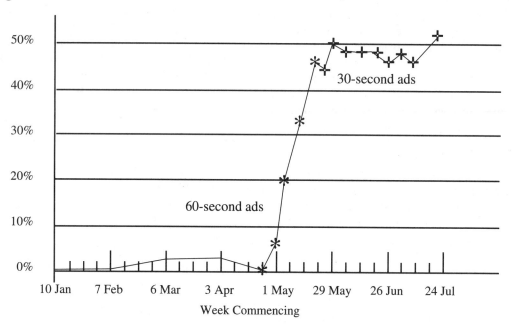

### B. Market share

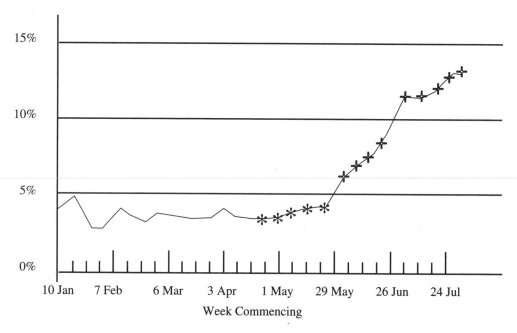

**FIGURE 20.2**

Continuous tracking results for the launch of a new brand of shampoo, showing the advertising cut-through (CPAR) trend in panel A and the market share trend (not rolled) in panel B.
*Source:* Proprietary.

the manager decided that the initial 60-second commercials were sufficiently exposed to the target audience and switched the media plan to less-expensive 30-second commercials, "lifts" from the longer versions. The lower graph, panel B, shows the brand's market share over the same tracking period. There was a steady rise in market share which continued after the switch to shorter ads, justifying the manager's campaign management decision—the manager would not see the market share data until some time after the cut-through data, which are available virtually instantly from continuous tracking, and thus the timing of the ad-unit switch, and indeed the switch itself, was a judgment call. As you can see, it is difficult to avoid the conclusion of causality from panel A to panel B and, provided that the manager also tracked promotions, price, and distribution (which he did), the manager would be correct in inferring that the campaign was working, and spectacularly so.

Although continuous tracking involves a strange mixture of good and bad features, rather reminiscent of academic purists' criticisms of qualitative research, we can only echo Bill Wells's famous comment in that context: "How could something so bad be so good?" But good it is. There is no doubt that continuous tracking represents the best compromise between the alternative methods of panel surveys and wave surveys: Its results are *sufficiently* causal and *sufficiently* reliable to direct managers to take action; moreover, because the results are available continuously and virtually instantly, this method allows the manager to take action immediately—and see the results of that action quickly.

The dynamic instant input and instant readout nature of continuous tracking has made it increasingly the tracking survey method of choice for advertisers.[18] Not only advertising effects, but the effects of distribution, price, promotions, and *all other IMC inputs,* including sponsorships and PR, can be tracked using this survey method.

### Market Survey Interview Methods

Tracking studies, strictly speaking, require personal (face-to-face) interviews because the interviewers have to show *ads* to respondents to measure processing (attention by the ad recognition method). Further, if the advertising communication model is a brand recognition model, the interviewers have to show *pictures of brands* or brand displays to respondents.

However, in countries such as the United States and Australia (in contrast with the United Kingdom, most of Europe, and Asia), telephone interviews are a much lower-cost alternative. The sacrifice when using telephone interviews is that measures of ad recognition, unless it's a radio campaign, and brand recognition, if that's the brand awareness objective, have to be verbally (orally) administered (without visual aids). The most valid way to do this is to conduct, beforehand, a small-scale *face-to-face prestudy* in which a sample of 30 or so target audience respondents are shown the ads and brands to be surveyed and asked to *describe* them in their own words. These descriptions are then summarized and used in the telephone interviews. It is worth noting that verbal ad recognition produces much lower scores (37 percent, on average) than visual ad recognition (61 percent, on average), and so the former results should be transformed if comparing across methods and if using this measure to track the "mental reach" of the campaign against media plan reach.[19]

### Order of Measures in the Market Survey

The recommended order of measures in tracking study market surveys is shown in Table 20.3. Note that the measures of processing (2, 4, and 10) and exposure (11) and action (5) are interspersed with the measures of communication effects. This is to prevent order bias—that is, answers to early questions affecting or "giving away" answers to later questions.

| **TABLE 20.3** |
| --- |

**TRACKING STUDY ORDER OF MEASURES IN THE MARKET SURVEY QUESTIONNAIRE**

1. Category need[a]
2. Category advertising cut-through
3. Brand awareness:
   a. Brand recall[a]
   b. Brand recognition[a]
4. Advertisement recall
5. Action (reported purchase or purchase-related behavior)
6. Brand purchase intention
7. Brand attitude
8. Brand attitude benefit beliefs
9. Purchase facilitation[a]
10. Advertisement recognition
11. Profile variables (especially media exposure)

[a]If an objective.

The order-of-measures rationale can best be explained with the aid of a *simplified* set of questions for IBM PCs, a product and brand used in some of our ad testing examples in Chapter 19.

*Category need* ("Do you intend to buy a personal computer?") comes first, before any brands are asked about. For the same reason, *category-prompted ad recall,* that is, cut-through ("What TV ads have you seen recently for personal computers?" "What magazine ads . . . ?"), must be placed early in the sequence, because it stems from a category cue. Respondents are, however, asked to name the brand in the CPAR questions, so now it is appropriate to move to brand questions.[20]

*Brand awareness* may require brand recognition measurement, brand recall measurement, or both (*if* both are objectives of the campaign). If both, then *brand recall* ("What brands of personal computer first come to mind?") should precede *brand recognition* ("Which of these brands have you seen before?"), as the first is "unaided" whereas the second is "aided" in that the brands are shown to (or named for) the respondent.

*Brand-prompted ad recall* ("What TV commercials have you seen recently for IBM Personal Computers?") is measured next. Even if we've measured brand recognition and thus "given" the respondent the brands, this doesn't matter, because the BPAR measure is *based* on the brand-as-cue (see the Colman-Brown BPAR measure described earlier).

*Action measures* are then taken. Depending on the action objectives, these may be purchase ("Which brand of personal computer have you bought recently?") or purchase-related ("Which personal computer stores or retail outlets have you visited?"). Quite logically, *brand purchase intention,* which is intended action, is the next measure ("If you were going to buy a personal computer for home use, how likely would you be to buy an IBM PC?").

*Brand attitude* ("Overall, how would you rank the IBM PC for home use—the single best, second best, or what?") and then brand attitude *benefit beliefs* ("How does the IBM PC rate on low price, good performance, adequate service support, and so on?") are then measured, with their order based on the avoidance of having the respondent "compute" a new overall attitude from considering the questionnaire-provided benefit beliefs.

*Ad recognition* ("Have you seen this commercial on TV before?" and if so, "How many times in to-tal?") occurs as the *last* processing measure—of in-media competitive attention—because now we're showing the respondent the ads (for example, the IBM "There is a difference" series for the IBM PC). To have shown the ads earlier would have biased every following measure.

Finally, target audience *profiling measures* are taken—at least periodically. While these usually include demographics, the most important is the *direct media exposure measure* (see Chapters 16 and 18) in which respondents report (in the IBM PC example) which TV programs they have watched and what magazines they have read and which Internet (World Wide Web) sites they have accessed. In the panel method, media exposure is measured by having each panelist maintain a *diary* of TV viewing habits, readership of magazines, Internet use, and so forth; and such questions would *not* appear on the questionnaire. Without a diary—that is, using the questionnaire method alone—only *types* of TV programs preferred or approximate frequency of exposure to regularly scheduled programs can be measured reliably, although print media exposure can be reported from memory quite accurately.

Obtaining direct media exposure (direct matching) data with the questionnaire method is very time-consuming for respondents and expensive in terms of interviewing costs. Also, media habits change quite slowly. Therefore, a practical solution is to do the direct matching survey as a separate study (same target population) every 6 months with a large wave sample.

## Analysis of Market Survey Results

For a *causal* analysis, market survey results should be analyzed at the *individual* level. Strictly speaking, individual-level causal analysis (over time) is possible only with *panel* surveys, that is, with the same respondents interviewed at time *t,* time $t + 1$, time $t + 2$, and so on, through to the end of the tracking. (Shortly, we will comment on what can be inferred if you used wave or continuous surveys.) At minimum, two interviews with the same respondents (most often the benchmark interview and one follow-up interview at the peak of or immediately after the campaign) would be required.

With a *panel* sample, the results are arrayed into a series of "turnover" tables, which link *successive pairs* of measures that represent the buyer response steps, or the more specific hierarchy of effects hypothesized for the campaign, for successive time periods. Turnover tables track what happened to respondents from time $t$ to time $t + 1$ and to successive time periods if surveyed—for example, whether exposure did or did not result in brand awareness, or whether brand attitude (given brand awareness) did or did not produce brand purchase intention—until all the steps of exposure $\rightarrow$ processing $\rightarrow$ communication effects (and thus brand position) $\rightarrow$ target audience action are linked. An example of a turnover table for *one* pair of hypothesized successive measures is shown in Table 20.4. The turnover incidence for each cell indicates which diagnosis of causality is appropriate. If the campaign is working (here, by increasing brand recognition), most (exposed) respondents should be in the top right-hand cell, indicating that (recent) exposure caused brand recognition. The lower right-hand cell shows the incidence of brand recognition due to *other* causes—such as advertising exposure prior to time $t$ or to in-store exposure to the brand.

More precisely deterministic statistical techniques, such as cross-lagged correlation and regression, can be applied to panel results. However, turnover analysis is simple for the manager to interpret, and it suffices for *reasonably safe* causal conclusions.

If, however, the market survey has employed *separate samples* (wave method or continuous method) rather than panel methodology, causal interpretation is rendered more tentative. All that can be said with separate samples is that a certain *percentage* of respondents showed brand awareness (or other processing or communication effects) at time $t$, another *percentage* showed it at time $t + 1$, and so forth, and that in each *simultaneous* time period a certain percentage purchased. That is, we are comparing aggregates with aggregates. What we cannot *strongly* conclude is that brand awareness (or other effects) at time $t$ *caused* purchase at time $t + 1$ or in any *later* time period, because we haven't tracked the same individuals over time.[21] With the *wave* tracking method,

causal inference is a major problem—and more so the further apart the waves are, as the chain of causes and effects are badly dislocated in time. With the *continuous* tracking method, however, the observations of inferred causes and effects are virtually continuous, and although different individuals are observed, causality is a *reasonable* conclusion. Managers who act on it will most of the time be right.

In practice, then, continuous tracking is the method we recommend. Valid *enough* inference about sequential campaign effects can be made from the less-than-strictly-causal survey procedure of continuous tracking. The aggregate trend relationships can usually detect any *major* causal movements (or conspicuous lack of them) in a campaign's progress through the six-step effects sequence, and the instant "reading" of the campaign more than makes up for the continuous method's causal shortcomings.

### Exposure-to-Sales Analysis

So far, we have assumed that the manager is interested in knowing completely *how* advertising works, through all six steps of the effects sequence. This requires market surveys with consumers or customers so as to document the full chain of effects.

However, the manager, once convinced that a good understanding of the likely causal process has been gained, may then choose to track at a more general level *without* market surveys. This we call partial (aggregate) tracking because it jumps from step 1 to step 5 or 6. Most often, it consists of relating one of the *gross exposure* measures (advertising expenditure rate or GRP attainment rate) to an *aggregated* marketing objective measure (sales or market share, brand equity, or profit).

Aggregate tracking requires some form of direct input-output analysis. Such analysis may range from an "eyeball" comparison of advertising input trends with sales output trends, to a quantitative model of the

---

**TABLE 20.4**

**TURNOVER ANALYSIS FOR INFERRING CAUSALITY IN MARKET SURVEY RESULTS (EXAMPLE).**

|  | Did not recognize brand at time $t + 1$ | Recognized brand at time $t + 1$ |
|---|---|---|
| **Exposed at time** $t$ | Campaign not working | Most of the *exposed* respondents should *end up in this cell* |
| **Not exposed at time** $t$ | Most of the *unexposed* respondents should be here | Campaign not the cause of brand recognition |

observed relationship and thus predicted future relationship. Quantitative models include BRANDAID and ADPULS, but these are beyond the mathematical scope of this book.[22] Actually, based on honest reports in the literature on "sales modeling" as to the subjectivity required, we remain to be convinced that these quantitative models are reliably better than eyeball analysis, at least for the most important campaign management decisions.[23]

## APPLICATIONS OF TRACKING

There are five main applications of tracking studies, ranging from major to minor:

1. Determining why the advertising communications, promotion, or IMC campaign is or is not working
2. Adjusting the budget
3. Adjusting the media plan
4. Adjusting the exposure ratio of individual ads in the pool
5. Making minor improvements in ads

### Determining Why the Campaign Is or Is Not Working

The most important application of tracking, at least initially, is to determine why the advertising communications, promotion, or IMC campaign is or is not working (meeting its marketing goal). Until the campaign is actually launched, the manager has been operating only with the advertising plan—which, all things considered, is no more than a *hypothesis* about how the advertising is *expected* to work. Sophisticated managers always will want to test this hypothesis (through continuous tracking or perhaps with panel methodology).

*Direct response* advertisers have a relatively easy tracking job (sales are relatively immediate and are inevitably caused by the ad). *IMC* advertisers using sponsorships, event marketing, publicity, and other "diffuse" advertising communication and promotion activities face a more difficult tracking job. We emphasize, however, that campaign tracking is still very useful for evaluating these types of campaigns. IMC tracking can be achieved as for mass media advertising tracking by recording the expenditure on, and estimated *reach* of, the IMC activities employed. Several case histories, such as an example of a carefully tracked "mailbox drop" brochure promotion campaign, can be found in the recent excellent book by Sutherland.[24]

### Adjusting the Budget

Media *budget* adjustments, that is, increases or decreases in the rate of advertising spending, can be made without conducting market surveys. Aggregate input-output tracking—such as advertising expenditure rate related to sales rate—is sufficient for this.

### Adjusting the Media Plan

*Gross* adjustments of the media plan, such as increasing or decreasing GRPs in various *geographic* markets, as in Schroer's method of budgeting (see Chapter 2), requires only aggregate analysis as above. However, *fine-tuning* of the media plan in terms of adjusting the reach and frequency to increase *effective* reach, requires continuous tracking or panel methodology.

Figure 20.3 shows a hypothetical example of how MEF/c can be checked and thus effective reach appropriately increased if necessary.[25] Number (claimed frequency) of ad exposures per advertising cycle is shown on the horizontal axis as the causal independent variable, and the proportion of target audience individuals who buy the brand during (or, as appropriate, following) that cycle is plotted on the vertical axis as the dependent effects measure. In this example, it appears that MEF/c = 4/c is the effective minimum frequency, and thus the manager should aim to maximize effective reach at that level, that is, to maximize the number of individuals at R4+/c.

### Adjusting the Exposure Ratio of Individual Ads in the Pool

Market surveys that include the processing measures, since these are individual-ad based, can use these results to adjust the exposure ratio of ads in the campaign's pool of ads. The "winner" in ad testing, for example, may turn out not to be significantly more effective in campaign conditions than the number two ad. Their exposures could therefore be equalized. Or, a new winner may be found, or losers discovered, that should be upweighted or downweighted, respectively. For example, American Express adjusted the ratio of its "Do You Know Me" TV commercials (Robert Ludlum, Mel Blanc, Benny Goodman, and others) to reflect their apparent effectiveness within the campaign. The company probably has done the same with the extensive pool of print ads employed in its more recent "Portraits" campaign as well.

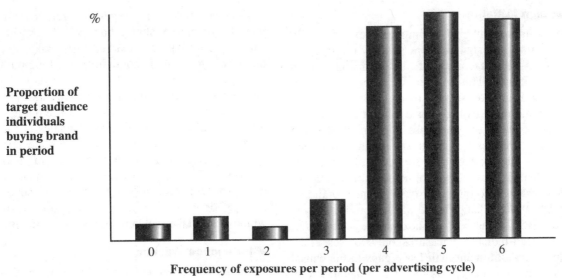

**FIGURE 20.3**
Checking MEF from continuous tracking or panel tracking results (hypothetical example).

With continuous tracking, ratio adjustments can be made frequently. This can help to forestall "wearout," as explained later in this chapter.

### Making Minor Improvements in Ads

The final and more emergency-initiated application of tracking research is to make small improvements in the executional content of particular advertisements while they are in the campaign. For example, a TV video "super" (text superimposed over the video images) can be added to reinforce a benefit claim, or the audio can be rerecorded to mention the brand name more often in association with the category need. Print ads are even easier to change. Magazine ads and outdoor ads and posters do have quite a long insertion commitment to the media, meaning that revised ads cannot appear immediately. However, changes in all other print and broadcast media, especially to newspapers and radio ads, can be made at short notice.

### HOW OFTEN TO TRACK

We've left the discussion of one of the biggest decisions until now: how often to track the campaign. Only by understanding the purpose and methods of tracking can this decision correctly be made.

Essentially, there are three campaign considerations that determine the frequency and the type of tracking research that should be conducted (Table 20.5): initiation, change, and maintenance.

**TABLE 20.5**

**HOW OFTEN TO TRACK AND WHAT TYPE OF TRACKING TO CONDUCT**

| Status of campaign | Frequency of tracking | Type of tracking |
|---|---|---|
| Initiation | Several purchase cycles[a] minimum | Complete causal: market surveys with panel methodology |
| Major change by competitor or in market | One purchase cycle[a] (two waves) initially, then several more if needed | Aggregate at first, then complete causal if serious problem |
| Maintenance | Monthly, with major review at midyear and end-of-year planning period | Aggregate |

[a]For long purchase-cycle products, the tracking waves should be done *monthly*.

### Campaign Initiation

When a new campaign is initiated—either a new brand's first campaign or a new strategy for an existing brand—the causality of the campaign's plan should be tested. This will require a complete set of measures, in market surveys using continuous tracking or panel methodology, for a minimum of several purchase cycles (for fmcg products and frequently purchased services) or about six months (for long purchase-cycle products and services). All measures are needed. (It is even wise to include brand recall as well as brand recognition in case the new brand or strategy causes a change in the way the product is purchased. Both measures are inexpensive to include.) Use of lead-indicator measures only, or less than complete measurement, will leave gaps in the causal chain. Total-market surveys with panel methodology should be used, with individual-level analysis; or continuous tracking, with aggregate trend analysis.

To establish reliable causal inferences, a sufficient time period of tracking must be allowed for campaign initiation. For *short* purchase-cycle products and services, the period should be at least three to four purchase cycles. For *long* purchase-cycle products and services, a reasonable campaign initiation measurement period is at least 6 months and, in the case of long decision-time products or services, 12 months. Six months or a year should mean that enough purchases have occurred to build up a causal picture of the campaign's effects.

Analysis is in terms of multiple turnover tables relating successive effects for successive time periods. For fmcg products, the "effects" time periods are *purchase* cycles. For long purchase-cycle products, *monthly* time periods should be used. Whereas the monthly effects period is arbitrary, it's a good starting point pending evidence that advertising in the category has substantial effects *only* over a longer period.

### Major Change

Major change does not refer to a major change by the advertised brand, which would be classified as initiation in our table. Rather, it refers to major changes that occur (1) in a competitor's strategy or (2) in the market itself, such as a new government regulation, or consumer boycotting of a product because of a health scare, or other adverse or perhaps fortuitously positive publicity. Any change likely to affect *our* brand's advertising performance should be tracked as soon as it occurs.

First, a quick and inexpensive *aggregate* assessment of the market should be made. Aggregate measures, notably sales and market shares, taken over one purchase cycle—or 1 month apart for long purchase-cycle products (two waves)—should be enough to decide whether the change is serious and likely to continue (hence the two waves, to measure the trend). If a substantial effect on our brand's sales is forecast, then complete *causal* tracking should be resumed, again for several purchase cycles or several months as applicable. This second phase is to determine whether our brand will need to react with a new advertising strategy or even with a new marketing strategy—which would take the campaign back to initiation.

### Maintenance Tracking

Certainly at the *aggregate* level, most often monitoring advertising expenditure rate and sales rate, maintenance tracking should be undertaken during the remaining periods of market "equilibrium." Aggregate data are easy to compile—the company usually *has* the necessary figures but managers neglect to *analyze* them.

This is where continuous data-review models such as BRANDAID come to the fore.[26] Graphic (not just numeric) reports or personal computer displays regularly signal whether the market is indeed in equilibrium and whether the company's advertising is proceeding as planned. The more sophisticated of these data-review models incorporate an expert system to statistically detect deviations from the normal effects pattern. Nevertheless, if you don't have such a model, major problems should be adequately evident from eyeballing the trends.

It is good management practice to schedule a major midyear and end-of-year review in which the client and agency are required to read and submit written comments on all available input, effects, and output trends, followed by a meeting. Regular reviews at intervals of at least 6 months serve to punctuate planning during maintenance periods. These regular reviews will help managers to decide when the current advertising campaign has run its course. This leads to our final topic in campaign evaluation: wearout.

### WHAT IS "WEAROUT"?

At a commonsense level, everyone knows what "wearout" is: when the advertising campaign is not working any more. (It is very possible, of course, for

CHAPTER 20: CAMPAIGN TRACKING AND EVALUATION **599**

*other* adlike communications and promotion offers to wear out if employed over a sustained period. The typical concern, though, is with advertising wearout, and that's what we will focus on here.) But from a managerial perspective, diagnosing wearout, and correcting it, is far more complicated than this.

We will see that there are three possible conclusions to be drawn when the advertising campaign does not seem to be working any more:

1. Advertising strategy obsolescence
2. Media plan slippage
3. Creative idea or execution wearout

To detect where the problem lies, and thus to draw the right conclusion and apply the right corrective actions, we need three types of audits, which cover (1) the marketing plan—to check for advertising strategy obsolescence; (2) the media plan—to check for media plan slippage; and (3) the ads themselves—to check for "advertising wearout" in its proper sense, that is, wearout of the *creative idea or the creative executions* themselves. The audits or checks should be conducted in the stated order, as explained in the following sections.

## FIRST CHECK: THE MARKETING PLAN

Before the manager can conclude that a sales decline is caused by advertising wearout, there are alternative causes to be considered. A complete *marketing audit* should be conducted because the problem may extend to the marketing plan rather than just the advertising plan. A marketing audit should be conducted *first* because, in a competitive market, the lead time for correction to stem the sales decline will usually be very short.

There are many reasons sales could decline without the brand's advertising having worn out in the conventional sense. These reasons fall under three headings: changes in the brand's marketing mix, changes in a competitor's marketing mix, and changes in consumer values.

### Changes in the Brand's Marketing Mix

A first set of reasons for a decline in sales, not due to advertising, is changes in (other) components of the brand's marketing mix. A change in product formulation or service, distribution, price, or promotion other than advertising could be the cause of the sales decline.

- If these changes have the effect of acting as purchase inhibitors, then the advertising strategy should be adapted to counter the inhibition. (See Chapter 5's discussion of purchase facilitation as a communication objective.) This is a minor correction within the same advertising strategy.
- A major, deliberate change in the brand's marketing mix would, of course, call for a completely revised advertising strategy.

New brands represent a special case. With new brands, a sales decline is often the result of the brand achieving its true repeat-purchase incidence and rate; that is, high initial sales in most cases represent the effect of a large incidence of trial purchases and an inflated purchase rate due to introductory deals, so that a drop-off occurs when less than 100 percent of the triers repeat, or when individual repeaters' rate of purchase without deals stabilizes to the brand's "true" repeat rate.[27]

- The true repeat effect for a new brand would not normally call for a change in advertising strategy, although it may signal an assessment of the promotion strategy if the repeat rate is too low (see Chapter 14's discussion of postpurchase and usage promotions).

### Changes in a Competitor's Marketing Mix

A second set of reasons for a sales decline is changes in a competitor's marketing mix. A major new brand introduction, such as Arm & Hammer Baking Soda toothpaste, can redefine the market and cause sales and market share declines for other brands. Or, a change in a competing brand's marketing mix, such as a large gain in distribution outlets through acquisition or merger, can produce declines for other brands.

Under the heading of changes in a competitor's marketing mix we include changes in a competing brand's *advertising strategy* (target audience or benefit positioning) but *not* changes in the competitor's *media* strategy *unless* the latter changes follow from a changed advertising strategy. Changes in a competitor's media strategy alone are discussed later.

- Changes in a competitor's *marketing mix other than advertising or promotion* that cause our brand's sales to decline will call for a revised *marketing* plan and, along with it, a completely revised advertising strategy.
- Changes in a competitor's *advertising (or promotion) strategy* that cause our brand's sales to decline

can, more narrowly, often be countered by a change in our brand's advertising (or promotion) strategy alone.

An example of the need for marketing plan revision would be the rush of many brands of personal computers to develop IBM compatibles (popularly known as "clones") when IBM became the dominant competitor in the personal computer market. A revised marketing plan became necessary; a revised advertising strategy alone would not have been sufficient to counter this trend. IBM began implementing a serious counterclone marketing plan in the 1990s, widening its distribution and reducing its prices to compete with the clone makers.

On the other hand, some years ago, when Miller Beer changed its advertising strategy (specifically its *positioning* strategy) to the "It's Miller Time" theme, which brought the Miller High-Life brand out of the doldrums in the beer market, rival Budweiser countered by simply revising *its positioning* strategy to reflect even broader situational use than Miller's, with the "When do *you* say Budweiser?" theme. Budweiser's counterstrategy suggested that a Bud is suitable at any time, not just after a hard day's work as Miller's advertising implied for Miller High-Life. In the soft-drink market, more recently, "Always Coca-Cola" is the epitome of this strategy of "all situations" positioning, which attempts to nullify other brands' *specific* situational positioning (the slogan also means "Always choose it [Coke]," an extension of "Coca-Cola is it," and is an example of central positioning by the market leader—see Chapter 6).

### Changes in Consumer Values

A third set of reasons for a sales decline is changes in consumers' "tastes" or values, manifest in altered importance or evaluation weights ($E_i$'s in our multiattribute formula for the I-D-U multiattribute model) placed on the attributes (more accurately, the benefits) that consumers seek in a product category. The toothpaste market, for instance, underwent changes in consumers' benefit importance with the emergence of decay prevention as a major consideration, and later, plaque reduction. Likewise, medically initiated sociocultural changes saw low tar emerge as a consumer benefit in the cigarette market, low alcohol content or fewer calories emerge as consumer benefits in the beer market, and a surge in health concern generally. And let's not forget Healthy Choice frozen dinners,

which launched with the right name at the right time in terms of consumer values.

Changes in consumer values resulting in altered benefit importance weights (including the emergence of a new benefit, such as baking soda in toothpaste, which, by definition, previously had no importance) can be addressed in two ways:

**1.** If the altered or new benefit threatens to *substantially repartition* the market (see Chapter 18), then the usual response will be to quickly seek a product reformulation or new formulation, resulting in a change in the *marketing* plan that will enable our brand to compete successfully in the new submarket (for example, Crest toothpaste bringing out its own baking soda version).

**2.** Alternatively, an adequate response may be to revise the advertising strategy: the target audience, benefit or user positioning, or both audience and benefit positioning. Our brand could focus on a more sharply defined target audience, such as *subcategory* users, and try to boost the importance of a previous benefit in the brand attitude communication objective (for example, Ultra-Brite and Close-Up continuing to go for the "cosmetic" segment of the market after the fluoridated toothpastes entered).

### Summary of External Causes

All of these "external" causes of a sales decline—changes in our brand's marketing mix, changes in a competitor's mix, and changes in the market itself via changes in consumer values—would be detected if the manager were conducting *complete* tracking research. Continuous tracking, in particular, is very good at picking up *non*advertising-induced changes, which stand out as deviations from the normally smooth trends other than when advertising cycles are spiking the short-term effects.

Such changes call for a complete marketing audit (which should take the form of a situation audit—see Chapter 18) in order to decide whether a revised *marketing* plan or, progressively less expensive, a revised *advertising* strategy, a revised creative strategy (new creative idea or new executions), or a revised promotion strategy is the appropriate solution.

**Advertising Strategy Obsolescence Rather Than "Wearout."** With external causes of a sales decline, the assessment is that the current advertising strategy is *obsolete* rather than that the current strategy has "worn out" in the proper meaning of the term. The proper meaning of "wearout" is that the current campaign is failing to work up to expectation (failing to achieve the sales or market-share goal) in the *absence* of external causes. Only if the marketing audit establishes that external causes are *not* responsible for the sales decline can we then consider advertising wearout (as opposed to advertising strategy obsolescence) to be the problem.

However, to isolate the exact internal cause or causes of advertising wearout, there is still further investigation to be done. We now know that the advertising *strategy* is still sound, but something could be wrong with the media plan, or with the way the creative executions are being scheduled in the media plan, or with the creative idea or the creative executions themselves. The best place to begin in detecting the *internal* cause or causes of wearout is with an audit of the *media* plan.

### SECOND CHECK: THE MEDIA PLAN

Logically, with internal causes of wearout, the problem must be occurring in the exposure step (step 1) or the processing step (step 2) of the six-step effects sequence. This is because, if the advertising strategy is still appropriate, something must be breaking down in the steps *leading to* the communication effects and brand position step (step 3) and the target audience action step (step 4). We begin with exposure, by checking the media plan.

### Changes in Media Vehicle Audiences

The pattern of exposures to the advertising could have changed because the delivery of the media plan itself has changed. Changes in media plan delivery are often obscured by the use of gross tracking indicators such as the dollar amount spent on advertising or total GRPs. It is quite possible to be spending the same amount, say, each quarter or to be achieving the same level of GRPs, yet to have a substantial change occur in the rate of effective reach—the number of target audience individuals reached at the minimum effective frequency level per advertising cycle.

Television programs, in particular, wax and wane in popularity, and seasonal differences in the ratings of established programs are remarkably large.[28] But the main reason for failing to achieve effective reach, almost certainly, is bulk buying of media by GRPs in-

stead of by specific programs (or by specific media vehicles in the general case). As we have emphasized, the advertiser needs to know about exposure to the *target* audience, and this knowledge is not obtainable in the grosser audience figures used to accumulate GRPs.

The first check for internal causes of campaign wearout, therefore, should be to *update the direct matching survey* of the target audience's media vehicle exposure. For a brand using demographic or psychographic matching rather than direct matching, the ability to detect media plan "slippage" is considerably lessened by the indirect fix on the target audience. Nevertheless, a media plan check is still required, and this would be a good time to institute a direct matching survey (see Chapters 17 and 18). At the very least, a recomputation of the match between the demographic or psychographic target audience and vehicle audiences should be conducted.

### Effective Frequency Check

As we stated in Chapter 16, the calculation of the minimum effective frequency per advertising cycle, MEF/c, is necessarily an estimate. The MEF/c estimate is usually made prior to testing the actual ads that the creative team produces; that is, it assumes "average" ads. However, the ads could be so weak or so strong that they require more (if weak) or less (if strong) frequency to achieve the brand's communication effects. If so, the MEF/c will need to be adjusted upward or downward, as appropriate. The main problem in terms of pseudo-wearout is running the ad at too low a frequency, so that it never "wears *in*." Wear-*in* refers to the tendency of an ad to require fewer exposures on successive flights to achieve its communication objectives[29]—presuming these flights reach the same people, of course.[30] In any event, it is worth the time to investigate "achieved" frequency during tracking.

MEF/c can be checked in tracking by asking respondents, in conjunction with the *ad recognition* question, the ad recognition *frequency* question: how many times they've seen or heard the ad in the last month or so.[31] Their reported frequency can be checked against the media plan's intended frequency for each advertising cycle. If too few report MEF, then chances are you're losing effective reach. This is likely to be due to the media schedule rather than to the ad losing attention, as very little attention is needed to report simply *seeing* (or hearing) an ad. It is also true, however, that *very* attention-getting ads will tend to have their frequency *over*reported, but that's a nice bonus—only rarely should you reduce the MEF, or reduce it by more than 1 per advertising cycle.

### "Maintenance" Plans

A related problem of exposure and media plan delivery —discussed in Chapter 16 but *well* worth repeating here—occurs after a heavy initial burst of advertising for a new brand or for a new campaign. After the heavy initial burst, the advertising is often cut back to a "maintenance" level. But usually too little thought is given to what the maintenance plan actually delivers. Again, gross statistics, such as "half the GRPs" (an especially common statistic) or "half the reach" or "half the average frequency" tell us nothing about what the plan is actually delivering. A so-called maintenance plan may look like it's achieving half the "impact" of the original plan, but in fact it may be delivering far below this, particularly if it drops nearly everyone below the minimum effective frequency level required in the advertising cycle.

There is also the question of *what* is being maintained—by way of communication objectives. It is one thing, for example, to maintain a target audience of brand loyals with relatively low frequency advertising, but quite another to attempt to maintain a target audience of brand switchers with the same maintenance plan. Yet such distinctions rarely enter into the evaluation of reduced media plans. Instead, all detailed consideration is buried in meaningless figures like GRPs, as though the target audience responds to advertising expenditure dispensed in any shape or form.

Make sure you know what "maintenance" means before you consider such a plan.

### Summary of Media Plan Causes

When internal campaign wearout is first signaled by a decline in sales in the *absence* of apparent causes *outside* the campaign, the manager should immediately request from the media planner a detailed accounting of the past and current delivery of the media plan. This accounting should be expressed in terms of the number of individuals reached in each advertising cycle (the purchase cycle should be checked, also, especially for new product categories) at the minimum effective frequency level. If this figure has not changed, then exposure can be ruled out as a cause, and the problem must reside in one or more of the processing responses to the ads themselves.

### FINAL CHECK: THE ADVERTISEMENTS THEMSELVES

Finally, we arrive at *advertising wearout* in the proper sense of the term: that the *creative idea* itself or the *creative executions* are no longer meeting the sales objective even though the advertising strategy is correct and the media plan is sound. The problems could be in the processing responses of attention, learning, or acceptance, or with emotional responses in learning and acceptance. We will see that the solutions may require changes in the creative executions *or* changes in the media plan.

### Attention Wearout

The first response in the processing of all advertisements is attention. Initial attention to ads was examined extensively in Chapter 10. *Diminished* attention to an advertisement, at the individual audience member level, after it has been processed several times, is a common cause of wearout.[32] Diminished attention is particularly likely to affect campaigns in print media where the easy response for the consumer or customer is to turn the page. It is less of a problem in broadcast media, particularly TV, where the easy response is to watch or listen. Nevertheless, attention wearout can occur for an ad in any medium.

To alleviate the problem of diminished attention to a campaign, slightly different advertising executions of the same advertising strategy (the same benefit positioning and creative idea) are the lowest-cost solution. Miller Lite was perhaps the first to do this on a comprehensive scale on TV, with its "ex-jock" pool of commercials, and Blue Nun was an early example on radio. But in print, where the problem of holding the reader's attention can be severe, advertisers have been somewhat slower to use variations on a theme.[33] Continuous tracking data from Millward Brown suggests that print ads (magazine and probably newspaper ads) experience a major drop in processing, as measured by brand-prompted ad recall (BPAR), which measures the proportion of people who link the ad to the *brand*, after 3 exposures.[34] *Note* that this may be considerably more than 3 *insertions*, depending on the reach pattern of the media schedule, as explained in Chapter 17; and it may be more *or* less than 3 insertions in a particular publication if multiple publications are used in the plan. Print advertisers who use multiple executions include Kraft Singles, liquor brands such as Chivas Regal and Johnny Walker, and cigarette brands such as Kent and True, which operate with about 10 different executions of the same underlying message strategy. Figure 20.4 shows variations on a theme for Heineken beer's international campaign; these ads are shown in *global* media vehicles, such as the world airline magazines, to communicate the positioning benefit (U in the I-D-U model) that Heineken is the *most* internationally preferred imported beer.

If executional variations don't seem to be sufficient to restore attention to the campaign (easily measurable in continuous tracking), then it is time to start looking for a new *creative idea.* As emphasized in Chapters 7 and 18, any contemplated new creative ideas must be thoroughly concept-developed and pretested to ensure that the idea selected does not depart from the brand's current positioning (a positioning change would be a change in advertising *strategy,* which is not the correction intended here).

### Learning (Interference) Wearout

Wearout can also occur in the second response in processing: (rote) learning. As explained in Chapter 8, rote learning is necessary for two communication effects—*brand awareness,* in which the consumer or customer must learn the connection between the category need and the brand; and *low-involvement brand attitude,* in which the consumer or customer must learn the connection between the brand and the main benefit or benefits that tap into the brand purchase motivation.

Learning failure is very often due to prior attention failure, in which case it would be diagnosed in the foregoing attention analysis. If so, the solution would be, as before, variations on a theme using new stimuli to regain attention. However, learning failure can also occur in its own right due to *interference* from learning produced by competing brands. Interference can readily occur when one or more major competitors change their media schedule to attain greater frequency against target audience individuals than previously (dominance); or change the ratio of ads in their pool, or even their advertising message execution slightly to achieve stronger associative learning of (the competitor's) brand awareness or brand attitude.

Changes in scheduling or changes in executional emphasis by a competitor can produce very significant interference effects.[35] An increase in effective frequency by an astute competitor, along the lines suggested in Chapter 16, could find the competitive brand dominating at the individual audience member level in terms of opportunities to learn the brand name as a top-of-mind response to the category need (brand recall) and simultaneously strengthening the connection between the brand and its benefit or benefits (brand attitude). Similarly, a competitor whose brand

**FIGURE 20.4**
Variations on a theme: global (more correctly, multinational) executions for Heineken beer's export campaign.
*Courtesy:* Heineken and Bartle Bogle Hegarty Ltd., London.

is chosen at the point of purchase (brand recognition) may increase its executional emphasis on package shots or improve its portrayal of benefits (brand attitude) and make large inroads on your brand—without the competitor altering its media expenditure or its advertising strategy at all.

Also, your brand's *previous* campaign can interfere for weeks or months after it has concluded when you introduce a new campaign (Figure 20.5). In this case, the interfering "competitor" is you! The solutions to this problem, however, are just the same as when an actual competitor is doing the interfering.

Interference is the major problem that affects *recall* in learning, which underlies brand recall awareness and low-involvement brand attitude. Interference is *not,* however, a very significant factor in *recognition* learning.[36] Rather, time-related decay, which is a very slow process, is the main cause of declining recognition. We point out this distinction in the causes of recall unlearning (interference) and

recognition unlearning (time-related decay) because the solutions to learning problems as causes of wearout depend on it.

- If *brand recall* is the appropriate type of brand awareness communication objective for the brand, then *dominance* in the advertising cycle (increasing MEF/c above that of the largest competitor—see Chapter 16) is the best corrective tactic. Note that if the media budget is to be held constant, this will require *wider spacing* of advertising cycles (flights[37]).
- If *brand recognition* is the objective, then *shortening the spacing between flights* is the best corrective tactic. However, as brand recognition is very long lasting once established, first make sure that the problem is not due to insufficient brand or package exposure *in* the ad itself.

As to the maximum interval (hiatus) *between* advertising cycles, or flights, some evidence suggests

**FIGURE 20.5**

A brand's previous campaign can interfere with advertising awareness (as measured here by CPAR) of its new campaign for a considerable time. The graphed curves show CPAR for both the first and the new ads. The vertical bars show GRPs, averaging about 100 per week while each ad was on-air. *Courtesy:* M. Sutherland; see note 1.

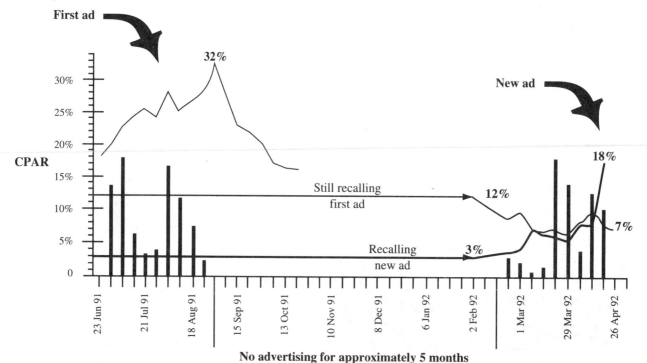

that, for a new brand, the delay should be no longer than 1 month, though for an established brand, delays of up to 3 months may be tolerated.[38] Theoretically, too, the *less brand loyal* the target audience, the *shorter* the hiatuses that should be allowed in the schedule.

### Acceptance (Overexposure) Wearout

Negative reactions due to overexposure are *most unlikely with print ads,* because the consumer or customer can simply turn the page (for a magazine or newspaper ad or figuratively for an interactive TV or PC ad), or look away (from a billboard or poster), or throw out the ad (direct mail). The wearout problem with print ads is almost certain to be attentional wearout, or possibly learning wearout caused by interference or decay, but not wearout due to overexposure. A consumer or customer is most unlikely to counterargue with a print ad.

On the other hand, *broadcast ads are very susceptible to overexposure wearout* because most people sit passively and attend to the ad. This is particularly true of television commercials, though less true of radio commercials because of radio's frequent use as a background medium. In fact, attitudinal wearout (negative shifts in attitude upon repeated exposures) has been demonstrated *only* with television commercials and not with advertising in any other medium.[39]

What corrective actions should be tried for advertising that has worn out due to overexposure to, and counterarguing and rejection by, too many members of the target audience?

- If the advertising is *low-involvement/informational,* *ignore* the rejection responses, as they are not relevant to this brand attitude strategy quadrant. If the advertising is *low-involvement/transformational,* however, *drop the ad immediately,* as negative reactions are fatal in this quadrant.
- For *high-involvement* brand attitude advertising, be it informational or transformational, the best solution is to implement *variations on a theme.* The advertiser has to remove offending elements, or not present them as often, so as to delay wearout, and replace them with interesting elements. This means different advertisements must be used. A related and less expensive but less satisfactory solution which may work in the short run is to *rotate* the individual ads more often.

- A particular solution applies to target audiences who have fully learned (low-involvement) or accepted (high-involvement) a favorable brand attitude—these would be *brand loyals* or *routinized favorable brand switchers*—and this is to use *shorter ads.*[40] Brief TV or radio commercials (10-second or 15-second spots) and smaller or reduced-copy print ads should serve to maintain brand awareness. Brand awareness should, in turn, "carry" the favorable brand attitude (by reminder) without the ad having to provide actual attitude-relevant content. Indeed, further exposure of *loyal* audiences to the full attitude content could fuel counterarguing and wearout.[41] However, shorter ads should be used *only* for favorable target audiences. They are *not* suitable for other audiences whose communication effects are not at full strength.

Before assuming overexposure is the cause, we again emphasize that in campaign tracking the advertiser has to be alert for the other internal causes of wearout, including exposure slippage (which is *not* wearout but rather constitutes a problem with the media plan), attention, and learning. Also, it should be evident that the advertiser must not lose sight of the advertising communication model and particularly the brand attitude strategy. Remember the Charmin example: acceptance measures of processing would almost surely have suggested that the Mr. Whipple commercial had worn out early; however, acceptance was irrelevant to the low-involvement/informational way in which this commercial worked.

## SUMMARY OF ADVERTISING WEAROUT SOLUTIONS

A summary of the varying causes of wearout and their respective solutions is appropriate.

First, there are the causes of sales declines that are *not* due to advertising wearout but *do* signal an advertising strategy's *obsolescence* and indeed the obsolescence of the advertising plan and the marketing plan. These sets of reasons are (1) changes in other components of the brand's marketing mix; (2) changes in competitors' marketing mixes, including their advertising strategy but not their media strategy alone; and (3) changes in consumer values, reflected in the altered importance of advertised benefits.

Second, another cause of sales decline that is not due to advertising wearout is (4) slippage in the brand's media plan. An update of the media plan to ensure that vehicles are selected to achieve the original effective reach goal is all that is required here. Again, this is not advertising wearout.

The final three causes of sales declines can legitimately be classified as *advertising wearout*, in that they represent a failure of the advertising in the absence of external causes—that is, in the absence of causes 1 to 4. The causes of advertising wearout are either (5) attentional problems, (6) learning problems, or (7) acceptance problems.

The manager must diagnose the problem correctly and should apply the solutions as indicated in Table 20.6.

Campaign evaluation, as we have seen, is not an easy task. Tracking studies can be expensive to conduct and difficult to analyze. Advertising wearout in particular is difficult to detect correctly although the solutions are straightforward, once the right cause has been detected. For the manager who is spending millions of dollars on the company's or brand's campaign, however, campaign tracking is a vital and necessary ongoing and concluding stage of advertising communications and promotion management.

## NOTES

1. The fact that most advertising campaigns are not formally evaluated is reinforced in an interesting article by P. R. Klein and M. Tainiter, Copy research validation: The advertiser's perspective, *Journal of Advertising Research,* 1983, *23* (5), pp. 9–17. These investigators followed up on 1,165 TV commercials, from 412 campaigns, tested by the McCollum Spielman testing service. Although many were very large budget campaigns, few were formally tracked. A likely reason for this, apart from money, is that managers almost inevitably fall prey to "hindsight bias"—that is, they believe they know (after the fact, of course) why a campaign did or did not work. Pressure for accountability in all areas of business, including advertising, is rapidly removing this excuse for not tracking campaigns. See T. B. C. Poietz and H. S. J. Robben, Individual reactions to advertising: Theoretical and methodological developments, *International Journal of Advertising,* 1994, *13* (1), pp. 25–53, for the observation on hindsight bias; and M. Sutherland, *Advertising and the Mind of the Consumer,* St. Leonard's, Australia: Allen & Unwin, 1993, for the diminishing excuse and sound business reasons for campaign tracking.

2. Based on an analysis of 78 TV advertising campaigns for fmcg products in the United States; see J. P. Jones, Advertising's woes and advertising accountability, *Admap,* September 1994, pp. 24–27. One in 10 produced "outstanding" long-term (1-year) effects; four in 10 produced a measurable long-term effect; two in 10 showed no long-term effect; and three in 10 a negative long-term effect.

3. Again, defining media broadly to include promotion offer delivery as media (see Chapter 15).

4. GRPs were defined in Chapter 16 (see Table 16.1). For promotion offers, *audience* can be taken as the number of samples delivered, coupons distributed, and so on. These are equivalent conceptually to advertising vehicle GRPs.

5. Remember from Chapter 19 (on ad testing) that the attempt to create a competitive media environment in an *ad test* by exposing the ad in a "standard" media excerpt, such as a TV program or simulated magazine, with competing ads, does not provide a good measure or predictor of its in-media attention. Such an "excerpt" represents a sample of size n = 1 from the *pop-*

---

**TABLE 20.6**

### ADVERTISING WEAROUT: CAUSES AND SOLUTIONS

| Cause of wearout | Corrective action |
|---|---|
| *Attention*—diminished attention (especially to print ads) | *Variations*—different executions of the same advertising message strategy, to hold attention |
| *Learning*—unlearning due to competitive interference (brand recall and *low-involvement* brand attitude) or to too long a delay or hiatus in the media schedule (brand recognition) | *Flighting*—to offset competitive interference, but with a relatively short hiatus of 1 to 3 months maximum between flights |
| *Acceptance*—rejection responses (especially to broadcast ads) emerging with prolonged repetition; affects category need, *high-involvement* brand attitude, *low-involvement/transformational* brand attitude, induced brand purchase intention, and purchase facilitation (when these are objectives) | *Variations*—different executions of the same advertising message strategy, to delay rejection of elements: *faster rotation* of existing ads, although this is only a short-term solution; also *shorter ads* for favorable target audience |

*ulation* of media environments that the ad will actually face. Campaign tracking is the place to test (to "posttest") whether the ad works in media.

6. Syndicated services offering advertisement recognition measures include the following: for TV commercials, Bruzzone Research Corporation (which mails out photoboards of TV commercials and has the questionnaires returned by mail); for radio commercials, Haug Associates (by phone); for magazine ads, Roper Starch (but *see note 8*); and for newspaper ads and trade magazine ads, Starch Ballot, Readex, and Harvey Communication Measurement Service.

7. M. Sutherland, same reference as in note 1, pp. 217–218.

8. A suspected attention problem due to the creative execution not holding up in media is the one situation where day-after recall (DAR) (for example, Burke, Gallup & Robinson, Mapes & Ross) makes sense because it is *known* that the respondents were exposed to the media vehicle (that is, the TV program). However, note that a valid test would require *multiple* DAR tests in a representative sample of programs used in the media plan, which becomes very expensive. Likewise, for magazine ads, the Starch recognition procedure is tied to a particular magazine, so diagnosis of creative attention for a magazine ad would require *multiple* Starch tests across a representative sample of magazines used in the media plan. Managers should hope that attention problems are sufficiently diagnosed in the ad testing phase—it's considerably cheaper!

9. S. Colman and G. Brown, Advertising tracking studies and sales effects, *Journal of the Market Research Society,* 1983, *25* (2), pp. 165–183. Also G. Brown, Tracking studies and sales effects: A U.K. perspective, *Journal of Advertising Research,* 1985, *25* (1), pp. 52–64. This is the main measure used by Millward Brown's tracking service.

10. If the campaign has used only one medium, or if the manager wants to track the campaign's advertising *by* media, the question can be narrowed accordingly, and in the latter case, repeated for each type of advertising —TV commercials, radio commercials, newspaper ads, and so on.

11. The "recently" is important, to locate the ad recall in the advertising cycles. It's usually taken as the last few weeks.

12. Somewhat remarkably, the Millward Brown tracking service uses only *claimed* recall, not proven recall, in its Awareness Index measure (see later). However, recalled content can still be used for diagnostic purposes.

13. Academic adherents of "associative network theory" are susceptible to the confusions described in this paragraph. The problem is that the network's *directional* associations or links are not equally strong and thus equally likely to be activated. Simple example: for most people, the link Des Moines → capital of Iowa is much stronger than the link Capital of Iowa → Des Moines.

Another trendy concept from the memory paradigm is "implicit memory," which is a reincarnation of the much older concept of "learning without awareness." In memory terminology, ad-based tracking measures (including CPAR and BPAR) are tests of "explicit" memory, because the consumer has to recall the learning event (the ad), whereas brand-based tracking measures (including brand awareness and brand attitude communication effects) are tests of "implicit" memory, because recall of the (usually) many learning events that caused the awareness or the attitude does not occur and indeed (usually) is an impossible task (unless the cause was a one-off direct response ad). There's no necessity to remember the ad or ads for *brand* effects to occur, and in fact brand awareness and brand attitude, the two universal communication effects, quite normally increase or decrease unconsciously or implicitly, without conscious or explicit memory of the events or processes. By labeling this normal process "implicit memory," non-practitioner academics think they've discovered some new way to measure advertising effects! See, for example, H. S. Krishnan and S. Shapiro, Comparing explicit and implicit memory for brand names from advertisements, *Journal of Experimental Psychology: Applied,* 1996, *2* (2), pp. 147–163.

14. For a similar opinion on target audience analysis in tracking, see C. McDonald, Point of view: The key is to understand consumer response, *Journal of Advertising Research,* 1993, *33* (5), pp. 63–69.

15. V. G. Morwitz, E. Johnson, and D. C. Schmittlain, Does measuring intent change behavior? *Journal of Consumer Research,* 1993, *20* (1), pp. 46–61.

16. For descriptions of the continuous tracking survey method, see S. Colman and G. Brown, same reference as in note 9; M. Sutherland, same reference as in note 1; and M. Sutherland and W. Harper, The use of moving averages: A case study in extracting information from data bases, *Australian Journal of Marketing Research,* 1994, *2* (2), pp. 19–34.

17. Shorter or longer roll periods, with consequently smaller or larger cumulative sample sizes, can be used to observe short-term versus long-term effects. See especially M. Sutherland and W. Harper, same reference as in note 16, for the rationale governing roll periods. Note that the roll is a simple (unweighted) moving average.

18. At the time of this writing, continuous tracking, led by Millward Brown, the research firm, is the fastest-growing market research technique in the United States. Market researchers in England (Millward Brown and others) and Australia (MarketMind and

others) have been using this technique for over a decade.

19. The 61 percent visual ad recognition estimate comes from TV ads surveyed in C. E. Young and M. Robinson, Guideline℠: Tracking the commercial viewer's wandering attention, *Journal of Advertising Research,* 1987, *27* (3), pp. 15–22, and is close to the 60 percent norm reported by Bruzzone Research Corporation (BRC). The 37 percent verbal ad recognition estimate comes from a study of 750 TV ad campaigns in which respondents were asked to recognize each ad after being read a verbal description of it, by D. Walker and M. F. von Gonten, Explaining related recall outcomes: New answers from a better model, *Journal of Advertising Research,* 1989, *29* (3), pp. 11–21.

20. The astute reader will notice that brands mentioned in the category advertising cut-through measure will bias the next measure, brand recall (if it is an objective). However, this bias is far less serious than if brand recall were to come first.

21. Causal interpretation can be inferred if we assume that individuals interviewed in each tracking wave are "clones" in that they are drawn from the same population of homogeneous respondents. Thus we are simulating the sampling of *one* person over time, as in a panel. This is a somewhat heroic assumption but it seems to hold *reasonably* well in practice.

22. See J. D. C. Little, BRANDAID: A marketing-mix model, part 1: Structure, *Operations Research,* 1975, *23* (4), pp. 628–673; H. Simon, ADPULS, an advertising model with wearout and pulsation, *Journal of Marketing Research,* 1982, *19* (3), pp. 352–363; and D. Horsky and L. S. Simon, Advertising and the diffusion of new products, *Marketing Science,* 1983, *2* (1), pp. 1–10.

23. See, for instance, Gordon Brown's revealing account of problems with Millward Brown's "Awareness Index," the main continuous tracking statistic in that company's popular campaign evaluation methodology, in G. Brown, Modelling advertising awareness, *The Statistician,* 1986, *35* (2), pp. 289–299; also see P. Feldwick, S. Carter, and L. Cook, How valuable is the Awareness Index? *Market Research Society (U.K.) Conference Proceedings,* 1991, pp. 137–140, and G. Brown, Modelling advertising awareness, *Admap,* April 1991, pp. 25–29, and G. Brown, J. Green, and A. Farr, A vigorous defence of the "awareness index and detailed recall" findings, in *People, Brands & Advertising,* Leamington Spa, U. K.: Millward Brown International Plc, 1992, pp. 49-59, and especially pp. 56–59. Millward Brown's experience with sales modeling is typical, we believe.

24. M. Sutherland, same reference as in note 1, chapter 19.

25. See also G. M. Fulgoni, The role of advertising—is there one?, *Admap,* April 1987, pp. 54–57; A. MacDonald, Quantifying the effect of advertising: The implication for advertising strategies, *Journal of Targeting, Measurement and Analysis for Marketing,* 1994, *3* (1), pp. 48–59; and A. Roberts, T.V. exposure, brand buying, and ad effects, *Admap,* June 1994, pp. 31–37.

26. See note 22.

27. See especially J. H. Parfitt and B. J. K. Collins, Use of consumer panels for brand share prediction, *Journal of Marketing Research,* 1968, *5* (2), pp. 131–146; and J. D. C. Little, Aggregate advertising models: The state of the art, *Operations Research,* 1979, *27* (4), pp. 629–667.

28. For instance, the average prime-time ratings by season were 13.8, 11.7, 9.6, and 12.9 for quarters 1, 2, 3, and 4 of 1993. See ADWEEK's *Marketers' Guide to Media,* 1994, *17* (1), p. 26.

29. M. Sutherland, same reference as in note 1, pp. 188–189.

30. They wouldn't in the "shifting reach" pattern, for instance.

31. For impressive evidence showing that people *automatically* encode event frequency, such as the number of times they have seen an ad, with a slight tendency to underestimate beyond three or four—hence, claimed frequency is conservative—see L. Hasher and R. T. Zacks, Automatic processing of fundamental information: The case of frequency of occurrence, *American Psychologist,* 1984, *39* (12), pp. 1372–1388.

32. C. S. Craig, B. Sternthal, and C. Leavitt, Advertising wearout: An experimental analysis, *Journal of Marketing Research,* 1976, *13* (4), pp. 365–372.

33. J. R. Rossiter, Visual imagery: Applications to advertising, in A. A. Mitchell, ed., *Advances in Consumer Research,* vol. 9, Provo, UT: Association for Consumer Research, 1982, pp. 101–106.

34. Starch Noted scores show that ad recognition remains remarkably constant over 5 or 6 exposures. However, it seems likely that brand attitude–relevant processing diminishes over successive exposures. Using the measure "Seen [brand] advertised recently," Gordon Brown of Millward Brown suggests that the diminution is as follows: 1 st exposure = 1.0, 2nd exposure = 1.0, 3rd exposure = 0.75, 4th exposure = 0.25, 5th or subsequent exposures = 0.1 each. This suggests rotation of print ads after 3 exposures (this may be more *or* less than 3 *insertions* in a particular publication, depending on the media plan's reach pattern). See G. Brown, The awareness problem: Attention and memory effects from TV and magazine advertising, *Admap,* January 1994, pp. 15–20; and also A. Farr,

How to harness the power of magazine advertising, *Admap,* December 1995, pp. 25–29.

35. Dramatic interference effects were demonstrated in a neatly designed experiment that varied the relative frequency (or "share of voice") of competitive advertising and also the creative effectiveness (or "reward value") of competing ads. Although this was a laboratory experiment, the conditions were quite similar to brand recall learning and low-involvement brand attitude learning in the real world, where competitive interference and not time between exposures is postulated to be the "unlearning" process. See L. A. Lo Sciuto, L. H. Strassmann, and W. D. Wells, Advertising weight and the reward value of the brand, *Journal of Advertising Research,* 1967, *7* (2), pp. 34–38.

36. W. A. Wickelgren, *Learning and Memory,* Englewood Cliffs, NJ: Prentice-Hall, 1977, chapter 15.

37. Notice that these are *flights* of advertising, that is, totally on then totally off cycles. It is not *pulsing,* which is "mostly on then partly off" cycles—the trimming from the on cycles being used in what would otherwise be off cycles (see Chapter 16). Pulsing is a common form of "maintenance" plan and is not recommended.

38. For example, see D. G. Clarke, Econometric measurement of the duration of advertising effect on sales, *Journal of Marketing Research,* 1976, *13* (4), pp. 345–347; and H. Simon, same reference as in note 22.

39. Some studies misleadingly suggest that counterarguing is rarely a problem with broadcast commercials because their presentation lasts such a short time and then is supplanted immediately by another commercial or by the program. The evidence for minimal counterarguing with broadcast commercials, however, has been based on *single-exposure* studies. With multiple exposures, as in the vast majority of actual campaigns, counterarguing and consequent rejection clearly can occur. For the two viewpoints and evidence, see P. L. Wright, Cognitive responses to mass media advocacy, in R. E. Petty, T. M. Ostrom, and T. C. Brock, eds., *Cognitive Responses in Persuasion,* Hillsdale, NJ: Lawrence Erlbaum Associates, 1981, pp. 263–282; and B. J. Calder and B. Sternthal, Television commercial wearout: An information processing view, *Journal of Marketing Research,* 1980, *17* (2), pp. 173–186.

40. Note that the recommendation of shorter ads is made for *low- or high*-involvement brand attitude, yet it is still designed to prevent acceptance wearout (solely a high-involvement phenomenon). Brand loyals and routinized favorable brand switchers probably have moved to low-involvement anyway in deciding to *repurchase* the brand. The idea is to stop them from going *back* into high-involvement (by reconsidering the purchase decision) through their irritation with the brand's advertising.

41. A recent test by the ABC network and the J. Walter Thompson agency of multiple 15-second commercials in a single pod or commercial break suggests an increased level of irritation as viewers realize there are more commercials. However, this presumes a major industry shift toward shorter commercials instead of selective use of them. Furthermore, the test audience was not analyzed for brand loyalty, to which our shorter-commercial recommendation applies. See L. G. Reiling, Mixed spot lengths increase effects of the longer, *Marketing News,* April 26, 1985, p. 6.

## DISCUSSION QUESTIONS

Although we recommend a project rather than discussion questions for Part Seven, below are some short-exercise questions for the three advertising research chapters.

**20.1.** Chapter 18: For McDonald's restaurants, prepare two summary advertising strategies aimed respectively at:
   **a.** Brand loyals
   **b.** Other-brand loyals

**20.2.** Chapter 18: Thinking carefully about probable target audience involvement and communication objectives, conduct a management judgment ad test (MJT) of the Audi 90 automobile advertisement shown in Figure 6.5.

**20.3.** Chapter 19: For the Häagen-Dazs ice cream ad reproduced in Figure 8.5, write a memorandum to the research company listing, in order, the ad testing measures you believe would constitute a valid procedure for testing this ad. Explain your selection of measures and the recommended order of measurement.

**20.4.** Chapter 19: In recent years, Coca-Cola has employed primarily a brand recognition *and* brand recall/low-involvement/informational *and* transformational advertising communication model. The two most recent campaigns, "It's the real thing," and "Coke is it!" seem transformational for brand loyals but informational (implied comparative) for brand switchers and other-brand loyals. In this complex situation, what specific measures would you recommend for testing these types of ads, and why?

**20.5.** Chapter 20: How can you prove that the target audience has been exposed to the ads in your campaign and, further, that the ads received at least initial attention?

**20.6.** Chapter 20: You have been running the same advertising campaign for 6 months. The rate of sales of your brand is starting to slow, and the other managers have recommended as the solution a fresh creative approach. What would be your recommendation?

**20.7.** Chapter 20: For magazine advertisements versus TV commercials, discuss the roles of attentional wearout and acceptance wearout, noting solutions in each of the four "cells" of your answer.

## FURTHER READING

There is only one good reference for campaign tracking as such: Max Sutherland's book, listed last. First, though, we recommend some readings that assist in the analysis of tracking study results and then some readings on advertising wearout.

Leckenby, J. D., and Wedding, N. *Advertising Management: Criteria, Analysis and Decision Making.* Columbus, OH: Grid, 1982.

Chapters 7 and 8 of this book contain an excellent introductory explanation of why lagged advertising analysis is necessary to interpret the exposure-to-sales relationship. Chapter 8 also contains a simplified but helpful description of BRANDAID.

Fitzroy, P. *Analytical Models for Marketing Management.* New York: McGraw-Hill, 1976.

This book offers a very good, relatively easy-to-follow explanation of mathematical models in marketing. For advertising applications, see especially chapter 2 (consumer buying behavior) and chapter 7 (advertising strategy).

Lilien, G., Kotler, P., and Moorthy, K. S. *Marketing Models.* Englewood Cliffs, NJ: Prentice-Hall, 1992.

This is the best of the current textbooks on mathematical models for marketing decisions. This very detailed how-to book covers basic to advanced models. Besides advertising models (chapter 6), the book is also noteworthy for its attention to sales promotion models (chapter 7). However, it is probably advisable to read the Fitzroy text first, as the size of this one may be daunting.

Most articles on wearout fail to identify whether the responses that are "wearing out" are relevant to the brand's advertising communication objectives. The following articles were selected because they specify the processing response that is wearing out and illustrate our three types of advertising wearout.

Haley, R. I. Sales effects of media weight. *Journal of Advertising Research,* 1978, *18*(3), pp. 9–18.

Attention wearout is the presumed process underlying the valuable case histories presented in Haley's article. The author argues that constant media weight produces diminishing sales returns due to attention wearout.

Lo Sciuto, L. A., Strassman, L. H., and Wells, W. D. Advertising weight and the reward value of the brand. *Journal of Advertising Research,* 1967, *7*(2), pp. 34–38.

Learning (interference) wearout is demonstrated in this well-designed series of laboratory experiments. Interference applies to brand recall and *low-involvement* brand attitude learning situations.

Sawyer, A. Repetition, cognitive responses, and persuasion. In Petty, R. E., Ostrom, T. M., and Brock, T. C., Eds. *Cognitive Responses in Persuasion.* Hillsdale, NJ: Lawrence Erlbaum Associates, 1981, pp. 263–282.

Acceptance (overexposure) wearout is carefully analyzed in this chapter. Although not noted by the author, overexposure only applies to *high-involvement* brand attitudes, when the target audience counterargues with the brand's benefit claims, and to low-involvement/ *transformational* advertising if the target audience begins to dislike the ad itself. It is *not* a problem for low-involvement/informational advertising.

Finally, the best (and only) practical book on campaign tracking is:

Sutherland, M. *Advertising and the Mind of the Consumer.* St. Leonard's, Australia: Allen & Unwin, 1993.

This book is thoughtful, entertaining, and full of campaign examples. It shows how to use continuous tracking to quickly detect how well the campaign is working, whether problems are arising, and what to do to correct them. Also, it is less technical than our book.

# The Advertising Communications and Promotion Plan

This appendix presents a managerial checklist for preparing the advertising communications and promotion plan. It presumes that you've read the book, and as such, has no explanatory text. Its purpose is to enable the manager to organize and summarize all that's been learned, from research and from the framework in the book, into an overall AC&P plan. The plan's format is applicable to any brand of product or service, or to the company as the brand for a corporate campaign. (See also Figure A.1, which summarizes "what's going on" in constructing the AC&P plan and reminds the manager of the total picture.)

The AC&P plan's sections correspond approximately with the manager's planning stages. The plan's sections are as follows:

A. Cover page and research checklist
B. Marketing objectives and budget
C. Target audience and action objectives
D. Communications objectives and brand positioning statement
E. Creative strategy
F. IMC strategy
G. Media strategy
H. Advertising strategy summary (creative brief)

In constructing the plan, two aspects must be kept in mind.

First, if you have more than one *target audience* for your advertising communications and promotions, then:

- If the target audiences are in *different* stages of the marketing channel (for example, retailers and consumers), then you must do a *full* AC&P plan (sections A through H) for each channel stage.
- If the target audiences are at the *same* stage of the marketing channel (for example, other-brand switchers and brand loyals at the end-customer or consumer stage), then you must do *sections C through H* separately for each.

Second, the brackets to the left of subsections B through G of the plan are for you to state your *degree of confidence* in the decision made for that subsection: write in the letter corresponding to low (L), medium (M), or high (H) confidence. This will help later, should the plan require revision, by indicating which parts of the plan were tentative to begin with.

## A. COVER PAGE AND RESEARCH CHECKLIST

1. **Plan identification details.** (Complete as appropriate.)

- Brand
- Target audience

| Media strategy | Creative and IMC strategy | Communication objectives and positioning | Target audience selection and action objectives | Marketing objectives and budget | |
|---|---|---|---|---|---|
| **Exposure** → | **Processing** → | **Communication effects and brand position** → | **Target audience action** → | **Sales or market share, and brand equity** → | **Profit** |
| Media attention (OTS) | Attention Learning Emotion Acceptance | Category need* Brand awareness* Brand attitude* Brand purchase intention Purchase facilitation *Brand position* | Trial Repeat purchase | | |
| Advertising strategy research | Concept development research and ad/promotion testing | | | Campaign tracking and evaluation | |

**FIGURE A.1**
Summary of advertising communications and promotion management.

- IMC plan or type of advertising communications or promotions emphasized
- Period covered by this plan
- Manager(s) responsible
- Date prepared

2. **Research checklist.** (Check all types of advertising research employed or *to be employed* in the formulation and implementation of the plan. If you wish, write in DONE, or to be done, TBD, respectively, instead of check marks. It is useful for future reference to make this the second page of the plan, summarizing the research methods; for example, three focus groups, customized ad test with cell sizes of 100 per ad, continuous tracking with 100 respondents weekly, and so forth. At minimum, check the applicable items.)

- Advertising strategy research: situation audit _____, qualitative ASR _____, quantitative ASR _____
- Creative research: concept development research _____, management judgment test _____, quantitative ad test _____
- Campaign evaluation: aggregate tracking _____, wave survey _____, panel survey _____, continuous tracking _____

## B. MARKETING OBJECTIVES AND BUDGET

[   ]
confidence

1. **Profit contributions of advertising communications (AC) and promotions (P).** (Complete each line that applies by writing in the *time horizon* for the objective: immediate (IMM), 1 year (1-YR), or long-run (LR). For the

first three items, a "blank" means that this factor is assumed to stay constant, that is, "maintained." Lastly, write in the profit goal if it is known.)

- Increase selling price: AC _____ P _____
- Lower costs: AC _____ P _____
- Increase sales volume *rate* (units): AC _____ P _____
- Profit goal, for period _____ (month, year) to _____ (month, year): $ _____

[   ]  2. **Sales goal required to yield the profit goal, and total AC&P budget to support this sales goal.** (Write in units and dollar amounts.)

- Current sales: units _____ $ _____
- Targeted sales at end of period: units _____ $ _____
- Budget for the period: $ _____
- Check the method or methods used to set the budget (if more than one method, write 1, 2, and so on):

Task method _____, IAF/5Q _____, Industry A/S ratio comparison _____, Peckham's 1.5 rule/order-of-entry method _____, Spending test _____, Statistical projection _____, Schroer's method _____, Task matrix method _____, Powers's formula _____

[   ]  3. **Market share: sales goal as percentage of category sales.** (Write in.)

- Market partitioning structure (diagram):

- Market (category) on which market share calculations are based: _____
  _____
- Market's annual growth rate (in *percent*): units _____% $ _____%
- Current market share (in *percent*): units _____% $ _____%
- Market share target to yield sales target (in *percent*): units _____% $ _____%

[   ]  4. **Brand equity objectives.** (Check one objective for each.)

- Value equity: increase _____ maintain _____
- Uniqueness equity: increase _____ maintain _____

## C. TARGET AUDIENCE AND ACTION OBJECTIVES

[   ]  1. **Target audience(s).** (Complete the details below for all relevant TAs: the
confidence  primary target audience and, if applicable, secondary and lower priority target audiences. If a demographic or other delineator is used, describe this too.

*Note:* If the campaign is aimed at different stages in the marketing channel, you must complete a separate AC&P plan for each.)

| | Brand loyalty status (NCU, OBL, OBS, FBS, BL, or subgroup) | Estimated number | Action's *current* status (e.g., brand purchase rate) | Action *objective* (e.g., targeted brand purchase rate) |
|---|---|---|---|---|
| • Primary TA (delineator) | _____ _____ | _____ | _____ | _____ |
| • Secondary TA (delineator) | _____ _____ | _____ | _____ | _____ |
| • Tertiary TA (delineator) | _____ _____ | _____ | _____ | _____ |

[  ]  **2. Behavioral sequence model.** (Construct table.)

| | Stage 1 | Stage 2 | Stage n |
|---|---|---|---|
| • Roles at each stage (who) | | | |
| • Locations (where) | | | |
| • Time and timing (when) | | | |
| • Stage decision summary (what) | | | |

[  ]  **3. Target decision role(s).** (There may be more than one important targeted role *within* the primary target audience, or within the secondary target audience, and so on. Specify the role or roles clearly. For the typical role-player in each case, provide as much personal profile information as possible but *avoid* speculation.)

| | Decision role(s) targeted | Personal profile (add more lines if needed) |
|---|---|---|
| • Primary TA | _____ _____ | _____ _____ |
| • Secondary TA | _____ _____ | _____ _____ |
| • Tertiary TA | _____ _____ | _____ _____ |

**D. COMMUNICATION OBJECTIVES AND BRAND POSITIONING STATEMENT (*NOTE:* A SEPARATE SET OF COMMUNICATION OBJECTIVES PLUS POSITIONING STATEMENT IS REQUIRED FOR EACH TARGET AUDIENCE. DUPLICATE THE HEADINGS IN SECTIONS *D THROUGH G* FOR EACH TA, AND COMPLETE THE SEPARATE SUBPLANS.)**

[  ]
confidence

**1. Category need.** (Specify category need, and check one option.)

• Category need description _____
• Omit _____
• Remind _____
• Sell _____

[ ]

**2. Brand awareness.** (Specify necessary brand identification, and check one option.)

- Brand identification description (exact name, package or logo that targeted role-player must identify) _____
- Brand recognition (at POP) _____
- Brand recall (prior to purchase) _____
- Both (if justified) _____

[ ]

**3a. Brand attitude objective.** (Choose one option.)

- Create (new attitude) _____
- Increase (make present attitude more positive than it is) _____
- Modify (connect to new motivation) _____
- Maintain (current attitude) _____
- Change (from negative to positive) _____

[ ]

**3b. Brand attitude strategy.** (Explain selection of quadrant, the brand purchase or usage motivation, and the specific emotion-shift process to achieve the motivation.)

- Brand attitude strategy quadrant (LI/I, LI/T, HI/I, HI/T) and why _____
  _____
- Motivation _____
- Emotion-shift _____

[ ]

**4. Brand purchase intention.** (Choose one option, and describe if it is to be generated.)

- Omit (soft-sell delayed) _____
- Generate (hard-sell immediate) _____
  How generated _____

[ ]

**5. Purchase facilitation.** (Choose one option, and describe if it is to be incorporated.)

- Omit _____
- Incorporate in campaign:
  Product _____ Price _____ Distribution _____ Selling _____ Publicity _____
  How incorporated _____
  _____

[ ]

**6. Positioning statement.** (Insert, in the format below, the specific target audience, the brand, the category need, and a full classification of the benefits per the I-D-U analysis. The italicized a-b-e specification can be omitted if this micro level of the brand's position is to be delegated to the agency.)

- To _____
- _____ is the brand of _____
- that (in its advertising):
  emphasizes _____
  (*with* _____ *focus*),
  must mention _____
  _____

trades off _____

_____

and omits _____

_____

## E. CREATIVE STRATEGY

[   ]
confidence

**1. Creative idea.** (The creative idea must be stated in sufficient detail to enable advertising executions to be made from it.)

_____

_____

_____

_____

[   ]

**2. Rossiter-Percy grid tactics.**

- Brand recognition checklist (if an objective):
  Category need is clearly mentioned and portrayed _____
  Brand identification stimulus is sufficiently exposed in ad(s) _____
  Brand identification stimulus: brand package _____, brand name _____, brand logo _____
- Brand recall checklist (if an objective):
  Main copy line associates category need with brand name _____
  Main copy line (or CN-BN association) is repeated _____
  Personal reference is explicit _____ or clearly implied _____
  Special presenter used for brand recall _____
  Interactive mnemonic device or jingle for brand recall _____
- Brand recall–boosted brand recognition checklist (if an objective):
  Brand package or logo shown with brand name clearly visible _____
  Main copy line associates category need with brand name _____
  Main copy line (or CN-BN association) is repeated _____
  Personal reference is explicit _____ or clearly implied _____
  Special presenter used for brand recall _____
  Interactive mnemonic device or jingle for brand recall _____
- Low-involvement/informational brand attitude checklist (if this strategy applies):
  Problem-solution format _____
  One emphasized benefit (preferable), _____ or two emphasized benefits (maximum) _____, or singular group of related benefits (with one overall benefit to be learned) _____
  Emphasized benefit claim(s) easily learned _____
  Emphasized benefit claim(s) made to (legal) extreme _____
- Low-involvement/transformational attitude checklist (if this strategy applies):
  Likable ad(s) _____
  Emotional execution is unique to brand _____
  Extreme emotional authenticity of emphasized benefit _____
- High-involvement/informational attitude checklist (if this strategy applies):

Correct emotional portrayal of category need if early in product category life cycle _____
Initial attitude taken into account _____
Maximum of seven benefits used to establish target attitude _____
Strongest benefits given first _____
Capstone (summary) benefit claim _____
All benefit claims are convincing (neither underclaimed nor overclaimed) _____

Presenter (company itself or in-ad presenter) is expert, objective _____
Refutational (if negative initial attitude) _____
Explicit comparative (if small brand with entrenched competitor) _____

- High-involvement/transformational attitude checklist (if this strategy applies):
Target audience will identify with brand's product portrayal in ad _____
Emotional authenticity tailored to lifestyle group(s) within target audience _____

Transformational benefits are overclaimed _____
Informational benefits (if included) are convincing _____

[   ]   **3. In-ad presenter (if presenter is to be used).**

- Purpose (check one):
Boost communication effects (as completed below) _____
Information overload "expert fallback" _____
- Visibility (if brand awareness is to be boosted). What percentage of the target audience will immediately recognize the presenter? _____%
How is the presenter expected to boost *either* BRGN, BRCL, or *both?*

_____

- Expertise (if either LI/I or HI/I brand attitude is to be boosted, or if "expert fallback" is to be used for overloaded decision maker).
Describe nature of presenter's expertise "hook" to the product or service.

_____

- Objectivity (if HI/I brand attitude is to be boosted). Describe presenter's reputation for objectivity and how this will be executed in the ad.

_____

- Likability (if LI/T brand attitude is to be boosted). Describe why the target audience likes or will like the presenter.

_____

- Similarly (if HI/T brand attitude is to be boosted). Describe how the presenter will be perceived as "equal or slightly better" than the typical decision maker's self-image, and the similarity "hook" if there is one.

_____

- Power (if brand purchase intention is to be boosted). Describe authoritative or commanding characteristics of the presenter.

_____

[    ]

4. **Attention tactics.** (Write in or check tactics for each type of advertising employed in plan.)

- TV commercials (see Table 10.2): video-story script type _____ (must be appropriate; see Table 10.3), audio script fits video script _____. AV "rhythm" appropriate (see Figure 10.1) _____, branding clear _____, main benefit claim clearly shown or stated (if informational) _____ *or* authentically portrayed (transformational) _____
- Radio commercials (see Table 10.5): very high interest opening device _____, high-imagery sentences or lyrics throughout _____, ends with a relevant punch _____
- Newspaper ads (see Table 10.8): ad size appropriate _____, color picture and logo _____, picture dominates (less so for HI/I) _____, complete headline (if LI) _____ *or* lead-in headline (if HI) _____, body copy less than 50 words (if LI) _____ *or* 50 to 200 words with block-listed benefits (if HI) _____, lowercase typeface _____, brand name in headline and repeated at bottom right (if LI) _____ *or* brand name or logo at bottom right (if HI) _____, brand name or logo prominent _____
- Magazine ads (see Table 10.12): large picture _____, picture has single dominant focal point _____, celebrity presenter (if used in picture) is named _____, complete headline of 1 to 8 words (if LI) _____ *or* lead-in headline of 1 to 5 words (if HI) _____, headline is positive (or justified negative) _____, personal words in headline _____, headline in or near picture (straight ad) _____ *or* below picture (visual conveyor ad) _____ *or* above picture (if headline is verbal conveyor) _____, body copy less than 50 words (if LI) _____, *or* 50 to 250 words (if HI) _____, short sentences _____, mainly short words _____, concrete (high imagery) words and phrases predominate in copy _____, brand name in headline or continues from it (LI) _____ *or* in headline or at end of copy (if HI) _____, pictorial logo (if used) is visible _____
- Directory ads (see Table 10.14): picture or sketch in ad (unless prohibited) _____, picture or sketch conveys right image for the company _____, lead-in headline of 1 to 5 words _____, body copy uses bullet-point benefit claims _____, brand name is prominent _____, phone number _____, address and location (if visits intended) _____, credit card options listed _____
- Outdoor ads and posters—mobile (see Table 10.16): large, nonconveyor picture _____, headline plan body copy is 1 to 5 words and complete _____, brand name or logo continues headline _____, and is prominent _____
- Outdoor ads and posters—stationary (see Table 10.16): complete headline (if short-copy ad) _____ *or* lead-in headline (if long-copy ad for HI brand choice) _____, body copy is 50 to 200 words _____, body copy is lowercase _____, brand name is in headline and repeated at bottom right (LI) _____ *or* at bottom right (HI) _____, brand name or logo is prominent _____
- Direct response ads (in *any* of above media; see Table 10.19): company is presented credibly _____, picture has image match with brand of product or service _____, headline has image match with brand of product or ser-

vice _____, body copy has fact match with benefits desired by target audience _____, response device matches dealer and is easy to use _____

- Direct response telemarketing (see Table 10.20): prospect or customer is "known" before calling _____, prepared one-minute opening script _____, benefits in rank of order of importance _____, one or two "added" benefits for closing _____, price made clear _____, restatement of benefits available if necessary to clarify _____, close will be attempted _____, recap buyer's exact commitment if close is made _____ *or* thank anyway _____

- TV or PC interactive ads (as for HI *DR magazine ads,* plus:) all banners are short lead-in type headlines pretested for high interest _____, navigation through ad site has been pretested to be logical and easy _____

## F. IMC STRATEGY (COMPLETE THIS SECTION IF PLAN USES CORPORATE ADVERTISING, ADLIKE COMMUNICATIONS, OR PROMOTIONS.)

[  ]
confidence

1. **Corporate advertising/adlike communications/promotions.** (Check all to be used, and write in communication objective[s] for each.)

| | | |
|---|---|---|
| Corporate identity program | _____ | _____ |
| Public relations (PR) | _____ | _____ |
| Corporate image advertising | _____ | _____ |
| Sponsorship | _____ | _____ |
| Event marketing | _____ | _____ |
| Publicity | _____ | _____ |
| Direct response advertising | _____ | _____ |
| Database marketing | _____ | _____ |
| Loyalty program | _____ | _____ |
| Sales-force nonmonetary promotion | _____ | _____ |
| Sales-force monetary incentive | _____ | _____ |
| Retail layout[a] | _____ | _____ |
| Feature ads[a] | _____ | _____ |
| POP displays[a] | _____ | _____ |
| Retail price-off[a] | _____ | _____ |
| Private labeling[a] | _____ | _____ |
| TV or PC interactive shopping[a] | _____ | _____ |

[  ]

2. **Trade promotions.** (Check all to be used, and write in communication objectives for each.)

| | | |
|---|---|---|
| New line fee | _____ | _____ |
| Introductory (trial) price-off | _____ | _____ |
| Returns (trial) | _____ | _____ |

_____

[a]If retailer, or company that sells at retail.

Price-off      _____   _____

Co-op allowance (e.g., for feature ads _____   _____
   or displays)

Sales contest      _____   _____

Sales education      _____   _____

[   ]   **3. End-customer/consumer promotions.** (Check all to be used, and write in communication objectives for each.)

Sampling (e.g., trade show,      _____   _____
   demonstration, free sample)

Refund or rebate (trial)      _____   _____

Bonus pack (trial)      _____   _____

Direct price-off (trial)      _____   _____

Warranty (trial)      _____   _____

Premium (trial)      _____   _____

Manufacturer's coupon (trial)      _____   _____

Next-purchase coupon      _____   _____

Multiunit coupon, refund, or rebate   _____   _____

Multiunit contest or sweepstakes    _____   _____

Multiunit premium      _____   _____

Packaging      _____   _____

With-sale (extra) service      _____   _____

After-sale (extra) service      _____   _____

[   ]   **4. IMC planning check.** (For all the IMC activities selected in F1 through F3, write a summary statement of how, together, they meet the three IMC principles.)

- Selection integration (task matrix achievement of communication objectives)

   _____
   _____
   _____
   _____

- Positioning integration (macropositioning consistency)

   _____
   _____
   _____
   _____

- Customer timeline integration (show sequence, or sequences if more than one target audience)

   _____
   _____
   _____
   _____

## G. MEDIA STRATEGY (ADVERTISING MEDIA AND, IF USED, IMC MEDIA. IMC MEDIA STRATEGY ASSUMES PRIOR USE OF TASK MATRIX METHOD, FOR WHICH CALCULATIONS SHOULD BE APPENDED.)

[  ]
confidence

1. **Media selection.** (Write in primary and secondary media selections and approximate percent of media budget for each. For secondary media, state purpose: for example, to boost specific communication objectives, imagery transfer, promotion, and so on.)

   - Primary medium     _____    _____%
   - Secondary media     _____    _____%_____
          _____    _____%_____
          _____    _____%_____
          _____    _____%_____
          _____    _____%_____

[  ]

2. **Reach pattern.** (Check which one is chosen. If a combination, write 1, 2 in sequence of use instead of checking.)

   Blitz _____           Regular purchase cycle _____
   Wedge _____         Awareness reach _____
   Reverse wedge/PI _____    Shifting reach _____
   Short fad _____        Seasonal priming _____

[  ]

3. **Minimum effective frequency.** (Complete the following for each geographic market if plan differs by region, and for each target audience if more than one target.)

   - Target audience purchase cycle for this product category _____ years/months/days
   - Number of *advertising* cycles in planning period _____
   - MEF/c required for each advertising cycle in period

   _____ _____ _____ _____ _____ _____ _____ _____

[  ]

4. **Effective reach.** (Complete for each geographic market and target audience as applicable.)

   - Estimated number of target audience consumers reached in each advertising cycle

   _____ _____ _____ _____ _____ _____ _____ _____

   - Probability of purchase when reached at MEF/c, for each advertising cycle (note that the purchase itself may be delayed after ad cycle)

   _____ _____ _____ _____ _____ _____ _____ _____

[  ]

5. **Media vehicles and ad units.** (Complete for each advertising cycle in turn.)

   - Advertising cycle # _____

| • Vehicles | Unit(s) | Contribution to MEF/c | Cost |
|---|---|---|---|
| _____ | _____ | _____ | _____ |
| _____ | _____ | _____ | _____ |
| _____ | _____ | _____ | _____ |
| _____ | _____ | _____ | _____ |
| _____ | _____ | _____ | _____ |

- Effective reach of combined placements \_\_\_\_\_ × probability of purchase \_\_\_\_\_ × margin \_\_\_\_\_ = total revenue $ \_\_\_\_\_ minus total cost of placements $ \_\_\_\_\_ = profit $ \_\_\_\_\_ *per advertising cycle*

[  ]

6. **Individual continuity.** (Take the perspective of the typical target audience member *reached one or more times at MEF during the period,* and estimate how many times the individual will see each ad over the advertising cycles in the period. The column totals and the column MEFs must fit the *reach pattern.*)

- Ad 1 \_\_\_\_ \_\_\_\_ \_\_\_\_ \_\_\_\_ \_\_\_\_ \_\_\_\_ \_\_\_\_ \_\_\_\_ total \_\_\_\_
- Ad 2 \_\_\_\_ \_\_\_\_ \_\_\_\_ \_\_\_\_ \_\_\_\_ \_\_\_\_ \_\_\_\_ \_\_\_\_ total \_\_\_\_
- Ad 3 \_\_\_\_ \_\_\_\_ \_\_\_\_ \_\_\_\_ \_\_\_\_ \_\_\_\_ \_\_\_\_ \_\_\_\_ total \_\_\_\_
- Ad 4 \_\_\_\_ \_\_\_\_ \_\_\_\_ \_\_\_\_ \_\_\_\_ \_\_\_\_ \_\_\_\_ \_\_\_\_ total \_\_\_\_
- Total \_\_\_\_ \_\_\_\_ \_\_\_\_ \_\_\_\_ \_\_\_\_ \_\_\_\_ \_\_\_\_ \_\_\_\_ total \_\_\_\_
- MEF \_\_\_\_ \_\_\_\_ \_\_\_\_ \_\_\_\_ \_\_\_\_ \_\_\_\_ \_\_\_\_ \_\_\_\_

(Allow for MEF contribution of brand's promotion activity in a particular advertising cycle.)

[  ]

7. **Wearout potential.** (Estimate the number of exposures to the typical target audience member before each ad wears out, then compare with total in 6.)

|  | Attention | Learning[b] | Acceptance |
|---|---|---|---|
| • Ad 1 | \_\_\_\_ | \_\_\_\_ | \_\_\_\_ |
| • Ad 2 | \_\_\_\_ | \_\_\_\_ | \_\_\_\_ |
| • Ad 3 | \_\_\_\_ | \_\_\_\_ | \_\_\_\_ |
| • Ad 4 | \_\_\_\_ | \_\_\_\_ | \_\_\_\_ |

[  ]

8. **Expected profit contribution of total media plan.** (Sum over all advertising cycles in plan.)

- Revenue $ _____
- Cost $ _____
- Profit $ _____

## H. ADVERTISING STRATEGY SUMMARY (CREATIVE BRIEF FOR THE ADVERTISING COMMUNICATIONS AND FOR PROMOTIONS. ADD BULLET POINTS AS NECESSARY, BUT BE CONCISE IN STATING EACH POINT.)

**Target audience** _____

**1. Exposure**

- 
- 

---

[b]Insert largest competitor's frequency per advertising cycle that will cause major interference.

2. **Processing (must include intended brand position)**

   - 
   - 
   - 

3. **Communication objectives**

   - 
   - 
   - 
   - 
   - 

4. **Action**

   - 
   -

# Subject index

AAS (always a share) products and services, 405–407, 408, 409, 415

a-b-e micromodel of benefit focus (*see* Positioning)

Acceptance measures (*see* Processing)

ACL (*see* Adjective checklist measure)

Action standards (*see* Ad testing)

Action, target audience:
in AC&P plan, 613–614, 623
action objectives and decision participant roles, 86–88
ad test measures of, 572
and campaign tracking, 589–590, 593, 594
consumer behaviors, 72
for corporate image advertising, 332
for database marketing, 409–411
for direct response advertising, 306
and effective frequency, 467–468
fourth step in effects sequence and buyer response steps, 11–16, 612
measures of, 515–516
specific target behaviors, 63–64
and the five buyer groups, 63–64
trade behaviors, 71–72

Active customer model (Schmittlein-Morrison), 409–411

Adjective checklist (ACL) measure, 565, 581(n)

Adlike communications, 5–6

Ad likability (*see* Likability)

ADPULS model, 596

Ad recall:
vs. day-after advertising recall, 587, 607(n)
brand-prompted ad recall (BPAR), 587–588, 589
category-prompted ad recall (CPAR), 588–589

Ad recognition, 587

AdTel technique (Burke), 572, 576(n), 583(n)

Ad testing:
action standards, 562–563
analysis of results, 562–563
buyer behavior (action) measures, 572
communication effects measures, 562, 566–571
cost of, 189, 204–205, 207, 550–551
definition, 538, 550–551
"degree of finish" of test ads, 557–559
design of ad tests, 556–557
in focus groups, 551–553
interview methods, 555–556
management judgment tests (MJTs), 538, 548–550

multinational ads, 554–555
number of exposures, 559
order and selection of measures, 560–562
processing measures, 564–566
sample size, 552, 556, 557
screening questions and pre-measures, 563–564
syndicated ad tests, 553–555
target audience for, 563–564
when to use, 548, 550, 612

Ad recall:
vs. day-after advertising recall, 587, 607(n)
brand-prompted ad recall (BPAR), 587–588, 589
category-prompted ad recall (CPAR), 588–589

Ad recognition, 587

Advertising:
business-to-business (*see* Industrial advertising)
classified, 192
consumer, local (*see* Consumer advertising, local)
consumer, national (*see* Consumer advertising, national)
communication models (*see* Advertising communication models)
cooperative (*see* Cooperative advertising allowances)
corporate image (*see* Corporate identity programs *and* Corporate image advertising)
definition, 3–5
direct response (*see* Direct response advertising)
effects (*see* Six-step effects sequence)
expenditure on, 5–7
general, 4, 324, 331
global (*see* multinational)
industrial (*see* Industrial advertising)
interactive (*see* Interactive TV or PC advertising)
legal restrictions on, 226, 232–233, 270–271, 390, 517
multinational, 97, 554–555
and reduction of selling costs, 27, 29–30
retail (*see* Retail advertising)
subconscious effects (*see* Subconscious processing of advertising)
subliminal (*see* Subliminal advertising)
trade (*see* Trade advertising)
wearout (*see* Advertising wearout)

Advertising carryover effect, 535(n), 598

Advertising communications
new term, xiv
definition, 3–7
(*see also* Advertising, and Adlike communications)

Advertising communication models, 212–213, 239(n), 555, 588

Advertising concept development research (*see* Concept development research)

Advertising content research (*see* Advertising strategy research)

Advertising content screening research (*see* Concept development research)

Advertising cycles (*see* Media strategy)

Advertising idea generation (*see* Concept development research)

Advertising communications and promotion (AC&P) plan, 611–623

Advertising recall, day-after (*see* Ad recall)

Advertising research (*see* Advertising strategy research; Concept development research; Management judgment tests; Ad testing; and Campaign tracking research)

Advertising strategy, defined, 599

Advertising strategy research:
advertising strategy summary, 532–534, 611, 622–623
definition, 505
qualitative research, 519–524
quantitative research, 524–532
situation audit, 505–519

Advertising strategy summary (*see* Advertising strategy research)

Advertising-to-sales (A/S) ratio, 38–39

Ad units:
adjustments for MEF, 279, 280–281, 284–285, 289–290, 292–295, 298–300, 300–302, 304
and advertising wearout, 605
and communication objectives, 488

Advertising wearout:
acceptance (overexposure) wearout, 605
in ad tests, 559
and advertising units, 605
attention wearout, 602–603
definition, 600–601, 602
learning (interference) wearout, 603–605
and maximum effective frequency, 458–459
prevention of, 602–606

AIDA formula, 309–310, 311

AIO (activities, interests, and opinions) inventories, 524, 530

ALEA model (*see* Processing)

Anxiety personality trait state, 97, 98, 484

ARS ad test, 235(n), 239–240(n), 554–555

Atmosphere (*see* Retailer's promotions)

Attention (*see* Processing)

Attitude toward the ad (*see* Likability, of the advertisement)

Attitudes (*see* Brand attitude)

Attractiveness of presenters (*see* Presenters, attraction)

Attributes:
vs. benefits, 152–153
multiattribute model, 142, 149–152, 161–165, 310, 600

Attributions, in processing promotion offers, 573–575

Audience overlap, 329
(*see also* Media vehicle selection, duplication of exposures)

Awareness-attitude-behavior approach (*see* Target audience, brand loyalty approach)

Awareness Index (Millward Brown's), 608(n)

Awareness reach pattern (*see* Reach patterns)

Bass model, 515–516, 534(n)

BBD-LD model, 495

BBD-LD REPEAT model, 495–497

Behavioral objectives (*see* Action, target audience)

Behavioral sequence models (BSMs), 83–91, 217, 450, 521–522

BehaviorScan technique (IRI's), 507, 508, 583(n)

Believability of advertising (*see* Benefit claims, and believability)

Benefit beliefs (*see* Brand attitude, benefit beliefs)

Benefit chaining technique, 523, 543

Benefit claims:
and believability, 215, 226–227, 228, 232–233, 244–245, 247–253, 259, 270–271, 564–565 (*see also* overclaiming; extreme claims; curious disbelief)
vs. benefits, 544
comparative approach, 254–255, 269–270
consumer language in, 527–528
curious disbelief, 226–227
extreme claims, 226–227, 228, 232–233
for high-involvement brand attitude, 244–259
and "initial attitude" in high-involvement brand attitude, 247–253

Benefit claims (*cont'd*)
for low-involvement brand attitude, 224–230
number of, 226, 227–228, 255
overclaiming, 251–252, 259
ratings of, 569–570
refutational approach, 253, 272(n)
"summary" benefit claim, 255
underclaiming, 252–253, 259
vs. use of a presenter, 268
Benefit segmentation, 509–512
Benefits:
a-b-e micromodel of benefit focus (*see* Positioning)
and brand equity, 170(n), 528–529
assessing importance of, 150, 228
changes in importance, 151, 164
choice rule (*see* Brand attitude)
I-D-U mesomodel of benefit emphasis (*see* Positioning)
Beta-binomial distribution (BBD), 497
Billboards (*see* Outdoor ads and posters)
Bizarre executions, 238(n)
Blitz reach pattern (*see* Reach patterns)
Boomerang effect (*see* Benefit claims, overclaiming)
Bonus packs for trial, 360–361
Brainstorming:
computer-assisted, 543–544
I-G-I method, 191, 197–198, 543
BRANDAID model, 519, 596, 598, 609
Brand attitude:
absolute attitude, 130–131
benefit beliefs, 122–123
benefit beliefs, measures of, 569–570
and brand equity, 131–132, 170(n), 528–529
choice rule, 120, 123–124
components of, 120–124
computed attitude, 130
definition, 110
freestanding emotions, 123
impersonal attitude, 131, 325
"initial attitude" in high-involvement brand attitude, 247–253
(*see also* Cognitive responses)
measures of, 568–569
and motives, 121–122, 212–213
multiattribute model of (*see* Positioning, I-D-U mesomodel)
objectives, 120, 124–125, 129
personal attitude, 131, 325
and positioning, 142
and promotions, 325–326
(*see also* Promotions, CFB presentations of)
relative attitude, 130–131
and repeat purchase, 68–69, 76
strategy (*see* Brand attitude strategy)
summary attitude, 130
superbelief, 120–121, 245
vulnerability, 93–94, 126
Brand attitude strategy:
and ad testing, 555, 556, 557–558, 559
and competing ads, 483–484
and effective frequency, 463, 464, 465

and media selection, 420, 422–424, 425, 426, 427–428, 429
and presenters, 263, 264–267
quadrants, 213, 224
Brand awareness:
and ad testing, 555, 560–561, 562
brand recall vs. ad recall, 588, 589
brand recall-boosted brand recognition, 118–119
brand recall and competing ads, 483, 603–605, 606
brand recall creative tactics, 219–223
brand recall, definition, 114–115, 117
brand recall measure, 571
brand recall and repetition, 221, 222, 231
brand recognition, auditory, 117, 444(n)
brand recognition creative tactics, 214–217
brand recognition, definition, 114–115, 116
brand recognition measure, 570–571
brand recognition and repetition, 219, 231
brand recognition and media scheduling, 604
and conveyors, 196–197
definition, 110
and effective frequency, 463, 464, 465
and encoding specificity, 217
general creative tactics, 216–217
importance of, 113–114
and interpersonal influence, 463
and learning, 214–215
and media selection, 419–422, 424–427, 428–429, 432
objectives, 113, 115–119, 129
and positioning, 142
and presence, 134
and presenters, 261–264
and promotions, 325, 258, 360, 361, 362, 365–366, 368, 370
and salience, 134
Brand equity:
and AC&P plan, 612, 613
benefit-based method of measuring, 528–529
and brand attitude, 131–132
brand awareness equity, 114
brand name equity, 131–132, 170(n), 528–529
definition, 131
in fifth step of effects sequence, 14, 612
as a marketing objective, 11, 12, 28–29
Moran's method of measuring, 28–29, 45–46, 513–515
uniqueness equity, 28, 45–46, 513–515
value equity, 28–29, 45–46, 513–515
Brand image (*see* Brand attitude, benefit beliefs)
Branding (*see* Brand awareness: brand recall creative tactics *and* brand recognition creative tactics)

Brand loyals (*see* Target audience, brand loyals (BLs))
Brand loyalty approach (*see* Target audience, brand loyalty approach)
Brand position:
in AC&P plan, 612, 615–616
and communication effects, 11–12
definition, 141, 160
and positioning, 140–141, 160
supercommunication effect, 141, 160
Brand purchase intention:
and acceptance, 126–128
and decision participant, 126
and direct response ads, 309
assumed, 127–128
definition, 110, 126
generated, 127–128
and long purchase-cycle products or services, 69
measures, 567–568, 581–582(n)
objectives, 127–128, 129
and point-of-purchase IMC media, 426
and presenters, 263, 267–268
and promotions, 326
Brand recall (*see* Brand awareness)
Brand recall-boosted brand recognition (*see* Brand awareness)
Brand recognition (*see* Brand awareness)
Brand switchers (*see* Target audience, brand switchers (BSs))
Brand-user image (*see* Positioning, user-as-hero)
Bruzzone Research Company (BRC) ad recognition measure, 607(n)
Brochures, 5
BSM (*see* Behavioral sequence models)
Budget:
in AC&P plan, 612–613
advertising communications and promotion (AC&P), overall budget for, 32–44, 46–47
and campaign evaluation, 596
IMC budget allocation, 328–331
and media selection, 428–430
percentage spent on creative and research, 189, 204–205, 208(n), 540
Budget-setting methods:
"Five Questions" (5Q) procedure, 36–37
IAF/5Q method, 35–37, 43
Industry A/S comparison method, 38–39, 43, 507
interaction assumption in, 35
management jury, 35–36
Peckham's 1.5 rule/order-of-entry method, 39–40, 43
Powers's formula, 330–331
quality-of-spending assumption in, 43–44
Schroer's method, 42–43, 448, 507
share-of-voice, 42–43
spending test, 41, 43
statistical projection, 41–42, 43
task matrix method for IMC budget-setting, 328–330
task method, 34–35, 37, 143

Brand loyals (*see* Target audience, brand loyals (BLs))
Burke day-after recall scores, 103(n), 312(n)
(*see also* Ad recall)
Business magazine ads, 5
Business-to-business advertising (*see* Industrial advertising)
Buyer behavior (*see* Action, target audience)
Buyer response steps, 12–14, 550, 590–591, 612
Buying amount, 63, 64, 69–71
Buying center (*see* Group decisions)
Buying rate, 63, 68–69, 75–77

CAAS advertising expert system, 209(n), 543, 544
Cable TV medium, 420–423, 429, 430, 431, 439, 440
CACI geodemographic service, 480
Calendars, 438, 439
Campaign tracking research:
adjusting the media budget, 596
adjusting the media plan, 596
adjusting the pool of ads, 596–597
advertising strategy obsolescence, 600–601
advertising wearout (*see* Advertising wearout)
aggregate vs. causal, 590, 595
analysis of tracking study results, 594–596
applications, 596–597
brand equity measures, 590
communication effects measures, 588–589
continuous method, 591–593, 595
definition, 585
exposure measures, 586
how often to track, 597–598
IMC tracking, 585, 593
improvements in ads, 597
interview methods in tracking studies, 593
market share measures, 590
market survey method, 590–591, 593
measures used in tracking, 585–590, 593
media plan slippage, 601–602
methodology, 590
order of measures in tracking studies, 593
panel method, 591, 594–595
processing measures, 586–588
profit measures, 590
sales measures, 590
sample composition for tracking studies, 590
target audience action measures, 589–590
wave method, 591, 595
when to use, 597–598
Carryover effect of advertising (*see* Advertising carryover effect)
Catalogs, 393
Category advertising "cut-through," (*see* Ad recall, category-prompted ad recall)
Category attitude, 112, 525–526, 566–567
Category awareness, 112, 566–567
Category benefit beliefs, 566

Category hierarchy (*see* Market, hierarchical definition of)
Category need:
and acceptance, 245, 564
and brand awareness, 115, 142
definition, 110, 111
and direct response ads, 308
measures, 566–567
and media selection, 423, 426–427, 434, 484–485, 468, 469
and motives, 110, 111, 121–122, 147–149
objectives, 111–113, 129
and positioning, 141–146
and promotions, 325, 484, 485
and purchase cycles, 335, 434, 468, 469, 485
(*see also* Reach patterns)
Category purchase intention, 112, 526, 566
Celebrity presenters (*see* Presenters, celebrity)
Choice rule (*see* Brand attitude, choice rule)
Cinema advertising, 5
Classified ads (*see* Advertising)
"Clutter-awareness" testing, 556, 579(n), 580(n)
Cognitive dissonance, 260, 357, 373, 376–377, 378–379(n)
Cognitive responses:
measure, 564–565, 581(n)
theory, 216, 244, 269
Colman-Brown measure of ad recall (*see* Ad recall, brand-prompted ad recall (BPAR))
Color:
in ads, 289, 290, 293, 298–299, 300–302, 304, 420–421, 422, 423
in retail environments, 386
Communication effects:
and brand position, 12, 14, 140
category-level, 112, 566–567
and the decision participant, 92–93
definitions of the five effects, 110
general definition, 109
measures, 566–571, 588–589
"mental bins" analogy, 109–110
of promotion, 324–327
theoretical origin of, 132–133
third step in effects sequence and buyer response steps, 12–14, 612
relative communication strengths of advertising communications and promotions, 324–327
(*see also* Category need; Brand awareness; Brand attitude; Brand purchase intention; Purchase facilitation; *and* Brand position)
Communication objectives:
in AC&P plan, 614–616, 623
and advertising units, 488
and brand position, 16–17, 140
from communication effects, 110, 113, 120, 124, 126, 128, 129
and effective frequency, 458–459, 462–463, 464, 465
and presenters, 261–268, 546–547
Comparative advertising (*see* Benefit claims, comparative approach)

Competitive advertising interference, 42–43, 219, 221, 222, 227, 229–230, 231–232, 462–463, 464, 465, 483–484, 601–605, 606
Competitive frame (*see* Market partitioning)
Competitive Market Structure Analysis (CMSA), 513
Competitor orientation (*see* Marketing, competitor orientation)
Computer-assisted brainstorming, 543–544
Concept development research (CDR):
creative idea generation, 542–543
definition of "concept," 541
general definition, 540
screening of concepts, 189, 191, 203–205, 214, 544–550
Confidence measure, 569, 582(n)
CONPAAD measurement, 571, 582–583(n)
Consumer advertising, local, 434–436
Consumer advertising, national, 5, 430–434
Consumer behavior (*see* Action, target audience)
Consumer life cycle (*see* Product life cycle, consumer life cycle)
Consumer magazine advertising, 5
Consumer promotion (*see* Manufacturer's promotions; Retailer's promotions; Direct marketing promotions)
Consumer values, changes in, 600
Contests and sweepstakes, 370
Continuity programs (*see* Loyalty programs)
Conversion model (*see* Brand attitude, vulnerability)
Cooperative advertising allowances, 355
Copy (*see* Verbal content in ads)
Corporate identity programs, 4, 324, 333–334, 343
Corporate image advertising, 4, 324, 334–339, 438–439
Cost lowering as a manufacturing objective, 27, 29–30
Cost-per-effective-rating-point (CPERP), 493
Cost-per-thousand (CPM), 492–493
Coupons:
general, 5,
for trial, 357, 364–367
for repeat purchase, 367, 368–370
retailer's coupons, 392
(*see also* FSIs)
Creative brief (*see* Advertising strategy summary)
Creative idea:
definition, 180–184
importance of, 178–180
long-term management, 198–199
RAM-Conveyor theory (*see* RAM-Conveyor theory of creative ideas)
theory of random creativity, 184–191, 202–207, 538
when to use, 177
(*see also* Concept development research)

Creative strategy:
in AC&P plan, 612, 616–619
sequence 177–178
Credibility of presenters (*see* Presenters, credibility)
Crisis and rumor management, 334, 343–346
Curious disbelief (*see* Benefit claims, curious disbelief)
Cusp-catastrophe model, 373, 376–377, 412
Customer franchise building (CFB) presentation of promotion offers:
bonus packs, 361
contests and sweepstakes, 370
coupons, 365–366, 369, 370
direct price-offs, 362, 375–376
general concept, 4, 131, 325–326
premiums, 363–364
refund offers, 360
samples, 358–359
warranties, 362–363
Customer timeline integration (*see* IMC, principles of)
Customer migration, in database marketing, 411

DAGMAR approach, 24, 47(n)
DAR (*see* Ad recall)
Database marketing, 4, 307, 308, 324, 404–411
Day-after recall (*see* Ad recall)
Decider role, 86, 87, 88
Decision participant profile variables, 92–99, 521
Decision participant roles, 83, 86–88, 521–522
Decision-making unit, 86
Decision roles (*see* Decision participant roles)
Defender model, 145
"Degree of finish" of test ads (*see* Ad testing)
Delphi method, 36, 50(n)
Demand:
price elasticity of (*see* Brand equity, Moran's method)
primary, 110
secondary, 110
Demographic matching (*see* Media vehicle selection)
Demographic delineation of target audiences, 59–60
Demographic profile variables, 95
De-partitioning (*see* Market partitioning)
Designing ads to suit the media vehicle, 286, 481, 482–483
Direct mail medium, 5, 7, 306, 307–310, 425, 426–428, 429, 432, 435, 437, 438, 439, 440, 441–442, 466
Direct marketing promotions, 4, 324, 404–415
Direct matching (*see* Media vehicle selection)
Directories, advertising in, 5, 300–303
Direct response advertising, 4, 5, 305–312, 425, 426–428, 429, 432, 433–434, 435, 436, 437, 439–442, 466, 467, 489, 491, 618–619

Displays (*see* Retailer's promotions)
Disposition to purchase, 457, 458–459, 562–563
Distribution strategy, 46, 71
Distributors (*see* Trade promotion)
"Dominance" in media scheduling (*see* Minimum effective frequency (MEF))
Duplication of exposures (*see* Media vehicle selection)

Econometric analysis of advertising effects (*see* Sales modelling)
Effective frequency (*see* Frequency)
Effective reach (*see* Reach)
Ehrenberg's method for trial goal-setting, 67, 75–77
Elasticity of demand (*see* Brand equity, Moran's method)
Electroencephalographic (EEG) measurement apparatus, 571, 582(n)
Emotional responses (*see* Processing, emotion)
Encoding specificity principle (*see* Brand awareness)
Endorsers (*see* Presenters)
Event marketing, 4, 5, 324, 339–340
Exhibitions (*see* Trade shows)
Experience curve, 30, 49(n)
Experimental-control design, 556–557, 560, 561–562, 564, 579(n)
Expert systems, 209(n), 389–390, 543–544
Expertise of presenters (*see* Presenters)
Exposure:
in AC&P plan, 622
of ads in ad tests, 551–552, 556–557, 560
and acceptance measures, 564–565
definition, 447, 457–458
and focus groups, 551–552
and media scheduling, 602–605
and OTS, 447, 457–458
as first step in effects sequence and buyer response steps, 11, 12, 13, 14, 612
duplication of exposures (*see* Media vehicle selection)
Exposure-to-sales analysis, 595–596
Eye-tracking technique, 571, 578(n)

Factor analysis, 530, 536(n)
Fad products (*see* Reach patterns)
Fast-moving consumer goods (fmcg) (*see* Reach patterns, regular purchase cycle pattern)
Fear appeals, 158–159
(*see also* Anxiety)
Five Questions (5Q) procedure (*see* Budget-setting methods)
Flighting (*see* Reach patterns)
Flyers (handbills), 4, 435, 432, 438
"Impulse" purchases, 116
Focus groups, 519–524, 551–553
Freestanding inserts (*see* FSIs)
Frequency:
definition, 447,
effective frequency, 457–459
(*see also* Minimum effective frequency; Maximum effective frequency)
frequency distributions, 460–461

FSIs (freestanding inserts), 6, 19, 366, 425, 426–427, 432, 433, 518

Gallup & Robinson day-after advertising recall measure, 607(n)
GENI brainstorming program, 543
Geodemographic delineation of target audiences, 59
Goals:
  in ad testing, 553, 562–563
  in budget-setting, 32–33, 34–40, 328–331
  vs. objectives, 25–26
  for repeat purchase, 68–71, 75–77
  for trial, 65–68, 75–77, 515–516
Group depth interviews (GDIs) (see Focus groups)
Gross rating points (GRPs), 447, 449, 453, 490, 586, 596, 601, 602, 606(n)
Group decisions, 86, 87, 101(n), 552

Handbills (see Fliers)
Hendry "bathtub" explanation, 68–69
Hierarchies of effects, 85–86, 245, 309–310
High-involvement purchase decisions (see Involvement in purchase decisions)
High-involvement/informational (HI/I) creative tactics, 246–255, 264–266
High-involvement/transformational (HI/T) creative tactics, 255–260, 267
HomeScan (or BrandScan) technique, 572
Humor in ads, 229, 241(n), 242(n), 288

I-D-U mesomodel of benefit emphasis (see Positioning, I-D-U mesomodel of)
Industry A/S ratio comparison (see Budget-setting methods)
"Information overload," 255, 261, 262
Innovativeness personality trait, 97
In/on packs, 365–366
Interference (see Advertising wearout)
Interpersonal influence (see Personal influence)
Introversion-extraversion personality trait, 97–98
Inventory transfer, 383–384
Image, corporate (see Corporate image advertising)
Imagery transfer, 287, 431–432
IMC (integrated marketing communications):
  in AC&P plan, 619–620
  budgeting for, 328–331
  definition, 6–7
  effects on planning, 7–8
  media for, point-of-decision, 425, 426–428, 429–430, 480
  media for, prepurchase, 424, 425–426, 429–430
  principles of, 323–328
  revolution in, xiii, xiv, 3–7
  strategy in manager's planning stages, 14, 17–19, 612
Impact scheduling, 484, 485–488

Incomplete satisfaction motive, 170
Independent Averaged Forecast (IAF) method (see Budget-setting methods)
Individual depth interviews (IDIs), 519–520
Industrial advertising, 5, 292–303, 436–438
Industrial magazine advertising, 298–300, 301
Informational motives:
  and ad testing, 556–560
  definition, 120–122
  emotional portrayal of, 225
  and positioning, 147–149
  and promotion offers, 573
  and Rossiter-Percy grid, 213
Information processing (see Processing)
Input-output analysis, 595–596
Integrated marketing communications (see IMC)
Intellectual stimulation or mastery motive, 121, 228, 442–443, 573, 575
Intelligence personality trait, 97
Interactive TV or PC advertising, 4, 5, 6, 19, 65, 247, 306, 308, 311, 358, 393–396, 403, 425–429, 432, 435, 436, 437, 440, 442, 443, 466–467, 480, 485, 491, 501(n), 557, 559, 561, 605
Internet (see Interactive TV or PC ads)
Interpurchase interval (see Purchase cycle)
Interpurchase time (see Purchase cycle)
Involvement in purchase decisions:
  and brand attitude vulnerability, 93–94
  and brand purchase intention, 126–127
  definition, 93, 126, 213, 224, 246
  high (see High-involvement)
  low (see Low-involvement)
  measurement of, 239(n), 522, 535(n)
  and media frequency, 463
  and target audience, 213
Irritating ads, 225–226
Issues management (see Crisis and rumor management)

Jingles, 222, 286, 287, 288

Kirton Adaption-Innovation Inventory (KAI), 97

Laddering technique, 170–171(n), 523
Lagged effects of advertising, 594–596
Largest competitor plus one (LC + I) scheduling (see Minimum effective frequency, estimation of)
Latitude of acceptance, in high-involvement brand attitude creative tactics, 247–253, 259
Layout (see Retail promotions)
Learning (see Processing)
Learning measures (see Processing)
Legal considerations (see Advertising, legal restrictions on)

Length of commercials, 280–281, 285, 605, 606
Leverage principle of target audience selection (see Target audience selection)
LFG (lost for good) products and services, 405–407, 408, 409, 415
Likability:
  of media vehicles, 482
  of the advertisement, 225–226, 229, 247, 258, 581(n)
  of presenters (see Presenters)
Lifestyle (see Psychographics)
Lifestyle segmentation, 256–258
Lifetime value (LTV) calculation, 408–409
Low-involvement purchase decisions (see Involvement in purchase decisions)
Low-involvement/informational (LI/I) creative tactics, 224–230, 266–267
Low-involvement/transformational (LI/T) creative tactics, 227–230, 266–267
Loyalty programs, 4, 5, 324, 411–413

Macropositioning (see Positioning)
Magazine advertising, 5, 7, 292–300, 602
Magazines medium, 420–423, 429, 432, 433, 437, 438, 439, 440, 442, 461–463, 484, 491
Main copy line, 220
Management-jury method (see Budget-setting methods)
Management judgment ad tests (MJTs) (see Ad testing)
Manufacturer's promotions:
  contests and sweepstakes, 370
  bonus packs, 360–361
  direct price-offs, 361–362, 375–376
  coupons, 364–367, 368–370
  packaging, 367–368
  premiums, 363–364, 370–371
  products or service sampling, 357–359
  refunds or rebates, 360, 369–370
  sales-force promotions, 352–354
  service, 371–373, 376–377
  trade promotions, 354–356
  trade shows, 5, 7, 357, 358, 375
  warranties, 362–363
Market:
  defined, 61, 508–509
  hierarchical definition of, 144–145, 509–513
Market segmentation, 8–9
Market share:
  in AC&P plan, 613
  budgeting for, 39–40, 42–43
  in fifth step in effects sequence, 14, 612
  measures of, 507–513
  vs. sales as objectives, 46–47
Market structure (see Market)
Market survey method in tracking studies (see Campaign tracking research)
Marketing:
  competitor orientation in, 9
  concept, 9

customer orientation in, 9
  mix, 8
  new mix, 9–10
  strategy principles, 8–9
Marketing objectives, 25–32
Marketing plan, 599–601
Market partitioning (see Market, hierarchical definition of)
Maximum effective frequency, 459, 498, 605
McCollum-Spielman ad test, 239–240(n), 553–554, 580(n)
"Media balloon," 448–449
Media buying, 479, 490, 492
Media exposure (see Media vehicle selection, direct matching)
Media, advertising (mainstream), 5, 420–423
Media, IMC, 5, 424–428
Media plan:
  flighting (see Reach patterns)
  frequency rate, 490, 492
  implementation of, 477–498
  "maintenance" plans, 449, 467–468, 602, 608(n)
  parameters of, 446–451
  reach and frequency rule, 492
  reach rule, 490, 492
  schedule implementation, large advertiser, 497–498
  schedule implementation, small advertiser, 495–497
  slippage in, 601
  trade-offs in, 446, 448–449
Media selection:
  and communication objectives, 419–428
  and media vehicles (see Media vehicle selection)
  primary medium, 428–429
  secondary media, 428, 429–430
Media strategy:
  in AC&P plan, 612, 621–622
  definition, 446
  and effective frequency, 457–468
  (see also Minimum effective frequency (MEF))
  and reach patterns, 451–457
  and scheduling over time, 468–469
  (see also Reach patterns)
Media vehicle selection
  ad unit effects (see Advertising units)
  competing ads in the vehicle, 481, 483–484
  demographic matching, 477–479
  direct matching, 477–481, 530–532
  duplication of exposures, 489–490, 491, 495–498
  impact scheduling (see Impact scheduling)
  and likability-dislikability of the vehicle (see Likability)
  and prestige of the vehicle, 482, 500(n)
  and profit, 492–493
  psychographic matching, 479
  "qualitative" effects of, 481–489
  second-stage, 481–489
  timing of vehicle, 484–485
  vehicle environment effects, 481, 482–483,

and vehicle-tailored ads, 482–483
Memory, 84, 130, 134(n), 233(n), 255, 288, 392, 507, 517, 587–589
"Mental bins" analogy (*see* Communication effects)
Merchandising, 390
Minimum effective frequency (MEF):
and advertising cycle (c), 461
and advertising units, (*see* Advertising units)
and individual continuity, 467–468
definition, 447, 459, 450
and "dominance," 447, 450, 604
estimation of, 461–467
and impact scheduling, 485–488
and "maintenance" plans, 449, 467–468, 602
and media vehicle selection, 461–462, 464, 465, 466, 467
Mesopositioning (*see* Positioning)
Micropositioning (*see* Positioning)
Mixed approach-avoidance motive, 121, 213, 225
MLI (Media Leverage Index) method, 531
Money-back offers (*see* Refunds or rebates; Warranties)
Motivation (*see* Motives for purchase)
Motivation research (*see* Motives for purchase and usage, assessment of)
Motives for purchase and usage:
assessment of, 522–524
and benefits, 120, 122–123, 153
and brand attitudes, 120–122, 163
and category need, 110,
and drive theory, 121–122, 136–137(n)
and emotions, 120, 153, 225, 228
informational (*see* negatively originated *and also* Informational motives)
negatively originated, 121,122
positively originated, 121–122
and positioning, 147–149
transformational (*see* positively originated *and also* Transformational motives)
(*see also* Problem removal; Problem avoidance; Incomplete satisfaction; Mixed approach-avoidance; Normal depletion; Sensory gratification; Intellectual stimulation or mastery; Social approval)
Moving-average "rolling" method, in campaign tracking, 591–592
MSW (*see* McCollum Spielman ad test)
Multiattribute attitude models (*see* Attributes)
Music in ads, 282, 285, 313(n)
(*see also* Jingles)
Music in retail environments, 386–387
Myers-Briggs Type Indicator, 103(n)
"Mystery ad" format, 221, 241(n), 283–284

Need for cognition personality trait, 104(n)
Neurolinguistic programming (NLP) personality traits, 98

New category users (*see* Target audience, new category users (NCUs))
New products, 37–40, 65–68, 451–453
NEWS model, 467
Newspaper ads, 5, 289–292
Newspaper medium, 420–423, 425, 429, 432–433, 434–435, 437, 438, 439, 440, 442, 491
Newspaper supplements, 290
Normal depletion motive, 121, 147, 225

Objectives:
definition, 25–36
management by, 47–48(n)
vs. goals, 25–26
Objectivity of presenters (see Presenters)
One-time purchased products, 68
Opinion leadership, 97
Opportunities to see (OTS), 447, 457–458
Order of entry, 39–40
Other-brand loyals (*see* Target audience, other-brand loyals (OBLs))
Other-brand switchers (*see* Target audiences, other-brand switchers (OBSs))
Outdoor ads and posters, 5, 303–305
Outdoor medium, 420–423, 429, 432, 433, 437, 438, 439, 491
Own-brands (*see* Retailer's promotions, private labeling)

PEAC attention test, 572, 583(n)
Packaging promotions (*see* Manufacturer's promotions)
Payback period, 41, 379
Peckham's 1.5 rule/order of entry method (*see* Budget-setting methods)
Penetration (*see* Ehrenberg's method)
Perceived risk (*see* Involvement, in purchase decisions)
Personal influence:
and advertising, 259
and effective frequency, 463–464, 465
and reach patterns, 452–453
and samples, 359
Personal reference, brand recall tactic, 221–222
Personal selling, 27, 30, 352–354, 385–386
Personality states, 98, 484–485
Personality traits, 96–99, 104(n)
Pioneer advantage (*see* Order of entry)
Planning stages, for the manager, 14–20
Point-of-purchase (POP) promotions medium, 425, 426–428, 431, 432, 433–434, 435
Point-of-purchase (POP) displays (*see* Retailer's promotions)
Pool of ads (or "poolout"), 183–184, 551, 602–603, 605, 606
POP (*see* Point-of-purchase)
Positioning:
a-b-e micromodel of benefit focus, 152–159
in AC&P plan, 612, 615–616
and brand position, 140–141

definition, 141
I-D-U mesomodel of benefit emphasis, 147–152, 169–170(n), 527, 528
product-as-hero, 146–147
statement, 141, 159–160
X-YZ macromodel of positioning location, 141–147
user-as-hero, 146, 259
Positioning statement (*see* Positioning)
Postpackaging medium, 425, 426–428, 432, 435, 436, 437
Posttesting of ads (*see* Campaign tracking research)
Power of presenters (*see* Presenters)
Powers's formula (*see* Budget-setting methods)
PR (public relations), 4, 5, 324, 333–334, 424–426, 436, 437, 438, 439
Premiums (*see* Manufacturer's promotions)
Pre-post design, 553–555, 556–557, 560, 562–563, 564
Pre-priced shippers (*see* Price packs)
Presenters:
animated characters, 229, 260, 261
attraction, 263, 264, 266–267
and brand awareness, 261, 263–264,
brand recall tactic, 220, 222
celebrity presenters, 263, 264–266, 281, 295–296, 316(n)
credibility, 263, 264–266
expertise, 220, 222, 263, 264, 265–266, 281, 295–206, 316(n)
how to select, 260–268
high-involvement/informational (HI/I) brand attitude tactic, 246, 253
and "information overload," 261, 262
legal requirements, 270–271
likability, 263, 264, 266–267
objectivity, 220, 222, 263, 264, 265–266, 270–271
power, 262, 263, 267–268
and Rossiter-Percy grid, 263, 264
similarity, 263, 264, 267–268
types of in-ad presenters, 261
visibility, 261–262, 263–264
when to use, 261–262
ratings of, 546–547
(*see also* VisCAP model of presenter characteristics)
Prestige of media vehicles, 482, 500(n)
Pretesting ads (*see* Ad testing)
Pretesting and posttesting promotion offers, 572–575
Price:
as a marketing objective, 26, 27, 28–29
reference price, 392
(*see also* Manufacturer's promotions; Retailer's promotions)
Price elasticity (*see also* Brand equity, Moran's method)
Price-off promotions (*see* Manufacturer's promotions; Retailer's promotions)
Price packs, 361
Price-related promotions, 6–7

Primacy and recency effects:
in brand recall, 221, 237(n)
and order of benefit claims, 255, 273(n)
Print ads 288–305
(*see also* Magazine ads; Newspaper ads; Outdoor and poster ads; Yellow Pages and directory ads)
Private labeling (*see* Retailer's promotions)
PRIZM geodemographic service, 480
Problem avoidance motive, 121, 147–148, 225
Problem detection analysis, 498, 523
Problem removal motive, 121, 147–148, 225
Problem-solution format in ads, 225
Processing:
in AC&P plan, 612, 623
acceptance, 244–246, 269
acceptance measures, 564–565
ALEA model of, 244–245
attention, 279–282, 284–285, 289–292, 292–298, 298–300, 301–303, 304, 308, 311, 572
attention measures, 571–572
attention to media vehicles, 461–462, 464, 465, 466, 473(n)
(*see also* 280, 284, 289, 293, 298, 299, 300, 302, 304, 308, 311)
attribution responses to promotion offers, 573–574
defined, 11, 580
emotion, 120, 122–123, 153–159, 225, 227–229, 245
learning, 214–216
learning measures, 565
processing measures in campaign tracking, 586–588
of promotion offers, 572–575
second step in effects sequence and buyer response steps, 11–14, 612
Product-as-hero (*see* Positioning)
Product category life cycle:
advertising communication and promotion emphasis in, 10–11
consumer life cycle, 247, 251–252, 271(n)
for "fad" products, 453
from situation audit, 515–516
and high-involvement/informational (HI/I) creative tactics, 246–247, 251–252
and target audience leverage, 61–62
Profile variables (*see* Decision maker profile variables)
Profit:
in AC&P plan, 612–613, 622
and campaign evaluation, 590
and corporate image advertising, 337
final step in effects sequence, 11–12, 14–15, 612–613
measures of, 506
and the media schedule, 493
and price-offs, 398–399
return on promotion offers, 575–576
Projective techniques, 165–166, 523–524

Promotions:
vs. advertising communications, 3–7
definition, 3, 4, 6, 21(n)
(*see* Manufacturer's promotions; Retailer's promotions; Direct marketing promotions)
Promotion offer testing, 572–576
Psychographics, 59–60, 96, 479, 524, 530, 536(n)
Psychographic matching (*see* Media vehicle selection)
Psycholinguistics (*see* Verbal content in ads)
Publicity, 4, 5, 324, 329, 339–341, 343–346, 424, 425–426, 437, 439
Public relations (*see* PR)
Public self-consciousness personality trait, 98
Pulsing (*see* Media plan, "maintenance" plans)
Pupillometric measurement, 571, 582(n)
Purchase cycle:
in behavioral sequence model (BSM), 89–90
in database marketing, 409–411
definition, 89, 447, 451
for grocery stores, 397
long cycles, 69, 436, 455–456
measurement of, 89–90
for fmcg products, 70, 76–77, 453–455
for new products, 451
for seasonal products, 456–457
Purchase-diary panels, 507, 508, 513
Purchase facilitation:
and advertising communications, 325, 326
and acceptance, 245
defined, 110, 128
and direct response ads measures, 570
objectives, 128–129, 132
and promotions, 325, 326
Purchase motivations (*see* Motives for purchase and usage)
"Push" and "pull" channel strategies, 27, 31–32

Qualitative research (*see* Advertising strategy research)
Quantitative research (*see* Advertising strategy research)
Q-sort procedure, 545–546, 576–577(n)

Radio commercials 5, 284–288, 557, 559
Radio medium, 420–423, 425, 427, 429, 431–432, 435, 436, 437, 440–441
RAM-Conveyor theory of creative ideas, 192–198, 261, 286–287, 296–297, 543
"Ratchet" effect of advertising followed by promotion, 468–469
Reach:
decisions, 448–469
definition, 447
effective reach, 447, 450
(*see also* Reach patterns)

geographic, 448
secondary media for hard-to-reach target audiences, 429, 431
Reach patterns:
awareness reach pattern, established product, 455
blitz pattern, new product, 451–452
definition, 447
flighting in, 449, 454–455, 604, 606, 608(n)
regular purchase cycle reach pattern, established product, 453–455
reverse-wedge/PI pattern, new product, 452–453, 480
media schedule implementation of, 492
seasonal priming pattern, established product, 456–457
shifting reach pattern, established product, 455–456
short fad pattern, new product, 453
wedge pattern, new product, 452
Reach-frequency-monetary value (RFM) calculation, 409–411
Reach rule (*see* Media plan)
Rebates (*see* Refunds or rebates)
Recall:
of ads (*see* Ad recall)
of brands (*see* Brand awareness)
Recognition:
of ads (*see* Ad recognition)
of brands (*see* Brand awareness)
Refunds or rebates (*see* Manufacturer's promotions)
Refutational advertising (*see* Benefit claims, refutational approach)
Regression analysis, 41, 42, 411, 528, 536(n), 595
Regular purchase cycle reach pattern (*see* Reach patterns)
Relationship marketing, 413
Reliability:
in qualitative research, 520, 552–553, 526
in questionnaire surveys or ad tests or concept screening research, 545, 552, 580(n), 581–582(n)
and sample or cell size, 552
Repeat audience (*see* Media vehicle selection, duplication of exposures)
Repeat purchase (*see* Action, target audience)
Repetition:
and brand attitude learning, 227, 229–230
and brand awareness learning, 216, 217–218, 219, 221, 222–223, 231
and introversion-extraversion, 97
in the media schedule (*see* Reach patterns)
within the ad (in-ad), 221
(*see also* Frequency)
Retail advertising, 5, 434–436, 437
Retailer's promotions:
action objectives, 382–383
atmosphere, 4, 384, 385–388
bait-and-switch tactic, 390
defined, 4, 324, 382
feature ads, 4, 388–390

high-low pricing tactic, 391, 399
inventory transfer objective, 383–384
layout, 4, 384–386
merchandising, 390
POP displays, 4, 390–391
price-offs, 375–376, 391–392, 397–400
private labeling, 4, 392–393
and trade promotions, 383, 389, 398–399, 400(n)
TV or PC interactive shopping, 4, 383, 393–395
Retail feature ads (*see* Retailer's promotions, feature ads)
Reverse wedge/PI reach pattern (*see* Reach patterns)
Rhetorical questions in copy, 287–288
Rossiter-Percy grid (*see* Advertising communication models)

Sales:
in AC&P plan, 612, 613
advertising's contribution, 14
exposure-to-sales analysis, 595–596
fifth step in effects sequence, 11, 12, 14–15, 612
vs. market share, 46–47
measures, 506–507
objectives, 30–32
and profit, 26–27, 47
Sales modelling, 228, 596, 608(n)
Sales-force promotions, 4, 324, 352–354
Sales response function, 36
Sample size (*see* Reliability)
Sampling or samples (*see* Manufacturer's promotions)
Satisfaction-dissatisfaction, 86, 377
Scanner data (*see* Sales, measures)
Schroer's method (*see* Budget-setting methods)
Seasonal reach pattern (*see* Reach patterns)
Selection integration (*see* IMC, principles of)
Self-image, 267
Self-monitoring personality trait, 104(n)
Semantic differential scales, 569–570, 582(n)
Sensory gratification motive, 121, 122, 147, 148, 194, 213, 228
Service as a repeat-purchase promotion, 371–373, 374, 376–377
Sex differences in persuasion, 98
Share of Voice (SOV), 39
Shelf height, 356
Shelf space, 356
Shelf tags (*see* Retailer's promotions)
Shifting reach pattern (*see* Reach patterns)
Short fad reach pattern (*see* Reach patterns)
"Single-source" syndicated media and product data, 532
Situation audit (*see* Advertising strategy research)
Situational approach to measuring motives and attitudes, 148, 527, 568

Six-step effects sequence, 11–12, 14–20, 585, 612
Size of ads, 289–290, 293, 298–299, 300–302, 304
Social approval motive, 121, 122, 146, 147, 148, 213, 228
Social class, 96
Solomon four-group design, 579(n)
Source effects, 260
SOM (*see* Market share)
SOV (*see* Share of Voice)
SPEEDBACK attention test, 572
Speed of response (*see* Action, target audience)
Sponsorships, 4, 5, 324, 339–341, 346–347, 424, 425–426, 429, 430, 432, 436, 437, 438, 439
Starch advertisement recognition measure, 295, 304, 315(n)
Store atmosphere (*see* Retailer's promotions, atmosphere)
Store brands (*see* Retailer's promotions, private labeling)
Store image advertising, 436
Strategy:
definition, 26
(*see also* Advertising strategy; Creative strategy; IMC strategy; Media strategy; Positioning statement)
Subconscious processing of advertising, 196, 201, 216 (n)
Subliminal effects of advertising, 165–166, 173(n)
Sweepstakes (*see* Contests and sweepstakes)
Syndicated ad tests (*see* Ad testing, syndicated)

Tactic-first approach, 182–183
Tactics, definition, 26
Target audience:
and ad testing, 563–564
and advertising units, 488, 605, 606
awareness-attitude-behavior approach (*see* brand loyalty approach)
brand loyalty approach, 57–63, 71, 74–75, 481
and concept screening, 545
and corporate advertising communications, 332–333
definition and database marketing, 57–59
distributors as, 71–72
effect of campaign on prospect group membership, 467–468, 589–590
five buyer groups (NCUs, OBLs, OBSs, FBLs, BLs), 57–59 (*see also* specific subgroups)
and high-involvement/informational (HI/I) brand attitude creative tactics, 247–254
and high-involvement/transformational (HI/T) brand attitude creative tactics, 256–258, 259, 267
and industrial advertising, 74
and minimum effective frequency (MEF), 462, 464, 465, 467–468
leverage principle in selection, 61–63, 521

measurement of, 521, 524, 525–527
and media vehicle selection (*see* Media vehicle selection, direct matching)
and promotion pretesting, 574
and purchase decision involvement, 213, 224, 246
selection, 61–63, 521
specific subgroups, 59, 61–62, 525–527
vs. target market, 61
vulnerability approach, 93–94
Target audience action objectives (*see* Action, target audience)
Telemarketing, 5, 6, 306, 307, 308, 310–311, 376, 425, 426–428, 441, 442
Television (TV) commercials, 5, 7, 280–284, 557–559
Television medium, 420–423, 428–432, 434, 435, 436, 437, 438, 439, 440, 491
Testimonials, 271, 283, 285, 295
Thought-starter lists, 542–543
Tracking studies (*see* Campaign tracking research)
Trade advertising (*see* Manufacturer's promotions, trade promotions)
Trade allowances or discounts
Trade promotions (*see* Manufacturer's promotions)

Trade publications, 5, 300, 436, 437, 438
Trade shows, (*see* Manufacturer's promotions)
Transformational motives:
and ad testing, 556–560
definition, 121–122,
emotional portrayal of, 227–229, 256–258
and positioning, 147–149
and promotion offers, 573
and Rossiter-Percy grid, 213
Trial (*see* Action, target audience)
Trustworthiness of presenters (*see* Presenters, objectivity)
Turnover analysis, 594–595
TV or PC interactive shopping (*see* Retailer's promotions)

Unconscious processing of advertising (*see* Subconscious processing of advertising)
Uniqueness:
of advertising executions, 228–229
of benefits (*see* Positioning, I-D-U mesomodel)
UPC scanners (*see* Scanner data)
Usage promotions (*see* Promotion, repeat-purchase promotions)

User-as-hero (*see* Positioning)
"USP" (Unique Selling Proposition) approach, 226
Validity:
in ad testing, 202–204, 580(n), 581–582(n), 584
in campaign tracking research, 586–588, 589, 606(n), 607(n)
in concept screening research, 189, 202–204, 547–548
and managers' intuition, 209(n)
in qualitative research, 519, 520, 551–552, 535(n), 536(n), 537
in quantitative research, 524, 527–528, 535(n), 536(n)
VALS lifestyle typology (SRI's), 104(n), 530
Vehicle selection (*see* Media vehicle selection)
Verbal content in ads, 97, 193, 196, 197–198, 200–202, 219–222, 231–232, 243, 251–255, 259, 266, 282–284, 286–288, 290–292, 295, 296–298, 300, 301, 302, 303, 305, 309–311, 316(n), 375–376, 399–400, 541, 543, 544, 554, 571–572
VIDEAC media model, 497–498
VisCAP model of presenter characteristics, 262–268, 546–547

Visual content in ads, 192–193, 196, 197–198, 200–202, 218, 254, 257, 258, 266, 281–282, 282–284, 290–291, 295, 298, 300, 301, 303, 305, 309–310, 311, 386, 541, 544, 557–559, 571–572
Visual imagery, 286–287, 231–232,
Visual imaging ability, 98
Voice-overs, in TV commercials, 266
Volume objectives (*see* Sales, objectives)

Warranties (*see* Manufacturer's promotions)
Wearout (*see* Advertising wearout)
Weather and media scheduling, 469
Wedge reach pattern (*see* Reach patterns)
Worldwide Web (*see* Interactive TV or PC ads)
Word-of-mouth communication (*see* Personal influence)

X-YZ macromodel of positioning location (*see* Positioning, macromodel of)

Yellow Pages and directory ads, 5, 7, 111, 114, 300–303, 483, 484

# Name index

A & P supermarkets, 316–317, 321, 335, 356
Aaker, D.A., 166, 208, 471, 581
ABB Electric company, 61, 74
ABC (American Broadcasting Company), 588, 609
Abelson, R.P., 217
Abernethy, A., xvi, 274, 314, 473
Abraham, M., 49, 208, 378
Abrams, B., 303
Abruzzo, J., 240
Absolut vodka, 183, 207, 229
Achenbaum, A.A., 448, 471
Achrol, R.S., 22
Ackoff, R.L., 242
Action Direct Marketing company, 319
Acura automobiles, 254
Acuvue disposable contact lenses, 90, 91
Ad Chart research service, 317
Ad News newspaper, 185, 186, 187, 188
Adams, A.J., 211, 240, 579
Adams, H.F., 210, 314
ADBANK company, 517
Adidas footwear, 347
Adler, Alfred, 102
AdTel, 472
AdvantEdge television advertising company, 313
Advertising Age magazine, 517
Advertising Research Foundation (ARF), 208, 314, 178
ADWEEK publishing company, 21, 312, 318, 444, 445, 491, 497, 501, 517, 608
AEI's music service, 401
Agassi, Andre, 146
Agriculture department (USDA), 232
Ahmed, S.A., 380
Ahtola, O.T., 136
AIDS (Acquired Immune Deficiency Syndrome), 156, 194, 351
Aim toothpaste, 144, 148, 221
Air Transport World magazine, 508
Ajax laundry detergent, 144, 370, 371
Ajzen (now Aizen), I., 137, 139
Alarm soap, 282
Alba, J.W., 135, 137, 138, 168, 239
Alden Catalog company, 409
Alexander's stores, 313
Alfa-Romeo automobiles, 368, 427
Ali, A., 380
Alka-Seltzer antacid remedy, 89, 111
Allcom agency, 543
Allen, C.T., 236, 237, 241, 315, 350, 401, 500
Allen, K., 186
Allenby, G.M., 514, 534
Allyson, June, 276
Almond Joy candy bar, 131
Alpert, D., xvi
Alpert, M., 150

Alpert, F.H., 51
Alpert M.I., 150, 169
Alreck, P.L., 87, 88, 101
Alsop, R., 276, 536
Ambler, T., 24
American Airlines, 254, 508
American Association of Advertising Agencies (AAAA), 180
American Association of Yellow Pages Publishers, 317
American Express Card, 52, 71, 112, 118, 125, 188, 220, 254, 262, 263, 271, 276, 430, 533, 596
American Express Travelers Checks, 158, 258
American Family Association, 482
American Marketing Association, 584
American Motors, 362
American Society for Quality Control, 138
Amidon, M.D., 276
Anderson windows, 508
Anderson's scuba school, 303
Anderson, B.B., 236
Anderson, E., 50
Anderson, J.R., 167
Anderson, P.F., 380, 474
Anderson, R.E., 103
Andrews, S., 319
Andronicus coffee, 150
Ang, L., xv, 192, 209, 210
Angin, K.T., 237, 238, 314
Anheuser-Busch company, 59
Aniero, H.J., 365, 378, 379
Anson, C., 48
ANZ bank, 577
Apollo Comedy Hour TV program, 496
Appel, D.L., 22
Appel, V., 500
Apple computers, 184, 231, 232, 248, 260, 358, 362, 512
Apple Macintosh computer, 248, 358
Apple retail outlets, 71
ARBOR research company, 545, 572, 581, 582
Areni, C.S., 241, 387, 401
Ariel laundry detergent, 345
Aristotle, 170
Arm & Hammer company, 6
Arm & Hammer laundry detergent, 5, 23
Armani aftershave lotion, 290
Armani Fragrances company, 291
Armani men's deodorant, 512
Armstrong, J.S., 50, 52
Armstrong, Louis, 263
Arndt, J., 52
Arnott's Australia Ltd, 219
Arnott's water crackers, 218, 219
Arons, L., 271
Aronson, E., 23, 104, 159, 171, 172, 173, 240, 271, 272, 274
Arzt, E.L., 67, 78

ASDA supermarkets, 393
Ashe, Arthur, 156
ASI research company, 578, 583
Assael, H., 479, 498
Association of Home Appliances, 508
Assuncao, N., 79
AT&T company, 75, 125, 154, 205, 206, 270, 276, 515, 540
AT&T long-distance telephone service, 516, 538, 539, 547
Athiyaman, A., 501
Atlanta Home Show, 358
Audi 90 automobile, 153, 154, 609
Audi A8 Sport automobile, 245, 246
Audi company, 154, 246, 254
Australian Consolidated Press, 315
Australian Direct Marketing Association, 307
Australian Tourist Commission (ATC), 455, 541, 542, 545, 546
Automotive News magazine, 508
Aversa, N., 79
Avis rental cars, 118, 182, 254
Avon company, 326, 342, 343, 350
Avon cosmetics, 24
"Avon ladies," 24, 358
Axelrod, J.N., 483
Aycrigg, R.H., 363, 379

Babb, E.M., 583
Bacall, Lauren, 274
Bacardi rum, 230
Backer Spielvogel Bates agency, 190, 201
Bacon, F.T., 227, 241
Badzinski, D.M., 210
Bagozzi, R.P., 127, 136, 137, 235, 236, 241, 474, 583
Bailey, E.B., 474, 534
Baker, G., 318
Baker, M.J., 274, 276
Baker, Stephen, 542, 576
Balasubramanian, S.K., 350
Baldinger, A.L., 77
Balenciaga Enterprises company, 196
Balenciaga's Talisman perfume, 196, 218
Bamossy, G.J., 242, 402
Banana Republic, 401
Banca di Roma, 184
Bandler, R., 104
Bank of America, 337, 338
Bankers Trust investment funds, 249
Banquet dinners, 15
Barczak, G.J., 378
Bargh, J.A., 138
Barlow, W.E., 444
Baron, P.H., 471
Barry, T.E., 272
Barter, J., 136
Bartges, D.W., 349
Bartle Bogle Hegarty agency, 202, 228, 603
Bartling, C.A., 135

Bartolini, T., 276
Barwise, T.P., 48, 80, 491, 500, 501
BASF company, 543
Bass, F.M., 40, 49, 51, 65, 134, 515, 516, 534
Bassman, E.S., 538, 576
Basu, A., 208
Bateson, J.E.G., 381
Bath & Body soap, 401
Bath & Body Works stores, 401
Batra, R., 136
Bauer, R.A., 239, 274
Baumgartner, J., 137
Bawa, K., 368, 380
Baxter, J.C., 581
Bayer pain remedy, 265
Bayus, B.L., 79, 80
BBDO agency, 222, 523
Beach Boys, The, 340
Beale, C., 238
Beard, J.D., 319
Bearden, W.O., 379, 381
Beattie, A.E., 343, 350
Beatty, S.E., 241, 276
Beck's beer, 114
Bee Gees, 222
Belafonte, Shari, 263, 276
Belch, G.E., 241
Belk, R.W., 88, 101, 380, 474, 583
Bell Atlantic Telephone Company, 262
Bell, S.S., 49, 77
Bellaire, A., 274
Bellenger, D.N., 535
Bellow, D.C., 378
Beltramini, R.F., 274
Benetton clothing, 157, 165, 172, 182, 260, 463, 566, 581
Bennett, P.D., 81
Bentham, Jeremy, 172
Beracs, J., 274
Bergen, M., 378
Berger, P.D., 169, 319
Berkowitz, E., 376, 380, 399, 402
Berkowitz, L., 138
Berlitz language courses, 310
Berlitz Publishing company, 310
Bernhardt, K.L., 474, 535
Berry, L., 381
Berry, Norman, 179
Berthon, P., 319
Bettman Archives, 543
Bettman, J.R., 134, 138, 173, 575, 583
Betty Crocker cake mix, 264
Bevins, J. agency, 237
Bhargava, M., 318
Bhatla, S., 238
Bic Disposable razors, 104
Biel, A., 49, 134
Binkert, B., xvi
Birdseye foods, 243, 502
Bishop, S.E., 276
Biswas, A., 400, 403

Bittner, M.J., 101
Black & Decker Dustbuster, 370
Black & Decker power tools, 510
Black Flag bug spray, 237
Black, P., 240
Blackston, M., 48
Blackwell, R.D., 401, 498
Blair, E.A., 375, 380
Blair, M.H., 43, 52, 144, 168, 178, 179, 204, 205, 207, 209, 211, 240, 578, 579
Blamires, C., 583
Blanc, Mel, 596
Blank, A., 233
Blattberg, R.C., 22, 51, 77, 383, 384, 400, 414, 415, 534
Blin, J.M, 536
Bloch, P.H., 101, 136, 260
Block, M.P., 381, 397, 398, 402
Blue Nun wine, 465, 602
BMW automobiles, 233, 254, 350
Bobinski, G.S., Jr., 349
Body by Jake Hip & Thigh Machine, 262
Bogart, Humphrey, 263
Bogart, L., 23, 137, 209, 238
Bold laundry detergent, 231, 465
Bolton, R., 381
Bond, James, 266
Bonfield, E.H., 233
Bonoma, T.V., 101, 207
Booz, Allen & Hamilton company, 42, 178, 207
Broadcast Advertisers' Reports, 462
Borden's dairy products, 289, 340, 390
Borden, N.H., 22, 391
Borg, Bjorn, 263
Bornstein, R.F., 135
Boston Consulting Group, The, 49, 51
Bottger, P.C., 101
Bounty candy bar, 131
Bower, G.H., 133, 235
Bowman, D., 168
Boya, U.O., 316
Boyd, B.K., 47
Boyd, J.H., 48, 349
Bozell & Jacobs agency, 28, 48, 349
Bradford, J.W., 513, 534
Brandes, W., 276
Bridges, Lloyd, 266
Brim coffee, 75, 80, 262
Brisoux, J.E., 126, 137
Bristol-Myers Squibb company, 265
British Aerospace company, 338
British Airways, 286
British Leyland company, 339
British Telecom (BT), 376
Britney, K.E.A., 414
Britt, S.H., 47, 169, 537
Broadbent, S., 53, 312, 473
Brock, J.T., 277
Brock, T.C., 133, 171, 241, 274, 565, 581, 609, 610
Brodie, R.J., 50
Brody, E.I., 474
Brookes, R., 100
Brooks Brothers stores, 393, 400
Brosnan, Pierce, 266
Brown, G.H., 317, 587, 607, 608
Brown, S.P., 135
Brownbride, G., 136

Brownlee, M.A., 521
Brundage, J., xvi
Bruvold, N.T., 316
Bruzzone Research Corporation (BRC), 236, 312, 607
Bruzzone, D.E., 581
Bryce, W.J., 314
Buchanan, B., 277
Buchanan, L., 208
Buck, S., 393, 402
Buckingham, C., 400
Buckley, William, F., Jr., 96
Bucklin, R.E., 400
Bud Light beer, 143
Budget Gourmet dinners, 168
Budweiser beer, 230, 518, 600
Budweiser company, 154
Buesing, T., 77
Bugelski, B.R., 233, 234, 500
Buhr, T.A., 276
Bumba, L.J., 445
Bundaberg rum, 485, 487, 500
Burbach, R., 535
Burger King restaurants, 143, 254, 578
Burke Marketing Research company, 572, 103, 312, 607
Burlace, W., 317
Burnett, Carol, 265
Burnett, J.J., 103
Burnett, Leo, 236
Burnkrant, R.E., 314
Burns, M.J., 170
Burroughs, J., 274
Burton, S., 400, 403
Busch, P.S., 474
Bush, A.J., 318
Bush, R.P., 318
Bushman, B.J., 104
Business Week magazine, 292
Buss, A.H., 104
Butaye, I., 234
Butcher, J.N., 137
Buzzell, R.D., 23, 40, 51, 178, 179, 207
Byers, L., 554, 579
Byrne, D., 173

Caballero, M.J., 276
CACI geodemographic service, 480
Cacioppo, J.T., 226, 239, 240, 241, 252, 272, 276, 277, 581
Cadillac automobiles, 258
Cadillac (General Motors) company, 210
Cadillac Eldorado automobile, 201
Cadillac Seville automobile, 174, 184, 201
Cahners Publishing company, 49, 317, 378
Calder, B.J., 344, 346, 350, 535, 537, 609
California Raisin Board, 202, 260
Calvin Klein jeans, 229, 287, 463, 464
Cam-2 motor oil, 364
Campbell's Soup company, 42, 71, 102, 169, 179, 207, 211, 227, 236
Campbell's soup, 579
Campbell, D.T., 210, 579
Campbell, L., 314
Campbell, Naomi, 261, 262, 264, 274

Campbell-Mithun-Esty agency, 18
Cannon, H., 479, 498, 499
Canon camera, 146
Capitol Records company, 445
Capon, N., 209
Carey, J.R., 381
Carillon importers, 207
Carli, L.L., 104
Carman, J.M., 471
Carmon, Z., 363, 379
Carnation company, 179, 207
Caron, R., 318
Carpenter, G.S., 51, 142, 143, 150, 154, 167, 168, 171, 174
Carpenter, P.A., 316
Carpet and Rug Institute, 508
Carpet Manufacturers' Marketing Association, 508
Carr, M., 237
Carroll, B., 414
Carroll, Diahann, 174
Carter, Jimmy, 264
Carter, S., 608
Carter, T., 51
Castrol motor oil, 282
Cataquet, H., 207
Cathay Pacific airlines, 336, 337
Cathey, A.S., 411, 412, 415
Cattell, R.B., 103
Cavedon, A., 238
Caywood, C., 500, 501
CBS (Columbia Broadcasting System), 444
Century 21 real estate company, 335
Cetola, H., 97, 99, 104
Chaiken, S., 138
Chalmers, J., 317
Chandrashakaran, M.V., 239
Chandrasekharan, R., 74, 80
Chanowitz, B., 233
Charlie perfume, 237, 262
"Charlie the Tuna," 263
Charmin toilet tissue, 225, 226, 247, 463
Chase, Chevy, 276
Chase, D., 168
Chaterjee, R., 49
Chattopadhyay, A., 102, 137, 239
Cheerios cereal, 87
Chen, R.D.H., 414
Cher (LaPierre), 281
Cherian, J., 318
Cheseborough-Ponds company, 78, 364
Chestnut, R.W., 77, 81
Chevalier, M., 400
Chevrolet automobiles, 508
Chevron company, 206, 211, 349
Chez Paul restaurant, 345
Chiang, J., 79
Chiclets chewing gum, 84
Chilton Research Services, 173
Chisolm, J., 315
Chivas Regal Scotch whiskey, 258, 603
Chow, S., xvi, 198, 210, 577
Christiansen, R.E., 317
Chrysler automobiles, 74, 360, 362, 386
Chudnoff, M.M., 575, 583
Church & Dwight company, 6
Churchill, G.A., Jr., 193, 209, 274, 276, 287, 314

Cialdini, R.B., 277, 378, 583
CIBA company, 543
Cinzano vermouth, 231
Circuit City stores, 475
CitiBank company, 508
Clairol hair products, 184, 202
Clancy, K.J., 173, 208, 409, 414, 534
Claritas geodemographic services, 480
Clark candy bar, 131
Clark, G.L., 317
Clark, L.A., 136
Clarke, D.G., 608
Clarke, P., 241
Classic Cola (Sainsbury's), 236
Clemenger agency, 312
Clemons, D.S., 170
Cleopatra, 243
Clicque, S.H., 381
Close, Glenn, 276
Close-up toothpaste, 148, 529, 600
Club Med resorts, 259
CMS company, 21
CNN Early Morning II TV program, 496
Coca-Cola company, 87, 113, 141, 157, 179, 207, 253, 277, 267, 287, 288, 289, 335, 343, 370, 431, 518, 609
Coe, B.J., 348, 578
Coffin, T., 287, 314
Cohen, D., 271, 278
Cohen, J.B., 241
Coke (Coca-Cola Classic) soft drink, 62, 87, 111, 114, 117, 133, 143, 144, 145, 205, 208, 211, 229, 226, 236, 253, 254, 270, 272, 287, 391, 466, 479, 482, 483, 518, 535, 556, 600, 609
Coke II soft drink, 143, 163, 164, 165, 255, 277
Cold Power detergent, 335
Cole, A., 102
Cole, C.A., 242
Coleman, E.B., 316
Coleman, R.P., 102
Colford, S.W., 277
Colgate toothpaste, 144, 243, 335, 513
Colgate-Palmolive company, 335
Colley, R.H., 24
Collins, B.J.K., 608
Collins, M.A., 501
Colman, S., 587, 607
Columbo, R.A., 74, 80
Comanor, W.S., 49
Communication Week magazine, 508
Compaq computers, 512
Competitive Media Reporting company, 517
ConAgra company, 12, 23, 253, 271, 369
Cone, Fairfax, 243
Conlin, R.P., 579
Connors, Jimmy, 264, 265
Consumer Reports magazine, 132
Contac cold remedy, 221
Cooil, B., 48, 49
Cook, B., 408
Cook, G., 350
Cook, L., 608
Cooper, C.L., 209
Cooper, R.G., 51

Cooper-Martin, E., 535
Coors Light beer, 143
Coppola, Francis Ford, 208
Corfman, K.P., 101, 350
Cornhill Insurance company, 339, 340, 425
Cornoldi, C., 238
Cortez, J.P., 51
Cosby, Bill, 254, 264, 265, 266, 267, 268, 278
Cosmopolitan magazine, 138
Costa, P.T., 137
Cotton, B.C., 583
Coucke, P., 350
Coulter, R.H., 236, 315
"Count Dracula," 226, 271
Cover Concepts Marketing company, 379
Cox, A.D., 401
Cox, D., 401
Cox, D.F., 239, 252, 271
Cox, J.M., 380
Cox, S., 238
Crafton, S.M., 400
Craig, C.S., 103, 498, 501, 502, 608
Craigen, J.G., 349
Crask, M.R., 166
Cravens, D.W., 474
Crawford, Cindy, 266, 267
Creative Artists Agency, 179
Crest toothpaste, 95, 144, 148, 238, 513, 527, 529, 600
Crimmins, J.C., 138
Crites, S.L., 581
"Crocker, Betty," 264
Cross-Linked Elastin skin cream, 250
CUB supermarkets, 66
Culligan, D., 349
Culliton, J., 22
Cummins, E.R., 394, 401
Cuneo, A.Z., 402
Curhan, R.C., 400
Currim, I.S., 79, 534
Curry, D.J., 101

D'Arcy Masius Benton & Bowles agency, 60, 201
Dabholkar, P.A., 411, 412, 415
Dagnoli, J., 207
Dahr, S.K., 348
Daley, D., 276
Danaher, P.J., 50
Dannon yogurt, 510, 511
Danzig, F., 210
Darby, M.R., 259
Darmon, R.Y., 380
Dataquest company, 512
Datril pain remedy, 254
Davids, M., 348
Davies, I., 236
Davies, T., 119, 135
Davis, J.J., 348, 403
Day, G.S., 22, 77, 165, 166, 173, 474, 534
Day After movie, The, 482
Daytona 500 World Sportscar Championship, 339
DDB Needham Worldwide agency, 49, 180, 207, 257, 288
Dealerscope Merchandising magazine, 508
Dean, J., 22
Dean, James, 263

de Bakey, Michael, 262
de Beni, R., 238
Debevec, K., 237, 276
DeBono, K.G., 103
Deese, J., 240
Deighton, J., 22, 137, 157, 172, 415
Dekimpe, M.G., 51
Delbecq, L., 209
Delsym cough medicine, 313
Delta airlines, 254
Demko, P.R., 133
Demtel International company, 307
Deneuve, Catherine, 264
DeNeve, R., 350
Denham, R., 185, 186, 187, 188, 189
DePaulo, P., 210, 272, 276
DePaulo, B.M., 276
Depend products, 276
Deveny, K., 243, 402
Devine, P.G., 138
Devinney, T., 48, 49
Dewar's Scotch whiskey, 174
Dhar, P., 349
Dial soap, 184, 202
Diamond, S.A., 278
Dickson, J.P., 102
Dickson, P.R., 24, 96, 134, 400, 583
Diet Coke soft drink, 111, 117, 118, 144, 167, 222
Diet Dr. Pepper soft drink, 276
Diet Pepsi soft drink, 111, 117, 141
Diet 7Up soft drink, 201
Diet Sunkist soft drink, 117
Digel antacid remedy, 40
Digital (DEC) computers, 475, 509
Digital Equipment Corporation, 512
Diners Card, 335
Dingena, M., 193, 210
Dinsmore, F., 349
Dirksen, C.J., 4
Dodd, T.H., 350
Dodson, J.A., 211, 474, 536
Domzal, T.J., xvi, 103, 104
Donaton, S., 21
Donnelley Marketing company, 21, 378, 379
Donnelly, J.H., 171
Donovan, R.J., 101, 135, 139, 233, 238, 317, 385, 401, 403, 578, 579
Donthu, N., 318
Doodle O's cheese snacks 390, 391
Doritos corn chips, 276
Dornoff, R.J., 238
Doubleclick Network company, 501
Douglas, Michael, 266
Dourlay, T., xvi
Dove soap, 231, 232
Dove chocolate, 276
Dow Chemical company, 260
Dowling, G.R., 22, 97, 103, 207, 348, 351
Doyle Dane Bernbach agency, 201, 202, 209, 291
Dr. Pepper soft drink, 81, 565
Dreyer's Grand Light Ice Cream, 265, 276
Droge, C., xvi, 101
Drucker, P., 22, 24
Dubas, M., 173
Dubitsky, T.M., 581
Duffy, M., 50

Dun & Bradstreet company, 378
Duncan, T., 500, 501
DuPont company, 116, 119, 134, 349, 364, 445
DuPont nylon carpets, 508
Duracell batteries, 147
Durgee, J.F., 243
Dutta, S., 378
Dwyer, F.R., 363, 379, 414
d'Ydewalle, G., 350

E.R. (Emergency Room) TV program, 492
E.F. Hutton company, 265
E.Y.E., Inc. research company, 571
Eagleson, G., 578, 581
Eagly, A.H., 104, 314
Easingwood, C.J., 22
East, R., 81
Eastwood, Clint, 265
Eddie Bauer retailers, 401
Edison, Thomas, 542
Edwards, K., 233
Edwards, W., 137, 169
Egeth, H., 240
Ehrenberg, A.S.C., 32, 49, 65, 67, 69, 73, 74, 76, 77, 78, 79, 80, 81, 135, 239, 242, 357, 378, 402, 491, 498, 499, 500, 501, 515, 516, 536
Ehrlichman, John, 265
Eighmey, J., 182, 201, 207, 210
Einstein, G.O., 238
Elfverson, M., 521
Ellerbee, Linda, 265
"Elsie the Cow," 289
Emmrich, S., 272
Empty Nest TV program, 496
Emshoff, J.R., 242
Energizer batteries, 147, 282
"Energizer Bunny," 147, 282, 313
Engel, J.F., 401, 498
Engel, R.W., 234, 241
Enjoli perfume, 237, 262
Enrico, D., 276
Eppen, G.D., 383, 384, 400
Eppright, D., xvi
Equifax geodemographic service, 480
Erhart-Babic's National Retail Tracking Index, 507, 508
Erickson, J.L., 313
Esch, F-R., 158, 209, 543, 544, 576
Eskin, G.J., 313, 471, 502
Esquire magazine, 138
Estes, W.K., 217, 235
Evans, I.G., 581
Ever-Ready batteries, 282
Evian water, 231
Excedrin pain remedy, 268
Exxon company, 231, 343
Eysenck, H.J., 103, 133, 137

Faberman, J., 380
Fabrigar, L.R., 581
Fader, P.S., 79
Fannin, R., 78
Fanta soft drink, 117
Farley, J.U., 534
Farmer, K.M., 313
Farquar, P.H., 210
Farr, A., 608
Farris, P.W., 23, 49, 71, 79, 378

Fazio, R.H., 135, 138, 169, 210, 221, 236, 237, 314
FCB (Foote Cone Belding) agency, 139, 185, 186, 187, 188, 189, 202, 239, 243
FCC (Federal Commications Commission), 539
Federal Express couriers, 95, 141, 143, 220, 518
Feick, L., 277
Feigin, B., 535
Fein, G., 536
Feinberg, R.A., 274, 401
Feldwick, P., 608
Fellini, Federico, 184, 208
Fenigstein, A., 104
Fennell, G, 139
Ferrell, O.C., 474
Ferster, C.B., 583
Fielden, J.S., 319
Finn, D.W., 187
Finn, A., 315
Firestone tires, 265
Fischer company, 132
Fishbein, M., 102, 137, 139
Fisher-Price toys, 138, 229
Fitzgerald, Ella, 237, 262
Fitzmaurice, J., 380
Fitzroy, P., 609
Fleischmann's margarine, 514
Fletcher, K., 381
Flower stores, 441
Folger's coffee, 75, 150, 154, 214, 266
Food and Drug Administration (FDA), 517
Ford automobiles, 74, 335
Ford Motor company, 220, 349
Ford, G.T., 169
Ford, Harrison, 266
Foreman, George, 278
Formula One motor racing, 347
Fornell, C., 40, 49, 51
Fortis company, 192, 194
Fortune magazine, 292
Foster Nunn Loveder agency, 154, 246
Foster, Jodie, 266
Foster's beer, 313, 315
Four-ex (XXXX) beer, 315
Fouss, J.M., 535
Fox Hollywood Theatre TV program, 496
"Fox Z. Doodle," 391
Fox, Michael, J., 277, 278
Fox, R.J., 21
Foxall, G., 88, 97, 102, 103
Frank Small & Associates research company, 273
Frank, R., 207
Fraser, C., 513, 534
Frazer, C.F., 167, 172
Freeman, L., 208, 395
Freud, Sigmund, 165, 166
Frey, K.P., 314
Friedmann, R., 402, 403
Frito-Lay food products, 8
Fryburger, V., 6
FTC (Federal Trade Commission), 169, 226, 233, 270, 361, 375, 391, 399, 402, 517
Fuji cameras, 146
Fuji film, 305

Fujitsu computers, 512
Fulgoni, G.M., 391, 401, 608
"Fuller Brush men," 358
Furse, D.H., 240, 272, 274, 313, 314, 315, 582

Gablinger's light beer, 167, 201
Gabor, A., 48
Gaeth, G.J., 102, 232, 242
Gaidis, W.C., 583
Galen, R., 314
Gallagher, J., 401
Gallagher, K., 313
Galloway, J., 135
Gallup & Robinson research company, 500, 607
Gallup surveys, 133
Gap stores, The, 393, 402
Gardial, S.F., 170
Gardner, M.P., 210, 272, 349
Garfield, B., 168
Garfinkle, N., 498, 502
Garner, James, 146, 267
Gaskin, S., 51, 168, 277
Gatignon, H., 168
Gaye, Marvin, 202
GE company, 118
Geissler, G.L., 21
Gelb, B.D., 241, 316
General Foods company, 78, 144, 479
General Mills company, 179
General Motors automobiles, 343
General Motors (GM) company, 49, 74, 210
General Motors Card, 412
Gensch, D.H., 60, 61, 74, 77, 536
George, Linda Day, 264
George, W.R., 171
Gerstner, E., 378, 390, 401
Ghosh, A., 498, 501, 502
Gibson, L.D., 208
Gibson, R., 401
Gibson, C., 315
Giles, W., 207
Gillette razors, 22
Gilson, E., 312
Girbaud (VF) jeans, 402
Givon, G.P., 134
Givon, M., 474
Givson, R., 243
Glad Bake baking paper, 193, 194
Glazer, R., 48, 150, 169, 171
Gleason, M., 554, 579
Goerne, C., 21
Gold Blend coffee, 536
Goldberg, M.E., 102, 169, 210, 232, 240, 242, 500
Golden, R.J., 575, 583
Golder, P.N., 50, 167
Goldman, A.E., 537
Goldstein, M H., 380
Goldstucker, J.L., 535
Gollin, J., 208
Good Housekeeping magazine, 260
Goodhardt, G.J., 79, 80, 499, 500, 501, 536
Goodman, Benny, 596
Goodyear tires, 579
Gopalakrishna, S., 49, 375, 378, 380
Gorn, G.J., 102, 169, 210, 500
Govender, R., 138
Graham, G.L., xvi, 51

Graham, P., 499, 536
Gram, D., 276
Granbois, D.H., xvi
Grant, K., 581
Grass, R.C., 349, 444, 582
Gray, J.I., 314
Gray, S., 210
Green Giant's "Giant," 229, 263
Green Giant's "Sprout," 229
Green, J., 608
Green, L., 579, 581
Green, P.E., 534, 536
Greene, W.F., 211, 500
Greenwald, A.G., 133, 171
Greer, L.S., 340, 349
Grey agency, 49, 146, 523
Griffen, A., 535
Grindler, J., 104
Gross, I., 185, 200, 208, 210, 211, 550, 578
Grossarth-Maticek, R., 137
Gruber, A., 582
Grueger, J.A., 233
Guadagni, P.M., 401
Gucci apparel, 71
Guiltinan, J.P., 378
Gulas, G.M., 380
Gullen, P., 473
Gumbel, Bryant, 327
Gupta, S., 70, 79, 101
Gustafson, D.H., 209
Guthrie, E.R., 235
Gutman, J., 170, 171, 535
Gyles, S., 311, 319

Häagen-Dazs ice cream, 228, 229, 287, 313
Häagen-Dazs company, 228
Haas, R.G., 274
Haas, R.W., 49
Hack, Shelley, 276
Hackman, Gene, 266
Hague, P.N., 21
Hague, S., 207
Hains, P., 402, 403
Hair, J.F., 474
Haire, M., 256
Haist, F., 235
Haley, K., 312
Haley, R.I., 149, 150, 169, 210, 471, 482, 499, 610
Halstead, D., 101
Hamill, Dorothy, 174
Hammond, K., 79
Hammond, L.J., 240
Hanawait, N.G., 135
Hanimex cameras, 305
Hansell, J.H., 240
Hanssens, D.M., 51
Hard Copy TV program, 492
Harkins, S.G., 581
Harper, Mike, 18, 174, 253, 271
Harper, W., 607
Harris, R.J., 104, 135, 234, 238
Hart, M., 221
Hartwick, J., 232, 240
Harvey Communication Measurement Service, 607
Harvey, A., 349
Hasher, L., 608
Hastak, M., 572, 583
Hastie, R., 137
Hastings, H., 22

Haugh Associates research company, 607
Haugh, L.J., 134, 365, 379, 380
Hauser, J.R., 23, 168, 238, 513, 534, 535, 536, 581
Hausknecht, D., xvi
Hawkins, S.A., 227, 241
Hayashi, A., 576
Hayes, Helen, 267
Haygood, R.C., 134, 501
Headen, R.S., 491, 501
Healthy Choice breakfasts, 369
Healthy Choice dinners, 12, 23, 52, 60, 65, 96, 113, 114, 123, 131, 141, 153, 161, 211, 218, 231, 234, 253, 271, 568, 600
Healthy Choice ice cream, 369
Healthy Portion dinners, 168
Healthy Request dinners, 168, 169
Hearst, E., 217
Heath, T.B., 277
Heatherley, S., 135
Hecker, S., 237, 238, 261
Heeler, R.M., 117, 135, 241, 535
Hefflin, D.T.A., 134, 501
Heineken beer, 114, 347, 509, 603
Heinz company, 78
Heinz ketchup, 499
Helmann's mayonnaise, 465
Helsen, K., 400, 471
Helson, H., 583
Henderson, C.M., 392, 401
Hendry Corporation, The, 51, 68, 69, 78, 509, 534
Herr, P.M., 135, 169, 210, 221, 236, 314, 474
Hershey's candy bars, 370, 372
Hertz, 254, 266
Hess, J.D., 378, 390, 401
Hewlett-Packard computers, 512
Hewlett-Packard consumer products, 146, 174, 445
Heyer, W.D., 402
Hickey, L., 316
High Point coffee, 75
Higie, R.A., 277, 380
Higson, C., 48
Hilgard, E.R., 133, 235
Hilton C.B., 319
Him, K., 501
Hirsch, A., 387, 401
Hirschman, E.C., 379, 583
Hitchon, J.M., 193, 209, 287, 314
Hite, C. Fraser, 135
Hite, R.E., 135
Hitler, Adolf, 185, 186
Hoch, S.J., 51, 227, 241, 384, 402
Hodges, A., 318
Hoffer, G.E., 400
Hogan, Paul, 455
Holbert, N.B., 378, 381, 382, 538, 554, 563, 575, 581, 583
Holbrook, M.B., 132, 138, 138, 379, 579, 583
Holden, S.J.S., 134, 235
Holland, O., 565, 581
Holman, R.H., 135, 237, 238, 241, 261, 403
Holmes, J.H., 379, 474
Homan, S., xvi
Homans, G.C., 583
Homer, P.M., 274
Honda automobiles, 413

Honomichl, J., 414
Hooley, G.J., 50
Hoover vacuum cleaners, 363, 364
Hope, Bob, 263, 267
Hopkins, Claude, 243, 348, 518
Horsky, D., 65, 78, 474, 608
Hotpoint company, 523
House Beautiful, 483
Houseman, John, 265
Houston, M.J., 102
Houston, Whitney, 276
Hovland, C.I., 171, 269, 277
Howard, D.J., 314, 385, 401
Howard, J.A., 79, 133, 271, 534
Howard-Brown, J., 318
Howe, H.E., 102, 137
Hoyer, W.D., 135, 234
Hoyt & Co, 378
Hoyt, Chris, 378
Hudson, Rock, 156
Hughes, G.D., 241, 314, 583
Hull, C.L., 132, 133
Hulse, S.H., 240, 242
Hulton Deutsch Collection, 543
Hume, S., 49
Hung, C.L., 50
Hunt, H.K., 103
Hunter, M., 186, 188
Hutchinson, J.W., 133, 138, 168
Hyman, M.R., 103
Hyundai automobiles, 231

Iacocca, Lee, 360
IBM company, 23, 105, 123, 144, 168, 234, 278, 289, 479, 515, 518
IBM computers, 120, 122, 123, 143, 144, 459, 509, 512, 567, 569, 594, 600
ICI company, 368, 380
Impact Market Watch newsletter, 145
Indianapolis 500 motor race, 346
Infosino, W.J., 516, 534, 582
Inman, J., 401, 402
Interfaces magazine, 540
International Dairy Food Association, 262
International Red Cross, 23
Internet Shopping Network, 394
IRI (Information Resources Inc.), 41, 80, 208, 356, 390, 391, 397, 402, 472, 480, 507, 508, 518, 531, 532, 536, 572
Irwin, F., 583
Irwin, H., 351
Ivory detergent, 144
Ivory soap, 154

J & B Scotch whiskey, 195
J.D. Power and Associates research company, 102
J. Walter Thompson agency, 49, 201, 202, 206, 312, 609
J.C. Penney, 394
Jacard, J., 536
Jack Daniels bourbon, 174
Jackson, B.B., 414, 415
Jackson, J.M., 135
Jackson, Mark ("Whacko"), 147
Jackson, Michael, 263
Jackson, Reggie, 261
Jacobs, L.W., 50
Jacoby, J., 77, 81

Jaguar, 339, 340
Jain, A., 385, 401
James, J.C., 188, 173
Janis, I.L., 269, 277
Janiszewski, C.A., 241
Jansen, David, 268
Jell-O gelatin desserts, 142, 143, 267
Jenkins, J.R.G., 473
Jennings, L., 581
Jessen, R.J., 52
Jif peanut butter, 96, 146
Jockey shorts, 345
John, G., 378
John Blair Marketing Company, 379
John Deere Tractors, 351
John Roedder, D., 315, 350, 401
John Singleton agency, 187
Johnny Walker Scotch whiskey, 182, 603
Johnson & Johnson (J & J) company, 49, 90, 91, 345
Johnson's Baby Shampoo, 125, 222
Johnson, Earvin ("Magic"), 156, 263
Johnson, B., 210
Johnson, E.J., 173, 607
Johnson, H., 473
Johnson, J.D., 101, 104
Johnston, W.J., 411, 412, 415
Jolson, M.A., 103, 319, 380
Jonas, K., 313
Jones, B., xvi
Jones, D., 102
Jones, J.P., 32, 49, 209, 461, 472, 578, 606
Jones, James Earl, 262
Jordan, James, Jr., 202, 222
Jordan, McGrath, Case & Taylor ad agency, 222, 238
Jordan, Michael, 262
Jorgensen, B.K., 350
Journal of Direct Marketing, 319
Journal of Retailing, 403
Journal of Targeting, Measurement and Analysis for Marketing, 319
Just, M.A., 316
Juster, T.F., 581, 582
JVC electronics company, 132

Kabanoff, B., 209, 576
Kable, M., 415
Kahle, L.R., 274
Kahn, B.E., 78, 79, 89, 102, 402
Kalapurakal, R., xv
Kalish, S., 78
Kalwani, M.U., 78, 134, 581
Kalyanarum, G., 239
Kamakura, W.A., 49, 534
Kamin, H., 499
Kamins, M.A., 51, 240, 276, 499
Kaminsky, P.F., 317
Kamp, E., 240
Kanetkar, V., 48
Kanouse, D.E., 243
Kardes, F.R., 103, 137, 169, 238, 474
Karni, E., 259
Karpis, S.L., 414
Kaspar, H., 372, 380
Kasper, H., 101
Kassarjian, H.H., 173, 240, 241
Kassarjian, W.M., 240
Katz, D., 136, 169, 172
Katz, H., 445, 501
Kaufmann, P.J., 402, 403
Keller, K.L., xvi, 138, 255, 444

Kelley, H.H., 277
Kellogg's cereals, 23, 264, 335
Kellogg's Complete cereal, 118
Kelly, G., 315
Kelly, J.P., 319, 380
Kelly, K., 173
Kelman, H.C., 274
Keng, K.A., 74, 80
Kenmore washing machines, 508
Kenny, C., xvi
Kent cigarettes, 603
Kent, R.J., 236, 500
Kentucky Fried Chicken (KFC), 268, 436
Keown, C.F., 50
Kerin, R.A., 384, 401
Kerker, R.M., 343, 350
Kernan, J.B., 103, 104, 276
Kerrigan, Nancy, 267
Key, W.B., 165, 173
KHBB agency, 319
Kieff, J.R, 535
Kiesler, T., 499
Kilbourne, W.E., 173
Killey & Withy and Punshon agency, 185
Kim, D., 49, 387, 401
Kim, J., 474
Kimberly-Clark company, 355
King, K.W., 210
King, S., 307
King, T.R., 207
Kingfisher Bay Resort, 258, 259
Kinnear, T.C., 188
Kintsch, W., 297, 316
Kirin beer, 266
Kirton, M.J., 97, 103
Kleenex tissues, 142, 143, 355
Klein, E.L., 313
Klein, P.R., 283, 313, 578, 579, 606
Klinger, M.R., 173
KLM Airlines, 441
Klompmaker, J.E., 491, 501
Klue, J., 444
Kmart department stores, 29
Kodak film, 266, 268, 515
Kool cigarettes, 363
Koten, J., 101, 313
Kotler, P., 24, 50, 53, 78, 81, 535, 609
Kover, A.J., 240, 536
Kowet, D., 304, 349
Kraft General Foods company, 50, 78, 145, 201, 220, 475
Kraft Singles cheese, 603
Kramer, A., 166, 173
Kraus, S.J., 271
Kresge, J., 276
Krishnan, H.N., 607
Kroeber-Riel, W., xv, 157, 158, 172, 209, 210, 543, 576
Kroeger, A., 4
Kroll, N.E.A., 237, 238, 314
Krugman, H.E., 233, 580
Kuritsky, A.P., 538, 576
Kuse, A.R., 577

L'Oreal cosmetics, 276
L.A. Law TV program, 492
L.L. Bean company, 132, 390
L.L. Bean outdoor clothing catalogue, 327
Lackey, S., 238
Laczniak, G.R., 380, 474

Ladd, Cheryl, 237
Lafayette, J., 209
Lal, R., 378
Lama, Dalai, 185, 186, 187, 188, 189
Lambert, D.M., 535
Lamons, B., 318
Lancaster, K., 445
Landon, E.L., 375, 380
Landon, Michael, 266
Landor Associates research company, 343
Lang, P.J., 136
Langer, E., 233
Lapersonne, E., 102
Lark cigarettes, 266
Laroche, M., 126, 137
Laskey, H.A., 166, 350
Lasorda, Tommy, 183, 184, 207, 208
Lastovicka, J.L., 233
Latham, G.P., 47
LaTour, M.S., 173
Lattin, J.M., 400
Laurent, G., 102
Lauterborn, R.F., 24, 351
Lautman, M.R., 103, 271, 545, 548, 576
Lava soap, 225
Lavenka, N.M., 131, 138
Lawrence, J., 210, 239
Le, N.T., 534
Leading National Advertisers (LNA) media service, 462
Lean Cuisine dinners, 15, 23, 65, 78, 161, 162, 168
Leavitt, C., 581, 608
Le Boutillier, J., 134
Le Boutillier, S., 134
Leckenby, J.D., 495, 501, 609
Ledowsky, H., 187
Lee, Archie, 535
Lee, H., 498, 523
Le Goff, J-J., 102
Lehmann, C., 238
Lehmann, D.R., 49, 101, 165, 173, 534
Leigh, J.H., 102, 103, 209, 234, 237, 313, 582, 583
Leighton, B.A., 381
Le Mans endurance race, 339
Lemmink, J., 101, 372, 380
Lenk, J., 534
Leno, Jay, 277
Leo Burnett agency, 49, 77, 201, 236, 243, 581
Leone, R.P., 388, 401
Leong, S.M., 234
Lett, J.D., 379, 474
Levenson, Sam, 288, 242
Leventhal, H., 173
Lever 2000 soap, 202
Lever Brothers (Unilever) company, 156, 202, 210
Levi Strauss clothing stores, 119
Levi's clothing, 142, 143, 184, 202, 238, 345
Levin, G., 207
Levin, I.P., 232, 242
Levy, S.J., 284
Lewis, St. Elmo, 319
Lexus automobile, 254
Lieberman, J., 383, 384, 400
Lieberman, M.B., 51
Liesse, J., 210
Life cereal, 463

Lifesavers candy, 243
Light 'n' Lively yogurt, 510
Likierman, A., 48
Lilien, G.L., xvi, 78, 81, 101, 209, 378, 380, 535, 609
Lin, L.Y.S., 534
Lincoln Mercury automobile, 264
Lindblom, C.E., 207
Lindzey, G., 23, 104, 240, 271, 274
Linkletter, Art, 262
Lintas agency, 22, 90
Lipman, J., 102, 238
Liquid Tide detergent, 225
Listermint mouthwash, 144, 254
Little, J.D.C., 50, 71, 401, 471, 538, 576, 608
Litvack, D., 102
LNA/Arbitron media service, 517
Locander, W., 136, 234
Lockard, J.S., 380
Locke, E.A., 47
Lodish, L.M., 36, 49, 50, 81, 208, 378, 471, 490
Loftus, E.F., 173, 237
Loftus, G.R., 237
Logan, M., 281, 313
London Fog rainwear, 485
Longman, K.A., 471, 476
Lonial, S.C., 102
Lopex, A., 243
Loren, Sophia, 278
Los Angeles Dodgers, 207
Lo Sciuto, L.A., 608, 610
Lovibond, P.F., 173
Low, G.S., 50, 347
Lowenbrau beer, 509
Lowenstein, G.F., 79
Lowrey, T.M., 317
Lubetkin, B., 81, 208, 471
Lubliner, M., 22
Lucas, D.B., 169, 537
Ludlum, Robert, 596
Lufthansa airlines, 254
Lugosi, Bela, 271
Luh, C.W., 580
Lusch, R.F., 380, 474
Luscher color chips, 386
Lutz, K.A., 237, 238
Lutz, R.J., 237, 238
Lux shampoo, 266
Lynch, J.G., Jr., 50, 134, 137, 138, 350
Lynn, M., 135, 154

M&M jewellers, 376
M&Ms candy, 182, 184, 202
MacCrimmon, K.R., 543, 576
MacDonald, A., 608
MacDonald, S., 101
MacInnis, D.J., 240
Macklin, M.C., 316
MacLachlan, D., 234
MacLachlan, J., 96, 102, 208, 281, 313, 578, 581
MacMillan, I.C., 381
Madden, T.J., 276
"Madge," 263
Madonna (Ciccone), 266
Magiera, M., 207
Magnavox TV sets, 92
Mahajan, V., 471, 474, 534
Mahaswaran, D., 168, 171
Maher, B., 303, 317, 318
Maidenform bra, 243

Majaro, S., 47
Malden, Karl, 262, 268
Mall of America, 395
Maloney, J., 240
Mandese, J., 21, 102
Manning, K.C., 277
Mantrala, M.K., 133
Mapes & Ross research company, 281, 607
March, J.G., 133
Marcoolyn, G., 101, 401 , 403
Mark, Marky, 463
Market Facts research company, 93, 102
Market Research Corporation of America (MRCA), 507
Market Research Corporation of America (MRCA) Menu Census, 508
Market Research Corporation of America (MRCA) National Consumer Panel, 508
MarketMind Technologies research company, 553, 607
Marks & Spencer stores, 393
Marks, L.J., 240
Marlboro cigarettes, 182, 184, 364
"Marlboro Cowboy," 229
Marmorstein, H., 137
Marone, M.J., 277
Mars Kal Kan dog and cat food, 479
Marschalk company, 240, 249
Marsh, P., 48
Marshall Fields stores, 394
Marshall, D., 349, 350
Marshner, D.C., 47
Martilla, J.A., 173
Martin, C.R. Jr., 102, 103, 209, 237, 313, 316, 582, 583
Martineau, P., 96, 102
Marx, Groucho, 271
Master Card, 113
Mathur, I., 102
Mathur, L.K., 102
Mathur, S., xv
Matoun, M.A., 103
Maxim coffee, 75, 80
Maxwell House coffee, 58, 59, 75, 80, 214, 215, 233, 499
May, M., 271
Mayer, M., 138
Mayer-Douglas company, 369
Mayor, J.D., 500
Mazda automobiles, 254
Mazurski, E.J., 173
Mazursky, D., 138
McAlister, L., 277, 401
McArthur, L.Z., 276
McCabe, E.A., 181
McCall's magazine, 500, 502
McCann, J.M., 81, 389, 401, 474
McCann-Erickson agency, 21, 49, 179, 201, 202, 337, 535
McCarter, M., 208
McCarthy, E., 24
McCarthy, M.S., 277
McCarthy, P.S., 74, 80
McCollum Spielman Worldwide (MSW) research company, 205, 206, 208, 234, 239, 312, 313, 314, 473, 553, 554, 555, 556, 558, 559, 569, 578, 579, 580, 581, 606
McConville, M., 581

McCorkell, G., 209, 411, 415
McCormick, L.J., 500
McCracken, G., 208
McCullough, J.E., 211
McDaniel, M.A., 238
McDonald's restaurants, 7, 8, 28, 118, 143, 168, 220, 221, 222, 254, 265, 343, 344, 345, 346, 368, 482, 578, 609
McDonald, C., 134, 313, 473, 607
McDonough, M., 186
McEnroe, John, 263
McFadden, D., 137
McGraw-Hill companies, 343
McGuire, W.J., 23, 104, 171, 240, 241, 271, 274
MCI long-distance telephone service, 75
McIntire, S., 50
McKinnon, G.F., 380
McLennan, M., 276
McMahon, Ed, 264
McOmish, M., 274
McQueen, J., 77, 172
McRae, R.R., 137
Mediamark research company, 499, 536
Meenaghan, T., 349, 350
Mehta, A., 581
Memorex audiotapes, 237, 261
Mendelsohn, G.A., 136
Mercedes-Benz automobiles, 89, 254
Mercedes SEL automobile, 259
Merrill Lynch company, 414
Mesak, H.I., 471
Metropolitan Transit Authority (New York), 125
Meyer, R.J., 79, 534
Miami International Boat & Sailboat show, 346
Michell, P.C.N., 179, 207
Michelob beer, 60, 61, 509
Mick, D.G., 208, 243
Midas mufflers, 351
Middleton, K.R., 349
Midgley, D.F., 22, 97, 103
Mieneke mufflers, 278
"Mikey," 463
Milky Way candy bar, 131
Millar, K.U., 172
Millar, M.G., 172
Miller beer, 600
Miller Genuine Draft beer, 167
Miller High Life beer, 167, 600
Miller Lite beer, 60, 143, 167, 184, 201, 463, 602
Miller Publishing company, 399
Miller, C., 21, 277, 380, 401
Miller, G.A., 255
Miller, G.R., 277
Miller, J.R., 297, 316
Milliman, R.E., 386, 387, 401
Millward Brown research company, 135, 602, 607, 608
Milton, F., 381
Miniard, P.W., 238, 277
Misra, S., 265, 276
Mitchell, A., 400
Mitchell, A.A., 314, 608
Mitchell, N.A., 210
Mitra, A., 474
Moberg, G., 152, 170
Mobil 1 motor oil, 347
Moccona coffee, 149

Modelo shoes, 266
Mohn, N.C., 534
Mohr, J.J., 50
Molloy, J.T., 385, 401
Mondroski, M., 209
Monitor Plus media service, 462
Monroe, K.B., 362, 379, 401
Montgomery, D.B., 51
Montgomery, J., 350
Moon, Y.S., 274
Moore, Demi, 266
Moore, K., 535
Moore, S.D., 77
Moore, S.P., 79
Moore, W.L., 22
Moorthy, K.S., 78, 81, 535, 609
Moran, W.T., 28, 44, 45, 46, 48, 52, 53, 134, 169, 170, 474, 513, 514, 528, 534, 569, 577, 582
Mord, M.S., 312
More, E., 351
Morris, B., 499
Morris, P.E., 350
Morrison, D.G., 50, 74, 78, 80, 409, 414, 581, 582
Morrison, P.D., 103
Morton, I., 186
Morwitz, V.G., 607
Mosatche, H.S., 166, 173
Moscowitz, H., 232, 243
Moss, Kate, 463
Motes, W.H., 319
Mothersbaugh, D.L., 277
Mountain Dew soft drink, 117, 335
Mowrer, O.H., 240
Moxie soft drink, 117
"Mr. Whipple," 225, 226, 247, 463
MRI research company, 532
"Mrs. Olson," 266
MTV, 346
Mucha, Z., 51
Mulhern, F.J., 401
Muller, E., 471, 474, 534
Murnane, K., 236
Murphy, I.P., 501
Murphy, J.H., 98, 104
Murphy, P.E., 376, 380, 474
Murray, G.B., 473
Mustang automobile, 231
MUZAK music service, 386
Myatt, G., xv
Myers, J.G., 208
Myers, J.H., 150, 169, 256
Myerson, S., 402

Nabisco cookies, 351
Nakamoto, K., 142, 143, 150, 167, 168, 169, 171, 174
Namath, Joe, 281
Nance, S.E., 133
Naples, M.J., 471, 473, 476
NARHEX company, 250
Nash, E.L., 415
Nash, M., 474
National Enquirer magazine, 344, 500
National Advertising Division of the Council of Better Business Bureaus, 254
National Advertising Review Board, 399
National Family Opinion (NFO) research company, 507
National Infomercial Marketing Association, 474

National Potato Promotion Board, 253, 255
National Purchase Diary (NPD) research company, 66, 507
National Retail Hardware Association, 508
NBC Sunday Night Movie TV program, 502
Nebergall, R.E., 271
NEC consumer products, 174, 350, 351
Nedungadi, P., 134
Neilsen's Local Market Household, 507
Nelson, P.E., 239
Nescafe coffee, 58, 75
Nescafe Gold Blend coffee, 202
Nesdale, A., 101, 401, 403
Neslin, S.A., 134, 365, 380
Networking Management magazine, 508
New Coke (Coke II), 143, 163, 164
New York Boat Show, 358
New York Times newspaper, 344
New York Yankees, 272
Newcombe, John, 146
Newell, H.H., 225, 240, 578
Newman, Paul, 8, 263
Newman's Own salad dressing, 8
Newsom, D., 501
Newspaper Advertising Bureau, 315, 552
Newsweek magazine, 485
Newton, D.A., 352, 377
New Yorker, The, 485
NFL (National Football League), 370
Nicholls, J.A.F., 350
Niefeld, J.S., 48, 337, 349
Nielsen (A.C.) company, 21, 39, 41, 95, 172, 208, 312, 366, 408, 444, 453, 472, 499, 500, 518, 531, 532, 536, 572, 578
Nielsen Drug Index, 507, 508
Nielsen Mass Merchandise Index, 507, 508
Nielsen SPACEMAN computer program, 384
Nieman-Marcus stores, 406, 407
Niemann, Y.F., 581
Nike footwear, 38, 387
Nile, Reverend Fred, 185
Nissan Infiniti automobile, 221
Nixon, Richard, 264, 265, 276
Nobel Peace Prize, 185
Nord, W.R., 234, 583
Norse, S., 350
Nunnally, J.C., 577
Nuprin pain reliever, 265, 276
NW Ayer agency, 201, 205
NYPD Blue TV program, 482

Obermiller, C., 173
O'Connor, G.C., 208, 578
O'Curry, S., 363, 379
Ogilvy & Mather agency, 48, 112, 179, 201, 240, 271
Ogilvy, David, 291
Oil of Ulan skin cream, 278, 335
Ojdana, E.S., 474
"Old Lonely," 263
Olins, W., 348
Oliva, T.A., 381
Oliver, R.C., 101
Oliver, R.L., 101, 136, 381, 583

Olson, J.C., 169, 171, 172, 173, 174, 535, 583
Olver, J., 49, 79
Olympic Games, 340, 351
OmniCom research company, 553
Omo Power laundry detergent, 345
O'Neal, Shaquille, 267
Opinion Research Corporation (ORC), 379
Oprah Winfrey TV program, 496
Optima True Grace Card, 254
Oral-B toothbrush, 183
Orange juice, 297
Orenstein, F., 23, 209
Orr, B.H., 98, 104
Ortmeyer, G., 402
Orwell, George, 184
Osborne, J.W., 238
Osgood, C.E., 210, 570, 582
O'Shaughnessy, J., 165, 173
Osherson, D.N., 243
Oshinsky, A., 317
Ostrom, T.M., 133, 241, 274, 565, 581, 609, 610
O'Sullivan, M., xvi
O'Toole, J., 180, 207
Outland, D., 378
Oxenfeldt, A.R., 22
Oxydol detergent, 40
Ozga, S.A., 464, 474

P & O shipping line, 221, 237
Packer, M., 103
Padgett, V.R., 171
Page, M.M., 137
Page, Patti, 271
Paine Webber company, 266
Painton, S., 173
PAL dog food, 265
Palmer, Arnold, 264
Palmolive detergent, 144
Palmolive dishwashing liquid, 263
Palmolive soap, 335
Pan Am airlines, 346
Panasonic electronics company, 132
Papazian, E., 444
Parasuraman, S., 381
Parfitt, J.H., 608
Park, B., 137,
Park, C.S., 528, 529, 536
Parker pens, 272
Parry, M., 40, 49, 51
Parsons, L.J., 51
Pathmark stores, 355
Patzer, G.L., 276
Paul, G.W., 378
Pavlish, M., 319
Pavlov, I.P., 241
Pawlowski, D.R., 210
Payne, J.W., 173
PEAC research company, 583
Pechmann, C., 270, 272, 277
Peckham, J.O., 39, 45, 50, 67, 507, 517
Peirce, C.S., 243
Pendergrast, M., 534, 535
People magazine, 500
Pepsi Free soft drink, 117, 229
Pepsi Max soft drink, 480
Pepsico company, 335, 343, 346, 407, 431
Pepsi-Cola soft drink, 62, 117, 133, 144, 145, 163, 164, 173, 253, 254, 255, 267, 270, 272, 277, 278, 335, 370, 391, 483

Perception Research Services, 571
Percy, L., 22, 103, 104, 105, 135, 139, 155, 170, 212, 213, 214, 230, 233, 234, 235, 236, 237, 238, 239, 241, 243, 245, 260, 271, 274, 278, 314, 315, 316, 317, 428, 450, 522, 535, 536, 537, 553, 555, 578, 579
Perdue chickens, 264
Perdue, Frank, 264
Perfect, T., 135
Performer Q rating service, 276
Perkins, Anthony, 156
Perkins, W.S., 171
Perloff, R.M., 277
Pernod drink, 243
Perrier soft drink, 8, 144, 145, 150, 226, 363, 364, 370
Persil Power laundry detergent, 345
Pert shampoo, 335
Peter, J.P., 174, 234, 583
Peters, Tom, 372
Petray, E.R., 424
Petrison, L., 347, 414, 415
Petty, R.E., 226, 239, 240, 241, 252, 272, 274, 276, 277, 565, 581, 609, 610
Peugeot automobiles, 543
Pfizer company, 78
Phelps, M.P., 236
Philips interactive compact disk (CD-I), 65, 124, 515
Philips company, 132, 335
Phillips, A., 315, 319
Piaget watches, 28
Piech, J.L., 349
Piercy, N., 207
Pillsbury cake mix, 363
"Pillsbury Doughboy," 263
"Pillsbury Doughboy" Collector's Plate, 363
Pincott, G., 500
Pitt, L.F., 319
Pitts, R.E., 343
Pledge polish, 231
Poietz, T.B.C., 606
Point-of-Purchase Advertising Institute (POPAI), 116, 119, 134, 364
Polaroid camera, 146, 267
Politz, A., 169
Pollay, R.W., 169, 210
Polo Crest cologne, 38
Polo deodorant, 512
Poltrack, D.F., 498
Polykoff, Shirley, 181, 202
Pomerantz, S.D., 276
"Popeye," 266
Porter, M.E., 49
Powell, M.C., 220, 236, 314
Powers, T.L., 330, 331, 348, 351, 358
Pra Baldi, A., 238
Prasad, V.K., 500
Pratkanis, A.R., 159, 171, 172, 173, 272
Pratto, F., 138
Prentice, R.M., 21, 347
Presley, Elvis, 263
Preston, R.H., 363, 379
Pretesting Company, The, 571
Price, L.L., 380
Pride, W.M., 276
Priemer, A.B., 471, 474, 476
Princess Diana, 271

Principal, Victoria, 281
Pringle, L.G., 450, 474
Prinkey, K., 97, 99, 104
Procter & Gamble (P&G) company, 32, 49, 67, 95, 96, 154, 156, 202, 225, 335, 343, 350, 364, 368, 543
Progressive Grocer magazine, 95, 356
Prudential insurance company, 158
Pryor, B., 276
Pung, G., 100
Purina pet foods, 282
Purk, M.E., 402
Purolator courier service, 143
Putler, D., xvi

Quadrant research company, 315
Quaker Oats, 266

R & V insurance company, 158, 165
R.J. Reynolds (RJR) cigarettes, 89
R.L. Polk research company, 74, 80
R.H. Bruskin Associates research company, 240
R.H. Donnelley company, 480
Rabino, D., 232, 243
Rabinowitz, J.C., 215
Raddatz, A., 303
Radio Advertising Bureau, 444
Radio Recall research company, 314
Radio Shack electronics stores, 28, 400
Radio TV Reports service, 517
Radner, Gilda, 267
Ragu sauces, 311
Raid bug spray, 232, 237, 286
Rajendran, K.N., 392, 401
Raju, J.S., 348
Raju, P.S., 102, 572, 583
Ralph Lauren men's clothing, 38, 260, 427
Ralph's Grocery company, 388
Ralston company, 282
Ralston Purina Cat Chow, 282
Raman, K., 133
Ramirez, G.G., 349
Ramsay, T., 350
Randolph, K., 407, 414
Ranganathan, S., 536
Rao, A.G., 78, 378, 534
Rao, V.R., 390, 401, 534
Rapp, S., 414
Ratneshwar, S., 235, 272
Ray, M.L., 79, 133, 173, 241, 581
R-C (Royal Crown) Cola soft drink, 62, 117, 145, 278, 483
RCA company, 132, 515
RCA TV sets, 264
Read, J-M., 187
Reader's Digest magazine, 316, 493, 500
Readex research service, 607
Real People TV program, 499
Redbook magazine, 483
Redken hair products, 8
Reebok footwear, 380
Reece, B., xvi
Reed, J.B., 24
Reeves, R., 132, 226, 240
Reggie candy bars, 261
Reibstein, D., 134
Reichheld, F.F., 49, 413, 414, 415
Reid, J., xvi
Reid, L.N., 209, 300, 317

Reidenbach, R.E., 349
Reiling, L.C., 609
Reilly, P.J., 187
Reinhard, Keith, 207
Renker, G., 312
Research Systems Corporation (ARS) research company, 178, 205, 208, 235, 239, 270, 553, 554, 555, 556, 577, 579, 580, 581, 584
Resnik, A.J., 170
Retton, Mary Lou, 265
Reunite wine, 499
Revlon company, 78, 266
Reynolds, T.J., 170, 171, 535
Rheem P200 industrial chemical drum, 380
Rheingold brewery, 167
Rhodes, T., 499
Ribaux, D., 380
Rice Krispies cereal, 69
Rice, J., 93, 102, 381, 495
Rice, M.D., 495, 501
Richins, M.L., 136, 260
Ridgway, N.M., 101
Ridley, D., 173
Ries, A., 166, 174, 207, 240
Riezebos, H.J., 138
Rink, D.R., 22
Riyait, S., 581
RJR/Nabisco company, 479
Robben, H.S.J., 606
Robert Timms coffee, 150
Roberts, A., 472, 474, 537, 608
Roberts, M.L., 319
Robertson, I.T., 209
Robertson, K., 231, 242
Robertson, T.S., 78, 133, 134, 173, 241, 471, 474
Robin Hood Trilogy TV program, 496
Robinson, E.D., 380
Robinson, J., 276
Robinson, M., 314, 607
Robinson, W.A., 365, 379, 380, 576, 583
Robinson, W.T., 40, 49, 51, 168, 277
Robotham, J., 512
Rodelius, W., 363, 379
Roediger III, H.L., 238
Rogers, J.C., 401
Rogers, J.L., 318
Rogers, R.W., 173
Rolaids antacid remedy, 40
Rollerblade in-line skates, 52
Rolling Stone magazine, 96, 485, 486
Rolloff, M.E., 277
Rolls-Royce automobiles, 143, 167, 291
Romeo, J.R., 237
Rosch, E., 133
Rose, R.L., 277
Rosenberg, K., 144, 168, 209
Rosenberg, M.J., 137
Roslow, S., 350
Rossi, P.R., 514, 534
Rossiter J.R., 101, 102, 104, 133, 135, 139, 155, 170, 192, 209, 211, 212, 213, 214, 230, 233, 234, 235, 236, 237, 238, 239, 241, 243, 245, 260, 271, 274, 278, 300, 314, 315, 316, 317, 385, 401, 402, 403, 428, 450, 522, 535, 536, 553, 555, 565, 576, 578, 579, 581, 608

Rotfeld, H.J., 314
Roth, 148, 151, 168
Rothaus, S.E., 379, 583
Rothschild, M.L., 231, 235, 236, 241, 250, 277, 401, 449, 473, 583
Rotter, J.B., 583
Rotzoll, K.B., 472, 476
Roy Morgan Research company, 531
Rozelle, R.M., 581
RSL-signpost research company, 318
Rubel, C., 401
Rubinson, J.R., 23, 66, 78, 80
Russell, G.J., 49, 534
Russell, J.A., 136
Russell, J.T., 209
Russo, J.E., 572, 583
Rust, R.T., 50, 491, 497, 501
Ruth, W.J., 165, 166, 173, 241
Ruud, J.E., 348, 381

Saari, L.M., 47
Sachs, W.S., 348
Saegert, J.G., 134
Safeguard soap, 386
Safeway supermarkets, 66, 396, 445
Sainsbury food stores 235, 393
Saintilan, P., 209, 211
Saks Fifth Avenue, 510
Salz, N., 207
SAMI-Burke's SamScan, 507, 508
SAMI-Burke's SAMI, 508
Sanbonmatsu, D.M., 138, 169
"Sanders, Colonel," 268
Sanft, H., 499
Sanka coffee, 75, 237, 262, 264, 509
Sara Lee company, 78
Sarel, D., 314
Sarnoff, I., 172
Sasser, W.E., 49, 414
Saturn automobiles, 343
Saucony footwear, 406, 407
Savin copiers, 254
Sawyer, A.G., 134, 241, 272, 583, 610
Scali, McCabe, Sloves agency, 181
Scammon, D., 209
Schank, R., 314
Schendel, D., 22
Schepaler, E.M., 237, 238, 314
Schier, M.F., 104
Schiller, Z., 102
Schindler, R.M., 137, 172, 379, 400, 403, 583
Schlinger, M.J., 577, 579, 581
Schlitz beer, 51
Schlossberg, H., 276
Schmidt, S.R., 238
Schmittlein, D.C., 50, 79, 89, 102, 400, 402, 409, 414, 471, 607
Schnarrs, S.P., 52
Schneider, L.G., 79
Schonfeld & Associates company, 38
Schonfeld, E.P., 48, 349
Schorin, G.A., 209
Schroer, J.C., 41, 42, 43, 45, 51, 53, 59, 448, 507
Schultz, D.E., xv, 22, 24, 330, 347, 348, 351, 365, 379, 380, 576, 583
Schultz, R.L., 51
Schumann, D.W., 170, 276, 348
Schwartz McDonald, S., 537
Schwarzenegger, Arnold, 195, 268
Schweppes' Stuff Cola soft drink, 480

Schwerin research company, 578
Schwerin, H.S., 225, 240, 578
Scope mouthwash, 254
Scott, C.A., 474
Scott, D.R., 349
Seamons, B.L., 499
Sears stores, 49, 85, 362, 510, 515
Sega video games, 347
Segal, M.N., 74, 79
Seinfeld TV (program), 430, 490
Seinfeld, Jerry, 276
Sen, S.K., 77
Sensor razors, 22
Sentis, K., 171, 172
Serafin, R., 210
Sethuraman, R., 30, 32, 49
Settle, R.B., 87, 88, 101
7-Eleven company, 79
7Up soft drink, 117, 144, 182, 184, 201, 226, 335, 466
Sewall, M.A., 361, 237, 314, 315, 380
Shabbabb, G., 499
Shaeffer's beer, 286
Shaffer, C.M., 536
Shaft, E., 243
Shake 'N Bake seasoning, 184, 201
Shanteau, J., 101
Shapiro, S., 607
Sharma, S., 474, 535
Sharp, B., 318
Shavitt, S., 136, 171
Shaw, K.N., 47
Sheay, C.L., 316
Sheen, Charlie, 266
Shepherd, Cybill, 276
Shergill, S., 7, 21
Sherif, C.W., 271
Sherif, M., 271
Sherrell, D.L., 101
Sherry, J.F., Jr., 317, 583
Sheth, J.N., 133, 474, 583
Shields, Brooke, 287, 463, 464
Shimamura, A.P., 235
Shimp, T.A., 234, 241, 316, 379, 380, 474
Shochu liquor, 266
Shocker, A.D., 235, 256, 534
Shoemaker, C., 380
Shoemaker, R.W., 368, 380
Shostack, L., 154, 171
Shuchman, A., 26
Shugan, S.M., 145, 148, 168
Shulman, R.S., 173, 409, 414, 534
Shuman, P.J., 349
Siddle, D.A.T., 173
Siepel, C.M., 583
Silk, A.J., 198, 210, 235, 236, 241, 538, 576, 581
Silkience shampoo, 445
Silver, C., 350
Silverstone, R.F., 48
Simmons mattresses, 180, 181
Simmons company, 181
Simmons Market Research Bureau (SMRB), 318, 498, 502, 532
Simon, C.J., 48, 49, 50
Simon, H., 608
Simon, H.A., 133
Simon, J., 274
Simon, J.L., 52, 390, 401, 471

Simon, L.S., 608
Simonson, I., 74, 79, 363, 379
Simpsons TV program, The, 492
Simpson, O.J., 263
Singh, S.N., 231, 236, 242, 449, 473
Sissors, J.Z., 445, 471, 481, 498
60 Minutes TV program, 340, 424, 471, 481, 485, 489, 490, 498, 499
Skil power tools, 510
Skinner, B.F., 233, 376, 583
Slama, M., 401
Slamecka, N.J, 238
Slim Fast Foods company, 207
Sloan, P., 210, 276
Smartfood popcorn, 8
Smidts, A., 274
Smirnoff vodka, 174
Smith Barney Shearson company, 278
Smith, E.E., 243
Smith, L.J., 500
Smith, N.C., 402
Smith, R.A., 137, 169
Smithoes, B.H., 277
Snell, M., 378
Snickers candy bar, 131
Snyder, M., 22, 103, 104
Snyder, R., 210, 272
Snyder, G., 196
Soley, L.C., 300, 317
Solomon, E., 535
Solomon, M.R., 135, 241, 403
Soni, P.K., 101
Sony consumer products, 475
Sony electronics company, 132, 263
Southcorp Packaging company, 368, 380
Southern Comfort bourbon whiskey, 475
Spangenberg, E., 387, 401
Speckman, R.E., 535
Speilberger, C.D., 137
Spence, K.W., 132, 133
Sperry Rand company, 167
Spivey, W.A., 136
Spray 'n' Wash prewash spray, 218
Sprint long-distance telephone service, 75, 267, 508
Sprite soft drink, 69, 117
Squire, L.R., 235
Srinivasan, V., 234, 528, 529, 536
Srivastava, R.K., 534
SSB agency, 172
Stabiner, K., 276
Staelin, R., 255, 378
Staffaroni, J., 580
Stafford, E.R., 274
Standard Brands, 261
Stankey, M.J., 491, 501
Stanley, J.C., 579
Stannard, C.I., 313
Star, S.H., 52, 53, 78, 166, 168, 174
Starch INRA Hooper (Roper Starch) research company, 234, 295, 304, 312, 315, 316, 318, 338, 349, 607, 608
Starch, Daniel, 4
Stargell, Willie, 276
Starr, Ringo, 263
State Farm insurance, 118, 413
Statistical Research Inc., 317
Staudte, V., xvi
Stayman, D., xvi, 103
Steckel, J.H., 101

Stefflre, V., 141, 160, 167, 174
Steiner, R.L., 78
Steinfeld, Jake, 262
Steinlager beer, 288
Steinway pianos, 118
Stephenson, W.C., 577
Stern, B.B., 241, 313
Stern, B.L., 170
Stern, L.W., 535
Stern, R., 208
Sternberg, R.J., 210
Sternthal, B., 103, 168, 171, 317, 344, 346, 350, 608, 609
Stevenson, T.H., 272
Stewart, D.W., 22, 32, 170, 210, 240, 271, 272, 274, 277, 313, 314, 315, 535, 582
Stewart, James, 265
Stewart, M.J., 49, 208
Stone, B., 50, 414, 422, 424, 625, 318, 444
Stouffer's company, 162, 168
Stouffer's Lean Cuisine products, 252
Stout, P.A., 104, 274, 340, 349
Strang, R.A., 10
Strassman, L.H., 608, 610
Streep, Meryl, 263
Streisand, Barbara, 271
Stroh's beer, 149
Strong, E.C., 241, 471
Strong, E.K., 319
Strong, J.T., 173
Strong, S.E., 500
Stuart, E.W., 234, 241
Suchard, H.T., 349
Suci, G., 210, 570, 582
Sugar, 172
Sujan, M., 168, 171
Sullivan, E., 581
Sullivan, M.M., 48, 49, 50
Sultan, F., 534
Sun-Maid Growers of California, 369
Sun-Maid raisins, 369, 370
Sunkist soft drink, 117
Sushan, J., 316
Sutherland, M., 119, 135, 587, 604, 606, 607, 608, 609, 610
Swan, J.E., 22, 101
Swayne, L.E., 272
Swenson, M.R., 473
Sykes, R.N., 350
Sylvester, A.K., 77
Synodinos, N.E., 50

Tab soft drink, 117, 141, 144
Tadlaoui, A., 389, 401
Tainiter, M., 578, 579, 606
Talbot's clothing company, 132, 146
Tamsin, F., 350
Tang breakfast drink, 499
Tannenbaum, P.H., 210, 570, 582
Tannenbaum, S.I., 24, 351
Tanner, J., 103
Tanner, V., 577
Tansey, R., 103
Target stores, 28
Tarkenton, Fran, 281
Tarlow, A., 380
Tarpey, L.X., 239
Tarr, A.G., 135
Taster's Choice coffee, 58, 75, 118, 184, 202, 536
Tauber, E.M., 535, 578
Taylor, Elizabeth, 267

Taylor, W.L., 316
TBWA agency, 183
TDK audiotapes, 237, 262
Ted Bates agency, 202, 240
Teinowitz, I., 77, 167
Telcom research service, 571
Telephony magazine, 508
Teleresearch company, 421, 444
Tellis, G., 30, 32, 49, 50, 79, 167, 392, 401
Terminator movies, 268, 282
Terminator 2 movie, 282
Texaco company, 263
Texas Instruments calculators, 375
TGI research company, 532
Thompson, C.P., 135
Thompson, D.M., 236
Thorson, E., 22, 235
3 Musketeers candy bar, 131
Tidd, K.L., 380
Tide laundry detergent, 40, 155, 156, 225 , 231
Tiffany's stores, 427
Tigert, D.J., 105, 479, 498
Time magazine, 502
Times newspaper, The, 290
TN AGB research company, 536
Today show TV program, 327
Tokura, T., xvi
Tolley, B.S., 23, 209
Tom, G., 282, 313
Tomlin, E.R., 570, 582
Tontine Bedding company, 306
Tontine Body Pillow, 305, 306
"Tony the Tiger," 264
Toohey's beer, 221, 288, 453
Total cereal, 87
Totten, J.C., 381, 397, 398, 402
Tourangeau, R., 210
Toyota automobiles, 336
Toyota company, 157
Trachtenberg, J.A., 350
Triandis, H.C., 137
Triplett, T., 312
Trout, J., 166, 174, 207, 240
True cigarettes, 603
Tuchman, S., 314
Tulving, E., 217, 235
Turk, P., 472, 476, 501
Turner, Kathleen, 276
Turner, Tina, 188
Tums antacid remedy, 40
TV Guide magazine, 496
Tybout, A.M., 344, 345, 346, 350
Tylenol pain reliever, 149, 150, 254, 265, 345, 346
Tyson, Mike, 263

Ublique company, 378
Udell, J.G., 10, 22
Ule, G.M., 50
Ultra Brite toothpaste, 231, 513, 600
Ultra Slim-Fast diet products, 15, 183, 184, 207, 231, 276
Uncles, M.D., 77, 78, 402, 415
Unilever company, 49, 179, 207, 311, 345, 350, 482

Unisys computers, 512
United Airlines, 157, 254
United Distillers company, 486
Unnava, H.R., 238
Urban, G.L., 23, 40, 51, 52, 53, 78, 166, 168, 174, 513, 534, 536, 581
Urbany, J.E., 400
USAir airline, 345
U.S. Department of Transportation, 137
U.S. Food and Drug Administration, 232
U.S. Internal Revenue Service, 278
U.S. Postal Service, 318
U.S. Steel company, 243
US West Hotels, 407
UV sunscreen products, 335

V&S Vin & Spirit company, 183
V-8 vegetable juice, 101
Vance, Coughlan & Woodward research service, 517
Vanden Abeele, P., 234, 350
Vanden Bergh, B.G., 209
Van den Bergh company, 311
van den Bulte, C., 22
van den Heiden, M., xvi
Van de Ven, A.H., 209
van Goten, M.F., 282, 313
van Raaji, W.F., 242, 402–403
Van Rensbergen, J., 350
van Riel, C.B.M., 348, 351
van Trijp, H.C.M., 402
Van Waterschoot, W., 22
Vaseline Intensive Care lotion, 364
Vaseline petroleum jelly, 167
Vaughan, R., 239
Vavra, T., 241
Veblen, T., 188
Veronis, Suhler & Associates company, 21
Video Storyboard Tests research company, 276
Vipat, P., 231, 242
Visa Card, 254
Visine eyedrops, 226
Vivitar cameras, 295, 296, 297, 316
Vivitar corporation, 296
VMS company, 517
Volkersz, S., xvi
Volksbanken Raiffeisenbanken company, 158
Volkswagen automobiles, 184, 201, 202, 257, 288, 291, 297
Volvo automobiles, 7, 159, 180, 222, 254, 340, 346, 347
von Gonten, M.F., 607
von Hippel, E., 103
VW Audi company, 257
VW Golf automobile, 257

Wagner, C., 543, 576
Wakshlag, J., 491, 501
Wall Street Journal, The, 490
Wal-Mart stores, 399
Walker, D., 282, 313, 581, 607

Walker, I., 581
Walker, R., 537
Wallace, E.S., 378
Wallace, W.H., 444, 582
Walton, J.R., 376, 380, 399, 402
Wang, P., 347, 414, 415
Wansink, B., 79, 581
Ward Automotive News magazine, 508
Ward, A.A., 102
Ward, S., 133
Wargo, J.R., 318
Warneford, P., 173
Warr, P., 136
Warshaw, P.R., 581
Wascoe, D., 65, 78, 135
Wasson, N., 276
Watkins, M.J., 233
Watson, D., 136
Watson, John B., 173
Watson, R.T., 319
Watson, Thomas, B., 518
Webster's Dictionary, 347
Webster, F.E., 101
Webster, J.C., 173
Wedding, N., 609
Weight Watchers dinners, 23, 78, 168, 409
Weigold, M.F., 137
Weinberg, C.B., 48, 380, 453, 471, 474
Weinberg, P., 209
Weinberger., M.G., 314
Weinblatt, L., 582
Weiss, A.M., 48, 136
Weiss, D.L., 48
Weiss, R.F., 133
Weitz, B.A., 50, 378
Wells, M., 313
Wells, W.D., 32, 49, 105, 228, 229, 230, 239, 241, 479, 498, 581, 593, 608, 610
Wendy's restaurants, 463, 578
Wenger, D.M., 343, 350
Wensley, R., 165, 173
Wentz, L., 207, 350
Wenzlaff, R., 343, 350
Wernerfelt, B., 239
West, D.C., 50, 209
Westbrook, R.A., 136
Westinghouse company, 335
Westover, K., xvi
Wheaties cereal, 262
Wheeler, C., 381
"Whipple, Mr.," 225, 226, 463, 605
White Diamonds perfume, 267
Whittle Communications company, 380, 386
Wickelgren, W.A., 136, 240, 608
Wicken., G., 315
Widrick, S.M., 121, 136
Wilcox, G.B., 340, 349
Wilkes, R.E., 103
Wilkie, O., 243
Wilkie, W.L., 173
Willemain, T.R., 208, 578

Williams, C., 101
Williams, D.L., 319
Williams, J.D., 349, 375, 378, 380
Williams, M., 402
Williams, T.G., 401
Williamson, D.A., 491, 501
Willis, Bruce, 263
Wilson, R., 479
Wilson, D.T., 101
Wilson, E.J., 74, 80, 101
Wilson, R.D., 474, 499
Wilson, T.A., 49
Wind, J.(Y.), 81, 101, 474
Windham, B., 276
Wineman, J.D., 401
Winter, F.W., 498
Winter, F.L., 402
Winters, L.C., 211, 349, 582
Winters, P., 277
Winzenberg, S., 312
Wisk laundry detergent, 155, 156, 222
Wisniewski, K., 534
Witcher, B., 349
Wolf, M.A., 534
Wollen, K.A., 238
Woodruff, R.B, 170
Woodside, A.G., 74, 80, 101, 134, 235, 241, 315, 444
Wright, G.P., 74, 80, 134
Wright, J., 381
Wright, P.L., 277, 609
Wrigley's company, 335
Wundt, W., 136
Wyer, R.S., 169, 582

Xerox copiers, 81, 141, 254, 509

Yalch, R.F., 222, 238, 314, 387, 401
Yandell, B., 350
Yankelovich Clancy Shulman research company, 208, 507
Yardley cosmetics, 347
Yetton, P.W., 101
Yi, Y., 137, 171
Yoplait yogurt, 124
Young & Rubicam agency, 185, 186, 187, 222, 268, 394
Young, C.E., 314, 607
Young, E., 552, 578
Young, Robert, 237, 262, 264, 268
Young, S., 520, 535
Yuspeh, S., 536

Zacks, R.T., 608
Zahra, S.A., 173
Zaichkowsky, J.L., 231, 241, 242
Zajonc, R.B., 135
Zaltman, G., 535
Zeithaml, V., 381
Zhang, Y., 241
Zielske, H., 472
Zillmann, D., 173
Zinkhan, G.M., 234, 241, 316
Zuckerman, M., 276